The Greenhorn's Guide™ to
Alaska Fishing Jobs

Mark Maricich

On the cover: Alaskan fishermen, on a Prince William Sound seiner, during the summer salmon fishing season.

Cover photo credit: Alamy

All inquiries should be addressed to:
King Salmon Communications, Inc.
P.O. Box 2942
Seal Beach, CA 90740

Or visit us via the Internet at:
www.AlaskaFishingJobs.com

Printed in the United States of America.
Copyright © 2020 Mark Maricich

10 9 8 7 6 5 4 3 2 1

Library of Congress Information:

ISBN-13:978-0-9892434-1-4

Maricich, Mark.
    The Greenhorn's Guide to Alaska Fishing Jobs: Step-by-step guide to employment in the Alaskan fisheries — salmon, halibut, crab, cod, pollack, deck hand & processor jobs — Plus: knots, nets & know-how — Complete with a listing of over 17,000 job contacts. Fully illustrated and contains dozens of action photos. / Mark Maricich

Reference.

Includes index.

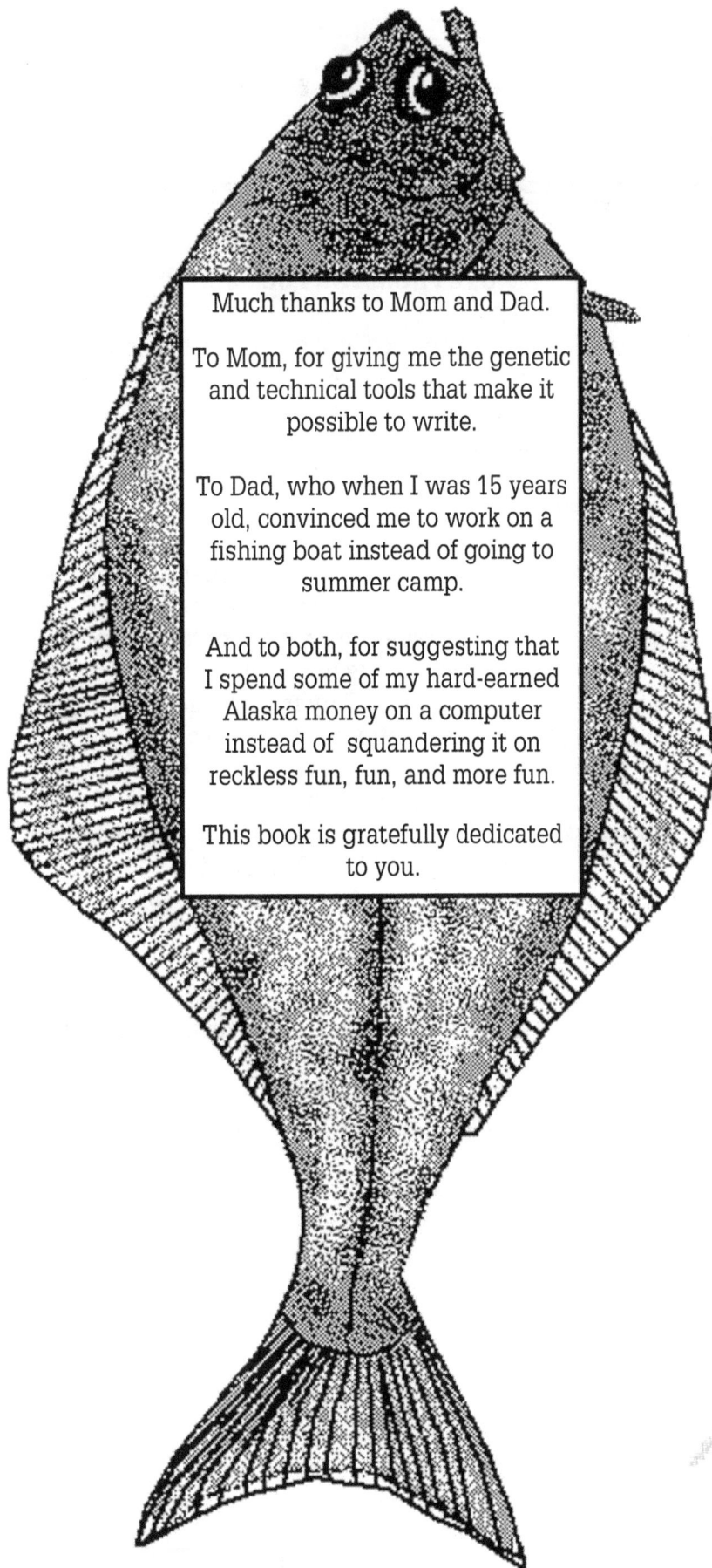

Much thanks to Mom and Dad.

To Mom, for giving me the genetic and technical tools that make it possible to write.

To Dad, who when I was 15 years old, convinced me to work on a fishing boat instead of going to summer camp.

And to both, for suggesting that I spend some of my hard-earned Alaska money on a computer instead of squandering it on reckless fun, fun, and more fun.

This book is gratefully dedicated to you.

A NOTE FROM THE PUBLISHER

This book is meant to be used as a guide to employment in the commercial fisheries. It neither encourages nor discourages employment in the fishing industry. Rather, it presents as much information as possible so the reader can decide for himself or herself whether to work on a fishing boat or processor, or in a cannery in the Alaskan commercial fishing industry.

Alaska fishing jobs can be dangerous, and the reader should be aware of this. The author, publisher, or marketer cannot be held responsible for any problems encountered as a result of the reader's own choice to pursue employment, or for problems that he or she may encounter due to any inaccurate information contained in this book. Total liability from the author, publisher or marketer regarding any matter related to this guide will not exceed the purchase price of this publication.

The facts presented herein were completely current when this book was published. Every effort has been taken to make this guide as accurate as possible. When dealing with such a large volume of material, however, it's likely that some of the information presented here may have changed. If you note any gross errors, we'd appreciate your contacting us so we can correct them.

The wages we estimate are based on past experience and are no guarantee that you'll make the same. Your remuneration will be based on the success of your boat, the area where you're fishing, the prices buyers are paying, and your crew share, or hourly wage.

green´horn. n. {prob. orig. with reference to a young animal with immature horns.}
1. an inexperienced person; beginner; novice.
2. a person easily deceived; dupe.
3. a recently arrived immigrant. {Colloq.}
{Humorous or patronizing in all senses.}

Dear Future Fisherman,

   Alaska is not only one of the most beautiful places on earth, but it's one of the most bountiful. It also offers many opportunities for men and women of all ages to make large amounts of money in short periods of time. Working as a fisherman, or as a processor worker, is an incredible adventure with high earning potential.

   The purpose of this guide is to help persons like yourself, who are interested in working as a fisherman, or as cannery or processor worker. PART 1 - The Harvesting Industry, will tell you what you'll need to know if you're interested in working as a deck hand on a boat. It will give you important information that only insiders usually have and will increase your chances of entering the elite and wealthy workforce of the Alaskan commercial fisherman. PART 2 - The Processing Industry, will help you on the road to employment in a cannery, or on a floating processor or factory trawler. This guide will supply you with enough facts so you can decide for yourself whether or not Alaskan employment is for you—and if it is, how to go about getting a job and making it the best experience possible.

   This book will provide you with some very important job-hunting advice from fishermen with over 25 years of experience. It's complete with illustrations and photos for your enjoyment and education. Also, with a list of over 17,000 contacts in the commercial fishing and processing industry, this book boasts many times the information found in other Alaska employment guides.

   All we can say is—if you decide to go to Alaska, great! Go for it! And even if you decide that working in Alaska isn't something you want to do, we hope you'll be informed and entertained by this book—and become a little bit more knowledge-able about the commercial fishing industry! Either way, do what you've got to do—and hopefully you'll make the right choice. Good luck! Happy fishing!

Sincerely,

King Salmon Communications, Inc.

Mark Maricich has spent 13 summers fishing salmon commercially in the waters of Kodiak and Southeast Alaska. His family has fished in Alaska and Washington for over 100 years. He's proud to bring you *The Greenhorn's Guide*™ and hopes it will help you with your fishing venture.

Additional thanks to:

Roy Maricich, Mike Maricich, Tim Maricich, Shawn Maricich, David Maricich, Janet Maricich, and all of my hundreds of relatives, especially the ones who picked me up at the airport or let me stay with them in Seattle. Also, Chad Leese, Jim Coger, Matt Castle, Noel Anthonysz, Clark Smith, Rick Eberle and to all my friends and fellow crew members past and present. Your knowledge and experience have contributed greatly to the writing of this book. Much thanks. See ya' at the river... when salmon run!

And of course, even more special thanks to my wife Victoria Maricich for her love and support during the countless hours I spent on this book.

TABLE OF CONTENTS

INTRODUCTION

Congratulations! By reading this book, you're taking the first step toward getting a job in Alaska! Commercial fishing is one of the most lucrative jobs available anywhere. In fact, during 13 seasons in Alaska, I grossed almost $200,000, the comparable equivilant of $500,000 based on current fish prices, by working eight to 12 weeks on a salmon fishing boat each summer. It was cash I needed to put myself through college—quite comfortably, I might add.

When people discover I've worked as an Alaskan commercial fisherman, they often ask me how they can get a job on a fishing boat. Usually, my first response is, "It helps to know somebody." Then I'll give them the phone numbers of a few boat skippers who might be interested in hiring them. And that's usually as far as it goes. Why? Because they don't pursue their job search any further.

Persistence is the whole key to getting a job on a fishing boat. If a person doesn't have enough perseverance to make a few phone calls or write a few letters to prospective employers, what good would they be on a boat where the skipper expects the crew to work 20 hours a day in 10-foot seas while the wind is blowing 40 knots? Persistence and endurance are what commercial fishing is all about. And when you get that one lump check for $20,000 or $50,000 at the end of the season, you'll know it was worth it!

The purpose of this book is to inform greenhorns of the best opportunities for them in the commercial fishing industry. Since the summer salmon fishing season offers the best chances for newcomers to get jobs, the majority of this book is dedicated to this fishery. Many of the topics that we cover in the salmon section, such as working, living and job hunting conditions, can also be applied to the other fisheries. The latter sections in this book will cover opportunities in the herring, halibut, groundfish, and crab fisheries. We'll also discuss working on floating processors, factory trawlers and in canneries.

For those who read this book and decide to work in Alaska, we'll present several job search plans to meet their specific needs. Some people may prefer to get a job months ahead of the fishing season, whereas others may prefer to travel to Alaska and get a job then. Just in case you prefer to job-hunt at the last minute—and because some people do get jobs this way—we'll provide a street-smart strategy for walking the docks. But make no mistake about it: we advise this approach only as a last resort. Instead, start your job search early by using the list of 17,000 contacts provided in this guide, and the job search plans we've organized for you. This strategy will help you get a job beforehand. Once again, if you decide that you'd like to work on a boat, pay special attention to the salmon chapters. Much of what you read there can be used to gain employment in the other fisheries.

NOTE ABOUT *DEADLIEST CATCH*

In this author's opinion, the TV show, *Deadliest Catch*, airing on the Discovery Channel, has had a positive impact on the commercial fishing industry in Alaska. Some Alaskan fisherman may scoff at this—after all, how could a TV show that simply documents what they do every day affect the commercial fisheries in Alaska? First of all, awareness.

The weekly airings of *Deadliest Catch* on the Discovery Channel have certainly helped promote wild Alaskan seafood, and the effort to produce this product was shown in *Deadliest Catch*.

Also, after *Deadliest Catch* began airing, there was an increase in people showing interest in pursuing Alaska fishing jobs, which has been good for skippers seeking crews. So, thanks to the fishing crews and producers of *Deadliest Catch* for helping to support the prosperity of the Alaskan fisheries.

And if you are a job seeker, be aware that commercial fishing is a real job, and not a TV show. Be prepared and know what you are getting into. Read and learn!

Photo published by permission of the f/v Northwestern

Greenhorn's Guide author Mark Maricich (center) onboard with the f/v Northwestern crew (from l to r, Norman Hansen, Edgar Hansen, Nick Mavar Jr., Matt Bradley) at Deadliest Catch's CatchCon 2011 in Seattle. Note the broken nose on Nick, where he got hit by the hook during opilio season — OUCH!

Check out Deadliest Catch online at:
https://go.discovery.com/tv-shows/deadliest-catch

Learn more about the f/v Northwestern at:
www.fvnorthwestern.com

PART 1

The Harvesting Industry

A DAY IN THE LIFE OF A FISHERMAN

So you're interested in working on a commercial fishing boat? Read this section to see if you can handle a day in the life of a salmon fisherman.

3:30 a.m. The alarm rings and you roll out of your bunk still half asleep. All your muscles are aching. You slowly put on your sweats and boots as your skipper yells at you to hurry and pick the anchor. You rush outside on the bow, begin pulling up the anchor, then realize it's pouring outside. After you take care of the anchor, you go back inside the galley and change into dry clothes, hanging up your wet clothes next to the stove to dry. You start a pot of coffee and yawn a lot.

4:02 a.m. Your boat makes its way from the sheltered bay to the open ocean. It's still dark and you realize that you'll be spending the day working in 10-foot seas and 30-knot winds. You wish you were home. You check the coffee and realize that the stove went out a half-hour ago. When you open the stove, there's a half-inch of diesel fuel sloshing back and forth. You grab a roll of paper towels, clean it up, relight the stove and wish you were home again.

4:05 a.m. You arrive at the fishing grounds and your skipper tells you to let the net go. The net is pulled off the deck by the skiff and stretched out for about 1,200 feet in the shape of a hook.

While the net is out, the skipper has you hit the water repeatedly with a large plunger pole to scare the fish into the net. You're having a hard time standing while you're plunging because the swells are so big. When the net has been stretched out for about 25 minutes, the boat and skiff meet, completely surrounding the salmon with the net. Once this happens, you help to connect the skiff end of the net to the boat. Then you pile the net on the back deck while the power block pulls it in for you. This operation takes about 20 cold, wet minutes. Your rain gear keeps you dry, but it's so windy your face gets drenched. Finally, you get to the end of the net and see you've caught about a hundred sockeye salmon. A hundred is a good haul when it comes to sockeyes!

5:00 a.m. The first little glow of sunlight is creeping over the mountains. While you're pitching the fish into the hatch, you're automatically calculating how much money you've just made. Let's see—one hundred sockeye, at an average weight of five pounds, equals 500 pounds. At a about a $1.30 a pound*, the boat just made $650. Since you're getting 10 percent of

Shelikof Straits, which is between Kodiak Island and the mainland, is known by mariners worldwide for its treacherous seas.

*Fish prices vary from season to season.

4

whatever the boat makes, you've just made $65! That's not bad for an hour's work! Your skipper tells you to let the net go again, so you do. You smell something burning and realize that the clothes you put next to the stove are now a little bit drier than you had previously intended.

5:15 a.m. You sit on the hatch cover in your rain gear and enjoy a nice, hot cup of coffee. Your fellow crew member volunteers to temporarily oversee the operation, allowing you to take a little break.

5:25 a.m. Your break is over and the skiff is making its way towards the boat, which means you'll be piling the net in a matter of minutes.

6:00 a.m. The net is brought aboard and you didn't catch one single fish. Therefore, you made nothing. Your boat travels to a different fishing area, so you go up to the tophouse to help the skipper steer the boat.

7:03 a.m. When the boat arrives at the new area, you climb down to the deck and let the net go. While it's being released, the net gets caught on a nail, ripping a huge hole in it. Your skipper screams and yells, but all you can do is hope that you don't lose any fish because of it.

8:00 a.m. The net is brought aboard and you were lucky! Even though there was a hole in the net, the fish didn't escape. You caught 100 fish, so you made another 65 bucks! You quickly fix the hole and let the net into the water again to catch some more fish.

8:30 a.m. The sun is out and it's getting a little brighter. You're finally fully awake. Breakfast is ready, but you only have five minutes to eat because you've got to bring the net aboard soon. The eggs are only half-cooked because the stove isn't working. You wish you were at Denny's. Then you remember how tough you are, living life on the edge in Alaska, so you eat every raw morsel of your breakfast.

8:57 a.m. This time you bag only 10 fish, so your skipper decides to move to a different area to catch a special tide.

11:15 a.m. You arrive at the new area and let out the net.

12:13 p.m. You bring the fish aboard. This time you caught 200 sockeye. Very good! You just made $130 with that set. So far you've made $260 since you woke up and it's only noon. You move to a new spot and let the net go.

12:45 p.m. The rain is coming down in sheets again and the wind is picking up. As you haul in the net, a jellyfish blows into

Although you're fishing for salmon, your net might also catch halibut, crab, pollock, ling cod, snapper and bass. You're not allowed to sell these fish. They are either thrown overboard while alive, or saved and eaten for dinner.

your face, stinging your face and eyes. But you have to tough it out and work for the next few minutes, even though you feel like you're on fire from the neck up. Eventually, your face stops stinging but your eyes remain sore.

1:10 p.m. The fish are brought aboard. There are only 50 of them. It isn't a huge payday, but it's still over 30 bucks an hour. Your skipper decides that you'll spend the rest of the day in the same area. You let the net go again.

2:13 p.m. This time you catch 75 salmon, which is more than last time. So you let the net go again.

3:20 p.m. You bring the net aboard, bagging 1,000 pollock and only 25 salmon. Since you don't get paid for pollock, you throw them overboard. Then you let the net go again.

4:10 p.m. While you're stacking the net on deck, you have to stop to pull a huge wad of kelp from it. Once you manage to do this, you continue bringing the net aboard.

4:25 p.m. Fifty fish are brought aboard. You let the net go again. The rain hasn't stopped and you're feeling miserable.

4:35 p.m. You realize that a whale just swam through your net.

4:50 p.m. As you're bringing the net aboard, you find a hole about as big as a semi-truck. You see the whale swimming off in the distance.

5:12 p.m. You haul in the net and there are no fish in it. They must have escaped through the hole. You wish you were lying on a sunny beach somewhere. You fix the hole and let the net go again.

6:05 p.m. The next set brings in 100 sockeye. Very good! You let the net go again. Dinner is ready, so you eat while the net is stretched out. You gobble down your baked salmon and get ready to pile the net.

7:10 p.m. You bring the fish aboard. This time you caught another hundred. Very good! That's another 65 bucks and it adds up after a while! The rain stops and the sun peeps out from behind the clouds. Everything is going good and everyone is happy. You let the net go again.

7:15 p.m. The net gets screwed up on the way out. Your skipper is screaming at everyone and the crew is mad. You back-haul the net and let it go again. Hopefully, there won't be any complications this time.

8:22 p.m. You bring the fish aboard. There are only 25 in the net. Even though it's almost 8:30 p.m., there's still plenty of sun-

Salmon fishermen will occasionally get stung by jellyfish that get trapped in the net. The stings are nothing serious though, just irritating enough to make the victim mad.

light left so you continue to fish.

10:35 p.m. You bring the net aboard, and there are only five salmon in it. It's not very inspiring, so your skipper calls it a day. It's still amazingly light out even though it'll be midnight in less than 90 minutes. You travel back into the bay.

11:15 p.m. You arrive at the tender, which is anchored in the bay. It's an 80-foot boat operated by the cannery that buys your fish. You begin unloading your catch. You throw the fish into a large net basket called a brailer so they can be weighed. When the fish are unloaded, you rinse out the hatch. Then you untie from the tender.

12:15 a.m. You drop anchor and shut off the engine. You sit at the galley table to unwind and figure out how much money you made that day. Since you caught 4,300 pounds of salmon, and are paid a $1.30 per pound, your boat made $5,590. Your crew share is 10 percent, so you just made over $500 for the day! That's not bad money for a day's work! Your skipper tells you to set the alarm clock for 3:30 a.m. You'll only get three hours sleep, but hopefully you'll make another $500 tomorrow. You scrub fish scales off your arms.

12:22 a.m. You lie down in your bunk and close your eyes.

12:23 a.m. You're fast asleep.

12:24 a.m. to 3:29 a.m. You dream of fish, fish, fish—and more fish.

3:30 a.m. The alarm rings. You don't want to get up, but you do. You put on your sweats and boots, and get ready to start a brand new day!

"Last summer we really malyhacked them! One day, we caught 5,000 reds, weighing 25,000 pounds, and made $3,250 each in 24 hours!"

—Matt, a college student from Washington who works summers as a deck hand.

THE BASICS OF FISHING

There's recently been much concern over tuna fishermen killing dolphins. Dolphins rarely get caught in salmon nets. If a seal or shark gets caught, they're usually released unhurt and alive.

Out of all of the fisheries, the salmon fishing industry offers the best opportunities for a greenhorn to get hired as a deck hand. Most jobs are on a type of salmon fishing boat called a "purse seiner." This chapter specifically refers to salmon, but the basic living, working and financial conditions discussed here can be applied to herring, halibut, groundfish and crab fishing, as well.

In purse-seine fishing, the basic idea is to surround the salmon with a net that's about a quarter of a mile long and about 50 feet deep. Once the fish are surrounded, the bottom of the net is drawn up with a purse line. This pulls the net into a bowl-like shape, trapping the fish. The catch is then brought aboard and put into the hatch for storage.

The salmon fishing season runs throughout the summer. The Alaska Department of Fish & Game regulates the days fishermen are allowed to fish. This schedule is based on the number of salmon that have escaped upstream to spawn. The first day of the fishing season usually falls between June 9 and June 25, depending on the area in Alaska where you're working. The last official day of the season is sometime in October, but most skippers call it quits around the end of August.

Usually, a skipper demands that his crew work on the boat two weeks prior to the opening day of the season. This will entail cleaning and painting the boat, buying groceries and stowing them away, loading the net and other gear onto the boat, fixing anything that needs attention mechanically or cosmetically, and traveling to the fishing grounds. You may live on the boat at this time, if it's approved by your skipper. Since you automatically agree to maintain the boat when you join a crew, you won't be paid for this preparatory work. When the season is over, you'll be required to remove all supplies from the boat and clean it again.

Transportation from your home to the port where the boat is berthed will be your responsibility. Don't expect your skipper to fly you to Seattle or Alaska from wherever you live. But once you make it to the boat and start working, you won't have any living expenses to worry about until the end of the season. When you're working on the boat, all your basic needs will be provided. Your food will be furnished at no cost to you until the end of the season when the bill will be divided equally among crew members and is deducted from your final earnings. Usually the food bill is around $1,000 per person, depending on how well your crew eats. There's also a fuel bill that's usually about $1,000 per person. You'll be given a bunk to sleep in, and the rent for living on the boat is FREEEE!!!

You'll need a commercial fishing license from the Department of Fish & Game. The cost is $200 for non-residents of Alaska, and $60 for residents. Your skipper might purchase it for you, then deduct the expense from your check at the end of the season. But if not the case, be prepared to pay beforehand.

The supplies you must provide for yourself include a sleeping bag, clothing, toiletries and fishing gear. A complete list is provided later in this guide.

Each crew is composed of four to seven people, depending on the size of your boat and the area where you'll be fishing. Each person has his or her own specific job. The skipper makes crucial decisions and his word is THE LAW on the boat. The deck hands not only work aboard the boat and pile the net, but have other duties such as cooking, repairing the boat, cleaning and navigation.

When it comes down to it, even though people have their own specific jobs, it's an overall team effort on a boat. If someone decides that he doesn't want to be a team player, he's going to have a miserable season and will probably get fired. The smartest thing to do is to keep yourself busy at all times and help your crew members, even though your own work may be done. This is the best way to get along on a boat and to contribute to the total team effort. With this attitude you'll be spoken of highly by your skipper and will undoubtedly be asked to come back the following year.

When you're working on a boat, you should expect to work all day, every day, for the duration of the two to three-month season. Your workdays will be 16 to 20 hours long, with an occasional 24-hour workday thrown in now and then. If you're fortunate enough to have an occasional day off due to bad weather or Department of Fish & Game closures, your time will probably be filled with many chores related to maintaining the boat. You will work very long hours, but you will get used to it.

When you're fishing, your boat is your home-away-from-home. You'll do everything on your boat—eat, sleep and work your ass off—rarely getting a chance to step on land. The boats used for purse seining are anywhere from 35-to 58-feet long, the latter

You don't get to take many showers while fishing, but you might get a chance to go on land and take a bath in a stream. If you do, look out for bears!

Many crew members develop The Aleutian Stare. It's a condition where deck hands become so home-sick that they stare hypnotically into the water, sometimes dazing for minutes at a time.

being the longest allowed by the Alaska Department of Fish & Game. These fishing vessels are usually made of fiberglass or wood, but there are a few steel boats out there, too.

While fishing, you'll be out of touch with society for most of the season. Every once in a while you'll have the chance to make a phone call—but this occasion is rare, unless there is a satellite phone on your boat. You may receive and send mail, which is usually delivered by the fishing tender, but you'll be in such isolated areas that you may not receive mail for weeks. When you go fishing it's recommended that you put a freeze on your bills, or have someone pay them for you until you get back home to pay them off with all the money you'll make.

The living conditions on the boat include being wet, cold and miserable. You'll work outdoors on deck 20 hours a day in awful weather. You'll be expected to work even though you're seasick and tired. You'll have to touch wet, slimy fish all day, but usually you won't be required to clean any unless you decide to have one for dinner. You'll be tired most of the time and will probably drink lots of coffee. You'll rarely get a chance to take a shower, sometimes going for weeks without one. You'll probably get yelled at a lot by your skipper, and occasionally be the brunt of short tempers among your crew members. Most of your food will be starchy and burnt. You'll get stung by lots of jellyfish. Sound like fun?

When the season is over you'll be paid a percentage of what the boat makes. Most percentages for deck hands range between 5 percent and 10 percent of the total gross boat stock. For example: If the boat grosses a total stock of $200,000 and your share is 10 percent, you'll have earned $20,000. Out of the $20,000, approximately $2,000 will be taken out of your check for your fishing license and your share of the food and fuel. So, in this case, the total amount you'll take home is $18,000.

Even though you work for your skipper, the Internal Revenue Service considers you a self-employed person, This means no taxes will be taken out of your check. Your skipper will provide you with a 1099 Form, which states the amount of money you've made during the season. When it's time to pay your taxes, it's all up to you—so make sure you save some of your bucks for Uncle Sam. It's best to talk to an accountant about these matters.

The bottom line is that you'll probably walk away from the

fishing season with a nice wad of cash in your pocket—and some great memories to recall for the rest of your life.

If you understand the basics of fishing and think you could bear the hard work and miserable living conditions to get to the big payoff, you should begin looking for a job now.

If you don't think that living on a small fishing boat is for you, but you would still like to work in Alaska, you should read PART 2 - The Processing Industry.

Some seasons, the crew share can reach $75,000 for three month's work. When this much is made, Uncle Sam could claim about $25,000 of it. OUCH!

WOMEN AND FISHING

Although it's still a very male-dominated occupation, the fishing industry is attracting more women every year. Now, it's getting to the point where one in 10 boats has at least one woman on the crew. In the past, these few women were either the wives or girlfriends of skippers. But now, many women with no relation to the boat owners are working on their crews. In fact, there are several boats where the actual skippers are women—a situation unheard of a few years ago. To top it off, these women are some of the best fishermen in Alaska.

Many women pull their share of the workload very well, since most of the labor involves finesse and persistence as opposed to sheer brute strength. Of course, opposite sexes living and working in such tight quarters does have its obvious drawbacks when it comes to privacy, harassment and such. But usually the novelty wears off fast, and men and women start treating each other as equals very quickly. If you're a woman or know a woman who's interested in fishing, there are opportunities for females in the fishing industry. But women, as well as men, must be prepared for the big challenges that are ahead.

11

WHAT IS A SALMON?

Salmon are one of the few fish that can live in both salt water and fresh water. They're hatched in rivers and lakes, spend their lives swimming in the sea, return to the fresh-water stream of their origin, then spawn and die. Similar in appearance to a very large trout, salmon live from two to seven years, depending on the species. The following is a list of the different types of salmon you may encounter in Alaska.

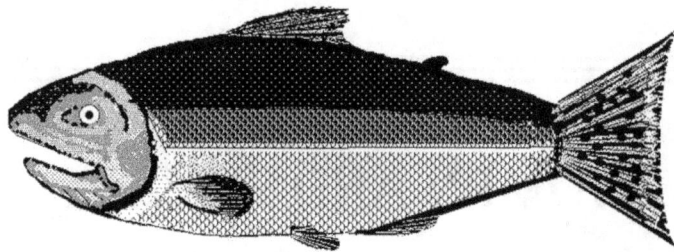

When working on a boat, you get used to the fishy smell in no time. As far as you're concerned, fish smell like money!

King or Chinook Salmon. This is the largest of all salmon, which is why it's called "king." Sometimes weighing as much as 70 pounds, the king usually averages about 20 pounds. Its life span is up to seven years. Kings are characterized by their substantial size, round body, large scales, black mouth and tongue, small eye pupils, black spots on the back, and gold- or silver-colored tail with black spots. Kings are the rarest of salmon. Buyers pay good money for them, but fishermen don't catch many. Worth up to $3.50/pound.

Silver or Coho Salmon. This fish has silver on its tail and body, so it's called "silver." It reaches weights up to 20 pounds, but most are in the eight- to 10-pound range. Its life span is three years. A silver is similar in appearance to a king salmon, with its round shape, large scales and small eye pupils. However, it has silver, not black spots, on its tail. This is a nice salmon, but underrated by buyers. As a result, it doesn't bring in as much money as it deserves. Worth up to $1.15/pound.

Dog or Chum Salmon. This fish is called a "dog" because it develops huge dog-like teeth when it reaches freshwater. It weighs up to 20 pounds, but most are about 10 pounds. Its life span is three to six years. Dogs are characterized by their large eye pupils, big head, sharp teeth, large scales and wide, non-spotted tails streaked with silver. When this fish reaches fresh water, it's very easy to identify because it develops large, red tiger-stripes on its sides. This salmon is a little less common than other species, depending on the area. It's not in extreme demand by buyers, so it's worth a little less than the more desirable salmon. Worth up to 80¢/pound.

Red or Sockeye Salmon. These fish are called "reds" because their skin turns this color when they reach fresh water. Also, their meat is bright red. Sockeyes reach weights up to 12 pounds. Most, however, are in the five-pound range. Its life span is four to seven years. Reds are characterized by their streamlined body, beautiful blue-green scales (which is the reason they're also called "bluebacks") and non-spotted tail. This salmon is fairly common. But it's a premium product and brings in higher prices. Worth up to $1.30/pound.

Pink or Humpback Salmon. Called "humpies" because of the hump on the backs of the male, and "pinks" because of their pink meat, these fish reach weights up to eight pounds. Most, however, are in the three-pound range. Their life span is two years. These salmon are characterized by their small size, small scales and humps. They have no silver on their tails—just black spots, which also appear on their backs. Humpies are the most common of all salmon. They're worth the least amount of money per pound. Worth up to 45¢/pound.

In recent years, the pink salmon runs have been quite successful. Some boats have recorded incredible catches of 120,000 pounds or 40,000 fish in one day and up to one million pounds of pinks for the summer!

HOW FISH ARE CAUGHT
BY PURSE SEINE

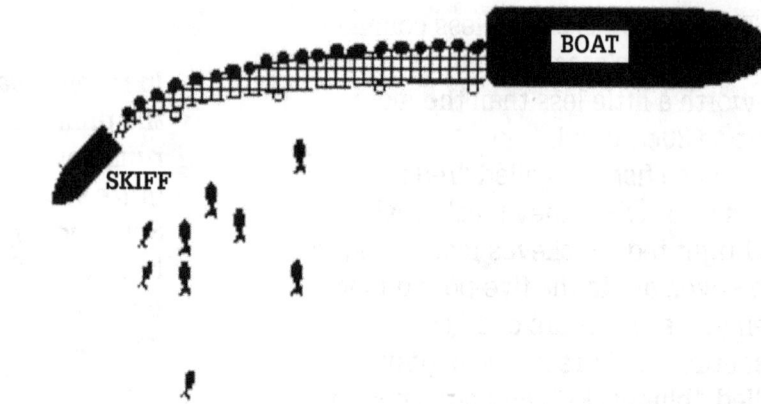

RIVER

1. The skiff is released near the beach with the net attached. The skiffman guides it to shore, where the river-bound salmon are intercepted.

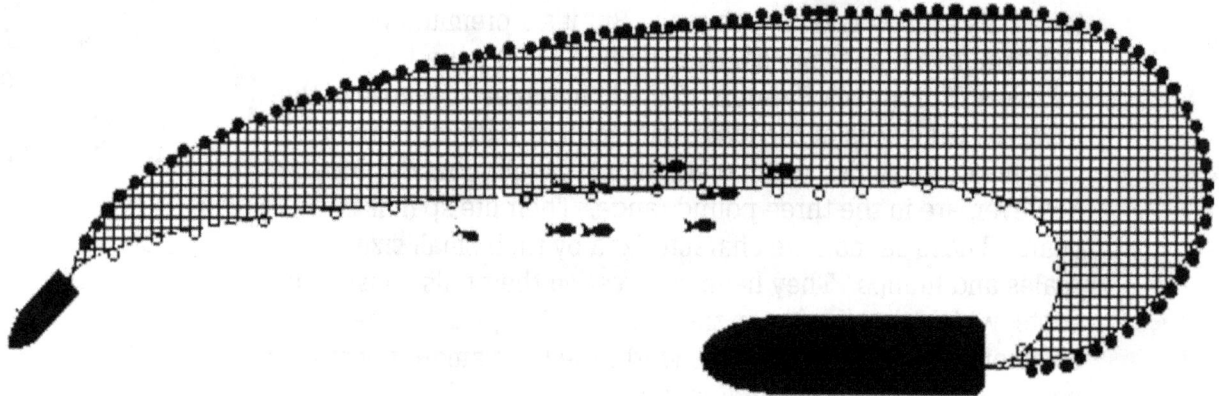

BOAT

SKIFF

2. The net is pulled into a hook shape by the boat. It acts as a scoop, trapping the fish.

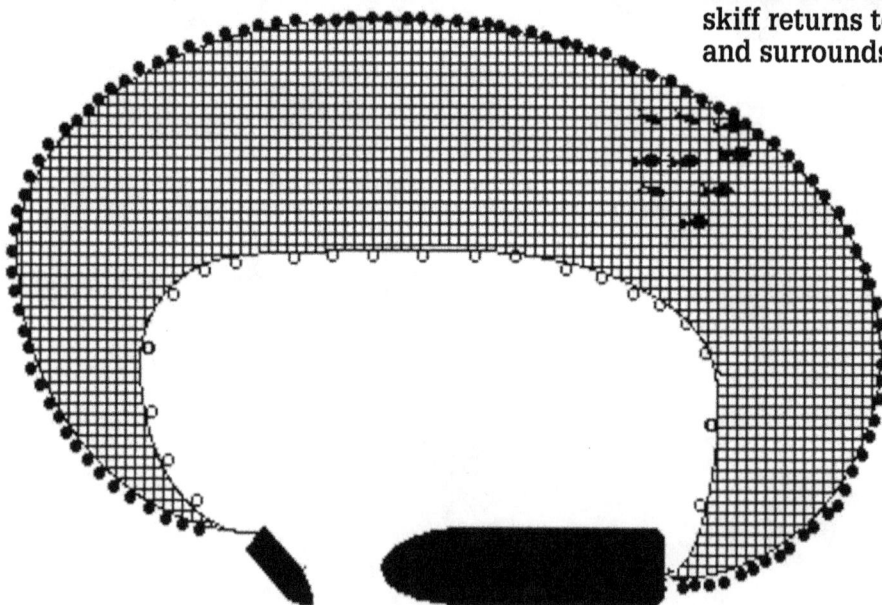

BEACH

3. After 25 minutes, the skiff returns to the boat and surrounds the salmon.

14

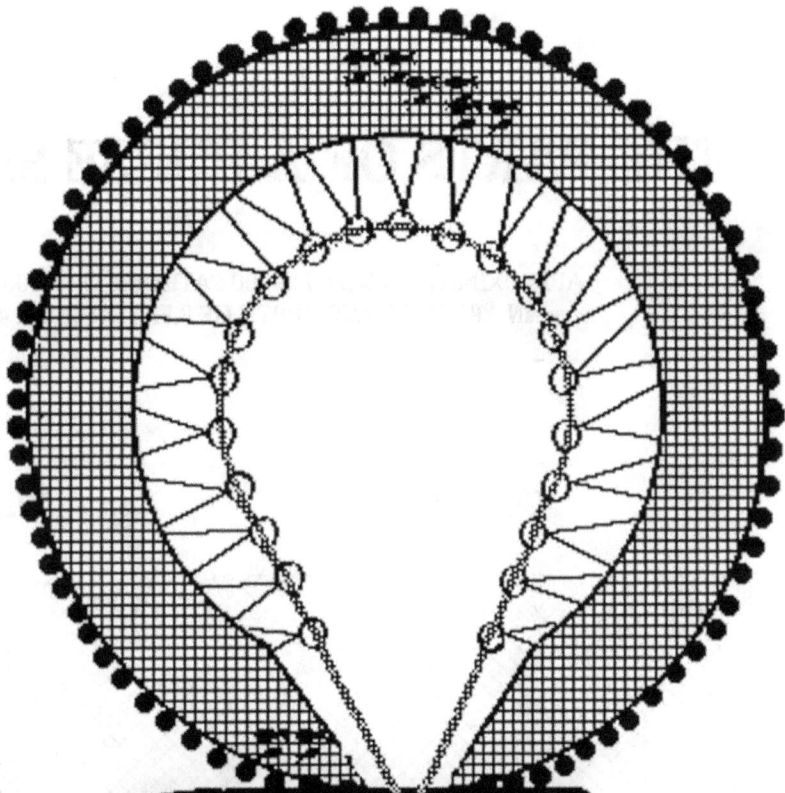

4. The boat begins pursing the net, while the skiff tows to compensate for the effect that the wind and swell have on the net.

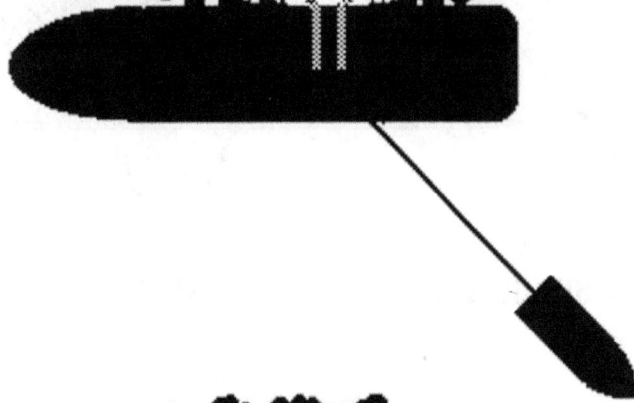

5. The bottom of the net is pursed up, trapping the fish inside. The salmon are then hauled aboard and placed into the hatch for storage.

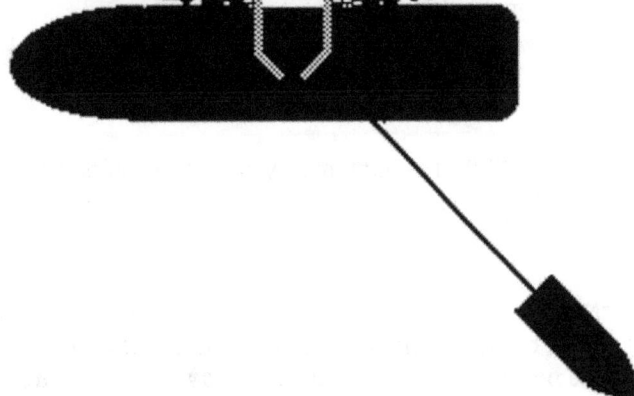

15

THE PARTS OF A PURSE SEINE NET

**APPROXIMATE LENGTH IS 200 FATHOMS OR 1,200 FEET, WITH
AN APPROXIMATE DEPTH OF 8 FATHOMS OR 48 FEET.***

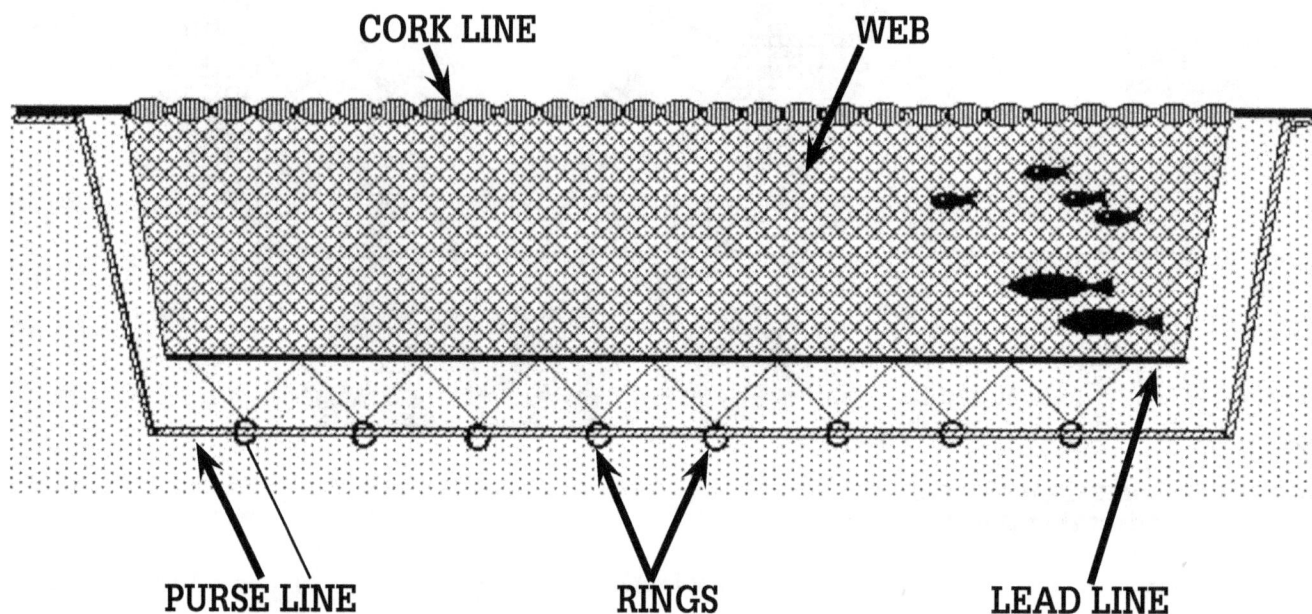

CORK LINE. The cork or Styrofoam part of the net that floats. Corks are approximately six inches in diameter.

LEAD LINE. The weighted part of the net that sinks to the ocean bottom.

PURSE LINE. The line that is used to draw or purse up the bottom of the net to trap the fish.

RINGS. Plastic or metal hoops, approximately 8 inches in diameter, through which the purse line is threaded.

WEB. The light, meshy, netted, nylon portion of the net, in which the fish get caught.

***NOTE:** This picture is not to scale. Most nets have over 1,500 corks and 25 or more rings, but this varies depending on the personal fishing styles of different skippers. The purpose of this chart is to display the basic parts of a purse seine net and should not be considered as an example of all nets.

SO...YOU WANT TO BE A SALMON FISHERMAN

Before you apply for a job on a fishing boat, you should know a little about the various positions available in a commercial salmon purse seine operation. On most boats, deck hands are assigned two specific duties: a primary job that's directly related to catching fish, and a secondary job that's related to maintaining the boat and contributing to daily living needs.

PRIMARY JOBS (on a purse seiner)

SKIFFMAN. This person is responsible for the operation and maintenance of the skiff, a small power boat that helps close up the net. He tows the net when it's stretched out and is responsible for surrounding the fish. He then tows the boat while the net is being hauled aboard. It's a very dangerous job since the skiff is a high-powered machine, and it's towing thousands of pounds of weight while trying to negotiate the high seas.

Being a skiffman is a very lonely job which requires spending 20 hours a day in a 15-foot boat by yourself. The fumes from the engine make some people nauseous and the loud sound of the engine can be dangerous to one's hearing. Since the skiffman is in the skiff all day, it's difficult for him to have a secondary job on the boat.

Working the skiff is physically easy compared to working on deck, and the skiffman's probably the only person on the boat who doesn't get stung by jellyfish. Since sitting in the skiff is so physically undemanding, many skiffmen add about 20 pounds to their guts during the summer just from their lack of exercise. It's a position of high stress and responsibility. The skiffman usually has many years of salmon-fishing and boat experience. Every boat has a skiffman. He's essential to the operation of the boat.

DECK BOSS. This person is a multifunctional deck hand who performs as an auxiliary helper to the the skipper and crew. In salmon fishing, the title "deck boss" is used even though it doesn't necessarily mean that the person in this position is anyone's boss or the most important person on the boat. In fact, the deck boss is more of an overall assistant than anything. He or she may help run the hydraulic controls, coil the purse line, or help pile the net on the back deck when it's windy. Anyone can be a deck boss, if they can pay attention to their surroundings and work hard. Not every boat has a deck boss; usually only the bigger boats have a need for this position.

"All mariners, all mariners, all mariners....this is WBH-29 Kodiak. We have gale warnings, gale warnings, seas to fifteen feet. Small craft advisory!"

—Peggy Dyson, a well known radio voice in the Kodiak area, had given her daily weather reports for over 25 years.

CORK PILER. This person is responsible for piling the cork portion of the net (the part that floats on top of the water) as it's hauled out of the ocean and onto the deck. This is a job that requires a lot of finesse. Many people like piling corks because it's probably the most creative of the deck jobs. In fact, some people's cork piles are works of art. Once mastered, this job can be a lot of fun. Many times the cork piler's secondary job is cook. Cork piling is a good job for someone with no experience. Every boat has a cork piler.

LEAD PILER. The lead piler is responsible for piling the heavy part of the net, known as the lead line, when it's hauled out of the water and onto the deck. The lead line is so called because it's a hollow rope filled with tiny lead pellets (pronounced leds) that help the net sink to the ocean bottom. Being a lead piler is the most physically demanding job on the boat since it involves piling weighted lead line all day. Some people consider this to be the worst position on the boat because the lead piler works the hardest, gets the wettest and gets slapped in the face by the most jellyfish. Others thrive on the challenge of being pushed to the edge physically. One thing's for sure: the lead piler comes out of the season with the most rippling muscles, which could be considered a hidden benefit. Piling the lead line is a difficult job to learn at first since it involves a unique combination of finesse and strength. No previous experience is necessary to become a lead piler, but you should be very strong and have a desire to work hard. Every boat needs a lead piler.

WEB PILER. This person is responsible for piling the web (net) portion of the net as it's hauled out of the water and onto the deck. This is a very easy job to learn. Many times the web will just pile itself and the piler barely moves a muscle. Other times, when it's windy, piling the web is the hardest job on the boat because the net billows like a huge sail. For the most part, though, it's an easy job and a good position for someone with no fishing experience. Many small boats don't have web pilers. Instead, the cork and lead pilers work together piling the web since it falls on deck between the two of them. Many of the larger boats, however, have a need for web pilers.

SECONDARY JOBS

The following are jobs assigned to crew members in addition to their primary jobs.

COOK. Being a cook on a fishing boat is a thankless job and everyone knows it. You have to cook for people whose only real joys in life are eating and sleeping. It's a big responsibility and, in addition to knowing how to cook, you have to be very organized. The menu doesn't have to be anything fancy. Meat-and-potatoes-type stuff or spaghetti usually satisfies a crew.

The cook's responsibilities include cooking three meals a day, buying and storing groceries, and cleaning and maintaining the stove and galley area. Every once in a while it's a nice gesture for the cook to make cookies or nachos to perk up the morale of the crew.

Many people don't like cooking because it takes away a lot of their free time. But there are some definite advantages to being the cook. For example, you can prepare what you feel like eating and you usually don't have to do the dishes (unless you're a nice guy). Also, cooking is probably the easiest way to get a job on a boat.

If you're a good cook and you've gotten a few rave reviews for your pot roast or meat loaf, your culinary expertise could go a long way toward helping you land a job on a fishing boat. It's difficult to master the art of cooking on a boat, though, since the cooking area is small, the stove doesn't always work and you've got to prepare meals while the boat is rolling back and forth. Most boats have just one person responsible for cooking, but some boats split up the cooking duties between two or three crew members.

ENGINEER. The engineer is a very important crew member whose principal duty is to maintain everything mechanical on the boat. It's essential for an engineer to be knowledgeable about diesel engines and electrical systems. Occasionally, there's some hydraulic work that has to be done, so it's good to know about hydraulics, too. Since many boats use refrigerated sea-water to keep the fish cold before they're sold, the engineer should be a refrigeration guy, too. Anyone with all these qualifications will be a highly sought-after individual and should have no problem getting a job on a fishing vessel. However, even if you're less qualified, but have good mechanical skills

"One summer, we traded a nice king salmon to a shrimper who gave us a five-gallon bucket full of the biggest shrimp you ever saw! Needless to say, with all the fresh halibut, king crab and venison we had, including the salmon berry pies, it was an incredible barbecue!"

—Dee Dee , a girl who's spent many summers at sea.

and are willing to learn and take on responsibility, you could be a good engineer.

SECOND SKIFFMAN. The second skiffman helps the skiffman while the net is stretched out to entrap the fish. Essentially, he's an apprentice to the skiffman and sometimes steers the skiff. He also "plunges," a monotonous job that entails hitting the water repeatedly with a long aluminum pole to scare fish into the net. Sometimes he's just there to keep the skiffman company. Being second skiffman is a fun job. People in this position learn a lot about running the skiff. When the net is ready to be closed up, the skiffman will drop the second skiffman off at the boat to help pile the net onto the deck. It usually isn't a necessary secondary job, but on many of the bigger boats it is.

SOMEBODY. "Somebody" is not an official secondary job title, but it's usually the person who doesn't have an immediate project to work on at the time. Since there may be three deck hands—one working as cook, the other as engineer and the third as skiffman, for example—and each one isn't busy all the time, there's always "somebody" who needs "something" to do. This is the person who's called to duty when the skipper says, "Will somebody please jump into the hatch and separate the fish?" Or when the cook says, "Will somebody please do the dishes so they're out of my way?" That's what "somebody" is all about. Get it? Got it? Good!

On a boat, there will always be those "somebody" jobs. It's a good idea to volunteer for these tasks. Not only will you show your skipper you're a hard worker, but you'll gain the important respect of your fellow crew members. Fishing is a team effort. Remember, on a boat, everybody is "somebody."

*NOTE: The jobs described in this chapter are specific to the salmon purse seine industry. Jobs on herring, halibut, groundfish, and crab fishing boats are different, but involve many of the same physical skills (refer to later chapters). Every fishing boat in Alaska has a cook and an engineer.

During the summer of the Exxon oil spill, salmon fishing was cancelled in many areas. Hundreds of skippers used their boats to help with the clean-up effort.

Fast action and concentration in the skiff.

The power block pulls in the net while the crew piles it on the back deck.

Three big kings for three big guys.

ALASKAN PURSE SEINER

LENGTH: 58 FEET
SPEED: 10 NAUTICAL MILES PER HOUR (KNOTS)
STORAGE: 40,000 LBS. OR 10,000 to 20,000 SALMON
CREW: 4 to 7 PERSONS, DEPENDING ON AREA

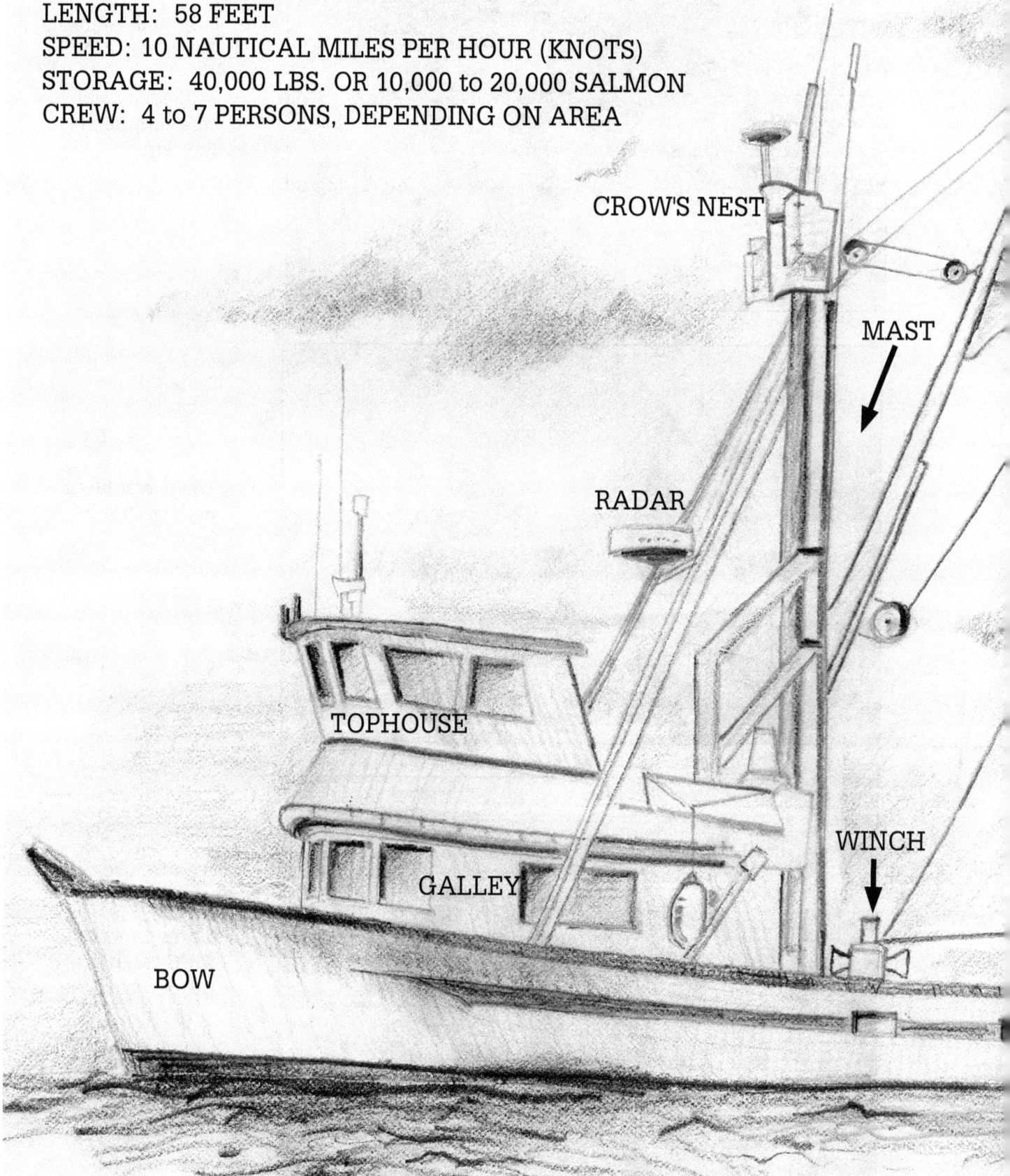

CROW'S NEST

MAST

RADAR

TOPHOUSE

WINCH

GALLEY

BOW

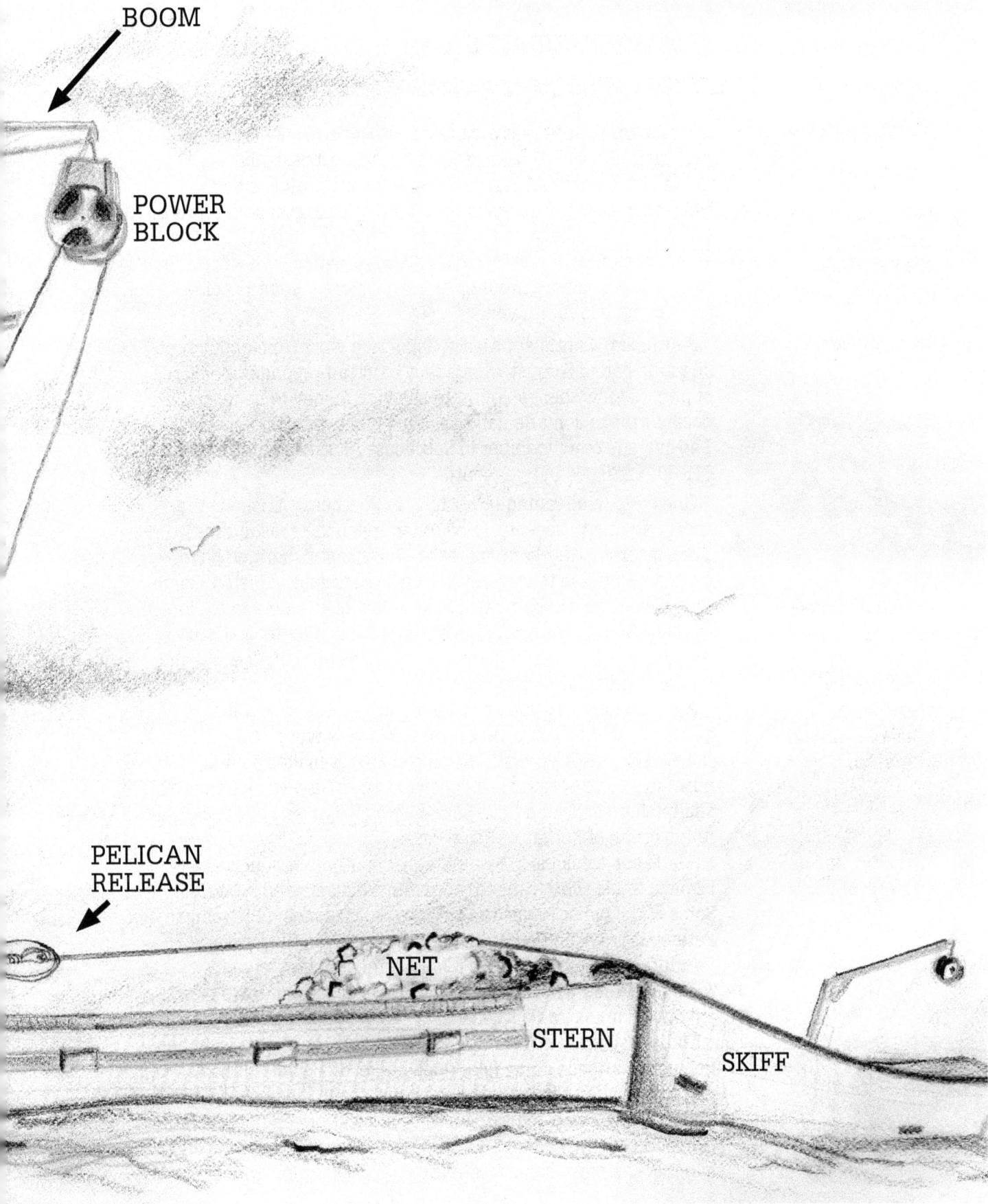

BOOM

POWER
BLOCK

PELICAN
RELEASE

NET

STERN

SKIFF

Illustration by Janet Maricich Loftus

THE DIFFERENT SALMON FISHING AREAS

There are six different areas in Alaska where salmon purse seining is allowed. These areas include Southeast Alaska, Kodiak Island, False Pass, Chignik, Cook Inlet, and Prince William Sound. Each area is different from the others in terms of the fishing methods used, the kinds of salmon caught, and the average amount of money crews make. If you know a little about each of these fishing grounds, it'll be easier for you to decide which area is right for you.

Southeast. Southeast Alaska fishermen work from about June 25 to the end of August. Since they catch a preponderance of pink salmon, there's not quite as much money to be made because pinks don't demand as much money as other species. The average crew member in Southeast Alaska can make about $15,000 - $20,000 in two months.

One definite advantage to fishing in Southeast Alaska is the short two-month season. In all other areas, the season runs three months. Another plus is that Southeast fishermen have more days off due to closures by the Department of Fish & Game. This means you probably will have some leisure time to explore your surroundings, including the towns and villages that are the final destinations of many luxury cruise ships. All this—and you're getting paid for it!

Another aspect of fishing in Southeast Alaska is that it's physically the easiest of all areas in which to work, except for the abundance of jellyfish, which sometimes makes fishing miserable. Furthermore, since you'll almost always be fishing in sheltered areas, you'll be in calm water as opposed to fishing the rough ocean of Kodiak or False Pass.

Southeast Alaska is breathtakingly beautiful with all its islands, trees, snow-capped mountains, glaciers and waterfalls. Some of the major towns in Southeast Alaska include Ketchikan, Petersburg and Juneau—although the latter isn't a very large port for purse seiners. Since it's the largest fishery area in Alaska, and most boats have large crews of six, there are many job opportunities in Southeast.

Kodiak Island. Kodiak offers the complete, hard-core, salmon fishing experience many fishermen crave. It's a very difficult place to fish, but there's lots of money to be made because Kodiak crews catch red salmon—the highest priced fish, with the exception of king salmon, which pays higher. The average crew member can make somewhere in the $25,000 range with some crew members making over $50,000 for a summer's work.

One thing Kodiak is known for is its long fishing seasons. The season usually starts around June 9 and sometimes doesn't end until the beginning of September. Another thing Kodiak is known for is its atrocious weather! It's very common to fish in 10-foot seas and 40-knot winds in Kodiak, but one gets used to it.

The raw, harsh, nature of Kodiak is incredible. Unlike Southeast Alaska, it has rolling tundra, jagged mountain peaks and few trees. Kodiak is the home of the Kodiak brown bear, the largest carnivore on earth. If you fish in this area, you'll become one with nature, which is quite a refreshing experience for a city-slicker. The city of Kodiak is the home port for many fishing boats, so it's a good place to walk the docks looking for a job.

False Pass. False Pass is the most isolated of all the fisheries. There are no big towns in this area and most of the boats are based out of Kodiak. Its geographic location in the Aleutian Islands makes it an attractive fishery for someone who really wants to get away from it all. False Pass is a difficult fishery due to its remote location and long fishing season, usually beginning in early June and ending in late August. The weather gets very rough here, so only the toughest of the tough will survive in this area. But there's good money to be made, since the catch is mostly red salmon.

Chignik. Chignik is one of the hotter areas to fish because of the incredible volume of red salmon. It's on the Aleutian Peninsula so the weather promises to be very nasty. Fishing begins here in early June and goes until the end of August. The money-making potential in Chignik is usually higher than the other fishing areas. If you get the opportunity to fish in this area, you should go no matter what!

Cook Inlet. There's the potential for making plenty of money in Cook Inlet since the catch is mostly red salmon. Fishing begins here in early June and goes through late August. Many of the seiners that fish in Cook Inlet are from Homer, a main town in the area. There are also a few boats from Kenai, another city in the area, but they're mostly smaller gill-netters.

Prince William Sound. Although the 1989 oil spill devastated much of the wildlife in Prince William Sound, it seems the salmon were not affected as much as they were originally believed to have been. Several years ago, so many fish were caught in this area that no one knew what to do with them.

In 1964, an 8.5 magnitude earthquake created a 100-foot tidal wave that wiped out much of Kodiak city.

"I met an Aleut native who let me borrow his wetsuit and surfboard. It was fun surfing the waves of Chiniak except that I got pretty worked. The board was water-logged, the water was freezing and my wetsuit leaked!"

—Dave, a Southern California surfer who spends his summers fishing in Alaska.

The majority of fish caught in the Prince William Sound are pink salmon. With the recent healthy salmon prices, and strong salmon runs, there is quite a bit of money to be made in this fishery. The fishing season starts here in the middle of June and ends in late August. The main towns in Prince William Sound are Cordova and Valdez.

Areas of Fisheries

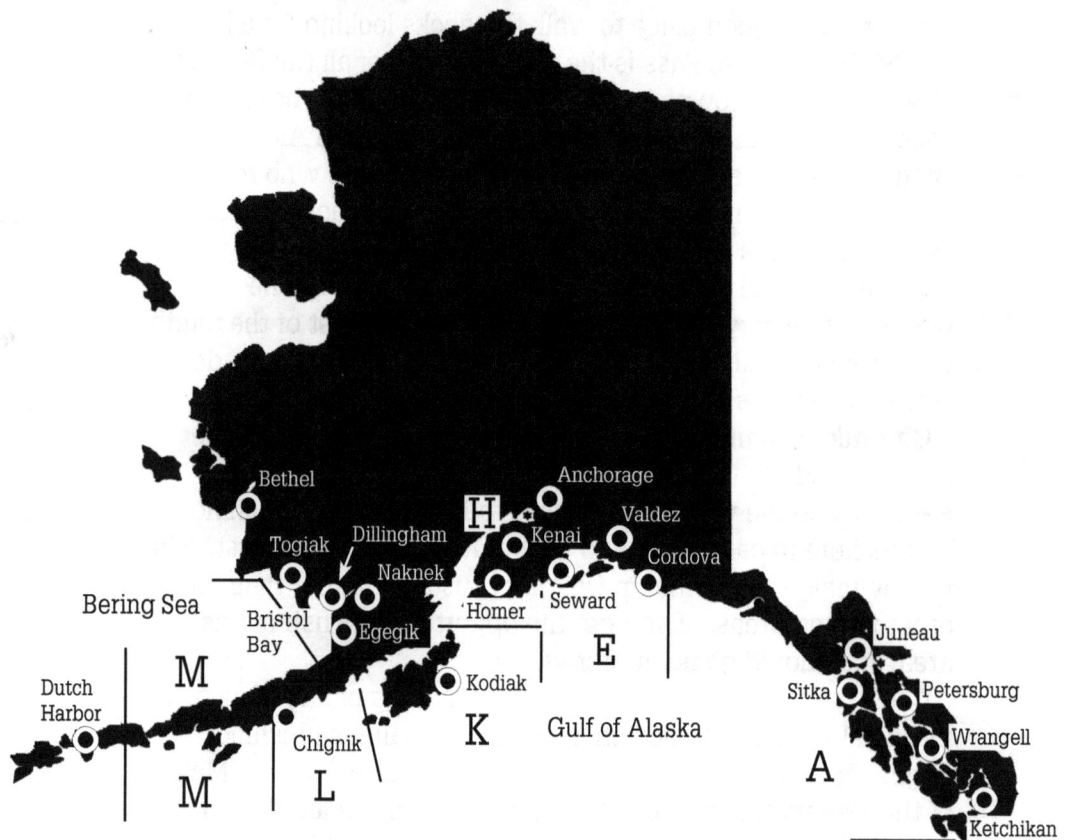

The Alaska Department of Fish & Game separates the entire Alaskan salmon purse seine fishery into six major areas.

—— Indicates area boundaries

A=Southeast
E=Prince William Sound
H=Cook Inlet

K=Kodiak
L=Chignik
M=False Pass

Top. Pulling a shark out of the net to freedom.
Bottom left. Piling the lead line.
Bottom right. "Look, Ma! Look what I caught!"

CHART OF ALASKAN WATERS

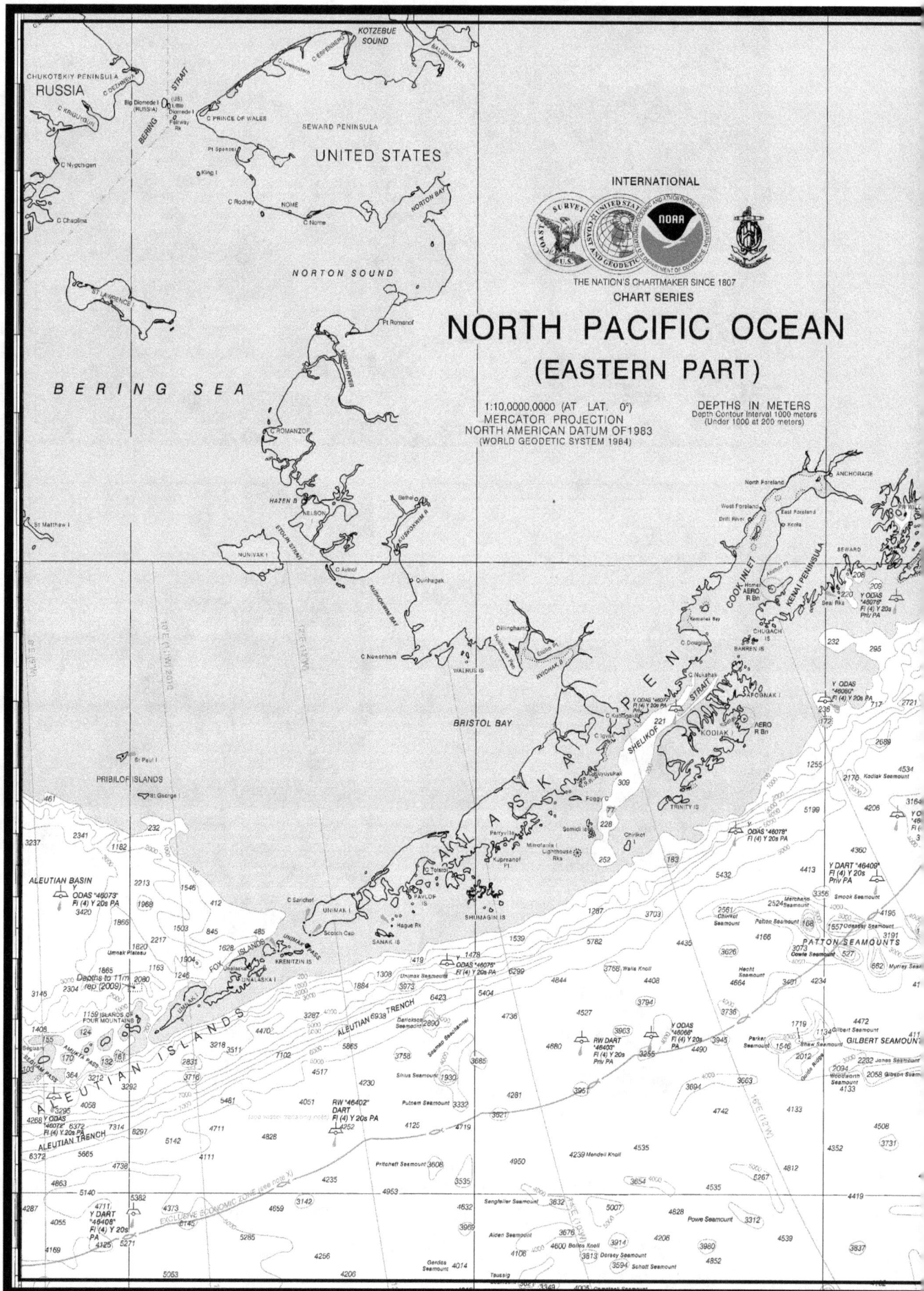

INTERNATIONAL

THE NATION'S CHARTMAKER SINCE 1807

CHART SERIES

NORTH PACIFIC OCEAN

(EASTERN PART)

1:10,0000,0000 (AT LAT. 0°)
MERCATOR PROJECTION
NORTH AMERICAN DATUM OF 1983
(WORLD GEODETIC SYSTEM 1984)

DEPTHS IN METERS
Depth Contour Interval 1000 meters
(Under 1000 at 200 meters)

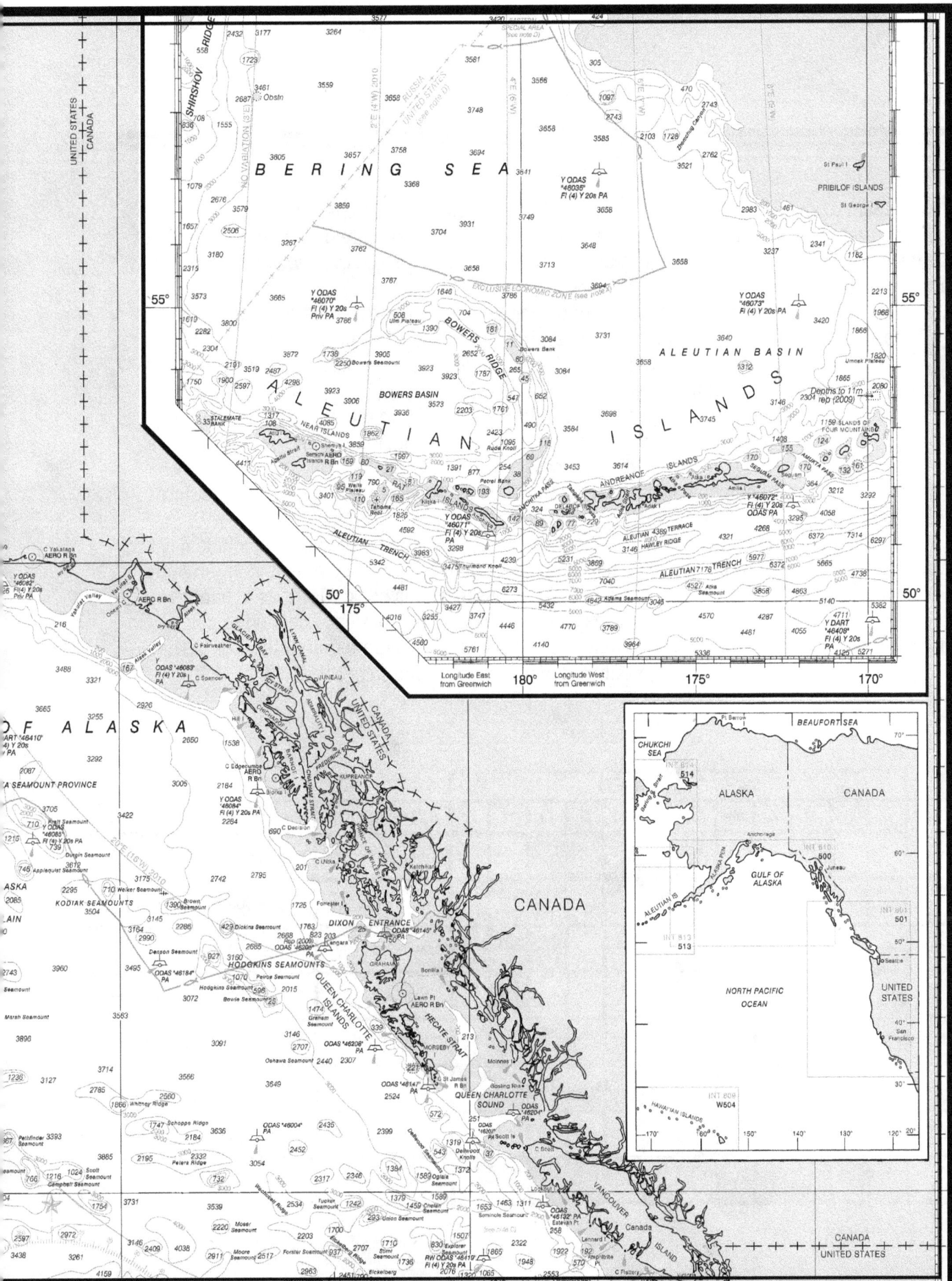

UNITED STATES
CANADA

SHIRSHOV RIDGE

B E R I N G   S E A

55°

PRIBILOF ISLANDS
St Paul I
St George I

EXCLUSIVE ECONOMIC ZONE (see note D)

Y ODAS "46035" Fl (4) Y 20s PA
Y ODAS "46070" Fl (4) Y 20s Priv PA
Y ODAS "46073" Fl (4) Y 20s PA

BOWERS RIDGE
Bowers Bank
Ulm Plateau
ALEUTIAN BASIN
Umnak Plateau
Depths to 11m rep (2009)

BOWERS SEAMOUNT
BOWERS BASIN

A L E U T I A N   I S L A N D S

ISLANDS OF FOUR MOUNTAINS

NEAR ISLANDS
STALEMATE BANK
Attu
Agattu Strait
Semichi Is
ABRO District R Bn
Rude Knoll
Petrel Bank
Walls Plateau
Tahoma Reef

AMCHITKA PASS
ANDREANOF ISLANDS
Adak I
Amlia
SEGUAM PASS
Seguam
AMUKTA PASS

Y "46072" Fl (4) Y 20s ODAS PA
DELAROF
Y ODAS "46071" Fl (4) Y 20s
ALEUTIAN TERRACE
HAWLEY RIDGE

ALEUTIAN TRENCH
Thuirmand Knoll

Atka Seamount
Azteca Seamount
ALEUTIAN TRENCH

50°

Y DART "46408" Fl (4) Y 20s PA

Longitude East from Greenwich   180°   Longitude West from Greenwich   175°   170°

C. Yakataga AERO R Bn
Y ODAS "46082" Fl(4) Y 20s Priv PA

OF ALASKA

Yakutat Bay
AERO R Bn
ODAS "46083" Fl (4) Y 20s PA
C Spencer
GLACIER BAY
JUNEAU
C Fairweather

SEAMOUNT PROVINCE
Pratt Seamount
Y ODAS "46085" Fl (4) Y 20s PA
Durgin Seamount
Applequist Seamount
Welker Seamount
KODIAK SEAMOUNTS
Brown Seamount
Denson Seamount
Dickins Seamount
HODGKINS SEAMOUNTS
Peirce Seamount
Hodgkins Seamount
Bowie Seamount

ALASKA
ART "46410" Fl (4) Y 20s PA

C Edgecumbe AERO R Bn
Biorka I
Y ODAS "46084" Fl (4) Y 20s PA
C Decision
Ketchikan
DIXON ENTRANCE
ODAS "46145" PA
ODAS "46208" PA
Langara I
GRAHAM
Bonilla I

QUEEN CHARLOTTE ISLANDS
Graham Seamount
Oshawa Seamount
Lawn Pt AERO R Bn
MORESBY
McInnes

HECATE STRAIT

CANADA

CANADA
UNITED STATES

Whitney Ridge
Schoppe Ridge
Pathfinder Seamount
Peters Ridge
Scott Seamount
Campbell Seamount

Moser Seamount
Tucker Seamount
Crelan Seamount
Union Seamount
Seminole Seamount
Forster Seamount
Moore Seamount
Stimi Seamount
Eickelberg Seamount

St James R Bn
Gosling Rock
QUEEN CHARLOTTE SOUND
ODAS "46204" PA
ODAS "46207" PA
Scott Is
C Scott
Dellwood Knolls
Ogden Seamount
ODAS "46147" PA

ODAS "46132" Estevan PA
Amphitrite
ODAS "46119" PA
Explorer
RW ODAS "46131" Fl (4) Y 20s PA

VANCOUVER ISLAND
C Flattery

CHUKCHI SEA
Pt Barrow
BEAUFORT SEA
ALASKA
CANADA
Bering Strait
Anchorage
ALEUTIAN IS
GULF OF ALASKA
Juneau
NORTH PACIFIC OCEAN
Seattle
UNITED STATES
San Francisco
HAWAIIAN ISLANDS

29

YEAR-ROUND OPPORTUNITIES

In addition to salmon fishing, there are other fisheries that offer excellent employment opportunities. Herring, halibut, groundfish, and crab fishing boats hire deck hands throughout the year. Floating processors, factory trawlers and canneries are also good ways to earn money and gain experience.

These opportunities offer a wide variety of fishing-related jobs. There are labor intensive deck jobs in addition to cooking, engineering and maintenance jobs. Most of the workers on floating processors or factory trawlers will be fish slimers or work on the freezer crew. Canneries offer a variety of land-based jobs.

The methods of job hunting in these other fisheries are similar to those used to get a salmon job. You may secure a job before the season, or wait until the last minute and walk the docks. However, if you plan to work on a floating processor or factory trawler, you must get hired before you go. These companies don't hire off the docks! Canneries, on the other hand, hire before and during the season.

In the following chapters, we'll discuss these opportunities in more detail, and include a list of over 17,000 skippers and companies. This should be a good tool to start you on your job hunt.

The following graph summarizes the fisheries discussed in this book. Use it as a handy reference: It covers the various fishing seasons, earnings, and experience needed to get hired. The contract times are the minimum times crew members are required to work in that particular fishery. Many times, it's possible to work longer, if one so chooses.

FISHERY	MONTHS FISHED												EXPERIENCE	EARNINGS	CONTRACT
	J	F	M	A	Ma	Jn	Jl	Au	S	O	N	D			
Salmon						■	■	■	■				Greenhorns OK	To $50,000	2 - 3 months
Dungeness Crab						■	■	■	■	■	■	■	Greenhorns OK	To $15,000	2 - 3 months
King Crab										■	■		Advanced Only	To $60,000	1 month
Tanner Crab	■	■	■	■					■				Advanced Only	To $50,000	2 - 3 months
Groundfish	■	■	■	■	■	■	■	■	■	■	■	■	Green to Adv	To $100,000	2 - 6 months
Halibut		■	■	■	■	■	■	■	■	■	■		Greenhorns OK	To $40,000	1 - 3 months
Herring		■	■	■	■								Green to Adv	To $40,000	1 - 3 months
Factory Trawler	■	■	■	■	■	■	■	■	■	■	■	■	Greenhorns OK	To $2,000 / wk	2 - 3 months

VARIOUS FISH THAT ARE HARVESTED IN ALASKAN WATERS

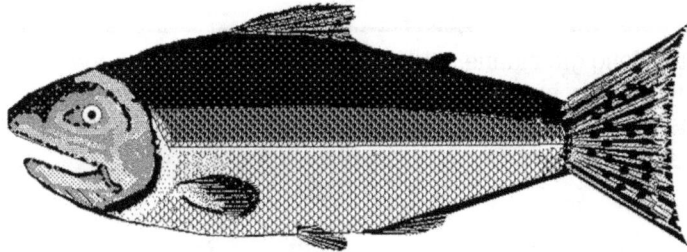

Salmon

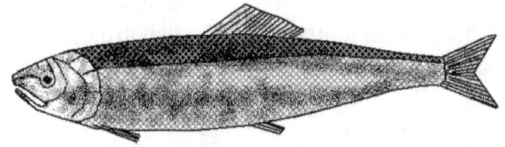

Herring

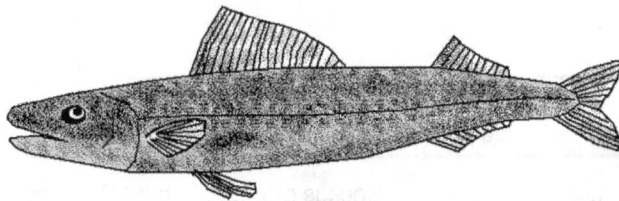

Black Cod

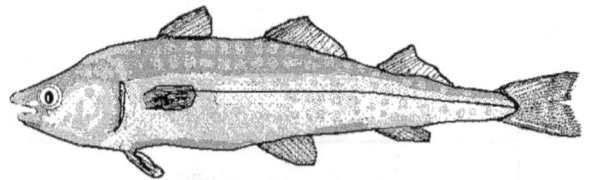

Pollock

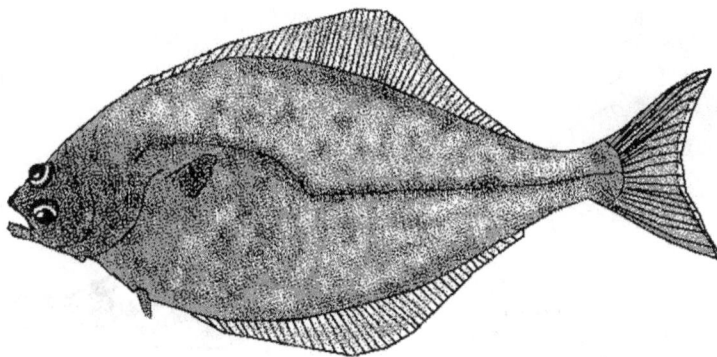

Halibut

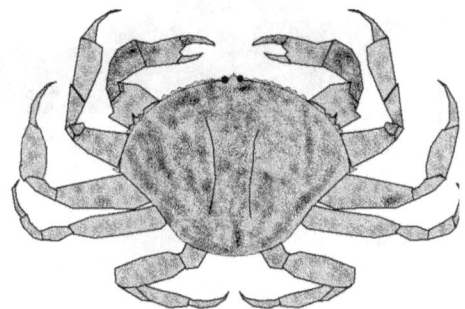

Dungeness Crab

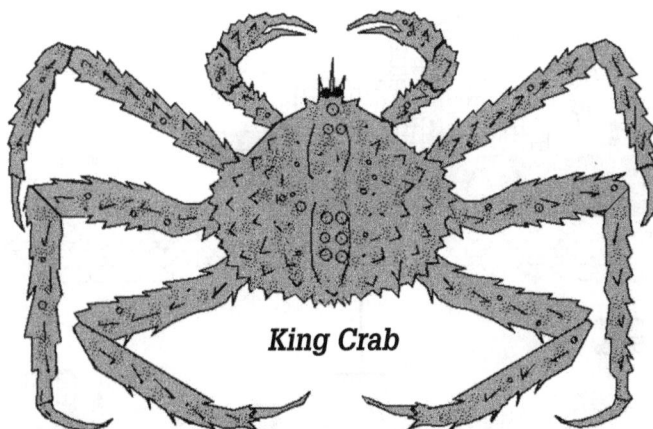

King Crab

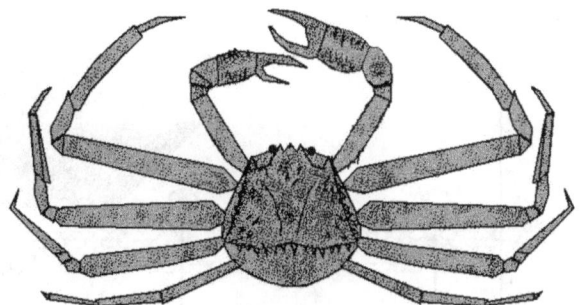

Opilio Crab

VARIOUS METHODS OF FISHING

In addition to purse seining and gillnetting, there are several other methods of fishing that are widely used:

LONGLINING: Baited hooks are connected to a long groundline. It's placed on the ocean floor between two anchors, and marked above the surface with a flag buoy. The groundline lays on the bottom for several hours while the fish are caught on the inviting hooks. The line and fish are winched aboard.

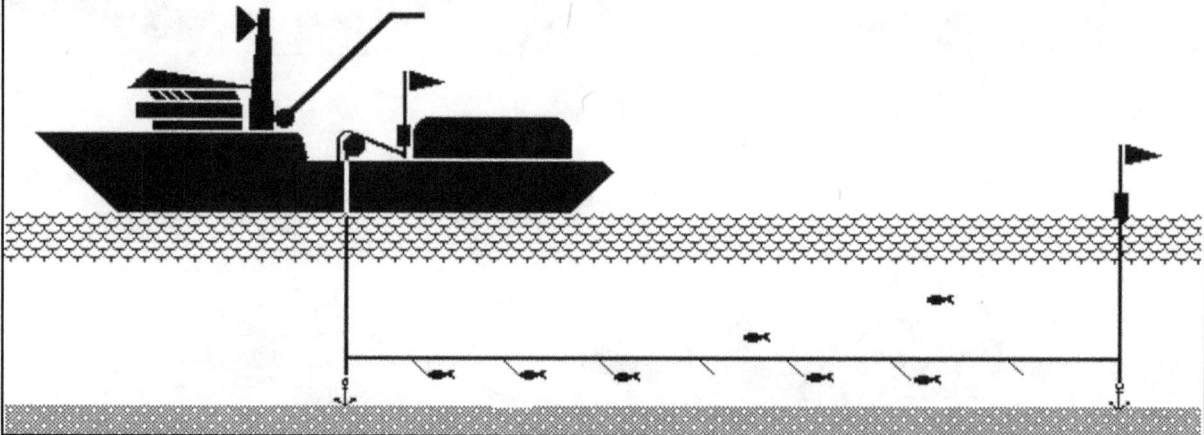

TRAWLING: In trawl fishing, a long net similar in shape to a large windsock is dragged behind the boat until it's full. This net may be 100 fathoms long and hold up to 110 tons of fish.

CRABBING: All crab are caught by a method called pot fishing. A baited, steel-and-mesh cage, called a "crab pot," is lowered to the bottom of the ocean and marked above the surface with a rubber bag buoy. When the bait attracts the crab, they enter the pot, are trapped, and then hoisted aboard.

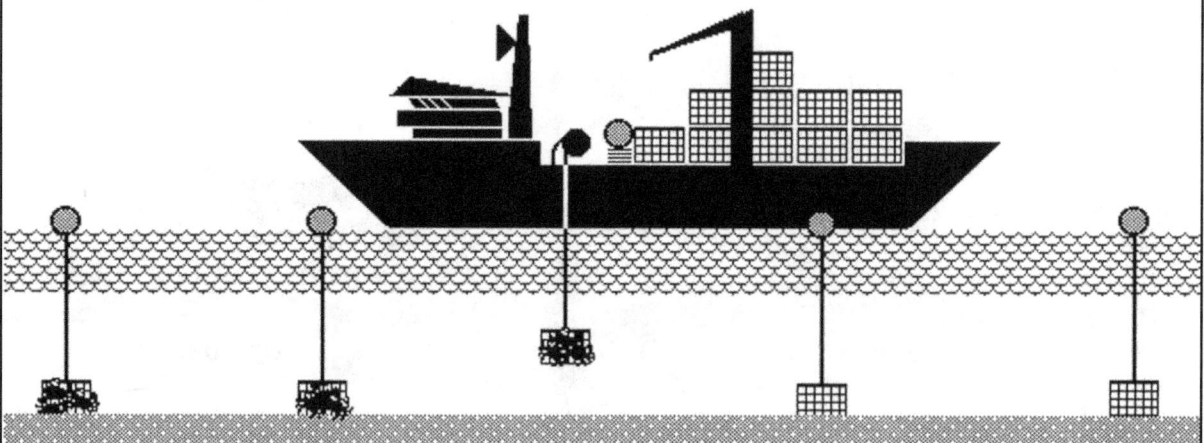

Your only sanctuary is a 2-foot by 6-foot bunk.

One of the many women who has earned her living by fishing for salmon in Alaska.

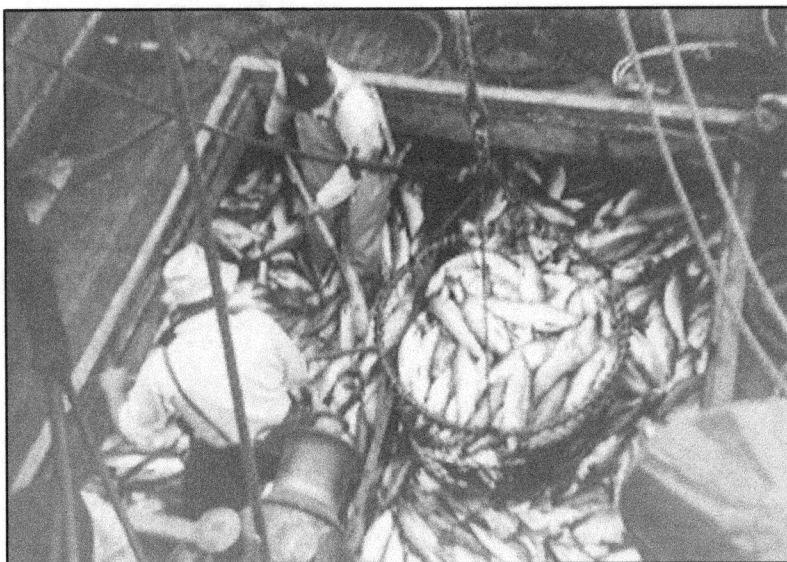

Filling the brailer with salmon to sell to the cannery.

Surfing Chiniak,
Kodiak, AK on a
day off.

Deckload! Just
made $2,000 for
an hour's work!

Hauling a couple
hundred sockeye
aboard.

SALMON DRIFT NET

Gillnetting is a method of salmon fishing used throughout Alaska. It's fairly simple work and a good way for greenhorns to gain experience.

A gillnet consists of a floating cork line at the top, and a lead line at the bottom with webbing in between them. When the net is stretched out in the water, the salmon swim into it and become entangled by their gills. The two basic gillnetting methods used are set net and drift net.

Set nets are stationary nets placed in permanent locations along the shore. This method is used primarily by native or family operations. It's rare for outsiders to get hired in this fishery.

The drift net method uses a small boat, 32 feet or less in length, that drifts while fishing. A drum is used to set the net and reel it back in after the proper amount of time has passed. The crew then picks the salmon out of the net by hand. Most drift net boats hire from one to three crew members depending on the area fished. Unlike the open ocean drift nets, these are much smaller and environmentally safe, rarely catching any fish but salmon.

The salmon drift net season runs for a couple of months during the summer. The season in Southeast Alaska extends from early July to mid-September. In Bristol Bay, the season lasts from the end of June until the beginning of August.

There is good money to be earned in the salmon drift net fishery. Bristol Bay is the most lucrative of the areas with most crew members earning 15 to 20 percent of the gross income, resulting in $15,000 to $25,000 in six weeks. Southeast Alaska crew members get 10 percent of the gross, earning an average of $10,000 to $15,000 for two months. Cook Inlet has produced well in the last few years and might be a good place to walk the docks due to its accessibility to Anchorage.

The best ports to pursue work in the salmon drift net fishery are Dillingham, Togiak, Naknek, Homer, Petersburg, Ketchikan, Valdez, Cordova, and Sitka.

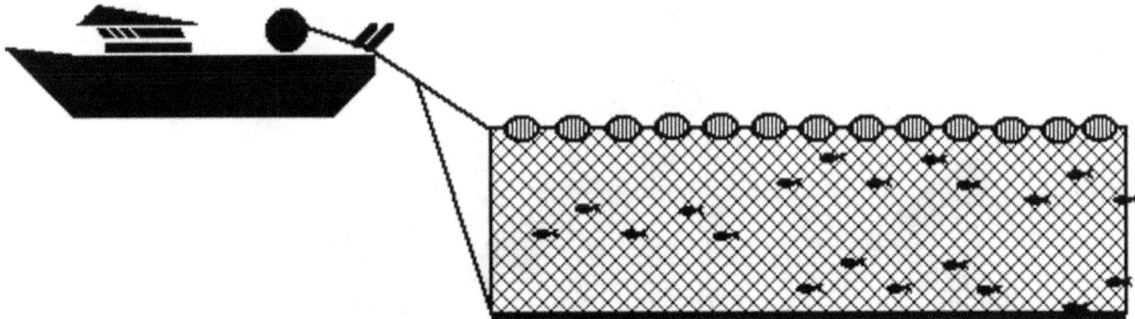

HALIBUT

Halibut are large, flatfish that weigh up to 300 pounds. They have delicious, white meat, which is in high demand by restaurants and seafood markets. Buyers will pay boats around $6 per pound for halibut.

Most halibut are caught by a method of fishing called "longline." This procedure employs baited hooks connected to a long groundline. It's placed on the ocean floor between two anchors, and marked above the surface with a flag buoy. The groundline lays on the bottom for several hours while the fish are caught on the inviting hooks. An average groundline is composed of five units of line, called "skates," which measure 1,800 feet each and carry 100 hooks each. These skates combine to provide a mile of fishable groundline, and the capability of catching 500 halibut. The line is winched aboard. Then the fish are gaffed, hauled on deck, hit on the head, gutted, and placed on ice, one after the other, after the other...

The sizes and types of halibut-longline boats vary throughout Alaska. Most can be identified by the flag buoys and tubs full of hooks on the back deck. The stern may also be covered by a wood or metal shed that's used to protect the crew from the elements. The main halibut boat ports are Kodiak, Homer, Seward, Sitka, Petersburg and Ketchikan.

The halibut fishing season takes place from March to November, and is regulated by the 'IFQ' (Individual Fisherman Quotas) system. Before IFQ, the entire halibut season would be composed of three, 24-hour fishing derbies for the entire year—a dangerous, and difficult approach to managing the fishery. IFQ helped to improve this. Plus, IFQ ensures that fresh, Alaskan halibut is available throughout most of the year, a key benefit.

Halibut fishing is fairly dangerous work that isn't recommended for the easily tired or weak of stomach. High seas, sharp knives and snaggy hooks add to the risk factor. It's a fast-paced, bloody, and messy job. The workers are expected to fish at least 24 hours straight with the possibility of a 48-hour shift. The total contract time can be anywhere from a week, to several months, depending on the boat. This includes boat preparation, fishing, and cleaning the boat after you're through.

The Alaskan halibut fishery provides an excellent opportunity for workers to make good money and good job contacts. The average crew member makes several hundred dollars per day, with some enjoying daily paydays up to $5,000, with seasonal earnings up to $40,000. Many halibut skippers have diversified to catch salmon and groundfish as well. The most successful deck hands will be offered work in these fisheries, too.

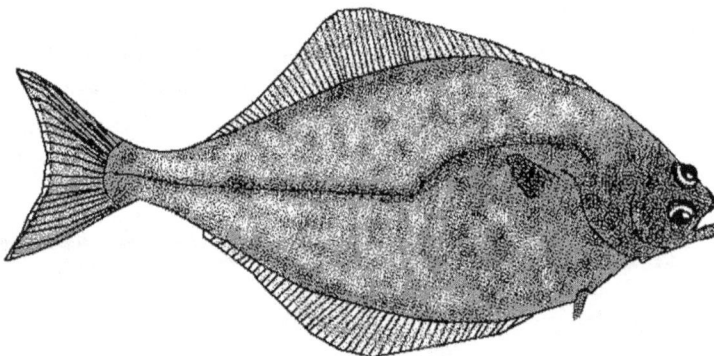

GROUNDFISH

Groundfish are a type of mid-water to bottom fish that include pollock, Pacific cod, black cod, sole and flounder. They're used in the mass production of white meat filets, roe, and "surimi," also known as imitation crab meat.

There are excellent opportunities in the groundfish industry, providing employment throughout the year. Pollock season is open twice a year—once from January 20 to late April, then again from September 1 to late October. Black cod are caught from mid-April to late October. Pacific cod, flounder and sole are caught throughout the year. There are over 13,000 deck hand jobs in the groundfish industry.

The most popular methods of catching groundfish are by longline and trawl. The longline method used for groundfish is the same as for halibut. In trawl fishing, a long net similar in shape to a large windsock is dragged behind the boat until it's full. This net may be 100 fathoms long and hold up to 110 tons of fish.

In both fisheries, the size and type of fishing boats may vary. They may be anywhere from 50 to 350 feet long. A longline boat is easy to distinguish by the flag buoys, tubs full of hooks, and shed on the back deck. Trawlers are distinguished by the big reel with a net wrapped around it that's stationed on the back deck.

Earnings for crew members differ from boat to boat. Longliners should be able to hack out a day-in, day-out grind and manage to earn a $10,000 to $15,000 monthly crew share with some boats making much more. The big money seems to be with the groundfish trawlers since they catch a huge volume of fish. Some pollock crew members make $50,000 for each three-month trip. With two pollock seasons (January to April, then June to October) they can make $100,000 if they work both trips! These fisheries are now tightly regulated by the Alaska Department of Fish and Game with not as many fish allowed to be caught—and not as much money to be made.

The average contract times vary among companies. Most boats sign their workers to a two-month contract. Even though there is fishing year round, most organizations prefer their crews to work two months on, then two months off, if the workers so choose. This way they'll always have fresh workers. It's best to ask each boat what its policy is and determine what's best for you. Longlining and trawling are incredibly intense work and may be too difficult for some people. For greenhorns, it's recommended that if you get a job on one of these boats, it should be during the calmer summer months.

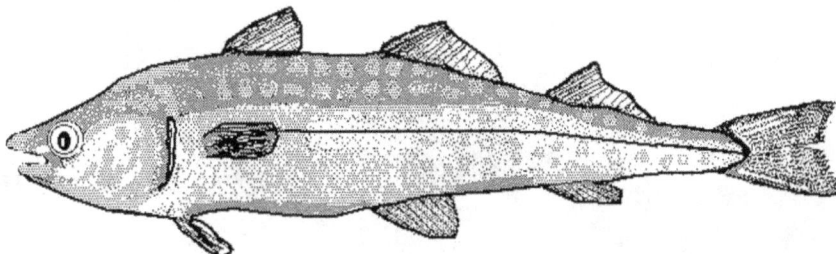

ALASKAN TRAWLER

LENGTH: 145 to 360 FEET
SPEED: 15 NAUTICAL MILES PER HOUR (KNOTS)
STORAGE: 1,500 TONS OF FINISHED PRODUCT
CREW: 25 to 50 PERSONS, DEPENDING ON SIZE

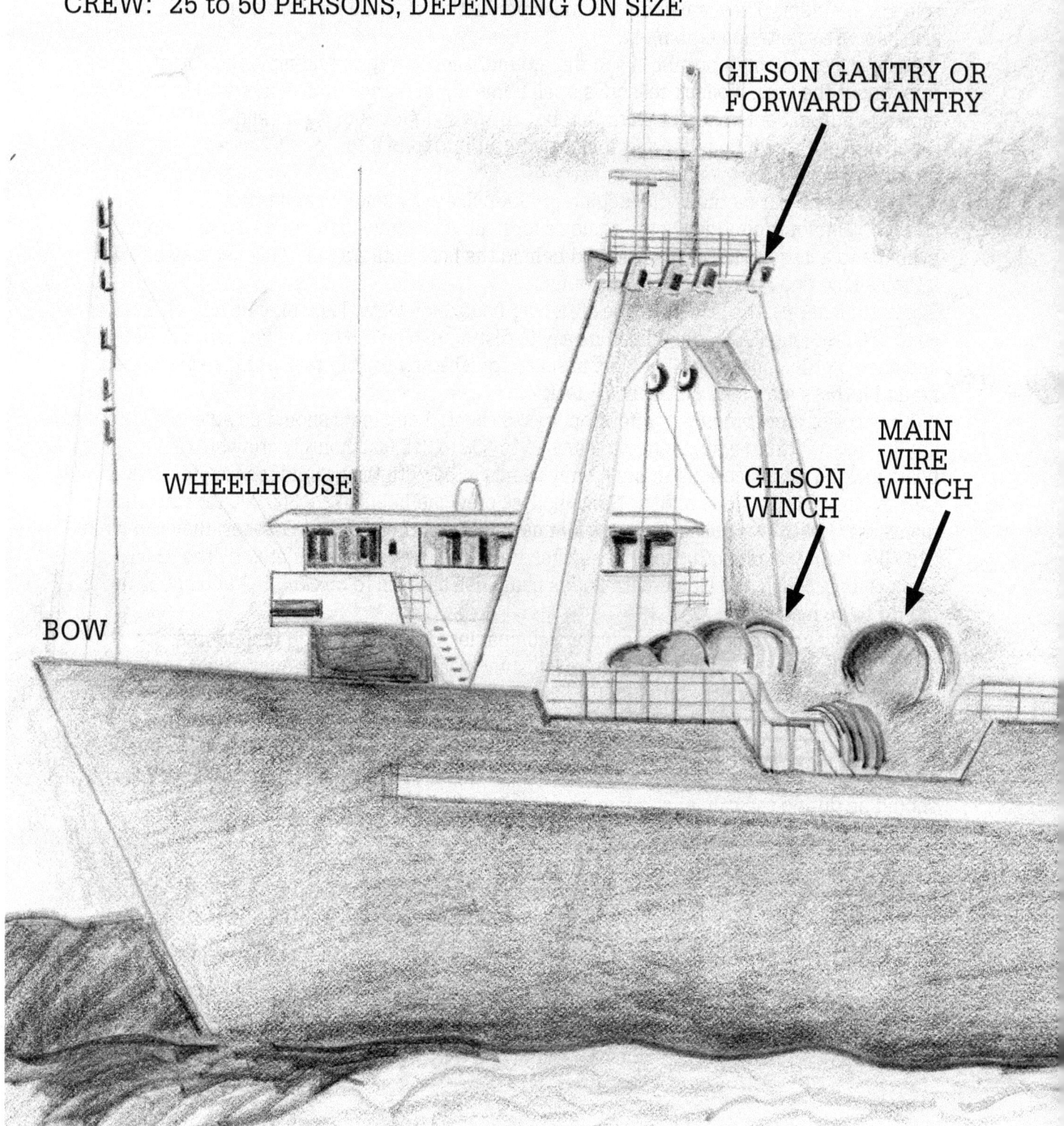

GILSON GANTRY OR
FORWARD GANTRY

MAIN
WIRE
WINCH

GILSON
WINCH

WHEELHOUSE

BOW

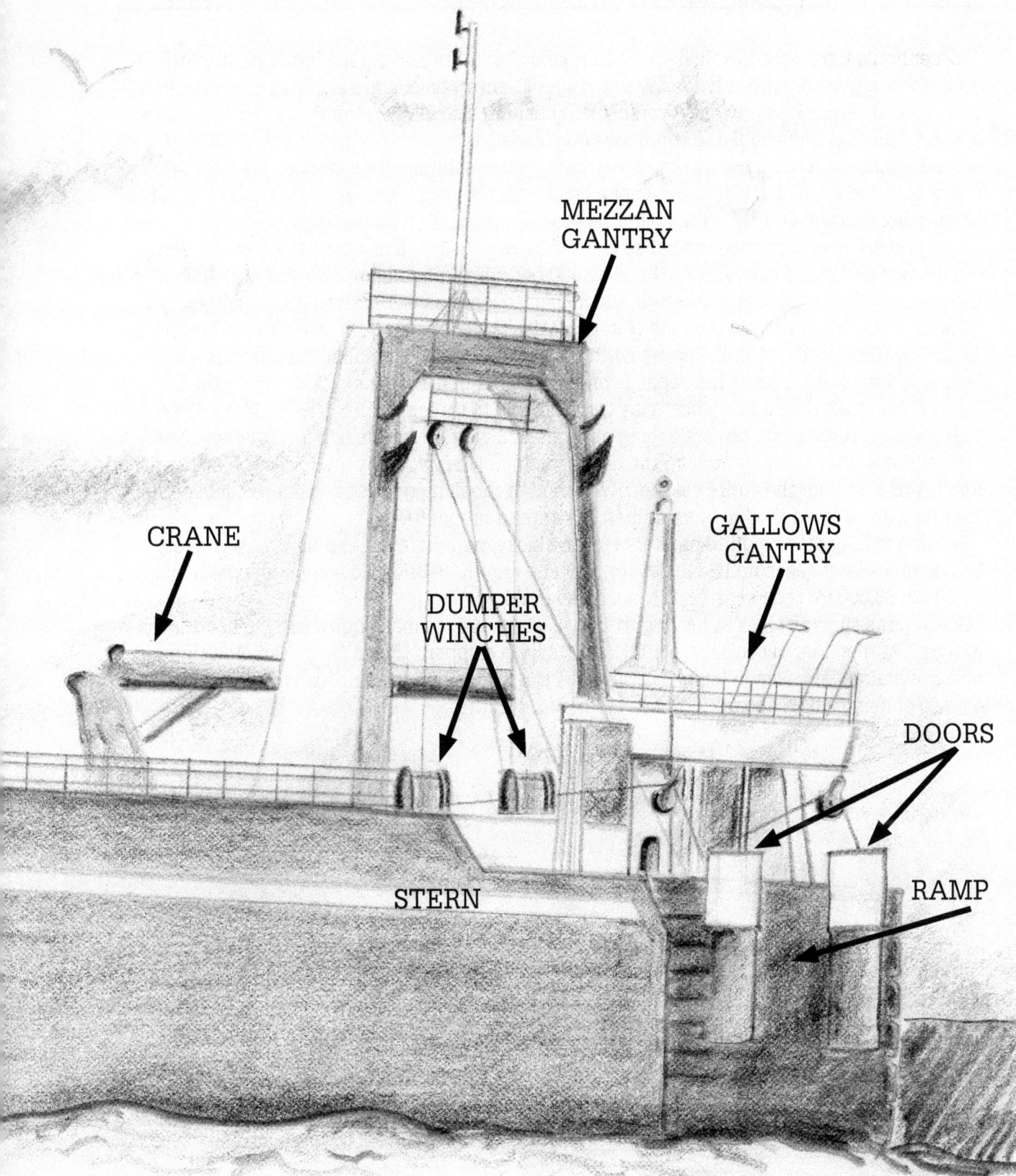

MEZZAN
GANTRY

CRANE

GALLOWS
GANTRY

DUMPER
WINCHES

DOORS

STERN

RAMP

Illustration by Janet Maricich Loftus

39

HERRING

Greenhorns interested in salmon or halibut jobs should try herring fishing first. Its slow pace offers a good opportunity for any newcomer to enter the commercial fishing industry as a deck hand. Since it's fairly easy work, herring fishing also allows ample time for a person to adjust to the working and living conditions on a boat.

The method most often used to catch herring is purse seining. It's essentially the same operation used in salmon seining, except a smaller net is used. Airplanes are used to spot the herring from above, and radio their sightings to their partner boats below.

The primary reason herring are fished is for their roe. In Japan, it's preferred over caviar. Buyers pay fishermen between $300 and $1,500 per ton, depending on the size and quality of the sac roe. The leftover meat is often sold as bait to longline and crab boats.

Herring are fished statewide in the waters of Alaska. The fishing season starts in Southeast Alaska in March and gradually moves north until mid-June. The amount of time a crew is committed to work varies. This depends on the number of areas where their boat fishes.

A crew contract on a herring boat may last from one to three months. The majority of this time involves traveling to remote fishing grounds and waiting for the fish to show up. The actual time a crew spends catching the fish is minimal. In fact, many areas allow boats to fish for only one hour for the entire season. Even though the fishing time is so limited, most crew members are still required to work at least a month in preparation.

Herring fishing may be quite profitable for the lucky, patient few. It's a hit or miss fishery. Some crew shares reach up to $40,000 for only one month's work! Most crew members make $4,000 to $8,000 for their share, but some make nothing.

Greenhorns shouldn't look at herring fishing as just a way to make quick cash. They should look at it as a builder of confidence and contacts with skippers. Since many herring skippers also run halibut and salmon boats, anyone who can prove their worthiness will have a good chance of being asked aboard for these other opportunities.

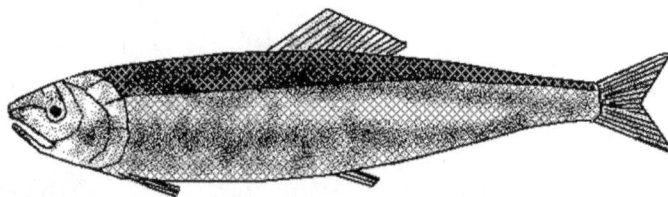

CRAB

The crabbing industry in Alaska provides year-round employment with high earning potential. The three types of crab fished are king, tanner (opilio crab) and dungeness.

King crab fishing offers the opportunity to make a huge amount of money in a very short period of time. It's possible to make up to $60,000 during the two-to-four week king crab season in October and November! The big money isn't as easy as it sounds: The work is very dangerous. Also, to get hired for the short king crab season, most skippers require that you work the long tanner crab season as well. King crab are caught primarily in the Bering Sea, Bristol Bay and the Aleutians, but there's also a fishery in Kodiak. The main ports are Dutch Harbor and Kodiak.

Tanner crab boats employ thousands of crew members each year during the long, cold winter months. The season lasts from mid-November to late-April. Some boats will have two separate crews, one at the beginning, and one at the end of the season. A deck hand on a tanner crab boat can make $50,000 for a two-month contract. Most skippers will hire only the most experienced seamen to work in this fishery. Much of the hiring is done out of Seattle at the Fisherman's Terminal. The main port for tanner crab fishing is Dutch Harbor.

Dungeness isn't as lucrative as tanner or king crab fishing, but it offers the best opportunity for greenhorns. Dungeness crab are primarily caught in the calm, inside waters of Southeast Alaska. It's a slower, safer pace than the king or tanner crab fisheries and therefore, easier for newcomers to catch on. You won't make a fortune fishing dungeness—maybe $15,000 for two months—but you might add to your earnings by occasionally catching other fish, too. Most skippers have diversified to fish salmon and groundfish as well. The season is open twice during the year—once from June through August, then again from October through November. The main ports for dungeness crab are Petersburg, Sitka, Ketchikan, Yakutat and Kodiak.

All crab are caught by a method called pot fishing. A baited, steel-and-mesh cage, called a "crab pot," is lowered to the bottom of the ocean and marked above the surface with a rubber bag buoy. When the bait attracts the crab, they enter the pot, are trapped, and then hoisted aboard. The sizes of crab pots vary, ranging from the 3-foot wide 70-pound dungeness pot, to the 8-foot wide 1,000-pound king crab pot. A crab fishing vessel is easy to distinguish since it usually has hundreds of these pots stacked on the back deck.

The work on a crab boat is extremely challenging with only the most tenacious deck hands meeting its demands. After stacking pots and coiling lines in 30-foot seas, one soon realizes why crabbing is rated as the number one most dangerous fishing job. The king crab and tanner crab fisheries should be left to experts with a lot of boat experience. However, dungeness crabbing in Southeast Alaska is something that a greenhorn may benefit from.

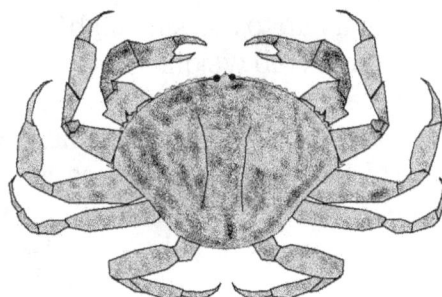

SO...YOU WANT TO BE A CRABBER

Many people are interested in working within the Alaskan crab fisheries but haven't a clue as to what is involved. All that they know about crab is what they see on *Deadliest Catch*—and that it's something you pay a pile of money for when you order it at Red Lobster. Yes, crab is expensive to the consuming public, but this is due to the difficulty factor related to the harvesting of these tasty crustaceans.

Crab fishing is incredibly dangerous and difficult work. Therefore, the crews must be paid well to compensate for their extreme efforts. Most of the fishing takes place during the winter months in the Bering Sea while crews encounter subfreezing weather conditions and hurricane force winds. To put it bluntly, it is not a fun time. Although the monetary reward is excellent (with some crews making $60,000 for a few weeks worth of king crab fishing), the sad truth is that a handful of these fishermen will never make it to shore to spend their money—a harsh reality about this dangerous job!

Crab fishing is definitely not something that an inexperienced seaman wants to try. Due to its danger factor, crabbing jobs are reserved for the salty dogs with a few years of fishing under their belts. For someone who is truly interested in crabbing, it is suggested that they first gain experience in the salmon fisheries — then give crabbing a try. It may be worth your while.

The Basics of Crabbing

Although there are several different crab fisheries in Alaska, the very basics of crab fishing remain the same among all.

Crab are caught by dropping a baited metal cage, or pot, into the water and letting it sit on the ocean floor long enough to attract the crab, lure them into the pot and trap them. The pot is then pulled on board and the crab are placed in a holding tank. The size of the pots vary from small, light pots used for dungeness crab in Southeast Alaska, too heavy 8-feet by 8-feet by 3-feet, 1,200 pound pots used for Bering Sea fishing. Each pot may contain up to 200 king crab weighing 12 pounds each or 1,000 tanner crab weighing 2 to 3 pounds each. Most crab boats don't exceed a total pot count of more than 250.

Crab fishing is a very difficult fishery in many different respects. For one thing, the weather is so awful that the conditions may make it nearly impossible to work. The Alaska

It's a little-known fact that Dutch harbor Alaska was attacked by the Japanese in World War II. Many people who look for jobs in Dutch Harbor will live in the old army bunkers until they find a boat that they can live and work on.

Department of Fish and Game manages the fishery with a set quota for allowable catch —the same type of IFQ system that is used with other fish. Once a boat catches their quota, their season is over. With some boats grossing over $1 million for several week's work, it usually isn't company policy to take the day off, even if it means working in 40-foot seas and 80-knot winds. Although most of the boats are built for rough weather, the 58-foot to 165-foot long vessels still take quite a beating.

The living conditions on most crab boats are basically miserable. Most crews average less than one hour of sleep a night during king crab season and less than four hours of sleep per night for tanner or opilio crab season. It is rare that you will ever get a cooked meal or enough time to eat one even if one were prepared. For many crab fishermen, their fishing-season diet consists primarily of Ding Dongs, Pringles and Pepsi.

Of course, for anyone to put up with this kind of misery, the final paycheck better be worth it, right? Many times it is for the crazy, elite fishermen that call themselves crabbers. For the short king crab season, it's possible for some crew members to make over $60,000! For the four-month tanner crab season, from January to April (it takes longer to fulfill the tanner crab quota), many crew members in the Bering Sea make in the neighborhood of $50,000.

It may seem that you should simply get a job for the short king crab season, make 60 grand, and then lay on the beach enjoying life for the rest of the year. Well, it's not quite that easy! To fish for king crab is a privilege that must be earned and most boats won't give you that opportunity unless you agree to fish the entire tanner crab season as well.

The pay scale for crew members on a crabber is as follows: You will be paid 4 percent to 6 percent of the total gross boat stock with the higher percentages being paid to the cook, engineer and first mate. When it comes to the fuel and food bill, many boats will not charge the crew for these expenses, but there are also those that will, so it all depends on the policy of the boat in question. And if it wasn't tough enough already, the crab must remain alive in order for you to get paid. If you deliver any dead crab to the the processor, you won't get paid for them.

There are many different duties on a crab boat. Some of these jobs include chopping bait and placing it in pots, sorting crab and stacking pots, running the hydraulics, chipping ice, and

For Bering Sea fishermen, telephone poles are a common unit of measurement when referring to the size of ocean swells. As in, "Those waves are higher than telephone poles!" (About 30-feet high.)

Steller sea lions love to play with the bags on crab pots, often popping them— resulting in lost pots, or entire strings of lost pots. r

much more. Some boats have specific deck duties, but many boats rotate these jobs.

The fact is that crabbing is dirty, hard, unpleasant, miserable work. Another fact is that you can make a huge amount of money doing it. If the money outweighs the pain, as it does for many people, crab fishing may be for you!

The Endless Flow of Work on a Crabber

Hour in and hour out for endless amounts of time you will repeat the same job over and over and over again on a crabber. Whether you're working the rail, or running the block, throwing the hook, running the coil or crane, stacking pots or throwing shots and bags, you will be working your tail off hour after hour after hour after hour to the point that your hands feel like they're going to fall off. The following steps represents the flow of work on a crab boat in the order performed by the crew:

1. Throwing the grappling hook.
2. Pulling it to the boat.
3. Putting the line through the power block in skinny block, and helping bags around and through the block.
4. Coiling by hand, or letting the coiler do it for you.
5. Attaching the pot to the picking boom gearmatic.
6. Hauling the pot on deck as it swings aboard.
7. Placing the pot on the launcher.
8. Opening the crab pot door.
9. Dumping crab on deck or on the sorting table.
10. Sorting and throwing the crab into the hole.
11. Chopping 50 pound blocks of frozen herring in a chopper and placing this in bait jars.
12. Dropping the pot in the water for further fishing (if fishing is good).

PARTS OF A CRAB POT

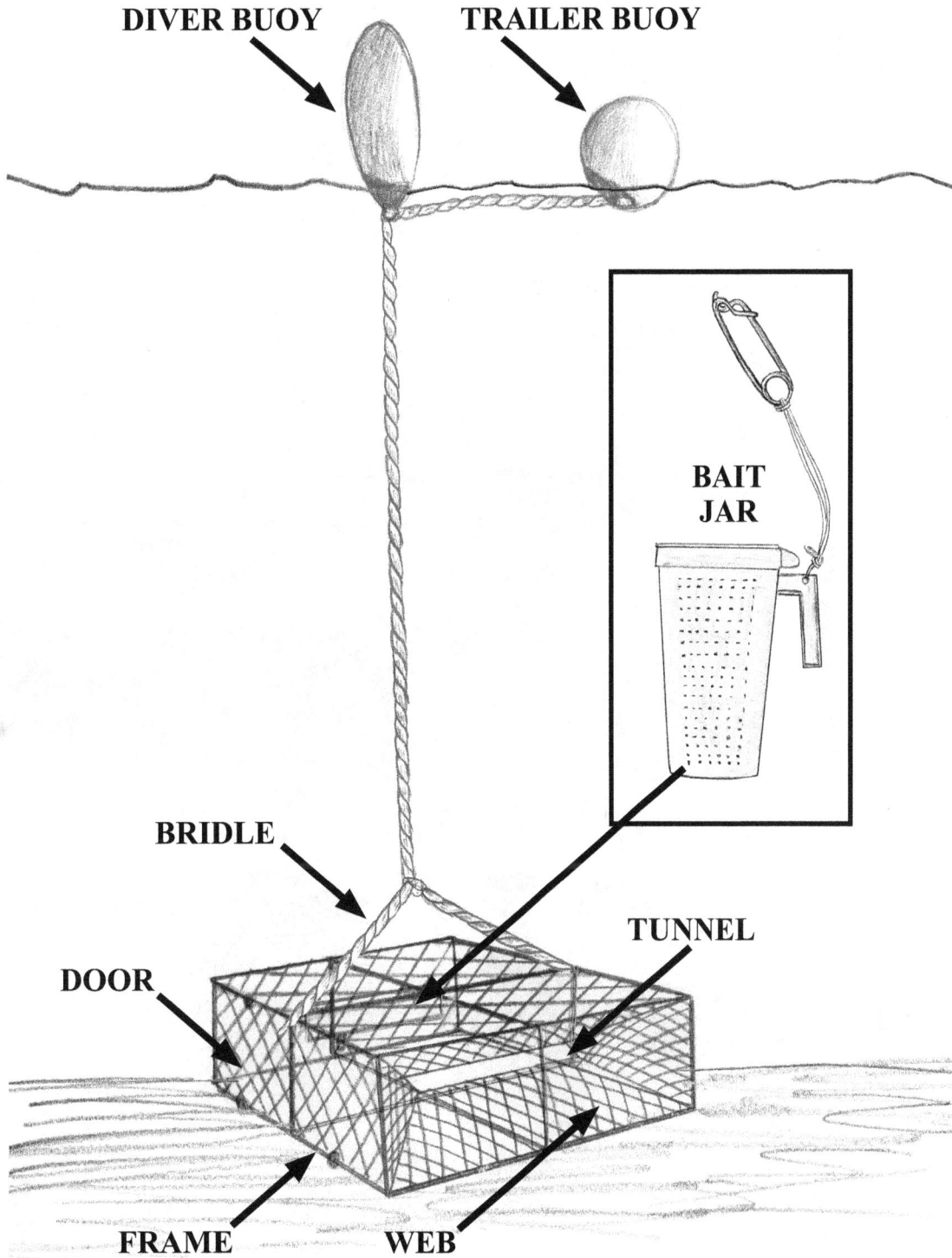

DIVER BUOY

TRAILER BUOY

BAIT JAR

BRIDLE

TUNNEL

DOOR

FRAME

WEB

ALASKAN CRABBER

LENGTH: 58 to 165 FEET
SPEED: 10 to 15 NAUTICAL MILES PER HOUR (KNOTS)
STORAGE: 100 TONS
CREW: 6 to 10 PERSONS, DEPENDING ON BOAT

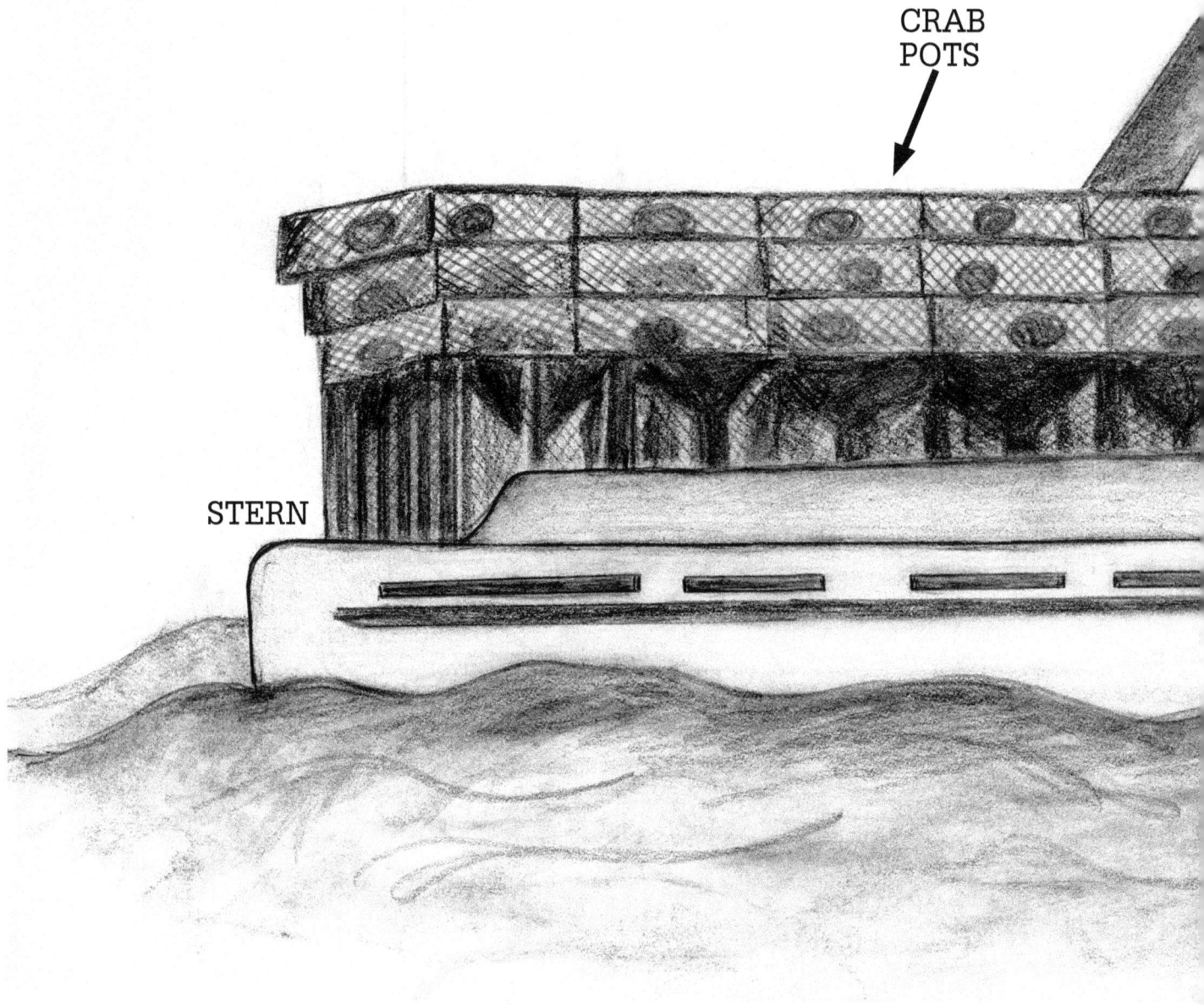

CRAB
POTS

STERN

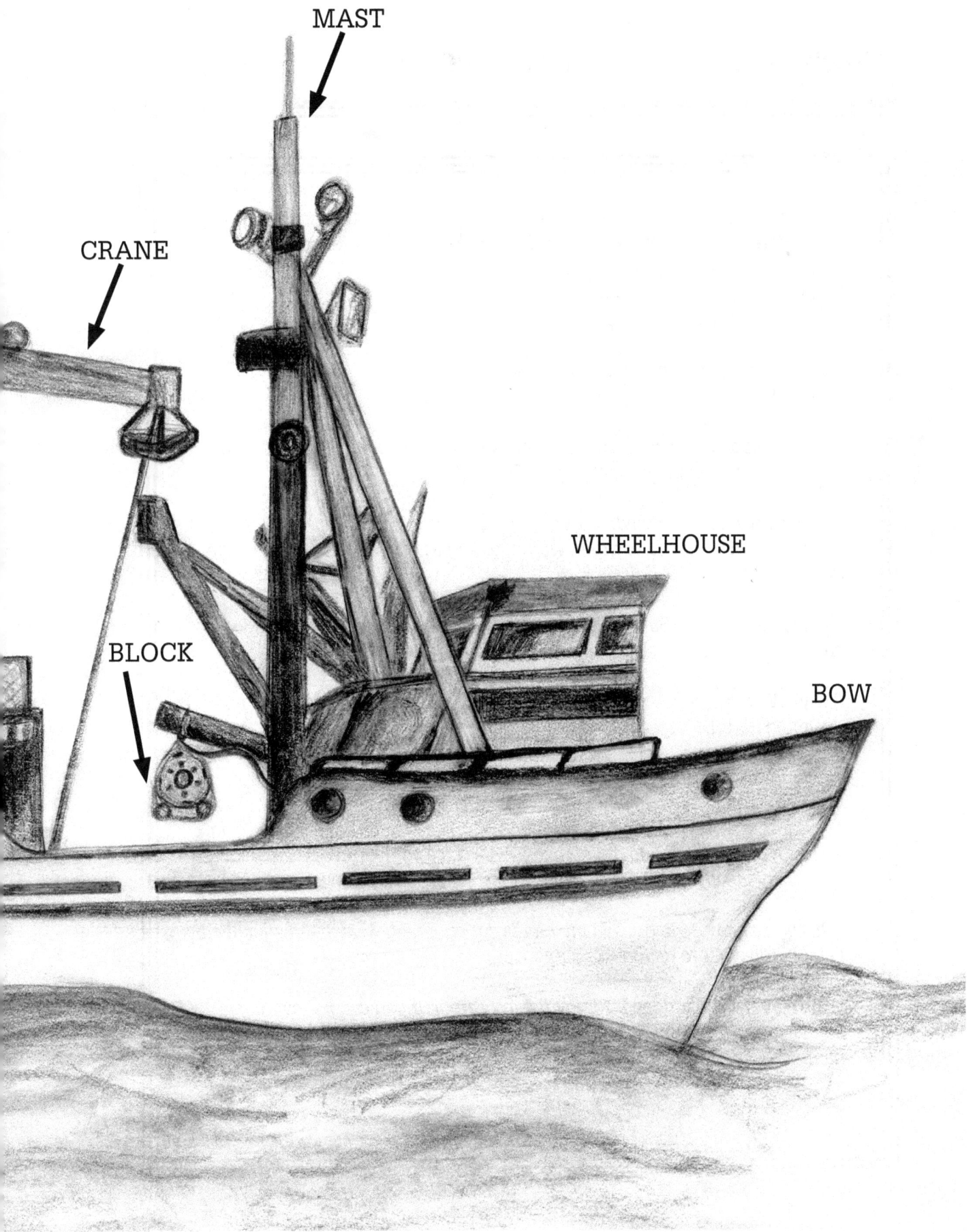

MAST

CRANE

WHEELHOUSE

BLOCK

BOW

Illustration by Zoë Fernandez

ANONYMOUS JOURNAL ENTRIES FROM ALASKAN CRABBERS

Commercial fishing is rated as one of the 10 most dangerous jobs you can have. Here are some anonymous journal entries from Alaskan crabbers.

"I never woke up with pain until I went crabbing. I went through a jar of Advil in a week."

"I never saw it rain once, but it snowed like crazy."

"This has to be better than any roller coaster in the world! The feeling of riding up in a wave, then dropping nearly 30 feet, is incredible! At the top, it feels as if you are weightless—just floating!"

"I always wanted to see what it was like to be in this type of weather—seeing this 25-foot wall of green water coming at you, knowing that you're going to eat it."

"Some boats are like Safeway with walk-in freezers and every type of ice cream. Other boats suck when it comes to food!"

"Why? Why did I want to come back up here?!! The human body was not designed for this!"

"Sometimes, I am so cold and my body hurts so bad that tears just start rolling down my face. I want to be anywhere but here and I know there is no chance in the world that it is going to happen. Then they start flowing. So I lean over the rail and get sprayed in the face so that no one else can see what is really going on. It is sad... But I just can't handle it anymore."

"On the last day, I almost had my hands cut off, and got my head squashed. I can hardly wait to get off this tub!"

"This may have just done it for my fishing career. If you can believe this, I actually thought about getting hurt so I can just get home. I am in so much pain—what's a little more?!"

A big brown bear with a big dog salmon, at McNeil Falls, AK.

At the tender, sucking up a huge load of herring.

Pulling a pot aboard.

MORE ALASKAN FISHING BOATS

SPORT FISHING
BOAT

LONGLINER

GILLNETTER

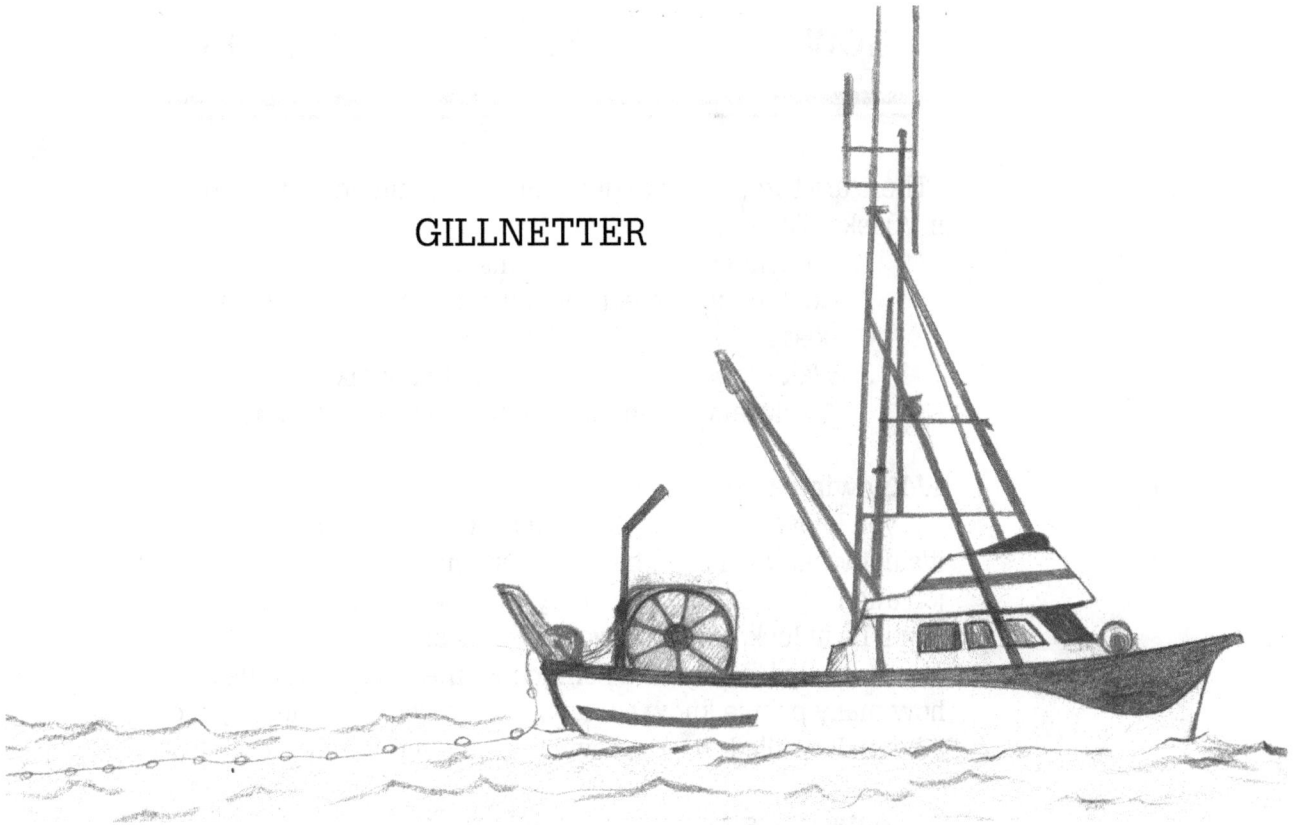

TROLLER

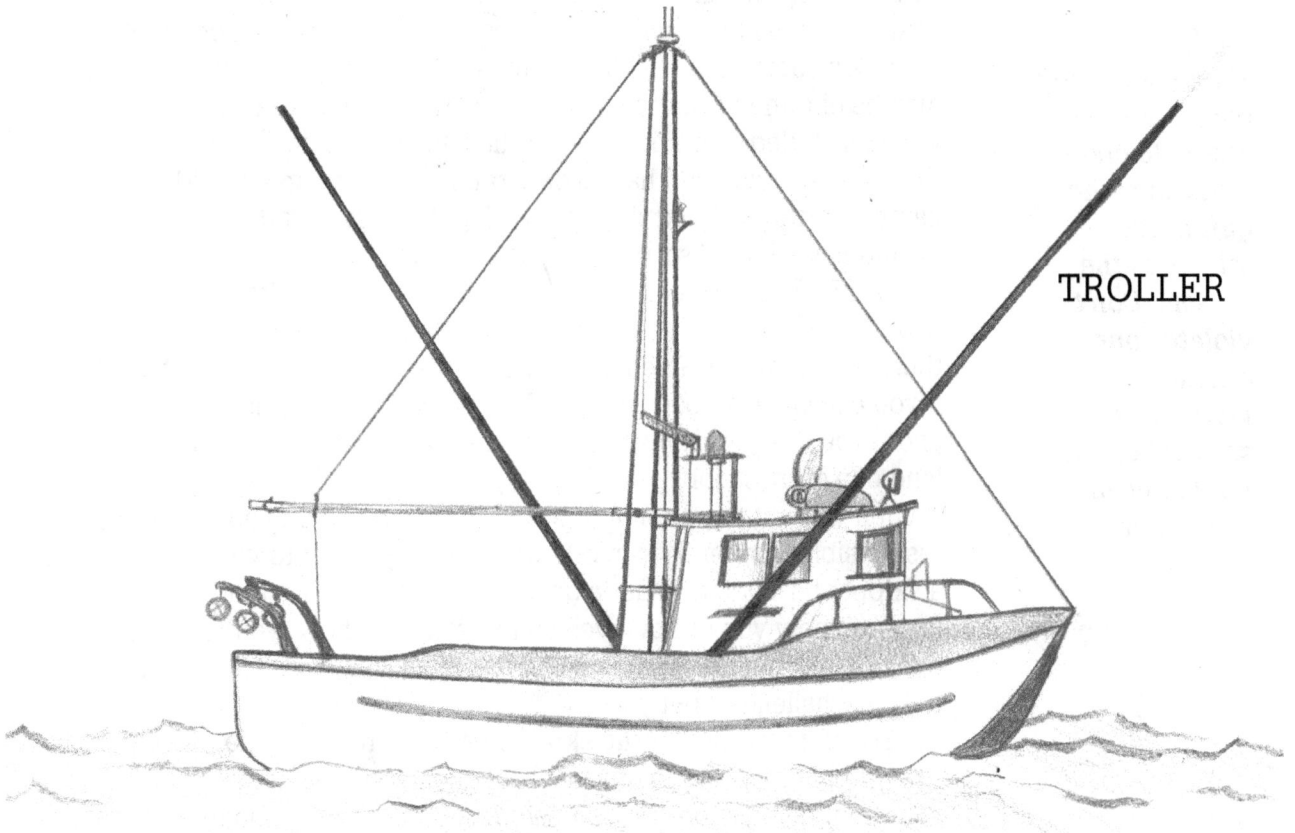

Illustration by Zoë Fernandez

HOW TO GET A JOB ON A FISHING BOAT

There are three ways to get a job on a commercial fishing boat in Alaska. They include:

1. Knowing someone who runs a boat.
2. Contacting someone you don't know who owns a boat and asking them for a job.
3. Waiting until the last minute, then walking the docks in Alaska and asking if anyone needs a deck hand.

1. Knowing a skipper.

If you know a skipper, you're in luck. As in many businesses, it's not what you know, but who you know. Ask your friend for a job and be persistent. Hopefully, he'll need a deck hand—and you'll be in luck. Also, tell your friends and relatives that you are currently looking for a fishing job in Alaska. You'd be surprised how many people know someone—who knows someone who runs a boat. It's called the "grapevine effect," and it may work for you.

2. Contacting a skipper you don't know.

Fortunately, for those who don't have personal contacts in the commercial fishing business, it's possible to obtain a list of people who own commercial fishing permits. This is public record and may be obtained from the Alaska Department of Fish & Game. We've included a complete list in the back of this book to save you the time, expense and hassle of obtaining it for yourself. With these names, addresses, and the tips you'll get by reading this guide, you should have a good start to finding a job on a fishing boat.

Over 17,000 commercial fishing permit holders are listed in this book. With an average of four crew positions available per boat, there are many possible jobs just from the people mentioned here. If you can write a good letter and compose a convincing resume— and if you're also very persistent—there's a good chance you could land one of these jobs.

When you put together your letter and resume, you should sound responsible, cooperative and hard-working. It's up to you to show a skipper he's going to get a good deal by hiring you. Since he doesn't know you or how well you'll work on a boat, you're going to have to convince him to give you a chance sight unseen. It's a difficult challenge—but you can do it.

✓ **You must convince the skipper you're a responsible person.** Draw from any past job or school-related experiences that make you seem responsible. You should include as many good references by respected persons as possible, including managers and

Skippers usually don't take too kindly to crew members who quit in the middle of the season. Don't violate your contract to work the whole season—or you might become shark bait.

professors. To verify that you're a hard worker, you should also include the starting and ending dates of your past employment, as well as the addresses and phone numbers of previous places you've worked. Also, if you try to stay out of trouble and are enthusiastic about life in general, you should convey this message. A good attitude is very important to many skippers.

✓ **You must persuade the skipper that you could be an asset to him on his boat.** You can do this by concentrating on your past positions and telling him how your experience could help on the boat. For instance, if you've worked in a restaurant as a waiter or chef, tell him you have a lot of good recipes in mind and would be willing to assume responsibility as the cook. If you've worked in a gas station and have some mechanical skills, tell him this. It's possible he'll sign you up as the engineer or to help out in the engine room. If you're very physically fit, participate in a lot of sports, and are strong, mention these facts. They'll help strengthen your case and make the skipper think of you as a capable person. Of course, if you have any previous boat experience, by all means, tell him!

✓ **You must convince the skipper he's going to get a good deal if he hires you.** There are several ways to do this. If your potential employer is from Seattle, tell him you'll travel there for two weeks during winter or spring break to help him get ready for the fishing season. He may not take you up on this offer, but at least he'll know you're enthusiastic about working. Above all, you need to let the skipper know you're flexible and willing to accommodate the boat's schedule. For example, if he wants you to start working in Alaska on May 15, you must be willing to deal with employers and professors so you can leave for Alaska when you're needed. Fortunately, some teachers and employers are quite understanding when it comes to commercial fishing jobs. In fact, most wish they could go themselves.

✓ **Offer to work at a half-share your first year.** What this means is you're willing to work as an apprentice. When you work for a half-share, you get paid at half the normal rate. For example, if the skipper usually pays a crew share of 10 percent, you'll get paid 5 percent. This doesn't mean you can work half as hard. Actually, it usually means you'll end up working twice as hard as everyone else.

Many people don't like the idea of working at a half-share, but you should look at salmon fishing as more than a one-season

The competition between the boats in Alaska is fierce. Commercial fishing is considered a sport by many skippers. The one who catches the most fish wins!

get-rich-quick scheme. In fact, many commercial fishermen start out their first year at a reduced rate. The author of this book, for example, made $16,000 working at a half-share during his first summer in Alaska, and made $35,000 a few summers later working at a full-share. You should view fishing as a seasonal job that has the potential to support you for the next few years.

A WAY TO GET HIRED

Offering to work at a half-share is probably the best, sure-fire way to get hired on a boat by someone you don't know. If you offer to cook and work at half-share—and if you're persistent and have a good attitude—you'll be virtually irresistible to skippers.

If you work at a half-share your first year, you'll get your foot in the door, meet other skippers and have a good chance of getting hired back the following year.

Think of it as an internship or apprenticeship—but instead of working for free as you would with these arrangements, you're working for a half-share. And even at that, you still may be able to make between $10,000 and $20,000 your first year. Of course, you should start out trying to get a job at full share. But if you're having a difficult time, tell the skipper you'll work for a half-share. It might be the key to a job!

One thing you should keep in mind is that skippers are professionals. No, they don't wear coats and ties when they go to work, but they have about a million dollars invested in their boats, gear and permits. For the most part, they're very shrewd businessmen. Many skippers have college degrees and a lot of them have other professions during the rest of the year. They take commercial fishing very seriously and expect their crews to take it seriously, too. As a result, they won't hire an inexperienced person unless they have some assurance that the applicant will be a good deck hand and an asset to the operation. You can convey this message to a potential employer in your resume.

When you put your letter and resume together, try to make them as neat and concise as possible. Take the time to make everything perfect. If you decide to write a form cover letter, make it sound like it isn't. And it's always a good idea to send a picture of yourself so potential employers can become more familiar with you.

With a little research, it may also be possible to reach potential employers by connecting with them on Facebook. If you choose to approach employers this way, it would be wise to make sure your own Facebook page doesn't have any negative postings that could ruin your chances of getting hired. Another online tool to consider when job hunting is Craigslist, as many skippers and seafood processors use this site to place job listings.

Most skippers are quality people who are equal opportunity employers as long as you're physically capable of handling the job. There are some skippers, however, who may discriminate openly when it comes to race or sex. Try not to let them phase you. Pass them up with dignity, and be glad you're not fishing with them. Living and working in an environment where you have to tolerate these backward attitudes wouldn't be worth your while for any amount of money. Don't let any kind of pre-judice discourage you from joining the many men and women of all races who are working hard to catch salmon and feed the world!

Be persistent! Don't give up! Write a million letters! Contact as many employers as you can! Hurry—don't waste any time! But if these tactics don't work, you still have the option of walking the docks to find work.

3. Walking the docks.

If it's late in the game and you still don't have a job, your only option may be to walk the docks. See the chapter entitled, "Walking the Docks For Salmon Jobs: The Strategic Approach" for some advice about this method of finding a job.

Go for it! Good luck!!!

A commercial fishing permit can cost a skipper between $20,000 and $100,000 to purchase, with some Southeast salmon permits running up to $250,000.

HOW TO WRITE A LETTER OF APPLICATION

Johnny Pukester
131313 Mockingbird Lane
Hangover, Maryland 00077
(202) 999-9999

February 19, 2013

Captain Clyde Yellalot
1234 Lettergo Lane
Bay of Pigs, WA 98991

Dear Clyde:

   My name is Johnny, and I'm <u>very</u> interested in working with you this summer on the Arctic Desperado. It's been a goal of mine to work on a purse seiner in Alaska for a long time, so I'm doing everything possible to land a job. I'm a sophomore at McGoo State U and am looking for a summer job that could keep me busy until I'm finished with graduate school.

   I realize that it's hard for you to consider me for a job since you have never met me, and especially since I've never worked on a salmon fishing boat before. As for my lack of fishing experience, my main disadvantage is being raised in an environment where the opportunity to work on a boat was not readily available. That's why I'm writing you this letter. I am one of the hardest workers you'll ever see, and I'd like to prove it.

   For my first year with you, I am willing to work at half-share. I've worked as a sous chef at Chez Puree restaurant in Kalamazoo, MD for the last two years, and if you give me the opportunity, I will most definitely be able to cook up some of the best boat food you've ever had. I also had the opportunity to work for five years at Ed's Gas Station in Hicksville, MD, where I became quite proficient at diesel and electrical repair. I have competed in several Mr. Olympia body-building contests, so I can assure you that I won't have any problem when it comes to physically handling the work. Also,   as a hobby, I frequently go on the deep-sea all-day fishing boat and I have no problem with seasickness.

   I will be driving to the state of Washington over spring break to further pursue a fishing job. Perhaps we could speak in person when I visit. At that time, I would be willing to help you with any work on the boat or gear that's needed. Please, Mr. Yellalot, give me the opportunity to fulfill my goal of fishing commercially for salmon in Alaska. I will look forward to talking with you. Hopefully we'll be catching a lot of salmon together this summer in Alaska!

Sincerely,

Johnny Pukester

Johnny Pukester

RESUME EXAMPLE

This is a sample resume. You may create your own by using this format, or another if you choose.

Johnny Pukester
131313 Mockingbird Lane
Hangover, MD 00077
(202) 999-9999
jonathanpukester@emailaddress.com

SKILLS:

- Accomplished chef in Greco-Roman contemporary cuisine.
- Able to work long hours while maintaining work quality.
- Get along well with people.
- Knowledgeable about boats and navigation.
- Mechanically skilled.

ACHIEVEMENTS:

- Lead cook at Chez Puree restaurant, manage crew of six.
- Completely restored an old John Deere diesel tractor.
- Won "Lineman of the Year Award" at McGoo State football.
- Placed in Mr. Olympia body-building contest.
- Supported self through school by starting a painting business.
- Raised $4,000 as a volunteer for homeless children.

WORK EXPERIENCE:

2008 to Present. Chez Puree Restaurant, Kalamazoo, MD.
Work as the lead cook. Won several awards for innovative cuisine.

2003 to 2008. Ed's Gas Station, Hicksville, MD. Worked as a mechanic. Learned all
about diesel repair.

2001 to 2003. Dodger Stadium, Los Angeles, CA. Cooked and sold Dodger dogs. Consistently
had highest sales.

EDUCATION: Currently obtaining degree in Business Administration from McGoo State.

High school diploma in 1995 from Salt Creek High School, Surf City, CA.

INTERESTS: Surfing, snow boarding, mountain biking, bowling, bungee cord jumping, Yatzee.

PHYSICAL STATS: Height: 6"2' Weight: 235 lbs. Birthdate: 6-12-87

WALKING THE DOCKS FOR SALMON JOBS:
THE STRATEGIC APPROACH

Well, you've sent out a million resumes and given it your best shot. But you've had no response. So what's the deal?

Like any other job search, nothing is guaranteed. It all depends on the people you contact, the time you reach them and how persistent you are. So if you've had no luck and you still want to go salmon fishing in the summer, what should you do? You might want to try walking the docks.

If this is your decision, it's best to start as early as possible. In this case, you should have a clear game plan in mind to increase your chances for employment. While there are many ways to go about it, here's one plan you may want to follow.

✓ **Spring Break.** Early spring is a good time to look for a job on the docks. In the middle or end of March, there are still hundreds of fishing vessels with openings for one or more crew members. Since many Alaskan purse seiners are home-based in Washington, the port cities in this state are a good place to start walking the docks.

Washington is more accessible than Alaska, and is only a 20-hour drive from anywhere in the western portion of the United States. Furthermore, it's a fun drive. So you may want to grab a friend and make this a job hunt/vacation!

There are several cities in Washington where you can walk the docks. They're mostly around the Seattle area or an hour or two away. On your must-visit list should be Seattle, Bellingham, Gig Harbor, Everett and Anacortes. When you visit these cities, just ask where the fishing boats are. Somebody will be able to help you out. You'll know what type of boat to look for since there's an illustration of a purse seiner in this guide.

In the spring when the weather's getting better, skippers often spend hours working on their boats in preparation for the summer fishing season. Chances are good that many will be on their boats and available to talk to you.

When you're looking for a job, ask everybody! Ask the people on the boats, the people on the docks and the people working on the nets. Be friendly and enthused about landing a job.

You may also want to hand out your resume with your picture on it, including the phone number of the hotel or youth hostel where you're staying. Some fishermen may laugh when you hand them a resume, but it'll show them you're serious about getting a job. Furthermore, if your resume has your picture on it, they'll remember who you are.

Alaska is one of the few places in the world where you can see a hundred bald eagles flying in the sky at the same time.

It's also important to let people know you're willing to start working right away. Explain to the skippers that you took a week off and traveled to Washington to get a job. Tell them you'd like to help them work on their boats for the remainder of your vacation if they can ensure you a summer job. Don't expect to be paid for this work, though. You're getting your foot in the door and showing a potential boss what a good worker you are.

It may also be a good idea to visit the employment offices of the Alaskan canneries based in Seattle. That way you'll have an option open if you don't end up working on a boat.

If your spring trip doesn't result in a job, don't give up! Just go home and plan to come back in May.

Note: There's also a small, limited salmon-fishing industry in the Puget Sound area of Washington. It's not as lucrative as the Alaskan fishery because the government restricts the number of days that boats can fish in Puget Sound even more rigorously than it restricts openings and closures in Alaska.

If you get hired by a boat in Washington, make sure its destination is Alaska. Puget Sound boats are easy to identify because they have a very large metal reel on their back decks. Called a "drum," this reel is used to wrap up the net and isn't allowed on Alaskan purse seiners.

✓ **May 15.** Now is the time to leave for Alaska to continue your job search. If you can't start looking until June, that's fine. But by beginning no later than May 15, you'll get a head start on your competition.

You should go back to Washington and visit the same docks in Seattle, Bellingham, Everett, Gig Harbor and Anacortes that you visited during your spring break. Many times things change right before the season starts and crew members quit for various reasons. Be persistent. Start in the early morning and don't quit until sundown. If you get a job, very good! If you try your hardest, spend a few days looking and still can't get a job, it's time to go to Alaska!

✓ **Travel to Kodiak.** An inexpensive way to travel to Alaska is to drive up the Al-Can Highway and take the Alaska Marine Highway System (state ferry) to the city of Kodiak. For more information, you can call the ferry at (907) 465-3941 or visit their website at www.dot.state.ak.us/amhs to get a schedule of departures and arrivals. Remember: The ferry operates on certain days only, so you need to check ahead for information.

A successful boat relies on the crew to perform as a team. If the workers don't get along well, then the operation suffers. That's why many skippers will hire crew members based solely on their personalities.

Kodiak Harbor is
home to dozens
of enormous sea
lions that swim
and feed next to
the city dock.

The reason we suggest you start in Kodiak is because it's the largest fishing port in the entire state of Alaska and the salmon fishing season opens here first. The best time to get to Kodiak is at the end of May until about June 7.

The halibut season is in full swing in May. During this time, it's possible to pay for your trip to Alaska by baiting hooks and performing tasks for skippers who are preparing for the halibut season.

By doing this work, you might land a job on a halibut boat. If you do, get ready for the experience of bloody, sleepless, miserable hell. Some greenhorns may find that halibut fishing is too difficult, but most just grin and bear it. It's also very lucrative, with opportunities to make up to $10,000 for a week's work. But earnings depend on your boat and success.

Many halibut skippers also fish for salmon. If you show them you're a good worker, they may hire you on their salmon crew for the summer, or at least recommend you to a skipper who's still hiring.

The salmon fishing season starts in Kodiak around the 9th of June. So if you don't have a job lined up in Kodiak by then, you should go to Cordova and look there. Again, remember that the Alaska State Ferry travels to Kodiak on certain days of the week. Therefore, you should adjust your schedule accordingly. If you're serious about getting a fishing job, you should be in Cordova around June 9.

✓ **Cordova.** Cordova is our next stop since it's a very large fishing port and the season starts here around June 15. Keep your ears open to find out exactly when the first day of the season is. If you don't land a job, and you notice that all the boats are leaving the harbor to go fishing, don't be discouraged. It's just time to go to Ketchikan to look for a job!

✓ **Ketchikan.** It may seem that you're going the wrong way since you're now traveling south instead of north. The reason for this itinerary is that the salmon fishing season starts in Southeast Alaska around June 23, and you should be there when it opens. Ketchikan, Sitka, and Petersburg are the major fishing ports in this area.

Since Southeastern fishermen have lots of time off due to Department of Fish & Game closures and will be tied to the docks during the month of July, you could easily continue your search here for the rest of the summer. Or you could get a job at a cannery. If you don't want to give up, then there's one last hope for you: Go back to Kodiak.

✓ **Back to Kodiak.** Most years the Department of Fish & Game closes Kodiak Island for fishing from about June 25 through July 5 for a Fourth of July break. This holiday marks the halfway point in the fishing action in Kodiak. This is a time when many crew members who didn't work out or couldn't handle the work decide to quit. For you, it's a very good time to look for a job on the docks because there's little competition from other dock-walkers. You see, most people don't have the inside scoop you have, and they don't realize that many Kodiak fishermen quit around the Fourth of July. If you don't get a job by the Fourth, you can either continue your hunt or get yourself a job in a cannery. If you work in a cannery you might make $5,000 to $7,000 in take-home pay, which would still make your summer worthwhile!

✓ **August 10 - October 31.** Whether you're still walking the docks or working in a cannery, keep your ears open since this is a good time to pick up late-season fishing jobs. Since they've already made a lot of money, many fishermen get homesick in August and quit. If you're working in a cannery and offered a fishing job, by all means take it! Late-season fishing isn't as lucrative as the summer jobs, but you'll still make more than if you were working in a cannery.

We are merely presenting this idea as an example of one of the many strategies you may create for yourself. The job search plan we have presented here concentrates primarily in the areas of Kodiak, Prince William Sound and Southeast Alaska. There are many other excellent cities and areas where you may want to search, including Cook Inlet and Bristol Bay (if you choose to work on a gillnetter). Just keep an open mind with your search, and realize that there are many areas where you can look.

Tongass National Forest in Southeast Alaska is considered a rainforest, with Ketchikan receiving an average of 160 inches—or more than 13 feet—of rainfall per year.

NEWSPAPERS AND PERIODICALS

Newspapers and periodicals relating to the fishing industry, or catering to the citizens of prominent fishing ports, may be an excellent source of information and job leads. Sometimes, these publications carry classified ads of companies or private skippers needing help. Additionally, you can place an ad of your own stating your desire to work. This latter method, however, works best when searching for a job as a deck hand.

If you place a "work wanted" ad, it might be answered by a skipper who is hiring a crew.

National Fisherman
P.O. Box 7438
Portland, Maine 04112
www.nationalfisherman.com

Wrangell Sentinel
P.O. Box 798
Wrangell, AK 99929
www.thewrangellsentinel.com

Ketchikan Daily News
P.O. Box 7900
Ketchikan, AK 99901
www.ketchikandailynews.com

Pacific Fishing Magazine
1000 Andover Park East
Seattle, WA 98188
www.pacificfishing.com

Daily Sitka Sentinel
112 Barracks St.
Sitka, Alaska 99835
www.sitkasentinel.com

Petersburg Pilot
P.O. Box 930
Petersburg, AK 99833
www.petersburgpilot.com

Anchorage Daily News
P.O. Box 149001
Anchorage, AK 99514
www.adn.com

Homer News
3482 Landings St.
Homer, AK 99603
www.homernews.com

Kodiak Daily Mirror
1419 Selig St.
Kodiak, AK 99615
www.kodiakdailymirror.com

Bristol Bay Times
P.O. Box 241582
Anchorage, AK 99524
www.thebristolbaytimes.com

Juneau Empire
3100 Channel Dr.
Juneau, AK 99801
www.juneauempire.com

Peninsula Clarion
150 Trading Bay Road
Kenai, AK 99611
www.peninsulaclarion.com

PART 2

The Processing Industry

HOW TO GET A JOB IN THE PROCESSING INDUSTRY

If you're interested in working in the processing industry, this section is for you. These steps should lead you to securing a job in a cannery or shore-based processor, or on a floating processor or factory trawler.

1) Decide which area of processing you wish to pursue. Would you rather work on shore or at sea?

2) After you've decided, contact the companies that you feel are best for you. Many companies will mail you a job application or have one posted on their websites.

3) If you decide to request for a job application by mail or email, create a simple note asking for one. There's no need to spend a lot of time on this letter. These companies aren't hiring you for your English skills; they're hiring you for your fish-gutting skills.

4) Send your notes requesting job applications to the companies that are on one of the three lists included in this section. You may want to send a self-addressed stamped envelope with your request. This may speed up the company's response. However, it is not required.

5) Not all companies will respond to your letter. Some companies don't send out applications and prefer you to call or view their website for information. A couple of weeks after sending out your request letters, you will have received the majority of your applications.

6) Fill out all of the applications and mail them back to the companies. They may contact you later with further instructions.

7) If, after sending out your request letter, you didn't get a very good response, or if you're curious about your job prospects after completing and returning an application, you may want to give the companies a few phone calls. It never hurts to be persistent.

(SAMPLE LETTER)

Johnny Pukester
131313 Mockingbird Lane
Hangover, MD 00077
January 17, 2013

Dear Sir/Madam:

I am very interested in employment as a fish gutter with your company. Please send me any job information or applications that you may have.

Thank you very much.

Sincerely,

Johnny Pukester

Johnny Pukester

A note to save you time: It's perfectly acceptable to write a form letter like this example, and make photocopies of it to send to companies. This will save you the time of individually writing a letter to every company you wish to contact. It would be a nice touch, though, to sign the letter.

8) If you're still looking for a summer job, and it's the beginning of June, there is a decision you have to make. Are you going to stay home and mow your dad's lawn for the keys to his car, and a roll of quarters to spend at the arcade? Or are you going to go for the gusto, and travel north to Alaska?

9) If you decide to travel north to get a job, we wish you the best of luck. The majority of cannery workers are people who are hired off the street, or from one of the Alaska Employment Service centers. We have provided a list of these centers for you.

CANNERIES AND SHORE-BASED PLANTS

If working on a fishing boat doesn't sound like something you'd like to do, you might consider working in a cannery or shore-based processing plant. You won't earn as much as you would fishing, but you still may be able to clear $7,000 for two month's work.

The average amount employees are paid is around $7 an hour. However, you may be paid overtime of time-and-a-half for any hours worked over 40 in a one-week period. During the peak of the season, you may work 120 hours per week. The earnings add up fast.

Getting to the job site is the responsibility of the employee. Some employers, however, will provide an end-of-season bonus to pay the employee's airfare back to Seattle. This is only provided if the employee completes the entire season contract with the company.

Most canneries provide some sort of housing to their employees. It is usually a dorm-style accommodation with a public shower. Meals may also be included. Sometimes employees sleep in a trailer or tent. Many times, housing is provided on a first-come, first-served basis. Some canneries provide free housing, but others will deduct up to $10 per day directly from the employee's paycheck. This may be refunded if the employee completes his or her contract.

There are a variety of jobs available in canneries for men and women over 18 years of age. Canneries and shore-based plants hire mechanics, cooks, custodians, accountants, nurses, forklift operators, secretaries, truck loaders, dock workers, and people in dozens of other occupations. The majority of jobs, however, are on the processing line, where the fish are sorted, gutted, canned, cooked, or frozen, and turned into Grade 'A' Alaskan seafood products. Employers may or may not provide raingear, boots and gloves—so be sure to ask about this.

Most companies hire out of their Seattle headquarters during the fall, winter, and spring months, and will hire at the cannery locations in Alaska during the summer months. During the non-summer months, you may send these companies your resume or a letter requesting an application. After you send them your application, they may call you to conduct a telephone interview, or schedule a personal interview in Seattle. During the summer months, you may walk in and apply directly at the cannery locations in Alaska. It is best to do this immediately prior to, or during the peak periods of the season. You may also be hired through the Alaska Employment Service in the town that the cannery is based. Remember to bring your proper I-9 identification to avoid delays in being hired.

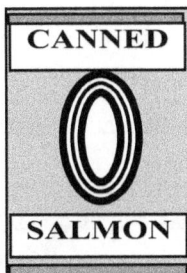

For more specific information regarding the different cannery locations and employee policies, contact the companies listed on the following pages:

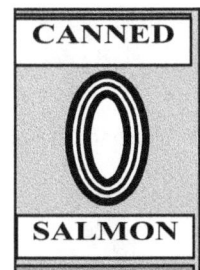

CANNERIES AND SHORE-BASED PLANTS

SHORE-BASED PROCESSORS

10th & M Seafoods
1020 M Street
Anchorage, AK 99501
www.10thandmseafoods.com

Alaskan Fish Factory LTD
800 Fish Dock Road
Homer, AK 99603
www.thefishfactory.net

Catch Sitka Seafood LLC
2614 Sawmill Creek Road
Sitka, AK 99835
www.northlineseafoods.com

57 Degrees North LLC
PO Box 288
St Paul Island, AK 99660
www.cbsfa.com57.html

Aleutia
PO Box 408
Sand Point, AK 99661
www.aleutia.org

Chugach Wild Salmon
PO Box 1125
Girdwood, AK 99587
www.alaskafishmarket.com

60° NORTH SEAFOODS LLC
PO Box 239
Cordova, AK 99574
www.sixtynorthseafoods.com

Alyeska Seafoods Inc
3015 112th AVE NE
Bellevue, WA 98004
www.westwardseafoods.com

Coal Point Trading Company
PO Box 674
Homer, AK 99603
www.welovefish.com

Alaska Blue Harvest Seafoods
2305 Watergate Way
Kenai, AK 99611
www.alaskablueharvestseafoods.com

APICDA Joint Venture Inc
302 Gold Street
Juneau, AK 99801
www.apicda.com

Coastal Cold Storage Inc
PO Box 307
Petersburg, AK 99833
www.coastalcoldstorage.com

Alaska General Seafoods
6425 NE 175TH ST
KENMORE, WA 98028
www.akgen.com

Aquatech Seafood LLC
6221 Petersburg Street
Anchorage, AK 99507
www.crabfactory.com

Copper River Fish Market
PO Box 2222
Cordova, AK 99574
www.copperriverfishmarket.com

Alaska Glacier Seafoods Inc
PO Box 34363
Juneau, AK 99803
www.alaskaglacierseafoods.com

Beachm Fishery Inc
PO Box 39
Kasilof, AK 99610
www.beachmfishery.com

Copper River Seafoods
1118 East 5TH Ave
Anchorage, AK 99501
www.copperriverseafoods.com

Alaska Wild Kenai Salmon LLC
831 Briny Circle
Anchorage, AK 99515
www.alaskawildkenaisalmon.com

Big Creek Fisheries LLC
3900 Railway Ave
Everett, WA 98201
www.deepseafisheries.com

Custom Seafoods
PO Box 2158
Soldotna, AK 99669
www.customseafoods.com

Alaska Wild Seafood Partners LLC
PO Box 1502
Cordova, AK 99574
www.alaskawildseafoodsllc.com

Captain Jacks Seafood Locker
PO Box 693
Seward, AK 99664
www.captainjacksalaska.com

DBA Wild Alaska Salmon & Seafood
PO Box 602
King Salmon, AK 99613
www.wildalaskasalmonandseafood.com

CANNERIES AND SHORE-BASED PLANTS

Dejon Delights Ltd
PO Box 712
Haines, AK 99827
www.dejondelights.com

Desire Fish Co Inc
2500 Donovan Ave
Bellingham, WA 98225
www.desirefish.com

E C Phillips & Son Inc
PO Box 7095
Ketchikan, AK 99901
www.ecphillipsalaska.com

Echo Lake Meats
PO Box 346
Soldotna, AK 99669
www.echolakemeats.com

Ekuk Fisheries LLC
2442 NW Market St #625
Seattle, WA 98107
www.ekukfisheries.com

False Pass Seafoods LLC
5303 Shilshole Ave NW
Seattle, WA 98107
www.tridentseafoods.com

Favco Inc
PO Box 190968
Anchorage, AK 99519
www.favcoinc.com

Fees Custom Seafood's
PO Box 790
Whittier, AK 99693
www.feescustomseafoods.com

Foodland Iga
615 W. Willourghby Ave
Juneau, AK 99801
www.foodland-iga.com

Golden Harvest Alaska Seafood LLC
2219 Rimland Drive
Bellingham, WA 98226
www.goldenharvestalaska.com

Haines Packing Co
PO Box 930
Haines, AK 99827
www.hainespacking.com

Homer Fish Processing
PO Box 2044
Homer, AK 99603
www.myalaskafish.com

Hooked Seafood
2315 Industrial Blvd
Juneau, AK 99801
www.hookedseafoodalaska.com

Icicle Seafoods Inc
PO Box 79003
Seattle, WA 98119
www.icicleseafoods.com

Icy Strait Seafoods Inc
2825 Roeder Ave
Bellingham, WA 98225
www.icystraitseafoods.com

International Seafoods of Alaska Inc.
PO Box 2997
Kodiak, AK 99615
www.isa-ak.com

Keta Seafoods
PO Box 1135
Craig, AK 99921
www.ketaseafoods.com

Kodiak Fresh Seafood
328B Shelikof Street
Kodiak, AK 99615
www.kodiakfreshseafood.com

Kodiak Wildsource
312 W Marine Way
Kodiak, AK 99615
www.kodiakwildsource.com

Kwikpak Fisheries LLC
2909 Arctic Blvd
Anchorage, AK 99503
www.kwikpakfisheries.com

LC Fisheries Inc
Po Box 17013
Seattle, WA 98127
www.leadercreekfisheries.com

Mystic Salmon
PO Box 126
Yakutat, AK 99689
www.mysticsalmon.com

North Pacific Seafoods Inc
4 Nickerson Street
Seattle, WA 98109
www.northpacificseafoods.com

Norton Sound Seafood Products
2701 Gambell Street
Anchorage, AK 99503
www.nortonsoundseafood.com

CANNERIES AND SHORE-BASED PLANTS

Northern Lights Smokeries LLC
PO Box 848
Petersburg, AK 99833
www.nlsmokeries.com

Seafood Producers Cooperative
2875 Roeder Ave Suite 2
Bellingham, WA 98225
www.spcsales.com

Whittier Seafood LLC
3 Lake Bellevue Drive
Bellevue, WA 98005
www.whittierseafood.com

Northport Fisheries INC
6105 61ST Ave SE
Snohomish, WA 98290
www.northportfisheries.com

Silver Bay Seafoods
208 Lake Street
Sitka, AK 99835
www.silverbayseafoods.com

Wild Premium Salmon LLC
PO Box 151
Raymond, WA 98577
www.wildpremiumsalmon.com

Ocean Beauty Seafoods
PO Box 70739
Seattle, WA 98127
www.oceanbeauty.com

Sitka Salmon Alaska Holdings LLC
216 Smith Street #B
Sitka, AK 99835
www.sitkasalmonshares.com

Wildfish Cannery LLC
PO BOX 93
Klawock, AK 99925
www.wildfishcannery.com

Pacific Seafood
317 Shelikof Street
Kodiak, AK 99615
www.pacificseafood.com

Tonka Seafoods Inc
PO Box 1420
Petersburg, AK 99833
www.tonkaseafoods.com

Yakutat Seafoods
900 Powell Ave SW
Renton, WA 98057
www.eefoods.com

Peter Pan Seafoods Inc
3015 112th Ave NE
Bellevue, WA 98004
www.ppsf.com

Trident Seafoods Corporation
5303 Shilshole Ave NW
Seattle, WA 98107
www.tridentseafoods.com

For the current, complete list of shore-based processors from the Alaska Department of Fish & Game, link to:

https://www.adfg.alaska.gov/index.cfm?adfg=fishlicense.holders

Pure Pacific Seafood Inc
7900 SE 28th Steet Suite 403
Mercer Island, WA 98040
www.dfbcompany.com

Unisea Inc
PO Box 97019
Redmond, WA 98073
www.unisea.com

Resurrection Bay Seafoods
PO Box1710
Seward, AK 99664
www.pacificseafood.com

Valdez Fisheries
PO Box 125
Valdez, AK 99686
www.valdezfisheries.org

Sea Level Seafoods LLC
PO Box 2085
Wrangell, AK 99929
www.pacificseafood.com

Western Alaska Fisheries
3015 112TH Ave NE
Bellevue, WA 98004
www.westwardseafoods.com

FLOATING PROCESSORS AND FACTORY TRAWLERS

Floating processors and factory trawlers are two types of large ships that process fish while afloat in the remote waters of Alaska. They can both exceed 300 feet in length and have crews of 100 or more workers each. The only difference between the two vessels is that factory trawlers catch most of the fish they process, whereas floating processors rely on other boats to deliver fish to them. The year-round function for both vessels is to process groundfish into filets, roe or surimi. They also process crab, herring and salmon.

The jobs on floating processors and factory trawlers are basically the same, except there are more deck-hand jobs on the trawlers. Most crew members are hired in non-deck positions, usually on the slime-line, where the fish are gutted and cleaned. Others will be roe-sorters or on the freezer crew. The pay for this type of work varies between $7 and $10 an hour. With lots of overtime, it's possible to earn $1,000 a week with some bonus potential. Since you're aboard ship for two to three months with no place to spend your wages, your savings add up.

There are many different policies regarding employment, food, room and travel expenses, which are set by the companies who own these ships. Some companies will pay for all expenses, while others will charge for meals, room and transportation. Also, some companies only allow their crews to work two months on, then two months off, but others will let their employees work as long as they want. Your best bet is to contact as many companies as possible to satisfy your particular needs. If you want to work on a floating processor or factory trawler, you must get hired before you go. These companies don't hire off the docks!

Working on a factory trawler or floating processor isn't very glamorous. You'll be working countless hours below the main deck, standing on your feet, gutting fish. You'll smell bad and get sick of looking at fish. It's monotonous, mindless work, which is the reason why there's such a high turnover rate in this industry.

There are many advantages to working on a processor or factory trawler. You'll make some good money and gain some valuable sea experience. After working for a few months, you'll know whether or not you want to pursue a fishing career by trying to get on a salmon or longline boat. There's also a chance that if you're a good worker on the slime line, you may be promoted to deck hand. These ships present year-round employment opportunities for almost 15,000 workers with many openings for greenhorns.

FLOATING PROCESSORS & CATCHER/PROCESSORS

FLOATING PROCESSORS

American Seafoods Co LLC
2025 First Ave - Suite 900
Seattle, WA 98121
https://www.americanseafoods.com

Beauty Bay of Washington LLC
23929 22nd Drive SE
Bothell, WA 98021

Cascade Fishing Inc
4201 21st Ave W
Seattle, WA 98199

Clipper Seafoods Ltd
641 West Ewing Street
Seattle, WA 98119
https://www.clipperseafoods.com/readme

East West Seafoods LLC
PO Box 124
Kodiak, AK 99615

F/V America's Finest
570 Kirkland Way
Kirkland, WA 98033
https://www.fishermensfinest.com/

Fishing Company of Alaska Inc
4201 21ST Ave W
Seattle, WA 98199
http://oceanpeaceinc.com/

FV Blue Gadus
2930 Westlake AVE N #300
Seattle, WA 98109
http://bluenorth.com/

Icicle Seafoods Inc
PO Box 79003
Seattle, WA 98119
http://www.icicleseafoods.com/

Kruzof Fisheries LLC
PO Box 3302
Seward, AK 99664
https://www.jrfisheries.com/contact.html

North Pacific Fishing Inc
570 Kirkland Way Suite 200
Kirkland, WA 98033
https://www.fishermensfinest.com/

Northline Seafoods
4690 Sawmill Creek Road
Sitka, AK 99835
https://www.northlineseafoods.com/

Ocean Fresh Seafood Co LLC
4257 24th Ave West
Seattle, WA 98199
http://signatureseafoods.com/contact-us/

Ocean Peace Inc
4201 21st Ave West
Seattle, WA 98199
http://oceanpeaceinc.com/

Paradigm Seafoods LLC
PO Box 1230
Cordova, AK 99574
https://www.paradigmseafoods.com/

Pavlof Fisheries LLC
3900 Railway Ave
Everett, WA 98201
https://www.deepseafisheries.com/

Pearl Bay Seafoods LLC
PO Box 1278
Homer, AK 99603
https://pearlbayseafoods.com/

PetersonPlus Wild Alaskan Foods
PO Box 1063
Kodiak, AK 99615
https://petersonplus.com/

Potters Own Fine Fish
PO Box 1472
Cordova, AK 99574

P/V Cape Greig
801 S Fidalgo Street
Seattle, WA 98108
https://www.eefoods.com

Sitka Wild Seafoods
PO Box 2016
Sitka, AK 99835
https://www.sitkawildseafoods.com/

Smackdown Salmon
1929 Sheridan Street
Port Townsend, WA 98368
https://www.smackdownsalmon.com/

Trident Seafoods Corporation
5303 Shilshole Ave NW
Seattle, WA 98107
https://www.tridentseafoods.com

US Fishing LLC
570 Kirkland Way Suite 200
Kirkland, WA 98033
https://www.fishermensfinest.com/

CATCHER/PROCESSORS

Alaska's Finest Seafoods
PO Box 6565
Sitka, AK 99835
https://www.alaskasfinestseafood.com/

Clipper Endeavor LLC
641 West Ewing Street
Seattle, WA 98119
https://www.clipperseafoods.com/

Fairweather Fish Co LLC
PO Box 6256
Sitka, AK 99835
https://www.fairweathersalmon.com/

FV Blue Ballard
2930 Westlake Ave N #300
Seattle, WA 98109
http://bluenorth.com/

Gulf Mist Inc
3900 Railway Avenue
Everett, WA 98201
https://www.deepseafisheries.com/

CATCHER/PROCESSORS & FACTORY TRAWLERS

Hartney Bay Seafood
PO Box 2416
Cordova, AK 99574
https://www.hartneybayseafood.com/

Seafreeze Alaska I LLC
1801 Fairview Ave East
Seattle, WA 98102
http://www.unitedstatesseafoods.com/

Shelfords Boat Ltd
PO Box 12946
Mill Creek, WA 98082
https://www.shelfordfisheries.com/

Sword Seafood Company LLC
236 Observatory Street
Sitka, AK 99835
https://www.swordseafood.com/

Trident Seafoods Corporation
5303 Shilshole Ave NW
Seattle, WA 98107
https://www.tridentseafoods.com/

FACTORY TRAWLERS

Alaska Longline LLC
2930 Westlake Ave N
Seattle, WA 98109
http://bluenorth.com/

Alaskan Leader Group LLC
8874 Bender Rd
Lynden, WA 98264
https://alaskanleader.com/

American Seafoods Company LLC
2025 1st Ave
Seattle, WA 98121
https://www.americanseafoods.com/

Arctic Fjord Inc
2727 Alaskan Way Pier 69
Seattle, WA 98121
https://www.arcticstorm.com/

Arctic Storm Inc
2727 Alaskan Way Pier 69
Seattle, WA 98121
https://www.arcticstorm.com/

Arica Vessel LLC
2320 West Commodore Way
Seattle, WA 98199
http://www.northstarfishing.com/

Bering Leader Fisheries LLC CO
8874 Bender Rd
Lynden, WA 98264
https://alaskanleader.com/

Blue North
2930 Westlake Ave N #300
Seattle, WA 98109
http://bluenorth.com/

Cape Horn Vessel LLC
2320 West Commodore Way
Seattle, WA 98199
http://www.northstarfishing.com/

Coastal Villages Longline LLC
711 H ST
Anchorage, AK 99501
http://www.coastalvillages.org/

Glacier Fish Co LLC
2320 West Commodore Way
Seattle, WA 98199
http://www.glacierfish.com/

Golden Alaska Seafoods LLC
2200 Alaskan Way
Seattle, WA 98121
http://www.goldenalaska.com/

Kodiak Fishing Partners Inc
8874 Bender Rd
Lynden, WA 98264
https://alaskanleader.com/the-fleet/
alaskan-leader

Liberator Fisheries LLC
2157 N Northlake Way
Seattle, WA 98103
http://starboats.com/

Northern Hawk LLC
711 H
Anchorage, AK 99501
https://www.coastalvillages.org/

Ohara Corporation
120 Tillson Ave Suite 1
Rockland, ME 04841
https://www.oharacorporation.com/

Phoenix Processor Ltd Partnership
333 First Ave West
Seattle, WA 98119
http://www.prempac.com/

Rebecca Irene Vessel LLC
2320 W Commodore Way
Seattle, WA 98199
http://www.northstarfishing.com/
vessels/ft-rebecca-irene/

Starbound LLC
2157 N Northlake Way
Seattle, WA 98103
http://starboats.com/

Unimak Vessel LLC
2320 W Commodore Way
Seattle, WA 98199
http://www.northstarfishing.com/

For the current, complete list of floating processors, catcher / processors and factory trawlers from the Alaska Department of Fish & Game, link to:

https://www.adfg.alaska.gov/index.cfm?adfg=fishlicense.holders

TYPES OF SEAFOOD PROCESSING JOBS

SHORE-BASED OR CANNERY JOBS

Belly slitters—use fillet knives to cut fish from throat to abdomen.

Head decapitators—cut the heads off of fish using a guillotine type of machine.

Gut pullers—remove fish guts and also pull out egg sacs, which are a premium product.

Spooners—clean out any leftover organs and gunk along the spine of the fish.

Washers—are in charge of running fish into a washer.

Fish graders—grade fish (excellent to poor) and sort them into bins.

Weighers—weigh the fish and sort them into bins according to size.

Sorters—place fish into the correct bins, based on species, grade, weight and size.

Tray stackers—clean, sort and the place the fish on freezer trays.

Freezer crew—works on a number of freezer-related duties and breaks frozen fish from trays.

Packing room workers—package fish, prep it for shipping, move pallets and label boxes.

Beach crew (dock crew)—helps to unload fish from boats, such as tenders and fishing vessels.

Ice and bait crew—help provide ice, bait, and other items to tenders and fishing boats.

Britestack workers—place cans on pallets, right-side-up of course.

Night clean up crew—clean bins, slime lines, and machinery to help reduce contamination.

Forklift drivers—move pallets by forklift, such as ice-filled totes, boxes, and heavy items.

Truck loaders—load vans and trucks with seafood product that is being transported to market.

Office staff workers—include roles such as receptionist, accounting, payroll, and administrative support.

Egg house workers—handle the careful processing of salmon roe and the boxing of product.

AT-SEA FLOATING PROCESSOR AND FACTORY TRAWLER JOBS

Factory trawler workers—are the "at-sea" version of those shore-based workers listed above.

Fillet machine operators—prepare pollock meat into filets using a machine.

Flippers and candlers—inspect filets for bones or parasites.

Extruders—process the finished surimi paste in preparation for freezing.

Cook and galley assistants—plan meals, cook, feed the crew and wash dishes.

Factory trawler deck hands—set and haul the net, which is one of the higher paying jobs.

Combies—mostly process fish below deck, but also help on deck when needed.

Factory foremen—oversee the entire processing operation, which is a higher paid position.

Seafood quality controllers—inspect the final seafood product to ensure it meets quality standards.

A Bering Sea crabber bucking tides and swells on its way to the fishing grounds.

An Alaskan factory trawler at 200-plus feet in length.

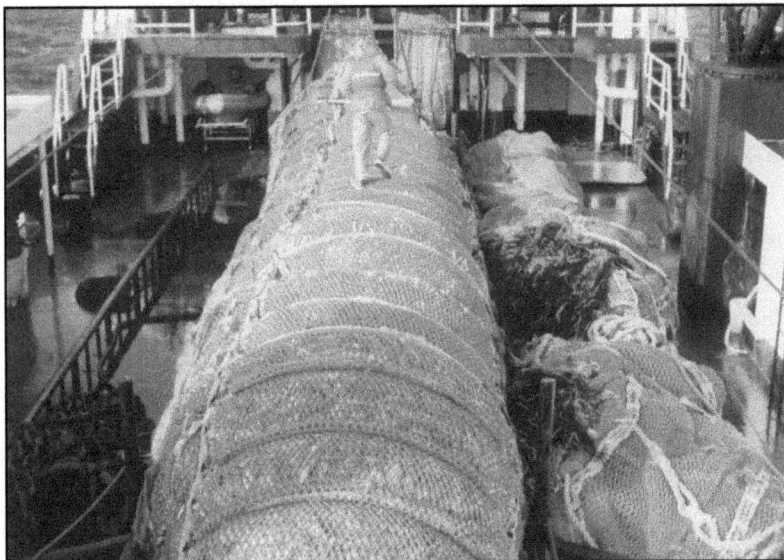

A nice codend stuffed with pollock, on its way to becoming fish sticks or surimi (also known as krab with a "k").

STATE OF ALASKA EMPLOYMENT SERVICE CENTERS

The State of Alaska Employment Service is an excellent source of information regarding current job openings in the seafood processing industry. The large majority of fishing-related jobs available through this state-run agency are positions in canneries and shore-based processors, or on floating processors and factory trawlers. Skippers of fishing boats rarely hire their crews through this service. If you wish to use this service in your job search, you may contact the centers on our list. However, they may not be of much help to you unless you are already in Alaska. If you travel to Alaska to look for a job, stop by one of these centers.

If you wish to be hired through the Alaska Job Service, you must apply in person. Be prepared and have the proper documentation with you, including:

1) Proper I-9 Identification. This includes at least one of the following:

   a) A United States passport.
   b) A picture I.D. (like a driver's license) and original Social Security card
   c) A birth certificate, or certificate of naturalization.
   d) A Green Card or unexpired INS employment authorization.

2) You may be asked to take a drug test.

Anchorage Employment Service
3301 Eagle St., Room #101
Anchorage, AK 99510
(907) 269-4746
24-HOUR SEAFOOD JOBLINE
(907) 269-4770
http://jobs.alaska.gov/

Bethel Employment Service
P.O. Box 187
Bethel, AK 99559
(907) 543-2210

Dillingham Employment Service
P.O. Box 1149
Dillingham, AK 99576
(907) 842-5579

Homer Employment Service
601 E. Pioneer Ave., #123
Homer, AK 99603
(907) 235-7200

Juneau Employment Service
10002 Glacier Hwy, #200
Juneau, AK 99801-8569
(907) 465-4562

Ketchikan Employment Service
2030 Sea Level Dr. #220
Ketchikan, AK 99901
(907) 225-3181

Kodiak Employment Service
309 Center St.
Kodiak, AK 99615
(907) 486-3105

Petersburg Employment Service
102 Haugen Dr.
Petersburg, AK 99833
(907) 772-3791

Seward Employment Service
P.O. Box 1009
Seward, AK 99664
(907) 224-5276

Sitka Employment Service
304 Lake, St., #101
Sitka, AK 99835
(907) 747-3423

Valdez Employment Service
P.O. Box 590
Valdez, AK 99686
(907) 835-4910

PROPER DOCUMENTATION

If you want to work in Alaska, or any place in the United States, your employer must verify your eligibility to work in the country. You must show them proper documentation.

PASSPORT

United States
of America

The Secretary of the United States of America hereby requests all whom it may concern to permit the citizen/national of the United States named herein to pass without delay or hindrance and in case of need to give all lawful aid and protection.

Johnny

Signature of Bearer

The United States of America
PASSPORT

Johnny Pukester
131313 Mockingbird Ln.
Hangover, MD 00077

Passport Agency
Washington D.C.

>>>>>>>>>>>>>>>>>>>>>>>>>>
>>>>>>>>>>>>>>>>>>>>>>>>>>

A United States Passport.

No other document is needed if you have this.

OR

Identification Card

Johnny Pukester
131313 Mockingbird Ln.
Hangover, MD 00077

Born 6-12-87

Johnny

SOCIAL SECURITY

123-45-6789

Johnny

If you have no Passport, you need to have a picture I.D. (like a driver's license) AND your <u>original</u> Social Security Card. No photocopies!!

OR

Identification Card
State of California

NAME: Pukester, Johnny
Birthdate: 6-12-87
Birthplace: Surf City General Hospital
Card Number: 123456789123456780

State Registrar Signature   X *Bill*

If you have no passport, picture I.D., or Social Security Card, you may show your employer a state-issued identification, birth certificate, or a certificate of naturalization. Employers will not accept hospital-issued birth certificates as verification.

If you do not have any of the items mentioned, show your employer a Green Card and unexpired I.N.S. authorization to work in this country. If you have none of these, please consult your local I.N.S. Department for instructions on how to obtain them.

SUMMER CANNERY JOBS: THE PEAK PERIODS

If you've decided to travel north to get a summer cannery job, you should know the peak periods of the salmon season in the different areas of Alaska. Of course, the peak periods are the best times to find a job. This information should be helpful when planning your job-search strategy.

AREA OF ALASKA	CITIES IN AREA	PEAK PERIODS

SOUTHEAST	Ketchikan
	Petersburg
	Sitka
	Wrangell
		Sockeye Salmon
		    July
		
		Pink Salmon
		    Late July through August
		
		Silver Salmon
		    July through early August

COOK INLET	Anchorage
	Kenai
	Homer
		Sockeye Salmon
		    Mid-July
		
		Pink Salmon
		    Late July through August

KODIAK	Kodiak	Sockeye Salmon
		    Late June through July
		
		Pink Salmon
		    Late July to mid-August

PRINCE WILLIAM SOUND	Seward
	Valdez
	Cordova
		Sockeye Salmon
		    Mid-July
		
		Pink Salmon
		    Late July through August

BRISTOL BAY	Dillingham Egegik Naknek	Sockeye Salmon First half of July

PART 3

Things You Need to Know

The Kodiak brown bear is the largest carnivore on earth and can reach heights of over 10 feet when standing upright.

If you've landed a fishing job in Alaska or you're planning to walk the docks to find one, you'll have to find your way to the last great frontier. If you don't fly to Alaska, we'd recommend that you drive a van there, taking the Al-Can Highway in combination with the Alaska State Ferry / Alaska Marine Highway, (907) 465-3941. When taking the Al-Can Highway, be prepared for a bumpy ride: most of the road is gravel. Since there aren't many gas stations along the way, you should also bring extra gas and a lot of tools to fix any mechanical problems you may have. A shotgun is also recommended since there are many wild animals that might want you for breakfast.

Most of the fishing towns along the route will have some sort of campground where you can park your van or set up your tent. The campgrounds usually charge between $15 and $25 per night. Some towns also have youth hostels, which charge around $15 a night.

THINGS TO KNOW WHEN YOU GET A JOB

Don't expect to be paid in full until about a month after the fishing season ends. You'll be allowed to take a draw on your earnings of probably $5,000 or so, but you'll have to wait for the canneries to pay the skipper before you get everything that's coming to you.

You should also be aware of "spring settlements." Many times the canneries send a bonus to the skippers in the springtime following the previous fishing season. You're entitled by law to receive your share of this bonus. If you don't receive a check by March of the following year, call your skipper and ask if you'll be receiving one. Often, the spring bonus is $2,000 to $4,000 per crew member, so it's definitely worth asking about.

While you're in these towns, you may be able to pick up odd jobs such as painting or cleaning boats, which will help subsidize the cost of your trip. All you have to do is offer to help. It's a good way to show people you're a hard worker—and maybe they'll recommend you for a fishing job.

The following is a list of some cities and towns that are good places to seek employment. Included is information about where you can stay overnight. For your convenience, we've noted the phone number of each city's youth hostel, if there is one.

WASHINGTON

Seattle	Youth Hostel (206) 622-5443
	https://www.americanhotelseattle.com/en-us/rooms
	Mobile Parks
Everett	Mobile Park
Gig Harbor & Tacoma	Mobile Parks
Anacortes	Camping

ALASKA

Anchorage	Youth Hostel (907) 276-3635
	www.hostelbookers.com
	Camping
Cordova	Camping
Homer	Camping
Juneau	Youth Hostel (907) 586-9559
	Camping
Ketchikan	Camping
Kodiak	Camping
Petersburg	Camping
Valdez	Camping
Seward	Camping
Kenai	Camping

SUPPLIES YOU NEED

So how should you pack for a few months at sea? For starters, only bring clothes you don't mind exposing to salt water and fish slime. Your best bet is to travel lightly and be ready for every possibility in weather and work. To be fully prepared for commercial fishing in Alaska, you should bring the following items with you. Of course, everything is tax-deductible!

DUFFEL BAG

The bigger the better. You can get one of these at any Army surplus store. You'll need a bag that's big enough to carry a whole season's supply of clothing and gear.

CLOTHING

✓ **One heavy jacket.**

It doesn't necessarily have to be heavy, but it does have to be warm. The coldest it gets in Alaska during the summer is the low 40s, and the winter has sub-zero temperatures, so be prepared. An old Gor-Tex jacket is ideal since it's lightweight, warm, and waterproof. Fishing is dirty work, so don't bring anything too nice.

✓ **Two hooded cotton pullover sweatshirts.**

You might not have room for a pillow in your duffel bag. If this is the case, just bring a pillow case, fill it with sweatshirts, and there you go—instant pillow! After all, where do you think you are, the Hilton? You're on a boat in Alaska! Rough it a little!!!

Two is a good number. That way, if one gets wet, you can have the other one drying in the engine room. It's suggested that you cut off the sleeves right below the elbow to prevent getting salt-water boils from wet clothing.

✓ **Four pair of cotton sweat pants.**

It's nice to have three pair to work in and an extra pair for backup when all the others are dirty. Patagonia makes some excellent pants that are wool and polypropylene. They cost about $80. If you want to spend the money, go for it. But if you don't, regular sweats should work just fine.

✓ **Two wool sweaters.**

Wool is always the best because it keeps you dry. The only drawback is that wool sweaters take up a lot of space in your duffel bag. Take at least one—and if you can manage it, take two.

✓ **Ten tee shirts.**

You'll wear many tee shirts. If possible, bring along a couple of long-sleeve versions of this clothing staple. You'll be glad you did.

✓ Ten pair of underwear

Actually, bring as many as you want. Since you won't get a chance do laundry very often, it's nice to have a few extra pair on to hand.

✓ Two pair of long underwear.

Two pair should be just fine. The polypropylene underwear is lightweight, stays dry and works great.

✓ Ten pair of lightweight wool socks.

Socks are very, very important. Cotton socks will make your life wet, cold and miserable. What you need are lightweight socks that keep you warm, repel water and stay pulled up without bunching around your toes and ankles. If it gets cold, doubling up two thin socks on each foot might give you a better fit than one pair of thick socks, but it's up to you. Wool or polypropylene is the only way to go. Socks that are recommended or sold as skiing socks are also good. Some people like to bring a few pair of heavy wool socks, but it basically comes down to what you prefer. A couple of pair of cotton athletic socks might be good for your days off.

✓ One pair of deck shoes.

Any pair of comfortable, rubber-soled (non-slip) shoes or boots will do just fine. What you need is something to put on when you aren't wearing your fishing boots. You'll want something comfortable to live in and work in when you have time off from fishing.

✓ Two baseball caps.

These will help keep water and jellyfish out of your face. You should bring one to use as your main hat and one to use when your main hat blows off and sinks into the water.

✓ One wool hat or Elmer-Fudd-type hat.

If it covers your ears and keeps them warm, it will make your life on the boat that much more bearable. This kind of hat is optional, but highly recommended.

✓ One bandanna.

If the jellyfish get bad, you might want to cover your face.

Bring a lot of clothes because you will get wet! It's always nice to have some dry clothes to change into.

FISHING GEAR

✓ **One pair of rain pants.**

Purchase either Grunden's or Helly-Hansen products. You'll be wasting your time and quality of life on anything else. Grunden's are heavy-duty, roomy and will last for several years. Helly-Hansen are very comfortable and lightweight, but might fall apart toward the end of the season Expect to pay $120 at the most for a pair of rain pants.

✓ **One raincoat.**

Again, Grunden's or Helly-Hansen is the only way to go. Expect to pay $120 at the most for a jacket.

✓ **One pair of Servus XtraTuf boots.**

Don't even waste your time with anything else. Xtratuf boots are an overall outstanding product with the best traction for working on deck. Ninety-nine percent of the fishermen in Alaska wear them, which has to tell you something. You can get them in plain or steel toe—whichever you prefer—for about $100.

✓ **One pair of felt boot liners.**

Even though the XtraTuf boots have good traction for working on deck, they can be very uncomfortable when you wear them for long periods of time. Boot liners and good socks will make your feet that much happier. A pair of boot liners costs about $10

✓ **Four pairs of Atlas Vinylove rubber gloves.**

Don't try to cut corners by using those rubber dishwashing gloves. They'll fall apart in your first 10 minutes at sea.

Don't waste your time buying inexpensive raingear that's supposed to work. It never does—and then your life is miserable. Spend the money and get the best raingear available!

AN IMPORTANT NOTE ABOUT FISHING GEAR

You're responsible for buying your own fishing gear. Don't get stuck on a boat without the proper gear or your life will be dismal!

Atlas gloves are a favorite of fishermen because of their durability, comfort and ability to grip things when wet. There are three different types: Model #620 is your basic glove that stops right above your wrist ($20); Model #640 is a glove that has sleeves running all the way up to your armpits to keep your arms dry and protect you from jellyfish ($40); and there are other models as well, which are suited for various needs. The only drawback with the sleeved gloves is that they may make you sweat, but it's better than saltwater and jellyfish. You might want to get two pair of the basic gloves and two pair with sleeves to see which ones you prefer. Ask for the orange Atlas gloves all the fishermen wear. Any marine supply store clerk will know what you're talking about.

✓ **Four pair of cotton glove liners.**

These liners are white, cotton-knit gloves. You can wear them underneath your rubber gloves to keep your hands warm and dry. Or you can wear them by themselves because they're good for gripping ($20).

✓ **One pocket knife.**

This is very important since you'll be using your knife a lot. An ideal knife is one that folds out and has a locking mechanism. The blade on the knife should be about three inches long so you can use it for a variety of purposes. You can spend between $10 and $1000 on a knife, but since there's a good chance you'll lose it overboard, don't spend too much. Some marine supply stores will sell a basic, steel pocket knife that runs about $5 and works well. Since some stores print their names on these knives as a kind of calling card, you may be able to get one free with a large order of gear. All you have to do is ask.

OTHER ITEMS

You should also bring a sleeping bag, glasses, sunglasses, personal items, hygiene items, stationery, stamps, books, tapes, camera, and a fishing pole for fun. Also, it's IMPORTANT to bring your Social Security Card and picture identification, or other I-9 documentation, cash and credit cards.

You might want to bring a fishing pole in case you get a little time off. Catching a salmon with a rod and reel is an unforgettable experience!

If you fly to Alaska, be sure to pack your pocket knife in your checked baggage (duffle bag). The TSA airport security workers will appreciate this.

With recent environmental awareness, it's evident that commercial fishermen are truly concerned about keeping our oceans clean. Instead of littering overboard, most boats store their trash and plastic waste until it can be properly disposed of on land.

OPTIONAL EQUIPMENT

✓ **One Grunden's Neptune suit.**

This is a waterproof nylon and PVC jumpsuit manufactured by Grunden's. It's an optional item for skiffmen and deck hands, but it's very nice to have. It will keep you warm, dry, and comfortable as you work on deck ($250).

✓ **One Mustang suit.**

This is optional equipment, but for skiffmen it's a good investment. A Mustang suit is a bright orange, insulated jumpsuit that's equipped with flotation devices. Another name for this type of suit is a "float suit." Mustang is a brand name ($350).

KING CRAB GEAR
What You'll Need if You're Gonna Be a Crabber

✓ **King crab gear. Additional items to consider if crabbing.**
- Bring <u>two</u> pair of <u>insulated</u> XtraTuf boots and extra felt boot liners
- Booties (optional)
- Bama socks (wool socks)
- Fox River Port wool socks (recommended by crabbers)
- Sweats: Helly Hansen fleece poly pants
- Gloves: ATLAS 460 <u>insulated</u> gloves
- Hats: Grunden's fleece hat with ear flaps
- Extra baseball caps
- One warm jacket for in town
- Ski goggles: Smith, Uvex or Oakley with clear lenses because it's always dark out. Bring extra lenses.
- Extra sweat shirts
- Raingear: Bring at least two new pair of raingear based on a two-month trip. You will always be trading one wet pair for a dry pair. It's not a bad idea to buy your raingear in Seattle, because it is more expensive in Dutch Harbor.

WHERE YOU CAN BUY YOUR GEAR

LFS Inc.
Bellingham, WA (360) 734-3336
Seattle, WA (206) 789-8110
Dutch Harbor, AK (907) 581-2178
https://www.go2marine.com/

- LFS Washington Locations:
  Bellingham, Poulsbo & Seattle

- LFS Alaska Locations:
  Anchorage, Dillingham, Dutch Harbor, Cordova,
  Kenai, Naknek, Sitka & Homer (Kachemak Gear Shed)

Cy's Sporting Goods
Kodiak, AK (907) 486-3900

Big Ray's
Kodiak, AK (907) 486-4276
(also in Anchorage & Fairbanks)
https://www.bigrays.com/

Kodiak Marine Supply
Kodiak, AK (907) 486-5752
www.kodiakmarinesupply.com

Seattle Marine
Seattle, WA (206) 285-5010
www.seamar.com

Tongass Trading Company
Ketchikan, AK (907) 225-5101
www.tongasstrading.com

Sutliff True Value Hardware
Kodiak, AK (907) 486-5797

Marine Supply & Hardware
Anacortes, WA (360) 293-3014
www.marinesupplyandhardware.com

For a more comprehensive listing of fishermen's supply stores, visit The Marine Yellow Pages online at www.MarineYellowPages.com

Dumping a stuffed pot- load of crab onto the sorting table.

Sorting opilio crab during a 30-hour grind.

Alaskan purse seiner bringing in a good haul.

THE PSYCHOLOGY OF FISHING

In many famous books and films, there's the story of the sea captain or crew member who was at sea for a long time and went completely crazy. One of the toughest things about working on a commercial fishing boat is the mental strain that one encounters while being at sea for long periods of time.

Living and working on a boat, not having any freedom, and being obliged to do everything the skipper says can get old real fast. Also, the farthest distance you can get away from your fellow crew members is the length of the boat, which is about 60 feet or more. Sometimes you don't get to walk on dry land for weeks at a time, which is enough to drive most people a little nuts. In addition, the physical isolation of working on a fishing boat evokes the same constrained feelings you'd have if you were a slave or a prisoner.

In order to maintain your sanity, it's important to learn how to play mind games with yourself. Furthermore, you should be aware of the psychology of fishing and apply it to your life at sea.

You should always try to maintain a good attitude. Sometimes this is very difficult to do, especially when fishing isn't very good and the weather is lousy. It seems as though a lot of people, including skippers, get in bad moods when the weather gets bad. Many times, the worse the weather, the worse people's attitudes get. So when you're completely drenched and you haven't seen the sun shine for two weeks and everyone's in a bad mood, it's important to understand why people are pissed.

Try to cheer them up a little or tell them a joke to get their minds off their misery. You should also try to cheer yourself up when you're feeling a little bit down by thinking about what a positive experience you're having—even though you're miserable, too. At least you're making some money and building your character.

When you're fishing, the high points are high and the low points are low. This is one of the most difficult facts to keep in mind when you're trying to maintain your overall sanity on a boat. For instance, if you catch a huge number of fish in one day, and personally make $3,000 for your work, it's natural that you'd be ecstatic thinking how easy it was to earn all that money in such a short period of time. Then, if you catch absolutely nothing for the next two weeks—not even a fish for

Some skippers have the Dr. Jeckyl and Mr. Hyde complex. They're perfectly normal people on land, but when they're on the water they go crazy.

87

dinner—it's not unlikely that you'd slip into a bad mood, get depressed and wonder if you'd ever catch another fish the entire season. But overall, during that two-week period, you still made $3,000 and averaged about $200 per day. Remember the old saying: "Not every day is Christmas!" It's a popular adage on the fishing grounds.

You have to look at fishing in a very broad sense so you don't get too psyched out by the daily variance in your earnings. Once the season is over, and you've left Alaska with a hefty check in your pocket, you're going to forget about the bad days anyway. So there's really no reason to make a big deal about them when you're actually experiencing misery on the fishing grounds. Bumming yourself out just ain't worth it!

Try not to take things too personally. Once in a while, things don't go as smoothly as they should and mistakes are made. If you screw up and people yell at you, try to remain calm and do your best to correct the problem. They're criticizing your performance, not you as a person. If the screaming really gets bad, pretend you're a duck and let the verbal abuse bead off you. Be tough and take it

Remember, when you point your finger at someone else, you've still got three pointing right back at you.

This may be difficult to do, but you've got to remember that you're only human and you'll make mistakes from time to time.

When something goes wrong, people may often be overwhelmed by the urgency of the moment and overreact. So it's important to realize what's going through their heads, as well as your own. Sometimes, people don't realize that what they're saying is offensive. When this happens, it sometimes results in a heated argument. This is a waste of time since arguments don't fix problems—they just hurt feelings. Watch what you say, and have patience with others. If tempers flare, as they often do on a boat, a prompt apology and a spirit of forgiveness can save the day.

Some more advice: Be careful not to point the finger at other people's faults and failings. They'll be sure to return the courtesy when you screw up. Never talk badly about your crew members behind their backs. It's a waste of time and may end up in a huge fight. Remember, no one's perfect!

Stick it out and be tough!!! Sometimes commercial fishing is extremely demanding on the body. Other times it's mentally draining and you feel like you cannot go another day without dropping dead or going insane. The best strategy is to convince yourself that you're tough and you can stick it out. Remember, your stay in Alaska is just a temporary thing and you'll be home soon.

When things are getting tough, it helps to make a game out of it by challenging yourself to prove how tough you are and how far you can push yourself.

Some people have a difficult time dealing with boat life in general and just can't handle it. Then there are the people who get homesick to the point where they're completely useless. This is not a good thing. Occasionally, people will quit because they can't handle the stress of living on a boat and being away from home.

Once I fished with a guy named Joe, who got depressed because we weren't catching any fish. He was homesick and missed his girlfriend a lot. So he quit in July without making a dime. By the end of the summer, the boat's luck had changed and each crew member made a $35,000 share. Do you think Joe would have liked making 35 grand for sticking it out an extra month? Damn right he would have! It's usually in one's best interest to hang in there and be strong!

To sum it up, you have to be tough mentally and capable of handling adverse situations. When it comes down to inter-personal communication among crew members, you're all in the same boat, literally. The Golden Rule really applies here—and is always appreciated. Good manners and an unselfish attitude can save the day.

Who would have thought that you'd learn so much about people and yourself by working on a fishing boat?

The most successful fishermen are the ones who can deal with the psychological aspects of the business.

DRUGS AND BOATS DON'T FLOAT!

Sure, we're all adults and can make our own decisions—but with regard to drug use on fishing boats, your smartest choice would be to 'just say no.' First of all, if the Coast Guard boards a boat and finds any illegal drugs, it can seize the boat and put the entire crew in jail. Secondly, you need to be able to think fast and act calmly—drugs impair this ability, cause people to overreact, result in injuries, and further complicate problems at hand. Plus, the pure, natural, incredible experience of Alaska is better than the false high that any drug could provide. Okay, okay... we're done preaching. But do yourself a favor and don't bring drugs!

HOW TO STAY ON GOOD TERMS WITH
YOUR SKIPPER AND FELLOW CREW MEMBERS

1. Notice what work needs to be done on the boat and do it without waiting to be asked.
2. Always volunteer for the scum jobs.
3. When you do any job, give it 100 percent.
4. Always try to help others.
5. Be considerate of your crew mates, which also includes being considerate of their privacy.
6. Don't be the "hands in pocket guy." Don't be the person who stands there while others work. Always be enthused and be a "hands on" type of person. Don't be the guy rinsing the boat while the others are scrubbing it. Everyone hates a rinser.
7. Keep a good attitude.
8. Don't spend too much time sleeping in the bunk.
9. When you have free time, hang out with the skipper in the tophouse. Listen, learn, and try to help.
10. Don't bad-mouth your crew members or skipper.
11. Don't take drugs.
12. If you drink while in town, do it moderately. There are lots of fights in Alaskan bars. Elbow Room Bar in Dutch Harbor was once known as the toughest bar in North America.
13. Don't include your skipper in intracrew squabbles.
14. Make a point of learning navigation and how to fix fishing gear.
15. Let the skipper make the decisions and be supportive of them.
16. Be eager to get up in the morning to catch a lot of fishies!!!
17. DON'T BE A CRYBABY!!!

KNOTS YOU NEED TO KNOW

CLOVE HITCH

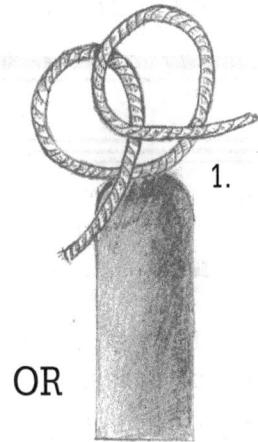

1.

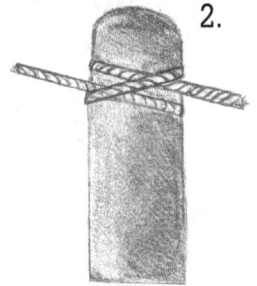

2.

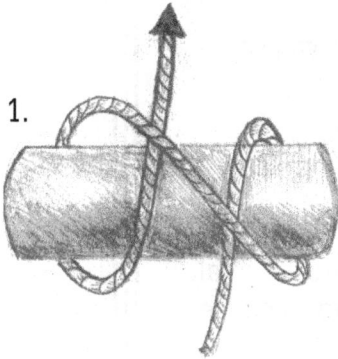

1.

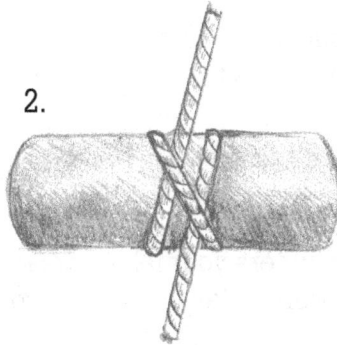

2.

OR

SHEET BEND

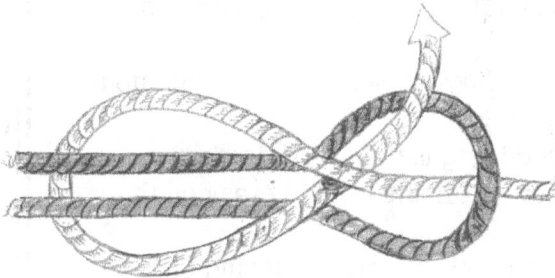

SQUARE KNOT

BOWLINE

1.

LOVER'S KNOT

2.

SAFETY TIPS: HOW TO SURVIVE ON A BOAT

Commercial fishing is rated as one of the 10 most dangerous jobs you can have. Be careful! Here's a list of things to watch out for.

1. Watch your step.
2. Keep the deck clean.
3. Keep your eye out for other's safety.
4. When traveling, always know where your fellow crew members are at all times. This way, if someone were to fall overboard, you'd have a chance to save them before it was too late and they were lost.
5. When dipping any buckets into the water to fill them, be careful! If the boat's moving, the bucket may act as a water parachute and pull you overboard.
6. Don't piss into the wind. (Not a safety tip, but good to know.)
7. Make sure everything in the rigging is tight. Tight is good. Anything loose on a boat is bad.
8. Make sure all loose ropes are put away. Loose lines can get wound up in the propeller and seize the engine. Not good!
9. Make sure the galley is clean and everything is put away. In bad weather, dishes tend to fly and peanut butter jars tend to break on the floor. Not fun!
10. Make sure all deck hatch covers are properly closed. A sinking boat isn't much fun either!
11. Be knowledgeable about how to operate the boat and its navigation equipment, including the Loran and radios.
12. Make sure your survival suit is easily accessible. Each boat should have one suit for each crew member.
13. Be able to recognize when things on the boat, including parts of the net, are worn and need to be fixed or replaced.
14. Keep your eyes open at all times.
15. Be aware of any strange noises or smells that may be cause for alarm.
16. Don't let any spare parts or supplies run out. Call attention to any shortages, deficiencies, or problems as soon as you notice them.

One of the many bald eagles in Alaska, doing what eagles do... catch fish!

Drift gillnetting salmon.

An official crab-pot launcher!

SEASICKNESS AND HEALTH TIPS

"In the last three years, I've seen four guys quit for health reasons. They all had such bad tooth-aches they had to fly south to get them fixed!"

—Mike, a Kodiak skipper.

Some seasick-prone mariners feel better by using special electronic wristbands, which help relieve the symptoms of seasickness.

Due to the nature of this subject, this is by far our grossest section. Anyone who feels woozy when discussing pimples or vomit should bypass this chapter, although it contains very worthwhile information.

Being in good health is one of the more important factors that will contribute to your overall success as a commercial fisherman. In Alaska, you'll find that having a health problem is a nightmare because the areas where most boats fish are too far away from civilization to do anything about it.

The best tactic is to visit your doctor and dentist before the season begins. This is the only way you can be certain you're in top-notch health. Then, if you have any strange diseases or your teeth are beginning to fall out, you can take care of the problem before it takes care of you. It's a much better strategy than waiting until you get to Alaska to see if your condition gets worse, then having to go by seaplane to the nearest hospital.

Seasickness. When you're on a boat, one of the first things you'll worry about is seasickness. Before you go to Alaska, you should purchase some Scopolamine seasick medication. You'll need a doctor's prescription for these little patches, which are stuck behind the ear to fight seasickness. They seem to work very well for most people, but for others they worsen the problem. So try them out and see if they work for you.

Another solution to help with seasickness is the use of specially designed wristbands that either generate weak electical fields, or are magnetized and designed to stimulate accupuncture pressure points.

A lot of times the worst part of seasickness is the awful feeling you get when you're trying to hold back from vomiting. If you're sick, you're sick. Barf in the water and feed the fish! No one cares!! You might get teased a bit, but remember: every fisherman has gotten seasick at least once in his or her life, so it's nothing to be embarrassed about.

Many times people get sick their first day on the boat, and once they're used to their new environment, they're fine for the rest of the season. Also, when one feels sick, it's always best to be outside in the fresh air or in the tophouse where you can see the waves that are rocking your world. The very worst place to be is in the bunk or galley. That's when you start losing the seasickness war.

Jellyfish. Jellyfish are another one of those irritating complications that sometimes make an Alaskan commercial fisherman's life not so much fun. For the most part, Alaskan jellyfish are not that big a deal. You can't die from them, butthey can make you uncomfortable. A jellyfish's sting will make your skin itch and burn. The irritation usually lasts about 15 minutes or so. It's just enough to be a bother. But if you get a jellyfish tentacle in your eye, it can be very painful.

There are many home remedies for jellyfish stings, including applying meat tenderizer or dry milk to the sting. Applying petroleum jelly to one's face each morning before the jellyfish get a chance to land on bare skin is supposed to help. Some of the more experienced fishermen may tell you that urinating on your hands is the best remedy for jellyfish stings. Don't believe them. They're just trying to get you to pee on your hands so they can tease you about it the rest of the season!!!

Salt-water boils. Salt-water boils are another problem fishermen try to avoid. These are pimple-like irritations that appear on the wrists and arms of people who are in constant contact with wet clothing. If you're a victim, don't try to pop these boils because they can become infected and very painful. First of all, you should cut off all your sleeves to the elbow since wet clothing causes these boils. Then you should apply hydrogen peroxide to the boils at least once a day to kill the germs. Although it may take a few weeks, they'll eventually go away.

Fish poisoning. Be very careful not to get any cuts while you're on the boat. This may be difficult to do since you'll be cutting things constantly—and with the rolling motion of the sea, a simple slip of the knife seems inevitable. When you get cut, put a lot of hydrogen peroxide on the wound, keep it as dry as possible and change the bandage every chance you get. Make sure not to get any fish slime—and yes, it's called that— in the cut because it might cause you to develop fish poisoning. This condition can actually be fatal, so take care. You can tell you have fish poisoning when you get a cut, then notice a big black streak running up your arm or leg a couple of weeks later. Eventually this black streak will make its way to your heart and you'll die. Sure, if you catch the problem in time you can take antibiotics to quell the infection, so don't worry too much. Basically, try not to cut yourself.

At times, your body will ache and you'll be miserable. But if you get a check for $20,000 at the end of the season, you might feel a little better!

Be careful when crawling into your bunk at night. That's when nine out of 10 serious leg cramps occur.

Leg cramps and carpel tunnel syndrome. Many commercial fisherman have problems with cramps in their legs and carpal tunnel syndrome in their hands and wrists. The most violent leg cramps I've ever had were on a boat. When your legs are in constant motion due to the movement of the sea, they'll eventually cramp up. Also, since you're constantly using your hands in a very repetitive, vigorous manner, carpal tunnel syndrome can set in and reduce circulation, feeling, and the ability to move one's fingers. There are medications available for both these conditions. They'd be worth investigating if you run into trouble with these problems.

Messy, flaky hands. Finally, hand lotion is one of a fisherman's best friends. By protecting your hands with Neutrogena or a similar product, you can prevent your fingers from getting huge, painful cracks in them—and stop your skin from peeling. Peeling hands may not sound like a big deal, but what tends to peel is the skin on the palms. It's a very ugly condition. Worst of all is returning to civilization with flaky hands. A simple handshake turns into a traumatic event for your friends since everyone is sure you've got some kind of funky skin-rot disease. Anyway, use lotion. It's a good idea.

Please consult your doctor about any of the suggestions made above. It's important that you seek the guidance of a physician who can help you maintain your health, evaluate your specific health problems and recommend the proper treatment.

YOUR CONTRACT WITH THE SKIPPER

When you get a job on a boat, it's always important that you and your skipper agree beforehand what your crew share will be. You and he should decide whether you'll receive a half-share or full-share, and if that share is 5 percent of the crew's gross earnings— or 10 percent, or more. Many times these contracts are verbal, but it's always best to get the terms in writing to avoid future complications.

HOW TO SPLICE A LINE

Splicing is an important skill that all fishermen should know. And if you can learn how to splice from the following drawings, you're a genius and should be a rocket scientist—not a fisherman. But these illustrations can point you in the right direction. When splicing, you should use a fid or a marling spike, both of which are tools to help make separating the braids of line a little easier. The tips of each braid are commonly taped with black electrical tape prior to splicing, which keeps each strand from fraying. Sometimes, using a cigarette lighter to burn the ends of each strand will melt the line, ensuring it won't become frayed when working with it.

The sad fact is that a very small percentage of crewmen actually learn how to splice. Those who master this craft are usually the ones who will be asked to come back on the best boats, year after year. So do yourself, and your fellow crew members and skipper a favor—learn how to splice.

EYE SPLICE

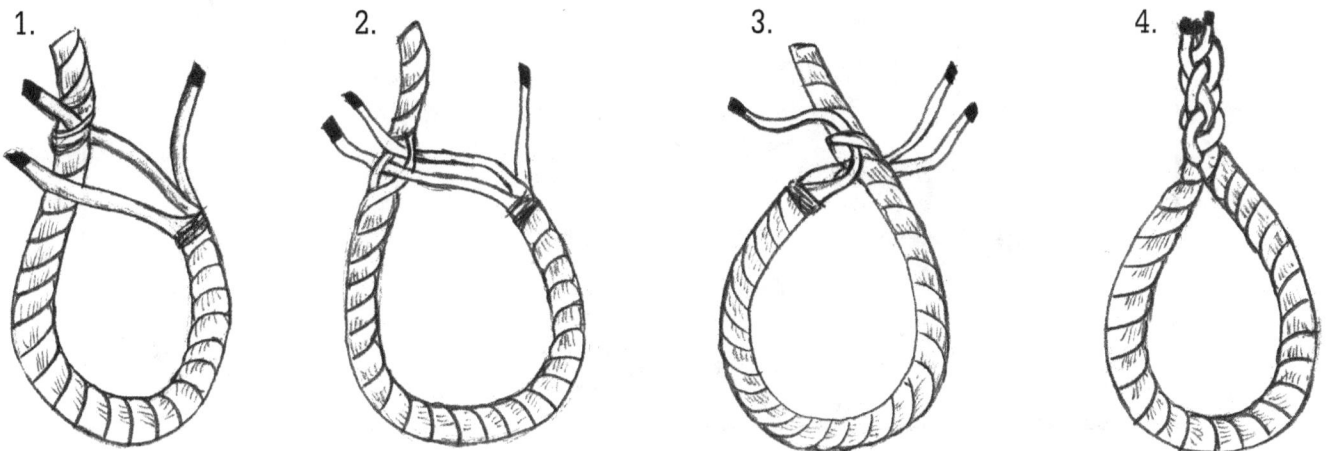

SHORT SPLICE

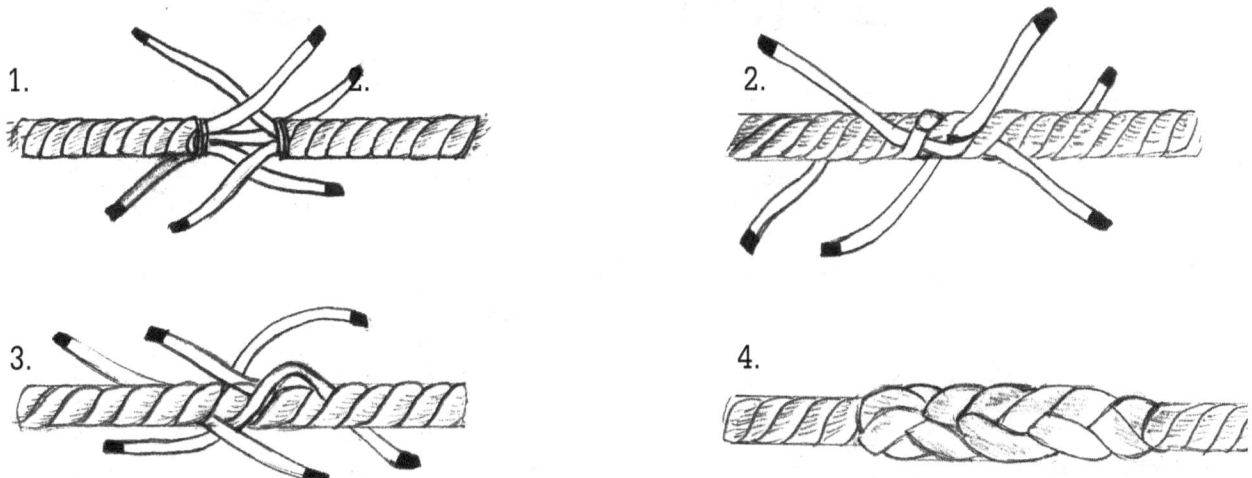

HOW TO SEW WEB

What happens when you get a hole in the web of a fishing net or crab pot? You lose fish and money. That's why you need to learn how to sew web. The ability to mend a net separates the fishing pros from the wannabes—and if you can fix that big rip, or even that small one-bar, you will be a valuable member of the crew. The following illustrations show the basics of fixing a hole and sewing web.

1.

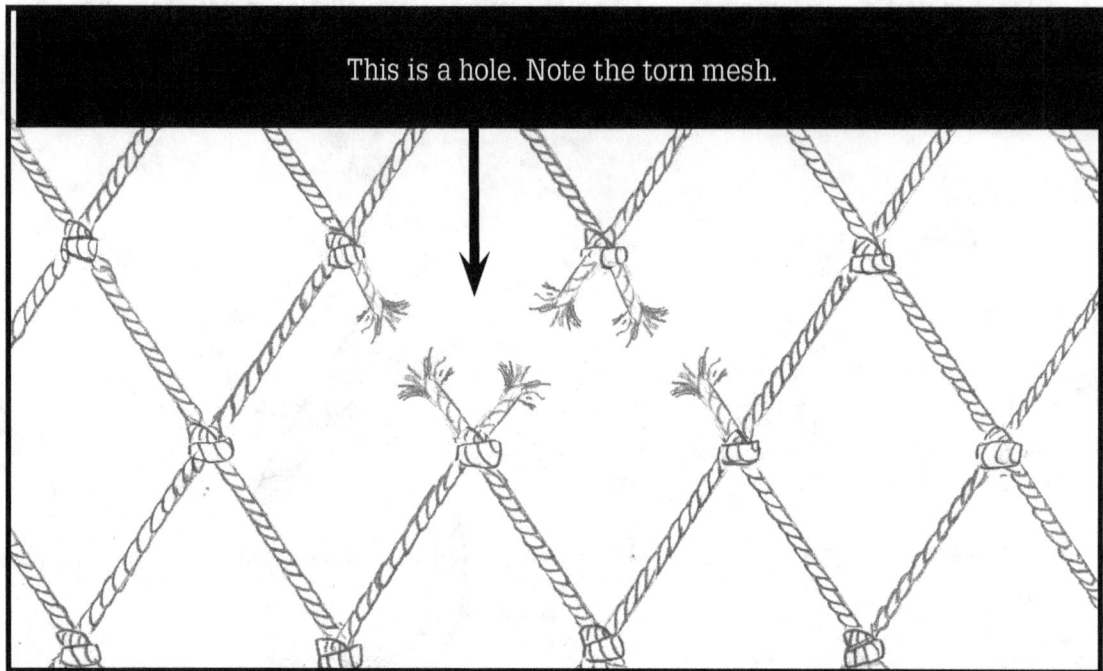

This is a hole. Note the torn mesh.

2.

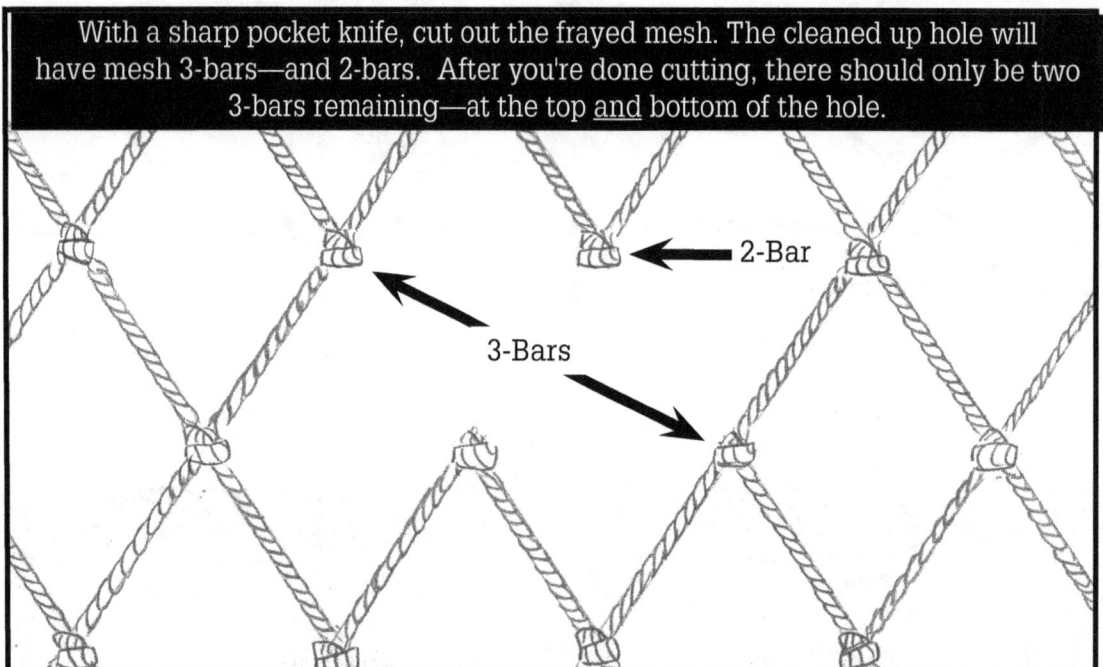

With a sharp pocket knife, cut out the frayed mesh. The cleaned up hole will have mesh 3-bars—and 2-bars. After you're done cutting, there should only be two 3-bars remaining—at the top <u>and</u> bottom of the hole.

2-Bar

3-Bars

3. Using a sewing needle with twine, tie two sheet bends to anchor the twine at the top 3-bar (Point A, Figure X), then continue with mesh knots at the 2-bars (Points B and C, Figures Y and Z)—finishing up by anchoring a clove hitch at 3-bar D.

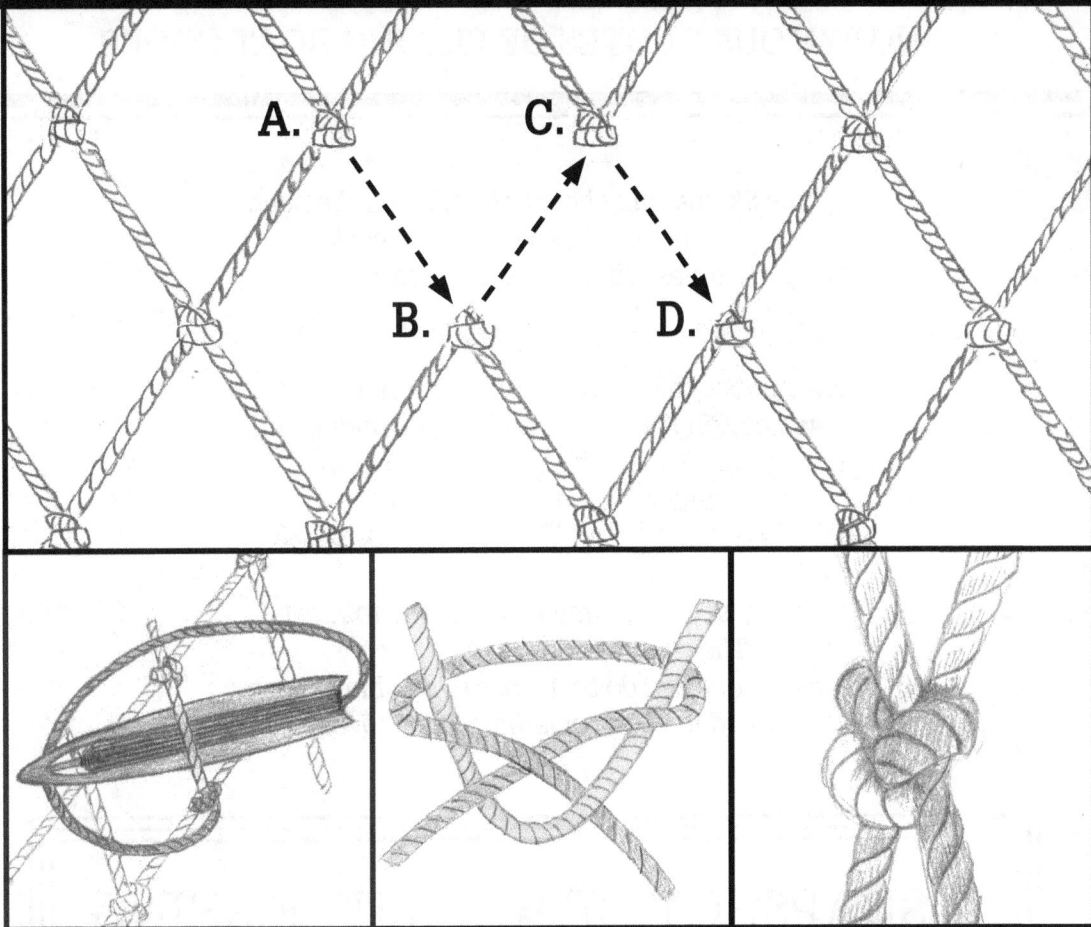

Figure X: Use a sewing needle, tie off the twine on a 3-bar, at the start of the hole—and also at the finish.

Figure Y: This is the mesh knot used for mending web,

Figure Z: Once the mesh knot is created, cinch down on the "V" of the existing web to make the knot

4. The hole is fixed! Now what are you waiting for?! Get back to work and catch some more fish!

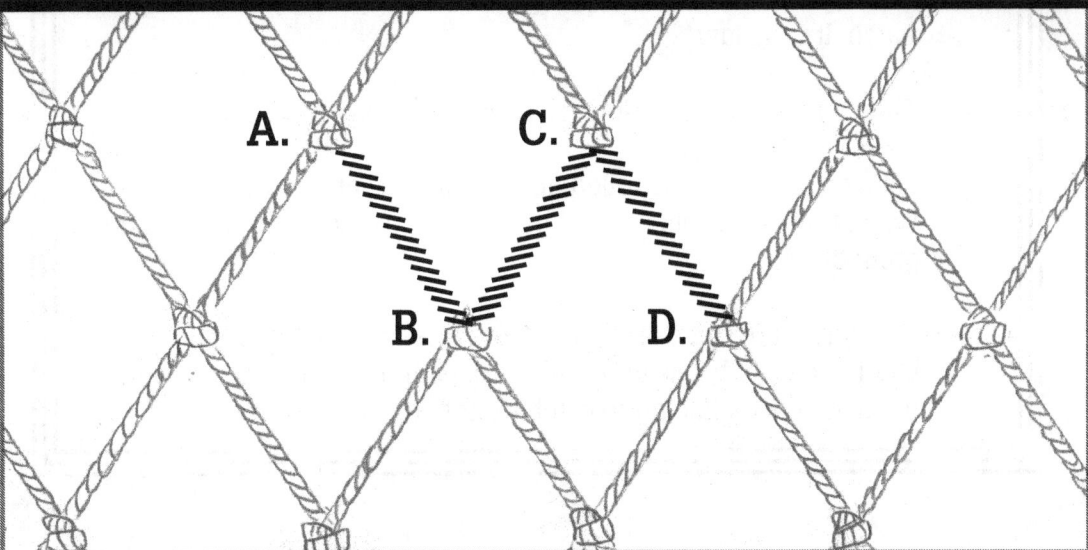

ANONYMOUS QUOTES OF FISHING BOAT COOKS

*"The Skipper may be number one on the boat,
but no one screws with the cook
unless they want to eat soap."*

*"Ever notice that the cook on a boat never eats his
own cooking? Kind of makes you wonder, huh?
Don't worry, nothing will happen
unless you piss off the chef."*

*"Many self-proclaimed chefs come to Alaska.
The trick is not to be a good cook,
as anyone can do that—but to be able to cook
good food on something that moves!"*

A SNAPSHOT OF HALIBUT FISHING AND LONGLINING

- When you're done halibut fishing, your clothes will smell forever.

- Many salmon skippers go out halibut fishing before salmon season, which is an opportunity to get hired for both fisheries.

- Each halibut is beheaded and gutted before being put into the hatch. It's the law.

- There are two types of longline gear, snap on and conventional.

- Snap on groundline is rolled up on a drum that's on the stern. When the hooks come in, the gangions are disconnected from the groundline.

- Longliners are some of the hardest working fisherman. They bait millions of hooks and run lots of gear, relying on the ancient method of hook fishing to catch their fish.

PART 4

Good Stuff from the Journal

UNCLE ROY'S SMOKED SALMON RECIPE

Here's a recipe for you that's worth the price of this book. Held top secret in the Maricich family for decades, it is now open to the public. This recipe is direct from the captain's log of Roy Maricich, who is known in history as one of the leading Alaskan salmon highliners ever to fish the waters of Kodiak and Southeast Alaska (see the Eagle of Dakavak story on page 114). To give full credit to its origins, Roy got the recipe directly from Aleut, native Alaskans, in Kodiak, Alaska. This recipe is the smoked-salmon equivilant of Kitty Eisenhower's fudge recipe, because it had been a closely-guarded secret for years, and was acclaimed for its culinary perfection.

Just a couple of tips for making the ultimate smoked salmon. Use alder wood and real wild Alaskan salmon, preferably king salmon. But other salmon will taste great, too (even the farmed stuff will work well). This recipe is so great, you could probably even smoke bullhead and it would taste incredible. But stick with the salmon, it will taste much better!

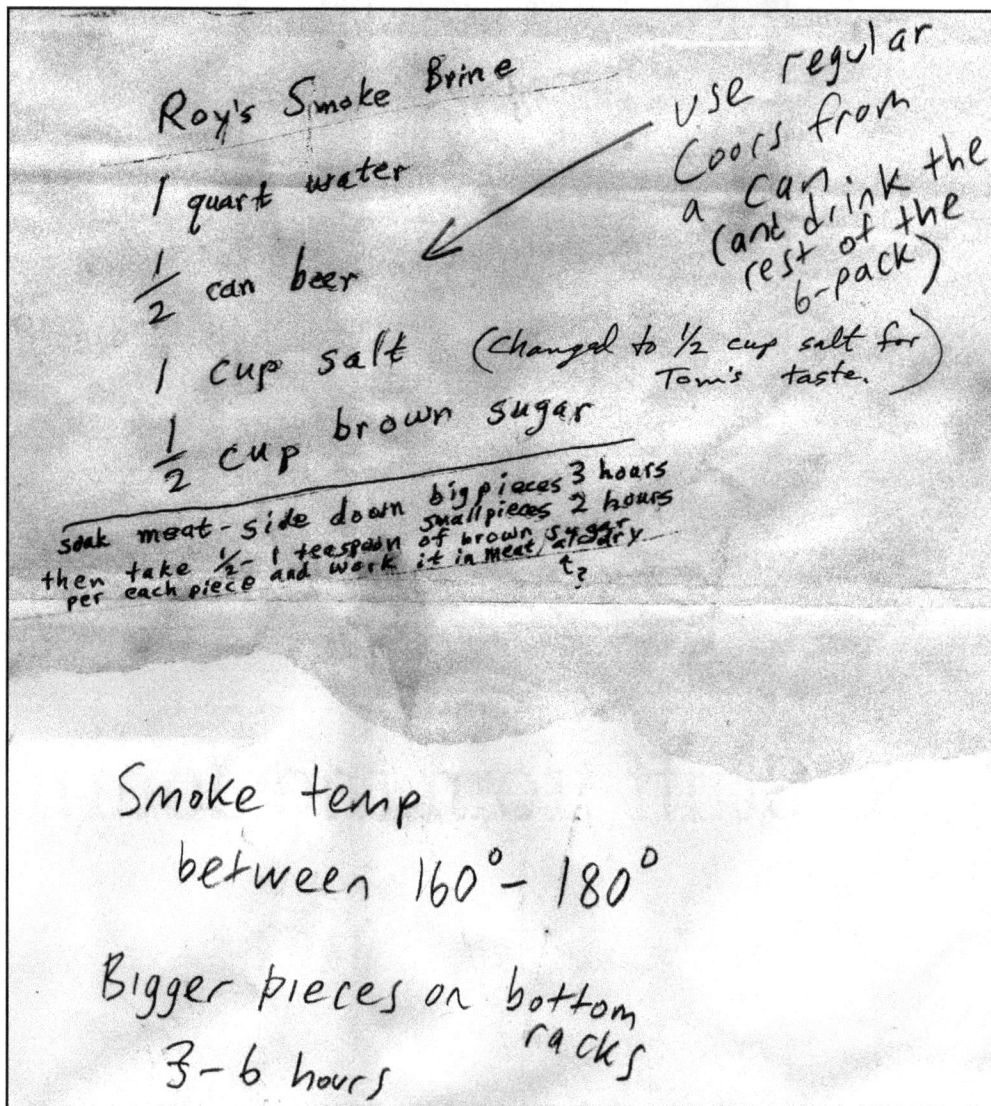

Roy's Smoke Brine

1 quart water

½ can beer ← use regular Coors from a can (and drink the rest of the 6-pack)

1 cup salt (Changed to ½ cup salt for Tom's taste.)

½ cup brown sugar

soak meat - side down big pieces 3 hours small pieces 2 hours
then take ½ - 1 teaspoon of brown sugar dry. per each piece and work it in meat.

Smoke temp between 160° - 180°

Bigger pieces on bottom racks 3 - 6 hours

THE SEASICK SAILOR
OR
CONVULSING COOK

A poem by Peter Maricich,
a fisherman, who is now a rocket scientist (for real)

I think that I shall never be, More wary of a nasty sea,
When it gets rough, God's rebuke, Would probably still not stop the puke.

Food goes in and churns about, Then comes on up and right back out.
But one good thing you have to say, I taste my meals six times a day.

The food goes down, each savored bite, Then flies on out in strickened flight.
I laugh about it now, but sigh. When I am sick I want to die.

Here is how the epic goes. When greasy food gets to the nose,
My brain it argues, tries to plead. But my stomach, will just not take heed.

My body tired of crashing bout, Screams and hollers – let it out!
For men far hardier than I, Have given up and let it fly.

Pretty soon my brain relents, My stomach thinks it's heaven sent.
My jaws relax, let pass a burp, A mouth screams out, "Where do I urp?"

Eyes soon search the room in pain, Legs propel me – half in vain.
My shipmates watch the clean scrubbed floor, Will Peter make it out the door?

Hands reach out, the boat just rocked, I hope the God damned door ain't locked,
I'd cursed the door, no doubt a sin, But does it open out or in?

(To those of you who think it's funny, I'll tell you puke is awful runny,
Once that juice is on the loose, You don't know who you're going to goose.)

My fingers finally reach the latch, I scramble out – up through the hatch.
But my foot it catches on a rag, Next time I'll steal that vomit bag.

At last I make it to the side, The puke swells up – it's bonafide.
My stomach muscles tighten up, Here comes another half a cup.

My mouth is open, jaws spread wide, Yes it did, it cleared the side.
But what's this stuff upon my sock, and still we haven't left the dock.

THE EAGLE OF DAKAVAK (a true story)

Fishing is much more than just a job. It ends up equating to a philosophy of life. When one spends months on the sea, away from their immediate family, friends and civilization, it gives a person a lot of time to think. Also, when faced with the hardships of nature and the grueling demands of fishing-boat life, people are forced to come to honest grips with themselves.

What are you made of? Who are you? What is your role on this planet? What is really important? And how much will you endure to reach a goal? These are all questions that in one way or another, a people tend to answer for themselves during a season, or a life, of commercial fishing.

One of the greatest lifelong lessons I learned was during one of the snottiest days of my entire 13-summer fishing career while fishing with Uncle Roy on the Mainland. The weather was horrible, we were extremely tired, we had a major equipment failure, and all of us just wanted to anchor up and take a nap. All of us, that is, except for the Eagle of Dakavak.

My uncle, Roy Maricich (1927-2009), had been a highliner salmon fisherman in Alaska for nearly 50 years. He claimed that his success was a result of hard work, luck, and learning from past mistakes. I'm convinced that his abilities were derived from more of a natural origin. As if he were born from Mother Nature herself and placed on this earth to fish, Roy's instinct was ever so apparent when the odds were against him. Like the wildest of animals, his will to survive was a driving force in his life. One thing was for sure, he would never quit, no matter how bad things looked.

It was the summer of '92, and the fishing at Afognak Island, Alaska was poor. Roy decided that we'd seen enough. We tightened up the rigging of the Lady Lyla, and traveled to the mainland. The trip across the Shelikof Strait was a bumpy one with with the seas building to more than 15 feet.

Not only was the weather crappy when we'd reached the fishing grounds off Dakavak, but Roy's worst nightmare had come true. While we'd wasted an entire day sifting water at Afognak, boats were catching 1,000 to 2,500 red salmon a haul in Dakavak. Some vessels had grossed $50,000 boat stocks in the time we'd been piddling around in the wrong area—resulting in earnings of about $5,000 per each deck hand for only a day's work on those boats. Roy was chewing toothpicks like a fiend, a habit he partook when the odds weren't in his favor. It was getting late in the day, but we had time to make one haul. While the net was in the water, the nightmare got worse. The engine in our power skiff died. Without it, we couldn't fish.

Our engineer, Jim Coger, pulled the valve covers off the old diesel engine and found the problem. Its push rods were severely bent. We'd recently had some work done at the cannery and the mechanics made an error during the engine's assembly. All odds were against us. It was the hottest salmon run of the season—and maybe the decade—and we got there late and had no skiff. To top things off, the parts we needed to fix it were only available in Kodiak city, which was 12 hours away.

It looked like we were going to have to quit and travel to Kodiak. I should have known better. If there's one word that Roy didn't have in his vocabulary, it was "quit". Before we knew it, Roy was eyeing a small, green dinghy that was tied up floating behind the tender. Our cook, Matt Castle, and I looked at each other in disbelief. "Uncle Roy couldn't actually be considering using that little boat as our skiff, could he?" we thought. It looked like something you might use to jig for bluegill in a lake somewhere—but certainly not something you'd picture yourself using to fight williwaws and peeling waves, fishing salmon off Mainland Alaska.

Roy, however, had complete confidence in his and his crew's ability—and the fishability of that sketchy dinghy. And before our skiff man, Chad Leese, knew it, he was sitting in his new skiff, which we swapped for the old one. It was a puke green colored, 10-foot, plastic trout-fishing boat, complete with Styrofoam insulation for maximum flotation. There was a good chance Chad would need it. The only thing missing were oars, which were probably included with it when it was new, about 50 years earlier. Several hours later, we awoke, picked the anchor and got ready for fishing. Matt and I said the "Hail Mary" for Chad. We laughed as he bailed a foot of water from his leaky skiff.

An overturned 5-gallon, Delo 400 oil bucket made an excellent seat as Chad started up his low-horsepower, circa-1945 Evinrude outboard engine. Chad just laughed with a crazed look in his eye. A smoldering Marlboro hung in the corner of his mouth as he listened to the powerless putt, putt, putt of our substitute skiff. We attempted to set the net, but our new skiff, nicknamed the Green Machine, didn't have enough power to pull our net off the deck. Matt and I grabbed the bunt of our seine with full arms and manhandled it into the water.

We thought everything was fine until, suddenly, the skiff was nearly flipped over by the tow line! Chad came close to swimming, but luckily had enough experience to escape the situation and corrected the problem. Chad was O.K., but our stand-in skiff wasn't; the outboard motor broke down. The sheer pin had snapped and disabled the propeller from spinning. We pulled 50 fathoms of our heavy net with the skiff attached to it, back to the boat by hand. There were jellyfish splattering everywhere and Uncle Roy was screaming. It wasn't a pretty scene. Chad just sat in the dinghy with his wet cigarette dangling from his lips.

Actual photo of Chad Leese hurling the heaving line to Jim Coger, while fishing reds with "The Green Machine" skiff, near Dakavak Bay.

It looked like we were out of luck and would most certainly have to gimp back to Kodiak with a broken skiff. It wasn't a good time for this to happen. Some boats were catching 500 a haul, which meant another hot day of fishing that we'd miss. With pure ingenuity, Coger managed to MacGyver a sheer pin out of an old welding rod. He made some extras too, just in case we'd need them later—and we would. It worked just fine and we were able to fish.

Then Roy got that look in his eye, the look of anger and

perseverance. He couldn't be defeated. We wouldn't quit. Roy carefully set his net and used his natural instinct to catch fish. Our replacement skiff lacked basic power and pulling ability, but Roy's perseverance and ability guided us to success. Roy was able to harness the forces of the wind and tides to fill our net with salmon.

We fished rather well the rest of the day. The sheer pin broke every hour or so, and Chad would stop everything, take apart the outboard motor, and fix it, so we could continue fishing. The day ended when the tide drifted us over a king crab pot and ripped a 150-fathom hole through our net. We weren't too upset though. We'd managed to catch over 15,000 pounds of beautiful, blue-backed sockeyes for an overall excellent day of fishing—representing about $2,000 for each of our crew for a hard day's work. If it weren't for Roy's persistence, we would've caught nothing.

We were creatures of nature with the will to survive. Our skiff had no power, so we used the wind and tides to shape our net. Our desire to buck the tides of failure was earthly. Yet, the inner force that helped us reach our goal was spiritual. The natural embrace of our animal and spirit was inspired by the sea.

A bald eagle flew in the distance, hunting for hours on end with extreme patience. It would glide with the wind and then fly against it. Eventually it spotted an unsuspecting salmon, which it would grab with its fierce talons and bring back to its nest. Roy once told me that if he were any animal besides human, he'd want to be an eagle. At Dakavak, and everywhere else he fished, he spread his wings, and soared as a highliner.

Roy Maricich on the f/v Lady Lyla,
chewing on his trademark toothpick.

Ahhh... another
beautiful day in
Shelikof Strait!

Fresh salmon,
iced and ready to
be eaten.

Inside a crab pot.

PART 5

Contact List of Skippers

and Permit Holders

CONTACT LIST OF SKIPPERS AND PERMIT HOLDERS

If you've decided that working on a commercial fishing boat is an opportunity you'd like to pursue, the following list should help you toward realizing your goal. It contains over 17,000 names and addresses of individuals who hold commercial fishing permits in Alaska. Besides walking the docks, contacting the people on this list is the only way for someone without experience or connections to get hired. Many of these people are skippers, own boats, or are related to people who run fishing boats.

An efficient way to contact skippers is by mailing them letters. But don't expect immediate responses. If the fishing season has already begun, you should focus on the next season. Advance planning, patience and a good resume will be most effective. Once skippers have your resume, a few follow-up phone calls might help, if you have access to or have been provided with their phone numbers.

Always show courtesy and consideration when trying to get in touch with the people on this list. Many skippers should be delighted to hear from you and happy to discuss employment with you or refer you to someone else. Don't be timid. Even though you're contacting strangers, they're normal people just like you, who share your common interest in fishing and making money.

The following will explain how to interpret the information in the following list:

Name:	Clyde Yellalot*
Address:	1234 Lettergo Lane
City, State, Zip:	Bay of Pigs, WA, 98991
Boat Name:	Arctic Desperado
(if available)	

*Note: Please don't write any letters or make any calls to Captain Clyde Yellalot. He's purely a fictitious character—but you probably already figured that out, huh?

Also, this list originates from the Alaska Department of Fish & Game commercial fishing permit holder database at: https://www.cfec.state.ak.us/plook/#downloads It is a complicated database to dig into, so the processed list we provide here may be easier to read.

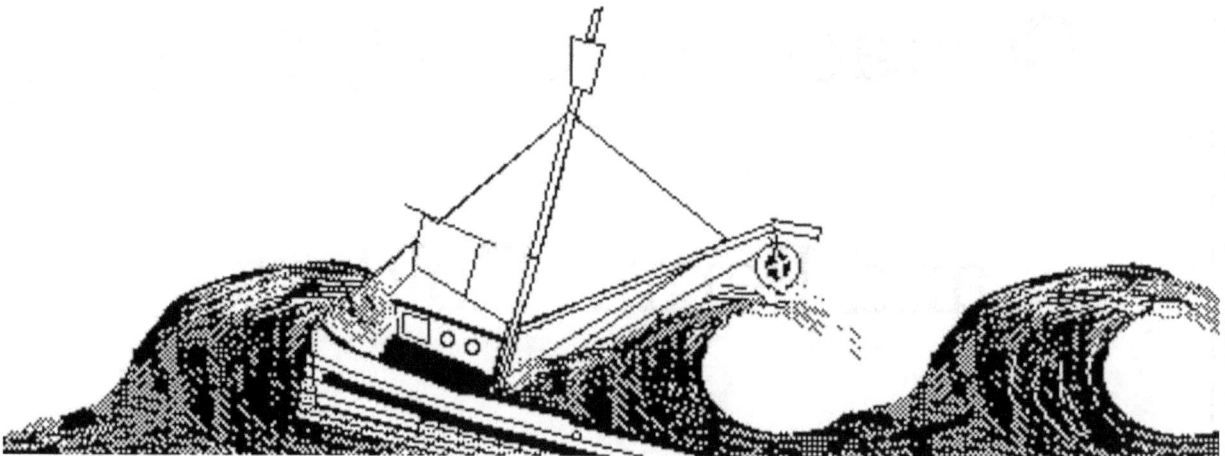

SALMON FISHING LIST—PURSE SEINE

SALMON, PURSE SEINE, SOUTHEAST

NINA ALBER, BOX 111, CORDOVA, AK 99574
ANTHONY ALFIERI, 1266 MOANA DR, SAN DIEGO, CA 92107
JOE ALFIERI, 1340 PLUM ST, SAN DIEGO, CA 92106
MICHAEL ALFIERI, 18120 196TH AVE SE, RENTON, WA 98058
JASPER ALLBRETT, BOX 2223, SITKA, AK 99835
PETER ANCICH, 2131 VAN KARAJAN DR, RANCHO PALOS VERDE, CA 90275
MARK ANDERSON, 49 NORTH STAR LN, FRIDAY HARBOR, WA 98250
NANCY ANDERSON, BOX 34, CHEHALIS, WA 98532
NORMAN ANDERSON, 620 W LAKE SAMISH, BELLINGHAM, WA 98229
TRAVIS ANDERSON, BOX 1623, SITKA, AK 99835
ROBERT ANK, 19316 133RD PL SE, RENTON, WA 98058
ANDREW BABICH, 8306 25TH AVE CT NW, GIG HARBOR, WA 98332
MICHAEL BABICH, 13510 GOODNOUGH DR NW, GIG HARBOR, WA 98332
NICK BABICH, 13310 PURDY DR NW, GIG HARBOR, WA 98332
RANDALL BABICH, BOX 429, LAKEBAY, WA 98349
JAMES BACON, 3357 S TONGASS HWY, KETCHIKAN, AK 99901
FRANK BALOVICH, BOX 1396, SITKA, AK 99835
TY BARKHOEFER, 103 SCARLETT WAY, SITKA, AK 99835
DAVIS BARRETT, BOX 842, PORT TOWNSEND, WA 98368
DAVID BARRY, 3980 N DOUGLAS HWY, JUNEAU, AK 99801
JOHN BARRY, 800 HALIBUT POINT RD #C, SITKA, AK 99835
DALE BARTELDS, 301 WORTMAN LP, SITKA, AK 99835
DAVID BEAUDIN, 430 S BLACK AVE, BOZEMAN, MT 59715
GLENN BECK, 127 CLARKS FALL RD, ASHAWAY, RI 2804
ROBERT BECKER, BOX 240238, DOUGLAS, AK 99824
WALTER BENKMAN, 10533 14TH AVE NW, SEATTLE, WA 98177
GREGORY BERITICH, 1810 23RD AVE CT SE, PUYALLUP, WA 98374
MITCHELL BERITICH, 2128 N FRACE, TACOMA, WA 98406
IVO BEZMALINOVIC, 1916 PIKE PL #1255, SEATTLE, WA 98101
DAVID BILL, 3042 CENTER RD, LOPEZ, WA 98261
ANDREW BLAIR, BOX 108, FOX ISLAND, WA 98333
BRIAN BLANDOV, BOX 436, METLAKATLA, AK 99926
BRIAN BLANKENSHIP, 4316 VALLHALLA DR, SITKA, AK 99835
ERIC BLANKENSHIP, 1808 EDGECUMBE DR, SITKA, AK 99835
JEFF BLANKENSHIP, 1709 HALIBUT POINT RD #12, SITKA, AK 99835
PAUL BLANKENSHIP, 500 LINCOLN ST #B6, SITKA, AK 99835
WALLACE BOTSFORD, 721 15TH ST, BELLINGHAM, WA 98225
TONY BOZANICH, 3534 168 AVE NE, BELLEVUE, WA 98008
JOHN BRANTUAS, BOX 1365, PETERSBURG, AK 99833
JARED BRIGHT, BOX 2097, PETERSBURG, AK 99833
TOBIAS BRIGHT, BOX 2097, PETERSBURG, AK 99833
JIM BRISCOE, 1714 WILSON AVE, BELLINGHAM, WA 98225
ROBERT BRISCOE, 1043 PEACE PORTAL DR, BLAINE, WA 98230
WILLIAM BROADHEAD, BOX 221, WILSON, WY 83014
JAMES BRUNSMAN, BOX 105, DAYVILLE, OR 97825
JAKOB BUECHE, 2023 E SIMS WAY #207, PORT TOWNSEND, WA 98368
JARED BURDETT.GROSS, 37 POTTER RD, KETCHIKAN, AK 99901
CHRISTIAN BUSCHMANN, BOX 898, PETERSBURG, AK 99833
RONN BUSCHMANN, BOX 1367, PETERSBURG, AK 99833
TEDDY BUTTLE, 8712 8TH AVE NW, SEATTLE, WA 98117
TODD CANNON, 7612 190TH NE, ARLINGTON, WA 98271
ARLENE CARLE, BOX 32, HYDABURG, AK 99922
JAN CARLE, BOX 1, HYDABURG, AK 99922
JOHN CARLE, BOX 1, HYDABURG, AK 99922
MATTHEW CARLE, BOX 32, HYDABURG, AK 99922
WESTON CARROLL, BOX 3013, HOMER, AK 99603
DANIEL CASTLE, 4430 S TONGASS HWY, KETCHIKAN, AK 99901
JAMES CASTLE, 87 SHOUP ST, KETCHIKAN, AK 99901
DOUGLAS CHANEY, 11719 MADERA DR SW, LAKEWOOD, WA 98499
SCOTT CHENEY, 3512 FIDALGO BAY RD, ANACORTES, WA 98221
CHARLES CHRISTENSEN, BOX 824, PETERSBURG, AK 99833
DALE CHRISTENSEN, 18912 88TH AVE W, EDMONDS, WA 98026
DAVID CHRISTENSEN, 7301 164TH PL SW, EDMONDS, WA 98026
JOE CISNEY, 994 REHBERG RD, GREENBANK, WA 98253

JAY CLIFTON, 3802 HALIBUT POINT RD, SITKA, AK 99835
RUSSELL COCKRUM, 5791 N TONGASS HWY, KETCHIKAN, AK 99901
RALPH COLE, 14084 MADRONA DR, ANACORTES, WA 98221
WILLIAM CONNOR, BOX 1124, PETERSBURG, AK 99833
CHRIS CORNWELL, 4220 CRYSTAL SPRINGS DR, BAINBRIDGE ISD, WA 98110
CRAIG COUNCILMAN, 11029 33RD DR SE, EVERETT, WA 98208
VERNON CRANE, 111 BAHRT CIR, SITKA, AK 99835
BRUCE CRESSWELL, BOX 219, TYRONE, NM 88065
DANIEL CROME, BOX 1010, WESTPORT, WA 98595
TIMOTHY CURRALL, 433 FRONT ST, KETCHIKAN, AK 99901
CLYDE CURRY, BOX 572, PETERSBURG, AK 99833
JOHN CURRY, 444 S STATE ST #409, BELLINGHAM, WA 98225
JULIANNE CURRY, BOX 2182, PETERSBURG, AK 99833
LANCE CURRY, 2198 FERNDALE TER, FERNDALE, WA 98248
JEROME DAHL, BOX 1275, PETERSBURG, AK 99833
JOHN DEGROEN, 9810 SW 148TH ST, VASHON, WA 98070
ARCHIE DEMMERT, BOX 223, KLAWOCK, AK 99925
ARTHUR DEMMERT, BOX 125, CRAIG, AK 99921
CURTIS DEMMERT, BOX 223, KLAWOCK, AK 99925
DAVID DEMMERT, BOX 6097, EDMONDS, WA 98026
JOSEPH DEMMERT, 7802 209TH ST SW, EDMONDS, WA 98026
KARL DEMMERT, BOX 556, CRAIG, AK 99921
LAWRENCE DEMMERT, 5775 SCHICKLES LN, BELLINGHAM, WA 98226
LONNIE DEMMERT, BOX 2683, STANWOOD, WA 98292
MICHAEL DEMMERT, BOX 391, CRAIG, AK 99921
NICHOLAS DEMMERT, BOX 1132, CRAIG, AK 99921
NICHOLAS DEMMERT, BOX 1132, CRAIG, AK 99921
STEVEN DEMMERT, 11700 MUKILTEO SPDWAY 201-1031, MUKILTEO, WA 98275
TROY DENKINGER, 2221 HALIBUT POINT RD, SITKA, AK 99835
RANDALL DOBRYDNIA, 69 W MATTLE RD, KETCHIKAN, AK 99901
KURT DOBSZINSKY, 1989 DRAKE AVE, POINT ROBERTS, WA 98281
LEIF DOBSZINSKY, BOX 752, FOX ISLAND, WA 98333
MARK DOBSZINSKY, 17002 12TH AVE SW, NORMANDY PARK, WA 98166
LARRY DONTOS, 2334 FAIRWAY LN, OAK HARBOR, WA 98277
RONALD DURGAN, BOX 340, CRAIG, AK 99921
SIDNEY EDENSHAW, BOX 352, HYDABURG, AK 99922
KEN EICHNER, 5166 SHORELINE DR N, KETCHIKAN, AK 99901
L EIDE, BOX 15, PETERSBURG, AK 99833
LANSING EIDE, BOX 15, PETERSBURG, AK 99833
MITCHELL EIDE, BOX 981, PETERSBURG, AK 99833
ED EINARSON, 9311 VALLEY VIEW RD, BLAINE, WA 98230
LARRY ENGBLOM, 11635 E OAKMONT DR, MUKILTEO, WA 98275
GLENDA ENLOE, 2609 HALIBUT POINT RD, SITKA, AK 99835
JEFF ERICKSON, BOX 53, PETERSBURG, AK 99833
ROCKY ERTZBERGER, BOX 298706, WASILLA, AK 99629
GEORGE ESQUIRO, BOX 1993, PORT TOWNSEND, WA 98368
IZAAK ESQUIRO, BOX 984, WARM SPRINGS, OR 97761
CHRIS EVENS, BOX 886, PETERSBURG, AK 99833
CRAIG EVENS, BOX 585, PETERSBURG, AK 99833
ERIC EVENS, BOX 1412, PETERSBURG, AK 99833
CHRISTINE FANNING, 2925 JACKSON RD, JUNEAU, AK 99801
JIM FARMER, BOX 692, CRAIG, AK 99921
ROBERT FELLOWS, 266 E BAYVIEW AVE, HOMER, AK 99603
MICHAEL FILE, BOX 1666, PETERSBURG, AK 99833
SCOTT FILE, 4515 TRAFALGAR, JUNEAU, AK 99801
PAUL FINNEY, 1588 HILLSIDE PL, HOMER, AK 99603
CHRIS FLINN, 927 15TH ST, BELLINGHAM, WA 98225
CHARLES FOGLE, 5722 CAMPBELL LAKE RD, ANACORTES, WA 98221
C.DAVID FRANKLIN, 3401 W LAWTON ST, SEATTLE, WA 98199
KYLE FRANKLIN, BOX 62, PETERSBURG, AK 99833
ANTHONY FRANULOVICH, 1302 N AVE, ANACORTES, WA 98221
GERALD GAMBLE, 3602 ENTRADA DR NE, OLYMPIA, WA 98506
RICHARD GEIST, 3401 W LAWTON ST, SEATTLE, WA 98199
CYNTHIA GENTHER, 3214 LILLY LAKE RD, BOW, WA 98232
ANTHONY GEORGE, 1916 LARRABEE AVE #B, BELLINGHAM, WA 98225

SALMON FISHING LIST—PURSE SEINE

MATTHEW GIAMBRONE, 410 CALHOUN AVE, JUNEAU, AK 99801
DEREK GIBB, BOX 1845, PETERSBURG, AK 99833
BRIAN GIERARD, BOX 7343, KETCHIKAN, AK 99901
DANIEL GILBERT, BOX 2531, KODIAK, AK 99615
MICHELLE GILBERTSEN, 19128 TRILOGY PARKWAY E, BONNEY LK, WA 98391
GENE GLAAB, 609 OJA ST, SITKA, AK 99835
JAMES GLENOVICH, 818 17TH ST, BELLINGHAM, WA 98225
ROBERT GLENOVICH, 480 S STATE ST #102, BELLINGHAM, WA 98225
JEFFREY GOLDEN, 8322 SILVER LAKE RD, MAPLE FALLS, WA 98266
STEVEN GOOD, BOX 85540, SEATTLE, WA 98145
DENNIS GOSPODINOVIC, 5087 ZANDER DR, BELLINGHAM, WA 98226
KEVIN GRANBERG, BOX 2002, PETERSBURG, AK 99833
KIRBY GREEN, 418 HIGHLAND DR #3, SEATTLE, WA 98109
RANDAL GREGG, BOX 20373, JUNEAU, AK 99802
JEFFREY GRIN, BOX 397, WRANGELL, AK 99929
BEN GROSS, 8012 POPPY CT, JUNEAU, AK 99801
MICHAEL GRUENHEIT, 2605 E ST, BELLINGHAM, WA 98225
R HALDANE, 4611 SUNNYSIDE AVE N, SEATTLE, WA 98103
DEAN HALTINER, BOX 443, PETERSBURG, AK 99833
FRED HALTINER, BOX 408, PETERSBURG, AK 99833
ROBERT HALTINER, BOX 808, PETERSBURG, AK 99833
KURT HANSEN, 5266 35TH AVE NE, SEATTLE, WA 98105
WILLIAM HANSEN, 7602 76TH AVE SW, LAKEWOOD, WA 98498
AUDREY HANSON, 4797 NETTLE LANE, BELLINGHAM, WA 98226
BRET HANSON, 2916 ST CLAIR ST, BELLINGHAM, WA 98226
JEFF HANSON, 5639 WHITEHORN WAY, BLAINE, WA 98230
BRADLEY HAYNES, 243 W MATTLE RD, KETCHIKAN, AK 99901
DANNY HAYNES, BOX 7036, KETCHIKAN, AK 99901
GARY HAYNES, 625 SUNSET DR, KETCHIKAN, AK 99901
BLAINE HAYWARD, BOX 256, METLAKATLA, AK 99926
ROYCE HAYWARD, BOX 161, METLAKATLA, AK 99926
RONALD HENRY, 2417 TONGASS AVE #111-141, KETCHIKAN, AK 99901
EDMOND HISAW, BOX 1179, TENINO, WA 98589
ALBERT HOFSTAD, BOX 1030, PETERSBURG, AK 99833
MICHAEL HOLMSTROM, 17952 MCLEAN RD, MOUNT VERNON, WA 98273
GEORGE HOOPER, 1900 W NICKERSON ST #116-68, SEATTLE, WA 98119
STEPHEN HUESTIS, 12704 471ST AVE SE, NORTH BEND, WA 98045
ROGER INGMAN, BOX 1155, SITKA, AK 99835
SARA JACKINSKY, BOX 1044, HOMER, AK 99603
ALAN JACKLET, 4521 325TH AVE NE, CARNATION, WA 98014
JEFFREY JACKSON, 3803 MCGINNIS DR, JUNEAU, AK 99803
MARY JACOBS, BOX 135, OPHIR, OR 97464
JOHN JAGER, 4114 MATIA DR, FERNDALE, WA 98248
GEORGE JAMES, 13622 N 98TH AVE #K LIMA COURT, SUN CITY, AZ 85351
DORIS JANOVICH, BOX 372, GIG HARBOR, WA 98335
HOLLIS JENNINGS, 1900 W NICKERSON ST #116-7, SEATTLE, WA 98119
BRAD JENSEN, 813 52ND ST, PORT TOWNSEND, WA 98368
DOUGLAS JENSEN, BOX 92535, ANCHORAGE, AK 99509
ERIC JENSEN, 17403 COLONY RD, BOW, WA 98232
JEREMY JENSEN, 2900 JACKSON RD, JUNEAU, AK 99801
MARC JERKOVICH, 3710 HARBORVIEW DR, GIG HARBOR, WA 98332
NICK JERKOVICH, 3710 HARBORVIEW DR, GIG HARBOR, WA 98332
JOHN JOHANSON, BOX 276, KLAWOCK, AK 99925
NICHOLAS JOHANSON, 1900 W NICKERSON ST #213, SEATTLE, WA 98119
RUDOLPH JOHANSON, 411 FRONT ST, KETCHIKAN, AK 99901
RUDY JOHANSON, BOX 5120, KETCHIKAN, AK 99901
JUSTNA JOHNS, BOX 726, CRAIG, AK 99921
LEROY JOHNS, BOX 1126, SISTERS, OR 97759
HANS JOHNSON, 520 14TH ST, BOULDER, CO 80302
JOSH JOHNSON, 103 HORIZON WAY, SITKA, AK 99835
MOSES JOHNSON, 1413 HALIBUT POINT RD, SITKA, AK 99835
RONALD JOHNSON, BOX 2232, WRANGELL, AK 99929
TIMOTHY JOLIBOIS, 3725 N 24TH ST, TACOMA, WA 98407
DAVID JONES, BOX 64, WINTHROP, WA 98862
KENNETH JONES, 4092 GINNETT RD, ANACORTES, WA 98221
MARIE JURLIN, 3312 45TH ST NW, GIG HARBOR, WA 98335

NICK JURLIN, 4622 E BRADFORD AVE, ORANGE, CA 92867
MICHELE JW.PFUNDT, BOX 1162, PETERSBURG, AK 99833
DELBERT KADAKE, BOX 554, KAKE, AK 99830
ANDREW KALK, 415 COLEMAN ST, JUNEAU, AK 99801
BRIAN KANDOLL, BOX 1363, PETERSBURG, AK 99833
DARRELL KAPP, 338 BAYSIDE RD, BELLINGHAM, WA 98225
RYAN KAPP, 2202 TEAL CT, BELLINGHAM, WA 98229
TRAVIS KAPP, 4723 S PONDEROSA PK RD, PRESCOTT, AZ 86303
AARON KESTERSON, 8235 LUSK RD, CONCRETE, WA 98292
MATTHEW KINNEY, 103 KRAMER AVE, SITKA, AK 99835
ANDREW KITTAMS, BOX 1544, PETERSBURG, AK 99833
ARNIE KJARSTAD, 16609 S WALL ST, MOUNT VERNON, WA 98273
JEFFREY KOETJE, 18180 DUNBAR RD, MOUNT VERNON, WA 98273
ERNEST KOHLHASE, BOX 240524, DOUGLAS, AK 99824
JASON KOHLHASE, 10753 HORIZON DR, JUNEAU, AK 99801
KENNETH KRIEGER, 36813 S WIND CREST DR, TUCSON, AZ 85739
GILBERT KRIGBAUM, BOX 2409, WESTPORT, WA 98595
MICHAEL KRIGBAUM, BOX 564, GRAYLAND, WA 98547
ADANNA KVERNVIK, BOX 1081, PETERSBURG, AK 99833
CAROLYN KVERNVIK, BOX 1081, PETERSBURG, AK 99833
BEN KYLE, 2817 MARTIN ST, BELLINGHAM, WA 98226
JAMES KYLE, 4102 LINNELL RD, DEMING, WA 98244
SHON LANDON, BOX 22, TOLEDO, WA 98511
LAUCHLIN LEACH, 2318 NE 105TH ST, SEATTLE, WA 98125
ROBERT LEEKLEY, BOX 217, PETERSBURG, AK 99833
WILLIAM LEESE, 1014 HOYT AVE, EVERETT, WA 98201
JOHN LIDDICOAT, 4115 BAKER AVE NW, SEATTLE, WA 98107
RICHARD LINDBLOM, 2971 TILLICUM BEACH DR, CAMANO ISLAND, WA 98282
LONNIE LINDEMUTH, BOX 2069, SNOHOMISH, WA 98291
MICHAEL LOCKABEY, BOX 1542, WRANGELL, AK 99929
GREGG LOVROVICH, 5310 72ND AVE NW, GIG HARBOR, WA 98335
PAULINE LOVROVICH, 3406 ROSEDALE ST, GIG HARBOR, WA 98335
TIM LOVROVICH, 7021 120TH ST CT NW, GIG HARBOR, WA 98332
TOM LOVROVICH, 9705 JACOBSEN LN, GIG HARBOR, WA 98332
LOREN LUNDQUIST, BOX 244, EASTSOUND, WA 98254
CLIFFORD MACDONALD, BOX 575, PETERSBURG, AK 99833
ERIC MACIAS, 1900 W NICKERSON ST # 116-82, SEATTLE, WA 98119
FREDERICK MAGILL, BOX 444, PETERSBURG, AK 99833
DANIEL MAJORS, BOX 5358, KETCHIKAN, AK 99901
JOHN MALICH, 7809 OLYMPIC VIEW DR, GIG HARBOR, WA 98335
KAI MALICOAT, BOX 2266, SITKA, AK 99835
VIC MANDICH, 2800 MORAINE WAY, OXNARD, CA 93030
BRUCE MANN, 363 NE 178TH ST, SHORELINE, WA 98155
EDWARD MANNING, 11170 RIDGERIM TRAIL SE, PORT ORCHARD, WA 98367
ANDREW MANOS, 3014 EMORY ST, ANCHORAGE, AK 99508
THOMAS MANOS, BOX 749, GIRDWOOD, AK 99587
WILLIAM MANOS, 10371 MIRA VISTA DR, SANTA ANA, CA 92705
WILLIAM MANOS, 1566 KEKAULIKE AVE, KULA, HI 96790
ROY MARICICH, BOX 819, ANACORTES, WA 98221
TIMOTHY MARICICH, 13680 DONNELL RD, ANACORTES, WA 98221
BRUCE MARIFERN, BOX 917, PETERSBURG, AK 99833
JEFF MARKUSEN, 9653 RONALD DR, BLAINE, WA 98230
KENNETH MARKUSEN, 572 N HARVEY RD, BLAINE, WA 98230
ANDREW MARRESE, 2442 NW MARKET ST PMB #411, SEATTLE, WA 98107
DANIEL MARSDEN, BOX 15, METLAKATLA, AK 99926
KIRT MARSH, BOX 1421, PETERSBURG, AK 99833
J.CHERIE MARTENS, BOX 623, PETERSBURG, AK 99833
MARTY MARTINEZ, BOX 513, METLAKATLA, AK 99926
VICTORIA MARVIN.DENKINGER, 2221 HALIBUT POINT RD, SITKA, AK 99835
SIGURD MATHISEN, BOX 1460, PETERSBURG, AK 99833
WAYNE MATHISEN, BOX 671, PETERSBURG, AK 99833
PAUL MATSON, 1752 NW MARKET ST #800, SEATTLE, WA 98107
RODERICK MCCAY, BOX 161, PETERSBURG, AK 99833
KENT MCCOLLUM, BOX 2096, PETERSBURG, AK 99833
CHARLES MCCULLOUGH, BOX 707, PETERSBURG, AK 99833
JEFFREY MCFADYEN, BOX 592, PETERSBURG, AK 99833

SALMON FISHING LIST—PURSE SEINE

GARY MCGEE, 40 DRAYTON CT, BLAINE, WA 98230
ROBERT MCILRAITH, BOX 1515, EATONVILLE, WA 98328
JOHN MCLEAN, BOX 2191, HOMER, AK 99603
LEE MCVICKER, BOX 2336, WRANGELL, AK 99929
HERMAN MEINERS, BOX 92669, ANCHORAGE, AK 99503
THOMAS MEINERS, BOX 21843, JUNEAU, AK 99802
ERIK MENTEN, BOX 506, TENAKEE, AK 99841
MERCURY MICHAEL, 14580 MADISON AVE NE, BAINBRIDGE ISLAND, WA 98110
AARON MILLER, BOX 2144, PETERSBURG, AK 99833
JAMES MILLER, BOX 1184, PETERSBURG, AK 99833
SPENCER MILLER, 241 W HAMPTON LN, OLYMPIA, WA 98512
RICHARD MOLLER, BOX 1081, GIG HARBOR, WA 98332
DARKO MOROVIC, BOX 756, WESTPORT, WA 98595
MATTHEW MUNKRES, 9508 N HARBORVIEW DR, GIG HARBOR, WA 98332
KEVIN MURPHY, 4492 S TONGASS, KETCHIKAN, AK 99901
ROSS NAGAMINE, 213 GARDEN LANE, KETCHIKAN, AK 99901
PAUL NASH, BOX 1761, FRIDAY HARBOR, WA 98250
NIKOULAS NEBL, 3828 EVERGREEN AVE, KETCHIKAN, AK 99901
NORVAL NELSON, 1625 FRITZ COVE RD, JUNEAU, AK 99801
TODD NEVERS, 712 SIRSTAD ST, SITKA, AK 99835
DONALD NEWMAN, 415 NW 120TH, SEATTLE, WA 98177
YANCEY NILSEN, BOX 1822, PETERSBURG, AK 99833
MARK NUGENT, BOX 5382, KETCHIKAN, AK 99901
MATTHEW NUGENT, 31605 NE 123RD ST, DUVALL, WA 98019
VIRGINIA OLNEY, BOX 2456, SITKA, AK 99835
BAE OLNEY.MILLER, 505 OCAIN ST, SITKA, AK 99835
NICK OLNEY.MILLER, 3006 BARKER ST, SITKA, AK 99835
NELS OLSON, 80872 S VALLEY RD, DUFUR, OR 97021
DENNIS ONEIL, BOX 1083, PETERSBURG, AK 99833
PATRICK ONEIL, 349 RAVEN HILL RD, LOPEZ ISLAND, WA 98261
ALAN OTNESS, BOX 317, PETERSBURG, AK 99833
NELS OTNESS, BOX 2058, PETERSBURG, AK 99833
KELLAN PATRICK, 521B 20TH AVE, SEATTLE, WA 98122
KEVIN PATRICK, 2888 S 355TH ST, FEDERAL WAY, WA 98003
DREW PATTERSON, BOX 897, CRAIG, AK 99921
THOMAS PAWLAK, 1900 W NICKERSON #116-203, SEATTLE, WA 98119
JOHN PECKHAM, BOX 8394, KETCHIKAN, AK 99901
ALFRED PEELER, BOX 761, PETERSBURG, AK 99833
JUSTIN PEELER, BOX 184, SITKA, AK 99835
BRUCE PETERMAN, 4139 WOODLAND ST, SANTA MARIA, CA 93455
CHAD PETERMAN, 178 KASNYKU LN, FRIDAY HARBOR, WA 98250
MCKENNA PETERSON, BOX 3982, KETCHUM, ID 83340
STEVE PETERSON, BOX 550, VASHON, WA 98070
CHARLES PETTICREW, BOX 971, WRANGELL, AK 99929
ALEC PFUNDT, BOX 1342, PETERSBURG, AK 99833
BRYON PFUNDT, BOX 1162, PETERSBURG, AK 99833
JEB PHILLIPS, BOX 1253, PETERSBURG, AK 99833
KENNETH PHIPPEN, 312 TILSON ST, SITKA, AK 99835
CHARLES PIECUCH, 4737 4TH AVE NE, SEATTLE, WA 98105
JUSTIN PIECUCH, 1923 NE LAURIE VIEW, POULSBO, WA 98370
JACOB PIPES, 2442 NW MARKET ST PMB 527, SEATTE, WA 98107
RONALD PORTER, BOX 957, WARD COVE, AK 99928
DARRELL POWERS, BOX 618, WRANGELL, AK 99929
JOSEPH PURATICH, BOX 272, GIG HARBOR, WA 98335
ROBERT PURATICH, BOX 1223, GIG HARBOR, WA 98335
DAVID PYLE, 17423 SCHALIT WAY, LAKE OSWEGO, OR 97035
ROBERT QUARTERMAN, 281 BLACKHAWK RD, YAKIMA, WA 98908
IAN RABB, 5125 N. DOUGLAS HWY, JUNEAU, AK 99801
JAMISON RAMSEY, BOX 9631, KETCHIKAN, AK 99901
ROYCE.TODD RANNIGER, 226 CRANBERRY RD, KETCHIKAN, AK 99901
RONALD RECORDS, BOX 1345, CRAIG, AK 99921
IVAN REIFENSTUHL, 218 SHOTGUN ALLEY, SITKA, AK 99835
HARTMUT REIMNITZ, 23505 80TH AVE SW, VASHON, WA 98070
DARRELL RIGGS, 1921 DODGE CIR, SITKA, AK 99835
DARREN ROBERTS, 111 S 44TH ST, BELLINGHAM, WA 98229

RICK ROCHELEAU, BOX 631, SITKA, AK 99835
RICHARD ROOD, BOX 3466, LYNNWOOD, WA 98046
JASON ROONEY, BOX 307, WRANGELL, AK 99929
PAUL ROSTAD, BOX 183, KAKE, AK 99830
ERIC ROSVOLD, BOX 1144, PETERSBURG, AK 99833
STANLEY SAVLAND, BOX 621, HOONAH, AK 99829
AMY SCHAUB, 500 BAWDEN ST, KETCHIKAN, AK 99901
MART SCHONBERG, 125 SPOTTED FAWN COURT, SEDONA, AZ 86351
PAUL SCHONBERG, BOX 1167, STANWOOD, WA 98292
PETER SCHONBERG, 75-816F HIONA ST, HOLUALOA, HI 96725
J.CARLOS SCHWANTES, BOX 2335, SITKA, AK 99835
BRADFORD SCUDDER, 266 S MOBLEY LN, BOISE, ID 83712
KEVIN SEABECK, 8555 30TH NW, SEATTLE, WA 98117
DOUGLAS SELIVANOFF, 3000 BIG MOUNTAIN RD, WHITEFISH, MT 59937
AARON SEVERSON, BOX 507, PETERSBURG, AK 99833
MARK SEVERSON, BOX 1502, PETERSBURG, AK 99833
ROLLO SHAQUANIE, BOX 288, KAKE, AK 99830
JAY SIMERKA, 1929 SHERIDAN ST, PORT TOWNSEND, WA 98368
BRIAN SIMPSON, 3104 PLYMOUTH DR, BELLINGHAM, WA 98225
GARY SLAVEN, BOX 205, PETERSBURG, AK 99833
DAVID SORENSEN, 9825 SUNRISE BEACH DR NW, GIG HARBOR, WA 98332
PAIGE SORENSEN, 510 OLMSTEAD LN SW, OLYMPIA, WA 98512
JAMES SPEARIN, BOX 1019, HOMER, AK 99603
FREDERICK STAGER, BOX 8243, KODIAK, AK 99615
MARK STEVENS, BOX 863, WRANGELL, AK 99929
RANDY STEWART, 11374 WALKER RD, MOUNT VERNON, WA 98273
SVEN STROOSMA, 18273 W BIG LAKE BLVD, MOUNT VERNON, WA 98274
REX STROUP, 2001 COVE PL, ANACORTES, WA 98221
ANTRIL SUYDAM, 75-5608 HIENALOLI RD #31, KAILUA-KONA, HI 96740
MICHAEL SVENSON, 104 SHARON DR, SITKA, AK 99835
MIKE SVENSON, 104 SHARON DR, SITKA, AK 99835
JOHN SVENSSON, BOX 2059, KALAMA, WA 98625
JOHN SWANSON, BOX 1546, PETERSBURG, AK 99833
ROBERT SWANSON, BOX 924, PETERSBURG, AK 99833
JONATHAN SWEIGERT, 4305 SE COOPER, PORTLAND, OR 97206
DOMINICK TARABOCHIA, 8021 SHIRLEY AVE, GIG HARBOR, WA 98332
TANNER THAIN, BOX 824, CRAIG, AK 99921
NYLE THOMAS, BOX 1744, PETERSBURG, AK 99833
JAY THOMASSEN, BOX 1451, PETERSBURG, AK 99833
STEVEN THOMASSEN, BOX 424, WRANGELL, AK 99929
TROY THOMASSEN, BOX 152, PETERSBURG, AK 99833
MAGNUS THORSTENSON, 829 GOLDBELT AVE, JUNEAU, AK 99801
PEDER THORSTENSON, 1660 HALLINAN ST, LAKE OSWEGO, OR 97034
ROBERT THORSTENSON, 410 CALHOUN AVE, JUNEAU, AK 99801
DEREK THYNES, BOX 1624, PETERSBURG, AK 99833
JAMES TISSYCHY, 554 EAST ST, KETCHIKAN, AK 99901
CHARLES TREINEN, 2054 ARLINGTON DR, ANCHORAGE, AK 99517
PAUL TROKA, 8602 SOBEK LN, CONCRETE, WA 98237
JOHN UNDERHILL, BOX 1012, SITKA, AK 99835
HOUSTON VAUGHAN, BOX 770, CRAIG, AK 99921
JAMES VAUGHAN, BOX 770, CRAIG, AK 99921
KELVIN VAUGHAN, BOX 1256, CRAIG, AK 99921
DANIEL VEERHUSEN, BOX 971, HOMER, AK 99603
GREGORY VEITEHANS, 210 24TH ST, PORT TOWNSEND, WA 98368
WILLIAM VELER, BOX 387, HOONAH, AK 99829
KORY VERSTEEG, BOX 1775, PETERSBURG, AK 99833
GARRET VINCENTZ, BOX 1572, WARD COVE, AK 99928
JANET VITALICH, 622 W LAKE SAMMISH DR, BELLINGHAM, WA 98229
BRUCE WALLACE, 410 CALHOUN AVE, JUNEAU, AK 99801
JAMES WALTZ, 1418 191ST DR SE, SNOHOMISH, WA 98290
WILLIAM WAMSER, BOX 2071, CORDOVA, AK 99574
FRANK WARFEL, BOX 1512, WRANGELL, AK 99929
ADAM WARTMAN, 2144 NW 204TH ST, SHORELINE, WA 98177
SHARON WARTMAN, 2144 NW 204TH ST, SHORELINE, WA 98177
DOUGLAS WELLS, 3642 W LAWTON ST, SEATTLE, WA 98199

SALMON FISHING LIST—PURSE SEINE

MARK WEYNANDS, 22332 GLENN RD, MOUNT VERNON, WA 98273
MICHAEL WEYNANDS, 13090 BRIDGEVIEW WAY, MOUNT VERNON, WA 98273
LUKE WHITETHORN, BOX 1716, PETERSBURG, AK 99833
MARY WILLIAMS, BOX 103, KAKE, AK 99830
CHARLES WILLS, BOX 7554, KETCHIKAN, AK 99901
NOE WINROD, BOX 1056, CRAIG, AK 99921
TITUS WINROD, BOX 1291, CRAIG, AK 99921
FRANK WRIGHT, BOX 497, HOONAH, AK 99829
PHILLIP WYMAN, BOX 2507, SITKA, AK 99835
SETH WYMAN, 5024 ROBINWOOD LN, BOW, WA 98232
LAWRENCE YOUNG, 224 MAKA HOU LP, WAILUKU, HI 96793
MARK YOUNG, BOX 2016, SITKA, AK 99835
CHRIS YSTAD, 104 CHIRIKOV DR, SITKA, AK 99835
ANDY ZUANICH, 812 W CONNECTICUT ST, BELLINGHAM, WA 98225
MICHELLE ZUANICH, 6727 37TH AVE NW, SEATTLE, WA 98117
SHIRLEY ZUANICH, 812 W CONNECTICUT ST, BELLINGHAM, WA 98225

SALMON, PURSE SEINE, PRINCE WILLIAM SOUND

WAYNE ACKERLUND, 831 N AGAVE CT, IRVINS, UT 84738
DEBRA ADAMS, BOX 194, CORDOVA, AK 99574
MARK ADAMS, 6606 N ASSEMBLY ST, SPOKANE, WA 99218
LOUIE ALBER, BOX 111, CORDOVA, AK 99574
JASON ALEXANDER, 18315 87TH AVE SE, SNOHOMISH, WA 98296
LESLIE ALLEN, BOX 984, VALDEZ, AK 99686
MYRA ALLEN, BOX 984, VALDEZ, AK 99686
RUSSELL ALLEN, BOX 1062, CORDOVA, AK 99574
STEVEN ALLEY, BOX 488, VALDEZ, AK 99686
DEAN ANDERSON, BOX 41, CHIGNIK LAGOON, AK 99565
KALE ANDERSON, 1193 BAY AVE, HOMER, AK 99603
JON ANDREWS, BOX 1034, SEWARD, AK 99664
DIONICE ANUFRIEV, BOX 2356, HOMER, AK 99603
RYAN ASA, BOX 1134, CORDOVA, AK 99574
BENJAMIN BABIC, BOX 1833, CORDOVA, AK 99574
MATHEW BABIC, BOX 988, CORDOVA, AK 99574
MICHAEL BABIC, BOX 1853, CORDOVA, AK 99574
ANDREW BABICH, 8306 25TH AVE CT NW, GIG HARBOR, WA 98332
MICHAEL BABICH, 13510 GOODNOUGH DR NW, GIG HARBOR, WA 98332
KOAL BACKLUND, BOX 2944, SEWARD, AK 99664
J BAILEY, 1413 SUNRISE DR, ANCHORAGE, AK 99508
JAMES BALDRIDGE, 38280 ROBINSON LP RD, STERLING, AK 99672
JAMES BALDRIDGE, BOX 3665, KENAI, AK 99611
DAVE BEAM, BOX 297, GIRDWOOD, AK 99587
DONALD BERGQUIST, 4922 S SMUGGLERS COVE RD, FREELAND, WA 98249
LARS BERGQUIST, 4922 S SMUGGLERS COVE RD, FREELAND, WA 98249
RODGER BERGQUIST, 4816 SARATOGA RD, LANGLEY, WA 98260
CHARLES BLACK, BOX 666, HOMER, AK 99603
CLIFFORD BLACK, 11620 OUR RD, ANCHORAGE, AK 99516
DEREK BLAKE, BOX 245, CORDOVA, AK 99574
HUGHIE BLAKE, BOX 2376, CORDOVA, AK 99574
RONALD BLAKE, BOX 1236, CORDOVA, AK 99574
RONDA BLOUGH, BOX 555, HOONAH, AK 99829
GREGG BOSICK, BOX 34, KASILOF, AK 99610
GREGORY BOSICK, BOX 390, KASILOF, AK 99610
CHRISTOPHER BOURGEOIS, BOX 1945, CORDOVA, AK 99574
RYAN BROUGHTON, BOX 264, SEWARD, AK 99664
EZEKIEL BROWN, BOX 782, CORDOVA, AK 99574
JAMES BURTON, BOX 41, CORDOVA, AK 99574
JEFFERY CABANA, BOX 26, HOMER, AK 99603
JEREMY CABANA, BOX 719, HOMER, AK 99603
KAMI CABANA, BOX 201, GIRDWOOD, AK 99587
LARRY CABANA, BOX 3388, HOMER, AK 99603
LEROY CABANA, BOX 49, HOMER, AK 99603
RUSSEL CABANA, BOX 201, GIRDWOOD, AK 99587
TIM CABANA, BOX 201, GIRDWOOD, AK 99587
ROBERT CAMERON, 2120 41ST ST, ANACORTES, WA 98221

JOSTEN CARLSON, BOX 3496, VALDEZ, AK 99686
DOUGLAS CARROLL, BOX 1071, CORDOVA, AK 99574
KIP CARROLL, BOX 1173, CORDOVA, AK 99574
WESTON CARROLL, BOX 3013, HOMER, AK 99603
JEFF CHAPPELL, BOX 1343, CORDOVA, AK 99574
WARREN CHAPPELL, BOX 743, CORDOVA, AK 99574
ELMER CHESHIER, BOX 2264, CORDOVA, AK 99574
DUSTIN CLINE, 2821 WILEY POST AVE, ANCHORAGE, AK 99517
KIMBERLY COLLINS, BOX 1734, CORDOVA, AK 99574
TORI CONNOR, BOX 1641, PETERSBURG, AK 99833
MEGAN CORAZZA, BOX 732, HOMER, AK 99603
RICHARD CORAZZA, BOX 1320, HOMER, AK 99603
RICHARD CORAZZA, 200 W 34TH AVE #932, ANCHORAGE, AK 99503
SONJA CORAZZA, BOX 1320, HOMER, AK 99603
KEVIN CORCORAN, BOX 1371, CORDOVA, AK 99574
NICHOLAS CRUMP, BOX 321, VALDEZ, AK 99686
WILLIAM CRUMP, BOX 3731, VALDEZ, AK 99686
BERNARD CULBERTSON, BOX 2906, VALDEZ, AK 99686
DAVID DANIELS, BOX 930, VALDEZ, AK 99686
BRANDON DARR, 925 SOUNDVIEW AVE, HOMER, AK 99603
WILLIAM DAVIS, BOX 1494, KODIAK, AK 99615
EDWARD DAY, BOX 534, VALDEZ, AK 99686
PATRICK DAY, BOX 788, VALDEZ, AK 99686
STUART DEAL, 7314 11TH AVE NW, SEATTLE, WA 98117
ELI DEXTER, 2606 38TH ST, BELLINGHAM, WA 98229
RODERICK DEXTER, 2602 38TH ST, BELLINGHAM, WA 98229
TYLER DILLON, BOX 1326, CORDOVA, AK 99574
MATTHEW DOHNER, 4321 BOBLETT RD, BLAINE, WA 98230
RODNEY DOHNER, BOX 1912, BLAINE, WA 98231
NATHAN DOLL, BOX 23, CORDOVA, AK 99574
MAXMILLIAN DURTSCHI, BOX 1012, GIRDWOOD, AK 99587
MICHAEL DURTSCHI, BOX 1012, GIRDWOOD, AK 99587
MATTHEW DZIEDZIC, 125 ELLA VITA CT, DURANGO, CO 81301
RICK EBERLE, 14547 GIBRALTER RD, ANACORTES, WA 98221
ROBERT ECKLEY, BOX 1274, CORDOVA, AK 99574
DAVID EDENS, BOX 3456, HOMER, AK 99603
MARK EDENS, BOX 641, HOMER, AK 99603
KENNETH ENGBLOM, BOX 1475, CHELAN, WA 98816
BRYAN ERICKSON, 8759 GUIDE MERIDIAN RD, LYNDEN, WA 98264
ROXY ESTES, BOX 1709, CORDOVA, AK 99574
STEVE ESTES, BOX 155, CORDOVA, AK 99574
STEVEN FEENSTRA, BOX 991, BELLINGHAM, WA 98227
ROBERT FISCHER, 4155 SWEET RD, BLAINE, WA 98230
ERIC FLEMING, 6948 FAIRWEATHER DR, ANCHORAGE, AK 99518
C.DAVID FRANKLIN, 3401 W LAWTON ST, SEATTLE, WA 98199
MARCUS FULLER, BOX 3205, VALDEZ, AK 99686
ROBERT FUNKHOUSER, 2911 PLYMOTH DR, BELLINGHAM, WA 98225
ANTHONY GABRIEL, BOX 137, KENAI, AK 99611
GREGORY GABRIEL, BOX 3392, SOLDOTNA, AK 99669
JAMES GABRIEL, 4041 WINCHESTER LOOP, ANCHORAGE, AK 99507
JOSEPH GANNON, BOX 1901, CORDOVA, AK 99574
GAYLE GILDNES, 15006 CHANNEL LN, LA CONNER, WA 98257
STEVEN GILDNES, BOX 2393, CORDOVA, AK 99574
SWEN GILDNES, BOX 519, CORDOVA, AK 99574
MICHAEL GLASEN, BOX 2532, CORDOVA, AK 99574
MICHAEL GLASEN, BOX 432, CORDOVA, AK 99574
DINA GREGG, BOX 20373, JUNEAU, AK 99802
QUINCY GREGG, BOX 20373, JUNEAU, AK 99802
MASON GROVES, 3705 ARTIC #570, ANCHORAGE, AK 99503
MICHAEL GRUENHEIT, 2605 E ST, BELLINGHAM, WA 98225
JEFFREY GUARD, BOX 856, CORDOVA, AK 99574
KENNETH HALPIN, BOX 1022, HOMER, AK 99603
PETER HAMRE, 19460 VILLAGES SCENIC PARKWAY, ANCHORAGE, AK 99516
MICHAEL HAND, BOX 2181, CORDOVA, AK 99574
RAYMOND HARRIS, BOX 1318, SEWARD, AK 99664
ARNE HATCH, BOX 346, SEWARD, AK 99664

SALMON FISHING LIST—PURSE SEINE

DAVID HATCH, 1049 B AVE, EDMONDS, WA 98020
PAIGE HATCH, 4331 S CARIE WAY, BOISE, ID 83709
MATTHEW HEGGE, BOX 848, KODIAK, AK 99615
ROBERT HENRICHS, BOX 1000, CORDOVA, AK 99574
CALE HERSCHLEB, BOX 1261, CORDOVA, AK 99574
TRAVIS HINES, BOX 2968, HOMER, AK 99603
RAYMOND HONKOLA, BOX 100, CORDOVA, AK 99574
ROBERT HONKOLA, BOX 124, CORDOVA, AK 99574
JOHN HOPKINS, BOX 343, CORDOVA, AK 99574
SHILA HOUGH, 3733 BEN WALTERS LN #2, HOMER, AK 99603
FLOYD HUTCHENS, 2421 W BUCK HORN CT, EAGLE, ID 83616
SARA JACKINSKY, BOX 1044, HOMER, AK 99603
DOUGLAS JENSEN, BOX 92535, ANCHORAGE, AK 99509
GORDON JENSEN, BOX 785, CORDOVA, AK 99574
ISAAC JENSEN, BOX 1582, CORDOVA, AK 99574
JAMES JENSEN, BOX 365, CORDOVA, AK 99574
RODERICK JENSEN, BOX 1614, CORDOVA, AK 99574
BENJAMIN JOHNSON, BOX 263, CORDOVA, AK 99574
CHELSA JOHNSON, 110 W FAIRVIEW AVE, HOMER, AK 99603
ELI JOHNSON, BOX 1089, CORDOVA, AK 99574
GERALD JOHNSON, BOX 1887, WESTPORT, WA 98595
HANS JOHNSON, 520 14TH ST, BOULDER, CO 80302
RYAN JOHNSON, BOX 2931, KODIAK, AK 99615
KENNETH JONES, BOX 615, CORDOVA, AK 99574
VICTOR JONES, BOX 1831, CORDOVA, AK 99574
PATRICIA KALLANDER, BOX 2272, CORDOVA, AK 99574
ALAN KAPP, BOX 3312, VALDEZ, AK 99686
DARRELL KAPP, 338 BAYSIDE RD, BELLINGHAM, WA 98225
TERRANCE KILBREATH, 31 PINE ST #210, EDMONDS, WA 98020
RICHARD KING, 4371 KAPUNA RD, KILAUEA, HI 96754
JACOB KOMPKOFF, BOX 1055, VALDEZ, AK 99686
HENDRIK KRUITHOF, BOX 1784, CORDOVA, AK 99574
MARTIN KULLER, BOX 312, CATHLAMET, WA 98612
DAVID LARSON, BOX 581, CONWAY, WA 98238
JAMES LARSON, 19003 COUNTY LINE RD, STANWOOD, WA 98292
MICHAEL LAUKITIS, 59065 MEADOW LN, HOMER, AK 99603
BRIAN LEE, 31250 W LEE DR, SUTTON, AK 99674
EVERETT LINDHOLM, 415 E PARK DR, ANACORTES, WA 98221
ROBERT LINDSEY, 3162 SPRUCE CAPE RD, KODIAK, AK 99615
JOSEPH LINVILLE, BOX 1753, SEWARD, AK 99664
ROBERT LINVILLE, BOX 1771, CORDOVA, AK 99574
TYEE LOHSE, BOX 1275, CORDOVA, AK 99574
ALEXANDER LOPEZ, BOX 1648, VALDEZ, AK 99686
THOMAS LOPEZ, BOX 991, VALDEZ, AK 99686
THOMAS LOPEZ, BOX 991, VALDEZ, AK 99686
JOHN LOVE, BOX 141, GIRDWOOD, AK 99587
AMBER LUKIN, BOX 2039, HOMER, AK 99603
JACOB LUNDLI, BOX 632, CORDOVA, AK 99574
BRIAN LYTLE, BOX 2433, CORDOVA, AK 99574
PETER MACDONALD, BOX 1062, ANACORTES, WA 98221
EDWARD MANNING, 11170 RIDGERIM TRAIL SE, PORT ORCHARD, WA 98367
THOMAS MANOS, BOX 749, GIRDWOOD, AK 99587
HAYDEN MARKUSEN, 9510 HARVEY RD, BLAINE, WA 98230
JEFF MARKUSEN, 9653 RONALD DR, BLAINE, WA 98230
ROB MARKUSEN, 7627 AVERY LN, CUSTER, WA 98240
MICHAEL MAURER, BOX 1433, CORDOVA, AK 99574
RAYMOND MAY, BOX 8985, KODIAK, AK 99615
MARTIN MCCALLUM, 4351 S DISCOVERY RD, PORT TOWNSEND, WA 98368
ROBERT MCDONNELL, 230 SHALLOW SHORE RD, BELLINGHAM, WA 98229
GILLIAN MCKENZIE, BOX 2071, CORDOVA, AK 99574
SCOTT MCKENZIE, BOX 2071, CORDOVA, AK 99574
DANNY MCLEAN, BOX 351, HOMER, AK 99603
JACOB MCLEAN, BOX 2191, HOMER, AK 99603
JERI MCLEAN, BOX 2191, HOMER, AK 99603
JOHN MCLEAN, BOX 2191, HOMER, AK 99603

MARK MEADOWS, 4894 WENDY LN, KELSEYVILLE, CA 95451
MICHAEL MEINTS, BOX 2402, CORDOVA, AK 99574
GALEN MEYER, BOX 514, CORDOVA, AK 99574
MICHAEL MICKELSON, BOX 1504, CORDOVA, AK 99574
RICHARD MILL, BOX 39861, NINILCHIK, AK 99639
THANE MILLER, BOX 2961, VALDEZ, AK 99686
TIMOTHY MOORE, BOX 1646, HOMER, AK 99603
GEORGE MORRIS, 3426 BELVIDERE AVE SW, SEATTLE, WA 98126
JAMIN MORRIS, BOX 1959, HOMER, AK 99603
EMIL NELSON, BOX 130, HOMER, AK 99603
GUNNAR NELSON, 528 BAYSIDE RD, BELLINGHAM, WA 98225
JESSIE NELSON, BOX 130, HOMER, AK 99603
ROBERT NELSON, BOX 205, KASILOF, AK 99610
THOMAS NELSON, BOX 1392, HOMER, AK 99603
ERIC NEWBURY, BOX 136, GIRDWOOD, AK 99587
JON NICHOLS, BOX 266, CORDOVA, AK 99574
PETER NORNES, 21316 92ND PL W, EDMONDS, WA 98020
KEITH OMEY, 1511 MILL AVE, BELLINGHAM, WA 98225
KEVIN OTOOLE, BOX 65, CORDOVA, AK 99574
MAKENA OTOOLE, BOX 1986, CORDOVA, AK 99574
JOHN PALMISANO, 7249 SHADOWBROOK DR, KIRTLAND, OH 44094
KENNETH PARKER, 9577 WEST 5 MILE RD, BRANCH, MI 49402
DANIEL PATTERSON, 1900 W NICKERSON #116 BOX 17, SEATTLE, WA 98119
MCKENNA PETERSON, BOX 3982, KETCHUM, ID 83340
AARON PETTINGILL, BOX 916, CORDOVA, AK 99574
BRICE PHILLIPS, BOX 581, CORDOVA, AK 99574
DOUGLAS PHILLIPS, BOX 795, CORDOVA, AK 99574
CHARLES PIECUCH, 4737 4TH AVE NE, SEATTLE, WA 98105
JOHN PLATT, BOX 1085, CORDOVA, AK 99574
BRUCE PRIVETT, 2001 WASILLA FISHHOOK RD, WASILLA, AK 99654
ROBERT PURATICH, BOX 1223, GIG HARBOR, WA 98335
ARMIN REIMNITZ, 9004 191ST PL SW, EDMONDS, WA 98026
JOHN RENNER, BOX 756, CORDOVA, AK 99574
RAYMOND RENNER, BOX 1181, CORDOVA, AK 99574
BRUCE RIZER, BOX 113003, ANCHORAGE, AK 99511
RYAN ROGERS, 1470 FLINTRIDGE AVE, EUGENE, OR 97401
CHRIS ROSAUER, BOX 78, GIRDWOOD, AK 99587
MALCOLM ROSS, BOX 3476, HOMER, AK 99603
NEIL RUSSELL, 4216 E INDIGO CT, NAMPA, ID 83687
JUSTIN RYAN, BOX 2374, CORDOVA, AK 99574
ETHAN SANDELIN, 20536 GLOUCESTER LN, BEND, OR 97701
LARRY SANDELIN, 409 LONGTIME LN, SEDRO WOOLLEY, WA 98284
SAMUEL SCHAEFER, BOX 1261, FORT COLLINS, CO 80522
BARRY SCHAUFF, 316 CENTER ST, KODIAK, AK 99615
RICHARD SCHOLLENBERG, BOX 264, ANCHOR POINT, AK 99556
ANDREW SCUDDER, 531 N 28TH ST, BOISE, ID 83702
BRADFORD SCUDDER, 266 S MOBLEY LN, BOISE, ID 83712
PATRICK SELANOFF, BOX 3397, VALDEZ, AK 99686
GERALD SMALLWOOD, BOX 453, CORDOVA, AK 99574
CHARLES SMITH, BOX 1976, CORDOVA, AK 99574
GREGORY SMITH, BOX 2235, VALDEZ, AK 99686
KRISTEN SMITH, BOX 2260, VALDEZ, AK 99686
SKYLER SMITH, BOX 2215, ANACORTES, WA 98221
WAYNE SMITH, BOX 419, CORDOVA, AK 99574
ALENA SOLNTCEVA, BOX 1976, CORDOVA, AK 99574
JAMES SPEARIN, BOX 1019, HOMER, AK 99603
MATTHEW SPRINGER, BOX 2882, HOMER, AK 99603
IVAN STONOROV, 41046 CRESTED CRANE ST, HOMER, AK 99603
JEFFREY STRONG, 2026 FIRCREST AVE, COUPEVILLE, WA 98239
PAUL SUTTON, 2647 W PALAIS DR, COUR D'ALENE, ID 83815
RAY SUTTON, BOX 2469, VALDEZ, AK 99686
LINDA SUYDAM, BOX 987, KODIAK, AK 99615
RYAN TARABOCHIA, 8145 17TH AVE SW, SEATTLE, WA 98016
BRYN TENNYSON, BOX 167, DILLINGHAM, AK 99576
JAY THOMASSEN, BOX 1451, PETERSBURG, AK 99833

SALMON FISHING LIST—PURSE SEINE

JONATHAN THOMASSEN, BOX 836, SEWARD, AK 99664
CAROLYN THORNE, BOX 711, CORDOVA, AK 99574
GERALD THORNE, BOX 1192, CORDOVA, AK 99574
RYAN THORNE, BOX 2394, CORDOVA, AK 99574
CHARLES TOTEMOFF, 3000 C ST #301, ANCHORAGE, AK 99503
SCOTT TRESSLER, BOX 1078, SEWARD, AK 99664
NATHAN TUELLER, BOX 913, GIRDWOOD, AK 99587
WENDY TUELLER, BOX 913, GIRDWOOD, AK 99587
COLTEN TUTT, 2175 STERLING HWY, HOMER, AK 99603
ERIC TUTT, BOX 2452, HOMER, AK 99603
JOEL TUTT, BOX 387, HOMER, AK 99603
STEVE TUTT, BOX 1105, HOMER, AK 99603
HERBERT UPTON, BOX 2854, HOMER, AK 99603
GONZALO VILLALON, BOX 2695, CORDOVA, AK 99574
SCOTT VORRATH, BOX 281, CORDOVA, AK 99574
WILLIAM WAMSER, BOX 2071, CORDOVA, AK 99574
ROBERT WARE, 33585 CUMULUS RD, EAGLE RIVER, AK 99577
SHAWN WATERS, 9680 W 34TH CREST, BLAINE, WA 98230
NATHAN WIDMANN, BOX 1883, CORDOVA, AK 99574
JOHN WIESE, BOX 1031, CORDOVA, AK 99574
ROBERT WIESE, BOX 864, CORDOVA, AK 99574
TIM WILKIE, BOX 1726, SEWARD, AK 99664
MORGAN WILLIAMS, 7362 W PARKS HWY #223, WASILLA, AK 99623
SHAWN WILLIAMS, BOX 672505, CHUGIAK, AK 99567
ZACHARY WILLIAMS, 19136 BIRCHWOOD LOOP RD, CHUGIAK, AK 99567
JEREMY WINN, 315 GARFIELD, HOQUIAM, WA 98550
JACOB WISE, 1930 EAST END RD #B, HOMER, AK 99603
MARK WISNER, BOX 314, ANCHOR POINT, AK 99556
SERGEY YAKUNIN, BOX 5044, NIKOLAEVSK, AK 99556

SALMON, PURSE SEINE, COOK INLET

MATTHEW ALWARD, 60082 CLARICE WAY, HOMER, AK 99603
FREDERICK ANDERSON, 1193 BAY AVE, HOMER, AK 99603
JOHN BARNARD, 64525 PITZMAN AVE, HOMER, AK 99603
MARVIN BELLAMY, BOX 6426, HALIBUT COVE, AK 99603
JOHN BLACKWELL, BOX 1063, WINCHESTER BAY, OR 97467
MARINA BOSICK, BOX 34, KASILOF, AK 99610
PHILIP BRUDIE, BOX 111, HOMER, AK 99603
JOSEPH BRUNNER, 475 RAINBOW CT, HOMER, AK 99603
NATHAN BUCHANAN, BOX 1306, SEWARD, AK 99664
THOMAS BUCHANAN, BOX 821, SEWARD, AK 99664
THOMAS BUCHANAN, BOX 925, SEWARD, AK 99664
BARI CABANA, BOX 201, GIRDWOOD, AK 99587
BARREN CABANA, BOX 201, GIRDWOOD, AK 99587
HILARY CABANA, BOX 719, HOMER, AK 99603
JENNIFER CABANA, BOX 3388, HOMER, AK 99603
KAMI CABANA, BOX 201, GIRDWOOD, AK 99587
KANNEN CABANA, BOX 26, HOMER, AK 99603
TAYLA CABANA, BOX 26, HOMER, AK 99603
ASHTON CALLAHAN, BOX 3090, HOMER, AK 99603
ALBERT CARROLL, 55090 BENJAMIN AVE #1, HOMER, AK 99603
WESTON CARROLL, BOX 3013, HOMER, AK 99603
KASEY CLAY, 115 W PRASCH AVE, YAKIMA, WA 98902
AUGUSTUS COTTEN, BOX 6428, HALIBUT COVE, AK 99603
SAM COTTEN, BOX 6432, HALIBUT COVE, AK 99603
KYLE DENTON, 8521 EMERALD ST, ANCHORAGE, AK 99502
NICK DOWNS, 2732 LYNN ST, BELLINGHAM, WA 98229
KENNETH DUFFUS, 20441 PTARMIGAN BLVD, EAGLE RIVER, AK 99577
MARK EDMINSTER, BOX 1874, HOMER, AK 99603
MORGAN EJ.JONES, BOX 3472, HOMER, AK 99603
LEONARD FABICH, BOX 1331, HOMER, AK 99603
BRENDA FARREN, 497 WESTWOOD AVE, HOMER, AK 99603
RUSSELL FITZWATER, BOX 576, GIRDWOOD, AK 99587
CAMRON HAGEN, BOX 2647, HOMER, AK 99603
MARK HALPIN, BOX 2483, HOMER, AK 99603
THERESA HALPIN, BOX 1022, HOMER, AK 99603

DAVID HATCH, 1049 B AVE, EDMONDS, WA 98020
DOUG KELLER, 39980 FERNWOOD DR, HOMER, AK 99603
ANDRE LOVETT, BOX 4243, HOMER, AK 99603
WILLIAM LOVETT, BOX 4243, HOMER, AK 99603
BRAD MARDEN, BOX 2856, HOMER, AK 99603
DAVID MARTIN, BOX 468, CLAM GULCH, AK 99568
MICHAEL MARTINSON, 18908 WHIRLAWAY RD, EAGLE RIVER, AK 99577
BARBARA MCBRIDE, BOX 1857, HOMER, AK 99603
PATRICK MCELROY, BOX 456, KASILOF, AK 99610
JACOB MCLEAN, BOX 2191, HOMER, AK 99603
RYAN MEGANACK, BOX 5526, PORT GRAHAM, AK 99603
SERAPHIM MEGANACK, 425 W REDOUBT AVE # 307, SOLDOTNA, AK 99669
GEORGE MILNE, BOX 1846, HOMER, AK 99603
WILLIAM MIOTKE, 4530 JADE DR, HOMER, AK 99603
JOHN MOONIN, BOX 8054, NANWALEK, AK 99603
NICHOLAS MOONIN, BOX 8035, ENGLISH BAY, AK 99603
CHRISTOPHER MOSS, BOX 1115, HOMER, AK 99603
EMIL NELSON, BOX 130, HOMER, AK 99603
JAKOB NELSON, BOX 1392, HOMER, AK 99603
JESSIE NELSON, BOX 130, HOMER, AK 99603
KATLIAN NELSON, BOX 205, KASILOF, AK 99610
KERRY NELSON, BOX 205, KASILOF, AK 99610
SONJA NELSON, BOX 1392, HOMER, AK 99603
ZACHARY NELSON, BOX 1071, HOMER, AK 99603
MARVIN NORMAN, 18253 CLEAR FALLS CIR, EAGLE RIVER, AK 99577
PATRICK NORMAN, BOX 5509, PORT GRAHAM, AK 99603
WAYNE NORMAN, BOX 5546, PORT GRAHAM, AK 99603
GILBERT OLSEN, 621 BILL ST, ANCHORAGE, AK 99515
CHRISTOPHER PERRY, BOX 1808, HOMER, AK 99603
PAUL RAYMOND, BOX 2755, HOMER, AK 99603
KENNETH ROGERS, 1060 JEFFREY AVE, HOMER, AK 99603
JOHN ROHR, BOX 2621, HOMER, AK 99603
ALEX ROTH, BOX 1002, HOMER, AK 99603
MARK ROTH, BOX 2008, HOMER, AK 99603
PAUL ROTH, BOX 3154, HOMER, AK 99603
ROBERT ROTH, BOX 1314, ANCHOR POINT, AK 99556
CHARLES RUPPENTHAL, 55951 TOM CAT DR, HOMER, AK 99603
EMILIE SPRINGER, BOX 2882, HOMER, AK 99603
WENDY TUELLER, BOX 913, GIRDWOOD, AK 99587
STEVE TUTT, BOX 1105, HOMER, AK 99603
RODERIC VAN.SAUN, BOX 39622, NINILCHIK, AK 99639
JEROLD VANTREASE, BOX 1730, HOMER, AK 99603
DARWIN WALDSMITH, BOX 39309, NINILCHIK, AK 99639
CHARLES WALKDEN, BOX 2017, HOMER, AK 99603
STEPHEN WEBB, BOX 1127, KASILOF, AK 99610
ROBERT WHITE, BOX 201, SEWARD, AK 99664
ERIC WINSLOW, BOX 1716, HOMER, AK 99603
JACOB WISE, 1930 EAST END RD #B, HOMER, AK 99603
RICHARD WISE, BOX 2896, HOMER, AK 99603
JOHN WOODRUFF, 914 NW 165TH PL, SHORELINE, WA 98177
THOMAS YOUNG, 2601 N TAHITI LP, ANCHORAGE, AK 99507

SALMON, PURSE SEINE, KODIAK

FRANK ABENA, 2080 BLOOMFIELD RD, SEBASTOPOL, CA 95472
BRAD AGA, BOX 176, LARSEN BAY, AK 99624
JOSE AGUILAR, 1315 28TH ST, ANACORTES, WA 98221
JASON ALEXANDER, 18315 87TH AVE SE, SNOHOMISH, WA 98296
PETER ALEXSON, BOX 661, HOMER, AK 99603
PETER ALLAN, BOX 2160, KODIAK, AK 99615
JAMES ALPIAK, BOX 8683, KODIAK, AK 99615
MATTHEW ALWARD, 60082 CLARICE WAY, HOMER, AK 99603
RENEE ALWARD, 60082 CLARICE WAY, HOMER, AK 99603
AL ANDERSON, BOX 10, CHIGNIK LAGOON, AK 99565
HERMAN ANDERSON, 2610 MILL BAY RD #C3, KODIAK, AK 99615
ROBERT ANDERSON, 2610 MILL BAY RD #A9, KODIAK, AK 99615

SALMON FISHING LIST—PURSE SEINE

STOSH ANDERSON, BOX 310, KODIAK, AK 99615
GERI ARNDT, BOX 2338, KODIAK, AK 99615
KENNETH ASCHBACHER, 2031 N 47TH ST, PHOENIX, AZ 85008
LAWRENCE ASHOUWAK, BOX 105, OLD HARBOR, AK 99643
NICK BABICH, 13310 PURDY DR NW, GIG HARBOR, WA 98332
KWIN BAILEY, 511 FREDRICKS DR, ANCHORAGE, AK 99504
DORLA BALDRIDGE, BOX 3665, KENAI, AK 99611
JAMES BALDRIDGE, 38280 ROBINSON LP RD, STERLING, AK 99672
WADE BALL, BOX 3361, KODIAK, AK 99615
ADAM BARKER, 126 E FAIRVIEW AVE, HOMER, AK 99603
CYNTHIA BARKER, 126 E FAIRVIEW AVE, HOMER, AK 99603
SANFORD BEACHY, BOX 800, HOMER, AK 99603
DYLAN BEAN, 11147 WOMENS BAY DR, KODIAK, AK 99615
JULIAN BEAN, BOX 2813, KODIAK, AK 99615
DON BEATTY, 7503 STATE RTE 20, ANACORTES, WA 98221
ANDY BERESTOFF, 3478 PUFFIN DR, KODIAK, AK 99615
JAMES BERNS, BOX 44, OLD HARBOR, AK 99643
TRAVIS BERNS, BOX 33, OLD HARBOR, AK 99643
DARRELL BERNTSEN, 8320 BARNETT DR, ANCHORAGE, AK 99518
ALBERT BIGLEY, BOX 1454, HOMER, AK 99603
RICHARD BLACK, BOX 8833, KODIAK, AK 99615
ANDREW BLAIR, BOX 108, FOX ISLAND, WA 98333
DANNY BLAIR, 11399 TULIN PARK LP, ANCHORAGE, AK 99516
RICK BLAIR, BOX 679, FOX ISLAND, WA 98333
EVAN BLANKENSHIP, BOX 3265, HOMER, AK 99603
BRADFORD BLONDIN, 1412 BARANOF ST, KODIAK, AK 99615
BRIAN BLONDIN, BOX 1521, KODIAK, AK 99615
DERRICK BLONDIN, 1412 BARANOF ST, KODIAK, AK 99615
JASON BLONDIN, 1415 BARANOF ST, KODIAK, AK 99615
RANDY BLONDIN, BOX 159, KODIAK, AK 99615
RONALD BLONDIN, 1412 BARANOF ST, KODIAK, AK 99615
HOWARD BODI, 3031 SPRUCE CAPE RD, KODIAK, AK 99615
JOHN BOGGS, BOX 1199, KODIAK, AK 99615
CURTIS BOLLINGER, BOX 2024, KODIAK, AK 99615
JON BOTZ, BOX 5538, KODIAK, AK 99615
NORMAN BOTZ, BOX 5508, CHINIAK, AK 99615
TIMOTHY BOTZ, BOX 5505, CHINIAK, AK 99615
JARED BOWERS, 3800 STERLING HWY, HOMER, AK 99603
BOB BOWHAY, BOX 187, KODIAK, AK 99615
RICHARD BOWHAY, 3515 E SMITH RD, BELLINGHAM, WA 98226
ROBERT BOWSER, BOX 280, LAKEBAY, WA 98349
JAMES BROWN, 901 S GUNNYSACK RD, PALMER, AK 99645
GERALD BUCKEY, BOX 1831, KODIAK, AK 99615
ROY BURTON, 9609 SUNRISE RD, BLAINE, WA 98230
CHRISTIAN BUSCHMANN, BOX 898, PETERSBURG, AK 99833
JAMES CALHOUN, 57177 ZULU CT, HOMER, AK 99603
JAMES CALHOUN, 4360 ANDERSON ST, HOMER, AK 99603
ROBERT CAMERON, 2120 41ST ST, ANACORTES, WA 98221
EMILY CAPJOHN, 326 COPE ST, KODIAK, AK 99615
JOSHUA CARDMAN.PEDEN, 34950 MOONRISE ST, HOMER, AK 99603
EILEEN CARLSEN, 2483 SPRUCE CAPE LOT 6, KODIAK, AK 99615
KURT CARLSON, BOX 8858, HOMER, AK 99603
LEONARD CARPENTER, BOX 1970, KODIAK, AK 99615
JANET CARROLL, BOX 883, HOMER, AK 99603
ROBERT CARTER, BOX 2817, KODIAK, AK 99615
CARMEL CARTY, BOX 2733, KODIAK, AK 99615
JASON CHANDLER, 569 LETA, KODIAK, AK 99615
WILLIAM CHOQUETTE, 629 L ST #101, ANCHORAGE, AK 99501
RANDY CHRISTENSEN, BOX 1, LARSEN BAY, AK 99624
AARON CHRISTIANSEN, 7362 W PARK'S HWY #553, WASILLA, AK 99623
CARL CHRISTIANSEN, 11721 12TH AVE NW, SEATTLE, WA 98177
CARL CHRISTIANSEN, BOX 779, KODIAK, AK 99615
DAVID CHRISTIANSEN, BOX 2, OLD HARBOR, AK 99643
EMIL CHRISTIANSEN, 8211 DEBARR RD, ANCHORAGE, AK 99504
FRED CHRISTIANSEN, 7051 CHAD ST, ANCHORAGE, AK 99518

HAROLD CHRISTIANSEN, 1311 A LARCH ST, KODIAK, AK 99615
HAROLD CHRISTIANSEN, BOX 129, OLD HARBOR, AK 99643
JERRY CHRISTIANSEN, BOX 1102, KODIAK, AK 99615
KENNETH CHRISTIANSEN, 1849 MARMOT DR, KODIAK, AK 99615
MILES CHRISTIANSEN, BOX 75, OLD HARBOR, AK 99643
JASON CLARK, 2310 CONTENTMENT CT, NORTH POLE, AK 99705
MICHAEL CLARK, BOX 2009, KODIAK, AK 99615
MICHAEL CLEMENS, 317 SHELIKOF ST, KODIAK, AK 99615
ROBERT CLOKE, BOX 1433, KODIAK, AK 99615
JAMES COBB, BOX 1289, HOMER, AK 99603
WILLIAM COOK, 605 BRANCH LINE RD, YUKON, OK 73099
NICHOLAS COOPER, 2701 STOVER ST #17, FORT COLLINS, CO 80525
BRIAN CORDER, BOX 321, KODIAK, AK 99615
DANIEL CORNELIUS, BOX 1863, KODIAK, AK 99615
JOHN COSTANTI, 600 S STATE ST #309, BELLINGHAM, WA 98225
FRANCIS COSTELLO, BOX 108, KODIAK, AK 99615
MAURICE COSTELLO, BOX 754, KODIAK, AK 99615
PATRICK COSTELLO, BOX 8831, KODIAK, AK 99615
WILLIAM COSTELLO, 315 THORSHEIM ST, KODIAK, AK 99615
ALFRED CRATTY, 3510 EDS WAY, KODIAK, AK 99615
ALFRED CRATTY, BOX 1, OLD HARBOR, AK 99643
WILLIE CREAMER, BOX 2003, HOMER, AK 99603
GLENN CROCETTI, 118 BANCROFT DR, KODIAK, AK 99615
MICHAEL DAVIS, 10720 WHIMBREL DR, ANCHORAGE, AK 99507
GREGORY DEANE, 15739 YOKEKO DR, ANACORTES, WA 98221
CRAIG DEHART, 819 LOWER MILL BAY RD, KODIAK, AK 99615
DAVID DENSMORE, BOX 223, KODIAK, AK 99615
DOUGLAS DEPLAZES, BOX 2923, KODIAK, AK 99615
HENRY DERA, BOX 66, ALLOWAY, NJ 8001
ROBERT DIERICH, BOX 720, KODIAK, AK 99615
STANLEY DUNCAN, BOX 639, KODIAK, AK 99615
VICTOR DUNCAN, BOX 414, GIRDWOOD, AK 99587
MICHAEL DURTSCHI, BOX 1012, GIRDWOOD, AK 99587
ALAN DYEKMAN, BOX 880, KODIAK, AK 99615
RICK EBERLE, 14547 GIBRALTER RD, ANACORTES, WA 98221
GREGORY EGLE, BOX 3274, KODIAK, AK 99615
KEN EICHNER, 5166 SHORELINE DR N, KETCHIKAN, AK 99901
JAMES EUFEMIO, BOX 907, KODIAK, AK 99615
TIM FASTABEND, 91922 HWY 202, ASTORIA, OR 97103
ROBERT FELLOWS, 266 E BAYVIEW AVE, HOMER, AK 99603
WALLACE FIELDS, BOX 1691, KODIAK, AK 99615
JACOB FINLEY, 468 LILLY DR, KODIAK, AK 99615
MARY FIORENTINO, 737 ELLIS AVE, LAKE OSWEGO, OR 97034
RYAN FLETCHER, BOX 8673, KODIAK, AK 99615
CHARLES FOGLE, 5722 CAMPBELL LAKE RD, ANACORTES, WA 98221
LEON FRANCISCO, BOX 483, KODIAK, AK 99615
ARTHUR GAGNE, 82103 KEITEL ST, INDIO, CA 92201
JOHN GALLIHER, 2933 SPRUCE CAPE RD, KODIAK, AK 99615
EDITH GILBERT, 12604 12TH AVE NW, MARYSVILLE, WA 98271
JOHN GILBERT, 33293 NEACUZIE LN, WARRENTON, OR 97146
DOUGLAS GILES, BOX 1, SELDOVIA, AK 99663
LESLIE GILES, BOX 275, SELDOVIA, AK 99663
MARK GLADU, 3829 N ROWEN CIR, MESA, AZ 85207
TIMOTHY GOSSETT, BOX 1277, KODIAK, AK 99615
DANIEL GRANT, 201 WALKER LN, KENAI, AK 99611
GARY GRAVES, 1340 4TH ST, COLUMBIA CITY, OR 97018
MICHAEL GRUNERT, BOX 187, CHIGNIK LAGOON, AK 99565
GEROLD GUGEL, BOX 671227, CHUGIAK, AK 99567
ROBERT GUNDERSON, 3614 SPRUCE CAPE RD, KODIAK, AK 99615
LEIF GUSTAFSON, 4111 E SUPERIOR ST, DULUTH, MN 55804
DAVID HAMMITT, BOX 1005, KODIAK, AK 99615
PETER HAMRE, 19460 VILLAGES SCENIC PARKWAY, ANCHORAGE, AK 99516
PETER HANNAH, BOX 647, KODIAK, AK 99615
JACOB HANOHANO, BOX 851, KODIAK, AK 99615
RANDALL HANSEN, 22628 N SAN RAMON DR, SUN CITY WEST, AZ 85375

SALMON FISHING LIST—PURSE SEINE

PAUL HARDER, BOX 48, NAALEHU, HI 96772
CHARLES HARRIS, BOX 283, KASILOF, AK 99610
LEROY HARRIS, BOX 262, CLAM GULCH, AK 99568
EDWARD HASKINS, BOX 667, GIRDWOOD, AK 99587
JAMES HAYDEN, BOX 8085, KODIAK, AK 99615
MATTHEW HEGGE, BOX 848, KODIAK, AK 99615
JON HENSON, BOX 176, KODIAK, AK 99615
ZACHARY HILL, 1016 NE FEDERAL ST, BEND, OR 97703
DENNIS HINTZ, 404 POPLAR ST, KODIAK, AK 99615
EDWARD HOCHMUTH, BOX 5, LARSEN BAY, AK 99624
ROBERT HOCHMUTH, BOX 74, LARSEN BAY, AK 99624
SIDNEY HOEDEL, 10563 SPINDRIFT LP, ANCHORAGE, AK 99515
NICHOLAS HOFFMAN, 2159 ISLAND CIR, KODIAK, AK 99615
DOROTHY HOLM, BOX 365, KODIAK, AK 99615
IVER HOLM, BOX 8938, KODIAK, AK 99615
OLIVER HOLM, BOX 8749, KODIAK, AK 99615
TODD HOPPE, BOX 2589, HOMER, AK 99603
BRYAN HORN, 1776 MISSION RD, KODIAK, AK 99615
DAVID HORN, 717 UPPER MILL BAY RD, KODIAK, AK 99615
JAMES HORN, 1776 MISSION RD, KODIAK, AK 99615
SHARON HORN, 1210 MISSION RD, KODIAK, AK 99615
STEVEN HORN, 1210 MISSION RD, KODIAK, AK 99615
SARAH HUNTER, 695 APPLE WAY, SELAH, WA 98942
CLIFTON IVANOFF, BOX 8883, KODIAK, AK 99615
IAN IVANOFF, 1327 MOUNTAIN VIEW DR, KODIAK, AK 99615
PETER IVANOFF, 1327 MOUNTIAN VIEW DR, KODIAK, AK 99615
REUBEN IVANOFF, BOX 8883, KODIAK, AK 99615
STEVEN IVANOFF, 1327 MOUNTAIN VIEW DR, KODIAK, AK 99615
SARA JACKINSKY, BOX 1044, HOMER, AK 99603
MARY JACOBS, BOX 135, OPHIR, OR 97464
CHARLES JOHNSON, BOX 15378, FRITZ CREEK, AK 99603
CHRISTOPHER JOHNSON, BOX 151, KODIAK, AK 99615
CLINT JOHNSON, BOX 909, KODIAK, AK 99615
DAVID JOHNSON, 7916 110TH AVE SE, NEWCASTLE, WA 98056
ERNIE JOHNSON, 2850 SPRUCE LN, HOMER, AK 99603
GREGORY JOHNSON, BOX 52, HOMER, AK 99603
MICHAEL JOHNSON, 224 W REZANOFF DR, KODIAK, AK 99615
MICHAEL JOHNSON, 795 W SWAPP DR, KANAB, UT 84741
NATE JOHNSON, 515 RANGE VIEW, HOMER, AK 99603
NORRIS JOHNSON, 275 MOUNTIAN VIEW DR, HOMER, AK 99603
THOMAS JOHNSON, BOX 2289, KODIAK, AK 99615
RONALD JOLIN, BOX 2022, KODIAK, AK 99615
KENNETH JONES, 4092 GINNETT RD, ANACORTES, WA 98221
JOHN JURKOVICH, 395 GUEMES IS RD, ANACORTES, WA 98221
VITOMIR KALCIC, BOX 1486, KODIAK, AK 99615
NICK KATELNIKOFF, BOX 170, OUZINKIE, AK 99644
RICK KATELNIKOFF, BOX 56, OUZINKIE, AK 99644
RONALD KAVANAUGH, 1533 SAWMILL CIR, KODIAK, AK 99615
SYLVIA KAVANAUGH, 719 COTTONWOOD CRK, KODIAK, AK 99615
DOUG KELLER, 39980 FERNWOOD DR, HOMER, AK 99603
PETER KENDRICK, BOX 2798, KODIAK, AK 99615
JACOB KEPLINGER, 1615 LYNDEN WAY #A, KODIAK, AK 99615
MATTHEW KEPLINGER, BOX 8527, KODIAK, AK 99615
MITCHELL KEPLINGER, BOX 1006, KODIAK, AK 99615
TERRANCE KILBREATH, 31 PINE ST #210, EDMONDS, WA 98020
CHARLES KING, BOX 1573, KODIAK, AK 99615
ROBERT KING, BOX 504, KODIAK, AK 99615
SIDNEY KINNEY, 103 KRAMER AVE, SITKA, AK 99835
COLIN KIRKPATRICK, 116 S 7TH, MOUNT VERNON, WA 98274
ALEXEI KNAGIN, BOX 873584, WASILLA, AK 99687
GARY KNAGIN, 1519 E REZANOF DR, KODIAK, AK 99615
MARK KNIGHT, 12620 NEHER RIDGE DR, ANCHORAGE, AK 99516
STEVEN KNOWLES, 1423 E KOUSKOV ST, KODIAK, AK 99615
CHARLES KRAMER, BOX 83, PORT LIONS, AK 99550
DAVID KUBIAK, 818 TAGURA ST, KODIAK, AK 99615
RONALD KUCZEK, BOX 91657, ANCHORAGE, AK 99509

MARTIN KULLER, BOX 312, CATHLAMET, WA 98612
BASIL LARIONOFF, BOX 9003, KODIAK, AK 99615
DARIK LARIONOFF, BOX 8694, KODIAK, AK 99615
SHELLY LAUKITIS, 59065 MEADOW LN, HOMER, AK 99603
DONALD LAWHEAD, 3915 E BLUE SAPPHIRE CT, WASILLA, AK 99654
ELLIOTT LAYFIELD, BOX 644, WINTHROP, WA 98862
KENNETH LAYFIELD, BOX 644, WINTHROP, WA 98862
LUTHER LECHNER, BOX 8538, KODIAK, AK 99615
LUKE LESTER, BOX 553, KODIAK, AK 99615
EVERETT LINDHOLM, 415 E PARK DR, ANACORTES, WA 98221
JOE LINDHOLM, 11355 WHISTLE LAKE RD, ANACORTES, WA 98221
ROBERT LINDSEY, 3162 SPRUCE CAPE RD, KODIAK, AK 99615
MICHAEL LONGRICH, BOX 730, KODIAK, AK 99615
DAVID LOUTREL, 1430 CRESCENT DR, ANCHORAGE, AK 99508
JEFFREY LUKIN, BOX 41, PORT LIONS, AK 99550
LESTER LUKIN, BOX 62, PORT LIONS, AK 99550
ANNA M.VAN.DER.CORPUT, BOX 900, CLOVERDALE, CA 95425
CHRIS MAGNUSEN, BOX 516, KODIAK, AK 99615
HAROLD MAGNUSSON, BOX 283, KODIAK, AK 99615
DAVID MANN, 73 WINWARD DR, BELLINGHAM, WA 98229
BRAD MARDEN, BOX 2856, HOMER, AK 99603
SHAWN MARICICH, BOX 528, ANACORTES, WA 98221
TIMOTHY MARICICH, 13680 DONNELL RD, ANACORTES, WA 98221
JERRY MARKOSKI, 165 GREEN RIVER RD, GREENFIELD, MA 1301
GEORGE MARSHALL, 11185 WOMENS BAY DR, KODIAK, AK 99615
MICHAEL MARTIN, BOX 1275, KODIAK, AK 99615
ANDREI MARTISHEV, BOX 1125, ANCHOR POINT, AK 99556
CHRISTINE MATTHEWS, BOX 73, OUZINKIE, AK 99644
STEVE MAUGHAN, 4404 LAUESEN AVE, NORTH POLE, AK 99705
RAYMOND MAY, BOX 8985, KODIAK, AK 99615
MICHAEL MAYO, 2808 SAWMILL CREEK RD, SITKA, AK 99835
BRENT MCCORMICK, BOX 5506, CHINIAK, AK 99615
DANIEL MCFARLAND, BOX 8632, KODIAK, AK 99615
DANNY MCLEAN, BOX 351, HOMER, AK 99603
JACOB MCLEAN, BOX 2191, HOMER, AK 99603
BRIAN MCWETHY, 3836 SUNSET DR, KODIAK, AK 99615
CHARLES MCWETHY, BOX 8552, KODIAK, AK 99615
QUINNAN MCWETHY, BOX 8552, KODIAK, AK 99615
HERMAN MEINERS, BOX 92669, ANCHORAGE, AK 99503
VICTOR MELOVEDOFF, BOX 82, OLD HARBOR, AK 99643
DANIEL MILLER, BOX 2865, KODIAK, AK 99615
EDWARD MONKIEWICZ, 1110 PURTOV ST, KODIAK, AK 99615
JAMES MONROE, BOX 1202, KODIAK, AK 99615
KIP MONROE, BOX 1432, KODIAK, AK 99615
ILKKA MONSON, 3429 HENNEPIN AVE S, MINNEAPOLIS, MN 55408
MIKE MONSON, BOX 1736, KODIAK, AK 99615
GEOFFREY MORGAN, BOX 191072, ANCHORAGE, AK 99519
ROBERT MOSS, BOX 3428, HOMER, AK 99603
ROBERT MOSS, 48480 GRANT AVE, KENAI, AK 99611
SAMUEL MUTCH, 210 B SHELIKOF, KODIAK, AK 99615
ANDREW NAULT, BOX 922, KODIAK, AK 99615
ARNIE NELSON, 3140 DEBORAH LYNN CIR, ANCHORAGE, AK 99507
ARNOLD NELSON, BOX 85, PORT LIONS, AK 99550
ELIZABETH NELSON, BOX 85, PORT LIONS, AK 99550
HARRY NELSON, BOX 87, PORT LIONS, AK 99550
MICHAEL NELSON, BOX 21, OLD HARBOR, AK 99643
THOMAS NELSON, BOX 101, PORT LIONS, AK 99550
AARON NEVIN, BOX 3251, KODIAK, AK 99615
JOHN NEVIN, BOX 2125, KODIAK, AK 99615
DAVID OBRIEN, 3700 PUFFIN DR, KODIAK, AK 99615
STEPHEN OBRIEN, BOX 8804, KODIAK, AK 99615
MAKOTO ODLIN, 295 NEVA WAY #A, KODIAK, AK 99615
CONSTANCE OLSEN, BOX 322, KODIAK, AK 99615
DANIEL OLSEN, BOX 1743, KODIAK, AK 99615
THORVOLD OLSEN, BOX 322, KODIAK, AK 99615
JACOB ORGAN, BOX 58, KODIAK, AK 99615

SALMON FISHING LIST—PURSE SEINE

HENRY ORTH, 3462 N PARADISE LN, WASILLA, AK 99623
WILLIAM PACK, BOX 2314, LONGVIEW, WA 98632
MARIA PAINTER, 3901 WOODLAND DR, KODIAK, AK 99615
ALEXANDER PANAMAROFF, BOX 6, LARSEN BAY, AK 99624
MARKO PATITUCCI, BOX 8918, KODIAK, AK 99615
MICHAEL PATITUCCI, BOX 1511, KODIAK, AK 99615
DANIEL PATTERSON, 1900 W NICKERSON #116 BOX 17, SEATTLE, WA 98119
RYAN PECARICH, 1903 E SUNSET DR, BELLINGHAM, WA 98226
KURT PEDERSEN, BOX 2405, KODIAK, AK 99615
LAURIE PEDERSEN, BOX 3084, KODIAK, AK 99615
STEVEN PENN, BOX 249, KODIAK, AK 99615
EDUARDO PEREZ, BOX 208, KODIAK, AK 99615
EDWARD PESTRIKOFF, BOX 56, OLD HARBOR, AK 99643
CHARLES PETERSON, 1850 THREE SISTERS WAY, KODIAK, AK 99615
HOWARD PETERSON, BOX 1063, KODIAK, AK 99615
DEANA PIKUS, BOX 2843, KODIAK, AK 99615
JEREMIE PIKUS, BOX 2843, KODIAK, AK 99615
PATRICK PIKUS, BOX 2843, KODIAK, AK 99615
LEVI PINGREE, #1 NE ARM UGANIK BAY, KODIAK, AK 99697
DRAKE PIPER, BOX 15233, FRITZ CREEK, AK 99603
STEPHAN PLANCICH, BOX 377355, OCEANVIEW, HI 96737
DARREN PLATT, BOX 1413, KODIAK, AK 99615
JOHN POHJOLA, 2811 IRIS ST, ANCHORAGE, AK 99517
GARY PRICE, BOX 63, OLD HARBOR, AK 99643
DALE PRUITT, BOX 2278, KODIAK, AK 99615
JOSEPH PURATICH, BOX 272, GIG HARBOR, WA 98335
CHERYL PYLE, BOX 336, STEVENSON, WA 98648
DANA REID, BOX 8935, KODIAK, AK 99615
MAX REID, 3772 MAPLEWOOD, MAR VISTA, CA 90066
HARTMUT REIMNITZ, 23505 80TH AVE SW, VASHON, WA 98070
SEVEREAN REUTOV, BOX 2230, HOMER, AK 99603
MICHELLE RITTENHOUSE, BOX KWP, KODIAK, AK 99615
SHAWNA RITTENHOUSE, BOX KWP, KODIAK, AK 99615
NATHANIEL ROSE, 3011 SPRUCE CAPE RD APT A, KODIAK, AK 99615
BARRY ROSENKRANZ, 290 OLD STAGE WAY, YAKIMA, WA 98908
PHILLIP ROSENKRANZ, 2141 MAPLEWAY RD, YAKIMA, WA 98908
ERIC ROSVOLD, BOX 1144, PETERSBURG, AK 99833
ALEX ROTH, BOX 1002, HOMER, AK 99603
RICHARD ROTH, 39142 SUCHAVIEW RD, HOMER, AK 99603
STEVEN ROTH, BOX 3171, HOMER, AK 99603
WILLIAM ROTH, BOX 3171, HOMER, AK 99603
GARY ROZELLE, BOX 5033, AKHIOK, AK 99615
RYDER RUOSS, BOX 1572, KODIAK, AK 99615
CASEY RUSSELL, 305 S BLUE HERON WAY, NAMPA, ID 83667
NEIL RUSSELL, 4216 E INDIGO CT, NAMPA, ID 83687
STEVEN RUSSELL, 3152 WOODY WAY LP, KODIAK, AK 99615
FRED SARGENT, 3177 WOODY WAY LP, KODIAK, AK 99615
STAN SARGENT, BOX 384119, WAIKOLOA, HI 96738
WALTER SARGENT, 1830 MISSION RD, KODIAK, AK 99615
BRUCE SCHACTLER, BOX 2254, KODIAK, AK 99615
JOSEPH SCHACTLER, BOX 2254, KODIAK, AK 99615
JAMES SCHAUFF, BOX 8150, KODIAK, AK 99615
WILLIAM SCHAUFF, BOX 8774, KODIAK, AK 99615
ALBERT SCHMEIL, BOX 164, KODIAK, AK 99615
ZACKARY SCHMEIL, BOX 2863, KODIAK, AK 99615
CRAIG SELVOG, 9490 ADRIAN LN, SEDRO WOOLLEY, WA 98284
SHILOH SEYMOUR, 201 PEACH TREE LN, SHELBYVILLE, KY 40065
NICHOLAI SHOLL, 3673 GULL DR, KODIAK, AK 99615
KELLY SIMEONOFF, 2711 VALLEY FORGE CIR, ANCHORAGE, AK 99502
DEVIN SKONBERG, 2930 WOODY WAY CIR #B, KODIAK, AK 99615
JAMES SKONBERG, BOX 70, OUZINKIE, AK 99644
WILLIAM SLINEY, BOX 1369, KODIAK, AK 99615
DENNIS SMEDLEY, 1064 E SCHWALD RD, WASILLA, AK 99654
DONOVAN SMEDLEY, BOX 8529, KODIAK, AK 99615
ROBERT SMITH, BOX 261, KASILOF, AK 99610

COLVER SONNENTAG, 13631 VENUS WAY, ANCHORAGE, AK 99515
FREDERICK STAGER, BOX 8243, KODIAK, AK 99615
WALTER STANLEY, 2971 SUNSPOT CIR, ANCHORAGE, AK 99507
MORGAN STARK, 1407 W LEMP ST, BOISE, ID 83702
DANIEL STIHL, BOX 3373, KODIAK, AK 99615
ELISABETH STIHL.WIRZ, BOX 3373, KODIAK, AK 99615
ANTRIL SUYDAM, 75-5608 HIENALOLI RD #31, KAILUA-KONA, HI 96740
GARY SUYDAM, BOX 2807, KODIAK, AK 99615
KEVIN SUYDAM, BOX 980, KODIAK, AK 99615
STEVEN SUYDAM, BOX 987, KODIAK, AK 99615
SCOTT SWITZER, BOX 2451, HOMER, AK 99603
BRIAN TARABOCHIA, BOX 2253, CORDOVA, AK 99574
MARK THOMAS, 2249 SELIEF LN, KODIAK, AK 99615
ERIC THOMPSON, BOX 3261, KODIAK, AK 99615
JANICE TORSEN, 2428 GLENWOOD, ANCHORAGE, AK 99508
JAMES TOTEFF, BOX 418, KALAMA, WA 98625
CHARLES TRAFTON, 13971 TRAFTON RD, ANACORTES, WA 98221
CHARLES TREINEN, 2054 ARLINGTON DR, ANCHORAGE, AK 99517
CHRISTIAN TROSVIG, 1841 MISSION RD, KODIAK, AK 99615
STANLEY VANMATRE, 3199 PENINSULA RD, KODIAK, AK 99615
ZACHARY VARGO, 11233 S RUSSIAN CREEK RD, KODIAK, AK 99615
JOHN VELSKO, BOX 2269, HOMER, AK 99603
DONALD VINBERG, BOX 9032, KODIAK, AK 99615
RAY WADSWORTH, 200 E MAIN ST, OALKEY, ID 83346
ARTHUR WARD, 6912 SEWELL DR, SALCHA, AK 99714
NELSON WARD, 6912 SEWELL DR, SALCHA, AK 99714
DOUGLAS WATERBURY, 3373 MELNITSA LN, KODIAK, AK 99615
TYSON WHITTOCK, 10601 ELLIS DR, ANCHORAGE, AK 99507
MILES WIEBE, 5201 GJOSUND DR, HOMER, AK 99603
WILLIAM WIEBE, 5201 GJOSUND DR, HOMER, AK 99603
ADAM WILKIE, BOX 1726, SEWARD, AK 99664
TIM WILKIE, BOX 1726, SEWARD, AK 99664
DUKE WILLIAMS, BOX 872425, WASILLA, AK 99687
SHAWN WILLIAMS, BOX 672505, CHUGIAK, AK 99567
ZACHARY WILLIAMS, 19136 BIRCHWOOD LOOP RD, CHUGIAK, AK 99567
DANIEL WILSON, BOX 2697, KODIAK, AK 99615
HUGH WISNER, BOX 2783, KODIAK, AK 99615
LINDA WISNER, BOX 2783, KODIAK, AK 99615
JERAMY YOUNG, BOX 806, KODIAK, AK 99615
CHRIS ZWOLINSKI, BOX 83218, FAIRBANKS, AK 99708

SALMON, PURSE SEINE, CHIGNIK

ALFREDO ABOUEID, BOX 26, CHIGNIK LAGOON, AK 99565
JASON ALEXANDER, 18315 87TH AVE SE, SNOHOMISH, WA 98296
SEAN ALEXANDER, 2120 REVERE CIR, ANCHORAGE, AK 99515
BENJAMIN ALLEN, BOX 84, CHIGNIK, AK 99564
AARON ANDERSON, BOX 43, CHIGNIK LAGOON, AK 99565
BILLY ANDERSON, BOX 12, CHIGNIK, AK 99564
DAVID ANDERSON, 171 MOUNTAIN VIEW DR B, HOMER, AK 99603
DEAN ANDERSON, BOX 41, CHIGNIK LAGOON, AK 99565
EUGENE ANDERSON, BOX 87, SEWARD, AK 99664
GEORGE ANDERSON, BOX 168, CHIGNIK LAGOON, AK 99565
H.GARY ANDERSON, BOX 47, CHIGNIK LAGOON, AK 99565
JEREMY ANDERSON, BOX 1, CHIGNIK LAGOON, AK 99565
JULIUS ANDERSON, BOX 30, CHIGNIK LAGOON, AK 99565
PETER ANDERSON, BOX 37, CHIGNIK, AK 99564
RODNEY ANDERSON, BOX 188, CHIGNIK LAGOON, AK 99565
RONALD ANDERSON, 39370 BRENMARK RD, HOMER, AK 99603
STOSH ANDERSON, BOX 310, KODIAK, AK 99615
RICHARD BLACK, BOX 8833, KODIAK, AK 99615
CLIFFORD BRANDAL, BOX 113, KODIAK, AK 99615
HENRY BRANDAL, BOX 22, CHIGNIK LAGOON, AK 99565
PETER BUMPUS, BOX 167, CHIGNIK LAGOON, AK 99565
GLEN BURKHART, 36426 MEANDERING RD, SOLDOTNA, AK 99669

SALMON FISHING LIST—PURSE SEINE

LAUNI CAMERON, 2120 41ST ST, ANACORTES, WA 98221
DALE CARLSON, BOX 3, CHIGNIK, AK 99564
ERNEST CARLSON, BOX 21, CHIGNIK, AK 99564
EUGENE CARLSON, 43633 SE 147TH LN, NORTH BEND, WA 98045
RODERICK CARLSON, BOX 70, CHIGNIK, AK 99564
BRANDON DAUGHERTY, BOX 26, CHIGNIK, AK 99564
MMERCE DEPARTMENT OF CO, BOX 110802, JUNEAU, AK 99811
HENRY ERICKSON, BOX 62, CHIGNIK LAGOON, AK 99565
RAYMOND ERICKSON, BOX 61, CHIGNIK LAGOON, AK 99565
MICHAEL GALLIGAN, BOX 1926, FRIDAY HARBOR, WA 98250
TIMOTHY GERVAIS, BOX 7, RUBY, AK 99768
TONY GREGORIO, BOX 24, CHIGNIK LAGOON, AK 99565
DAN GRUNERT, BOX 28, CHIGNIK LAGOON, AK 99565
FRANK GRUNERT, 4954 W NORTHERN ROSE LN, WASILLA, AK 99623
MICHAEL GRUNERT, BOX 187, CHIGNIK LAGOON, AK 99565
ARNE HATCH, BOX 346, SEWARD, AK 99664
WALLACE HINDERER, 311 HANSEN RD, PORT ANGELES, WA 98363
PAUL JOHNSON, 102 SHIPYARD RD, DECATUR ISLAND, WA 98221
RYAN JOHNSON, BOX 2931, KODIAK, AK 99615
JOHN JONES, BOX 56, CHIGNIK LAGOON, AK 99565
JOHN JONES, BOX 149, CHIGNIK LAGOON, AK 99565
WILLIAM JONES, 100 SHIPYARD RD, DECATUR ISLAND, WA 98221
ARCHIE KALMAKOFF, BOX 69, PERRYVILLE, AK 99648
HARRY KALMAKOFF, BOX 48008, CHIGNIK LAKE, AK 99548
JOAN KALMAKOFF, BOX 133, PERRYVILLE, AK 99648
JOSEPH KALMAKOFF, 19720 LINDEN AVE N # 514, SHORELINE, WA 98133
OLGA KALMAKOFF, 9499 BRAYTON DR #266, ANCHORAGE, AK 99507
WILLIAM KASHEVAROF, BOX 52, SELDOVIA, AK 99663
ALOYS KOPUN, BOX 74, CHIGNIK, AK 99564
AXEL KOPUN, 16435 NICOLI WAY, EAGLE RIVER, AK 99577
BORIS KOSBRUK, BOX 111, PERRYVILLE, AK 99648
HARRY KOSBRUK, BOX 87, PERRYVILLE, AK 99648
PATRICK KOSBRUK, BOX 110, PERRYVILLE, AK 99648
ROBB KULIN, BOX 1293, GIRDWOOD, AK 99587
ELLIOT LIND, BOX 2396, HOMER, AK 99603
MITCHELL LIND, 320 LAKEVIEW DR, CHIGNIK LAKE, AK 99548
BRETT LOUNSBURY, BOX 8947, KODIAK, AK 99615
RICHARD LOUNSBURY, 601 W 20TH AVE, ANCHORAGE, AK 99503
MICHAEL MACALUSO, BOX 871624, WASILLA, AK 99687
PETER MCCARTHY, BOX 2733, KODIAK, AK 99615
GABRIEL MCKILLY, BOX 190344, ANCHORAGE, AK 99519
DANNY MCLEAN, BOX 351, HOMER, AK 99603
TIMOTHY MURPHY, BOX 242071, ANCHORAGE, AK 99524
SAMUEL MUTCH, 210 B SHELIKOF, KODIAK, AK 99615
BONNIE NELSON, 840 SW 162ND ST, BURIEN, WA 98166
GARRETT OLSEN, 3107 SW 171ST, BURIEN, WA 98166
KNUD OLSEN, 114 2ND AVE S #201, EDMONDS, WA 98020
SHIRLEY OLSEN, 6815 MADRONA DR NW, TULALIP, WA 98271
GEORGE ORLOFF, 118 MARJONETTE WAY, CHIGNIK, AK 99564
AUGUST PEDERSEN, BOX 72, CHIGNIK LAGOON, AK 99565
ALDEN ROSS, BOX 3476, HOMER, AK 99603
AXEL ROWLAND, BOX 393, UNALASKA, AK 99685
ROGER ROWLAND, BOX 393, UNALASKA, AK 99685
AUSTIN SHANGIN, BOX 73, PERRYVILLE, AK 99648
CLEMENT SHANGIN, 435 E 10TH #3, ANCHORAGE, AK 99501
EDGAR SHANGIN, BOX 110574, ANCHORAGE, AK 99511
JACOB.J.L SHANGIN, BOX 112112, ANCHORAGE, AK 99511
RUSSELL SHANGIN, 2440 E TUDOR RD #272, ANCHORAGE, AK 99507
STEPHEN SHANGIN, 10308 THIMBLEBERRY DR, ANCHORAGE, AK 99515
MATTHEW SIEMION, 3028 ALDERWOOD AVE, BELLINGHAM, WA 98225
ARNOLD SKONBERG, BOX 8601, KODIAK, AK 99615
MINNIE SKONBERG, BOX 5, CHIGNIK, AK 99564
ROBERT SMITH, BOX 261, KASILOF, AK 99610
ANDREW STEPANOFF, BOX 521914, BIG LAKE, AK 99652
LINDA SUYDAM, BOX 987, KODIAK, AK 99615
MARCELLA SUYDAM, BOX 3246, HOMER, AK 99603

DANIEL VEERHUSEN, BOX 971, HOMER, AK 99603
TIM WILKIE, BOX 1726, SEWARD, AK 99664
MARVIN YAGIE, BOX 125, PERRYVILLE, AK 99648

SALMON, PURSE SEINE, ALASKA PENINSULA

MICHAEL ALFIERI, 18120 196TH AVE SE, RENTON, WA 98058
MARK ANDERSON, 49 NORTH STAR LN, FRIDAY HARBOR, WA 98250
STOSH ANDERSON, BOX 310, KODIAK, AK 99615
JOHN BARRY, 800 HALIBUT POINT RD #C, SITKA, AK 99835
WALTER BENKMAN, 10533 14TH AVE NW, SEATTLE, WA 98177
JACK BERNTSEN, BOX 98, SAND POINT, AK 99661
LOUIS BERNTSEN, BOX 255, SAND POINT, AK 99661
PATRICK BROWN, BOX 69, SAND POINT, AK 99661
LAWSON BUNDRANT, 20530 RICHMOND BCH DR NW, SHORELINE, WA 98177
CARL CARLSON, BOX 44, SAND POINT, AK 99661
NICK CARLSON, 3781 WILEY POST LP, ANCHORAGE, AK 99517
JOSEPH CARR, 10241 STROGANOF DR, ANCHORAGE, AK 99507
JEFFREY COUNTS, 1957 COUNTRY GROVE LN, ENCINITAS, CA 92024
WILLIAM CUMBERLIDGE, BOX 110, SAND POINT, AK 99661
JOHANNES DEBAKKER, 8642 LIBBY RD NE, OLYMPIA, WA 98506
TROY DENKINGER, 2221 HALIBUT POINT RD, SITKA, AK 99835
MICHAEL DURTSCHI, BOX 1012, GIRDWOOD, AK 99587
RUDY DUSHKIN, 8820 VERNON ST, ANCHORAGE, AK 99515
WILLIAM DUSHKIN, BOX 135, SAND POINT, AK 99661
ANDREW FOSTER, BOX 162, SAND POINT, AK 99661
BRUCE FOSTER, BOX 46, SAND POINT, AK 99661
CAROL FOSTER, BOX 162, SAND POINT, AK 99661
DWAIN FOSTER, BOX 162, SAND POINT, AK 99661
JACK FOSTER, BOX 254, SAND POINT, AK 99661
JOHN FOSTER, BOX 225, SAND POINT, AK 99661
C.DAVID FRANKLIN, 3401 W LAWTON ST, SEATTLE, WA 98199
MICHAEL GALLIGAN, BOX 1926, FRIDAY HARBOR, WA 98250
STEVEN GALOVIN, BOX 215, SAND POINT, AK 99661
JOHN GALVIN, BOX 171, SAND POINT, AK 99661
GLEN GARDNER, BOX 444, SAND POINT, AK 99661
RICHARD GEORGE, 955 MARINE DR, BELLINGHAM, WA 98225
DEAN GOULD, BOX 124, KING COVE, AK 99612
ROBERT GOULD, BOX 234, KING COVE, AK 99612
ROBERT GOULD, BOX 307, KING COVE, AK 99612
GLORIA GRONHOLDT, BOX 14, SAND POINT, AK 99661
CHARLES GUNDERSEN, BOX 24, SAND POINT, AK 99661
GEORGE GUNDERSEN, BOX 51, SAND POINT, AK 99661
MARTIN GUNDERSEN, BOX 50, SAND POINT, AK 99661
PAUL GUNDERSEN, BOX 91, SAND POINT, AK 99661
MICHAEL HARVIE, 507 CLARK RD, BELLINGHAM, WA 98225
KURT HASTINGS, 2097 E MILLMAN RD, LANGLEY, WA 98260
RICHARD HASTINGS, 1308 DINES POINT RD, GREENBANK, WA 98253
DYLAN HATFIELD, BOX 1143, PETERSBURG, AK 99833
TIMOTHY HEUKER, BOX 98, CASCADE LOCKS, OR 97014
IVAN HOBLET, BOX 62, FALSE PASS, AK 99583
TOM HOBLET, BOX 108, FALSE PASS, AK 99583
TRAVIS HOBLET, BOX 12, FALSE PASS, AK 99583
ARTHUR HOLMBERG, BOX 78, SAND POINT, AK 99661
FRED HOLMBERG, 8017 HAMLET LN, EVERETT, WA 98203
JOHN HOLMBERG, BOX 85, SAND POINT, AK 99661
LEONARD HOLMBERG, BOX 223, SAND POINT, AK 99661
PAUL HOLMBERG, BOX 3233, PALMER, AK 99645
CHARLES JACKSON, BOX 54, SAND POINT, AK 99661
GEORGE JACKSON, BOX 166, SAND POINT, AK 99661
ROBERT JACKSON, BOX 5011 #146, FERNDALE, WA 98248
ANDREW JACOBSEN, BOX 125, UNALASKA, AK 99685
DICK JACOBSEN, BOX 307, SAND POINT, AK 99661
NORMAN JOHANNESSEN, BOX 1638, OROVILLE, WA 98844
DAVID JOHNSON, BOX 15252, FRITZ CREEK, AK 99603
DAVID JONES, BOX 64, WINTHROP, WA 98862

SALMON FISHING LIST—BEACH SEINE / DRIFT GILLNET

DARRELL KAPP, 338 BAYSIDE RD, BELLINGHAM, WA 98225
LOUANN KOSO, BOX 131, KING COVE, AK 99612
RAYMOND KOSO, BOX 877309, WASILLA, AK 99687
TRAVIS KOSO, 2800 N ALMA DR, WASILLA, AK 99623
MICHAEL KURTZ, BOX 32265, BELLINGHAM, WA 98228
NICHOLAS KURTZ, BOX 32265, BELLINGHAM, WA 98228
NORMAN KUZAKIN, BOX 105, KING COVE, AK 99612
MELVIN LARSEN, BOX 33, SAND POINT, AK 99661
NORMAN LARSEN, BOX 52, SAND POINT, AK 99661
ROBIN LARSEN, BOX 264, SAND POINT, AK 99661
SHELLY LAUKITIS, 59065 MEADOW LN, HOMER, AK 99603
JOE LUDVICK, BOX 74, SAND POINT, AK 99661
TAYLOR LUNDGREN, BOX 216, SAND POINT, AK 99661
KENNETH MACK, BOX 182, KING COVE, AK 99612
KENNETH MACK, BOX 176, KING COVE, AK 99612
FREDERICK MAGILL, BOX 444, PETERSBURG, AK 99833
ANDREW MANOS, 3014 EMORY ST, ANCHORAGE, AK 99508
JULIAN MANOS, BOX 749, GIRDWOOD, AK 99587
THOMAS MANOS, BOX 749, GIRDWOOD, AK 99587
JEFF MARKUSEN, 9653 RONALD DR, BLAINE, WA 98230
KENNETH MARKUSEN, 572 N HARVEY RD, BLAINE, WA 98230
MATTHEW MARTUSHEV, BOX 3603, HOMER, AK 99603
VICTORIA MARVIN.DENKINGER, 2221 HALIBUT POINT RD, SITKA, AK 99835
DON MCCALLUM, BOX 185, KING COVE, AK 99612
HUBERT MCCALLUM, BOX 434, SAND POINT, AK 99661
MARIAH MCCALLUM, BOX 185, KING COVE, AK 99612
FRANK MELSETH, BOX 66, SAND POINT, AK 99661
ERIK MENTEN, BOX 506, TENAKEE, AK 99841
LARSEN METTLER, 8316 25TH AVE NW, SEATTLE, WA 98117
ALLEN MITCHELL, 41 STRAWBERRY PT RD, BELLINGHAM, WA 98229
JOHN MITCHELL, 41 STRAWBERRY PT RD, BELLINGHAM, WA 98229
EMIL MOBECK, BOX 121, SAND POINT, AK 99661
ALVIN NEWMAN, BOX 248, KING COVE, AK 99612
RAYMOND NUTT, BOX 122, SAND POINT, AK 99661
ALVIN OSTERBACK, BOX 104, SAND POINT, AK 99661
DAVID OSTERBACK, BOX 144, SAND POINT, AK 99661
STEVEN OVERA, 19417 2ND AVE SE, BOTHELL, WA 98012
DALE PEDERSEN, 9218 CAMPBELL TERRACE DR, ANCHORAGE, AK 99502
DEAN PEDERSEN, BOX 877325, WASILLA, AK 99687
CHARLES PIECUCH, 4737 4TH AVE NE, SEATTLE, WA 98105
JOSEPH PURATICH, BOX 272, GIG HARBOR, WA 98335
ERIC SAMUELSON, BOX 66, KING COVE, AK 99612
HERMAN SAMUELSON, 8 MAIN ST, KING COVE, AK 99612
PETER SCHONBERG, 75-816F HIONA ST, HOLUALOA, HI 96725
DOUG SHELFORD, 16212 BOTHELL EVERETT HWY #340, MILL CRK, WA 98102
WILLIAM SHELLIKOFF, GEN DEL, FALSE PASS, AK 99583
DAVID SORENSEN, 9825 SUNRISE BEACH DR NW, GIG HARBOR, WA 98332
DAN THOMAS, BOX 1623, BLAINE, WA 98231
KILEY THOMPSON, BOX 116, SAND POINT, AK 99661
SCOTT THORNE, BOX 717, PICABO, ID 83348
DANIEL VEERHUSEN, BOX 971, HOMER, AK 99603
WILLIAM WIEBE, 5201 GJOSUND DR, HOMER, AK 99603
TIM WILKIE, BOX 1726, SEWARD, AK 99664
KEITH WILLIAMS, 1924 E COLGATE DR, TEMPE, AZ 85283
ANDREW WILSON, BOX 127, KING COVE, AK 99612
COREY WILSON, BOX 267, KING COVE, AK 99612
DAVID WILSON, BOX 333, SAND POINT, AK 99661
DAVID WILSON, BOX 6114, EDMONDS, WA 98026
JUSTIN WILSON, BOX 267, KING COVE, AK 99612
OSCAR WILSON, BOX 144, KING COVE, AK 99612
VERNON WILSON, BOX 308, KING COVE, AK 99612
MARK YOUNG, BOX 2016, SITKA, AK 99835
ROBERT ZUANICH, 2200 6TH AVE STE 806, SEATTLE, WA 98121

SALMON, BEACH SEINE, KODIAK

CHAD AGA, BOX 116, LARSEN BAY, AK 99624
JOHN BARTOLINO, BOX 73, OUZINKIE, AK 99644
RHONDA BOWERS, 6632 E 12TH AVE, ANCHORAGE, AK 99504
LANI CARLSEN, BOX 3300, KODIAK, AK 99615
TERESA CARLSON, BOX 114, LARSEN BAY, AK 99624
ANDRE COSSETTE, BOX 8670, KODIAK, AK 99615
RICHARD COURCHANE, BOX 264, CUSTER, WA 98240
ANTHONY DEL.REAL, 3506 N 438TH AVE, TONOPAH, AZ 85354
DONALD DUMM, BOX 1723, KODIAK, AK 99615
WESTON FIELDS, BOX 25, KODIAK, AK 99615
LOCKE FINLEY, BOX 8649, KODIAK, AK 99615
GEORGE HARTMAN, 412 SARGENT DR, KODIAK, AK 99615
NICHOLAS HOFFMAN, 2159 ISLAND CIR, KODIAK, AK 99615
EVA HOLM, BOX 8749, KODIAK, AK 99615
ROY JONES, BOX 90, LARSEN BAY, AK 99624
JERRY LAKTONEN, BOX 392, GRANITE FALLS, WA 98252
MARK LARSEN, 3628 KNIK AVE, ANCHORAGE, AK 99517
KIMBERLY LESTER, BOX 553, KODIAK, AK 99615
MICHAEL LIND, 1850 LIBERTY LN, THORNFIELD, MO 65762
ROBERT MAY, BOX 90, PORT LIONS, AK 99550
RICHARD METZGER, 2725 WILLEYS LAKE RD, CUSTER, WA 98240
KEITH OMLID, 1220 GWINN ST E, MONMOUTH, OR 97361
KRIS OMLID, 20644 BEAUMONT DR, BEND, OR 97701
MARK OMLID, BOX 7304, LOVELAND, CO 80537
AARON OSWALT, BOX 722, KODIAK, AK 99615
ALLEN PANAMAROFF, BOX 145, LARSEN BAY, AK 99624
FRIEDA PANAMAROFF, BOX 25, LARSEN BAY, AK 99624
SUSAN PAYNE, BOX 1903, KODIAK, AK 99615
LAWRENCE RADONSKI, BOX 237, KODIAK, AK 99615
KIMBERLY RIEDEL.BYLER, BOX KZB, KODIAK, AK 99697
EARL SMITH, 154 HUMMINGBIRD CIR, FLORISSANT, CO 80820
ROBERT TOLL, BOX 96, KASILOF, AK 99610
EDWARD TYSON, BOX 401, ANCHOR POINT, AK 99556
EDWARD WALTON, BOX 3123, KODIAK, AK 99615
JANE WIEBE, 5201 GJOSUND DR, HOMER, AK 99603
CHRIS ZWOLINSKI, BOX 83218, FAIRBANKS, AK 99708

SALMON, DRIFT GILLNET, SOUTHEAST

CYNTHIA ADAMS, BOX 1007, HAINES, AK 99827
DAVID ADAMS, 825 S DIOMEDE, PALMER, AK 99645
WILLIAM ADICKES, 1401 EDGECUMBE DR, SITKA, AK 99835
GARY ADKISON, BOX 873, CRAIG, AK 99921
GABRIEL ALAMILLO, BOX 1421, HAINES, AK 99827
GERALD ALBECKER, BOX 1207, HAINES, AK 99827
BRUCE ALEXANDER, 5127 SUNNYSIDE BLVD, MARYSVILLE, WA 98270
CESAR ALVARADO, 8011 SECLUSION DR, ANCHORAGE, AK 99504
ROBERT ANDERSON, 17824 MARINE DR, STANWOOD, WA 98292
KEITH ANUNDI, 42121 MT PLEASANT DR, SCIO, OR 97374
JOSHUA ARNOLD, 106 SHOTGUN ALLEY, SITKA, AK 99835
WILLIAM AUGER, BOX 9335, KETCHIKAN, AK 99901
PAUL AXELSON, 15001 N TONGASS, KETCHIKAN, AK 99901
BRAD BADGER, BOX 684, HAINES, AK 99827
JESSIE BADGER, BOX 542, HAINES, AK 99827
HAROLD BAILEY, BOX 887, WRANGELL, AK 99929
TODD BAILEY, 511 KENNEDY ST, JUNEAU, AK 99801
ARNOLD BAKKE, BOX 1482, WRANGELL, AK 99929
TRAVIS BANGS, BOX 403, WRANGELL, AK 99929
ROBERT BARCAS, BOX 784, NEW MEADOWS, ID 83654
DOUGLAS BARKER, BOX 813, WRANGELL, AK 99929
RANDALL BATES, BOX 34624, JUNEAU, AK 99803
DAVID BAXTER, 4455 MORESBY WAY, FERNDALE, WA 98248
JAYME BAXTER, 723 17TH ST, BELLINGHAM, WA 98225
THOMAS BAZER, BOX 95, PETERSBURG, AK 99833

SALMON FISHING LIST—DRIFT GILLNET

JAMES BECKER, BOX 240522, DOUGLAS, AK 99824
PAUL BEESE, BOX 770, WESTPORT, WA 98595
JACOB BELL, BOX 1682, HAINES, AK 99827
JAMES BENSON, BOX 8742, KETCHIKAN, AK 99901
HEIDI BERG, BOX 1392, PETERSBURG, AK 99833
DALTON BERGMAN, 108 HERB DIDRICKSON ST, SITKA, AK 99835
CLAY BEZENEK, 1617 WATER ST, KETCHIKAN, AK 99901
ERIC BEZENEK, 1617 WATER ST, KETCHIKAN, AK 99901
HAROLD BIELESKI, BOX 924, HAINES, AK 99827
FRED BIGSBY, BOX 157, HAINES, AK 99827
GREG BIRCHELL, BOX 183, PETERSBURG, AK 99833
BRIAN BITZ, BOX 627, HOONAH, AK 99829
HARLEY BLACK, BOX 19103, THORNE BAY, AK 99919
DOUG BLACKWELL, 1900 W NICKERSON ST #116 PMB 111, SEATTLE, WA 98119
CHARLES BLATTNER, BOX 33916, JUNEAU, AK 99803
DOUGLAS BLUMER, 6058 AZALEA DR, ANCHORAGE, AK 99516
BURKE BOHNSACK, 300 W 9TH ST, JUNEAU, AK 99801
HANS BORVE, 2138 THORNTON RD, FERNDALE, WA 98248
DALE BOSWORTH, BOX 45, PETERSBURG, AK 99833
TRISTAN BOTSFORD, BOX 211, WRANGELL, AK 99929
BLAKE BOUSLEY, BOX 8643, KETCHIKAN, AK 99901
WILLIAM BOUSLEY, BOX 8643, KETCHIKAN, AK 99901
STEVEN BOX, 1512 LING CT, JUNEAU, AK 99801
KAREN BOYCE, BOX 564, HAINES, AK 99827
JOSHUA BRANDENBURG, 5673 OHELO RD, KAPAA, HI 96746
DAVID BRAY, 3816 BARANOF AVE, KETCHIKAN, AK 99901
THOMAS BRAYTON, 145 BEHRENDS AVE, JUNEAU, AK 99801
MARK BUCHKOSKI, BOX 34026, JUNEAU, AK 99803
MICHAEL BUJACICH, 3815 VERNHARDSON ST, GIG HARBOR, WA 98332
STEVEN BURRELL, BOX 275, PETERSBURG, AK 99833
ANTHONY BYFORD, 4222 PTARMIGAN ST, JUNEAU, AK 99801
LEE BYRD, BOX 46, WRANGELL, AK 99929
ROBERT CASHEN, 300 HERMIT ST #4, JUNEAU, AK 99801
BRIAN CASTLE, BOX 243, CRAIG, AK 99921
WAYNE CHAMBERS, BOX 227, HAINES, AK 99827
BRIAN CHAMPLAIN, 7335 WILLOW ST, SEBASTOPOL, CA 95472
LARRY CHARRIER, 201 BEACH DR, NORDLAND, WA 98358
ROBERT CHICHESTER, 620 EAGLE VIEW DR, GRANITE FALLS, WA 98252
HARRY CHURCHILL, BOX 606, WRANGELL, AK 99929
RANDY CHURCHILL, BOX 152, WRANGELL, AK 99929
STEPHEN CLARK, 1412 R ST, PORT TOWNSEND, WA 98368
CHARLES CLEMENT, BOX 282, METLAKATLA, AK 99926
CHARLES CLEMENT, 1242 WALDON PT RD BOX 302, METLAKATLA, AK 99926
SOMMERS COLE, 4024 RIDGE WAY, JUNEAU, AK 99801
DAVID COLEMAN, BOX 6082, SITKA, AK 99835
MICHAEL COLEMAN, BOX 2054, SITKA, AK 99835
SAMUEL COLITO, 4846 N 7TH, TACOMA, WA 98406
JOSHUA CONN, BOX 593, PETERSBURG, AK 99833
RYAN COOK, BOX 963, HAINES, AK 99827
JEFF COYNE, 1898 SWANTOWN RD, OAK HARBOR, WA 98277
VERNE CRAIG, BOX 1238, PETERSBURG, AK 99833
ELLIS CROPPER, BOX 241, FRIDAY HARBOR, WA 98250
CHRIS CROWE, BOX 211304, AUKE BAY, AK 99821
THOMAS CROY, 1936 BIRCH AVE, REEDSPORT, OR 97467
RICHARD CURRIER, 12020 CROSS ST, JUNEAU, AK 99801
TROY CURTISS, BOX 1532, PETERSBURG, AK 99833
JOHN CVETICH, 420 ROBINHOOD DR, HAILEY, ID 83333
WOODY CYR, 1308 SAWMILL CREEK ROAD, SITKA, AK 99835
ALAN DALE, 926 NORDSTROM DR, KETCHIKAN, AK 99901
ANTHONY DAOUST, 3875 GEIST RD STE PMB 452, FAIRBANKS, AK 99709
ERIC DAUGHERTY, BOX 34602, JUNEAU, AK 99803
RICHARD DAUGHERTY, BOX 34864, JUNEAU, AK 99803
T.ATLIN DAUGHERTY, 9223 N DOUGLAS HWY, JUNEAU, AK 99801
TODD DAUGHERTY, BOX 32705, JUNEAU, AK 99802
ROBERT DAVID, BOX 174, HAINES, AK 99827
WINSTON DAVIES, BOX 1695, WRANGELL, AK 99929

G.WILLIAM DAVIS, BOX 762, SKAGWAY, AK 99840
MATT DAVIS, BOX 451, HAINES, AK 99827
RICHARD DAVIS, 2347 KEVIN CT, JUNEAU, AK 99801
THEODORE DEATS, BOX 20517, JUNEAU, AK 99801
JOHN DEBUSE, BOX 20815, JUNEAU, AK 99802
CRAIG DECKER, BOX 2138, WRANGELL, AK 99929
BRIAN DELAY, 16955 GLACIER HWY, JUNEAU, AK 99801
SAM DEMMERT, BOX 187, YAKUTAT, AK 99689
MICHAEL DENTLER, BOX 9054, KETCHIKAN, AK 99901
CHARLES DEWITT, BOX 128, HAINES, AK 99827
STUART DEWITT, BOX 117, HAINES, AK 99827
ROBERT DICKINSON, 235 N STATE ST, BELLINGHAM, WA 98225
TIMOTHY DIMOND, BOX 240692, DOUGLAS, AK 99824
JAMESZON DOGGETT, 1302 SAWMILL CREEK RD #29, SITKA, AK 99835
ROBERT DOLAN, BOX 1062, PETERSBURG, AK 99833
PHILIP DRAGE, BOX 706, WARRENTON, OR 97146
JIM DUNBAR, BOX 299, CRAIG, AK 99921
PATRICK DUNBAR, 327 1ST AVE, HAINES, AK 99827
DOUGLAS DUNCAN, 1034 W 14TH ST, PORT ANGELES, WA 98363
TERRY DURKIN, BOX 114, PETERSBURG, AK 99833
BRENNON EAGLE, BOX 576, WRANGELL, AK 99929
WAYNE EASTERLY, BOX 335, WRANGELL, AK 99929
DANIEL EDMONDSON, BOX 211549, AUKE BAY, AK 99821
RICHARD ELIASON, 8475 E GOLD BULLION BLVD, PALMER, AK 99645
ARNOLD ENGE, BOX 2113, PETERSBURG, AK 99833
DAVID ERICKSON, BOX 14509, FRIDAY HARBOR, WA 98250
DAWSON EVENDEN, BOX 244, HAINES, AK 99827
DAVID EVENS, BOX 87, PETERSBURG, AK 99833
LYNN EWING, BOX 1335, PETERSBURG, AK 99833
LUKE FANNING, 2925 JACKSON RD, JUNEAU, AK 99801
SEAN FANSLER, 5036 7TH AVE NE, SEATTLE, WA 98105
ORION FENNER, BOX 476, PETERSBURG, AK 99833
TYSON FICK, 9831 NINE MILE CREEK RD, JUNEAU, AK 99801
TOM FISHER, BOX 1928, WRANGELL, AK 99929
DANIEL FLICKINGER, BOX 707, WRANGELL, AK 99929
SILAS FLOR, BOX 396, PETERSBURG, AK 99833
OTTO FLORSCHUTZ, BOX 547, WRANGELL, AK 99929
STEVEN FOSSMAN, BOX 532, HAINES, AK 99827
RUDY FRANULOVICH, BOX 5433, KETCHIKAN, AK 99901
STEFAN FRITZ, 1417 206 AVE CT KPN, LAKEBAY, WA 98349
TYLER GARBISCH, 1116 W PALO VERDE DR, CHANDLER, AZ 85224
JOHN GARRISON, 16 BEAR MEADOWS LN, ABERDEEN, WA 98520
ERIC GERALD, BOX 2084, WRANGELL, AK 99929
JERRY GERMAIN, BOX 272, CRAIG, AK 99921
DAVE GIBSON, 127 W 7TH ST, JUNEAU, AK 99801
ALBERT GIDDINGS, BOX 758, HAINES, AK 99827
JOSEPH GIL, BOX 5, POINT BAKER, AK 99927
WILLIAM GILBERT, BOX 5705, BELLINGHAM, WA 98227
LEE GILPIN, BOX 1511, PETERSBURG, AK 99833
KARL GLADSJO, BOX 462, WRANGELL, AK 99929
GARY GRAHAM, BOX 1067, HAINES, AK 99827
DAVID GREEN, 5583 KNIGHT RD, BELLINGHAM, WA 98226
RYAN GREEN, 1021 ARCTIC BLVD, JUNEAU, AK 99801
RICHARD GREGG, BOX 20669, JUNEAU, AK 99802
WILLIAM GREVSTAD, BOX 8844, KETCHIKAN, AK 99901
ALAN GROSS, BOX 1828, PETERSBURG, AK 99833
JARED GROSS, BOX 1374, WRANGELL, AK 99929
STEPHANIE GROSS, 326 4TH ST #808, JUNEAU, AK 99801
MATTHEW GRUENING, 325 3RD ST #B, JUNEAU, AK 99801
NATHAN GRUENING, BOX 20662, JUNEAU, AK 99802
TERRANCE GRUMMETT, 1724 B DOUGLAS HWY, JUNEAU, AK 99801
CODY GRUSSENDORF, 9386 RIVERCOURT WAY, JUNEAU, AK 99801
TIM GRUSSENDORF, 9386 RIVERCOURT WAY, JUNEAU, AK 99801
TY GRUSSENDORF, 9386 RIVERCOURT WAY, JUNEAU, AK 99801
FABIAN GRUTTER, 711 ETOLIN ST, SITKA, AK 99835
IVAN GRUTTER, 3205 HALIBUT POINT RD, SITKA, AK 99835

SALMON FISHING LIST—DRIFT GILLNET

CLIFTON GUDGEL, BOX 1543, PETERSBURG, AK 99833

MIKALEA GUDMUNDSON, BOX 652, HAINES, AK 99827

ROBERT GUDMUNDSON, 2500 DONOVAN AVE, BELLINGHAM, WA 98225

CHRISTOPHER GUGGENBICKLER, BOX 1491, WRANGELL, AK 99929

STANLEY GUGGENBICKLER, BOX 985, WRANGELL, AK 99929

RYAN GULLUFSEN, BOX 22003, JUNEAU, AK 99802

OLE GUNDERSEN, 8103 N TONGASS HWY, KETCHIKAN, AK 99901

GILBERT GUNDERSON, BOX 1408, WRANGELL, AK 99929

LARRY HAGWOOD, BOX 43, HAINES, AK 99827

MIKE HAMAR, 303 DISTIN AVE, JUNEAU, AK 99801

JACOB HAMMER, BOX 97, PETERSBURG, AK 99833

TIMOTHY HANNON, BOX 47, HAINES, AK 99827

EDWARD HANSEN, 1008 FISH CREEK RD, JUNEAU, AK 99801

BRET HANSON, 2916 ST CLAIR ST, BELLINGHAM, WA 98226

DONALD HASELTINE, BOX 152, CRAIG, AK 99921

SHAUN HASELTINE, BOX 484, KLAWOCK, AK 99925

DAVID HASHAGEN, BOX 8311, KETCHIKAN, AK 99901

JEFFREY HAY, BOX 1373, WRANGELL, AK 99929

DENNIS HEIMDAHL, BOX 256, PETERSBURG, AK 99833

SAMUEL HEIMDAHL, BOX 21047, JUNEAU, AK 99802

SCOTT HEITMAN, BOX 1039, WARD COVE, AK 99928

JAY HENDRICKS, 2001 HUGHES WAY, JUNEAU, AK 99801

JEFFREY HENDRICKS, BOX 225, TOK, AK 99780

MELISSA HENSHAW, 1727 EDGECUMBE DR, SITKA, AK 99835

CARL HERNANDEZ, BOX 48, POINT BAKER, AK 99927

DONALD HERNANDEZ, BOX 48, POINT BAKER, AK 99927

DANIEL HERR, 975 GENEVA ST, BELLINGHAM, WA 98229

LEWIS HIATT, BOX 6277, KETCHIKAN, AK 99901

MICHAEL HIGGINS, 109 DIGBY RD, MOUNT VERNON, WA 98274

DAVID HILDRE, 6330 N DOUGLAS, JUNEAU, AK 99801

MARK HOFSTAD, BOX 1397, PETERSBURG, AK 99833

MELINDA HOFSTAD, BOX 1030, PETERSBURG, AK 99833

RUSSELL HOLBROOK, BOX 18145, COFFMAN COVE, AK 99918

HERB HOLCOMB, BOX 114, YAKUTAT, AK 99689

JAMES HOLCOMB, BOX 206, YAKUTAT, AK 99689

NICK HOLCOMB, BOX 105, YAKUTAT, AK 99689

FORREST HOLLOWAY, 3343 PARK PL, JUNEAU, AK 99801

PAUL HOLM, 11008 N DEER DR, WOODWAY, WA 98020

HANS HOLUM, 730 PARK AVE, KETCHIKAN, AK 99901

SHANE HOSTETLER, BOX 943, LAKEBAY, WA 98349

DANIEL HOTCH, BOX 778, HAINES, AK 99827

KEVIN HUDSON, BOX 581, METLAKATLA, AK 99926

RICHARD HUDSON, BOX 194, METLAKATLA, AK 99926

NORMAN HUGHES, BOX 1136, HAINES, AK 99827

ROBERT HULSE, 639 DEERMOUNT ST, KETCHIKAN, AK 99901

ROGER INGMAN, BOX 1155, SITKA, AK 99835

ENVER ISAKOVIC, 4212 E OREGON ST, BELLINGHAM, WA 98226

CLINTON IVERS, 9620 MUSKET BALL CIR, ANCHORAGE, AK 99507

JAKE JABUSCH, BOX 1228, PETERSBURG, AK 99833

BRENDA JACKINSKY, BOX 39127, NINILCHIK, AK 99639

ROBERT JACKSON, BOX 5011 #146, FERNDALE, WA 98248

EDDIE JASPER, 1613 WETMORE AVE, EVERETT, WA 98201

JAMES JENKINS, BOX 947, WRANGELL, AK 99929

JOSHUA JENKINS, BOX 947, WRANGELL, AK 99929

MARK JENSEN, BOX 457, PETERSBURG, AK 99833

LEIF JOHANSEN, 3191 AMBER AVE, FAIRBANKS, AK 99709

MARK JOHANSEN, 13617 AVON ALLEN RD, MOUNT VERNON, WA 98273

CHRISTOPHER JOHNSON, BOX 2183, WRANGELL, AK 99929

JENNER JOHNSON, 406 HIRST ST APT B, SITKA, AK 99835

KARL JOHNSON, BOX 821, HAINES, AK 99827

MARTIN JOHNSON, 1807 SAWMILL CREEK, SITKA, AK 99835

BILL JOHNSTON, BOX 134, PETERSBURG, AK 99833

HENRY JONES, 3003 SAINT CLAIR, BELLINGHAM, WA 98226

IVAN JONES, 12644 BELLEFLOWER LN, FREDERICKSBURG, VA 22407

KENNETH JUDSON, 5875 GLACIER HWY #34, JUNEAU, AK 99801

DOUGLAS KAINO, 12722 39TH AVE NE, SEATTLE, WA 98125

MICHAEL KAMPNICH, BOX 119, CRAIG, AK 99921

JOHN KATZEEK, BOX 997, HAINES, AK 99827

ERIK KEGEL, BOX 118, PETERSBURG, AK 99833

GREGORY KENDALL, BOX 535, PETERSBURG, AK 99833

BRANDON KENFIELD, BOX 245, WRANGELL, AK 99929

ROBERT KENNEY, 8182 THUNDER ST, JUNEAU, AK 99801

PETER KEUTMANN, BOX 263, PETERSBURG, AK 99833

BYRON KING, 28005 203RD AVE SE, KENT, WA 98042

DUANE KING, BOX 1043, WRANGELL, AK 99929

JEFFERY KLANOTT, BOX 808, HAINES, AK 99827

DAVID KLEPSER, BOX 8946, KETCHIKAN, AK 99901

DONALD KLEPSER, 821 COUNTRYSIDE BLVD, HAILEY, ID 83333

KEVIN KLEPSER, BOX 5341, KETCHUM, ID 83340

WILLIAM KNECHT, BOX 259, WRANGELL, AK 99929

ALEX KNIGHT, BOX 615, HAINES, AK 99827

ANDREW KNIGHT, BOX 1658, PETERSBURG, AK 99833

JOHN KNIGHT, BOX 1133, PETERSBURG, AK 99833

JONAH KNUTSON, 700 S TRENTON ST, SEATTLE, WA 98108

MORGAN KNUTSON, BOX 785, HAINES, AK 99827

PETER KNUTSON, 4602 SW FRONTENAC ST, SEATTLE, WA 98136

ERNEST KOHLHASE, BOX 240524, DOUGLAS, AK 99824

JON KOHLHASE, BOX 240524, DOUGLAS, AK 99824

ROBERT KUNTZ, BOX 455, WRANGELL, AK 99929

DAVID LAING, 2653 NORTH SHORE RD, BELLINGHAM, WA 98226

CLARENCE LAITI, BOX 20147, JUNEAU, AK 99802

FRANK LAMBERT, BOX 32202, JUNEAU, AK 99803

TYLER LAPPETITO, 4429 WEBSTER ST, OAKLAND, CA 94609

BRIAN LARSEN, 333 45TH PL, SEA ISLE CITY, NJ 8243

ERIC LARSON, BOX 301, PETERSBURG, AK 99833

MARILYN LARSON, 6661 HOLLY PL SW, SEATTLE, WA 98136

LEONARD LEACH, BOX 6017, KETCHIKAN, AK 99901

DANIEL LENGSTORF, BOX 1147, SKAGWAY, AK 99840

SCOTT LESH, BOX 715, SKAGWAY, AK 99840

TED LEWIS, BOX 2103, VASHON, WA 98070

MARK LIGHT, BOX 132, HAINES, AK 99827

RONALD LINDSEY, BOX 1344, PETERSBURG, AK 99833

JEANIE LITTLEJOHN, BOX 647, WRANGELL, AK 99929

EVAN LOVE, 104 KUHNLE DR, SITKA, AK 99835

GREG LUTTON, BOX 1924, PETERSBURG, AK 99833

JOSEPH LYKKEN, BOX 71, WRANGELL, AK 99929

NELS LYNCH, BOX 425, HAINES, AK 99827

DRAKE LYONS, BOX 527, PETERSBURG, AK 99833

RALPH MACKIE, BOX 252, CRAIG, AK 99921

CHRISTOPHER MACKOVJAK, 3703 SE 65TH AVE UNIT B, PORTLAND, OR 97206

CURTIS MANGUSSO, BOX 240573, DOUGLAS, AK 99824

JOHN MANGUSSO, BOX 240573, DOUGLAS, AK 99824

MICHAEL MANN, BOX 32653, JUNEAU, AK 99803

CHRISTINE MANNING, BOX 501, WRANGELL, AK 99929

RYAN MANNING, 8005 SHIRLEY AVE, GIG HARBOR, WA 98332

DANIEL MARTIN, BOX 708, HAINES, AK 99827

DAVID MARTIN, BOX 88, PETERSBURG, AK 99833

NICHOLAS MARTIN, BOX 8312, KETCHIKAN, AK 99901

ROBERT MARTIN, BOX 357, PETERSBURG, AK 99833

RONALD MARTIN, BOX 526, HAINES, AK 99827

SHANE MARTIN, BOX 284, HAINES, AK 99827

GUENTER MATH, BOX 20571, JUNEAU, AK 99802

STEPHEN MATHEWS, BOX 18126, COFFMAN COVE, AK 99918

BRIAN MATTSON, BOX 1168, PETERSBURG, AK 99833

MORRIS MATTSON, BOX 1168, PETERSBURG, AK 99833

FRED MAY, BOX 514, METLAKATLA, AK 99926

NOAH MAYO, 2800 SAWMILL CREEK RD, SITKA, AK 99835

IVAN MCCALLISTER, BOX 8954, KETCHIKAN, AK 99901

ALBERT MCDONNELL, 7888 SE 46TH AVE, PORTLAND, OR 97206

KEVIN MCDOUGALL, BOX 240714, DOUGLAS, AK 99824

SALMON FISHING LIST—DRIFT GILLNET

MICHAEL MCGOVERN, 900 DECKER RD, PASCO, WA 99301
RAPHAEL MCGUIRE, BOX 578, HAINES, AK 99827
MICHAEL MCHENRY, 3829 MELROSE ST, JUNEAU, AK 99801
ABRAHAM MCINTYRE, BOX 1994, WRANGELL, AK 99929
PAUL MCINTYRE, BOX 1994, WRANGELL, AK 99929
JEFF MCKEAN, 1683 S NANSEA LN, HAMMETT, ID 83627
CHRISTOPHER MCMURREN, BOX 312, WRANGELL, AK 99929
HOWARD MCVICKER, 1015 GROVE PL, COSTA MESA, CA 92627
LEE MCVICKER, BOX 2336, WRANGELL, AK 99929
MICHAEL MEDALEN, BOX 969, PETERSBURG, AK 99833
DAVID MEINERS, 1013 WEE BURN, JUNEAU, AK 99801
GEORGE MEINTEL, 1704 S COLORADO AVE, BOISE, ID 83706
PAUL MENISH, BOX 33, PETERSBURG, AK 99833
BRIAN MERRITT, BOX 401, WRANGELL, AK 99929
CHATHAM MILLER, BOX 240441, DOUGLAS, AK 99824
DAWSON MILLER, BOX 2231, WRANGELL, AK 99929
SAM MILLER, BOX 240441, DOUGLAS, AK 99824
CLAYTON MILTON, BOX 184, METLAKATLA, AK 99926
DUKE MITCHELL, BOX 80, WRANGELL, AK 99929
JOHN MOLLER, BOX 32425, JUNEAU, AK 99803
PETER MOORE, BOX 7573, KETCHIKAN, AK 99901
KRISTOPHER MORDEN, BOX 32, HAINES, AK 99827
MIKE MORTELL, BOX 53, POINT BAKER, AK 99927
JOSEPH MOSER, 291 E SMITH RD, BELLINGHAM, WA 98226
ROBERT MOSHER, 11985 MENDENHALL LP RD, JUNEAU, AK 99801
LUCAS MULLEN, BOX 543, PETERSBURG, AK 99833
JERRY NANKERVIS, BOX 34831, JUNEAU, AK 99803
ED NEAL, 2928 FRITZ COVE RD, JUNEAU, AK 99801
NICHOLAS NEKEFEROFF, 3416 HALIBUT POINT RD #A, SITKA, AK 99835
SCOTT NEWMAN, BOX 1348, PETERSBURG, AK 99833
MAMIE NILSEN, BOX 532, PETERSBURG, AK 99833
MATT NILSEN, BOX 1463, PETERSBURG, AK 99833
GUNNAR NOREEN, BOX 240367, DOUGLAS, AK 99824
JAMES ODEGAARD, 2309 CEDAR CT, MOUNT VERNON, WA 98273
ROBERT ODMARK, BOX 7594, KETCHIKAN, AK 99901
CHRISTOPHER OLSEN, BOX 378, HAINES, AK 99827
YNGVE OLSSON, BOX 605, HAINES, AK 99827
HELEN OPHEIM, BOX 2118, WRANGELL, AK 99929
BRIAN ORILEY, BOX 772, HAINES, AK 99827
DONALD OSTLIE, BOX 2637, VASHON, WA 98070
CHRIS OTTESEN, BOX 2011, WRANGELL, AK 99929
WOODY PAHL, BOX 1581, HAINES, AK 99827
DANNY PARDEE, 2223 FRITZ COVE RD, JUNEAU, AK 99801
STEVE PARIS, 9716 CRESCENT VALLEY NW, GIG HARBOR, WA 98332
HUNT PARR, BOX 418, PETERSBURG, AK 99833
JOEL PASQUAN, BOX 845, HAINES, AK 99827
BRYAN PEREZ, BOX 7991, KETCHIKAN, AK 99901
TIMOTHY PEROV, BOX 33321, JUNEAU, AK 99803
GEOFF PETERSEN, BOX 870883, WASILLA, AK 99687
CARL PETERSON, BOX 22834, JUNEAU, AK 99801
GEORGE PETERSON, 5785 S TONGASS, KETCHIKAN, AK 99901
RICHARD PHILLIPS, BOX 522, WRANGELL, AK 99929
DUANE PIATT, 48215 LAKESIDE DR, SOLDOTNA, AK 99669
LANCE PIHLMAN, BOX 5322, KETCHIKAN, AK 99901
LANNY PIHLMAN, BOX 778, WARD COVE, AK 99928
PAUL PIPES, 4105 NE 60TH, SEATTLE, WA 98115
DAVID POPE, 2417 TONGASS AVE SUITE 111-344, KETCHIKAN, AK 99901
JONATHAN POWELL, BOX 1733, WRANGELL, AK 99929
WILLIAM PRISCIANDARO, BOX 1716, HAINES, AK 99827
ROBERT PROULX, BOX 1736, WRANGELL, AK 99929
SAM PRYSUNKA, BOX 2294, WRANGELL, AK 99929
JOEL RANDRUP, BOX 1231, PETERSBURG, AK 99833
JOHN REAR, BOX 240497, DOUGLAS, AK 99824
AUTUMN RECORDS, BOX 7111, KETCHIKAN, AK 99901
ALAN REEVES, BOX 741, WRANGELL, AK 99929
RYAN REEVES, BOX 758, WRANGELL, AK 99929

WILLIAM RHODES, BOX 268, CRAIG, AK 99921
SPENCER RICHTER, BOX 1011, CRAIG, AK 99921
MICHAEL RIEDERER, 9309 GLACIER HWY A101, JUNEAU, AK 99801
ERIC RIEMER, BOX 23458, KETCHIKAN, AK 99901
JACOB RODRIGUEZ, BOX 5691, KETCHIKAN, AK 99901
HELEN ROTH, BOX 1451, HAINES, AK 99827
JOHN ROTH, BOX 2771, HAINES, AK 99827
JOSEPH ROTH, 16169 WATERFALL RD, KETCHIKAN, AK 99901
STEVE ROTTLER, 159 WESTERN AVE W #454, SEATTLE, WA 98119
ZEEKUAL ROULSTON, BOX 154, POINT BAKER, AK 99927
JAMES ROWLAND, BOX 970, WRANGELL, AK 99929
MARK SALDI, BOX 287, SKAGWAY, AK 99840
ENOCH SCHERTEL, BOX 43, YAKUTAT, AK 99689
ANN SCHMID, 3442 DENALI AVE, KETCHIKAN, AK 99901
JEREMY SCHRUMM, 2417 TONGASS AVE #111-321, KETCHIKAN, AK 99901
MICHAEL SCHWARTZ, BOX 434, PETERSBURG, AK 99833
ROBERT SCHWARTZ, BOX 1533, PETERSBURG, AK 99833
DAN SCHWEITZER, BOX 1667, PETERSBURG, AK 99833
JAMES SCUDERO, BOX 551, METLAKATLA, AK 99926
JERRY SCUDERO, 955 FOREST AVE, KETCHIKAN, AK 99901
JEV SHELTON, 1670 EVERGREEN AVE, JUNEAU, AK 99801
TORY SHIER, BOX 861, METLAKATLA, AK 99926
ANTONIO SILVA, BOX 602, WRANGELL, AK 99929
ANTHONEY SINE, BOX 32132, JUNEAU, AK 99803
KARL SJODIN, 714 148TH ST NE, ARLINGTON, WA 98223
KURT SJODIN, 1253 N 143RD, SEATTLE, WA 98133
JOHN SKEELE, 262 KAAGWAANTAAN ST, SITKA, AK 99835
DAVID SKRZYNSKI, BOX 813, DOUGLAS, AK 99824
MILAN SLIPCEVIC, 156 WINDWARD DR, BELLINGHAM, WA 98229
ROBERT SLITER, BOX 240543, DOUGLAS, AK 99824
ROBERT SLITER, BOX 240543, DOUGLAS, AK 99824
CHAD SMITH, BOX 1741, WRANGELL, AK 99929
DANIEL SMITH, BOX 911, WRANGELL, AK 99929
JAMES SMITH, BOX 251, CORDOVA, AK 99574
MARTY SMITH, BOX 228, HAINES, AK 99827
SAMUEL SMITH, BOX 210651, AUKE BAY, AK 99821
TANNER SMITH, BOX 1379, WRANGELL, AK 99929
SHANE SNYDER, 106 KINCROFT, SITKA, AK 99835
PAUL SOUTHLAND, BOX 257, WRANGELL, AK 99929
EVANS SPARKS, 100 DONNA DR, SITKA, AK 99835
EVANS SPARKS, 101 PEACE LN, SITKA, AK 99835
RON SPARKS, BOX 1087, HAINES, AK 99827
BYRON SPENCE, 2908 COTTONWOOD AVE, BELLINGHAM, WA 98225
RICHARD SPRAGUE, BOX 567, PETERSBURG, AK 99833
BARBARA STAAKE, BOX 843, PETERSBURG, AK 99833
MICHAEL STAINBROOK, BOX 2052, PETERSBURG, AK 99833
LARS STANGELAND, 222 FRONT ST #600, JUNEAU, AK 99801
MITCHELL STAUFFER, 77-6703 NOHEALANI PL, KAILUA-KONA, HI 96740
ROBERT STEDMAN, 45 MONTGOMERY LN, ABERDEEN, WA 98502
KEVIN STELL, BOX 21965, JUNEAU, AK 99802
DAVID STICKLER, BOX 685, HAINES, AK 99827
JAMES STICKLER, BOX 974, HAINES, AK 99827
RAY STONER, BOX 394, PETERSBURG, AK 99833
RALPH STRICKLAND, BOX 292, PETERSBURG, AK 99833
JAMES STROMDAHL, BOX 1326, PETERSBURG, AK 99833
MIKE STUART, BOX 58, HAINES, AK 99827
TRAVIS STUART, BOX 58, HAINES, AK 99827
MARTIN SVENSON, 14861 N TONGASS, KETCHIKAN, AK 99901
MIKE SVENSON, 104 SHARON DR, SITKA, AK 99835
STEVE SVENSSON, BOX 1207, MARYSVILLE, WA 98270
DYLAN SWAINSON, BOX 2125, PETERSBURG, AK 99833
JAMES SZYMANSKI, BOX 418, HAINES, AK 99827
EDWARD TAGABAN, BOX 1492, PETERSBURG, AK 99833
ANTHONY TAIBER, BOX 1861, PETERSBURG, AK 99833
CAULLEN TAYLOR, BOX 1278, HAINES, AK 99827
CODY TAYLOR, BOX 897, HAINES, AK 99827

SALMON FISHING LIST—DRIFT GILLNET

LEE TAYLOR, BOX 1077, HAINES, AK 99827
CHARLES TEAL, BOX 1637, WARD COVE, AK 99928
TERRANCE THOMAS, BOX 33301, JUNEAU, AK 99803
WILLIAM THOMAS, BOX 942, HAINES, AK 99827
NORMAN THOMPSON, 2520 OAKES AVE, ANACORTES, WA 98221
RICHARD THOMPSON, 443 WINDWARD WAY, DAVENPORT, FL 33837
JAMES THOMSEN, BOX 621, HAINES, AK 99827
KENNETH THOMSEN, BOX 191, HAINES, AK 99827
ARTHUR THURN, 2323 G ST, BELLINGHAM, WA 98225
CHARLES THYNES, BOX 1517, PETERSBURG, AK 99833
DAVID THYNES, BOX 533, PETERSBURG, AK 99833
STEVEN THYNES, BOX 193, PETERSBURG, AK 99833
JACK TURNER, 118 MCKINLEY ST, BURLINGTON, WA 98233
ZACHARY TURNER, BOX 1112, SKAGWAY, AK 99840
ERICA TYAS, 703 E NORTH ST, BELLINGHAM, WA 98225
MICHAEL TYAS, 703 E NORTH ST, BELLINGHAM, WA 98225
SHAYAR VALANDRO, BOX 210966, AUKE BAY, AK 99821
JAMES VANDEBUNTE, BOX 1222, WRANGELL, AK 99929
SHANNON VANDERVEST, BOX 1392, PETERSBURG, AK 99833
CHRISTIAN VAUGHAN, BOX 7621, KETCHIKAN, AK 99901
BRIAN VAUGHN, BOX 34086, JUNEAU, AK 99802
JOHN VERHEY, BOX 2281, WRANGELL, AK 99929
NICHOLAS VERSTEEG, BOX 1752, PETERSBURG, AK 99833
RICK VERSTEEG, BOX 63, PETERSBURG, AK 99833
DANIEL VICK, BOX 1271, PETERSBURG, AK 99833
GANNON VICK, BOX 842, PETERSBURG, AK 99833
STEWART VICK, BOX 1271, PETERSBURG, AK 99833
FELIX VILLARMA, BOX 938, WRANGELL, AK 99929
STEVEN VLAHOVICH, 1068 SW 325TH CT, FEDERAL WAY, WA 98023
MICHAEL WALLACE, 1537 PRIMROSE CR, LYNDEN, WA 98264
CHAD WALLING, 17285 LENA LOOP RD, JUNEAU, AK 99801
JAY WALLING, 16765 LENA LOOP RD, JUNEAU, AK 99801
ROGER WALLING, 17285 LENA LP RD, JUNEAU, AK 99801
MICHAEL WARD, BOX 1691, HAINES, AK 99827
ERIC WEATHERS, BOX 1791, CORDOVA, AK 99574
ALEXANDER WEISSBERG, 311 CASCADE ST, SITKA, AK 99835
STEVE WEISSBERG, 455 CHARTERIS ST, SITKA, AK 99835
JERRY WELCH, BOX 1686, PETERSBURG, AK 99833
NICHOLAS WELCH, BOX 1873, PETERSBURG, AK 99833
TODD WELCH, BOX 1686, PETERSBURG, AK 99833
DAVID WENZLAU, 1901 FRITZ COVE RD, JUNEAU, AK 99801
CHRISTOPHER WERTZ, BOX 283, ANCHOR POINT, AK 99556
JEFFREY WHICKER, BOX 774, WARD COVE, AK 99928
DAVID WHITE, 189 POTTER RD, KETCHIKAN, AK 99901
JAMES WHITE, BOX 32892, JUNEAU, AK 99803
JAMES WHITETHORN, BOX 94, PETERSBURG, AK 99833
CHRISTOPHER WHITTLESEY, BOX 809, PETERSBURG, AK 99833
COLE WILBURN, BOX 240056, DOUGLAS, AK 99824
JOE WILLIS, BOX 43, PETERSBURG, AK 99833
BRUCE WILSON, 743 N 184TH ST, SHORELINE, WA 98133
JEFF WOLFE, BOX 381, SITKA, AK 99835
GLORIANNE WOLLEN, BOX 1076, PETERSBURG, AK 99833
DAVID WOLTEN, BOX 501, WRANGELL, AK 99929
MATTHEW WOLTEN, BOX 501, WRANGELL, AK 99929
FLOYD WOOD, 8012 GLADSTONE ST, JUNEAU, AK 99801
GEORGE WOOD, BOX 902, PETERSBURG, AK 99833
KARSTEN WOOD, BOX 2195, PETERSBURG, AK 99833
AARON WOODROW, 17875 POINT STEPHENS RD, JUNEAU, AK 99801
MAXIMILIAN WORHATCH, BOX 407, PETERSBURG, AK 99833
ZACHARY WORRELL, 155 CORDOVA ST, JUNEAU, AK 99801
ANDY WRIGHT, BOX 1432, PETERSBURG, AK 99833
TODD WYMAN, 2176 HALIBUT POINT RD, SITKA, AK 99835
ALAN YOUNG, 4932 WREN DR, JUNEAU, AK 99801
LARRY YOUNG, BOX 922, PETERSBURG, AK 99833
MONTE YOUNG, 2413 SAWMILL CREEK RD, SITKA, AK 99835

MICHAEL ZIMNY, 13127 45TH AVE W, MUKILTEO, WA 98275
BRIAN ZWICK, 801 PETERSON ST, KETCHIKAN, AK 99901

SALMON, DRIFT GILLNET, PRINCE WILLIAM SOUND

STEVE ABERLE, 7041 POTTER HEIGHTS DR, ANCHORAGE, AK 99516
ROLLY ACOBA, BOX 2174, CORDOVA, AK 99574
ROMEO ACOBA, BOX 2025, CORDOVA, AK 99574
DEBRA ADAMS, BOX 194, CORDOVA, AK 99574
MARK ADAMS, 6606 N ASSEMBLY ST, SPOKANE, WA 99218
MICHAEL ADAMS, BOX 961, CORDOVA, AK 99574
DAVID AERS, BOX 2045, HOMER, AK 99603
IVAN AFONIN, BOX 875588, WASILLA, AK 99687
MAKSIM AFONIN, 7645 HWY 291, FORD, WA 99013
VIC AFONIN, BOX 2733, HOMER, AK 99603
LOUIE ALBER, BOX 111, CORDOVA, AK 99574
LESLIE ALLEN, BOX 984, VALDEZ, AK 99686
RUSSELL ALLEN, BOX 1062, CORDOVA, AK 99574
SPENCER ALLEN, 1240 EAGLE VIEW DR, HOMER, AK 99603
LEO AMERICUS, BOX 2112, CORDOVA, AK 99574
KALE ANDERSON, 1193 BAY AVE, HOMER, AK 99603
KRIS ANDERSON, BOX 892, CORDOVA, AK 99574
MARK ANDERSON, 11321 WILLENE DR, ANCHORAGE, AK 99516
JON ANDREWS, BOX 1034, SEWARD, AK 99664
DIONICE ANUFRIEV, BOX 2356, HOMER, AK 99603
KARP ANUFRIEV, BOX 1718, HOMER, AK 99603
HEIDI BABIC, BOX 1208, CORDOVA, AK 99574
MATHEW BABIC, BOX 988, CORDOVA, AK 99574
MICHAEL BABIC, BOX 1853, CORDOVA, AK 99574
RUSSELL BABIC, BOX 1833, CORDOVA, AK 99574
KABAN BACKLUND, 48178 SEWARD HWY, MOOSE PASS, AK 99631
KARL BACKLUND, 48178 SEWARD HWY, MOOSE PASS, AK 99631
KARL BACKLUND, BOX 43, MOOSE PASS, AK 99631
KOAL BACKLUND, BOX 2944, SEWARD, AK 99664
DONALD BAILEY, BOX 412, CORDOVA, AK 99574
J BAILEY, 1413 SUNRISE DR, ANCHORAGE, AK 99508
WILLIAM BAILEY, BOX 1190, CORDOVA, AK 99574
VICTORIA BAKER, BOX 600, CORDOVA, AK 99574
SETH BALINT, BOX 783, CORDOVA, AK 99574
RICK BALLAS, BOX 352, CORDOVA, AK 99574
JOHN BANKS, BOX 2462, CORDOVA, AK 99574
LOREN BANKS, BOX 2431, CORDOVA, AK 99574
ANTHONY BARNES, BOX 3221, PALMER, AK 99645
STEPHEN BARNES, BOX 332, CORDOVA, AK 99574
JAMES BARR, 733 FLINT ROCK WAY, IVINS, UT 84738
MORGAN BARROWCLIFF, BOX 10, ANCHOR POINT, AK 99556
GEORGE BASARGIN, BOX 305, FORD, WA 99013
GEORGI BASARGIN, BOX 343, NINE MILE FALLS, WA 99026
PETRO BASARGIN, BOX 2126, HOMER, AK 99603
PLATON BASARGIN, BOX 875402, WASILLA, AK 99687
YAKOV BASARGIN, 37534 KETTLE VIEW AVE, HOMER, AK 99603
ROBERT BEEDLE, BOX 1242, CORDOVA, AK 99574
KRISTINE BERAN, 15435 GROTLE RD NE, BAINBRIDGE ISLAND, WA 98110
DONALD BERGQUIST, 4922 S SMUGGLERS COVE RD, FREELAND, WA 98249
RODGER BERGQUIST, 4816 SARATOGA RD, LANGLEY, WA 98260
DAN BILDERBACK, 4623 CAMPUS CIR, ANCHORAGE, AK 99507
WILLIAM BLACK, BOX 204, CORDOVA, AK 99574
DAVID BLAKE, BOX 374, MARYSVILLE, WA 98270
KORY BLAKE, BOX 1122, CORDOVA, AK 99574
PETER BLAKE, BOX 718, CORDOVA, AK 99574
DAVID BLANCHARD, BOX 904, SOLDOTNA, AK 99669
DAVID BLOUNT, 1905 E 19TH ST, ROSWELL, NM 88201
MICHAEL BLUME, 5675 N DOUGLAS HWY, JUNEAU, AK 99801
JOHN BOCCI, BOX 1312, CORDOVA, AK 99574
ALEXANDER BODUNOV, BOX 603, WILLOW, AK 99688

SALMON FISHING LIST—DRIFT GILLNET

EROFAY BODUNOV, BOX 196, WILLOW, AK 99688
SERGEY BOGATCHEV, BOX 1533, CORDOVA, AK 99574
GLENN BORODKIN, BOX 423, CORDOVA, AK 99574
GARRETT BOSICK, BOX 34, KASILOF, AK 99610
GREGORY BOSICK, BOX 390, KASILOF, AK 99610
GREGORY BOTTJEN, 1150 S COLONY WAY STE 3-406, PALMER, AK 99645
SCOTT BOTTOMS, 189 E NELSON AVE #225, WASILLA, AK 99654
CHRISTOPHER BOURGEOIS, BOX 1945, CORDOVA, AK 99574
MICHAEL BOWEN, 2150 INNES CIR, ANCHORAGE, AK 99515
KEITH BOYLE, POX 870295, WASILLA, AK 99687
BRET BRADFORD, BOX 1235, CORDOVA, AK 99574
DAVID BRANSHAW, BOX 2241, CORDOVA, AK 99574
DERRICK BRANSON, BOX 3404, SEWARD, AK 99664
RICHARD BRAY, 101 W CHENAULT AVE, HOQUIAM, WA 98550
RUSSELL BRAY, 504 BANK ST #5, WALLACE, ID 83873
TERRY BRAY, BOX 1189, CORDOVA, AK 99574
PETE BROCKERT, BOX 2326, CORDOVA, AK 99574
ANDREW BRODERS, 5743 OLD GARDINER RD, PORT TOWNSEND, WA 98368
JACK BROUGHTON, BOX 264, SEWARD, AK 99664
RYAN BROUGHTON, BOX 264, SEWARD, AK 99664
EZEKIEL BROWN, BOX 782, CORDOVA, AK 99574
CLINTON BUCHHOLZ, 2331 GREENRIDGE CIR #2, ANCHORAGE, AK 99507
MARK BUCHKOSKI, BOX 34026, JUNEAU, AK 99803
MARK BUCHNER, BOX 7819, BEND, OR 97708
MARTIN BUDNICK, 89603 HWY 101, WARRENTON, OR 97146
CARL BURTON, BOX 81, CORDOVA, AK 99574
CARL BURTON, BOX 1404, CORDOVA, AK 99574
JAMES BURTON, BOX 41, CORDOVA, AK 99574
WES BUSBY, 915 SOUNDVIEW AVE, HOMER, AK 99603
WADE BUSCHER, BOX 1032, CORDOVA, AK 99574
JOHN BUTLER, BOX 315, CORDOVA, AK 99574
KADE BUTLER, BOX 2383, CORDOVA, AK 99574
NORMAN CAMPBELL, BOX 1346, CORDOVA, AK 99574
HERBERT CARINO, BOX 1064, CORDOVA, AK 99574
DAVID CARLSON, BOX 500, CORDOVA, AK 99574
HENRY CARLSON, BOX 500, CORDOVA, AK 99574
KENNETH CARLSON, 2926 MADISON WAY, ANCHORAGE, AK 99508
DANNY CARPENTER, BOX 1430, CORDOVA, AK 99574
ERIC CARPENTER, 5432 E NORTHERN LTS BLVD #666, ANCHORAGE, AK 99508
MARC CARREL, BOX 461, CORDOVA, AK 99574
JACOB CARROLL, 12219 NE 136TH PL, KIRKLAND, WA 98034
KIP CARROLL, BOX 1173, CORDOVA, AK 99574
RICHARD CASCIANO, BOX 584, CORDOVA, AK 99574
JOSE CEBALLOS, BOX 2606, CORDOVA, AK 99574
JEFF CHAPPELL, BOX 1343, CORDOVA, AK 99574
WARREN CHAPPELL, BOX 743, CORDOVA, AK 99574
GREG CHEREMNOV, 29095 S DRYLAND RD, CANBY, OR 97013
KLEMENTA CHERNISHOFF, 7971 ST CHARLES ST, KEIZER, OR 97303
GRIGORY CHERNISHOV, 10589 S TOLIVER RD, MOLALLA, OR 97038
DYLAN CHESHIER, BOX 2264, CORDOVA, AK 99574
ELMER CHESHIER, BOX 2264, CORDOVA, AK 99574
RAYMOND COFFEY, 1701 ENTIAT RIVER RD, ENTIAT, WA 98822
GARRETT COLLINS, BOX 472, CORDOVA, AK 99574
LEE COLLINS, BOX 1734, CORDOVA, AK 99574
JOE COOK, BOX 215, CORDOVA, AK 99574
WILLIAM COOK, 605 BRANCH LINE RD, YUKON, OK 73099
STEVEN COPELAND, 421 E AMHERST CIR, SATELLITE BEACH, FL 32937
LIAM CORCORAN, BOX 1371, CORDOVA, AK 99574
GEORGE COVEL, BOX 984, LEWISTOWN, MT 59457
WILLIAM CRAIG, BOX 110401, ANCHORAGE, AK 99511
BYRON CULLENBERG, BOX 688, PALMER, AK 99645
GERALD CUNNINGHAM, BOX 1451, CORDOVA, AK 99574
ROBERT CUNNINGHAM, BOX 22, CORDOVA, AK 99574
HARRY CURRAN, BOX 42, CORDOVA, AK 99574
BENJAMIN DAIGLE, BOX 4013, HOMER, AK 99603
JEFFREY DAVIS, BOX 173, CORDOVA, AK 99574

JAMES DAY, 1002 BROWNS POINT BLVD, TACOMA, WA 98422
STEPHEN DAY, 8830 GLORALEE ST, ANCHORAGE, AK 99502
CHARLES DEATON, BOX 874, CORDOVA, AK 99574
SETH DENSMORE, 3655 S OLD GLENN HWY PMB #A, PALMER, AK 99645
CHARLES DEVILLE, BOX 6, WALTON, OR 97490
TIM DILLON, BOX 2576, CORDOVA, AK 99574
TIM DILLON, BOX 1014, CORDOVA, AK 99574
TYLER DILLON, BOX 1326, CORDOVA, AK 99574
ELAINE DINNOCENZO, BOX 806, KASILOF, AK 99610
NATHAN DOLL, BOX 23, CORDOVA, AK 99574
PAUL DUNATOV, 11321 36TH ST NE, LAKE STEVENS, WA 98258
JAMES DUNDAS, BOX 133, CORDOVA, AK 99574
NATHAN DUNTON, 4 LADERA PLACE, SANTA FE, NM 87508
WESLEY E.F.WOODS, BOX 463, CORDOVA, AK 99574
ANDREW ECKLEY, BOX 2014, CORDOVA, AK 99574
ROBERT ECKLEY, BOX 1274, CORDOVA, AK 99574
LINDA ECOLANO, BOX 1593, CORDOVA, AK 99574
KEITH EDENS, BOX 641, HOMER, AK 99603
EFREIM EFIMOFF, 27246 S PRIMROSE PATH, CAUBY, OR 97013
VASILY EFIMOFF, 8017 3RD ST NE, LAKE STEVENS, WA 98258
DAVID EIKE, BOX 2305, CORDOVA, AK 99574
JONATHAN ERICKSON, BOX 3695, HOMER, AK 99603
MICAH ESS, BOX 1353, CORDOVA, AK 99574
STEVE ESTES, BOX 155, CORDOVA, AK 99574
WILLIAM EVANS, BOX 643, MONTESANO, WA 98563
MILOS FALTA, 27 LILINOE ST, HILO, HI 96720
JACK FARRELL, 212 ORCA INLET DR #1744, CORDOVA, AK 99574
EDESY FEFELOV, BOX 2686, HOMER, AK 99603
PHILIP FILLINGHAM, BOX 1824, CORDOVA, AK 99574
DENISE FJORTOFT, 3718 SHOREWOOD AVE, GREENBACK, WA 98253
JENS FJORTOFT, 3718 SHOREWOOD AVE, GREENBANK, WA 98253
MARK FLANAGAN, BOX 3673, SEWARD, AK 99664
JOSEPH FLEMING, 6948 FAIRWEATHER DR, ANCHORAGE, AK 99518
MICHAEL GALE, 3800 MCMAHON AVE, ANCHORAGE, AK 99516
GAYLE GILDNES, 15006 CHANNEL LN, LA CONNER, WA 98257
STEVEN GILDNES, BOX 2393, CORDOVA, AK 99574
SWEN GILDNES, BOX 519, CORDOVA, AK 99574
LANNY GILLESPIE, BOX 2312, CORDOVA, AK 99574
DARIN GILMAN, BOX 223, CORDOVA, AK 99574
SHAWN GILMAN, BOX 223, CORDOVA, AK 99574
DAVID GLASEN, BOX 2202, CORDOVA, AK 99574
MICHAEL GLASEN, BOX 2532, CORDOVA, AK 99574
MICHAEL GLASEN, BOX 432, CORDOVA, AK 99574
TONI GODES, BOX 943, CORDOVA, AK 99574
KURT GOETZINGER, BOX 1268, CORDOVA, AK 99574
VASILII GORDEEV, BOX 531, ANCHOR POINT, AK 99556
JAMES GORESEN, 10206 JAMESTOWN DR #C, ANCHORAGE, AK 99507
JOHN GRAHAM, BOX 1078, CORDOVA, AK 99574
TERRY GRANGER, BOX 1018, CORDOVA, AK 99574
JOHN GROCOTT, BOX 59, ILWACO, WA 98624
GEOFF GROSS, BOX 1986, GIRDWOOD, AK 99587
ROBERT HAGER, BOX 1552, CORDOVA, AK 99574
KEVIN HAISMAN, BOX 174, CORDOVA, AK 99574
CHRIS HAMILTON, BOX 893, CORDOVA, AK 99574
WILLIAM HAMMER, BOX 1324, CORDOVA, AK 99574
RANDY HAMSON, 5392 290TH ST, CUSHING, MN 56443
ELEANOR HAND, BOX 2181, CORDOVA, AK 99574
BENJAMIN HANDLEY, BOX 900, HOMER, AK 99603
ARDY HANSON, BOX 2485, CORDOVA, AK 99574
MARK HAZELTINE, 3200 STAYSAIL DR, ANCHORAGE, AK 99516
PAUL HEARN, BOX 2091, CORDOVA, AK 99574
MARK HEIDBRINK, BOX 2084, CORDOVA, AK 99574
DOUGLAS HEIMBUCH, BOX 4502, SOLDOTNA, AK 99669
ROBERT HENRICHS, BOX 1000, CORDOVA, AK 99574
ALEC HERSCHLEB, BOX 1744, GIRDWOOD, AK 99587
CURTIS HERSCHLEB, BOX 1622, CORDOVA, AK 99574

SALMON FISHING LIST—DRIFT GILLNET

JOHN HERSCHLEB, 440 E 56TH AVE #A, ANCHORAGE, AK 99518
KENT HERSCHLEB, 7536 SW 34TH AVE, PORTLAND, OR 97219
CAMERON HESSE, BOX 1251, CORDOVA, AK 99574
RUSTY HIGGINS, BOX 526, CORDOVA, AK 99574
ANNALEE HILL, 7001 E LAKE CIR, PALMER, AK 99645
HANS HILL, 2424 N WILLOW DR, WASILLA, AK 99654
RONALD HINDE, BOX 166, CORDOVA, AK 99574
THOMAS HLAVNICKA, BOX 131, HOONAH, AK 99829
TUAN HO, BOX 1502, CORDOVA, AK 99574
PETER HOEPFNER, BOX 1204, CORDOVA, AK 99574
JAMES HONKOLA, BOX 1813, CORDOVA, AK 99574
MATT HONKOLA, BOX 132, CORDOVA, AK 99574
RAYMOND HONKOLA, BOX 100, CORDOVA, AK 99574
HAYLEY HOOVER, BOX 2302, CORDOVA, AK 99574
ROBERT HOOVER, BOX 1039, CORDOVA, AK 99574
JOHN HOPKINS, BOX 343, CORDOVA, AK 99574
TOM HUFFER, 11551 TARGHEE LP, EAGLE RIVER, AK 99577
ALLEN HUGHES, BOX 55, CORDOVA, AK 99574
EFIM IVANOV, BOX 870096, WASILLA, AK 99687
ULIANA IVANOV, BOX 147, HUBBARD, OR 97032
JAMES IVERSON, 43530 ROSS DR, SOLDOTNA, AK 99669
WILLIAM JARRELL, BOX MYK, GLENNALLEN, AK 99588
PETER JENKINS, 2400 TASHA DR, ANCHORAGE, AK 99502
HERBERT JENSEN, BOX 294, CORDOVA, AK 99574
JEFFEREY JENSEN, BOX 770955, EAGLE RIVER, AK 99577
KAREN JOHNS, 20913 33RD DR SE, BOTHELL, WA 98021
CHRIS JOHNSON, 2638 EMPIRE AVE, MELBOURNE, FL 32934
JAMES JOHNSON, BOX 263, CORDOVA, AK 99574
JOHN JOHNSON, BOX 1179, CORDOVA, AK 99574
RANDALL JOHNSON, 5575 E ROSEBUD CT, WASILLA, AK 99654
STEVEN JOHNSON, BOX 894, CORDOVA, AK 99574
KENNETH JONES, BOX 615, CORDOVA, AK 99574
KURT JONES, BOX 1221, CORDOVA, AK 99574
MIKEL JONES, BOX 2566, SEWARD, AK 99664
VICTOR JONES, BOX 1831, CORDOVA, AK 99574
DANIEL JORY, 28 GEORGE ST, ILION, NY 13357
KYLE KAIN, BOX 1824, SEWARD, AK 99664
GRIGORY KASACHEV, BOX 874232, WASILLA, AK 99687
IVAN KASACHEV, BOX 879244, WASILLA, AK 99687
PETER KASACHEV, BOX 4082, HOMER, AK 99603
JERRY KENNEDY, 28924 48TH AVE NW, STANWOOD, WA 98292
MEGHAN KING, 25 CASSAL RD, WINTHROP, WA 98862
RANDALL KOCHER, 370 PATRICK RD, COBLESKILL, NY 12043
RODGER KOECHLING, BOX 533, CORDOVA, AK 99574
ERIK KOKBORG, BOX 1754, CORDOVA, AK 99574
DYLAN KOMPKOFF, BOX 1602, KENAI, AK 99611
MICHAEL KOMPKOFF, 4700 CANTERBURY WAY, ANCHORAGE, AK 99503
ARSENY KONEV, BOX 873816, WASILLA, AK 99687
EVGENY KONEV, BOX 879644, WASILLA, AK 99687
PETER KONOVALOV, BOX 3122, HOMER, AK 99603
DEAN KRAMER, BOX 966, CORDOVA, AK 99574
KURT KRAMER, BOX 1138, GIRDWOOD, AK 99587
JOHN KRANING, BOX 982, HOMER, AK 99603
KENNETH KRITCHEN, BOX 625, BAKER CITY, OR 97814
LYLE KRITCHEN, BOX 935, CORDOVA, AK 99574
SIMEAO KUSNETSOV, BOX 874394, WASILLA, AK 99654
ALEXANDER KUZMIN, BOX 3009, HOMER, AK 99603
DANIEL KUZMIN, BOX 2494, HOMER, AK 99603
DAVID KUZMIN, BOX 820, HOMER, AK 99603
DAVID KUZMIN, 16727 LEARY RD, WOODBURN, OR 97071
DEOMID KUZMIN, BOX 1542, DELTA JUNCTION, AK 99737
DIMITRY KUZMIN, BOX 820, HOMER, AK 99603
DIMITRY KUZMIN, BOX 2192, HOMER, AK 99603
ELISAY KUZMIN, BOX 879381, WASILLA, AK 99687
FALILEY KUZMIN, BOX 3360, HOMER, AK 99603

FIERCE KUZMIN, BOX 3696, HOMER, AK 99603
ILIA KUZMIN, 6785 PIERCE CT N, KEIZER, OR 97303
IRENE KUZMIN, BOX 1046, DELTA JUNCTION, AK 99737
KALLISTRAT KUZMIN, BOX 896, DELTA JUNCTION, AK 99737
KIRIL KUZMIN, BOX 12525 450TH ST SE, FERTILE, MN 56540
KONDRA KUZMIN, 8002 W MINTZ LN, WASILLA, AK 99623
LARION KUZMIN, BOX 2192, HOMER, AK 99603
LAZARY KUZMIN, BOX 1766, CORDOVA, AK 99574
LEONTEY KUZMIN, BOX 1542, DELTA JUNCTION, AK 99737
MAKSIM KUZMIN, BOX 2192, HOMER, AK 99603
MAXIM KUZMIN, BOX 2506, HOMER, AK 99603
MIHAEL KUZMIN, BOX 2494, HOMER, AK 99603
VICTOR KUZMIN, BOX 2495, HOMER, AK 99603
VLADIMIR KUZMIN, BOX 772, DELTA JUNCTION, AK 99737
ZINON KUZMIN, BOX 873414, WASILLA, AK 99687
PAUL LACA, BOX 523, GIRDWOOD, AK 99587
TODD LADD, BOX 1306, CORDOVA, AK 99574
RONALD LAHN, 2609 GALA RD N APT# 104, KISSIMME, FL 34746
KYLE LAKEY, 16812 2ND ST, GALESVILLE, WI 54630
SABIN LANDALUCE, BOX 2026, CORDOVA, AK 99574
STEVEN LANGEBARTEL, BOX 2095, CORDOVA, AK 99574
GLEN LANKARD, BOX 456, CORDOVA, AK 99574
ANDREW LARSON, 19003 COUNTY LINE RD, STANWOOD, WA 98292
DAVID LARSON, BOX 581, CONWAY, WA 98238
WILLARD LARSON, 1523 S 12TH, MOUNT VERNON, WA 98273
JOEL LATHBURY, 6006 ADAGIO LANE, APOLLO BEACH, FL 33572
JOHN LAYMAN, 15299 HIGHWAY DD, MILLER, MO 65707
BRIAN LEE, 31250 W LEE DR, SUTTON, AK 99674
JASON LEE, BOX 1441, CORDOVA, AK 99574
KYLE LEE, 8239 SKY MOUNTAIN CIR, ANCHORAGE, AK 99502
TRAVIS LEE, 189 E NELSON AVE PMB #274, WASILLA, AK 99654
MICHAEL LEESE, BOX 1941, GIRDWOOD, AK 99587
HAL LEWIS, BOX 920571, DUTCH HARBOR, AK 99692
ERIC LIAN, BOX 1025, CORDOVA, AK 99574
WILLIAM LINDOW, BOX 1612, CORDOVA, AK 99574
IAN LINDSAY, 20610 MAINLAND VIEW LN NE, SUQUAMISH, WA 98392
ROBERT LINVILLE, BOX 1771, CORDOVA, AK 99574
ANATOLIE LISOV, 407 E SHORE RD, NINE MILE FALLS, WA 99026
GREGORY LOFORTE, BOX 865, CORDOVA, AK 99574
RALPH LOHSE, BOX 14, CORDOVA, AK 99574
ROBERT LOHSE, HC 60 BOX 310, COPPER CENTER, AK 99573
TEAL LOHSE, BOX 2464, CORDOVA, AK 99574
TRAE LOHSE, BOX 2378, CORDOVA, AK 99574
TYEE LOHSE, BOX 1275, CORDOVA, AK 99574
JOHN LORENTZEN, BOX 464, CORDOVA, AK 99574
THOMAS LOVE, BOX 881, GIRDWOOD, AK 99587
MATT LUKIN, BOX 1450, HOMER, AK 99603
BENJAMIN LUSTIG, BOX 311, GIRDWOOD, AK 99587
BRIAN LYTLE, BOX 2433, CORDOVA, AK 99574
JAMES LYTLE, 1606 W 7TH, ABERDEEN, WA 98520
KENNETH LYTLE, 10633 BRIANHURST AVE, LAS VEGAS, NV 89144
MICHAEL LYTLE, 98 VALLEY RD, HOQUIAM, WA 98550
DENNIS MAGNUSON, BOX 1732, SEWARD, AK 99664
TRAVIS MAGNUSSON, BOX 177, GIRDWOOD, AK 99587
MICHAEL MAHONEY, BOX 2416, CORDOVA, AK 99574
JOSEPH MALATESTA, BOX 2228, SOLDOTNA, AK 99669
FRED MALUTIN, BOX 492, CORDOVA, AK 99574
REGAN MANN, BOX 1523, CORDOVA, AK 99574
KEN MANNING, 6325 WOODHILL DR, GIG HARBOR, WA 98332
GREGORY MANS, BOX 1342, CORDOVA, AK 99574
FRED MARINKOVICH, 8721 137TH ST NW, GIG HARBOR, WA 98329
WILLIAM MARKOWITZ, BOX 2201, CORDOVA, AK 99574
WILLIAM MARKOWITZ, BOX 141, CORDOVA, AK 99574
ROBERT MARTINSON, BOX 815, VERNON, AZ 85940
NIKOLI MARTISHEV, 260 ESCORT ST, MOLALLA, OR 97038

SALMON FISHING LIST—DRIFT GILLNET

WALTER MARTISHEV, 3150 7TH ST, HUBBARD, OR 97032
ANTHONY MATVEEV, BOX 877197, WASILLA, AK 99687
EVTROPII MATVEEV, BOX 2139, HOMER, AK 99603
FRED MATVEEV, 8440 RYOAKS PL, ANCHORAGE, AK 99504
KIRIL MATVEEV, BOX 2327, HOMER, AK 99603
MAXIM MATVEEV, BOX 2582, HOMER, AK 99603
NIKIT MATVEEV, BOX 2139, HOMER, AK 99603
CHRISTOPHER MAXCY, 7945 FOWLER LN, BOZEMAN, MT 59718
BRANDON MAXWELL, BOX 1574, CORDOVA, AK 99574
MATTHEW MAXWELL, BOX 344, CORDOVA, AK 99574
ROBERT MAXWELL, BOX 344, CORDOVA, AK 99574
MICHAEL MCCARTHY, BOX 1685, CORDOVA, AK 99574
GERALD MCCUNE, BOX 372, CORDOVA, AK 99574
GERALD MCCUNE, BOX 131, CORDOVA, AK 99574
DAVID MCKENZIE, BOX 1304, CORDOVA, AK 99574
SCOTT MCKENZIE, BOX 2071, CORDOVA, AK 99574
KIMBERLY MENSTER, BOX 2142, CORDOVA, AK 99574
JOSEPH MEREDITH, BOX 1731, CORDOVA, AK 99574
JAMES MERRITT, 3150 AMIGO DR, LAKE HAVASU CITY, AZ 86404
NICK MERRITT, BOX 2216, CORDOVA, AK 99574
RANDY MERRITT, BOX 646, CORDOVA, AK 99574
TERRY MERRITT, BOX 2082, CORDOVA, AK 99574
JASON METZ, 37104 TINY RD, SOLDOTNA, AK 99669
TIMOTHY METZ, 1593 OLD BRICELAND RD, GARBERVILLE, CA 95542
MICHAEL MICKELSON, BOX 1504, CORDOVA, AK 99574
ROBERT MIELKE, BOX 870988, WASILLA, AK 99687
DANIEL MILLER, BOX 2865, KODIAK, AK 99615
THOMAS MISSEL, BOX 637, SEWARD, AK 99664
JOSHUA MITCHELL, 440 HAZEL MILL RD, ASHEVILLE, NC 28806
RUSSELL MOBLEY, GEN DEL, WHITTIER, AK 99693
SIMON MOLODIH, 9801 WAGON RD, MOUNT ANGEL, OR 97362
LLOYD MONTGOMERY, BOX 1188, CORDOVA, AK 99574
JAMES MYKLAND, BOX 1241, CORDOVA, AK 99574
MICHAEL NAK, 782 N JACKSON AVE, OGDEN, UT 84404
NICHOLAS NEBESKY, 200 W 34 AVE #277, ANCHORAGE, AK 99503
CRAIG NEWBURY, 17103 MARLE DR, BURLINGTON, WA 98233
ERIC NEWBURY, BOX 136, GIRDWOOD, AK 99587
FREDERICK NEWIRTH, BOX 1102, CORDOVA, AK 99574
FREDERICK NEWIRTH, BOX 105, CORDOVA, AK 99574
CALEB NICHOLS, BOX 235, CORDOVA, AK 99574
DANIEL NICHOLS, BOX 235, CORDOVA, AK 99574
JON NICHOLS, BOX 266, CORDOVA, AK 99574
JOEL NIMMER, N4886 CTH V, FOND DU LAC, WI 54937
PER NOLAN, BOX 924, CORDOVA, AK 99574
OTTO NORDTVEIT, 1417 NW 205TH, SHORELINE, WA 98177
MITCHELL NOWICKI, BOX 2232, CORDOVA, AK 99574
TRACEY NUZZI, BOX 396, CORDOVA, AK 99574
PATRICK OBRIEN, 7261 EVANDER DR, ANCHORAGE, AK 99518
JEFFREY OLSEN, BOX 2362, CORDOVA, AK 99574
STANLEY OLSEN, 28129 235TH AVE SE, MAPLE VALLEY, WA 98038
PHILIP OMAN, BOX 1494, LONG BEACH, WA 98631
KELSEY OPSTAD, 3500 TAIGA DR, ANCHORAGE, AK 99516
IVAN ORLOV, BOX 891, DEER PARK, WA 99006
ANASTACIO OVCHINNIKOV, BOX 875663, WASILLA, AK 99687
JAMES PAHL, BOX 179, CORDOVA, AK 99574
KENNETH PARKER, 9577 WEST 5 MILE RD, BRANCH, MI 49402
SARA PARKER, BOX 1986, CORDOVA, AK 99574
BRITT PEDICORD, 1809 S PENNSYLVANIA ST, DENVER, CO 80210
LARI PERRON, 389 S 650TH E, DIETRICH, ID 83324
SCOTT PERRON, BOX 2024, CORDOVA, AK 99574
JOEL PETRZELKA, 14349 HIDDEN RIDGE LN, BOW, WA 98232
JON PETRZELKA, 17165 SKYRIDGE CT, MOUNT VERNON, WA 98274
PAUL PETRZELKA, 804 QUINNAT DR, BURLINGTON, WA 98233
LATHAN PETSKA, 81570 475TH AVE, ORD, NE 68862
MACON PETSKA, 81570 475TH AVE, ORD, NE 68862
GREG PETTINGILL, BOX 916, CORDOVA, AK 99574

DOUGLAS PETTIT, BOX 745, CORDOVA, AK 99574
BRICE PHILLIPS, BOX 581, CORDOVA, AK 99574
JEFFREY PHILLIPS, BOX 35, CORDOVA, AK 99574
KRIS PHILLIPS, BOX 2295, CORDOVA, AK 99574
JASON PLATT, BOX 1434, CORDOVA, AK 99574
JOHN PLATT, BOX 1085, CORDOVA, AK 99574
ANFISA POLUSHKIN, BOX 62, HOMER, AK 99603
MARKIAN POLUSHKIN, BOX 879276, WASILLA, AK 99687
ASHTON POOLE, BOX 2186, HOMER, AK 99603
MICHAEL POOLE, BOX 2186, HOMER, AK 99603
LYNN POTTER, BOX 1472, CORDOVA, AK 99574
STEPHEN POTTER, 17995 MARIES COUNTY RD #538, ROLLA, MO 65401
JACOB PRIVAT, 1101 17TH AVE #204, SEATTLE, WA 98122
NATHANIEL QUINLEY, 1365 W SIERRA AVE, COTATI, CA 94931
GREG RANKIN, BOX 985, CORDOVA, AK 99574
GARY RAYMOND, BOX 596, CORDOVA, AK 99574
JAMES REED, BOX 1796, HOMER, AK 99603
JOHN RENNER, BOX 756, CORDOVA, AK 99574
KENNETH RENNER, BOX 6, CORDOVA, AK 99574
RAYMOND RENNER, BOX 1181, CORDOVA, AK 99574
KYLE RENNIE, BOX 2298, VALDEZ, AK 99686
AFANACY REUTOV, BOX 870528, WASILLA, AK 99687
ALIMPI REUTOV, 8537 W CARMEL RD, WASILLA, AK 99623
ANATOLY REUTOV, BOX 595, STERLING, AK 99672
ANTIP REUTOV, BOX 1204, STERLING, AK 99672
AVTANOM REUTOV, BOX 1056, HOMER, AK 99603
DANIEL REUTOV, 28390 S DRY LAND RD, CANBY, OR 97013
DAVID REUTOV, 31818 S ONA WAY, MOLALLA, OR 97038
DIO REUTOV, BOX 874717, WASILLA, AK 99687
EFERY REUTOV, BOX 283, WILLOW, AK 99688
EVGENY REUTOV, BOX 3021, SOLDOTNA, AK 99669
FEODOR REUTOV, BOX 1388, HOMER, AK 99603
FOMA REUTOV, BOX 3058, HOMER, AK 99603
FRED REUTOV, 27246 S PRIMROSE PATH, CANBY, OR 97013
ILIA REUTOV, BOX 823, WILLOW, AK 99688
IONA REUTOV, BOX 873462, WASILLA, AK 99687
IOSIF REUTOV, 28390 S DRYLAND RD, CANBY, OR 97013
IRMIL REUTOV, BOX 1338, HOMER, AK 99603
IVAN REUTOV, 8262 S MONTE CRISTO, WOODBURN, OR 97071
JOE REUTOV, BOX 44, AURORA, OR 97002
JONAH REUTOV, BOX 3058, HOMER, AK 99603
JULIAN REUTOV, BOX 2197, HOMER, AK 99603
KERIL REUTOV, BOX 529, HOMER, AK 99603
KIRIL REUTOV, 4861 S BINNICLE DR #1, WASILLA, AK 99623
MARIA REUTOV, 27246 S PRIMROSE PATH, CANBY, OR 97013
MELETEY REUTOV, BOX 875749, WASILLA, AK 99654
MICHAEL REUTOV, BOX 3021, SOLDOTNA, AK 99669
NIKOLAI REUTOV, BOX 2342, HOMER, AK 99603
ONICIFOR REUTOV, BOX 2197, HOMER, AK 99603
PAHISI REUTOV, BOX 1500, HOMER, AK 99603
PAVIL REUTOV, BOX 3537, HOMER, AK 99603
PETER REUTOV, BOX 1204, STERLING, AK 99672
PHILIP REUTOV, 20837 YUKON ST NE, AURORA, OR 97002
SAMSON REUTOV, BOX 486, REARDAN, WA 99029
SERGEI REUTOV, BOX 759, HOMER, AK 99603
STEPHAN REUTOV, 27246 S PRIMROSE PATH, CANBY, OR 97013
TIMOFEY REUTOV, 27246 SPRIMROSE PATH, CANBY, OR 97013
VASILY REUTOV, BOX 1204, STERLING, AK 99672
VLADIMIR REUTOV, BOX 1130, STERLING, AK 99672
BRAD REYNOLDS, BOX 1936, CORDOVA, AK 99574
OLIN RINDAL, BOX 3302, SEWARD, AK 99664
WILLIAM ROBERTSON, BOX 2296, PALMER, AK 99645
PATRICK ROCKWELL, 581 PINE CREST LOOP, SANDPOINT, ID 83864
ANTHONY RODRIGUES, BOX 163, CORDOVA, AK 99574
PHILIP ROPER, BOX 877948, WASILLA, AK 99687
JAKE ROSAUER, BOX 78, GIRDWOOD, AK 99587

SALMON FISHING LIST—DRIFT GILLNET

JOSE RUBIO, BOX 1109, CORDOVA, AK 99574
BRIAN RUTZER, BOX 2371, CORDOVA, AK 99574
WILLIAM S.EVANS, 3411 WILLOW PLACE, ANCHORAGE, AK 99517
DAVID SAIGET, BOX 1093, CORDOVA, AK 99574
BRADLEY SAPP, BOX 2543, CORDOVA, AK 99574
MELVIN SARY, 1206 E MCLEOD RD, BELLINGHAM, WA 98226
PAUL SAUNDERS, BOX 451, CORDOVA, AK 99574
TIM SCHLOESSER, BOX 35, ANCHOR POINT, AK 99556
WALTER SCHNEUER, BOX 1344, CORDOVA, AK 99574
STEVE SCHOONMAKER, BOX 218, KASILOF, AK 99610
RICHARD SCHULTZ, BOX 1291, CORDOVA, AK 99574
ERIK SCOTT, 51305 BISCAYEN DR, KENAI, AK 99611
TYRELL SEAVEY, BOX 265, SEWARD, AK 99664
PATRICK SELANOFF, BOX 3397, VALDEZ, AK 99686
TERENTY SELEDKOV, 2390 MEADOW LN, WOODBURN, OR 97071
BRIAN SHAW, BOX 2319, CORDOVA, AK 99574
FREDRICK SHIPMAN, BOX 1471, CORDOVA, AK 99574
HARRY SHIPMAN, BOX 1985, CORDOVA, AK 99574
RAYMOND SHIPMAN, BOX 631, CORDOVA, AK 99574
ROBERT SILVEIRA, BOX 801, CORDOVA, AK 99574
MICHAEL SIMPSON, 17209 FOOTHILL AVE, EAGLE RIVER, AK 99577
CHARLES SKEEK, BOX 742, PETERSBURG, AK 99833
ROBERT SMITH, BOX 251, CORDOVA, AK 99574
WAYNE SMITH, BOX 419, CORDOVA, AK 99574
BRENT SONGER, BOX 1019, CORDOVA, AK 99574
JOHN STACK, BOX 1983, CORDOVA, AK 99574
CRYSTAL STAMPER, BOX 1068, CORDOVA, AK 99574
DIRK STEGEMAN, 5870 HOGAN DR, BLAINE, WA 98230
JACK STEVENSON, BOX 1099, CORDOVA, AK 99574
AUSTIN STEWART, BOX 1571, CORDOVA, AK 99574
MICHAEL STOLTZ, BOX 85285, FAIRBANKS, AK 99708
JORDAN STOVER, 54545 E END RD, HOMER, AK 99603
STEVEN SWARTZBART, BOX 233, CORDOVA, AK 99574
EDGAR TABILAS, BOX 1874, CORDOVA, AK 99574
GARY TAYLOR, BOX 112241, ANCHORAGE, AK 99511
JAMES TEICH, BOX 102, CHITINA, AK 99566
CHRISTOPHER THOMAS, 1852 E 24TH AVE, ANCHORAGE, AK 99508
JOHN THOMAS, BOX 284, CORDOVA, AK 99574
THEA THOMAS, BOX 1566, CORDOVA, AK 99574
RON THOMSON, 143 WILD ROSE LN, TOLEDO, WA 98591
CAROLYN THORNE, BOX 711, CORDOVA, AK 99574
GERALD THORNE, BOX 1192, CORDOVA, AK 99574
GERY THORNE, BOX 2215, CORDOVA, AK 99574
RYAN THORNE, BOX 2394, CORDOVA, AK 99574
LOUIS TINER, BOX 1223, SEWARD, AK 99664
ARVO TOMRDLE, 51183 BUOY AVE, KENAI, AK 99611
THOMAS TOMRDLE, BOX 1482, KENAI, AK 99611
CHARLES TOTEMOFF, 3000 C ST #301, ANCHORAGE, AK 99503
JENNIE TOTEMOFF, BOX 221, DILLINGHAM, AK 99576
MICHAEL TOWLE, BOX 2234, CORDOVA, AK 99574
DAREN TRAXINGER, BOX 1822, CORDOVA, AK 99574
ROBIN TRAXINGER, BOX 1822, CORDOVA, AK 99574
ANDREW TRESNESS, BOX 2046, CORDOVA, AK 99574
BENJAMIN TROCKI, BOX 703, GIRDWOOD, AK 99587
MCKYER TRUMBLEE, BOX 1094, CORDOVA, AK 99574
STEVE TUTT, BOX 1105, HOMER, AK 99603
GLENN UJIOKA, BOX 932, CORDOVA, AK 99574
KENNETH UTTERSON, 38281 HWY 27, HILLMAN, MN 56338
GABRIEL VALIHOV, 10515 S ROSEWOOD WAY, MOLALLA, OR 97038
BENJAMIN VANDYCK, BOX 473, CORDOVA, AK 99574
JEFFERY VANDYCK, BOX 473, CORDOVA, AK 99574
KORRY VARGO, 7 TURNER LN, LYME, NH 3768
SIDOR VASILE, 51686 139TH AVE, GONVICK, MN 56535
KEVIN VESEL, BOX 669, SEWARD, AK 99664
STEVE VICAN, BOX 1653, CORDOVA, AK 99574

GONZALO VILLALON, BOX 2695, CORDOVA, AK 99574
THAI VU, BOX 1502, CORDOVA, AK 99574
STEVEN WALTERS, BOX 487, GIRDWOOD, AK 99587
CLIFFORD WARD, BOX 264, CORDOVA, AK 99574
RICK WARRA, 544 ST RT 4, NASELLE, WA 98638
JAMES WEBBER, BOX 934, CORDOVA, AK 99574
MICHAEL WEBBER, BOX 1711, CORDOVA, AK 99574
RYAN WEBBER, BOX 1592, CORDOVA, AK 99574
WILLIAM WEBBER, BOX 1230, CORDOVA, AK 99574
WILLIAM WEBBER, 2000 POWER CK RD, CORDOVA, AK 99574
HANS WERNER, BOX 212, CORDOVA, AK 99574
RICHARD WHEELER, BOX 256, ARDENVOIR, WA 98811
FRANK WHITE, BOX 1474, HAINES, AK 99827
GARY WHITE, 11534 GREEN CT, CONIFER, CO 80433
NATHAN WIDMANN, BOX 1883, CORDOVA, AK 99574
HENRY WIESE, BOX 1708, CORDOVA, AK 99574
JOHN WIESE, 4160 EDINBURGH DR, ANCHORAGE, AK 99502
JOHN WIESE, BOX 1031, CORDOVA, AK 99574
ROBERT WIESE, BOX 864, CORDOVA, AK 99574
JOHN WILLIAMS, BOX 1991, CORDOVA, AK 99574
SHAWNA WILLIAMS.BUCHANA, BOX 672505, CHUGIAK, AK 99567
JOHN WINDER, 4610 2ND NW, SEATTLE, WA 98107
KENNETH WIRKKALA, BOX 795, ILWACO, WA 98624
RICHARD WISE, BOX 2896, HOMER, AK 99603
GENE WOODEN, BOX 2203, CORDOVA, AK 99574
DENNIS ZADRA, BOX 2348, CORDOVA, AK 99574

SALMON, DRIFT GILLNET, COOK INLET

JON ADAMS, 4706 ASTER AVE, MCKINLEYVILLE, CA 95519
KEITH ADAMS, 13670 KITTY HAWK LN, REDDING, CA 96003
TRAVIS ADAMS, 4706 ASTER AVE, MCKINLEYVILLE, CA 95519
WAYNE ADAMS, 4670 ASTER RD, MCKINLEYVILLE, CA 95519
BILL AFONIN, BOX 1472, HOMER, AK 99603
DAN ANDERSON, 41140 CHINA POOT ST, HOMER, AK 99603
ERIK ANDERSON, 2100 ROGUE RIVER HWY, GRANTS PASS, OR 97527
MARK ASHLEY, 23 DOYLE RD, RAYMOND, WA 98557
ROBERT BACKMAN, BOX 1894, ABERDEEN, WA 98520
DAN BAETEN, BOX 7026, NIKISKI, AK 99635
THOMAS BAGNOLI, 1717B ALENCASTRE ST, HONOLULU, HI 96816
BRIAN BAKER, 34285 KHAMSIN ST, SOLDOTNA, AK 99669
LANCE BARNETT, BOX 1267, ASTORIA, OR 97103
ALEXEI BASARGIN, 5561 E ALDER DR, WASILLA, AK 99654
ALEXEY BASARGIN, BOX 1709, HOMER, AK 99603
ANDREAN BASARGIN, BOX 1393, HOMER, AK 99603
JOSEPH BASARGIN, BOX 2313, HOMER, AK 99603
KRISTINA BASARGIN, BOX 1777, HOMER, AK 99603
SIVERYAN BASARGIN, BOX 171, HOMER, AK 99603
ZINAIDA BASARGIN, BOX 1777, HOMER, AK 99603
DAVID BECK, BOX 6410, HALIBUT COVE, AK 99603
CARL BELL, 1501 LEGENDARY CT, GRAND PRARIE, TX 75050
ANNETTE BELLAMY, BOX 6426, HALIBUT COVE, AK 99603
MARVIN BELLAMY, BOX 6426, HALIBUT COVE, AK 99603
RAYMOND BELLAMY, 3801 JAMES DR, ANCHORAGE, AK 99504
JOHN BENSON, 12730 240TH ST NE, ARLINGTON, WA 98223
LOREN BERGH, 3045 198TH SE, ISSAQUAH, WA 98027
JESSE BJORKMAN, BOX 8293, NIKISKI, AK 99635
JOSHUA BLACK, 2060 N EUGENE DR, PALMER, AK 99645
FREDDIE BLEVINS, 2372 MT OLIVET RD, PULASKI, VA 24301
BILL BONDIETTI, BOX 2445, HOMER, AK 99603
TODD BOONSTRA, 37203 SPECKLEBELLY CIR, KENAI, AK 99611
FRANCIS BOWE, BOX 435, HOMER, AK 99603
FRANK BOWERS, 4200 MEADOW DR, TROY, NY 12180
CHARLES BRADY, 367 W ARLINGTON AVE, SOLDOTNA, AK 99669
LEVI BRAS, 41748 TISCHER AVE, SOLDOTNA, AK 99669

SALMON FISHING LIST—DRIFT GILLNET

CHRISTOPHER BRAUN, 10581 LAKE RD, PIERZ, MN 56364
DONALD BRIDGES, BOX 963, KENAI, AK 99611
SAMUEL BROW, BOX 1161, SOLDOTNA, AK 99669
MOLLY BROWN, 1134 E 3RD ST, PORT ANGELES, WA 98362
BILL BUCHKOSKI, 286 SR 105, RAYMOND, WA 98577
JESSE BURNHAM, 510 STATE ST, SUMNER, WA 98390
GERALD BYRNE, 131 SIERRA HEIGHTS, SOLDOTNA, AK 99669
ASHTON CALLAHAN, BOX 3090, HOMER, AK 99603
JORDAN CAMERON, BOX 99, SELDOVIA, AK 99663
CARL CARLSON, BOX 12, HYDABURG, AK 99922
DALLIN CARLSON, 27110 TAYLOR, KASILOF, AK 99610
JAMES CARLSON, 27110 TAYLOR AVE, KASILOF, AK 99610
RONI CARMON, 51995 ARNESS RD, KENAI, AK 99611
JEREMIAH CARR, 3236 LAKE ST, HOMER, AK 99603
MARK CASSERI, BOX 342, KASILOF, AK 99610
CATHERINE CASSIDY, BOX 599, KASILOF, AK 99610
BRYAN CHAPMAN, BOX 31, SOLDOTNA, AK 99669
BRYAN CHAPMAN, BOX 31, SOLDOTNA, AK 99669
ANDREI CHASCHIN, 9599 BRAYTON DR #408, ANCHORAGE, AK 99507
CHARLES CHEZIK, BOX 188, SOLDOTNA, AK 99669
LANE CHILMAN, 3020 E HOQUIAM RD, HOQUIAM, WA 98550
STEPHEN CHOPP, BOX 6424, HALIBUT COVE, AK 99603
BARTON CHOW, BOX 2044, HOMER, AK 99603
STEVEN CLARK, BOX C, CHINOOK, WA 98614
TOM COCKLIN, 2378 HARBOR LANDING CIR, ANCHORAGE, AK 99515
RANDALL COLLINS, 15620 SE 312TH AVE, BORING, OR 97009
BENJAMIN COLLMAN, BOX 22940, JUNEAU, AK 99802
RODNEY COLLMAN, 13515 SE RICHEY RD, BORING, OR 97009
L.LINDSAY CONKLIN, 1375 HAYWARD ST S, SALEM, OR 97306
LARRY CONKLIN, 212 W HARRIMAN, ABERDEEN, WA 98520
WILLARD CONLEY, BOX 422, LONGVIEW, WA 98632
GEORGE CONNER, 35555 SPUR HWY PMB 267, SOLDOTNA, AK 99669
JAMES CONNER, BOX 959, STERLING, AK 99672
MARY CONNER, 35555 SPUR HWY PMB 267, SOLDOTNA, AK 99669
ROBERT CORREIA, BOX 729, KASILOF, AK 99610
GARY COVEY, BOX 39331, NINILCHIK, AK 99639
JUSTIN CRAMER, 12302 WINTER PARK PLACE, EAGLE RIVER, AK 99577
BERNICE CRANDALL, 37225 CETACEA LN, KENAI, AK 99611
KIM CRESAP, BOX 110330, ANCHORAGE, AK 99516
MERRILL DANNA, BOX 8215, NIKISKI, AK 99635
MICHAEL DAUGHERTY, BOX 148, STERLING, AK 99672
LLOYD DAVIS, 48390 INDEPENDENCE AVE, SOLDOTNA, AK 99669
MALINDA DAVIS, BOX 38, GERVAIS, OR 97026
TERRY DAVIS, 1325 LARCH ST, KODIAK, AK 99615
J DEGRAFFENRIED, 1139 DEGRAFFENRIED CT, HOMER, AK 99603
PETER DELUCA, 24988 RED FOX LN, KASILOF, AK 99610
RUEBEN DEMIDOFF, 36646 LEIF ST, STERLING, AK 99672
MATTHEW DITCH, 35636 LITTLE WALLUSKI LN, ASTORIA, OR 97103
ROBERT DOLAN, BOX 687, KENAI, AK 99611
BEN DOUMIT, 22815 65TH AVE E, SPANAWAY, WA 98387
MARK DOUMIT, 3918 CORTEZ LP SW, OLYMPIA, WA 98512
MATTHEW DOUMIT, 1100 LAMB RD, TROY, ID 83871
JOSEPH DRAGSETH, BOX 408, KENAI, AK 99611
KENNETH DUFFUS, 20441 PTARMIGAN BLVD, EAGLE RIVER, AK 99577
REGINALD DUFFUS, 5351 RAYMA DR, JACOBUS, PA 17407
JARED DUNCAN, BOX 533, KASILOF, AK 99610
CHARLES EDWIN.WELLES, 106 SHERIDAN AVE, TAKOMA PARK, MD 20912
FOMA EFIMOV, BOX 2296, HOMER, AK 99603
DOMINIK EFTA, 48115 GRANT AVE, KENAI, AK 99611
LEONARD EFTA, BOX 353, KENAI, AK 99611
SCOTT ELY, BOX 2031, PAHOA, HI 96778
JAMES ENGEBRETSEN, BOX 5072, NIKOLAEVSK, AK 99556
TAYLOR EVENSON, 4020 CROSSON DR, ANCHORAGE, AK 99517
THOR EVENSON, 1300 W 7TH AVE #208, ANCHORAGE, AK 99501
ANATOLI FEFELOV, BOX 5070, NIKOLAEVSK, AK 99556
ELIZABETH FEFELOV, BOX 5113, NIKOLAEVSK, AK 99556

NIKIT FEFELOV, BOX 5111, NIKOLAEVSK, AK 99556
KEITH FINDLEY, 805 NW BUCKEYE AVE, EARLHAM, IA 50072
PAUL FINNEY, 1588 HILLSIDE PL, HOMER, AK 99603
PAUL FLEENOR, BOX 3505, HOMER, AK 99603
DAVID FLYNN, 9800 TOLSONA CIR, ANCHORAGE, AK 99515
GALE FLYNN, 49390 GEORGINE CT, KENAI, AK 99611
THOMAS FLYNN, BOX 8036, NIKISKI, AK 99635
JOHN FORD, 14295 MINORCA COVE, DEL MAR, CA 92014
KRISTINA FORSBERG, 16315 NE 36TH ST, VANCOUVER, WA 98682
FEODOR FROLOV, BOX 1236, DELTA JUNCTION, AK 99737
BRUCE GABRYS, 10229 BAFFIN ST, EAGLE RIVER, AK 99577
KEITH GAIN, BOX 132, SELDOVIA, AK 99663
CHRIS GARCIA, BOX 203, KENAI, AK 99611
CASEY GAZE, 6575 KENAI SPUR HWY, KENAI, AK 99611
TOM GILMARTIN, 46677 LAKE ST #2, KENAI, AK 99611
NEIL GORDEEV, BOX 531, ANCHOR POINT, AK 99556
ELIZABETH GORDON, 2124 S AINSWORTH AVE, TACOMA, WA 98405
MAXIM GOSTEVSKYH, BOX 5151, NIKOLAEVSK, AK 99556
STANLEY GRANGER, BOX 1162, SOLDOTNA, AK 99669
WILLIAM GRANGER, BOX 1162, SOLDOTNA, AK 99669
STEPHEN GRAVELLE, 53090 BORGEN AVE, KENAI, AK 99611
KENNETH GRIMES, 4115 CIMARRON RD, FALLON, NV 89406
OMAR GUCER, BOX 1386, HOMER, AK 99603
MARK GUERTIN, BOX 25, GARDEN, MI 49835
BYRON HAGGREN, 1 THIRD ST #105, ASTORIA, OR 97103
MATTHEW HAGGREN, 155 SKYLINE AVE, ASTORIA, OR 97103
MIKE HAGGREN, 1 THIRD ST #105, ASTORIA, OR 97103
BRIAN HAINES, 3 OAK ST, ALBANY, NY 12205
DANIEL HAKKINEN, BOX 1398, KENAI, AK 99611
RICKY HALLETT, BOX 1185, STERLING, AK 99672
RONALD HALSEY, BOX 323, SOLDOTNA, AK 99669
ANDREW HANRAHAN, 48395 JOHNS RD, SOLDOTNA, AK 99669
THOMAS HANSON, 32506 236TH AVE SE, BLACK DIAMOND, WA 98010
WYATT HANSON, 32506 236TH AVE SE, BLACK DIAMOND, WA 98010
JAMIE HARRIS, BOX 8227, NIKISKI, AK 99635
BRIAN HARRISON, 1065 LARKSPUR CT, HOMER, AK 99603
RYAN HATT, 322 W REDOUBT #5, SOLDOTNA, AK 99669
CARL HATTEN, BOX 305, KASILOF, AK 99610
JACKIE HATTEN, BOX 305, KASILOF, AK 99610
MICHAEL HATTEN, 352 CHUGACH DR, SOLDOTNA, AK 99669
NELSON HAUTANEN, 3157 W 64TH, ANCHORAGE, AK 99502
GEORGE HEAVERLEY, 33440 PHYLLIS CIR, SOLDOTNA, AK 99669
STEVEN HEIDEMANN, 7431 MARGARET CIR, ANCHORAGE, AK 99518
HANNAH HEIMBUCH, 4540 ANDERSON ST, HOMER, AK 99603
IVAN HEIMBUCH, 4540 ANDERSON ST, HOMER, AK 99603
MICHAEL HEIMBUCH, 4540 ANDERSON ST, HOMER, AK 99603
PAUL HEIMBUCH, GEN DEL, WHITTIER, AK 99693
MARTIN HERMANSEN, 710 BONANZA AVE, ANCHORAGE, AK 99518
JOHN HERRICK, BOX 87, ANCHOR POINT, AK 99556
JOHNATHAN HILLSTRAND, BOX 3186, HOMER, AK 99603
P.NEAL HILLSTRAND, BOX 1312, ANCHOR POINT, AK 99556
RUSTIN HITCHCOCK, BOX 3122, KENAI, AK 99611
MATTHEW HOCKEMA, BOX 15386, FRITZ CREEK, AK 99603
JEFF HODDER, BOX 448, STERLING, AK 99672
KEVIN HOGAN, 4501 ICE DOCK RD, HOMER, AK 99603
RICKI HOISTAD, BOX 221, FORMAN, ND 58032
LARRY HOLLAND, BOX 212, CATHLAMET, WA 98612
FRED HOLMBERG, 245 W GOLDENWOOD ST, WASILLA, AK 99654
WILLIAM HOLT, BOX 794, KASILOF, AK 99610
DEL HOPTOWIT, BOX 748, MABTON, WA 98935
C HOUGH, 3733 BEN WALTERS LN #2, HOMER, AK 99603
ERIK HUEBSCH, BOX 599, KASILOF, AK 99610
JACK HUGHES, BOX 1401, CRESTED BUTTE, CO 81224
DAVID HULIEN, 725 W KYLE WILLIAMS CIR, WASILLA, AK 99654
WESLEY HUMBYRD, 860 WILLOW DR, HOMER, AK 99603
KIRK IHANDER, 63235 NE TOWN CT, BEND, OR 97701

SALMON FISHING LIST—DRIFT GILLNET

MARK IHANDER, 92146 LEWIS & CLARK RD, ASTORIA, OR 97103

ANATOLY IVANOV, BOX 118, HOMER, AK 99603

GREGORY IVANOV, 2789 BROOKLAKE RD NE, SALEM, OR 97303

LAVRO IVANOV, 6127 S SCHNEIDER RD, WOODBURN, OR 97071

NESTOR IVANOV, BOX 15316, FRITZ CREEK, AK 99603

SAVIN IVANOV, 802 STARK ST, SILVERTON, OR 97381

MICHAEL JAHRIG, 10205 35TH AVE SW, SEATTLE, WA 98146

VERN JAMISON, 1628 NW SUGARMAPLE CT, MCMINNVILLE, OR 97128

DAVID JEWELL, 135 S LEIBROCK ST, SOLDOTNA, AK 99669

ASA JOHNSON, 24590 YUKON RD, KASILOF, AK 99610

CHELSA JOHNSON, 110 W FAIRVIEW AVE, HOMER, AK 99603

MARK JOHNSON, 2430 W STONEBRIDGE DR, WASILLA, AK 99654

MICHAEL JOHNSON, 795 W SWAPP DR, KANAB, UT 84741

DAVID JONES, 39730 SHELBY KAY RD, HOMER, AK 99603

KRISTIN JONES, BOX 323, SOLDOTNA, AK 99669

ROLAND JONES, 250 PHILLIPS DR, KENAI, AK 99611

DANIEL JORGENSEN, 819 4TH ST SW, SPENCER, IA 51301

DANIEL JORGENSEN, 819 4TH ST SW, SPENCER, IA 51301

ALEX KALUGIN, 6098 TOPAZ ST NE, SALEM, OR 97305

ALEX KALUGIN, BOX 16, HOMER, AK 99603

ALEXANDER KALUGIN, BOX 16, HOMER, AK 99603

AVRAAM KALUGIN, BOX 2846, HOMER, AK 99603

CHRISTOPHER KALUGIN, BOX 5111, NIKOLAEVSK, AK 99556

GAVRIL KALUGIN, BOX 3046, HOMER, AK 99603

IVAN KALUGIN, BOX 4282, HOMER, AK 99603

KIPRIAN KALUGIN, BOX 711, HOMER, AK 99603

MAKEY KALUGIN, BOX 396, GERVAIS, OR 97026

NESTOR KALUGIN, BOX 3046, HOMER, AK 99603

STEVE KALUGIN, BOX 4302, HOMER, AK 99603

TROPHILY KALUGIN, 32707 VOZNESENKA LOOP RD, HOMER, AK 99603

TAYLOR KARNIKIS, BOX 230411, ANCHORAGE, AK 99523

ANDREY KAYA, 13177 PORTLAND RD NE, GERVAIS, OR 97026

DOUGLAS KAYSER, 2120 NE 20TH AVE, CANBY, OR 97013

BRENTLEY KEENE, 64765 PITZMAN AVE, HOMER, AK 99603

CHRIS KEMPF, 36100 BORE TIDE DR, KENAI, AK 99611

LEE KEMPF, 36100 BORE TIDE DR, KENAI, AK 99611

SCOTT KEMPF, 38405 HOMEWOOD AVE, STERLING, AK 99672

GAVIN KEOHANE, BOX 481, KENAI, AK 99611

TIMOTHY KEOHANE, 35555 SPUR HWY #290, SOLDOTNA, AK 99669

JASON KIMBALL, 900 SPANISH TRAIL DR, SPARVIS, NV 89441

WARD KINCHEN, BOX 127, ALBANY, LA 70711

THOMAS KLINKER, 408 NO VIEW AVE, HOMER, AK 99603

TATIANA KONEV, BOX 508, HOMER, AK 99603

NICHOLAS KORNILKIN, BOX 1303, MOLALLA, OR 97038

MARIA KULIKOV, BOX 1185, HOMER, AK 99603

JOHNNY KULJIS, BOX 196, CLAM GULCH, AK 99568

ALENTINA KUSNETSOV, BOX 1355, HOMER, AK 99603

ARTEM KUZMIN, BOX 5103, NIKOLAEVSK, AK 99556

DIONISII KUZMIN, 46743 GOLDEN VIEW CIR, HOMER, AK 99603

FADEY KUZMIN, BOX 3009, HOMER, AK 99603

ILIA KUZMIN, BOX 3433, HOMER, AK 99603

KIRIAN KUZMIN, BOX 1520, HOMER, AK 99603

KLAUDIA KUZMIN, BOX 2494, HOMER, AK 99603

NIKITA KUZMIN, BOX 1542, DELTA JUNCTION, AK 99737

PAVEL KUZMIN, BOX 1669, KODIAK, AK 99615

PETER KUZMIN, BOX 2494, HOMER, AK 99603

SAMSON KUZMIN, BOX 27, DELTA JUNCTION, AK 99737

SERGI KUZMIN, BOX 264, DELTA JUNCTION, AK 99737

SIVERIAN KUZMIN, BOX 264, DELTA JUNCTION, AK 99737

VARLAAM KUZMIN, BOX 1184, HOMER, AK 99603

VASILY KUZMIN, BOX 1599, DELTA JUNCTION, AK 99737

YAKOV KUZMIN, BOX 3433, HOMER, AK 99603

KELLIE KVASNIKOFF, BOX 39242, NINILCHIK, AK 99639

PETER LABARBERA, 52662 WARREN AVE, KENAI, AK 99611

ALEXANDER LADUTKO, 9599 BRAYTON DR #408, ANCHORAGE, AK 99507

BRETT LAICHAK, 4802 HUNTER DR, ANCHORAGE, AK 99502

GARY LAMM, BOX 2934, KENAI, AK 99611

PATRICK LANGDON, 4296 CLAUDIA ST, HOMER, AK 99603

SAMUEL LARSEN, 41430 GERRARD AVE, SOLDOTNA, AK 99669

JONATHAN LARSON, 39841 FERNWOOD DR, HOMER, AK 99603

RONALD LARSON, 680 N 13TH AVE, WALLA WALLA, WA 99362

DONALD LEACH, 4521 N AUTUMN LN, WASILLA, AK 99623

ROBBIN LEVENHAGEN, BOX 143, KASILOF, AK 99610

ANTHONY LINDOW, 41633 E LAKE AVE, SOLDOTNA, AK 99669

ERIK LINDOW, 51315 SEA QUEST DR, KENAI, AK 99611

JEFFREY LINDOW, 8220 OPAL DR, ANCHORAGE, AK 99502

CHARLES LINDSAY, BOX 15428, FRITZ CREEK, AK 99603

IVAN LISOV, 46743 GOLDEN VIEW CIR, HOMER, AK 99603

TONY LITTLE, BOX 864, EUFAULA, OK 74432

ALEKSANDER LITVIN, BOX 2848, HOMER, AK 99603

CORY LOOS, 5199 SLAVIN DR, HOMER, AK 99603

CORY LOOS, 5199 SLAVIN DR, HOMER, AK 99603

KEVIN LORAN, 5432 E NORTHERN LIGHTS BVLD #346, ANCHORAGE, AK 99508

MARK MAHAN, BOX 2405, HOMER, AK 99603

MATTHEW MAHAN, 907 WOODSTOVE RD, PORT TOWNSEND, WA 98368

MCKENZIE MAHAN, BOX 2405, HOMER, AK 99603

TERRY MAHAN, BOX 122, KASILOF, AK 99610

JOSEPH MALATESTA, 18144 CANAL COURT, GULFPORT, MS 39503

JOSEPH MALATESTA, 18144 CANAL COURT, GULFPORT, MS 39503

DALE MALCHOFF, BOX 5538, PORT GRAHAM, AK 99603

KEVIN MANN, BOX 32653, JUNEAU, AK 99803

DAVID MARTIN, BOX 468, CLAM GULCH, AK 99568

LEE MARTIN, BOX 743, HOMER, AK 99603

ROBERT MARTIN, 5462 VINEWOOD, FALLON, NV 89406

DAVID MARTISHEV, BOX 1660, HOMER, AK 99603

IOSIF MARTISHEV, BOX 2906, HOMER, AK 99603

VARVARA MARTISHEV, BOX 1660, HOMER, AK 99603

VENIAMIN MARTISHEV, 1195 TIERRA LYNN DR, WOODBURN, OR 97071

AKAKY MARTUSHEV, BOX 1744, HOMER, AK 99603

ANISIFOR MARTUSHEV, 5640 S WHISKEY HILL RD, HUBBARD, OR 97032

DOMNIN MARTUSHEV, BOX 5006, NIKOLAEVSK, AK 99556

DOROFEY MARTUSHEV, BOX 368, HOMER, AK 99603

MARY MARTUSHEV, BOX 805, HOMER, AK 99603

NIKIT MARTUSHEV, BOX 1939, HOMER, AK 99603

PETR MARTUSHEV, BOX 452, ANCHOR POINT, AK 99556

TROFIM MARTUSHEV, BOX 879298, WASILLA, AK 99687

VARSONOFY MARTUSHEV, BOX 5148, NIKOLAEVSK, AK 99556

ZENON MARTUSHEV, BOX 1011, HOMER, AK 99603

FAEENA MARTUSHOFF, BOX 2887, HOMER, AK 99603

FEDOS MARTUSHOFF, BOX 865, STERLING, AK 99672

SOFRONY MARTUSHOFF, BOX 4041, HOMER, AK 99603

SPIRIDON MARTUSHOFF, BOX 2135, HOMER, AK 99603

JOSEPH MASUI, BOX 3185, HOMER, AK 99603

GLEN MATHEW, BOX 2452, SOLDOTNA, AK 99669

GLEN MATHEW, BOX 2452, SOLDOTNA, AK 99669

ROLAND MAW, BOX 64, KASILOF, AK 99610

JOHN MCCOMBS, BOX 39087, NINILCHIK, AK 99639

RONALD MEEHAN, BOX 1670, SOLDOTNA, AK 99669

DIMITRY MELKOMUKOV, BOX 5016, NIKOLAEVSK, AK 99556

MARKELL MELKOMUKOV, 51240 SEA QUEST DR, KENAI, AK 99611

VASILY MELKOMUKOV, 1028 DEER RUN LN, WOODBURN, OR 97071

ROBERT MERCHANT, 36260 WREN DR, KENAI, AK 99611

TRAVIS MERCIER, 37975 HARBIN AVE, STERLING, AK 99672

J MERCURIO, 26994 JOHANSEN DR, KASILOF, AK 99610

PETER MICCICHE, BOX 1544, SOLDOTNA, AK 99669

BRIAN MILLER, BOX 1717, HOMER, AK 99603

NORBERT MILLER, BOX 39083, NINILCHIK, AK 99639

CASEY MITCHELL, 317 ROCKWELL AVE, SOLDOTNA, AK 99669

CHRISTOPHER MOSS, BOX 1115, HOMER, AK 99603

ALEKSANDRO MURACHEV, BOX 2259, HOMER, AK 99603

SALMON FISHING LIST—DRIFT GILLNET

JERE MURRAY, BOX 237, SELDOVIA, AK 99663
GREG MUSSMAN, 12156 E MASON RD, MAPLE, WI 54854
CLAYTON NELSON, 546 SOUNDVIEW AVE, HOMER, AK 99603
RUSSELL NEWBERRY, 184 W FAIRVIEW AVE, HOMER, AK 99603
FRANK NEWTON, 260 JULIUSSEN ST, KENAI, AK 99611
JACOB NEWTON, BOX 8096, NIKISKI, AK 99635
JOSHUA NEWTON, 34791 LIBRA CT, SOLDOTNA, AK 99669
ANGELA NIEMI, 53908 TIEGA WAY, KENAI, AK 99611
PATRICK NOLAN, 6001 S HALLIE DR, WASILLA, AK 99623
MARTIN NORMAN, BOX 5574, PORT GRAHAM, AK 99603
VINCENT NOVAK, BOX 220892, ANCHORAGE, AK 99522
ERIC NYCE, 1850 KUSKOKWIM ST, ANCHORAGE, AK 99508
ANDREW ODONNELL, 420 2ND AVE, ABERDEEN, WA 98520
RICHARD OLDHAM, BOX 15175, FRITZ CREEK, AK 99603
DALE OLSGARD, BOX 999, HOMER, AK 99603
ANDREW ONEIL, BOX 615, BUCKNER, MO 64016
BRIAN ONEIL, 1531 LAKE CITY VALLEY RD, BUCKNER, MO 64016
MATTHEW OXFORD, BOX 15201, FRITZ CREEK, AK 99603
WALTER PAGE, BOX 2816, KENAI, AK 99611
MATTHEW PANCRATZ, BOX 5054, NIKOLAEVSK, AK 99556
DAVID PATCHETT, BOX 428, KASILOF, AK 99610
THOMAS PATTERSON, 203 KINGSTON WAY, WALNUT CREEK, CA 94597
REUBIN PAYNE, BOX 1171, SOLDOTNA, AK 99669
MARK PEDERSEN, 8512 RAINBOW ROW, JUNEAU, AK 99801
GREGORY PERKINS, 1255 TIERRA GRANDE PL, WASILLA, AK 99654
GIAMBATTIST PERONE, 1807 W 1ST ST, SAN PEDRO, CA 90732
CHRISTOPHER PERRY, BOX 1808, HOMER, AK 99603
JOHN PERRY, BOX 1597, KENAI, AK 99611
RAYMOND PETERKIN, BOX 7244, NIKISKI, AK 99635
RALPH PETTERSON, 1007 MISSION AVE, KENAI, AK 99611
FEODOR PIATKOFF, 51686 139TH AVE, GONVICK, MN 56644
TIMOFEY PIATKOFF, 507 2ND AVE S, ERSKINE, MN 56535
GORDON PITZMAN, BOX 3135, HOMER, AK 99603
IAN PITZMAN, 4254 SVEDLUND CIR, HOMER, AK 99603
KATHERINE PITZMAN, 4254 SVEDLUND CIR, HOMER, AK 99603
KATHERINE PITZMAN, 4254 SVEDLUND CIR, HOMER, AK 99603
STEPHEN POLLACK, BOX 120, SELDOVIA, AK 99663
GILKERIA POLUSHKIN, BOX 104, HOMER, AK 99603
KORNILY POLUSHKIN, BOX 851, HOMER, AK 99603
LAZAR POLUSHKIN, BOX 3510, HOMER, AK 99603
ABRAHAM PORTER, BOX 1018, KENAI, AK 99611
ELIJAH PORTER, BOX 7048, NIKISKI, AK 99635
ROBERT PORTER, BOX 7081, NIKISKI, AK 99635
J POWELL, BOX 124, STERLING, AK 99672
KEVIN PRENTICE, BOX 1532, EUFAULA, OK 74432
MATTHEW RAFFERTY, 39307 SUCHAVIEW RD, HOMER, AK 99603
BRIAN RANGUETTE, BOX 7181, NIKISKI, AK 99635
ERIC RANGUETTE, 34760 POPPY WOOD ST, SOLDOTNA, AK 99669
MICHAEL RANGUETTE, 6864 SEACOVE AVE W, ST AUGUSTINE, FL 32086
THOMAS RANGUETTE, BOX 111, GARDEN, MI 49835
PAUL RAYMOND, BOX 2755, HOMER, AK 99603
ARTHUR REITH, 820 D ST, GEARHART, OR 97138
BRIAN REITH, 52535 WINWOOD CT, KENAI, AK 99611
JAMES REITH, 35106 REITH LARSON LN, ASTORIA, OR 97103
BUDDY RENNER, BOX 878, KASILOF, AK 99610
DARREL RENNER, 51724 ABRAM AVE, KASILOF, AK 99610
AFANASY REUTOV, 8266 S MONTE CRISTO RD, WOODBURN, OR 97071
AFANASY REUTOV, BOX 3125, HOMER, AK 99603
ALEXANDER REUTOV, 7362 W PARKS HWY # 340, WASILLA, AK 99623
ALEXANDER REUTOV, 602 KIMBERLY CT, MOLALLA, OR 97038
ALEXANDER REUTOV, BOX 687, SOLDOTNA, AK 99669
ANDREY REUTOV, BOX 2212, HOMER, AK 99603
ANTON REUTOV, 10853 S RIDGETOP DR, MOLALLA, OR 97038
ARIANDA REUTOV, BOX 1879, KODIAK, AK 99615
ARSENY REUTOV, BOX 2845, HOMER, AK 99603
AVRAAMY REUTOV, BOX 3207, HOMER, AK 99603

CHRISTOPHER REUTOV, BOX 3116, HOMER, AK 99603
DAVID REUTOV, BOX 458, HOMER, AK 99603
DAVID REUTOV, 4295 TIFFANY PLACE NE, KEIZER, OR 97303
DENNIS REUTOV, 10271 S ROSEWOOD WAY, MOLALLA, OR 97038
DIMITRY REUTOV, BOX 2063, HOMER, AK 99603
DIONICI REUTOV, BOX 4251, HOMER, AK 99603
EOICIFI REUTOV, 2000 BRANDON AVE NE, KEIZER, OR 97303
FRED REUTOV, 10271 S ROSEWOOD WY, MOLALLA, OR 97038
GEORGE REUTOV, 7750 S MARK RD, CANBY, OR 97013
HARETINA REUTOV, BOX 3490, HOMER, AK 99603
IVAN REUTOV, BOX 1294, STERLING, AK 99672
IVAN REUTOV, BOX 4092, HOMER, AK 99603
IVONE REUTOV, BOX 5053, NIKOLAEVSK, AK 99556
KONSTANTIN REUTOV, BOX 1190, HOMER, AK 99603
KONSTANTIN REUTOV, BOX 1190, HOMER, AK 99603
LAVRENTII REUTOV, BOX 1190, HOMER, AK 99603
LAZAR REUTOV, BOX 258, HOMER, AK 99603
MARKIAN REUTOV, BOX 2557, HOMER, AK 99603
MAURICE REUTOV, BOX 893, WILLOW, AK 99688
MIHEI REUTOV, BOX 877256, WASILLA, AK 99687
MIHEY REUTOV, 154 CAMBRIDGE AVE, SILVERTON, OR 97381
NIKIT REUTOV, BOX 46, STERLING, AK 99672
PAISY REUTOV, BOX 893, WILLOW, AK 99688
PAUL REUTOV, BOX 3366, HOMER, AK 99603
PAVEL REUTOV, 11110 S RIDGE TOP DR, MOLALLA, OR 97038
PELAGIA REUTOV, BOX 2342, HOMER, AK 99603
STEFAN REUTOV, BOX 1251, STERLING, AK 99672
STEVE REUTOV, BOX 1463, HOMER, AK 99603
VENEDIM REUTOV, BOX 877691, WASILLA, AK 99687
ZINAIDA REUTOV, BOX 529, HOMER, AK 99603
ZINAVIDA REUTOV, 7750 S MARK RD, CANBY, OR 97013
ANN ROBERTS, 2442 MCKENZIE DR, ANCHORAGE, AK 99517
ROYCE ROBERTS, BOX 612, KENAI, AK 99611
W.SCOTT ROGERS, 7415 87TH ST E, PUYALLUP, WA 98372
JERRY ROGERSS, 1751 E 53RD AVE UNIT B, ANCHORAGE, AK 99507
PAUL ROLLER, BOX 3229, PALMER, AK 99645
EUGENE ROSENQUIST, BOX 225, KASILOF, AK 99610
ALEXANDER ROSS, BOX 6976, NIKISKI, AK 99635
JOHN RUMMERY, 1275 OCEAN DRIVE, HOMER, AK 99603
JOHN RUMMERY, 1275 OCEAN DR, HOMER, AK 99603
GARY RUSHTON, 740 ST RT 109, HOQUIAM, WA 98550
REVELLE RUSSELL, 60143 LOOKOUT MT LN, HOMER, AK 99603
RONALD RUSSELL, BOX 2, CLAM GULCH, AK 99568
RONALD RUST, BOX 2082, KENAI, AK 99611
EDWIN SALTZ, 162 FOOTHILL RD, SOLDOTNA, AK 99669
MAXIM SAMOILOV, BOX 807, SILVERTON, OR 97381
AFANASIA SANAROV, BOX 2175, HOMER, AK 99603
ALEX SANAROV, BOX 2175, HOMER, AK 99603
ARTEMY SANAROV, 910 BROWN ST, WOODBURN, OR 97071
FELEMON SANAROV, BOX 3432, HOMER, AK 99603
KIRIL SANAROV, BOX 1519, HOMER, AK 99603
VLADIMIR SANAROV, BOX 2175, HOMER, AK 99603
JON SAUERBREY, 40291 BOULDER PARK LN, SOLDOTNA, AK 99669
GEORGE SAVELIEFF, 6896 WACONDA RD NE, SALEM, OR 97305
CRAIG SCHLOESSER, BOX 356, ANCHOR POINT, AK 99556
JAY SCHMELZENBACH, 37903 PEACEFUL CIR, STERLING, AK 99672
JIMMIE SECREST, 9718 E MARGARET DR, TERRE HAUTE, IN 47803
GREGORY SEDY, 43 MEADOW LN, RAYMOND, WA 98577
TIMOTHY SEEKER, 1172 SR 4, NASELLE, WA 98638
GARY SEIMS, BOX 4213, HOMER, AK 99603
SHARON SELBY, BOX 78, ANCHOR POINT, AK 99556
ONUFRY SELEDKOV, BOX 960, WOODBURN, OR 97071
IONA SEREBREKOFF, BOX 1283, HOMER, AK 99603
SERGEY SEREBREKOFF, BOX 4052, HOMER, AK 99603
VASILISA SEREBREKOFF, BOX 4052, HOMER, AK 99603
SETH SHERRITT, BOX 2267, HOMER, AK 99603

SALMON FISHING LIST—DRIFT GILLNET

CASEY SIEKANIEC, BOX 1275, HOMER, AK 99603
DANIEL SMITH, BOX 421, KASILOF, AK 99610
JESSICA SMITH, 405 N GILL ST #1, KENAI, AK 99611
KENNETH SMITH, BOX 82 EAST SIDE STATION, BINGHAMTON, NY 13904
NATHAN SMITH, BOX 82 EASTSIDE STATION, BINGHAMTON, NY 13904
ARTEMI SNEGIREV, 33133 S HWY 213, MOLOLLA, OR 97038
CRISTY SOMERS, 468 RAINBOW CT, HOMER, AK 99603
DREW SPARLIN, 37020 CANNERY RD, KENAI, AK 99611
COLE SPRINKLE, 6741 W BARTLETT DR, WASILLA, AK 99623
GARY SPRUILL, BOX 161, KASILOF, AK 99610
KADEN SPURGEON, 26115 WILD FLOWER CIRCLE, EAGLE RIVER, AK 99577
DAVID SQUIRES, 4610 SUNSET DR W, TACOMA, WA 98466
PHILIP SQUIRES, BOX 1231, KENAI, AK 99611
STEPHEN SQUIRES, 4525 N DOUGLAS HWY, JUNEAU, AK 99801
TIMOTHY STAGE, BOX 1970, HOMER, AK 99603
DONALD STANDEFER, 51086 KARLUK AVE, KENAI, AK 99611
SCOTT STEGER, 39039 SHIRLY ST, STERLING, AK 99672
MARK STENSLAND, 1726 SE 159, PORTLAND, OR 97233
RONALD STENSLAND, 5510 NE 43RD CT, VANCOUVER, WA 98661
MARK STEWART, 8953 GARRETT WOODSON CIR, PALMER, AK 99645
AMY STONOROV, 41046 CRESTED CRANE ST, HOMER, AK 99603
QUINN STOOPS, 940 E DELLWOOD ST, WASILLA, AK 99654
DAVID STREUBEL, 5115 WOOD HALL DR, ANCHORAGE, AK 99516
BRENDA STROTHER, BOX 3498, KENAI, AK 99611
THOMAS STROTHER, BOX 2060, KENAI, AK 99611
W SULLIVAN, BOX 943, KENAI, AK 99611
NATHAN SWEARINGEN, BOX 1666, SITKA, AK 99835
WILLIAM SWEARINGEN, BOX 190, KENAI, AK 99611
LEVI TATROW, 15680 16TH RD, GARDEN, MI 49835
A.CARL TAURIAINEN, BOX 8004, NIKISKI, AK 99635
ALFRED TELLMAN, 190 E ASPEN AVE, WASILLA, AK 99654
DARRELL TEPP, 2715 WATERGATE WAY, KENAI, AK 99611
ROBERT TEPP, 2715 WATERGATE WAY, KENAI, AK 99611
DAVID TERPSTRA, 34160 GAS WELLS RD, SOLDOTNA, AK 99669
MARGARET TESTARMATA, BOX 864, SEWARD, AK 99664
JUSTIN THERIOT, 56531 EAST END RD, HOMER, AK 99603
DANNY THOMPSON, 34850 YALE ST #1, SOLDOTNA, AK 99669
RICHARD THOMPSON, 35555 SPUR HWY #390, SOLDOTNA, AK 99669
TOK THOMPSON, 1721 BELMONT AVE, PASADENA, CA 91103
LELAND TODD, BOX 466, SOLDOTNA, AK 99669
TIM TOLAR, 1201 EQUINOX WAY, KENAI, AK 99611
THOMAS TOMRDLE, BOX 698, KENAI, AK 99611
BRIAN TOSTE, BOX 392, WESTPORT, WA 98595
JOSEPH TOSTE, BOX 1141, WESTPORT, WA 98595
PAUL TOSTE, BOX 692, GRAYLAND, WA 98547
RAYMOND TOSTE, BOX 685, WESTPORT, WA 98595
MICKEY TOWNSEND, 47485 CLARANCE DR, SOLDOTNA, AK 99669
SANDRA TRAXINGER, 50040 TRAXINGER PL, KENAI, AK 99611
STEVE TVENSTRUP, 4928 BEAVER LP, KENAI, AK 99611
ANDREW UMLAUF, 5060 INGLEWOOD DR, LANGLEY, WA 98260
HERBERT UPTON, BOX 2854, HOMER, AK 99603
ZBIGNIEW URBANIAK, 9806 21ST AVE SE, EVERETT, WA 98208
JEFFREY VAN.SKY, 53842 TIAGA WAY, KENAI, AK 99611
DYER VANDEVERE, BOX 504, KASILOF, AK 99610
RION VANEK, BOX 39251, NINILCHIK, AK 99639
STEPHEN VANEK, BOX 39103, NINILCHIK, AK 99639
LAWRENCE WADDELL, 1427 S BUCHANEN PL, KENNEWICK, WA 99338
DAVID WADE, 308 E LOCHWOOD DR, CAMANO ISLAND, WA 98282
MARK WADE, 5103 CHUCKANUT DR, BOW, WA 98232
MICHAEL WADE, 1329 CROWNMILL AVE, MUKILTEO, WA 98275
CHARLES WALKDEN, BOX 2017, HOMER, AK 99603
DARRELL WALKER, 57060 E END RD, HOMER, AK 99603
ELBRIDGE WALKER, 6107 E WINDSTONE TRAIL, CAVE CREEK, AZ 85331
MARK WALKER, 3525 N GREY WOLF DR, WASILLA, AK 99654
PAUL WARNER, BOX 1015, KASILOF, AK 99610

JIMMY WEAVER, BOX 664, HOMER, AK 99603
STEPHEN WEBB, BOX 1127, KASILOF, AK 99610
KIMBERLY WEGDAHL, BOX 877858, WASILLA, AK 99687
MICHAEL WEGDAHL, 973 ELOCHOMAN VALLEY RD, CATHLAMET, WA 98612
KURT WEICHHAND, 5655 SCENIC PL, HOMER, AK 99603
JASON WELLS, BOX 2676, KEY WEST, FL 33045
BRENT WESTERN, 13021 MONTEGO CIR, ANCHORAGE, AK 99516
KIRT WESTERN, 3704 E 74TH AVE, ANCHORAGE, AK 99507
BRADFORD WHIPPLE, 4501 SW 44TH AVE, FT LAUDERDALE, FL 33314
DALLAS WHITE, 35775 RYAN LN, SOLDOTNA, AK 99669
MARTIN WHITE, BOX 62, KING SALMON, AK 99613
TY WICKLINE, 9828 E KANSAS AVE, AURORA, CO 80247
JEFFREY WIDMAN, 3431 CHERRY ST, ANCHORAGE, AK 99504
RICKY WIK, 1122 INLET WOODS DR, KENAI, AK 99611
SHANE WIK, BOX 7675, NIKISKI, AK 99635
LARRY WILLARD, BOX 955, KASILOF, AK 99610
JAMES WILLIAMSON, 255 ASPEN DR, SOLDOTNA, AK 99669
DON WILLOBY, 121 HICKRY STICK LN, EUFAULA, OK 74432
JERRE WILLS, 41370 ALAN DR, HOMER, AK 99603
WAYNE WILSON, 212 LINWOOD LN, KENAI, AK 99611
DANIEL WINN, BOX 1272, HOMER, AK 99603
JOHN WINNINGHAM, 32285 SALMON RUN DR, SOLDOTNA, AK 99669
ROBERT WITMAN, E10974 EULRICH RD, CLINTONVILLE, WI 54929
ROBERT WOLFE, BOX 1125, GIRDWOOD, AK 99587
DAVID WOO, 62084 SKYLINE DR, HOMER, AK 99603
NORMAN WOOD, BOX 169, GRANITE FALLS, WA 98252
CHRISTOPHER WORLEY, BOX 168, SELDOVIA, AK 99663
THOMAS WRIGHT, 1412 BARABARA, KENAI, AK 99611
ZETTA WULF, 53585 GERBER CT, KASILOF, AK 99610
GRIGORY YAKUNIN, BOX 1513, HOMER, AK 99603
JONAH YAKUNIN, BOX 752772, FAIRBANKS, AK 99712
NIKOLAI YAKUNIN, BOX 5043, ANCHOR POINT, AK 99556
VASILY YAKUNIN, BOX 5035, NIKOLAEVSK, AK 99556
VICTOR YAKUNIN, BOX 5009, NIKOLAEVSK, AK 99556
CAMERON YOURKOWSKI, 1924 SE 46TH AVE, PORTLAND, OR 97215
ALEX ZENUHIN, BOX 331, MOUNT ANGEL, OR 97362
MICHAEL ZENUHIN, 3660 VICTOR POINT RD NE, SILVERTON, OR 97381
MARC ZIMMERMAN, 36225 MERE CIRCLE, SOLDOTNA, AK 99669

SALMON, DRIFT GILLNET, ALASKA PENINSULA

MARK ANDRICH, 4898 SHARPE RD, ANACORTES, WA 98221
ALEXANDER ANFILOFEV, BOX 879118, WASILLA, AK 99687
STACY ARBELOVSKY, BOX 373, KASILOF, AK 99610
DONALD AUS, BOX 151, UNALASKA, AK 99685
REANNA B.MARIE.HEUKER, BOX 98, CASCADE LOCKS, OR 97014
RANDALL BAIN, BOX 347, SAND POINT, AK 99661
BRAD BARR, BOX 658, CARLSBORG, WA 98324
CHRISTOPHER BASARGIN, 52818 OLD EAST END RD, HOMER, AK 99603
NIKOLA BASARGIN, BOX 3264, HOMER, AK 99603
CLIFF BENDIXEN, BOX 36, KING COVE, AK 99612
CRAIG BENDIXEN, BOX 36, KING COVE, AK 99612
THOMAS BERTMAN, 201 BRIGADOON BLVD, SEQUIM, WA 98382
LEO BROWN, 35717 WALKABOUT RD, HOMER, AK 99603
ANTONIO CARINI, 43392 DODARO DR, TEMECULA, CA 92592
CHARLES CETAK, 6448 41ST AVE NW, OLYMPIA, WA 98502
RANDY CHESHIER, 1418 RIDDELL AVE NE, ORTING, WA 98360
THEO CHESLEY, 101 SEASHORE LN, NELSON LAGOON, AK 99571
RICHARD CHIABAI, 4309 BLUE HERON CIR #108 D, ANACORTES, WA 98221
VALENTINO CHIABAI, BOX 3039, ANACORTES, WA 98221
LARRY CHRISTENSEN, 1487 OLYMPIC HEIGHTS LN, FREELAND, WA 98249
CHRISTOPHER CLEMENS, BOX 1618, SEWARD, AK 99664
PATRICK COLLINS, 45000 GALLATIN RD, GALLATIN GATEWAY, MT 59730
PETER COSTANTI, 4 COSTANTI LN, SEDRO WOOLLEY, WA 98284
CRAIG DANIELSON, BOX 3034, PORT ANGELES, WA 98362

SALMON FISHING LIST—DRIFT GILLNET

DONALD DANIELSON, 3416 FEDERAL AVE, EVERETT, WA 98201
JARED DANIELSON, 23424 SE 240TH PL, MAPLE VALLEY, WA 98038
KURT DANIELSON, 3416 FEDERAL AVE, EVERETT, WA 98201
ESIAH DUSHKIN, BOX 215, KING COVE, AK 99612
MARK EDMINSTER, BOX 1874, HOMER, AK 99603
IVAN FEFELOV, BOX 684, HOMER, AK 99603
ROBERT GOULD, BOX 234, KING COVE, AK 99612
STEVEN GOULD, BOX 375, KING COVE, AK 99612
NOAH GRAHAM.MILLER, 13423 STANDISH DR, POWAY, CA 92064
TODD GRANGER, BOX 5174, BELLINGHAM, WA 98227
JAY GREENWOOD, 4001 32ND AVE W, SEATTLE, WA 98199
PETER GRONHOLDT, BOX 87, SAND POINT, AK 99661
GLEN HAAGENSEN, 933 KATHY PLACE, ANCHORAGE, AK 99504
QUINN HAGG, 63 KULSHAN CIR, LA CONNER, WA 98257
DONALD HALL, BOX 3084, HOMER, AK 99603
JOHN HANANGER, BOX 306, DILLINGHAM, AK 99576
BRIAN HARTMAN, BOX 928, NELSON LAGOON, AK 99571
BRUCE HENDRICKSON, 1060 MILLER LN, HOMER, AK 99603
MICHAEL HEUKER, BOX 98, CASCADE LOCKS, OR 97014
TALON HEUKER, BOX 98, CASCADE LOCKS, OR 97014
TIMOTHY HEUKER, BOX 98, CASCADE LOCKS, OR 97014
TOM HEUKER, BOX 98, CASCADE LOCKS, OR 97014
JOE HINTON, BOX 2543, SEWARD, AK 99664
TRAVIS HOBLET, BOX 12, FALSE PASS, AK 99583
DAG JENSHUS, BOX 642, WHITEFISH, MT 59937
DANIEL JOHNSON, BOX 924, NELSON LAGOON, AK 99571
HAROLD JOHNSON, BOX 909, NELSON LAGOON, AK 99571
TOMMY JOHNSON, BOX 914, NELSON LAGOON, AK 99571
BRANKO JURKOVICH, 3015 W 3RD PL, ANACORTES, WA 98221
PAOLO JURKOVICH, 3015 W 3RD PL, ANACORTES, WA 98221
ALICIA KOCHUTEN, BOX 921377, DUTCH HARBOR, AK 99692
ALEXANDRE KUSNETSOV, BOX 1719, HOMER, AK 99603
AVTONOM KUSNETSOV, BOX 875329, WASILLA, AK 99687
IVAN KUSNETSOV, BOX 1355, HOMER, AK 99603
LAURENTI KUSNETSOV, BOX 445, HOMER, AK 99603
MICHAEL KUSNETSOV, BOX 1719, HOMER, AK 99603
PAVEL KUSNETSOV, BOX 2627, HOMER, AK 99603
SAFRON KUSNETSOV, BOX 1719, HOMER, AK 99603
SIMEAO KUSNETSOV, BOX 874394, WASILLA, AK 99654
DIA KUZMIN, BOX 758, DELTA JUNCTION, AK 99737
VASILY KUZMIN, 16727 LEARY RD, WOODBURN, OR 97071
KIRIK KUZNETSOV, BOX 315, HOMER, AK 99603
LAZARO KUZNETSOV, BOX 315, HOMER, AK 99603
TAISIA KUZNETSOV, BOX 315, HOMER, AK 99603
BRETT LITTLE, 4754 LAKERIDGE DR E, LAKE TAPPS, WA 98391
SEVILLA LOVE, 6501 TESHLAR DR, ANCHORAGE, AK 99507
JOHN LUDVICK, 1819 S SHAWNEE TRL, COTTONWOOD, AZ 86326
PAUL LUDVICK, BOX 74, SAND POINT, AK 99661
JOSHUA LUPAC, 3416 FEDERAL AVE, EVERETT, WA 98201
EDWARD MACK, 8710 CARTER CIR, ANCHORAGE, AK 99507
ROBERT MACK, 12100 WOOWARD DR, ANCHORAGE, AK 99516
STANLEY MACK, BOX 303, SAND POINT, AK 99661
IOSIF MARTISHEV, BOX 1660, HOMER, AK 99603
BORIS MARTUSHEV, BOX 3432, HOMER, AK 99603
ILIA MARTUSHEV, BOX 2330, HOMER, AK 99603
ALEX MARTUSHOFF, BOX 1353, HOMER, AK 99603
ALEXANDER MARTUSHOFF, BOX 1353, HOMER, AK 99603
DAVID MARTUSHOFF, BOX 1354, HOMER, AK 99603
PAUL MARTUSHOFF, BOX 478, REARDAN, WA 99029
JOHN MCDEVITT, 1133 RED FIR RD, HOPE, ID 83836
SAMANTHA MCNELEY, 925 BERING SEA BEACH, NELSON LAGOON, AK 99571
ALAN MELLING, BOX 791, EVERETT, WA 98206
DAVE MELLING, 3909 V AVE, ANACORTES, WA 98221
WALTER MEZICH, 3233 LAKE PARK CIR, ANCHORAGE, AK 99517
TARY MIDDLESWORTH, 22814 FENBY LN, SWAN LAKE, MT 59911
ALLEN MILLER, BOX 56, KING COVE, AK 99612

BLAKE MONROE, 626 HILLCREST DR, ANACORTES, WA 98221
GUY MORGAN, BOX 161, MCGRATH, AK 99627
JESSE MOSICH, 2819 WHITE CLOUD AVE NW, GIG HARBOR, WA 98335
MARK MOSICH, 2819 WHITE CLOUD AVE NW, GIG HARBOR, WA 98335
MICHAEL MOSICH, 2819 WHITE CLOUD AVE NW, GIG HARBOR, WA 98335
THOMAS MURTHA, 115 MASHES SANDS, PANACEA, FL 32346
JOHNNY NELSON, BOX 948, NELSON LAGOON, AK 99571
LEONA NELSON, BOX 916, NELSON LAGOON, AK 99571
CHRISTOPHER NEWTON, BOX 363, KING COVE, AK 99612
GRANT NEWTON, BOX 51, KING COVE, AK 99612
MARK NEWTON, BOX 4, KING COVE, AK 99612
JOHN NILES, 9240 2ND AVE SW #112D, SEATTLE, WA 98106
MARK NORBISRATH, BOX 355, BEAVER, WA 98305
RICHARD NUCCI, 21436 PETER GRUBB RD SE, RENTON, WA 98058
ROBERT NYBERG, BOX 161, SAND POINT, AK 99661
BRANKO OGLESBEE, 608 LONGVIEW AVE, ANACORTES, WA 98221
SCOTT OGLESBEE, 701 7TH AVE S, EDMONDS, WA 98020
PAUL OLSON, 808 DANA DR, SEDRO WOOLLEY, WA 98284
WILLIAM OSTERBACK, BOX 144, SAND POINT, AK 99661
TONY PARRA, 514 AMERICAS WAY #9428, BOX ELDER, SD 57719
LEO PENDERGRAFT, BOX 242, SAND POINT, AK 99661
ANDREY POLUSHKIN, BOX 2458, HOMER, AK 99603
ARSENY POLUSHKIN, BOX 62, HOMER, AK 99603
DAVID POLUSHKIN, 690 KNIK GOOSE BAY RD #246, WASILLA, AK 99654
ILARION POLUSHKIN, BOX 3466, HOMER, AK 99603
LEONTY POLUSHKIN, BOX 3466, HOMER, AK 99603
VLADIMIR POLUSHKIN, BOX 879276, WASILLA, AK 99687
RAYBURN PRIDE, 528 PETER DANA POINT RD, PRINCETON, ME 4668
PAUL RANDALL, BOX 1333, ANCHOR POINT, AK 99556
CRAIG RAWLINSON, BOX 878, ELLENSBURG, WA 98926
DAVID RECTOR, 22407 61ST AVE SE, BOTHELL, WA 98021
ALEXANDER REUTOV, BOX 2272, HOMER, AK 99603
ANDREY REUTOV, BOX 2212, HOMER, AK 99603
ARSENY REUTOV, BOX 2845, HOMER, AK 99603
CORNILY REUTOV, BOX 3523, HOMER, AK 99603
DAVID REUTOV, BOX 3609, HOMER, AK 99603
ELESEY REUTOV, BOX 1251, STERLING, AK 99672
FEODOR REUTOV, BOX 390, KODIAK, AK 99615
GEORGE REUTOV, 7750 S MARK RD, CANBY, OR 97013
GEORGE REUTOV, BOX 1276, HOMER, AK 99603
GREGORY REUTOV, BOX 2597, HOMER, AK 99603
KIRICK REUTOV, BOX 563, HOMER, AK 99603
MAVRIK REUTOV, BOX 910, HOMER, AK 99603
MOISEY REUTOV, BOX 3609, HOMER, AK 99603
SERGEI REUTOV, BOX 1144, KODIAK, AK 99615
SOFRON REUTOV, BOX 563, HOMER, AK 99603
TIMON REUTOV, BOX 563, HOMER, AK 99603
YAKOV REUTOV, BOX 1251, STERLING, AK 99672
FRANCISCO RIVERA, BOX 926, ANCHOR POINT, AK 99556
RICHARD RYSEWYK, 429 N MAIN ST, NELSON LAGOON, AK 99571
BILL SAGER, BOX 202, KING COVE, AK 99612
KENNETH SEEBECK, 3301 PARK LANE #B, MOUNT VERNON, WA 98274
RONALD SHERIN, 1020 HADDON RD, ANACORTES, WA 98221
GARY SNARSKI, 3507 N PUGET SOUND, TACOMA, WA 98407
ANDREI SNEGIREV, BOX 2089, HOMER, AK 99603
VARIFALAMEI SNEGIREV, BOX 2487, HOMER, AK 99603
PATRICK SPRINGER, 11054 E STEARN AVE, MESA, AZ 85212
RIDGLEY STIER, 2183 SKYLINE DR, HOMER, AK 99603
MATTHEW STOVER, BOX 921, HOMER, AK 99603
RONALD TAVIS, BOX 402, GREENBANK, WA 98253
MICHAEL TRUMBLE, 2810 TAMARAK AVE, WASILLA, AK 99654
FRED TURKHEIMER, 6089 CRYSTAL SPRGS DR NE, BAINBRIDGE ID, WA 98110
CHRISTOPHER WENZEL, 3806 W TAPPS DR E, LAKE TAPPS, WA 98391
RANDY WESTENDORF, 38611 264TH AVE SE, ENUMCLAW, WA 98022
RYAN WESTENDORF, 38611 264TH AVE SW, ENUMCLAW, WA 98022
DAVID WILSON, BOX 6114, EDMONDS, WA 98026

SALMON FISHING LIST—DRIFT GILLNET

DEREK WILSON, BOX 151, KING COVE, AK 99612
WARREN WILSON, BOX 151, KING COVE, AK 99612
MICHAEL WOODING, 18809 3RD ST E, LAKE TAPPS, WA 98391
RICHARD WOODING, 2305 SUMNER TAPPS HWY E, LAKE TAPPS, WA 98391
TIMOTHY WOODING, 4449 185TH AVE E, LAKE TAPPS, WA 98391
TUCKER WOODING, 4449 185TH AVE E, LAKE TAPPS, WA 98391
TYLER WOODING, 4406 185TH AVE E, LAKE TAPPS, WA 98391
ZACHARY WOODING, 2305 SUMNER TAPPS HWY E, LAKE TAPPS, WA 98391
ROBERT WRIGHT, 801 41ST PL, EVERETT, WA 98201

SALMON, DRIFT GILLNET, BRISTOL BAY

CHARLES ABALAMA, BOX 3, EGEGIK, AK 99579
CURTIS ABALAMA, BOX 144, DILLINGHAM, AK 99576
DAREN ABELLA, 3422 38TH AVE SW, SEATTLE, WA 98126
JOBE ABRAHAM, BOX 71, CHEFORNAK, AK 99561
MIKE ABYO, BOX 445, PILOT POINT, AK 99649
ALLAN ACHESON, 2613 PINE ST, EVERETT, WA 98201
JAMES ACOVAK, BOX 137, NEW STUYAHOK, AK 99636
DOMINIC ADAMS, 595 LEIGIB COURT, GALT, CA 95632
ANDREW AGEN, 14145 AVON ALLEN, MOUNT VERNON, WA 98273
DANIEL AGEN, 14145 AVON ALLEN, MOUNT VERNON, WA 98273
DWAYNE AGLI, 7416 E 4TH, ANCHORAGE, AK 99504
JESSE AGNER, BOX 565, PETERSBURG, AK 99833
JACK AIELLO, 1563 MENDOCINO DR, CONCORD, CA 94521
RICHARD AIELLO, 120 VIA DEL MILAGRO, MONTEREY, CA 93940
SALVATORE AIELLO, 5397 BREEZEWOOD DR, PARADISE, CA 95969
GUSTY AKELKOK, BOX 1245, DILLINGHAM, AK 99576
LUKI AKELKOK, BOX 1245, DILLINGHAM, AK 99576
LUKI AKELKOK, BOX 1245, DILLINGHAM, AK 99576
AUSTIN ALAKAYAK, BOX 27, TOGIAK, AK 99678
LOUIE ALAKAYAK, BOX 27, MANOKOTAK, AK 99628
NICOLAI ALAKAYAK, BOX 10, MANOKOTAK, AK 99628
BRYAN ALBERT, 2264 S ST JOHN CT, WASILLA, AK 99654
MARC ALBERT, 6408 E KEYNOTE ST, LONG BEACH, CA 90808
DUANE ALBRIGHT, BOX 132, EGEGIK, AK 99579
JOE ALEXIE, BOX 86, TOGIAK, AK 99678
GASPARE ALIOTTI, 3057 BOSTICK AVE, MARINA, CA 93933
GIOVANNI ALIOTTI, 5041 SUNSET VISTA DR, SEASIDE, CA 93955
JOSEPH ALIOTTI, BOX 3325, MONTEREY, CA 93942
PAUL ALIOTTI, 1071 TRAPPERS TRAIL, PEBBLE BEACH, CA 93953
ROBERT ALIOTTI, 462 JACKSON ST, MONTEREY, CA 93940
SALVATORE ALIOTTI, 1238 BUENA VISTA AVE, PACIFIC GROVE, CA 93950
THOMAS ALIOTTI, BOX 32148, BELLINGHAM, WA 98228
JOSHUA ALIRKAR, 101 DESCHOUT RD, TOKSOOK BAY, AK 99637
MILES ALLEN, BOX 770788, EAGLE RIVER, AK 99577
BRIAN ALLISON, BOX 2245, OAK HARBOR, WA 98277
DAVID ALOTRICO, 16583 KAMB RD, MOUNT VERNON, WA 98273
RANDOLPH ALVAREZ, BOX 4012, IGIUGIG, AK 99613
DAVID AMIK, BOX 1033, BETHEL, AK 99559
IAN AMITIN, BOX 96124, PORTLAND, OR 97296
FRED ANAVER, BOX 236, KIPNUK, AK 99614
JONES ANAVER, BOX 2, KWIGILLINGOK, AK 99622
DENNIS ANDERSEN, 2709 SKILLMAN LN, PETALUMA, CA 94952
AMOS ANDERSON, 3501 E 42ND APT # 105, ANCHORAGE, AK 99508
BRUCE ANDERSON, BOX 70045, SOUTH NAKNEK, AK 99670
CHAD ANDERSON, BOX 224, NAKNEK, AK 99633
CONNOR ANDERSON, 11278 SAHALIE RD, LA CONNER, WA 98257
DARRIN ANDERSON, 3290 S LAKESHORE LP, PALMER, AK 99645
DEAN ANDERSON, 1521 134TH DR SE, SNOHOMISH, WA 98290
HAAKEN ANDERSON, BOX 335, DILLINGHAM, AK 99576
JOHN ANDERSON, BOX 1264, GRAND MARAIS, MN 55604
KAILEY ANDERSON, 113 BANCROFT, KODIAK, AK 99615
KAVIK ANDERSON, BOX 310, KODIAK, AK 99615
KEITH ANDERSON, 2256 SOUNDVIEW DR, LANGLEY, WA 98260

NORMAN ANDERSON, 620 W LAKE SAMISH, BELLINGHAM, WA 98229
SCOTT ANDERSON, BOX 49027, PORT HEIDEN, AK 99549
STOSH ANDERSON, BOX 310, KODIAK, AK 99615
TY ANDERSON, BOX 310, KODIAK, AK 99615
JOSEPH ANDREW, BOX 102, TOGIAK, AK 99678
KRISTINA ANDREW, BOX 146, DILLINGHAM, AK 99576
PETER ANDREW, BOX 1074, DILLINGHAM, AK 99576
RICHARD ANDREW, BOX 105, ALEKNAGIK, AK 99555
ROY ANDREW, BOX 137, TOGIAK, AK 99678
RYAN ANDREW, BOX 14, LEVELOCK, AK 99625
SHAWN ANDREW, BOX 154, NEW STUYAHOK, AK 99636
TREFIM ANDREW, BOX 12, ILIAMNA, AK 99606
WASSILLIE ANDREW, BOX 103, KWIGILLINGOK, AK 99622
CLINTON ANDREWS, 1750 ADAMS CIR, ANCHORAGE, AK 99515
JAMES ANDREWS, BOX 82, ALEKNAGIK, AK 99555
JOSEPH ANDREWS, BOX 103, TOGIAK, AK 99678
RAYMOND ANDREWS, BOX 54, ALEKNAGIK, AK 99555
WASSILLIE ANDREWS, BOX 92, NEW STUYAHOK, AK 99636
MATTHEW ANELON, BOX 246, NEWHALEN, AK 99606
TIM ANELON, BOX 167, ILIAMNA, AK 99606
BRAD ANGASAN, 3521 W 79TH AVE, ANCHORAGE, AK 99502
CHRISTOPHER ANGASAN, BOX 70131, SOUTH NAKNEK, AK 99670
FRED ANGASAN, BOX 70069, SOUTH NAKNEK, AK 99670
MARK ANGASAN, BOX 532, KING SALMON, AK 99613
RALPH ANGASAN, BOX 633, KING SALMON, AK 99613
RALPH ANGASAN, BOX 334, KING SALMON, AK 99613
STEVEN ANGASAN, BOX 193, NAKNEK, AK 99633
PHILLIP ANTHONY, 4804 DARLINGTON LN, EVERETT, WA 98203
RODNEY ANTTILA, 825 ISLAND VIEW DR NE, BEMIDJI, MN 56601
PAVILLA APALAYAK, BOX 21, MANOKOTAK, AK 99628
BRIAN APOKEDAK, BOX 11, LEVELOCK, AK 99625
RANDY ARDUSER, BOX 110833, ANCHORAGE, AK 99511
DANIEL ARMSTRONG, 6261 WEST TREE, ANCHORAGE, AK 99507
IVAN ARNARIAK, BOX 95, TOGIAK, AK 99678
JULINE ARNARIAK, BOX 95, TOGIAK, AK 99678
LARRY ARNARIAK, BOX 226, TOGIAK, AK 99678
JOHN ARNESTAD, 4907 RUCKER, EVERETT, WA 98203
KATIE ARNESTAD, 6014 96TH ST SW, MUKILTEO, WA 98275
LUCAS ARNESTAD, 4907 RUCKER AVE, EVERETT, WA 98203
PETER ARNESTAD, 2312 KENILWORTH PL, EVERETT, WA 98203
RYAN ARNESTAD, 17330 43 DR NW, STANWOOD, WA 98292
JUSTIN ARNOLD, BOX 577, HOMER, AK 99603
ANDREW ASARO, 798 LIGHTHOUSE AVE #119, MONTEREY, CA 93940
PATRICK ASHBY, 15015 MCKENDREE, PACIFIC PALISADES, CA 92072
RYAN ASHWORTH, 16 SEPTEMBER DR, MISSOULA, MT 59802
ALVIN ASPELUND, 320 BAWDEN ST #316, KETCHIKAN, AK 99901
ROGER ASPELUND, 2891 S LAKESHORE LP, PALMER, AK 99645
RYAN ASPELUND, 16500 VIRGO AVE, ANCHORAGE, AK 99516
BRADLEY ATAKITLIG, BOX 55, TOGIAK, AK 99678
ROBERT ATKINSON, 900 BROWN ST, ANCHORAGE, AK 99501
SAMUEL ATTI, BOX 42, KWIGILLINGOK, AK 99622
MICHAEL AUBLE, BOX 287, GLENNALLEN, AK 99588
DAVID AUGUSTUS, 2523 OXMOOR BLVD SW, HUNTSVILLE, AL 35803
BILLY AYOJIAK, BOX 61, MANOKOTAK, AK 99628
MARTIN AYOJIAK, BOX 132, TOGIAK, AK 99678
NORMA AYOJIAK, BOX 67, TOGIAK, AK 99678
TY BABB, BOX 510, TENANTS HARBOR, ME 4860
ZOLTAN BABOS, 5405 183RD DR NE, MARYSVILLE, WA 98271
CRAIG BACKLUND, 601 HEVLY RD, ARLINGTON, WA 98223
HUNTER BACKLUND, 601 HEVLY RD, ARLINGTON, WA 98223
GARY BACKMAN, BOX 799, CATHLAMET, WA 98612
GARY BACKMAN, 301 E BIRNIE SLOUGH RD, CATHLAMET, WA 98612
CHARLES BAKER, 3595 SUNRISE WAY, LUMMI ISLAND, WA 98262
CORY BAKER, 417 PEARL DR, BELGRADE, MT 59714
PATRICK BAKER, 1124 E BEACHVIEW PL, BELLINGHAM, WA 98226

SALMON FISHING LIST—DRIFT GILLNET

W BAKER, 417 PEARL DR, BELGRADE, MT 59714
DALE BAKK, BOX 6884, NIKISKI, AK 99635
DARREL BAKK, 54035 WILDERNESS LN, HOMER, AK 99603
DAVID BAKK, BOX 278, COOK, MN 55723
DONALD BAKK, BOX 8315, NIKISKI, AK 99635
JASON BAKK, 701 E FALKIRK CR, WASILLA, AK 99654
PETER BALCH, BOX 83453, FAIRBANKS, AK 99708
PETER BALESTERI, 13 HEATHER CT, SEASIDE, CA 93955
FRED BALL, 513 SW 3RD ST, COLLEGE PLACE, WA 99324
KEIRAN BANGS, BOX 26, PETERSBURG, AK 99833
BRAD BARBER, 19647 ARBOR LN, MT VERNON, WA 98274
EDWARD BARBER, BOX 925, GIRDWOOD, AK 99587
KYLE BARBER, 1550 RALEIGH ST APT 139, DENVER, CO 80204
DAVE BARKER, 126 E FAIRVEIW AVE, HOMER, AK 99603
TYLER BARKER, 584 S RENA RD, OLDTOWN, ID 83822
HARRY BARNES, BOX 111, DILLINGHAM, AK 99576
DAN BARR, 2408 NOB HILL AVE N, SEATTLE, WA 98109
DENNIS BARTLETT, BOX 876819, WASILLA, AK 99687
WALLACE BARTLETT, 3762 GLACIER DR, PITTSBURG, CA 94565
ALEXANDER BASARGIN, BOX 879099, WASILLA, AK 99687
ANDREY BASARGIN, BOX 3363, HOMER, AK 99603
AVTONOM BASARGIN, BOX 329, REARDAN, WA 99029
BORIS BASARGIN, BOX 1305, HOMER, AK 99603
DANIEL BASARGIN, BOX 1865, HOMER, AK 99603
DAVID BASARGIN, BOX 1089, HOMER, AK 99603
DIONISY BASARGIN, BOX 2325, HOMER, AK 99603
FILIMON BASARGIN, BOX 2884, HOMER, AK 99603
GAVRIIL BASARGIN, BOX 197, HOMER, AK 99603
GEORGE BASARGIN, BOX 879127, WASILLA, AK 99687
GREGORY BASARGIN, BOX 2676, HOMER, AK 99603
HARITON BASARGIN, BOX 2884, HOMER, AK 99603
IONA BASARGIN, BOX 879386, WASILLA, AK 99687
IOSIF BASARGIN, BOX 3376, HOMER, AK 99603
IULIAN BASARGIN, 15155, HOMER, AK 99603
IVAN BASARGIN, BOX 873163, WASILLA, AK 99687
IVAN BASARGIN, BOX 324, HOMER, AK 99603
IVAN BASARGIN, BOX 3495, HOMER, AK 99603
KALISTRAT BASARGIN, BOX 1305, HOMER, AK 99603
KIRIL BASARGIN, BOX 2395, HOMER, AK 99603
MAKSIM BASARGIN, BOX 324, HOMER, AK 99603
MARKEL BASARGIN, BOX 991, HOMER, AK 99603
MICHAEL BASARGIN, BOX 3363, HOMER, AK 99603
MICHAEL BASARGIN, BOX 2000, HOMER, AK 99603
MIHEY BASARGIN, BOX 875797, WASILLA, AK 99687
NIKIFER BASARGIN, BOX 197, HOMER, AK 99603
NIKITA BASARGIN, BOX 2057, HOMER, AK 99603
NIKITA BASARGIN, BOX 1788, HOMER, AK 99603
NIKOLAI BASARGIN, BOX 1145, HOMER, AK 99603
PETER BASARGIN, BOX 1709, HOMER, AK 99603
SAFRON BASARGIN, BOX 1764, HOMER, AK 99603
SELIVAN BASARGIN, BOX 2395, HOMER, AK 99603
SIVERYAN BASARGIN, BOX 171, HOMER, AK 99603
VARNAVY BASARGIN, BOX 1788, HOMER, AK 99603
ANTE BASKOVIC, 13 HILLCREST MANOR, ROLLING HILLS EST, CA 90274
TRAVIS BATTREAL, 415 S MAIN, RISING STAR, TX 76471
JIM BAUMGART, 210 BAYSIDE PL, BELLINGHAM, WA 98225
KURT BAUMGART, 3876 GRIFFITH AVE, BELLINGHAM, WA 98225
PAUL BAUR, 191 LAKEVIEW DR, DEFUNIAK SPRINGS, FL 32433
DERICK BAVILLA, BOX 71, TOGIAK, AK 99678
HENRY BAVILLA, BOX 111, TOGIAK, AK 99678
HENRY BAVILLA, BOX 114, TOGIAK, AK 99678
STEVEN BAVILLA, GEN DEL, ALEKNAGIK, AK 99555
BURTON BAXTER, 1718 RAINIER AVE, BELLINGHAM, WA 98229
JAYME BAXTER, 723 17TH ST, BELLINGHAM, WA 98225
KOHL BAXTER, 318 BAYSIDE RD, BELLINGHAM, WA 98225
PAULINE BAYAYOK, 4101 E 20TH AVE #1, ANCHORAGE, AK 99508

ERIC BEAMER, 1000 W CASCADE LN, LYNDEN, WA 98264
JENNIFER BECK, 3111 S 273RD ST, AUBURN, WA 98001
MATT BECK, 9705 W WESLEY AVE, LAKEWOOD, CO 80227
THOMAS BECK, 2102 32ND ST, ANACORTES, WA 98221
CELESTE BECK.GOODELL, BOX 3108, KODIAK, AK 99615
MARK BECKER, 1395 SANTA RITA CIR, SANTA BARBARA, CA 93109
MATTHEW BECKER, 1395 SANTA RITA CIR, SANTA BARBARA, CA 93109
DANIEL BEISHLINE, BOX 211447, AUKE BAY, AK 99821
SOFIA BEISHLINE, 444 WASHINGTON ST, BATH, ME 4530
KEITH BELL, 3712 ROALD AMUNDSEN, ANCHORAGE, AK 99517
MICHAEL BELL, BOX 849, CRAIG, AK 99921
RICHARD BELL, GENERAL DELIVERY, DILLINGHAM, AK 99576
JORDAN BELMONT, 1206 S 10TH ST, MOUNT VERNON, WA 98273
PATRICK BELT, BOX 1696, MARYSVILLE, WA 98252
ALAN BENEDICT, 15818 14TH AVE W, LYNNWOOD, WA 98087
DAVID BENEDICT, 17099 W SHADY POOL CT, SURPRISE, AZ 85387
BRIAN BENNETT, 2729 NW AVE, BELLINGHAM, WA 98225
DILLON BENNETT, BOX 575, DILLINGHAM, AK 99576
GEORGE BENNETT, 103 16TH ST, HOQUIAM, WA 98550
JOHN BENNETT, 17900 S GABLER LN, CORONA DE TUCSON, AZ 85641
GIFFORD BENOIT, 612 W 20TH AVE, ANCHORAGE, AK 99502
TERRY BENSON, 64 KILLAPIE BEACH RD, PORT LUDLOW, WA 98365
MICHAEL BENTON, BOX 30872, ANAHOLA, HI 96703
ELSA BENTZ, 4382 GLENWOOD DR, BOZEMAN, MT 59718
GARRETT BERG, 1241 DENALI ST #106, ANCHORAGE, AK 99501
GUNNAR BERG, 1241 DENALI ST #106, ANCHORAGE, AK 99501
JAMES BERG, BOX 93, OAKVILLE, WA 98568
DAVID BERLIN, 7910 LADASA PL, ANCHORAGE, AK 99507
ROBERT BERNTSEN, 4315 SW HOLGATE, SEATTLE, WA 98116
JORDAN BERRY, 12800 MARINE DR, ANACORTES, WA 98221
STEVE BERTELSEN, 1801 NAGLER RD, SELAH, WA 98942
JAYMI BETHEA, 1719 SELIEF LN, KODIAK, AK 99615
JONATHAN BETZ, 5824 US HWY 97, PESHASTIN, WA 98847
PATRICK BETZ, 5824 HWY 97, PESHASTIN, WA 98847
GLENN BIERNACKI, 1508 W CONNECTICUT, BELLINGHAM, WA 98225
JOSHUA BIGHAM, BOX 1371, FERNDALE, CA 95536
SOLOMON BILL, 316 TODD WAY, MILL VALLEY, CA 94941
JAMES BINGMAN, BOX 82, DILLINGHAM, AK 99576
IAN BITTNER, BOX 271, CHINOOK, WA 98614
RENATA BJAZEVICH, 1700 E LOPEZ CT, BELLINGHAM, WA 98229
ROBERT BJAZEVICH, 1700 E LOPEZ COURT, BELLINGHAM, WA 98229
DANIEL BLAKEY, 8045 12TH AVE NW, SEATTLE, WA 98117
NICK BLAKEY, 2924 NE STANTON ST, PORTLAND, OR 97212
TODD BLANCHARD, 16717 NE 182ND AVE, BRUSH PRAIRIE, WA 98606
JOHN BLETH, 610 SE DATE AVE, COLLEGE PLACE, WA 99324
ARTHUR BLOOM, 4506 PROSPECT WAY, JUNEAU, AK 99801
STEVEN BLOOM, 2636 NW 57TH ST #3, SEATTLE, WA 98107
ETHAN BLOUGH, BOX 555, HOONAH, AK 99829
ROBERT BLOUGH, BOX 555, HOONAH, AK 99829
BILLY BLUE, BOX 135, TOGIAK, AK 99678
ELDON BLUE, BOX 267, TOGIAK, AK 99678
BLUNKA BLUNKA, BOX 115, NEW STUYAHOK, AK 99636
WASSILLIE BLUNKA, BOX 55, NEW STUYAHOK, AK 99636
JOSEPH BOENISH, 6550 HUMPHREY RD, CLINTON, WA 98236
RAYMOND BOLL, BOX 122, KING COVE, AK 99612
ALFONSO BONANNO, 1644 SIERRA AVE, SEASIDE, CA 93955
ROBERT BONANNO, 4552 WILDCAT CIR, ANTIOCH, CA 94531
BRADY BOONE, BOX 3160, HOMER, AK 99603
COREY BOONE, 5504 PROSPECT DR, MISSOULA, MT 59808
MARCIA BOONE, BOX 396, HOMER, AK 99603
DYLAN BORDEN.DEAL, 7314 11TH AVE NW, SEATTLE, WA 98117
ROWAN BORDEN.DEAL, BOX 1975, CORDOVA, AK 99574
ANNA BORLAND.IVY, BOX 2219, HOMER, AK 99603
JON BOROVINA, 834 GRAND AVE, EVERETT, WA 98201
JOSEPH BOROVINA, 834 GRAND AVE, EVERETT, WA 98201
WILLIAM BOTHE, 1104 STILLWATER DR, JUPITER, FL 33458

SALMON FISHING LIST—DRIFT GILLNET

GEOFFREY BOWSER, 14971 WILBUR RD, LA CONNER, WA 98257

BRUCE BRAMEL, 971 MEDIO RD, SANTA BARBARA, CA 93103

EDWARD BRANDON, BOX 1016, DILLINGHAM, AK 99576

SEAN BRANDON, BOX 1406, DILLINGHAM, AK 99576

CHARLES BRANDT, 2715 E CONNECTICUT ST, BELLINGHAM, WA 98226

LOGAN BRANSTITER, 5572 S ANAURA PL, BOISE, ID 83709

JERROLD BRASWELL, BOX 138, DILLINGHAM, AK 99576

CHRISTOPHER BRAUN, 10581 LAKE RD, PIERZ, MN 56364

DAMIAN BRAVO, 5811 HAROLD WAY #1, HOLLYWOOD, CA 90028

TIERNA BRAVO.BUCHMAYR, BOX 60026, SEATTLE, WA 98160

ANDREW BRECKENRIDGE, BOX 185, MOUNT VERNON, WA 98237

GENEVA BRIGHT, BOX 100116, ANCHORAGE, AK 99510

ANGELO BRITO, BOX 564, DILLINGHAM, AK 99576

BRONSON BRITO, BOX 565, DILLINGHAM, AK 99576

DUSTIN BRITO, BOX 8041, NIKISKI, AK 99635

MANUEL BRITO, BOX 1006, DILLINGHAM, AK 99576

EDWARD BROCK, 22845 ROSE RD, MOUNT VERNON, WA 98274

ROBERT BROCKHOFF, BOX 894, WESTPORT, WA 98595

NICK BROCKMAN, 2440 E TUDOR RD PMB 132, ANCHORAGE, AK 99507

EBEN BROWN, 205 CREGO HILL RD, CHEHALIS, WA 98532

ILLAYANA BROWN, 205 CREGO HILL RD, CHEHALIS, WA 98532

MELVIN BROWN, BOX 111566, ANCHORAGE, AK 99511

KELLY BROYLES, 7060 BLACKHAWK LN, FOREST HILL, CA 95631

JAKE BRUNDRIDGE, BOX 396, SCOTTS MILL, OR 97375

ROBERT BUCHMAYR, BOX 60026, SEATTLE, WA 98160

JOHN BUERGER, BOX 210846, AUKE BAY, AK 99821

LAWSON BUNDRANT, 20530 RICHMOND BCH DR NW, SHORELINE, WA 98177

SHANNON BUNDY, BOX 325, WESTPORT, WA 98026

KEN BURGER, 12619 SW COVE RD, VASHON, WA 98070

MARION BURGRAFF, BOX 380, KING SALMON, AK 99613

ANFIM BURKOFF, 528 FENTAN AVE UNIT C, MOLALLA, OR 97038

SCOTT BURNFIELD, 561 E EAGLE RIDGE DR, SHELTON, WA 98584

DERICK BURNS, 207 FRIDAY CREEK RD, BELLINGHAM, WA 98229

GRAHAM BURNSIDE, 418 MILL BAY RD, KODIAK, AK 99615

FRANCES BURSCH, BOX 2314, CRESTED BUTTE, CO 81224

MARGARET BURSCH, 723 N FOREST ST #201, BELLINGHAM, WA 98225

THOMAS BURSCH, 2233 MOUNT AUGUSTINE DR, HOMER, AK 99603

MARCUS BURTNER, 425 E 6TH AVE #5, DURANGO, CO 81301

JEFFERY BURWELL, 3836 E COUNTRY FIELD CIR, WASILLA, AK 99654

MURRAY BUYS, 11201 MEYERS LN, LIVE OAK, CA 95953

DARREN BYAYUK, BOX 171, TOGIAK, AK 99678

WILLIAM BYAYUK, BOX 171, TOGIAK, AK 99678

KIRK CABANILLA, 14857 PIERCE RD, BYRON, MI 48418

CHRIS CAMERON, 450 ALAMEDA, ASTORIA, OR 97103

ANTHONY CAMPO, BOX 374, GONZALES, CA 93926

PETER CANNON, BOX 1038, FRIDAY HARBOR, WA 98250

MICHAEL CAPRI, 255 NW 17TH ST, NEWPORT, OR 97365

REX CAPRI, 255 NW 17TH ST, NEWPORT, OR 97365

MADELINE CARBO, 140 SE 5TH AVE #548, BOCA RATON, FL 33432

STEPHEN CARDINALLI, 1099 ROSITA RD, DEL REY OAKS, CA 93940

SAMUEL CARL, BOX 001, KIPNUK, AK 99614

GERRIT CARLOS, 74 SANDY LANE, WALNUT CREEK, CA 94597

SEAN CARLOS, BOX 552, DILLINGHAM, AK 99576

ROBERT CARLSON, 5923 E HWY 61, HOVLAND, MN 55606

CHARLES CARPENTER, 4739 MERMONT PL, EVERETT, WA 98203

LANDON CARPENTER, 1107 DIAMOND ST, SAN FRANCISCO, CA 94114

DREW CARR, 4746 E MERCER WAY, MERCER ISLAND, WA 98040

JEREMIAH CARR, 3236 LAKE ST, HOMER, AK 99603

MICHAEL CARR, 4461 GARDINER RD, PORT TOWNSEND, WA 98368

RITCH CARR, 4461 OLD GARDNER RD, PORT TOWNSEND, WA 98368

PASQUALE CARRIGLIO, 4158 EL BOSQUE DR, PEBBLE BEACH, CA 93953

KATHERINE CARSCALLEN, BOX 398, DILLINGHAM, AK 99576

COLTON CASTO, 16120 DUBUQUE RD, SNOHOMISH, WA 98290

GLENN CASTO, 16120 DUTIGUE RD, SNOHOMISH, WA 98290

MARK CASTO, 23929 22ND DR SE, BOTHELL, WA 98021

WALTER CASTO, 19618 61ST AVE SE, SNOHOMISH, WA 98290

DAMIEN CATALA, 1780 LARCH AVE NE #102, ISSAQUAH, WA 98029

JOHN CATALANO, 799 SPENCER ST #B, MONTEREY, CA 93940

BRENT CATHEY, BOX 15166, FRITZ CREEK, AK 99603

AARON CEXTON, 1904 7TH AVE E, WILLISTON, ND 58801

JOHN CHAKUCHIN, BOX 2632, BETHEL, AK 99559

BRETT CHAMBERS, 3296 ALDERGROVE RD, FERNDALE, WA 98248

FRANK CHAMBERS, 3296 ALDERGROVE RD, FERNDALE, WA 98248

NOAH CHAMBERS, BOX 151, NAKNEK, AK 99633

TRISTON CHANEY, BOX 25, DILLINGHAM, AK 99576

BRUCE CHARLES, BOX 6037, BOZEMAN, MT 59771

EVERETT CHARLIE, BOX 1998, BETHEL, AK 99559

BRYAN CHARTIER, BOX 233, SELDOVIA, AK 99663

WILFRED CHASE, BOX 43, NUNAPITCHUK, AK 99641

BRIAN CHELEDINAS, BOX 2061, SELAH, WA 98942

SCOTT CHELEDINAS, BOX 6424, BOZEMAN, MT 59771

BEN CHERNIKOFF, BOX 4, EGEGIK, AK 99579

CURTIS CHEVALIER, 920 21ST AVE, SEATTLE, WA 98122

MATTHEW CHEVALIER, 169 TERRACE DR, FRIDAY HARBOR, WA 98250

JOSEPH CHILDERS, BOX 1908, QUINCY, CA 95971

GUST CHOCKNOK, BOX 1171, DILLINGHAM, AK 99576

WASSILLIE CHOCKNOK, BOX 48, MANOKOTAK, AK 99628

EMIL CHRISTENSEN, BOX 49009, PORT HEIDEN, AK 99549

HENRY CHRISTENSEN, 1487 OLYMPIC HEIGHTS LN, FREELAND, WA 98249

JAMES CHRISTENSEN, BOX 49090, PORT HEIDEN, AK 99549

JOHN CHRISTENSEN, 1001 TRAPPER HILL RD, PORT HEIDEN, AK 99549

LARRY CHRISTENSEN, 1487 OLYMPIC HEIGHTS LN, FREELAND, WA 98249

LARRY CHRISTENSEN, 1487 OLYMPIC HEIGHTS LN, FREELAND, WA 98249

MACARLO CHRISTENSEN, 413 HAINES AVE, FAIRBANKS, AK 99701

NICK CHRISTENSEN, BOX 203, DILLINGHAM, AK 99576

ANTHONY CHRISTOPHER, HUD ST BOX 17, NEW STUYAHOK, AK 99636

PETER CHRISTOPHER, BOX 33, NEW STUYAHOK, AK 99636

CHRISTIAN CHUCKWUK, BOX 22, ALEKNAGIK, AK 99555

SERGIE CHUKWAK, BOX 338, NAKNEK, AK 99633

DONALD CHURCHILL, BOX 1061, HAINES, AK 99827

CRAIG CHYTHLOOK, 3020 MOOSE MT RD, FAIRBANKS, AK 99709

DANIEL CHYTHLOOK, BOX 11, ALEKNAGIK, AK 99555

JOSEPH CHYTHLOOK, BOX 692, DILLINGHAM, AK 99576

LEON CHYTHLOOK, BOX 2815, SOLDOTNA, AK 99669

MOSES CHYTHLOOK, BOX 145, DILLINGHAM, AK 99576

GAYLORD CLARK, 1704 HILLSIDE RD, STEVENSON, MD 21153

JACK CLARK, BOX 32412, JUNEAU, AK 99803

KAY CLARK, 1095 MISSION RD, HOMER, AK 99603

MICHAEL CLARK, 27 HOWARD RD, CATHLAMET, WA 98612

ROBERT CLARK, BOX 822, DILLINGHAM, AK 99576

RONALD CLARK, 13255 HWY 441 SE, OKEECHOBEE, FL 34974

TAYLOR CLARKSON, 1923 26TH AVE E, SEATTLE, WA 98112

JAKE CLEMENS, 2246 RIVERSIDE DR, LYONS, CO 80540

GARY CLINE, BOX 837, DILLINGHAM, AK 99576

DANIEL CLOUD, 318 CAROLYN ST, KODIAK, AK 99615

DONNA COFFEEN, 317 OHIMA DR, WALLA WALLA, WA 99362

KRISTEN COFFEEN, 105 OHIMA DR, WALLA WALLA, WA 98362

NAT COFFEEN, 105 OHIMA DR, WALLA WALLA, WA 99362

LESTER COLE, BOX 194, CUSICK, WA 99119

CHANCELAN COLLIER, BOX 122, SELDOVIA, AK 99663

DANIEL COLLINS, BOX 1504, KETCHUM, ID 83340

PHILLIP CONIJN, 22209 MT VERNON BIG LAKE RD, MT VERNON, WA 98274

DAVID CONNOR, BOX 622, NAKNEK, AK 99633

DOUGLAS CONNOR, 5 HILLSIDE RD, CONCORD, NH 3301

DUSTIN CONNOR, BOX 1372, PETERSBURG, AK 99833

HAROLD COOK, 11021 WING POINT WY NE, BAINBRIDGE ISLAND, WA 98110

JODY COOK, 2115 NW 12TH ST, BATTLE GROUND, WA 98604

MATHEWS COOK, BOX 644, KINGSTON, WA 98346

PHILLIP COOK, 22448 BULSON RD, MOUNT VERNON, WA 98274

TIM COOK, 3901 TAIGA DR, ANCHORAGE, AK 99516

SALMON FISHING LIST—DRIFT GILLNET

TREVOR COOK, 38 HYLAND STRINGER RD, RAYMOND, WA 98577

TRISHA COOK, 22448 BULSON RD, MT VERNON, WA 98274

RICHARD COOKE, BOX 950, CEDAR KEY, FL 32625

BENJAMIN COOPCHIAK, BOX 251, TOGIAK, AK 99678

BOBBY COOPCHIAK, BOX 181, TOGIAK, AK 99678

JIMMY COOPCHIAK, BOX 187, TOGIAK, AK 99678

RICHARD COOPCHIAK, BOX 51, TOGIAK, AK 99678

TEDDY COOPCHIAK, BOX 84, TOGIAK, AK 99678

KENNETH COOPER, BOX 85, SANDPOINT, ID 83864

MICHAEL CORL, 2616 ERIE ST, BELLINGHAM, WA 98226

JEFFREY CORRICK, 222 DECATUR ST NW, OLYMPIA, WA 98502

BRUCE CORSON, 205 E DIMOND BLVD #395, ANCHORAGE, AK 99515

ANDRE COSSETTE, BOX 8670, KODIAK, AK 99615

LEROY COSSETTE, BOX 8670, KODIAK, AK 99615

GIUSEPPE COSTA, 22 VIA DEL REY, MONTEREY, CA 93940

VINCENZO COSTA, 695 ELM AVE, SEASIDE, CA 93955

PETER COSTANTI, 4 COSTANTI LN, SEDRO WOOLLEY, WA 98284

CONOR COSTELLO, 207 FRIDAY CREEK RD, BELLINGHAM, WA 98229

CAMERON COUCH, 1216 RAYMOND, BELLINGHAM, WA 98229

DAVID COUCH, BOX 99 C/O NPS, NAKNEK, AK 99633

CASEY COUPCHIAK, BOX 128, TOGIAK, AK 99678

DENNIS COURTNEY, 4854 W GLENHAVEN DR, EVERETT, WA 98203

MARSHALL COURTNEY, 4854 W GLENHAVEN DR, EVERETT, WA 98203

JOHN COURTOIS, 409 S DIVISION ST, CASHMERE, WA 98815

JAMES COYLE, BOX 1170, HAILEY, ID 83333

GIUSEPPE CRACCHIOLO, 40056 GLEN IVY ST, MURRIETA, CA 92563

VICTOR CRAMER, 7890 FLETCHER BAY RD NE, BAINBRIDGE ID, WA 98110

VICTOR CRAMER, 7890 FLETCHER BAY RD NE, BAINBRIDGE ID, WA 98110

FRANK CRANBOURNE, BOX 608, DEMING, WA 98244

ANN CRANE, 2335 DOME VIEW AVE, FAIRBANKS, AK 99709

CAROLYN CRANE, BOX 15368, FRITZ CREEK, AK 99603

JAMES CRICHTON, 318 SUNDSTROM LN, FRIDAY HARBOR, WA 98250

MOLLY CRIMIN, 17330 43RD DR NW, STANWOOD, WA 98292

DARREN CROOKSHANKS, 6130 WILLOW GROVE RD, LONGVIEW, WA 98632

TONIA CROOKSHANKS, 6130 WILLOW GROVE RD, LONGVIEW, WA 98632

JOHN CROSBIE, BOX 1987, HOMER, AK 99603

FRED CROTHAMEL, 7217 SE 29TH ST, MERCER ISLAND, WA 98040

MADDISON CROTHAMEL, 7217 SE 29TH ST, MERCER ISLAND, WA 98040

MICHAEL CROUSE, 126 W SUNNY SANDS RD, CATHLAMET, WA 98612

RANDY CROZIER, 4311 212 ST CT E, SPANAWAY, WA 98387

DAVID CUBERT, 258 CAMP ONE RD, RAYMOND, WA 98577

JOHN CULMINE, 804 PUGET ST, BELLINGHAM, WA 98229

TODD CURREY, BOX 96, FORT SHAW, MT 59443

KEVIN CURRIER, 17 ANDREAS CT, NOVATO, CA 94945

ZACHARY CURRY, 16156 TOAD LN, BOW, WA 98232

JACOB CURTIS, 2005 WILLOW CREEK DR SPACE 2066, AUSTIN, TX 78741

STANLEY DAHL, 305 GROWLERS GULCH, CASTLE ROCK, WA 98611

JOSHUA DALTON, 5720 E FAIR PL, CENTENNIAL, CO 80111

NICOLAUS DAMMARELL, 418 79TH AVE SE, LAKE STEVENS, WA 98258

DAVID DANESE, 5060 LONGVIEW RD, ELMORE, AL 36025

JONATHAN DANESE, 5060 LONGVIEW RD, ELMORE, AL 36025

MICHAEL DANESE, 5060 LONGVIEW RD, ELMORE, AL 36025

SARA DANESE, 5060 LONGVIEW RD, ELMORE, AL 36025

JEREMY DARCANGELO, BOX 188, MANOKOTAK, AK 99628

NED DARONE, 47-688 ALAWIKI ST, KANEOHE, HI 96744

DEREK DAU, 480 SI VIEW PL SE, NORTH BEND, WA 98045

BENJAMIN DAUBER, 1809 TAYLOR AVE, BELLINGHAM, WA 98225

GEORGE DAUBER, 1809 TAYLOR AVE, BELLINGHAM, WA 98225

FRANCESCO DAVI, 746 NEWTON ST, MONTEREY, CA 93940

THOMAS DAVI, 19530 REDDING DR, SALINAS, CA 98908

BARRY DAVIS, 200 W 34TH AVE #556, ANCHORAGE, AK 99503

JEFFREY DAVIS, 548 SR 401, NASELLE, WA 98638

MICHAEL DAVIS, BOX 155, DILLINGHAM, AK 99576

BRENT DAWSON, BOX 803, DILLINGHAM, AK 99576

STEVE DAWSON, 8521 59TH ST NW, GIG HARBOR, WA 98335

KARL DEBOER, 1051 JUNIPER BEACH RD, CAMANO ISLAND, WA 98282

ERIC DEBRUIN, 10161 ROBIN HILL LN, DALLAS, TX 75238

TODD DECOSTA, BOX 8553, LACY, WA 98509

PARASCOVIA DEIGH, BOX 40, EGEGIK, AK 99579

ERIKA DELAROSA, 420 E HOWELL ST, SEATTLE, WA 98122

RUSSELL DELGROSSO, 4653 E VIA DONA RD, CAVE CREEK, AZ 85331

JOHN DELZOMPO, 4052 VIA LA PAZ, NAPA, CA 94558

HARVEY DEMANTLE, 300 AVEC RD HUD#8 BOX 97, NEW STUYAHOK, AK 99636

ERNEST DEMOSKI, 1037 W JONES DR, WASILLA, AK 99654

DANIEL DENNIS, 212 OCOTILLO PL, OCEANSIDE, CA 92057

DEREK DEPIERO, BOX 912, WILSON, WY 83014

BOZHO DERANJA, 665 W 9TH ST #B, SAN PEDRO, CA 90731

MIHO DERANJA, 1214 WESTERN AVE, GLENDALE, CA 91201

FREDERICK DEVEAU, BOX 12, DILLINGHAM, AK 99576

BRYAN DEVRIES, 4566 NOON RD, BELLINGHAM, WA 98226

MATTHEW DEWITTE, 14818 8TH AVE SE, MILL CREEK, WA 98012

JAY DEYO, 11544 DOWNEY RD, LA CONNER, WA 98257

SALVATORE DIMAGGIO, 60 EL CAMINO DEL SUR, MONTEREY, CA 93940

KATHERINE DINON, BOX 468, CRAIG, AK 99921

SHAWN DOCHTERMANN, BOX 866, KODIAK, AK 99615

THOMAS DOCK, BOX 203, TOGIAK, AK 99678

JORDAN DODSON.HUFF, 2216 FRANKLIN ST, BELLINGHAM, WA 98225

JACK DOERTY, BOX 1458, KALAMA, WA 98265

KEVIN DOERTY, BOX 1458, KALAMA, WA 98625

GLORIA DORIO, 1177 W PASEO DEL MAR, SAN PEDRO, CA 90731

JACK DOUGLAS, 2270 KELLY RD, BELLINGHAM, WA 98226

STEVEN DOUMIT, BOX 406, CATHLAMET, WA 98612

NICK DOWNS, 2732 LYNN ST, BELLINGHAM, WA 98229

DAVID DRISCOLL, BOX 385, KING SALMON, AK 99613

ADAM DUBAY, BOX 245, NAKNEK, AK 99633

BLINN DULL, BOX 465, DILLINGHAM, AK 99576

DUFFY DUNCAN, 1798 SE WALL ST, ASTORIA, OR 97103

HEIDI DUNLAP, 26 YOUNG ST, ASHEVILLE, NC 28801

KEN DUNSMORE, 225 RUE ORLEANS ST, BAYTOWN, TX 77520

DYLAN DURST, BOX 425, PETERSBURG, AK 99833

ROBERT DUTTON, 505 49TH ST SW, EVERETT, WA 98203

RUSSELL DYASUK, 1215 HESS AVE, FAIRBANKS, AK 99708

SAMSON DYASUK, BOX 12, TOGIAK, AK 99678

JORDAN DYER, BOX 1260, HOMER, AK 99603

ROBERT DYKEMAN, 1196 ARDEN CT, CHINO VALLEY, AZ 86323

BARBARA E.T.VUKAS, A MARBLE BEACH RD NW, GIG HARBOR, WA 98332

RICHARD ECHUCK, BOX 213, TOGIAK, AK 99678

JOHN EDLING, 4844 BROADWAY ST, BLAINE, WA 98230

JON EDSON, 19808 PARSONS CREEK RD, SEDRO WOOLLEY, WA 98284

NICHOLAS EDSON, 19808 PARSON CREEK RD, SEDRO WOLLEY, WA 98284

MIKE EGELAND, BOX 246, DILLINGHAM, AK 99576

KIRK EID, 349 W HEMMI RD, BELLINGHAM, WA 98226

ELIJAH EKNATY, BOX 1046, KOKHANOK, AK 99606

SAMUEL EKWURTZEL, 206 HUNGARY RD, GRANBY, CT 6035

JEFFREY ELBIE, 2510 WINTERCHASE CIR, ANCHORAGE, AK 99516

GENE ELLIOT, 92334 WALLUSKI LP, ASTORIA, OR 97103

DOUGLAS ELWELL, 4016 MERIDIAN AVE N, MARYSVILLE, WA 98271

SPENCER ELWELL, 4016 MERIDIAN AVE N, MARYSVILLE, WA 98271

BRADLEY EMERSON, 4904 197TH AVE E, BONNEY LAKE, WA 98391

LYDIA EMORY, BOX 486, NAKNEK, AK 99633

VINCENT ENGBRETSON, 35622 TUCKER CREEK LN, ASTORIA, OR 97103

JIM ENGLAND, 210 S 223 ST, DES MOINES, WA 98198

FEODOR EROFEEFF, BOX 937, WOODBURN, OR 97071

PETER EROFEEFF, BOX 937, WOODBURN, OR 97071

GAGE ETHINGTON, 562 S 100 W, AMERICAN FORK, UT 84003

JOHN.MICHAEL ETUCKMELRA, BOX 64, MANOKOTAK, AK 99628

KIM EUFEMIO, 1327 MYLARK LN, KODIAK, AK 99615

COLIN EVANS, 6043 NE KELDEN PL, SEATTLE, WA 98105

DEAN EVANS, 127 1/2 40TH ST, NEWPORT BEACH, CA 92661

DYLAN EVANS, 6043 NE KELDEN, SEATTLE, WA 98105

JOSHUA EVANS, 153 SUNSET DR, OAK HARBOR, WA 98277

W.LYNN EVANS, 9025 116TH ST NE, ARLINGTON, WA 98223

SALMON FISHING LIST—DRIFT GILLNET

NELS EVENS, BOX 585, PETERSBURG, AK 99833

ALVIN EVON, BOX 31, MANOKOTAK, AK 99628

KIM EWERS, 615 E WELLS FARGO DR, BROOKSIDE, UT 84782

ALINA FAIRBANKS, BOX 52057, FAIRBANKS, AK 99701

JOHN FAIRBANKS, 437 15TH ST, BELLINGHAM, WA 98225

JOSEPH FAITH, BOX 1316, DILLINGHAM, AK 99576

TAD FALK, 940 W CLATSOP AVE, ASTORIA, OR 97103

MIKE FALLEUR, 1401 OSTER RD, GEARHART, OR 97138

MILOS FALTA, 27 LILINOE ST, HILO, HI 96720

SARAH FARLOW, 2901 NEVADA ST, BELLINGHAM, WA 98226

KOMBIZ FAROKHPOUR, 1637 NADOWA ST, SOUTH LAKE TAHOE, CA 96150

DANIEL FARREN, 497 WESTWOOD AVE, HOMER, AK 99603

STEPHANIE FAUSER, BOX 336, LAKE OSWEGO, OR 97034

JOSEPH FERNANDEZ, 215 S SANTA CRUZ, VENTURA, CA 93001

SALVATORE FERRANTE, BOX 52, MONTEREY, CA 93942

BRYAN FERRASCI, BOX 18, CAMEL VALLEY, CA 93924

LEONARD FERRIGNO, 2387 ROLLING HILLS DR, CLARKSTON, WA 99403

BRYAN FERRIS, 3408 HARLEQUIN CT, KODIAK, AK 99615

CURTIS FERRIS, 915 30TH AVE #105, FAIRBANKS, AK 99701

WALLACE FIELDS, BOX 1691, KODIAK, AK 99615

TRULS FINBRATEN, 23220 49TH AVE SE, BOTHELL, WA 98021

JAMES FINCH, BOX 5042, KETCHIKAN, AK 99901

HENRY FISCHER, BOX 526, NAKNEK, AK 99633

NICHOLAS FITZGERALD, 115 POINTE PL, HILLSBOROUGH, NC 27278

ED FLANNERY, BOX 220145, ANCHORAGE, AK 99522

OLIVIA FLANNERY, BOX 220145, ANCHORAGE, AK 99522

HUGH FLEMING, BOX 1267, PETERSBURG, AK 99833

JOHN FLEMING, 11640 ELLEN AVE, ANCHORAGE, AK 99515

AUGUST FLENSBURG, BOX 3182, KENAI, AK 99611

CARL FLENSBURG, BOX 972, DILLINGHAM, AK 99576

GEORGE FLENSBURG, BOX 77, DILLINGHAM, AK 99576

OSCAR FLENSBURG, BOX 174, DILLINGHAM, AK 99576

EVAN FLETCHER, BOX 867, DILLINGHAM, AK 99576

LOUIS FLORA, 64535 SHEEP DR, HOMER, AK 99603

MIKE FLORA, 34710 MOONRISE ST, HOMER, AK 99603

FRANCISCO FLORESTA, BOX 413, DILLINGHAM, AK 99576

MARIANO FLORESTA, BOX 35, CLARKS POINT, AK 99569

BRENDAN FLYNN, 371 SCHOOL RD, LOPEZ ISLAND, WA 98261

JAMES FOLSOM, BOX 444, DILLINGHAM, AK 99576

RAYMOND FONDSE, BOX 335, SILVANA, WA 98287

JAMES FORD, BOX 70027, SOUTH NAKNEK, AK 99670

DENNIS FORSBERG, 1417 SE BLAIR RD, WASHOUGAL, WA 98671

VERNON FORSBERG, 28811 NW MAIN, RIDGEFIELD, WA 98642

STEVEN FOSSO, 4116 R AVE, ANACORTES, WA 98221

MIKE FOURTNER, BOX 361, NAPAVINE, WA 98565

LEROY FOX, BOX 136, TOGIAK, AK 99678

MARCUS FOX, 5 MERION CIRCLE, NAPA, CA 94558

MICHAEL FOX, 8117 FREDERICK PL, EDMONDS, WA 98026

MORGAN FOX, 1001 TRAPPER HILL RD, PORT HEIDEN, AK 99549

SEAN FOX, 2644 NW 87TH ST, SEATTLE, WA 98117

STEVEN FOX, 7034 DIBBLE AVE NW, SEATTLE, WA 98117

NOAH FRANCIS, 1363 E WESTMINSTER AVE, SALT LAKE CITY, UT 84105

PAUL FRANCIS, 1363 WESTMINSTER AVE, SALT LAKE CITY, UT 84105

PETER FRANCIS, 1363 E WESTMINSTER, SALT LAKE CITY, UT 84105

AIDAN FRANKLIN, 7942 RENIC DR, SEDRO WOOLLEY, WA 98284

CLAYTON FRANKLIN, 7942 RENIC DR, SEDRO WOOLLEY, WA 98284

JONATHAN FRANKLIN, BOX 154, MANOKOTAK, AK 99628

ELENA FRANKS, 3565 SAILBOARD CIRCLE, ANCHORAGE, AK 99516

MICHAEL FRANKS, 3565 SAILBOARD CIR, ANCHORAGE, AK 99516

DANIEL FRAZER, BOX 1284, CHOTEAU, MT 59422

SATANTA FREDENBERG, 1306 S ST, ANCHORAGE, AK 99501

DENNIS FREED, BOX 100, COLBERT, WA 99005

ERIKA FREITAS, BOX 14509, MILL CREEK, WA 98082

MICHAEL FRICCERO, BOX 2187, KODIAK, AK 99615

JOHN FRIIS.MIKKELSEN, 13009 7TH AVE NW, SEATTLE, WA 98177

PAUL FRIIS.MIKKELSEN, BOX 276, DILLINGHAM, AK 99576

BRYAN FRITZE, BOX 129, ALAKANUK, AK 99554

AARON FROST, BOX 176, TOGIAK, AK 99678

KNUT FROSTAD, BOX 923, PETERSBURG, AK 99833

RYAN FRY, BOX 52, PALMER, AK 99645

SPENCER FUENTES, BOX 251, SILVANA, WA 98287

JOHN FULTON, BOX 114, KING SALMON, AK 99613

JACOB GAGNER, 1727 EDGECUMBE DR, SITKA, AK 99835

KEITH GAIN, BOX 132, SELDOVIA, AK 99663

RICHARD GALGANO, 5105 ELDRIDGE ST, GOLDEN, CO 80403

JOSEPH GAMECHO, 945 FOREST AVE, PACIFIC GROVE, CA 93950

TERENCE GAMECHUK, BOX 66, MANOKOTAK, AK 99628

WASSILLIE GAMECHUK, BOX 165, MANOKOTAK, AK 99628

THOMAS GARDINER, BOX 1031, DILLINGHAM, AK 99576

DONALD GARDNER, 6902 FORD DR NW, GIG HARBOR, WA 98335

JACOB GARDNER, 4685 PINEWOOD CIR, LANGLEY, WA 98260

KY GARDNER, 2005 COMBIE RD, MEADOW VISTA, CA 95722

LUKE GARDNER, BOX 62, NASELLE, WA 98638

WILLIAM GARDNER, 2611 NW 54TH, SEATTLE, WA 98107

JASON GATES, 3707 ROSEDALE ST, GIG HARBOR, WA 98335

PHILLIP GAUTHIER, 21 AUBURN, ASTORIA, OR 97103

RUSSELL GEAGEL, BOX 4, SELDOVIA, AK 99663

GEORGE GEORGE, 13650 23RD ST, DADE CITY, FL 33525

MORRIS GEORGE, BOX 41, CLARKS POINT, AK 99569

MEGHAN GERVAIS, 40894 MCLAY, HOMER, AK 99603

ANTHONY GIACALONE, BOX 446, HOMER, AK 99603

VINCE GIAMMANCO, 9292 E CORRINE DR, SCOTTSDALE, AZ 85260

WARREN GIBBONS, 430 PARKRIDGE RD, BELLINGHAM, WA 98225

JOHN GIRVAN, 6440 S WASATCH BLVD STE 340, SALT LAKE CITY, UT 84121

PETE GIRVAN, 4809 S QUAIL POINT DR, SALT LAKE CITY, UT 84124

GEORGE GJERTSEN, 4825 91ST CT SW, MUKILTEO, WA 98275

TOM GLASS, BOX 258, DILLINGHAM, AK 99576

SCOTT GLEGOR, 92761 SIMONSEN RD, ASTORIA, OR 97103

FRANK GLOKO, BOX 52, MANOKOTAK, AK 99628

NORMAN GLOKO, BOX 71, MANOKOTAK, AK 99628

PAUL GLOKO, BOX 74, MANOKOTAK, AK 99628

JOHN GLOTFELTY, 28 TODILTO LN, DURANGO, CO 81301

SILAS GNAEDINGER, BOX 2246, HOMER, AK 99603

ELLIS GNYP, 5456 N W RD, BELLINGHAM, WA 98226

ANNIE GOLIA, BOX 1004, DILLINGHAM, AK 99576

PETER GOLIA, BOX 663, DILLINGHAM, AK 99576

JAMES GOODMAN, 1814 E REZANOF DR, KODIAK, AK 99615

TRAVIS GOODRICH, BOX 574, FRIDAY HARBOR, WA 98250

SAM GOSUK, BOX 177, TOGIAK, AK 99678

PERRY GRAHAM, 564 JOHN'S RIVER RD, ABERDEEN, WA 98520

TODD GRANGER, BOX 5174, BELLINGHAM, WA 98227

CHRISTOPHER GRANT, BOX 1170, HAILEY, ID 83333

FRANK GRAY, 1101 E 17TH, ANCHORAGE, AK 99501

LANCE GRAY, BOX 188, CHINOOK, WA 98614

ROBERT GRAY, BOX 28595, BELLINGHAM, WA 98228

BRIAN GREEN, BOX 283, MONITOR, WA 98836

COOPER GREEN, BOX 283, MONITOR, WA 98836

JORDAN GREEN, 2611 32ND AVE W, SEATTLE, WA 98199

OLIN GREEN, BOX 12547, SALEM, OR 97309

KENNETH GREENFIELD, BOX 237, CHINOOK, WA 98614

JOHNNY GREENLEY, BOX 295, TOGIAK, AK 99678

RANDAL GREGG, BOX 20373, JUNEAU, AK 99802

RICHARD GREGG, BOX 20669, JUNEAU, AK 99802

BEATRICE GREWAL, BOX 996, DILLINGHAM, AK 99576

DENNIS GRIECHEN, BOX 450, PILOT POINT, AK 99649

RONALD GRIFFIN, BOX 1953, KINGSTON, WA 98346

RYAN GRIFFIN, BOX 1953, KINGSTON, WA 98346

STEPHEN GRIFFING, 133 BANGSBERG RD, PORT CHARLOTTE, FL 33952

FRANK GRILLO, 899 DRAKE AVE, MONTEREY, CA 93940

GUY GROAT, BOX 29, NAKNEK, AK 99633

SALMON FISHING LIST—DRIFT GILLNET

BURT GRONN, BOX 963, KODIAK, AK 99615
COREY GRONN, 3901 WOLVERINE WAY, KODIAK, AK 99615
HUNTER GRUNHURD, 2583 MOUNTAIN VIEW RD, FERNDALE, WA 98248
KAEGAN GUDMUNDSON, 5973 RUTSATZ RD, DEMING, WA 98244
MIKALEA GUDMUNDSON, BOX 652, HAINES, AK 99827
THOR GUDMUNDSON, 2733 ORLEANS ST, BELLINGHAM, WA 98226
JOHN GUERRA, 27328 BAVELLA WAY, SALINAS, CA 93908
SEAN GUFFEY, 11245 ST RT E, ROLLA, MO 65401
GEROLD GUGEL, BOX 671227, CHUGIAK, AK 99567
JOSEPH GUGEL, 4788 E CRANE RD, WASILLA, AK 99654
RYAN GUIGGEY, 7163 WATERMILL WAY, SALT LAKE CITY, UT 84121
JACOB GULL, 78-1004 BISHOP RD, HOLUALOA, HI 96725
HERBERT GULLIFORD, 2661 N PEARL ST #292, TACOMA, WA 98407
GUSTAVIS GUMLICKPUK, BOX 26, NEW STUYAHOK, AK 99636
IVAN GUMLICKPUK, BOX 5051, KOLIGANEK, AK 99576
JUSTIN GUMLICKPUK, BOX 118, NEW STUYAHOK, AK 99636
WILLIAM GUMLICKPUK, BOX 71, NEW STUYAHOK, AK 99636
LANCE GUST, BOX 24, NEW STUYAHOK, AK 99636
GLENN GUSTAFSON, BOX 101962, ANCHORAGE, AK 99510
GRANT GUSTAFSON, BOX 101962, ANCHORAGE, AK 99510
DAMON HACHIYA, 67467 ENDLESS VIEW LP, HOMER, AK 99603
CHRISTOPHER HAGER, 11808 NE 162ND CT, BOTHELL, WA 98011
CHARLES HAGLUND, 93354 SVENSON ISLAND RD, ASTORIA, OR 97103
ROCK HAGLUND, 37759 LIBERTY LN, ASTORIA, OR 97103
MATTHEW HAKALA, 104 E PIONEER AVE, HOMER, AK 99603
DANIEL HALL, BOX 1164, PALMER, AK 99645
RAY HALL, 84654 TELEPHONE POLE RD, MILTON FREEWATER, OR 97862
TRAVIS HALL, BOX 501, HOMER, AK 99603
DAVID HAMBURG, 800 12TH AVE N, EDMONDS, WA 98020
ARVE HAMMER, 3616 166 PL SW, LYNNWOOD, WA 98037
KENNETH HAMMER, 2464 NW 198TH ST, SHORELINE, WA 98177
NICHOLAS HAMMING, BOX 262, GIRDWOOD, AK 99587
LUCAS HANCOX, 108 WHEELER MTN WAY, GALLATIN GATEWAY, MT 59730
STEVEN HANEY, 3700 E. PALMDALE DR, WASILLA, AK 99654
COLE HANSEN, 824 E VICTORIA AVE, BURLINGTON, WA 98233
FREDERICK HANSEN, BOX 3799, PALMER, AK 99645
GREGORY HANSEN, 1515 WILLIWAW WAY, WASILLA, AK 99654
KARL HANSEN, 439 NW 196TH PL, SEATTLE, WA 98177
OLAF HANSEN, BOX 3, NAKNEK, AK 99633
PAUL HANSEN, BOX 82, NAKNEK, AK 99633
JOHN HANSON, BOX 25, CHINOOK, WA 98614
ROBERT HANSON, 3705 ARCTIC BLVD PMB 2086, ANCHORAGE, AK 99503
JIM HARA, 930 WINTERSTONE DR, LEWISVILLE, TX 75067
BRADY HARANG, 122 ANNA DR, SITKA, AK 99835
WILLIAM HARGRAVE, BOX 250, NAVARRO, CA 95463
THOMAS HARMAN, 16131 BLACK BEAR DR, ANCHORAGE, AK 99516
DAVID HARSILA, 20103 23RD AVE NW, SHORELINE, WA 98177
JANIS HARSILA, 20103 23RD AVE NW, SHORELINE, WA 98177
KENT HART, 220 ST ANNS AVE, DOUGLAS, AK 99824
RON HART, 108 CAMPO VISTA DR, SANTA BARBARA, CA 93111
WARREN HART, 540 RIVERSHORE DR, ROSEBURG, OR 97470
ANDREW HARTINGER, 16544 27TH AVE NE, SHORELINE, WA 98155
JOHN HARVATH, 2501 MAYLEN CIR, ANCHORAGE, AK 99516
DANIEL HASTINGS, BOX 3324, SOLDOTNA, AK 99669
BRYCE HATCH, BOX 730, COEUR DE ALENE, ID 83816
GRANT HATCH, 939 16TH ST, CLARKSTON, WA 99403
JERRY HATTON, 378 RACCOON RD, OAKLAND, OR 97462
KEVIN HATTON, 2422 EVERGREEN PARK RD, GRAYLAND, WA 98547
EDDIE HAUGEN, 632 N 201ST LN, SHORELINE, WA 98133
LARRY HAVENS, BOX 769, CATHLAMET, WA 98612
DEVIN HEATH, 418 STATE ROUTE 105, RAYMOND, WA 98577
GUY HEBERT, 5010 YELLOW BRICK RD, BELLINGHAM, WA 98226
JERRY HEICHEL, BOX 425, STANWOOD, WA 98292
TODD HEICHEL, 4414 290TH ST NW, STANWOOD, WA 98292
BRAD HEIL, 41627 GLADYS CT, HOMER, AK 99603
TANNER HEIL, 41627 GLADYS CT, HOMER, AK 99603

MARK HEILALA, 7715 45TH PL W, MUKILTEO, WA 98275
RYAN HEILALA, 1120 HUFFMAN RD SUITE 24 PMB 213, ANCHORAGE, AK 99515
KARL HEIMBUCH, 987 KEYSTONE, SOLDOTNA, AK 99669
KARL HELLBERG, BOX 302, WARRENTON, OR 97146
BRETT HELLER, 17712 NE 189TH ST, BRUSH PRAIRIE, WA 98606
JEFF HENDRICKS, 5930 LAUREL SHAW CT, FERNDALE, WA 98248
RICHARD HENDRICKS, 3975 TUSTIN DR, PALMER, AK 99645
DANIEL HENDRICKSON, 8702 90TH AVE NW, GIG HARBOR, WA 98332
DANIEL HENDRICKSON, 4911 NE 44TH AVE, VANCOUVER, WA 98661
DAVID HENDRICKSON, 4505 NORTH 9TH ST, TACOMA, WA 98406
ELIJAH HENRY, BOX 1442, WESTPORT, WA 98595
JOSEPH HENRY, BOX 37006, TOKSOOK BAY, AK 99637
THOMAS HENSHAW, 1727 EDGECUMBE DR, SITKA, AK 99835
KJ HERMAN, BOX 3350, KODIAK, AK 99615
JAIME HERNANDEZ, BOX 8841, MOMMOTH LAKES, CA 93546
MICHAEL HERNANDEZ, BOX 58013, FAIRBANKS, AK 99711
BOONE HERR, 109 HOLLY POINTE, WARNER ROBINS, GA 31088
SHAYNE HERR, 7956 N WOLVERINE RD, PALMER, AK 99645
LEONARD HERZOG, 916 DELANEY ST, ANCHORAGE, AK 99501
ERIC HESSELROTH, 1001 DUCHESS RD, BOTHELL, WA 98012
CASEY HEUKER, BOX 98, CASCADE LOCKS, OR 97014
DAN HEUKER, BOX 98, CASCADE LOCKS, OR 97014
KORBIN HEUKER, BOX 98, CASCADE LOCKS, OR 97014
TIMOTHY HEUKER, BOX 98, CASCADE LOCKS, OR 97014
MINDY HEYANO, BOX 1409, DILLINGHAM, AK 99576
PETER HEYANO, BOX 730, DILLINGHAM, AK 99576
ROBERT HEYANO, BOX 1409, DILLINGHAM, AK 99576
LARRY HIGGINS, BOX 106, LA CONNER, WA 98257
SCOTT HIGLEY, 17015 THREE LAKES RD, SNOHOMISH, WA 98290
KARL HILL, BOX 4046, IGIUGIG, AK 99613
ROBERT HILL, BOX 623, NAKNEK, AK 99633
WILLIAM HILL, BOX 483, NAKNEK, AK 99633
DAVID HILLEY, BOX 1411, DILLINGHAM, AK 99576
DAVID HILLSTRAND, 4110 MAIN ST, HOMER, AK 99603
TARA HINES, BOX 161934, BIG SKY, MT 59716
LOUIS HIRATSUKA, 901 WILDROSE CT, ANCHORAGE, AK 99518
RICHARD HIRATSUKA, BOX 312, DILLINGHAM, AK 99576
EDMOND HISAW, BOX 1179, TENINO, WA 98589
KARLTON HISAW, BOX 1179, TENINO, WA 98589
BRYAN HODGSON, BOX 42, ALEKNAGIK, AK 99555
FRANK HOFF, 21930 453RD AVE, ARLINGTON, SD 57212
FRANK HOFF, 21930 453RD AVE, ARLINGTON, SD 57212
PATRICK HOGAN, BOX 1009, KODIAK, AK 99615
DOUGLAS HOGEN, 3099 SPRUCE CAPE RD, KODIAK, AK 99615
VINCE HOIBY, 3121 WAVE DR, EVERETT, WA 98203
DAVID HOLLINGSWORTH, 20 OLD WESTPORT RD, ABERDEEN, WA 98520
MICHAEL HOLM, 1500 E COLLEGE WAY #A PMB492, MT VERNON, WA 98273
PHILIP HOLMES, 973 GRAYS CREEK RD, INDIAN VALLEY, ID 83632
MILO HOLSTON, BOX 862, WINTHROP, WA 98862
MARK HOLUM, 12701 SAUNDERS RD, ANCHORAGE, AK 99516
ROMMIE HOOPER, BOX 71, TUNUNAK, AK 99681
ANNA HOOVER, BOX 167, NAKNEK, AK 99633
THOMAS HOSETH, BOX 1193, DILLINGHAM, AK 99576
CODY HOWSON, 2018 M AVE, ANACORTES, WA 98221
CLAYTON HOY, 3563 BRECKINRIDGE RD, EVERSON, WA 98247
GUY HOY, 3563 BRECKENRIDGE RD, EVERSON, WA 98247
STEPHEN HUBBARD, 2904 S COUNTY LINE RD, ALBANY, GA 31705
CHAD HUDDLESTON, 91580 YOUNGS RIVER RD, ASTORIA, OR 97103
ERIC HUDDLESTON, BOX 233, CANNON BEACH, OR 97110
ROBERT HUFF, 4602 ACADEMY ST, BELLINGHAM, WA 98226
CHARLES HUGHES, BOX 110693, ANCHORAGE, AK 99511
WADE HUGHES, 3360 ORBIT DR, ANCHORAGE, AK 99517
JOHN HULJEV, 2824 GAFFEY ST, SAN PEDRO, CA 90731
OTIS HUNSINGER, 92669 LEO DR, ASTORIA, OR 97103
WILLIAM HUNSINGER, BOX 1237, ASTORIA, OR 97103
JERRY HUNT, BOX 595, DILLINGHAM, AK 99576

SALMON FISHING LIST—DRIFT GILLNET

ASHTON HURLBURT, 11601 BARR RD, ANCHORAGE, AK 99516
DON HUSE, BOX 373, PETERSBURG, AK 99833
JIMMY HUTCHENS, 20282 ENGLISH RD, MOUNT VERNON, WA 98274
SAMUEL HUTCHENS, 20282 ENGLISH RD, MOUNT VERNON, WA 98274
DAVID IANI, BOX 549, KODIAK, AK 99615
PETER IANI, 236 4TH AVE S #302, EDMONDS, WA 98020
BRUCE ILUTSIK, BOX 52, ALEKNAGIK, AK 99555
GUSTY ILUTSIK, BOX 24, ALEKNAGIK, AK 99555
GIOVANNI INCAVIGLIA, 27618 TARRASA DR, PALOS VERDES, CA 90275
JAMES INGRAM, BOX 851, DILLINGHAM, AK 99576
ANGUS ISAAC, BOX 953, ANCHOR POINT, AK 99556
GARY ISAKSEN, 7419 25TH ST NE, LAKE STEVENS, WA 98258
KARL ISAKSEN, 1314 E LAS OLAS BLVD #1207, FORT LAUDERDALE, FL 33301
NATALIA ISHNOOK, BOX 5029, KOLIGANEK, AK 99576
CHRISTIAN ITUMULRIA, BOX 1162, DILLINGHAM, AK 99576
DICK ITUMULRIA, BOX 16, MANOKOTAK, AK 99628
BLAINE IVANOFF, 5816 34TH ST NW, GIG HARBOR, WA 98335
DAVID IVANOV, BOX 15316, HOMER, AK 99603
IAKOV IVANOV, BOX 40, MOLALLA, OR 97038
ANDREW IVERSEN, 23279 ALDO RD NW, POULSBO, WA 98370
PETE IVICEVICH, 3220 HEIGHTS PL, BELLINGHAM, WA 98226
DAVID IVY, BOX 2219, HOMER, AK 99603
TREYTON J.J.U.MARTIN, BOX 85, TOGIAK, AK 99678
WALTER JACKINSKY, 2217 W 46TH AVE, ANCHORAGE, AK 99517
MARK JACKSON, 1442 CHENA RIDGE RD CABIN, FAIRBANKS, AK 99709
MICHAEL JACKSON, 615 12TH ST, BELLINGHAM, WA 98225
MARIE JACOBS, 465 DAILEY AVE F30, ANCHORAGE, AK 99515
DANIEL JACOBSON, BOX 404, NAKNEK, AK 99633
JAKE JACOBY, 2030 GLACIER HWY, JUNEAU, AK 99801
DAVID JAMIESON, 523 OLD FORGE RD, MADISON, VA 22727
DAN JANSEN, 10915 59TH AVE W, MUKILTEO, WA 98275
DAVID JENNINGS, 2522 TAFT DR, LUMMI ISLAND, WA 98262
LEO JENNINGS, 500 LOCHER RD, TOUCHET, WA 99360
JEREMY JENSEN, 2900 JACKSON RD, JUNEAU, AK 99801
KRISTOPHER JENSEN, 405 BENNETT ST, SEDRO WOOLLEY, WA 98284
TIM JENSEN, BOX 30878, SEATTLE, WA 98133
ALEXIE JIMMIE, BOX 37127, TOKSOOK BAY, AK 99637
DAVID JIMMY, 5901 E 6TH AVE #160, ANCHORAGE, AK 99504
JOHN JIMMY, BOX 32, CHEFORNAK, AK 99561
JORDAN JIRA, 5407 7TH AVE NE, TULALIP, WA 98271
HELEN JOHN, 3833 SCENIC VIEW DR, ANCHORAGE, AK 99504
KIKO JOHN, BOX 126, MANOKOTAK, AK 99628
LOUIE JOHN, BOX 126, MANOKOTAK, AK 99628
MARK JOHN, 3833 SCENIC VIEW DR, ANCHORAGE, AK 99504
MYRON JOHN, BOX 69, MANOKOTAK, AK 99628
NATHAN JOHN, BOX 53, MANOKOTAK, AK 99628
RALPH JOHN, BOX 37061, TOKSOOK BAY, AK 99637
SIMEON JOHN, BOX 37051, TOKSOOK BAY, AK 99637
CONNER JOHNS, 2492 NORTHVIEW ST, BOZEMAN, MT 59715
BASIL JOHNSON, 1331 W 82ND, ANCHORAGE, AK 99518
CALEB JOHNSON, BOX 1014, DILLINGHAM, AK 99576
CARY JOHNSON, 92080 JOHN DAY RIVER RD, ASTORIA, OR 97103
CHRIS JOHNSON, 2013 DENELL WAY, BOISE, ID 83709
DAVID JOHNSON, 7916 110TH AVE SE, NEWCASTLE, WA 98056
DONALD JOHNSON, 762 SHELTER BAY DR, LA CONNER, WA 98257
FRITZ JOHNSON, BOX 1129, DILLINGHAM, AK 99576
GRAHAM JOHNSON, BOX 1744, WHITE SALMON, WA 98672
HERMAN JOHNSON, BOX 5010, KOLIGANEK, AK 99576
JOHN JOHNSON, BOX 2678, PALMER, AK 99645
KEVIN JOHNSON, BOX 78, DILLINGHAM, AK 99576
KURT JOHNSON, 22421 57TH AVE SE, BOTHELL, WA 98021
LUDWIG JOHNSON, BOX 278, DILLINGHAM, AK 99576
MATTHEW JOHNSON, 401 9TH AVE N APT 411, SEATTLE, WA 98109
MICHAEL JOHNSON, 4322 NW DR, BELLINGHAM, WA 98226
MICHAEL JOHNSON, BOX 70032, SOUTH NAKNEK, AK 99670

MYRTLE JOHNSON, BOX 608, NOME, AK 99762
NICK JOHNSON, BOX 5048, KOLIGANEK, AK 99576
ROGER JOHNSON, 43 RACE LN, ABERDEEN, WA 98520
RONALD JOHNSON, 12022 275TH AVE SE, MONROE, WA 98272
SASHA JOHNSON, 400 CAPRICORN CIR, ANCHORAGE, AK 99508
STANLEY JOHNSON, 92732 FERN HILL RD, ASTORIA, OR 97103
TREY JOHNSON, 516 GLEN AVE, SNOHOMISH, WA 98290
TROY JOHNSON, 98 SKYLINE AVE, ASTORIA, OR 97103
WILLIAM JOHNSON, BOX 1178, DILLINGHAM, AK 99576
WILLIAM JOHNSON, BOX 193, DILLINGHAM, AK 99576
AARON JOHNSTON, BOX 1656, HOMER, AK 99603
BRUCE JOLMA, 460 NE ALDER ST, CLATSKANIE, OR 97016
NATHAN JOLMA, 5815 N MONTANA AVE, PORTLAND, OR 97217
FORBES JONASSON, 1297 GARDNER WAY, MEDFORD, OR 97504
ALEXANDER JONES, BOX 64, WINTHROP, WA 98862
LAVONA JONES, 4133 MERIDIAN AVE N, MARYSVILLE, WA 98271
LIEF JONES, 3003 SAINT CLAIR, BELLINGHAM, WA 98226
RANDY JONES, 4133 MERIDIAN AVE N, MARYSVILLE, WA 98271
ROBERT JONES, 3705 ARCTIC BLVD #2059, ANCHORAGE, AK 99503
ROBERT JONES, 832 KLINE RD, BELLINGHAM, WA 98226
TYLER JONES, 3003 ST CLAIR, BELLINGHAM, WA 98226
MICHAEL JONROWE, BOX 272, WILLOW, AK 99688
ANDREW JORDAN, BOX 98, MANOKOTAK, AK 99628
NICHOLAS JORDAN, 4916 MORGAN DR, BLAINE, WA 98230
BRANDEN JORDON, 705 198TH PL SE, BOTHELL, WA 98012
JON JORGENSON, 1273 NE MCWILLIAMS RD, BREMERTON, WA 98311
VIOLA JOSEPH, BOX 472, NAKNEK, AK 99633
M.BLANCHE KALLSTROM, BOX 550, DILLINGHAM, AK 99576
TED KALLSTROM, 7146 RD 8 NW, EPHRATA, WA 98823
ALEXANDER KALUGIN, BOX 1131, HOMER, AK 99603
ANTANINA KALUGIN, BOX 3046, HOMER, AK 99603
AVRAM KALUGIN, BOX 3046, HOMER, AK 99603
CORNILY KALUGIN, 46810 GOLDEN VIEW CIR, HOMER, AK 99603
DAVID KALUGIN, BOX 3027, HOMER, AK 99603
DAVID KALUGIN, BOX 4282, HOMER, AK 99603
DIMITIAN KALUGIN, BOX 1624, HOMER, AK 99603
ILESAY KALUGIN, BOX 2727, HOMER, AK 99603
IVAN KALUGIN, BOX 3168, HOMER, AK 99603
IVAN KALUGIN, BOX 4282, HOMER, AK 99603
NIKOLA KALUGIN, BOX 598, HOMER, AK 99603
PHILIP KALUGIN, BOX 3161, HOMER, AK 99603
SAFRON KALUGIN, BOX 1921, HOMER, AK 99603
VLADIMIR KALUGIN, BOX 2480, HOMER, AK 99603
ZAHARY KALUGIN, BOX 1137, HOMER, AK 99603
ZINA KALUGIN, BOX 1131, HOMER, AK 99603
SHAWN KAMKAHPAK, BOX 142, TOGIAK, AK 99678
MATTHEW KANDOLL, BOX 2091, PETERSBURG, AK 99833
SCOT KANDOLL, BOX 2154, PETERSBURG, AK 99833
WILLIAM KANUK, BOX 2008, BETHEL, AK 99559
J.P KANULIE, 12431 HACE ST, ANCHORAGE, AK 99515
WALTER KANULIE, BOX 133, TOGIAK, AK 99678
EDWARD KAPATAK, BOX 5002, KOLIGANEK, AK 99576
CHARLIE KAPOTAK, BOX 5033, KOLIGANEK, AK 99576
LENA KAPOTAK, BOX 716, DILLINGHAM, AK 99576
EVAN KARL, BOX 8, DEERING, AK 99736
HARRY KARSHEKOFF, BOX 035, NONDALTON, AK 99640
KYLE KARVIA, 8704 NE 17TH ST, VANCOUVER, WA 98664
NORBERT KASHATOK, BOX 182, TULUKSAK, AK 99679
FISCHER KASS, 10244 GOODNEWS CIR, ANCHORAGE, AK 99515
KELLY KASS, 10244 GOODNEWS CIR, ANCHORAGE, AK 99515
NICHOLAS KATO, 1161 STATE ROUTE 4, NASELLE, WA 98638
FRANCES KAUL, BOX 64, WINTHROP, WA 98862
LARRY KAYOUKLUK, BOX 5026, KOLIGANEK, AK 99576
BRIAN KEAGY, 8260 HILLSIDE RD, ALTA LOMA, CA 91701
ACE KEIM, 1321 GRAM CIRCLE, ANCHORAGE, AK 99518

SALMON FISHING LIST—DRIFT GILLNET

MICHAEL KELLEY, 40349 PORTLOCK DR, HOMER, AK 99603

JOHN KELLY, 2011 W MACARTHUR ST, RANCHO PALOS VERDE, CA 90275

SHIRLEY KELLY, 1951 EARLY VIEW DR, ANCHORAGE, AK 99504

JAMES KEMMER, BOX 6, CHINOOK, WA 98614

PETER KENDRICK, BOX 2798, KODIAK, AK 99615

SAMMIE KESTER, BOX 4068, BELLINGHAM, WA 98227

SEIRAH KEVAL, 3036 LANDIS ST, SAN DIEGO, CA 92104

AUSTIN KILMER.MORRIS, 1418 EAST ISAACS AVE, WALLAWALLA, WA 99362

ROBERT KING, 15705 NE 194TH CT, BRUSH PRAIRIE, WA 98606

WILDON KING, 83072 LOWER DRY CREEK RD, MILTON FREEWATER, OR 97862

DANIEL KINGSLEY, BOX 4631, PILOT POINT, AK 99649

MITCHELL KINK, 2429 FRANKLIN ST, BELLINGHAM, WA 98225

CHRISTIAN KIRK, 18504 RIDGEFIELD RD NW, SEATTLE, WA 98177

GEORGE KIRK, BOX 2796, KODIAK, AK 99615

WILLIAM KIRK, 2011 W MACARTHUR ST, RANCHO PALOS VERDE, CA 90275

MICHAEL KLECKA, 202 6TH AVE, ROCHELLE, IL 61068

JOSHUA KLEIN, 1817 EAST 38TH LOOP, VANCOUVER, WA 98663

ABBEY KNIGHT, 610 W 9TH ST, JUNEAU, AK 99801

CASEY KNIGHT, BOX 942, PETERSBURG, AK 99833

CHRIS KNIGHT, BOX 22365, JUNEAU, AK 99802

KYLE KNIGHT, BOX 1133, PETERSBURG, AK 99833

STEVEN KNOWLES, 1423 E KOUSKOV ST, KODIAK, AK 99615

AUGUST KNUTSEN, 11670 WILDERNESS DR, ANCHORAGE, AK 99516

MURPHY KNUTSEN, BOX 187, DILLINGHAM, AK 99576

HOWARD KNUTSON, BOX 91456, ANCHORAGE, AK 99509

GREG KOETJE, 23 280TH ST NE, ARLINGTON, WA 98223

RICK KOETJE, 206 STATE AVE, MARYSVILLE, WA 98270

DOTTY KOGER, 4116 226TH PL NE, ARLINGTON, WA 98223

WILL KOGER, 4116 226TH PL NE, ARLINGTON, WA 98223

STEVEN KOHLER, BOX 83, ALEKNAGIK, AK 99555

JASON KOHLHASE, 10753 HORIZON DR, JUNEAU, AK 99801

BRIAN KOHLWES, 8112 126TH PLACE NE, KIRKLAND, WA 98033

GARY KOHLWES, 5960 CEDAR ST, FREELAND, WA 98249

GARY KOHLWES, 5960 CEDAR ST, FREELAND, WA 98249

MARIO KOLICH, 818 S PATTON AVE #1, SAN PEDRO, CA 90731

JASON KOONTZ, 53585 GERBER CT, KASILOF, AK 99610

DAVID KOPRA, BOX 1047, HOMER, AK 99603

DAN KORTHUIS, 782 1600 RD, DELTA, CO 81416

MATTHEW KORZENASKI, 903 ORANGE ST, SELINSGROVE, PA 17870

IVAN KRAABEL, 23220 49TH AVE SE, BOTHELL, WA 98021

BENJAMIN KRAMER, BOX 374, COPPER CENTER, AK 99573

PETER KRAMER, BOX 374, COPPER CENTER, AK 99573

FRED KRAUN, 4752 354TH AVE SE, FALL CITY, WA 98024

GARY KREIDER, 4829 OUTRIGGER LP, BLAINE, WA 98230

MOSES KRITZ, BOX 245, DILLINGHAM, AK 99576

MARYANNA KROEZE, 4081 EDWARDS DR NE, MOSES LAKE, WA 98837

RANDELL KROEZE, 4081 EDWARDS DR NE, MOSES LAKE, WA 98837

LOREN KROON, 1131 MCADOO WAY, WASILLA, AK 99654

WILLIAM KROONTJE, BOX 231, LYNDEN, WA 98264

JACOB KROPF, 5757 C MILLER RD, HUBBARD, OR 97032

VICKI KULLER, BOX 312, CATHLAMET, WA 98612

WHITNEY KULLER, BOX 312, CATHLAMET, WA 98612

JERRET KUMMER, BOX 1522, WESTPORT, WA 98595

WILLIAM KUNZWEILER, 5420 LBJ FREEWAY #515, DALLAS, TX 75240

STEVE KURIAN, 87 SCHOOLHOUSE LN, BLOOMSBURG, PA 17815

ALEXANDER KURTZ, BOX 32265, BELLINGHAM, WA 98228

MARK KURTZ, 1724 SW 5TH ST, FORT LAUDERDALE, FL 33312

ALENTINA KUSNETSOV, BOX 1355, HOMER, AK 99603

DOMIAN KUZMIN, BOX 367, DELTA JUNCTION, AK 99737

EVDOKIA KUZMIN, 16727 LEARY RD, WOODBURN, OR 97071

IOAN KUZMIN, BOX 272, DELTA JUNCTION, AK 99737

IOSIF KUZMIN, 709 PINTAIL ST, SILVERTON, OR 97381

CAROLYN KVERNVIK, BOX 1081, PETERSBURG, AK 99833

KURT KVERNVIK, BOX 1081, PETERSBURG, AK 99833

JORN KVINGE, 2321 WINDJAMMER CT NW, OLYMPIA, WA 98502

ALEXUS KWACHKA, 326 COPE ST, KODIAK, AK 99615

IVO LABAR, 1235 W 13TH ST, SAN PEDRO, CA 90731

CHARLES LABORDE, 12411 76TH AVE NW, MARYSVILLE, WA 98271

GENE LACHELT, 546 EMBASSY CIR, HENDERSON, NV 89015

PHILIP LAFATA, 1555 HARKSELL RD, FERNDALE, WA 98248

STEVEN LAINE, 20 RANGILA RD, NASELLE, WA 98638

JOSEPH LAKE, BOX 371, HOOPER BAY, AK 99604

TAYLOR LANDRUD, 18636 277ND PL S, COVINGTON, WA 98042

CYNTHIA LANER, 533 FRONTIER AVE, PAGOSA SPRINGS, CO 81147

JOHN LANER, 533 FRONTIER AVE, PAGUSA SPRINGS, CO 81147

KEITH LANGMAN, 815 RAMONA AVE, SPRING VALLEY, CA 91977

PRESTON LANUM, BOX 3404, HOMER, AK 99603

PARKER LARRIEU, 2085 LONG COVE DRIVE, OXNARD, CA 93036

BRADLEY LARSEN, 3071 N EDGEWATER DR, WASILLA, AK 99623

CURT LARSEN, 777 SCENIC DR, TWO HARBORS, MN 55616

RANDY LARSEN, 8079 SKEENA WAY, BLAINE, WA 98230

ALBERT LARSON, BOX 702, DILLINGHAM, AK 99576

BOICE LARSON, BOX 112, DILLINGHAM, AK 99576

BRET LARSON, 2766 SE TEAL AVE, GRESHAM, OR 97080

CHAD LARSON, 5026 259TH ST NE, ARLINGTON, WA 98223

WILLIAM LARSON, BOX 1181, DILLINGHAM, AK 99576

MICHAEL LARUSSA, 12650 BLAKELY PL NW, SEATTLE, WA 98177

TONY LARUSSA, 4041 33RD AVE W, SEATTLE, WA 98199

DON LATSHA, BOX 1628, MILTON, WA 98354

DONALD LAWHEAD, 3915 E BLUE SAPPHIRE CT, WASILLA, AK 99654

JON LAWLER, 215 FAWN CT, ANCHORAGE, AK 99515

JON LAWLER, 22128 STATE ROUTE 9 LOT 88, MOUNT VERNON, WA 98274

SIMON LAWRENCE, BOX 183, KWETHLUK, AK 99621

ELIJAH LAWSON, 543 N 82ND ST, SEATTLE, WA 98103

MICHAEL LEACH, 2100 GLACIER HWY, JUNEAU, AK 99801

GARRETT LEBLANC, 5988 W GREEN ACRES ST, HOMOSASSA, FL 34446

ROBERT LEBOVIC, 257 RIVERVIEW DR, ASHEVILLE, NC 28806

GABRIELLE LEDOUX, 8859 CROSS POINTE LP, ANCHORAGE, AK 99504

DOMINIC LEE, BOX 1635, MOAB, UT 84532

NILS LEE, 6252 NE LINCOLN RD E, POULSBO, WA 98370

SKYLR LEE, 22212 BOND RD NE, POULSBO, WA 98370

TROY LELAND, 2261 LUMMI SHORE RD, BELLINGHAM, WA 98226

ERIK LEMBKE, BOX 652, HAINES, AK 99827

RYAN LENON, 522 SUT LASRSEN WAY, KODIAK, AK 99615

ERIK LEONNIG, BOX 5581, CHINIAK, AK 99615

CROSBY LEVEEN, BOX 1662, CORDOVA, AK 99574

CLIFF LEWIS, BOX 1095, CANNON BEACH, OR 97110

JOSHUA LEWIS, 1120 HUFFMAN RD #24-466, ANCHORAGE, AK 99515

SAM LEWIS, 70 TIMBER TRAIL, BOULDER, CO 80302

STEVEN LEWIS, 7001 SEAVIEW AVE NW STE 160, SEATTLE, WA 98117

WALTER LEWIS, BOX 2, CHEFORNAK, AK 99561

JUSTIN LIBBY, 5110 SPRUCE CREEK CIR, ANCHORAGE, AK 99507

LANDON LIBBY, 11680 CANGE ST, ANCHORAGE, AK 99516

JACK LIBERATI, BOX 524, KING SALMON, AK 99613

VITO LIBERATI, 88 EDGEWATER PL, PITTSBURG, CA 94565

JERRY LIBOFF, BOX 646, DILLINGHAM, AK 99576

PALMER LIE, 21727 96TH AVE W, EDMONDS, WA 98020

KONAN LIND, BOX 870467, WASILLA, AK 99687

SIGNE LINDBERG, 2925 SAINT CLAIR, BELLINGHAM, WA 98226

THEODORE LINDLEY, BOX 1584, BETHEL, AK 99559

ZACHARY LINDOR, 210 PATTEE CANYON DR, MISSOULA, MT 59803

DAVID LINDSTROM, 689 LEXINGTON, ASTORIA, OR 97103

CALEB LINS, BOX 2152, AVALON, CA 90704

HAYDEN LINSCHEID, BOX 441, ALMA, CO 80420

KYLE LINTS, 64900 BERRY PAIL DR, HOMER, AK 99603

CHANTELLE LITTLE, 807 S MOUNTAIN AVE, ASHLAND, OR 97520

JOHN LITTLE, 807 S MOUNTAIN AVE, ASHLAND, OR 97520

RYAN LITTLETON, BOX 2143, PETERSBURG, AK 99833

MARC LLEWELLYN, 517 B MAPLE AVE, LA CONNER, WA 98257

HERBERT LOCKUK, BOX 194, TOGIAK, AK 99678

PETER LOCKUK, BOX 88, TOGIAK, AK 99678

CRAIG LOGUSAK, BOX 116, TOGIAK, AK 99678

SALMON FISHING LIST—DRIFT GILLNET

FRANK LOGUSAK, BOX 278, TOGIAK, AK 99678
SHANE LOHR, BOX 765, PETERSBURG, AK 99833
COLTON LONG, 2224 N 600 W, PLEASANT GROVE, UT 84062
JIM LONG, BOX 172, CHINOOK, WA 98614
BROGAN LONT, BOX 275, QUILCENE, WA 98376
BARBARA LOPEZ, BOX 906, DILLINGHAM, AK 99576
DAVID LORENZ, BOX 2382, KODIAK, AK 99615
WILLIAM LOWDER, 920 37TH ST, BOUDLER, CO 80303
CHAD LOWENBERG, 451 SEXTON RD, SEBASTOPOL, CA 95472
JOHN LOWRANCE, 3900 W HOOKER ST, SEATTLE, WA 98199
BENJAMIN LUCK, 605 BROWN AVE, FORT COLLINS, CO 90525
MATTHEW LUCK, BOX 4997, KETCHUM, ID 83340
CLAYTON LUDWIG, BOX 328, SILVANA, WA 98287
JEFFREY LUDWIG, 4018 226TH PL NE, ARLINGTON, WA 98223
JOEL LUDWIG, 4018 226TH PL NE, ARLINGTON, WA 98223
MARK LUDWIG, 16300 38TH AVE NW, STANWOOD, WA 98292
PETER LUDWIG, 4018 226TH PL NE, ARLINGTON, WA 98223
STEVEN LUDWIG, BOX 328, SILVANA, WA 98287
SUSAN LUDWIG, 4018 226TH PLACE NE, ARLINGTON, WA 98223
JOHN LUNDGREN, 921 AUTUMN LN #243, BELLINGHAM, WA 98229
KEITH LUTZ, 7812 HUETTER CT SW, OLYMPIA, WA 98512
YAKOBI LYON, 50884 MOUNTAIN GLACIER CT, HOMER, AK 99603
ERON MACARTNEY, 740 E KELLOGG RD, BELLINGHAM, WA 98226
DANIEL MACDONALD, BOX 5993, BELLINGHAM, WA 98227
JAEGER MACH, 18817 89TH AVE W, EDMONDS, WA 98026
LADISLAV MACH, 10830 24TH DR SE, EVERETT, WA 98208
PAUL MACH, 8257 16TH AVE NE, SEATTLE, WA 98115
JOE MACKENZIE, 3811 TERRACE DR, ANACORTES, WA 98221
WESTIN MACKENZIE, 3811 TERRACE DR, ANACORTES, WA 98221
JESSE MADDEN, 1425 E 10TH AVE, SPOKANE, WA 99202
FREDERICK MAGILL, BOX 444, PETERSBURG, AK 99833
STEPHEN MAHER, 26 YOUNG ST, ASHEVILLE, NC 28801
MICHAEL MALLOY, 11609 28TH ST SE, EVERETT, WA 98258
EUGENE MALTZEFF, 3805 56TH NE, OLYMPIA, WA 98506
KURT MANCHESTER, BOX 70867, SEATTLE, WA 98127
WILLIAM MANCHESTER, BOX 70867, SEATTLE, WA 98127
RALPH MANCUSO, BOX 181, NAKNEK, AK 99633
DAVID MANDICH, 31 BOURSAW AVE, HOQUIAM, WA 98550
BRUCE MANN, 363 NE 178TH ST, SHORELINE, WA 98155
NATASHA MANN, 363 NE 178TH ST, SHORELINE, WA 98155
DAVID MANNES, 325 E 77TH ST #5D, NEW YORK, NY 10075
DARRIN MANOR, 868 CHERRY AVE, BAINBRIDGE ISLAND, WA 98110
JORDAN MANOR, 868 CHERRY AVE NE, BAINBRIDGE ISLAND, WA 98110
ARI MANOS, 5224 VARCO RD NE, TACOMA, WA 98422
CURT MARBLE, 11278 SAHALIE RD, LA CONNER, WA 98257
ERIC MARBLE, 11278 SAHALIE RD, LA CONNER, WA 98257
NICHOLAS MARCOUX.KAMIS, BOX 2069, HOMER, AK 99603
JOHN MARDESICH, BOX 601, NAKNEK, AK 99633
MATTHEW MARDESICH, 525 KLAMATH DR, LA CONNER, WA 98257
NIKOLAS MARDESICH, 5101 GUEMES ISLAND RD, ANACORTES, WA 98221
EDWARD MARES, 211 PLYMOUTH DR, VISTA, CA 92083
SAMANTHA MARIFERN, BOX 917, PETERSBURG, AK 99833
KEVIN MARILLEY, 18155 JOY PL, BURLINGTON, WA 98233
FRANK MARINKOVICH, 2901 WHITE CLOUD AVE NW, GIG HARBOR, WA 98335
LUKE MARINKOVICH, 2901 WHITE CLOUD AVE NW, GIG HARBOR, WA 98335
MASON MARINKOVICH, 8721 137TH ST NW 616, HARBOR, WA 98329
MATTHEW MARINKOVICH, BOX 2084, FRIDAY HARBOR, WA 98250
OLIVER MARK, BOX 4004, TWIN HILLS, AK 99576
DARLENE MARTIN, 3811 MINNESOTA DR #313, ANCHORAGE, AK 99508
MAX MARTIN, BOX 1038, DILLINGHAM, AK 99576
TIMOTHY MARTIN, BOX 1912, VALDEZ, AK 99686
WARREN MARTIN, 5415 BELLWEST DR, BELLINGHAM, WA 98226
DONALD MARTINSON, 15105 59TH PL W, EDMONDS, WA 98026
DENNIS MARTISHEV, BOX 879026, WASILLA, AK 99687
ALEXAY MARTUSHEV, BOX 1765, HOMER, AK 99603

ANDREY MARTUSHEV, BOX 3113, HOMER, AK 99603
DAVID MARTUSHEV, BOX 1765, HOMER, AK 99603
FILIP MARTUSHEV, BOX 1886, HOMER, AK 99603
JOSIPH MARTUSHEV, BOX 5, GERVAIS, OR 97026
KIRIL MARTUSHEV, BOX 1939, HOMER, AK 99603
MATTHEW MARTUSHEV, BOX 3603, HOMER, AK 99603
MIHAEL MARTUSHEV, BOX 513, MOUNT ANGEL, OR 97362
MIHAEL MARTUSHEV, BOX 374, HOMER, AK 99603
NICKOLAI MARTUSHEV, BOX 9163, SALEM, OR 97305
SERGEI MARTUSHEV, BOX 1299, HOMER, AK 99603
TANYA MARTUSHEV, BOX 2595, HOMER, AK 99603
ZENON MARTUSHEV, BOX 1011, HOMER, AK 99603
GAVIN MASLEN, BOX 463, GLENNALLEN, AK 99588
ALLEN MATHEWS, 3450 CATHEDRAL ROCK RD, MALAGA, WA 98828
JASON MATHEWS, 3327 OHIO AVE, ST LOUIS, MO 63118
STEVEN MATHIEU, 1721 MISSION RD, KODIAK, AK 99615
JAKOB MATHISEN, 11753 SUNRISE DR NE, BAINBRIDGE ISLAND, WA 98110
MIKAL MATHISEN, 11753 SUNRISE DR NE, BAINBRIDGE ISLAND, WA 98110
JOHN MATSON, BOX 49001, PORT HEIDEN, AK 99549
MELVIN MATTHEWS, BOX 675, GLENNALLEN, AK 99588
ANDY MATTSON, 11312 E HULA CT, SPOKANE VALLEY, WA 99206
C.THEODORE MATTSON, N 10794 KARNOPP RD, WAUSAUKEE, WI 54177
JERRY MATZEN, BOX 9, LONG BEACH, WA 98631
WILLIAM MAUD, 905 RICHARDSON VISTA RD #297, ANCHORAGE, AK 99501
ERIK MAUDSLIEN, 225 NE 65TH ST #403, SEATTLE, WA 98115
PAUL MAUDSLIEN, 6631 TROON LANE SE, OLYMPIA, WA 98501
FELETI MAUGATAI, 3203 NE 198TH PLACE, LAKE FOREST PARK, WA 98155
BRIAN MAVAR, 604 SAINT MARYS DR, ANACORTES, WA 98221
JOHN MAVAR, BOX 1468, ANACORTES, WA 98221
NICK MAVAR, 4909 CROATION WAY, ANACORTES, WA 98221
ROBERT MAYER, BOX 186, DILLINGHAM, AK 99576
MICHAEL MAYO, 2808 SAWMILL CREEK RD, SITKA, AK 99835
FELICIA MCAULEY, BOX 915, CRAIG, AK 99921
JUSTIN MCAULEY, 3216 ALDERWOOD AVE, BELLINGHAM, WA 98225
SEAN MCCABE, 2106 VINING DR, BELLINGHAM, WA 98226
SETH MCCALLUM, BOX 191, PETERSBURG, AK 99833
GUSTY MCCARR, BOX 5020, KOLIGANEK, AK 99576
LAWRENCE MCCONNELL, 34 LA CANADA RD, EL PRADO, NM 87529
MARK MCCUTCHEON, 595 UNIVERSITY RD, FRIDAY HARBOR, WA 98250
JOHN MCDONALD, 7710 S 106TH ST, SEATTLE, WA 98178
ROSS MCDONALD, 57889 LEE VALLEY RD, COQUILLE, OR 97423
JACK MCDOUGALL, 915 W HERON, ABERDEEN, WA 98520
MONICA MCGILL, BOX 481, DILLINGHAM, AK 99576
BRYAN MCHALE, 6413 SANDRIDGE RD, LONG BEACH, WA 98631
MONTY MCINTYRE, 585 PLEASANT BAY, BELLINGHAM, WA 98229
MARK MCKEOWN, 6237 CHARING CROSS LN #E, MIDDLETON, WI 53562
JASON MCKLINLEY, 313 W MAIN ST, STANFORD, KY 40484
ROBERT MCLEAN, BOX 251965, LOS ANGELES, CA 90025
BRYAN MCMAHAN, BOX 209, GAKONA, AK 99586
JOHNNY MCMAHAN, BOX 184, GAKONA, AK 99586
KRISTIE MCMAHON, 20145 FOREST PARK DR NE, SHORELINE, WA 98155
MIKE MCMAHON, 20145 FOREST PARK DR NE, SHORELINE, WA 98155
GREG MCMILLAN, 15 KASANDRA LN, NASELLE, WA 98638
MICHAEL MCNEIL, 41218 N GROVE RD, DEER PARK, WA 99006
DANIEL MCPHERSON, 1002 NE 112TH ST, VANCOUVER, WA 98685
STUART MCTAGGART, 420 E HOWELL ST, SEATTLE, WA 98122
JAN MEDHAUG, 18038 3RD AVE NE, SHORELINE, WA 98155
TERRY MEDJO, 4426 DRAKE LN, GRAND ISLAND, NE 68801
ALEXANDER MEDLEY, 37920 RAINBOW DR, SOLDOTNA, AK 99669
FRITZ MENISH, 1343 MARION ST, ENUMCLAW, WA 98022
SAM MERCURIO, 1298 SYLVAN RD, MONTEREY, CA 93940
JAMES MERRINER, BOX 203, GALENA, AK 99741
PHILIP MERSHON, BOX 536, COLLEGE PLACE, WA 99324
CHESTER MESAK, BOX 176, KIPNUK, AK 99614
JACOB METZGER, 2725 WILLEYS LAKE RD, CUSTER, WA 98240

SALMON FISHING LIST—DRIFT GILLNET

CAMERON MEYER, 725 SLICK ROCK CREEK RD, OTIS, OR 97368
AMBER MICHALSON, 910 PARK ST, ASHLAND, OR 97520
RUSSELL MIDGETT, 278 BEECHER DALTON RD, SYLVA, NC 28779
JOEL MIDKIFF, 51 EAST COOK PL, SHELTON, WA 98584
ALEJANDRO MIGUEL, 1701 BROADWAY #M, VANCOUVER, WA 98663
NICK MIKE, BOX 1086, KOKHANOK, AK 99606
CALEB MIKKELSEN, 1260 N RAINBOW PARK DR, WASILLA, AK 99623
GLENN MIKKELSEN, 9124 MAIN ST, EDMONDS, WA 98026
LAURA MIKKELSEN, 1260 N RAINBOW PARK DR, WASILLA, AK 99623
LEIF MIKKELSEN, 9124 MAIN ST, EDMONDS, WA 98026
ROGER MIKKELSEN, BOX 403, WRANGELL, AK 99929
TIMOTHY MIKKELSEN, 1260 N RAINBOW PARK DR, WASILLA, AK 99623
JORDAN MILLAR, 6435 N VILLARD AVE, PORTLAND, OR 97217
AARON MILLER, BOX 334, NASELLE, WA 98638
ALAN MILLER, 1567 W RIVER DR, EAGLE RIVER, AK 99577
CHRISTOPHER MILLER, BOX 20897, JUNEAU, AK 99802
MICHAEL MILLER, BOX 319, NAKNEK, AK 99633
MOLLY MILLER, BOX 2037, KODIAK, AK 99615
THOMAS MILLER, BOX 1931, KODIAK, AK 99615
TIMOTHY MILLER, 11900 CANGE ST, ANCHORAGE, AK 99516
CURTIS MILLETT, 12700 NAUTILUS CT, ANCHORAGE, AK 99515
CHARLES MINCHER, BOX 131, DILLINGHAM, AK 99576
ANTHONY MIRKOVICH, 1649 ELM ST, SAN CARLOS, CA 94070
THEODORE MISCHAIKOV, 309 HIGHLAND DR, BELLINGHAM, WA 98225
ANDREW MITBY, 2768 ST RT 105, GRAYLAND, WA 98547
ERIC MITBY, BOX 551, TOKELAND, WA 98590
ANNA MITCHELL, 9242 ASHWORTH AVE N #A203, SEATTLE, WA 98103
CHRISTOPHER MITCHELL, 2932 LYNN ST, BELLINGHAM, WA 98225
MEGAN MITCHELL, 2315 HENRY ST, BELLINGHAM, WA 98225
STEVEN MITCHELL, BOX 471, CLINTON, WA 98236
MELVIN MONSEN, BOX 4-1894, ANCHORAGE, AK 99509
JOHN MONTECUCCO, BOX 2938, VASHON, WA 98070
THOMAS MONTECUCCO, 9806 N AUSTIN LN, SPOKANE, WA 99208
RICHARD MOODY, BOX 876351, WASILLA, AK 99687
EVERETT MOORCROFT, BOX 44, KING SALMON, AK 99613
HARRY MOORE, BOX 246, TOGIAK, AK 99678
HARRY MOORE, BOX 10, PALMER, AK 99645
JEHRA MOORE, 204 PUGET ST, SEDRO WOOLLEY, WA 98284
LOULARE MOORE, BOX 4063, TWIN HILLS, AK 99576
ROSELEEN MOORE, 5140 KACHEMAK DR, HOMER, AK 99603
JOSEPH MORAN, 930 13TH ST, BELLINGHAM, WA 98225
DOUGLAS MORGAN, 16339 HEADLANDS CIR, ANCHORAGE, AK 99516
GEOFFREY MORGAN, BOX 191072, ANCHORAGE, AK 99519
MICHAEL MORGAN, BOX 754, LANGLEY, WA 98260
TREVOR MORGAN, BOX 503, LANGLEY, WA 98260
RICHARD MORTON, BOX 1418, MUKILTEO, WA 98275
KELLY MOSELER, BOX 12, LANGLEY, WA 98260
CHARLES MOSES, BOX 37125, TOKSOOK BAY, AK 99637
ALEX MOST, 1815 MCGILVRA BLVD, SEATTLE, WA 98122
CHARLES MOST, BOX 325, WESTPORT, WA 98595
DYLAN MOST, BOX 325, WESTPORT, WA 98595
PEGGY MOST, 3812 E MCGRAW ST, SEATTLE, WA 98112
PETER MOST, 91 MAIN ST, EGEGIK, AK 99579
ANNA MOUNSEY, BOX 746, SNOQUAMIE, WA 98065
JERRY MUCHA, BOX 90793, ANCHORAGE, AK 99509
BRENDAN MULHOLLAND, 4978 HIGHLAND DR, BLAINE, WA 98230
MARTIN MULHOLLAND, 4978 HIGHLAND DR, BLAINE, WA 98230
PATRICK MULHOLLAND, 2144 S WALNUT ST #13, BOULDER, CO 80302
BRYAN MULLEN, 36508 SE 25TH ST, FALL CITY, WA 98024
CHRISTOPHER MULLEN, 35 FREMONT ST, MACHIAS, ME 4654
FREDERIK MUNRO, BOX 1971, HOMER, AK 99603
MARK MUNRO, BOX 1971, HOMER, AK 99603
THOREY MUNRO, BOX 1260, HOMER, AK 99603
TANNOR.T.J MUNROE, 3823 CYCLONE DR, BELLINGHAM, WA 98225
THOMAS MUNROE, 3823 CYCLONE DR, BELLINGHAM, WA 98225
GREGORY MUNSON, 16707 57TH AVE SE, SNOHOMISH, WA 98296

ANDREA MURPHY, 354 DIANE LN, SOLDOTNA, AK 99669
RICHARD MURPHY, BOX 732, DILLINGHAM, AK 99576
GREGORY MUSTOLA, 80190 ALSTON MAYGER RD, CLATSKANIE, OR 97016
PAUL MUTCH, 200 W 34TH AVE PMB #981, ANCHORAGE, AK 99503
DAVID MUTE, BOX 2267, BETHEL, AK 99559
WILLIE MUTE, BOX 5101, KONGIGANAK, AK 99545
DALE MYERS, BOX 433, KING SALMON, AK 99613
JAMES MYERS, BOX 197, NAKNEK, AK 99633
JEFFERY MYERS, 2950 W TELEQUANA DR, WASILLA, AK 99623
ANECIA NANALOOK, BOX 184, TOGIAK, AK 99678
MAURICE NANALOOK, BOX 2763, BETHEL, AK 99559
PETER NANALOOK, BOX 95, MANOKOTAK, AK 99628
GLEN NASH, 824 SUNDOWN LN, CAMANO ISLAND, WA 98282
JAMES NASH, 22448 BULSON RD, MOUNT VERNON, WA 98274
NECIA NASH, 22448 BULSON RD, MOUNT VERNON, WA 98274
PATRICK NASH, 193 SALMONBERRY LN, FRIDAY HARBOR, WA 98250
PETER NASH, 1545 NW 57TH ST #630, SEATTLE, WA 98107
ANDREW NASON, BOX 57, LOPEZ ISLAND, WA 98261
MARK NAUMANN, BOX 1635, MOAB, UT 84532
MICHAEL NEESE, BOX 2947, HOMER, AK 99603
ROBERT NEHUS, 210 W BAYVIEW, HOMER, AK 99603
ZACHARY NEHUS, BOX 1334, UNALASKA, AK 99685
JACK NELSEN, BOX 113, ANGLE INLET, MN 56711
THOMAS NELSEN, 8355 NW WILDCAT LAKE RD, BREMERTON, WA 98312
HERMAN NELSON, BOX 5005, KOLIGANEK, AK 99576
PARRY NELSON, BOX 92, KODIAK, AK 99615
WILLIAM NELSON, BOX 33, EKWOK, AK 99580
RANDALL NETTLES, BOX 551, CATHLAMET, WA 98612
GIOVANNI NEVOLOSO, 1514 KIMBALL AVE, SEASIDE, CA 93955
BRADLEY NEWELL, 2925 ST CLAIR ST, BELLINGHAM, WA 98226
FOREST NEWELL, 421 AUDUBON BLVD, SEVERANCE, CO 80550
BRIAN NEWMAN, BOX 893, PETERSBURG, AK 99833
DAVID NEWSON, 217 141ST AVE NE, BELLEVUE, WA 98007
GARY NICHOLAI, BOX 87, TOGIAK, AK 99678
BRANDON NICHOLSON, 525 S BEGICH DR, WASILLA, AK 99654
HANS NICHOLSON, 5301 E SHENNUM DR, WASILLA, AK 99654
MARK NICHOLSON, 2106 STOCKDALE CIR, ANCHORAGE, AK 99515
SHERISE NICHOLSON, 9499 BRAYTON DR #129, ANCHORAGE, AK 99507
WILLIAM NICHOLSON, 14439 TERRACE LN #A, EAGLE RIVER, AK 99577
LLOYD NICK, BOX 252, TOGIAK, AK 99678
FRANK NICKOLAI, BOX 75, EKWOK, AK 99580
DONALD NIELSEN, BOX 70151, SOUTH NAKNEK, AK 99670
GARITH NIELSEN, BOX 1089, KOKHANOK, AK 99606
PHILIP NIENHUIS, 3095 N HUNT RD, OAK HARBOR, WA 98277
TAYLOR NIENHUIS, 3095 N HUNT RD, OAK HARBOR, WA 98277
MICHAEL NILSEN, BOX 2069, PETERSBURG, AK 99833
FRANKLIN NISSEN, 250 E LAKE ELBERT DR NE, WINTER HAVEN, FL 33881
BRYCE NIVER, 955 LOCH NESS CT, WASILLA, AK 99654
MARK NIVER, 955 LOCHNESS CT, WASILLA, AK 99654
SCOT NIVER, BOX 2975, PALMER, AK 99645
DANIEL NOLAN, 6001 S HALLIE DR, WASILLA, AK 99623
SAM NOLAN, 9454 HERBERT PL, JUNEAU, AK 99801
BARRY NORTHCUTT, 17530 DUNBAR RD, MOUNT VERNON, WA 98273
ERIK NOSTE, 20825 BULSON RD, MOUNT VERNON, WA 98274
JOHN NOSTE, 121 WOODGROVE LN, CAMANO ISLAND, WA 98282
KURTIS NOSTE, 121 WOODGROVE LN, CAMANO ISLAND, WA 98292
MARK NOSTE, 311 MARINE DR, COUPEVILLE, WA 98239
PAUL NOSTE, 14849 VALLEY VIEW DR, MOUNT VERNON, WA 98273
TODD NOSTE, 2409 HUNTINGTOWNE FARMS LN, CHARLOTTE, NC 28210
STEIN NYHAMMER, 18504 RIDGEFIELD RD NW, SHORELINE, WA 98177
DOREEN NYSTROM, 23988 N WESTVIEW RD, MOUNT VERNON, WA 98274
KELLY OBLAD, 267 OXBOW RD, RAYMOND, WA 98577
ALLISON OBRIEN, BOX 1331, DILLINGHAM, AK 99576
DAVID OBRIEN, 3700 PUFFIN DR, KODIAK, AK 99615
MARCQUES OCONNELL, BOX 331, DILLINGHAM, AK 99576
MATHIAS OCONNELL, BOX 331, DILLINGHAM, AK 99576

SALMON FISHING LIST—DRIFT GILLNET

SOPHIE OCONNELL, BOX 331, DILLINGHAM, AK 99576
ALEX OCZKEWICZ, 18543 VALENTINE RD, MT VERNON, WA 98273
EDWARD OCZKEWICZ, 18268 VALENTINE RD, MOUNT VERNON, WA 98273
MILES OCZKEWICZ, 18268 VALENTINE RD, MOUNT VERNON, WA 98273
JOSEPH ODONNOGHUE, 1080 SGT CREEK RD, KODIAK, AK 99615
BRUCE OGREN, BOX 214, SOUTH BEND, WA 98586
ERIC OHLSEN, 3353 LAKEWOOD AVE S, SEATTLE, WA 98144
KENNETH OLDHAM, 3650 LAKE OTIS PKWY #102, ANCHORAGE, AK 99508
ANDERS OLIN, BOX 1634, MUKILTEO, WA 98275
JON OLSEN, 365 UTSALADY ROAD, CAMANO ISLAND, WA 98282
MARVIN OLSEN, BOX 133, EGEGIK, AK 99579
THOMAS OLSEN, BOX 856, DILLINGHAM, AK 99576
DANNY OLSON, 206 66TH AVE CT E, FIFE, WA 98424
DENNIS OLSON, BOX 537, DILLINGHAM, AK 99576
ERIC OLSON, 10741 LULIAD CIR, ANCHORAGE, AK 99507
HJALMAR OLSON, 17410 LULIAD CIR, ANCHORAGE, AK 99501
LEONARD OLSON, 900 W 5TH AVE #525, ANCHORAGE, AK 99501
ROBERT OLSON, 1647 VIEW HAVEN DR, OAK HARBOR, WA 98277
RUDOLPH OLSON, BOX 547, DILLINGHAM, AK 99576
HENRY OLYMPIC, BOX 35, ILIAMNA, AK 99606
KARL OMAN, BOX 1494, LONG BEACH, WA 98631
PATRICK ONEILL, BOX 1095, SOLDOTNA, AK 99669
MARK ORAVETZ, 100 SUNLAND DR, SEQUIM, WA 98382
TERRY OSTLING, 196 JACOBSON RD #33, CATHLAMET, WA 98612
JAMES OSTROM, 22018 N SADDLE MOUNTAIN LN, COLBERT, WA 99005
TODD OVERBY, BOX 304, LAKEBAY, WA 98349
LYNIQUE OVESON, 71849 DAUGHERTY LP, WALLOWA, OR 97885
DAVID OWENS, BOX 1853, PETERSBURG, AK 99833
BRYCIN PACHECO, BOX 113, NAKNEK, AK 99633
RICHARD PALMBY, 124 NORTH SHORE RD, BELLINGHAM, WA 98229
SALVATORE PAPETTI, BOX T, BELLINGHAM, WA 98227
SAVIOR PAPETTI, BOX 330203, SAN FRANCISCO, CA 94133
FABRIZIO PAPPALARDO, 283 WATSON ST APT D, MONTEREY, CA 93940
JAMES PARKER, BOX 12176, EVERETT, WA 98206
KRISTIN PARKER, 2830 ARBORVIEW DR #8, TRAVERSE CITY, MI 49685
DENNIS PARSONS, BOX 204, CRAIG, AK 99921
MICHAEL PATE, BOX 257, HOMER, AK 99603
ERIC PATTON, 48 STEPHENS RD, ELMA, WA 98541
DAN PAUK, BOX 82, MANOKOTAK, AK 99628
TEODORO PAUK, BOX 282, TOGIAK, AK 99678
HERMAN PAUL, BOX 166, TOGIAK, AK 99678
JOE PAUL, BOX 166, KIPNUK, AK 99614
TIMMY PAVELLA, BOX 38, NEW STUYAHOK, AK 99636
ANTHONY PAVONE, 244 GRANT ST, MARINA, CA 93933
JARED PAYNE, 42 TARTE RD, FRIDAY HARBOR, WA 98250
DREW PEARSON, 75 HYLAND STRINGER RD, RAYMOND, WA 98577
JAY PEARSON, 75 HYLAND STRINGER RD, RAYMOND, WA 98577
JON PEARSON, 38 HYLAND STRINGER RD, RAYMOND, WA 98577
DAVID PEDERSEN, 1150 S COLONY WAY #3 250, PALMER, AK 99645
MAXWELL PEELER, BOX 761, PETERSBURG, AK 99833
ANDREW PEITSCH, 43234 PENTTILA LN, ASTORIA, OR 97103
JUAN.CARLOS PENALOZA, 3155 SPRUCE CAPE RD, KODIAK, AK 99615
MICHAEL PENNYLEGION, 6364 WOODLYN RD, FERNDALE, WA 98428
DEAN PEPER, 3408 ROCKEFELLER AVE, EVERETT, WA 98201
BACCI PERATA, BOX 372, HONAVNAV, HI 96726
PAUL PEREZ, 1502 CRESTLINE DR, SANTA BARBARA, CA 93105
KYLE PETERS, BOX 144, NAKNEK, AK 99633
ANDERS PETERSON, 8302 FREDERICK PL, EDMONDS, WA 98026
ARTHUR PETERSON, BOX 382, NAKNEK, AK 99633
GREG PETERSON, 8302 FREDERICK PL, EDMONDS, WA 98026
LUKE PETERSON, 9208 BANK RD, VASHON, WA 98070
MARK PETERSON, 14250 130TH AVE NE, KIRKLAND, WA 98034
SIDNEY PETERSON, 2840 KITTITAS HWY, ELLENSBURG, WA 98926
ERIC PETIT, BOX 524, SOUTH BEND, WA 98586
JERRY PETLA, BOX 24, EKWOK, AK 99580

JIMMIE PETLA, BOX 8126, NIKISKI, AK 99635
OLEANNA PETLA, BOX 1114, DILLINGHAM, AK 99576
TANNER PETRY, 4792 PINEWOOD CIR, LANGLEY, WA 98260
KARL PETTERSEN, 1424 NW 201ST NW, SHORELINE, WA 98177
TRISTAN PETTIGREW, BOX 5772, KETCHUM, ID 83340
MINH PHAM, 706 S 104TH ST, SEATTLE, WA 98168
RUSSELL PHELPS, BOX 135, NAKNEK, AK 99633
ERIC PHILLIP, BOX 5055, KONGIGANAK, AK 99545
ALBERT PHILLIPS, 80610 WAGON WHEEL LP, IRRIGON, OR 97844
JOHN PHILLIPS, BOX 3650, HAILEY, ID 83333
WILLIAM PHILLIPS, 19633 MARINE VIEW DR SW, NORMONDY PARK, WA 98166
KENNETH PHILPOTT, 2526 LAKERIDGE DR, FERNDALE, WA 98248
ABRAM PIATKOFF, 316 BRANDT AVE N, FOSSTON, MN 56542
CHRIS PIATT, 4314 N AIRFIELD ST, WASILLA, AK 99654
MATTHEW PIATT, 4150 E PALMDALE DR, WASILLA, AK 99654
MICHAEL PIATT, 4585 SARATOGA AVE, SAN DIEGO, CA 92107
JOSEPH PICHA, 8401 NE KOURA RD, BAINBRIDGE ISLAND, WA 98110
GUY PIERCEY, 720 CEDAR ST, EDMONDS, WA 98020
JOSHUA PIERSON, 48 MAIN ST, SOTHBOROUGH, MA 1772
FRED PIKE, BOX 5, NAKNEK, AK 99633
JEFFERY PIKE, 1020 11TH ST #10, BELLINGHAM, WA 98227
CHRISTOPHER PILOSSOPH, BOX 19472, SEATTLE, WA 98109
ANDREW PITTARD, BOX 233, CANNON BEACH, OR 97110
JUSTIN PLEIER, 5675 E MOOSE ST, WASILLA, AK 99654
JAMES PLYMIRE, BOX 1183, HOMER, AK 99603
HTOO.HTOO PO, 4685 PINEWOOD CIR, LANGLEY, WA 98260
JAMES POLLACK, BOX 3726, HOMER, AK 99603
MATTHEW POLLACK, BOX 3726, HOMER, AK 99603
CHRISTOPHER POPA, 2268 AQUA HILL RD, FALLBROOK, CA 92028
SILVIA POPA, 14245 HANCOCK DR, ANCHORAGE, AK 99515
VICTOR POPA, 2268 AQUA HILL RD, FALLBROOK, CA 92028
DARRYL POPE, 3106 EDWARDS ST, BELLINGHAM, WA 98229
MARK PRATER, 24 ROY ST #296, SEATTLE, WA 98109
TYLER PRICE, 308 E BREWSTER, FAIRFIELD, WA 99012
JOSEPH PRINCEN, 36005 6TH AVE SW, FEDERAL WAY, WA 98023
DAVE PRITCHARD, 10790 PETER ANDERSON RD, BURLINGTON, WA 98233
JAMES PRUITT, BOX 1791, KODIAK, AK 99615
TOMAS PSTROSS, BOX 2614, CORDOVA, AK 99574
DONALD PULLEY, 10112 226TH AVE CT E, BUCKLEY, WA 98321
EDWARD PULLEY, 11310 202ND AVE E, BONNEY LAKE, WA 98391
MARC PULLEY, 1945 HARDING ST, ENUMCLAW, WA 98022
DAVID QUASHNICK, 92296 WILLOW RD, ASTORIA, OR 97103
DAVID QUASHNICK, 37574 GRIMSTAD LN, ASTORIA, OR 97103
JOSEPH QUASHNICK, 35277 LITTLE WALLUSKI LANE, ASTORIA, OR 99649
RICHARD QUASHNICK, 548 SR 401, NASELLE, WA 98638
JEFFREY QUINN, 225 N 160TH ST, SHORELINE, WA 98133
DAVID RAMIREZ, 4810 WOODSMAN LP, PLACERVILLE, CA 95667
JAMISON RAMSEY, BOX 9631, KETCHIKAN, AK 99901
JON.KEVIN RASAR, 17684 ALLEN RD, BOW, WA 98232
KARL RASMUSSEN, 12332 19TH AVE SE, EVERETT, WA 98208
ROY RASMUSSEN, 12332 19TH AVE SE, EVERETT, WA 98208
RYAN RASMUSSEN, 4496 RURAL AVE, BELLINGHAM, WA 98225
TYLER RASMUSSEN, BOX 565, VERDI, NV 89439
JOHN RATCLIFFE, 2114 141ST PL NE, MARYSVILLE, WA 98271
RAIU.KAI RAYMOND, 3353 LAKEWOOD AVE S, SEATTLE, WA 98144
TYONE RAYMOND, BOX 2331, VASHON, WA 98070
MICHELLE REAKOFF, BOX 68, HOMER, AK 99603
STEVEN RECTOR, 14623 N 154TH LN, SUPRISE, AZ 85379
JUSTIN REED, 1003 COLE AVE, SHOHOMISH, WA 98290
CHAD REEL, 3001 E KIBBY DR, WASILLA, AK 99654
SHAUN REEL, 1405 W BALLARD, SPOKANE, WA 99208
ANDREAS REFVIK, 19 CHANNEL CAY RD, KEY LARGO, FL 33037
OLAV REFVIK, 19 CHANNEL CAY RD, KEY LARGO, FL 33037
STEFFEN REFVIK, 19 CHANNEL CAY RD, KEY LARGO, FL 33037
CLINT REIGH, BOX 965, DILLINGHAM, AK 99576

SALMON FISHING LIST—DRIFT GILLNET

MICHAEL REITZ, BOX 10756, FAIRBANKS, AK 99710
ANTHONY RESETARITS, 111 E POTTER #1, ANCHORAGE, AK 99518
CHRISTIAN RESETARITS, 401 ATLANTIS AVE, ANCHORAGE, AK 99518
DANIEL RESETARITS, 199 ARGENT WAY, BLUFFTON, SC 29909
DOUGLAS RESETARITS, BOX 3063, HOMER, AK 99603
JOSEPH RESETARITS, 611 W 32ND AVE APT 100, ANCHORAGE, AK 99503
MELISSA RESETARITS, BOX 3063, HOMER, AK 99603
PETER RESETARITS, 605 CHURCHILL DOWNS DR, ABERDEEN, NC 28315
ALIZAR REUTOV, 1295 PRAIRIE CLOVER AVE NE, KEIZER, OR 97303
AVTANOM REUTOV, BOX 1056, HOMER, AK 99603
DANIEL REUTOV, BOX 466, HOMER, AK 99603
DAVID REUTOV, BOX 458, HOMER, AK 99603
EVSEVY REUTOV, BOX 3490, HOMER, AK 99603
JULIAN REUTOV, BOX 1887, HOMER, AK 99603
KONSTONTIN REUTOV, BOX 793, HOMER, AK 99603
MARK REUTOV, BOX 3322, HOMER, AK 99603
MIHEY REUTOV, BOX 2063, HOMER, AK 99603
PHILIP REUTOV, BOX 4041, HOMER, AK 99603
TRIFILYI REUTOV, BOX 793, HOMER, AK 99603
VAVIL REUTOV, BOX 809, HOMER, AK 99603
WLAS REUTOV, BOX 4041, HOMER, AK 99603
ZAHAR REUTOV, BOX 3005, HOMER, AK 99603
THOMAS REYNOLDS, BOX 246, CORTEZ, FL 34215
CHRISTOPHER RHOADS, 1436 CANE CREEK DR, GARNER, NC 27529
CODY RICE, BOX 1315, GIRDWOOD, AK 99587
VICTOR RICHARTE, 13024 SE 309TH PL, AUBURN, WA 98092
CALVIN RIDDLE, BOX 203, NAKNEK, AK 99633
KYLE RIDLEY, 18717 OLYMPIC VIEW DR, EDMONDS, WA 98020
CARMEN RIEDERER, 22928 SE 406TH ST, ENUMCLAW, WA 98022
DWIGHT RIEDERER, 22928 SE 406TH ST, ENUMCLAW, WA 98022
JAMES RIGGLE, 5301 LEARY AVE NW, SEATTLE, WA 98107
TRISTAN RIGGLE, 5301 LEARY AVE NW, SEATTLE, WA 98107
WALTER RILEY, 10320 COMPASS CIR, ANCHORAGE, AK 99515
DINO RINAUDO, 20244 PALOU DR, SALINAS, CA 93908
ALBERT RING, BOX 74, NAKNEK, AK 99633
KJELL RISDAL, 17274 SCAUP DR, BEND, OR 97707
BRAD ROBERTS, 562 S 100 W, AMERICAN FORK, UT 84003
JACOB ROBERTSON, 690 S. KINK GOOSE BAY #272, WASILLA, AK 99654
JOSEPH ROBERTSON, 690 S. KINK GOOSE BAY RD #272, WASILLA, AK 99654
RALPH ROBERTSON, 35248 LEIGH LN, ASTORIA, OR 97103
RANDALL ROBERTSON, BOX 62, NAKNEK, AK 99633
NORMAN ROCKNESS, 8526 WARREN DR NW, GIG HARBOR, WA 98335
TOR ROCKNESS, 1437 NE EUCLID AVE, PORTLAND, OR 97213
HANS RODVIK, 8301 BERRY PATCH DR, ANCHORAGE, AK 99502
HELEN ROE, 616 ORVIS AVE, SAN JOSE, CA 95112
ALBERT ROGOTZKE, 2631 155TH ST, CHARLES CITY, IA 50616
DAVID ROGOTZKE, 3094 WHITESIDE RD, DULUTH, MN 55804
JAY ROGOTZKE, 27090 320TH ST, SLEEPY EYE, MN 56085
ROGER ROGOTZKE, 27090 320TH ST, SLEEPY EYE, MN 56085
TOM ROGOTZKE, 1141 BLACKBIRD DR SW, HUTCHINSON, MN 55350
JOHN ROHR, BOX 2621, HOMER, AK 99603
ANDREW ROSAS, 511 SCHWARTZ RD, NORDLAND, WA 98358
WILLIAM ROSS, BOX 153, EGEGIK, AK 99579
FARLEY ROSSITER, 1262 BROADWAY #1A, BROOKLYN, NY 11221
MICHAEL ROTHAUS, 18224 SUNSET WAY, EDMONDS, WA 98026
MATTHEW RUDLOFF, 37 JARRETT ST, ASHEVILLE, NC 28806
JUDITH RUNYON, BOX 874781, WASILLA, AK 99687
RYDER RUOSS, BOX 1572, KODIAK, AK 99615
PARKER RUSH, 108 N 55TH ST, SEATTLE, WA 98103
CAMERON RUSSELL, 10403 122ND AVE KPN, GIG HARBOR, WA 98329
JARED RUSSELL, 3105 LAURELWOOD AVE, BELLINGHAM, WA 98225
MAKENZIE RUSSELL, BOX 524, SOUTH BEND, WA 98586
ANTHONY RUSSO, BOX 502, MOSS LANDING, CA 95039
JOSEPH RUSSO, 48 SAN PEDRO ST, SALINAS, CA 93901
LENNY RUSSO, 6 FLEETWOOD DR, GLOUCESTER, MA 1930
SALVATORE RUSSO, 3755 ACOCADO BLVD #354, LA MESA, CA 91941

RANDY RUZICH, 301 30TH ST STE B, ANACORTES, WA 98221
TIMOTHY S.M.CHRISTENSEN, 413 HAINES AVE, FAIRBANKS, AK 99701
MIKE SAARHEIM, 36608 VALLEY VISTA LN, ASTORIA, OR 97103
ERICK SABO, 17920 W NARRAMORE RD, GOODYEAR, AZ 85338
ROY SADLER, 359 S TOUTLE RD, TOUTLE, WA 98649
KEVIN SAIN, 413 FILLMORE, HOQUIAM, WA 98550
MADELEINE SALISBURY, 209 DUNES ST #4, MORROW BAY, CA 93442
DANIEL SALMON, BOX 4003, IGIUGIG, AK 99613
JEREMY SALMON, BOX 4003, IGIUGIG, AK 99613
HAROLD SAMUELSEN, BOX 412, DILLINGHAM, AK 99576
HECTOR SANCHEZ, 1713 MILL AVE, BELLINGHAM, WA 98225
WILLIAM SANCHEZ, BOX 256, TOGIAK, AK 99678
ERIC SANDVIG, 2460 GOSHEN RD, BELLINGHAM, WA 98226
RANDALL SANDVIK, 901 SHAW RD E, PUYALLUP, WA 98372
MACLEAN SATHER, 703.5 NORTH FOREST ST, BELLINGHAM, WA 98225
MICHAEL SATHER, 703 PRIEST POINT RD N W, TULALIP, WA 98271
RYAN SAVO, BOX 382, DILLINGHAM, AK 99576
JUSTIN SAWYER, 22 S MAUGHAN RIVER RD, WINTHROP, WA 98862
KONRAD SCHAAD, 53200 N MCNEIL PT, HOMER, AK 99603
MIRO SCHAAD, 53200 N MCNEIL PT, HOMER, AK 99603
SIMON SCHAAD, 624 YARROW CIR, FORT COLLINS, CO 80524
RYAN SCHAFF, 7401 N CRESTLINE, SPOKANE, WA 99217
PETER SCHELL, 18218 PALATINE, SHORELINE, WA 98133
CAMERON SCHILLE, 20044 BAGLEY DR N APT Y307, SHORELINE, WA 98133
MICHAEL SCHILLE, 6244 WINDFALL RD, CLINTON, WA 98236
COLE SCHLAGEL, BOX 714, DILLINGHAM, AK 99576
JEAN SCHLOSSER, 6820 TALL SPRUCE DR, ANCHORAGE, AK 99502
JORG SCHMEISSER, BOX 1791, KODIAK, AK 99615
EVERT SCHMELZENBACH, 92 S LANCASTER DR, NAMPA, ID 83651
LEEANN SCHMELZENBACH, 92 LANCASTER DR, NAMPA, ID 83651
DYLAN SCHOLS, 24607 W RED ROBIN DR, WITTMANN, AZ 85361
MICHAEL SCHOLS, 24607 W RED ROBIN DR, WITTMANN, AZ 85361
JASON SCHONBERG, BOX 1167, STANWOOD, WA 98292
KRISTIAN SCHONBERG, BOX 866, ALLYN, WA 98524
HUGH SCHROEDER, BOX 102, DILLINGHAM, AK 99576
ROSCOE SCHROEDER, 16533 OLD GLENN HWY #1, CHUGIAK, AK 99567
JACKSON SCHROYER, 3619 JULIA AVE, BELLINGHAM, WA 98229
RICHARD SCHUERGER, BOX 23143, KETCHIKAN, AK 99901
LUKE SCHWANTES, 41 E GREEN VALLEY RD, OAK HARBOR, WA 98277
MARK SCHWANTES, BOX 1387, DILLINGHAM, AK 99576
DYLAN SCOTT, 3266 Y ROAD, BELLINGHAM, WA 98226
JEFFREY SCOTT, 616 MOE RD, CAMANO ISLAND, WA 98282
ERIC SEABERG, 15616 VIRGINIA PT RD, POULSBO, WA 98370
AARON SEAMAN, 1618 PAYNES POINT RD, NEENAH, WI 54956
ALAN SEE, BOX 99, NASELLE, WA 98638
ERIC SEE, BOX 58, ROSBURG, WA 98643
GABRIEL SEE, BOX 99, NASELLE, WA 98638
ROBERT SEGAL, BOX 583, KING SALMON, AK 99613
ROBERT SEID, 3036 LANDIS ST, SAN DIEGO, CA 92104
BOYD SELANOFF, 2668 SW 41ST ST, GRESHAM, OR 97080
QUINN SELITSCH, 645 G ST #100-681, ANCHORAGE, AK 99501
DAMIAN SEREBREKOFF, BOX 4052, HOMER, AK 99603
NIKITA SEREBREKOFF, BOX 1126, HOMER, AK 99603
ZOSIMA SEREBREKOFF, BOX 753, HOMER, AK 99603
CAMERON SEVERSON, BOX 2118, PETERSBURG, AK 99833
MITCHELL SEYBERT, 700 COHO WAY, PORT HEIDEN, AK 99549
SHILOH SEYMOUR, 201 PEACH TREE LN, SHELBYVILLE, KY 40065
NIKITA SHARABARIN, 6363 S ZIMMERMAN RD, AURORA, OR 97002
DAVID SHARP, 1212 RAYMOND ST, BELLINGHAM, WA 98229
MICKEY SHARP, BOX 4013, TWIN HILLS, AK 99576
NOAH SHARP, 1212 RAYMOND ST, BELLINGHAM, WA 98229
ARNOLD SHAVINGS, 3922 SCENIC VIEW DR, ANCHORAGE, AK 99504
GRANT SHAW, 3800 NE 78TH AVE, PORTLAND, OR 97213
CORINNA SHERMAN, 12650 BLAKELY PLACE NW, SEATTLE, WA 98117
JARED SHERMAN, 39126 WAHL ST, STERLING, AK 99672
KENT SHERMAN, 39126 WAHL ST, STERLING, AK 99672

SALMON FISHING LIST—DRIFT GILLNET

BRENDAN SHERRER, 1791 POLNELL RD, OAK HARBOR, WA 98277

BENJAMIN SHERRETT.TEMPLE, 6415 SW JAGUAR AVE, REDMOND, OR 97756

JEFFREY SHOSTAD, 36008 49TH AVE S, AUBURN, WA 98001

FRANK SHUGHART, 301 E TORRANCE LN, OAK HARBOR, WA 98277

BRYAN SIFSOF, BOX 1465, DILLINGHAM, AK 99576

JANE SIFSOF, BOX 815, DILLINGHAM, AK 99576

LINDSEY SIFSOF, BOX 1250, DILLINGHAM, AK 99576

VICTOR SIFSOF, BOX 815, DILLINGHAM, AK 99576

DAVID SIMPSON, 5409 SULLIVAN RD, TALLAHASSEE, FL 32310

HARRY SINZ, BOX 110985, ANCHORAGE, AK 99511

FRANCIS SIPARY, BOX 37102, TOKSOOK BAY, AK 99637

JENNIFER SKARADA, BOX 213, DILLINGHAM, AK 99576

BRUCE SKOLNICK, 145 S BOUNDARY ST, SOLDOTNA, AK 99669

MARTIN SKRIVANICH, 3911 VERNHARDSON, GIG HARBOR, WA 98332

ERIC SLOTTEN, BOX 3783, HAILEY, ID 83333

NEAL SLOTVIG, 1358 N 150TH, SHORELINE, WA 98133

STANLEY SMALL, BOX 1536, DILLINGHAM, AK 99576

SUN SMALL, BOX 1536, DILLINGHAM, AK 99576

JOHN SMEATON, BOX 895, DILLINGHAM, AK 99576

MARTIN SMEATON, BOX 917, DILLINGHAM, AK 99576

NICK SMEATON, BOX 1205, DILLINGHAM, AK 99576

CAROLYN SMITH, BOX 116, ALEKNAGIK, AK 99555

CONNOR SMITH, 2750 STERLING HWY, HOMER, AK 99603

DANIEL SMITH, 252 NE AZALEA DRIVE, CORVALLIS, OR 97330

DAVID SMITH, BOX 1790, DILLINGHAM, AK 99576

DELBERT SMITH, 316 SE PIONEER WAY #560, OAK HARBOR, WA 98277

LUKE SMITH, 2923 LILY ST #A, ANCHORAGE, AK 99508

MARK SMITH, 11200 JEROME ST, ANCHORAGE, AK 99516

RORY SMITH, 310 NARRAGANSETT ST NE, PALM BAY, FL 32907

ROY SMITH, BOX 20481, JUNEAU, AK 99802

STEVE SMITH, 758 6TH, ASTORIA, OR 97103

JACK SNYDER, BOX 4021, TWIN HILLS, AK 99576

MICHAEL SODERLUND, BOX 2269, MAPLE FALLS, WA 98266

CARLEY SOLBERG, 2517 IRON ST, BELLINGHAM, WA 98225

LANGE SOLBERG, 2517 IRON ST, BELLINGHAM, WA 98225

MYRON SOLLID, BOX 544, STANWOOD, WA 98292

DAVID SOMERVILLE, BOX 163, PETERSBURG, AK 99833

JEFFERY SONGSTAD, 4804 DARLINGTON LN, EVERETT, WA 98204

CHAD SORENSON, 354 DIANE LN, SOLDOTNA, AK 99669

GIUSEPPE SPADARO, 50 VIA ENCINA, MONTEREY, CA 93940

JOHN SPANGLER, 3111 S 273RD ST, AUBURN, WA 98001

MARTIN SPEAK, 15439 85TH AVE NE, KENMORE, WA 98028

KARL SPIELMAN, 7104 GREENWOOD AVE N, SEATTLE, WA 98103

DOMINIC SPINALE, 4445 ROCK ISLAND DR, ANTIOCH, CA 94509

LARRY SPRY, BOX 203, GRAND PORTAGE, MN 55605

VINCENT STACEY, 2716 TAYLOR AVE, LONGVIEW, WA 98632

LOUIS STADEM, 250 E FIREWEED AVE, PALMER, AK 99645

NORMAN STADEM, 1826 E 26TH AVE, ANCHORAGE, AK 99508

TIMOTHY STAGE, BOX 1970, HOMER, AK 99603

LESLIE STAMBAUGH, BOX 604, NAKNEK, AK 99633

LOWELL STAMBAUGH, 47 HUNGRY HARBOR LN, NASELLE, WA 98638

BEN STAMMERJOHAN, BOX 2127, KINGSTON, WA 98346

BERT STAMMERJOHAN, BOX 762, CORDOVA, AK 99574

DUSTIN STARR, BOX 126, LONG BEACH, WA 98631

TERRY STEBEN, 1596 W SEQUIM BAY RD, SEQUIM, WA 98382

COLE STEFFENS, 4206 79TH PL NW, TULALIP, WA 98271

DAVID STEINBRUECK, 251 LIMES RD, LOPEZ ISLAND, WA 98261

KEITH STEINKE, 312 NE 88TH, SEATTLE, WA 98115

LUTHER STENBERG, 2422 FRIENDLY GROVE RD NE, OLYMPIA, WA 98506

DUANE STENSLAND, 817 NW 107TH ST, SEATTLE, WA 98177

ERICK STEVENS, 5762 STORR RD, FERNDALE, WA 98248

GEOFFREY STEVENS, 11 BEACH LN SW, LAKEWOOD, WA 98498

MARTIN STEVENS, 15823 WILDAIRE DR SE, YELM, WA 98597

WYATT STEVENS, 15823 WILDAIRE DR SE, YELM, WA 98597

KELLY STIER, BOX 449, NAKNEK, AK 99633

KENYON STIER, 7021 DRIFTWOOD ST, ANCHORAGE, AK 99518

ROBB STILNOVICH, 1012 CORONA DR, FIRCREST, WA 98466

VINCE STONE, 2707 GRAND AVE, EVERETT, WA 98201

ERIC STRAIN, 1984 S VIEW ST, SALT LAKE CITY, UT 84105

AUBERIN STRICKLAND, 5992 N NODDING AVE, PALMER, AK 99645

AUSTIN STRICKLAND, BOX 292, PETERSBURG, AK 99833

DUNEDIN STRICKLAND, 5992 N NODDING AVE, PALMER, AK 99645

LUKAS STRICKLAND, 5992 N NODDING AVE, PALMER, AK 99645

CLINTON STRONG, BOX 571, PAHALA, HI 96777

TUIE STRONG, BOX 513, PAHALA, HI 96777

CASEY STROOSMA, 18273 W BIG LAKE BLVD, MOUNT VERNON, WA 98274

ERWIN STROOSMA, 1226 S 10TH ST, MOUNT VERNON, WA 98274

HENRY STRUB, BOX 493, DILLINGHAM, AK 99576

ROBERT STRUB, BOX 1696, TONASKET, WA 98855

CHAD STUDEBAKER, 877 PETERSON RD, BURLINGTON, WA 98233

ABRAHAM SULLIVAN, 17710 TEKLANIKA DR, EAGLE RIVER, AK 99577

KURT SVASAND, 15812 71ST AVE NE, KENMORE, WA 98028

ADAM SVENSEN, BOX 716, ASTORIA, OR 97103

KRISTOPHER SVENSEN, BOX 274, ASTORIA, OR 97103

THOMAS SVENSEN, BOX 274, ASTORIA, OR 97103

DANIEL SWAB, 130 IVES RD, MASON, MI 48854

LUKE SWAB, 2728 COWART ST, CHATTANGOOGA, TN 37408

ADAM SWANSON, BOX 2151, PETERSBURG, AK 99833

KEITH SWICK, BOX 42, SELDOVIA, AK 99663

WILLIAM SWIMELAR, 601 SACHEEN TERRACE DR, NEWPORT, WA 99156

HEATHER TALBOT, 1204 SE MILLER ST, PORTLAND, OR 97202

ALEXANDER TALLEKPALEK, BOX 13, LEVELOCK, AK 99625

GUSTIE TALLEKPALEK, BOX 16, LEVELOCK, AK 99625

RYAN TALVI, 1110 SKYLINE DR, FAIRBANKS, AK 99712

BRIAN TARABOCHIA, 36573 VALLEY VISTA LN, ASTORIA, OR 97103

DANIEL TARABOCHIA, 7613 ELM CT SE, OLYMPIA, WA 98503

MARK TARABOCHIA, BOX 1757, NORTH PLAINS, OR 97133

RYAN TARABOCHIA, 92735 HAWTHORNE RD, ASTORIA, OR 97103

TERANCE TARABOCHIA, 219 LOOP RD, GRAYS RIVER, WA 98621

THOMAS TARABOCHIA, 156 MCDONALD RD, KELSO, WA 98626

REBECCA TEMPLE, 488 ELDERBERRY DR, HOMER, AK 99603

CHAD TENNYSON, 2851 PRIBILOF ST, ANCHORAGE, AK 99517

REED TENNYSON, BOX 167, DILLINGHAM, AK 99576

RICHARD TENNYSON, BOX 167, DILLINGHAM, AK 99576

RAYMOND THAYER, 626 VAN WYCK RD, BELLINGHAM, WA 98226

DEREK THERCHIK, BOX 37022, TOKSOOK BAY, AK 99637

RAYMOND THERCHIK, 2605 ASPEN HEIGHTS LP, ANCHORAGE, AK 99508

CARL THIELE, BOX ACR, ANCHORAGE, AK 99501

ISAAC THISTLE, 2223 MICHIGAN ST, BELLINGHAM, WA 98229

ERIC THOMAS, BOX 1165, PORT TOWNSEND, WA 98368

BRENT THOMPSON, 937 N 200TH ST #B305, SHORELINE, WA 98133

CHARLES THOMPSON, 875 OLD GARDINER RD, SEQUIM, WA 98382

CHRISTINA THOMPSON, 875 OLD GARDINER RD, SEQUIM, WA 98382

DENNIS THOMPSON, 19509 67TH AVE SE, SNOHOMISH, WA 98296

EVERETT THOMPSON, BOX 151, NAKNEK, AK 99633

HAILEY THOMPSON, BOX 3037, KODIAK, AK 99615

PETER THOMPSON, BOX 3037, KODIAK, AK 99615

SHERRY THOMPSON, 12662 SHORE ST, LEAVENWORTH, WA 98826

HENRY THOREEN, 928 195TH PLACE SW, LYNNWOOD, WA 98036

JAMES THOREEN, 2400 NW 80TH ST #111, SEATTLE, WA 98117

AMBER THORSON, BOX 1130, DILLINGHAM, AK 99576

MATTHEW THORSON, BOX 455, DILLINGHAM, AK 99576

RAYMOND THORSON, B0X 1130, DILLINGHAM, AK 99576

THERON THORSON, BOX 10232, DILLINGHAM, AK 99576

CONNOR THORSTENSON, 1660 HALLINAN ST, LAKE OSWEGO, OR 97034

PEDER THORSTENSON, 1660 HALLINAN ST, LAKE OSWEGO, OR 97034

JAMES TIKIUN, BOX 131, NUNAPITCHUK, AK 99641

THOMAS TILDEN, BOX 786, DILLINGHAM, AK 99576

JAMES TILLY, BOX 1081, KOKHANOK, AK 99606

DANIEL TIMMERMAN, BOX 475, DILLINGHAM, AK 99576

SALMON FISHING LIST—DRIFT GILLNET

RANDY TINKER, BOX 41, ALEKNAGIK, AK 99555
TROY TIRRELL, BOX 600, CORDOVA, AK 99574
TRAVIS TOBIN, 14314 HANCOCK LN, ANCHORAGE, AK 99515
KARI TOIVOLA, 3754 S BAY DR, SEDRO WOOLLEY, WA 98284
KRISTJAN TOIVOLA, 3754 S BAY DR, SEDRO WOLLEY, WA 98284
WITHERS TOLBERT, BOX 324, KING SALMON, AK 99613
RUSSELL TOLSMA, 2887 ALDERGROVE RD, FERNDALE, WA 98248
JACK TOM, BOX 5583, NEWTOK, AK 99559
NICK TOM, BOX 90061, NIGHTMUTE, AK 99690
MARITA TOMLINSON, BOX 111828, ANCHORAGE, AK 99511
AUSTIN TOMPKINS, 735 PARK ST, FRIDAY HARBOR, WA 98250
GREG TOPPING, BOX 759, KODIAK, AK 99615
AKATY TORAN, 17811 BOONES FERRY RD, HUBBARD, OR 97032
ROLF TORGERSON, 5118 167TH AVE CT, LONGBRANCH, WA 98351
THOMAS TORMALA, BOX 8829, KODIAK, AK 99615
THOMAS TORMALA, 1592 MONASHKA CIR, KODIAK, AK 99615
ANTONINO TORRENTE, 6 APPLE ST, GLOUCESTER, MA 1930
MARK TOWLE, 564 JOHNS RIVER RD, ABERDEEN, WA 98520
MOSES TOYUKAK, BOX 30, MANOKOTAK, AK 99628
MATTHEW TRACEY, BOX 628, FORT DUCHESNE, UT 84026
ROSS TRAINOR, 345 MAIN ST, VASSALBORO, ME 4989
TAM TRAN, 500 FOULKSTONE WAY, VALLEJO, CA 94591
CHARLES TREINEN, 2054 ARLINGTON DR, ANCHORAGE, AK 99517
KRISTINA TRETIKOFF, BOX 11, ILIAMNA, AK 99606
PATRICIA TREYDTE, BOX 398, DILLINGHAM, AK 99576
HEINZ TROSKA, 6721 DICKERSON DR, ANCHORAGE, AK 99504
GEORGE TROTT, 308 E LITTLE ISLAND RD, CATHLAMET, WA 98612
JOE TROTTER, BOX 5010, GLACIER, WA 98244
NICHOLAS TROXELL, 1615 LARCH ST, KODIAK, AK 99615
KATHRYN TSE, BOX 58, ROSBURG, WA 98643
WASSILLIE TUGATUK, BOX 189, MANOKOTAK, AK 99628
TODD TUKAYA, BOX 276, TOGIAK, AK 99678
WASSILLIE TUKAYA, BOX 165, TOGIAK, AK 99678
GUST TUNGUING, BOX 5040, KOLIGANEK, AK 99576
GUSTY TUNGUING, BOX 5038, KOLIGANEK, AK 99576
TRAVIS TUNGUING, BOX 5035, KOLIGANEK, AK 99576
GILBERT URATA, BOX 518, CORDOVA, AK 99574
DAVID URE, BOX 1950, KODIAK, AK 99615
JANICE URE, BOX 2361, KODIAK, AK 99615
JOHN URE, BOX 302, KODIAK, AK 99615
NELS URE, BOX 302, KODIAK, AK 99615
THOMAS URE, 1120 HUFFMAN RD #24 462, ANCHORAGE, AK 99515
ALEXANDER URIE, 2815 247TH AVE SE, SAMMAMISH, WA 98075
ANTHONY URIE, 18130 MIDVALE AVE N, SHORELINE, WA 98133
MICHAEL UTT, BOX 22200, SEATTLE, WA 98122
PSINGA VAENUKU, 1363 WESTMINSTER AVE, SALT LAKE CITY, UT 84105
JOSEPH VAN.ARSDEL, 12022 FARMINGTON RD, FARMINGTON, WA 99128
MALCOLM VANCE, BOX MXY #12, GLENNALLEN, AK 99588
BLAKE VANDER.LIND, 900 PEQUES ST #3402, SAN MARCOS, TX 78666
LARRY VANDER.LIND, 353 COURTNEY ST, ASHLAND, OR 97520
LAUREN VANDER.LIND, 1403 NE 65TH ST, VANCOUVER, WA 98665
JAMES VANOSS, 47850 E END, HOMER, AK 99603
JEROLD VANTREASE, BOX 1730, HOMER, AK 99603
JOSHUA VANTREASE, BOX 1730, HOMER, AK 99603
DAVID VARDY, 6232 185TH ST NW, STANWOOD, WA 98292
LINDA VARDY, BOX 129, LAKEWOOD, WA 98259
TIM VARDY, BOX 129, LAKEWOOD, WA 98259
TIM VEAL, 47113 STEVEN ST, KENAI, AK 99611
BRETT VEERHUSEN, 1122 E. PIKE S #761, SEATTLE, WA 98122
ERIK VELSKO, 780 DAYBREEZE CT, HOMER, AK 99603
GEORGE VENEROSO, BOX 83, WHITE HAVEN, PA 18661
JEFF VERVOORT, 830 SE MEADOWVALE DR, PULLMAN, WA 99163
TYSON VERVOORT, 1809 LYDIA AVE W, ROSEVILLE, MN 55133
PATRICK VILLANI, BOX 385, DILLINGHAM, AK 99576
IAN VINCENT, 16404 38TH AVE NW, STANWOOD, WA 98292
TIMOTHY VINCENT, 16404 38TH AVE NW, STANWOOD, WA 98292

KRISTEN VITTONE.ELWELL, 4016 MERIDIAN AVE N, MARYSVILLE, WA 98271
ANTHONY VLAHOVICH, BOX 515, SITKA, AK 99835
BERNIE VOLESKY, 22600 WINTERGREEN ST NW, BETHEL, MN 55005
CHRISTOPHER VOSS, 1743 SAN MARCUS PASS, SANTA BARBARA, CA 93105
JAMES VOSS, 1743 SAN MARCOS PASS, SANTA BARBARA, CA 93105
JOHN VUKAS, 4 MARBLE BEACH RD NW, GIG HARBOR, WA 98332
MAXWELL VUKAS, 4 MARBLE BEACH RD NW, GIG HARBOR, WA 98332
ANTE VUKIC, BOX 4726, SUNLAND, CA 91041
DANISLAV VUKICH, BOX 177, NAKNEK, AK 99633
DALE WADDELL, 930 OAK POINT RD, LONGVIEW, WA 98632
FOREST WAGNER, BOX 210845, AUKE BAY, AK 99821
GUST WAHL, BOX 949, DILLINGHAM, AK 99576
MARK WALATKA, 3933 BORLAND DR, ANCHORAGE, AK 99517
MICKIA WALCOTT, BOX 134, NEW STUYAHOK, AK 99636
PHILIP WALCOTT, BOX 106, NEW STUYAHOK, AK 99636
SPENCER WALCOTT, BOX 63, NEW STUYAHOK, AK 99636
FRANKLIN WALDRON, BOX 39093, NINILCHIK, AK 99639
JOAN WALDRON, 1160 W WATERLOO RD, OAK HARBOR, WA 98277
KYLE WALDRON, 1721 SW WATERSIDE CT, OAK HARBOR, WA 98277
STEVEN WALDRON, 1160 W WATERLOO RD, OAK HARBOR, WA 98277
VINTON WALDRON, 3511 SW BALDA ST, OAK HARBOR, WA 98277
VINTON WALDRON, 965 WALKER HEIGHTS PL, OAK HARBOR, WA 98277
ANTOINETTE WALKER, 1721 MISSION RD, KODIAK, AK 99615
BRIAN WALKER, 3901 SW AUSTIN ST, SEATTLE, WA 98136
MACGREGOR WALKER, BOX 17032, PORTLAND, OR 97217
ALEXANDER WALL, 273 N 1550 E, LAYTON, UT 84040
DEREK WALL, 92416 SVENSEN MARKET RD, ASTORIA, OR 97103
RANDALL WALL, 92416 SVENSEN MARKET RD, ASTORIA, OR 97103
DARROLD WALLONA, 4110 DEBARR #F29, ANCHORAGE, AK 99508
THOMAS WALSH, 157 SAN LUIS WAY, NOVATO, CA 94945
BRISTOL WALTON, 38725 GAVIN CIR, SOLDOTNA, AK 99669
DAGEN WALTON, 1747 N 460 W #101, LOGAN, UT 84341
INDY WALTON, 38725 GAVIN CIR, SOLDOTNA, AK 99669
MICHAEL WALVATNE, BOX 1221, LYNNWOOD, WA 98046
KRISTIAN WARFEL, BOX 2394, BELLINGHAM, WA 98227
JACK WARM, 24001 SE 243RD ST, MAPLE VALLEY, WA 98038
ADRIAN WARNESS, 19540 FREMONT AVE N, SHORELINE, WA 98133
GUSTY WASSILLIE, 11205 VIA BALBOA, ANCHORAGE, AK 99515
LENNY WASSILLIE, BOX 202, TOGIAK, AK 99678
TERRY WASSILLIE, BOX 14, ILIAMNA, AK 99606
WILLIE WASSILLIE, BOX 28, TOGIAK, AK 99678
GUSTY WASSILY, BOX 12, CLARKS POINT, AK 99569
HARRY WASSILY, BOX 105, CLARKS POINT, AK 99569
HENRY WASSILY, BOX 36, CLARKS POINT, AK 99569
STEVE WASSILY, BOX 458, DILLINGHAM, AK 99576
CHRISTOPHER WATERS, BOX 32063, BELLINGHAM, WA 98228
LANCE WATKINS, 537 S 39TH ST, BELLINGHAM, WA 98229
MARC WATSON, BOX 150, NAKNEK, AK 99633
RICHARD WATTERS, BOX 614, NAKNEK, AK 99633
SANDERS WEAVER, 1545 HOYT ST #63, ANCHORAGE, AK 99508
JOHN WEBB, 92615 ASTOR RD, ASTORIA, OR 97103
STEPHEN WEBB, BOX 1127, KASILOF, AK 99610
CLAUDE WEBSTER, BOX 121, KING SALMON, AK 99613
LINDA WEIST, 4904 197TH AVE E, BONNEY LAKE, WA 98391
JAMES WELLS, 40969 GRAND VIEW LN, ASTORIA, OR 97103
ALAN WELSH, 13020 FOSTER RD, ANCHORAGE, AK 99516
ZACH WERMERS, BOX 6245, BOZEMAN, MT 59771
MARK WEST, BOX 1664, SITKA, AK 99835
TYLER WESTLUND, 150 NW OREGON AVE, BEND, OR 97703
JAMES WHEELER, BOX 305, CLAM GULCH, AK 99568
ERIC WHITAKER, BOX 1323, WOODINVILLE, WA 98072
JAMES WHITCHER, 13244 THOMAS LN, ANACORTES, WA 98221
BRIAN WHITE, 5525 SW CAMERON RD, PORTLAND, OR 97221
CHRISTOPHER WHITE, 953 JANISH DR, SANDPOINT, ID 83864
RAYMOND WHITE, BOX 28, EEK, AK 99578
TARAN WHITE, 204 N 4TH AVE #85, SAND POINT, ID 83864

SALMON FISHING LIST—DRIFT GILLNET / SET GILLNET

BRUCE WHITING, 1302 W MUKILTEO BLVD, EVERETT, WA 98203
GABRIELLE WHITING, 4908 61ST DR NE, MARYSVILLE, WA 98270
STEPHEN WHITING, 4908 61ST DR NE, MARYSVILLE, WA 98270
JULIAN WHITSETT, 130 SE KING AVE, WARRENTON, OR 97146
C.KEITH WHITTERN, 7490 W 350 N, SHIPSHEWANA, IN 46565
TOM WHITTINGHAM, 1294 HARTZOG LP, NORTH POLE, AK 99705
PATRICK WHITTLESEY, 16121 PENINSULA RD, STANWOOD, WA 98292
FREDERICK WHYMN, BOX 14, TOGIAK, AK 99678
JONNY WICKER, 1818 FOOTHILL RD, KALISPELL, MT 59901
CHRISTOPHER WIDING, BOX 1659, EDMONDS, WA 98020
BAE WIDMIER, 3406 HALIBUT PT RD, SITKA, AK 99835
MATTHEW WIEBE, 369 MONTEZUMA ST #248, SANTA FE, NM 87501
JESSICA WIKSTROM, 6467 KAWAIHAU RD UNIT E, KAPAA, HI 96746
MARYJANE WILCOX, BOX 147, TOGIAK, AK 99678
LYLE WILDER, 110 N EASY ST, PORT ALSWORTH, AK 99653
RAYMOND WILLARD, BOX 870302, WASILLA, AK 99687
ABE WILLIAMS, 5116 W 80TH AVE #A, ANCHORAGE, AK 99502
BRADEN WILLIAMS, 5116 W 80TH AVE #A, ANCHORAGE, AK 99502
RICKEY WILLIAMS, BOX 1321, PETERSBURG, AK 99833
ROBERT WILLIAMS, 8706 CONWHIT LN SW, PORT ORCHARD, WA 98367
CANYON WILLIS, 16483 SW LONGVIEW ST, BEND, OR 97702
NOLAN WILLIS, 8877 KAK ISLAND ST, EAGLE RIVER, AK 99577
TIM WILLIS, 61483 SW LONGVIEW ST, BEND, OR 97702
VICTOR WILLIS, 25628 BENDILENT CIR, EAGLE RIVER, AK 99577
CHESTER WILSON, BOX 234, NAKNEK, AK 99633
DENNIS WILSON, BOX 142, DILLINGHAM, AK 99576
DUSTIN WILSON, BOX 234, NAKNEK, AK 99633
GEORGE WILSON, BOX 575, NAKNEK, AK 99633
JAMES WILSON, 13481 BAYWIND DR, ANCHORAGE, AK 99516
KENNY WILSON, BOX 1371, DILLINGHAM, AK 99576
KEVIN WILSON, 15689 EUCLID AVE, BAINBRIDGE, WA 98110
MIKE WILSON, 181 KEVINA RD, ELLENSBURG, WA 98926
RICHARD WILSON, BOX 237, NAKNEK, AK 99633
VERNER WILSON, BOX 905, DILLINGHAM, AK 99576
WADE WILSON, 13481 BAYWIND DR, ANCHORAGE, AK 99516
KURT WINTERHALTER, 5219 220TH NW, STANWOOD, WA 98292
ROBERT WINTERS, BOX 475, TWISP, WA 98856
DREW WISE, 10805 23RD DR SE, EVERETT, WA 98208
JOHN WISE, BOX 32, NAKNEK, AK 99633
MONICA WITTORFF, 352 STATE ROUTE HWY 105, RAYMOND, WA 98577
KRISTIAN WITTSTOCK, BOX 501, PETERSBURG, AK 99833
AURTHER WOINOWSKY, 301 PTARMIGAN RD, UGASHIK, AK 99613
WILLIAM WOLF, 17 ANDREAS CT, NAVATO, CA 94945
DAVID WOLFF, 644 1ST AVE, MENDOTA HEIGHTS, MN 55118
TOM WOLLAN, BOX 1198, DILLINGHAM, AK 99576
EVAN WONHOLA, BOX 51, NEW STUYAHOK, AK 99636
TIMOTHY WONHOLA, BOX 4042, TWIN HILLS, AK 99576
ANTHONY WOOD, BOX 602, KING SALMON, AK 99613
JASON WOOD, 569 S STORRS AVE, AMERICAN FORK, UT 84003
JUSTIN WOODIN, BOX 4469, DURANGO, CO 81302
FRANK WOODS, BOX 713, DILLINGHAM, AK 99576
ALEXANDER WORHATCH, BOX 614, PETERSBURG, AK 99833
ANDY WORHATCH, BOX 614, PETERSBURG, AK 99833
TRAVIS WREN, 78382 CALLE LAS RAMBLAS, LA QUINTA, CA 92253
WILLIAM WREN, 35669 AVE E, YUCAIPA, CA 92399
BOBBY WYAGON, BOX 5024, KOLIGANEK, AK 99576
GEOFFREY WYMAN, 349 RICHARD RD, OAK HARBOR, WA 98277
JASPAR WYMAN, 4822 S GRAHAM ST, SEATTLE, WA 98118
JOHN WYMAN, 4822 S GRAHAM ST, SEATTLE, WA 98118
MARY WYMAN, 349 RICHARD RD, OAK HARBOR, WA 98277
TREFON YAKO, BOX 1444, DILLINGHAM, AK 99576
FRED YECK, BOX 871, NEWPORT, OR 97365
ASHLEY YOUNG, BOX 151, HYDER, AK 99923
ROBERT YOUNG, BOX 3494, SOLDOTNA, AK 99669
PHILIP ZANDER, BOX 465, HOMER, AK 99603

AMANDA ZHAROFF, 1751 E 57TH CIR, ANCHORAGE, AK 99507
CARL ZIMIN, BOX 387, NAKNEK, AK 99633
KYLE ZIMIN, BOX 387, NAKNEK, AK 99633
LAURA ZIMIN, BOX 387, NAKNEK, AK 99633
RALPH ZIMIN, BOX 242, KING SALMON, AK 99613
NICHOLAS ZUANICH, 1578 BROOKEDGE CT, BELLINGHAM, WA 98226

SALMON, SET GILLNET, YAKUTAT

DANIEL ADAMS, BOX 487, YAKUTAT, AK 99689
RODNEY ANDERSON, BOX 364, YAKUTAT, AK 99689
ERIC BAKER, 2212 SE SPARROW ST, MILWAUKIE, OR 97222
SANORA BELL, BOX 245, YAKUTAT, AK 99689
FRED BEMIS, BOX 33, YAKUTAT, AK 99689
LARRY BEMIS, BOX 192, YAKUTAT, AK 99689
TIFFANY BEMIS, BOX 167, YAKUTAT, AK 99689
RUSSELL BOGREN, BOX 401, YAKUTAT, AK 99689
MICHAEL BORING, 3202 E PERSHING AVE, PHOENIX, AZ 85032
FRANK BRANTLEY, BOX 553, SITKA, AK 99835
ALLEN BREMNER, BOX 216, YAKUTAT, AK 99689
HOWARD BREMNER, BOX 53, YAKUTAT, AK 99689
JAMES BREMNER, BOX 53, YAKUTAT, AK 99689
JOHN BRESEMAN, 431 A ANDREWS ST, SITKA, AK 99835
DAVID BROWN, BOX 171, YAKUTAT, AK 99689
DAVID BROWN, BOX 35111, JUNEAU, AK 99803
CADIE BUCKLEY, BOX 1438, HAINES, AK 99827
ROBERT BULARD, BOX 241, YAKUTAT, AK 99689
BETTY BULLER, BOX 208, YAKUTAT, AK 99689
JOHN BULLER, BOX 238, YAKUTAT, AK 99689
MARY CARR, BOX 13162, TRAPPER CREEK, AK 99683
ARTHUR CHURCH, BOX 1044, WILLOW, AK 99688
LOREN CLARK, BOX 331, YAKUTAT, AK 99689
RONNIE CONVERSE, BOX 172, YAKUTAT, AK 99689
VICTORIA DEMMERT, BOX 366, YAKUTAT, AK 99689
GREG DIERICK, BOX 421, YAKUTAT, AK 99689
KYLE DIERICK, BOX 421, YAKUTAT, AK 99689
LARRY DIXON, BOX 265, WILLOW, AK 99688
MARK DONOHUE, 1078 CORONADO DR, ROCKLEDGE, FL 32955
PATRICIA DUNKELBERGER, 531 E 10TH, ANCHORAGE, AK 99501
BERTINA EDWARDS, BOX 38, YAKUTAT, AK 99689
MELISSA ENDICOTT, BOX 506, YAKUTAT, AK 99689
NATHANIEL ENDICOTT, BOX 170, YAKUTAT, AK 99689
GARY FELTS, 9300 E BOYD RD, PALMER, AK 99645
KEVIN FIRESTACK, 12271 W HAZEL, WASILLA, AK 99623
J FIVECOAT, BOX 10, BANKS, OR 97106
HAROLD FLOWERS, 116 DEARBORN, CALDWELL, ID 83605
JEFFREY FRAKER, BOX 517, YAKUTAT, AK 99689
ROSE.MARIE FRAKER, BOX 313, YAKUTAT, AK 99689
ANTHONY GLAZIER, BOX 275, YAKUTAT, AK 99689
BRANDT GRABER, BOX 202, YAKUTAT, AK 99689
ANDREW GRAY, BOX 1586, BARROW, AK 99723
GARY GRAY, BOX 304, YAKUTAT, AK 99689
HAROLD GRAY, BOX 13, YAKUTAT, AK 99689
ELI HANLON, BOX 183, YAKUTAT, AK 99689
VERNON HANSEN, BOX 106, YAKUTAT, AK 99689
ERNEST HARRY, BOX 24, YAKUTAT, AK 99689
PHILIP HARRY, BOX 515, YAKUTAT, AK 99689
MARK HAWNEY, 1036 W SCRIVNER RD, PORT ANGELES, WA 98362
ARLEEN HENRY, BOX 401, YAKUTAT, AK 99689
RUSSELL HENRY, BOX 102, YAKUTAT, AK 99689
RUSSELL HENSLER, BOX 145, SATSOP, WA 98583
HEATHER HOLCOMB, BOX 206, YAKUTAT, AK 99689
LES HOLCOMB, BOX 143, YAKUTAT, AK 99689
SONYA HOLCOMB, BOX 143, YAKUTAT, AK 99689
JERALD HOLMES, 1405 S 250TH, DES MOINES, WA 98198
DOREEN INGLE, 3208 HALIBUT POINT RD SPC 12, SITKA, AK 99835

SALMON FISHING LIST—SET GILLNET

GLENN ISRAELSON, BOX 64, YAKUTAT, AK 99689
EDWIN ITEN, BOX 344, KOTZEBUE, AK 99752
ELLEN IVERS, 9620 MUSKET BALL CIR, ANCHORAGE, AK 99507
VINCENT JACOBSON, BOX 28, YAKUTAT, AK 99689
DARYL JAMES, BOX 411, YAKUTAT, AK 99689
JEREMIAH JAMES, BOX 507, YAKUTAT, AK 99689
ERIC JENSEN, BOX 155, YAKUTAT, AK 99689
JAMES JENSEN, BOX 316, YAKUTAT, AK 99689
JONATHAN JENSEN, BOX 446, YAKUTAT, AK 99689
MICHAEL JENSEN, BOX 481, YAKUTAT, AK 99689
ADAM JOHNSON, BOX 313, YAKUTAT, AK 99689
ALEX JOHNSON, 1309 ANACOPPER RD, ANACORTES, WA 98221
RALPH JOHNSON, 2215 GREAT WESTERN ST #I, DOUGLAS, AK 99824
SAMUEL JOHNSON, BOX 412, YAKUTAT, AK 99689
KRISTOPHER KARSUNKY, 312 CHARTERIS ST, SITKA, AK 99835
TAYLOR KIMBAROW, BOX 1626, CORDOVA, AK 99574
CHARLES KLUSHKAN, BOX 57, YAKUTAT, AK 99689
GABRIEL KLUSHKAN, BOX 45, YAKUTAT, AK 99689
ADAM KOHNE, BOX 161, YAKUTAT, AK 99689
RICHARD KOROCH, 2425 41ST AVE E #K 126, SEATTLE, WA 98112
GRACE LEE, BOX 1441, CORDOVA, AK 99574
TARA LEE.MASON, 16526 GLACIER HWY, JUNEAU, AK 99801
ASHLEY LEKANOF, BOX 288, YAKUTAT, AK 99689
ROBERT LEKANOF, BOX 288, YAKUTAT, AK 99689
ERIC LEUSCH, GENERAL DELIVERY, STEBBINS, AK 99671
DAMIEN LONG, BOX 54, YAKUTAT, AK 99689
JANICE LOWENSTEIN, 18524 1ST NW, SHORELINE, WA 98177
JAY LOWENSTEIN, 13214 HARBOR HEIGHTS DR, MUKILTEO, WA 98275
JEFF LOWENSTEIN, 17385 GLACIER HWY, JUNEAU, AK 99801
JOHN LOWENSTEIN, 18524 1ST AVE NW, SEATTLE, WA 98177
BYRON MALLOTT, BOX 317, YAKUTAT, AK 99689
CASEY MAPES, BOX 215, YAKUTAT, AK 99689
CASEY MAPES, BOX 215, YAKUTAT, AK 99689
CHARLES MASON, 16526 GLACIER HWY, JUNEAU, AK 99801
DELANEY MASON, 16526 GLACIER HWY, JUNEAU, AK 99801
DEREK MASON, 16526 GLACIER HWY, JUNEAU, AK 99801
DEVEN MASON, 16526 GLACIER HWY, JUNEAU, AK 99801
JOHN MATSKO, BOX 458, YAKUTAT, AK 99689
CHRISTOPHER MILLER, 605 NE OLD BELFAIR HWY, BELFAIRURG, WA 98528
ROBERT MILLER, BOX 425, YAKUTAT, AK 99689
TANIS MILLER, BOX 425, YAKUTAT, AK 99689
TODD MILLER, BOX 1626, SITKA, AK 99835
TYLER MILLER, BOX 1626, SITKA, AK 99835
DANELLE MILLS, BOX 248, YAKUTAT, AK 99689
JOE MOODY, 11221 S 51ST #1003, PHOENIX, AZ 85044
DAVID MORTENSEN, 4820 KALENKA CIR, ANCHORAGE, AK 99502
SCOTT MORTENSEN, 4000 TAZLINA AVE, ANCHORAGE, AK 99517
DAVID NEGUS, BOX 126, YAKUTAT, AK 99689
SHANNON NEGUS, BOX 126, YAKUTAT, AK 99689
JAMES NELSON, BOX 449, YAKUTAT, AK 99689
JASON NELSON, 8061 SPORTSMAN CLUB RD NE, BAINBRIGDE ID, WA 98110
LISA NELSON, BOX 507, YAKUTAT, AK 99689
SHERI NELSON, BOX 117, YAKUTAT, AK 99689
RICK NEWLUN, BOX 291, YAKUTAT, AK 99689
DONALD PATE, BOX 402, YAKUTAT, AK 99689
ANDREW PAVLIK, BOX 307, YAKUTAT, AK 99689
JEREMIAH PAVLIK, BOX 191, YAKUTAT, AK 99689
JESSICA PAVLIK, BOX 191, YAKUTAT, AK 99689
JOHN PAVLIK, BOX 32, YAKUTAT, AK 99689
JONATHAN PAVLIK, BOX 293, YAKUTAT, AK 99689
PAUL PAVLIK, BOX 11, YAKUTAT, AK 99689
RUDY PAVLIK, BOX 11, YAKUTAT, AK 99689
RICHARD PELKEY, BOX 351, YAKUTAT, AK 99689
MARK PELLETT, 72 GREENWOOD AVE, WINTHROP, ME 4364
PATRICK PELLETT, 3208 HALIBUT POINT RD SPC 12, SITKA, AK 99835
MICHAEL PERRY, BOX 319, WAVERLY, WA 99039

LOWELL PETERSEN, BOX 62, YAKUTAT, AK 99689
EDUARDO PRECIADO, BOX 505, YAKUTAT, AK 99689
BLAIR RADOC, 10297 POINT REYES CIR, STOCKTON, CA 95209
GAYLE RANNEY, BOX 2349, CORDOVA, AK 99574
ESTHER REINECKE, BOX 281, YAKUTAT, AK 99689
CALEB ROBBINS, BOX 6256, SITKA, AK 99835
HAROLD ROBBINS, BOX 69, YAKUTAT, AK 99689
PATRICK ROBBINS, BOX 202, YAKUTAT, AK 99689
BENJAMEN ROCKWOOD, BOX 477, YAKUTAT, AK 99689
ROBERT ROCKWOOD, BOX 477, YAKUTAT, AK 99689
THOMAS ROHLOFF, BOX 154, YAKUTAT, AK 99689
DOUGLAS ROSS, BOX 1066, PRIEST RIVER, ID 83856
TRAVIS ROSS, BOX 352, YAKUTAT, AK 99689
KALANI RUSSELL, BOX 482, YAKUTAT, AK 99689
ENOCH SCHERTEL, BOX 43, YAKUTAT, AK 99689
ANTHONY SCHMIDT, BOX 464, YAKUTAT, AK 99689
ASHTON SCHMIDT, BOX 243, YAKUTAT, AK 99689
DENNSON SCHUMACHER, BOX 25, YAKUTAT, AK 99689
VERNON SCHUMACHER, BOX 1269, TOLEDO, WA 98591
VIRGIL SCHUMACHER, BOX 168, YAKUTAT, AK 99689
LEE SHELFORD, BOX 12840, MILL CREEK, WA 98082
JAMES SLATER, BOX 63, PELICAN, AK 99832
KELLY SMITH, 2163 E WINGED FOOT DR, CHANDLER, AZ 85249
KELLY SMITH, 2163 E WINGED FOOT DR, CHANDLER, AZ 85249
REBECCA SMITH, 2163 E WINGED FOOT DR, CHANDLER, AZ 85249
ROXANNE STEWART, 100 ROSS WAY, JUNEAU, AK 99801
BRAD SWANSON, BOX 202, YAKUTAT, AK 99689
JACOB TAYLOR, 9620 STINKIN ST, JUNEAU, AK 99801
RICARDO TEJEDA, BOX 82, YAKUTAT, AK 99689
TRACY THACK, BOX 292, YAKUTAT, AK 99689
TRACY THACK, BOX 292, YAKUTAT, AK 99689
WESLEY THOMPSON, BOX 2216, CORDOVA, AK 99574
OLAF TOTLAND, BOX 373, YAKUTAT, AK 99689
JOHN VALE, BOX 193, YAKUTAT, AK 99689
GEORGE VALLE, BOX 87, YAKUTAT, AK 99689
JONATHAN VALLE, BOX 503, YAKUTAT, AK 99689
ANDREW VARNI, 13788 E GERONIMO RD, SCOTTSDALE, AZ 85259
JOSHUA WEEKLY, 3175 JUNIPER ST, SAN DIEGO, CA 92104
MARCOS WEINRICK, BOX 473, YAKUTAT, AK 99689
LUCAS WHEELER, BOX 353, YAKUTAT, AK 99689
FREDERICK WHITE, 6590 GLACIER HWY #48, JUNEAU, AK 99801
ARNOLD WILLIAMS, BOX 465, YAKUTAT, AK 99689
RICHARD WILLIAMS, BOX 176, YAKUTAT, AK 99689
KATHLEEN WILLIAMSON, BOX 32383, JUNEAU, AK 99803
JAMES WILSON, 1201 CALLISTA AVE, VALRICO, FL 33596
JAMES WOODBURY, BOX 76, YAKUTAT, AK 99689
JOHANNA YOUNG, BOX 611, PELICAN, AK 99832
DAVID ZIMMER, 101 ANGELO PL, WALLA WALLA, WA 99362

SALMON, SET GILLNET, PRINCE WILLIAM SOUND

MICHAEL BROWN, 720 BURTON ST, SHERIDAN, WY 82801
DAVID FLEMING, 6948 FAIRWEATHER DR, ANCHORAGE, AK 99518
JOSEPH FLEMING, 400 W BLUEJAY DR, CHANDLER, AZ 85286
JOSH GRUMBLIS, 1832 BELLEVUE LP, ANCHORAGE, AK 99515
ZACHARY GRUMBLIS, 7420 SAND LAKE RD, ANCHORAGE, AK 99502
JOSEPH HALL, 14702 WATER FRONT LANE, EAGLE RIVER, AK 99577
MAX HARVEY, 1636 MOSS CREEK AVE, ANCHORAGE, AK 99507
ELLIOTT IRVIN, 100 DUNDEE MOUNTAIN RD, CENTER CONWAY, NH 93813
THOMAS JAMES, 40732 WATERMAN RD, HOMER, AK 99603
FOREST JENKINS, W25126 SULLIVAN RD, TREMPEALEAU, WI 54661
LYLE KRITCHEN, BOX 935, CORDOVA, AK 99574
ELEANOR MALA, BOX 2288, SEWARD, AK 99664
DYLAN MALONEY, BOX 1576, CORDOVA, AK 99574
TIM MILLER, BOX 1020, CORDOVA, AK 99574
LAUREN MOSS, BOX 1465, GIRDWOOD, AK 99587

SALMON FISHING LIST—SET GILLNET

JARON MURPHY, 3201 WOODRUFF LP, WASILLA, AK 99654
EMMA OWECKE, W 25376 SULLIVAN RD, TREMPEALEAU, WI 54661
PAUL OWECKE, W 25376 SULLIVAN RD, TREMPEALEAU, WI 54661
GUNNAR PERSON, 4322 BAYVIEW CT, HOMER, AK 99603
LISA RAGLAND, 17100 KINGS WAY, ANCHORAGE, AK 99516
MICHAEL SPAETGENS, 56760 EAST END RD, HOMER, AK 99603
CHRISTOPHER THOMAS, 1852 E 24TH AVE, ANCHORAGE, AK 99508
JOANN THOMAS, BOX 284, CORDOVA, AK 99574
CHARLES TOTEMOFF, 3000 C ST #301, ANCHORAGE, AK 99503
PARKER WHALEY, BOX 750849, FAIRBANKS, AK 99701
IAN WILLIAMS, 7141 LINDEN DR, ANCHORAGE, AK 99502
MICHELLE WILLIAMS, 7141 LINDEN DR, ANCHORAGE, AK 99502
LYNNETTE WRIGHT, 13-3354 LUANA ST, PAHOA, HI 96778
NEIL WRIGHT, 13-3354 LUANA ST, PAHOA, HI 96778
IOLA YOUNG, 429 W TENTH, JUNEAU, AK 99801

SALMON, SET GILLNET, ATKA/AMLIA ISLANDS
MOLLY CHINGLIAK, BOX 28, GOODNEWS BAY, AK 99589
ALEX KUDRIN, BOX 229, SAINT PAUL ISLAND, AK 99660

SALMON, SET GILLNET, COOK INLET
WILLIAM ABFALTER, 3746 PETERKIN AVE, ANCHORAGE, AK 99508
JAMES AHRENS, 3406 N WELLINGTON PL, SPOKANE, WA 99205
JOHN ALLARDICE, BOX 182, SELDOVIA, AK 99663
LANCE ALLDRIN, 3864 DUSTY LN, CHICO, CA 95973
LUKE ALLDRIN, 3864 DUSTY LN, CHICO, CA 95973
HANNAH ALLEN, 1411 DRY CREEK RD, ASHLAND CITY, TN 37015
PAULA AM.KULHANEK, BOX 3002, HOMER, AK 99603
CARRIE ANDERSON, 51985 KOALA LN, KENAI, AK 99611
MARK ANDERSON, 51985 KOALA LN, KENAI, AK 99611
SHAYLA ANDERSON, 11620 NE 150TH PL, KIRKLAND, WA 98034
JAMES ARNESS, 51910 ARNESS RD, KENAI, AK 99611
JOSEPH ARNESS, BOX 1470, KENAI, AK 99611
REBECCA ARNESS, 51910 ARNESS RD, KENAI, AK 99611
ROBERT ARNOLD, 20433 LUCAS AVE, EAGLE RIVER, AK 99577
DON BAILEY, BOX 416, ANCHOR POINT, AK 99556
FRANK BAILEY, 693 EVANS RD, MCKINLEYVILLE, CA 95519
GLORIA BAILEY, BOX 416, ANCHOR POINT, AK 99556
GREGORY BAILEY, 3206 OREGON DR #1, ANCHORAGE, AK 99517
JAMES BAILEY, 693 EVANS RD, MCKINLEYVILLE, CA 95519
JOHN BAILEY, 693 EVANS RD, MCKINLEYVILLE, CA 95519
JUSTIN BAILEY, 6727 STURTEVANT DR #B, PENNGROVE, CA 94951
LANCE BAILEY, BOX 416, ANCHOR POINT, AK 99556
EDWARD BARBER, BOX 925, GIRDWOOD, AK 99587
KEVIN BARKSDALE, BOX 244894, ANCHORAGE, AK 99524
MARILYN BARKSDALE, BOX 876865, WASILLA, AK 99687
H BARNES, 45915 KENAI SPUR HWY, KENAI, AK 99611
ANNE BARNETT, 8101 E 18TH AVE, ANCHORAGE, AK 99504
SERA BAXTER, BOX 182, SELDOVIA, AK 99663
JEFF BEAUDOIN, BOX 75, KASILOF, AK 99610
TOM BECK, BOX 37, HOMER, AK 99603
CALEB BECKER, 50083 S 700 RD, COLCORD, OK 74338
LESLIE BENJAMIN, BOX 1062, KASILOF, AK 99610
JOHN BENNETT, 9361 N BLUE FOX DR, PALMER, AK 99645
LOVERNE BERCEE, BOX 465, GIRDWOOD, AK 99587
AMY BERGA, BOX 165, KASILOF, AK 99610
ETHAN BERGA, BOX 165, KASILOF, AK 99610
DANIEL BILLMAN, 9700 PROSPECT DR, ANCHORAGE, AK 99516
FREDERICK BISMARK, BOX 82085, TYONEK, AK 99682
ROBERT BISMARK, BOX 82093, TYONEK, AK 99682
DAVID BLANCHARD, 1133 ACADIAN DR, HOUMA, LA 70363
HORACE BLANCHARD, 1133 ACADIAN DR, HOUMA, LA 70363
LAURA BLANCHARD, 1133 ACADIAN DR, HOUMA, LA 70363

LORENA BLANCHARD, 1133 ACADIAN DR, HOUMA, LA 70363
SETH BLANCHARD, 812 AUK ST, KENAI, AK 99611
BRENDAN BLOSSOM, BOX 3975, SOLDOTNA, AK 99669
BRITTANI BLOSSOM, BOX 3975, SOLDOTNA, AK 99669
DEBRA BLOSSOM, BOX 129, CLAM GULCH, AK 99568
DOUGLAS BLOSSOM, BOX 3975, SOLDOTNA, AK 99669
MARY BLOSSOM, BOX 3975, SOLDOTNA, AK 99669
CODY BLOSSOM.ADOLF, BOX 129, CLAM GULCH, AK 99568
GRETCHEN BOGARD, 45060 BOGARD CT, KENAI, AK 99611
JARRODD BOHN, 20366 KLAHANI DR, BEND, OR 97702
KRISTIN BOOCK, 11501 TOMASITA CT NE, ALBURQUERQUE, NM 87112
GEORGE BOUSSELAIRE, BOX 244254, ANCHORAGE, AK 99524
CHRISTINE BRANDT, BOX 504, SOLDOTNA, AK 99669
STEPHEN BRAUND, 2409 MARILAINE DR, ANCHORAGE, AK 99503
JEROLD BRENNEMAN, BOX 194, KASILOF, AK 99610
BERNICE BROWN, 2505 MCRAE RD, ANCHORAGE, AK 99517
EUDELL BROWN, 127 FIARWOOD LN, MENA, AR 71953
WARREN BROWN, BOX 77, SELDOVIA, AK 99663
WILLIAM BRUN, BOX 212, SELDOVIA, AK 99663
DANIEL BUNKER, BOX 875275, WASILLA, AK 99687
EMILY BUNKER, BOX 875275, WASILLA, AK 99687
TAMMY BUNKER, BOX 875275, WASILLA, AK 99687
TRAVIS BUNKER, BOX 875275, WASILLA, AK 99687
JOSEPH BURRIS, BOX 298032, WASILLA, AK 99654
JORDAN BYRNE, 9030 INDIAN BLUFF RD, GEORGETOWN, IN 47122
KAYLA CARAWAY, 10231 W FOREST HILLS CIR, WASILLA, AK 99623
KELLY CARAWAY, 10231 W FOREST HILLS CIR, WASILLA, AK 99623
TIMOTHY CARAWAY, 10231 W FOREST HILLS CIR, WASILLA, AK 99623
TITUS CARAWAY, 10231 W FOREST HILLS CIR, WASILLA, AK 99623
HAILEY CARLSON, 14800 S 1300 W, BLUFFDALE, UT 84065
MICHAEL CARLSON, 647 STATE RD 48, LUCK, WI 54853
MICHAEL CARLSON, 14800 S 1300 W, BLUFFDALE, UT 84065
SUSAN CARLSON, 647 STATE RD 48, LUCK, WI 54853
JUSTIN CARR, BOX 108, KENAI, AK 99611
NICOLE CARR, BOX 108, KENAI, AK 99611
BENJAMIN CARSWELL, BOX 82087, TYONEK, AK 99682
ELAINE CHALUP, BOX 406, HOMER, AK 99603
EMILY CHALUP, BOX 406, HOMER, AK 99603
BRENDA CHARLES, BOX 521131, BIG LAKE, AK 99652
RANDY CHARLES, BOX 521131, BIG LAKE, AK 99652
WILFORD CHARLES, BOX 521131, BIG LAKE, AK 99652
JEVON CHARTIER, BOX 2, SELDOVIA, AK 99663
ELIZABETH CHASE, BOX 39, KASILOF, AK 99610
MICHAEL CHASE, BOX 39, KASILOF, AK 99610
DAVID CHESSIK, BOX 1824, KENAI, AK 99611
ELIZABETH CHESSIK, BOX 1155, KENAI, AK 99611
NORBERT CHESSIK, BOX 1155, KENAI, AK 99611
LEONARD CHICKALUSION, BOX 82045, TYONEK, AK 99682
GUY CHOW, 1242 OCEAN DR, HOMER, AK 99603
LECON CHUITT, BOX 82118, TYONEK, AK 99682
CAYLEIGH CLARK, 117 DEEPWOOD CT, KENAI, AK 99611
CHERYN CLARK, 27067 REICHERT SUMMERFIELD RD, HEAVENER, OK 74937
RUSSELL CLARK, 27067 REICHERT SUMMER FIELD RD, HEAVENER, OK 74937
LESTER CLAYTON, BOX 133, KASILOF, AK 99610
BRYNDA CLEVELAND, 3050 AMBER BAY LP, ANCHORAGE, AK 99515
CAMILLE CLUCAS, 35401 PARSONAGE ST, SOLDOTNA, AK 99669
JON CLUCAS, 8589 CANNON RD, SEAFORD, DE 19973
MARK CLUCAS, 72886 STERLING HWY, CLAM GULCH, AK 99568
RITA CLUCAS, 8589 CANNON RD, SEAFORD, DE 19973
ROBERT CLUCAS, 72886 STERLING HWY, CLAM GULCH, AK 99568
ROBERT CLUCAS, 1509 RANDEE LANE, KENAI, AK 99611
TIMOTHY COHEN, 4220 NORTH POINT DR, ANCHORAGE, AK 99502
KENNETH COLEMAN, 35565 BARANOF ST, KENAI, AK 99611
VICTORIA COLEMAN, 35565 BARANOF ST, KENAI, AK 99611
LLOYD COLLINS, BOX 1409, KENAI, AK 99611

SALMON FISHING LIST—SET GILLNET

LISA CONFER, 1330 N CEDAR HILLS DR, PALMER, AK 99645
CORNELL CONSTANTINE, 35760 POPPYRIDGE RD, SOLDOTNA, AK 99669
FEDORA CONSTANTINE, BOX 82054, TYONEK, AK 99682
GARY COOPER, BOX 39042, NINILCHIK, AK 99639
DAVID CORAY, BOX 3234, SOLDOTNA, AK 99669
GARY CORDER, BOX 3646, SOLDOTNA, AK 99669
LORI.ANN CORESON, BOX 56, KENAI, AK 99611
TEAGUN CORESON, BOX 56, KENAI, AK 99611
TERRY CORESON, BOX 56, KENAI, AK 99611
ANTHONY CORREIA, BOX 456, CLAM GULCH, AK 99568
CAROLINE CORREIA, BOX 456, CLAM GULCH, AK 99568
RAY CORREIA, BOX 456, CLAM GULCH, AK 99568
ROBERT CORREIA, BOX 456, CLAM GULCH, AK 99568
TYRRELL CORREIA, BOX 456, CLAM GULCH, AK 99568
CHRISTOPHER CRAVER, BOX 29, TALKEETNA, AK 99676
ALAN CROOKSTON, 265 N MAIN ST #D165, KAYSVILLE, UT 84037
NINA CROOKSTON, 265 N MAIN ST #D165, KAYSVILLE, UT 84037
TED CROOKSTON, 265 N MAIN ST #D165, KAYSVILLE, UT 84037
CRAIG CUSACK, 430 ENDICOTT DR, SOLDOTNA, AK 99669
ANN DAIGLE, BOX 4013, HOMER, AK 99603
NAOMI DAIGLE, BOX 4013, HOMER, AK 99603
PATRICK DAIGLE, BOX 4013, HOMER, AK 99603
SIMEON DAIGLE, BOX 4013, HOMER, AK 99603
THOMAS DALRYMPLE, BOX 1502, SOLDOTNA, AK 99669
ALYSSA DARCH, BOX 108, KENAI, AK 99611
JAN DARCH, BOX 108, KENAI, AK 99611
NORMAN DARCH, BOX 108, KENAI, AK 99611
GARY DEIMAN, BOX 39224, NINILCHIK, AK 99639
KELSEY DEIMAN, BOX 39224, NINILCHIK, AK 99639
AMY DEJAX, 35000 JAMES ST, SOLDOTNA, AK 99669
CLIFFORD DEJAX, 35000 JAMES ST, SOLDOTNA, AK 99669
PERRIN DEJAX, 35000 JAMES ST, SOLDOTNA, AK 99669
CONOR DEMPSEY, BOX 8014, NIKISKI, AK 99635
MICHAEL DENBLEYKER, 3307 CHERRYWOOD AVE, BELLINGHAM, WA 98225
JEFF DENT, BOX 2233, KENAI, AK 99611
AARON DEXHEIMER, 1222 REED AVE #15, SAN DIEGO, CA 92109
EDWARD DILLON, BOX 8426, NIKISKI, AK 99635
WILLIAM DILLON, BOX 7588, NIKISKI, AK 99635
LINDSAY DOLIFKA, BOX 2833, KENAI, AK 99611
AUDRA DONER, 210 BREE AVE, ANCHORAGE, AK 99515
JOEL DONER, 210 BREE AVE, ANCHORAGE, AK 99515
JOHANNA DONER, 1925 N BATTERY CIR, PALMER, AK 99645
MARK DONER, 1925 N BATTERY CIR, PALMER, AK 99645
MERRY DONER, 1925 N BATTERY CIR, PALMER, AK 99645
STERLING DONER, 210 BREE AVE, ANCHORAGE, AK 99515
TANYA DONER, 5737 BIG BEND LP, ANCHORAGE, AK 99502
TIMOTHY DONER, 5737 BIG BEND LP, ANCHORAGE, AK 99502
AARON DUCKER, BOX 155, KASILOF, AK 99610
BRANDON DUCKER, 23259 COHOE LP RD, KASILOF, AK 99610
DANELL DUCKER, 22838 COHOE LOOP RD, KASILOF, AK 99610
JEANNETTE DUCKER, 22838 COHOE LP RD, KASILOF, AK 99610
MARK DUCKER, 23259 COHOE LP RD, KASILOF, AK 99610
SAMANTHA DUCKER, 22838 COHOE LP RD, KASILOF, AK 99610
SUZANNE DUCKER, 23259 COHOE LP RD, KASILOF, AK 99610
JACK DUCLOS, 16962 BEDFORD CHASE CIR, ANCHORAGE, AK 99516
JACOB DUENAS, 3108 GLENN DON DR, ANCHORAGE, AK 99504
DIANA DUNCAN, BOX 533, KASILOF, AK 99610
DENNIS EFFENBECK, 37275 MOSER ST, SOLDOTNA, AK 99669
CLAYTON ELDREDGE, GEN DEL, KETCHIKAN, AK 99901
FRED ELVSAAS, 5250 W BEVERLY LAKE RD, WASILLA, AK 99623
IVAN ENCELEWSKI, BOX 39773, NINILCHIK, AK 99639
RICHARD ENCELEWSKI, BOX 39066, NINILCHIK, AK 99639
KENNETH EVANS, 4826 JUMAR AVE, ANCHORAGE, AK 99516
MATTHEW EVANS, 4826 JUMAR AVE, ANCHORAGE, AK 99516
AMBER EVERY, 360 DOLCHOK, KENAI, AK 99611
KRISTEN EVERY, 2720 SET NET CT, KENAI, AK 99611

LORRAINE EVERY, 37033 MINKE DR, KENAI, AK 99611
MARILYN EVERY, 58132 KENAI SPUR HWY, KENAI, AK 99611
TRAVIS EVERY, 360 DOLCHOK, KENAI, AK 99611
WILLIAM FAULKNER, BOX 554, CLAM GULCH, AK 99568
WILLIAM FIELD, 50550 KENAI SPUR HWY, KENAI, AK 99611
ERNEST FINCH, 3401 SHAMROCK ST, ANCHORAGE, AK 99504
ROBERT FINCH, 11238 TULIN PARK LP, ANCHORAGE, AK 99516
ROGER FRANCISCO, BOX 201, KENAI, AK 99611
BRIAN GABRIEL, 2305 WATERGATE WAY, KENAI, AK 99611
LISA GABRIEL, 2305 WATERGATE WAY, KENAI, AK 99611
AGUSTUS GAETKE, 51655 IRIS CIR, KENAI, AK 99611
WILLIAM GALLIAND, BOX 75, SELDOVIA, AK 99663
DEMERY GARRANT, BOX 107, KASILOF, AK 99610
RONALD GARRANT, BOX 107, KASILOF, AK 99610
SHEILA GARRANT, BOX 107, KASILOF, AK 99610
MICHAEL GATLING, BOX 401, KENAI, AK 99611
BETTY GILCRIST, BOX 4256, SOLDOTNA, AK 99669
JOHN GILCRIST, BOX 4256, SOLDOTNA, AK 99669
TOM GORDON, 35900 LAKE RD, SOLDOTNA, AK 99669
ALFRED GRANGER, 837 AMANITA RD, FAIRBANKS, AK 99712
AMY GRANNUM, 5120 33RD AVE W, EVERETT, WA 98201
JACK GRANNUM, 5120 33RD AVE W, EVERETT, WA 98203
NATALIE GRANNUM, 5120 33RD AVE W, EVERETT, WA 98203
ROBERT GRANNUM, 5120 33RD AVE W, EVERETT, WA 98201
BRYSON GUARIN, 414 BONANZA ST, HOMER, AK 99603
SANDRA HAINES, 309 BEAN HILL RD, ENDICOTT, NY 13760
GEORGE HALL, BOX 771663, EAGLE RIVER, AK 99577
MELISSA HALL, BOX 771663, EAGLE RIVER, AK 99577
REILLY HALL, BOX 771663, EAGLE RIVER, AK 99577
DEBBIE HALSEY, BOX 323, SOLDOTNA, AK 99669
RONALD HALSEY, BOX 323, SOLDOTNA, AK 99669
MINDY HALVERSON, BOX 165, KASILOF, AK 99610
JOHN HAMILTON, 1113 KAKNU WAY, KENAI, AK 99611
RICHARD HAMILTON, BOX 252, WILLOW, AK 99688
CHEYENNE HANNAMAN, 14114 95TH AVE NW, GIG HARBOR, WA 98329
MARTHA HANSEN, BOX 101885, ANCHORAGE, AK 99510
CRAIG HARRISON, 19445 NORMANDY PARK DR SW, NORMANDY PK, WA 98166
STEPHEN HARRISON, BOX 193, TALKEETNA, AK 99676
KEVIN HARTLEY, BOX 2324, PALMER, AK 99645
KIRK HARTLEY, BOX 2324, PALMER, AK 99645
TONI HARTLEY, BOX 2324, PALMER, AK 99645
THOMAS HASBROUCK, 3001 E REGAL CT, WASILLA, AK 99654
BRANDON HATCH, 320 N 11TH AVE, POCATELLO, ID 83201
GREGORY HAYES, BOX 874264, WASILLA, AK 99687
OSCAR HAYNES, 4677 N CHARLEY DR, WASILLA, AK 99654
JULIE HECKERT, BOX 6941, NIKISKI, AK 99635
DOROTHY HERMANSEN, BOX 235, KASILOF, AK 99610
LAURA HERMANSEN, 205 E DIMOND BLVD PMB 507, ANCHORAGE, AK 99515
MARIE.ELISE HERMANSEN, BOX 1168, KASILOF, AK 99610
MARTIN HERMANSEN, 710 BONANZA AVE, ANCHORAGE, AK 99518
SUSAN HERMANSEN.JENT, 4721 JUMAR AVE, ANCHORAGE, AK 99516
JARED HERMON, 15255 E ROBIN LN, PALMER, AK 99645
KENT HERMON, 16455 E MAUD RD, PALMER, AK 99645
MARK HERMON, BOX 2394, BARROW, AK 99723
THOMAS HERMON, 15255 E ROBIN LN, PALMER, AK 99645
PAGE HERRING, BOX 1169, HOMER, AK 99603
RICHARD HILLEARY, BOX 8301, NIKISKI, AK 99635
NANCY HILLSTRAND, BOX 674, HOMER, AK 99603
ROMAYNE HINDMAN, BOX 2368, KENAI, AK 99611
THOMAS HINDMAN, BOX 2368, KENAI, AK 99611
NATHAN HOFF, 4116 W 88TH AVE #1, ANCHORAGE, AK 99502
CARRIE HOLLIER, 36045 REEF DR, KENAI, AK 99611
GARY HOLLIER, 36045 REEF DR, KENAI, AK 99611
JOANNA HOLLIER, 36045 REEF DR, KENAI, AK 99611
GAVIN HUDKINS, 11620 NE 150TH PL, KIRKLAND, WA 98034
JASON HUDKINS, 11620 NE 150TH PL, KIRKLAND, WA 98034

SALMON FISHING LIST—SET GILLNET

SARAH HUDKINS, 11620 NE 150TH PL, KIRKLAND, WA 98034
BRUCE HUDSON, BOX 82, TALKEETNA, AK 99676
CHARLES HUDSON, BOX 418, TALKEETNA, AK 99676
MICHAEL HUHNDORF, BOX 2557, KENAI, AK 99611
SHELIA ISAAK, BOX 1341, SOLDOTNA, AK 99669
BENJAMIN JACKINSKY, BOX 20, KASILOF, AK 99610
JOANN JACKINSKY, BOX 1025, KASILOF, AK 99610
LEAH JACKSON, 52500 LEAH ST, KENAI, AK 99611
TONY JACKSON, 52500 LEAH ST, KENAI, AK 99611
RONALD JACOB, BOX 451, KASILOF, AK 99610
TYLER JANOWSKI, 12346 SHENANDOAH RD, ANCHORAGE, AK 99516
SETH JARAMILLO, BOX 554, CLAM GULCH, AK 99568
JOHN JENT, 4721 JUMAR AVE, ANCHORAGE, AK 99516
ANDREA JOACHIM, 42010 FUNNY RIVER RD, SOLDOTNA, AK 99669
DONALD JOACHIM, 42010 FUNNY RIVER RD, SOLDOTNA, AK 99669
ARNOLD JOHNSON, BOX 39268, NINILCHIK, AK 99639
BENJAMIN JOHNSON, 139 S 200 W, HYRUM, UT 84319
BRENT JOHNSON, 20773 PORCUPINE LN, CLAM GULCH, AK 99568
CHARINE JOHNSON, BOX 1194, KASILOF, AK 99610
CYNTHIA JOHNSON, BOX 39268, NINILCHIK, AK 99639
DEBORAH JOHNSON, 819 GEISSLER RD, MONTESANO, WA 98563
GINGER JOHNSON, 20773 PORCUPINE LN, CLAM GULCH, AK 99568
GREG JOHNSON, 12400 NE 8TH CT, VANCOUVER, WA 98685
JUDITH JOHNSON, 20773 PORCUPINE LN, CLAM GULCH, AK 99568
MERRICK JOHNSON, 12400 NE 8TH COURT, VANCOUVER, WA 98685
PATRICIA JOHNSON, 12400 NE 8TH COURT, VANCOUVER, WA 98685
TYLER JOHNSON, 819 GEISSLER RD, MONTESANO, WA 98563
VIOLET JOHNSON, 20773 PORCUPINE LN, CLAM GULCH, AK 99568
SHARON JOHNSON.DEIMAN, BOX 39224, NINILCHIK, AK 99639
MELVIN JOHNSTON, 732 NASH ST, FRIDAY HARBOR, WA 98250
BRANDON JONES, 212 SHIRLEY ST, MOLALLA, OR 97038
MARK JONES, 13488 PASEO TERRANO, SALINAS, CA 93908
SHAWN JONES, 46975 BASE RD, SOLDOTNA, AK 99669
ERNEST JORDAN, BOX 90, KENAI, AK 99611
JACOB JORDAN, 16455 E MAUD RD, PALMER, AK 99645
JAMES JORGENSEN, 3237 S TREASURE COVE PL, TUCSON, AZ 85713
KATHERINE JULIUSSEN, 2090 6TH AVE APT 12, KENAI, AK 99611
MICHAEL JULIUSSEN, 1117 2ND ST, KENAI, AK 99611
CLINTON KEENER, BOX 2833, KENAI, AK 99611
MARILYN KEENER, BOX 2833, KENAI, AK 99611
TIMOTHY KEENER, BOX 2833, KENAI, AK 99611
CYNTHIA KIRCHER, BOX 95, KASILOF, AK 99610
KARL KIRCHER, BOX 95, KASILOF, AK 99610
NICOLE KLONIZOS, 36566 SHORT CIR, KENAI, AK 99611
AVERY KORNSTAD, 46701 JOYCE CIR, KENAI, AK 99611
JANEECE KORNSTAD, 46695 JOYCE CIR, KENAI, AK 99611
REID KORNSTAD, 46701 JOYCE CIR, KENAI, AK 99611
VERN KORNSTAD, 46695 JOYCE CIR, KENAI, AK 99611
BRIAN KOSKI, BOX 342, SOLDOTNA, AK 99669
GARY KOSKI, BOX 342, SOLDOTNA, AK 99669
KEARY KOSKI, BOX 342, SOLDOTNA, AK 99669
BRIAN KRAGER, 1084 CARMEL CT, SHOREVIEW, MN 54126
JOAN KRAGER, BOX 949, KENAI, AK 99611
SUSAN KRAGER, 4890 CHURCHILL ST, SHOREVIEW, MN 55126
HENRY KROLL, 26571 HEAVY DOWN DR, SOLDOTNA, AK 99669
MARY KROLL, 26571 HEAVY DAWN DR, SOLDOTNA, AK 99669
JEFF KUK, 860 SET NET DR, KENAI, AK 99611
ISABEL KULHANEK, BOX 3002, HOMER, AK 99603
JON KULHANEK, BOX 3002, HOMER, AK 99603
HELEN KURTZ, 2125 N OLD GLENN HWY, PALMER, AK 99645
STEVEN KURTZ, 7010 CHAD ST, ANCHORAGE, AK 99518
DANIEL KVASNIKOFF, BOX 8073, NANWALEK, AK 99603
EMERSON KVASNIKOFF, BOX 8044, NANWALEK, AK 99603
ERIC KVASNIKOFF, BOX 8029, NANWALEK, AK 99603
JAMES KVASNIKOFF, 37700 DIANE ST, STERLING, AK 99672

JAMES LAMSON, BOX 520765, BIG LAKE, AK 99652
LEWIS LAMSON, 18221 TEDROW CIR, EAGLE RIVER, AK 99577
BRAD LANGVARDT, BOX 213, SELDOVIA, AK 99663
JAMES LANIER, 19643 TENADA AVE, CHUGIAK, AK 99567
STEPHEN LAROSA, 5722 BIG BEND LP, ANCHORAGE, AK 99502
GREGORY LAWALTER, 1930 N BATTERY CIR, PALMER, AK 99645
JAMES LAZAR, 39805 SMITH RD, SOLDOTNA, AK 99669
BOYD LEMAN, 11675 STERLING HWY, NINILCHIK, AK 99639
CAROLYN LEMAN, 2699 NATHANIEL CT, ANCHORAGE, AK 99517
ERICA LEMAN, 12101 GRAIFF ST, ANCHORAGE, AK 99507
ERIK LEMAN, BOX 582, NAKNEK, AK 99633
HARRY LEMAN, BOX 39154, NINILCHIK, AK 99639
JOSEPH LEMAN, 12101 GRAIFF ST, ANCHORAGE, AK 99507
LOREN LEMAN, 2699 NATHANIEL CT, ANCHORAGE, AK 99517
SHELLE LEMAN, BOX 929, KASILOF, AK 99610
MATT LETZRING, BOX 6, KASILOF, AK 99610
JOHN LIGHT, 4300 NATRONA AVE, ANCHORAGE, AK 99516
PAUL LILEY, 835 W 9TH AVE, ANCHORAGE, AK 99501
DEBORAH LIMACHER, BOX 3001, HOMER, AK 99603
CHRISTOPHER LITTLE, BOX 8133, NIKISKI, AK 99635
IAN LLESHI, BOX 1346, KENAI, AK 99611
DENALI LOCKWOOD, BOX 1566, KENAI, AK 99611
MARK LOCKWOOD, BOX 1566, KENAI, AK 99611
MICHAEL LOCKWOOD, BOX 2709, KENAI, AK 99611
SUSAN LOCKWOOD, BOX 2709, KENAI, AK 99611
PATRICK LORENTZ, 3910 CROSSON DR, ANCHORAGE, AK 99517
MELISSA M.PIATT, 48215 LAKESIDFE AVE, SOLDOTNA, AK 99669
ADAM MACCABEE, 410 SPRING LN, SEDRO WOOLLEY, WA 98284
GEORGE MACCABEE, 2221 MULDOON #545, ANCHORAGE, AK 99504
BRUCE MANLEY, BOX 371, KASILOF, AK 99610
JOHN MANLEY, BOX 3047, KENAI, AK 99611
PAMELA MANLEY, BOX 735, KASILOF, AK 99610
JULIE MARCINKOWSKI, BOX 7428, NIKISKI, AK 99635
LEON MARCINKOWSKI, BOX 7428, NIKISKI, AK 99635
FRANCIS MARINER, 63650 STERLING HWY, CLAM GULCH, AK 99568
DANE MARKHAM, BOX 2357, KENAI, AK 99611
MICHAEL MARKHAM, BOX 2357, KENAI, AK 99611
MICHELE MARKHAM, 6209 E BASELINE RD, MESA, AZ 85206
ZACHARY MARKHAM, 6209 E BASELINE RD, MESA, AZ 85206
BRUCE MARKWOOD, 4451 NATRONA AVE, ANCHORAGE, AK 99516
HANNAH MARKWOOD, 4451 NATRONA AVE, ANCHORAGE, AK 99516
PAMELA MARKWOOD, 4451 NATRONA AVE, ANCHORAGE, AK 99516
EVAN MARTHEDAL, 6334 S ORANGE AVE, FRESNO, CA 93725
DARREN MARTIN, 32212 NW LACENTER RD, RIDGEFIELD, WA 98642
JACK MARTIN, BOX 816, SOLDOTNA, AK 99669
LANDON MARTIN, 32212 NW LACENTER RD, RIDGEFIELD, WA 98642
SHAREE MARTIN, 32212 NW LACENTER, RIDGEFIELD, WA 98642
LARRY MATSON, BOX 39034, NINILCHIK, AK 99639
DAVID MATTOX, 47 PARK VALE AVE #12, ALLSTON, MA 2134
JUSTIN MCCASLIN, 8111 LAKONIA DR, ANCHORAGE, AK 99516
WAYNE MCCORD, BOX 82075, TYONEK, AK 99682
MERRILL MCGAHAN, BOX 8022, NIKISKI, AK 99635
MERRILL MCGAHAN, BOX 7146, NIKISKI, AK 99635
JAMES MCGRATH, BOX 611, NINILCHIK, AK 99639
KRISTI MCLEAN, BOX 213, SELDOVIA, AK 99663
JUANITA MEIER, BOX 165, KASILOF, AK 99610
RANDY MEIER, BOX 165, KASILOF, AK 99610
PETER MELENCHEK, 14122 SNOWDRIFT WY, ANCHORAGE, AK 99515
MICHAEL METTEER, BOX 109, KENAI, AK 99611
DANIEL MEYER, 47430 DOUGLAS LN, KENAI, AK 99611
RORY MILLAR, BOX 213, SELDOVIA, AK 99663
JAMES MILLER, 3362 330TH ST, WELLMAN, IA 52356
JOHN MILLS, BOX 260, KASILOF, AK 99610
MARIAH MILLS, 115 N KOBUK, SOLDOTNA, AK 99669
PAULINE MILLS, BOX 260, KASILOF, AK 99610

SALMON FISHING LIST—SET GILLNET

DARRELL MISNER, BOX 1250, KASILOF, AK 99610
CHRISTOPHER MONFOR, BOX 2942, KENAI, AK 99611
CLARA MOONIN, BOX 75, SELDOVIA, AK 99663
EUGENE MOORE, 16151 NICKLEEN ST, ANCHORAGE, AK 99511
KENNETH MOORE, BOX 4192, HOMER, AK 99603
TODD MOORE, BOX 4152, SOLDOTNA, AK 99669
DALLAS MOULTRIE, 15817 W WHITEHOUSE LN, CHENEY, WA 99004
MICHAEL NAKADA, BOX 1838, HOMER, AK 99603
BYRON NALOS, BOX 7581, NIKISKI, AK 99635
MARIA NALOS, BOX 7581, NIKISKI, AK 99635
BRADEN NASH, 1851 NW 4TH AVE, ONTERIO, OR 97914
SHEA NASH, 151 SHADY LN, SOLDOTNA, AK 99669
BRIAN NELSON, BOX 7204, NIKISKI, AK 99635
BRIAN NELSON, 5300 SECLUDED CIR, ANCHORAGE, AK 99516
CHASE NELSON, 3697 FRENCHMAN RD, FAIRBANKS, AK 99709
GUNNAR NELSON, 5300 SECLUDED CIR, ANCHORAGE, AK 99516
PAUL NELSON, 21531 RENAULT ST, KASILOF, AK 99610
TERESA NELSON, BOX 7204, NIKISKI, AK 99635
TODD NELSON, BOX 8325, NIKISKI, AK 99635
ZACHARY NELSON, 5300 SECLUDED CR, ANCHORAGE, AK 99516
JULIE NICHOLS, 23545 S COHOE LP RD, KASILOF, AK 99610
KEITH NICHOLS, 23545 S COHOE LP RD, KASILOF, AK 99610
KIEL NICHOLS, 23545 S COHOE LP RD, KASILOF, AK 99610
JEREMY NOET, 1050 LARRABLE AVE #104 PMB 368, BELLINGHAM, WA 98225
MAGAN NOET, 1050 LARRABLE AVE #104 PMB 368, BELLINGHAM, WA 98225
DANIEL NORMAN, 36045 REEF DR, KENAI, AK 99611
GEORGE NYCE, BOX 401, KENAI, AK 99611
JESSICA NYCE, 1850 KUSKOKWIM ST, ANCHORAGE, AK 99508
ROBERTA NYCE, BOX 401, KENAI, AK 99611
SUSAN OAKLEY, 750 INDIAN RD, INDIAN, AK 99540
ROYCE ODER, BOX 389, KASILOF, AK 99610
STEPHEN OKKONEN, BOX 1025, KASILOF, AK 99610
PATRICIA OLENDER, 48077 GRANT AVE, KENAI, AK 99611
DEAN OSMAR, BOX 32, CLAM GULCH, AK 99568
MYDZUNG OSMAR, BOX 32, CLAM GULCH, AK 99568
TIMOTHY OSMAR, BOX 382, KASILOF, AK 99610
DANIEL OWEN, 33150 BAYLOR ST, SOLDOTNA, AK 99669
DEBBI PALM, 55140 E CHINOOK RD, KENAI, AK 99611
EUGENE PALM, 55140 E CHINOOK RD, KENAI, AK 99611
DEBORAH PALMER, 1140 N PINION DR, WASILLA, AK 99654
CHRISTOPHER PARKER, BOX 2724, KENAI, AK 99611
NATHANIEL PATSOS, 28172 SPRUCE PARK CIR, SOLDOTNA, AK 99669
TAMARA PELLEGROM, 113 DEEPWOOD CT, KENAI, AK 99611
JOSEPH PERSON, BOX 873, ANCHOR POINT, AK 99556
LILLIAN PERSON, 24120 RAMBLERS RD #A, CHUGIAK, AK 99567
MATTHEW PERSON, 24120 RAMBLERS RD, CHUGIAK, AK 99567
RICHARD PERSON, 24120 RAMBLERS RD, CHUGIAK, AK 99567
SAMUEL PETER, 6830 GOLD KINGS CIR #B, ANCHORAGE, AK 99504
CHRISTINE PETERS, 3406 N WELLINGTON PL, SPOKANE, WA 99205
DOUGLAS PETERSEN, 1757 APACHE DR, LARAMIE, WY 82072
W.BRYAN PETERSEN, 824 LAKEVIEW, STANSBURY PARK, UT 84074
RYAN PETERSON, 2900 WENTWORTH, ANCHORAGE, AK 99508
RALPH PETTERSON, 1007 MISSION AVE, KENAI, AK 99611
ALEX PFOFF, BOX 82087, TYONEK, AK 99682
JENNIFER PORTER, BOX 7081, NIKISKI, AK 99635
JEREMY POWERS, 10703 S OLD GLEN HWY, PALMER, AK 99645
KEITH PRESLEY, BOX 39370, NINILCHIK, AK 99639
TYLER PRESLEY, BOX 39370, NINILCHIK, AK 99639
ROBERTA PROCTOR, BOX 28, ANCHOR POINT, AK 99556
CHARLES PULLIAM, 4827 GRINSTEAD PL, NACHVILLE, TN 37216
HELEN QUIJANCE, BOX 79, SELDOVIA, AK 99663
LEE RAFTER, BOX 1772, KENAI, AK 99611
CRAIG RALSTON, 51655 IRIS CIR, KENAI, AK 99611
JOHNATHAN RALSTON, 51655 IRIS CIR, KENAI, AK 99611
LINDA RALSTON, 51655 IRIS CIR, KENAI, AK 99611
ERIC RANDALL, BOX 149, ANCHOR POINT, AK 99556

BENJAMIN RANSOM, BOX 74, KASILOF, AK 99610
GERALYNN RANSOM, BOX 74, KASILOF, AK 99610
MADELINE RANSOM, BOX 74, KASILOF, AK 99610
BRUNO RATHKE, BOX 319, KASILOF, AK 99610
GREGORY RAZO, 2939 DARTMOUTH DR, ANCHORAGE, AK 99508
RAYMOND REDINGTON, BOX 877653, WASILLA, AK 99687
ROBERT REDMOND, BOX 494, GIRDWOOD, AK 99587
CHAD RENNER, 14305 CHAWA CIR, ANCHORAGE, AK 99516
CINDY RENNER, 14310 CHAWA CIR, ANCHORAGE, AK 99516
TYRELL RENNER, BOX 211, KASILOF, AK 99610
NANCY RICHAR, BOX 13191, TRAPPER CREEK, AK 99683
MATTHEW RICHARD, 317 MAJOR WAY, SUN PRARIE, WI 53590
CORAL RICKETTS.YOTTER, BOX 6436, HALIBUT COVE, AK 99603
BRANDON RIDER, BOX 1359, ANCHOR POINT, AK 99556
ANN RODGERS, 5433 W 73RD, ANCHORAGE, AK 99502
CALVIN RODGERS, 7333 BASEL ST, ANCHORAGE, AK 99507
KENNY RODGERS, 7333 BASEL ST, ANCHORAGE, AK 99507
RAY RODGERS, 5433 W 73RD, ANCHORAGE, AK 99502
ADRIA ROLLMAN, BOX 7073, NIKISKI, AK 99635
TREVOR ROLLMAN, BOX 7073, NIKISKI, AK 99635
ROBERT ROOD, 99 TUNAPUNA LN, CORONADO, CA 92118
SEAN ROOD, 3241 NUGGET LN, ANCHORAGE, AK 99516
LAWRENCE RORRISON, BOX 250, KENAI, AK 99611
JOHN ROSS, BOX 86, SELDOVIA, AK 99663
MARK ROSS, 56335 GLENN RD, HOMER, AK 99603
LARRY ROZAK, BOX 1179, HOMER, AK 99603
CURT RUDD, 5603 DALZELL CR, ANCHORAGE, AK 99507
KEVIN RULLMAN, 7209 FOXRIDGE CIRCLE #1, ANCHORAGE, AK 99518
RENO RUTTUM, 3307 DORIS ST, ANCHORAGE, AK 99517
RIC RUTTUM, 3307 DORIS ST, ANCHORAGE, AK 99517
ANDY RUTTY, 1944 OLD STEESE CABIN B, FAIRBANKS, AK 99712
HOWARD RYHERD, 101 LINDA LN, SOLDOTNA, AK 99669
JAMES RYHERD, 3330 N EDGEWATER DR, WASILLA, AK 99623
STACEY RYHERD, 3330 N EDGEWATER DR, WASILLA, AK 99623
SUSAN RYHERD, 101 LINDA LN, SOLDOTNA, AK 99669
KYLE SARVELA, BOX 7572, NIKISKI, AK 99635
SUZANNE SAXON, 2409 MARILAINE DR, ANCHORAGE, AK 99517
ADAM SCHEER, BOX 298581, WASILLA, AK 99629
DAVID SCHEER, BOX 298581, WASILLA, AK 99629
ARMIN SCHMIDT, 36371 K BEACH RD UNIT A, KENAI, AK 99611
DAVID SCHMIDT, BOX 2288, KENAI, AK 99611
MARCIA SCHOOLEY, 26547 S COHOE LP, KASILOF, AK 99610
GREG SCHUMACHER, 9320 AUTUMN RIDGE CIR, ANCHORAGE, AK 99507
JOSEPH SCHWARTZ, 35555 SPUR HWY #142, SOLDOTNA, AK 99669
BRIAN SCOW, 2402 RIO BRANCA, HACIENDA, CA 91745
NANCY SCOW, 2402 RIO BRANCA, HACIENDA, CA 91745
CALLESTA SEATER, BOX 7552, NIKISKI, AK 99635
CHARLES SEATER, BOX 7552, NIKISKI, AK 99635
DYLAN SEATER, BOX 7552, NIKISKI, AK 99635
KATRINA SEATER, 13250 STEPHENSON ST, ANCHORAGE, AK 99515
KIMBERLY SEATER, 4501 SW 100TH ST, SEATTLE, WA 98146
LEE SEATER, 537 TIMBERLAKE DR, ASHLAND, OR 97520
ANTHONY SEE, 3240 W 71ST AVE, ANCHORAGE, AK 99502
EDWARD SEILER, 362 CULOMBINE ST, SOLDOTNA, AK 99669
KEVIN SEVILLE, BOX 8051, NANWALEK, AK 99603
CHRISTINA SHADURA, BOX 1632, KENAI, AK 99611
ELIZAVETA SHADURA, BOX 985, KASILOF, AK 99610
PAUL SHADURA, BOX 1632, KENAI, AK 99611
VIRGINIA SHADURA, BOX 1632, KENAI, AK 99611
ELI SHERIDAN, BOX 4136, SOLDOTNA, AK 99669
PHILIP SHERIDAN, BOX 4136, SOLDOTNA, AK 99669
DANIEL SHILLING, 1821 BLUEGRASS CIR, ANCHORAGE, AK 99502
BENNETT SIPES, 950 WOLVERINE DR, WOLVERINE LAKE, MI 48390
ANGELA SMITH, BOX 1710, KENAI, AK 99611
CHARLES SMITH, BOX 1710, KENAI, AK 99611
DARRELL SMITH, BOX 903, KASILOF, AK 99610

SALMON FISHING LIST—SET GILLNET

EVELYN SMITH, BOX 877563, WASILLA, AK 99687
KAHLENE SMITH, BOX 1710, KENAI, AK 99611
LORI SMITH, BOX 951, KENAI, AK 99611
MEGAN SMITH, BOX 951, KENAI, AK 99611
ROBERT SMITH, BOX 1343, STERLING, AK 99672
ROCKWELL SMITH, BOX 951, KENAI, AK 99611
STEVEN SMITH, BOX 877563, WASILLA, AK 99687
TODD SMITH, BOX 951, KENAI, AK 99611
DUSTIN SOLBERG, BOX 2052, CORDOVA, AK 99574
STEPHEN SPECK, BOX 13146, TRAPPER CREEK, AK 99683
DONALD STANDIFER, BOX 82001, TYONEK, AK 99682
DONALD STANDIFER, BOX 82051, TYONEK, AK 99682
ERNEST STANDIFER, BOX 82024, TYONEK, AK 99682
FRANK STANDIFER, BOX 82048, TYONEK, AK 99682
JOHN STANDIFER, BOX 82064, TYONEK, AK 99682
RANDY STANDIFER, BOX 82071, TYONEK, AK 99682
RONALD STANEK, 3623 LYNN DR, ANCHORAGE, AK 99508
BRENDAN STASSEL, 1217 E KLATT RD, ANCHORAGE, AK 99515
FRED STASSEL, BOX 112226, ANCHORAGE, AK 99511
RYAN STASSEL, 1217 E KLATT RD, ANCHORAGE, AK 99515
STEVEN STASSEL, 1217 E KLATT RD, ANCHORAGE, AK 99515
GRANT STEELE, 195 OCEAN PARK DR, ANCHORAGE, AK 99515
JOHN STEIBLE, 1753 CHEROKEE CT, MARYVILLE, TN 37801
MATTHEW STEIBLE, 3602 PARSONS AVENUE, ANCHORAGE, AK 99508
JEFFRY STEIG, 2300 N COTTONWOOD LP, WASILLA, AK 99654
SUSAN STEINBACH, BOX 312, KASILOF, AK 99610
ROBERT STENEHJEM, 48060 WOKEN CT, KENAI, AK 99611
ISAAC STEPHAN, 101 SW EVANS AVE, PORT ST LUCIE, FL 34984
LESTER STEPHAN, 7505 BOUNDRY #5, ANCHORAGE, AK 99504
MICHAEL STEPHAN, 6200 CAMROSE DR, ANCHORAGE, AK 99504
ELLIOT STEWART, 6405 OLD SEWARD HWY, ANCHORAGE, AK 99518
JOSHUA STINNETT, BOX 514, KASILOF, AK 99610
MICHAEL STRATTON, BOX 2468, PALMER, AK 99645
CATHERINE STURMAN, 386 W VINE ST, SOLDOTNA, AK 99669
MARY STURMAN, BOX 513, SOLDOTNA, AK 99669
STEVE STURMAN, 43535 EDDIES WAY, KENAI, AK 99611
SCOTT SUMMERS, BOX 948, SOLDOTNA, AK 99669
KRISTA SUTTON, 11675 STERLING HWY, NINILCHIK, AK 99639
MICHAEL SUTTON, BOX 39214, NINILCHIK, AK 99639
GARY SWAN, 875 N LUCUS RD #A, WASILLA, AK 99654
PAUL SWENNING, BOX 8072, NANWALEK, AK 99603
ALEXANDRIA SWICK, BOX 112, SELDOVIA, AK 99663
GRIFFIN SWICK, BOX 112, SELDOVIA, AK 99663
KENNETH SWICK, BOX 112, SELDOVIA, AK 99663
ROBERTA SWICK, BOX 112, SELDOVIA, AK 99663
JACK SWISS, 533 W 2ND AVE, ANCHORAGE, AK 99501
JOHN SWISS, 6920 KITLISA DR, ANCHORAGE, AK 99502
LEAH SWISS, 6920 KITLISA DR, ANCHORAGE, AK 99502
LINDA SWISS, 6920 KITLISA DR, ANCHORAGE, AK 99502
JACQUELYN TAYLOR, 50495 ONSLOW AVE, KENAI, AK 99611
NANCY TAYLOR, 7617 E 4TH AVE, ANCHORAGE, AK 99504
RAY TESSARO, BOX 304, CLAM GULCH, AK 99568
DANIEL THISTLE, 9793 W TRIMOTER ST, WASILLA, AK 99654
LEVI THISTLE, 140 EAGLE ST #302, ANCHORAGE, AK 99501
RICHARD THISTLE, 6379 S RAINS DR, WASILLA, AK 99623
FREDERICK THOERNER, 9033 WASHBURN ST #1, ANCHORAGE, AK 99502
ARNE TIKKA, BOX 2324, SOLDOTNA, AK 99669
GARRETT TIKKA, BOX 2324, SOLDOTNA, AK 99669
MATTHEW TIKKA, 311 CULUMBINE, SOLDOTNA, AK 99669
NATHAN TIKKA, BOX 2324, SOLDOTNA, AK 99669
SHARON TIKKA, 311 COLUMBINE ST, SOLDOTNA, AK 99669
MARY TOLL, BOX 725, KASILOF, AK 99610
ROBERT TOLL, BOX 96, KASILOF, AK 99610
GEORGE TOWNSEND, BOX 817, KENAI, AK 99611
HANA TREKELL, 1545 S SAINT PAUL ST, DENVER, CO 80210

LIAN TREKELL, 233 CERVANTES BLVD #102, SAN FRANCISCO, CA 94123
HEINZ TROSKA, 6721 DICKERSON DR, ANCHORAGE, AK 99504
VICKIE TYLER, BOX 109, KENAI, AK 99611
VICTOR TYLER, BOX 96, KENAI, AK 99611
LEONARD URICK, BOX 220182, ANCHORAGE, AK 99522
KRISTI VAN.HOOSE, 312 LUPINE ST, SOLDOTNA, AK 99669
WILLIAM VAN.HOOSE, 312 LUPINE ST, SOLDOTNA, AK 99669
DYER VANDEVERE, BOX 504, KASILOF, AK 99610
MATTHEW VANHOOSE, 30520 STUBBLEFIELD DR, SOLDOTNA, AK 99669
WILLIAM VANHOOSE, BOX 424, CLAM GULCH, AK 99568
DUSTY VANMETER, BOX 427, KASILOF, AK 99610
EVELYN VANMETER, BOX 498, KASILOF, AK 99610
BONNIE VAUGHN, 5722 BIG BEND LP, ANCHORAGE, AK 99502
JAKE VERSTEEG, BOX 64, GIRDWOOD, AK 99587
CARLEE VINCENT, 324 LYNNWOOD DR #1, ANCHORAGE, AK 99518
MARK VINCENT, 324 LYNNWOOD DR #1, ANCHORAGE, AK 99518
AMANDA WAGGONER, BOX 2445, KENAI, AK 99611
CARL WAGGONER, BOX 2445, KENAI, AK 99611
CHAD WAGGONER, BOX 2445, KENAI, AK 99611
DANN WAGGONER, BOX 2445, KENAI, AK 99611
HEATHER WAINAMO, 18532 CHEKOK CR, EAGLE RIVER, AK 99577
JESSE WALLACE, BOX 39771, NINILCHIK, AK 99639
DAVID WATSON, 23031 S COHOE LP, KASILOF, AK 99610
DAWNITA WATSON, 23031 S COHOE LP, KASILOF, AK 99610
STEPHEN WEBB, BOX 1127, KASILOF, AK 99610
KAREN WEBBER.WING, 9210 ELGIN CIR, ANCHORAGE, AK 99502
RANDY WEDDEL, 11565 DISCOVERY PARK, ANCHORAGE, AK 99515
SUSAN WELLS, 37305 CETACEA LN, KENAI, AK 99611
WALTER WELZ, BOX 665, HOMER, AK 99603
BROOKE WHIP, 11320 POLAR DR, ANCHORAGE, AK 99516
KATHLEEN WHIP, 1120 E HUFFMAN RD #24 PMB 301, ANCHORAGE, AK 99515
DANIEL WICHERS, 3347 N WILSON RD, OAK HARBOR, WA 98277
DAVID WICHERS, 3347 N WILSON RD, OAK HARBOR, WA 98277
JO.ANN WICHERS, 3347 N WILSON RD, OAK HARBOR, WA 98277
HOLLY WILEY, 63325 STERLING HWY, CLAM GULCH, AK 99568
HEIDI WILEY.WONG, 63650 STERLING HWY, CLAM GULCH, AK 99568
JANE WILKES, 9354 NASH RD, BOZEMAN, MT 59715
TIMOTHY WILKES, 9354 NASH RD, BOZEMAN, MT 59715
KRYSTINA WILLIAMS, BOX 206, KASILOF, AK 99610
ROBERT WILLIAMS, BOX 206, KASILOF, AK 99610
TOM WILLIAMSON, 9730 S 700 E, SANDY, UT 84104
SHARON WILLIFORD, BOX 1335, KENAI, AK 99611
JARETT WILSON, BOX 2303, KENAI, AK 99611
MARILYN WILSON, BOX 2303, KENAI, AK 99611
RUDOLPH WILSON, BOX 2303, KENAI, AK 99611
SARAH WILSON, 1851 NW 4TH AVE, ONTARIO, OR 97914
JOSH WISNIEWSKI, BOX 474, SITKA, AK 99835
LOKENI WONG, 63650 STERLING HWY, CLAM GULCH, AK 99568
MAKAYLA WONG, 63650 STERLING HWY, CLAM GULCH, AK 99568
MIKAELE WONG, 63650 STERLING HWY, CLAM GULCH, AK 99568
WAYNE WONG, 63650 STERLING HWY, CLAM GULCH, AK 99568
MICHAEL WOOD, BOX 773, TALKEETNA, AK 99676
MONTY WORTHINGTON, 15131 ECHO CANYON RD, ANCHORAGE, AK 99516
DOUGLAS WRATE, BOX 912, KASILOF, AK 99610
DANIEL WYSOCKI, 731 HIGH VIEW DR, ANCHORAGE, AK 99515
MONICA ZAPPA, BOX 382, KASILOF, AK 99610
BRIAN ZINCK, BOX 8201, NIKISKI, AK 99635
KRISTI ZURFLUH, 7601 E INDIAN BEND RD #1006, SCOTTSDALE, AZ 85250

SALMON, SET GILLNET, KODIAK
SUZANNE ABRAHAM, BOX 511, KODIAK, AK 99615
VIRGINIA ADAMS, BOX 8905, KODIAK, AK 99615
ROBERT ALLEN, 2303 PERKINS LN W, SEATTLE, WA 98199
ILA AMOS, 1031 ELDORADO, KLAMATH FALLS, OR 97601

SALMON FISHING LIST—SET GILLNET

THOMAS AMOS, 1031 ELDORADO, KLAMATH FALLS, OR 97601
JOHN ANGST, 13530 SEABREEZE CIR, ANCHORAGE, AK 99516
SHERRY BALL, BOX 3361, KODIAK, AK 99615
WADE BALL, BOX 3361, KODIAK, AK 99615
JEFFREY BASSETT, 5000 E 98TH, ANCHORAGE, AK 99507
LAURI BASSETT, 5000 E 98TH AVE, ANCHORAGE, AK 99507
JOSHUA BATEMAN, 12667 SOUTH RUSSIAN CRK RD, KODIAK, AK 99615
MARK BEARDSLEY, BOX 8776, KODIAK, AK 99615
SHEILA BEARDSLEY, BOX 8776, KODIAK, AK 99615
WENDY BECK, BOX 2790, KODIAK, AK 99615
CHRISTOPHER BERNS, BOX 23, KODIAK, AK 99615
GALEN BERNS, 1620 KRISTIN WY, MCKINLEYVILLE, CA 95519
LACEY BERNS, 1620 KRISTIN WAY, MCKINLEYVILLE, CA 95579
MADALYN BIGLER, 11038 CHANNELSIDE DR, GULFPORT, MS 39503
FERYLL BLANC, 13589 TRUMPETER LN, MOUNT VERNON, WA 98273
RICHARD BLANC, 13589 TRUMPETER LN, MOUNT VERNON, WA 98273
PHILIP BRINDLE, 12918 172ND AVE SE, RENTON, WA 98059
GABRIEL BROWN, 35717 WALKABOUT RD, HOMER, AK 99603
DANA BUCKINGHAM, BOX 166, JENNER, CA 95450
BLAKE BURKHOLDER, 11038 CHANNELSIDE DR, GULFPORT, MS 39503
KIMBERLY BURKHOLDER, 11038 CHANNELSIDE DR, GULFPORT, MS 39503
MARIANNE BURKHOLDER, 215 W SUNNY SANDS RD, CATHLAMET, WA 98612
NINA BURKHOLDER, 35717 WALKABOUT RD, HOMER, AK 99603
ANDREW CARSTENS, 11493 WOMANS BAY DR, KODIAK, AK 99615
WENDY CARSTENS, 11493 WOMENS BAY DR, KODIAK, AK 99615
DAVID CHRISTIANSEN, BOX 2, OLD HARBOR, AK 99643
HEATHER CORRIERE, BOX 8753, KODIAK, AK 99615
SIMON CORRIERE, BOX 8753, KODIAK, AK 99615
JUDY COTA, BOX 64, LARSEN BAY, AK 99624
MANDI COX, 12702 NOCH DR, KODIAK, AK 99615
PATRICIA COX, 12702 NOCH DR, KODIAK, AK 99615
JOHN CRATTY, BOX 166, JENNER, CA 95450
MAYA CURTIS, 1518 HIDDEN LN, ANCHORAGE, AK 99507
JANET DANELSKI, BOX 2333, KODIAK, AK 99615
PETER DANELSKI, BOX 2333, KODIAK, AK 99615
PETER DANELSKI, 2069 RIDGE CIR, KODIAK, AK 99615
WILLIAM DANELSKI, 2069 RIDGE CIR, KODIAK, AK 99615
MCKAY DEWEY, 1386 PHELPS LAKE DR, ROCKWALL, TX 75087
ERIC DIETERS, 455 PALMITAS ST, SOLANA BEACH, CA 92075
RITA DIETERS, 550 N LINCOLN AVE #334, LOVELAND, CO 80537
BRYAN DUFF, BOX 1330, RATHDRUM, ID 83858
DONALD DUMM, BOX 1723, KODIAK, AK 99615
HOMER DUNN, 9325 VIEW DR, JUNEAU, AK 99801
DANIEL EARLE, 5642 40TH AVE W, SEATTLE, WA 98199
SANDRA EARLE, 5642 40TH AVE W, SEATTLE, WA 98199
GABRIEL EDWARDS, BOX 8905, KODIAK, AK 99615
JONATHAN EDWARDS, BOX 8905, KODIAK, AK 99615
RICHARD ELLINGSON, BOX 633, KODIAK, AK 99615
BRYAN ELLSWORTH, 1948 MARMOT DR, KODIAK, AK 99615
CHARLES EVANS, BOX 233, NOORVIK, AK 99763
KENT EVANS, BOX 233, NOORVIK, AK 99763
ABRAHAM FIELDS, BOX 25, KODIAK, AK 99615
BETH FIELDS, BOX 25, KODIAK, AK 99615
DUNCAN FIELDS, BOX 25, KODIAK, AK 99615
LESLIE FIELDS, BOX 25, KODIAK, AK 99615
MICAH FIELDS, BOX 25, KODIAK, AK 99615
WALLACE FIELDS, BOX 1691, KODIAK, AK 99615
WESTON FIELDS, BOX 25, KODIAK, AK 99615
EDWIN FISHER, 38414 LABISKE LN, ASTORIA, OR 97103
JUDY FISHER, 38414 LABISKE LN, ASTORIA, OR 97103
KEVIN FISHER, BOX ALZ, KODIAK, AK 99697
HARVEY GOODELL, BOX 3108, KODIAK, AK 99615
LEIGH GORMAN.THOMET, BOX 3258, KODIAK, AK 99615
BRANDON GRAVES, 4430 CANYON VIEW PL, WENATCHEE, WA 98801
ERIC GRAVES, 4430 CANYON VIEW PL, WENATCHEE, WA 98801
JARL GUSTAFSON, BOX 952, HOMER, AK 99603

KATHLEEN GUSTAFSON, BOX 952, HOMER, AK 99603
JAMES HAMILTON, 1435 H ST, ANCHORAGE, AK 99501
JACK HANNAH, BOX 1803, KODIAK, AK 99615
PETER HANNAH, BOX 647, KODIAK, AK 99615
PAUL HARDER, BOX 48, NAALEHU, HI 96772
DANIEL HASLETT, 2600 BERRYMAN LN #B, ANCHORAGE, AK 99502
CLAIRE HAUGHEY, 2496 GARNER FIELD RD, UVALDE, TX 78801
LAUREN HAUGHEY, 2496 GARNER FIELD RD, WALDE, TX 78801
REBECCA HAUGHEY, 2496 GARNER FIELD RD, UVALDE, TX 78801
SAMUEL HAUGHEY, 2496 GARNER FIELD RD, UVALDE, TX 78801
PERSHING HILL, 8615 CORMORANT COVE, ANCHORAGE, AK 99507
EVA HOLM, BOX 8749, KODIAK, AK 99615
MALINA HOLM, BOX 8798, KODIAK, AK 99615
JOHN JASKOSKI, 1103 W 30TH AVE, ANCHORAGE, AK 99503
SUSAN JEFFREY, BOX 3363, KODIAK, AK 99615
GORDON JENSEN, BOX 548, KODIAK, AK 99615
NELS JENSEN, 3701 GULL DR, KODIAK, AK 99615
DARLENE JOHNSON, BOX 15, LARSEN BAY, AK 99624
JANISSA JOHNSON, BOX 15, LARSEN BAY, AK 99624
GLENN JORGENSEN, 15115 12TH DR SE, MILL CREEK, WA 98012
LARS JORGENSEN, 15115 12TH DR SE, MILL CREEK, WA 98012
C.ROSS KENDALL, 18151 WALDOW RD, OREGON CITY, OR 97045
PAUL KENDALL, 18151 WALDOW RD, OREGON CITY, OR 97045
KATHERINE KESLING, 1211 REZANOF DR, KODIAK, AK 99615
BROOK KOUREMETIS, BOX 2658, KODIAK, AK 99615
CHRISTIAN KOUREMETIS, 3378 SPRUCE CAPE RD, KODIAK, AK 99615
ELISABETH KOUREMETIS, BOX 424, KODIAK, AK 99615
LEO KOUREMETIS, BOX 424, KODIAK, AK 99615
TOM KOUREMETIS, BOX 1392, KODIAK, AK 99615
MARK KURKA, 5019 CRESCENT RIDGE DR, KILN, MS 39556
BRIAN LARGE, 517 CAROLYN ST, KODIAK, AK 99615
MARK LARSEN, 3628 KNIK AVE, ANCHORAGE, AK 99517
CALEB LEYLAND, BOX 25, KODIAK, AK 99615
DAVID LITTLE, BOX KWP, KODIAK, AK 99697
SARA LOEWEN.DANELSKI, 2069 RIDGE CIR, KODIAK, AK 99615
GEORGE MACEY, 185 W 400 N #A, SALT LAKE CITY, UT 84103
KODI METZGER, 2725 WILLEYS LAKE RD, CUSTER, WA 98240
RICHARD METZGER, 2725 WILLEYS LAKE RD, CUSTER, WA 98240
MICHAEL MILLER, 468 N MILLER ST, MESA, AZ 85203
JESSE MINGUS, BOX 1330, RATHDRUM, ID 83858
SHIRLEY MONROE, BOX 1202, KODIAK, AK 99615
TOLLEF MONSON, BOX 2971, KODIAK, AK 99615
KEITH MOORE, 14441 VAIL CUTOFF, RAINIER, WA 98576
SEAN MOORE, 14441 VAIL CUTOFF, RAINIER, WA 98576
ROBERT MUNSEY, 137 TIMBER LAKES, HERBER CITY, UT 84032
DOREECE MUTCH, 210 B SHELIKOF, KODIAK, AK 99615
SAMUEL MUTCH, 210 B SHELIKOF, KODIAK, AK 99615
SYDNEY MUTCH, 210 B SHELIKOF ST, KODIAK, AK 99615
ADELIA MYRICK, BOX 2971, KODIAK, AK 99615
ALFRED NAUMOFF, 1315 N MONTANA CIR, PALMER, AK 99645
EUGENE NAUMOFF, 1315 N MONTANA CIR, PALMER, AK 99645
NICHOLAS NEKEFEROFF, 3416 HALIBUT POINT RD #A, SITKA, AK 99835
PEGGY NEKEFEROFF, BOX 194, KODIAK, AK 99615
EDWIN NELSON, 1324 BARANOF, KODIAK, AK 99615
GUNNAR NELSON, BOX 26, PORT LIONS, AK 99550
NICK NELSON, BOX 26, PORT LIONS, AK 99550
RICKY NELSON, 413 ERSKINE, KODIAK, AK 99615
STANLEY NESS, BOX 1311, KODIAK, AK 99615
J.MICHAEL NUGENT, BOX 1937, KODIAK, AK 99615
ELLA OBRIEN, 1518 HIDDEN LN, ANCHORAGE, AK 99501
ERIK OBRIEN, 1518 HIDDEN LN, ANCHORAGE, AK 99501
STEPHEN OBRIEN, BOX 8804, KODIAK, AK 99615
JAMES OCONNOR, 2214 N 66TH ST, SCOTTSDALE, AZ 85257
DAN OGG, BOX 2754, KODIAK, AK 99615
ALLISON OMLID, 1220 GWINN ST E, MONMOUTH, OR 97361
CELESTINE OMLID, BOX 545, KODIAK, AK 99615

SALMON FISHING LIST—SET GILLNET

KEITH OMLID, 1220 GWINN ST E, MONMOUTH, OR 97361
KENDRA OMLID, BOX 7304, LOVELAND, CO 80537
MARK OMLID, BOX 7304, LOVELAND, CO 80537
OLUF OMLID, BOX 545, KODIAK, AK 99615
SUSAN PAYNE, BOX 1903, KODIAK, AK 99615
CHARLES PETERSON, 1850 THREE SISTERS WAY, KODIAK, AK 99615
DONALD PETERSON, 9325 VIEW DR, JUNEAU, AK 99801
JAMES PETERSON, 9325 VIEW DR, JUNEAU, AK 99801
KIMBERLY PETERSON, 9325 VIEW DR, JUNEAU, AK 99801
MARY PETERSON, 5028 MILLS DR, ANCHORAGE, AK 99508
THERESA PETERSON, 1850 THREE SISTERS WAY, KODIAK, AK 99615
JANE PETRICH, BOX 52, LARSEN BAY, AK 99624
GEOFFREY POPE, BOX 1760, BAYFIELD, CO 81122
GABRIEL PRICE.HALL, 2016 GOLF COURSE RD, BAYSIDE, CA 95524
ALF PRYOR, 1217 LARCH ST, KODIAK, AK 99615
JAMES PRYOR, 1012 STELLER WAY, KODIAK, AK 99615
PAUL RENTKO, 414 17TH PL, SNOHOMISH, WA 98290
DONNA RHODES, 91 SEAVIEW ST, CHATHAM, MA 2633
STEVE RITTENHOUSE, BOX KWP, KODIAK, AK 99615
THOMAS SCHWANTES, BOX 1911, KODIAK, AK 99615
ALEX SHUGAK, BOX 123, OLD HARBOR, AK 99643
CHASE SHUGAK, BOX 123, OLD HARBOR, AK 99643
ALBERT SIMEONOFF, BOX 5038, AKHIOK, AK 99615
CLAUDE SLATER, BOX 460, CARLSBORG, WA 98324
JANELLE SOMAN, 1254 MONARCH DR, LONGMONT, CO 80504
TERRI SPRINGER, BOX 1790, KODIAK, AK 99615
THOMAS SPRINGER, BOX 1790, KODIAK, AK 99615
LISA SQUARTSOFF, BOX 70, PORT LIONS, AK 99550
THEODORE SQUARTSOFF, BOX 77, OUZINKIE, AK 99644
MICHAEL STAPLEY, 1422 NE 20TH AVE, GAINSVILLE, FL 32609
ALAN STOVER, BOX 727, KODIAK, AK 99615
TOBY SULLIVAN, BOX 3047, KODIAK, AK 99615
KEVIN THOMET, BOX 3258, KODIAK, AK 99615
BRADLEY UNDERWOOD, 17800 ASHLAND DR, ANCHORAGE, AK 99516
KAY UNDERWOOD, 7140 BIG MOUNTAIN DR, ANCHORAGE, AK 99516
PAUL VICK, BOX 82651, FAIRBANKS, AK 99708
LEE WALTERS, 472 NE JACKSON ST, HILLSBORO, OR 97124
CORINA WATT, 38414 LABISKE LN, ASTORIA, OR 97103
JASON WATT, 38414 LABISKE LN, ASTORIA, OR 97103
PALMER WATT, 38414 LABISKE LANE, ASTORIA, OR 97103
HEATHER WEST, 2474 SPRUCE CAPE RD, KODIAK, AK 99615
DEBRA WILEY, BOX 1811, KODIAK, AK 99615
JASON WILEY, BOX 1811, KODIAK, AK 99615
WES WILEY, BOX 1811, KODIAK, AK 99615
ANITRA WINKLER, BOX 85, CANTWELL, AK 99729
ADAM WISCHER, BOX 202, KODIAK, AK 99615
LYNSEY WISCHER, BOX 202, KODIAK, AK 99615
THOMAS WISCHER, BOX 202, KODIAK, AK 99615
KALEB WRIGHT, 3042 KOTEEK CT, EUREKA, CA 99501

SALMON, SET GILLNET, ALASKA PENINSULA
DAVID ADAMS, BOX 1, SAND POINT, AK 99661
MARCUS ADAMS, BOX 1, SAND POINT, AK 99661
REANNA B.MARIE.HEUKER, BOX 98, CASCADE LOCKS, OR 97014
ROBERT BARNETT, BOX 274, SAND POINT, AK 99661
LARRY BEAR, BOX 228, KING COVE, AK 99612
BERT BENDIXEN, 16300 E SULLIVAN AVE, PALMER, AK 99645
LONNIE BRANDELL, BOX 68, KING COVE, AK 99612
PATRICK BROWN, BOX 69, SAND POINT, AK 99661
JON BRUNEAU, 13121 S CAMPBELL RD, ROCKFORD, WA 99301
LAWRENCE CALUGAN, 8710 CARTER CIR, ANCHORAGE, AK 99507
PAULA CALUGAN, BOX 78, SAND POINT, AK 99661
CARL CARLSON, BOX 261, SAND POINT, AK 99661
NICK CARLSON, 3781 WILEY POST LP, ANCHORAGE, AK 99517

RICHARD CARLSON, 72 SANAK ST, SAND POINT, AK 99661
TERRY CHRISTENSEN, 1200 W DIMOND #832, ANCHORAGE, AK 99515
DANNY CUMBERLIDGE, BOX 93, SAND POINT, AK 99661
EDMOND CUMBERLIDGE, BOX 110, SAND POINT, AK 99661
BRAD DEERING, BOX 12, SAND POINT, AK 99661
ESIAH DUSHKIN, BOX 215, KING COVE, AK 99612
RICHARD EASTLICK, BOX 147, SAND POINT, AK 99661
DONALD EUBANK, BOX 272, SAND POINT, AK 99661
AMY FOSTER, BOX 254, SAND POINT, AK 99661
ANDREW FOSTER, BOX 162, SAND POINT, AK 99661
BRUCE FOSTER, BOX 46, SAND POINT, AK 99661
DWAIN FOSTER, BOX 162, SAND POINT, AK 99661
JACK FOSTER, BOX 254, SAND POINT, AK 99661
JOHN FOSTER, BOX 225, SAND POINT, AK 99661
JOHN GALVIN, BOX 171, SAND POINT, AK 99661
ARTHUR GANACIAS, 12629 SE 208TH ST, KENT, WA 98031
GLEN GARDNER, BOX 444, SAND POINT, AK 99661
JOHN GARDNER, BOX 95, SAND POINT, AK 99661
ROBERT GOULD, BOX 234, KING COVE, AK 99612
ARLENE GUNDERSEN, BOX 51, SAND POINT, AK 99661
CHARLES GUNDERSEN, BOX 24, SAND POINT, AK 99661
GEORGE GUNDERSEN, BOX 51, SAND POINT, AK 99661
KIM GUNDERSEN, BOX 148, SAND POINT, AK 99661
MARTIN GUNDERSEN, BOX 50, SAND POINT, AK 99661
PAUL GUNDERSEN, BOX 91, SAND POINT, AK 99661
WAYNE GUNDERSEN, BOX 89, SAND POINT, AK 99661
JOHN HAMIK, 4002 KACHEMAK WY, HOMER, AK 99603
BRIAN HARTMAN, BOX 928, NELSON LAGOON, AK 99571
LOUDEN HARTMAN, 2430 CLEO AVE, ANCHORAGE, AK 99516
MERYLE HAYTER, 4038 W 88TH AVE, ANCHORAGE, AK 99502
BERNIE HEUKER, BOX 98, CASCADE LOCKS, OR 97014
COLTON HEUKER, BOX 98, CASADE LOCKS, OR 97014
HEIDI HEUKER, BOX 98, CASCADE LOCKS, OR 97014
HERMAN HEUKER, BOX 98, CASCADE LOCKS, OR 97014
MICHAEL HEUKER, BOX 98, CASCADE LOCKS, OR 97014
TALON HEUKER, BOX 98, CASCADE LOCKS, OR 97014
TIMOTHY HEUKER, BOX 98, CASCADE LOCKS, OR 97014
TOM HEUKER, BOX 98, CASCADE LOCKS, OR 97014
WESTON HEUKER, BOX 98, CASCADE LOCKS, OR 97014
DOUGLAS HOLMBERG, BOX 241, SAND POINT, AK 99661
RAYMOND HOLMBERG, BOX 266, SAND POINT, AK 99661
GEORGE JACKSON, BOX 166, SAND POINT, AK 99661
JOHN JAEGER, BOX 7030, OCEANVIEW, HI 96737
ROBERT JOHANSEN, BOX 15, SAND POINT, AK 99661
ANGELA JOHNSON, BOX 912, NELSON LAGOON, AK 99571
ELVIS JOHNSON, BOX 14, NELSON LAGOON, AK 99571
HAROLD JOHNSON, BOX 909, NELSON LAGOON, AK 99571
HERBERT JOHNSON, BOX 18, NELSON LAGOON, AK 99571
JENNY JOHNSON, BOX 909, NELSON LAGOON, AK 99571
TOMMY JOHNSON, BOX 914, NELSON LAGOON, AK 99571
ARTEMIE KALMAKOFF, BOX 286, SAND POINT, AK 99661
DUANE KAPP, BOX 304, SAND POINT, AK 99661
HELEN KOSO, 641 W 92ND AVE, ANCHORAGE, AK 99515
MELVIN KOSO, BOX 131, KING COVE, AK 99612
RICHARD KOSO, BOX 111053, ANCHORAGE, AK 99511
NORMAN KUZAKIN, BOX 105, KING COVE, AK 99612
NORMAN LARSEN, BOX 52, SAND POINT, AK 99661
PAULETTE LARSEN, BOX 226, SAND POINT, AK 99661
SHARLENE LOUK, BOX 916, NELSON LAGOON, AK 99571
LUKE LUDVICK, 1980 N FINGER COVE DR, PALMER, AK 99645
GARY MACK, 308 E SQUIRREL RD, KING COVE, AK 99612
HENRY MACK, 101 CHURCH RD BOX 224, KING COVE, AK 99612
JASON MACK, BOX 83, KING COVE, AK 99612
JEREMY MACK, 227 WINDY WAY, KING COVE, AK 99612
BRADY MARUNDE, 14918 E CROWN AVE, SPOKANE, WA 99216

SALMON FISHING LIST—SET GILLNET

GABE MCGLASHAN, BOX 62, SAND POINT, AK 99661
LOUIS MCGLASHAN, BOX 186, SAND POINT, AK 99661
JOSE MEDINA, 1659 MOSS CREEK AVE, ANCHORAGE, AK 99507
BENJAMIN MOBECK, BOX 57, SAND POINT, AK 99661
BENJAMIN MOBECK, BOX 11, SAND POINT, AK 99661
ERNEST MOBECK, BOX 932, NELSON LAGOON, AK 99571
SCOTT MORGAN, BOX 393, SAND POINT, AK 99661
CONNOR MURPHY, 408 LILLY DR, KODIAK, AK 99615
JAMES NELSON, BOX 948, NELSON LAGOON, AK 99571
CHRISTOPHER NEWTON, BOX 363, KING COVE, AK 99612
GRANT NEWTON, BOX 51, KING COVE, AK 99612
TYLER NICHOLSON, 1193 OVERLAND DR, SPRING HILL, FL 34608
HENRY NIELSEN, BOX 42, UNALAKLEET, AK 99684
DUKE OGATA, BOX 181, SAND POINT, AK 99661
RAYMOND OGATA, 1980 N FINGER COVE DR, PALMER, AK 99645
ERNEST ORLOFF, 900 W 5TH AVE #525, ANCHORAGE, AK 99501
ALVIN OSTERBACK, BOX 104, SAND POINT, AK 99661
DALE PEDERSEN, 9218 CAMPBELL TERRACE DR, ANCHORAGE, AK 99502
VIRGIL PORTER, BOX 73, SAND POINT, AK 99661
JON POWERS, 602 W TRIEN LAKE RD PMB 143, LAKE CHARLES, LA 70605
BRIAN RUSSELL, 705 HOSPITAL RD, DAWSON, KY 42408
SHIRLEY RUSSELL, 2870 KNIK, ANCHORAGE, AK 99503
CRAIG RYSEWYK, BOX 931, NELSON LAGOON, AK 99571
DERRICK RYSEWYK, 10212 W 12TH RD, COLEMAN, WI 54112
PAUL SCHAACK, BOX 32, COLD BAY, AK 99571
PETER SHURAVLOFF, 28 RED COVE RD, SAND POINT, AK 99661
BRANDON SMITH, BOX 354, SAND POINT, AK 99661
EDGAR SMITH, 2011 TERREBONNE LP, ANCHORAGE, AK 99502
JIM SMITH, BOX 354, SAND POINT, AK 99661
R.DREW SPARLIN, BOX 126, SAND POINT, AK 99661
RHY VERG.IN, 19415 LINDA LN, KASILOF, AK 99610
MARK WAGNER, BOX 1502, KINGSTON, WA 98346
ERIC WEBER, 3657 EASTWIND DR, ANCHORAGE, AK 99516
DAVID WILSON, BOX 6114, EDMONDS, WA 98026
OSCAR WILSON, BOX 82, KING COVE, AK 99612
VERNON WILSON, BOX 308, KING COVE, AK 99612

SALMON, GILLNET, UPPER YUKON

WESLEY ALEXANDER, BOX 62, NENANA, AK 99760
JAMES ANDERSON, ST RT BOX 93, BEMIDJI, MN 56671
PHILIP ARGALL, BOX 00286, NENANA, AK 99760
RIGORBERTO BARBAZA, 318 W 4TH AVE, NORTH POLE, AK 99705
DOUGLAS BISHOP, 3741 FRENCHMAN RD, FAIRBANKS, AK 99709
CECELIA BURGETT, BOX 85, GALENA, AK 99741
KENNETH CARLO, 1030 JOYCE DR, FAIRBANKS, AK 99701
WALTER CARLO, 1918 CENTRAL AVE, FAIRBANKS, AK 99709
BARBARA CARSON, BOX 232, NENANA, AK 99760
TERRENCE CLARK, BOX 357, NENANA, AK 99760
STEVEN CONATSER, BOX 81153, FAIRBANKS, AK 99708
MARVIN COX, BOX 871473, WASILLA, AK 99687
DAVID DAUSEL, BOX 80291, FAIRBANKS, AK 99708
JAY DE.LIMA, BOX 70, RUBY, AK 99768
DOLLY DEACON, GEN DEL, GRAYLING, AK 99590
HENRY DEACON, 8441 WILLIWA CIR, ANCHORAGE, AK 99504
ROBERT DENTLER, BOX 35, KALTAG, AK 99748
NEIL EKLUND, BOX 10987, FAIRBANKS, AK 99710
HUGH FATE, 750 FARMERS LOOP RD, FAIRBANKS, AK 99712
JESSE FLIRIS, 2001 S CHILLIGAN DR, WASILLA, AK 99654
JAMES FOLGER, BOX 216, TANANA, AK 99777
KILBOURN GEORGE, GEN DEL, STEVENS VILLAGE, AK 99774
ROBERT GOCHENAUER, 2607 LAUREN CREEK LP, ANCHORAGE, AK 99507
DIAN GURTLER, BOX 52, MANLEY HOT SPRINGS, AK 99756
MARY HAILEY, 2082 LAKEVIEW TER, FAIRBANKS, AK 99701
EDGAR HONEA, BOX 324, GALENA, AK 99741
SALLY HUDSON, BOX 71111, FAIRBANKS, AK 99701

MAX HUHNDORF, 9500 APHRODITE DR, ANCHORAGE, AK 99515
ANGELA HUNTINGTON, BOX 49, GALENA, AK 99741
HEATHER KOPONEN, 687 CHENA RIDGE, FAIRBANKS, AK 99709
THEODORE KRUGER, BOX 218, MCGRATH, AK 99627
JIM KUBANYI, 93 TIMBERLAND DR, FAIRBANKS, AK 99701
GEORGIANNA LINCOLN, 4625 EMERALD CIR, ANCHORAGE, AK 99502
THOMAS LIPSCOMB, BOX 71022, FAIRBANKS, AK 99707
PATRICK LOVELL, BOX 80403, FAIRBANKS, AK 99708
FRANKLIN MADROS, BOX 49, KALTAG, AK 99748
ALVIN MAILLELLE, BOX 25, GRAYLING, AK 99590
DAVID MARTINI, 902 DOVE ST, ST AUGUSTINE, FL 32084
CLYDE MAYO, 1618 KASSI CT, FAIRBANKS, AK 99709
FREDERICK MAYO, 1131 MERGANSER ST, FAIRBANKS, AK 99709
CHERYL MAYO.KRISKA, 4903 DRAKE ST, FAIRBANKS, AK 99709
WILLIAM MCLAUGHLIN, 1412 BIRCHWOOD DR, FAIRBANKS, AK 99709
PETER MERRY, 1293 SHYPOKE DR, FAIRBANKS, AK 99709
DONNA MILLER, BOX 138, ANVIK, AK 99558
MARIE MONROE, BOX 242, NENANA, AK 99760
DONALD MOORE, BOX 10989 STEESE BRANCH, FAIRBANKS, AK 99710
GABRIEL NICHOLI, GEN DEL, GRAYLING, AK 99590
RICHARD ODEGARD, 607 OLD STEESE HWY B #347, FAIRBANKS, AK 99701
PAUL ONEIL, 12512 CHANDLER BLVD #302, VALLEY VILLAGE, CA 91607
MARGARET PATRICK, BOX 66, GALENA, AK 99741
JENNY PELKOLA, BOX 227, GALENA, AK 99741
NORMAN PHILLIPS, BOX 83771, FAIRBANKS, AK 99708
GERALD PITKA, 7520 MARYLAND AVE, ANCHORAGE, AK 99504
MARI RAITTO, 5801 OLD VALDEZ TRAIL, SALCHA, AK 99714
GARY RICHARDSON, BOX 101, ANVIK, AK 99558
RICHARD ROBINSON, 703 BENTLEY DR, FAIRBANKS, AK 99701
SUSAN ROBINSON, 1911 SOUTHERN AVE, FAIRBANKS, AK 99709
JOEL SANBEI, BOX 162, ANIAK, AK 99557
GILBERT SEMAKEN, 230 W 14TH AVE #100, ANCHORAGE, AK 99501
RICHARD SMITH, 2230 OLD ELLIOTT HWY, FAIRBANKS, AK 99712
ROBERT SPARKS, BOX 71774, FAIRBANKS, AK 99701
ARNIE SUNNYBOY, BOX 72713, FAIRBANKS, AK 99707
JOEL SWEETSIR, BOX 584, NENANA, AK 99760
SANDRA TAYLOR, 2101 CARR AVE, FAIRBANKS, AK 99709
ARLENE TURNER, BOX 61, HOLY CROSS, AK 99602
DARRYL WALKER, BOX 72, HOLY CROSS, AK 99602
HENRY WIEHL, BOX 84358, FAIRBANKS, AK 99708
MARYJANE WIEHL, #5 BLUES WAY, RAMPART, AK 99767
RUSSELL WOOD, 607 OLD STEESE HWY STE B #712, FAIRBANKS, AK 99701
JOHN WOODS, BOX 104, MANLEY HOT SPRINGS, AK 99756
JACK WRIGHT, BOX 27, MANLEY HOT SPRINGS, AK 99756
PEGGY WRIGHT, BOX 72, RAMPART, AK 99767
ROXANNA WRIGHT, BOX 10578, FAIRBANKS, AK 99710
LEONARD YOUNG, BOX 3116, PALMER, AK 99645
JOSEPH ZURAY, BOX 123, TANANA, AK 99777

SALMON, SET GILLNET, BRISTOL BAY

AADEN AABERG, BOX 879554, WASILLA, AK 99687
AARON AABERG, BOX 34, NONDALTON, AK 99640
ILEAH AABERG, BOX 43, NONDALTON, AK 99640
NORMAN AABERG, 7124 E 17TH AVE, ANCHORAGE, AK 99504
RONALD AABERG, BOX 47005, PEDRO BAY, AK 99647
ROBERT ABRAMS, 386 LITTLE FIERY RD, SEQUATCHIE, TN 37374
EDWARD ACTIVE, 1400 E 4TH AVE, ANCHORAGE, AK 99501
FRANK ACTIVE, BOX 81, TOGIAK, AK 99678
STANLEY ACTIVE, BOX 131, TOGIAK, AK 99678
JANNELLE ADAMS, BOX 241, KING SALMON, AK 99613
HELEN ADERMAN, BOX 1124, DILLINGHAM, AK 99576
ANDRIA AGLI, 7416 E 4TH AVE, ANCHORAGE, AK 99504
ETHAN AGLI, BOX 359, NAKNEK, AK 99633
THOMAS AGONEY, 3500 E 72ND AVE, ANCHORAGE, AK 99507
BENJAMIN AHRENS, 2709 S BODENBERG LP, PALMER, AK 99645

SALMON FISHING LIST—SET GILLNET

CHRISTOPHER ALAKAYAK, BOX 62, MANOKOTAK, AK 99628
DESMOND ALAKAYAK, BOX 56, MANOKOTAK, AK 99628
MICHAEL ALAKAYAK, BOX 56, MANOKOTAK, AK 99628
SAM ALAKAYAK, BOX 62, MANOKOTAK, AK 99628
HATTIE ALBECKER, 101 OLGA LN, UGASHIK, AK 99613
WILLIAM ALBECKER, 101 OLGA LN, UGASHIK, AK 99613
DONALD ALBRIGHT, BOX 81, EGEGIK, AK 99579
DONALD ALBRIGHT, BOX 132, EGEGIK, AK 99579
DUANE ALBRIGHT, BOX 132, EGEGIK, AK 99579
WINIFRED ALFORD, BOX 133, NAKNEK, AK 99633
MARILYN ALFRED, BOX 323, TOGIAK, AK 99678
JACK ALLEN, BOX 1226, DILLINGHAM, AK 99576
JOHN ALLSPACH, 400 CANNON ST, CHESTERTOWN, MD 21620
DONALD ALVARADO, 725 PALMHAVEN AVE, SAN JOSE, CA 95125
KATIE ANDERSEN, BOX 886, DILLINGHAM, AK 99576
FREDRICK ANDERSON, BOX 276, NAKNEK, AK 99633
LUKE ANDERSON, 574 RIVER BEND RD, ROSEBURG, OR 97471
MARC ANDRES, 594 BORREGAS AVE, SUNNYVALE, CA 94085
GAYLE ANDREW, BOX 46, MANOKOTAK, AK 99628
CAROL ANDREWS, BOX 76, TOGIAK, AK 99678
CHRISTINE ANDREWS, BOX 215, TOGIAK, AK 99678
DANIEL ANDREWS, BOX 23, KASIGLUK, AK 99609
DONALD ANDREWS, BOX 87, ALEKNAGIK, AK 99555
JASPER ANDREWS, BOX 272, TOGIAK, AK 99678
KAY ANDREWS, BOX 87, ALEKNAGIK, AK 99555
KAYLA ANDREWS, BOX 1546, DILLINGHAM, AK 99576
WILLIAM ANDREWS, BOX 333, TOGIAK, AK 99678
DWIGHT ANELON, BOX 22, ILIAMNA, AK 99606
MARY ANELON, BOX 45, NEWHALEN, AK 99606
WILLIAM ANGAIAK, BOX 2501, BETHEL, AK 99559
NOLA ANGASAN, BOX 193, NAKNEK, AK 99633
RALPH ANGASAN, BOX 632, KING SALMON, AK 99613
FREDERICK ANTONE, BOX 144, TOGIAK, AK 99678
HANS APOKEDAK, BOX 37, LEVELOCK, AK 99625
PATRICIA APOKEDAK.ANDREW, BOX 210676, ANCHORAGE, AK 99521
NEIL ARMSTRONG, BOX 898, DILLINGHAM, AK 99576
ROSS ARMSTRONG, BOX 898, DILLINGHAM, AK 99576
NORA ARMSTRONG.JOHNSO, 1075 TERRACE VIEW DR, ALBERTON, MT 59820
JESSIE ARNARIAK, BOX 95, TOGIAK, AK 99678
COREY ARNOLD, 6930 SE HAROLD ST, PORTLAND, OR 97206
MATHEW ASKOAK, BOX 128, NEWHALEN, AK 99606
ALLAN ASPELUND, BOX 84, NAKNEK, AK 99633
CANDY ASPELUND, BOX 221, NAKNEK, AK 99633
DARRELL ASPELUND, BOX 360, NAKNEK, AK 99633
GAIL ASPELUND, BOX 235, NAKNEK, AK 99633
JENNIFER ASPELUND, BOX 25355, SEATTLE, WA 98165
LINDSEY ASPELUND, 3819 S BEAN RD, PORT ANGELES, WA 98363
MARY ASPELUND, BOX 84, NAKNEK, AK 99633
NORTH ASPELUND, BOX 25355, SEATTLE, WA 98165
SUSAN ASPELUND, 2920 CEDAR AVE, LUMMI ISLAND, WA 98262
ZACKARY ASPELUND, BOX 221, NAKNEK, AK 99633
WILLIE ATTI, BOX 55, KWIGILLINGOK, AK 99622
ANUSKA AYOJIAK, BOX 104, TOGIAK, AK 99678
HENRY AYOJIAK, BOX 147, MANOKOTAK, AK 99628
HOWARD AYOJIAK, BOX 122, MANOKOTAK, AK 99628
MARTIN AYOJIAK, BOX 83, TOGIAK, AK 99678
BASIL BACKFORD, BOX 388, DILLINGHAM, AK 99576
IDA BACKFORD, BOX 388, DILLINGHAM, AK 99576
CHERYL BACKMAN, 301 E BIRNE SL RD, CATHLAMET, WA 98612
HARLAN BAILEY, 1061 PALM AVE, MARTINEZ, CA 94553
MARTINA BAILEY, 6544 11TH AVE NW, SEATTLE, WA 98117
SAMUEL BAIN, 40 W SWANEY ST, PORT HADLOCK, WA 98339
CONNIE BAKER, 9678 W 900 N, COMMISKEY, IN 47227
GARY BAKER, 9678 W 900 N, COMMISKEY, IN 47227
BENJAMIN BAKK, 54035 WILODERNESS LN, HOMER, AK 99603

ALBERT BALL, BOX 671527, CHUGIAK, AK 99567
CAROLYN BALL, 24314 140TH AVE SE, KENT, WA 98042
CHRISTINA BALL, 131 OCEAN PARK DR, ANCHORAGE, AK 99515
FRED BALL, 513 SW 3RD ST, COLLEGE PLACE, WA 99324
GERALD BALL, BOX 542, DILLINGHAM, AK 99576
JASON BALL, 131 OCEAN PARK DR, ANCHORAGE, AK 99515
JUSTIN BALL, BOX 542, DILLINGHAM, AK 99576
LLOANN BALL, 513 SW 3RD ST, COLLEGE PLACE, WA 99324
TRAVIS BALL, BOX 4, DILLINGHAM, AK 99576
CHESTER BALLUTA, BOX 170, ILIAMNA, AK 99606
CLEMENT BALLUTA, BOX 51, NONDALTON, AK 99640
FEDOSIA BALLUTA, BOX 170, ILIAMNA, AK 99606
WASSIE BALLUTA, BOX 170, ILIAMNA, AK 99606
JOHN BANDLE, 3451 HILAND DR, ANCHORAGE, AK 99504
ADRIAN BARHAN, 6A OAK RD, CIRCLE PINES, MN 55014
DAVID BARHAN, 5801 RIDGE CREEK RD, SHOREVIEW, MN 55126
TAYLOR BARHAN, 6A OAK RD, CIRCLE PINES, MN 55014
DEE BARKER, 12921 39TH AVE SE #2, EVERETT, WA 98208
DAISY BARNES, BOX 111, DILLINGHAM, AK 99576
MARY BARNES, BOX 1435, DILLINGHAM, AK 99576
ADAM BARTLUM, 5117 NE 74TH CT, VANCOUVER, WA 98662
DAKOTA BARTLUM, 8508 NE 61ST AVE, VANCOUVER, WA 98662
MELANIE BARTLUM, 3024 BONIFACE PARKWAY, ANCHORAGE, AK 99504
BILLY BARTMAN, BOX 2, MANOKOTAK, AK 99628
ERNEST BARTMAN, BOX 2, MANOKOTAK, AK 99628
LARRY BARTMAN, BOX 86, MANOKOTAK, AK 99628
LAYNE BARTMAN, BOX 86, MANOKOTAK, AK 99628
VIRGINIA BARTMAN, BOX 3, MANOKOTAK, AK 99628
WELLS BAUMANN, BOX 1720, HOOD RIVER, OR 97031
STANLEY BEANS, BOX 70164, SOUTH NAKNEK, AK 99670
STEVEN BECKER, BOX 701, WILLOW, AK 99688
STANLEY BEEBE, 20626 SCOFIELD DR, CUPERTINO, CA 95014
CRYSTAL BEEMAN, BOX 1443, HOMER, AK 99603
ERIC BEEMAN, BOX 1443, HOMER, AK 99603
ROBBI BEHR, 100 S QUEEN ST, CHESTERTOWN, MD 21620
ROJI BEHR, 427 LAGUNITAS AVE #101, OAKLAND, CA 94602
ISAAK BELL, 1650 S COUNTRYWOOD DR, WASILLA, AK 99623
KYLE BELLEQUE, BOX 488, DILLINGHAM, AK 99576
BENJAMIN BENEDETTI, 5812 78TH AVE NW, GIG HARBOR, WA 98335
DINAH BENNETT, BOX 468, DILLINGHAM, AK 99576
JASON BENNIS, BOX 106, DILLINGHAM, AK 99576
JOHN BENNIS, BOX 406, DILLINGHAM, AK 99576
JOSEPH BENTON, 14057 MILBANK ST #2, SHERMAN OAKS, CA 91423
DANIEL BERG, 311 LINDEN CIR, CABONDALE, CO 81623
LOREN BERGSENG, BOX 469, CATHLAMET, WA 98612
ROBERT BETTS, 5095 S TEN MILE RD, MERIDIAN, ID 83642
KATHLEEN BIEGER, 1600 GRAND AVE, ST PAUL, MN 55419
DILLON BIENIEK, 931 89TH AVE, COON RAPIDS, MN 55433
BRENNA BIGELOW, 19541 CICUTTA WAY, EAGLE RIVER, AK 99577
RAVEN BIRKHOLZ, 7840 CRANBERRY ST, ANCHORAGE, AK 99502
GEORGE BISHOP, BOX 1047, HOMER, AK 99603
SHELBI BISHOP, BOX 1047, HOMER, AK 99603
STEPHEN BISHOP, BOX 1047, HOMER, AK 99603
JOHN BISKEY, 59731 410TH AVE, SWATARA, MN 55785
DANNY BISSONETTE, 18715 DUELL ST, AZUSA, CA 91702
SIDNEY BISSONETTE, 2103 W 46TH AVE, ANCHORAGE, AK 99503
TRAVIS BLACK, BOX 123, MANOKOTAK, AK 99628
DONALD BLAIR, 2906 DAWSON ST #8, ANCHORAGE, AK 99501
SAEJIN BLAIR, 1116 N MORGAN ST, PORTLAND, OR 97217
BARBARA BLANC, 38725 GAVIN CIR, SOLDOTNA, AK 99669
MATTHEW BLOCK, 3203 W DISCOVERY LP, WASILLA, AK 99654
MYRON BLUE, BOX 207, TOGIAK, AK 99678
GLEN BOGART, 2510 CHESTNUT, EVERETT, WA 98201
CHARLES BORBRIDGE, 603 W 10TH ST, JUNEAU, AK 99801
JOHN BORBRIDGE, 27481 210TH AVE SE, MAPLE VALLEY, WA 98038

SALMON FISHING LIST—SET GILLNET

THEODORE BORBRIDGE, BOX 5, MANOKOTAK, AK 99628

MARY BOSKOFSKY, BOX 48024, CHIGNIK LAKE, AK 99548

JENNIFER BOUFFIOU, 4715 NE 203RD ST, LAKE FOREST PARK, WA 98155

SEAN BOUFFIOU, 4715 NE 203RD ST, LAKE FOREST PARK, WA 98155

INA BOUKER, BOX 326, DILLINGHAM, AK 99576

JOHN BOUKER, BOX 326, DILLINGHAM, AK 99576

JOHN BOUKER, BOX 1135, DILLINGHAM, AK 99576

JOHNNA BOUKER, BOX 326, DILLINGHAM, AK 99576

NICHOLAS BOUKER, BOX 326, DILLINGHAM, AK 99576

KATHLEEN BRAGG, 23519 EAGLE RIVER RD, EAGLE RIVER, AK 99577

KEVIN BRAGG, 23519 EAGLE RIVER RD, EAGLE RIVER, AK 99577

GERALD BRAMAN, HC 31 BOX 5117, WASILLA, AK 99654

NOLAN BRAMAN, 3381 E GODFREY DR, WASILLA, AK 99654

SEAN BRAMAN, 3381 GODFREY DR, WASILLA, AK 99654

TAMMY BRAMAN, 3381 E GODFREY DR, WASILLA, AK 99654

LEON BRASWELL, BOX 990, DILLINGHAM, AK 99576

DYLAN BRAUND, BOX 50, HOMER, AK 99603

FINLEY BRAUND, BOX 50, HOMER, AK 99603

SARAH BRAUND, BOX 1898, HOMER, AK 99603

JOHN BRIGHT, BOX 100116, ANCHORAGE, AK 99510

HENRY BRODERICK, BOX 1032, CANNON BEACH, OR 97110

JONATHAN BRODERICK, BOX 1032, CANNON BEACH, OR 97110

MAX BRODERICK, BOX 423, CANNON BEACH, OR 97110

PERRY BRODERICK, 3663 SE 38TH AVE, PORTLAND, OR 97202

ZACHARY BROOKOVER, BOX 884, DILLINGHAM, AK 99576

COREY BROST, 205 WYOMING CT, SPEARFISH, SD 57783

FISCHER BROST, 205 WYOMING CT, SPEARFISH, SD 57783

KATHERINE BROWN, BOX 111566, ANCHORAGE, AK 99511

MELANIE BROWN, 2651 BROOK STONE LP, ANCHORAGE, AK 99515

WILLIAM BROWN, BOX 344, NAKNEK, AK 99633

GABRIELLE BUCCI, BOX 930, GIRDWOOD, AK 99587

SOPHIE BULLARD, 3120 NE WILLAMETTE AVE, CORVALLIS, OR 97330

DAVID BURKHARDT, BOX 1303, DILLINGHAM, AK 99576

KESLYNN BURKHARDT, 4343 SAN ROBERTO AVE #5, ANCHORAGE, AK 99508

CHRISTINA CACKLER, 2714 JEFFERSON AVE, REDWOOD CITY, CA 94062

CHRISTOPHER CALAMITA, 38 WOODLAWN ST, HAMDEN, CT 6517

TIMOTHY CAPO, BOX 638, NAKNEK, AK 99633

CAROLYN CARLOS, BOX 28, TOGIAK, AK 99678

HOMER CARNEY, 7611 MARRIETTA RD SE, NEW LEXINGTON, OH 43764

BRANDY CARPENTER, BOX 872177, WASILLA, AK 99687

DUANE CARPENTER, BOX 872177, WASILLA, AK 99687

JOHN CARPER, 19 MIDDLE RIVER RD, VERONA, VA 24482

TYLER CARR, BOX 102, GOVERMENT CAMP, OR 97028

ANNETTE CARUSO, BOX 398, KING SALMON, AK 99613

JUAN CASTANEDA, 2526 W BROADWAY, SPOKANE, WA 99201

KYLE CATALONE, 1200 W DIAMOND BLVD #601, ANCHORAGE, AK 99515

BRIAN CATO, BOX 452, PILOT POINT, AK 99649

MICHAEL CENCI, BOX 307, NASELLE, WA 98638

TAMARA CHARRON, BOX 245, NAKNEK, AK 99633

BRADLEY CHASE, BOX 672538, CHUGIAK, AK 99567

EVELYN CHASE, BOX 672538, CHUGIAK, AK 99567

ELIZABETH CHIKLAK, BOX 1281, DILLINGHAM, AK 99576

AMELIA CHRISTENSEN, BOX 203, DILLINGHAM, AK 99576

ANGELA CHRISTENSEN, 19331 KLONDIKE ST #3, CHUGIAK, AK 99567

SCOTT CHRISTENSEN, 225 HILLCREST ST, SPEARFISH, SD 57783

TERRY CHRISTENSEN, 1200 W DIMOND #832, ANCHORAGE, AK 99515

WILLIAM CHRISTENSEN, BOX 203, DILLINGHAM, AK 99576

KRISTIN CHRISTOFFERSON, BOX 1219, KODIAK, AK 99615

NATALIA CHRISTOPHER, BOX 115, NEW STUYAHOK, AK 99636

JEFF CIAMPAGLIA, 1618 N 170TH ST, SHORELINE, WA 98133

CLYDE CLARK, BOX 167, NAKNEK, AK 99633

EVELYN CLARK, 27 HOWARD RD, CATHLAMET, WA 98612

LEAH CLARK, 27 HOWARD RD, CATHLAMET, WA 98612

PEGGY CLARK, 185 N WELCOME SLOUGH RD, CATHLAMET, WA 98612

STACEY CLARK, BOX 1203, HOMER, AK 99603

CHRISTOPHER CLEMETSON, 326 KRANE DR, ANCHORAGE, AK 99504

DAVID CLEVELAND, BOX 4074, TWIN HILLS, AK 99576

LORRI COCKRELL, 1249 SKY HIGH TERRACE, EFFORT, PA 18330

JEREMY COGHILL, BOX 3171, PALMER, AK 99645

JORDAN COGHILL, BOX 115, NAKNEK, AK 99633

RYAN COLE, 4801 SPORTSMAN DR, ANCHORAGE, AK 99502

JOSH CONRAD, 3326 W 3400 N, MOORE, ID 83255

EVELYN COOPCHIAK, BOX 187, TOGIAK, AK 99678

LOUISE COOPCHIAK, BOX 317, TOGIAK, AK 99678

DANIEL COOPER, BOX A, ANGWIN, CA 84508

DOUGLAS COOPER, BOX A, ANGWIN, CA 94508

BRENT CORNELISON, 1996 E SEASONS RD, ATHOL, ID 83801

ETHAN CORNELISON, 1996 E SEASONS RD, ATHOL, ID 83801

SHERYL CORNELISON, 1996 E SEASON RD, ATHOL, ID 83801

NOAH CORP, BOX 132, JUNCTION CITY, CA 96048

KEVIN COSSAIRT, 6685 NEZ PERCE, BONNERS FERRY, ID 83805

DAVID COUPCHIAK, BOX 101, TOGIAK, AK 99678

ELIZABETH COURTNEY, 4854 W GLENHAVEN DR, EVERETT, WA 98203

JAMES CRIMP, 36 HARDEN AVE, CAMDEN, ME 4843

MATTHEW CRIMP, 1011 YERBA BEUNA AVE, OAKLAND, CA 94608

KATHLEEN CRONEN, BOX 930, GIRDWOOD, AK 99587

CHRISTOPHER CROOKHAM, BOX 43, NONDALTON, AK 99640

SUSAN CULLEN, 213 OREGON HWY, LONGVIEW, WA 98632

ALFRED CUMMINGS, BOX 940334, HOUSTON, AK 99694

GLORIA CUNNINGHAM, BOX 1451, CORDOVA, AK 99574

SHIANNE CURREY, BOX 96, FORT SHAW, MT 59443

TODD CURREY, BOX 96, FORT SHAW, MT 59443

JUNE CURTIS, 9933 LA JOLLA CIR S, SUN CITY, AZ 85358

JEANNE CUSMA, BOX 43, NONDALTON, AK 99640

JEREMY DARCANGELO, BOX 188, MANOKOTAK, AK 99628

DEVIN DARROUGH, BOX 1034, DILLINGHAM, AK 99576

RACHEL DARROUGH, BOX 1034, DILLINGHAM, AK 99576

MICHAEL DAVIS, BOX 155, DILLINGHAM, AK 99576

PAULINE DAVIS, 4511 FOLKER ST #37A, ANCHORAGE, AK 99507

CONRAD DAY, 2449 CR 127, TUSCOLA, TX 79562

HEATHER DEBOLT, BOX 1449, HOMER, AK 99603

BERNICE DECKER, 926 ALOHA WAY, LADY LAKE, FL 32159

JEFFREY DELKITTIE, BOX 1101, KOKHANOK, AK 99606

JOANN DELKITTIE, 3336 E 16TH AVE, ANCHORAGE, AK 99508

MARY DELKITTIE, BOX 52, NONDALTON, AK 99640

VIRGIL DELKITTIE, BOX 52, NONDALTON, AK 99640

RUDOLPH DEMOSKI, 3127 S. ST MIHIEL CIR, WASILLA, AK 99654

ZOYA DENURE, BOX 731, DELTA JUNCTION, AK 99737

MICHAEL DEVANEY, BOX 612, HOMER, AK 99603

OLGA DICK, BOX 28, MANOKOTAK, AK 99628

WILLIAM DIERSHAW, 2061 SHAVANO PL, LOVELAND, CO 80538

LAURI DISARRO, BOX WWP, KETCHIKAN, AK 99950

WALTER DISARRO, BOX WWP, KETCHIKAN, AK 99950

WAYNE DISARRO, BOX WWP, KETCHIKAN, AK 99950

LYDIA DOHERTY, 2641 N STEESE HWY #3, FAIRBANKS, AK 99712

JOHN DORE, 7014 65TH AVE SE, SNOHOMISH, WA 98290

MICHAEL DORE, 29976 RASH RD NE, KINGSTON, WA 98346

PATRICK DORE, 6206 27TH AVE NE, SEATTLE, WA 98115

THOMAS DORE, 9104 NE KIWI LN, KINGSTON, WA 98346

AMBER DOWIE, 435 EBERHART ST, LARAMIE, WY 82070

AUDRAH DOWIE, 435 EBERHART ST, LARAMIE, WY 82070

NICHOLAS DOWIE, BOX 2684, KODIAK, AK 99615

PRISCILLA DRAY, BOX 457, DILLINGHAM, AK 99576

LAWRENCE DREW, BOX 146, NAKNEK, AK 99633

NATALIE DREW, BOX 243, NAKNEK, AK 99633

JENNIFER DREW.TURPIN, BOX 146, NAKNEK, AK 99633

ADAM DUBAY, BOX 245, NAKNEK, AK 99633

ROBERT DUNNING, BOX 22, NAKNEK, AK 99633

BRADY DURGIN, 3800 OVERDALE DR, BILLETTE, WY 82718

EMILY DUTA, 333 NW 87TH ST, SEATTLE, WA 98117

MIHAIL DUTA, 333 NW 87TH ST, SEATTLE, WA 98117

LOUIE DYASUK, BOX 152, TOGIAK, AK 99678

SALMON FISHING LIST—SET GILLNET

JORDAN DYKES, BOX 6652, VAIL, CO 81658
ERIN DYNES, HC 1 BOX 3125, HEALY, AK 99743
TYLER DYNES, HC1 BOX 3125, HEALY, AK 99743
JAKOB EASTON, 2210 MEADOW AVE, BOULDER, CO 80304
ADAM EBNET, BOX 110370, ANCHORAGE, AK 99511
MARVIN EBNET, BOX 110370, ANCHORAGE, AK 99511
JOE ECHO.HAWK, 407 NELSON DR, BILLINGS, MT 59102
GEORGE ECKLEY, 179 WILSON HEIGHTS, KALISPELL, MT 59901
TRUDY ECKLEY, 179 WILSON HEIGHTS, KALISPELL, MT 59901
GALEN EGGLESTON, 5305 DORBRANDT ST #2, ANCHORAGE, AK 99518
DOMINICK EKAMRAK, BOX 51101, AKIACHAK, AK 99551
ANISHIA ELBIE, BOX 70002, SOUTH NAKNEK, AK 99670
JEFFREY ELBIE, BOX 70002, SOUTH NAKNEK, AK 99670
SHANNON ELDRIDGE, BOX 285, NAKNEK, AK 99633
LYDIA EMORY, BOX 486, NAKNEK, AK 99633
MAURICE ENRIGHT, 101 MY WAY, UGASHIK, AK 99613
CARL ERICKSON, 1309 TAYLOR AVE, BELLINGHAM, WA 98225
RUDY ERICKSON, 1309 TAYLOR AVE, BELLINGHAM, WA 98225
CHRISTOPHER ERPELDING, 1951 EARLY VIEW DR, ANCHORAGE, AK 99504
JOSHUA ESTES.KEMMERER, 133 ELMWOOD LN, HELENA, MT 59601
GLADYS EVANOFF, GEN DEL, NONDALTON, AK 99640
ORIN EVANOFF, BOX 474, PILOT POINT, AK 99649
SUZANNE EVANOFF, BOX 474, PILOT POINT, AK 99649
COREY EVANS, BOX 1092, DILLINGHAM, AK 99576
LORRAINE EVANS, 9425 ENDICOTT, ANCHORAGE, AK 99502
ANDREW EVON, BOX 45, MANOKOTAK, AK 99628
KEITH FAYER, BOX 182, TOGIAK, AK 99678
GARY FAYETTE, 8224 QUINAULT RD, BLAINE, WA 98230
BRET FELSENTHAL, 1248 S SUNSET DR, YUMA, AZ 85364
ALEXANDER FERNANDEZ, 4910 33RD AVE N, GOLDEN VALLEY, MN 55422
NANCY FLENSBURG, BOX 8998, KING SALMON, AK 99613
LUCY FLETCHER, 900 W 5TH #525, ANCHORAGE, AK 99501
VICTOR FLORES, BOX 153, TOGIAK, AK 99678
CHRISTOPHER FLORESTA, BOX 35, CLARKS POINT, AK 99569
MARY FLORESTA, 200 W 34TH AVE #174, ANCHORAGE, AK 99503
BRUCE FOERCH, 660 MASON ST, SAUGATUCK, MI 49453
EUGENE FOERCH, BOX 111, TOGIAK, AK 99678
KRYSTAL FOOTE, 3829 SE HARRISON ST, PORTLAND, OR 97214
SHANNON FORD, 1420 NW GILMAN BLVD #2136, ISSAQUAH, WA 98027
JOSHUA FORTUNE, BOX 521529, BIG LAKE, AK 99652
DAVID FOSTER, BOX 4003, TWIN HILLS, AK 99576
HELEN FOSTER, BOX 976, DILLINGHAM, AK 99576
KEVIN FOSTER, 19092 RIVER WOODS DR, BEND, OR 97702
MICKEY FOSTER, BOX 976, DILLINGHAM, AK 99576
REBECCA FOUNTAIN, 7940 SHORE ACRES DR NE, OLYMPIA, WA 98506
THOMAS FOUNTAIN, 7940 SHORE ACRES DR NE, OLYMPIA, WA 98506
MARTHA FOX, BOX 136, TOGIAK, AK 99678
HARVEY FRANKLIN, BOX 255, TOGIAK, AK 99678
CODY FRANSEN, 1859 KOK RD, LYNDEN, WA 98264
GREG FRANSEN, 1859 KOK RD, LYNDEN, WA 98264
KAREN FREEMAN, BOX 556, COOPER LANDING, AK 99572
AVI FRIEDMAN, 6109 PIMLICO RD, BALTIMORE, MD 21209
LAURA FROST, BOX 229, TOGIAK, AK 99678
ALEX FULLER, 833 W COMMERCIAL DR, WASILLA, AK 99654
NINA FURMAN, 801 W HOLIDAY DR, WASILLA, AK 99654
STEPHEN FURMAN, 801 W HOLIDAY DR, WASILLA, AK 99654
DIANA GAMECHUK, BOX 73, MANOKOTAK, AK 99628
LILLIAN GAMECHUK, BOX 111, MANOKOTAK, AK 99628
IRENE GAMECHUK.OLES, BOX 76, MANOKOTAK, AK 99628
ANNA GARDINER, BOX 34, CLARKS POINT, AK 99569
RYAN GEAGEL, BOX 4, SELDOVIA, AK 99663
LORENA GEERHART, BOX 91, MANOKOTAK, AK 99628
STEPHEN GERRY, 191 CROSS RD, ALAMO, CA 94507
CODY GILL, 7613 KINGPOST LP, HELENA, MT 59602
LEVI GILL, 2010 AVE C, BILLINGS, MT 59102

KORY GLICK, 352 E BLUEBERRY AVE #26, PALMER, AK 99645
LUCY GLOKO, BOX 113, MANOKOTAK, AK 99628
WILLIAM GLOKO, BOX 113, MANOKOTAK, AK 99628
JONAH GOLDEN, 3100 LAKEWOOD AVE S, SEATTLE, WA 98144
BRANDON GOODWINE, 2450 W 3965 SOUTH, WEST VALLEY CITY, UT 84119
THOMAS GORE, 21 BAYVIEW TER, MILL VALLEY, CA 94941
ALBERT GOSUK, BOX 73, TOGIAK, AK 99678
KAYTLYN GOSUK, BOX 237, TOGIAK, AK 99678
HEIDI GOULD, 6927 ROVENNA ST, ANCHORAGE, AK 99518
ROBERT GOULD, BOX 52, KING COVE, AK 99612
JESSE GREER, BOX 1621, GRANTS PASS, OR 97528
LARRY GREER, BOX 1621, GRANTS PASS, OR 97528
DANIEL GREISEN, 2114 WEATHERBY WAY, PETALUMA, CA 94954
BARRETT GRIBBLE, BOX 843, HOMER, AK 99603
SHIRLIE GRIBBLE, BOX 843, HOMER, AK 99603
GUST GRIECHEN, BOX 490, PILOT POINT, AK 99649
MOLLY GRIECHEN, BOX 588, DILLINGHAM, AK 99576
TIMOTHY GRIFFY, 9105 SE WASHINGTON ST, PORTLAND, OR 97216
DARLENE GROAT, BOX 29, NAKNEK, AK 99633
GUY GROAT, BOX 29, NAKNEK, AK 99633
LYNSEY GROAT, BOX 29, NAKNEK, AK 99633
AGOSTINO GROSSI, 21 MT HAMILTON COURT, CLAYTON, CA 94517
ENRICO GROSSI, 293 DRIFTWOOD DR, BAY POINT, CA 94565
JOHN GURZO, 435 EBERHART ST, LARAMIE, WY 82070
MOLLY GUST, BOX 231, TOGIAK, AK 99678
VINCE GUST, BOX 25, NEW STUYAHOK, AK 99636
ROBERT HADFIELD, BOX 416, KING SALMON, AK 99613
RENETTA HAGGARD, 2951 S BANK CIR, WASILLA, AK 99654
LEONA HAKALA, BOX 672387, CHUGIAK, AK 99567
JARED HAKKINEN, BOX 701, KASILOF, AK 99610
KIRK HAMILTON, 13065 RING LANE, LA CONNER, WA 98257
HEIDI HAMMOND, 16210 CHASEWOOD LN, ANCHORAGE, AK 99516
SAMANTHA HAMMONS, 181 WINDY RIDGE DR, LONGVIEW, WA 98632
HANK HANIGAN, 4208 S GREYSONE LN, SPOKANE, WA 98223
MARILYN HANSEN, BOX 82, NAKNEK, AK 99633
KENNETH HARBESON, 18351 BELDING BIRCH DR, CHUGIAK, AK 99567
GREGORY HARRIS, BOX 294, NAKNEK, AK 99633
BRANDON HARRISON, BOX 803, COOPER LANDING, AK 99572
DAVID HART, BOX 71, VAUGHN, WA 98394
SHARON HART, BOX 322, PORT HADLOCK, WA 98339
LYLE HEATH, BOX 100, NAKNEK, AK 99633
ALEC HEAVENER, 10261 CRESTVIEW LN, EAGLE RIVER, AK 99577
MIA HEAVENER, 7087 FAIRWEATHER PARK LP, ANCHORAGE, AK 99518
NINA HEAVENER, BOX 1003, DILLINGHAM, AK 99576
ROBERT HEAVENER, BOX 1003, DILLINGHAM, AK 99576
TAYT HELMER, 2290 CANYON RD, SPRINGVILLE, UT 84663
LARRY HENRY, 10452 CHAIN OF ROCK, EAGLE RIVER, AK 99577
JOHN HERRITY, BOX 433, WINDSOR, CO 80550
CAROL HESTER, BOX 267, NAKNEK, AK 99633
CASEY HEUKER, BOX 98, CASCADE LOCKS, OR 97014
DAVID HEYANO, BOX 190503, ANCHORAGE, AK 99523
EDWARD HEYANO, BOX 288, DILLINGHAM, AK 99576
ROSA HEYANO, BOX 190503, ANCHORAGE, AK 99519
STEVEN HICKS, 2816 28TH AVE SE, OLYMPIA, WA 98501
NATHAN HILL, BOX 1105, KOKHANOK, AK 99606
ELIZABETH HILLENBRAND, 10545 HOMEWARD LN, GRASS VALLEY, CA 95945
EARL HILLMAN, BOX 402, WASKISH, MN 56685
JAN HINKLE, 4480 SW 185TH AVE, BEAVERTON, OR 97078
GALACIA HIRATSUKA, BOX 428, DILLINGHAM, AK 99576
HANNAH HIRATSUKA, BOX 593, DILLINGHAM, AK 99576
JOANN HIRATSUKA, BOX 767, DILLINGHAM, AK 99576
DOLLY HOBSON, BOX 74, NONDALTON, AK 99640
MACY HOBSON, GEN DEL, NONDALTON, AK 99640
DAMIEN HOELSCHER, BOX 177, HOOPER BAY, AK 99604
JUSTIN HOFF, 21972 453RD AVE, ARLINGTON, SD 57212

SALMON FISHING LIST—GILLNET

BILLIE HOFFMAN, 1906 LANDES ST, PORT TOWNSEND, WA 98368
CALVIN HOFFMAN, 3434 CAMPBELL AIRSTRIP RD, ANCHORAGE, AK 99504
CRYSTAL HOFFMAN, 3434 CAMPBELL AIRSTRIP RD, ANCHORAGE, AK 99504
RONALD HOFFMAN, 3434 CAMPBELL AIRSTRIP RD, ANCHORAGE, AK 99504
MICHAEL HOLM, BOX 877210, WASILLA, AK 99687
JUSTINA HOLSTROM, BOX 156, NAKNEK, AK 99633
MICHAEL HOLSTROM, BOX 135, NAKNEK, AK 99633
HUNTER HONGSLO, 1650 S. COUNTRYWOOD DR, WASILLA, AK 99623
CALEB HOPKINS, 7450 E WALDRON COVE CT, PALMER, AK 99645
KIMBERLY HOPKINS, 7450 E WALDRON COVE CT, PALMER, AK 99645
LEVI HOPKINS, 7450 E WALDRON COVE CT, PALMER, AK 99645
TODD HOPKINS, 7450 E WALDRON COVE CT, PALMER, AK 99645
KALYN HUBERT, 17636 TEKLANIKA DR, EAGLE RIVER, AK 99577
KIM HUBERT, 17636 TEKLANIKA DR, EAGLE RIVER, AK 99577
JOHN HUFFER, 17603 RACHEL CIR, EAGLE RIVER, AK 99577
JOYCE HUFFER, 11551 TARGHEE LP, EAGLE RIVER, AK 99577
TOM HUFFER, 18207 SANCTUARY DR, EAGLE RIVER, AK 99577
DONALD HUIZENGA, 5481 DINKEL RD, BELLINGHAM, WA 98226
TOMMY HUIZENGA, 5481 DINKEL RD, BELLINGHAM, WA 98226
BRETT HULL, 1065 HEFLEY ST, GRANTS PASS, OR 97526
MEGAN HURLBURT, BOX 546, DILLINGHAM, AK 99576
ALANNAH HURLEY, BOX 1488, DILLINGHAM, AK 99576
ANDREA HURLEY, BOX 198, DILLINGHAM, AK 99576
KYLE HURLEY, 13 FERN HILL RD, CATHLAMENT, WA 98612
JUSTINA ILUTSIK, 2821 BELUGA BAY CIR, ANCHORAGE, AK 99507
DAVID ION, 25 LARSON RD, ESKO, MN 55733
ADAM ITUMULRIA, BOX 15, MANOKOTAK, AK 99628
JOANNE ITUMULRIA, BOX 16, MANOKOTAK, AK 99628
JUDY IVANOFF, BOX 7, NAKNEK, AK 99633
CHARLES IVY, 35341 RAINTREE CIR, SOLDOTNA, AK 99669
MARY.JEAN IVY, 35341 RAINTREE CIR, SOLDOTNA, AK 99669
CHARLEEN IVY.OGUINN, BOX 3729, SOLDOTNA, AK 99669
DANIELE JACOBS, 231 E LITTLE ISLAND RD, CATHLAMET, WA 98612
KURT JAEHNING, 1511 WEST BEACH RD, OAK HARBOR, WA 98277
LARRY JALLEN, BOX 70104, SOUTH NAKNEK, AK 99670
ELLIE JAMES, 128 N VISTA WAY, KELSO, WA 98626
MARGARET JAMISON, 1006 ALOHA WAY, LADY LAKE, FL 93644
ESTHER JEFFERY, BOX 808, BARROW, AK 99723
JORDAN JEFFERY, 590 25TH AVE #2, SAN FRANCISCO, CA 94121
MARY JOE, 203 HEINTZLEMAN DR, ANCHORAGE, AK 99503
FREDDIE JOHN, BOX 24, CLARKS POINT, AK 99569
GLADYS JOHN, BOX 656, DILLINGHAM, AK 99576
LAURA JOHN, BOX 185, MANOKOTAK, AK 99628
ANGELINA JOHNSON, BOX 145, NAKNEK, AK 99633
ANNETTE JOHNSON, 181 WINDY RIDGE DR, LONGVIEW, WA 98632
BRYAN JOHNSON, BOX 1538, DILLINGHAM, AK 99576
FORREST JOHNSON, BOX 291, KNIFE RIVER, MN 55609
HARRY JOHNSON, GEN DEL, KOLIGANEK, AK 99576
KEVIN JOHNSON, BOX 907, DILLINGHAM, AK 99576
LEON JOHNSON, BOX 226, DILLINGHAM, AK 99576
LYNN JOHNSON, BOX 145, NAKNEK, AK 99633
MATILDA JOHNSON, BOX 807, DILLINGHAM, AK 99576
ROBERT JOHNSON, 181 WINDY RIDGE DR, LONGVIEW, WA 98632
STEPHANIE JOHNSON, BOX 731, CATHLAMET, WA 98612
WILLIAM JOHNSON, BOX 551, CATHLAMET, WA 98612
DEBORAH JONES, BOX 46, NAKNEK, AK 99633
JEREMIAH JONES, 5800 TRAPPERS TRAIL, ANCHORAGE, AK 99516
SAMUEL JONES, BOX 323, NAKNEK, AK 99633
STEPHEN JONES, BOX 323, NAKNEK, AK 99633
SYLVESTER JONES, BOX 46, NAKNEK, AK 99633
BRADY JOSEPHSEN, 20417 US HWY 81, ARLINGTON, SD 57212
GEORGE JOY, BOX 167, NAKNEK, AK 99633
JOSHUA JUDD, 4847 WHITTIER RD, CLAYTON, WA 99110
TIMOTHY JURMU, 231 SONGBIRD LN, LONGVIEW, WA 98632
JAYDEN KAI.MAYER, BOX 186, DILLINGHAM, AK 99576
DONALD KALK, BOX EXI, JUNEAU, AK 99850

JACKIE KALMAKOFF, BOX 55, NAKNEK, AK 99633
HENRY KANULIE, BOX 61, TOGIAK, AK 99678
MAYA KANULIE, BOX 284, TOGIAK, AK 99678
NORMAN KASAK, BOX 228, TOGIAK, AK 99678
SUSIE KASAK, BOX 74, TOGIAK, AK 99678
JACKIE KEENE, BOX 288, TOGIAK, AK 99678
SCOTT KEHRLI, 285 STATE HWY 409, CATHLAMET, WA 98612
CONOR KELLY, 286 S 2ND ST #2D, BROOKLYN, NY 11211
WANDA KIE.MILLER, BOX 319, NAKNEK, AK 99633
BUDDA KIIMECHUK, 1276 E 113TH Q201, TAMPA, FL 33612
AUSTIN KING, BOX 344, KING SALMON, AK 99613
HANNELORE KIRKMAN, BOX 661, BROADUS, MT 59317
CORINA KOHUK, BOX 175, TOGIAK, AK 99678
DANIEL KOHUK, BOX 253, TOGIAK, AK 99678
SAMSON KOHUK, BOX 253, TOGIAK, AK 99678
CHARLES KOPP, 12010 SHORE CIR, ANCHORAGE, AK 99515
DAVID KOPRA, BOX 1047, HOMER, AK 99603
MAXWELL KORBUS, BOX 1877, MENDOCINO, CA 95460
LEVI KORTHUIS, 7250 LANKHOAR RD, LYNDEN, WA 98264
GERDA KOSBRUK, 8213 TUNDRA DR, PORT HEIDEN, AK 99549
KATHRYN KOTEN, BOX 874781, WASILLA, AK 99687
ELAINE KRAUN, 4752 354TH AVE SE, FALL CITY, WA 98024
EARLING KRAUSE, BOX 75, MANOKOTAK, AK 99628
LISA KREBS, BOX 1971, HOMER, AK 99603
ELI KRIEGH, 4490 DONALD ST, EUGENE, OR 97405
MOSES KRITZ, BOX 83, TOGIAK, AK 99678
EDMOND KROENER, 19331 KLONDIKE ST #3, CHUGIAK, AK 99567
HILDA KROENER, BOX 670394, CHUGIAK, AK 99567
LINA KUNZ, 418 STATE ROUTE 105, RAYMOND, WA 98577
TOBIN KUNZ, 418 STATE ROUTE 105, RAYMOND, WA 98577
KRISTINA KURTZ, BOX 92895, ANCHORAGE, AK 99509
MARTHA KVAMME, BOX 26, TOGIAK, AK 99678
BRAD LA.ROCK, BOX 845, COOPER LANDING, AK 99572
DAVID LAKE, BOX 173, HOOPER BAY, AK 99604
KATHERINE LAMSON, BOX 12, DILLINGHAM, AK 99576
JERRY LANG, 3102 N GREEN RD, OAK HARBOR, WA 98277
JASEN LARSGAARD, BOX 1567, DILLINGHAM, AK 99576
CARL LARSON, BOX 190906, ANCHORAGE, AK 99519
ROSEANN LARSON, BOX 264, DILLINGHAM, AK 99576
RYAN LARSON, BOX 834, DILLINGHAM, AK 99576
ANGELA LAWRENCE, 7100 CLAIRMONT CIR, ANCHORAGE, AK 99507
BRUCE LAWRENCE, 7100 CLAIRMONT CIR, ANCHORAGE, AK 99507
LINDSAY LAYLAND, BOX 1306, DILLINGHAM, AK 99576
TAYLOR LAYLAND, 2800 E MATTERHORN DR, FLAGSTAFF, AZ 86004
JAIME LEBARON, BOX 4, SELDOVIA, AK 99663
SHAUN LEBARON, 3434 CAMPBELL AIRSTRIP RD, ANCHORAGE, AK 99504
ERIK LEMAN, BOX 582, NAKNEK, AK 99633
JEFFREY LEMAN, BOX 582, NAKNEK, AK 99633
RYAN LEONHARDT, 10822 32ND ST E, EDGEWOOD, WA 98372
ANDREW LERVAAG, 2820 PORCUPINE TRAIL RD, ANCHORAGE, AK 99516
JONAH LERVAAG, 2820 PORCUPINE TRAIL, ANCHORAGE, AK 99516
CEARA LEWIS, BOX 1095, CANNON BEACH, OR 97110
ECOLA LEWIS.COLLIER, BOX 207, SELDOVIA, AK 99663
CHRISTINA LIBBY, 10981 TRAIL'S END RD, ANCHORAGE, AK 99507
JAMES LIBBY, 11680 CANGE ST, ANCHORAGE, AK 99516
KATRINA LIBBY, 11680 CANGE ST, ANCHORAGE, AK 99516
PAMELA LIBBY, 11680 CANGE ST, ANCHORAGE, AK 99516
STEPHEN LIBBY, 10981 TRAIL'S END RD, ANCHORAGE, AK 99507
WARREN LIBBY, 12621 BONA KIM LP, ANCHORAGE, AK 99515
JASON LICHTENBERG, 1716 WILSON AVE, SAINT PAUL, MN 55106
SAMUEL LINCOLN, BOX 158, DILLINGHAM, AK 99576
COREY LOCKBEAM, 8508 NE 61ST ST, VANCOUVER, WA 98662
ELENA LOCKUK, BOX 125, TOGIAK, AK 99678
MARTHA LOCKUK, 4516 E 9TH AVE, ANCHORAGE, AK 99508
ANDREA LOGUSAK, BOX 301, TOGIAK, AK 99678
FANNIE LOGUSAK, BOX 278, TOGIAK, AK 99678

SALMON FISHING LIST—GILLNET

BERTRAM LUCKHURST, BOX 405, DILLINGHAM, AK 99576
PETER LUDVICK, BOX 208, ILIAMNA, AK 99606
SHIRLEY LUDVICK, BOX 208, ILIAMNA, AK 99606
LEILANI LUHRS, BOX 25, TOGIAK, AK 99678
DANIEL MACCARONE, 6600 E SKYHAWK CIR, WASILLA, AK 99654
DANIEL MACDONALD, BOX 5993, BELLINGHAM, WA 98227
JOHN MACDONALD, BOX 5993, BELLINGHAM, WA 98227
KEVIN MACDONALD, 3656 WOODLAKE RD, BELLINGHAM, WA 98226
MARTIN MACHADO, 1236 CHESTNUT ST, SAN FRANCISCO, CA 94109
BEN MACK, BOX 70121, SOUTH NAKNEK, AK 99670
DONALD MACK, BOX 870235, WASILLA, AK 99687
JACOB MACK, BOX 70121, SOUTH NAKNEK, AK 99670
PAMELA MACK, BOX 870235, WASILLA, AK 99687
ERICA MADISON, 3753 W 44TH ST, ANCHORAGE, AK 99517
KATHRYN MADSON, 53921 GABRIEL CT, MILTON FREEWATER, OR 97862
RICHARD MADSON, 53921 GABRIEL CT, MILTON FREEWATER, OR 97862
FREDERICK MAGILL, BOX 444, PETERSBURG, AK 99833
ABIGAIL MARTIN, BOX 661, BROADUS, MT 59317
CLARA MARTIN, BOX 242, TOGIAK, AK 99678
DARRELL MARTIN, 4790 S EASTERN #170, LAS VEGAS, NV 89119
WILLIAM MARTIN, BOX 24, EGEGIK, AK 99579
ERIC MARXMILLER, 1751 26TH AVE, SAN FRANCISCO, CA 94122
GREGORY MARXMILLER, BOX 862, DILLINGHAM, AK 99576
JIM MARXMILLER, 20626 SCOFIELD DR, CUPERTINO, CA 95014
JUDY MATSON, BOX 552, NAKNEK, AK 99633
BURT MAUD, BOX 315, TOGIAK, AK 99678
DYLAN MCBRIDE, 126 W PIONEER AVE #4, HOMER, AK 99603
KEVIN MCCAMBLY, 12814 CHAPEL DR, ANCHORAGE, AK 99501
BODI MCCASKILL, 112 SW M ST, GRANTS PASS, OR 97526
REUBEN MCCRUM, BOX 1720, HOOD RIVER, OR 97031
BRYAN MCKIMSON, 1375 W SANDS DR, WASILLA, AK 99654
LANCE MCKIMSON, 1375 W SANDS DR, WASILLA, AK 99654
NATHANIEL MCKIMSON, 1375 W SANDS DR, WASILLA, AK 99654
DOUG MCRAE, BOX 82, MOOSE PASS, AK 99631
SETH MCSWAIN, 12630 RYA RD, ANCHORAGE, AK 99516
RODNEY MEEKS, 1515 W 15TH AVE, ANCHORAGE, AK 99501
BARBARA MEGGITT, BOX 60106, FAIRBANKS, AK 99706
CHARLES MEGGITT, BOX 60106, FAIRBANKS, AK 99706
RONALD MEGGITT, 1161 S BETTINIA WAY, WASILLA, AK 99623
SYLVIA MEJORADA, BOX 296, NAKNEK, AK 99633
BART MEYER, 210 SHOTGUN ALLEY, SITKA, AK 99835
ERIC MEYER, BOX 655, AVILA BEACH, CA 93424
JACOB MEYER, 36538 LAKEVIEW ST, STERLING, AK 99672
KEVIN MEYER, BOX 655, AVILA BEACH, CA 93424
CHERYL MIKE, BOX 1073, DILLINGHAM, AK 99576
DIANE MILLAR, 12630 RYA RD, ANCHORAGE, AK 99516
JONATHON MILLAR, 1011 E VICTORY RD, BOISE, ID 83706
MATTHEW MILLAR, 12630 RYA RD, ANCHORAGE, AK 99516
RICK MILLAR, 12630 RYA RD, ANCHORAGE, AK 99516
SHUREE MILLAR.HARTVIGSO, 12630 RYA RD, ANCHORAGE, AK 99516
KAYLA MILLER, BOX 645, DILLINGHAM, AK 99576
NORA MILLER, 11900 CANGE ST, ANCHORAGE, AK 99516
PATRICIA MINARD, BOX 1096, HILLSBORO, OR 97123
JEFFERY MITCHELL, 960 E SUSITNA DR, WASILLA, AK 99623
SHAWN MITCHELL, 9913 RELIANCE DR, ANCHORAGE, AK 99507
ALEXANDER MOCHIN, BOX 33, MANOKOTAK, AK 99628
BYRON MOCHIN, BOX 14, MANOKOTAK, AK 99628
JOHN MOEN, 4131 GRAND AVE, EVERETT, WA 98203
PAULA MONSEN, BOX 113, NAKNEK, AK 99633
RENNITA MONSEN, BOX 124, KING SALMON, AK 99613
ROLAND MONSEN, BOX 124, KING SALMON, AK 99613
ANTHONY MOORE, 13037 RIDGEVIEW DR, ANCHORAGE, AK 99516
BARBARA MOORE, BOX 88, MANOKOTAK, AK 99628
ELIZABETH MOORE, 1618 N 170TH ST, SHORELINE, WA 98133
MORGAN MOORE, 3434 CAMPBELL AIRSTRIP RD, ANCHORAGE, AK 99504

OWEN MOORE, BOX 552, EL GRANADA, CA 94018
PATRICK MOORE, 8950 N KIMBALL AVE, PORTLAND, OR 97203
ZACHARY MOORE, 13037 RIDGEVIEW DR, ANCHORAGE, AK 99518
MICHAEL MORAN, BOX 1798, CHICO, CA 95927
ADRIAN MORARESCU, 818 NE 106 ST APT 311, SEATTLE, WA 98125
GRAHAM MORRISON, 1 MAIN ST, KING SALMON, AK 99613
LANEY MOSES, BOX 23, LEVELOCK, AK 99625
CHARLES MOST, BOX 325, WESTPORT, WA 98595
CHRISTIE MOST, 7745 33RD AVE NW, SEATTLE, WA 98117
KEEFA MOXIE, 802 PRICE ST #3, ANCHORAGE, AK 99508
HOWARD MOZEN, 823 W 19TH AVE, ANCHORAGE, AK 99503
CONNOR MUIR, 5800 TRAPPERS TRAIL RD, ANCHORAGE, AK 99516
ROBBIE MUIR, 5800 TRAPPERS TRAIL, ANCHORAGE, AK 99516
CHRISTIAN MUNDORF, 1395 MAPLEWOOD DR, SALINE, MI 48176
EARL MUNDORF, 102 AMESBURY LN, CARY, NC 27511
GEORGE MUNDORF, 1395 MAPLEWOOD DR, SALINE, MI 48176
FREDERICK MUNRO, BOX 1971, HOMER, AK 99603
MONTE MURPHY, BOX 218, DILLINGHAM, AK 99576
PAMELA MURPHY, BOX 218, DILLINGHAM, AK 99576
JOHN MURRAY, BOX 212, CLARKSTON, WA 99403
REMIE MURRAY, BOX 1793, GIRDWOOD, AK 99587
REMIE MURRAY, 3586 ASOTIN CREEK RD, ASOTIN, WA 99402
WILLIAM MUSTARD, 240 MCDUFFIE DR, ATHENS, GA 30605
KATHLEEN MYERS, BOX 433, KING SALMON, AK 99613
MARGOT MYERS, 205 GRAND AVE, BELLINGHAM, WA 98225
KENNETH NANALOOK, BOX 5, TOGIAK, AK 99678
RAY NANALOOK, BOX 162, MANOKOTAK, AK 99628
ANECIA NANOK.OUYA, BOX 96, GOODNEWS BAY, AK 99589
RICHARD NANUK, BOX 83, HOOPER BAY, AK 99604
LESLIE NASHOOKPUK, BOX 38, NAKNEK, AK 99633
GWEN NEAL, BOX 3368, HOMER, AK 99603
TONY NEAL, BOX 3368, HOMER, AK 99603
CURTIS NELSON, 1317 SKY AVE, COLLEGE PLACE, WA 99324
GEORGE NELSON, BOX 5006, KOLIGANEK, AK 99576
ORYANNA NELSON, #8 1776 CT, LONGVIEW, WA 98632
WANDA NELSON, 1317 SKY AVE, COLLEGE PLACE, WA 99324
ALEX NEWMAN, 3730 MCCLELLAN RD, PENSACOLA, FL 32503
BOBBY NICHOLSON, BOX 177, DILLINGHAM, AK 99576
JANET NICHOLSON, 5800 LAKE OTIS #324, ANCHORAGE, AK 99507
WILLIAM NICHOLSON, 14439 TERRACE LN #A, EAGLE RIVER, AK 99577
EDWARD NICK, BOX 110, MANOKOTAK, AK 99628
JOHN NICK, BOX 124, TOGIAK, AK 99678
TIMOTHY NICK, BOX 753816, FAIRBANKS, AK 99701
TRAVIS NICK, BOX 252, TOGIAK, AK 99678
VICTOR NICK, BOX 88, KWETHLUK, AK 99621
JOSHUA NICKERSON, BOX 194, MANOKOTAK, AK 99628
TESSA NICKERSON, BOX 194, MANOKOTAK, AK 99628
DANYA NICKETA, 5500 N BONNIE DR, PALMER, AK 99645
CAMERON NICOLSON, 32 COMANCHE TRL, GREAT FALLS, MT 59404
CHRISTOPHER NICOLSON, 952 BROOKLYN AVE, BROOKLYN, NY 11203
DONALD NIELSEN, BOX 70151, SOUTH NAKNEK, AK 99670
JENS NIELSEN, BOX 93, NAKNEK, AK 99633
MARTHA NIELSEN, BOX 1089, KOKHANOK, AK 99606
NILS NIELSEN, BOX 1089, KOKHANOK, AK 99606
BARTHOLOMEW NIENHUIS, BOX 24, SOUTH NAKNEK, AK 99670
DUANE NIENHUIS, BOX 70024, SOUTH NAKNEK, AK 99670
MAIO NISHKIAN, 3202 W DISCOVERY LP, WASILLA, AK 99654
BOB NOBUHARA, BOX 1404, MOUNTAIN VIEW, CA 94042
MARK NODEN, 3500 MT. VIEW DR #8, ANCHORAGE, AK 99508
TIFFANY NOGG, 2420 LAKE GEORGE RD, ANCHORAGE, AK 99504
CHARLES NOLAY, 4045 E 20TH UNIT 71, ANCHORAGE, AK 99508
CHAD NORRIS, 1010 DOANE RD, BOZEMAN, MT 59718
PAUL NUKUSUK, BOX 153, HOOPER BAY, AK 99604
KENNETH NUKWAK, BOX 127, MANOKOTAK, AK 99628
BARBARA NUNN, BOX 158, DILLINGHAM, AK 99576

SALMON FISHING LIST—GILLNET

DEMETRI OAKS, BOX 83, HOOPER BAY, AK 99604
IRMA OBRIEN, BOX 507, INDIANOLA, WA 98342
WILLIAM OBRIEN, BOX 1037, DILLINGHAM, AK 99576
CHRISTINE OCONNOR, 2800 N PARK DR, WASILLA, AK 99654
JOHN OCONNOR, 2800 N PARK DR, WASILLA, AK 99654
LLOYD OCONNOR, BOX 546, DILLINGHAM, AK 99576
RENE OCONNOR, BOX 546, DILLINGHAM, AK 99576
RICHARD OCONNOR, BOX 1256, DILLINGHAM, AK 99576
TATIANA OCONNOR, BOX 1256, DILLINGHAM, AK 99576
TARYN OCONNOR.BRITO, BOX 546, DILLINGHAM, AK 99576
ADAM OGUINN, BOX 3729, SOLDOTNA, AK 99669
IVY OGUINN, BOX 3729, SOLDOTNA, AK 99669
MARTHA OHLSON, BOX 1720, HOOD RIVER, OR 97031
SHAWN OLES, BOX 76, MANOKOTAK, AK 99628
CHRISTOPHER OLSON, BOX 517, DILLINGHAM, AK 99576
CURTIS OLSON, BOX 661, BROADUS, MT 59317
LAWRENCE OLSON, BOX 82, CLARKS POINT, AK 99569
LORNA OLSON, BOX 15, DILLINGHAM, AK 99576
TOM OLSON, BOX 125, DILLINGHAM, AK 99576
DAVID OLTMAN, 604 LOWE ST, WENATCHEE, WA 98801
SARAH ONEILL, BOX 3368, HOMER, AK 99603
LUKE OWENS, 4070 SUMMIT CT NE, ROCKFORD, MI 49341
PAUL OWENS, 200 HUNTERS LN, ROCKFORD, MI 49341
BUD OWINGS, 1253 PHEASANT DR, NORTH POLE, AK 99705
JO OXENTENKO, BOX 671527, CHUGIAK, AK 99567
BRYDIN PACHECO, BOX 113, NAKNEK, AK 99633
JAMES PALIN, BOX 550, DILLINGHAM, AK 99576
TODD PALIN, 1140 W PARKS HWY, WASILLA, AK 99654
ALFONSO PALMA, 3200 S RAPID CIR, WASILLA, AK 99654
DOMINIC PAPETTI, 3151 WILD MUSTANG PASS, WICKENBURG, AZ 85390
KAREN PAPETTI, 3151 WILD MUSTANG PASS, WICKENBURG, AZ 85390
MARIE PAPETTI, 2610 ERIE ST, BELLINGHAM, WA 98225
SAVIOR PAPETTI, 5481 DINKLE RD, BELLINGHAM, WA 98226
MICHAEL PAPPAS, 20626 SCOFIELD DRIVE, CUPERTINO, CA 95014
DOLLY PARKER, 421 E 10TH, ANCHORAGE, AK 99501
JOHN PARKER, BOX 191, TOGIAK, AK 99678
SUSAN PASQUARIELLO, BOX 1354, DILLINGHAM, AK 99576
ERLINE PAT, BOX 87, MANOKOTAK, AK 99628
WILLIAM PATON, 4036 VANCE DR, ANCHORAGE, AK 99508
AGNES PAUK, BOX 36, MANOKOTAK, AK 99628
DANIEL PAUL, BOX 166, TOGIAK, AK 99678
SIDNEY PAVIAN, BOX 194, TOGIAK, AK 99678
NOYUK PEACOCK, 1621 WICHERSHAM DR, ANCHORAGE, AK 99507
BILLY PEEK, BOX 2, CATHLAMET, WA 98612
JEWELINE PELAGIO, BOX 1155, DILLINGHAM, AK 99576
CHRIS PENNEBAKER, 4705 SUMMER AVE NE, ALBUQUERQUE, NM 87110
MATTHEW PERKINS, BOX 42, MOOSE PASS, AK 99631
RICK PERLEBERG, 30571 SR 231 N, REARDSON, WA 99029
DALE PETERS, BOX 144, NAKNEK, AK 99633
ERIN PETERS, BOX 144, NAKNEK, AK 99633
HARLAN PETERSEN, BOX 429, NACHES, WA 98937
JACOB PETERSEN, BOX 70145, SOUTH NAKNEK, AK 99670
JEAN PETERSEN, BOX 70145, SOUTH NAKNEK, AK 99670
JENNIFER PETERSEN, BOX 70145, SOUTH NAKNEK, AK 99670
TED PETERSEN, BOX 70145, SOUTH NAKNEK, AK 99670
BENJAMIN PETERSON, 3450 STANFORD DR, ANCHORAGE, AK 99508
BESSIE PETERSON, 1747 LOGAN ST, ANCHORAGE, AK 99504
CHRISTOPHER PETERSON, 9245 KIRKWALL CIR, ANCHORAGE, AK 99502
JOHN PETERSON, 3450 STANFORD DR, ANCHORAGE, AK 99508
KAREN PETERSON, 3450 STANFORD DR, ANCHORAGE, AK 99508
DARREN PETLA, BOX 1257, DILLINGHAM, AK 99576
NIKOLAI PETTICREW, 18630 N LOWRIE LP, EAGLE RIVER, AK 99577
TATIANA PETTICREW, BOX 70133, SOUTH NAKNEK, AK 99670
DAVID PHARR, 97 W BIRNIE SLOUGH RD, CATHLAMET, WA 98612
LOGAN PHELPS, BOX 135, NAKNEK, AK 99633
MEADOW PHELPS, BOX 135, NAKNEK, AK 99633

RUSSELL PHELPS, BOX 135, NAKNEK, AK 99633
YVONNE PHELPS, BOX 135, NAKNEK, AK 99633
JEANETTE PHILLIPS, BOX 39574, NINILCHIK, AK 99639
JUDITH PHILLIPS, 11240 WOMENS BAY RD, KODIAK, AK 99615
PATRICIA PHILLIPS, BOX 215, DILLINGHAM, AK 99576
ERNEST PIERCE, BOX 556, COOPER LANDING, AK 99572
LUKE PIETRON, 28546 60TH AVE, CUSHING, MN 56443
ROGER PIETRON, 28546 60TH AVE, CUSHING, MN 56443
GEORGE PIGG, 5380 I-25 S, PUEBLO, CO 81004
BO PINGREE, 1738 SHELTON RD, WALLA WALLA, WA 99362
DANIEL PINGREE, 203 PINGREE CIR, UGASHIK, AK 99613
IDA PINGREE, 5309 KINGS WAY, ANACORTES, WA 98221
AURORA PLANT, BOX 1034, DILLINGHAM, AK 99576
TERRI POPA, 2268 AQUA HILL RD, FALLBROOK, CA 92028
VICTOR POPA, 2268 AQUA HILL RD, FALLBROOK, CA 92028
VICTORIA POPA, 3849 KLAHINE DR SE #6305, ISSAQUAH, WA 98029
CHARLES POST, BOX 90015, NIGHTMUTE, AK 99690
CHRIS POULSEN, BOX 938, PETERSBURG, AK 99833
CHRISTINE POULSEN, BOX 236, TOGIAK, AK 99678
MORGAN POULSEN, BOX 116, TOGIAK, AK 99678
RICHARD POULSEN, BOX 67, TOGIAK, AK 99678
CHRISTINE PRICE, BOX 1130, DILLINGHAM, AK 99576
BARBARA RALSTON, 51655 IRIS CIR, KENAI, AK 99611
CRAIG RALSTON, 51655 IRIS CIR, KENAI, AK 99611
REBEKAH RALSTON.SAVO, 51655 IRIS CIR, KENAI, AK 99611
MARSI RAMIREZ, 48947 ROSIE LN, KENAI, AK 99611
HELEN RAMONDOS, 10320 COMPASS CIR, ANCHORAGE, AK 99515
JOSHUA RANDICH, BOX 1322, GIRDWOOD, AK 99587
DAVID RANNEY, 12340 N US HWY 101, SHELTON, WA 98584
ERIN RANNEY, 12520 N US HWY 101, SHELTON, WA 98584
JUSTINE RANNEY, 3614 LINDEN AVE N APT 102, SEATTLE, WA 98103
LAURA RANNEY, 11240 WOMENS BAY DR, KODIAK, AK 99615
MEGHAN RANNEY, 12340 N US HWY 101, SHELTON, WA 98584
JEFFERY RASCO, 22 KNIGHT AVE, SEQUIM, WA 98382
RENEE RASCO, 783 SAN ANDREAS RD, LA SELVA BEACH, CA 95076
ROBERT RASCO, 783 SAN ANDREAS RD, LA SELVA BEACH, CA 95076
VICTORIA RAUSTEIN, BOX 574, KING SALMON, AK 99613
SAVANNAH RAWLS, BOX 1029, KOKHANOK, AK 99606
CLINT RAWLS.ROEHL, BOX 1063, KOKHANOK, AK 99606
MARLON RAY, BOX 243, NAKNEK, AK 99633
JACK REAKOFF, 114 NEWHOUSE, WISEMAN, AK 99790
MICHELLE REAKOFF, BOX 68, HOMER, AK 99603
MARK REAMEY, 3411 CHUTHMOK RD, DILLINGHAM, AK 99576
HANS REED, BOX 50, HOMER, AK 99603
DENISE REYNOLDS, 10151 SWEDE CREEK RD, PALO CEDRO, CA 96073
EARL REYNOLDS, 1170 SE VISTA PL, COLLEGE PLACE, WA 99324
ERICKA REYNOLDS, BOX 492, PILOT POINT, AK 99649
FREDERICK REYNOLDS, BOX 492, PILOT POINT, AK 99649
JOEL REYNOLDS, 1170 SE VISTA PL, COLLEGE PLACE, WA 99324
DEBRA RICE, BOX 331, GIRDWOOD, AK 99587
KIM RICE, BOX 331, GIRDWOOD, AK 99587
NICOLE RIGA, 3381 GODREY DR, WASILLA, AK 99654
NATHAN RISPLER, 6314 NE TILLAMOOK ST, PORTLAND, OR 97213
CHRISTOPHER ROACH, 210 3RD ST NE, LITTLE FALLS, MN 56345
BOYD ROBERTS, 4026 217TH ST SE, BOTHELL, WA 98012
ELIZABETH ROBERTS, 4026 217TH ST SE, BOTHELL, WA 98021
JACOB ROBERTS, 4026 217TH ST SE, BOTHELL, WA 98021
SHAYAN ROHANI, 4066 NE 12TH AVE, PORTLAND, OR 97212
BRYSON ROLLMAN, 19541 CICUTTA WAY, EAGLE RIVER, AK 99577
LEVI ROLLMAN, 1650 S COUNTRYWOOD DR, WASILLA, AK 99654
THOMAS ROLLMAN, 19541 CICUTTA WAY, EAGLE RIVER, AK 99577
TOM ROLLMAN, BOX 770778, EAGLE RIVER, AK 99577
COLBY ROOT, 442 HAGELBARGER AVE, FAIRBANKS, AK 99712
LAURA ROOTVIK, 958 SE LARCH AVE, COLLEGE PLACE, WA 98324
SONJA ROOTVIK, 958 SE LARCH AVE, COLLEGE PLACE, WA 99324
FELKA ROSCOE, 1281 E 19TH #A-102, ANCHORAGE, AK 99501

SALMON FISHING LIST—GILLNET

ADAM ROSE, 4105 W 4600 S, ROY, UT 84067
DAVID ROSE, 2170 S 1450 W, WELLSVILLE, UT 94339
GERAD ROSE, 2170 S 1450 W, WELLSVILLE, UT 94339
JALEN ROSE, 2170 SOUTH 1450 WEST, WELLSVILLE, UT 84339
JAYCE ROSE, 2779 W GORDON AVE, LAYTON, UT 84041
SASSA RUBY, BOX 341, DILLINGHAM, AK 99576
ZACHARY RUIZ, 450 BOAS DRIVE, SANTA ROSA, CA 95409
BROCK RUSSELL, 8501 OLD SAN ISABEL RD, RYE, CO 81069
CALEB RYNNING, 12512 MARINE DR, MARYSVILLE, WA 98271
KYLE RYNNING, 12512 MARINE DR, MARYSVILLE, WA 98271
NATHAN RYNNING, 12512 MARINE DR, MARYSVILLE, WA 98271
KYLE S.A.GREGORY, BOX 212, DILLINGHAM, AK 99576
DEBBIE SALMON, 134 COPPER CREEK RD, WOODLAND, WA 98674
DAVID SALMON.HART, BOX 71, VAUGHN, WA 98394
PAT SALVUCCI, 5240 E 142ND AVE, ANCHORAGE, AK 99516
RENEE SALVUCCI, 5420 E 142ND AVE, ANCHORAGE, AK 99516
SARAH SALVUCCI, 5240 E 142ND AVE, ANCHORAGE, AK 99516
GRAYSON SANBORN, 305 MIDWAY BLVD, BROOMFIELD, CO 80020
ROBERT SANBORN, BOX 5913, BELLINGHAM, WA 98227
WILLIAM SARANDRIA, 17495 PT LENA LP RD, JUNEAU, AK 99801
ALEX SAVO, BOX 109, NAKNEK, AK 99633
BRUCE SAVO, BOX 507, DILLINGHAM, AK 99576
DANIEL SAVO, BOX 507, DILLINGHAM, AK 99576
DAVID SAVO, BOX 123, KING SALMON, AK 99613
JOHN SAVO, BOX 109, NAKNEK, AK 99633
SCOTTY SAVO, BOX 109, NAKNEK, AK 99633
JOHN SCHANDELMEIER, HC 02 BOX 7193, GAKONA, AK 99586
JANET SCHLAGEL, BOX 714, DILLINGHAM, AK 99576
JASON SCHLEIZER, 1003 DENNIS DR, HANAHAN, SC 29410
KEVIN SCHMIDT, 24455 HICKORY RD, FERGUS FALLS, MN 56537
STEPHANIE SCHMIDT, 24455 HICKORY RD, FERGUS FALLS, MN 56537
AARON SCHRIER, 1010 W BABCOCK, BOZEMAN, MT 59715
DAVID SCHRIER, BOX 1051, SOLDOTNA, AK 99669
KEVIN SCHRIER, 7030 NW CHURCHILL WAY, CORVALLIS, OR 97330
HUGH SCHROEDER, BOX 402, DILLINGHAM, AK 99576
JEFFREY SCHROEDER, BOX 70091, SOUTH NAKNEK, AK 99670
JACOB SCHUG, 453 CEDAR RIDGE RD, PORTOLA, CA 96122
CARL SCOTT, BOX 51, CUSTER, SD 57730
CHRISTIAN SCOTT, 911 N SHIELDS ST, FORT COLLINS, CO 80521
DOUGLAS SHADE, BOX 156, DILLINGHAM, AK 99576
JUSTIN SHARP, BOX 54, MANOKOTAK, AK 99628
FRANK SHAWCROFT, 1359 JORDYNE ST, FAIRBANKS, AK 99701
MATT SHAWCROFT, BOX 10605, FAIRBANKS, AK 99710
NANCY SHERRER, 1791 POLNELL RD, OAK HARBOR, WA 98277
FRANK SIMPSON, BOX 1928, VALDEZ, AK 99686
KARYN SLOTTEN, BOX 3783, HAILEY, ID 83333
MOSI SLOTTEN, BOX 3783, HAILEY, ID 83333
BENJAMIN SMITH, 1754 EASTRIDGE DR, ANCHORAGE, AK 99501
ERNEST SMITH, BOX 183, HOOPER BAY, AK 99604
GEOFFREY SMITH, BOX 2364, KODIAK, AK 99615
LARRY SMITH, BOX 1391, DEER PARK, WA 99006
LYLE.TIEL SMITH, 1754 EASTRIDGE DR, ANCHORAGE, AK 99501
DANIEL SMOOT, 10046 CARIBOU ST, EAGLE RIVER, AK 99577
MARIE SNYDER, BOX 45, TOGIAK, AK 99678
MICHELLE SNYDER, 3100 BRIDLE LN, ANCHORAGE, AK 99517
HANS SOLIE, 14981 FISK RD, YAKIMA, WA 98908
INGEMAR SONNERUP, 3000 NW 64TH ST, SEATTLE, WA 98107
ALLAN SORENSEN, 265 KINNEY AVE, DETROIT, OR 97342
AUSTIN SORENSON, 354 DIANE LN, SOLDOTNA, AK 99669
CAMERON SORENSON, 354 DIANE LN, SOLDOTNA, AK 99669
JEANNE SORENSON, 51454 OCEAN ENTRANCE DR, KENAI, AK 99611
PAUL SORENSON, 51454 OCEAN ENTRANCE DR, KENAI, AK 99611
LANCE SPENCER, 134 COPPER CREEK RD, WOODLAND, WA 98674
JAY STANFORD, 1 MILLER CREEK, PORT ALSWORTH, AK 99653
LAUREN STANFORD, 16210 CHASEWOOD LANE, ANCHORAGE, AK 99516

MARY STEELE, 12441 BEACHCOMBER DR, ANCHORAGE, AK 99505
SAMUEL STEEN, BOX 16512, DEVER, CO 80216
CAROL.ANN STEFFENSEN, 1462 MT VIEW DR, KODIAK, AK 99615
STEVEN STEFFENSEN, 1462 MT VIEW DR, KODIAK, AK 99615
KEVIN STEPAN, BOX 167, MANOKOTAK, AK 99628
TYLER STERLING, 6847 S MEADOW DWNS WY, COTTONWOOD HTS, UT 94121
TERRI STONE, BOX 4, DILLINGHAM, AK 99576
KERRY STRAUB, BOX 607, DILLINGHAM, AK 99576
KRIS STRAUB, 4851 EIELSON FARM RD, NORTH POLE, AK 99705
AIYING SUN, 301 N BAILEY ST, PALMER, AK 99645
PAULINE SUPSOOK, BOX 486, PILOT POINT, AK 99649
NATALIA SUSKUK, GEN DEL, KOLIGANEK, AK 99576
NICK SUSKUK, BOX 14, NEW STUYAHOK, AK 99636
OLIA SUTTON, BOX 52, TOGIAK, AK 99678
THEODORE SUTTON, BOX 52, TOGIAK, AK 99678
MATTHEW SWANSON, 100 S QUEEN ST, CHESTERTOWN, MD 21620
GLADYS TANNER, BOX 107, MANOKOTAK, AK 99628
LAURA TARTER, 520 ILIMANO ST, KAILNA, HI 96734
EMILIA TAYLOR, 40909 SOLSTICE, HOMER, AK 99603
EMILY TAYLOR, 7221 SETTER DR, ANCHORAGE, AK 99502
KEVIN TAYLOR, 7221 SETTER DR, ANCHORAGE, AK 99502
REID TEN.KLEY, 17118 NE STONEY MEADOWS DR., VANCOUVER, WA 98682
RIAN TEN.KLEY, 17200 NE 40TH ST, VANCOUVER, WA 98682
ALLISON TENNYSON, BOX 167, DILLINGHAM, AK 99576
C TERPENING, BOX 442, HOMER, AK 99603
TRAVELER TERPENING, BOX 442, HOMER, AK 99603
CATHY THEODORSON, 7014 65TH AVE SE, SNOHOMISH, WA 98290
BENJAMIN THOMAS, 3326 NE 63RD AVE, PORTLAND, OR 97213
NELLIE THOMAS, BOX 146, TOGIAK, AK 99678
CHARLES THOMPSON, BOX 431, PILOT POINT, AK 99649
ESTHER THOMPSON, BOX 263, TOGIAK, AK 99678
DAWNIELLE THORNBURGH, 1146 MONTECELLO RD, NAPA, CA 94558
KATHLEEN THORNBURGH, 1146 MONTICELLO RD, NAPA, CA 94558
GLORIA THORSON, BOX 1270, DILLINGHAM, AK 99576
MARILYNN THORSON, BOX 1130, DILLINGHAM, AK 99576
MATTHEW THORSON, BOX 455, DILLINGHAM, AK 99576
GEORGE TIBBETTS, BOX 220992, ANCHORAGE, AK 99522
GEORGE TIBBETTS, BOX 105, NAKNEK, AK 99633
KEN TIBBETTS, 12500 CLIPPERSHIP DR, ANCHORAGE, AK 99515
M.ELAINE TIBBETTS, 12500 CLIPPERSHIP DR, ANCHORAGE, AK 99515
WES TIBBETTS, 12500 CLIPPERSHIP DR, ANCHORAGE, AK 99515
NINA TINKER, BOX 26, ALEKNAGIK, AK 99555
SALLY TINKER, BOX 806, DILLINGHAM, AK 99576
GARVIE TOBIN, 11900 CANGE ST, ANCHORAGE, AK 99516
DANNY TOGIAK, BOX 192, ALEKNAGIK, AK 99555
INA TOGIAK, BOX 232, TOGIAK, AK 99678
SOCOLI TOGIAK, BOX 232, TOGIAK, AK 99678
JADEN TOLIVER, 14510 LEMOYNE BLVD APT 2003, BILOXI, MS 39532
PETER TOMMY, BOX 34, TOGIAK, AK 99678
CLARA TORRISON, BOX 671656, CHUGIAK, AK 99567
PATRICK TOYUKAK, BOX 22, MANOKOTAK, AK 99628
EDWARD TREFON, BOX 38, ILIAMNA, AK 99606
MICHAEL TREFON, BOX 95, NONDALTON, AK 99640
JAMES TROTT, 231 E LITTLE ISLAND RD, CATHLAMET, WA 98612
NANCY TROTT, 239 E LITTLE ISLAND RD, CATHLAMET, WA 98612
DANIEL TUGATUK, BOX 115, MANOKOTAK, AK 99628
WASSILLIE TUGATUK, BOX 65, MANOKOTAK, AK 99628
MATTHEW TUGGLE, 271 CLERMONT AVE #1, BROOKLYN, NY 11205
DIANNE TUNNO, 574 RIVER BEND RD, ROSEBURG, OR 97471
FRANK TUNNO, 574 RIVER BEND RD, ROSEBURG, OR 97471
JODIE TUPUOLA, 1102 RAMONA ST, ANCHORAGE, AK 99515
MISIPATI TUPUOLA, 1102 RAMONA ST, ANCHORAGE, AK 99515
ALANNAH TURNER, BOX 433, GIRDWOOD, AK 99587
GRANT TURNER, BOX 433, GIRDWOOD, AK 99587
ETHAN TWOMEY, 30655 GREEN ARBOR DR, MURRIETA, WA 92563

SALMON FISHING LIST—GILLNET

TIM TWOMEY, 1410 NUNAKA DR, ANCHORAGE, AK 99504
ANTHONY UNDERWOOD, 13433 DIGGINDS DR, ANCHORAGE, AK 99515
MARY UNDERWOOD, 5141 SPRUCE CREEK CIR, ANCHORAGE, AK 99507
RALPH UNDERWOOD, 5141 SPRUCE CREEK CIR, ANCHORAGE, AK 99507
SASSA UNREIN, BOX 193, SEWARD, AK 99664
NICHOLAS VANASSE, 10246 TURTLE RIVER LAKE RD NE, BEMIDJI, MN 56601
JOHN VANNATTA, 1000 NICKAJACK LNDG, SOUTH PITTSBURG, TN 37380
NANCY VEAL, 47437 STEVEN ST, KENAI, AK 99611
NAOMI VEAL, 47113 STEVEN ST, KENAI, AK 99611
TIM VEAL, 47437 STEVEN ST, KENAI, AK 99611
JOHNNY VEENHOUWER, 45 NE WASHINGTON AVE #3, CHEHALIS, WA 98532
KODI VETSCH, BOX 321, RANCHESTER, WY 82839
ROD VETSCH, BOX 321, RANCHESTER, WY 82839
TAMMY VETSCH, BOX 1004, NACHES, WA 98937
LUKE VILLNAVE, BOX 891, DILLINGHAM, AK 99576
PAVEL VITEK, BOX 643, KASILOF, AK 99610
DAVID VOLENTINE, BOX 3, RYE, CO 81069
CRAIG VOLIGNY, 634 E HUSTON ST, BARBERTON, OH 44203
PAUL VOORHIS, BOX 1445, PALMER, AK 99645
MARK WAGNER, 11224 COUNTY LINE RD E, EDGEWOOD, WA 98372
SCOTT WAKEFIELD, BOX 402, WASKISH, MN 56685
JOSEPH WALKER, 400 7TH AVE, PORT HADLOCK, WA 98339
DENNIS WALLACE, HC 60 BOX 340G, COPPER CENTER, AK 99573
THOMAS WALLACE, 14109 NE 202 AVE, BRUSH PRAIRIE, WA 98606
MARINA WALTON, 38725 GAVIN CIRCLE, SOLDOTNA, AK 99669
ANDREW WAPPETT, BOX 10585, FAIRBANKS, AK 99710
TRICIA WARD, 14209 56TH AVE S, TUCKWILA, WA 98168
BRANDIE WARE, BOX 7479, NIKISKI, AK 99635
JOEL WARE, BOX 7479, NIKISKI, AK 99635
EVAN WASSILLIE, BOX 42, TOGIAK, AK 99678
FREDDIE WASSILLIE, BOX 46, NEWHALEN, AK 99606
GLENN WASSILLIE, BOX 100940, ANCHORAGE, AK 99501
RONALD WASSILLIE, BOX 46, NEWHALEN, AK 99606
JOSEPH WASSILY, BOX 52, CLARKS POINT, AK 99569
STACEY WAYNE, 210 SHOTGUN ALLEY, SITKA, AK 99835
REISE WAYNER, 13801 VENUS WAY, ANCHORAGE, AK 99511
RHONDA WAYNER, BOX 113014, ANCHORAGE, AK 99511
JOHN WEBER, 406 HAWTHORN AVE, KALISPELL, MT 59901
VICTORIA WEBER, 406 HAWTHORN AVE, KALISPELL, MT 59901
CLAUDE WEBSTER, BOX 121, KING SALMON, AK 99613
DEREK WEBSTER, BOX 121, KING SALMON, AK 99613
NATHAN WEBSTER, BOX 121, KING SALMON, AK 99613
SHERYL WEBSTER, BOX 121, KING SALMON, AK 99613
GEORGE WECKERLE, 4884 PINELEDGE DRIVE W, CLARENCE, NY 14031
DALE WEESE, 5702 S 2ND AVE, EVERETT, WA 98203
DUSTIN WEESE, 5716 S 2ND AVE, EVERETT, WA 98203
HAL WEESE, 17105 24TH PL NE, SNOHOMISH, WA 98290
MICHAEL WEESE, 17105 24TH PL NE, SNOHOMISH, WA 98290
TAMI WEESE, 5716 S 2ND AVE, EVERETT, WA 98203
NATHAN WEGNER, BOX 70063, SOUTH NAKNEK, AK 99670
TERRY WEGNER, 1980 DEVILLE DR, BREMERTON, WA 98312
JACK WEINBERG, 1532 FAIR GLEN RD, EL CAJON, CA 92019
PAUL WEINBERG, 33355 LOUISE RD, WINCHESTER, CA 92596
ROBERT WEINBERG, 1241 LOG CABIN CT, FAIRBANKS, AK 99701
GEFFREY WERNING, 11516 COUNTY ROAD 36, PLATTEVILLE, CO 80651
ALAN WEST, 985 BEAVER CREEK RD, CATHLAMET, WA 98612
ALLAN WEST, BOX 605, ANCHOR POINT, AK 99556
CATIGAN WEST, GEN DEL, KING SALMON, AK 99613
MARY WEST, BOX 452, PILOT POINT, AK 99649
VERYLE WEST, 958 BEAVER CREEK RD, CATHLAMET, WA 98612
KALEB WESTFALL, BOX 993, DILLINGHAM, AK 99576
KEITH WESTFALL, BOX 520164, BIG LAKE, AK 99652
CARTER WESTLUND, BOX 121 C/O VINCE WEBSTER, KING SALMON, AK 99613
BRENT WETTER, BOX 336, DILLINGHAM, AK 99576
DIANE WETTER, BOX 336, DILLINGHAM, AK 99576
EMMA WETTER, BOX 336, DILLINGHAM, AK 99576

ANI WHITE, BOX 326, DILLINGHAM, AK 99576
MARTIN WHITE, BOX 62, KING SALMON, AK 99613
NIA WHITE, BOX 326, DILLINGHAM, AK 99576
TYGA WHITE, BOX R, BONNERS FERRY, ID 83805
SEAN WHITLEY, BOX 176, MANOKOTAK, AK 99628
STEVIE WILBUR, 3922 DANDELION WINE CIR, ANCHORAGE, AK 99507
LATISHA WILKINSON, 14510 LEMOYNE BLVD APT 2003, BILOXI, MS 39532
BRADLEY WILLIAMS, 922 NE 63RD AVE, PORTLAND, OR 97213
DANA WILLIAMS, BOX 7009, RUIDOSO, NM 88345
DEVEN WILLIAMS, 14840 WILDIEN DR, ANCHORAGE, AK 99516
MARCUS WILLIAMS, BOX 7009, RUIDOSO, NM 88355
MARK WILLIAMS, BOX 7009, RUIDOSO, NM 88355
SAMUEL WILLIAMS, BOX 7009, RUIDOSO, NM 88555
DECKER WILLSON, BOX 1685, LIVINGSTON, MT 59047
RYAN WILLSON, BOX 434, NAKNEK, AK 99633
TIMOTHY WILLSON, 117 SO N ST, LIVINGSTON, MT 59047
VIOLET WILLSON, BOX 221, NAKNEK, AK 99633
BRYON WILSON, 1889 HUNTER LN, MENDOTA, MN 55118
DANICA WILSON, BOX 237, NAKNEK, AK 99633
FLOYD WILSON, BOX 133, KING SALMON, AK 99613
GEORGE WILSON, BOX 202, NAKNEK, AK 99633
IRENE WILSON, BOX 1032, KOKHANOK, AK 99606
KEITH WILSON, BOX 202, NAKNEK, AK 99633
LUKE WILSON, BOX 202, NAKNEK, AK 99633
RICHARD WILSON, BOX 237, NAKNEK, AK 99633
SHARON WILSON, BOX 237, NAKNEK, AK 99633
MOLLY WISE, BOX 429, PILOT POINT, AK 99649
PRESTON WOODS, BOX 543, DILLINGHAM, AK 99576
DAVID WRIGHT, 6507 GUNPOWDER LN, PROSPECT, KY 40059
MALCOLM WRIGHT, BOX 695, DILLINGHAM, AK 99576
SAMUEL WRIGHT, BOX 695, DILLINGHAM, AK 99576
DARLENE WYAGON, BOX 5024, KOLIGANEK, AK 99576
GLEN WYSOCKI, BOX 5015, KOLIGANEK, AK 99576
HOLLY WYSOCKI, BOX 175, DILLINGHAM, AK 99576
RICK WYSOCKI, BOX 175, DILLINGHAM, AK 99576
PAUL ZACZKOWSKI, BOX 403, TOK, AK 99780
DYLAN ZHAROFF, 259 MOUNTAIN VIEW DR, HOMER, AK 99603
GABRIEL ZHAROFF, BOX 14, EGEGIK, AK 99579
MALLORY ZHAROFF, 259 MOUNTAIN VIEW DR, HOMER, AK 99603
DALLAS ZIMIN, BOX 387, NAKNEK, AK 99633
JUSTIN ZIMIN, 4070 N FORESTWOOD DR, PALMER, AK 99645
KARISSA ZIMIN, 1281 S VINE RD, WASILLA, AK 99654
RYANN ZIMIN, BOX 70003, SOUTH NAKNEK, AK 99670
ALEXANDER ZORTMAN, 4600 EIELSON FARM RD, NORTH POLE, AK 99705
RYAN ZORTMAN, 4600 EISLON FARM RD, NORTH POLE, AK 99705
PRESTON A.W.J.PAINE, BOX 51143, AKIACHAK, AK 99551

SALMON, GILLNET, KUSKOKWIM

ARTHUR ABALAMA, BOX 2182, BETHEL, AK 99559
JAMES ACTIVE, BOX 152, KIPNUK, AK 99614
OSCAR ACTIVE, BOX 5032, KONGIGANAK, AK 99545
PETER ACTIVE, BOX 15, KASIGLUK, AK 99609
DANIEL ALBRITE, BOX 2774, BETHEL, AK 99559
AARON ALEXIE, BOX 51112, AKIACHAK, AK 99551
BRENDA ALEXIE, BOX 05, TULUKSAK, AK 99679
CARVALENA ALEXIE, BOX 401, BETHEL, AK 99559
DAVID ALEXIE, GEN DEL, AKIACHAK, AK 99551
DAVID ALEXIE, BOX 5, KWIGILLINGOK, AK 99622
ELLEPH ALEXIE, BOX 591, BETHEL, AK 99559
EUGENE ALEXIE, BOX 64, EEK, AK 99578
GEORGE ALEXIE, BOX 91, EEK, AK 99578
HANS ALEXIE, BOX 2308, BETHEL, AK 99559
HARRY ALEXIE, BOX 2424, BETHEL, AK 99559
HENRY ALEXIE, BOX 94, TULUKSAK, AK 99679
JESSICA ALEXIE, BOX 138, QUINHAGAK, AK 99655

SALMON FISHING LIST—GILLNET

KENYON ALEXIE, BOX 11, NUNAPITCHUK, AK 99641
MOSES ALEXIE, BOX 51134, AKIACHAK, AK 99551
NICHOLAI ALEXIE, BOX 116, TULUKSAK, AK 99679
OSCAR ALEXIE, BOX 708, BETHEL, AK 99559
PETER ALEXIE, BOX 43, KWETHLUK, AK 99621
PHILLIP ALEXIE, BOX 122, NUNAPITCHUK, AK 99641
RAYMOND ALEXIE, BOX 45, NUNAPITCHUK, AK 99641
ROY ALEXIE, BOX 1017, BETHEL, AK 99559
SAM ALEXIE, BOX 2153, BETHEL, AK 99559
STEVEN ALEXIE, BOX 46, NUNAPITCHUK, AK 99641
MORGAN ALFRED, BOX 3, QUINHAGAK, AK 99655
CHARLES ALLEN, BOX 2476, BETHEL, AK 99559
SAMANTHA ALORALREA, BOX 280, CHEVAK, AK 99563
ALECK ALOYSIUS, BOX 29, LOWER KALSKAG, AK 99626
ALEXANDER ALOYSIUS, BOX 1022, BETHEL, AK 99559
PETER ALUSKA, BOX 392, BETHEL, AK 99559
DAVID AMIK, BOX 1033, BETHEL, AK 99559
ABRAHAM ANDREW, BOX 2272, BETHEL, AK 99559
ADAM ANDREW, BOX 75, KASIGLUK, AK 99609
ANDREW ANDREW, BOX 8069, TUNTUTULIAK, AK 99680
ARCHIE ANDREW, BOX 2628, BETHEL, AK 99559
CARL ANDREW, BOX 34014, NAPAKIAK, AK 99634
CARL ANDREW, BOX 55, KWETHLUK, AK 99621
CARL ANDREW, BOX 8056, TUNTUTULIAK, AK 99680
CHARLIE ANDREW, BOX 8124, TUNTUTULIAK, AK 99680
DELLA ANDREW, BOX 124, TULUKSAK, AK 99679
HARRY ANDREW, BOX 64, NUNAPITCHUK, AK 99641
JIMMY ANDREW, BOX 5033, KONGIGANAK, AK 99545
JOEL ANDREW, BOX 155, KWETHLUK, AK 99621
JOHN ANDREW, 6121 PROSPERITY DR, ANCHORAGE, AK 99504
JOHN ANDREW, BOX 1066, BETHEL, AK 99559
JOHN ANDREW, 134 PLEASANT DR, QUINHAGAK, AK 99655
JOHN ANDREW, BOX 57, MANOKOTAK, AK 99628
JOSEPH ANDREW, BOX 75, KASIGLUK, AK 99609
JOSEPH ANDREW, BOX 202586, ANCHORAGE, AK 99520
LLOYD ANDREW, BOX 71, NUNAPITCHUK, AK 99641
MARTIN ANDREW, BOX 201, KWETHLUK, AK 99621
MELVIN ANDREW, BOX 34095, NAPAKIAK, AK 99634
NOAH ANDREW, BOX 28, KWIGILLINGOK, AK 99622
NOAH ANDREW, BOX 61, TULUKSAK, AK 99679
PETER ANDREW, BOX 25, TULUKSAK, AK 99679
STEVEN ANDREW, BOX 34077, NAPAKIAK, AK 99634
TOMMY ANDREW, BOX 48, KWIGILLINGOK, AK 99622
WILLIE ANDREW, BOX 168, KWETHLUK, AK 99621
WILSON ANDREW, GEN DEL, ATMAUTLUAK, AK 99559
WILSON ANDREW, BOX 18, NUNAPITCHUK, AK 99641
YEAKO ANDREW, BOX 6014, NAPASKIAK, AK 99559
MAX ANGELLAN, BOX 77, KWETHLUK, AK 99621
ALEXANDER ANVIL, BOX 1443, BETHEL, AK 99559
CARL ANVIL, BOX 1285, BETHEL, AK 99559
KENNETH ANVIL, BOX 52, BETHEL, AK 99559
KAREN ATSERIAK, BOX 43, QUINHAGAK, AK 99655
KAY ATTIE, BOX 93, KIPNUK, AK 99614
NOAH ATTIE, BOX 155, KIPNUK, AK 99614
DANIEL AUSDAHL, BOX 21, UPPER KALSKAG, AK 99607
DAVID AUSDAHL, BOX 940214, HOUSTON, AK 99694
JOE AVUGIAK, BOX 62, CHEFORNAK, AK 99561
JOHN AVUGIAK, BOX 109, CHEFORNAK, AK 99561
CARL AYAGALRIA, BOX 8067, TUNTUTULIAK, AK 99680
JASON AYAGALRIA, BOX 34055, NAPAKIAK, AK 99634
MOSES AYAGALRIA, BOX 2078, BETHEL, AK 99559
NORMAN AYAGALRIA, BOX 2705, BETHEL, AK 99559
LARRY AYAPAN, BOX 2672, BETHEL, AK 99559
NICK AYAPAN, BOX 36, KWETHLUK, AK 99621
WALTER AYOJIAK, BOX 026, GOODNEWS BAY, AK 99589

BRANDON AZEAN, BOX 5090, KONGIGANAK, AK 99545
EVON AZEAN, BOX 5095, KONGIGANAK, AK 99545
GERALD BEAN, BOX 67, BETHEL, AK 99559
DANIEL BEAVER, BOX 2887, BETHEL, AK 99559
JESSE BEAVER, BOX 13, GOODNEWS BAY, AK 99589
MOSES BEAVER, BOX 33, BETHEL, AK 99559
SAMUEL BEAVER, BOX 129, BETHEL, AK 99559
TIMOTHY BEAVER, BOX 32, KASIGLUK, AK 99609
WILSON BEAVER, BOX 6034, NAPASKIAK, AK 99559
CARLIE BEEBE, BOX 73, EEK, AK 99578
EDNA BEEBE, BOX 35, EEK, AK 99578
FRITZ BEEBE, BOX 131, EEK, AK 99578
JACOB BEEBE, 3887 GALACTICA DR, ANCHORAGE, AK 99517
TIMOTHY BEEBE, BOX 115, QUINHAGAK, AK 99655
FRANK BEREZKIN, BOX 6097, NAPASKIAK, AK 99559
JULIA BEREZKIN, BOX 125, QUINHAGAK, AK 99655
AMY BERLIN, 7910 LADASA PL, ANCHORAGE, AK 99507
CARL BERLIN, BOX 159, KASIGLUK, AK 99609
DANIEL BERLIN, BOX 61, KASIGLUK, AK 99609
JAMES BERLIN, BOX 118, NUNAPITCHUK, AK 99641
JOHN BERLIN, BOX 152, NUNAPITCHUK, AK 99641
JOSEPH BERLIN, BOX 12, NUNAPITCHUK, AK 99641
KENNETH BERLIN, BOX 1441, BETHEL, AK 99559
PETER BERLIN, BOX 109, NUNAPITCHUK, AK 99641
SAMUEL BERLIN, BOX 2735, BETHEL, AK 99559
STANLEY BERLIN, BOX 43, KASIGLUK, AK 99609
WILSON BERLIN, BOX 174, KASIGLUK, AK 99609
JAMES BILLY, BOX 34076, NAPAKIAK, AK 99634
SALLY BILLY, BOX 34088, NAPAKIAK, AK 99634
LAWRENCE BLACK, BOX 34073, NAPAKIAK, AK 99634
NORMAN BLACK, BOX 34016, NAPAKIAK, AK 99634
PATRICK BLACK, BOX 34021, NAPAKIAK, AK 99634
MICHAEL BORATKO, BOX 131, HOMER, AK 99603
JOHN BOROWSKI, BOX 287, ANIAK, AK 99557
ANNIE BRIGHT, BOX 116, GOODNEWS BAY, AK 99589
GEORGE BRIGHT, BOX 145, GOODNEWS BAY, AK 99589
JAMES BRIGHT, BOX 02, GOODNEWS BAY, AK 99589
ARNOLD BRINK, BOX 132, KASIGLUK, AK 99609
FRANKLIN BRINK, BOX 35, NUNAPITCHUK, AK 99641
GOLGA BRINK, BOX 13, KASIGLUK, AK 99609
GREGORY BRINK, BOX 34092, NAPAKIAK, AK 99634
IRVIN BRINK, BOX 36, KASIGLUK, AK 99609
PETER BRINK, BOX 3154, BETHEL, AK 99559
YAKO BRINK, BOX 003, KASIGLUK, AK 99609
CASSIUS BROWN, BOX 5105, KONGIGANAK, AK 99545
COLLIN BROWN, BOX 09, QUINHAGAK, AK 99655
DENNIS BROWN, BOX 9, QUINHAGAK, AK 99655
ERIC BROWN, BOX 123, QUINHAGAK, AK 99655
FRANK BROWN, BOX 053, EEK, AK 99578
JOSEPH BROWN, BOX 5104, KONGIGANAK, AK 99545
JOSHUA BROWN, BOX 92, QUINHAGAK, AK 99655
NICKY BROWN, BOX 054, EEK, AK 99578
RICHARD BROWN, BOX 093, EEK, AK 99578
SUSAN BROWN, BOX 9, QUINHAGAK, AK 99655
THEODORE BROWN, BOX 107, EEK, AK 99578
THOMAS BROWN, BOX 22, QUINHAGAK, AK 99655
TONY BROWN, BOX 67, EEK, AK 99578
VERNON BROWN, BOX 013, EEK, AK 99578
WALTER BROWN, BOX 88, EEK, AK 99578
WAYNE BROWN, BOX 013, EEK, AK 99578
RAYMOND C.W.ALEXIE, BOX 2424, BETHEL, AK 99559
TRAVIS CARL, BOX 8083, TUNTUTULIAK, AK 99680
ADOLPH CARTER, BOX 016, EEK, AK 99578
EMMA CARTER, BOX 005, EEK, AK 99578
FERDINAND CARTER, BOX 014, EEK, AK 99578

SALMON FISHING LIST—GILLNET

JOE CARTER, BOX 135, QUINHAGAK, AK 99655
NICK CARTER, BOX 3, EEK, AK 99578
JAMES CHALIAK, BOX 2271, BETHEL, AK 99559
ZECHARIAH CHALIAK, BOX 103, NUNAPITCHUK, AK 99641
STEVE CHAMBERLAIN, BOX 295, ANIAK, AK 99557
DANIEL CHARLES, BOX 175, KASIGLUK, AK 99609
DANNY CHARLES, BOX 5, BETHEL, AK 99559
DARREN CHARLES, BOX 83, NUNAPITCHUK, AK 99641
JAMES CHARLES, BOX 8044, TUNTUTULIAK, AK 99680
JESSE CHARLES, BOX 8044, TUNTUTULIAK, AK 99680
NICHOLAS CHARLES, BOX 876463, WASILLA, AK 99687
PETER CHARLES, 8131 LAMPLIGHTER CT, ANCHORAGE, AK 99502
JOHN CHARLIE, BOX 2376, BETHEL, AK 99559
MARTHA CHARLIE, BOX 791, BETHEL, AK 99559
RAY CHARLIE, BOX 8064, TUNTUTULIAK, AK 99680
THOMAS CHARLIE, BOX 8064, TUNTUTULIAK, AK 99680
LARRY CHASE, BOX 1981, BETHEL, AK 99559
NICK CHASE, BOX 3026, BETHEL, AK 99559
THOMAS CHASE, BOX 2795, BETHEL, AK 99559
VERNON CHASE, BOX 2552, BETHEL, AK 99559
JOSEPH CHIEF, BOX 1841, BETHEL, AK 99559
HELEN CHIMEGALREA, 3215 MADISON WAY, ANCHORAGE, AK 99509
JESSE CHIMEGALREA, BOX 1266, BETHEL, AK 99559
SAMMY CHIMEGALREA, BOX 24, BETHEL, AK 99559
SOPHIE CHIMEGALREA, BOX 16, KWETHLUK, AK 99621
FRANK CHINGLIAK, BOX 51123, AKIACHAK, AK 99551
MOLLY CHINGLIAK, BOX 28, GOODNEWS BAY, AK 99589
ZACHARIAH CHRIS, BOX 8084, TUNTUTULIAK, AK 99680
WADE CHURCH, BOX 124, QUINHAGAK, AK 99655
WILLARD CHURCH, BOX 124, QUINHAGAK, AK 99655
WASSILLIE CLARK, BOX 6062, NAPASKIAK, AK 99559
ALBERT CLEVELAND, BOX 96, QUINHAGAK, AK 99655
ELTON CLEVELAND, BOX 126, QUINHAGAK, AK 99655
EMMA CLEVELAND, BOX 45, QUINHAGAK, AK 99655
FERDINAND CLEVELAND, BOX 46, QUINHAGAK, AK 99655
FRANK CLEVELAND, BOX 45, QUINHAGAK, AK 99655
HAROLD CLEVELAND, BOX 44, EEK, AK 99578
JOHN CLEVELAND, BOX 88, QUINHAGAK, AK 99655
NORMAN CLEVELAND, BOX 72, QUINHAGAK, AK 99655
PAUL CLEVELAND, BOX 2172, BETHEL, AK 99559
RICHARD CLEVELAND, BOX 45, QUINHAGAK, AK 99655
NICHOLAS COOKE, BOX 690, BETHEL, AK 99559
JOHN COOLIDGE, BOX 89, NUNAPITCHUK, AK 99641
LUCY CROW, BOX 567, BETHEL, AK 99559
HAZEL CURRAN, 116 E LAUREL AVE, HOWEY IN THE HILLS, FL 34737
PATRICK CYRIL, BOX 6047, NAPASKIAK, AK 99559
AYAGIAG D.S.ANAVER, BOX 108, QUINHAGAK, AK 99655
CLARENCE DANIEL, BOX 2541, BETHEL, AK 99559
JOHN DANIEL, BOX 8047, TUNTUTULIAK, AK 99680
PETER DANIEL, BOX 5044, KONGIGANAK, AK 99545
RAY DANIEL, BOX 2541, BETHEL, AK 99559
DAVID DAVID, BOX 35, KWETHLUK, AK 99621
EDDIE DAVID, BOX 5086, KONGIGANAK, AK 99545
NICK DAVID, BOX 8011, TUNTUTULIAK, AK 99680
RYAN DAVID, BOX 92, KWIGILLINGOK, AK 99622
DEXTER DEMANTLE, BOX 156, AKIAK, AK 99552
ERNEST DEMANTLE, BOX 65, AKIAK, AK 99552
JOE DEMANTLE, BOX 62, TULUKSAK, AK 99679
CARTER DEMENTI, 7956 MOOSE RUN CIR, ANCHORAGE, AK 99507
GERALD DEMIENTIEFF, BOX 533, BETHEL, AK 99559
KAYLEE DEMIENTIEFF, BOX 3723, PALMER, AK 99645
OSCAR DEMIENTIEFF, BOX 1044, BETHEL, AK 99559
JACK DEVLIN, 9450 STRATHMORE DR, ANCHORAGE, AK 99502
PAUL DOCK, BOX 216, KIPNUK, AK 99614
SAMMY DOCK, BOX 015, KIPNUK, AK 99614
GERALD DOMNICK, BOX 2724, BETHEL, AK 99559

JOHN DONAHUK, BOX 97, QUINHAGAK, AK 99655
WILLIAM EDWARDS, BOX 98, NAPAKIAK, AK 99634
DARRELL EGOAK, BOX 6604, ATMAUTLUAK, AK 99559
JOSEPH EGOAK, BOX 6064, NAPASKIAK, AK 99559
LOTT EGOAK, BOX 52015, AKIAK, AK 99552
MOSES EGOAK, BOX 6571, ATMAUTLUAK, AK 99559
WILLIAM EGOAK, BOX 236, KWETHLUK, AK 99621
ABRAHAM EKAMRAK, BOX 141, AKIACHAK, AK 99551
CARLIE EKAMRAK, BOX 2835, BETHEL, AK 99559
JOSEPH EKAMRAK, BOX 51055, AKIACHAK, AK 99551
NATHAN EKAMRAK, BOX 51088, AKIACHAK, AK 99551
PETER EKAMRAK, BOX 51008, AKIACHAK, AK 99551
RILEY EKAMRAK, 2379 BELL CT #80, MEDFORD, OR 97504
WILLIE EKAMRAK, BOX 51101, AKIACHAK, AK 99551
KATHLEEN ENOCH, BOX 8054, TUNTUTULIAK, AK 99680
LINCOLN ENOCH, BOX 8033, TUNTUTULIAK, AK 99680
MATTHEW ENOCH, BOX 56, NUNAPITCHUK, AK 99641
PATLUSKA ENOCH, BOX 8054, TUNTUTULIAK, AK 99680
STEPHEN ENOCH, BOX 8033, TUNTUTULIAK, AK 99680
ZACHARY ENOCH, BOX 8113, TUNTUTULIAK, AK 99680
CHARITON EPCHOOK, BOX 126, KWETHLUK, AK 99621
JONATHAN EPCHOOK, BOX 192, KWETHLUK, AK 99621
CARLOTTA EVAN, BOX 8051, TUNTUTULIAK, AK 99680
DAVID EVAN, BOX 8111, TUNTUTULIAK, AK 99680
DENNIS EVAN, BOX 81, AKIACHAK, AK 99551
EVON EVAN, BOX 8121, TUNTUTULIAK, AK 99680
FRANK EVAN, BOX 13, AKIAK, AK 99552
GARY EVAN, BOX 44, GOODNEWS BAY, AK 99589
JEFFREY EVAN, BOX 44, GOODNEWS BAY, AK 99589
JOSHUA EVAN, BOX 6006, NAPASKIAK, AK 99559
KALELA EVAN, BOX 488, BETHEL, AK 99559
KATHY EVAN, BOX 146, GOODNEWS BAY, AK 99589
KEVIN EVAN, BOX 146, GOODNEWS BAY, AK 99589
NATHAN EVAN, BOX 34005, NAPASKIAK, AK 99634
PAVILA EVAN, BOX 8121, TUNTUTULIAK, AK 99680
RUTH EVAN, BOX 6013, NAPASKIAK, AK 99559
TRISTEN EVAN, BOX 2056, BETHEL, AK 99559
YAGO EVAN, BOX 6117, NAPASKIAK, AK 99559
DAVID EVANS, BOX 9, GOODNEWS BAY, AK 99589
MATILDA EVANS, BOX 109, QUINHAGAK, AK 99655
BENJAMIN EVON, BOX 3289, BETHEL, AK 99559
JAMES EVON, BOX 172, BETHEL, AK 99559
JEFFREY EVON, BOX 1133, BETHEL, AK 99559
TONY EVON, BOX 1013, BETHEL, AK 99559
WILLIAM EVON, BOX 1, BETHEL, AK 99559
MOSES F.G.ANVIL, BOX 6001, NAPASKIAK, AK 99559
CAULINE FERGUSON, BOX 209, BETHEL, AK 99559
WILLIAM FERGUSON, BOX 209, BETHEL, AK 99559
ELIA FISHER, BOX 22, KWETHLUK, AK 99621
JOHN FITKA, BOX 8101, TUNTUTULIAK, AK 99680
JOHN FLYNN, BOX 2732, BETHEL, AK 99559
ALEXIE FORD, BOX 155, QUINHAGAK, AK 99655
EVON FORD, BOX 143, QUINHAGAK, AK 99655
BENJAMIN FOSTER, BOX 15, QUINHAGAK, AK 99655
JOHN FOSTER, BOX 92, QUINHAGAK, AK 99655
MARTHA FOSTER, BOX 93, QUINHAGAK, AK 99655
NATHAN FOSTER, BOX 56, QUINHAGAK, AK 99655
DARREN FOX, BOX 70, GOODNEWS BAY, AK 99589
ESTHER FOX, BOX 70, GOODNEWS BAY, AK 99589
EVON FOX, BOX 612, BETHEL, AK 99559
JOHN FOX, BOX 67, QUINHAGAK, AK 99655
JOHN FOX, BOX 91, QUINHAGAK, AK 99655
MARY FOX, BOX 91, QUINHAGAK, AK 99655
RANDY FOX, BOX 4, PLATINUM, AK 99651
PAUL FRANCIS, BOX 262, BETHEL, AK 99559
ANDREW FRANK, BOX 8104, TUNTUTULIAK, AK 99680

SALMON FISHING LIST—GILLNET

MATTHEW FRANK, BOX 8007, TUNTUTULIAK, AK 99680
WASSILLIE FRANK, BOX 55, NUNAPITCHUK, AK 99641
WILLIE FRANK, BOX 8021, TUNTUTULIAK, AK 99680
GOLGA FREDERICK, BOX 87, NUNAPITCHUK, AK 99641
HERMAN FREDERICK, BOX 51162, AKIACHAK, AK 99551
WILLIE FREDERICK, BOX 51187, AKIACHAK, AK 99551
BYRON FRIDAY, BOX 8103, TUNTUTULIAK, AK 99680
JOHNNY FRIEND, BOX 46, KWIGILLINGOK, AK 99622
LEROY FRIENDLY, BOX 8017, TUNTUTULIAK, AK 99680
THOMAS FRIENDLY, BOX 8017, TUNTUTULIAK, AK 99680
JAMES FRYE, BOX 1104, ENNIS, TX 75119
HOMER GALILA, BOX 85, GOODNEWS BAY, AK 99589
LESTER GALILA, BOX 90, GOODNEWS BAY, AK 99589
NORMA GALILA, BOX 145, QUINHAGAK, AK 99655
DARRELL GARRISON, BOX 1963, BETHEL, AK 99559
ABRAHAM GEORGE, BOX 51149, AKIACHAK, AK 99551
DARREN GEORGE, BOX 51002, AKIACHAK, AK 99551
EDWARD GEORGE, BOX 51103, AKIACHAK, AK 99551
FRED GEORGE, BOX 154, AKIACHAK, AK 99551
FRITZ GEORGE, BOX 51062, AKIACHAK, AK 99551
JASON GEORGE, BOX 51085, AKIACHAK, AK 99551
JOSEPH GEORGE, BOX 51067, AKIACHAK, AK 99551
KURTIS GEORGE, BOX 52123, AKIAK, AK 99552
NORMAN GEORGE, BOX 62, AKIACHAK, AK 99551
SAMUEL GEORGE, BOX 51085, AKIACHAK, AK 99551
THOMAS GEORGE, BOX 51103, AKIACHAK, AK 99551
WALTER GEORGE, BOX 146, AKIACHAK, AK 99551
WASKA GEORGE, BOX 74, NUNAPITCHUK, AK 99641
WASSILLIE GEORGE, BOX 125, KWETHLUK, AK 99621
MARK GILBERT, BOX 874504, WASILLA, AK 99687
DAVID GILILA, BOX 53, AKIAK, AK 99552
NICK GILILA, 5343 E 42ND AVE, ANCHORAGE, AK 99508
JOSHUA GILL, BOX 2186, BETHEL, AK 99559
CARL GREEN, BOX 118, EEK, AK 99578
PETER GREEN, BOX 2366, BETHEL, AK 99559
ROLAND GREEN, BOX 55, EEK, AK 99578
PAUL GREGORY, BOX 1333, BETHEL, AK 99559
ROBERT GREGORY, GEN DEL, BETHEL, AK 99559
WASSILLIE GREGORY, BOX 204, BETHEL, AK 99559
JANE GRIFFIN, 1335 S WILLIWAW DR, PALMER, AK 99645
CHARLES GUEST, BOX 534, BETHEL, AK 99559
GEORGE GUEST, BOX 2845, BETHEL, AK 99559
JAMES GUY, BOX 11, KWETHLUK, AK 99621
PAUL GUY, BOX 85, KWETHLUK, AK 99621
WILLIAM GUY, BOX 231, KWETHLUK, AK 99621
JOB HALE, BOX 3274, BETHEL, AK 99559
HANS HALVERSON, BOX 94, BETHEL, AK 99559
RICHARD HANSON, BOX 22, BETHEL, AK 99559
ADOLPH HAWK, BOX 82, EEK, AK 99578
JERRY HAWK, BOX 66, TULUKSAK, AK 99679
LAWRENCE HAWK, BOX 82, EEK, AK 99578
SETH HEAKIN, BOX 27, EEK, AK 99578
ALEXIE HENRY, BOX 78, QUINHAGAK, AK 99655
ANDREW HENRY, BOX 5065, KONGIGANAK, AK 99545
JACOB HENRY, BOX 51063, AKIACHAK, AK 99551
JULIUS HENRY, BOX 111, QUINHAGAK, AK 99655
KENNETH HENRY, BOX 97, EEK, AK 99578
MARK HENRY, BOX 34108, NAPAKIAK, AK 99634
WASSILIE HENRY, BOX 2444, BETHEL, AK 99559
SAM HERMAN, 7030 HUNT AVE, ANCHORAGE, AK 99504
ROBERT HERRON, BOX 602, BETHEL, AK 99559
FRANK HILL, BOX 21, QUINHAGAK, AK 99655
HENRY HILL, BOX 17, SLEETMUTE, AK 99668
JOHN HILL, BOX 65, QUINHAGAK, AK 99655
MINNIE HILL, BOX 5, ANIAK, AK 99557

PETER HILL, GEN DEL, QUINHAGAK, AK 99655
JOHN HINZ, BOX 112, KIPNUK, AK 99614
GEORGE HOFFMAN, BOX 22, EEK, AK 99578
GREGORY HOFFMAN, BOX 971, BETHEL, AK 99559
JAMES HOFFMAN, BOX 1442, BETHEL, AK 99559
JAMES HOFFMAN, BOX 164, BETHEL, AK 99559
JEFFREY HOFFMAN, BOX 1081, BETHEL, AK 99559
LYMAN HOFFMAN, BOX 763, BETHEL, AK 99559
ROBERT HOFFMAN, BOX 983, BETHEL, AK 99559
RONALD HOFFMAN, BOX 1181, BETHEL, AK 99559
STANLEY HOFFMAN, BOX 2374, BETHEL, AK 99559
WILLIAM HOFFMAN, BOX 862, BETHEL, AK 99559
LEVI HOOVER, BOX 137, KASIGLUK, AK 99609
TIMOTHY HOOVER, BOX 5, KASIGLUK, AK 99609
ANDREW HUNTER, BOX 2223, BETHEL, AK 99559
FRANK HUNTER, BOX 147, QUINHAGAK, AK 99655
JONATHEN HUNTER, BOX 58, QUINHAGAK, AK 99655
JOSEPH HUNTER, BOX 723, BETHEL, AK 99559
ROBERT HUNTER, BOX 663, BETHEL, AK 99559
JESSE IGKURAK, BOX 64, KWIGILLINGOK, AK 99622
LEROY IGKURAK, BOX 5017, KONGIGANAK, AK 99545
SHERMAN IGKURAK, BOX 5010, KONGIGANAK, AK 99545
WILLIAM IGKURAK, BOX 23, KWIGILLINGOK, AK 99622
ALEXIE ISAAC, BOX 1735, BETHEL, AK 99559
JACKIE ISAAC, BOX 135, KASIGLUK, AK 99609
WASSILLIE ISAAC, BOX 413, BETHEL, AK 99559
TOM IVAN, BOX 52106, AKIAK, AK 99552
TIMOTHY IVON, BOX 5103, KONGIGANAK, AK 99545
DANIEL JACKSON, BOX 62, KWETHLUK, AK 99621
PETER JACKSON, BOX 65, KWETHLUK, AK 99621
VARLAAM JACKSON, BOX 32, KWETHLUK, AK 99621
VLADIMIR JACKSON, BOX 246, KWETHLUK, AK 99621
WILLIAM JACKSON, BOX 51076, AKIACHAK, AK 99551
CHRIS JACOB, BOX 494, BETHEL, AK 99559
DAVID JACOB, BOX 6121, NAPASKIAK, AK 99559
JAMES JACOB, BOX 6534, ATMAUTLUAK, AK 99559
JAMES JACOBS, BOX 128, NUNAPITCHUK, AK 99641
DOUGLAS JAMES, BOX 25, PLATINUM, AK 99651
JOHN JAMES, BOX 25, PLATINUM, AK 99651
NORMAN JAMES, BOX 25, PLATINUM, AK 99651
DIANE JAPHET, BOX 146, BETHEL, AK 99559
NELSON JASPER, BOX 52068, AKIAK, AK 99552
BETSY JENKINS, BOX 6563, ATMAUTLUAK, AK 99559
EUGENE JENKINS, BOX 714, BETHEL, AK 99559
FORREST JENKINS, BOX 1553, BETHEL, AK 99559
JOHN JENKINS, BOX 34120, NAPAKIAK, AK 99634
JOSEPH JERRY, BOX 143, BETHEL, AK 99559
ALVIN JIMMIE, BOX 1934, BETHEL, AK 99559
CLIFFORD JIMMIE, BOX 2815, BETHEL, AK 99559
JERRY JIMMIE, BOX 8154, TUNTUTULIAK, AK 99680
NORMAN JIMMIE, BOX 8067, TUNTUTULIAK, AK 99680
PAUL JIMMIE, BOX 8015, TUNTUTULIAK, AK 99680
RALPH JIMMIE, BOX 34051, NAPAKIAK, AK 99634
GEORGE JIMMY, BOX 73, CHEFORNAK, AK 99561
VALENTINO JIMMY, BOX 34064, NAPAKIAK, AK 99634
ALEXANDER JOEKAY, BOX 6033, NAPASKIAK, AK 99559
JAMES JOEKAY, BOX 6031, NAPASKIAK, AK 99559
MINNIE JOEKAY, BOX 2795, BETHEL, AK 99559
DAVID JOHN, BOX 24, KWIGILLINGOK, AK 99622
NORMAN JOHN, BOX 68, KWIGILLINGOK, AK 99622
WILSON JOHN, BOX 117, EEK, AK 99578
ADOLPH JOHNSON, BOX 127, QUINHAGAK, AK 99655
CARL JOHNSON, BOX 142, QUINHAGAK, AK 99655
WALTER JOHNSON, GEN DEL, QUINHAGAK, AK 99655
WALTER JOHNSON, BOX 6088, NAPASKIAK, AK 99559

SALMON FISHING LIST—GILLNET

HENRY JONES, BOX 93, QUINHAGAK, AK 99655
MAX JOSEPH, BOX 8003, TUNTUTULIAK, AK 99680
PETER JOSEPH, BOX 8046, TUNTUTULIAK, AK 99680
WALTER JOSHUA, BOX 096, EEK, AK 99578
RONALD KAISER, BOX 122, BETHEL, AK 99559
ISAAC KALISTOOK, BOX 941, BETHEL, AK 99559
LARRY KALISTOOK, BOX 1771, BETHEL, AK 99559
JOSHUA KAMEROFF, BOX 305, ANIAK, AK 99557
WILSON KANUK, BOX 2008, BETHEL, AK 99559
DEMETRIOS KARGAS, BOX 1528, BETHEL, AK 99559
ANTHONY KASAYULIE, BOX 29, AKIACHAK, AK 99551
JESSE KASSEL, BOX 37, KASIGLUK, AK 99609
FRANK KAWAGLEY, GEN DEL, AKIAK, AK 99552
JAMES KEENE, BOX 144, KASIGLUK, AK 99609
WASSILLIE KEENE, BOX 133, KASIGLUK, AK 99609
WILSON KEENE, BOX 1547, BETHEL, AK 99559
MALCOLM KENNEY, 2811 IRIS ST, ANCHORAGE, AK 99517
ALBERT KERNAK, 2221 MULDOON RD SPC 365, ANCHORAGE, AK 99504
JULIA KERNAK, BOX 84, EEK, AK 99578
WILLIE KERNAK, BOX 34035, NAPAKIAK, AK 99634
GARY KILBUCK, BOX 11, PLATINUM, AK 99651
ERIC KINEGAK, BOX 2166, BETHEL, AK 99559
LOUIE KINEGAK, BOX 51155, AKIACHAK, AK 99551
NELSON KINEGAK, BOX 51071, AKIACHAK, AK 99551
SAMUEL KINEGAK, BOX 64, KONGIGANAK, AK 99545
THOMAS KINEGAK, BOX 51052, AKIACHAK, AK 99551
GABRIEL KING, BOX 2227, BETHEL, AK 99559
PAUL KIUNYA, 5001 ROGER DR, ANCHORAGE, AK 99507
RALPH KIUNYA, BOX 5087, KONGIGANAK, AK 99545
RALPH KYLOOK, GEN DEL, TUNUNAK, AK 99681
GREGORY LAKE, BOX 23, AKIAK, AK 99552
ROBERT LAKE, BOX 85, AKIAK, AK 99552
RUSSELL LAMONT, BOX 552, BETHEL, AK 99559
COLLEEN LARAUX, BOX 975, BETHEL, AK 99559
ALEXANDER LARSON, BOX 51128, AKIACHAK, AK 99551
ELENA LARSON, BOX 122, KWETHLUK, AK 99621
FRANCIS LARSON, BOX 92, KWETHLUK, AK 99621
FRITZ LARSON, BOX 6037, NAPASKIAK, AK 99559
GREGORY LARSON, BOX 6055, NAPASKIAK, AK 99559
JACKIE LARSON, BOX 6132, NAPASKIAK, AK 99559
JOSEPH LARSON, BOX 6074, NAPASKIAK, AK 99559
OSCAR LARSON, BOX 34, KWETHLUK, AK 99621
WALTER LARSON, BOX 132, BETHEL, AK 99559
WILLIE LARSON, BOX 122, KWETHLUK, AK 99621
BRENT LATHAM, BOX 2841, BETHEL, AK 99559
WALTER LEE, BOX 153, TOGIAK, AK 99678
ROBERT LEKANDER, BOX 1577, BETHEL, AK 99559
CHARLIE LEWIS, BOX 30, KWIGILLINGOK, AK 99622
KACY LEWIS, BOX 8045, TUNTUTULIAK, AK 99680
HERMAN LIN, 801 S GARFIELD AVE #208, ALHAMBRA, CA 91801
THEODORE LINDLEY, BOX 1584, BETHEL, AK 99559
BRUCE LINDSEY, BOX 622, BETHEL, AK 99559
RUTH LISKEY, BOX 74, TULUKSAK, AK 99679
LARRY LITTLE, BOX 733, BETHEL, AK 99559
HENRY LOMACK, BOX 51013, AKIACHAK, AK 99551
JONATHAN LOMACK, BOX 114, AKIACHAK, AK 99551
MICHAEL LOMACK, BOX 832, BETHEL, AK 99559
WILLIAM LONG, BOX 723, COMSTOCK, TX 78837
FRANKLIN LOTT, BOX 52016, AKIAK, AK 99552
LEVI LOTT, BOX 51031, AKIACHAK, AK 99551
LOTT LOTT, BOX 113, BETHEL, AK 99559
ADOLPH LUPIE, BOX 8051, TUNTUTULIAK, AK 99680
BENJAMIN LUPIE, BOX 5088, KONGIGANAK, AK 99545
HENRY LUPIE, BOX 8062, TUNTUTULIAK, AK 99680
ISAAC LUPIE, GEN DEL, TUNTUTULIAK, AK 99680
JAMES LUPIE, BOX 8055, TUNTUTULIAK, AK 99680

JIMMIE LUPIE, BOX 8105, TUNTUTULIAK, AK 99680
NASTASIA LUPIE, BOX 8121, TUNTUTULIAK, AK 99680
LOUIE MANUTOLI, BOX 51027, AKIACHAK, AK 99551
CHRISTIAN MARK, BOX 96, QUINHAGAK, AK 99655
GEORGE MARK, BOX 16, QUINHAGAK, AK 99655
HENRY MARK, 633 HODSDON RD, POWNAL, ME 4069
JOHN MARK, BOX 16, QUINHAGAK, AK 99655
NICHOLAI MARK, BOX 70, QUINHAGAK, AK 99655
PAUL MARK, BOX 143, GOODNEWS BAY, AK 99589
RICHARD MARK, BOX 124, EEK, AK 99578
ROY MARK, BOX 87, QUINHAGAK, AK 99655
WILLIAM MARK, BOX 143, GOODNEWS BAY, AK 99589
CURTIS MARTIN, BOX 113, GOODNEWS BAY, AK 99589
DAVID MARTIN, BOX 16, KASIGLUK, AK 99609
KYLE MARTIN, BOX 22, GOODNEWS BAY, AK 99589
MICHAEL MARTIN, BOX 16, KASIGLUK, AK 99609
MOSES MARTIN, BOX 57, KWIGILLINGOK, AK 99622
THEODORE MARTIN, BOX 133, GOODNEWS BAY, AK 99589
DELORES MATTER, BOX 267, ANIAK, AK 99557
JOSEPH MATTER, BOX 267, ANIAK, AK 99557
FRANK MATTHEW, PITMALLEQ HEIGHTS HOUSE 72, QUINHAGAK, AK 99655
PETER MATTHEW, BOX 04, QUINHAGAK, AK 99655
TIMOTHY MATTHEW, BOX 4, QUINHAGAK, AK 99655
TIMOTHY MATTHEW, BOX 102, QUINHAGAK, AK 99655
JASON MAXIE, BOX 264, KWETHLUK, AK 99621
PAUL MAXIE, BOX 6002, NAPASKIAK, AK 99559
STEPHEN MAXIE, BOX 6092, NAPASKIAK, AK 99559
FRANK MAZZARO, BOX 1291, BETHEL, AK 99559
FLORENCE MCINTYRE, BOX 125, EEK, AK 99578
JOHN MCINTYRE, BOX 544, BETHEL, AK 99559
KEVIN MCINTYRE, BOX 8031, TUNTUTULIAK, AK 99680
MARIE MEADE, 4342 E 4TH ST, ANCHORAGE, AK 99508
JAMES MERRITT, BOX 154, QUINHAGAK, AK 99655
JASON MICHAEL, BOX 105, KWETHLUK, AK 99621
NICK MICHAEL, BOX 162, KWETHLUK, AK 99621
SETH MICHAEL, BOX 3, KWETHLUK, AK 99621
NORMAN MICHAELS, BOX 484, BETHEL, AK 99559
CURTIS MILLER, BOX 5076, KONGIGANAK, AK 99545
FRANK MILLER, BOX 15, EEK, AK 99578
JOEY MILLER, 101 BUNNELL APT 1B, ANCHORAGE, AK 99508
BOBBY MOCHIN, BOX 112, NUNAPITCHUK, AK 99641
MARCUS MOCHIN, BOX 6533, ATMAUTLUAK, AK 99559
FRANK MOJIN, BOX 645, BETHEL, AK 99559
JOHN MOJIN, BOX 1073, BETHEL, AK 99559
MICHAEL MOJIN, BOX 52, NUNAPITCHUK, AK 99641
VERLA MOJIN, 12022 ANCHOR PL, ANCHORAGE, AK 99515
FRANK MOORE, BOX 113, EEK, AK 99578
RENO MOORE, BOX 38, QUINHAGAK, AK 99655
SIXTY MOORE, BOX 13, QUINHAGAK, AK 99655
ERIC MORGAN, GEN DEL, CHUATHBALUK, AK 99557
HERMAN MORGAN, BOX 78, ANIAK, AK 99557
JOLI MORGAN, BOX 844, BETHEL, AK 99559
KENNETH MORGAN, BOX 90, KALSKAG, AK 99607
ALEXIE MORRIS, BOX 29, KWETHLUK, AK 99621
AXEL MOSES, 6409 SPRUCE ST, ANCHORAGE, AK 99507
CARL MOSES, BOX 51178, AKIACHAK, AK 99551
DALE MOSES, BOX 51044, AKIACHAK, AK 99551
EDDIE MOSES, BOX 92, AKIACHAK, AK 99551
FLOYD MOSES, BOX 744, BETHEL, AK 99559
SAMUEL MOSES, BOX 51044, AKIACHAK, AK 99551
TRAVIS MOSES, BOX 263, BETHEL, AK 99559
CARL MOTGIN, BOX 34062, NAPAKIAK, AK 99634
MARK MOYLE, BOX 14, PLATINUM, AK 99651
AARON MUTE, BOX 2275, BETHEL, AK 99559
JAMES MUTE, BOX 1982, BETHEL, AK 99559
JOHN MUTE, BOX 474, BETHEL, AK 99559

170

SALMON FISHING LIST—GILLNET

PAUL MUTE, BOX 474, BETHEL, AK 99559
CHRIS NAPOKA, BOX 22, TULUKSAK, AK 99679
COLIN NAPOKA, BOX 112, TULUKSAK, AK 99679
FRED NAPOKA, BOX 153, TULUKSAK, AK 99679
HELENA NAPOKA, BOX 81, TULUKSAK, AK 99679
LISA NAPOKA, BOX 8111, TUNTUTULIAK, AK 99680
NELSON NAPOKA, BOX 41, TULUKSAK, AK 99679
ANNA NECK, BOX 164, KASIGLUK, AK 99609
JOAN NECK, BOX 69, BETHEL, AK 99559
CURT NELSON, BOX 38, KALSKAG, AK 99607
FRANK NELSON, BOX 34115, NAPAKIAK, AK 99634
GARRETT NELSON, BOX 752, BETHEL, AK 99559
JONATHAN NELSON, BOX 34101, NAPAKIAK, AK 99634
SCOTT NELSON, BOX 34084, NAPAKIAK, AK 99634
VERNON NELSON, BOX 9, BETHEL, AK 99559
MICHAEL NERBY, BOX 1224, BETHEL, AK 99559
ALEXIE NICHOLAI, BOX 6085, NAPASKIAK, AK 99559
ANITA NICHOLAI, BOX 231, KWETHLUK, AK 99621
CURTIS NICHOLAI, BOX 148, NUNAPITCHUK, AK 99641
EDWARD NICHOLAI, GEN DEL, ATMAUTLUAK, AK 99559
ELENA NICHOLAI, BOX 903, BETHEL, AK 99559
GEORGE NICHOLAI, 834 N UPSTREAM PL, PALMER, AK 99645
JAMES NICHOLAI, BOX 6049, NAPASKIAK, AK 99559
JOHN NICHOLAI, BOX 6552, ATMAUTLUAK, AK 99559
JOSEPH NICHOLAI, BOX 6547, ATMAUTLUAK, AK 99559
WILLIE NICHOLAI, BOX 84, QUINHAGAK, AK 99655
LEVI NICHOLAS, BOX 191, KASIGLUK, AK 99609
MARIA NICHOLAS, BOX 53, KASIGLUK, AK 99609
NICHOLAI NICHOLAS, BOX 66, KASIGLUK, AK 99609
PETER NICHOLAS, BOX 56, KASIGLUK, AK 99609
YEAKO NICHOLAS, BOX 157, KASIGLUK, AK 99609
ZACHARIAS NICHOLAS, BOX 31, KWETHLUK, AK 99621
EUGENE NICHOLS, BOX 33, KASIGLUK, AK 99609
JASON NICHOLS, BOX 121, EEK, AK 99578
DIANE NICK, BOX 95, NUNAPITCHUK, AK 99641
JOSEPH NICK, BOX 6556, ATMAUTLUAK, AK 99559
KALILA NICK, BOX 6514, ATMAUTLUAK, AK 99559
MICHAEL NICK, BOX 116, NUNAPITCHUK, AK 99641
NICHOLAI NICK, BOX 95, NUNAPITCHUK, AK 99641
OLRICK NICK, BOX 483, BETHEL, AK 99559
PATRICK NICK, BOX 8085, TUNTUTULIAK, AK 99680
TOM NICK, BOX 7, NUNAPITCHUK, AK 99641
ADAM NICOLAI, BOX 33, KWETHLUK, AK 99621
EUGENE NICOLAI, BOX 124, KWETHLUK, AK 99621
ILARION NICOLAI, BOX 205, KWETHLUK, AK 99621
JAMES NICOLAI, BOX 35, AKIAK, AK 99552
JOHN NICOLAI, BOX 165, KWETHLUK, AK 99621
MARTIN NICOLAI, BOX 70, KWETHLUK, AK 99621
MICHAEL NICOLAI, BOX 51024, AKIACHAK, AK 99551
MOSES NICOLAI, BOX 108, KWETHLUK, AK 99621
PAUL NICOLAI, BOX 202, KWETHLUK, AK 99621
SAMUEL NICOLAI, BOX 138, AKIAK, AK 99552
WILLIAM NICOLAI, BOX 81, KWETHLUK, AK 99621
WILSON NICOLAI, BOX 61, KWETHLUK, AK 99621
ALEXANDER NICORI, BOX 72, KWETHLUK, AK 99621
ARNOLD NICORI, BOX 18, KWETHLUK, AK 99621
CHRISTOPHER NICORI, BOX 52, QUINHAGAK, AK 99655
FRANK NICORI, BOX 877790, WASILLA, AK 99687
JAMES NICORI, BOX 41, KWETHLUK, AK 99621
NELSON NICORI, BOX 213, KWETHLUK, AK 99621
THOMAS NICORI, GEN DEL, QUINHAGAK, AK 99655
JOHN NOATAK, BOX 51032, AKIACHAK, AK 99551
ALICE NOES, BOX 222, BETHEL, AK 99559
PHILLIP NOES, BOX 222, BETHEL, AK 99559
GEORGINE NORMAN, 1531 PLANTERS RIDGE LN, ALPHARETTA, GA 30004

FRED NOSE, BOX 51097, AKIACHAK, AK 99551
MARTIN NOSE, BOX 95, AKIACHAK, AK 99551
RANDY NOSE, BOX 51030, AKIACHAK, AK 99551
RAY NOSE, BOX 132, AKIACHAK, AK 99551
ROBERT NOSE, BOX 37123, TOKSOOK BAY, AK 99637
ROBERT NOSE, BOX 51124, AKIACHAK, AK 99551
ROLAND NOSE, BOX 117, AKIACHAK, AK 99551
RONALD NOSE, BOX 51151, AKIACHAK, AK 99551
ROSANE NOSE, BOX 51030, AKIACHAK, AK 99551
RYAN NOSE, BOX 30, AKIACHAK, AK 99551
EVAN OLICK, BOX 96, KWETHLUK, AK 99621
GABRIEL OLICK, BOX 8036, TUNTUTULIAK, AK 99680
MAX OLICK, BOX 56, KWETHLUK, AK 99621
MAX OLICK, BOX 56, KWETHLUK, AK 99621
JIMMIE OSCAR, BOX 104, BETHEL, AK 99559
NICHOLAI OSCAR, BOX 1558, BETHEL, AK 99559
WASKA OSCAR, GEN DEL, TUNUNAK, AK 99681
RICHARD OTTO, BOX 5015, KONGIGANAK, AK 99545
ROBERT OTTO, BOX 5043, KONGIGANAK, AK 99545
ADOLPH OUYA, BOX 96, GOODNEWS BAY, AK 99589
JOHN OWENS, BOX 3325, BETHEL, AK 99559
MICHAEL OWENS, BOX 193, KWETHLUK, AK 99621
TRAVIS OWENS, BOX 37, ANIAK, AK 99557
MARVIN PAINE, BOX 51005, AKIACHAK, AK 99551
CHUCK PARKS, BOX 24, NUNAPITCHUK, AK 99641
ZACHARIAH PARKS, BOX 135, NUNAPITCHUK, AK 99641
GEORGE PASITNAK, BOX 51150, AKIACHAK, AK 99551
HENRY PASITNAK, BOX 116, AKIACHAK, AK 99551
KEN PASITNAK, BOX 51164, AKIACHAK, AK 99551
ROBERT PASITNAK, BOX 102, AKIACHAK, AK 99551
BURT PAUL, BOX 115, KIPNUK, AK 99614
CARL PAUL, BOX 44, KIPNUK, AK 99614
JAMES PAUL, BOX 6087, NAPASKIAK, AK 99559
JOHN PAUL, BOX 45, KWIGILLINGOK, AK 99622
NACE PAUL, BOX 315, KIPNUK, AK 99614
NICHOLAS PAUL, BOX 34082, NAPAKIAK, AK 99634
PAUL PAUL, BOX 5034, KONGIGANAK, AK 99545
SAM PAUL, BOX 196, KIPNUK, AK 99614
STEVEN PAUL, BOX 34087, NAPAKIAK, AK 99634
WASSILLIE PAUL, BOX 121, KWETHLUK, AK 99621
JEFFREY PAVIL, BOX 2492, BETHEL, AK 99559
JEFF PAVILA, BOX 8112, TUNTUTULIAK, AK 99680
JONATHAN PAVILA, BOX 8151, TUNTUTULIAK, AK 99680
KATHERINE PAVILA, BOX 8151, TUNTUTULIAK, AK 99680
LAWRENCE PAVILA, BOX 8053, TUNTUTULIAK, AK 99680
PATRICK PAVILA, BOX 8131, TUNTUTULIAK, AK 99680
PETER PAVILA, BOX 8053, TUNTUTULIAK, AK 99680
YAKO PAVILA, BOX 8005, TUNTUTULIAK, AK 99680
CARLINE PAVILLA, BOX 6522, ATMAUTLUAK, AK 99559
FRED PAVILLA, BOX 184, TULUKSAK, AK 99679
HAROLD PAVILLA, BOX 113, KASIGLUK, AK 99609
JOSEPH PAVILLA, BOX 6587, ATMAUTLUAK, AK 99559
LAWRENCE PAVILLA, BOX 6521, ATMAUTLUAK, AK 99559
LEWIS PAVILLA, BOX 132, KWETHLUK, AK 99621
MICHAEL PAVILLA, BOX 6521, ATMAUTLUAK, AK 99559
MOSES PAVILLA, BOX 6544, ATMAUTLUAK, AK 99559
NICK PAVILLA, BOX 6596, ATMAUTLUAK, AK 99559
OSCAR PAVILLA, BOX 6551, ATMAUTLUAK, AK 99559
SKYLAR PAVILLA, BOX 6501, ATMAUTLUAK, AK 99559
WASSILLIE PAVILLA, BOX 34002, NAPAKIAK, AK 99634
JOHNETTE PETE, BOX 2065, BETHEL, AK 99559
CARL PETER, BOX 67, TULUKSAK, AK 99679
CLAYTON PETER, BOX 108, AKIACHAK, AK 99551
EDWARD PETER, BOX 135, AKIACHAK, AK 99551
GEORGE PETER, BOX 51018, AKIACHAK, AK 99551

SALMON FISHING LIST—GILLNET

HENRY PETER, BOX 2144, BETHEL, AK 99559
ISAAC PETER, BOX 51025, AKIACHAK, AK 99551
JACOB PETER, BOX 51004, AKIACHAK, AK 99551
KEVIN PETER, BOX 75, TULUKSAK, AK 99679
LINCOLN PETER, BOX 110, AKIACHAK, AK 99551
PHILLIP PETER, BOX 51057, AKIACHAK, AK 99551
ROMAN PETER, BOX 75, TULUKSAK, AK 99679
SAMMY PETER, BOX 35, TULUKSAK, AK 99679
TOM PETER, BOX 51045, AKIACHAK, AK 99551
TOMMY PETER, BOX 2224, BETHEL, AK 99559
WILLIAM PETERSON, BOX 44, NEW STUYAHOK, AK 99636
ADAM PETLUSKA, BOX 113, QUINHAGAK, AK 99655
ANNA PETLUSKA, BOX 6053, NAPASKIAK, AK 99559
JACKIE PETLUSKA, BOX 083, EEK, AK 99578
WALTER PETLUSKA, BOX 023, EEK, AK 99578
MURPHY PHILIP, BOX 5046, KONGIGANAK, AK 99545
BESSIE PHILLIP, BOX 82, TULUKSAK, AK 99679
DANIEL PHILLIP, BOX 51083, AKIACHAK, AK 99551
ERIC PHILLIP, BOX 51125, AKIACHAK, AK 99551
EVANGELINE PHILLIP, BOX 51125, AKIACHAK, AK 99551
GILBERT PHILLIP, BOX 173, AKIAK, AK 99552
JASON PHILLIP, BOX 5031, KONGIGANAK, AK 99545
JIMMY PHILLIP, BOX 8, KWIGILLINGOK, AK 99622
LETISHA PHILLIP, BOX 5053, KONGIGANAK, AK 99545
NICK PHILLIP, BOX 5007, KONGIGANAK, AK 99545
TONY PHILLIP, BOX 9, KWIGILLINGOK, AK 99622
VERNON PHILLIP, BOX 53, BETHEL, AK 99559
WILLIE PHILLIP, BOX 6, TULUKSAK, AK 99679
NICHOLAI PHILLIPS, BOX 2111, BETHEL, AK 99559
ALEXIE PLEASANT, 5130 TAKU DR #2, ANCHORAGE, AK 99508
ALICE PLEASANT, BOX 84, QUINHAGAK, AK 99655
CHRISTOPHER PLEASANT, BOX 85, NUNAPITCHUK, AK 99641
CURTIS PLEASANT, GENERAL DELIVERY, QUINHAGAK, AK 99655
FERDINAND PLEASANT, BOX 116, QUINHAGAK, AK 99655
JEFFEREY PLEASANT, BOX 51, QUINHAGAK, AK 99655
LONNIE PLEASANT, BOX 74, QUINHAGAK, AK 99655
SAM PLEASANT, BOX 84, QUINHAGAK, AK 99655
WILLIE PLEASANT, BOX 74, QUINHAGAK, AK 99655
WILLIE PLEASANT, BOX 4011, TWIN HILLS, AK 99576
WILLIAM R.E.CHARLES, BOX 2473, BETHEL, AK 99559
FRANCIS REICH, BOX 94, BETHEL, AK 99559
MARTIN ROACH, BOX 792, BETHEL, AK 99559
MARTIN ROACH, BOX 54, QUINHAGAK, AK 99655
RICHARD ROBB, BOX 1195, BETHEL, AK 99559
MOSES ROBERT.PETER, BOX 21, KWIGILLINGOK, AK 99622
AARON ROBERTS, BOX 131, QUINHAGAK, AK 99655
FRANK ROBERTS, BOX 131, QUINHAGAK, AK 99655
HERBERT ROBERTS, BOX 31, QUINHAGAK, AK 99655
JAMES ROBERTS, GEN DEL, QUINHAGAK, AK 99655
JAMES ROBERTS, BOX 54, GOODNEWS BAY, AK 99589
PETER ROBERTS, BOX 108, GOODNEWS BAY, AK 99589
ROBERT ROBERTS, BOX 122, QUINHAGAK, AK 99655
WILLIAM ROBERTS, BOX 64, GOODNEWS BAY, AK 99589
CURTIS ROBINETT, BOX 271, ANIAK, AK 99557
STANLEY RODGERS, BOX 542, BETHEL, AK 99559
WILLIAM ROLAND, BOX 2016, BETHEL, AK 99559
ELSIE ROSS, BOX 144, GOODNEWS BAY, AK 99589
WALTER SALLISON, BOX 10, NUNAPITCHUK, AK 99641
TIMOTHY SAMSON, BOX 077, KIPNUK, AK 99614
JOHN SAMUEL, BOX 48, PLATINUM, AK 99651
EARL SAMUELSON, BOX 6061-PKA, NAPASKIAK, AK 99559
LINDA SAMUELSON, BOX 313, BETHEL, AK 99559
EVELYN SARA, BOX 298521, WASILLA, AK 99623
DARRYL SERGIE, BOX 86, NUNAPITCHUK, AK 99641
ELIA SERGIE, BOX 92, LOWER KALSKAG, AK 99626
GERTRUDE SERRADELL, BOX 62, NUNAPITCHUK, AK 99641

MICHAEL SHANTZ, BOX 51, BETHEL, AK 99559
CARLIE SHARP, BOX 26, QUINHAGAK, AK 99655
GARY SHARP, BOX 118, QUINHAGAK, AK 99655
WILLIAM SHARP, BOX 26, QUINHAGAK, AK 99655
JOHN SIMON, BOX 118, QUINHAGAK, AK 99655
LETHA SIMON, BOX 24, BETHEL, AK 99559
STANLEY SIMONSON, BOX 73, GOLD BAR, WA 98251
DAVID SIMS, BOX 6605, ATMAUTLUAK, AK 99559
PAUL SLIM, BOX 184, KASIGLUK, AK 99609
LOUIE SMALL, BOX 152, QUINHAGAK, AK 99655
WILLIS SMALL, BOX 105, QUINHAGAK, AK 99655
DANIEL SMITH, BOX 24, GOODNEWS BAY, AK 99589
JASON SMITH, BOX 38, BETHEL, AK 99559
LLOYD SMITH, BOX 95, GOODNEWS BAY, AK 99589
ROBERT SNYDER, 28 PHILLIPS ST, AKIACHAK, AK 99551
TOM SNYDER, BOX 51153, AKIACHAK, AK 99551
HENRY SPEIN, BOX 78, KWETHLUK, AK 99621
ELIZABETH STEVEN, BOX 6126, NAPASKIAK, AK 99559
JOSEPH STEVEN, BOX 6095, NAPASKIAK, AK 99559
NICHOLAI STEVEN, BOX 6066, NAPASKIAK, AK 99559
BENJAMIN STEVENS, BOX 74, NUNAPITCHUK, AK 99641
JIMMY STEVENS, BOX 74, NUNAPITCHUK, AK 99641
JIMMY STONE, BOX 8103, TUNTUTULIAK, AK 99680
RICK STRAUSS, BOX 5012, KONGIGANAK, AK 99545
LARRY STRUNK, BOX 94, QUINHAGAK, AK 99655
FRANK SUMI, BOX 94, NUNAPITCHUK, AK 99641
EDDIE TEELUK, BOX 63, QUINHAGAK, AK 99655
JAMES THOMAS, BOX 2726, BETHEL, AK 99559
ALBERT TIKIUN, BOX 283, BEREA, OH 44017
HENRY TIKIUN, BOX 6562, ATMAUTLUAK, AK 99559
JOSEPH TIKIUN, BOX 34, TULUKSAK, AK 99679
HOWARD TINKER, BOX 81, KASIGLUK, AK 99609
MICHAEL TINKER, BOX 62, KASIGLUK, AK 99609
YAKO TINKER, BOX 163, KASIGLUK, AK 99609
JACOB TOBELUK, BOX 102, NUNAPITCHUK, AK 99641
WILLIE TOBELUK, BOX 51, NUNAPITCHUK, AK 99641
CHRISTOPHER TOM, BOX 153, QUINHAGAK, AK 99655
ALBERT TONIAK, BOX 75, GOODNEWS BAY, AK 99589
KEVIN TSIKOYAK, 28954 HIGHWAY W, MEADVILLE, MO 64659
ESAI TWITCHELL, BOX 121, KASIGLUK, AK 99609
GARY VANASSE, BOX 1544, BETHEL, AK 99559
ELENA VENES, BOX 901, BETHEL, AK 99559
JOSEPH VENES, BOX 1223, BETHEL, AK 99559
ROBERT VENES, BOX 402, BETHEL, AK 99559
ALEXANDER WASIERSKI, BOX 573, BETHEL, AK 99559
EVON WASKA, BOX 1965, BETHEL, AK 99559
FRANK WASSILIE, BOX 58, AKIACHAK, AK 99551
GABRIEL WASSILIE, BOX 1771, BETHEL, AK 99559
GEORGIANN WASSILIE, BOX 29, AKIACHAK, AK 99551
JACOB WASSILIE, BOX 29, AKIACHAK, AK 99551
LLOYD WASSILIE, BOX 51148, AKIACHAK, AK 99551
MATTHEW WASSILIE, BOX 42, AKIACHAK, AK 99551
SCHOUVILLER WASSILIE, BOX 51104, AKIACHAK, AK 99551
ANDREW WASSILLIE, BOX 7, NUNAPITCHUK, AK 99641
ARTHUR WASSILLIE, BOX 34031, NAPAKIAK, AK 99634
ELI WASSILLIE, BOX 189, NUNAPITCHUK, AK 99641
ELLIOT WASSILLIE, BOX 22, NUNAPITCHUK, AK 99641
ESTHER WASSILLIE, BOX 57, AKIACHAK, AK 99551
JERRY WASSILLIE, BOX 229, NUNAPITCHUK, AK 99641
OSCAR WASSILLIE, BOX 34083, NAPAKIAK, AK 99634
FREDERICK WATSON, BOX 2336, BETHEL, AK 99559
ISAAC WESTCOAST, 802 N PRICE ST #2, ANCHORAGE, AK 99508
RAMY WESTDAHL, BOX 2451, BETHEL, AK 99559
RICHARD WESTDAHL, BOX 153, BETHEL, AK 99559
FREDERICK WHEELER, BOX 93, BETHEL, AK 99559
ANTHONY WHITE, BOX 8085, TUNTUTULIAK, AK 99680

SALMON FISHING LIST—GILLNET

CARL WHITE, BOX 2965, BETHEL, AK 99559
EDWARD WHITE, BOX 28, EEK, AK 99578
HENRY WHITE, BOX 34018, NAPAKIAK, AK 99634
JOHN WHITE, BOX 024, EEK, AK 99578
JOHN WHITE, BOX 190, BETHEL, AK 99559
KEVIN WHITE, BOX 18, BETHEL, AK 99559
MOSES WHITE, BOX 54, KASIGLUK, AK 99609
PAUL WHITE, BOX 8013, TUNTUTULIAK, AK 99680
PETER WHITE, BOX 95, EEK, AK 99578
RICHARD WHITE, BOX 34065, NAPAKIAK, AK 99634
ROBERT WHITE, GEN DEL, QUINHAGAK, AK 99655
ROLAND WHITE, BOX 8014, TUNTUTULIAK, AK 99680
TIMOTHY WHITE, BOX 30, EEK, AK 99578
TONY WHITE, BOX 35, NUNAPITCHUK, AK 99641
RONALD WHITTOM, BOX 411, BETHEL, AK 99559
BRUCE WILLIAMS, BOX 128, AKIAK, AK 99552
CHARLES WILLIAMS, BOX 91061, ATQASUK, AK 99791
CINDY WILLIAMS, BOX 1861, BETHEL, AK 99559
EVAN WILLIAMS, BOX 6082, NAPASKIAK, AK 99559
HARRY WILLIAMS, BOX 6094, NAPASKIAK, AK 99559
JAMES WILLIAMS, BOX 10, QUINHAGAK, AK 99655
MICHAEL WILLIAMS, BOX 27, AKIAK, AK 99552
ROBERT WILLIAMS, BOX 124, AKIAK, AK 99552
SAMMY WILLIAMS, BOX 52004, AKIAK, AK 99552
SHAWN WILLIAMS, BOX 10, QUINHAGAK, AK 99655
SINKA WILLIAMS, BOX 6, LOWER KALSKAG, AK 99626
VERNON WILLIAMS, BOX 128, AKIAK, AK 99552
HUEY WILLIE, BOX 34037, NAPAKIAK, AK 99634
JOHN WILLIE, GEN DEL, NAPASKIAK, AK 99559
JOHN WILLIE, BOX 34068, NAPAKIAK, AK 99634
NANCY WORM, BOX 34033, NAPAKIAK, AK 99634
JOSEPH WP.EVAN, BOX 8111, TUNTUTULIAK, AK 99680
JOHN WUYA, BOX 2928, BETHEL, AK 99559

SALMON, GILLNET, KOTZEBUE

GUY ADAMS, BOX 627, KOTZEBUE, AK 99752
LANGFORD ADAMS, BOX 148, KOTZEBUE, AK 99752
PATRICK ADAMS, BOX 148, KOTZEBUE, AK 99752
ALLEN AHNANGNATOGU, BOX 1043, HOMER, AK 99603
MARY AHNANGNATOGU, 4019 SAN ERNESTO AVE #A4, ANCHORAGE, AK 99508
CLARENCE ALLEN, BOX 254, KOTZEBUE, AK 99752
ROBERT ALLEN, BOX 209, KOTZEBUE, AK 99752
ROGER ALLEN, BOX 209, KOTZEBUE, AK 99752
STEPHEN APGAR, BOX 4622, WEST RICHLAND, WA 99353
DWIGHT ARNOLD, BOX 28, NOATAK, AK 99761
JOHN BAKER, BOX 831, KOTZEBUE, AK 99752
TAMMY BAKER, BOX 425, KOTZEBUE, AK 99752
HARRY BALDWIN, BOX 1037, KOTZEBUE, AK 99752
BLAINE BARGER, BOX 222, KOTZEBUE, AK 99752
CARL BARGER, BOX 77, NOATAK, AK 99761
DONALD BARGER, BOX 249, KOTZEBUE, AK 99752
HERMAN BARGER, BOX 682, KOTZEBUE, AK 99752
DELANO BARR, BOX 005, SHISHMAREF, AK 99772
GILBERT BARR, BOX 13, DEERING, AK 99736
ROSIE BARR, 4120 JAMES DR, ANCHORAGE, AK 99504
ALFRED BEAVER, BOX 71673, FAIRBANKS, AK 99707
FRANK BEECROFT, 3543 MT VIEW DR #31, ANCHORAGE, AK 99504
MATTHEW BERGAN, BOX 1164, KOTZEBUE, AK 99752
JEFF BONACCI, 2317 W 7095 S, WEST JORDAN, UT 84084
EDWIN BOOTH, BOX 50031, KIVALINA, AK 99750
HENRY BOOTH, BOX 291, KOTZEBUE, AK 99752
PHILLIP BOOTH, BOX 125, NOATAK, AK 99761
ROLAND BOOTH, BOX 75, NOATAK, AK 99761
RAYMOND BROWN, BOX 1278, KOTZEBUE, AK 99752

RONALD BROWN, BOX 14, KOTZEBUE, AK 99752
JOE CARTER, BOX 8, NOORVIK, AK 99763
JOE CARTER, BOX 52, NOORVIK, AK 99763
HARRY CLARK, BOX 215, KOTZEBUE, AK 99752
JONAS CLEVELAND, BOX 143, AMBLER, AK 99786
BESSIE COFFIN, BOX 25, NOORVIK, AK 99763
CHRISTOPHER COLLINS, BOX 1375, KOTZEBUE, AK 99752
RAYMOND COPPOCK, BOX 152, KOTZEBUE, AK 99752
JOHN CRAIGHEAD, 216 LIVINGSTON, MISSOULA, MT 59803
FRANK DAVIDOVICS, BOX 628, KOTZEBUE, AK 99752
PAUL DONAGHY, BOX 700, EL PRADO, NM 87529
THOMAS DUBLIN, BOX 333, KOTZEBUE, AK 99752
LOUIS EDENSHAW, BOX 571, KOTZEBUE, AK 99752
JOHN EVANS, BOX 1198, KOTZEBUE, AK 99752
ARCHIE FERGUSON, BOX 835, KOTZEBUE, AK 99752
CHARLES FERREIRA, BOX 114, KOTZEBUE, AK 99752
AMOS FOSTER, BOX 237, KOTZEBUE, AK 99752
STAHELI FOSTER, BOX 973, KOTZEBUE, AK 99752
WILLIAM FOSTER, BOX 37, KOTZEBUE, AK 99752
KAREN FRANKLIN, BOX 776, KOTZEBUE, AK 99752
CHARLEEN GAIR, 370 PIONEER PKWY, PALMER, AK 99645
JAMES GALL, 5002 DARTMOUTH RD #20, FAIRBANKS, AK 99709
DONALD GALLAHORN, BOX 909, KOTZEBUE, AK 99752
GARY GALLAHORN, BOX 170, NOORVIK, AK 99763
JOEY GALLAHORN, BOX 678, KOTZEBUE, AK 99752
KARAN GALLAHORN, BOX 83, KOTZEBUE, AK 99752
KENNETH GALLAHORN, BOX 946, KOTZEBUE, AK 99752
MARVIN GALLAHORN, BOX 61, KOTZEBUE, AK 99752
AYAGIAQ GOODWIN, BOX 88, KOTZEBUE, AK 99752
HENRY GOODWIN, BOX 334, KOTZEBUE, AK 99752
PEARL GOODWIN, BOX 413, KOTZEBUE, AK 99752
ADAM GREENE, BOX 1077, KOTZEBUE, AK 99752
AMOS GREENE, BOX 183, KOTZEBUE, AK 99752
ANDREW GREENE, BOX 421, KOTZEBUE, AK 99752
CHARLES GREENE, BOX 302, KOTZEBUE, AK 99752
LEO GREENE, BOX 66, KOTZEBUE, AK 99752
CHARLIE GREGG, BOX 144, KOTZEBUE, AK 99752
LILA GREGG, BOX 257, KOTZEBUE, AK 99752
GERALD GREIST, BOX 268, KOTZEBUE, AK 99752
WILLIAM GREIST, 2892 MIDWAY PLACER RD, FAIRBANKS, AK 99701
JOSEPH GROVES, BOX 685, KOTZEBUE, AK 99752
KAREN HADLEY, BOX 155, KOTZEBUE, AK 99752
GABRIEL HANSEN, BOX 815, KOTZEBUE, AK 99752
BRIAN HARRIS, BOX 3400-J, WASILLA, AK 99687
LEVI HARRIS, BOX 889, KOTZEBUE, AK 99752
BOB HAWLEY, BOX 65, KIVALINA, AK 99750
LAVONNE HENDRICKS, 200 W 34TH ST #903, ANCHORAGE, AK 99503
CARL HENRY, BOX 245, KOTZEBUE, AK 99752
DONALD HENRY, BOX 846, KOTZEBUE, AK 99752
PHILLIP HENRY, BOX 744, KOTZEBUE, AK 99752
DANIEL HENSLEY, BOX 157, KOTZEBUE, AK 99752
MICHAEL HENSLEY, BOX 1266, KOTZEBUE, AK 99752
WILSON HESS, BOX 307, KOTZEBUE, AK 99752
EDITH HILTS, BOX 144, SELDOVIA, AK 99663
RODNEY HILTS, BOX 144, SELDOVIA, AK 99663
RONDAL HOGAN, BOX 193, KOTZEBUE, AK 99752
RONDAL HOGAN, BOX 542, TALKEETNA, AK 99676
ART HOURIHAN, 512 EYAK DR ROOM #12, ANCHORAGE, AK 99501
KIRK HOWARTH, BOX 1212, KOTZEBUE, AK 99752
KIRK HOWARTH, BOX 214, KOTZEBUE, AK 99752
QUINN ITEN, BOX 344, KOTZEBUE, AK 99752
RUTH ITEN, BOX 344, KOTZEBUE, AK 99752
PAUL IYATUNGUK, BOX 1084, KOTZEBUE, AK 99752
JOSEPH JACKSON, BOX 110605, ANCHORAGE, AK 99511
SHERRELL JACKSON, BOX 232, NOORVIK, AK 99763

SALMON FISHING LIST—GILLNET

ALANNAH JONES, BOX 838, KOTZEBUE, AK 99752
CHARLES JONES, BOX 463, KOTZEBUE, AK 99752
FRED JONES, BOX 951, KOTZEBUE, AK 99752
KEITH JONES, 48008 S FORK DR, THREE RIVERS, CA 93271
TONY JONES, BOX 73, BUCKLAND, AK 99727
VICTOR JONES, BOX 691, KOTZEBUE, AK 99752
CHINA KANTNER, BOX 804, KOTZEBUE, AK 99752
SETH KANTNER, BOX 804, KOTZEBUE, AK 99752
GILBERT KARMUN, 4915 E 6TH AVE, ANCHORAGE, AK 99508
KATHERINE KEITH, BOX 831, KOTZEBUE, AK 99752
FRANK KENWORTHY, BOX 332, KOTZEBUE, AK 99752
OTTO KENWORTHY, BOX 14, KOTZEBUE, AK 99752
ORAN KNOX, BOX 50045, KIVALINA, AK 99750
NATHAN KOTCH, BOX 96, KOTZEBUE, AK 99752
DONALD KOUTCHAK, BOX 137, KOTZEBUE, AK 99752
LANCE KRAMER, BOX 1384, KOTZEBUE, AK 99752
DAVID L.L.GALLAHORN, BOX 909, KOTZEBUE, AK 99752
ROBERT LATHROP, 333 M ST #208, ANCHORAGE, AK 99501
DUSTIN LIE, BOX 98, KIANA, AK 99749
HAROLD LIE, BOX 1218, KOTZEBUE, AK 99752
THOR LIE, BOX 307, KOTZEBUE, AK 99752
RODNEY LINCOLN, 6374 PROMINENCE POINTE DR, ANCHORAGE, AK 99516
JEREMY LISBOURNE, BOX 611, KOTZEBUE, AK 99752
DEAN LUKIN, BOX 1350, KOTZEBUE, AK 99752
PETER LUTHER, BOX 70, NOATAK, AK 99761
AURORA MADSEN, BOX 627, KOTZEBUE, AK 99752
JAMES MAGDANZ, BOX 278, KOTZEBUE, AK 99752
JEROME MCCALL, BOX 748, KOTZEBUE, AK 99752
JAMES MCCLELLAN, BOX 311, KOTZEBUE, AK 99752
THOMAS MCDONALD, BOX 58, NOATAK, AK 99761
MYRNA MENDENHALL, BOX 146, KOTZEBUE, AK 99752
AXEL MILLS, BOX 21, NOATAK, AK 99761
GILBERT MILLS, BOX 45, NOATAK, AK 99761
WILLIAM MINERVA, 2918 CHENA HOT SPRINGS RD, FAIRBANKS, AK 99712
ROGER MITCHELL, BOX 64, NOATAK, AK 99761
JEFFREY MONROE, BOX 189, KOTZEBUE, AK 99752
RONALD MONSON, BOX 763, KOTZEBUE, AK 99752
EMERSON MOTO, BOX 36037, DEERING, AK 99736
ALFRED NANOUK, BOX 310, KOTZEBUE, AK 99752
DEREK NANOUK, BOX 1285, KOTZEBUE, AK 99752
ANTHONY NELSON, BOX 1051, KOTZEBUE, AK 99752
ARVID NELSON, BOX 25, KOTZEBUE, AK 99752
BERGMAN NELSON, BOX 404, KOTZEBUE, AK 99752
DARIN NELSON, BOX 87, KOTZEBUE, AK 99752
DEREK NELSON, BOX 25, KOTZEBUE, AK 99752
PETER NELSON, 8311 SPRUCE ST #2, ANCHORAGE, AK 99507
RICKY NELSON, BOX 33, KOTZEBUE, AK 99752
SVEN NELSON, BOX 327, KOTZEBUE, AK 99752
TRAVIS NELSON, BOX 32, KOTZEBUE, AK 99752
VERNON NELSON, BOX 973, KOTZEBUE, AK 99752
MAGGIE NEWLIN, BOX 85, NOORVIK, AK 99763
BRUCE NEWMAN, 8251 HESS AVE, LA GRANGE, IL 60525
CHAD NORDLUM, BOX 482, KOTZEBUE, AK 99752
CYRUS NORTON, BOX 192, KOTZEBUE, AK 99752
DICK NORTON, BOX 63, KOTZEBUE, AK 99752
ERNEST NORTON, BOX 361, KOTZEBUE, AK 99752
FRED NORTON, BOX 63, KOTZEBUE, AK 99752
PAUL NORTON, BOX 128, NOATAK, AK 99761
STANLEY NORTON, BOX 412, KOTZEBUE, AK 99752
RONALD OAKLEY, 2782 E MIKEY CIR, WASILLA, AK 99654
LESLIE OUTWATER, BOX 174, KOTZEBUE, AK 99752
WILLARD OUTWATER, BOX 625, PALMER, AK 99645
STACEY PHILLIPS, BOX 3651, PALMER, AK 99645
JOHN RAE, BOX 857, KOTZEBUE, AK 99752
JOHN RAE, BOX 857, KOTZEBUE, AK 99752
CHARLIE REED, BOX 334, KOTZEBUE, AK 99752

FLOYD REED, BOX 1048, KOTZEBUE, AK 99752
JOSEPH REICH, BOX 298, KOTZEBUE, AK 99752
PETER REICH, BOX 402, KOTZEBUE, AK 99752
WILLIAM REICH, BOX 576, KOTZEBUE, AK 99752
HENRY RICHARDS, BOX 695, KOTZEBUE, AK 99752
ROBERT RICHARDS, BOX 695, KOTZEBUE, AK 99752
ROBERT RICHARDS, BOX 184, KOTZEBUE, AK 99752
VERNON RICHARDS, BOX 184, KOTZEBUE, AK 99752
CLARENCE ROSSELL, BOX 64, KOTZEBUE, AK 99752
BURTON RUSSELL, BOX 274, KOTZEBUE, AK 99752
WALTER RUSSELL, BOX 963, KOTZEBUE, AK 99752
LUKE SAMPSON, BOX 833, KOTZEBUE, AK 99752
CALVIN SCHAEFFER, BOX 721, KOTZEBUE, AK 99752
FREDERICA SCHAEFFER, BOX 1, NOATAK, AK 99761
JAMES SCHAEFFER, BOX 293, KOTZEBUE, AK 99752
KEVIN SCHAEFFER, BOX 322, KOTZEBUE, AK 99752
MICHAEL SCHAEFFER, BOX 294, KOTZEBUE, AK 99752
RAY SCHAEFFER, BOX 1385, KOTZEBUE, AK 99752
ROBERT SCHAEFFER, BOX 1148, KOTZEBUE, AK 99752
ROSWELL SCHAEFFER, BOX 1359, KOTZEBUE, AK 99752
WARREN SCHAEFFER, BOX 1187, KOTZEBUE, AK 99752
WAYNE SCHAEFFER, BOX 70, NOORVIK, AK 99763
MICHAEL SCHIEBER, BOX 562, HEALY, AK 99743
NEIL SCHIEBER, BOX 562, HEALY, AK 99743
RICHARD SCOTT, BOX 15, DEERING, AK 99736
BILLY SHELDON, BOX 1307, KOTZEBUE, AK 99752
DEVIN SHELDON, BOX 1063, KOTZEBUE, AK 99752
FRANCIS SHELDON, BOX 132, KOTZEBUE, AK 99752
FRANCIS SHELDON, BOX 1307, KOTZEBUE, AK 99752
ENOCH SHIEDT, BOX 234, KOTZEBUE, AK 99752
HARLEY SHIELD, BOX 977, KOTZEBUE, AK 99752
BOBBY SMITH, BOX 875, KOTZEBUE, AK 99752
DONALD SMITH, BOX 96, KIANA, AK 99749
EUGENE SMITH, BOX 1158, KOTZEBUE, AK 99752
FRED SMITH, BOX 1197, KOTZEBUE, AK 99752
LOUIS SMITH, BOX 1065, KOTZEBUE, AK 99752
CARL SNYDER, BOX 122, KOTZEBUE, AK 99752
DANIEL SNYDER, BOX 877584, WASILLA, AK 99687
JACKSON SNYDER, BOX 1166, KOTZEBUE, AK 99752
ALAN SOURS, BOX 1286, KOTZEBUE, AK 99752
JOSHUA SOURS, BOX 485, KOTZEBUE, AK 99752
ENOCH STALKER, BOX 971, KOTZEBUE, AK 99752
JUDITH STEIN, BOX 113, KOTZEBUE, AK 99752
KENNETH STEIN, BOX 113, KOTZEBUE, AK 99752
STEPHANIE STEIN, BOX 1354, KOTZEBUE, AK 99752
JOSEPH SWAN, BOX 50017, KIVALINA, AK 99750
TIMOTHY THRAPP, BOX 100986, ANCHORAGE, AK 99510
KENNETH TIKIK, BOX 67, KOTZEBUE, AK 99752
MAHLON UHL, BOX 366, KOTZEBUE, AK 99752
ALLEN UPICKSOUN, BOX 664, KOTZEBUE, AK 99752
EDWIN VIGLIONE, BOX 81, KOTZEBUE, AK 99752
JOHN WALKER, BOX 285, KOTZEBUE, AK 99752
OSCAR WALKER, BOX 103, BUCKLAND, AK 99727
DAVID WASHINGTON, BOX 1376, KOTZEBUE, AK 99752
CHARLES WEIDNER, 3605 ARCTIC BLV #2012, ANCHORAGE, AK 99503
DOUGLAS WICKEN, BOX 1078, KOTZEBUE, AK 99752
EVA WICKEN, BOX 968, KOTZEBUE, AK 99752
MARK WILLETTE, BOX 1813, CORDOVA, AK 99574
JAMES WILSON, BOX 754, KOTZEBUE, AK 99752
ROGER WRIGHT, BOX 209, KOTZEBUE, AK 99752
MICHAEL ZAGARS, BOX 201, KOTZEBUE, AK 99752
BEVERLY ZIBELL, BOX 121, NOORVIK, AK 99763
MARCUS A.R.REDFOX, BOX 232, EMMONAK, AK 99581

SALMON FISHING LIST—GILLNET

SALMON, GILLNET, LOWER YUKON

BERNARD AFCAN, BOX 56, NUNAM IQUA, AK 99666
BRANDON AFCAN, BOX 215, EMMONAK, AK 99581
JAMES AFCAN, BOX 1404, PALMER, AK 99645
JENNIFER AFCAN, BOX 142, SAINT MARYS, AK 99658
ALBERT AGATHLUK, BOX 214, EMMONAK, AK 99581
JEFFREY AGATHLUK, BOX 235, EMMONAK, AK 99581
RANDELL AGATHLUK, BOX 235, EMMONAK, AK 99581
STEPHANIE AGATHLUK, BOX 48, EMMONAK, AK 99581
JOSEPH AGAYAR, BOX 134, ALAKANUK, AK 99554
MAX AGAYAR, BOX 134, ALAKANUK, AK 99554
MAXINE AGAYAR, BOX 136, ALAKANUK, AK 99554
RICHARD AGAYAR, BOX 69, ALAKANUK, AK 99554
TIFFANY AGAYAR, BOX 63, ALAKANUK, AK 99554
BRANDON AGUCHAK, BOX 133, SCAMMON BAY, AK 99662
ERIC.B.M. AGUCHAK, BOX 41, SCAMMON BAY, AK 99662
ANTONIA AGWIAK, BOX 32083, MOUNTAIN VILLAGE, AK 99632
BERT AGWIAK, BOX 32083, MOUNTAIN VILLAGE, AK 99632
JAMIE AGWIAK, BOX 45, EMMONAK, AK 99581
JOHN AGWIAK, BOX 32324, MOUNTAIN VILLAGE, AK 99632
IRENE AKARAN, BOX 20086, KOTLIK, AK 99620
RICHARD AKARAN, BOX 20103, KOTLIK, AK 99620
THEODORE AKARAN, BOX 20135, KOTLIK, AK 99620
MICHAEL AKERELREA, BOX 5, SCAMMON BAY, AK 99662
SEAN AKERELREA, 424 S HAMILTON ST, PAINTED POST, NY 14870
CHRISTOPHER AKETACHUNAK, BOX 20071, KOTLIK, AK 99620
DEON AKETACHUNAK, BOX 20051, KOTLIK, AK 99620
JAMES AKETACHUNAK, BOX 20051, KOTLIK, AK 99620
JIMMY AKETACHUNAK, BOX 20057, KOTLIK, AK 99620
EUNICE ALEXIE, BOX 192, SAINT MARYS, AK 99658
HARVEY ALEXIE, BOX 32111, MOUNTAIN VILLAGE, AK 99632
LLOYD ALEXIE, BOX 32077, MOUNTAIN VILLAGE, AK 99632
MATTHEW ALEXIE, BOX 32191, MOUNTAIN VILLAGE, AK 99632
RAYMOND ALEXIE, BOX 32227, MOUNTAIN VILLAGE, AK 99632
ROBERTA ALEXIE, BOX 32111, MOUNTAIN VILLAGE, AK 99632
BENJAMIN ALICK, BOX 5116, PILOT STATION, AK 99650
JOSEPH ALICK, BOX 5036, PILOT STATION, AK 99650
MELISSA ALICK, BOX 5071, PILOT STATION, AK 99650
ETHAN ALORALREA, BOX 1384, BETHEL, AK 99559
JOHN ALOYSIUS, BOX 27, HOLY CROSS, AK 99602
APRIL ALSTROM, BOX 252, ALAKANUK, AK 99554
AXEL ALSTROM, 4961 E ALDER DR, WASILLA, AK 99654
DALE ALSTROM, 9499 BRAYTON DR #110, ANCHORAGE, AK 99507
DORIS ALSTROM, BOX 112, ALAKANUK, AK 99554
EARL ALSTROM, BOX 384, SAINT MARYS, AK 99658
ERIC ALSTROM, BOX 243, SAINT MARYS, AK 99658
ETHAN ALSTROM, BOX 317, SAINT MARYS, AK 99658
FRANK ALSTROM, BOX 169, ALAKANUK, AK 99554
HAZEL ALSTROM, BOX 317, SAINT MARYS, AK 99658
JAMAL ALSTROM, BOX 169, ALAKANUK, AK 99554
LATRELL ALSTROM, BOX 112, ALAKANUK, AK 99554
PENNY ALSTROM, 5161 W STACY ST #48, WASILLA, AK 99623
RAGNAR ALSTROM, BOX 112, ALAKANUK, AK 99554
RICHARD ALSTROM, BOX 8, SAINT MARYS, AK 99658
ROBERT ALSTROM, 2940 CAPSTAN DR, ANCHORAGE, AK 99516
SHAUN ALSTROM, BOX 150, ALAKANUK, AK 99554
THOMAS ALSTROM, BOX 46, ALAKANUK, AK 99554
WILLIAM ALSTROM, BOX 317, SAINT MARYS, AK 99658
AYDEN ALSTROM.BEANS, BOX 314, SAINT MARYS, AK 99658
RONALD ALSTROM.BEANS, BOX 314, SAINT MARYS, AK 99658
DAVID AMIK, BOX 1033, BETHEL, AK 99559
ERIC AMUKON, BOX 131, SCAMMON BAY, AK 99662
GEORGE AMUKON, BOX 43, SCAMMON BAY, AK 99662
DAVID ANDREW, BOX 53, MARSHALL, AK 99585
JOHN ANDREW, BOX 88, MARSHALL, AK 99585

NICK ANDREW, BOX 127, MARSHALL, AK 99585
ALFRED ANDREWS, BOX 20064, KOTLIK, AK 99620
ARTHUR ANDREWS, BOX 20092, KOTLIK, AK 99620
BRIAN ANDREWS, BOX 20328, KOTLIK, AK 99620
CHARLES ANDREWS, BOX 32136, MOUNTAIN VILLAGE, AK 99632
FREDRICK ANDREWS, BOX 93, EMMONAK, AK 99581
GABRIEL ANDREWS, BOX 20016, KOTLIK, AK 99620
HAROLD ANDREWS, BOX 32253, MOUNTAIN VILLAGE, AK 99632
HAZEL ANDREWS, BOX 32253, MOUNTAIN VILLAGE, AK 99632
KENNETH ANDREWS, BOX 20067, KOTLIK, AK 99620
LAWRENCE ANDREWS, BOX 102, SAINT MARYS, AK 99658
NANCY ANDREWS, BOX 20049, KOTLIK, AK 99620
PAUL ANDREWS, BOX 165, EMMONAK, AK 99581
PHILIP ANDREWS, BOX 169, EMMONAK, AK 99581
RICK ANDREWS, BOX 08, EMMONAK, AK 99581
ROBERT ANDREWS, BOX 18, EMMONAK, AK 99581
SIMON ANDREWS, BOX 32001, MOUNTAIN VILLAGE, AK 99632
ALLEN ANDY, BOX 5526, NEWTOK, AK 99559
FRANCINE APAREZUK, BOX 20029, KOTLIK, AK 99620
DAVID ASKOAK, BOX 225, NEWHALEN, AK 99606
NICEPHORE ASKOAK, BOX 2, RUSSIAN MISSION, AK 99657
DAISY ATTIE, BOX 32132, MOUNTAIN VILLAGE, AK 99632
CYPRIAN AUGLINE, BOX 153, ALAKANUK, AK 99554
MATTHEW AUGLINE, BOX 171, ALAKANUK, AK 99554
SHIRLEY AUGLINE, BOX 94, ALAKANUK, AK 99554
TERRENCE AUGLINE, BOX 243, ALAKANUK, AK 99554
LEONARD AUGUSTINE, BOX 3307, BETHEL, AK 99559
TRACY AUGUSTINE, BOX 43, EMMONAK, AK 99581
CLARA AUSTIN, BOX 110, SAINT MICHAEL, AK 99659
JOHN AYUNERAK, BOX 195, ALAKANUK, AK 99554
THOMAS BARCLAY, 12739 S GOOSE CREEK RD, WASILLA, AK 99623
ALBERT BEANS, BOX 5121, PILOT STATION, AK 99650
CARL BEANS, BOX 32036, MOUNTAIN VILLAGE, AK 99632
CHRISTOPHER BEANS, BOX 5004, PILOT STATION, AK 99650
CLETUS BEANS, BOX 32266, MOUNTAIN VILLAGE, AK 99632
DAVID BEANS, BOX 314, SAINT MARYS, AK 99658
DOMINIC BEANS, BOX 5065, PILOT STATION, AK 99650
ELMER BEANS, BOX 32356, MOUNTAIN VILLAGE, AK 99632
FRANCIS BEANS, BOX 325, SAINT MARYS, AK 99658
FREDERICK BEANS, BOX 32313, MOUNTAIN VILLAGE, AK 99632
GEORGE BEANS, BOX 153, SAINT MARYS, AK 99658
JACOB BEANS, BOX 32013, MOUNTAIN VILLAGE, AK 99632
JOEL BEANS, 1311 BALFOUR DR #4, ANCHORAGE, AK 99515
JOHN BEANS, BOX 315, MOUNTAIN VILLAGE, AK 99632
JOSEPH BEANS, BOX 32152, MOUNTAIN VILLAGE, AK 99632
MICHAEL BEANS, BOX 145, SAINT MARYS, AK 99658
NANCY BEANS, BOX 354, MOUNTAIN VILLAGE, AK 99632
NATHAN BEANS, BOX 5052, PILOT STATION, AK 99650
NORMAN BEANS, BOX 32174, MOUNTAIN VILLAGE, AK 99632
OLAN BEANS, BOX 246, SAINT MARYS, AK 99658
RAPHAEL BEANS, BOX 32063, MOUNTAIN VILLAGE, AK 99632
RODERICK BEANS, BOX 333, SAINT MARYS, AK 99658
WILLIE BEANS, BOX 5052, PILOT STATION, AK 99650
LEONA BERGMAN, BOX 32352, MOUNTAIN VILLAGE, AK 99632
CLARA BIRD, BOX 18, EMMONAK, AK 99581
DEREK BIRD, BOX 57, EMMONAK, AK 99581
JOHN BIRD, BOX 227, EMMONAK, AK 99581
MARTINA BIRD, BOX 141, EMMONAK, AK 99581
TASHA BIRD, BOX 204, SAINT MARYS, AK 99658
PETER BLACK, 536 W CRESTWOOD AVE, WASILLA, AK 99654
RODERICK BLANKET, BOX 32135, MOUNTAIN VILLAGE, AK 99632
BRENDA BOB, 3205 CASSIUS CT, ANCHORAGE, AK 99508
RUSSELL BODEY, 4905 83RD AVE SE, SNOHOMISH, WA 98290
ALAN BOLIVER, BOX 75, MARSHALL, AK 99585
ANDREW BOOTS, BOX 97, MARSHALL, AK 99585

SALMON FISHING LIST—GILLNET

MARCIA BOOTS, BOX 104, MARSHALL, AK 99585
MICHAEL BORATKO, BOX 131, HOMER, AK 99603
ALVIN BROWN, BOX 9, EMMONAK, AK 99581
ANDREW BROWN, BOX 32187, MOUNTAIN VILLAGE, AK 99632
CLARA BROWN, 100 W 13TH AVE, ANCHORAGE, AK 99501
PAUL BROWN, BOX 32163, MOUNTAIN VILLAGE, AK 99632
AGNES BUSTER, BOX 213, ALAKANUK, AK 99554
RAYMOND BUSTER, BOX 206, EMMONAK, AK 99581
KENNETH C.P.FITKA, BOX 52, MARSHALL, AK 99585
FRANK CAMILLE, BOX 41, NUNAM IQUA, AK 99666
JOHN CANOE, BOX 13, NUNAM IQUA, AK 99666
LENORA CARPLUK, BOX 83043, FAIRBANKS, AK 99708
CHARLENE CHANEY, BOX 198, EMMONAK, AK 99581
BILLY CHARLES, BOX 41, EMMONAK, AK 99581
ISAIAH CHARLES, BOX 41, EMMONAK, AK 99581
BRENT CHARLIE, BOX 32362, MOUNTAIN VILLAGE, AK 99632
RICHARD CHARLIE, BOX 175, SCAMMON BAY, AK 99662
OLE CHIEF, BOX 32082, MOUNTAIN VILLAGE, AK 99632
ARTHUR CHIKIGAK, BOX 64, ALAKANUK, AK 99554
CELIA CHIKIGAK, BOX 21, ALAKANUK, AK 99554
VERNON CHIKIGAK, BOX 147, ALAKANUK, AK 99554
ZITA CHIKIGAK, BOX 64, ALAKANUK, AK 99554
ANTHONY CHIKLAK, BOX 295, MOUNTAIN VILLAGE, AK 99632
JAMIE CHIKLAK, BOX 32286, MOUNTAIN VILLAGE, AK 99632
WILMA CHRISTENSEN, 1715 TAMARRA CIR, ANCHORAGE, AK 99508
URSULA CLAUNCH, BOX 37, EMMONAK, AK 99581
NICK COFFEE, BOX 2, MARSHALL, AK 99585
PATRICK COFFEE, BOX 131, MARSHALL, AK 99585
RAYMOND COFFEE, BOX 41, MARSHALL, AK 99585
DARRYL COFFEY, BOX 93, STEBBINS, AK 99671
GORDON COFFEY, BOX 71038, STEBBINS, AK 99671
JAMES COOK, BOX 174, ALAKANUK, AK 99554
DEWAYNE COOPER, 527 HOYT ST, ANCHORAGE, AK 99508
PHILIP COVLASKY, BOX 170, EMMONAK, AK 99581
ANTHONY COWBOY, BOX 211, SAINT MARYS, AK 99658
JOEL CRANE, BOX 271, EMMONAK, AK 99581
JOHN CRANE, BOX 228, EMMONAK, AK 99581
PAUL CRANE, BOX 271, EMMONAK, AK 99581
FRANCIS DAMIAN, BOX 114, ALAKANUK, AK 99554
JONATHAN DAMIAN, BOX 81, ALAKANUK, AK 99554
THOMAS DAMIAN, 3930 GARDNER ST #C, ANCHORAGE, AK 99508
JEREMY DAUPHINEE, BOX 94, SAINT MARYS, AK 99658
JEFF DEMIENTIEFF, BOX 51, HOLY CROSS, AK 99602
LEONARD DEMIENTIEFF, BOX 18, HOLY CROSS, AK 99602
PATRICIA DEMIENTIEFF, BOX 51, HOLY CROSS, AK 99602
GEORGE DONART, 917 W 20TH AVE, ANCHORAGE, AK 99503
AARON DOTOMAIN, BOX 870029, WASILLA, AK 99687
JAMES DUFFY, BOX 54, RUSSIAN MISSION, AK 99657
BILLIE.JO DUNY, BOX 03, EMMONAK, AK 99581
DEBRA DUNY, BOX 102, MARSHALL, AK 99585
IRENE DUNY, BOX 102, MARSHALL, AK 99585
MICHAEL DUNY, BOX 77, MARSHALL, AK 99585
WILLIAM DUNY, BOX 31, ALAKANUK, AK 99554
SETH E.AGUCHAK, BOX 8, SCAMMON BAY, AK 99662
ALLEN EDMUND, BOX 176, ALAKANUK, AK 99554
CLYDE EDMUND, BOX 164, ALAKANUK, AK 99554
JOSEPHINE EDMUND, BOX 253, ALAKANUK, AK 99554
SHELBY EDMUND, BOX 253, ALAKANUK, AK 99554
CALVIN EDWARDS, BOX 196, SAINT MARYS, AK 99658
CYPRIAN EDWARDS, BOX 251, EMMONAK, AK 99581
JAMES EDWARDS, BOX 144, SAINT MARYS, AK 99658
JESSE EDWARDS, BOX 5027, PILOT STATION, AK 99650
LEON EDWARDS, BOX 96, MARSHALL, AK 99585
MYRON EDWARDS, BOX 115, RUSSIAN MISSION, AK 99657
WALTER EDWARDS, BOX 35, MARSHALL, AK 99585
CURTIS ELACHIK, BOX 20015, KOTLIK, AK 99620

AARON ELIA, BOX 132, SAINT MARYS, AK 99658
JOHN ELIA, BOX 85, SAINT MARYS, AK 99658
AMVROSSY EVAN, BOX 268, SAINT MARYS, AK 99658
GARRETT EVAN, BOX 17, MARSHALL, AK 99585
GREGORY EVAN, BOX 37, MARSHALL, AK 99585
NORMA EVAN, BOX 108, MARSHALL, AK 99585
OLGA EVAN, BOX 110, RUSSIAN MISSION, AK 99657
CRYSTAL FANCYBOY, BOX 5105, PILOT STATION, AK 99650
FRANK FANCYBOY, BOX 5164, PILOT STATION, AK 99650
KATHY FANCYBOY, BOX 5123, PILOT STATION, AK 99650
PAUL FANCYBOY, BOX 5006, PILOT STATION, AK 99650
STELLA FANCYBOY, BOX 20132, KOTLIK, AK 99620
TODD FANCYBOY, BOX 5094, PILOT STATION, AK 99650
WILBERT FANCYBOY, BOX 5105, PILOT STATION, AK 99650
WILLIE FANCYBOY, BOX 5123, PILOT STATION, AK 99650
AARON FITKA, BOX 155, MARSHALL, AK 99585
CHARLIE FITKA, BOX 59056, SAINT MICHAEL, AK 99659
DANIEL FITKA, BOX 52, MARSHALL, AK 99585
FRED FITKA, BOX 84, MARSHALL, AK 99585
JAYLENE FITKA, BOX 71, MARSHALL, AK 99585
WILLIAM FITKA, BOX 91, MARSHALL, AK 99585
WILLIE FITKA, BOX 154, MARSHALL, AK 99585
ANDREW FOXIE, BLUEBERRY ST #4112, STEBBINS, AK 99671
DAVID FRANCIS, BOX 5047, PILOT STATION, AK 99650
PAUL FRANCIS, BOX 188, EMMONAK, AK 99581
RUDOLPH FRANCIS, BOX 25, SAINT MARYS, AK 99658
ZENA FRANCIS.HUNT, BOX 293, SAINT MARYS, AK 99658
GREGORY FRATIS, BOX 218, EMMONAK, AK 99581
JOSEPH FRIDAY, 154 SUBDIVISION RD, CHEVAK, AK 99563
ALOYSIUS GEORGE, BOX 5168, PILOT STATION, AK 99650
DMITRI GEORGE, BOX 20166, KOTLIK, AK 99620
EUGENE GEORGE, BOX 5048, PILOT STATION, AK 99650
GLORIA GEORGE, BOX 32084, MOUNTAIN VILLAGE, AK 99632
IGNATIUS GEORGE, BOX 45, ALAKANUK, AK 99554
PETER GEORGE, 220 HILLSIDE ROAD, SCAMMON BAY, AK 99662
RAYMOND GEORGE, BOX 151, SAINT MARYS, AK 99658
STANLEY GEORGE, BOX 32005, MOUNTAIN VILLAGE, AK 99632
THOMAS GEORGE, BOX 13, SAINT MARYS, AK 99658
VERNON GEORGE, BOX 121, SAINT MARYS, AK 99658
JOSEPH GERARD, 11150 E LUPINE, PALMER, AK 99645
DANIELLE GREENE, BOX 5055, PILOT STATION, AK 99650
KAREN GREENE, BOX 5158, PILOT STATION, AK 99650
LINDA GREENE, BOX 5063, PILOT STATION, AK 99650
MORRIS GREENE, BOX 5158, PILOT STATION, AK 99650
SHAWN GREENE, BOX 5045, PILOT STATION, AK 99650
FRANK GREGORY, BOX 254, MOUNTAIN VILLAGE, AK 99632
HAROLD GREGORY, BOX 131, EMMONAK, AK 99581
MELVIN GREGORY, BOX 34, EMMONAK, AK 99581
ADELE GRIFFITH, BOX 5371, NAVARRE, FL 32566
WILLIAM GUIDRY, BOX 155, SAINT MARYS, AK 99658
L HAGELAND, 5500 YUKON CHARLIE LP, ANCHORAGE, AK 99502
EVAN HAMILTON, BOX 195, EMMONAK, AK 99581
THEODORE HAMILTON, BOX 7, EMMONAK, AK 99581
WILLIAM HAMILTON, 101 YUKON WAY, EMMONAK, AK 99581
ALLEN HANSON, BOX 212, ALAKANUK, AK 99554
RYAN HANSON, 5831 JORDAN CR, ANCHORAGE, AK 99504
THOMAS HART, BOX 136, SAINT MARYS, AK 99658
GARY HAUGEN, 7707 STANLEY DR, ANCHORAGE, AK 99518
ARTHUR HECKMAN, BOX 60, PILOT STATION, AK 99650
ARTHUR HECKMAN, BOX 5160, PILOT STATION, AK 99650
BRIAN HECKMAN, BOX 5147, PILOT STATION, AK 99650
CANDACE HECKMAN, BOX 5141, PILOT STATION, AK 99650
CHARLES HECKMAN, BOX 5172, PILOT STATION, AK 99650
DARIN HECKMAN, BOX 5013, PILOT STATION, AK 99650
GABRIEL HECKMAN, BOX 5157, PILOT STATION, AK 99650
LLOYD HECKMAN, BOX 60, PILOT STATION, AK 99650

SALMON FISHING LIST—GILLNET

STANLEY HECKMAN, BOX 5010, PILOT STATION, AK 99650
SUZANNE HECKMAN, BOX 5128, PILOT STATION, AK 99650
TROY HECKMAN, BOX 5049, PILOT STATION, AK 99650
JOHNNY HENRY, BOX 190, SCAMMON BAY, AK 99662
DAVID HERBERT, BOX 287, SAINT MARYS, AK 99658
JOHN HESS, BOX 32385, MOUNTAIN VILLAGE, AK 99632
SCOTT HESS, BOX 164, MOUNTAIN VILLAGE, AK 99632
STEPHEN HILL, BOX 5, ANIAK, AK 99557
ANTHONY HOOTCH, BOX 226, EMMONAK, AK 99581
DOUGLAS HOOTCH, BOX 132, EMMONAK, AK 99581
LINDA HOOTCH, BOX 5, EMMONAK, AK 99581
RANDY HOOTCH, BOX 294, EMMONAK, AK 99581
RUDOLPH HOOTCH, BOX 20105, KOTLIK, AK 99620
JUSTIN HOOVER, BOX 5073, PILOT STATION, AK 99650
PIUS HOOVER, BOX 311, EMMONAK, AK 99581
DOUGLAS HORN, BOX 63, EMMONAK, AK 99581
PHILIP HORN, BOX 163, EMMONAK, AK 99581
NORMAN HOUSLER, BOX 84, RUSSIAN MISSION, AK 99657
RYAN HOUSLER, BOX 41, RUSSIAN MISSION, AK 99657
AARON HUNT, BOX 20065, KOTLIK, AK 99620
BERNARD HUNT, BOX 20077, KOTLIK, AK 99620
DOMINIC HUNT, BOX 36, EMMONAK, AK 99581
EVAN HUNT, BOX 20025, KOTLIK, AK 99620
FRANCIS HUNT, BOX 20014, KOTLIK, AK 99620
HERMES HUNT, BOX 20011, KOTLIK, AK 99620
JIMMY HUNT, BOX 92, SHAKTOOLIK, AK 99771
JOEL HUNT, BOX 75, EMMONAK, AK 99581
MARTIN HUNT, BOX 20062, KOTLIK, AK 99620
MATT HUNT, BOX 20138, KOTLIK, AK 99620
ROBERT HUNT, BOX 20083, KOTLIK, AK 99620
ASHLEY HUNTER, BOX 117, MARSHALL, AK 99585
DOLORES HUNTER, 3730 CHAFFEE CIRCLE, ANCHORAGE, AK 99517
DONALD HUNTER, BOX 83, MARSHALL, AK 99585
GARY HUNTER, BOX 21, SCAMMON BAY, AK 99662
GERALD HUNTER, BOX 408, HOOPER BAY, AK 99604
HELEN HUNTER, BOX 103, SCAMMON BAY, AK 99662
LARSON HUNTER, BOX 161, SCAMMON BAY, AK 99662
LESLIE HUNTER, BOX 50, MARSHALL, AK 99585
LESLIE HUNTER, 4331 VANCE DR #B6, ANCHORAGE, AK 99508
MATTHEW IGNATIUS, BOX 57, NUNAM IQUA, AK 99666
JACOB ISAAC, BOX 142, MARSHALL, AK 99585
JULIUS ISAAC, BOX 85, MARSHALL, AK 99585
MAXIE ISAAC, BOX 166, MARSHALL, AK 99585
JAMES ISIDORE, BOX 216, ALAKANUK, AK 99554
DANIEL J.R.TEELUK, BOX 20141, KOTLIK, AK 99620
CHRISTOPHER JAMES, BOX 104, ALAKANUK, AK 99554
MICHAEL JAMES, BOX 168, ALAKANUK, AK 99554
RON JENNINGS, BOX 21, EMMONAK, AK 99581
CHARLES JERUE, 3431 WILEY POST LP, ANCHORAGE, AK 99517
MICHAEL JIMMY, BOX 72, EMMONAK, AK 99581
STAN JIMMY, GENERAL DEL, EMMONAK, AK 99581
BERNARD JOE, BOX 32321, MOUNTAIN VILLAGE, AK 99632
GREGORY JOE, BOX 32016, MOUNTAIN VILLAGE, AK 99632
JASON JOE, BOX 172, ALAKANUK, AK 99554
MARIE JOE, 9780 STANLEY DR, WASILLA, AK 99623
ALEX JOHNSON, BOX 24, NUNAM IQUA, AK 99666
CLARENCE JOHNSON, BOX 367, SAINT MARYS, AK 99658
DAVID JOHNSON, BOX 67, EMMONAK, AK 99581
DONALD JOHNSON, BOX 2640, BETHEL, AK 99559
GEORGE.OT. JOHNSON, BOX 32079, MOUNTAIN VILLAGE, AK 99632
HENRY JOHNSON, BOX 211, EMMONAK, AK 99581
JORDAN JOHNSON, BOX 20058, KOTLIK, AK 99620
JOSEPH JOHNSON, BOX 20058, KOTLIK, AK 99620
NEIL JOHNSON, 131 TYSON STREET, SAINT MARYS, AK 99658
OSCAR JOHNSON, BOX 32255, MOUNTAIN VILLAGE, AK 99632

WILLIE JOHNSON, BOX 218, EMMONAK, AK 99581
BRANDON JOHNSON.EDWARDS, BOX 251, EMMONAK, AK 99581
CYPRIAN JOHNSON.EDWARDS, BOX 251, EMMONAK, AK 99581
NATHAN JOHNSON.EDWARDS, BOX 251, EMMONAK, AK 99581
DANIEL JORGENSEN, 16232 CLINE ST #C, EAGLE RIVER, AK 99577
CHRISTOPHER JOSEPH, 4306 COPE ST APT 3, ANCHORAGE, AK 99503
DAMIAN JOSEPH, BOX 210, ALAKANUK, AK 99554
JOHN JOSEPH, BOX 142, ALAKANUK, AK 99554
KEVIN JOSEPH, BOX 166, ALAKANUK, AK 99554
LORRAINE JOSEPH, BOX 183, ALAKANUK, AK 99554
MATTHEW JOSEPH, BOX 5084, PILOT STATION, AK 99650
RAYMOND JOSEPH, BOX 26, ALAKANUK, AK 99554
RONALD JOSEPH, BOX 206, ALAKANUK, AK 99554
XAVIER JOSEPH, BOX 166, ALAKANUK, AK 99554
ALMIRA KAGANAK, BOX 95, SCAMMON BAY, AK 99662
CHARLIE KAGANAK, BOX 192, SCAMMON BAY, AK 99662
CLIFFORD KAGANAK, BOX 27, SCAMMON BAY, AK 99662
JAMES KAGANAK, BOX 12, SCAMMON BAY, AK 99662
KEITH KAGANAK, BOX 214, SCAMMON BAY, AK 99662
KIMMIE KAGANAK, BOX 88, SCAMMON BAY, AK 99662
MARCUS KAGANAK, BOX 123, SCAMMON BAY, AK 99662
NAAMAN KAGANAK, BOX 35, SCAMMON BAY, AK 99662
SCOTT KAGANAK, BOX 07, SCAMMON BAY, AK 99662
WYBON KAGANAK, BOX 112, SCAMMON BAY, AK 99662
BRANDON KAMEROFF, BOX 83, EMMONAK, AK 99581
FREDERICK KAMEROFF, BOX 60703, FAIRBANKS, AK 99706
HAROLD KAMEROFF, BOX 104, EMMONAK, AK 99581
JAMES KAMEROFF, BOX 87, EMMONAK, AK 99581
JOSEPH KAMEROFF, BOX 141, EMMONAK, AK 99581
JUSTIN KAMEROFF, BOX 35, EMMONAK, AK 99581
LEON KAMEROFF, BOX 177, EMMONAK, AK 99581
PERRY KAMEROFF, BOX 193, SAINT MARYS, AK 99658
ROBERT KAMEROFF, BOX 81, EMMONAK, AK 99581
RYAN KAMEROFF, BOX 87, EMMONAK, AK 99581
TERESA KAMEROFF, BOX 34, MARSHALL, AK 99585
CLIFFORD KAMKOFF, BOX 20167, KOTLIK, AK 99620
RICHARD KAMKOFF, BOX 20249, KOTLIK, AK 99620
WILLIE KAMUCK, BOX 6, SAINT MARYS, AK 99658
ANDREW KASAYULI, BOX 04, SCAMMON BAY, AK 99662
PAUL KASSOCK, BOX 86, ALAKANUK, AK 99554
WILFRED KATCHEAK, BOX 71048, STEBBINS, AK 99671
ABRAHAM KELLY, BOX 5080, PILOT STATION, AK 99650
ANDREW KELLY, BOX 222, EMMONAK, AK 99581
ELIAS KELLY, BOX 5093, PILOT STATION, AK 99650
MARTHA KELLY, BOX 84, EMMONAK, AK 99581
YOLANDA KELLY, BOX 222, EMMONAK, AK 99581
ELLEN KEYES, BOX 203, EMMONAK, AK 99581
HUMPHREY KEYES, BOX 203, EMMONAK, AK 99581
MARY KEYES, BOX 20149, KOTLIK, AK 99620
PHILOMENA KEYES, BOX 20170, KOTLIK, AK 99620
XAVIER KEYES, BOX 32185, MOUNTAIN VILLAGE, AK 99632
ZENA KILANGAK, BOX 71, EMMONAK, AK 99581
WILLIAM KINZY, 1010 NELCHINA ST, ANCHORAGE, AK 99501
HAROLD KITSICK, BOX 20070, KOTLIK, AK 99620
VERNON KITSICK, BOX 20097, KOTLIK, AK 99620
DENNIS KLINE, 18541 TALARIK DR, EAGLE RIVER, AK 99577
ANDREW KLINGBEIL, 9866 S DOG SLED ST, WASILLA, AK 99623
EDWARD KOKRINE, BOX 32076, MOUNTAIN VILLAGE, AK 99632
RICHARD KOKRINE, BOX 32153, MOUNTAIN VILLAGE, AK 99632
STANLEY KOKRINE, BOX 251, ALAKANUK, AK 99554
STEVEN KOKRINE, BOX 175, ALAKANUK, AK 99554
FRANCIS KOZEVENIKOFF, BOX 52, EMMONAK, AK 99581
RODERICK KOZEVENIKOFF, BOX 232, EMMONAK, AK 99581
THOMAS KOZEVNIKOFF, 320 E 46TH AVE APT 2, ANCHORAGE, AK 99501
EDWIN LAITY, 1619 LOT 1 SAWMILL CK RD, SITKA, AK 99835

SALMON FISHING LIST—GILLNET

FRED LAMONT, BOX 32348, MOUNTAIN VILLAGE, AK 99632
GERALD LAMONT, BOX 244, EMMONAK, AK 99581
JOHN LAMONT, 7051 W WINDSOR DR, WASILLA, AK 99623
KATHLEEN LAMONT, BOX 168, EMMONAK, AK 99581
GEORGE LANDLORD, BOX 65, MARSHALL, AK 99585
JAMES LANDLORD, BOX 32168, MOUNTAIN VILLAGE, AK 99632
THOMAS LAPP, 56846 E END RD, HOMER, AK 99603
KENNETH LARAUX, BOX 903, BETHEL, AK 99559
HERBERT LAWRENCE, BOX 32037, MOUNTAIN VILLAGE, AK 99632
MARVIN LAWRENCE, 1529 PRIMROSE ST #A, ANCHORAGE, AK 99508
MATHILDA LAWRENCE, 211 BUNN ST, ANCHORAGE, AK 99508
KENNETH LEE, BOX 122, ALAKANUK, AK 99554
JAMES LEOPOLD, BOX 118, ALAKANUK, AK 99554
RICHARD LEVI, BOX 31, SAINT MICHAEL, AK 99659
MELISSA LEWIS, BOX 10161, FAIRBANKS, AK 99710
DAVID LOCKWOOD, BOX 84, UNALAKLEET, AK 99684
CHARLES LONG, BOX 32303, MOUNTAIN VILLAGE, AK 99632
NICHOLAS LONG, BOX 32053, MOUNTAIN VILLAGE, AK 99632
NICHOLAS LONG, BOX 33664, JUNEAU, AK 99803
PAUL LONG, BOX 32345, MOUNTAIN VILLAGE, AK 99632
WILLIE LONG, BOX 213, SAINT MARYS, AK 99658
LAMARR LOWE, BOX 49, ALAKANUK, AK 99554
MARIO LUJAN, BOX 879088, WASILLA, AK 99687
ALBERT LUKE, 6003 BUCKNER DR, ANCHORAGE, AK 99504
JOHANNA LUKE, BOX 32094, MOUNTAIN VILLAGE, AK 99632
WILLIAM LUKE, BOX 101, SAINT MARYS, AK 99658
MICHAEL LUKUDAK, BOX 17, EMMONAK, AK 99581
ANDREW MAKAILY, BOX 5012, PILOT STATION, AK 99650
ANDREW MAKAILY, BOX 5088, PILOT STATION, AK 99650
DARYL MANUMIK, BOX 53, NUNAM IQUA, AK 99666
HENRY MANUMIK, BOX 73, EMMONAK, AK 99581
JAMAL MANUMIK, BOX 53, NUNAM IQUA, AK 99666
JOSEPH MANUMIK, BOX 54, NUNAM IQUA, AK 99666
PAUL MANUMIK, BOX 44, NUNAM IQUA, AK 99666
MARY MARTINEZ, 11215 TRAILS END RD, ANCHORAGE, AK 99507
CLEMENT MATTHIAS, BOX 20150, KOTLIK, AK 99620
RONALD MCCALLISTER, 631 RUTH ESTATES RD, FAIRBANKS, AK 99712
CHRISTOPHER MIKE, BOX 96, SAINT MARYS, AK 99658
DAVID MIKE, BOX 20130, KOTLIK, AK 99620
EMIL MIKE, BOX 20130, KOTLIK, AK 99620
GREGORY MIKE, BOX 71041, STEBBINS, AK 99671
NIMERON MIKE, BOX 71088, STEBBINS, AK 99671
ROGER MIKE, BOX 71078, STEBBINS, AK 99671
HENRY MINOCK, BOX 5007, PILOT STATION, AK 99650
MARTIN MINOCK, BOX 5078, PILOT STATION, AK 99650
PETER MINOCK, BOX 85, RUSSIAN MISSION, AK 99657
SHEILA MINOCK, BOX 85, RUSSIAN MISSION, AK 99657
JASON MOEN, 5510 E RUTAN AVE, WASILLA, AK 99654
ALLEN MOORE, BOX 61, EMMONAK, AK 99581
CALVIN MOORE, BOX 167, EMMONAK, AK 99581
FREDRICK MOORE, BOX 68, EMMONAK, AK 99581
MARTIN MOORE, BOX 103, EMMONAK, AK 99581
MARTIN MOORE, BOX 116, EMMONAK, AK 99581
MORGAN MOORE, BOX 68, EMMONAK, AK 99581
ROBERT MOORE, BOX 55, EMMONAK, AK 99581
JOHN MOSES, BOX 32038, MOUNTAIN VILLAGE, AK 99632
STANLEY MOSES, BOX 215, ALAKANUK, AK 99554
JOHN MOXIE, GEN DEL, MARSHALL, AK 99585
FRANKLIN MURPHY, BOX 117, EMMONAK, AK 99581
GEORGE MURPHY, BOX 117, EMMONAK, AK 99581
JOSEPH MURPHY, BOX 21, SHELDON POINT, AK 99666
LORRAINE MURPHY, BOX 56, ALAKANUK, AK 99554
MATTHEW MURPHY, BOX 51, NUNAM IQUA, AK 99666
NOLAN MURPHY, BOX 20157, KOTLIK, AK 99620
BILLY MYERS, BOX 5113, PILOT STATION, AK 99650
NICKY MYERS, BOX 5144, PILOT STATION, AK 99650

SARAH MYERS, BOX 5023, PILOT STATION, AK 99650
THOMAS MYOMICK, BOX 66, EMMONAK, AK 99581
KENNETH N.H.VASKA, BOX 64, RUSSIAN MISSION, AK 99657
MYRON NANENG, BOX 1226, BETHEL, AK 99559
CLINT NASHOANAK, BOX 232, SAINT MARYS, AK 99658
ARLENE NICK, BOX 5081, PILOT STATION, AK 99650
DIMITRI NICK, BOX 5087, PILOT STATION, AK 99650
EXODUS NICK, BOX 5087, PILOT STATION, AK 99650
JONATHAN NICK, BOX 5053, PILOT STATION, AK 99650
LUTHER NICK, BOX 2172, BETHEL, AK 99559
MARIA NICK, BOX 5087, PILOT STATION, AK 99650
MARTIN NICK, BOX 67, RUSSIAN MISSION, AK 99657
PATRICK NICK, BOX 5064, PILOT STATION, AK 99650
REX NICK, BOX 5087, PILOT STATION, AK 99650
CAROLINE NOBLE, BOX 10, NUNAM IQUA, AK 99666
DANIEL ODINZOFF, BOX 20027, KOTLIK, AK 99620
JOSEPH ODINZOFF, BOX 20053, KOTLIK, AK 99620
CYRIL OKITKUN, BOX 20117, KOTLIK, AK 99620
CYRIL OKITKUN, BOX 20178, KOTLIK, AK 99620
DARRYL OKITKUN, BOX 20118, KOTLIK, AK 99620
DONOVAN OKITKUN, BOX 20142, KOTLIK, AK 99620
DUNCAN OKITKUN, BOX 20142, KOTLIK, AK 99620
GERALDINE OKITKUN, BOX 20105, KOTLIK, AK 99620
HARRY OKITKUN, BOX 20054, KOTLIK, AK 99620
LEWIS OKITKUN, BOX 20104, KOTLIK, AK 99620
MARVIN OKITKUN, BOX 20142, KOTLIK, AK 99620
PETER OKITKUN, BOX 20036, KOTLIK, AK 99620
REYNOLD OKITKUN, BOX 20104, KOTLIK, AK 99620
WAYNE OKITKUN, BOX 20137, KOTLIK, AK 99620
JOHN OKTOYAK, BOX 11, EMMONAK, AK 99581
LANNY OKTOYAK, BOX 202, EMMONAK, AK 99581
MATILDA OKTOYAK, BOX 11, EMMONAK, AK 99581
TILLIE OKTOYUK, BOX 51, EMMONAK, AK 99581
IRWIN ONEY, BOX 18, ALAKANUK, AK 99554
JACOB OTTEN, BOX 64, SAINT MICHAEL, AK 99659
MARTHA OUTWATER, BOX 711, NOME, AK 99762
ROBERT OWLETUCK, BOX 101, MARSHALL, AK 99585
MELVIN P.R.TEELUK, BOX 20068, KOTLIK, AK 99620
AMY PANIPTCHUK, BOX 262, MOUNTAIN VILLAGE, AK 99632
SAUL PANIPTCHUK, BOX 54, SHAKTOOLIK, AK 99771
MICHAEL PAPP, BOX 121, MARSHALL, AK 99585
ALOYSIUS PATRICK, BOX 124, ALAKANUK, AK 99554
LEONARD PATTON, BOX 116, BETHEL, AK 99559
BRENT PAUKAN, BOX 71, SAINT MARYS, AK 99658
DAWSON PAUKAN, BOX 205, SAINT MARYS, AK 99658
JAMES PAUKAN, BOX 76, SAINT MARYS, AK 99658
JOHN PAUKAN, BOX 116, SAINT MARYS, AK 99658
RENA PAUKAN, BOX 177, SAINT MARYS, AK 99658
RORY PAUKAN, BOX 141, SAINT MARYS, AK 99658
SVEN PAUKAN, BOX 141, SAINT MARYS, AK 99658
KENNETH PAUL, BOX 15, EMMONAK, AK 99581
MARVIN PAUL, BOX 85, ALAKANUK, AK 99554
RODNEY PAUL, BOX 91, ALAKANUK, AK 99554
RONNIE PAUL, BOX 5112, PILOT STATION, AK 99650
ALPHONSUS PETE, BOX 11, NUNAM IQUA, AK 99666
DALE PETE, BOX 15, NUNAM IQUA, AK 99666
DARLENE PETE, BOX 15, NUNAM IQUA, AK 99666
FREDERICK PETE, BOX 71089, STEBBINS, AK 99671
JOHN PETE, BOX 96, STEBBINS, AK 99671
STANLEY PETE, BOX 15, NUNAM IQUA, AK 99666
CHERYL PETEROFF, BOX 117, MARSHALL, AK 99585
LEROY PETERS, BOX 91, HOLY CROSS, AK 99602
RICHARD PETERS, 1613 WASHINGTON DR #B, FAIRBANKS, AK 99709
DAVID PETERSON, BOX 32040, MOUNTAIN VILLAGE, AK 99632
DAVID PETERSON, BOX 32194, MOUNTAIN VILLAGE, AK 99632
FREDERICK PETERSON, BOX 82, SAINT MARYS, AK 99658

SALMON FISHING LIST—GILLNET

GEORGE PETERSON, BOX 356, SAINT MARYS, AK 99658
HOWARD PETERSON, BOX 32263, MOUNTAIN VILLAGE, AK 99632
SARAH PETERSON, BOX 32222, MOUNTAIN VILLAGE, AK 99632
BENJAMIN PHILLIP, BOX 287, ALAKANUK, AK 99554
EDWARD PHILLIP, BOX 87, ALAKANUK, AK 99554
PIUS PHILLIP, BOX 185, ALAKANUK, AK 99554
SIMEON PHILLIP, BOX 42, ALAKANUK, AK 99554
TRACEY PHILLIP, BOX 255, ALAKANUK, AK 99554
YAGO PITKA, BOX 92, RUSSIAN MISSION, AK 99657
ELIAS POLTY, BOX 41, SAINT MARYS, AK 99658
HEATHER POLTY, 6130 BLACKBERRY ST #B, ANCHORAGE, AK 99502
LESTER POLTY, BOX 5002, PILOT STATION, AK 99650
SAGE PORTER, BOX 112, ALAKANUK, AK 99554
KEITH POST, BOX 233, ALAKANUK, AK 99554
TASHA POST, BOX 233, ALAKANUK, AK 99554
ANTHONY PRINCE, BOX 20128, KOTLIK, AK 99620
CHARLES PRINCE, BOX 216, SAINT MARYS, AK 99658
FRANCIS PRINCE, BOX 20084, KOTLIK, AK 99620
FRANCIS PRINCE, BOX 20084, KOTLIK, AK 99620
JAKE PRINCE, BOX 125, SAINT MARYS, AK 99658
JESSICA PRINCE, BOX 20247, KOTLIK, AK 99620
JOSEPH PRINCE, BOX 5092, PILOT STATION, AK 99650
LAURIE PRINCE, BOX 20112, KOTLIK, AK 99620
RYAN PRINCE, BOX 20084, KOTLIK, AK 99620
SIMEON PRINCE, BOX 327, SAINT MARYS, AK 99658
THOMAS PRINCE, BOX 20061, KOTLIK, AK 99620
JOHN QUEENIE, BOX 32334, MOUNTAIN VILLAGE, AK 99632
IRENE R.K.WILLIAMS, BOX 20002, KOTLIK, AK 99620
LEONARD RAMOTH, BOX 33, SCAMMON BAY, AK 99662
ANTHONY RAPHAEL, BOX 51, SHELDON POINT, AK 99666
PAUL RAPHAEL, BOX 18, NUNAM IQUA, AK 99666
WILFRED RAPHAEL, GENERAL DELIVERY, NUNAM IQUA, AK 99666
ADAM RAYMOND, BOX 106, STEBBINS, AK 99671
NITA REARDEN, 1284 LAKESHORE DR, HOMER, AK 99603
ARTHUR REDFOX, BOX 105, EMMONAK, AK 99581
CAROL REDFOX, BOX 32067, MOUNTAIN VILLAGE, AK 99632
CHARLES REDFOX, BOX 282, EMMONAK, AK 99581
CHRISTOPHER REDFOX, BOX 32067, MOUNTAIN VILLAGE, AK 99632
DOUGLAS REDFOX, BOX 232, EMMONAK, AK 99581
JACOB REDFOX, BOX 194, EMMONAK, AK 99581
MARGARET REDFOX, BOX 97, EMMONAK, AK 99581
SCOTT RILEY, BOX 15, SAINT MARYS, AK 99658
WILLIAM RILEY, BOX 326, SAINT MARYS, AK 99658
BILLY RIVERS, BOX 73, SCAMMON BAY, AK 99662
ISAAC RIVERS, BOX 64, SCAMMON BAY, AK 99662
OSCAR RIVERS, BOX 143, KWETHLUK, AK 99621
TYRONE ROBINSON, 2207 ROOSEVELT DR #8, ANCHORAGE, AK 99517
KEONI S.W.PRINCE, BOX 20247, KOTLIK, AK 99620
RALPH SACCHEUS, BOX 57, ELIM, AK 99739
DAVID SALLISON, BOX 296, SAINT MARYS, AK 99658
CAROLINE SANDERS, BOX 527, BETHEL, AK 99559
JEFFREY SANDERS, BOX 527, BETHEL, AK 99559
ROBERT SAVETILIK, BOX 20125, KOTLIK, AK 99620
ROGER SEAVOY, BOX 3, MCGRATH, AK 99627
TIMOTHY SERGIE, 7333 LINDEN DR, ANCHORAGE, AK 99502
VASILLY SERGIE, BOX 87, MARSHALL, AK 99585
PATRICK SETON, BOX 20032, KOTLIK, AK 99620
DENIS SHELDEN, BOX 103, ALAKANUK, AK 99554
ANTHONY SHEPPARD, BOX 32140, MOUNTAIN VILLAGE, AK 99632
STANISLAUS SHEPPARD, BOX 32154, MOUNTAIN VILLAGE, AK 99632
TRINA SHEPPARD, 3240 PENLAND PKWY #274, ANCHORAGE, AK 99508
AMBROSE SHORTY, BOX 95, EMMONAK, AK 99581
ANDREA SHORTY, BOX 146, MARSHALL, AK 99585
ELIZABETH SHORTY, BOX 46, MARSHALL, AK 99585
CHAZ SIMS, 2810 W NORTHERN LIGHTS #10, ANCHORAGE, AK 99517

EUGENE SINKA, BOX 20107, KOTLIK, AK 99620
THOMAS SINKA, BOX 20133, KOTLIK, AK 99620
DARRYL SIPARY, BOX 203, SAINT MARYS, AK 99658
DEREK SIPARY, BOX 222, SAINT MARYS, AK 99658
OTIS SIPARY, BOX 182 LOT 6 BLK 6 SIPARY RD, SAINT MARYS, AK 99658
ALOYSIUS SMITH, BOX 51, SCAMMON BAY, AK 99662
CHARLES SMITH, BOX 07, EMMONAK, AK 99581
AARON STANISLAUS, BOX 152, ALAKANUK, AK 99554
HARRY STANISLAUS, BOX 223, ALAKANUK, AK 99554
ANDREW STEPHANOFF, BOX 27, RUSSIAN MISSION, AK 99657
BYRON STEPHANOFF, BOX 105, RUSSIAN MISSION, AK 99657
ANDREW STERN, BOX 62, NUNAM IQUA, AK 99666
DANIEL STEVENS, BOX 339, SAINT MARYS, AK 99658
EUGENE STEVENS, BOX 32138, MOUNTAIN VILLAGE, AK 99632
WILFRED STEVENS, BOX 231, SAINT MARYS, AK 99658
GEORGE STRONGHEART, 4031 LORE RD SPC #7, ANCHORAGE, AK 99507
JAMES STRONGHEART, GEN DEL, ALAKANUK, AK 99554
JOHN STRONGHEART, BOX 43, NUNAM IQUA, AK 99666
JOHN STRONGHEART, BOX 82, ALAKANUK, AK 99554
JOHN STRONGHEART, BOX 43, SHELDON POINT, AK 99666
MARY STRONGHEART, BOX 82, ALAKANUK, AK 99554
OLE STRONGHEART, LOWER YUKON RIVER GEN DEL, ALAKANUK, AK 99554
NICK SUGAR, LOWER YUKON RIVER, EMMONAK, AK 99581
HERSCHEL SUNDOWN, BOX 152, SCAMMON BAY, AK 99662
THOMAS SUNDOWN, BOX 67, SCAMMON BAY, AK 99662
WALTER SUOMELA, BOX 3092, HOMER, AK 99603
JEFFERY SUTTER, BOX 32071, MOUNTAIN VILLAGE, AK 99632
PIUS TEELUK, BOX 20114, KOTLIK, AK 99620
CHARLIE TEGANLAKLA, BOX 43, MARSHALL, AK 99585
DAVID TEGANLAKLA, BOX 242, EMMONAK, AK 99581
KAMERON TEGANLAKLA, BOX 242, EMMONAK, AK 99581
GREGORY TEVE, 5018 SOUTH HAMPTON DR, ANCHORAGE, AK 99503
ANDREW THOMPSON, BOX 111, SAINT MARYS, AK 99658
DUANE THOMPSON, BOX 32171, MOUNTAIN VILLAGE, AK 99632
FRANCIS THOMPSON, BOX 111, SAINT MARYS, AK 99658
KYLE THOMPSON, BOX 111, SAINT MARYS, AK 99658
LYLE THOMPSON, BOX 363, SAINT MARYS, AK 99658
NICHOLAS THOMPSON, BOX 208, SAINT MARYS, AK 99658
PAUL THOMPSON, BOX 86, SAINT MARYS, AK 99658
TROY THOMPSON, BOX 208, SAINT MARYS, AK 99658
CHARLOTTE TIKIUN, BOX 32004, MOUNTAIN VILLAGE, AK 99632
CHRISTOPHER TINKER, BOX 92, SAINT MARYS, AK 99658
ELIA TINKER, BOX 194, SAINT MARYS, AK 99658
JOHN TINKER, BOX 5106, PILOT STATION, AK 99650
TITUS TOMAGANUK, BOX 98, HOOPER BAY, AK 99604
JOHN TONUCHUK, BOX 20153, KOTLIK, AK 99620
KADEN TONUCHUK, 3930 E GLENDALE, WASILLA, AK 99654
WALTER TONUCHUK, BOX 20156, KOTLIK, AK 99620
WILBUR TONUCHUK, BOX 20088, KOTLIK, AK 99620
PAUL TONY, BOX 20078, KOTLIK, AK 99620
RONALD TRADER, BOX 243, EMMONAK, AK 99581
GABRIEL TUCKER, BOX 86, EMMONAK, AK 99581
MAGGIE TUCKER, BOX 38, EMMONAK, AK 99581
NICHOLAS TUCKER, BOX 25, EMMONAK, AK 99581
NICHOLAS TUCKER, BOX 178, EMMONAK, AK 99581
DAVID TUNUTMOAK, BOX 157, SCAMMON BAY, AK 99662
WILLIAM TWETO, BOX 225, SAINT MARYS, AK 99658
CYRIL TYSON, BOX 152, ALAKANUK, AK 99554
ESTHER TYSON, BOX 52, SAINT MARYS, AK 99658
FRANCIS TYSON, BOX 211, ALAKANUK, AK 99554
JOHN TYSON, BOX 42, SAINT MARYS, AK 99658
JULIAN TYSON, BOX 221, SAINT MARYS, AK 99658
PETER TYSON, BOX 52, SAINT MARYS, AK 99658
JOSEPH UISOK, BOX 20087, KOTLIK, AK 99620
ROBERT UISOK, %EVAN UISOK BOX 132, EMMONAK, AK 99581

SALMON FISHING LIST—GILLNET

SIMEON UISOK, BOX 187, EMMONAK, AK 99581
BYRON ULAK, BOX 102, SCAMMON BAY, AK 99662
SIMEON ULAK, BOX 29, SCAMMON BAY, AK 99662
JEFFERY UNOK, BOX 20075, KOTLIK, AK 99620
JOHN UNOK, BOX 20076, KOTLIK, AK 99620
MINNIE UNOK, 5058 A HOLLIS AVE, FT CAMPBELL, KY 42223
WILLIAM UNOK, BOX 20034, KOTLIK, AK 99620
CAROLYN UTTEREYUK, BOX 191, SCAMMON BAY, AK 99662
JOHN UTTEREYUK, BOX 191, SCAMMON BAY, AK 99662
LAWRENCE UTTEREYUK, BOX 25, SCAMMON BAY, AK 99662
ARTHUR VASKA, BOX 14, RUSSIAN MISSION, AK 99657
RHY VERG.IN, 19415 LINDA LN, KASILOF, AK 99610
MARLIN VIRG.IN, BOX 232095, ANCHORAGE, AK 99523
GEORGE WAGNER, 825 MULCHATNA DR, WASILLA, AK 99654
HAROLD WALKER, 2760 RUBY DR, ANCHORAGE, AK 99502
JAMES WALKER, BOX 168, HOLY CROSS, AK 99602
CLIFFORD WALTERS, BOX 341, MOUNTAIN VILLAGE, AK 99632
GLENN WALTERS, BOX 32167, MOUNTAIN VILLAGE, AK 99632
FRANCINE WASKA, BOX 98, EMMONAK, AK 99581
GEORGE WASKA, BOX 20023, KOTLIK, AK 99620
RALPH WASKA, BOX 20021, KOTLIK, AK 99620
RAYMOND WASKA, BOX 46, EMMONAK, AK 99581
RAYMOND WASKA, BOX 98, EMMONAK, AK 99581
STANLEY WASKA, BOX 236, EMMONAK, AK 99581
BARBARA WASKEY, BOX 32310, MOUNTAIN VILLAGE, AK 99632
MATHEW WASKEY, BOX 32355, MOUNTAIN VILLAGE, AK 99632
MITCHELL WASKEY, BOX 20328, KOTLIK, AK 99620
THOMAS WASKEY, BOX 312, MOUNTAIN VILLAGE, AK 99632
JESAN WASKEY.WALKER, BOX 32287, MOUNTAIN VILLAGE, AK 99632
ALICE WASKY, BOX 117, ALAKANUK, AK 99554
VERONICA WASSILI, 1427 INLET PL, ANCHORAGE, AK 99501
STEPHANIE WEAVER, BOX 207, ALAKANUK, AK 99554
CHRIS WEINGARTH, BOX 74, SAINT MARYS, AK 99658
ERIK WEINGARTH, BOX 74, SAINT MARYS, AK 99658
NITA WEINGARTH, BOX 74, SAINT MARYS, AK 99658
CLIFFORD WESTDAHL, BOX 218, SAINT MARYS, AK 99658
WILLIAM WESTDAHL, 8637 VERNON ST, ANCHORAGE, AK 99502
BILLY WESTLOCK, BOX 184, EMMONAK, AK 99581
JOHN WESTLOCK, BOX 44, EMMONAK, AK 99581
TONY WESTLOCK, BOX 184, EMMONAK, AK 99581
ANDREW WHITE, BOX 58, MARSHALL, AK 99585
ANITA WIGLEY, BOX 95, RUSSIAN MISSION, AK 99657
JACK WILDE, BOX 32226, MOUNTAIN VILLAGE, AK 99632
LAQUISHA WILLIAMS, BOX 123, SCAMMON BAY, AK 99662
RUDOLPH WILLIAMS, BOX 20002, KOTLIK, AK 99620
ALICE WILSON, 1206 E 8TH AVE #1040, ANCHORAGE, AK 99501
CASSANDRA WILSON, BOX 91750, ANCHORAGE, AK 99509
CLARENCE WILSON, BOX 172, HOOPER BAY, AK 99604
GABRIEL WILSON, BOX 148, SCAMMON BAY, AK 99662
MARK WILSON, 9780 W STANLEY DR, WASILLA, AK 99623
GALEN XAVIER, BOX 245, ALAKANUK, AK 99554
NORMAN XAVIER, BOX 5005, PILOT STATION, AK 99650
PEARL YUNAK, BOX 5121, PILOT STATION, AK 99650
JACK YUPANIK, BOX 3, EMMONAK, AK 99581
PHILIP YUPANIK, BOX 58, EMMONAK, AK 99581

SALMON, GILLNET, NORTON SOUND

ARTHUR AMAKTOOLIK, BOX 1856, NOME, AK 99762
DORIS AMAKTOOLIK, BOX 39067, ELIM, AK 99739
MARY.LOU AMAKTOOLIK, BOX 62052, GOLOVIN, AK 99762
STANLEY AMAROK, BOX 62011, GOLOVIN, AK 99762
ERIC AMUKTOOLIK, BOX 62101, GOLOVIN, AK 99762
GABRIEL ANAGICK, BOX 87, UNALAKLEET, AK 99684
WILSON ANGNABOOGUK, 6001 ACHESON LN, ANCHORAGE, AK 99504
JAY ASICKSIK, BOX 71035, SHAKTOOLIK, AK 99771
DUANE AUKON, BOX 39003, ELIM, AK 99739

DONALD AULIYE, BOX 96, SHAKTOOLIK, AK 99771
RITA AULIYE, BOX 96, SHAKTOOLIK, AK 99771
JOHN BAHNKE, BOX 1873, NOME, AK 99762
KEVIN BAHNKE, BOX 1792, NOME, AK 99762
SIMON BEKOALOK, BOX 83, SHAKTOOLIK, AK 99771
ROY BRADLEY, BOX 67, ELIM, AK 99739
BOYD BRANCH, BOX 277, UNALAKLEET, AK 99684
CHARLIE BROWN, BOX 62112, GOLOVIN, AK 99762
MELVIN BROWN, BOX 16, UNALAKLEET, AK 99684
CAROL CHARLES, BOX 177, UNALAKLEET, AK 99684
EMMANUEL CHARLES, BOX 53103, KOYUK, AK 99753
LEO CHARLES, BOX 53048, KOYUK, AK 99753
WILLIAM CHRISTENSEN, BOX 287, SUTTON, AK 99674
ALFRED COMMACK, BOX 81, UNALAKLEET, AK 99684
PAYTON COMMACK, BOX 81, UNALAKLEET, AK 99684
THOMAS D.A.SACCHEUS, BOX 39053, ELIM, AK 99739
BENJAMIN DANIELS, BOX 31, ELIM, AK 99739
ERIC DANIELS, BOX 39083, ELIM, AK 99739
HARRY DANIELS, BOX 39037, ELIM, AK 99739
JERRY DANIELS, 35305 RAVENWOOD ST, SOLDOTNA, AK 99669
KATIE DANIELS, BOX 203, UNALAKLEET, AK 99684
RONALD DAVENA, 2946 BRITTANY PL, ANCHORAGE, AK 99504
LAWRENCE DAVIS, 12631 TANADA LOOP, ANCHORAGE, AK 99515
CHARLES DEGNAN, BOX 180, UNALAKLEET, AK 99684
BRANDON DEWEY, BOX 53138, KOYUK, AK 99753
JOHN DEXTER, BOX 33, POINT HOPE, AK 99766
GALEN DOTY, BOX 308, UNALAKLEET, AK 99684
BEN EAKON, BOX 61, UNALAKLEET, AK 99684
GORDON EAKON, BOX 75, UNALAKLEET, AK 99684
JEFFREY ERICKSON, BOX 301, UNALAKLEET, AK 99684
KAREN ERICKSON, BOX 216, UNALAKLEET, AK 99684
KARL ERICKSON, BOX 154, UNALAKLEET, AK 99684
CYRUS ETAGEAK, BOX 71032, SHAKTOOLIK, AK 99771
LARRY FAGERSTROM, BOX 62065, GOLOVIN, AK 99762
HOWARD FARLEY, BOX 1423, NOME, AK 99762
FRANKLIN FOCIA, BOX 187, UNALAKLEET, AK 99684
PETE G.J.KATONGAN, BOX 105, UNALAKLEET, AK 99684
JOSEPH GAJDOSIK, BOX 39, UNALAKLEET, AK 99684
JAMES HANSEN, 242 MULDOON RD, ANCHORAGE, AK 99504
BRICE HARDY, 214 E KING APT B, NOME, AK 99762
ROBIN HARPER.CAUDILL, BOX 172, UNALAKLEET, AK 99684
ANTHONY HAUGEN, BOX 122, UNALAKLEET, AK 99684
NORMAN HAUGEN, BOX 145, UNALAKLEET, AK 99684
MERLIN HENRY, BOX 53024, KOYUK, AK 99753
WAYNE HENRY, BOX 62043, GOLOVIN, AK 99762
HARLAND HOLLY, GEN DEL, COUNCIL, AK 99762
KENNETH HUGHES, BOX 1430, NOME, AK 99762
PATRICIA HUHTA, BOX 355, UNALAKLEET, AK 99684
REESE HUHTA, BOX 355, UNALAKLEET, AK 99684
ELLEN HUNT, BOX 92, SHAKTOOLIK, AK 99771
NELSON HYKES, 1812 CINDYLEE LN, ANCHORAGE, AK 99507
GUY IONE, BOX 52, WHITE MOUNTAIN, AK 99784
ALEXANDER IVANOFF, BOX 68, UNALAKLEET, AK 99684
ALLEN IVANOFF, BOX 73, UNALAKLEET, AK 99684
BURKHER IVANOFF, BOX 177, UNALAKLEET, AK 99684
DEAN IVANOFF, BOX 134, UNALAKLEET, AK 99684
DYLAN IVANOFF, BOX 196, UNALAKLEET, AK 99684
FRED IVANOFF, BOX 306, UNALAKLEET, AK 99684
HENRY IVANOFF, BOX 196, UNALAKLEET, AK 99684
JACOB IVANOFF, BOX 337, UNALAKLEET, AK 99684
JERRY IVANOFF, BOX 102, UNALAKLEET, AK 99684
LARRY IVANOFF, BOX 37, UNALAKLEET, AK 99684
RALPH IVANOFF, BOX 96, UNALAKLEET, AK 99684
RALPH IVANOFF, BOX 235, UNALAKLEET, AK 99684
RYAN IVANOFF, BOX 39103, ELIM, AK 99739
SERGEI IVANOFF, BOX 34, UNALAKLEET, AK 99684

SALMON FISHING LIST—GILLNET

SHERILEE IVANOFF, PMB 68, UNALAKLEET, AK 99684
STEPHEN IVANOFF, BOX 235, UNALAKLEET, AK 99684
WEAVER IVANOFF, BOX 113, UNALAKLEET, AK 99684
YANNITA IVANOFF, BOX 306, UNALAKLEET, AK 99684
ZACHARY IVANOFF, BOX 73, UNALAKLEET, AK 99684
EDWARD JACKSON, BOX 71111, SHAKTOOLIK, AK 99771
GEORGE JACKSON, BOX 112, UNALAKLEET, AK 99684
MATTHEW JACKSON, BOX 71004, SHAKTOOLIK, AK 99771
CHRISTINE JEMEWOUK, BOX 77, ELIM, AK 99739
JOHNNY JEMEWOUK, BOX 39077, ELIM, AK 99739
FRANK JOHNSON, BOX 117, UNALAKLEET, AK 99684
HARRY JOHNSON, BOX 56, UNALAKLEET, AK 99684
MYRTLE JOHNSON, BOX 608, NOME, AK 99762
SIKULIK JOHNSON, BOX 222, UNALAKLEET, AK 99684
TRAEGER JOHNSON, BOX 56, UNALAKLEET, AK 99684
JEFFERY JONES, BOX 396, UNALAKLEET, AK 99684
WESLEY JONES, BOX 343, UNALAKLEET, AK 99684
JALEN KATCHATAG, BOX 343, UNALAKLEET, AK 99684
JERRY KATCHATAG, BOX 62103, GOLOVIN, AK 99762
JOSEPH KATCHATAG, BOX 165, UNALAKLEET, AK 99684
SHELDON KATCHATAG, BOX 159, UNALAKLEET, AK 99684
VAN KATCHATAG, BOX 73, SHAKTOOLIK, AK 99771
FRANK KAVAIRLOOK, BOX 91, ELIM, AK 99739
SCOTT KENT, BOX 85, NOME, AK 99762
PATRICK KIMOKTOAK, BOX 53116, KOYUK, AK 99753
STEVEN KIMOKTOAK, BOX 53055, KOYUK, AK 99753
PHILLIP KNISELEY, 2813 KIMBERLIE CT #1, ANCHORAGE, AK 99508
GABRIEL KOTONGAN, BOX 39006, ELIM, AK 99739
KENNETH KOTONGAN, BOX 39012, ELIM, AK 99739
KOLLIN KOTONGAN, BOX 303, UNALAKLEET, AK 99684
WAYNE KOTONGAN, BOX 233, UNALAKLEET, AK 99684
WILLIAM KOUTCHAK, BOX 155, UNALAKLEET, AK 99684
JUNE KUGELMANN, 17500 POINT LENA LOOP RD, JUNEAU, AK 99801
SHANE L.C.SACCHEUS, BOX 39026, ELIM, AK 99739
ERIC LARSEN, BOX 684, NOME, AK 99762
CHARLES LEWIS, BOX 62035, GOLOVIN, AK 99762
THERESA LINCOLN, 10260 SEXTANT CIR, ANCHORAGE, AK 99515
CHARLES LOCKWOOD, BOX 84, UNALAKLEET, AK 99684
MAGGIE LUDWIG, BOX 1152, NOME, AK 99762
KEVIN MCDONALD, BOX 53062, KOYUK, AK 99753
KEVIN MICHAEL, BOX 241931, ANCHORAGE, AK 99524
CHESTER MILLETT, BOX 353, UNALAKLEET, AK 99684
RACHEL MOORE, BOX 56, SHAKTOOLIK, AK 99771
TIMOTHY MOORE, BOX 39092, ELIM, AK 99739
ENOCH MOSES, GEN DEL, ELIM, AK 99739
MAUDE MOSES, BOX 62062, GOLOVIN, AK 99762
JEFFREY MURRAY, BOX 72, ELIM, AK 99739
NATHAN MURRAY, BOX 39087, ELIM, AK 99739
PAUL NAGARUK, BOX 31, ELIM, AK 99739
ANDREW NAKARAK, BOX 71028, SHAKTOOLIK, AK 99771
LARRY NAKARAK, BOX 17, UNALAKLEET, AK 99684
MORRIS NAKARAK, BOX 39061, ELIM, AK 99739
HENRY NANOUK, BOX 43, UNALAKLEET, AK 99684
JOLENE NANOUK, BOX 343, UNALAKLEET, AK 99684
MARTIN NANOUK, BOX 843, KOTZEBUE, AK 99752
AARON NASSUK, BOX 73, KOYUK, AK 99753
CHRISTOPHER NASSUK, BOX 53034, KOYUK, AK 99753
RICHARD NASSUK, BOX 53037, KOYUK, AK 99753
ROGER NASSUK, BOX 52, KOYUK, AK 99753
MICHAEL NICHOLS, BOX 272, NOME, AK 99762
JOHN NOFFSKER, BOX 1171, NOME, AK 99762
DONALD OLIVER, BOX 62027, GOLOVIN, AK 99762
MARGARET OLSON, BOX 1798, NOME, AK 99762
ERIC OSBORNE, BOX 1761, NOME, AK 99762
JOSHUA OSBORNE, BOX 1561, NOME, AK 99762

MALA OTTON, BOX 53136, KOYUK, AK 99753
TROY OTTON, BOX 53044, KOYUK, AK 99753
MARILYN OYOUMICK, BOX 112, UNALAKLEET, AK 99684
EVERSON PANIPTCHUK, BOX 102, SHAKTOOLIK, AK 99771
HERBERT PANIPTCHUK, BOX 24, UNALAKLEET, AK 99684
JOSEPH PANIPTCHUK, BOX 81, UNALAKLEET, AK 99684
REUBEN PANIPTCHUK, BOX 102, SHAKTOOLIK, AK 99771
ROY PANIPTCHUK, BOX 3, SHAKTOOLIK, AK 99771
SAUL PANIPTCHUK, BOX 54, SHAKTOOLIK, AK 99771
SILAS PANIPTCHUK, BOX 25, SHAKTOOLIK, AK 99771
CARL PAUL, BOX 66, ELIM, AK 99739
MARLIN PAUL, BOX 39066, ELIM, AK 99739
CLARK PEARSON, BOX 1733, CORDOVA, AK 99574
STEVEN PERRY, BOX 71102, SHAKTOOLIK, AK 99771
DEAN PETERSON, BOX 62032, GOLOVIN, AK 99762
JASON PETERSON, 4332 BIRCH RUN DR, ANCHORAGE, AK 99507
JOHN PETERSON, BOX 62032, GOLOVIN, AK 99762
JORY PETERSON, BOX 387, UNALAKLEET, AK 99684
STUART ROCK, BOX 18, SHAKTOOLIK, AK 99771
KYLE RYAN, BOX 254, UNALAKLEET, AK 99684
ADAM SACCHEUS, BOX 39038, ELIM, AK 99739
ALBERT SACCHEUS, BOX 87, UNALAKLEET, AK 99684
CHARLES SACCHEUS, 515 EAST 12TH #8, ANCHORAGE, AK 99501
CHARLES SACCHEUS, BOX 39090, ELIM, AK 99739
RUSSELL SACCHEUS, BOX 117, ELIM, AK 99739
FRED SAGOONICK, BOX 45, SHAKTOOLIK, AK 99771
MELANIE SAGOONICK, BOX 195, UNALAKLEET, AK 99684
THOMAS SAGOONICK, BOX 71031, SHAKTOOLIK, AK 99771
TONIA SAGOONICK, BOX 12, SHAKTOOLIK, AK 99771
LANCE SAMPSON, BOX 62041, GOLOVIN, AK 99762
THOMAS SAMPSON, BOX 71082, SHAKTOOLIK, AK 99771
CLARENCE SAVETILIK, BOX 14, SHAKTOOLIK, AK 99771
TREVOR SAVETILIK, BOX 108, SHAKTOOLIK, AK 99771
CASEY SHERMAN, BOX 1184, NOME, AK 99762
CODY SHERMAN, BOX 1184, NOME, AK 99762
MIKAEL SHERMAN, BOX 117, UNALAKLEET, AK 99684
LUKE SMITH, BOX 84074, WHITE MOUNTAIN, AK 99784
COREY SOCKPEALUK, BOX 53014, KOYUK, AK 99753
DALE SOOKIAYAK, BOX 78, SHAKTOOLIK, AK 99771
LARS SOOKIAYAK, BOX 71042, SHAKTOOLIK, AK 99771
MARLIN SOOKIAYAK, BOX 71058, SHAKTOOLIK, AK 99771
RUBY SOOSUK, 1200 W DIMOND #1442, ANCHORAGE, AK 99501
CLIFF SOPER, BOX 208, CANTWELL, AK 99729
JASON TAKAK, BOX 87, ELIM, AK 99739
KENNETH TAKAK, BOX 39074, ELIM, AK 99739
KIMBERLY TAKAK, BOX 113, ELIM, AK 99739
MARVIN TAKAK, BOX 113, ELIM, AK 99739
RANDALL TAKAK, BOX 108, SHAKTOOLIK, AK 99771
ROY TAKAK, BOX 71017, SHAKTOOLIK, AK 99771
ALICE TOSHAVIK, BOX 132, UNALAKLEET, AK 99684
JASON TOSHAVIK, BOX 132, UNALAKLEET, AK 99684
AMBROSE TOWARAK, BOX 89, UNALAKLEET, AK 99684
CLARENCE TOWARAK, BOX 175, UNALAKLEET, AK 99684
DONALD TOWARAK, BOX 175, UNALAKLEET, AK 99684
ISAIAH TOWARAK, BOX 40, UNALAKLEET, AK 99684
MERLE TOWARAK, BOX 273, UNALAKLEET, AK 99684
TYRONE TOWARAK, BOX 89, UNALAKLEET, AK 99684
REID TULLOCH, BOX 291, UNALAKLEET, AK 99684
GEORGE TURNER, BOX 205, UNALAKLEET, AK 99684
LORETTA TWETO, BOX 207, UNALAKLEET, AK 99684
JAMES WEST, BOX 1074, NOME, AK 99762
DARLENE WHITNEY, BOX 1861, NOME, AK 99762
LEONARD WILLOYA, BOX 93, GOLOVIN, AK 99762
JOHN WILSON, BOX 352, UNALAKLEET, AK 99684
GEORGE WOODS, BOX 72, UNALAKLEET, AK 99684

SALMON FISHING LIST—HAND TROLL

GEORGE ABBOTT, 364 VILLAGE ST, JUNEAU, AK 99801
CASIMERO ACEVEDA, BOX 311, KAKE, AK 99830
MANUEL ACEVEDA, BOX 154, KAKE, AK 99830
STEPHEN ACTOR, BOX 240146, DOUGLAS, AK 99824
CLIFFORD ADAMS, CANADIAN SIDE BOX 205, KAKE, AK 99830
HARLAN ADAMS, BOX 2652, SITKA, AK 99835
RICHARD ADAMS, BOX 497, CRAIG, AK 99921
STANLEY ADAMS, BOX 162, KAKE, AK 99830
CLIFFORD ADAMSON, BOX 18075, COFFMAN COVE, AK 99918
WILSON AEGERTER, BOX 1061, WARD COVE, AK 99928
MANUEL AGUILAR, 241 FRONT ST, JUNEAU, AK 99801
RICHARD AHO, BOX 1272, PETERSBURG, AK 99833
GLENN AKINS, 1500 E PUSCH WILDERNESS DR #16205, ORO VALLY, AZ 85737
WILLIAM AKINS, BOX 493, KLAWOCK, AK 99925
GERALD ALBECKER, BOX 1207, HAINES, AK 99827
LAWRENCE ALBECKER, BOX 503, WARD COVE, AK 99928
KIRK ALBRECHT, 101 BURKHART DR APT F 42, SITKA, AK 99835
KIRK ALBRECHT, BOX 1853, SITKA, AK 99835
MARIYAN ALEKSIEV, BOX 853, WRANGELL, AK 99929
JAMES ALLAN, 443 RAMOLA ST, FAIRBANKS, AK 99709
HAROLD ALLARD, BOX 27, PELICAN, AK 99832
FREDRIC ALLEN, 31 MARBLEMOUNT PL, REPUBLIC, WA 99166
MICHAEL ALLEN, BOX 451, WRANGELL, AK 99929
DONALD ALSUP, BOX WWP, KETCHIKAN, AK 99950
JONATHAN ALSUP, BOX 486, TOK, AK 99780
DAVID AMES, 101 DEERFIELD PL, CHEHALIS, WA 98532
BRANZON ANANIA, BOX 8072, PORT ALEXANDER, AK 99836
AARON ANDERSON, 737 HARRIS ST, KETCHIKAN, AK 99901
EDWARD ANDERSON, 14046 N TONGASS HWY, KETCHIKAN, AK 99901
GILBERT ANDERSON, BOX 83, CRAIG, AK 99921
JEROLD ANDERSON, BOX 34, TENAKEE, AK 99841
JOSEPH ANDERSON, BOX 2206, SITKA, AK 99835
RICHARD ANDERSON, 19224 HALWOOD RD, GLENWOOD, MN 56334
ROBERT ANDERSON, 1720 DIKE RD, MOUNT VERNON, WA 98273
ROGER ANDERSON, BOX 2386, REDWOOD CITY, CA 94064
STANLEY ANDERSON, BOX 1705, JUNEAU, AK 99801
SUSAN ANDERSON, 1440 E ST #3, ANCHORAGE, AK 99501
TROY ANDERSON, BOX 837, PETERSBURG, AK 99833
ERIC ANDERSTROM, BOX 879622, WASILLA, AK 99687
MICHAEL ANDRUSS, 47653 ROCKY RD, HALFWAY, OR 97834
PETER ANDRUSS, 20131 COHEN DR, JUNEAU, AK 99801
FREDERICK ANGERMAN, BOX 1, WRANGELL, AK 99929
JOHN ANGERMAN, BOX 849, WRANGELL, AK 99929
LEONARD ANGERMAN, BOX 136, WRANGELL, AK 99929
MERCEDES ANGERMAN, BOX 1, WRANGELL, AK 99929
RUSSELL ANSAY, BOX 102036, ANCHORAGE, AK 99510
BROOKS ARESON, BOX 1356, SITKA, AK 99835
ROBERT ARMSTRONG, BOX 21826, JUNEAU, AK 99802
SUSAN ARRINGTON, BOX 1903, SITKA, AK 99835
BILL ASHBY, BOX 210241, AUKE BAY, AK 99821
MATTHEW ASHENFELTER, BOX 527, KAKE, AK 99830
FLOYD ASHFORD, 985 CLEAR ST, NORTH POLE, AK 99705
EVERETT ATHORP, BOX 526, KLAWOCK, AK 99925
ALEXANDER ATKINSON, BOX 162, METLAKATLA, AK 99926
GARY ATKINSON, BOX 1953, SITKA, AK 99835
RUSTY ATWOOD, BOX 549, CRAIG, AK 99921
ARNOLD AUSTIN, BOX 151, KAKE, AK 99830
RICHARD AUSTIN, GEN DEL, KAKE, AK 99830
ROSS AVILA, 215 WHITE CLIFF AVE, KETCHIKAN, AK 99901
JOHN BABAROVICH, 2027 N AVE, ANACORTES, WA 98221
RICHARD BABAROVICH, 1902 ISLAND VIEW PL, ANACORTES, WA 98221
CURTIS BACH, BOX 32514, JUNEAU, AK 99803
DONALD BAGGS, BOX 343, DOUGLAS, AK 99824
HAROLD BAILEY, BOX 887, WRANGELL, AK 99929
MICHAEL BAINES, 1640 FRITZ COVE RD, JUNEAU, AK 99801

WILLIAM BAINES, BOX 82, METLAKATLA, AK 99926
DAVID BAINTER, BOX 611, GRAYLAND, WA 98547
CURTIS BAIRD, 111 FINN ALLEY, SITKA, AK 99835
KARL BAKER, 417 W 21ST ST, WILMINGTON, DE 19802
MYRON BAKER, BOX 24, POINT BAKER, AK 99927
CHARLES BALDERSON, 7025 ALTA VISTA DR SW, PORT ORCHARD, WA 98366
DEAN BALDWIN, BOX 7212, KETCHIKAN, AK 99901
DREW BAMBER, GEN DEL, SITKA, AK 99835
MARK BAMBER, 353 E NORTH CAMANO DR, CAMANO ISLAND, WA 98282
TIMOTHY BANASZAK, BOX 34915, JUNEAU, AK 99803
JERRY BARBER, BOX 6491, SITKA, AK 99835
DOUGLAS BARKER, BOX 813, WRANGELL, AK 99929
PATRICK BARKER, 204 SHOTGUN ALLEY, SITKA, AK 99835
PATRICK BARKER, 603 SAWMILL CREEK RD, SITKA, AK 99835
LEO BARLOW, 3121 SPINNAKER DR, ANCHORAGE, AK 99516
A BARND, BOX 624, ANACORTES, WA 98221
LOUIS BARR, BOX 210361, AUKE BAY, AK 99821
GAYLORD BARRON, BOX 5706, KETCHIKAN, AK 99901
JAMES BARRY, BOX 135, JUNEAU, AK 99802
CHARLEEN BARTELS, 8044 DAVIDSON AVE, EDNA BAY, AK 99950
DAVID BARTH, BOX 371, SULTAN, WA 98294
GENE BARTOLABA, BOX 501, SITKA, AK 99835
RAYMOND BARTOO, 1745 MENDENHALL PENN RD, JUNEAU, AK 99801
LOUIS BARTOS, 705 COOK ST, KETCHIKAN, AK 99901
FRED BASS, 4794 BUCEY AVE, KETCHIKAN, AK 99901
RANDALL BATES, BOX 34624, JUNEAU, AK 99803
BRUCE BAUER, HC 60 BOX 2892, HAINES, AK 99827
MICHAEL BAUER, BOX 1897, WRANGELL, AK 99929
JAMES BAUMANN, BOX 33, SITKA, AK 99835
TROY BAYNE, BOX 1541, SITKA, AK 99835
RICHARD BEAL, BOX 561, PETERSBURG, AK 99833
JOHN BEALEY, 54070 BEAR CREEK RD, BANDON, OR 97411
ANDREW BEAN, BOX 593, KAKE, AK 99830
CORNELL BEAN, BOX 150, KAKE, AK 99830
HENRICH BEAN, GEN DEL, HOONAH, AK 99829
HENRICH BEAN, BOX 165, KAKE, AK 99830
JOHN BEAN, BOX 5337, KETCHIKAN, AK 99901
JOHN BEAN, BOX PPV, KETCHIKAN, AK 99950
VICTOR BEAN, BOX 171, HOONAH, AK 99829
VICTOR BEAN, BOX 635, HOONAH, AK 99829
WILLIAM BEAN, BOX 122, KAKE, AK 99830
JOHN BECKER, BOX 33082, JUNEAU, AK 99803
JOSEPH BECKS, BOX 2425, JUNEAU, AK 99803
JAY BEEDLE, 9435 GLACIER HWY, JUNEAU, AK 99801
FREDERICK BEGLEY, BOX 535, WARD COVE, AK 99928
JUAN BELCHER, BOX 2300, SITKA, AK 99835
GARY BELL, 3143 LINDEN DR, ANCHORAGE, AK 99502
GARY BELL, BOX 240064, DOUGLAS, AK 99824
ORLANDO BELL, BOX 1609, PETERSBURG, AK 99833
ROBERT BELL, BOX 115, ELFIN COVE, AK 99825
LARRY BEMIS, BOX 192, YAKUTAT, AK 99689
WILLIAM BENDIXEN, BOX 1197, JUNEAU, AK 99802
GERALD BENNETT, 5876 LUND ST, JUNEAU, AK 99801
EMMET BENOLKEN, BOX 1263, CRAIG, AK 99921
KENNETH BENSON, BOX 7031, KETCHIKAN, AK 99901
LEE BENSON, BOX 152, YAKUTAT, AK 99689
HUGH BENTON, BOX 62, ELFIN COVE, AK 99825
CLIFFORD BENZEL, 8707 GAIL AVE, JUNEAU, AK 99801
ROBERT BERCELI, BOX 2092, CORDOVA, AK 99574
CHARLES BERG, 15401 W VERDE LN, GOODYEAR, AZ 85395
CLIFFORD BERG, BOX 21328, JUNEAU, AK 99802
JEFFREY BERG, BOX 890, PETERSBURG, AK 99833
THOMAS BERGERON, 814 PETERSON, KETCHIKAN, AK 99901
ALVIN BERGMANN, 1210 MENDENHALL PENINSULA RD, JUNEAU, AK 99801
ALBERT BERGSENG, 100 E SUNNYSANDS RD, CATHLAMET, WA 98612
DENNIS BERKELEY, 3208 HALIBUT POINT RD SOLLARS #8, SITKA, AK 99835

SALMON FISHING LIST—HAND TROLL

GILBERT BERKEY, 143 RASPBERRY LN N, KETCHIKAN, AK 99901
BENJAMIN BERKLEY, BOX 23, PETERSBURG, AK 99833
EDWARD BERNEY, BOX 19267, THORNE BAY, AK 99919
ERNEST BERNHARDT, BOX 1312, SITKA, AK 99835
FRANCIS BERNHOFT, BOX 1775, SITKA, AK 99835
ALFRED BERRY, 2740 3RD AVE, KETCHIKAN, AK 99901
BRUCE BERRYHILL, 90 SPRUCE ST #202, JUNEAU, AK 99801
ROBERT BERRYHILL, 157 BEHRENDS AVE, JUNEAU, AK 99801
RONALD BERTSCH, 155 N PHEASANT RUN, COUPEVILLE, WA 98239
DAVID BESEAU, BOX 966, CRAIG, AK 99921
ASTRID BETHERS, BOX 210003, AUKE BAY, AK 99821
RUSSELL BETTERTON, 2150 HALIPUT PT RD, SITKA, AK 99835
JOSEPH BETTIS, 1327 SCENIC AVE, BELLINGHAM, WA 98225
DEREK BEZEMER, BOX 885, CRAIG, AK 99921
CHARLES BIASTOCH, BOX 1589, WRANGELL, AK 99929
RICHARD BIERSCHENK, 456 1/2 N PLANK RD, NEWBURGH, NY 12550
LANCE BIFOSS, BOX 23189, KETCHIKAN, AK 99901
KEITH BILLI, BOX 1003, PETERSBURG, AK 99833
JAMES BILLINGSLEY, BOX 4497, MOUNT EDGECUMBE, AK 99835
ANN BILLS, 415 ARROWHEAD ST, SITKA, AK 99835
JAMES BIRCH, BOX 1475, PETERSBURG, AK 99833
DANIEL BIRD, BOX 1628, PETERSBURG, AK 99833
ALBERT BIXBY, 5030 THANE RD, JUNEAU, AK 99801
GILBERT BIXBY, BOX 32, JUNEAU, AK 99802
EDWARD BLACK, 2869 HORSEHEAD BAY DR, GIG HARBOR, WA 98335
GREG BLACK, BOX 1521, WARD COVE, AK 99928
HARLEY BLACK, BOX 19103, THORNE BAY, AK 99919
JOHN BLACK, BOX 585, HOONAH, AK 99829
WILLIAM BLACKBURN, 4143 ASPEN ST, JUNEAU, AK 99801
RYAN BLACKWELL, 8105 CIRCLE DR, JUNEAU, AK 99801
ALBERT BLAIR, BOX 27, SEQUIM, WA 98382
CHRISTOPHER BLANC, BOX 186, CRAIG, AK 99921
CHARLES BLANKENSHIP, 401 ANGUS WAY, JUNEAU, AK 99801
JEFF BLANKENSHIP, 1709 HALIBUT POINT RD #12, SITKA, AK 99835
WILLIAM BLATCHLEY, BOX 307, CRAWFORDSVILLE, OR 97336
WILLIAM BLOOM, BOX 1283, WRANGELL, AK 99929
CLARENCE BLOOMQUIST, 1720 VALLEY CT #75, JUNEAU, AK 99801
WILLIAM BLOOMQUIST, 7026 E BLUE SKY DR, SCOTTSDALE, AZ 85266
TONY BOARIO, 221 E 7TH AVE #207, ANCHORAGE, AK 99501
GERALD BODDING, 2111 2ND AVE, KETCHIKAN, AK 99901
JACK BODDY, 1731 EDGECUMBE DR #A, SITKA, AK 99835
JAMES BODDY, 205 AIRPORT RD A6, SITKA, AK 99835
GEORGE BOGREN, BOX 392, YAKUTAT, AK 99689
JOHN BOHAN, 9510 N DOUGLAS HWY, JUNEAU, AK 99801
RICHARD BOON, BOX 3039, KETCHIKAN, AK 99901
GILBERT BOOTH, BOX 34, METLAKATLA, AK 99926
THEODORE BORBRIDGE, 7820 MAYFAIR #B, ANCHORAGE, AK 99502
JOSEPH BORCHICK, BOX 210143, AUKE BAY, AK 99821
MERLIN BOST, 11142 E MARCH PT RD, ANACORTES, WA 98221
ROGER BOTNEN, BOX 946, CRAIG, AK 99921
THOMAS BOTTS, BOX 424, HOONAH, AK 99829
DICK BOUSLEY, BOX 206, METLAKATLA, AK 99926
RICHARD BOUSSOM, BOX 304, SITKA, AK 99835
CHARLES BOWEN, BOX 1933, SITKA, AK 99835
PAUL BOWEN, BOX 68, PETERSBURG, AK 99833
MICHAEL BOWER, BOX 1254, WRANGELL, AK 99929
DARREL BRADY, BOX 191, WRANGELL, AK 99929
KEITH BRADY, BOX 1843, WRANGELL, AK 99929
LENORD BRADY, BOX 19308, THORNE BAY, AK 99919
MELVIN BRADY, BOX 103, WRANGELL, AK 99929
WILLIAM BRADY, 1890 GLACIER HWY #204, JUNEAU, AK 99801
WILLIAM BRADY, BOX 904, SITKA, AK 99835
GERALD BRAGER, 110 JARVIS ST, SITKA, AK 99835
ERVIL BRAMAN, BOX 272, GUSTAVUS, AK 99826
STEVE BRANDOW, 10713 GENA RD N, KETCHIKAN, AK 99901

FRANK BRANN, BOX 7, METLAKATLA, AK 99926
VERNON BRANTLY, BOX 1411, WRANGELL, AK 99929
ROLLO BRAY, 1764 1ST AVE, KETCHIKAN, AK 99901
TYLER BRAY, 324 ALDER ST, KETCHIKAN, AK 99901
JOHN BREMNER, BOX 20161, JUNEAU, AK 99802
HENRY BRENDIBLE, BOX 476, METLAKATLA, AK 99926
LES BRENDIBLE, 206 GARDEN LN, KETCHIKAN, AK 99901
LESLIE BRENDIBLE, BOX 29362, BELLINGHAM, WA 98228
THOMAS BRENDIBLE, BOX 55, METLAKATLA, AK 99926
BONNIE BRESEMAN, BOX 203, PELICAN, AK 99832
JOHN BRESEMAN, 431 A ANDREWS ST, SITKA, AK 99835
CHRISTOPHER BREWTON, 7 MAKSOUTOFF ST, SITKA, AK 99835
ROLAND BRICE, 2236 SE MIGNONETTE CT, GRESHAM, OR 97080
ROGER BRILEY, BOX 9259, KETCHIKAN, AK 99901
JOSEPH BRINDLE, RT 1 BOX 1062, KETCHIKAN, AK 99901
HANS BROADLAND, BOX 130, PETERSBURG, AK 99833
RICHARD BROLSMA, 402 ETOLIN WAY #10, SITKA, AK 99835
WALLY BROMMELS, 6590 GLACIER HWY #281, JUNEAU, AK 99801
DANA BROOKS, BOX 214, CRAIG, AK 99921
MICHAEL BROOKS, BOX 6964, KETCHIKAN, AK 99901
JAMES BROSCHAT, 215 KIMSHAM, SITKA, AK 99835
CAROL BROWN, BOX 14, MEYERS CHUCK, AK 99903
DANIEL BROWN, BOX 101, ELFIN COVE, AK 99825
DAVID BROWN, 230 VITSKARI ST #B, SITKA, AK 99835
DAVID BROWN, BOX 171, YAKUTAT, AK 99689
DUANE BROWN, BOX 213, KAKE, AK 99830
EVA BROWN, BOX 456, POINT BAKER, AK 99927
JUSTIN BROWN, 103 METLAKATLA ST, SITKA, AK 99835
LENA BROWN, 230 S FRANKLIN ST #804, JUNEAU, AK 99801
LLOYD BROWN, 17827 131 AVE SE, SNOHOMISH, WA 98290
ROBERT BROWN, GEN DEL, HOONAH, AK 99829
STEVAN BROWN, 2025 GREENBROOK BLVD, RICHLAND, WA 99352
WESLEY BROWN, BOX 196, KAKE, AK 99830
WILLIAM BROWN, GEN DEL, HOONAH, AK 99829
ARON BRUNDIDGE, 1619 SAWMILL CREEK RD #4, SITKA, AK 99835
JOYCE BRYNER, BOX 408, WRANGELL, AK 99929
MATTHEW BRYNER, BOX 1642, PETERSBURG, AK 99833
EVERETT BUCHANAN, 6026 DOUGLAS HWY, JUNEAU, AK 99801
JAMES BUCHANAN, BOX 2642, JUNEAU, AK 99803
MARK BUCK, 16487 DEERWOOD RD, GARDEN CITY, MN 56034
THOMAS BUDD, 1718 EDGECUMBE DR, SITKA, AK 99835
ROBERT BULARD, BOX 241, YAKUTAT, AK 99689
DALE BUNDY, BOX 1585, JUNEAU, AK 99802
GEORGE BUNTING, BOX 341514, ARLETA, CA 91334
HELEN BURD, BOX 22950, JUNEAU, AK 99802
WALTER BURKHARDT, 8539 STEEP PL, JUNEAU, AK 99801
STEVEN BURRELL, BOX 275, PETERSBURG, AK 99833
BENJAMIN BURTON, 130 BRYANT #113, KETCHIKAN, AK 99901
CLYDE BURTON, BOX 915, POINT BAKER, AK 99927
HENRY BURTON, 2716 HALIBUT POINT RD #35, SITKA, AK 99835
CATHERINE BUTLER, 3198 OLD HWY 13, PARK FALLS, WI 54552
ROGER BUTTRAM, BOX 242, GUSTAVUS, AK 99826
GLENN BYINGTON, BOX 021541, JUNEAU, AK 99802
TED BYLSMA, BOX 1064, BLAINE, WA 98230
DONALD BYRD, 2701 HALIBUT POINT RD, SITKA, AK 99835
LEE BYRD, BOX 46, WRANGELL, AK 99929
OLCAY CAF, 1003 BONNIE DOON, JUNEAU, AK 99801
KENNETH CALHOON, BOX 491, PETERSBURG, AK 99833
MATTHEW CALLAHAN, 2008 HALIBUT POINT RD, SITKA, AK 99835
DAVID CALLISTINI, 103 BURKHART DR #D29, SITKA, AK 99835
WILLIAM CAMERON, 4217 MENDENHALL BLVD, JUNEAU, AK 99801
CLYDE CAMPBELL, BOX 8889, KETCHIKAN, AK 99901
JIMMIE CAMPBELL, RR 1 BOX 209, ARCO, ID 83213
SARA CAMPBELL, BOX 2013, PETERSBURG, AK 99833
BENJAMIN CAMPEN, BOX 372, SITKA, AK 99835

SALMON FISHING LIST—HAND TROLL

GARY CAMPEN, BOX 161, PORT HADLOCK, WA 98339
JAMES CANARY, 2333 PROSPECT AVE, CHELAN, WA 98816
ANTHONY CANDELARIO, BOX 541, TENAKEE, AK 99841
JESSE CANNON, 3016 S TONGASS HWY, KETCHIKAN, AK 99901
SONNY CANNON, 3016 S TONGASS, KETCHIKAN, AK 99901
MARK CANONICA, 619 E 84TH, TACOMA, WA 98445
JAMES CARIELLO, BOX 562, PETERSBURG, AK 99833
GEORGE CARLE, BOX 316, HYDABURG, AK 99922
SVEIN CARLSEN, 428 MADISON, KETCHIKAN, AK 99901
BENNETT CARLSON, BOX 2936, SITKA, AK 99835
CRAIG CARLSON, BOX 2066, WRANGELL, AK 99929
FRANCIS CARLSON, BOX 613, DOUGLAS, AK 99824
GARY CARLSON, 3235 TONGASS, KETCHIKAN, AK 99901
KURT CARLSON, 338 MAIN ST, KETCHIKAN, AK 99901
LYNETTE CARLSON, BOX 19214, THORNE BAY, AK 99919
RAY CARLSON, BOX 110, POINT BAKER, AK 99927
CANUTE CARLSTROM, BOX 903, WARD COVE, AK 99928
WAYNE CARNES, BOX 240258, DOUGLAS, AK 99824
DANIEL CAROTHERS, BOX 240917, DOUGLAS, AK 99824
JOHN CARPENTER, 3215 BENNETT DR, BELLINGHAM, WA 98225
MICHAEL CARPENTER, BOX 1365, PETERSBURG, AK 99833
ROBERT CARPENTER, 4137 BIRCH LN, JUNEAU, AK 99801
RICHARD CARR, BOX 603, PETERSBURG, AK 99833
LAWRENCE CARSON, BOX 37, MEYERS CHUCK, AK 99903
JAMES CARTMILL, BOX 210294, AUKE BAY, AK 99821
ROBERT CARTMILL, BOX 210294, AUKE BAY, AK 99821
ROBERT CARTWRIGHT, 203 AIRPORT RD #A13, SITKA, AK 99835
FRANK CASE, 1231 S 2ND, PASCO, WA 99301
WAYNE CASEY, 5612 S 133, SEATTLE, WA 98168
KEVIN CASTLE, BOX 1110, CRAIG, AK 99921
RONALD CASTLE, GEN DEL, CRAIG, AK 99921
STEPHEN CASTOR, BOX 407, CRAIG, AK 99921
RICHARD CATRETT, 3446 MEANDER WAY, JUNEAU, AK 99801
EUGENE CAVANAUGH, BOX 550, KAKE, AK 99830
RICHARD CAVANAUGH, BOX 227, KAKE, AK 99830
LEN CEDER, 17105 GLACIER HWY, JUNEAU, AK 99801
KERMIT CESAR, BOX 34482, JUNEAU, AK 99803
CLARENCE CHALMERS, BOX 443, METLAKATLA, AK 99926
MIKE CHAMBERS, 3311 HALIBUT POINT ROAD, SITKA, AK 99835
RAYMOND CHAPMAN, GEN DEL, MEYERS CHUCK, AK 99903
TIMOTHY CHAPMAN, GEN DEL, MEYERS CHUCK, AK 99903
GAROLD CHARLES, RT 2 BOX 11, KETCHIKAN, AK 99901
IVAN CHARLES, BOX 271, DOT LAKE, AK 99737
MARVIN CHARLES, RT 2 BOX 7, KETCHIKAN, AK 99901
MATTHEW CHARLES, 2222 EASTVIEW DR, BREMERTON, WA 98310
MATTHEW CHARLES, BOX 38, HYDABURG, AK 99922
MELVIN CHARLES, BOX 27, HYDABURG, AK 99922
SETH CHARLTON, 2009 SAWMILL CREEK RD #C, SITKA, AK 99835
HENRY CHARTRAND, BOX 1992, SITKA, AK 99835
DONALD CHASE, BOX 35684, JUNEAU, AK 99803
WILLIAM CHEESEMAN, 6725 GRAY ST, JUNEAU, AK 99801
NORMAN CHENEY, BOX 1156, PETERSBURG, AK 99833
DONALD CHENHALL, BOX 1062, WARD COVE, AK 99928
JOSH CHEVALIER, 2513 SAWMILL CREEK RD, SITKA, AK 99835
MARC CHOQUETTE, 5921 LUND ST, JUNEAU, AK 99801
BARRY CHRISTENSEN, 3409 BAILY BLVD, KETCHIKAN, AK 99901
MICHAEL CHRISTIAN, BOX 1034, WRANGELL, AK 99929
JEFF CHRISTOPHER, BOX 265, CAPE MAY POINT, NJ 8212
PAUL CHULIK, BOX 224, SITKA, AK 99835
JOHN CHURCH, BOX 801, WRANGELL, AK 99929
RANDY CHURCHILL, BOX 606, WRANGELL, AK 99929
ADELBERT CLARK, BOX 403, CRAIG, AK 99921
GERALD CLARK, BOX 225, CRAIG, AK 99921
LARRY CLARK, BOX 3515, JUNEAU, AK 99803
WILLIAM CLARK, BOX 993, SILVERDALE, WA 98383
CHARLES CLAYTON, BOX 116, HAINES, AK 99827

STEPHEN CLAYTON, BOX 2476, SITKA, AK 99835
WALTER CLAYTON, BOX 364, HAINES, AK 99827
JOSEPH CLERGET, BOX 342, HOONAH, AK 99829
LARRY CLERGET, 16504 SHELDON LN SW, ROCHESTER, WA 98579
JAY CLIFTON, 3802 HALIBUT POINT RD, SITKA, AK 99835
BRIAN CLOOSE, 1417 JAY WEST RD, CARLTON, MN 55718
DENNIS COCHLIN, BOX 7201, KETCHIKAN, AK 99901
PAULINE COFFEY, 2840 KATALLA CIRCLE, ANCHORAGE, AK 99518
JAMES COLE, 7300 MADRONA DR NE, BAINBRIDGE IS, WA 98110
DAVID COLEMAN, BOX 713, SITKA, AK 99835
DANIEL COLLIER, BOX 582, WRANGELL, AK 99929
ARNOLD COLLINS, 315 3RD ST, JUNEAU, AK 99801
SPENCER COMBS, 503 CHARTERIS ST, SITKA, AK 99835
EDWARD COMRADA, BOX 304, KAKE, AK 99830
DUSTIN CONNOR, BOX 1372, PETERSBURG, AK 99833
ROBERT CONVERSE, BOX 26, YAKUTAT, AK 99689
VICKI CONVERSE, BOX 37, TENAKEE, AK 99841
WILBUR CONVERSE, BOX 276, JUNEAU, AK 99802
WILLIAM CONYERS, BOX 3171, JUNEAU, AK 99803
JODY COOK, 2115 NW 12TH ST, BATTLE GROUND, WA 98604
LARRY COOKE, BOX 1343, PETERSBURG, AK 99833
GALEN COOLEY, 2573 NEWMARK AVE, NORTH BEND, OR 97459
RICHARD COOPER, 1627 33RD AVE NE, OLYMPIA, WA 98506
WALTER CORAM, 5202 PINE ST, BELLAIRE, TX 77401
DENNY CORBIN, BOX 765, PELICAN, AK 99832
DOUGLAS CORL, BOX 1570, PETERSBURG, AK 99833
JOSEPH CORNELL, BOX 8560, KETCHIKAN, AK 99901
ROBERT CORPUZ, 520 6TH ST, JUNEAU, AK 99802
JAMES COSTALES, 878 JACKSON ST, KETCHIKAN, AK 99901
DAVE COTTRELL, BOX 947, PETERSBURG, AK 99833
HAROLD COWAN, BOX 1073, WARD COVE, AK 99928
MITCH COWAN, 2716 HALIBUT POINT RD #13, SITKA, AK 99835
ROBERT COWAN, BOX 1135, WARD COVE, AK 99928
CHRISTOPHER COX, 2442 NW MARKET ST PMB 425, SEATTLE, WA 98107
LINDON COX, BOX 625, WARD COVE, AK 99928
LARRY CRABILL, 1412 N LAKE VIEW DR, OKLAHOMA CITY, OK 73127
BRIXIE CRABTREE, BOX 1271, WRANGELL, AK 99929
APRIL CRADER, POUCH A G CAPE POLE, KETCHIKAN, AK 99901
EDWARD CRAIN, 268 NARCISSA PL, WALLA WALLA, WA 99362
THOMAS CRANE, 2511 SAWMILL CREEK RD, SITKA, AK 99835
LORIN CRANSON, BOX 5272, KALISPELL, MT 59903
STEPHEN CRAPO, 9347 BETTY CT, JUNEAU, AK 99801
EDWARD CRAWFORD, 370 NE CAMANO DR #375, CAMANO ISLAND, WA 98282
BRADLEY CRAYNE, BOX 569, CRAIG, AK 99921
THOMAS CRESS, BOX 607, VALDEZ, AK 99686
FRED CRICK, 41233 212TH AVE SE, ENUMCLAW, WA 98022
ALFRED CROGAN, 806 15TH AVE SE, ABERDEEN, SD 57401
JIM CROGAN, 570 SEATTER #2, JUNEAU, AK 99801
ELLIS CROPPER, BOX 241, FRIDAY HARBOR, WA 98250
JOHN CROSS, 1900 W NICKERSON ST #213, SEATTLE, WA 98119
MATTHEW CROSSETT, BOX 417, YAKUTAT, AK 99689
CHRIS CROWE, BOX 211304, AUKE BAY, AK 99821
MARK CROZIER, 4366 TAKU BVLD, JUNEAU, AK 99801
CARL CRUIKSHANK, BOX 390, CRAIG, AK 99921
MICHAEL CUDDIHY, 15614 UPLANDS WAY SE, NORTH BEND, WA 98045
JAMES CUFLEY, 3506 NE 182ND ST, SEATTLE, WA 98155
ANGUS CUMMING, BOX 210448, AUKE BAY, AK 99821
DUANE CUMMINGS, 9158 SKYWOOD LN, JUNEAU, AK 99801
ROB CUMMINGS, BOX 1754, PETERSBURG, AK 99833
ROGER CUMMINGS, BOX 8804, KETCHIKAN, AK 99901
GEOFFREY CURRALL, 4384 S TONGASS HWY, KETCHIKAN, AK 99901
RICHARD CURRAN, BOX 1336, SITKA, AK 99835
CRAIG CURTISS, BOX 693, PETERSBURG, AK 99833
NANCY CURTISS, 18601 INDIAN CREEK RD, WILLAMINA, OR 97396
TROY CURTISS, BOX 1532, PETERSBURG, AK 99833
THOMAS DADE, 18650 FENDELL RD, WILLAMINA, OR 97396

SALMON FISHING LIST—HAND TROLL

GARY DAETWILER, 1800 NORTHWOOD DR #I-72, JUNEAU, AK 99801
CHRIS DAHL, 1000 SEAWEED LN, POINT BAKER, AK 99927
JEROME DAHL, BOX 1275, PETERSBURG, AK 99833
JEROME DAHL, BOX 128, PETERSBURG, AK 99833
MICHAEL DAHLBERG, BOX 945, AUKE BAY, AK 99821
DONALD DAHMAN, 3892 SE BLOOMFIELD RD, SHELTON, WA 98584
TERRENCE DAIGNAULT, BOX 08, PETERSBURG, AK 99833
ALAN DALE, 926 NORDSTROM DR, KETCHIKAN, AK 99901
DEVIN DALIN, 7937 WILLIAMS RD, KETCHIKAN, AK 99901
GEORGE DALTON, BOX 175, HOONAH, AK 99829
RICHARD DALTON, BOX 407, HOONAH, AK 99829
GENO DALY, 5500 E 38TH CT #3, ANCHORAGE, AK 99504
VICTOR DAMIAN, BOX 546, PETERSBURG, AK 99833
JOE DANIELS, BOX 7932, KETCHIKAN, AK 99901
MARK DANIELS, BOX 351, HYDABURG, AK 99922
LINNUS DANNER, BOX 724, HAINES, AK 99827
MARKO DAPCEVICH, 221 LINCOLN ST, SITKA, AK 99835
DICKIE DAU, BOX 210206, AUKE BAY, AK 99821
TOM DAUGHERTY, 9640 N DOUGLAS, JUNEAU, AK 99801
MAYNARD DAUM, BOX 906, POINT BAKER, AK 99927
GEORGE DAVENPORT, BOX 100342, ANCHORAGE, AK 99510
WILLIAM DAVIDSON, BOX 1336, PETERSBURG, AK 99833
DWAYNE DAVIES, BOX 313, KAKE, AK 99830
IRVIN DAVIES, 1701 CENTRAL, JUNEAU, AK 99801
LARRY DAVIES, 9096 N DOUGLAS, JUNEAU, AK 99801
ALAN DAVIS, BOX 306, KAKE, AK 99830
ALBERT DAVIS, 314 KATLIAN ST, SITKA, AK 99835
HENRY DAVIS, 3116 164TH ST SW #214, LYNWOOD, WA 98037
HERMAN DAVIS, BOX 395, SITKA, AK 99835
NICHOLAS DAVIS, BOX 234, KAKE, AK 99830
RANDY DAVIS, BOX 592, HOONAH, AK 99829
ROBERT DAVIS, 895 W 12TH ST #223, JUNEAU, AK 99801
WESLEY DAVIS, BOX 1393, PETERSBURG, AK 99833
WILLIAM DAVIS, BOX 287, HOONAH, AK 99829
DAVID DAWLEY, BOX 830, CRAIG, AK 99921
RICHARD DEAKINS, BOX 2977, JUNEAU, AK 99803
JEFFREY DEAN, BOX 264, HUSUM, WA 98623
THEODORE DEATS, BOX 20517, JUNEAU, AK 99801
JAMES DEBOER, BOX 1196, ELMA, WA 98541
HAROLD DEMMERT, BOX 22, ANGOON, AK 99820
OSCAR DEMMERT, BOX 274, KAKE, AK 99830
PAUL DEMMERT, BOX 274, KAKE, AK 99830
ROBERT DEMMERT, BOX 214, ANGOON, AK 99820
SAMSON DEMMERT, BOX 516, YAKUTAT, AK 99689
WILLIAM DEMMERT, 860 COHO WY #5, BELLINGHAM, WA 98225
DONALD DEMUTH, BOX 21, TALKEETNA, AK 99676
JOHN DEMUTH, BOX 456, DOUGLAS, AK 99824
VINCENT DEMUTH, BOX 456, DOUGLAS, AK 99824
LUTHER DENNIS, 905 LAKE ST, SITKA, AK 99835
RICHARD DENOVA, 620 SAWMILL CREEK RD, SITKA, AK 99835
GARRY DESROSIERS, BOX EXI, JUNEAU, AK 99850
FRANK DEVERAUX, BOX 7, YAKUTAT, AK 99689
HARRY DIAMOND, BOX 1152, WARD COVE, AK 99928
STEVEN DICE, BOX 442, YAKUTAT, AK 99689
HAROLD DICK, BOX 362, HOONAH, AK 99829
JACQUELINE DICK, BOX 390, HOONAH, AK 99829
RONALD DICK, BOX 92, PELICAN, AK 99832
JACK DIEBAG, BOX 875252, WASILLA, AK 99687
DENNIS DILLON, BOX 6673, KETCHIKAN, AK 99901
WILLIAM DIMOND, BOX 1101, SITKA, AK 99835
WAYNE DISARRO, BOX WWP, KETCHIKAN, AK 99950
THOMAS DIXON, BOX 417, KLAWOCK, AK 99925
HENRY DOAK, RT 2 BOX 664, KAMIAH, ID 83536
HERMAN DOBROVOLSKY, BOX 1106, PETERSBURG, AK 99833
GEORGE DODDINGTON, 3850 YORKSHIRE AVE, EUGENE, OR 97405

BILL DODSON, BOX EDB, EDNA BAY, AK 99950
JERRY DODSON, BOX 63, POINT BAKER, AK 99927
JOHN DODSON, BOX EDB, EDNA BAY, AK 99950
MICHAEL DOGGETT, 1306 EDGECUMBE DR, SITKA, AK 99835
ROBERT DOLAN, BOX 1062, PETERSBURG, AK 99833
LOREN DOMKE, BOX 1216, JUNEAU, AK 99802
WILLIS DONNALLY, 105 SHULER DR, SITKA, AK 99835
DAVID DOREN, BOX 83595, FAIRBANKS, AK 99708
DICK DORSTEN, BOX 662, LACONNER, WA 98257
ELWOOD DOUGLAS, 3362 HAWKIN, KETCHIKAN, AK 99901
JOSEPH DOUPE, RT 1 BOX 321-A, OCEAN PARK, WA 98640
RONALD DOUVILLE, BOX 604, CRAIG, AK 99921
RILEY DOWD, 3519 HARBOR VIEW DR #1, GIG HARBOR, WA 98332
BARBARA DOWE, 39092 KINGS VALLEY HWY, MONMOUTH, OR 97361
CHRIS DOWLING, 711 COOK ST, KETCHIKAN, AK 99901
MICHAEL DUBY, 7220 GLACIER HWY, JUNEAU, AK 99811
KENNETH DUCKETT, BOX 23178, KETCHIKAN, AK 99901
DANIEL DUGAQUA, BOX 168, KAKE, AK 99830
CLARENCE DULL, 112 OCEAN VEIW ST, SITKA, AK 99835
LARRY DUMMER, 9216 LONG RUN DR, JUNEAU, AK 99801
ALBERT DUNCAN, 721 LAKE ST, SITKA, AK 99835
DANIEL DUNCAN, BOX 19264, THORNE BAY, AK 99919
ELMER DUNCAN, BOX 33212, JUNEAU, AK 99803
GIDEON DUNCAN, BOX 91, HYDABURG, AK 99922
JOHNNY DUNCAN, 2906 SAWMILL CREEK RD, SITKA, AK 99835
PETER DUNCAN, BOX 43, ANGOON, AK 99820
ROBERT DUNCANSON, BOX 92, MEYERS CHUCK, AK 99903
RICHARD DUNDAS, BOX 22, METLAKATLA, AK 99926
CHARLES DUNNE, BOX 41, METLAKATLA, AK 99926
DELBURT DUNNE, BOX 599, METLAKATLA, AK 99926
DENNIS DUNNE, BOX 224, METLAKATLA, AK 99926
FRANCIS DUNNE, 5915 SUNSET, JUNEAU, AK 99801
JOHN DUPREE, BOX 684, PETERSBURG, AK 99833
KENT DURAND, 2157 W 17TH CT, EUGENE, OR 97402
EARL DURDLE, BOX 8071, PORT ALEXANDER, AK 99836
EUGENE DURKEE, 1050 SALMON CREEK LN #A101, JUNEAU, AK 99801
TERRY DURKIN, BOX 114, PETERSBURG, AK 99833
LARRY DURST, BOX 164, PETERSBURG, AK 99833
DAVID DUSINA, BOX EXI, EXCURSION INLET, AK 99850
HENRY DUVERNOY, BOX 21166, JUNEAU, AK 99802
ALEK DYAKANOFF, BOX 7111, KETCHIKAN, AK 99901
JOHAN DYBDAHL, 5984 NORTH ST, JUNEAU, AK 99801
JOSH DYBDAHL, BOX 266, HOONAH, AK 99829
JAMES EARLY, BOX 466, WRANGELL, AK 99929
BERNICE EASTERLY, BOX 197, HOONAH, AK 99829
RANDALL EASTERLY, BOX 1524, WRANGELL, AK 99929
BENJAMIN EATON, BOX 364, METLAKATLA, AK 99926
MICHAEL EBERHARDT, BOX 22361, JUNEAU, AK 99802
JOHN EBONA, BOX 21149, JUNEAU, AK 99802
ROGER EDDY, 2898 SAWMILL CREEK ST RT, SITKA, AK 99835
DARREN EDENSHAW, BOX 25, HYDABURG, AK 99922
DOUG EDENSHAW, BOX 179, KLAWOCK, AK 99925
LOUIS EDENSHAW, BOX 571, KOTZEBUE, AK 99752
WILLIAM EDENSHAW, BOX 201, HYDABURG, AK 99922
JAMES EDGARS, BOX 1814, PETERSBURG, AK 99833
EDWIN EDWARDS, BOX 138, WRANGELL, AK 99929
ERNEST EGGLESTON, 401 MILLS ST, SITKA, AK 99835
KEN EICHNER, 5166 SHORELINE DR N, KETCHIKAN, AK 99901
L EIDE, BOX 15, PETERSBURG, AK 99833
BRIAN ELKINS, 14329 JORDAN RD, ARLINGTON, WA 98223
SEAN ELLIOTT, 2695 DAVID ST APT #2, JUNEAU, AK 99801
HANS ELLIOTT.PETAJA, 2695 DAVID ST APT #2, JUNEAU, AK 99801
CHRIS ELLIS, BOX 2135, WRANGELL, AK 99929
ERNEST ELLISON, BOX 69, KLAWOCK, AK 99925
MICHAEL ELSTAD, BOX 1562, SITKA, AK 99835

SALMON FISHING LIST—HAND TROLL

ERIC EMBREE, 1350 PEYTON PLACE, KETCHIKAN, AK 99901
RICHARD EMBREE, BOX 506, TOKELAND, WA 98590
JOHN EMEL, 721 ALDER ST, EDMONDS, WA 98020
JOSEPH EMEL, 9485 MISERY POINT RD NW, SEABECK, WA 98380
JOHN ENGE, 712 E ELLENDALE AVE, DALLAS, OR 97338
VERN ENGESATH, 66 SHALE RD, PORT ANGLES, WA 98362
LARRY ENGLUND, BOX 240298, DOUGLAS, AK 99824
ALLAN ENGSTROM, 1627 EVERGREEN AVE, JUNEAU, AK 99801
PATRICK ERCOLIN, BOX 1001, WRANGELL, AK 99929
CHARLES ERICKSON, BOX 553, SITKA, AK 99835
PETER ESQUIRO, 108 SAND DOLLAR DR, SITKA, AK 99835
JOHN ESTES, 2652 DOUGLAS HWY, JUNEAU, AK 99801
FELIVERTO ESTRADA, 212 SHOTGUN ALLEY, SITKA, AK 99835
JOSHUA ETCHER, BOX 1952, PETERSBURG, AK 99833
VANCE ETCHER, BOX 1025, PETERSBURG, AK 99833
KIRK ETTLES, 4410 SESAME ST, JUNEAU, AK 99801
LEO EVANS, BOX 902, SITKA, AK 99835
ROBERT EVANS, 113 METLAKATLA NORTH #4, SITKA, AK 99835
RAYMOND EVENS, BOX 197, PETERSBURG, AK 99833
ROBERT EWERS, 4093 BEACH BLUFF RD, BEACH BLUFF, TN 38313
LYNN EWING, BOX 1335, PETERSBURG, AK 99833
VICTOR EXTON, 18340 S SPRINGWATER RD, ESTACADA, OR 97023
ROBERT EZELL, BOX 762, MI WUK, CA 95346
MARION EZRRE, BOX 20208, JUNEAU, AK 99802
DANIEL FABRELLO, 2476 O DAY DR, JUNEAU, AK 99801
LINDA FABRELLO, BOX 1590, WRANGELL, AK 99929
JUSTIN FAGER, 206 1/2 LAKEVIEW DR, SITKA, AK 99835
DARIN FAGERSTROM, 1105 MENDENHALL PENINSULA RD, JUNEAU, AK 99801
JOHN FAIN, 679 BLUEBERRY DR #A, KETCHIKAN, AK 99901
MIKE FAIR, BOX 70128, FAIRBANKS, AK 99707
RONALD FAIRBANKS, BOX 467, KLAWOCK, AK 99925
NICHOLAS FAMA, BOX 19436, THORNE BAY, AK 99919
LENA FARKAS, BOX 253, YAKUTAT, AK 99689
JOHN FARLEIGH, 1319 H ST, ANCHORAGE, AK 99501
JOHN FARNAN, BOX 727, SKAGWAY, AK 99840
ALLAN FAWCETT, BOX 622, METLAKATLA, AK 99926
JOHN FAWCETT, BOX 44, METLAKATLA, AK 99926
WILLIAM FAWCETT, 6026 N DOUGLAS, JUNEAU, AK 99801
STANLEY FELSMAN, GEN DEL, WRANGELL, AK 99929
JERRY FELTON, 2518 E TUDOR #205, ANCHORAGE, AK 99507
RANDALL FERDINAND, BOX 1846, WRANGELL, AK 99929
KELLY FERGUSON, 3880 HALIBUT POINT RD, SITKA, AK 99835
ROBERT FERNBACH, BOX 6316, KETCHIKAN, AK 99901
TYSON FICK, 9831 NINE MILE CREEK RD, JUNEAU, AK 99801
RICHARD FIELDS, BOX 5981, KETCHIKAN, AK 99901
MICHAEL FILE, BOX 1666, PETERSBURG, AK 99833
MICHAEL FINK, 26 BARANOF, FAIRBANKS, AK 99701
BRANDON FINN, 105 LANCE DR APT F, SITKA, AK 99835
DEAN FIRESTACK, BOX 258, YAKUTAT, AK 99689
KEVIN FIRESTACK, 12271 W HAZEL, WASILLA, AK 99623
STEVEN FISH, BOX 6448, SITKA, AK 99835
PATRICK FISHER, 1413 QUEEN ANNE #12, SEATTLE, WA 98109
TOM FISHER, BOX 1928, WRANGELL, AK 99929
MARK FITZJARRALD, BOX 22982, JUNEAU, AK 99802
PATRICK FLANERY, BOX 2005, SITKA, AK 99835
FORREST FLEENOR, 100 PACIFIC CT, KETCHIKAN, AK 99901
TODD FLEMING, 1107 EDGECUMBE DR, SITKA, AK 99835
HENRY FLETCHER, 3221 MOOHEAU AVE, HONOLULU, HI 96816
LORENZO FLORENDO, BOX 308, HOONAH, AK 99829
WALTER FONTAINE, BOX 47, CRAIG, AK 99921
DAVID FORBES, 206 PRINCESS WY, CENTRAL POINT, OR 97502
RAY FORD, BOX 924, WRANGELL, AK 99929
ROBERT FORD, BOX 338, SAINT IGNATIUS, MT 59865
STEVEN FORREST, BOX 308, WRANGELL, AK 99929
VICTOR FORRESTER, BOX 5225, KETCHIKAN, AK 99901
JEFFREY FORTUNE, BOX 35024, JUNEAU, AK 99803

EDWARD FOSTER, BOX 655, DOUGLAS, AK 99824
RICHARD FOSTER, GEN DEL, AKUTAN, AK 99553
DAVID FOWLER, BOX 2164, PETERSBURG, AK 99833
CARL FOX, BOX 42, METLAKATLA, AK 99926
HERBERT FOX, BOX 234, JUNEAU, AK 99802
LESTER FRAGNER, BOX 1061, SITKA, AK 99835
JEFFREY FRAKER, BOX 517, YAKUTAT, AK 99689
ROBERT FRAKER, BOX 284, YAKUTAT, AK 99689
ALBERT FRANK, BOX 1854, PINE RIDGE, SD 57770
HAROLD FRANK, BOX 167, ANGOON, AK 99820
KEVIN FRANK, BOX 184, ANGOON, AK 99820
LAVERNE FRANK, 8728 GAIL AVE, JUNEAU, AK 99801
WALLY FRANK, BOX 32005, JUNEAU, AK 99803
KYLE FRANKLIN, BOX 62, PETERSBURG, AK 99833
STEFFEN FRAZIER, 9361 TURN ST, JUNEAU, AK 99801
JAMES FREDERICK, 2007 COVE PL, ANACORTES, WA 98221
ALEXANDER FREDRICK, BOX 21852, JUNEAU, AK 99802
ALBIN FREDRICKSON, 3410 FOSTER AVE #F11, JUNEAU, AK 99801
ROGER FRENCH, 1919 DODGE CIR, SITKA, AK 99835
KEVIN FRIDAY, BOX 72, HOONAH, AK 99829
GEORGE FRIEND, BOX 1212, WARD COVE, AK 99928
RYAN FRIEND, 4322 CORE PL, JUNEAU, AK 99801
TERRY FRISKE, 117 DARRIN DR, SITKA, AK 99835
PETER FROEHLICH, 1785 EVERGREEN AVE, JUNEAU, AK 99801
ERICK FUGLVOG, BOX 131, PETERSBURG, AK 99833
JAMES FUHRMANN, BOX 4503, SOLDOTNA, AK 99669
JEFFREY FUJIOKA, BOX 210628, AUKE BAY, AK 99821
KAREN FULLER, 1009 MURIEL ST NE, ALBUQUERQUE, NM 87112
DONALD FUNK, BOX 2031, TUALATIN, OR 97062
ISTVAN FUZAK, BOX 1137, CRAIG, AK 99921
THOMAS GAFFNEY, BOX 6701, KETCHIKAN, AK 99901
DAN GAGNON, BOX 792, CORDOVA, AK 99574
DAVID GALANIN, BOX 146, SITKA, AK 99835
JERROD GALANIN, BOX 1804, SITKA, AK 99835
RONALD GALDABINI, 2409 UMPQUA HWY 99, DRAIN, OR 97435
MERLE GALLAGHER, 146 THOMAS ST, KETCHIKAN, AK 99901
CHARLES GAMBLE, 1038 CAPITOL AVE, JUNEAU, AK 99801
LAURENCE GAMMAN, 9342 BETTY CT, JUNEAU, AK 99801
FORREST GANGLE, 612 ETOLIN ST, SITKA, AK 99835
JERRY GARDINER, 596 SCHOENBAR RD, KETCHIKAN, AK 99901
PATRICK GARDNER, BOX 1, CRAIG, AK 99921
GARRY GARRISON, BOX 9290, KETCHIKAN, AK 99901
KEVEN GARRISON, BOX 65, ELFIN COVE, AK 99825
JOAN GATES, BOX 531, TENAKEE, AK 99841
JOHN GATES, BOX 196, YAKUTAT, AK 99689
J.MICHAEL GAYLE, 7730 STEILACOOM RD SE #13, OLYMPIA, WA 98503
JONATHAN GEARY, 1630 MENDENHALL PENINSULA, JUNEAU, AK 99801
GABRIEL GEORGE, BOX 95, ANGOON, AK 99820
PETER GEORGE, 3208 HALIBUT POINT RD #21, SITKA, AK 99835
THOMAS GEORGE, BOX 022082, JUNEAU, AK 99802
WILLIAM GEORGE, 9014 GEE ST, JUNEAU, AK 99801
CLARENCE GERMAIN, BOX 7518, KETCHIKAN, AK 99901
STEPHEN GIANARELLI, BOX 957, CRAIG, AK 99921
DELLA GIBB, BOX 794, FOSTER, OR 97345
RICHARD GIBB, BOX 794, FOSTER, OR 97345
HARRY GIBBS, BOX 457, CRAIG, AK 99921
ERIC GIDEON, GEN DEL, PORT TOWNSEND, WA 98368
SHANE GILLEN, BOX 2096, WRANGELL, AK 99929
LEE GILPIN, BOX 1511, PETERSBURG, AK 99833
JOHNY GILSON, 3857 FAIRVIEW, KETCHIKAN, AK 99901
FRANK GIOFFRE, BOX 2814, SITKA, AK 99835
CLARENCE GISSE, 2118 2ND AVE, KETCHIKAN, AK 99901
JOHN GITKOV, 22745 GLACIER HWY, JUNEAU, AK 99801
ANNA GJERDE, 15720 83RD AVE E, PUYALLUP, WA 98373
HAFTOR GJERDE, BOX 722, PETERSBURG, AK 99833
MELVIN GJERDE, BOX 1116, PETERSBURG, AK 99833

SALMON FISHING LIST—HAND TROLL

KARL GLADSJO, BOX 462, WRANGELL, AK 99929
WAYNE GLANDER, BOX 643, WRANGELL, AK 99929
ANTHONY GLAZIER, BOX 275, YAKUTAT, AK 99689
DOUGLAS GLESSING, BOX 191, ANGOON, AK 99820
RAYMOND GLINIECKI, BOX 020236, JUNEAU, AK 99802
PATRICK GLOVER, BOX 522, HOONAH, AK 99829
WILLIAM GLOVER, 4914 CEDARWOOD LN NW, GIG HARBOR, WA 98335
JASON GOINS, BOX 741, HOONAH, AK 99829
JEFFREY GOLDEN, 8322 SILVER LAKE RD, MAPLE FALLS, WA 98266
LEO GOLDEN, BOX 2767, SITKA, AK 99835
MATTHEW GONZALEZ, BOX 306, HOONAH, AK 99829
SUSAN GONZALEZ, BOX 256, HOONAH, AK 99829
GALE GOOD, 12175 GLACIER HWY #E404, JUNEAU, AK 99801
TERRY GOODWIN, 4245 S PINNACLE PEAK DR, WASILLA, AK 99623
FRANK GORDON, BOX 142, KAKE, AK 99830
FREDERICK GORDON, BOX 107, KAKE, AK 99830
JAMES GRAHAM, 3250 DENALI #27, KETCHIKAN, AK 99901
JARED GRAMS, BOX 437, HOONAH, AK 99829
ALFRED GRANT, GEN DEL, JUNEAU, AK 99802
DAVID GRANT, BOX 84, HYDABURG, AK 99922
EDWARD GRANT, 8196 THREADNEEDLE ST, JUNEAU, AK 99801
KENNETH GRANT, BOX 402, HOONAH, AK 99829
MARVIN GRANT, BOX 1558, SITKA, AK 99835
MORRIS GRANT, BOX 105, KAKE, AK 99830
ROBERT GRANT, BOX 397, BELLINGHAM, WA 98227
WILLIE GRANT, BOX 403, HOONAH, AK 99829
ERVING GRASS, BOX 475, YAKUTAT, AK 99689
ANDREW GRAY, BOX 1586, BARROW, AK 99723
KENNETH GRAY, BOX 814, SITKA, AK 99835
ROBERT GRAY, BOX 317, HOONAH, AK 99829
KARL GREENEWALD, BOX 181, HOONAH, AK 99829
JAMES GREENOUGH, 9965 SW JURGENS LN, TUALATIN, OR 97062
WAYNE GREENSTREET, BOX 33, SKAGWAY, AK 99840
GORDON GREENWALD, BOX 231, HOONAH, AK 99829
ALEC GREGORIOFF, BOX 157, METLAKATLA, AK 99926
MICHAEL GREGORY, 3816 KIOWA DR, JUNEAU, AK 99801
MIKE GREGORY, 3816 KIOWA DR, JUNEAU, AK 99801
ROBERT GREGOVICH, 202 TROY AVE, JUNEAU, AK 99801
THOMAS GREINIER, BOX 34742, JUNEAU, AK 99803
RICHARD GRESETH, BOX 70, PETERSBURG, AK 99833
DENNIS GRIMM, 1220 GLACIER AVE #201, JUNEAU, AK 99801
RICK GROSHONG, BOX 401, HOONAH, AK 99829
ALAN GROSS, BOX 1828, PETERSBURG, AK 99833
DAVID GROSS, BOX 74, SITKA, AK 99835
DONNA GROVER, BOX 942, WRANGELL, AK 99929
TIMOTHY GRZESKOWIAK, BOX 367, YAKUTAT, AK 99689
DAVID GUBSER, 7005 W BIRDSELL CIR, WASILLA, AK 99623
PAUL GUGGENBICKLE, BOX 63, PELICAN, AK 99832
CHRISTOPHER GUGGENBICKLER, BOX 1491, WRANGELL, AK 99929
JAMES GUINEY, BOX 1244, PETERSBURG, AK 99833
SALLY GUINEY, BOX 1244, PETERSBURG, AK 99833
WILLIAM GURSKE, BOX 291, PETERSBURG, AK 99833
ROBERT GUSTAFSON, 11322 S RUSSIAN CREEK RD, KODIAK, AK 99615
BRUCE GUTHRIE, BOX 185, METLAKATLA, AK 99926
EDWARD GUTHRIE, BOX 447, METLAKATLA, AK 99926
SOLOMON GUTHRIE, BOX 447, METLAKATLA, AK 99926
SOLOMON GUTHRIE, BOX 765, METLAKATLA, AK 99926
VICTOR GUTHRIE, BOX 1128, PETERSBURG, AK 99833
WILLIAM GUY, 416 NELLIS RD, BOTHELL, WA 98012
KEITH HAAS, 14028 2ND AVE NW, MARYSVILLE, WA 98270
KEVIN HACK, 1621 TONGASS AVE #100, KETCHIKAN, AK 99901
MARK HACKETT, 500 LINCOLN B4, SITKA, AK 99835
ED HAFFNER, BOX 32614, JUNEAU, AK 99803
HERMAN HAFFNER, 2710 ENGINEERS CUTOFF RD, JUNEAU, AK 99801
ERVIN HAGERUP, BOX 14, AUKE BAY, AK 99821

DAVID HAIDER, BOX 513, CHINOOK, MT 59523
MICHAEL HAILEY, BOX 974, CRAIG, AK 99921
JACK HAINEY, GEN DEL, POINT BAKER, AK 99927
VICTOR HALDANE, BOX 44, HYDABURG, AK 99922
MICHELLE HALE, 4431 TAKU BLVD, JUNEAU, AK 99801
ROBERT HALE, BOX 8072, KETCHIKAN, AK 99901
CHRISTOPHER HALL, 2408 WALTER DR, MODESTO, CA 95351
CLIFFORD HALL, BOX 333, FOX ISLAND, WA 98333
DAVID HALL, BOX 2563, JUNEAU, AK 99803
RICHARD HALL, 2120 E 36TH, ANCHORAGE, AK 99508
ANTHONY HALLMANN, 3043 CREST AVE, KETCHIKAN, AK 99901
FRED HALTINER, BOX 408, PETERSBURG, AK 99833
JEREMY HAMBERGER, 1148 PARK AVE, KETCHIKAN, AK 99901
FRANCIS HAMERSKY, 6590 GLACIER HWY # 281, JUNEAU, AK 99801
ZACHARY HAMILTON, BOX 1664, WARD COVE, AK 99928
CHARLES HAMLEY, BOX 467, WRANGELL, AK 99929
STANLEY HAMLIN, 612 W 10TH ST, JUNEAU, AK 99801
KENNETH HAMMER, BOX 1446, PETERSBURG, AK 99833
ROGER HAMMER, 2005 W MICHIGAN AVE, MIDLAND, TX 79701
AUSTIN HAMMOND, BOX 728, HAINES, AK 99827
ERNEST HAMMOND, POUCH B, KETCHIKAN, AK 99901
HELEN HAMMOND, POUCH B, KETCHIKAN, AK 99901
DAVID HAMMONDS, BOX 158, GUSTAVUS, AK 99826
CHARLES HANAS, 62 LODE LANE S, KETCHIKAN, AK 99901
EUGENE HANCOCK, 3619 MENDENHALL LP RD, JUNEAU, AK 99801
ELI HANLON, BOX 183, YAKUTAT, AK 99689
JOHN HANLON, 8610 MARILYN, JUNEAU, AK 99801
STEPHEN HANLON, BOX 91, HOONAH, AK 99829
TIMOTHY HANN, BOX 162, YAKUTAT, AK 99689
DANNY HANSEN, 895 W 12TH ST, JUNEAU, AK 99801
DICK HANSEN, BOX 9821, KETCHIKAN, AK 99901
EDWIN HANSEN, 229 NW 56TH, SEATTLE, WA 98107
ERNEST HANSEN, 51 S DIAMOND SHORE LN, SEQUIM, WA 98382
RICHARD HANSEN, BOX 253, PETERSBURG, AK 99833
RICHARD HANSEN, BOX 194, PETERSBURG, AK 99833
PHILLIP HANSON, 10905 MENDENHALL LP RD, JUNEAU, AK 99801
HERSHEL HARDING, BOX 304, WRANGELL, AK 99929
HAROLD HARGRAVE, 3772 JULEP ST, JUNEAU, AK 99801
CHARLES HARRIGAN, BOX 1596, JUNEAU, AK 99802
JAMES HARRIGAN, 1610 DAVIDOFF, SITKA, AK 99835
BRENT HARRINGTON, 188 COUNTY RD #121, OAKLAND, AR 72661
CATHERINE HARRIS, BOX 555, PETERSBURG, AK 99833
CHARLES HARRIS, BOX 555, PETERSBURG, AK 99833
MARY HARROP, BOX 985, PETERSBURG, AK 99833
ERNEST HARRY, BOX 24, YAKUTAT, AK 99689
JOSEPH HARSHMAN, 167 CREST DR, FAIRBANKS, AK 99712
PATRICIA HARTLAND, 10370 JOHNSON WY, JUNEAU, AK 99801
LESLIE HARTLEY, BOX 495, YAKUTAT, AK 99689
WILLIAM HARTSOCK, BOX 585, DOUGLAS, AK 99824
DAVE HARTUNG, BOX 1664, WRANGELL, AK 99929
DEWEY HARWOOD, BOX 9404, KETCHIKAN, AK 99901
NICK HASHAGEN, BOX 7033, KETCHIKAN, AK 99901
ANTHONY HASKINS, 1805 EDGECUMBE DR, SITKA, AK 99835
MARY HASTINGS, BOX 5893, KETCHIKAN, AK 99901
JAMES HATFIELD, 119 AUSTIN ST # 1109, KETCHIKAN, AK 99901
ARNOLD HAUBE, BOX 736, PETERSBURG, AK 99833
LONNIE HAUGHTON, 7 ELINOR AVE, MILL VALLEY, CA 94941
JAMES HAWKINS, BOX 163, SITKA, AK 99835
MARK HAWNEY, 1036 W SCRIVNER RD, PORT ANGELES, WA 98362
DALTON HAY, BOX 392, HAINES, AK 99827
DAVID HAY, BOX 52, HOONAH, AK 99829
RICHARD HAY, BOX 205, PELICAN, AK 99832
CALVIN HAYASHI, BOX 1003, SITKA, AK 99835
MURRAY HAYES, 224 GRANT ST, PORT TOWNSEND, WA 98368
PATRICK HAYES, 5453 DOREN RD, ACME, WA 98220

SALMON FISHING LIST—HAND TROLL

EDWIN HAYNES, 308 4TH AVE S #227, SEATTLE, WA 98104
LONNIE HAYWARD, BOX 9443, KETCHIKAN, AK 99901
ALEXANDER HAZELTON, 531 5TH ST, JUNEAU, AK 99801
EDRA HEBBRING, BOX 467, POINT BAKER, AK 99927
DENNIS HEIMDAHL, BOX 256, PETERSBURG, AK 99833
HAROLD HELFRICH, 2450 TONGASS AVE #232, KETCHIKAN, AK 99901
GERARD HELGESEN, BOX 34, HYDABURG, AK 99922
JAMES HEMBREE, BOX 177, HOONAH, AK 99829
OLAF HEMNES, BOX 175, RYDERWOOD, WA 98581
ANTHONY HENDERSHOT, 20191 GLADSTONE AVE, PT CHARLOTTE, FL 33952
VIRGIL HENKE, ST RT 2105 SAWMILL CREEK RD, SITKA, AK 99835
FREDERICK HENRY, BOX 165, YAKUTAT, AK 99689
JERALDINE HENRY, BOX 607, HOONAH, AK 99829
LAWRENCE HENRY, BOX 296, METLAKATLA, AK 99926
RONNIE HENRY, BOX 493, METLAKATLA, AK 99926
RUSSELL HENRY, BOX 102, YAKUTAT, AK 99689
RANDOLPH HENSLEY, BOX 53, GUSTAVUS, AK 99826
ARLENE HEPLER, BOX 1322, SITKA, AK 99835
GARY HERALD, BOX 785, ANACORTES, WA 98221
F HERFF, BOX 1186, PETERSBURG, AK 99833
DOUGLAS HERGERT, BOX 433, WRANGELL, AK 99929
DONALD HERNANDEZ, BOX 48, POINT BAKER, AK 99927
HERBERT HERT, BOX 723, WARD COVE, AK 99928
MARK HESSEE, BOX 117, DOUGLAS, AK 99824
JAMES HESSON, 601 W WILLOUGHBY, JUNEAU, AK 99801
GERALD HEWLETT, BOX 55, PELICAN, AK 99832
RANDY HIATT, BOX 210891, AUKE BAY, AK 99821
DAVID HIEBERT, BOX 2203, SITKA, AK 99835
MERWYN HIEBERT, 514 A ST NE, AUBURN, WA 98002
JANICE HIGHFIELD, BOX 701, HAINES, AK 99827
GARY HILDITCH, BOX 6, EDNA BAY, AK 99950
GERALD HILEY, 3884 GALA LP RD, BELLINGHAM, WA 98226
DAVID HILL, 105 FINN ALLEY, SITKA, AK 99835
ROYAL HILL, BOX 67, HOONAH, AK 99829
ERNEST HILLMAN, BOX 624, HOONAH, AK 99829
ERNEST HILLMAN, 1744 GLACIER AVE, JUNEAU, AK 99801
JARRETT HIRAI, BOX 1906, SITKA, AK 99835
WILLIAM HIXSON, #1 THE POINT, FUNTER BAY, AK 99850
THOMAS HLAVNICKA, BOX 131, HOONAH, AK 99829
TIMOTHY HLAVNICKA, BOX 248, HOONAH, AK 99829
JOHN HODGES, 318 COLEMAN ST, JUNEAU, AK 99801
JAMES HODGMAN, 415 A FRONT ST, KETCHIKAN, AK 99901
RICHARD HOFFMAN, 2684 SILVER CREEK DR, GREEN COVE, FL 32043
MARK HOFSTAD, BOX 1397, PETERSBURG, AK 99833
THOMAS HOGAN, BOX 1648, HOMER, AK 99603
PATRICK HOLLYWOOD, BOX 535, METLAKATLA, AK 99926
WILLIAM HOLLYWOOD, RT 1 BOX 3, KETCHIKAN, AK 99901
CARL HOLM, 2318 2ND AVE, SEATTLE, WA 98121
MICHAEL HOLMAN, 700 WATER ST UPPER, KETCHIKAN, AK 99901
SHARON HOLT, BOX 9224, KETCHIKAN, AK 99901
DUANE HORN, BOX 32803, JUNEAU, AK 99803
WILLIAM HORTON, BOX 020505, JUNEAU, AK 99802
PATRICK HORWATH, RT 2 BOX 42, KETCHIKAN, AK 99901
ABBY HOSIER, GENERAL DELIVERY, PORT ALEXANDER, AK 99836
LEO HOUSTON, 9144 PARKWOOD DR, JUNEAU, AK 99801
ERIC HOUTARY, 700 FAIRBANKS ST # 229, FAIRBANKS, AK 99701
PAUL HOVIK, BOX 23321, KETCHIKAN, AK 99901
SY HOVIK, BOX 23321, KETCHIKAN, AK 99901
ALBERT HOWARD, BOX 362, ANGOON, AK 99820
GEORGE HOWARD, BOX 1833, SITKA, AK 99835
GLENN HOWARD, 602 MERRILL ST, SITKA, AK 99835
JOHN HOWARD, BOX 29, ANGOON, AK 99820
WOODROW HOWARD, BOX 651, SITKA, AK 99835
GREGORY HOWE, BOX 336, GUSTAVUS, AK 99826
ROBERT HOWE, 783 N YAKIMA, WASILLA, AK 99654
MIKE HUCK, BOX 604, WARD COVE, AK 99928

JOHN HUDSON, BOX 629, METLAKATLA, AK 99926
MILNE HUDSON, BOX 8971, KETCHIKAN, AK 99901
MITCHELL HUDSON, BOX 483, METLAKATLA, AK 99926
RICHARD HUDSON, BOX 194, METLAKATLA, AK 99926
NATALIA HUFFMAN, BOX 806, SITKA, AK 99835
TERRY HUGO, BOX 9507, KETCHIKAN, AK 99901
GRANVILLE HULETT, 615 NE JESSUP, PORTLAND, OR 97211
JEFF HUME, 5212 KLAHANIE DR NW, OLYMPIA, WA 98502
DONALD HUMENIK, BOX 81457, FAIRBANKS, AK 99708
ELLWOOD HUNT, 4410 JULEP ST, JUNEAU, AK 99801
FLOYD HUNT, BOX 133, HOONAH, AK 99829
KENNETH HUNTER, BOX 164, ANGOON, AK 99820
RODNEY HUNTER, BOX 8, ANGOON, AK 99820
JEREMY HURD, BOX 1446, WARD COVE, AK 99928
DEBORAH HURLEY, BOX 1551, PETERSBURG, AK 99833
EMERY HURLEY, BOX 993, WARD COVE, AK 99928
MALCOLM HURSH, 1345 FRITZ COVE RD, JUNEAU, AK 99801
DON HUSE, BOX 373, PETERSBURG, AK 99833
RICHARD HUSE, BOX 272, PETERSBURG, AK 99833
FRANCIS IHNAT, 10050 MENDENHALL LOOP RD, JUNEAU, AK 99801
MICHAEL IHNAT, BOX 396, HOONAH, AK 99829
CHARLES INGALLS, BOX 158, REXFORD, MT 59930
DOROTHY INGLE, BOX 315, PETERSBURG, AK 99833
JULIA INGRAM, 407 13TH ST #300, BELLINGHAM, WA 98225
GEORGE INMAN, BOX 1073, SITKA, AK 99835
JOHN INMAN, 7011 E CORREGITOR RD, VANCOUVER, WA 98664
JOHN ISAAK, BOX 240316, DOUGLAS, AK 99824
LAWRENCE ISHII, 310 PETERSON, SITKA, AK 99835
GLENN ISRAELSON, BOX 64, YAKUTAT, AK 99689
SPENCER ISRAELSON, BOX 565, PETERSBURG, AK 99833
ROY ISTURIS, BOX 020766, JUNEAU, AK 99802
DUANE JACK, BOX 581, HOONAH, AK 99829
EDDIE JACK, BOX 39, ANGOON, AK 99820
EDWARD JACK, 613 CHINOOK WAY, ANGOON, AK 99820
ERNEST JACK, BOX 94, HOONAH, AK 99829
JOHNNY JACK, BOX 115, ANGOON, AK 99820
WALTER JACK, BOX 45, ANGOON, AK 99820
DAVID JACKMAN, 111 S WHITTIER #5100, WICHITA, KS 67207
ALEX JACKOWSKI, 1615 E 34TH ST, TACOMA, WA 98404
ALLEN JACKSON, BOX 241, KAKE, AK 99830
BEN JACKSON, 6590 GLACIER HWY #215, JUNEAU, AK 99801
BRUCE JACKSON, BOX 141, KAKE, AK 99830
CARLOS JACKSON, 2417 TONGASS AVE 111-251, KETCHIKAN, AK 99901
CLARENCE JACKSON, BOX 301, KAKE, AK 99830
DALE JACKSON, BOX 202-352 KEKU RD, KAKE, AK 99830
GEORGE JACKSON, BOX 6117, KETCHIKAN, AK 99901
HAROLD JACKSON, BOX 73912, FAIRBANKS, AK 99707
JEFFREY JACKSON, 3803 MCGINNIS DR, JUNEAU, AK 99803
LOREN JACKSON, BOX 211, KAKE, AK 99830
NORMAN JACKSON, 835 E SESAME ST, KETCHIKAN, AK 99901
ROYAL JACKSON, BOX 255, KAKE, AK 99830
THOMAS JACKSON, BOX 106, KAKE, AK 99830
WILLIAM JACKSON, 4408 N RIVERSIDE, JUNEAU, AK 99801
WILLIS JACKSON, BOX 241, KAKE, AK 99830
VINCENT JACOBSON, BOX 28, YAKUTAT, AK 99689
HENRY JAEGER, BOX 967, CRAIG, AK 99921
TIMOTHY JAGUSCH, BOX 692, WARD COVE, AK 99928
ROBERT JAHNKE, BOX 991, WARD COVE, AK 99928
CHESTER JAMES, BOX 115, KAKE, AK 99830
CLIFFORD JAMES, BOX 1709, PETERSBURG, AK 99833
DARYL JAMES, BOX 411, YAKUTAT, AK 99689
DONALD JAMES, BOX 284, KAKE, AK 99830
KENNETH JAMES, BOX 590, PETERSBURG, AK 99833
MELVIN JAMES, 1600 S 30TH LOT 201, ESCANABA, MI 49829
OWEN JAMES, BOX 645, HOONAH, AK 99829
PHILIP JAMES, BOX 2113, SITKA, AK 99835

SALMON FISHING LIST—HAND TROLL

ROBERT JAMES, BOX 63, ANGOON, AK 99820
ROBERT JAMES, BOX 453, CRAIG, AK 99921
RUSSELL JAMES, BOX 192, KAKE, AK 99830
THOMAS JAMES, BOX 441, HOONAH, AK 99829
DAVID JANZEN, BOX 2106, PETERSBURG, AK 99833
DEAN JAQUISH, BOX 545, WRANGELL, AK 99929
SID JARRELL, 1007 HALIBUT POINT RD, SITKA, AK 99835
RYAN JARVILL, 137 SHELIKOF WAY, SITKA, AK 99835
AGNES JAUSSAUD, 231 KATLIAN #3 2, SITKA, AK 99835
WILFORD JAUSSAUD, 231 KATLIAN #3-2, SITKA, AK 99835
FRANK JAYNES, 33 POWER HOUSE RD STG, KETCHIKAN, AK 99901
CHRISTINE JENKINS, BOX 194, WRANGELL, AK 99929
JAMES JENNINGS, BOX 902, DOUGLAS, AK 99824
KENNETH JENNINGS, BOX 1351, WRANGELL, AK 99929
DAVID JENNY, 716 KATLIAN ST #3, SITKA, AK 99835
ERVIN JENSEN, 881 NW SELBO RD, BREMERTON, WA 98310
JAMES JENSEN, BOX 213, YAKUTAT, AK 99689
JERRY JENSEN, 414 SHELIKOF ST, KODIAK, AK 99615
MARK JENSEN, BOX 457, PETERSBURG, AK 99833
MICHAEL JENSEN, 4901 BUCKINGHAM WAY, ANCHORAGE, AK 99503
ROLLAND JESKE, 3516 H P R, SITKA, AK 99835
FLOYD JIM, BOX 82, ANGOON, AK 99820
FRANK JIM, BOX 3, ANGOON, AK 99820
JOSEPH JIM, BOX 82, ANGOON, AK 99820
ERNEST JOHN, BOX 115, ANGOON, AK 99820
RICHARD JOHN, BOX 6716, KETCHIKAN, AK 99901
WILLIAM JOHN, BOX 62, ANGOON, AK 99820
AUGUST JOHNNIE, BOX 022003, JUNEAU, AK 99802
DUSTY JOHNS, BOX 1393, JUNEAU, AK 99802
EDGAR JOHNS, 4236 PTARMIGAN ST, JUNEAU, AK 99801
GLENN JOHNS, BOX 34462, JUNEAU, AK 99803
GREG JOHNS, BOX 214, KLAWOCK, AK 99925
ANTHONY JOHNSON, BOX 51, YAKUTAT, AK 99689
BILL JOHNSON, BOX 20944, JUNEAU, AK 99801
BRADLEY JOHNSON, BOX 100, MEYERS CHUCK, AK 99903
CHARLES JOHNSON, BOX 3, SITKA, AK 99835
CLIFFORD JOHNSON, 9505 ANTLER WY, JUNEAU, AK 99801
DAVID JOHNSON, 815 PHERSON ST, SITKA, AK 99835
DAVID JOHNSON, 6590 GLACIER HWY #137, JUNEAU, AK 99801
DEVIN JOHNSON, 4202 HALIBUT POINT RD, SITKA, AK 99835
EARLE JOHNSON, 300 PETERSON AVE APT A, SITKA, AK 99835
ERIC JOHNSON, BOX 23507, KETCHIKAN, AK 99901
GEORGE JOHNSON, BOX 37, ANGOON, AK 99820
JAMES JOHNSON, 2200 DUVOY CT, ANCHORAGE, AK 99502
JOSEPH JOHNSON, BOX 374, YAKUTAT, AK 99689
JOSEPH JOHNSON, BOX 88, ANGOON, AK 99820
KENNETH JOHNSON, BOX 145, ANGOON, AK 99820
KENNETH JOHNSON, BOX 145, ANGOON, AK 99820
KYLE JOHNSON, 1503 EDGECUMBE DR, SITKA, AK 99835
MARTIN JOHNSON, 1807 SAWMILL CREEK, SITKA, AK 99835
MAXWELL JOHNSON, 110 FINN ALLEY, SITKA, AK 99835
MICHAEL JOHNSON, BOX 1344, SITKA, AK 99835
NOEL JOHNSON, BOX 6232, SITKA, AK 99835
OLIVER JOHNSON, BOX PPV, KETCHIKAN, AK 99950
RALPH JOHNSON, BOX 2672, SITKA, AK 99835
RANDALL JOHNSON, BOX 1029, CRAIG, AK 99921
RAYMOND JOHNSON, 245 IRWIN ST, JUNEAU, AK 99801
RONALD JOHNSON, BOX 2232, WRANGELL, AK 99929
SAMUEL JOHNSON, BOX 412, YAKUTAT, AK 99689
SKIP JOHNSON, BOX 5, YAKUTAT, AK 99689
STANLEY JOHNSON, 405 LOUISE CT, SITKA, AK 99835
STEVEN JOHNSON, 4168 N TONGASS, KETCHIKAN, AK 99901
THOMAS JOHNSON, BOX 1821, PETERSBURG, AK 99833
WALTER JOHNSON, 7640 PLEASURE VIEW CT, ANCHORAGE, AK 99507
WILBER JOHNSON, BOX 34, ANGOON, AK 99820

WILFRED JOHNSON, BOX 237, HOONAH, AK 99829
GARITT JOHNSTON, BOX 134, PETERSBURG, AK 99833
RALPH JOHNSTON, BOX 9, PETERSBURG, AK 99833
BRUCE JOHNSTONE, 3353 1ST ST #A, KETCHIKAN, AK 99901
DUSTIN JONES, BOX 152, KLAWOCK, AK 99925
GERALD JONES, BOX 29, DOUGLAS, AK 99824
HENRY JONES, 3003 SAINT CLAIR, BELLINGHAM, WA 98226
JAMES JONES, BOX 9107, KETCHIKAN, AK 99901
LESTER JONES, BOX 893, WRANGELL, AK 99929
LOUIS JONES, BOX KXA, KASAAN, AK 99950
LYNN JONES, BOX 650, CRAIG, AK 99921
MICHAEL JONES, BOX 897, PETERSBURG, AK 99833
MICHAEL JONES, BOX 46, PETERSBURG, AK 99833
WALTER JONES, 8311 ASPEN AVE, JUNEAU, AK 99801
WILLARD JONES, BOX 575, WARD COVE, AK 99928
WILLIAM JONES, BOX 6794, KETCHIKAN, AK 99901
WILLIAM JONES, BOX 872, CRAIG, AK 99921
DENNIS JORGENSEN, 331 GASTINEAU #B-4, JUNEAU, AK 99801
GENE JORGENSEN, BOX 210648, AUKE BAY, AK 99821
CHARLIE JOSEPH, BOX 684, SITKA, AK 99835
FRANK JOSEPH, BOX 185, ANGOON, AK 99820
JEAN JOSEPH, BOX 684, SITKA, AK 99835
MATTHEW JOSEPH, GEN DEL, TENAKEE, AK 99841
RICHARD JOSEPH, 3208 HALIBUT POINT RD #3, SITKA, AK 99835
CLINTON JUDKINS, RT 2 BOX 2127, PROSSER, WA 99350
ERIKA JUDSON, BOX 210565, AUKE BAY, AK 99821
NORMAN JUDSON, BOX 240931, DOUGLAS, AK 99824
NORMAN JUDSON, BOX 1134, ANCHOR POINT, AK 99556
TIMOTHY JURCZAK, 242 SEAWATCH DR, KETCHIKAN, AK 99901
WILLIAM KACENAS, 1010 POND REEF RD, KETCHIKAN, AK 99901
LORETTA KADAKE, BOX 193, KAKE, AK 99830
MARVIN KADAKE, BOX 193, KAKE, AK 99830
WAYNE KAER, BOX 954, WRANGELL, AK 99929
JOSEPH KAHKLEN, BOX 135, ANGOON, AK 99820
TEDDY KAINO, BOX 265, PETERSBURG, AK 99833
HARRY KALBUS, BOX 63, MINERAL, WA 98355
GUY KALKINS, BOX 2053, WRANGELL, AK 99929
DALE KANEN, 9050 ROCKY COVE DR, ANCHORAGE, AK 99507
WILLIAM KANTOLA, 7811 S WHEELING #A, TULSA, OK 74136
STEVEN KANTOR, 1010 WATER ST, KETCHIKAN, AK 99901
CHARLES KARELLA, HC01 BOX 1726, GLENNALLEN, AK 99588
RHONDA KARLS, 5728 156TH S W, EDMONDS, WA 98020
ERNEST KARRAS, 6370 #2 GLACIER HWY, JUNEAU, AK 99801
PETER KARRAS, 230 KOGWANTON ST, SITKA, AK 99835
ALEX KARSUNKY, BOX 331, YAKUTAT, AK 99689
JAMES KASE, 6231 E MT GOAT CIRCLE, WASILLA, AK 99654
JEFF KASPER, 3523 FOREST GORVE DR, JUNEAU, AK 99801
LEONARD KATO, BOX 43, KLAWOCK, AK 99925
JOE KAWASHIMA, BOX 281, PETERSBURG, AK 99833
DEAN KAYLER, 22411 286TH AVE SE, MAPLE VALLEY, WA 98038
CHARLES KAZE, BOX 337, HOONAH, AK 99829
KEN KEARNEY, 624 W 9TH ST, JUNEAU, AK 99801
JAMES KEARNS, BOX 148, GUSTAVUS, AK 99826
KENNETH KEARNS, BOX 44, GUSTAVUS, AK 99826
JIM KEELINE, BOX 10, YAKUTAT, AK 99689
LINDEL KEIGHTLEY, 600 LAKE ST, SITKA, AK 99835
HARRY KEIM, 11585 MENDENHALL LP RD, JUNEAU, AK 99801
PAUL KEITHAHN, 17242 POINT LENA LOOP RD, JUNEAU, AK 99801
ROMAN KELESKE, BOX 32, POINT BAKER, AK 99927
HARRY KELLER, BOX 2442, JUNEAU, AK 99803
THORPE KELLY, W 518 23RD, SPOKANE, WA 98203
WILLIAM KEMPERMAN, BOX 19265, THORNE BAY, AK 99919
BERNARD KENDALL, BOX 91779, ANCHORAGE, AK 99509
KEITH KENDALL, 1724 THUNDERBIRD PL, ANCHORAGE, AK 99508
ROBERT KENNEDY, BOX 6, KLAWOCK, AK 99925

SALMON FISHING LIST—HAND TROLL

JOE KENOYER, RT 1 BOX 181, KETCHIKAN, AK 99901
GLEASON KENT, BOX 2797, JUNEAU, AK 99803
RICHARD KEOWN, 9679 MORAINE WAY, JUNEAU, AK 99801
MICHAEL KERNIN, BOX 274, SITKA, AK 99835
RODNEY KIESEL, 4444 MOUNTAINSIDE DR, JUNEAU, AK 99801
JERRY KIFFER, RT 1 BOX 941, KETCHIKAN, AK 99901
HERMAN KILLIAN, BOX 6283, KETCHIKAN, AK 99901
JOE KINCH, BOX 783, JUNEAU, AK 99801
CINTHIA KINDLER, BOX 381, ANACORTES, WA 98221
DALE KING, BOX 241 547 LAKEVIEW, METLAKATLA, AK 99926
JERRY KING, BOX 725, HOONAH, AK 99829
TIM KINGWELL, 147 PRICE ST #A, SITKA, AK 99835
ROBERT KINVILLE, 2309 #5 HALIBUT POINT RD, SITKA, AK 99835
EVERETT KIRCHHOFER, 9356 GLACIER HWY, JUNEAU, AK 99801
JOHN KISER, BOX 1011, WARD COVE, AK 99928
KIM KLANG, 2262 BUTLER CREEK RD, SEDRO WOOLLEY, WA 98284
KENNETH KLEIN, BOX 9609, KETCHIKAN, AK 99901
VICTOR KLOSE, 2729 TONGASS AVE #210, KETCHIKAN, AK 99901
EARL KLOSTER, 2126 2ND ST, DOUGLAS, AK 99824
ANDREW KNIGHT, BOX 1658, PETERSBURG, AK 99833
DAVID KNIGHT, BOX 251, HAINES, AK 99827
JOHN KNIGHT, 8689 DUDLEY ST, JUNEAU, AK 99801
JOHN KNIGHT, BOX 1133, PETERSBURG, AK 99833
HAROLD KNIGHTLINGER, BOX 34025, JUNEAU, AK 99803
HOWARD KNUDSON, BOX 437, HOONAH, AK 99829
RALPH KNUDSON, 6590 GLACIER HWY #34, JUNEAU, AK 99801
VICTOR KOBETICH, BOX 284, WRANGELL, AK 99929
DANIEL KOCSIS, BOX 692, HAINES, AK 99827
TIMOTHY KOENEMAN, BOX 1324, PETERSBURG, AK 99833
JOEL KOENIG, BOX 311, HOONAH, AK 99829
DAVID KOESTER, 2740 SE BENSON AVE, NEWPORT, OR 97365
JEFFREY KOETJE, 18180 DUNBAR RD, MOUNT VERNON, WA 98273
LEO KONDRO, BOX 278, KAKE, AK 99830
JACQUELINE KOOKESH, BOX 102, ANGOON, AK 99820
SALLY KOOKESH, BOX 91, ANGOON, AK 99820
STEVEN KORTIE, BOX 111062, ANCHORAGE, AK 99511
K KOSKI, 1899 SW ABERDEEN CT, OAK HARBOR, WA 98277
KOLE KOSKI, 4399 ABBY WAY, JUNEAU, AK 99801
CORWIN KOZMINSKI, BOX 5835, KETCHIKAN, AK 99901
RICHARD KRAFT, 106 DONNA DR, SITKA, AK 99835
LEE KRAUSE, BOX 1150, SITKA, AK 99835
MARVIN KRAUSE, BOX 1065, SITKA, AK 99835
ANN KREKELBERG, 17550 LENA LP RD, JUNEAU, AK 99801
LLOYD KRESTENSEN, BOX 41, TWO RIVERS, AK 99716
KENNETH KRIEGER, 36813 S WIND CREST DR, TUCSON, AZ 85739
REGINALD KRKOVICH, BOX 478, YAKUTAT, AK 99689
DALE KUBIK, BOX 224, CRAIG, AK 99921
LAWRENCE KUEHNE, BOX 305, HOONAH, AK 99829
JACK KVALE, 1776 COPPERFIELD CT, CLARKSVILLE, TN 37042
JACK KVALE, BOX 186, WRANGELL, AK 99929
JESSE KVALE, 8351 E MAGNIFICENT VIEW DR, PALMER, AK 99645
PHOEBE KVALE, BOX 186, WRANGELL, AK 99929
KURT KVERNVIK, BOX 1081, PETERSBURG, AK 99833
ROY KYLE, BOX PPV, KETCHIKAN, AK 99950
BRIAN LACEY, 9330 MINER DR, JUNEAU, AK 99801
GARY LACEY, BOX 1049, PETERSBURG, AK 99833
DARREN LACHAPELLE, BOX 2058, PETERSBURG, AK 99833
RICHARD LACKEY, PIER 45 SHED B, SAN FRANCISCO, CA 94133
WILLIAM LACKEY, 1030 PEDRO ST, FAIRBANKS, AK 99701
EDWIN LAITY, 1619 LOT 1 SAWMILL CK RD, SITKA, AK 99835
RONALD LAKEY, 3048 EAGLE LN, MCKINLEYVILLE, CA 95519
RICHARD LAMPE, BOX 21833, JUNEAU, AK 99802
ROBERT LAMPE, BOX 413, HOONAH, AK 99829
WILLIAM LAMPE, BOX 1833, JUNEAU, AK 99801
DOLAN LANCASTER, 1830 DAVIS AVE, JUNEAU, AK 99801
EDWARD LANDER, BOX 426, CRAIG, AK 99921

DAVID LANDINGHAM, 2771 MENDENHALL PEN RD, JUNEAU, AK 99801
FRANK LANE, BOX 103, ANGOON, AK 99820
JAMES LANGE, BOX 8114, PORT ALEXANDER, AK 99836
SANDRA LANGE, BOX 16174, TWO RIVERS, AK 99716
CARMEN LANTIEGNE, BOX 596, PETERSBURG, AK 99833
STEPHEN LAPOSKI, BOX 1471, PETERSBURG, AK 99833
ANDREW LARSEN, BOX 361, YAKUTAT, AK 99689
ARTHUR LARSEN, BOX 571, WRANGELL, AK 99929
CARL LARSEN, BOX 1019, SITKA, AK 99835
GAYLE LARSEN, BOX 1439, WRANGELL, AK 99929
BARBARA LARSON, BOX 1462, WRANGELL, AK 99929
DARLENE LARSON, BOX 70, POINT BAKER, AK 99927
JOHN LARSON, 5959 S TONGASS HWY, KETCHIKAN, AK 99901
ANTHONY LATZEL, BOX 297, YAKUTAT, AK 99689
FREDERICK LAUTH, BOX 17065, SEATTLE, WA 98107
DENNIS LAVIGNE, 4300 MARION DR, JUNEAU, AK 99801
DAVID LAWLER, BOX 1243, LA CONNER, WA 98257
NATHAN LAWNICKI, BOX 4, CRAIG, AK 99921
NELS LAWSON, 411 A VERSTOVIA, SITKA, AK 99835
TIMOTHY LEACH, BOX PPV LOT #29, KETCHIKAN, AK 99950
BERNICE LEAF, 7607 44TH W, TACOMA, WA 98466
DANIEL LEAF, 3323 MEANDER WY, JUNEAU, AK 99801
GARY LEASK, BOX 759, WARD COVE, AK 99928
IRVING LEASK, 8400 FREDERICK PL, EDMONDS, WA 98026
WALLACE LEASK, BOX 176, METLAKATLA, AK 99926
ALDEN LEATHERMAN, 3748 LEHMAN RD, LAINGSBURG, MI 48848
EULA LEBO, BOX 23, POINT BAKER, AK 99927
WILLIS LEBO, BOX 486, POINT BAKER, AK 99927
MICHAEL LEBOKI, 4409 NE 192ND CIR, RIDGEFIELD, WA 98642
GARY LEBOWITZ, BOX 95, HOONAH, AK 99829
ANDRE LECORNU, BOX 8853, KETCHIKAN, AK 99901
ERIC LEE, BOX 858, PETERSBURG, AK 99833
JACK LEE, BOX 1081, WARD COVE, AK 99928
JACK LEE, BOX 536, HOONAH, AK 99829
TERRY LEE, 1612 SMC, SITKA, AK 99835
WILLIAM LEE, BOX 15, HOONAH, AK 99829
ROBERT LEEKLEY, BOX 217, PETERSBURG, AK 99833
ANTHONY LEICHTY, BOX 47, CRAIG, AK 99921
WILLIAM LEMKE, BOX 611, PETERSBURG, AK 99833
GARY LENOX, 9324 VIEW DR, JUNEAU, AK 99801
PAUL LERMA, 9445 BERNERS AVE #18, JUNEAU, AK 99801
HAROLD LERVICK, 392 E BIRNIE SLOUGH RD, CATHLAMET, WA 98612
JAMES LESH, GEN DEL, GUSTAVUS, AK 99826
EARL LETSINGER, 1756 1ST & TONGASS, KETCHIKAN, AK 99901
RICHARD LEVITT, BOX 102, GUSTAVUS, AK 99826
ERIC LEWIS, BOX 2046, PETERSBURG, AK 99833
JAMES LEWIS, BOX 37, ELFIN COVE, AK 99825
LEO LEWIS, BOX 124, YAKUTAT, AK 99689
TRAVIS LEWIS, BOX 45, ELFIN COVE, AK 99825
TRUEMAN LEWIS, BOX 521, KAKE, AK 99830
MATTHEW LICHTENSTEIN, BOX 643, PETERSBURG, AK 99833
LEIF LIE, BOX 2861, JUNEAU, AK 99803
LLOYD LINDEGAARD, BOX 210142, AUKE BAY, AK 99821
JASON LINDLEY, 4401 ABBY WAY, JUNEAU, AK 99801
FRANKLIN LINDOFF, BOX 71, HOONAH, AK 99829
MIKE LINDOFF, BOX 289, HOONAH, AK 99829
JERRY LISTOWSKI, 234 7TH ST, JUNEAU, AK 99801
STEVEN LITTLE, BOX 301, GUSTAVUS, AK 99826
VICTOR LITTLEFIELD, 103 LITTLEBYRD WAY, SITKA, AK 99835
ROCKY LITTLETON, BOX 1373, PETERSBURG, AK 99833
RODNEY LITTLETON, BOX 1427, PETERSBURG, AK 99833
MICHAEL LOCKABEY, BOX 1542, WRANGELL, AK 99929
GREGORY LOCKWOOD, 4936 HUMMINGBIRD LN, JUNEAU, AK 99801
RALPH LOHSE, BOX 14, CORDOVA, AK 99574
CRAIG LONG, 3850 KILLEWICH DR, JUNEAU, AK 99801
GEORGE LONG, 9159 PARKWOOD DR, JUNEAU, AK 99803

SALMON FISHING LIST—HAND TROLL

JARED LONG, BOX EXI, JUNEAU, AK 99850
JERALD LOOMIS, BOX 332, HAINES, AK 99827
MARY LORD.WILD, BOX 109, ELFIN COVE, AK 99825
PAUL LORIS, BOX 2035, PRIEST RIVER, ID 83856
LEIF LOSETH, BOX 1164, PETERSBURG, AK 99833
FRANK LOVE, BOX 5243, KETCHIKAN, AK 99901
WILLIAM LOVE, BOX 1983, PETERSBURG, AK 99833
FREDERICK LOW, BOX 265, SIXES, OR 97476
FRANK LOWE, 4503 86TH SE, MERCER ISLAND, WA 98040
LEONARD LOWELL, 301 HIGHLAND DR, JUNEAU, AK 99801
PAUL LUBOMIRSKI, 3919 OLD PALI RD, HONOLULU, HI 96817
EDWARD LUDLOW, 1506 DAVIDOFF ST, SITKA, AK 99835
RICHARD LUDLOW, BOX 803 TRACT B, PORT ALEXANDER, AK 99836
DUARD LUDWIG, 9025 217TH ST SW, EDMONDS, WA 98026
RUSTY LUKINICH, BOX 1042, WRANGELL, AK 99929
DRUE LUNA, 102 EDGECLIFF WAY, KETCHIKAN, AK 99901
PAUL LUND, BOX 266, PETERSBURG, AK 99833
ROY LUND, BOX 266, PETERSBURG, AK 99833
GEORGE LUNDA, 9675 MORAINE WAY, JUNEAU, AK 99801
ROBERT LUNDA, BOX 204, HOONAH, AK 99829
MARK LUNDAMO, 237 CRANBERRY RD, KETCHIKAN, AK 99901
JAMES LUNZ, 1625 INTERLAKEN PL E, SEATTLE, WA 98112
JAMES LUTHER, 635 DEERMOUNT ST, KETCHIKAN, AK 99901
ANN LYONS, BOX 931, PETERSBURG, AK 99833
ANTHONY LYONS, BOX 309, QUILCENE, WA 98376
DEBORAH LYONS, BOX 379, SITKA, AK 99835
DRAKE LYONS, BOX 527, PETERSBURG, AK 99833
JACK LYONS, BOX 527, PETERSBURG, AK 99833
NEIL LYONS, BOX 527, PETERSBURG, AK 99833
WILLIAM LYONS, BOX 725, PETERSBURG, AK 99833
JAMES MACDONALD, 2718 LEE ST, ANCHORAGE, AK 99504
JUDITH MACDONALD, BOX 634, TENAKEE, AK 99841
TIMOTHY MACDONALD, BOX 1252, CRAIG, AK 99921
STUART MACH, BOX 303, KAKE, AK 99830
NORMAN MACKENZIE, BOX 95, HOONAH, AK 99829
RALPH MACKIE, BOX 252, CRAIG, AK 99921
THOMAS MACKIE, BOX 1050, CRAIG, AK 99921
RODNEY MADDOX, BOX 1165, JACKSONVILLE, OR 97530
KENNETH MADSEN, BOX 918, PETERSBURG, AK 99833
TIMOTHY MAGUIRE, BOX 32692, JUNEAU, AK 99803
MICHAEL MAHER, BOX 21175, JUNEAU, AK 99802
PATRICK MAHER, GEN DEL, IMNAHA, OR 97842
ANDREW MAKAILY, 8998 LONGRUN DR, JUNEAU, AK 99803
BYRON MALLOTT, 102 CORDOVA ST, JUNEAU, AK 99801
RONALD MANEVAL, BOX 104, SEABECK, WA 98380
STACEY MANK, BOX 488, KLAWOCK, AK 99925
RODNEY MANKINS, BOX 34041, JUNEAU, AK 99803
VANCE MANKINS, 2328 113 PLACE N, SEATTLE, WA 98133
DENNIS MANN, BOX 873, WRANGELL, AK 99929
JASON MANNEY, BOX 32265, JUNEAU, AK 99803
RAY MANSFIELD, BOX 336, DOUGLAS, AK 99824
BARBARA MAPES, BOX 1, YAKUTAT, AK 99689
RAYMOND MAPES, BOX 1, YAKUTAT, AK 99689
PAUL MARESH, BOX 3123, KETCHIKAN, AK 99901
CHARLES MARIOTTI, BOX 2633, SITKA, AK 99835
JOHN MARKLE, 7321 HARDING DR, SALCHA, AK 99714
PAUL MARKS, BOX 21376, JUNEAU, AK 99802
HAROLD MARKUSON, 838 HARDING ST, KETCHIKAN, AK 99901
BRIAN MARTENS, 2420 SIXTH AVE, KETCHIKAN, AK 99901
BERNHARDT MARTIN, BOX 526, WRANGELL, AK 99929
ELTON MARTIN, BOX 135, METLAKATLA, AK 99926
GENE MARTIN, BOX 417, HAINES, AK 99827
KENNETH MARTIN, BOX 286, KAKE, AK 99830
LYLE MARTIN, 2800 POSTAL WAY I-3, JUNEAU, AK 99801
MICHAEL MARTIN, 14714 GOODRICH DR NW, GIG HARBOR, WA 98329

MITCHELL MARTIN, 8477 THUNDER MOUNTAIN RD #4, JUNEAU, AK 99801
ROBERT MARTIN, 3441 MEANDER WY, JUNEAU, AK 99801
ROLAND MARTIN, BOX 272, KAKE, AK 99830
ROY MARTIN, BOX 406, WRANGELL, AK 99929
RYAN MARTIN, BOX 8143, PORT ALEXANDER, AK 99836
SHELBY MARTIN, 3109 NATIONAL PARK SERVICE RD A-7, JUNEAU, AK 99801
SYDNEY MARTIN, BOX 1301, WRANGELL, AK 99929
TIMOTHY MARTIN, 280 W KAGY BLVD #D, BOZEMAN, MT 59715
WADE MARTIN, BOX 1865, SITKA, AK 99835
HAROLD MARTINDALE, BOX 2197, WRANGELL, AK 99929
JAMES MARTINSEN, BOX 385, PETERSBURG, AK 99833
HELWIG MARTINSON, BOX 1082, PETERSBURG, AK 99833
DONALD MARVIN, BOX 42, KLAWOCK, AK 99925
RICHARD MARVIN, 621 MERRILL ST, SITKA, AK 99835
JOHN MASON, BOX 37, HAINES, AK 99827
ERIC MASTERS, BOX 564, DOUGLAS, AK 99824
HENRY MASTERS, 3230 NOWELL AVE, JUNEAU, AK 99801
DONALD MASTERSON, 8614 EVERGREEN PARK RD, JUNEAU, AK 99801
TOM MATHEWS, 4154 48TH AVE, SEATTLE, WA 98116
TYLER MATHEWS, 9950 STEPHEN RICHARDS DR 118, JUNEAU, AK 99801
ELMER MATNEY, BOX 949, WRANGELL, AK 99929
MORRIS MATTSON, BOX 1168, PETERSBURG, AK 99833
SHELTON MAVES, BOX 117, CRAIG, AK 99921
JAMES MAYER, BOX 33212, JUNEAU, AK 99803
DAVID MAYNARD.LOSH, BOX 195, HOONAH, AK 99829
MICHAEL MAYO, 2808 SAWMILL CREEK RD, SITKA, AK 99835
ALTON MCALLISTER, POUCH Y, KETCHIKAN, AK 99901
WILLIAM MCATEE, BOX 4388, BELLINGHAM, WA 98227
SETH MCCALLUM, BOX 191, PETERSBURG, AK 99833
JOHN MCCASLIN, BOX 3-5000, JUNEAU, AK 99802
ALAN MCCAY, BOX 513, WRANGELL, AK 99929
BERT MCCAY, BOX 78, WRANGELL, AK 99929
R MCCLINTOCK, 102 BARONOF ST, SITKA, AK 99835
CHARLES MCCLOSKEY, BOX 1728 SITKUME RT, MYRTLE POINT, OR 97458
DOUG MCCLOSKEY, BOX 493, WRANGELL, AK 99929
KENT MCCOLLUM, BOX 2096, PETERSBURG, AK 99833
SHAWN MCCONNELL, BOX 184, HOONAH, AK 99829
WYMAN MCCONNELL, BOX 121, HOONAH, AK 99829
CRAIG MCCORMICK, BOX 130, SKAGWAY, AK 99840
JAMES MCCRACKEN, BOX 691, SEWARD, AK 99664
GARY MCCULLOUGH, BOX 707, PETERSBURG, AK 99833
HARRY MCDONALD, 264 DERN DRAW, KALISPELL, MT 59901
JOHN MCDONALD, 907 LEMON CK RD, JUNEAU, AK 99802
MARY MCDONALD, RT 1 BOX 903, KETCHIKAN, AK 99901
DAVID MCFADDEN, BOX 668, PETERSBURG, AK 99833
MONTE MCFARLAND, 4314 VALLHALLA, SITKA, AK 99835
KENNETH MCGEE, BOX 021046, JUNEAU, AK 99802
FREEMAN MCGILTON, BOX 201, METLAKATLA, AK 99926
JAMES MCGOWAN, 202 KATLIAN ST #A, SITKA, AK 99835
DONALD MCGRAW, BOX 324, SITKA, AK 99835
ROBERT MCGRAW, 201 NEW ARCHANGEL ST, SITKA, AK 99835
JAMES MCHALEY, BOX 1148, PETERSBURG, AK 99833
MICHAEL MCHENRY, 3829 MELROSE ST, JUNEAU, AK 99801
WAYNE MCHOLLAND, BOX 2233, WRANGELL, AK 99929
JEFF MCIRVIN, 3560 KNOWLES RD, WENATCHEE, WA 98801
DANIEL MCKAY, BOX 261, PETERSBURG, AK 99833
ERIC MCKEE, 1455 THOMPSON AVE, SANTA CRUZ, CA 95062
SEAN MCKEOWN, BOX 210388, AUKE BAY, AK 99821
ALFRED MCKINLEY, BOX 021713, JUNEAU, AK 99802
JAMES MCLAUGHLIN, 6725 MARGUARITE ST, JUNEAU, AK 99801
ROBERT MCLAUGHLIN, BOX 1657, SITKA, AK 99835
CAROLYN MCLEOD, 785 HARRIS ST, KETCHIKAN, AK 99901
GEORGE MCLEOD, 6236 S MULLEN, TACOMA, WA 98409
GARY MCMASTER, 1722 EDGECUMBE DR, SITKA, AK 99835
KEVIN MCNAMEE, BOX 6243, SITKA, AK 99835

SALMON FISHING LIST—HAND TROLL

JOSEPH MCNEILL, BOX 67, KLAWOCK, AK 99925
LARRY MCQUARRIE, BOX 9618, KETCHIKAN, AK 99901
MICHAEL MEDALEN, BOX 969, PETERSBURG, AK 99833
JOSEPH MEEK, 2658 DOUGLAS HWY, JUNEAU, AK 99801
LEWIS MEEK, BOX 62, KLAWOCK, AK 99925
PHILLIP MEEKS, BOX 1514, PETERSBURG, AK 99833
THOMAS MEGOWN, 4106 HALIBUT PT RD, SITKA, AK 99835
VERNON MEISSNER, BOX 286, WRANGELL, AK 99929
MICHAEL MELENDREZ, BOX 222, CRAIG, AK 99921
HARVEY MENEZES, BOX 2148, PETERSBURG, AK 99833
SCOT MENZIES, 10972 BRENTWOOD LN NTG, KETCHIKAN, AK 99901
DON MERCER, BOX 97, POINT BAKER, AK 99927
EDWIN MERCER, 113 WOLFF DR, SITKA, AK 99835
HERBERT MERCER, BOX 1606, JUNEAU, AK 99801
TERENTY MERCULIEF, BOX 1545, SITKA, AK 99835
GERALD MERRIGAN, BOX 1065, PETERSBURG, AK 99833
CARROLL MERRITT, BOX 2301, WRANGELL, AK 99929
CARLOS METCALF, 8707 N LP WY, JUNEAU, AK 99801
ROBERT METER, 619 NO HANNIFIN, BISMARCK, ND 58501
ROBERT MEYER, BOX WWP, KETCHIKAN, AK 99950
RONALD MEYER, 45509 SE 150TH ST, NORTH BEND, WA 98045
CHAD MICKEL, 10805 N TONGASS HWY, KETCHIKAN, AK 99901
MAX MIELKE, 5930 LEMON ST, JUNEAU, AK 99801
JOSHUA MIETHE, BOX 2031, WRANGELL, AK 99929
LON MIKKELSEN, 4420 RIORDAN HILL DR, HOOD RIVER, OR 97031
KENNY MILAM, GEN DEL, SITKA, AK 99835
MICHAEL MILLAR, 4510 PROSPECT WY, JUNEAU, AK 99801
DOUGLAS MILLER, BOX 36, TENAKEE, AK 99841
FRANCIS MILLER, 241 W HAMPTON LN SW, OLYMPIA, WA 98512
KATHY MILLER, BOX 9602, KETCHIKAN, AK 99901
KIRK MILLER, BOX 351, AUKE BAY, AK 99821
LEROY MILLER, 1116 PARK AVE #3, KETCHIKAN, AK 99901
MAI MILLER, BOX 7982, KETCHIKAN, AK 99901
NORMAN MILLER, 1220 GLACIER AVE #312, JUNEAU, AK 99801
WILLIAM MILLER, BOX 8131, KETCHIKAN, AK 99901
JEFFREY MILLS, BOX 457, HOONAH, AK 99829
ROBERT MILLS, BOX 141024, ANCHORAGE, AK 99514
THOMAS MILLS, BOX 259, HOONAH, AK 99829
DONALD MILNES, 8243 ASPEN AVE, JUNEAU, AK 99801
CAROL MINER, 1310 34TH, ANACORTES, WA 98221
DANIEL MINER, 1406 34TH ST, ANACORTES, WA 98221
WALTER MINGE, 5295 N DOUGLAS HWY, DOUGLAS, AK 99824
JOHN MINNICH, BOX 5685, KETCHIKAN, AK 99901
KATHLEEN MOATS, 1720 DOUGLAS HWY, DOUGLAS, AK 99824
JOHN MODENE, 2895 MENDENHALL LOOP RD #51, JUNEAU, AK 99801
DENNIS MOEN, BOX 771047, EAGLE RIVER, AK 99577
ARTHUR MOLL, 2309 2ND AVE, KETCHIKAN, AK 99901
RALPH MOLL, 223 OBSERVATORY ST, SITKA, AK 99835
PETER MONDICH, 278 FIREWEED LN, KETCHIKAN, AK 99901
TODD MONTALBO, 9396 N DOUGLAS HWY, JUNEAU, AK 99801
CHRISTOPHER MOORE, BOX 8888, KETCHIKAN, AK 99901
EDWARD MOORE, 5994 LEMON ST, JUNEAU, AK 99801
JOHN MOORE, BOX 20534, JUNEAU, AK 99802
OLAN MOORE, BOX 893, SITKA, AK 99835
THOMAS MOORE, BOX 9317, KETCHIKAN, AK 99901
WILLIAM MOORE, BOX 300, CRAIG, AK 99921
DAN MORENO, BOX 1432, SITKA, AK 99835
PAUL MORENO, 127 S FRANKLIN ST #301, JUNEAU, AK 99801
SHAWN MOREY, 3229 TIMBERLINE CT, KETCHIKAN, AK 99901
DONALD MORGAN, BOX 561, TENAKEE, AK 99841
ERNEST MORGAN, BOX 582, TENAKEE, AK 99841
ROBERT MORGAN, 8048 KOSCIVSCKO DR, EDNA BAY, AK 99950
RYAN MORIN, BOX 8164, KETCHIKAN, AK 99901
DEVIN MORITZ, BOX 42, HOONAH, AK 99829
FREDERICK MORK, 108 RUDOLPH WALTON CIR, SITKA, AK 99835
ARDIS MORRIS, BOX 679, SITKA, AK 99835

MARY MORRIS, BOX 1049, CRAIG, AK 99921
WILLIAM MORRIS, BOX 240332, DOUGLAS, AK 99824
KEVIN MORRISON, BOX 4623, SOLDOTNA, AK 99669
WILLIAM MORRISON, 4039 #D S TONGASS, KETCHIKAN, AK 99901
JAMES MORTELL, BOX 42, POINT BAKER, AK 99927
MIKE MORTELL, BOX 53, POINT BAKER, AK 99927
RICHARD MOSSBURG, 2716 HALIBUT POINT RD #34, SITKA, AK 99835
JAMES MOTHERSHEAD, 8935 HAFFNER CT, JUNEAU, AK 99801
VICTOR MOY, 8213 CEDAR ST, JUNEAU, AK 99803
GARY MUEHLBERGER, BOX PPV, KETCHIKAN, AK 99950
JOSEPH MUELLER, B0X 210011, AUKE BAY, AK 99821
MILES MUNHOVEN, BOX 6335, KETCHIKAN, AK 99901
LAURA MURPH, 2309 2ND AVE, KETCHIKAN, AK 99901
FRANCIS MURPHY, BOX 1158, WARD COVE, AK 99928
JOHN MURPHY, BOX 1263, WARD COVE, AK 99928
STEVEN MURPHY, BOX 572, WRANGELL, AK 99929
TAM MURPHY, BOX 1175, WARD COVE, AK 99928
CLARENCE MURRAY, 216 VITSKARI ST SPC 4, SITKA, AK 99835
EARL MURRY, POUCH B WHALE PASS, KETCHIKAN, AK 99901
HARRY MUSEWSKI, BOX 155, PETERSBURG, AK 99833
MICHAEL MUSEWSKI, 403 SPRUCE ST, SITKA, AK 99835
BENJAMIN MUSIELAK, BOX 34773, JUNEAU, AK 99803
RICHARD MYERS, 102 DEERFIELD AVE, WATERBURY, CT 6708
JAMES MYRICK, 320 TLINGIT DR #30, JUNEAU, AK 99801
ERNIE NAKAMURA, BOX 32784, JUNEAU, AK 99803
WILLIAM NASH, 1680 FRITZ COVE RD, JUNEAU, AK 99801
DANIEL NATHAN, BOX 8651, KETCHIKAN, AK 99901
FRANK NATKONG, BOX 203, HYDABURG, AK 99922
WALTER NATKONG, BOX 61, HYDABURG, AK 99922
THOMAS NAVE, 1619 SMC #6, SITKA, AK 99835
ED NEAL, 2928 FRITZ COVE RD, JUNEAU, AK 99801
MICHAEL NEALSON, 181 DOGWOOD LN, BRINNON, WA 98320
OLAUS NEBL, 1111 DUNTON ST, KETCHIKAN, AK 99901
JAMES NEILSON, BOX 12, MEYERS CHUCK, AK 99903
NICHOLAS NEKEFEROFF, 3416 HALIBUT POINT RD #A, SITKA, AK 99835
C.GENE NELSON, BOX 1251, PORT ANGELES, WA 98362
CHARLENE NELSON, BOX 23305, KETCHIKAN, AK 99901
CHARLES NELSON, BOX 8836, KETCHIKAN, AK 99901
CHARLES NELSON, 3721 EL CAMINO ST, JUNEAU, AK 99801
DANIEL NELSON, BOX 919 PCC, PALMER, AK 99645
DARREN NELSON, 73 CLOVER VIEW CT, KETCHIKAN, AK 99901
ERIC NELSON, BOX 240073, DOUGLAS, AK 99824
GILBERT NELSON, BOX 43, METLAKATLA, AK 99926
HARRY NELSON, 8849 GAIL AVE, JUNEAU, AK 99801
JOHN NELSON, BOX 109, CRAIG, AK 99921
SUSAN NELSON, BOX 672, HAINES, AK 99827
WILLIAM NELSON, BOX 38, ANGOON, AK 99820
PETER N. JOHNSON, 2417 TONGASS AVE #111-324, KETCHIKAN, AK 99901
NEIL NEWLUN, BOX 957, PETERSBURG, AK 99833
JOSEPH NEWMAN, 5660 N DOUGLAS HWY, JUNEAU, AK 99801
SAM NEWMAN, 555 D ST, DOUGLAS, AK 99824
LEEROY NEWTON, BOX 1364, PETERSBURG, AK 99833
YANCY NICHOL, 11 DEER VALLEY DR, GLENWOOD SPRINGS, CO 81601
MICHAEL NICHOLS, BOX 122, POINT BAKER, AK 99927
RICHARD NICHOLS, BOX 312, YAKUTAT, AK 99689
VANCE NICHOLS, 1825 NE 4TH ST, E WENATCHEE, WA 98801
WILLIAM NICHOLS, 9112 284TH ST NE, ARLINGTON, WA 98223
JAMES NIELSEN, BOX 4201, MOUNT EDGECUMBE, AK 99835
MICHAEL NIGRO, BOX 81, GUSTAVUS, AK 99826
MATT NILSEN, BOX 1463, PETERSBURG, AK 99833
MICHAEL NILSEN, BOX 2069, PETERSBURG, AK 99833
PETER NILSEN, BOX 427, PETERSBURG, AK 99833
ROBERT NISBET, 722 LAKE ST, SITKA, AK 99835
ANTHONY NIZICH, 3045 FRITZ COVE RD, JUNEAU, AK 99801
MICHAEL NIZICH, 1860 FRITZ COVE RD, JUNEAU, AK 99801
GARY NOLT, BOX 9548, KETCHIKAN, AK 99901

SALMON FISHING LIST—HAND TROLL

DEAN NORDENSON, BOX 210025, AUKE BAY, AK 99821
THOMAS NORDTVEDT, 75288 TROY RD, WALLOWA, OR 97885
THOMAS NORDTVEDT, 126 GIMBAL LN, KETCHIKAN, AK 99901
PALMER NORE, BOX 404, WRANGELL, AK 99929
LADD NORHEIM, BOX 935, PETERSBURG, AK 99833
DAVID NORMAN, BOX 1327, CRAIG, AK 99921
JAMES NORRIS, BOX 483, HOONAH, AK 99829
KENNETH NORRIS, BOX 2036, SITKA, AK 99835
DENNIS NORTHRUP, BOX 1159, WARD COVE, AK 99928
WAYNE NORTHRUP, BOX 1177, WARD COVE, AK 99928
LEO NORTON, 8302 S TONGASS HWY, KETCHIKAN, AK 99901
JACQUES NORVELL, BOX 240314, DOUGLAS, AK 99824
TODD NOTTINGHAM, BOX 34425, JUNEAU, AK 99803
CHARLES NOWLIN, BOX 020283, JUNEAU, AK 99802
EHREN OBERNDORFER, BOX 6528, SITKA, AK 99835
BRIAN OBERREUTER, 1938 DODGE CIR, SITKA, AK 99835
JAMES OCONNOR, 6030 CHATHAM DR, JUNEAU, AK 99801
JOSEPH OFFUTT, BOX 662, DOUGLAS, AK 99824
SHAWN OGIMACHI, BOX 281, KLAWOCK, AK 99925
GEORGE OGLE, BOX 381, YAKUTAT, AK 99689
NEIL OHASHI, 223 STEDMAN ST, KETCHIKAN, AK 99901
MICHAEL OHLSON, BOX 3039, ARIZONA CITY, AZ 85123
GEORGE OKEGAWA, 8419 DECOY BLVD, JUNEAU, AK 99801
RONALD OKEGAWA, 3400 EUREKA #304, ANCHORAGE, AK 99501
HENRY OKSVOLL, BOX 2845, SITKA, AK 99835
CARL OLIVER, BOX 243, HOONAH, AK 99829
ERLING OLSEN, 3028 NOWELL AVE, JUNEAU, AK 99801
ANNETTE OLSON, BOX 814, PETERSBURG, AK 99833
DARRYL OLSON, BOX 1304, PETERSBURG, AK 99833
DUANE OLSON, 5750 SILVER STAR RD, BELLINGHAM, WA 98226
HELMER OLSON, BOX 814, PETERSBURG, AK 99833
MARIE OLSON, BOX 33556, JUNEAU, AK 99803
RONALD OLSON, BOX 123, KLAWOCK, AK 99925
STEVEN OLSON, 714 CHATHAM AVE #2, KETCHIKAN, AK 99901
RICHARD OLTMAN, 370 MIDDLEPOINT, PORT TOWNSEND, WA 98368
BRIAN OMANN, 285 BON JON VIEW WAY, SEQUIM, WA 98382
ROY OMOHUNDRO, RT 1 BOX 67, SUMMERVILLE, OR 97376
DANIEL ONEIL, BOX 1455, PETERSBURG, AK 99833
DENNIS ONEIL, BOX 1083, PETERSBURG, AK 99833
ALLEN ONEILL, BOX 753, PELICAN, AK 99832
LARRY OREAR, BOX 115, PETERSBURG, AK 99833
NATHAN ORR, BOX 1409, SEWARD, AK 99664
CHARLES ORSBORN, BOX 210893, AUKE BAY, AK 99821
CARL OSBAKKEN, ST RT 1719 SMC, SITKA, AK 99835
WILLIAM OSBEKOFF, 238 LAKEVIEW DR, SITKA, AK 99835
DAVID OTTE, 938 W SESAME ST, KETCHIKAN, AK 99901
CHARLES OUELLETTE, BOX 735, SITKA, AK 99835
BARRY OYLER, PPV, KETCHIKAN, AK 99950
MONTE OYLER, BOX 1, POINT BAKER, AK 99927
NORMAN OYLER, BOX 4128, EASTSIDE, OR 97420
ROBERT OZAWA, BOX 1707, SITKA, AK 99835
CHRISTOPHER PACE, BOX 33594, JUNEAU, AK 99803
LANCE PACKER, BOX 592, SITKA, AK 99835
LOGAN PADGETT, BOX 205, PETERSBURG, AK 99833
GEORGE PAGE, BOX 49, PETERSBURG, AK 99833
DAVID PALMER, BOX PPV, KETCHIKAN, AK 99950
VICTOR PALMER, BOX 63, HAINES, AK 99827
JOHN PALMES, BOX 20454, JUNEAU, AK 99802
MATTHEW PANCRATZ, BOX 5054, NIKOLAEVSK, AK 99556
DENNIS PARENT, 11291 BAYVIEW EDISON RD, MOUNT VERNON, WA 98273
MARILYN PARKS, BOX 565, WARD COVE, AK 99928
ALLEN PARMENTER, BOX 9091, KETCHIKAN, AK 99901
FOREST PARSLEY, BOX 475, PETERSBURG, AK 99833
CAROLYN PARSONS, BOX 55, CRAIG, AK 99921
BOBBY PATE, BOX 402, YAKUTAT, AK 99689

DONALD PATE, BOX 402, YAKUTAT, AK 99689
ROGER PATTEN, 1215 SW 149TH, SEATTLE, WA 98166
ALEXANDER PATTERSON, BOX 45, METLAKATLA, AK 99926
JAMES PATTERSON, BOX 443, SITKA, AK 99835
WILLIAM PATTERSON, 14435 AGUA VISTA RD N, JACKSONVILLE, FL 32224
JESSICA PAVLIK, BOX 191, YAKUTAT, AK 99689
PAUL PEARSON, BOX 1195, SITKA, AK 99835
THOMAS PEARSON, 603 DEERMOUNT, KETCHIKAN, AK 99901
CLINT PEAVEY, BOX 8344, KETCHIKAN, AK 99901
DAN PEAVEY, BOX 19228, THORNE BAY, AK 99919
ROBERT PEAVEY, 119 AUSTIN # 210, KETCHIKAN, AK 99901
ROBERT PECK, BOX 76, ANGOON, AK 99820
MARK PEDERSEN, 8512 RAINBOW ROW, JUNEAU, AK 99801
GERALD PEELE, BOX 46, HYDABURG, AK 99922
CHARLES PEEP, BOX 1603, HAINES, AK 99827
RICHARD PELKEY, BOX 351, YAKUTAT, AK 99689
WARREN PELLETT, BOX 885, SITKA, AK 99835
JAMES PENNY, 2013 SAWMILL CREEK RD #6, SITKA, AK 99835
LINCOLN PERATROVICH, BOX 3, KLAWOCK, AK 99925
PETER PEREZ, 4300 N DOUGLAS, JUNEAU, AK 99801
ALFRED PERKINS, BOX 683, SITKA, AK 99835
JAMES PERKINS, BOX 909, PACIFIC CITY, OR 97135
DAVID PERRY, 2417 TONGASS AVE # 111-143, KETCHIKAN, AK 99901
JAMES PERRY, 5975 LEMON ST, JUNEAU, AK 99801
DAVID PETERKIN, BOX 5441, KETCHIKAN, AK 99901
RYAN PETERS, 110 LANCE DR, SITKA, AK 99835
WALTER PETERS, BOX 494, WRANGELL, AK 99929
FRANKLIN PETERSEN, BOX 020513, JUNEAU, AK 99802
LOWELL PETERSEN, BOX 62, YAKUTAT, AK 99689
ERIK PETERSON, BOX 75, PELICAN, AK 99832
FLOYD PETERSON, BOX 245, HOONAH, AK 99829
GERALD PETERSON, BOX 523, HOONAH, AK 99829
JOE PETERSON, 4274 ROSS CT, ANCHORAGE, AK 99504
KIRK PETERSON, BOX 172, CRAIG, AK 99921
LESLIE PETERSON, BOX 551, KAKE, AK 99830
LORRAINE PETERSON, BOX 114, KAKE, AK 99830
MELANIE PETERSON, BOX 6604, KETCHIKAN, AK 99901
RALPH PETERSON, BOX 2027, PETERSBURG, AK 99833
ROBERT PETERSON, BOX 403, PETERSBURG, AK 99833
WILLIAM PETERSON, BOX 137, HOONAH, AK 99829
STEVE PETTY, BOX 202, GUSTAVUS, AK 99826
WILLIAM PFEIFER, 2901 BARANOF AVE, KETCHIKAN, AK 99901
CAVEN PFEIFFER, 236 OBSERVATORY ST, SITKA, AK 99835
JEFFREY PFUNDT, BOX 855, PETERSBURG, AK 99833
J PHETTEPLACE, 1013 W 6TH, THE DALLES, OR 97058
TRUEMAN PHILBRICK, 1501 DAVIDOFF ST, SITKA, AK 99835
FREDERICK PHILLIPS, BOX 020987, JUNEAU, AK 99802
JAMES PHILLIPS, 18195 TRAILS END DR, JUNEAU, AK 99801
LELAND PHILLIPS, BOX 1251, WRANGELL, AK 99929
RONALD PHILLIPS, 1500 S COTTEN DR, WASILLA, AK 99654
VERNON PHILLIPS, BOX 522, WRANGELL, AK 99929
DUANE PIATT, 48215 LAKESIDE DR, SOLDOTNA, AK 99669
JESS PIBURN, POUCH B, KETCHIKAN, AK 99901
KENNETH PIERCE, BOX 8004, PORT ALEXANDER, AK 99836
CHARLES PIERCY, BOX 1025, WARD COVE, AK 99928
WILLIAM PIERRE, BOX 460, ORONDO, WA 98843
DENNIS PIKE, BOX 846, CORDOVA, AK 99574
SHARON PILLEN, BOX 671672, CHUGIAK, AK 99567
ARTHUR PIM, 620 112TH SE #131, EVERETT, WA 98204
TIMOTHY PINE, 3705 ARCTIC BLVD #209, ANCHORAGE, AK 99503
GERALD PITCHER, 871 GOLDMINE TRAIL, FAIRBANKS, AK 99712
STEPHEN PITELL, 3501 PREBLE ST, BREMERTON, WA 98312
TOM PITTMAN, 173 BEHRENDS AVE, JUNEAU, AK 99801
GARY PLUMB, BOX 8234, KETCHIKAN, AK 99901
JOHN POLIVKA, 311 WORTMAN LP, SITKA, AK 99835

SALMON FISHING LIST—HAND TROLL

LARRY POLLOCK, BOX 4134, MOUNT EDGECUMBE, AK 99835
GERALD POND, 5227 MADRONA HTS, SILVERTON, OR 97381
ALBERT PORTER, BOX 175, YAKUTAT, AK 99689
CARL PORTER, BOX 7844, KETCHIKAN, AK 99901
DAVID POTTS, 23511 19TH DR SE, BOTHELL, WA 98021
AARON POWELL, BOX 499, WRANGELL, AK 99929
CAROLINE POWELL, BOX 159, YAKUTAT, AK 99689
WARREN POWERS, BOX 150, POINT BAKER, AK 99927
JACOB PRATT, BOX 202, HOONAH, AK 99829
STEVE PRESTON, BOX 869, PORT ALEXANDER, AK 99836
ROBERT PRICE, BOX 54, HYDABURG, AK 99922
ROGER PRICE, BOX 60372, FAIRBANKS, AK 99706
JOHN PRIDDY, BOX 647, CRAIG, AK 99921
GERALD PRIMMER, 1215 SAYLES ST, KETCHIKAN, AK 99901
WILLIAM PRIVETT, BOX 775, WRANGELL, AK 99929
JAMES PROCTOR, BOX 31, GUSTAVUS, AK 99826
BRUCE PUCKETT, 6685 W LEOPOLD LP, WASILLA, AK 99623
VERNON PULJU, BOX 3040, KETCHIKAN, AK 99901
ERIN PURPLE, 59-258 PUPUKEA RD, HALEIWA, HI 96712
ARVID PUUSTINEN, BOX 531, HOONAH, AK 99829
JACK QUERY, 8866 N DOUGLAS HWY, JUNEAU, AK 99801
RICHARD QUINN, BOX 94, MARBLEMOUNT, WA 98267
MARCELO QUINTO, BOX 20583, JUNEAU, AK 99802
AZA RALPH, 6842 ROOSEEVELT DR, KETCHIKAN, AK 99901
DAVID RAMOS, 4651 REKA DR #24, ANCHORAGE, AK 99508
GEORGE RAMOS, BOX 128, YAKUTAT, AK 99689
DON RANDALL, POUCH E, KETCHIKAN, AK 99901
JOHN RANWEILER, BOX 2118, EL PRADO, NM 87529
STEVEN RASMUSSEN, 2741 ENGINEERS CUTOFF RD, JUNEAU, AK 99801
SVEND RASMUSSEN, 336 S 185TH ST, SEATTLE, WA 98148
DAVID RATHBONE, BOX 863, WRANGELL, AK 99929
BOBBY RATLIFF, BOX 1343, PETERSBURG, AK 99833
PEGGY RAUWOLF, 7942 S TONGASS HWY, KETCHIKAN, AK 99901
JEFFERY RAY, BOX 1864, PETERSBURG, AK 99833
GREGORY REAVES, 434 3RD ST, JUNEAU, AK 99801
DOUGLAS REDBURN, BOX 240488, DOUGLAS, AK 99824
HARLEN REED, 6630 LIBBY RD, OLYMPIA, WA 98506
ALAN REEVES, BOX 741, WRANGELL, AK 99929
RYAN REEVES, BOX 758, WRANGELL, AK 99929
BRIAN REID, BOX 32012, JUNEAU, AK 99803
LESLIE REID, BOX 32012, JUNEAU, AK 99803
JEFFREY REINHARDT, 2025 HALIBUT POINT RD, SITKA, AK 99835
BRUCE REITER, BOX 1039, DELTA JUNCTION, AK 99737
MARTY REMUND, BOX 1295, HAINES, AK 99827
MELVIN RENER, BOX 104, YAKUTAT, AK 99689
LESLIE RENO, BOX 677, WARD COVE, AK 99928
RICHARD REYNOLDS, 112 DODGE LN, PORT LUDLOW, WA 98365
KENNETH RHEA, 11213 NW 25TH CRT, VANCOUVER, WA 98685
COLE RHODEN, BOX 630, PETERSBURG, AK 99833
RONALD RHODES, 710 LAKE ST, SITKA, AK 99835
THOMAS RHYNER, 505 ROBIN DR, KENAI, AK 99611
ELI RIBICH, BOX 110, PETERSBURG, AK 99833
GLEN RICE, ISLAND D, MEYERS CHUCK, AK 99903
JOHN RICE, BOX 18131, COFFMAN COVE, AK 99918
ALLEN RICHARDS, BOX 944, PETERSBURG, AK 99833
DONALD RICHARDS, BOX 1764, PETERSBURG, AK 99833
GEORGE RICHTER, BOX 1 EDB, KETCHIKAN, AK 99950
PATRICK RICHTER, 1508 HIS WAY LN, EDNA BAY, AK 99950
RICKY RICHTER, 2500 HALIBUT POINT RD, SITKA, AK 99835
RONALD RICHTER, 5329 LAKEMOUNT BLVD SE #823, BELLEVUE, WA 98006
WAYNE RICHTER, 2500 HALIBUT POINT RD, SITKA, AK 99835
GERALD RICKARD, BOX 66, PETERSBURG, AK 99833
WILLIS RIDLEY, BOX 527, METLAKATLA, AK 99926
RAFE RIECH, 805 CHARLES ST, SITKA, AK 99835
EDWARD RILATOS, BOX 781, WRANGELL, AK 99929
RONALD RIMA, POSTAL AMEX 2009 113 W G STREET, SAN DIEGO, CA 99821

ROBERT RINEHART, BOX 5442, KETCHIKAN, AK 99901
CRAIG RING, 578 N POINT HIGGINS, KETCHIKAN, AK 99901
DAMION RIPLEY, 3512 ALASKA AVE, KETCHIKAN, AK 99901
WALTER RITCHIE, BOX 46520, SEATTLE, WA 98126
RICHARD RITTER, BOX 691, DOUGLAS, AK 99824
KENNETH RIVEST, 2339 MEADOW LN, JUNEAU, AK 99801
RONALD RIVETT, 1910 8TH AVE NE, ABERDEEN, SD 57401
CLAUDE ROBERTS, 9029 LONGRUN DR, JUNEAU, AK 99801
DANIEL ROBERTS, 3136 N TRUWOOD DR #A, PRESCOTT VALLEY, AZ 86314
DONALD ROBERTS, 2415 HEMLOCK #308, KETCHIKAN, AK 99901
INA ROBERTS, 2415 HEMLOCK #209, KETCHIKAN, AK 99901
TOM ROBERTS, 5311 NE 207TH AVE, VANCOUVER, WA 98662
WAYNE ROBERTS, 9452 B LAPEROUSE, JUNEAU, AK 99801
YOTE ROBERTSON, BOX 1072, DILLINGHAM, AK 99576
BETHANY ROBICHAUD, BOX 116, GUSTAVUS, AK 99826
BRENT ROBINSON, BOX 1549, WARD COVE, AK 99928
MAX ROBISON, BOX 481, LA CONNER, WA 98257
LARRAE ROCHELEAU, 1202 SEWARD AVE, SITKA, AK 99835
THOMAS ROCKNE, BOX 1305, PETERSBURG, AK 99833
ROBERT ROCKWOOD, BOX 477, YAKUTAT, AK 99689
BRYAN ROESING, 5766 MEGO DR, ANCHORAGE, AK 99507
LAUREN ROGERS, BOX 842, WRANGELL, AK 99929
GERALD ROMINE, 2120 BROADWAY, BAKER, OR 97814
MARVIN RONIMOUS, BOX 1246, PETERSBURG, AK 99833
LEWIS ROOKER, 638 SEWARD ST, JUNEAU, AK 99801
PAUL ROOP, BOX 480, CRAIG, AK 99921
CLARENCE ROSE, BOX 176, ANGOON, AK 99820
HAROLD ROSE, BOX 161, KAKE, AK 99830
JOHN ROSS, 517 NELSON ST, JUNEAU, AK 99801
TIMOTHY ROSS, BOX 371, YAKUTAT, AK 99689
WILLIAM ROSS, BOX 371, YAKUTAT, AK 99689
RICHARD ROSTAD, BOX 183, KAKE, AK 99830
SCOTT ROTH, 3648 MARY ANN CT, ANCHORAGE, AK 99502
JERRY ROUNSLEY, 10890 MENDENHALL LP RD, JUNEAU, AK 99801
TERRY ROWLAND, BOX 605, WRANGELL, AK 99929
MILAN RUCKA, 1912 SE 125TH CT, VANCOUVER, WA 98683
JACK RUDER, 1942 S COLFAX ST, GRIFFITH, IN 46319
GABRIEL RUFF, BOX 4501, MOUNT EDGECUMBE, AK 99835
MICHAEL RUGO, BOX 1424, WRANGELL, AK 99929
WILLIAM RUHLE, 2655 N CERRITOS, PALM SPRINGS, CA 92262
MAXWELL RULE, 110 DONNA DR, SITKA, AK 99835
JOHN RUOPP, 323 POLARIS CIRCLE, BISHOP, CA 93514
DAVID RUSSELL, 9198 W PARKVIEW TERRACE LP, EAGLE RIVER, AK 99577
DOUGLAS RUSSELL, BOX 524, THORNE BAY, AK 99919
ERIC RUSSELL, HC 33 BOX 2969, WASILLA, AK 99654
JACKIE RUSSELL, 7943 N DOUGLAS HWY, JUNEAU, AK 99802
JAMES RUSSELL, BOX 301, YAKUTAT, AK 99689
SIGURD RUTTER, 310 TILSON, SITKA, AK 99835
PETER RUZGIS, BOX 22, KLAWOCK, AK 99925
RODERICK RYLL, BOX 2273, WRANGELL, AK 99929
DAVID RYNO, BOX 367, KLAWOCK, AK 99925
FRANK RYNO, 1240 W BEYLUND LP, PALMER, AK 99645
KEITH SAHL, 208 BEHRENDS AVE, JUNEAU, AK 99801
GREGORY SALES, BOX 2377, SITKA, AK 99835
MAC SALING, BOX 6696, KETCHIKAN, AK 99901
ROGER SALMI, 12004 SHADOW BROOK RD, SW OLYMPIA, WA 98502
ROGER SAMPSON, BOX 332, METLAKATLA, AK 99926
CECIL SAMSON, BOX 169, METLAKATLA, AK 99926
GAINHART SAMUELSON, BOX 449, PETERSBURG, AK 99833
ERIC SAND, BOX 1238, PETERSBURG, AK 99833
JOHN SANDERSON, BOX 021031, JUNEAU, AK 99802
ROBERT SANTI, 263 OHINA PL, KIHEI, HI 96753
BRUCE SARFF, BOX 1613, WRANGELL, AK 99929
MICHAEL SATHER, 703 PRIEST POINT RD N W, TULALIP, WA 98271
BRYCE SAVIERS, 2600 ENGINEERS CUTOFF, JUNEAU, AK 99801
FRANCIS SAVIERS, 2556 ENGINEERS CUTOFF, JUNEAU, AK 99801

SALMON FISHING LIST—HAND TROLL

RICHARD SAVIERS, BOX 3091, JUNEAU, AK 99803
STANLEY SAVLAND, BOX 621, HOONAH, AK 99829
DANIEL SAVONE, 15431 TOBOGGAN RD, PINE, CO 80470
EZRA SBONEK, BOX PPV, KETCHIKAN, AK 99950
JEFFREY SBONEK, BOX 16, POINT BAKER, AK 99927
ROBERT SCHAEFER, BOX 6307, SITKA, AK 99835
LUKE SCHEIDECKER, BOX 338, CRAIG, AK 99921
WILLIAM SCHENKER, BOX 022108, JUNEAU, AK 99802
ENOCH SCHERTEL, BOX 43, YAKUTAT, AK 99689
TIM SCHERTEL, 408 HOGAN DR, LIBBY, MT 59923
BOYD SCHIESS, 236 W 4000 S, LOGAN, UT 84321
DAN SCHIMELPFENIG, BOX 198, YAKUTAT, AK 99689
ANTHONY SCHMIDT, BOX 464, YAKUTAT, AK 99689
MICHAEL SCHMIT, 648 BUREN RD, KETCHIKAN, AK 99901
ALAN SCHOLL, 5388 NIKULA RD, EMBARRASS, MN 55732
KENNETH SCHOONOVER, BOX 373, HOONAH, AK 99829
PAUL SCHREIBER, 231 KATLIAN #A10, SITKA, AK 99835
ROBERT SCHROTH, BOX 1104, JUNEAU, AK 99801
RUSSELL SCHULTZ, BOX 240562, DOUGLAS, AK 99824
BRITTANEY SCHUNZEL, 1823 EASTLAKE AVE #463, SEATTLE, WA 98102
STEVEN SCHUTTE, BOX 10837, FAIRBANKS, AK 99710
RONN SCHUTTIE, 6126 SHOAL PL, KETCHIKAN, AK 99901
MICHAEL SCHWARTZ, BOX 434, PETERSBURG, AK 99833
KELLY SCOTT, BOX 738, ANCHOR POINT, AK 99556
JONATHAN SCRIBNER, 9502 RADCLIFFE CT, JUNEAU, AK 99801
ROBERT SEARING, BOX 147, POINT BAKER, AK 99927
LAVELLE SEARS, RT 1 BOX 675, KETCHIKAN, AK 99901
GEORGE SEE, 6590 GLACIER HWY #275, JUNEAU, AK 99801
GLADYS SEEDS, BOX 33, TENAKEE, AK 99841
RONNIE SEGO, BOX 7784, KETCHIKAN, AK 99901
ARMAND SEGUIN, 141 NEWCASTLE DR, VALLEJO, CA 94591
JASON SEIFERT, 6490 N DOUGLAS HWY, JUNEAU, AK 99801
JOHN SEINES, BOX 931, WRANGELL, AK 99929
LOUIS SELTZER, BOX 2575, HOMER, AK 99603
RODNEY SELVIG, BOX 981, MEADOW VISTA, CA 95722
MARK SEVERSON, BOX 1502, PETERSBURG, AK 99833
HELEN SEYFERLICH, W 2390 SUNSET BEACH DR, ELMA, WA 98541
GEOFFREY SEYMOUR, BOX 25, PELICAN, AK 99832
DAVID SHAPLEY, 2120 33RD AVE, ANACORTES, WA 98221
RAYMOND SHAPLEY, BOX 189, CRAIG, AK 99921
ROLLO SHAQUANIE, BOX 288, KAKE, AK 99830
DANIEL SHARCLANE, BOX 122, HOONAH, AK 99829
DEAN SHARCLANE, C/O PO BOX 114, HOONAH, AK 99829
JOHN SHARCLANE, 3405 FOSTER AVE #149, JUNEAU, AK 99801
PHIL SHARCLANE, BOX 405, HOONAH, AK 99829
CHRIS SHARPSTEEN, 2527 ROUTE JJ, ROCKY COMFORT, MO 64861
ELLEN SHARPSTEEN, BOX 1255, PETERSBURG, AK 99833
MARK SHAW, 832 BUREN #96, KETCHIKAN, AK 99901
CLIFFORD SHEA, 835 E SESAME, KETCHIKAN, AK 99901
LAWRENCE SHEARER, BOX 305, METLAKATLA, AK 99926
MICHAEL SHELDON, BOX 1285, PETERSBURG, AK 99833
JOHN SHELTON, BOX 101, HOONAH, AK 99829
BRIAN SHILTS, BOX 367, WRANGELL, AK 99929
DAVID SHILTS, BOX 19264, THORNE BAY, AK 99919
MICHAEL SHILTS, BOX 1341, WRANGELL, AK 99929
ROBERT SHILTS, 934 BROWN DEER RD, KETCHIKAN, AK 99901
ARTHUR SHOEMAKER, BOX 3-6000 #127, JUNEAU, AK 99801
BILL SHORT, BOX 177, KAKE, AK 99830
JOSEPH SHORT, BOX 1224, PETERSBURG, AK 99833
MARK SHORT, BOX 342, CRAIG, AK 99921
ARNOLD SHRYOCK, BOX 188, NAMPA, ID 83653
LEWIE SILVA, BOX 58, PETERSBURG, AK 99833
RON SILVA, BOX 210007, AUKE BAY, AK 99821
RYAN SILVA, 608 MONASTERY ST, SITKA, AK 99835
JOHN SIMONS, 342 ENDRESON, HOQUIAM, WA 98550

JAMES SIMPSON, BOX 45, HYDER, AK 99923
JOHN SIMPSON, BOX 1773, SITKA, AK 99835
JOHN SIMPSON, 3315 MEANDER WY, JUNEAU, AK 99801
LOUIE SIMPSON, BOX 766, SITKA, AK 99835
LYLE SIMPSON, BOX 7213, KETCHIKAN, AK 99901
DANIEL SIMS, 41801 UPPER BERLIN DR, LEBANON, OR 97355
TOM SIMS, BOX 1553, WRANGELL, AK 99929
JACK SIREVOG, 1106 PARK AVE, KETCHIKAN, AK 99901
GARY SJOROOS, BOX 966, JUNEAU, AK 99802
ALF SKAFLESTAD, BOX 177, HOONAH, AK 99829
ALF SKAFLESTAD, BOX 490, HOONAH, AK 99829
ARLEN SKAFLESTAD, BOX 381, YAKUTAT, AK 99689
KOLBJORN SKAFLESTAD, BOX 471, HOONAH, AK 99829
WENDELL SKAFLESTAD, BOX 214, HOONAH, AK 99829
DEWEY SKAN, BOX 34, KLAWOCK, AK 99925
THOMAS SKEEK, BOX 242, KAKE, AK 99830
WILBUR SKEEK, BOX 593, HOONAH, AK 99829
JOHN SKEELE, 262 KAAGWAANTAAN ST, SITKA, AK 99835
MICHAEL SKRZYNSKI, BOX 240813, DOUGLAS, AK 99824
COLBY SLANAKER, 66 GARLAND CT, KETCHIKAN, AK 99901
DAVID SLATE, BOX 236, SITKA, AK 99835
FRANCES SLATE, BOX 236, SITKA, AK 99835
RONALD SLATTERY, 206 W MATTLE RD, KETCHIKAN, AK 99901
GARY SLAVEN, BOX 205, PETERSBURG, AK 99833
ANDREW SLAVIN, BOX 489, PETERSBURG, AK 99833
DANIEL SLOAN, BOX 1967, PETERSBURG, AK 99833
JOEL SMALLEY, BOX 496, WRANGELL, AK 99929
ROBERT SMART, BOX 420, NAUKATI BAY, AK 99950
DAVID SMILEY, 1302 SAWMILL CREEK RD #28, SITKA, AK 99835
ALVIN SMITH, BOX 3739, WINNEMUCCA, NV 89446
DENNIS SMITH, 2006 HALIBUT PT RD, SITKA, AK 99835
ERNEST SMITH, BOX 1641, SUSANVILLE, CA 96130
GARRETT SMITH, 113 NAOMI KANOSH LN, SITKA, AK 99835
GLEN SMITH, BOX 8044, PORT ALEXANDER, AK 99836
HENRY SMITH, BOX 481, SITKA, AK 99835
LAWREN SMITH, BOX 32305, JUNEAU, AK 99803
LESTER SMITH, 5755 GLACIER HWY, JUNEAU, AK 99801
MICHAEL SMITH, 832 BUREN #113, KETCHIKAN, AK 99901
PATRICK SMITH, 504 NW 77TH ST, VANCOUVER, WA 98665
PAUL SMITH, BOX 8131, KETCHIKAN, AK 99901
RAY SMITH, 230 W 14TH # 401, ANCHORAGE, AK 99501
ROGER SMITH, BOX 245, OROVILLE, WA 98844
ROSSER SMITH, BOX 475, HOONAH, AK 99829
SCOTT SMITH, 5901 E 6TH #238, ANCHORAGE, AK 99504
WILLIAM SMITH, 2806 MARSHA AVE, JUNEAU, AK 99803
STEPHEN SNAPP, 290 10TH ST, PORT TOWNSEND, WA 98368
WILLIAM SNIDER, BOX 1307, PETERSBURG, AK 99833
J SNYDER, BOX 82352, FAIRBANKS, AK 99708
LESLIE SNYDER, BOX 1076, PETERSBURG, AK 99833
ROSS SOBOLEFF, BOX 240632, DOUGLAS, AK 99824
HENRY SONDIE, 207 WASHINGTON, KETCHIKAN, AK 99901
GREGORY SORENSON, BOX 109, HOPE, AK 99605
PAUL SOUTHLAND, BOX 257, WRANGELL, AK 99929
ROD SOWARDS, 8489 THUNDER MNT RD, JUNEAU, AK 99801
CORALIE SPARKS, BOX 387, ST IGNATIUS, MT 59865
RALPH SPEAR, 832 BUREN #116, KETCHIKAN, AK 99901
JAMES SPETEN, 7432 N DAVENPORT ST, DALTON GARDENS, ID 83815
DONALD SPIGELMYRE, BOX 611, PETERSBURG, AK 99833
ANTHONY SPRAGUE, 12841 JOHNS RD, ANCHORAGE, AK 99515
RICHARD SPRAGUE, BOX 567, PETERSBURG, AK 99833
BARBARA STAAKE, BOX 843, PETERSBURG, AK 99833
SCOTT STAFFORD, 911 PAXTON RD SW, ROCHESTER, MN 55902
EDWARD STAHL, 1140 WOODLAND AVE, KETCHIKAN, AK 99901
EDWARD STAHL, 651 DEERBERRY CT, KETCHIKAN, AK 99901
LEONARD STAIGLE, 27035 S SKINNER, ESTACADA, OR 97023

SALMON FISHING LIST—HAND TROLL

LUCAS STAMM, BOX 5663, KETCHIKAN, AK 99901
NORMAN STANDLEY, BOX 1601, SNOHOMISH, WA 98291
HOWARD STARBARD, 4452 WOOD DUCK AVE, JUNEAU, AK 99801
DENNIS STARR, 6009 GULL WAY, JUNEAU, AK 99801
ALAN STEIN, GEN DEL, POINT BAKER, AK 99927
FRANK STEINER, 83 POWERHOUSE RD STG, KETCHIKAN, AK 99901
WILLIAM STELLER, BOX 1723, HOMER, AK 99603
KEVIN STELMACH, BOX 621, PETERSBURG, AK 99833
LEIF STENFJORD, 117 NW 181ST ST, SHORELINE, WA 98177
LEE STEPHENS, 6655 N DOUGLAS HWY, JUNEAU, AK 99801
MICHAEL STEPHENS, BOX PPV, KETCHIKAN, AK 99950
DONALD STEVENS, BOX 1393, WRANGELL, AK 99929
JOHN STEVENS, BOX 2256, JUNEAU, AK 99803
SCHUYLER STEVENS, 9227 LONG RUN DR, JUNEAU, AK 99801
ALLEN STEWART, BOX 606, PELICAN, AK 99832
ERNEST STEWART, RT 1 BOX 1047, KETCHIKAN, AK 99901
HOMER STEWART, BOX 1287, GLOBE, AZ 85501
MICAH STICKWAN, BOX 5041, KETCHIKAN, AK 99901
DONALD STINE, BOX 247, KAKE, AK 99830
DAN STOCKEL, BOX 1172, SITKA, AK 99835
EARL STOKES, BOX 512, WRANGELL, AK 99929
DAVID STONE, BOX 204, YAKUTAT, AK 99689
RAY STONER, BOX 394, PETERSBURG, AK 99833
STEVEN STORM, 4757 MOSQUITO LAKE RD, DEMING, WA 98244
CHARLES STOTTS, BOX 13, TENAKEE, AK 99841
JAMES STOUGH, BOX 1320, WRANGELL, AK 99929
JHEA STOUT, BOX 9011, KETCHIKAN, AK 99901
CHARLES STOVALL, 2396 ODAY DR, JUNEAU, AK 99801
MARY STRAHM, BOX 723, PELICAN, AK 99832
PATRICK STRAM, BOX 210086, AUKE BAY, AK 99821
JOHN STRANGE, 1200 W DIMOND #1424, ANCHORAGE, AK 99515
RICHARD STRATY, BOX 210211, AUKE BAY, AK 99821
AUSTIN STRICKLAND, BOX 292, PETERSBURG, AK 99833
JOHN STRICKLING, 22-1/2 RIKER ST, SALINAS, CA 93901
JAMES STROMDAHL, BOX 1326, PETERSBURG, AK 99833
LEIF STROMDAHL, BOX 523, PETERSBURG, AK 99833
WALTER STUART, BOX 2196, WRANGELL, AK 99929
RICHARD STUBBE, 35600 SINGLTON RD, CALINESA, CA 92320
SUSAN STURM, 617 KATLIAN #A10, SITKA, AK 99835
DENNIS SUCH, BOX 3115, KETCHIKAN, AK 99901
PETER SULLIVAN, BOX 020874, JUNEAU, AK 99802
IRENIO SUMAUANG, 220 LANCE DR, SITKA, AK 99835
JOSEPH SUNNEN, BOX 2095, PETERSBURG, AK 99833
DAVID SVENDSEN, BOX 1123, WRANGELL, AK 99929
AXEL SVENSON, 283 S POINT HIGGINS, KETCHIKAN, AK 99901
MICHAEL SVENSON, 104 SHARON DR, SITKA, AK 99835
FARRELL SWAIN, BOX 3082, SITKA, AK 99835
DYLAN SWANBERG, BOX 3053, SITKA, AK 99835
ADAM SWANSON, BOX 2151, PETERSBURG, AK 99833
ERIC SWANSON, BOX 6330, SITKA, AK 99835
FLOYD SWANSON, BOX KXA, KETCHIKAN, AK 99950
RICHARD SWANSON, BOX 39286, NINILCHIK, AK 99639
ROBERT SWANSON, BOX 924, PETERSBURG, AK 99833
JAMES SWIFT, BOX 1193, SITKA, AK 99835
TROY SWOFFORD, 923 GLACIER AVE, JUNEAU, AK 99801
ROGER SYLVESTER, 2620 FRITZ COVE RD, JUNEAU, AK 99801
ARCADIO TAGABAN, 175 GASTINEAU AVE #A, JUNEAU, AK 99801
LARRY TALLEY, 3041 DOUGLAS HWY, JUNEAU, AK 99801
HENRY TALLMAN, BOX 402, THORNE BAY, AK 99919
GEORGE TANINO, BOX 5577, KETCHIKAN, AK 99901
J TANNER, 215 5TH ST, DOUGLAS, AK 99824
JIMMY TATSUDA, BOX 7442, KETCHIKAN, AK 99901
WILLIAM TATSUDA, 525 GRANT ST, KETCHIKAN, AK 99901
JOHN TATUM, BOX 5294, KETCHIKAN, AK 99901
JON TATUM, BOX 252, SITKA, AK 99835
GORDON TAYLOR, 5555 THANE RD, JUNEAU, AK 99801

HAL TAYLOR, BOX 586, SITKA, AK 99835
JERRY TAYLOR, BOX 7893, KETCHIKAN, AK 99901
PATRICK TAYLOR, BOX 33818, JUNEAU, AK 99803
RICHARD TAYLOR, BOX 171, THORNE BAY, AK 99919
ROBERT TAYLOR, BOX 1234, BOZEMAN, MT 59715
STANLEY TAYLOR, BOX 5313, KETCHIKAN, AK 99901
LEOPOLDO TEJEDA, BOX 283, YAKUTAT, AK 99689
HERBERT TENNELL, BOX 1772, SITKA, AK 99835
DONALD TENNEY, BOX 8063, PORT ALEXANDER, AK 99836
DEAN TERRY, BOX 46, PETERSBURG, AK 99833
JOEL TEUNE, 6239 S TONGASS AVE, KETCHIKAN, AK 99901
ROGER THAYER, BOX 313, YAKUTAT, AK 99689
JERRY THEROS, 6840 ROBERTSON BLVD, CHARLESTON, OR 97420
TODD THINGVALL, BOX 375, HOONAH, AK 99829
DONALD THOMAS, GEN DEL, ISSAQUAH, WA 98027
FRED THOMAS, BOX 181, NORDLAND, WA 98358
GERALD THOMAS, BOX 245, SITKA, AK 99835
JAMES THOMAS, BOX 217, KAKE, AK 99830
JAMES THOMAS, 2026 HALIBUT POINT RD #D, SITKA, AK 99835
JASON THOMAS, 73 CLOVER VIEW CT, KETCHIKAN, AK 99901
PAUL THOMAS, BOX 104, ANGOON, AK 99820
RICHARD THOMAS, BOX 212, KAKE, AK 99830
ROBERT THOMAS, 5275 SHORELINE DR N, KETCHIKAN, AK 99901
WILLIAM THOMAS, BOX 5196, KETCHIKAN, AK 99901
LINDA THOMASSEN, BOX 742, WRANGELL, AK 99929
PALMER THOMASSEN, BOX 608, PETERSBURG, AK 99833
ROBERT THOMASSEN, BOX 1265, PETERSBURG, AK 99833
CHESTER THOMPSON, 684 D 2 LP RD N, KETCHIKAN, AK 99901
CODY THOMPSON, BOX 324, KLAWOCK, AK 99925
DANIEL THOMPSON, BOX 464, WRANGELL, AK 99929
DONNA THOMPSON, 938 W SESAME ST, KETCHIKAN, AK 99901
DOUGLAS THOMPSON, 3817 EVERGREEN AVE, KETCHIKAN, AK 99901
JAMES THOMPSON, BOX 1260, WRANGELL, AK 99929
WILLIAM THOMPSON, BOX 924, WARD COVE, AK 99928
ED THORSEN, BOX 784, PETERSBURG, AK 99833
DONALD THORSTEINSON, BOX 728, PETERSBURG, AK 99833
DONALD THURSTON, 9310 LOHRER LN NE, OLYMPIA, WA 98516
KENNETH THYNES, BOX 791, PETERSBURG, AK 99833
STEVEN THYNES, BOX 193, PETERSBURG, AK 99833
LARRY TILLOTSON, BOX 518, WARD COVE, AK 99928
ARNOLD TISCH, BOX 32457, JUNEAU, AK 99803
JAMES TITUS, BOX 512 1/2, THORNE BAY, AK 99919
BRYAN TODD, BOX 181, GUSTAVUS, AK 99826
KIM TOLAND, BOX 1037, PETERSBURG, AK 99833
MARK TOLLFELDT, BOX 578, KLAWOCK, AK 99925
ROBERT TOLSON, BOX 88, HYDABURG, AK 99922
JOHN TOMARO, 2564 MEADOW LN, JUNEAU, AK 99801
SEAN TOMKINSON, BOX 244, KLAWOCK, AK 99925
WILLIAM TOMPKINS, 416 6TH ST, JUNEAU, AK 99801
PAUL TORGRAMSEN, BOX 1959, WRANGELL, AK 99929
INGWALD TOTLAND, BOX 27, YAKUTAT, AK 99689
OLAF TOTLAND, BOX 373, YAKUTAT, AK 99689
ALBERT TRACY, BOX 51, SITKA, AK 99835
JON TRAIBUSH, BOX 55, GUSTAVUS, AK 99826
THOMAS TRAIBUSH, 1300 PEACE PORTAL DR #206, BLAINE, WA 98230
LARRY TRAMBITAS, BOX 210331, AUKE BAY, AK 99821
WALTER TRENT, 3870 HALIBUT PT HWY, SITKA, AK 99835
DAVID TROUT, BOX 1094, HAINES, AK 99827
MARC TUCHSCHERER, 9015 GEE ST, JUNEAU, AK 99801
SHAWN TUCKER, 9174 JAMES BLVD, JUNEAU, AK 99801
BRYAN TURNER, BOX 1226, WARD COVE, AK 99928
SHELDON TURNER, 115 JAMESTOWN DR, SITKA, AK 99835
GEORGE TURNMIRE, BOX 26, ANGOON, AK 99820
TIMOTHY TWADDLE, BOX 1825, SITKA, AK 99835
FRED UMBARGER, 8477 THUNDER MOUNTAIN RD #36, JUNEAU, AK 99801
ROY UNDERDAHL, 3021 CREST AVE S, KETCHIKAN, AK 99901

SALMON FISHING LIST—HAND TROLL

DOUGLAS UNRUH, RT 1 BOX 57, PERRYTON, TX 79070
JACK URATA, BOX 907, WRANGELL, AK 99929
JOHN VALE, BOX 193, YAKUTAT, AK 99689
SHIRLIE VALE, BOX 509, YAKUTAT, AK 99689
STEPHEN VALE, BOX 92, YAKUTAT, AK 99689
ARCHIE VALENTINE, BOX 55724, NORTH POLE, AK 99705
GEORGE VALLE, BOX 44, YAKUTAT, AK 99689
THEODORE VALLE, BOX 272, YAKUTAT, AK 99689
DARRELL VANDERGRIFF, 412 D1 LOOP RD N, KETCHIKAN, AK 99901
SHANNON VANDERVEST, BOX 1392, PETERSBURG, AK 99833
JAMES VANDERWEELE, BOX 6116, KETCHIKAN, AK 99901
JOANNE VANDERWEELE, BOX 6116, KETCHIKAN, AK 99901
JOE VANDERZANDEN, BOX 122, GUSTAVUS, AK 99826
PAUL VANDOR, BOX 240502, DOUGLAS, AK 99824
DAVID VANOOSTENBUR, BOX 9391, KETCHIKAN, AK 99901
MICHAEL VAUGHN, 1304 GEORGESON LP, SITKA, AK 99835
JAMES VEAZEY, BOX 8576, KETCHIKAN, AK 99901
WILLIAM VELER, BOX 387, HOONAH, AK 99829
STEPHEN VERTREES, BOX 1963, PETERSBURG, AK 99833
ARTUR VESHTI, 410 SPRUCE ST A, SITKA, AK 99835
DANIEL VICK, BOX 1271, PETERSBURG, AK 99833
GANNON VICK, BOX 842, PETERSBURG, AK 99833
JAMES VICK, BOX 613, PETERSBURG, AK 99833
FELIX VILLARMA, BOX 938, WRANGELL, AK 99929
SEFERINO VILLARREAL, BOX 533, HOONAH, AK 99829
EDWARD VILORIA, BOX 696, PETERSBURG, AK 99833
PETER VINCENT, BOX 344, HOONAH, AK 99829
EDWARD VOLK, BOX 1564, PETERSBURG, AK 99833
ROBERT VOLK, BOX 576, PETERSBURG, AK 99833
SAMUEL VOLK, 7011 TAMIR AVE, ANCHORAGE, AK 99504
SANDRA VOLK, BOX 554, PETERSBURG, AK 99833
RAYMOND VOLZKE, BOX 3089, KETCHIKAN, AK 99901
JOE VON.DOLOSKI, BOX 8117, PORT ALEXANDER, AK 99836
JOSEPH WABEY, 15618 42ND DR NW, STANWOOD, WA 98292
HUGH WADE, BOX 939, AUKE BAY, AK 99821
SEVARD WAGENIUS, BOX 9375, KETCHIKAN, AK 99901
THOMAS WAGGONER, BOX 5706, KETCHIKAN, AK 99901
WALTER WAGNER, BOX 107, METLAKATLA, AK 99926
FRANK WAITE, BOX 1647, PETERSBURG, AK 99833
JOHN WAITE, 125 MAIN ST #113, KETCHIKAN, AK 99901
WILLIAM WALDER, BOX 11, ELFIN COVE, AK 99825
ARNOLD WALKER, GEN DEL, ANGOON, AK 99820
JONATHAN WALKER, BOX 553, WARD COVE, AK 99928
MURRAY WALSH, 3219 TONGASS BLVD, JUNEAU, AK 99801
DONALD WANIE, BOX 65, DOUGLAS, AK 99824
BRUCE WANSTALL, BOX 19332, THORNE BAY, AK 99919
MONTE WARBIS, 12100 ELDERBERRY LN NTG, KETCHIKAN, AK 99901
ROLAND WARD, AK PIONEERS HOME, SITKA, AK 99835
BRUCE WARDEN, BOX 1783, SITKA, AK 99835
WILLIAM WARE, BOX 672, PETERSBURG, AK 99833
FRANK WARFEL, BOX 517, WRANGELL, AK 99929
LUKE WARMAN, 9015 GEE ST, JUNEAU, AK 99801
BRIAN WARMUTH, BOX 6382, KETCHIKAN, AK 99901
RONALD WARREN, BOX 2664, SITKA, AK 99835
ARNOLD WASVICK, BOX 493, PETERSBURG, AK 99833
CHARLES WATSON, 10533 INTERLAKE AVE N, SEATTLE, WA 98133
DANIEL WEATHERLY, BOX 1018, HOMER, AK 99603
MARJORIE WEATHERS, BOX 133, HOPE, AK 99605
BRETT WEAVER, 104 PEACE LN, SITKA, AK 99835
MARK WEAVER, BOX 1181, PETERSBURG, AK 99833
VICTOR WEAVER, BOX 2034, SITKA, AK 99835
JOSEPH WEBB, 507 KATLIAN ST, SITKA, AK 99835
JAY WEBBER, 516 PARADISE RAIL, HAMILTON, MT 59840
JOHN WEEMES, BOX 197, UNALAKLEET, AK 99684
ROY WEGAND, BOX 357, KLAWOCK, AK 99925

JEFFREY WEGENER, BOX 2078, PETERSBURG, AK 99833
KENT WEGENER, BOX 594, PETERSBURG, AK 99833
ARNOLD WEIMER, 635 W 12TH ST, JUNEAU, AK 99801
DAVID WEIS, 1961 HAMPTON RD, WAUCHULA, FL 33873
KEITH WEISS, BOX 534, TENAKEE, AK 99841
CLYDE WELCH, 6010 N DOUGLAS HWY, JUNEAU, AK 99801
DENNIS WELCH, BOX 1611, HOMER, AK 99603
DOUGLAS WELDE, BOX 875, PETERSBURG, AK 99833
VIRDEN WELDE, 12221 48TH ST E, EDGEWOOD, WA 98372
WAYNE WELDE, 10812 153RD ST CT E, PUYALLUP, WA 98374
ROBERT WELKER, BOX 1247, FORKS, WA 98331
KENNETH WELLS, BOX 4, YAKUTAT, AK 99689
MARK WELLS, C/O 395 HWY 101 W, PORT ANGELES, WA 87362
GERALD WENTWORTH, BOX 101, CRAIG, AK 99921
BRENT WENTZEL, BOX 111, ONALASKA, WA 98570
LAWRENCE WEST, BOX 627, METLAKATLA, AK 99926
LEROY WEST, 419 12TH ST, JUNEAU, AK 99801
WILLIAM WEST, 5894 PINE ST, JUNEAU, AK 99801
JAMES WESTERVELT, BOX 3482, MONTROSE, CO 81402
JOHN WESTLUND, 4810 TANYA CIR, ANCHORAGE, AK 99502
GEORGE WESTMAN, BOX 534, HOONAH, AK 99829
JANELLE WEYHMILLER, BOX 147, CRAIG, AK 99921
CHARLES WHEATON, BOX 21662, JUNEAU, AK 99802
MATT WHEELER, BOX 135, YAKUTAT, AK 99689
TED WHITBECK, 9099 SHEIYE WY, JUNEAU, AK 99801
DANA WHITE, GEN DEL, JUNEAU, AK 99801
FRANK WHITE, GEN DEL, KAKE, AK 99830
IRENE WHITE, BOX 586, PETERSBURG, AK 99833
JAMES WHITE, 245B W MATTLE RD, KETCHIKAN, AK 99901
TODD WHITE, BOX 523, WRANGELL, AK 99929
TRAVIS WHITE, BOX 864, CRAIG, AK 99921
ULEY WHITE, BOX 586, PETERSBURG, AK 99833
PAUL WHITEHEAD, 5300 BLUEBERRY LN, JUNEAU, AK 99801
ELMER WHITETHORN, BOX 885, PETERSBURG, AK 99833
GERALD WHITETHORN, BOX 1550, PETERSBURG, AK 99833
JOE WHITSON, BOX 1018, SITKA, AK 99835
CHESTER WICK, BOX 149, POINT BAKER, AK 99927
ALLAN WICKENS, 2417 TONGASS AVE #111-336, KETCHIKAN, AK 99901
DANIEL WICKMAN, BOX 894, WRANGELL, AK 99929
TOM WICKMAN, BOX 1513, WRANGELL, AK 99929
KENNETH WICKS, BOX 34017, JUNEAU, AK 99803
GEOFFREY WIDDOWS, BOX 342, YAKUTAT, AK 99689
KENNETH WIDMYER, BOX 242, EDNA BAY, AK 99950
DETLEF WIECK, 2270 D MILLAR RD, FRIDAY HARBOR, WA 98250
LUKE WIEDEL, 4650 QUAY ST, WHEAT RIDGE, CO 80033
RICHARD WIEDERSPOHN, BOX 965, WRANGELL, AK 99929
TRAVIS WILCOX, BOX 1376, WARD COVE, AK 99928
LINCOLN WILD, BOX 1673, SITKA, AK 99835
LINDA WILD, BOX 020704, JUNEAU, AK 99802
GERALD WILKERSON, 4635 S SPRUCE, WHITE CLOUD, MI 49349
RUSSELL WILKES, BOX 830, SITKA, AK 99835
WAYNE WILKINSON, 98445 E LN, BROOKINGS, OR 97415
LAWRENCE WILLARD, BOX 194, HAINES, AK 99827
ALVIN WILLIAMS, BOX 33381, JUNEAU, AK 99803
ANTHONY WILLIAMS, BOX 15, ANGOON, AK 99820
BILLY WILLIAMS, 8322 GLADSTONE ST, JUNEAU, AK 99801
CHARLES WILLIAMS, 7001 E B ST, TACOMA, WA 98404
CHARLES WILLIAMS, CEDAR SPRINGS BYTE, EDNA BAY, AK 99950
DANIEL WILLIAMS, BOX KXA, KETCHIKAN, AK 99950
DANIEL WILLIAMS, 800 SIRSTAD, SITKA, AK 99835
DWIGHT WILLIAMS, BOX 2674, JUNEAU, AK 99803
JEFF WILLIAMS, BOX 21744, JUNEAU, AK 99802
JOHN WILLIAMS, 511 W 10TH ST, JUNEAU, AK 99801
JON WILLIAMS, BOX 615, PELICAN, AK 99832
MELVIN WILLIAMS, BOX 278, HOONAH, AK 99829

SALMON FISHING LIST—HAND TROLL / FISH WHEEL

RICHARD WILLIAMS, 9253 GEE ST, JUNEAU, AK 99801
ROGER WILLIAMS, BOX 118, ANGOON, AK 99820
SYLVESTER WILLIAMS, BOX 127, KLAWOCK, AK 99925
WALLACE WILLIAMS, BOX 765, DOUGLAS, AK 99824
ZENITH WILLIAMS, 288 VILLAGE ST, JUNEAU, AK 99801
JACK WILLIS, BOX 202, PETERSBURG, AK 99833
JOHN WILLIS, BOX 534, KAKE, AK 99830
R.STEPHEN WILLIS, BOX 426, HOONAH, AK 99829
ROY WILLIS, 5020 POWERS ST, JUNEAU, AK 99801
FRED WILLOCKS, RT 3 BOX 508, MARYVILLE, TN 37801
CHARLES WILLS, BOX 7554, KETCHIKAN, AK 99901
RODNEY WILLS, BOX 6271, KETCHIKAN, AK 99901
MICHAEL WILLYERD, BOX 9342, KETCHIKAN, AK 99901
CALVIN WILSON, BOX 261, KAKE, AK 99830
CALVIN WILSON, BOX 181, KAKE, AK 99830
CHARLES WILSON, BOX 314, METLAKATLA, AK 99926
ELIZABETH WILSON, BOX 240434, DOUGLAS, AK 99824
FRANK WILSON, BOX 472, DOUGLAS, AK 99824
GARY WILSON, BOX 021091, JUNEAU, AK 99802
MATTHEW WILSON, 617 KATLIAN ST, SITKA, AK 99835
NORMAN WILSON, 111 SAND DOLLAR DR, SITKA, AK 99835
RANDALL WILSON, BOX 108, KAKE, AK 99830
GREG WINEGAR, 4477 MOUNTAINSIDE DR, JUNEAU, AK 99801
KENNETH WINGO, BOX 020284, JUNEAU, AK 99802
CHAD WINNOP, 100 KINCROFT WAY #A, SITKA, AK 99835
IRA WINOGRAD, 435 KENNEDY ST, JUNEAU, AK 99801
JOHN WINTHER, BOX 509, PETERSBURG, AK 99833
ROLAND WIRTH, 612 MONASTERY ST, SITKA, AK 99835
MICHAEL WISNEWSKI, 201 W MATTLE RD N, KETCHIKAN, AK 99901
KURT WOHLHUETER, BOX 1312, PETERSBURG, AK 99833
JEFF WOLFE, BOX 381, SITKA, AK 99835
SHARON WOLFE, BOX 9171, KETCHIKAN, AK 99901
KENNETH WOLFF, BOX 94, PELICAN, AK 99832
JAMES WOMACK, BOX 1506, SITKA, AK 99835
CRAIG WONG, 7115 CORREGIDOR RD, VANCOUVER, WA 98664
CHARLES WOOD, BOX 383, PETERSBURG, AK 99833
MICHAEL WOOD, 6590 GLACIER HWY #118, JUNEAU, AK 99801
PATRICK WOOD, 10 MELTON RD, PORT ANGELES, WA 98363
THOMAS WOOD, 1752 14TH AVE S, SEATTLE, WA 98144
BRETT WOODBURY, BOX 2121, WRANGELL, AK 99929
GEORGE WOODS, BOX 292, KLAWOCK, AK 99925
GREGORY WOODS, BOX 4, KLAWOCK, AK 99925
WILLIAM WOODS, BOX 4, KLAWOCK, AK 99925
CHARLES WOOLSEY, 2309 HALIBUT POINT RD #38, SITKA, AK 99835
ROB WORDEN, BOX 21154, AUKE BAY, AK 99821
ANDY WORHATCH, BOX 614, PETERSBURG, AK 99833
NYAL WORSHAM, 2660 DOUGLAS HWY, JUNEAU, AK 99801
RANDALL WORTMAN, BOX 271, CRAIG, AK 99921
ANDY WRIGHT, BOX 1432, PETERSBURG, AK 99833
FRANK WRIGHT, BOX 75, HOONAH, AK 99829
FRANK WRIGHT, BOX 497, HOONAH, AK 99829
GORDON WROBEL, 961 NEBRASKA AVE W, SAINT PAUL, MN 55117
LARRY WYCKOFF, 368 ROAD D, WILLOWS, CA 95988
JOHN WYNN, 6050 N DOUGLAS HWY, JUNEAU, AK 99801
LYLE YANCEY, BOX 1738, WRANGELL, AK 99929
DAVID YEISLEY, 8365 N TONGASS HWY, KETCHIKAN, AK 99901
CLAUDE YOUNG, 722 WHISPERING PINES LN, COEURD ALENE, ID 83815
RALPH YOUNG, 1645 LEES CREEK RD, MYRTLE CREEK, OR 97457
ROBERT YOUNG, BOX KXA KASAAN, KETCHIKAN, AK 99950
ROBIN YOUNG, BOX 1194, PETERSBURG, AK 99833
THOMAS YOUNG, 495 INDIAN RIVER RD, SITKA, AK 99835
WILLIAM YOUNG, 2389 KA SEE ANN DR, JUNEAU, AK 99801
JOHN YOUNGER, BOX 6324, SITKA, AK 99835
JOHN YUREK, BOX 84735, FAIRBANKS, AK 99708
NICHOLAS YURKO, 9412 LONG RUN DR, JUNEAU, AK 99801
CHARLES ZIESKE, BOX 70, POINT BAKER, AK 99927

ARTHUR ZINK, BOX 125, KLAWOCK, AK 99925
FRANK ZINN, BOX 7235, KETCHIKAN, AK 99901
CARMELITA ZWICK, MARBLE IS 3 NKI 426, NAUKATI BAY, AK 99950

SALMON, FISH WHEEL, UPPER YUKON
HENRY AGNES, BOX 1, NULATO, AK 99765
VICTORIA AGNES, BOX 3537, VALDEZ, AK 99686
GEORGE ALBERT, BOX 34, RUBY, AK 99768
BRIAN ASPLUND, 406 W MCNAIR RD, WINNEBAGO, IL 61088
KAREN ATTLA, BOX 3588, KENAI, AK 99611
MARY BEAL, 2701 TURNER ST #4C, FAIRBANKS, AK 99701
DARLENE BISHOP, 3365 SANDVIK ST, FAIRBANKS, AK 99709
DEBORAH BOOTH, BOX 65, ANVIK, AK 99558
CHARLIE BOULDING, BOX 89, MANLEY HOT SPRINGS, AK 99756
VALERIE BRAIRTON, 1638 MARBURGER DR, FAIRBANKS, AK 99712
CECELIA BURGETT, BOX 85, GALENA, AK 99741
RONALD BURGETT, BOX 185, GALENA, AK 99741
RICHARD BURNHAM, BOX 8, KALTAG, AK 99748
C CAMPBELL, BOX 111, TANANA, AK 99777
WALTER CARLO, 1918 CENTRAL AVE, FAIRBANKS, AK 99709
WILLIAM CARLO, 1601 MARIKA #3, FAIRBANKS, AK 99709
RONALD CARTER, BOX 463, NENANA, AK 99760
KENNETH CHASE, BOX 41, ANVIK, AK 99558
TIMOTHY CHASE, 4109 GARFIELD ST #A, ANCHORAGE, AK 99503
SHANNON CHASE.JENSEN, BOX 151, ANVIK, AK 99558
SHAWN CLARK, BOX 357, NENANA, AK 99760
TERRENCE CLARK, BOX 357, NENANA, AK 99760
ROSE.ANN DAYTON, BOX 353, GALENA, AK 99741
GINGER DE.LIMA, BOX 70, RUBY, AK 99768
MARVIN DEACON, BOX 45, GRAYLING, AK 99590
NELSON DEACON, BOX 4, GRAYLING, AK 99590
DIANE DEMOSKI, 3207 CHIMNEY SWIFT LN, RICHMOND, TX 77469
ERNEST DEMOSKI, 1037 W JONES DR, WASILLA, AK 99654
FLORA DEMOSKI, 1261 BRADWAY RD, NORTH POLE, AK 99705
MARTHA DEMOSKI, BOX 13, NULATO, AK 99765
WILLIAM DEMOSKI, BOX 273, GALENA, AK 99741
LILLER DIEMONT, 5818 SUTTER AVE, RICHMOND, CA 94804
LINA EDWIN, BOX 5, KALTAG, AK 99748
AARON EKADA, BOX 68, NULATO, AK 99765
CURTIS ERHART, 2647 GREBE AVE, FAIRBANKS, AK 99709
LESTER ERHART, BOX 213, TANANA, AK 99777
REBECCA ERHART, BOX 263, TANANA, AK 99777
TERRENCE ESAU, BOX 00143, NENANA, AK 99760
AUSTIN ESMAILKA, BOX 25, KALTAG, AK 99748
EARL ESMAILKA, BOX 82, KALTAG, AK 99748
FLORENCE ESMAILKA, BOX 29, RUBY, AK 99768
HAROLD ESMAILKA, BOX 29, RUBY, AK 99768
LAWRENCE ESMAILKA, BOX 65072, NULATO, AK 99765
CHARLES EVANS, BOX 42, STEVENS VILLAGE, AK 99774
DAVID EVANS, BOX 72548, FAIRBANKS, AK 99707
LINDA EVANS, BOX 73431, FAIRBANKS, AK 99707
DAVID FERRIERA, 2131 YELLOWSNOW RD, FAIRBANKS, AK 99709
JAMES FOLGER, BOX 216, TANANA, AK 99777
RUSSELL FOLGER, BOX 216, TANANA, AK 99777
RICKI FREIREICH, BOX 26, GRAYLING, AK 99590
BEVERLY GEORGE, 3288 ADAMS DR #114, FAIRBANKS, AK 99709
JESSICA GOFF, 901 YOKUM ST, FAIRBANKS, AK 99709
GAIL GREGORY, BOX 316, GALENA, AK 99741
JOHN HAKALA, BOX 771226, EAGLE RIVER, AK 99577
JOSH HANSON, BOX 172, NENANA, AK 99760
LARRY HAUSMANN, BOX 18, GALENA, AK 99741
ANITA HENRY, 1707 TURNER ST #102, FAIRBANKS, AK 99701
ANNIE HILDEBRAND, BOX 65050, NULATO, AK 99765
EDDIE HILDEBRAND, BOX 65050, NULATO, AK 99765
JAMES HONEA, BOX 324, GALENA, AK 99741

SALMON FISHING LIST—FISH WHEEL / POWER TROLL

GILBERT HUNTINGTON, BOX 264, GALENA, AK 99741
GLENDA HUNTINGTON, BOX 124, GALENA, AK 99741
JOHN HUNTINGTON, BOX 209, TANANA, AK 99777
LEONARD HUNTINGTON, 601 CHENA RIDGE RD, FAIRBANKS, AK 99709
LOIS HUNTINGTON, BOX 209, TANANA, AK 99777
ORVILLE HUNTINGTON, BOX 107, HUSLIA, AK 99746
STANLEY HUNTINGTON, BOX 54, GALENA, AK 99741
TOM HUNTINGTON, BOX 57111, NORTH POLE, AK 99705
CARL JERUE, BOX 30, ANVIK, AK 99558
HENRY KANAYURAK, BOX 764, BARROW, AK 99723
IRENE KANGAS, BOX 74168, FAIRBANKS, AK 99707
PHILIP KENNEDY, BOX 103, TANANA, AK 99777
JOSEPH KETZLER, 269 SHANNON DR APT A, FAIRBANKS, AK 99701
STEVEN KETZLER, BOX 145, NENANA, AK 99760
MARY KLEINSCHMIDT, BOX 318, NENANA, AK 99760
EILEEN KOZEVNIKOFF, BOX 84358, FAIRBANKS, AK 99708
JOHN KRIEG, BOX 56515, NORTH POLE, AK 99705
RONALD KRUGER, BOX 34, ANVIK, AK 99558
TED KRUGER, BOX 121, ANVIK, AK 99558
THEODORE KRUGER, BOX 218, MCGRATH, AK 99627
JUDY LEE, 1725 ROSEMARY CT, ANCHORAGE, AK 99508
PRISCILLA LEGG, 1917 9TH ST, ANACORTES, WA 98221
EDMUND LORD, BOX 26, NENANA, AK 99760
EDMUND LORD, BOX 183, NENANA, AK 99760
KAREN LORD, BOX 183, NENANA, AK 99760
VICTOR LORD, BOX 374, NENANA, AK 99760
ANDY LUDECKER, BOX 81844, FAIRBANKS, AK 99708
JENNY LUDECKER, BOX 81844, FAIRBANKS, AK 99708
ANDREW LUDECKER.JONES, BOX 81844, FAIRBANKS, AK 99708
RICK MACKEY, BOX 368, NENANA, AK 99760
JOHNNY MADROS, BOX 87, KALTAG, AK 99748
VAN MADROS, BOX 45013, HUGHES, AK 99745
DAVID MAILLELLE, BOX 56, GRAYLING, AK 99590
HERBERT MAILLELLE, GEN DEL, GRAYLING, AK 99590
FREDERICK MAYO, 1131 MERGANSER ST, FAIRBANKS, AK 99709
RANDY MAYO, BOX 70866, FAIRBANKS, AK 99707
PATRICK MCCARTY, BOX 12, RUBY, AK 99768
JOSEPHINE MCGINTY, BOX 65036, NULATO, AK 99765
WILLIAM MCLAUGHLIN, 1412 BIRCHWOOD DR, FAIRBANKS, AK 99709
JORDAN MICHEL, BOX 65131, NULATO, AK 99765
CHARLES MILLER, JOHNSON HENRY LN #2, GALENA, AK 99741
LUCY MILLER, BOX 3444, VALDEZ, AK 99686
MARIE MONROE, BOX 242, NENANA, AK 99760
PATRICK MOORE, BOX 61, TANANA, AK 99777
ROBERTA MORRISON.BOULDIN, BOX 89, MANLEY HOT SPRINGS, AK 99756
DENISE NEWMAN, 1729 KENNEDY ST, FAIRBANKS, AK 99709
JACQUELINE NICHOLAS, BOX 2, KALTAG, AK 99748
NICK NICHOLAS, BOX 106, GRAYLING, AK 99590
VICTOR NICHOLAS, BOX 65069, NULATO, AK 99765
TODD NICKOLI, 938 GILMORE ST APT F, FAIRBANKS, AK 99701
WAYNE NICKOLI, BOX 55, GRAYLING, AK 99590
ALFRED NOLLNER, BOX 1, GALENA, AK 99741
EDGAR NOLLNER, BOX 34, GALENA, AK 99741
STEPHEN OBRIEN, BOX 42, MANLEY HOT SPRINGS, AK 99756
LOREEN PARKER, 3705 ARCTIC BLVD #2073, ANCHORAGE, AK 99509
DANIEL PATRICK, BOX 66, GALENA, AK 99741
JERRY PEARSON, 624 FRONT ST, FAIRBANKS, AK 99701
EMMITT PETERS, BOX 129, RUBY, AK 99768
ROBERT PIERCE, BOX 614, NENANA, AK 99760
TERRY PITKA, BOX 27, GALENA, AK 99741
GAYLE RAMEY, BOX 38, NENANA, AK 99760
LYDENE RAY, BOX 73, KALTAG, AK 99748
JIMMIE RICKS, BOX 73416, FAIRBANKS, AK 99701
MADELINE RILEY, BOX 80951, FAIRBANKS, AK 99708
FRANCIS ROBERTS, BOX 77041, TANANA, AK 99777

MOSES SAMUELSON, 631 NOYES ST, FAIRBANKS, AK 99701
KEVIN SAUNDERS, BOX 103, KALTAG, AK 99748
GOODWIN SEMAKEN, BOX 14, KALTAG, AK 99748
ANTHONY SHEWFELT, BOX 202, FORT YUKON, AK 99740
ROBERT SIMPSON, 3384 SE WOODWARD, PORTLAND, OR 97202
HORACE SMOKE, BOX 74028, STEVENS VILLAGE, AK 99774
GABRIEL SOLOMON, BOX 63, KALTAG, AK 99748
ARLENE SOMMER, BOX 175, GALENA, AK 99741
FRED SOMMER, BOX 60295, FAIRBANKS, AK 99706
NEIL SOMMER, BOX 83, NULATO, AK 99765
RUDY SOMMER, BOX 3, TANANA, AK 99777
TRAVIS SOMMER, BOX 60632, FAIRBANKS, AK 99706
JOHN STAM, BOX 21, GALENA, AK 99741
CHARLES STEVENS, BOX 38, NENANA, AK 99760
WAYNE STICKMAN, BOX 65, NULATO, AK 99765
HARVEY STRASSBURG, BOX 109, GALENA, AK 99741
THEODORE SUCKLING, BOX 55, NENANA, AK 99760
DALE SWARTZENTRUBER, 5607 IRISH RD, SCHUYLER, VA 22969
EDWARD SWEAT, 1121 19TH AVE, FAIRBANKS, AK 99701
MILFORD SWEAT, 1977 MELANIE LN, FAIRBANKS, AK 99709
LESTER SWEETSIR, 205 KODY DR, FAIRBANKS, AK 99701
PAT SWEETSIR, 455 3RD AVE #606, FAIRBANKS, AK 99701
GREGORY TAYLOR, BOX 81572, FAIRBANKS, AK 99709
CALVIN THURMOND, 4433 SANERNESTO AVE #112, ANCHORAGE, AK 99508
GARY THURMOND, BOX 305, GALENA, AK 99741
JOSEPH TURNER, BOX 65066, NULATO, AK 99765
MIKE TURNER, BOX 646, NENANA, AK 99760
ERIC UMPHENOUR, 888 LYNNWOOD WAY, NORTH POLE, AK 99705
CHARLES VERBY, 1977 POLK BARRON ST, COMSTOCK, WI 54826
MARGIE WALKER, BOX 50, GRAYLING, AK 99590
ROBERT WALKER, BOX 149, ANVIK, AK 99558
ANESHA WALLACE, 1735 THUNDERBIRD PL, ANCHORAGE, AK 99508
ARCHIE WHOLECHEESE, BOX 2, GALENA, AK 99741
LARRY WHOLECHEESE, BOX 358, GALENA, AK 99741
ALFRED WIEHL, 2825 ROLAND RD, FAIRBANKS, AK 99709
JENNIFER WILSON, BOX 172, NENANA, AK 99760
RUSSELL WOOD, 607 OLD STEESE HWY STE B #712, FAIRBANKS, AK 99701
RAYMOND WOODS, BOX 74, MANLEY HOT SPRINGS, AK 99756
STAN ZURAY, BOX 172, TANANA, AK 99777

SALMON, POWER TROLL, STATEWIDE

HAROLD ABBOTT, BOX 185, PETERSBURG, AK 99833
MARVIN ADAMS, 2984 BRANDYWINE AVE, ANCHORAGE, AK 99502
WILLIAM ADICKES, 1401 EDGECUMBE DR, SITKA, AK 99835
KIRK ALBRECHT, BOX 1853, SITKA, AK 99835
KALEB ALDRED, BOX 6123, SITKA, AK 99835
HAROLD ALLARD, BOX 410, PELICAN, AK 99832
MICHAEL ALLARD, BOX 733, PELICAN, AK 99832
DREW ALLEN, BOX 211122, AUKE BAY, AK 99821
RAFE ALLENSWORTH, BOX 862, SITKA, AK 99835
NORMAN ALSUP, 15008 N TONGASS HWY, KETCHIKAN, AK 99901
RODERICK ALTON, BOX 62, HOONAH, AK 99829
JEFF AMBROSIER, BOX 39558, NINILCHIK, AK 99639
TOM AMOS, 90 FINN HALL RD, PORT ANGELES, WA 98362
ALAN ANDERSEN, 2041 HALIBUT PT RD, SITKA, AK 99835
JASON ANDERSEN, BOX 99, SITKA, AK 99835
BRADLEY ANDERSON, 3112 HALIBUT PT RD, SITKA, AK 99835
ERIC ANDERSON, BOX 23496, KETCHIKAN, AK 99901
RYAN ANDREE, BOX 72, GUSTAVUS, AK 99826
TOM ANDREWS, BOX 735, PELICAN, AK 99832
JEFFREY ANGELO, BOX 151, SAMOA, CA 95564
ALAN ANTHONY, 507 KATLIAN ST, SITKA, AK 99835
BASRI ARITAN, GENERAL DELIVERY, SITKA, AK 99835
JACK ARMER, BOX 6252, SITKA, AK 99835

SALMON FISHING LIST—POWER TROLL

FRED ATHORP, BOX 792, WARD COVE, AK 99928
CHRISTOPHER ATTWOOD, 5114 PICNIC POINT RD, EDMONDS, WA 98026
BEN ATWOOD, BOX 583, WARD COVE, AK 99928
DAVID AXMAKER, BOX 836, PETERSBURG, AK 99833
HANS BAERTLE, BOX 240266, DOUGLAS, AK 99824
DAVID BAILEY, BOX 21431, JUNEAU, AK 99802
JOHN BAILEY, 48 BADDY RD, LAWRENCEBURG, TN 38464
WILLIAM BAILEY, BOX 271, WRANGELL, AK 99929
ROBERT BAIRD, BOX 197, DEER HARBOR, WA 98243
BRADLEY BALDWIN, 4029 DEBORAH DR, JUNEAU, AK 99801
FRANK BALOVICH, BOX 1396, SITKA, AK 99835
MARK BAMBER, 353 E NORTH CAMANO DR, CAMANO ISLAND, WA 98282
RONALD BARBER, 11105 18TH ST NE, LAKE STEVENS, WA 98258
NORMAN BARBRE, 1679 5TH ST, LOS OSOS, CA 93402
KENT BARKHAU, 123 RIGGS RD, SITKA, AK 99835
JAMES BARNES, BOX 45, CRAIG, AK 99921
LOUIS BARR, BOX 210361, AUKE BAY, AK 99821
JOSEPH BARRETT, 1772 ATTERBERRY RD, SEQUIM, WA 98382
DAVID BARTH, BOX 371, SULTAN, WA 98294
JAMES BATEMAN, 331 DEERMOUNT ST, KETCHIKAN, AK 99901
ROBERT BATEMAN, 331 DEERMOUNT ST, KETCHIKAN, AK 99901
KENNETH BATES, BOX 660, EUREKA, CA 95502
BRUCE BAUER, HC 60 BOX 2892, HAINES, AK 99827
PATRICK BAUM, 4825 THANE RD, JUNEAU, AK 99801
BRANT BAXTER, BOX 1023, OAK HARBOR, WA 98277
KENNETH BAXTER, 1130 TIMBERLINE CT, JUNEAU, AK 99801
JAMES BEAL, BOX 442, METLAKATLA, AK 99926
KEVIN BEAM, 2309 HALIBUT POINT RD #8, SITKA, AK 99835
MARTIN BEAM, 35628 WHITNAH LN, RICHLAND, OR 97870
CORNELL BEAN, BOX 150, KAKE, AK 99830
JOHN BEAN, BOX PPV, KETCHIKAN, AK 99950
LELAND BEAN, BOX PPV, KETCHIKAN, AK 99950
RUSSELL BEARD, 30551 NAVARRO RIDGE RD, ALBION, CA 95410
RANDALL BEASON, BOX 240552, DOUGLAS, AK 99824
THEODORE BEESE, BOX 1042, WESTPORT, WA 98595
ALEXANDER BEHARY, BOX 2041, PETERSBURG, AK 99833
NANCY BEHNKEN, 117 JEFF DAVIS ST, SITKA, AK 99835
RICHARD BELL, 2033 MILKY WAY, CERES, CA 95307
ROBERT BELL, BOX 115, ELFIN COVE, AK 99825
RYLAND BELL, BOX 115, ELFIN COVE, AK 99825
TAIGA BELL, 1012 WEE BURN DR, JUNEAU, AK 99801
ROBERT BENSON, BOX 1297, CRAIG, AK 99921
CHARLES BENTLEY, BOX 1305, WARD COVE, AK 99928
BERT BERGMAN, 801 CHARLES #A, SITKA, AK 99835
DAVID BERNHARDT, BOX 1791, SITKA, AK 99835
LEE BERZANSKE, BOX 1072, KASILOF, AK 99610
JON BETZINA, CALLE 14 APT F-103 QUINTAS DE CUP, SAN JUAN, PR 926
KIM BETZINA, BOX 628, PETERSBURG, AK 99833
RORY BIFOSS, 3817 MOON CREEK RD, MILES CITY, MT 59301
C BIGELOW, BOX 6355, SITKA, AK 99835
JOHN BISSON, 49 DOUBLE EAGLE LANE, KETCHIKAN, AK 99901
FRANK BITONTI, 8035 BLUFFS EDGE ST NW, ALBUQUERQUE, NM 87120
JOHN BLACK, BOX 585, HOONAH, AK 99829
THOMAS BLAKE, BOX 925, CRAIG, AK 99921
JOHN BLENZ, BOX 817, WARD COVE, AK 99928
MIKE BOBO, BOX 373, CRAIG, AK 99921
GARY BODDY, 1731 EDGECOMBE DR, SITKA, AK 99835
DARYL BOGARDUS, BOX 5729, CHARLESTON, OR 97420
STEVEN BOOTH, RR 2 BOX 46, KETCHIKAN, AK 99901
DALE BOSWORTH, BOX 45, PETERSBURG, AK 99833
THOMAS BOTTS, BOX 424, HOONAH, AK 99829
CHARLIE BOWER, BOX 1295, HAINES, AK 99827
MARK BRADLEY, 218 LAKEVEIW DR, SITKA, AK 99835
KEITH BRADY, BOX 1843, WRANGELL, AK 99929
STEPHEN BRADY, BOX 2362, SITKA, AK 99835

FORREST BRALEY, BOX 172, ANGOON, AK 99820
JAMES BRAY, 324 ALDER ST, KETCHIKAN, AK 99901
MIKE BRECKON, BOX 2351, FERNDALE, WA 98248
RAYMOND BRESSLER, BOX 308, INDIANOLA, WA 98342
DAVID BRICKELL, BOX 81672, FAIRBANKS, AK 99708
DANIEL BRIGHAM, BOX 1842, SITKA, AK 99835
ALBERT BROCK, BOX 373, WRANGELL, AK 99929
CARL BRODERSEN, 16294 POINT LENA LOOP RD, JUNEAU, AK 99801
KURT BRODERSEN, BOX 23, MEYERS CHUCK, AK 99903
JONATHAN BROUWER, BOX 22927, JUNEAU, AK 99802
FRANK BRUNO, 10 BOB WHITE, OAKLEY, CA 94561
KAREN BUCHKOSKI, BOX 34326, JUNEAU, AK 99803
HOWARD BUCKBEE, BOX 3112, SITKA, AK 99835
THOMAS BUDD, 1718 EDGECUMBE DR, SITKA, AK 99835
JONATHAN BUNT, BOX 1364, SITKA, AK 99835
RON BURDICK, 1415 RANDOLPH AVE, STEILACOOM, WA 98388
ROSEMARY BURNETT, 119 LILLIAN DR, SITKA, AK 99835
TODD BUTLER, 1245 WATER ST, KETCHIKAN, AK 99901
JAMES BUTTON, 2212 HALIBUT POINT RD, SITKA, AK 99835
DANIEL BYRON, BOX 95, PORT LIONS, AK 99550
HUNTER BYRON, BOX 95, PORT LIONS, AK 99550
RICHARD CABE, BOX 19122, THORNE BAY, AK 99919
BRUCE CADY, BOX 391, PETERSBURG, AK 99833
ANDY CALLISTINI, 106 NAOMI KANOSH LN, SITKA, AK 99835
ERIC CALVIN, 210 BRADY ST, SITKA, AK 99835
KRIS CALVIN, BOX 807, SISTERS, OR 97759
WILLIAM CAMERON, 3640 TONGASS BLVD, JUNEAU, AK 99801
THOMAS CAMPANELLI, 12215 64TH AVENUE CT NW, GIG HARBOR, WA 98332
BENJAMIN CAMPEN, BOX 372, SITKA, AK 99835
ADAM CANIK, BOX 43, PETERSBURG, AK 99833
CLIFTON CARLE, BOX 98, HYDABURG, AK 99922
JAMES CARLE, BOX 1163, CRAIG, AK 99921
JOHN CARLSON, BOX 240366, DOUGLAS, AK 99824
CHRISTOPHER CARROLL, 107 EBERHARDT DR, SITKA, AK 99835
JACOB CARTE, 8493 FOREST LN, JUNEAU, AK 99801
JASON CARTER, BOX 57, TENAKEE, AK 99841
ROBERT CARTWRIGHT, 203 AIRPORT RD #A13, SITKA, AK 99835
SCOTT CASSEDY, 116 OSPREY ST, SITKA, AK 99835
JOSEF CASTLE, BOX 82328, FAIRBANKS, AK 99709
STEPHEN CASTOR, BOX 407, CRAIG, AK 99921
RICHARD CATRETT, 3446 MEANDER WAY, JUNEAU, AK 99801
BRIAN CATTERALL, 1123 E MARKET ST, ABERDEEN, WA 98520
WILLIS CAVANAUGH, BOX 113, KAKE, AK 99830
SEAN CAVLAN, 224 KATLIAN ST, SITKA, AK 99835
KERMIT CESAR, BOX 34482, JUNEAU, AK 99803
JOHN CESSNUN, BOX 1203, CRAIG, AK 99921
SCOTT CHADWICK, BOX 2, YAKUTAT, AK 99689
MICHAEL CHAPMAN, BOX 425, PATEROS, WA 98846
ARTHUR CHASE, BOX 33921, JUNEAU, AK 99803
WESTON CHAVEZ, BOX 6289, SITKA, AK 99835
RICHARD CHRISTENSEN, BOX 563, CANBY, OR 97013
BRIAN CHRISTIAN, BOX 1581, WRANGELL, AK 99929
LUTHER CHRISTOPHER, 426 12TH ST, TELL CITY, IN 47586
FRANKLIN CHURCHILL, BOX 1590, WRANGELL, AK 99929
CHESTON CLARK, BOX 242, SITKA, AK 99835
COY CLARK, 8366 S TONGASS, KETCHIKAN, AK 99901
DAVID CLARK, 507 KATLIAN ST, SITKA, AK 99835
LOREN CLARK, BOX 331, YAKUTAT, AK 99689
ROBERT CLARK, BOX 95, HOONAH, AK 99829
DAVID CLARKE, 1225 E SUNSET DR #727, BELLINGHAM, WA 98225
JOHN CLEAVER, 100 BAHOVEC CT, SITKA, AK 99835
LARRY CLERGET, 16504 SHELDON LN SW, ROCHESTER, WA 98579
JAY CLIFTON, 3802 HALIBUT POINT RD, SITKA, AK 99835
CHARLES COHEN, BOX 20670, JUNEAU, AK 99802
MATT COLE, BOX 240493, DOUGLAS, AK 99824

SALMON FISHING LIST—POWER TROLL

DAVID COLEMAN, BOX 6082, SITKA, AK 99835
FOREST COLLINS, BOX 664, CRAIG, AK 99921
WARREN COLLINS, BOX 1247, CRAIG, AK 99921
CHRISTOPHER COMBS, 503 CHARTERIS ST, SITKA, AK 99835
WILLIAM COMBS, BOX 401, PELICAN, AK 99832
RONALD CONATSER, 3656 F BECK RD, RICE, WA 99167
MARCUS CONTAG, BOX 8008, PORT ALEXANDER, AK 99836
WILBUR COOPER, BOX 597, GIRDWOOD, AK 99587
THOMAS COPELAND, 420 FOREST PARK DR S, KETCHIKAN, AK 99901
CODY COWAN, BOX 8602, KETCHIKAN, AK 99901
DAN CRANE, BOX 15368, FRITZ CREEK, AK 99603
ROBERT CRANSTON, 1808 EDGECUMBE DR, SITKA, AK 99835
BRIAN CRAPO, 9347 BETTY CT, JUNEAU, AK 99801
JAY CREASY, 860 FOREST PARK, KETCHIKAN, AK 99901
PATRICK CRENNA, 3486 HALIBUT POINT RD, SITKA, AK 99835
CARL CROME, BOX 466, PETERSBURG, AK 99833
IAN CRYAN, 1822 MARK ALAN, JUNEAU, AK 99801
MICHAEL CUMMINGS, 5038 N TONGASS HWY, KETCHIKAN, AK 99901
RONALD CUNNINGHAM, BOX 6114, SITKA, AK 99835
RICHARD CURRAN, BOX 1336, SITKA, AK 99835
CAL CURT, 649 E SAGE BRUSH ST, GILBERT, AZ 85296
TROY CURTISS, BOX 1532, PETERSBURG, AK 99833
AARON CUSHING, BOX 1321, SITKA, AK 99835
DANIEL CUSHING, 116 B HARVEST WAY, SITKA, AK 99835
ARNE DAHL, GEN DEL, POINT BAKER, AK 99927
ERIC DAHL, 16984 HERIGSTAD RD NE, SILVERTON, OR 97381
SAMUEL DALIN, 7937 WILLIAMS RD, KETCHIKAN, AK 99901
DANIEL DALLEY, BOX 220710, CENTERFIELD, UT 84622
MIKE DALY, 501 CHARTERIS ST #A, SITKA, AK 99835
DUGAN DANIELS, 507 KATLIAN ST, SITKA, AK 99835
JAMES DANIELS, BOX 707, PELICAN, AK 99832
JOSEPH DANIELS, 507 KATLIAN ST, SITKA, AK 99835
MARK DANIELSON, BOX 782, SITKA, AK 99835
LINDA DANNER, BOX 1313, SITKA, AK 99835
ROBERT DARRINGTON, BOX 210048, AUKE BAY, AK 99821
KEVIN DAU, BOX 219, CRAIG, AK 99921
PAUL DAU, BOX 20995, JUNEAU, AK 99802
RICHARD DAUGHERTY, BOX 34864, JUNEAU, AK 99803
TOM DAUGHERTY, 9640 N DOUGLAS, JUNEAU, AK 99801
CULLEN DAVIS, 1407 GEORGESON LP, SITKA, AK 99835
GARETT DAVIS, BOX 511, YAKUTAT, AK 99689
RICHARD DAVIS, 2347 KEVIN CT, JUNEAU, AK 99801
DAVID DAWLEY, BOX 830, CRAIG, AK 99921
PAUL DE.MONTIGNY, BOX 1584, PETERSBURG, AK 99833
LOIS DEBOER, BOX 455, PETERSBURG, AK 99833
ANDREW DEERING, BOX 1334, CRAIG, AK 99921
PETER DEJONGH, 507 KATLIAN ST, SITKA, AK 99835
ARTHUR DEMMERT, BOX 125, CRAIG, AK 99921
SAM DEMMERT, BOX 366, YAKUTAT, AK 99689
SAM DEMMERT, BOX 187, YAKUTAT, AK 99689
TIMOTHY DEMMERT, BOX 220, KLAWOCK, AK 99925
JAMES DENNIS, BOX 591, CRAIG, AK 99921
DAVID DENSMORE, BOX 223, KODIAK, AK 99615
MMERCE DEPARTMENT OF CO, BOX 110802, JUNEAU, AK 99811
HALEY DESROSIERS, BOX 1954, PETERSBURG, AK 99833
DENNIS DIAMOND, BOX 8937, KETCHIKAN, AK 99901
JAMES DICICCO, BOX 1066, SITKA, AK 99835
KYLE DIERICK, BOX 421, YAKUTAT, AK 99689
CASEY DIGENNARO, 208 PARK ST, SITKA, AK 99835
PAUL DILLON, 8267 N DOUGLAS HWY, JUNEAU, AK 99801
TIMOTHY DIMOND, BOX 240692, DOUGLAS, AK 99824
MICHAEL DIVERTY, BOX 214, SITKA, AK 99835
DAN DOAK, BOX 677, WRANGELL, AK 99929
FORREST DODSON, 263 KATLIAN, SITKA, AK 99835
JAMES DOGGETT, 1306 EDGECUMBE DR, SITKA, AK 99835
JAMESZON DOGGETT, 1302 SAWMILL CREEK RD #29, SITKA, AK 99835

JULIE DOGGETT, 1328 CANNON ISLAND DR, SITKA, AK 99835
ROBERT DOLAN, BOX 1062, PETERSBURG, AK 99833
CARL DOMINICKS, 320 CASCADE ST, SITKA, AK 99835
MATTHEW DONOHOE, BOX 3114, SITKA, AK 99835
JOSEPH DONOHUE, BOX 20652, JUNEAU, AK 99802
ANTHONY DOTY, BOX 688, CLINTON, WA 98236
DENIS DOUGLAS, 37776 GRAYLING CT, SOLDOTNA, AK 99669
MICHAEL DOUVILLE, BOX 68, CRAIG, AK 99921
RAYMOND DOUVILLE, BOX 66, CRAIG, AK 99921
MICHAEL DOVE, BOX 8083, PORT ALEXANDER, AK 99836
J DOWNER, BOX 1045, HAINES, AK 99827
RANDY DRAKE, 1504 DAVIDOFF ST, SITKA, AK 99835
DONALD DRUMM, BOX 5810, CHARLESTON, OR 97420
ROBERT DUKES, 11087 NW PIONEER RD, SEABECK, WA 98380
AMANDA DUNAWAY, BOX 2053, PETERSBURG, AK 99833
DONALD DURGAN, BOX 340, CRAIG, AK 99921
KELLY DURGAN, BOX 950, CRAIG, AK 99921
JAMES DYBDAHL, BOX 47, HOONAH, AK 99829
KENNETH EARNST, 27871 MINKLER RD, SEDRO WOOLLEY, WA 98284
JUSTIN EBERHARD, BOX 1361, SITKA, AK 99835
ROBERT EDENSO, 608 BIORKA ST, SITKA, AK 99835
DUANE EDWARDS, BOX 2088, NEWPORT, OR 97365
THOMAS EDWARDS, 10617 RIVIERA DR, ANDERSON ISLAND, WA 98303
ARTHUR EELLS, BOX 853, SITKA, AK 99835
ARTHUR EELLS, 1935 ANNA CIR, SITKA, AK 99835
BRANDON EELLS, 706 MONASTERY ST #A, SITKA, AK 99835
CLEVELAND EELLS, BOX 853, SITKA, AK 99835
D.JEFFREY EELLS, BOX 1811, OREGON CITY, OR 97045
TYLER EELLS, 114 DARRIN DR2, SITKA, AK 99835
GARY EGERTON, 3278 BROOKS HILL RD, LANGLEY, WA 98260
AJAX EGGLESTON, BOX 1305, HAINES, AK 99827
LEVI EILEY, BOX 20062, JUNEAU, AK 99802
GEORGE ELIASON, 105 SAND DOLLAR DR, SITKA, AK 99835
RICHARD ELIASON, 8475 E GOLD BULLION BLVD, PALMER, AK 99645
WAYNE ELLIS, BOX 2135, WRANGELL, AK 99929
TRACEY EMANUEL, BOX 6358, SITKA, AK 99835
JOSEPH EMERSON, BOX 35736, JUNEAU, AK 99803
THOMAS EMERSON, 10410 DOCK ST, JUNEAU, AK 99801
THOMAS EMERSON, BOX 102, KEYPORT, WA 98345
HOLLY ENDERLE, BOX 30, ELFIN COVE, AK 99825
STEVEN ENGE, BOX 422, PETERSBURG, AK 99833
JOHN ENGLE, BOX 9296, KETCHIKAN, AK 99901
LEWIS ENGLISHBEE, BOX 609, KILA, MT 59920
FRED ENSIGN, BOX 238, CRAIG, AK 99921
MICHAEL ERB, 16461 ST JAMES CIR, ANCHORAGE, AK 99516
JAMES ERICKSON, BOX 366, HOONAH, AK 99829
JAY ERICKSON, BOX 633, HOONAH, AK 99829
MIKE ERICKSON, BOX 34363, JUNEAU, AK 99803
STEVEN ERICKSON, BOX 319, THORNE BAY, AK 99919
JAY ERIE, BOX 1126, SITKA, AK 99835
JOHN ERP, BOX 1041, SITKA, AK 99835
MARK EVANOFF, BOX 8612, KETCHIKAN, AK 99901
DOUG EVENDEN, BOX 244, HAINES, AK 99827
MELVIN FAIRBANKS, 2417 TONGASS AVE # 111-127, KETCHIKAN, AK 99901
EUGENE FARLEY, BOX 251, HOONAH, AK 99829
JIM FARMER, BOX 692, CRAIG, AK 99921
WILLIAM FARMER, BOX 336, CRAIG, AK 99921
JEFFERY FARVOUR, 439 VERSTOVIA AVE, SITKA, AK 99835
FRED FAYETTE, BOX 6338, SITKA, AK 99835
RANDALL FERDINAND, BOX 1846, WRANGELL, AK 99929
ROBERT FERGUSON, 7101 N DOUGLAS HWY, JUNEAU, AK 99801
DEVON FERNANDEZ, BOX 270, YAKUTAT, AK 99689
LANCE FINCH, BOX 64, THERMOPOLIS, WY 82443
DAVID FINIFROCK, BOX 446, VAUGHN, WA 98394
ROBERT FINZEL, BOX 3088, OREGON CITY, OR 97045
JAMES FISCHER, 1802 ALDER WAY #A, SITKA, AK 99835

SALMON FISHING LIST—POWER TROLL

STEVEN FISH, BOX 6448, SITKA, AK 99835
ALAN FISHER, 9195 JAMES BLVD, JUNEAU, AK 99801
ALLAN FISHER, BOX PPV, KETCHIKAN, AK 99950
GEORGE FISHER, BOX 539, HOONAH, AK 99829
THOMAS FISHER, 4465 COLUMBIA BLVD, JUNEAU, AK 99801
RYAN FITZGERALD, BOX 704, CRAIG, AK 99921
FORREST FLEENOR, 100 PACIFIC CT, KETCHIKAN, AK 99901
DOUGLAS FLEMING, BOX 1267, PETERSBURG, AK 99833
TIMOTHY FLEMING, BOX 354, ORCAS, WA 98280
WILLIAM FLOR, BOX 262, PETERSBURG, AK 99833
OTTO FLORSCHUTZ, BOX 547, WRANGELL, AK 99929
BENJAMIN FLOYD, 122 KNUTSON DR, SITKA, AK 99835
TRAVIS FOLKERTS, 2004 S 14TH ST, UNION GAP, WA 98903
ARTHUR FORBES, 143 THOMPSON RD, SEQUIM, WA 98382
YOUNES FOROOZIN, BOX 6394, SITKA, AK 99835
ZACHARY FOSS, 1820 EDGECUMBE DR, SITKA, AK 99835
BENNIE FOSSUM, BOX 5, HOONAH, AK 99829
ROBERT FRAKER, BOX 284, YAKUTAT, AK 99689
JOSHUA FRAME, 80 ARROWHEAD, MISSOULA, MT 59801
WILLIAM FRANKLIN, 3133 JERNS RD, SEDRO WOOLLEY, WA 98284
MARTIN FREDRICKSON, 714 SIRSTAD ST, SITKA, AK 99835
ROD FREW, 12107 NW 8TH AVE, VANCOUVER, WA 98685
CLAY FRICK, BOX 1222, HAINES, AK 99827
GREG FRIEDRICHS, 1450 30TH ST, PORT TOWNSEND, WA 98368
TERRY FRISKE, 117 DARRIN DR, SITKA, AK 99835
TAD FUJIOKA, 214 SHOTGUN ALLEY, SITKA, AK 99835
CHAD FULTON, BOX 3, CRAIG, AK 99921
ROBERT FULTON, BOX 43, CRAIG, AK 99921
BILLY GADDIS, BOX 507, KAKE, AK 99830
JON GAEDKE, BOX 134, ROLLING BAY, WA 98061
DANIEL GALLACHER, 341 N SHORE BLVD, FOX ISLAND, WA 98333
STEVEN GARNICK, 2619 N SADDLE VISTA RD, TONOPAH, AZ 85354
MARY GEBHARD, 2635 STELLAR WAY, FAIRBANKS, AK 99712
DARREN GEE, 8460 KIMBERLY ST, JUNEAU, AK 99801
JEFF GEORGE, 2280 INDUSTRIAL BLVD, JUNEAU, AK 99801
THOMAS GEORGE, BOX 1, KLAWOCK, AK 99925
WILLIAM GEORGE, 9014 GEE ST, JUNEAU, AK 99801
JERRY GERMAIN, BOX 272, CRAIG, AK 99921
FOREST GERMAN, BOX 6393, SITKA, AK 99835
ZANE GIBBONS, 998 C ARTMAN GIBSON RD, CORVILLE, WA 99114
CORY GIFFORD, BOX 8030, PORT ALEXANDER, AK 99836
DAVID GIFFORD, BOX 8125, PORT ALEXANDER, AK 99836
GENE GILDEN, 8362 SHADOW LANE, ANACORTES, WA 98221
JOHNY GILSON, 3857 FAIRVIEW, KETCHIKAN, AK 99901
ERIC GJERTSEN, 221 S GARDEN ST, BELLINGHAM, WA 98225
JASON GJERTSEN, 714 ETOLIN ST, SITKA, AK 99835
DAVID GLAZIER, BOX 2091, SITKA, AK 99835
JASON GLENN, BOX 31, GUSTAVUS, AK 99826
JOHN GODFREY, 329 KATLIAN ST, SITKA, AK 99835
IVAN GONZALEZ, BOX 256, HOONAH, AK 99829
DANIEL GOODWIN, 4245 S PINNACLE PEAK DR, WASILLA, AK 99623
JORGE GORYN, BOX 473, HAINES, AK 99827
MARTIN GOWDY, 9815 15TH NW, SEATTLE, WA 98117
GREG GRASSER, BOX 1026, CRAIG, AK 99921
DENNIS GRAY, BOX 617, HOONAH, AK 99829
EDWARD GRAY, BOX 401, SITKA, AK 99835
DAVID GREEN, 5583 KNIGHT RD, BELLINGHAM, WA 98226
DONALD GREEN, BOX 681, HOONAH, AK 99829
TYLER GREEN, 322 WACHUSETTS, SITKA, AK 99835
JAMES GREENFIELD, BOX 1673, PETERSBURG, AK 99833
ROGER GREGG, BOX 3, WRANGELL, AK 99929
KEITH GREINER, 424 VERSTOVIA, SITKA, AK 99835
RICHARD GRESETH, BOX 70, PETERSBURG, AK 99833
JOHN GROENENDYK, 35478 SOLITUDE, SOLDOTNA, AK 99669
ROGER GROSS, 172 LIBBY ST, SEQUIM, WA 98382
NATHAN GRUENING, BOX 20662, JUNEAU, AK 99802

ERIC GRUNDBERG, BOX 2193, PETERSBURG, AK 99833
ANTHONY GUGGENBICKLER, BOX 393, WRANGELL, AK 99929
STANLEY GUGGENBICKLER, BOX 985, WRANGELL, AK 99929
RICHARD GUHL, 721 SIRSTAD ST, SITKA, AK 99835
BRUCE H.M.WHITE, BOX 252, NENANA, AK 99760
GREG HAAG, BOX 6447, SITKA, AK 99835
ADAM HACKETT, 228 LAKEVIEW DR, SITKA, AK 99835
MATTHEW HAFFNER, 18216 PT STEHENS RD, JUNEAU, AK 99801
JOHN HAGEN, BOX 1153, CRAIG, AK 99921
RICHARD HAGEN, BOX 421, CRAIG, AK 99921
ROBERT HAGEN, BOX 2334, SITKA, AK 99835
TRAVIS HAGEN, BOX 421, CRAIG, AK 99921
DYLAN HALEY, 500 LINCOLN ST B1, SITKA, AK 99835
JACOB HALLINGSTAD, BOX 295, KAKE, AK 99830
FRED HAMILTON, BOX 661, CRAIG, AK 99921
FREDERICK HAMILTON, BOX 106, CRAIG, AK 99921
JEFFREY HAMMER, 3715 Q AVE, ANACORTES, WA 98221
CHARLES HANAS, 62 LODE LANE S, KETCHIKAN, AK 99901
DANIEL HAND, BOX 47, TENAKEE, AK 99841
ROBERT HANSEN, BOX 6161, SITKA, AK 99835
CHRISTOPHER HANSON, BOX 2283, SITKA, AK 99835
ALDWIN HARDER, BOX 714, HOONAH, AK 99829
BRADEN HARDING, BOX 1278, CRAIG, AK 99921
DAVID HARMAN, 2132 LAWSON CREEK RD, DOUGLAS, AK 99824
JAMES HARRIGAN, 1610 DAVIDOFF, SITKA, AK 99835
BRENT HARRINGTON, 188 COUNTY RD #121, OAKLAND, AR 72661
DAVE HARTUNG, BOX 1664, WRANGELL, AK 99929
SHAUN HASELTINE, BOX 484, KLAWOCK, AK 99925
REID HAWKINS, 6545 HUASNA TOWNSITE RD, ARROYO GRANDE, CA 93420
CHARLES HAWKS, BOX 93, CRAIG, AK 99921
CALVIN HAYASHI, BOX 1003, SITKA, AK 99835
MURRAY HAYES, 224 GRANT ST, PORT TOWNSEND, WA 98368
ROBERT HAYES, BOX 886, WRANGELL, AK 99929
DAVID HAYS, 119 AUSTIN ST #1111, KETCHIKAN, AK 99901
MIKE HEAD, BOX 330, CRAIG, AK 99921
THOMAS HEATH, 304 LAKE ST #103, SITKA, AK 99835
KEITH HELLER, BOX 304, PELICAN, AK 99832
MATTHEW HEMENWAY, BOX 228, PETERSBURG, AK 99833
THOMAS HENSHAW, 1727 EDGECUMBE DR, SITKA, AK 99835
LEWIS HIATT, BOX 6277, KETCHIKAN, AK 99901
DANIEL HICKMAN, BOX 108, PETERSBURG, AK 99833
DAN HIGGINS, BOX 14, MEYERS CHUCK, AK 99903
VERNON HILL, BOX 433, HOONAH, AK 99829
STANLEY HJORT, BOX 828, PETERSBURG, AK 99833
RICHARD HOFFMAN, 2684 SILVER CREEK DR, GREEN COVE, FL 32043
MARK HOFMANN, 1042 OBSTRUCTION PASS RD, OLGA, WA 98279
MARK HOFSTAD, BOX 1397, PETERSBURG, AK 99833
HERB HOLCOMB, BOX 114, YAKUTAT, AK 99689
JAMES HOLCOMB, BOX 206, YAKUTAT, AK 99689
LES HOLCOMB, BOX 143, YAKUTAT, AK 99689
NICK HOLCOMB, BOX 105, YAKUTAT, AK 99689
JAMES HOLIEN, BOX 443, KLAWOCK, AK 99925
BLAISE HOLLY, BOX 34, PORT HADLOCK, WA 98339
JASON HOLST, 1400 EDGECUMBE DR, SITKA, AK 99835
MICHAEL HORNAMAN, BOX 1235, SITKA, AK 99835
MATTHEW HOUSER, BOX 1392, WRANGELL, AK 99929
SEAN HOVIK, BOX 6312, SITKA, AK 99835
COURTNEY HOWARD, 1809 EDGECUMBE DR, SITKA, AK 99835
SHAPLEIGH HOWELL, BOX 1926, WRANGELL, AK 99929
HERBERT HOWEY, 1064 ADELIA ST #B, BLAINE, WA 98230
GARY HUGHES, BOX 6455, SITKA, AK 99835
JAMES HUGHES, 507 KATLIAN ST, SITKA, AK 99835
ROBERT HUNLEY, BOX 7, MEYERS CHUCK, AK 99903
MICHAEL IHNAT, BOX 396, HOONAH, AK 99829
GREGORY INDRELAND, BOX 413, YAKUTAT, AK 99689
FRANK INFERRERA, 1745 SOMMERFELD ST, SANTA CRUZ, CA 95062

SALMON FISHING LIST—POWER TROLL

ROGER INGMAN, BOX 1155, SITKA, AK 99835
WALTER INGRAM, 407 13TH ST #300, BELLINGHAM, WA 98225
PAUL IPOCK, 1504 B EDGECUMBE DR, SITKA, AK 99835
WAYNE IVERS, BOX 42, YAKUTAT, AK 99689
PATRICK J.KEEGAN.MARRS, BOX 6552, SITKA, AK 99835
FRANK JACK, 365 PINE ST, ANCHORAGE, AK 99508
CLARENCE JACKSON, BOX 301, KAKE, AK 99830
RANDELL JACKSON, BOX 867, HAINES, AK 99827
SIMON JACOBI, BOX 1065, SITKA, AK 99835
LARRY JACOBSON, BOX 109, POINT BAKER, AK 99927
TIMOTHY JAGUSCH, BOX 692, WARD COVE, AK 99928
TYLER JANSSEN, BOX 1982, WRANGELL, AK 99929
ROBBY JARVILL, BOX 32546, JUNEAU, AK 99803
RYAN JARVILL, 137 SHELIKOF WAY, SITKA, AK 99835
BRADEN JAY, BOX 202, SITKA, AK 99835
UTE JEFFERIS, BOX PPV, KETCHIKAN, AK 99950
DOUGLAS JENNY, 709 SAWMILL CREEK RD, SITKA, AK 99835
JAMES JENSEN, BOX 316, YAKUTAT, AK 99689
JONATHAN JENSEN, BOX 446, YAKUTAT, AK 99689
DONALD JESKE, 2308 HALIBUT POINT RD, SITKA, AK 99835
JESSE JESKE, 203 BRADY ST, SITKA, AK 99835
JAY JETTER, BOX 6083, SITKA, AK 99835
MICHAEL JEWETT, 3220 1ST, KETCHIKAN, AK 99901
DAVID JOHN, 1821 WICKERSHAM DR, JUNEAU, AK 99801
GREG JOHNS, BOX 214, KLAWOCK, AK 99925
CHRISTOPHER JOHNSON, BOX 2183, WRANGELL, AK 99929
EARLE JOHNSON, 300 PETERSON AVE APT A, SITKA, AK 99835
JAY JOHNSON, BOX 468, YAKUTAT, AK 99689
KENNETH JOHNSON, BOX 6591, SITKA, AK 99835
LINDSAY JOHNSON, BOX 1032, HAINES, AK 99827
MOSES JOHNSON, 1413 HALIBUT POINT RD, SITKA, AK 99835
PAUL JOHNSON, BOX 1083, SITKA, AK 99835
TIMOTHY JOHNSON, 8267 ASPEN AVE, JUNEAU, AK 99801
BILL JOHNSTON, BOX 134, PETERSBURG, AK 99833
GREGG JONES, 4016 HALIBUT POINT RD, SITKA, AK 99835
LYNN JONES, BOX 650, CRAIG, AK 99921
NICKOLAS JONES, BOX 108, CRAIG, AK 99921
RYAN JONES, BOX 1166, SITKA, AK 99835
TOM JONES, BOX 23712, KETCHIKAN, AK 99901
EVAN JONJAK, BOX 2257, WRANGELL, AK 99929
ERIC JORDAN, 103 GIBSON PL, SITKA, AK 99835
KARL JORDAN, 101 DONNA DR, SITKA, AK 99835
ROBERT JURRIES, BOX 177, CRAIG, AK 99921
JOHN KAER, BOX 716, PETERSBURG, AK 99833
KEITH KAGEE, BOX 1766, WRANGELL, AK 99929
G.KEVIN KAMBAK, BOX 426, SITKA, AK 99835
GAVIN KAMBAK, BOX 426, SITKA, AK 99835
JEFFREY KASEMAN, 38315 LA RUE WAY, DAVIS, CA 95616
RANDY KATZENMEYER, BOX 48, HAINES, AK 99827
JOEL KAWAHARA, 3652 LINDSAY HILL RD, QUILCENE, WA 98376
DAN KAYSER, BOX 2153, PETERSBURG, AK 99833
KIPP KEIM, BOX 826, WHITEHALL, MT 59759
RYAN KELLY, BOX 442, ASOTIN, WA 99402
WILLIAM KEMPERMAN, BOX 19265, THORNE BAY, AK 99919
JAMES KING, 111 CYRESS MILL CT, BRUNSWICK, GA 31520
SHAYNE KING, BOX 18157, COFFMAN COVE, AK 99918
DENISE KLINGLER, 603 ETOLIN ST, SITKA, AK 99835
GARY KLUSHKAN, BOX 45, YAKUTAT, AK 99689
MICHAEL KNAUSS, BOX 211, SITKA, AK 99835
ALAN KNETTEL, 2417 TONGASS AVE #111-359, KETCHIKAN, AK 99901
GILBERT KNUTSON, 231 KATLIAN ST B-12, SITKA, AK 99835
JON KOEFOD, 22449 MONTICOLA, WORELY, ID 83876
DAVID KOESTER, 2740 SE BENSON AVE, NEWPORT, OR 97365
CINDY KOETJE, 16536 MOBERG RD, MOUNT VERNON, WA 98273
ERNEST KOHLHASE, BOX 240524, DOUGLAS, AK 99824
ADAM KOHNE, BOX 161, YAKUTAT, AK 99689

MATTHEW KONOSKE, BOX 1943, SITKA, AK 99835
RANDY KONRAD, HC 60 BOX 2895, HAINES, AK 99827
JOHNNY KOONS, BOX 10, CALLIHAN, TX 78007
STEVE KORT, BOX 8096, PORT ALEXANDER, AK 99836
TODD KORTH, 2154 VIZCAYA CIR, CAMPBELL, CA 95008
KURT KORTHALS, 2908 LUSITANA CT, LIVERMORE, CA 94550
KIT KRAFT, BOX 446, CRAIG, AK 99921
JAKE KRANZ, 1713 EDGECUMBE DR, SITKA, AK 99835
DAVID KRAUSE, BOX 1065, SITKA, AK 99835
JAY KRAUSE, BOX 951, SITKA, AK 99835
JON KRISTJANSSON, 3044 TONGASS BLVD, JUNEAU, AK 99801
REGINALD KRKOVICH, BOX 478, YAKUTAT, AK 99689
GARRETT KROSCHEL, HC60 BOX 2848, HAINES, AK 99827
PETER KROVINA, BOX 6027, SITKA, AK 99835
JAKE KUMMA, 14610 200TH AVE SE, RENTON, WA 98059
ROBERT KUNTZ, BOX 455, WRANGELL, AK 99929
FRANK KYLE, BOX 6586, SITKA, AK 99835
BRIAN LACEY, 9330 MINER DR, JUNEAU, AK 99801
CALE LADUKE, BOX 1216, SITKA, AK 99835
ARTHUR LARSEN, BOX 571, WRANGELL, AK 99929
GEORGE LARSEN, BOX 2234, WRANGELL, AK 99929
NOAH LARSON, BOX 220, CARLTON, WA 98814
BEN LAWRIE, 339 WORTMAN LP, SITKA, AK 99835
MATTHEW LAWRIE, BOX 6006, SITKA, AK 99835
STEPHEN LAWRIE, 312 WORTMAN LOOP, SITKA, AK 99835
SCOTT LAWSON, BOX 204, OAK HARBOR, WA 98277
GARY LEASK, BOX 759, WARD COVE, AK 99928
JAMES LECRONE, 1972 HALIBUT POINT RD, SITKA, AK 99835
ADAM LEE, BOX 34306, JUNEAU, AK 99803
ANTHONY LEICHTY, BOX 47, CRAIG, AK 99921
JAMES LEIGH, 30398 LEIGH LN, PARMA, ID 83660
HENRY LEON, BOX 10402, BAINBRIDGE ISLAND, WA 98110
WILLIAM LEWIS, BOX 6181, SITKA, AK 99835
JACOB LICARI, 112 SAND DOLLAR DR, SITKA, AK 99835
MATTHEW LICHTENSTEIN, BOX 643, PETERSBURG, AK 99833
ANCHOR LINDHOLM, 5405 EDENS RD, ANACORTES, WA 98221
JANE LINDSEY, BOX 240632, DOUGLAS, AK 99824
PATRICK LINDSEY, 17330 MOORS AVE, FRASER, MI 48026
MICHAEL LOCKABEY, BOX 1542, WRANGELL, AK 99929
LOUIS LONGMIRE, BOX 111, YAKUTAT, AK 99689
DENNIS LONGSTRETH, 330 WACHUSETTS ST, SITKA, AK 99835
JACK LORRIGAN, 2300 N LAUREL DR, PALMER, AK 99645
DAVID LOUTREL, 1430 CRESCENT DR, ANCHORAGE, AK 99508
RICHARD LUNDAHL, BOX 718, PELICAN, AK 99832
RONALD LUNDAMO, 657 N POINT HIGGINS RD, KETCHIKAN, AK 99901
GREG LUTTON, BOX 1924, PETERSBURG, AK 99833
DAVID LYONS, BOX 379, SITKA, AK 99835
CARTER MABRY, BOX 6511, SITKA, AK 99835
MATT MAGIE, 1410 D SAWMILL CREEK RD, SITKA, AK 99835
DAVID MAGNUS, BOX 135, SITKA, AK 99835
FRANK MAGNUSON, 209 MILLS ST A, SITKA, AK 99835
JOHN MAGNUSON, BOX 55, POINT BAKER, AK 99927
BYRON MALLOTT, BOX 317, YAKUTAT, AK 99689
JASON MANNEY, BOX 32265, JUNEAU, AK 99803
CASEY MAPES, BOX 215, YAKUTAT, AK 99689
JAMES MARKER, BOX 267, CRAIG, AK 99921
DONALD MARSH, BOX 217, MOSIER, OR 97040
WALTER MARSH, 717 CANYON RD, KETCHIKAN, AK 99901
GREGORY MARTIN, 218 VITSKARI ST, SITKA, AK 99835
MICHAEL MARTIN, 14714 GOODRICH DR NW, GIG HARBOR, WA 98329
KARL MARTINSEN, 306 WORTMAN LP #A, SITKA, AK 99835
CHARLES MASON, 16526 GLACIER HWY, JUNEAU, AK 99801
DEVEN MASON, 16526 GLACIER HWY, JUNEAU, AK 99801
KELVIN MATHESON, 107 E JONTHAN AVE, OMAK, WA 98841
ERNEST MATTESON, BOX 6304, SITKA, AK 99835
JERRY MATTHEWS, BOX 2543, SITKA, AK 99835

SALMON FISHING LIST—POWER TROLL

MORRIS MATTSON, BOX 1168, PETERSBURG, AK 99833
SHELTON MAVES, BOX 117, CRAIG, AK 99921
MICHAEL MAYO, 2808 SAWMILL CREEK RD, SITKA, AK 99835
PATRICK MCCARTHY, BOX 5204, KETCHIKAN, AK 99901
LUCAS MCCONNELL, 2575 SAWMILL CREEK RD, SITKA, AK 99835
LANCE MCCUTCHEON, BOX 6253, SITKA, AK 99835
JOHN MCDONALD, BOX 466, MIMBRES, NM 88049
GREGG MCENTIRE, BOX 15164, HOMER, AK 99603
JEFFRY MCENTIRE, BOX 833, HAINES, AK 99827
MONTE MCFARLAND, 4314 VALLHALLA, SITKA, AK 99835
KENNETH MCGEE, 2390 ENGINEERS CUT OFF, JUNEAU, AK 99801
PATRICK MCGRATH, BOX 2060, PETERSBURG, AK 99833
CHUCK MCGRAW, BOX 234, SITKA, AK 99835
JOSH MCGRAW, 1204 EDGECOMBE DR, SITKA, AK 99835
DENNIS MCGUIRE, BOX 133, ANGOON, AK 99820
WAYNE MCHOLLAND, BOX 2233, WRANGELL, AK 99929
BARRY MCKEE, 1111 HALIBUT POINT RD, SITKA, AK 99835
ERIC MCKEE, 1455 THOMPSON AVE, SANTA CRUZ, CA 95062
KENNETH MCLEOD, BOX 434, SITKA, AK 99835
GARY MCMASTER, 1722 EDGECUMBE DR, SITKA, AK 99835
STEVE MCMURRY, BOX 6391, SITKA, AK 99835
RODNEY MCVICKER, 24411 GRACEY TRAIL LN NE, POULSBO, WA 98370
DANIEL MELLING, 5581 HEART LAKE PL, ANACORTES, WA 98221
NELSON MERRELL, 1323 GLACIER HWY, JUNEAU, AK 99801
THEODORE MERRELL, 3240 FRITZ COVE RD, JUNEAU, AK 99801
BRIAN MERRITT, BOX 401, WRANGELL, AK 99929
RONALD MERRITT, BOX 912, WRANGELL, AK 99929
STEVEN MERRITT, BOX 1138, CRAIG, AK 99921
EDWARD MERTZ, BOX 3105, SITKA, AK 99835
ERIC MEYER, BOX 655, AVILA BEACH, CA 93424
MARK MEYER, BOX 1, TENAKEE, AK 99841
ROBERT MEYER, BOX 10, MEYERS CHUCK, AK 99903
GARY MEYERS, 3208 HALIBUT POINT RD #23, SITKA, AK 99835
CHAD MICKEL, 10805 N TONGASS HWY, KETCHIKAN, AK 99901
MAX MIELKE, 5930 LEMON ST, JUNEAU, AK 99801
CALEB MIETHE, BOX 2031, WRANGELL, AK 99929
JOSHUA MIETHE, BOX 2031, WRANGELL, AK 99929
LANCE MIETHE, BOX PPV, KETCHIKAN, AK 99950
BRENT MILLER, 2919 PASCOE LN, NAMPA, ID 83686
JACOB MILLER, BOX 21708, JUNEAU, AK 99802
JAY MILLER, BOX 6565, SITKA, AK 99835
MARCUS MILLER, BOX 1218, HAINES, AK 99827
RUSSELL MILLER, 350 SOLARIS LN, BAYSIDE, CA 95524
DUKE MITCHELL, BOX 80, WRANGELL, AK 99929
TYRUS MOFFITT, BOX 1165, SITKA, AK 99835
ANDREW MONTGOMERY, 274 POLK ST, EUGENE, OR 97402
DENNIS MONTGOMERY, BOX 48, ELFIN COVE, AK 99825
DENNIS MOODY, 3022 CREST AVE, KETCHIKAN, AK 99901
HENRY MOORE, BOX 2372, SITKA, AK 99835
JAMES MOORE, BOX 770, HAINES, AK 99827
JONATHAN MOORE, 3464 SHERMAN ST, PORT TOWNSEND, WA 98368
JOSHUA MOORE, BOX 2015, PETERSBURG, AK 99833
GEORGE MORFORD, 507 KATLIAN ST, SITKA, AK 99835
JAMES MORGAN, BOX 6167, SITKA, AK 99835
FREDERICK MORK, 108 RUDOLPH WALTON CIR, SITKA, AK 99835
JAMISON MORK, BOX 44, PELICAN, AK 99832
J MORRISON, BOX 2514, SITKA, AK 99835
RALEIGH MORRISON, BOX 74, HYDABURG, AK 99922
JAMES MOSSBURG, 5423 MOSQUITO LAKE RD, DEMING, WA 98244
GARY MUEHLBERGER, BOX PPV, KETCHIKAN, AK 99950
LUCAS MULLEN, BOX 543, PETERSBURG, AK 99833
CHAD MULLIGAN, 224 MARINE ST, SITKA, AK 99835
GARY MULLIGAN, 224 MARINE ST #A, SITKA, AK 99835
RICHARD MULLIGAN, 107 SHELIKOF WAY, SITKA, AK 99835
RYAN MULLIGAN, BOX 8007, PORT ALEXANDER, AK 99836

KATHLEEN MURPHY, 142 BECKETT POINT RD, PORT TOWNSEND, WA 98368
FRANK MURRAY, BOX 34, CRAIG, AK 99921
JOHN MURRAY, 224 OBSERVATORY ST, SITKA, AK 99835
TROY MUTZ, BOX 42, ELFIN COVE, AK 99825
RICHARD MYERS, 102 DEERFIELD AVE, WATERBURY, CT 6708
PHILIP NAGL, BOX 6116, SITKA, AK 99835
CHRISTOPHER NASH, BOX 6493, SITKA, AK 99835
DAVID NASH, 1267 FRITZ COVE RD, JUNEAU, AK 99801
DONALD NASH, BOX 1167, HAINES, AK 99827
LEE NASH, HC 60 BOX 3842, HAINES, AK 99827
DOUGLAS NEAL, 5426 HANNEGAN RD, BELLINGHAM, WA 98226
ED NEAL, 2928 FRITZ COVE RD, JUNEAU, AK 99801
IZAAK NEEDHAM, BOX 6382, SITKA, AK 99835
FRANK NEIDIFFER, BOX 1746, PETERSBURG, AK 99833
MARK NEIDIFFER, BOX 1913, PETERSBURG, AK 99833
JAMES NELSON, BOX 449, YAKUTAT, AK 99689
KENNETH NELSON, BOX 6098, SITKA, AK 99835
DARELL NESS, BOX 240454, DOUGLAS, AK 99824
TODD NEVERS, 712 SIRSTAD ST, SITKA, AK 99835
PETER N. JOHNSON, 2417 TONGASS AVE #111-324, KETCHIKAN, AK 99901
ROBERT NEWCOMB, BOX 76, CRAIG, AK 99921
NEIL NEWLUN, BOX 957, PETERSBURG, AK 99833
MAXINE NEYMAN, BOX 1606, WRANGELL, AK 99929
CASSIUS NICHOLS, 35075 BOND RD, LEBANON, OR 97355
MICHAEL NICHOLS, BOX 122, POINT BAKER, AK 99927
RYAN NICHOLS, 305 ISLANDER DR, SITKA, AK 99835
MICHAEL NILSEN, BOX 1084, PETERSBURG, AK 99833
BRIAN NOLTE, BOX 7409, BROOKINGS, OR 97415
EVAN NORBISRATH, 3725 S AIRPORT RD, PORT ANGELES, WA 98363
THOMAS NORDTVEDT, 126 GIMBAL LN, KETCHIKAN, AK 99901
CRAIG NORMAN, 4112 HALIBUT POINT RD, SITKA, AK 99835
KURT NORMAN, 250 WILCOX LN, CORVALLIS, MT 59840
DENNIS NORTHRUP, BOX 1159, WARD COVE, AK 99928
WAYNE NORTHRUP, BOX 1177, WARD COVE, AK 99928
RONALD NYMAN, 2395 AURORA CT, JUNEAU, AK 99801
TIMOTHY OCONNOR, BOX 1225, CRAIG, AK 99921
DAVID OEN, BOX 2473, SITKA, AK 99835
ERIC OEN, BOX 2026, SITKA, AK 99835
TREVOR OESTER, BOX 81977, FAIRBANKS, AK 99708
DOUGLAS OGILVY, BOX 323, GUSTAVUS, AK 99826
SARA OHLIN, 507 KATLIAN ST, SITKA, AK 99835
REX OLANDER, 210 DEBBIE LN, SHELTER COVE, CA 95589
JOHNNY OLSEN, 4005 161ST AVE SE, BELLEVUE, WA 98006
DANIEL OLSON, 1035 COUNTY LINE RD, GRAYLAND, WA 98547
DARRYL OLSON, BOX 1304, PETERSBURG, AK 99833
KENNETH OLSON, BOX 1557, PETERSBURG, AK 99833
PAUL OLSON, 606 MERILL ST, SITKA, AK 99835
RICHARD OLSON, 359 OHLSON LN, KETCHIKAN, AK 99901
RONALD OLSON, BOX 123, KLAWOCK, AK 99925
ZACHARY OLSON, BOX 2451, SITKA, AK 99835
RICHARD OLTMAN, 370 MIDDLEPOINT, PORT TOWNSEND, WA 98368
RONALD ONEIL, #53 WWP, KETCHIKAN, AK 99950
RON OPHEIM, BOX 2118, WRANGELL, AK 99929
ARTHUR OSBORNE, BOX 240925, DOUGLAS, AK 99824
DAVID OTTE, 2417 TONGASS AVE #111 PMB139, KETCHIKAN, AK 99901
GREGORY OWENS, BOX 1091, SITKA, AK 99835
HERBERT OYLER, BOX 2135, PETERSBURG, AK 99833
ROBERT OYLER, 263 SUNDAY LN, KALISPELL, MT 59901
CHRISTOPHER PACE, BOX 33594, JUNEAU, AK 99803
BRADELLE PADON, 740 5TH ST, JUNEAU, AK 99801
DEBRA PAGE, BOX 115, ELFIN COVE, AK 99825
JONATHAN PARKER, BOX 406, PETERSBURG, AK 99833
NATHAN PARKER, BOX 972, PETERSBURG, AK 99833
WAYNE PARKS, BOX 985, PETERSBURG, AK 99833
PAT PARRISH, BOX 2895, SITKA, AK 99835

SALMON FISHING LIST—POWER TROLL

WALTER PASTERNAK, BOX 830, SITKA, AK 99835

KIM PATOTZKA, BOX 827, CRAIG, AK 99921

DARREN PATRICK, BOX 226, GUSTAVUS, AK 99826

WILLIAM PATRICK, 2003 ANNA CIR, SITKA, AK 99835

MICHAEL PATTISON, 246 STRAWBERRY RD, KETCHIKAN, AK 99901

MATTHEW PEARSON, BOX 1427, PORT ARANSAS, TX 78373

DAN PEAVEY, BOX 19228, THORNE BAY, AK 99919

MATTHEW PEAVEY, BOX 442, CRAIG, AK 99921

STEVEN PEAVEY, BOX 5, MEYERS CHUCK, AK 99903

JEFF PEDERSEN, 16315 NE UNION RD, RIDGEFIELD, WA 98642

CHARLES PEEP, BOX 1603, HAINES, AK 99827

DAVID PENDARVIS, BOX NKI, KETCHIKAN, AK 99950

HOWARD PENDELL, BOX 1615, SITKA, AK 99835

BRYAN PEREZ, BOX 7991, KETCHIKAN, AK 99901

THOMAS PERKINS, BOX 5393, KETCHIKAN, AK 99901

WILLIAM PERKINS, BOX 6071, SITKA, AK 99835

WARD PERSON, BOX 1295, ANCHOR POINT, AK 99556

BENJAMIN PETERS, BOX 1424, PORT ANGELS, WA 98362

DUSTIN PETERS, BOX 726, WARD COVE, AK 99928

PAUL PETERS, BOX 902, HAINES, AK 99827

RYAN PETERS, 110 LANCE DR, SITKA, AK 99835

MARK PETERSEN, 8405 NUGGET DR, JUNEAU, AK 99801

BRUCE PETERSON, 507 KATLIAN ST, SITKA, AK 99835

CARL PETERSON, BOX 593, SITKA, AK 99835

CHRIS PETERSON, BOX 6025, SITKA, AK 99835

ERIC PETERSON, BOX 2976, SITKA, AK 99835

ERIK PETERSON, BOX 75, PELICAN, AK 99832

GERALD PETERSON, BOX 523, HOONAH, AK 99829

RALPH PETERSON, BOX 2027, PETERSBURG, AK 99833

RENA PETERSON, 7475 ADDENDA CT, ANCHORAGE, AK 99507

JOHN PETRABORG, BOX 6067, SITKA, AK 99835

ALEX PEURA, 3739 S TONGASS HWY, KETCHIKAN, AK 99901

CAVEN PFEIFFER, 236 OBSERVATORY ST, SITKA, AK 99835

TRUEMAN PHILBRICK, 1501 DAVIDOFF ST, SITKA, AK 99835

CARL PHILLIPS, BOX 74, PELICAN, AK 99832

FREDERICK PHILLIPS, 1210 EDGECOMB DR, SITKA, AK 99835

ABEL PIERCY, BOX 1025, WARD COVE, AK 99928

CHARLES PIERCY, BOX 1025, WARD COVE, AK 99928

LANNY PIHLMAN, BOX 778, WARD COVE, AK 99928

STEPHEN PITELL, 3501 PREBLE ST, BREMERTON, WA 98312

BEN PLATT, BOX 1894, WINDSOR, CA 95492

LESLIE PLY, BOX 64, ELFIN COVE, AK 99825

JOHN POLIVKA, 311 WORTMAN LP, SITKA, AK 99835

LAURA POLLARD, BOX 8046, PORT ALEXANDER, AK 99836

NATHAN POLLOCK, 21000 NE 67TH AVE, BATTLEGROUND, WA 98604

THOMAS POPE, 323 W 3RD ST, PORT ANGELES, WA 98362

JOEL POWER, 5 LAST LAKE LN, BELLINGHAM, WA 98229

LANCE PRESTON, BOX 6416, SITKA, AK 99835

JAMES PROCTOR, BOX 810, KLAMATH, CA 95548

JAMES PROCTOR, BOX 31, GUSTAVUS, AK 99826

JERRY PUCKETT, BOX 3131, SITKA, AK 99835

SEAN PULLIAM, BOX 2422, YUCCA VALLEY, CA 92286

MIKE QUANDT, 80 JENSEN RD, PORT TOWNSEND, WA 98368

JAMES QUIGLEY, BOX 80, CRAIG, AK 99921

IAN RABB, 5125 N. DOUGLAS HWY, JUNEAU, AK 99801

RON RADER, BOX 7862, KETCHIKAN, AK 99901

ROBERT RAE, BOX 67, HUNTERS, WA 99137

DANIEL RASMUSSEN, 110 CHERRY AVE, CHIMACUM, WA 98325

JOHN RASMUSSEN, 3186 HORSEHEAD BAY DR NW, GIG HARBOR, WA 98335

PEGGY RAUWOLF, 7942 S TONGASS HWY, KETCHIKAN, AK 99901

DANIEL REAR, 1007 HALIBUT POINT RD, SITKA, AK 99835

JOHN REAR, BOX 240497, DOUGLAS, AK 99824

RONALD REED, BOX 1437, PETERSBURG, AK 99833

GERALD REINHOLDT, 62313 S CANAAN RD, ST HELENS, OR 97051

SANFORD REISBICK, 10415 STARDUST LN SE, OLYMPIA, WA 98501

JESSE REMUND, 330 WACHUSETTS ST, SITKA, AK 99835

MARTY REMUND, BOX 1295, HAINES, AK 99827

MICHAEL RENTEL, BOX 33406, JUNEAU, AK 99803

ISAAC REYNOLDS, 205 A CASCADE CREEK RD, SITKA, AK 99835

JOSHUA RHOADES, BOX 6211, SITKA, AK 99835

BONNIE RICHARDS, BOX 933, SITKA, AK 99835

DONALD RICHARDS, BOX 1764, PETERSBURG, AK 99833

RONALD RICHARDS, 124 TOWNSHIP LINE RD, PORT ANGELES, WA 98362

DAVID RICHEY, BOX 6204, SITKA, AK 99835

ROBERT RIGGS, BOX 1290, WRANGELL, AK 99929

TRACY RIVERA, BOX 541, TENAKEE, AK 99841

RONALD RIVETT, 1910 8TH AVE NE, ABERDEEN, SD 57401

CALEB ROBBINS, BOX 6256, SITKA, AK 99835

PATRICK ROBBINS, BOX 202, YAKUTAT, AK 99689

BRIAN ROBERTS, 177 TELEGRAPH RD #356, BELLINGHAM, WA 98226

MARK ROBERTS, BOX 246, PETERSBURG, AK 99833

SEAN ROBERTS, BOX 583, WARD COVE, AK 99928

CALVIN ROBINSON, BOX 2225, SITKA, AK 99835

ERIC ROBINSON, 1006 HALIBUT POINT RD, SITKA, AK 99835

JEFFREY ROBINSON, BOX 633, PETERSBURG, AK 99833

TAYLOR ROBISON, BOX 329, CRAIG, AK 99921

PETER RODDY, BOX 6436, SITKA, AK 99835

JENA ROETZER, 14126 240TH ST NE, ARLINGTON, WA 98223

RICHARD ROGERS, BOX 258, KAKE, AK 99830

DAVID ROJCEWICZ, BOX 954, PETERSBURG, AK 99833

C.ALAN ROSS, BOX 19376, THORNE BAY, AK 99919

JOHN ROSS, 517 NELSON ST, JUNEAU, AK 99801

PAUL ROSTAD, BOX 183, KAKE, AK 99830

LEROY ROTH, 2306 2ND AVE, KETCHIKAN, AK 99901

MICHAEL ROWSE, BOX 36, HOONAH, AK 99829

MICHAEL RUGO, BOX 1424, WRANGELL, AK 99929

STEVE RUNNION, 427 VERSTOVIA ST, SITKA, AK 99835

RONALD RUSHER, BOX 18072, COFFMAN COVE, AK 99918

CHARLES RUSSELL, BOX NKI #8, KETCHIKAN, AK 99950

JAMES RYMAN, BOX 1032, SITKA, AK 99835

DAVID RYNO, BOX 368, CRAIG, AK 99921

BRAD SAALSAA, BOX 9382, KETCHIKAN, AK 99901

HARDY SAFFOLD, BOX 8097, PORT ALEXANDER, AK 99836

DUANE SAMATO, BOX 77, ANGOON, AK 99820

HARRY SAMATO, 1220 GLACIER AVE #307B, JUNEAU, AK 99801

EDWARD SANDERSON, BOX 91, HYDABURG, AK 99922

JOHN SANTI, BOX 3247, SITKA, AK 99835

ROBERT SANTI, 263 OHINA PL, KIHEI, HI 96753

MARK SAPPINGTON, BOX 302, YAKUTAT, AK 99689

JOSEPH SARCEDA, 1085 SWEETWOOD CIR, NAMPA, ID 83651

JASON SARGENT, BOX 1045, SITKA, AK 99835

SVEN SAVLAND, BOX 621, HOONAH, AK 99829

E.KEVIN SCHADE, 12200 STONE AVE N #34, SEATTLE, WA 98133

STEVE SCHALLBERGER, LOT 3 BLOCK 8, EDNA BAY, AK 99950

THOMAS SCHEIDT, 3918 HALIBUT POINT RD, SITKA, AK 99835

ROBERT SCHELL, BOX 1367, SITKA, AK 99835

CRAIG SCHLEY, 161 GLENWAY RD, BROOKLYN, WI 53521

JEFFERY SCHMIDT, BOX 615, KITTITAS, WA 98934

KENNETH SCHOONOVER, BOX 373, HOONAH, AK 99829

ALEC SCHRAMEK, BOX 124, PETERSBURG, AK 99833

PAUL SCHREIBER, 231 KATLIAN #A10, SITKA, AK 99835

LEWIS SCHUMEJDA, BOX 2182, SITKA, AK 99835

DAN SCHWEITZER, BOX 1667, PETERSBURG, AK 99833

ANDREW SCORZELLI, BOX 6416, SITKA, AK 99835

WILBERT SCOTT, BOX 6054, KETCHIKAN, AK 99901

EVAN SEAGER, 301 PALANEHE ST, KIHEI, HI 96753

NANCY SEAGER, 8714 54TH PL W, MUKILTEO, WA 98275

HEATHER SEARS, 30551 NAVARRO RIDGE RD, ALBION, CA 95410

ELSA SEBASTIAN, BOX 964, HAINES, AK 99827

FOREST SEBASTIAN, BOX 1990, PETERSBURG, AK 99833

JOSEPH SEBASTIAN, BOX 1990, PETERSBURG, AK 99833

JAMES SEE, BOX 281, CRAIG, AK 99921

SALMON FISHING LIST—POWER TROLL

DONOVAN SEESZ, 114 HARBOR MOUNTAIN RD, SITKA, AK 99835
SPENCER SEVERSON, BOX 6224, SITKA, AK 99835
IAN SEWARD, BOX 1644, HAINES, AK 99827
DANIEL SEWELL, BOX 355, NETARTS, OR 97143
TIM SEXTON, BOX 6426, SITKA, AK 99835
GREGORY SHAPLEY, BOX 85, CRAIG, AK 99921
DAVID SHILTS, BOX 19264, THORNE BAY, AK 99919
MICHAEL SHILTS, BOX 1341, WRANGELL, AK 99929
KARL SHLAUDEMAN, BOX 6473, KETCHIKAN, AK 99901
KELLAN SHOEMAKER, 106 GIBSON PL, SITKA, AK 99835
ROBERT SHOREY, BOX 240452, DOUGLAS, AK 99824
MARK SHORT, BOX 393, SITKA, AK 99835
DAVID SILVA, BOX 602, WRANGELL, AK 99929
DIANNE SILVA, BOX 602, WRANGELL, AK 99929
TOM SIMS, BOX 1553, WRANGELL, AK 99929
ALF SKAFLESTAD, BOX 177, HOONAH, AK 99829
KOLBJORN SKAFLESTAD, BOX 471, HOONAH, AK 99829
MARSH SKEELE, 216 SMITH ST. UNIT B, SITKA, AK 99835
KELSEY SKORDAHL, 109C LANCE DR, SITKA, AK 99835
LUCAS SKORDAHL, 110 HARBOR MOUNTAIN DR, SITKA, AK 99835
CLARK SLANAKER, 3136 TIDE AVE, KETCHIKAN, AK 99901
JAMES SLATER, BOX 63, PELICAN, AK 99832
WESLEY SLATTERY, 206 W MATTLE RD, KETCHIKAN, AK 99901
CHRIS SLAUGHTER, BOX 1933, FERNDALE, WA 98248
GARY SLAVEN, BOX 205, PETERSBURG, AK 99833
BRUCE SMITH, BOX 273, GUSTAVUS, AK 99826
OTTO SMITH, BOX 1981, PORT TOWNSEND, WA 98368
TODD SMITH, BOX 111, GUSTAVUS, AK 99826
VOLNEY SMITH, 2318 HALIBUT POINT RD, SITKA, AK 99835
WAYNE SMITH, BOX 875548, WASILLA, AK 99687
RICHARD SMITHA, 15284 DECEPTION RD, ANACORTES, WA 98221
NICK SMOLKA, 2417 TONGASS AVE # 111-335, KETCHIKAN, AK 99901
RUSSELL SMOOT, BOX 337, VALLEYFORD, WA 99036
RUSSELL SNELL, BOX 6425, SITKA, AK 99835
DONALD SNOW, 7593 SW SURFLAND ST, SOUTH BEACH, OR 97366
ROSS SOBOLEFF, BOX 240632, DOUGLAS, AK 99824
HARRY SODEMAN, 12519 PARKSIDE LN, MOUNT VERNON, WA 98273
MICHAEL SOFOULIS, BOX 210551, AUKE BAY, AK 99821
JEFFREY SOLES, BOX 74, WRANGELL, AK 99929
AUSTIN SOLLARS, BOX 32424, JUNEAU, AK 99803
EVANS SPARKS, 100 DONNA DR, SITKA, AK 99835
DALE STANLEY, BOX 7442, KETCHIKAN, AK 99901
SHANE STANLEY, BOX 19531, THORNE BAY, AK 99919
HOWARD STARBARD, 4452 WOOD DUCK AVE, JUNEAU, AK 99801
GEORGE STATON, 1923 WHITE POINT RD, FRIDAY HARBOR, WA 98250
SHERMAN STATON, 507 KATLIAN ST, SITKA, AK 99835
WAYNE STAUFFER, 3285 FRITZ COVE RD, JUNEAU, AK 99801
JAMES STEDMAN, 47 MONTGOMERY LN, ABERDEEN, WA 98520
JOEL STEENSTRA, BOX 1367, CRAIG, AK 99921
RICHARD STEFFEY, 5320 S 093 E, WOLCOTTVILLE, IN 46795
ZACH STENSON, 1508 GLACIER AVE, JUNEAU, AK 99801
DEREK STEWART, BOX 102, PELICAN, AK 99832
JEFF STEWART, BOX 6546, SITKA, AK 99835
WILLIAM STEWART, BOX 201, GUSTAVUS, AK 99826
LYNN STEYAART, BOX 545, PETERSBURG, AK 99833
WENDI STICKWAN, BOX 5041, KETCHIKAN, AK 99901
BRETT STILLWAUGH, BOX 1552, WRANGELL, AK 99929
RAY STONER, BOX 394, PETERSBURG, AK 99833
JHEA STOUT, BOX 9011, KETCHIKAN, AK 99901
STEPHEN STRASBURGER, BOX 1422, WRANGELL, AK 99929
BENJAMIN STROECKER, BOX 52, GUSTAVUS, AK 99826
MATTHEW STROEMER, 1403 EDGECUMBE DR, SITKA, AK 99835
STEVE STROMME, BOX 22985, JUNEAU, AK 99801
URIAH STRONG, BOX 65, TENAKEE, AK 99841
ZEB STRONG, 3213 S 166TH ST, SEATAC, WA 98188

JACOB STRUBBE, BOX 130, SONOITA, AZ 85637
WALTER STUART, BOX 2196, WRANGELL, AK 99929
JAMES STUKEY, BOX 144, CRAIG, AK 99921
KELSEY SULLIVAN, 501 YORK ST, BELLINGHAM, WA 98225
RICHARD SUMMERS, BOX 227, CRAIG, AK 99921
SOREN SUNDET, BOX 711, JUNEAU, AK 99801
MICHAEL SUTTON, 104 SOMER DR, SITKA, AK 99835
DYLAN SWANBERG, BOX 3053, SITKA, AK 99835
BRAD SWANSON, BOX 202, YAKUTAT, AK 99689
ERIC SWANSON, BOX 6330, SITKA, AK 99835
LONNIE SWANSON, BOX 552, SITKA, AK 99835
SCOTT SWANSON, 9779 NINE MILE RD, JUNEAU, AK 99801
EDWARD TEAGUE, BOX 131, WRANGELL, AK 99929
DAN TEAS, BOX 246, SITKA, AK 99835
BRUCE TENNEY, 9363 N DOUGLAS HWY SIDE A, JUNEAU, AK 99802
ANDREW TERHAAR, BOX 6475, SITKA, AK 99835
JOHN TERRY, 1018 E WISHKAH PMB #334, ABERDEEN, WA 98520
SHERRY THIERFELDER, 11816 ISLAND DR, ANDERSON ISLAND, WA 98303
JEFF THOMAS, 55784 HWY 112, PORT ANGELES, WA 98363
KIM THOMPSON, BOX 195, HOONAH, AK 99829
STEVEN THYNES, BOX 193, PETERSBURG, AK 99833
DONALD TORGESON, 101 HAVEN LANE #2, SITKA, AK 99835
BRIAN TREKELL, BOX 2641, SOLDOTNA, AK 99669
JONATHAN TULLY, BOX 5513, KETCHIKAN, AK 99901
DAVID TURCOTT, 102 DARRIN DR, SITKA, AK 99835
GREG TURNER, BOX 684, DELTA JUNCTION, AK 99737
JEFFREY TURNER, 329 KATLIAN ST, SITKA, AK 99835
PEDR TURNER, BOX 217, GUSTAVUS, AK 99826
PATRICK TYNER, BOX 541, CRAIG, AK 99921
ROY UBER, 1502 DAVIDOFF ST, SITKA, AK 99835
SHANE ULERY, BOX 19197, THORNE BAY, AK 99919
BRUCE ULRICH, BOX 736, SITKA, AK 99835
HOWARD ULRICH, BOX 6107, SITKA, AK 99835
MELVIN VAN.RONK, 1004 LARABEE CREEK RD, REDCREST, CA 95569
RICHARD VAN.RONK, 1498 17TH ST, OCEANO, CA 93445
RYAN VANDERPOPPEN, 4300 134TH AVE, HAMILTON, MI 49419
EDWARD VANDOR, 7595 N DOUGLAS HWY, JUNEAU, AK 99801
DANIEL VERNETTI, 8477 THUNDER MOUNTAIN RD #54, JUNEAU, AK 99801
GARRET VINCENTZ, BOX 1572, WARD COVE, AK 99928
SCOTT VISSCHER, HC 60 BOX 2842, HAINES, AK 99827
HARRIET WADLEY, BOX 318, CRAIG, AK 99921
ROBERT WAGNER, BOX 264, HOONAH, AK 99829
WALTER WAGNER, BOX 107, METLAKATLA, AK 99926
WILLIAM WALDER, BOX 11, ELFIN COVE, AK 99825
ELDON WALKER, 3848 MELROSE ST, JUNEAU, AK 99801
MICHAEL WALSH, 5855 N DOUGLAS HWY, JUNEAU, AK 99801
CONLEY WARD, 2309 HALIBUT POINT RD #13, SITKA, AK 99835
KATHLEEN WARM, 507 KATLIAN ST, SITKA, AK 99835
BRIAN WARMUTH, BOX 6382, KETCHIKAN, AK 99901
DENNIS WATSON, BOX 134, CRAIG, AK 99921
FORTCH WAYNE, 6 BLACKBEAR LN, MEYERS CHUCK, AK 99903
STUART WEATHERS, BOX 1734, SITKA, AK 99835
STEVE WEISSBERG, 455 CHARTERIS ST, SITKA, AK 99835
DONALD WELBORN, BOX 6285, LOS OSOS, CA 93412
CELESTE WELLER, BOX 64, PELICAN, AK 99832
JOHN WELSH, 409 DE ARMOND #B, SITKA, AK 99835
BRENT WENTZEL, BOX 111, ONALASKA, WA 98570
MARK WEST, BOX 1664, SITKA, AK 99835
MICHAEL WEST, BOX 6412, SITKA, AK 99835
ROY WEST, 507 KATLIAN ST, SITKA, AK 99835
JOHN WEYHMILLER, BOX 98, CRAIG, AK 99921
JOSEPH WEYHMILLER, BOX 413, TWISP, WA 98856
MICHAEL WEYHMILLER, BOX 191, CRAIG, AK 99921
MATT WHEELER, BOX 135, YAKUTAT, AK 99689
FRANK WHITE, BOX 1474, HAINES, AK 99827

HERRING ROE—PURSE SEINE

JAMES WHITE, 245B W MATTLE RD, KETCHIKAN, AK 99901
JAMES WHITE, BOX 32892, JUNEAU, AK 99803
DANNY WHITSON, BOX 6291, SITKA, AK 99835
ALLAN WICKENS, 2417 TONGASS AVE #111-336, KETCHIKAN, AK 99901
JESSE WIDMYER, BOX 7100, KETCHIKAN, AK 99901
ROBERT WIDMYER, BOX 6603, KETCHIKAN, AK 99901
WENDY WIDMYER, BOX 242, EDNA BAY, AK 99950
BRANT WIDNESS, BOX 7773, KETCHIKAN, AK 99901
MATTHEW WIEDEMANN, BOX 32, ELFIN COVE, AK 99825
HANS WIENBERG, BOX 164, SITKA, AK 99835
SHERMAN WIGLE, BOX 2038, PETERSBURG, AK 99833
CHARLES WILBER, 705 ETOLIN, SITKA, AK 99835
JAMES WILD, BOX 109, ELFIN COVE, AK 99825
ERIC WILKERSON, 2840 ENGINEERS CUTOFF, JUNEAU, AK 99801
KENNETH WILKINSON, 203 AIRPORT RD #A12, SITKA, AK 99835
TERRANCE WILLBURN, BOX 19389, THORNE BAY, AK 99919
BILLY WILLIAMS, 8322 GLADSTONE ST, JUNEAU, AK 99801
DAVID WILLIAMS, BOX 10191, FAIRBANKS, AK 99710
DAVID WILLIAMS, 1912 SAWMILL CREEK RD, SITKA, AK 99835
DENA WILLIAMS, 2202 CRESTLINE CT, GRAND JUNCTION, CO 81507
CLYDE WILLIAMSON, PMB 336 150 S HWY 160 #8, PAHRUMP, NV 89048
RYAN WILSON, BOX 414, SITKA, AK 99835
WILLIAM WILSON, BOX 602, TENAKEE, AK 99841
WAYNE WINTHER, BOX 505, SITKA, AK 99835
GARRETT WOOD, BOX 1696, KODIAK, AK 99615
LES WOODWARD, BOX 2059, WRANGELL, AK 99929
RANDALL WORTMAN, BOX 271, CRAIG, AK 99921
ANDY WRIGHT, BOX 1432, PETERSBURG, AK 99833
JOSEPH WROBLEWSKI, 640-545 IRIS RD, MCARTHUR, CA 96056
ERIC WYATT, BOX 369, CRAIG, AK 99921
DONALD YATES, BOX 614, CRAIG, AK 99921
SHAWN YATES, BOX 481, KLAWOCK, AK 99925
BRETT YOUNG, BOX 1971, WRANGELL, AK 99929
MARK YOUNG, BOX 2016, SITKA, AK 99835
STEVE YOUNG, BOX 745, PELICAN, AK 99832
TIM YOUNG, BOX 63, HYDABURG, AK 99922
VERNE YOUNG, BOX 611, PELICAN, AK 99832
EVERETT YOUNGBERG, BOX 2056, PETERSBURG, AK 99833
BRETT ZAENGLEIN, 403 MILLS ST, SITKA, AK 99835
GUTHRIE ZASTROW, 3930 S TONGASS HWY, KETCHIKAN, AK 99901
MICHAEL ZIARA, 30 WOODMAN RD, PORT TOWNSEND, WA 98368
BRIAN ZIEL, BOX 44, TENAKEE, AK 99841
RUDOLF ZIEL, BOX 44, TENAKEE, AK 99841
CLAUDE ZIMMERLE, 410 COOK STREET, KETCHIKAN, AK 99901

SALMON, SPECIAL HARVEST AREA, SOUTHEAST
HATCHERY SHELDON JACKSON, 834 LINCOLN ST #200, SITKA, AK 99835

HERRING ROE, PURSE SEINE, SOUTHEAST
LOUIE ALBER, BOX 111, CORDOVA, AK 99574
JOHN BARRY, 800 HALIBUT POINT RD #C, SITKA, AK 99835
DALE BARTELDS, 301 WORTMAN LP, SITKA, AK 99835
HUGHIE BLAKE, BOX 2376, CORDOVA, AK 99574
RONALD BLAKE, BOX 1236, CORDOVA, AK 99574
JIM BODDING, 1911 8TH ST, ANACORTES, WA 98221
JOHN CARLE, BOX 1, HYDABURG, AK 99922
DANIEL CASTLE, 4430 S TONGASS HWY, KETCHIKAN, AK 99901
JULIANNE CURRY, BOX 2182, PETERSBURG, AK 99833
TROY DENKINGER, 2221 HALIBUT POINT RD, SITKA, AK 99835
KEN EICHNER, 5166 SHORELINE DR N, KETCHIKAN, AK 99901
MITCHELL EIDE, BOX 981, PETERSBURG, AK 99833
ROBERT FELLOWS, 266 E BAYVIEW AVE, HOMER, AK 99603
CHARLES FOGLE, 5722 CAMPBELL LAKE RD, ANACORTES, WA 98221
DEAN HALTINER, BOX 443, PETERSBURG, AK 99833

GARY HAYNES, 625 SUNSET DR, KETCHIKAN, AK 99901
ROYCE HAYWARD, BOX 161, METLAKATLA, AK 99926
MICHAEL HOLMSTROM, 17952 MCLEAN RD, MOUNT VERNON, WA 98273
SARA JACKINSKY, BOX 1044, HOMER, AK 99603
LEROY JOHNS, BOX 1126, SISTERS, OR 97759
VICTOR JONES, BOX 1831, CORDOVA, AK 99574
DARRELL KAPP, 338 BAYSIDE RD, BELLINGHAM, WA 98225
MITCHELL KEPLINGER, BOX 1006, KODIAK, AK 99615
TERRANCE KILBREATH, 31 PINE ST #210, EDMONDS, WA 98020
SIDNEY KINNEY, 103 KRAMER AVE, SITKA, AK 99835
ANDREW KITTAMS, BOX 1544, PETERSBURG, AK 99833
MICHAEL KURTZ, BOX 32265, BELLINGHAM, WA 98228
LUKE LESTER, BOX 553, KODIAK, AK 99615
EVERETT LINDHOLM, 415 E PARK DR, ANACORTES, WA 98221
CLIFF LIU, 13320 MULHOLLAND DR, BEVERLY HILLS, CA 90210
NELS LYNCH, BOX 425, HAINES, AK 99827
TOMI MARSH, 2417 TONGASS AVE # 111-176, KETCHIKAN, AK 99901
RAYMOND MAY, BOX 8985, KODIAK, AK 99615
WILLIAM MENISH, BOX 877, PETERSBURG, AK 99833
JOSHUA MILLER, BOX 252, PETERSBURG, AK 99833
SAMUEL MUTCH, 210 B SHELIKOF, KODIAK, AK 99615
MARCUS NELSON, BOX 792, METLAKATLA, AK 99926
NICK NELSON, 3380 PARK PLACE, JUNEAU, AK 99801
NORVAL NELSON, 1625 FRITZ COVE RD, JUNEAU, AK 99801
ROBERT NELSON, BOX 205, KASILOF, AK 99610
THOMAS NELSON, BOX 1392, HOMER, AK 99603
CHARLES OLSON, 3009 HALIBUT POINT RD, SITKA, AK 99835
ALAN OTNESS, BOX 317, PETERSBURG, AK 99833
NELS OTNESS, BOX 366, PETERSBURG, AK 99833
JUSTIN PEELER, BOX 184, SITKA, AK 99835
RONALD PORTER, BOX 957, WARD COVE, AK 99928
MALCOLM ROSS, BOX 3476, HOMER, AK 99603
J.CARLOS SCHWANTES, BOX 2335, SITKA, AK 99835
CHARLES SKEEK, BOX 742, PETERSBURG, AK 99833
THOMAS STAFFORD, BOX 3403, HOMER, AK 99603
CHARLES TREINEN, 2054 ARLINGTON DR, ANCHORAGE, AK 99517

HERRING ROE, PURSE SEINE, PRINCE WILLIAM SOUND
LOUIE ALBER, BOX 111, CORDOVA, AK 99574
MYRA ALLEN, BOX 984, VALDEZ, AK 99686
RUSSELL ALLEN, BOX 1062, CORDOVA, AK 99574
THOMAS ALLEN, 16420 SANDPIPER DR, ANCHORAGE, AK 99516
H.GARY ANDERSON, BOX 47, CHIGNIK LAGOON, AK 99565
RONALD ANDERSON, 1222 101ST AVE CT, GREELEY, CO 80634
STOSH ANDERSON, BOX 310, KODIAK, AK 99615
MATHEW BABIC, BOX 988, CORDOVA, AK 99574
SANFORD BEACHY, BOX 800, HOMER, AK 99603
DONALD BERGQUIST, 4922 S SMUGGLERS COVE RD, FREELAND, WA 98249
HUGHIE BLAKE, BOX 2376, CORDOVA, AK 99574
RONALD BLAKE, BOX 1236, CORDOVA, AK 99574
SHERYL BLAKE, BOX 1212, CORDOVA, AK 99574
CARL BURTON, BOX 81, CORDOVA, AK 99574
TRAVIS BUTLER, BOX 332, CONWAY, WA 98238
LEROY CABANA, BOX 49, HOMER, AK 99603
DONALD CALHOON, 11001 E EQUESTRIAN ST, PALMER, AK 99645
JAMES CALHOUN, 4360 ANDERSON ST, HOMER, AK 99603
VIRGIL CARROLL, BOX 319, CORDOVA, AK 99574
KENNETH CASTNER, BOX 558, HOMER, AK 99603
MEAGAN CHRISTIANSEN, 1849 MARMOT DR, KODIAK, AK 99615
CLYDE CURRY, BOX 572, PETERSBURG, AK 99833
DAVID DANIELS, BOX 930, VALDEZ, AK 99686
PHYLLIS DAY, 2020 MULDOON RD #317, ANCHORAGE, AK 99504
VICTOR DUNCAN, BOX 414, GIRDWOOD, AK 99587
MICHAEL DURTSCHI, BOX 1012, GIRDWOOD, AK 99587
LINDA ECOLANO, BOX 1593, CORDOVA, AK 99574

HERRING ROE & FOOT BAIT—PURSE SEINE

HAROLD ENGEBRETSEN, BOX 534, HOMER, AK 99603
HARLEY ETHELBAH, 86 APPALOOSA LN, BELLINGHAM, WA 98229
ROBERT FELLOWS, 266 E BAYVIEW AVE, HOMER, AK 99603
OLIVER FLYNN, BOX 2106, HOMER, AK 99603
GRANT FRITZ, BOX 13, KASILOF, AK 99610
STEVEN GILDNES, BOX 2393, CORDOVA, AK 99574
SWEN GILDNES, BOX 519, CORDOVA, AK 99574
DOUGLAS GILES, BOX 1, SELDOVIA, AK 99663
LESLIE GILES, BOX 275, SELDOVIA, AK 99663
DARIN GILMAN, BOX 223, CORDOVA, AK 99574
GEROLD GUGEL, BOX 671227, CHUGIAK, AK 99567
KENNETH HALPIN, BOX 1022, HOMER, AK 99603
RANDALL HANSEN, 22628 N SAN RAMON DR, SUN CITY WEST, AZ 85375
ARNE HATCH, BOX 346, SEWARD, AK 99664
JOHN HERSCHLEB, 440 E 56TH AVE #A, ANCHORAGE, AK 99518
ROBERT HEYANO, BOX 1409, DILLINGHAM, AK 99576
LAURIE HONKOLA, 4354 BIRCH RUN DR, ANCHORAGE, AK 99507
RAYMOND HONKOLA, BOX 100, CORDOVA, AK 99574
ROBERT HOOVER, BOX 1039, CORDOVA, AK 99574
C HOUGH, 3733 BEN WALTERS LN #2, HOMER, AK 99603
SARA JACKINSKY, BOX 1044, HOMER, AK 99603
MARY JACOBS, BOX 135, OPHIR, OR 97464
BARBARA JENSEN, BOX 294, CORDOVA, AK 99574
DOUGLAS JENSEN, BOX 92535, ANCHORAGE, AK 99509
SUANNA JOHANNESSEN, BOX 474, CORDOVA, AK 99574
KENNETH JONES, BOX 615, CORDOVA, AK 99574
VICTOR JONES, BOX 1831, CORDOVA, AK 99574
BRANKO JURKOVICH, 608 LONGVIEW AVE, ANACORTES, WA 98221
VITOMIR KALCIC, BOX 1486, KODIAK, AK 99615
WILLIAM KASHEVAROF, BOX 52, SELDOVIA, AK 99663
TIMOTHY KENNEDY, BOX 1662, CORDOVA, AK 99574
MITCHELL KEPLINGER, BOX 1006, KODIAK, AK 99615
TERRANCE KILBREATH, 31 PINE ST #210, EDMONDS, WA 98020
MARK KISER, 6436 DOW LN, ANACORTES, WA 98221
GERALD KOLSCHOWSKY, 1143 HALLADAY CT, BATAVIA, IL 60510
MICHAEL KURTZ, BOX 32265, BELLINGHAM, WA 98228
CARL LANE, 2106 LUMMI VIEW DR, BELLINGHAM, WA 98226
EVERETT LINDHOLM, 415 E PARK DR, ANACORTES, WA 98221
LINDA LINDHOLM, 415 E PARK DR, ANACORTES, WA 98221
FREDERIC LOVE, 1830 E 3900 S, SALT LAKE CITY, UT 84124
MATTHEW LUCK, BOX 4997, KETCHUM, ID 83340
THOMAS MCALLISTER, 9156 N DOUGLAS HWY, JUNEAU, AK 99802
CHARLES MCCRACKEN, BOX 940, CORDOVA, AK 99574
SCOTT MCKENZIE, BOX 2071, CORDOVA, AK 99574
RODNEY MCLAY, BOX 504, HOMER, AK 99603
DANNY MCLEAN, BOX 351, HOMER, AK 99603
JOHN MCLEAN, BOX 2191, HOMER, AK 99603
MIKE MCMAHON, 20145 FOREST PARK DR NE, SHORELINE, WA 98155
WILLIAM MENISH, BOX 877, PETERSBURG, AK 99833
ROSELEEN MOORE, 5140 KACHEMAK DR, HOMER, AK 99603
ROBERT MOSS, BOX 3428, HOMER, AK 99603
SAMUEL MUTCH, 210 B SHELIKOF, KODIAK, AK 99615
THOMAS NELSEN, 8227 200 ST SW, EDMONDS, WA 98026
JESSIE NELSON, BOX 130, HOMER, AK 99603
ROBERT NELSON, BOX 205, KASILOF, AK 99610
THOMAS NELSON, BOX 1392, HOMER, AK 99603
MICHAEL NOKLEBY, 2903 ROZEWOOD DR, BREMERTON, WA 98310
LEONARD OGLE, 1122 B AVE S, EDMONDS, WA 98020
CHARLES OLSON, 3009 HALIBUT POINT RD, SITKA, AK 99835
THORNE POPELKA, BOX 577, KLAWOCK, AK 99925
GARY RAYMOND, BOX 596, CORDOVA, AK 99574
MALCOLM ROSS, BOX 3476, HOMER, AK 99603
RICHARD SCHOLLENBERG, BOX 264, ANCHOR POINT, AK 99556
KRIS STRAUB, 4851 EIELSON FARM RD, NORTH POLE, AK 99705
ANTRIL SUYDAM, 75-5608 HIENALOLI RD #31, KAILUA-KONA, HI 96740

GARY SUYDAM, BOX 2807, KODIAK, AK 99615
KEVIN SUYDAM, BOX 980, KODIAK, AK 99615
MARCELLA SUYDAM, BOX 3246, HOMER, AK 99603
STEVEN SUYDAM, BOX 987, KODIAK, AK 99615
GARY TAYLOR, BOX 112241, ANCHORAGE, AK 99511
CAROLYN THORNE, BOX 711, CORDOVA, AK 99574
CHARLES TREINEN, 2054 ARLINGTON DR, ANCHORAGE, AK 99517
GARY TRIEWEILER, BOX 2905, HOMER, AK 99603
GILBERT URATA, BOX 518, CORDOVA, AK 99574
WILLIAM WEBBER, 2000 POWER CK RD, CORDOVA, AK 99574
JAMES WICKERSHAM, 15723 18TH AVE W, LYNNWOOD, WA 98037
ROBERT WIESE, BOX 864, CORDOVA, AK 99574
TIM WILKIE, BOX 1726, SEWARD, AK 99664

HERRING ROE & FOOD/BAIT, PURSE SEINE, COOK INLET

JASON ALEXANDER, 18315 87TH AVE SE, SNOHOMISH, WA 98296
PETER ALEXSON, BOX 661, HOMER, AK 99603
H.GARY ANDERSON, BOX 47, CHIGNIK LAGOON, AK 99565
RONALD ANDERSON, 39370 BRENMARK RD, HOMER, AK 99603
DOUGLAS BLOSSOM, BOX 289, CLAM GULCH, AK 99568
TIM CABANA, BOX 201, GIRDWOOD, AK 99587
DONALD CALHOON, 11001 E EQUESTERIAN ST, PALMER, AK 99645
JAMES CALHOUN, 4360 ANDERSON ST, HOMER, AK 99603
GLEN CARROLL, BOX 551, HOMER, AK 99603
KENNETH CASTNER, BOX 558, HOMER, AK 99603
KENNETH CHRISTIANSEN, 1849 MARMOT DR, KODIAK, AK 99615
TERRY CRATTY, 3805 E COTTONWOOD WAY, WASILLA, AK 99654
JOSEPH DRAGSETH, BOX 408, KENAI, AK 99611
MARVIN DRAGSETH, BOX 224, KENAI, AK 99611
HAROLD ENGEBRETSEN, BOX 534, HOMER, AK 99603
JERRY EVERMAN, 258 W LITTLE ISLAND, CATHLAMET, WA 98612
ROBERT FELLOWS, 266 E BAYVIEW AVE, HOMER, AK 99603
KEITH FINDLEY, 805 NW BUCKEYE AVE, EARLHAM, IA 50072
CHARLES FOGLE, 5722 CAMPBELL LAKE RD, ANACORTES, WA 98221
JIM FRARY, BOX 1019, HOMER, AK 99603
GRANT FRITZ, BOX 13, KASILOF, AK 99610
LESLIE GILES, BOX 275, SELDOVIA, AK 99663
DARIN GILMAN, BOX 223, CORDOVA, AK 99574
PAUL GRONHOLDT, BOX 288, SAND POINT, AK 99661
GEROLD GUGEL, BOX 671227, CHUGIAK, AK 99567
KENNETH HALPIN, BOX 1022, HOMER, AK 99603
RANDALL HANSEN, 22628 N SAN RAMON DR, SUN CITY WEST, AZ 85375
ARNE HATCH, BOX 346, SEWARD, AK 99664
KENNETH HILL, BOX 1290, CORDOVA, AK 99574
C HOUGH, 3733 BEN WALTERS LN #2, HOMER, AK 99603
SHILA HOUGH, 3733 BEN WALTERS LN #2, HOMER, AK 99603
SARA JACKINSKY, BOX 1044, HOMER, AK 99603
STEVEN KARABACH, 42465 DEER HEIGHTS DR N, DAVENPORT, WA 99122
WILLIAM KASHEVAROF, BOX 52, SELDOVIA, AK 99663
MITCHELL KEPLINGER, BOX 1006, KODIAK, AK 99615
TERRANCE KILBREATH, 31 PINE ST #210, EDMONDS, WA 98020
MARK KISER, 6436 DOW LN, ANACORTES, WA 98221
GERALD KOLSCHOWSKY, 1143 HALLADAY CT, BATAVIA, IL 60510
MICHAEL KURTZ, BOX 32265, BELLINGHAM, WA 98228
CARL LANE, 2106 LUMMI VIEW DR, BELLINGHAM, WA 98226
EVERETT LINDHOLM, 415 E PARK DR, ANACORTES, WA 98221
FREDERIC LOVE, 1830 E 3900 S, SALT LAKE CITY, UT 84124
WILLIAM MANOS, 1566 KEKAULIKE AVE, KULA, HI 96790
DAVID MARTIN, BOX 468, CLAM GULCH, AK 99568
RODNEY MCLAY, BOX 504, HOMER, AK 99603
DANNY MCLEAN, BOX 351, HOMER, AK 99603
JOHN MCLEAN, BOX 2191, HOMER, AK 99603
ALVIN MCLENAGHAN, 1035 9TH AVE S, EDMONDS, WA 98020
MICHAEL MCNEIL, 41218 N GROVE RD, DEER PARK, WA 99006

HERRING ROE—PURSE SEINE

SUSAN MITCHELL, 41 STRAWBERRY PT RD, BELLINGHAM, WA 98229
EDWARD MONKIEWICZ, 1110 PURTOV ST, KODIAK, AK 99615
TIMOTHY MOORE, BOX 1646, HOMER, AK 99603
ROBERT MOSS, BOX 3428, HOMER, AK 99603
THOMAS NELSEN, 8227 200 ST SW, EDMONDS, WA 98026
ARNOLD NELSON, BOX 85, PORT LIONS, AK 99550
ROBERT NELSON, BOX 205, KASILOF, AK 99610
THOMAS NELSON, BOX 1392, HOMER, AK 99603
MICHAEL NOKLEBY, 2903 ROZEWOOD DR, BREMERTON, WA 98310
LEONARD OGLE, 1122 B AVE S, EDMONDS, WA 98020
CHARLES OLSON, 3009 HALIBUT POINT RD, SITKA, AK 99835
RODNEY RISLEY, 3649 OLD PACIFIC HWY S, KELSO, WA 98626
MALCOLM ROSS, BOX 3476, HOMER, AK 99603
BRUCE SCHACTLER, BOX 2254, KODIAK, AK 99615
THOMAS STAFFORD, BOX 3403, HOMER, AK 99603
KRIS STRAUB, 4851 EIELSON FARM RD, NORTH POLE, AK 99705
GARY SUYDAM, BOX 2807, KODIAK, AK 99615
KEVIN SUYDAM, BOX 980, KODIAK, AK 99615
MARCELLA SUYDAM, BOX 3246, HOMER, AK 99603
CHARLES TREINEN, 2054 ARLINGTON DR, ANCHORAGE, AK 99517
GARY TRIEWEILER, BOX 2905, HOMER, AK 99603
JUNELLA TRIEWEILER, BOX 2905, HOMER, AK 99603
GILBERT URATA, BOX 518, CORDOVA, AK 99574
JEROLD VANTREASE, BOX 1730, HOMER, AK 99603
DANIEL VEERHUSEN, BOX 971, HOMER, AK 99603
RAY WADSWORTH, 200 E MAIN ST, OALKEY, ID 83346

HERRING ROE, PURSE SEINE, KODIAK

LOUIE ALBER, BOX 111, CORDOVA, AK 99574
PETER ALEXSON, BOX 661, HOMER, AK 99603
MATTHEW ALWARD, 60082 CLARICE WAY, HOMER, AK 99603
H.GARY ANDERSON, BOX 47, CHIGNIK LAGOON, AK 99565
STOSH ANDERSON, BOX 310, KODIAK, AK 99615
VERNON ANDERSON, BOX 3254, KODIAK, AK 99615
ADAM BARKER, 126 E FAIRVIEW AVE, HOMER, AK 99603
JAMES BELL, 62-1214 OHINA ST, KANEOHE, HI 96743
GENE BENSON, 16020 169TH AVE SE, MONROE, WA 98272
JAMES BERNS, BOX 44, OLD HARBOR, AK 99643
TRAVIS BERNS, BOX 33, OLD HARBOR, AK 99643
ALBERT BIGLEY, BOX 1454, HOMER, AK 99603
ANDREW BLAIR, BOX 108, FOX ISLAND, WA 98333
BRIAN BLONDIN, BOX 1521, KODIAK, AK 99615
JAMES CALHOUN, 4360 ANDERSON ST, HOMER, AK 99603
CARMEL CARTY, BOX 2733, KODIAK, AK 99615
CARL CHRISTIANSEN, 11721 12TH AVE NW, SEATTLE, WA 98177
EMIL CHRISTIANSEN, 8211 DEBARR RD, ANCHORAGE, AK 99504
FRED CHRISTIANSEN, 7051 CHAD ST, ANCHORAGE, AK 99518
HAROLD CHRISTIANSEN, BOX 129, OLD HARBOR, AK 99643
KENNETH CHRISTIANSEN, 1849 MARMOT DR, KODIAK, AK 99615
ALFRED CRATTY, BOX 1, OLD HARBOR, AK 99643
LARRY DOOLEY, BOX 13389, TRAPPER CREEK, AK 99683
MARK EDENS, BOX 641, HOMER, AK 99603
MORGAN EJ JONES, BOX 3472, HOMER, AK 99603
ROBERT FELLOWS, 266 E BAYVIEW AVE, HOMER, AK 99603
WALLACE FIELDS, BOX 1691, KODIAK, AK 99615
DONALD FLYNN, BOX 623, HOMER, AK 99603
OLIVER FLYNN, BOX 2106, HOMER, AK 99603
CHARLES FOGLE, 5722 CAMPBELL LAKE RD, ANACORTES, WA 98221
DANIEL GILBERT, BOX 2531, KODIAK, AK 99615
JOEL GREY, 3403 STEAMBOAT ISLAND RD #432, OLYMPIA, WA 98502
GEROLD GUGEL, BOX 671227, CHUGIAK, AK 99567
ROBERT GUNDERSON, 3614 SPRUCE CAPE RD, KODIAK, AK 99615
KENNETH HALPIN, BOX 1022, HOMER, AK 99603
KENNETH HALPIN, BOX 2448, HOMER, AK 99603
JOHN HANCOCK, BOX 938, VASHON, WA 98070

LARS HANSEN, 205 E DIMOND BLVD #158, ANCHORAGE, AK 99515
RANDALL HANSEN, 22628 N SAN RAMON DR, SUN CITY WEST, AZ 85375
MATTHEW HEGGE, BOX 848, KODIAK, AK 99615
OLIVER HOLM, BOX 8749, KODIAK, AK 99615
BRYAN HORN, 1776 MISSION RD, KODIAK, AK 99615
JAMES HORN, 1776 MISSION RD, KODIAK, AK 99615
MARY JACOBS, BOX 135, OPHIR, OR 97464
HERBERT JENSEN, BOX 294, CORDOVA, AK 99574
JAMES JENSEN, BOX 365, CORDOVA, AK 99574
AARON JOLIN, BOX 2022, KODIAK, AK 99615
MITCHELL KEPLINGER, BOX 1006, KODIAK, AK 99615
TERRANCE KILBREATH, 31 PINE ST #210, EDMONDS, WA 98020
MARK KISER, 6436 DOW LN, ANACORTES, WA 98221
MICHAEL KURTZ, BOX 32265, BELLINGHAM, WA 98228
WAYNE KVASNIKOFF, 633 GILTNER LN, EDMONDS, WA 98020
LUKE LESTER, BOX 553, KODIAK, AK 99615
EVERETT LINDHOLM, 415 E PARK DR, ANACORTES, WA 98221
MARY LYNCH, BOX 415, DIXON, NM 87527
MARK MAHAN, BOX 2405, HOMER, AK 99603
IVER MALUTIN, BOX 8501, KODIAK, AK 99615
RAYMOND MAY, BOX 8985, KODIAK, AK 99615
DANNY MCLEAN, BOX 351, HOMER, AK 99603
JOHN MCLEAN, BOX 2191, HOMER, AK 99603
JOHN MITCHELL, 41 STRAWBERRY PT RD, BELLINGHAM, WA 98229
JAMES MONROE, BOX 1202, KODIAK, AK 99615
SAMUEL MUTCH, 210 B SHELIKOF, KODIAK, AK 99615
ARNOLD NELSON, BOX 85, PORT LIONS, AK 99550
ROBERT NELSON, BOX 205, KASILOF, AK 99610
LEONARD OGLE, 1122 B AVE S, EDMONDS, WA 98020
DANIEL OLSEN, BOX 1743, KODIAK, AK 99615
MARK OLSEN, 1111 PURTOV ST, KODIAK, AK 99615
ARTHUR PEDERSEN, BOX 224, SUTTON, AK 99674
DARREN PLATT, BOX 1413, KODIAK, AK 99615
SHAWNA RITTENHOUSE, BOX KWP, KODIAK, AK 99615
MALCOLM ROSS, BOX 3476, HOMER, AK 99603
BRUCE SCHACTLER, BOX 2254, KODIAK, AK 99615
BARRY SCHAUFF, 316 CENTER ST, KODIAK, AK 99615
THOMAS STAFFORD, BOX 3403, HOMER, AK 99603
FLOYD SUYDAM, BOX 2987, HOMER, AK 99603
GARY SUYDAM, BOX 2807, KODIAK, AK 99615
STEVEN SUYDAM, BOX 987, KODIAK, AK 99615
ANDREW TEUBER, BOX 1544, KODIAK, AK 99615
WAYNE TREAT, RT 5 BOX 368 B, HARRISON, AR 72601
CHARLES TREINEN, 2054 ARLINGTON DR, ANCHORAGE, AK 99517
RAY WADSWORTH, 200 E MAIN ST, OALKEY, ID 83346
JAMES WICKERSHAM, 15723 18TH AVE W, LYNNWOOD, WA 98037
WILLIAM WIEBE, 5201 GJOSUND DR, HOMER, AK 99603
GORDON WILSON, BOX 2697, KODIAK, AK 99615

HERRING ROE, PURSE SEINE, CHIGNIK

MICHAEL GRUNERT, BOX 187, CHIGNIK LAGOON, AK 99565

HERRING ROE, PURSE SEINE, ALASKA PENINSULA

ROBERT FELLOWS, 266 E BAYVIEW AVE, HOMER, AK 99603
TOM HOBLET, BOX 108, FALSE PASS, AK 99583
MITCHELL KEPLINGER, BOX 1006, KODIAK, AK 99615
MICHAEL KURTZ, BOX 32265, BELLINGHAM, WA 98228
LUKE LESTER, BOX 553, KODIAK, AK 99615
JOHN MCLEAN, BOX 2191, HOMER, AK 99603
ROBERT NELSON, BOX 205, KASILOF, AK 99610
MALCOLM ROSS, BOX 3476, HOMER, AK 99603
BRUCE SCHACTLER, BOX 2254, KODIAK, AK 99615

HERRING ROE—BEACH SEINE

HERRING ROE, PURSE SEINE, BRISTOL BAY
PETER ALEXSON, BOX 661, HOMER, AK 99603
JODY COOK, 2115 NW 12TH ST, BATTLE GROUND, WA 98604
ROBERT FELLOWS, 266 E BAYVIEW AVE, HOMER, AK 99603
ROBERT HEYANO, BOX 1409, DILLINGHAM, AK 99576
TOM HOBLET, BOX 108, FALSE PASS, AK 99583
STEVEN HORN, 1210 MISSION RD, KODIAK, AK 99615
MITCHELL KEPLINGER, BOX 1006, KODIAK, AK 99615
MICHAEL KURTZ, BOX 32265, BELLINGHAM, WA 98228
LUKE LESTER, BOX 553, KODIAK, AK 99615
BRUCE MARIFERN, BOX 917, PETERSBURG, AK 99833
JOHN MCLEAN, BOX 2191, HOMER, AK 99603
ROBERT NELSON, BOX 205, KASILOF, AK 99610
THOMAS NELSON, BOX 1392, HOMER, AK 99603
MALCOLM ROSS, BOX 3476, HOMER, AK 99603
ERIC ROSVOLD, BOX 1144, PETERSBURG, AK 99833
BRUCE SCHACTLER, BOX 2254, KODIAK, AK 99615

HERRING ROE, BEACH SEINE, NORTON SOUND
PETER DESMOND, 2877 23RD ST, SAN FRANCISCO, CA 94110
SUSAN ENTSMINGER, HC 72 BOX 800, TOK, AK 99780
PAUL FRIIS.MIKKELSEN, BOX 276, DILLINGHAM, AK 99576
TOM HENDEL, BOX 1804, KODIAK, AK 99615
BRIAN KANDOLL, BOX 1363, PETERSBURG, AK 99833
LARRY LAWSON, 20324 CHAUTAUQUA BCH DR SW, VASHON, WA 98070
RUTH MITCHELL, 41 STRAWBERRY POINT RD, BELLINGHAM, WA 98226
JOHN SWANSON, BOX 1546, PETERSBURG, AK 99833
CHARLES TREINEN, 2054 ARLINGTON DR, ANCHORAGE, AK 99517

HERRING ROE, GILLNET & PURSE SEINE, KODIAK
RICHARD METZGER, 2725 WILLEYS LAKE RD, CUSTER, WA 98240
EDWARD MONKIEWICZ, 1110 PURTOV ST, KODIAK, AK 99615

HERRING ROE & FOOD/BAIT, GILLNET, SOUTHEAST
ARNOLD BAKKE, BOX 1482, WRANGELL, AK 99929
JIM BAUMGART, 210 BAYSIDE PL, BELLINGHAM, WA 98225
KURT BAUMGART, 3876 GRIFFITH AVE, BELLINGHAM, WA 98225
GARY BAXTER, 7569 BIRCH BAY DR, BLAINE, WA 98230
ROBERT BECKER, BOX 240238, DOUGLAS, AK 99824
MIKE BETHEL, BOX 111, METLAKATLA, AK 99926
CLAY BEZENEK, 1617 WATER ST, KETCHIKAN, AK 99901
GREG BIRCHELL, BOX 183, PETERSBURG, AK 99833
CHRISTOPHER BOOTH, BOX 576, METLAKATLA, AK 99926
STEVEN BOOTH, BOX 395, METLAKATLA, AK 99926
DALE BOSWORTH, BOX 45, PETERSBURG, AK 99833
ALEX BRENDIBLE, BOX 619, METLAKATLA, AK 99926
MATTHEW BRYNER, BOX 1642, PETERSBURG, AK 99833
CHRISTIAN BUSCHMANN, BOX 898, PETERSBURG, AK 99833
BEVERLY CHALMERS, BOX 443, METLAKATLA, AK 99926
CHARLES CLEMENT, BOX 282, METLAKATLA, AK 99926
CHARLES CLEMENT, 1242 WALDON PT RD BOX 302, METLAKATLA, AK 99926
AARON COOK, BOX 313, METLAKATLA, AK 99926
KARL COOK, BOX 492, METLAKATLA, AK 99926
DOUGLAS CORL, BOX 1570, PETERSBURG, AK 99833
JUDITH CROME, BOX 466, PETERSBURG, AK 99833
LORNA DICKINSON, 235 N STATE ST, BELLINGHAM, WA 98225
RONALD DURGAN, BOX 340, CRAIG, AK 99921
KEN EICHNER, 5166 SHORELINE DR N, KETCHIKAN, AK 99901
RICHARD ELIASON, 8475 E GOLD BULLION BLVD, PALMER, AK 99645
ARNOLD ENGE, BOX 2113, PETERSBURG, AK 99833
STEVEN ENGE, BOX 422, PETERSBURG, AK 99833
JEFF ERICKSON, BOX 53, PETERSBURG, AK 99833

SIERRA GOLDEN, 8322 SILVER LAKE RD, MAPLE FALLS, WA 98266
ROGER GREGG, BOX 3, WRANGELL, AK 99929
MIKE HAMAR, 303 DISTIN AVE, JUNEAU, AK 99801
DANNY HAYNES, BOX 7036, KETCHIKAN, AK 99901
GARY HAYNES, 625 SUNSET DR, KETCHIKAN, AK 99901
JOYCE HAYNES, 2051 SEA LEVEL DR #301, KETCHIKAN, AK 99901
BLAINE HAYWARD, BOX 256, METLAKATLA, AK 99926
BYRON HAYWARD, BOX 446, METLAKATLA, AK 99926
MICHAEL HOLMSTROM, 17952 MCLEAN RD, MOUNT VERNON, WA 98273
HANS HOLUM, 730 PARK AVE, KETCHIKAN, AK 99901
CLIFFORD HUDSON, BOX 480, METLAKATLA, AK 99926
RICHARD HUDSON, BOX 194, METLAKATLA, AK 99926
ROGER INGMAN, BOX 1155, SITKA, AK 99835
ANTE IVCEVIC, 200 BAYSIDE PL, BELLINGHAM, WA 98225
TRINITY JACKSON, BOX 758, METLAKATLA, AK 99926
J.R. JENSEN, 3022 WOODUCK, JUNEAU, AK 99801
RUDY JOHANSON, BOX 5120, KETCHIKAN, AK 99901
CHRISTOPHER JOHNSON, BOX 2183, WRANGELL, AK 99929
DALE JOHNSON, 32988 SNYDER HILL, POLSON, MT 59860
MATTHEW KANDOLL, BOX 2091, PETERSBURG, AK 99833
KURT KIVISTO, BOX 1036, PETERSBURG, AK 99833
DAVID KLEPSER, BOX 8946, KETCHIKAN, AK 99901
DONALD KLEPSER, 821 COUNTRYSIDE BLVD, HAILEY, ID 83333
KEVIN KLEPSER, BOX 5341, KETCHUM, ID 83340
MELISSA KLEPSER, BOX 8946, KETCHIKAN, AK 99901
CASEY KNIGHT, BOX 942, PETERSBURG, AK 99833
JOHN KNIGHT, BOX 1133, PETERSBURG, AK 99833
KYLE KNIGHT, BOX 1133, PETERSBURG, AK 99833
H.ERVIN KOERTH, 1105 GOLF COURSE RD, GATESVILLE, TX 76528
CINDY KOETJE, 16536 MOBERG RD, MOUNT VERNON, WA 98273
JASON KOHLHASE, 10753 HORIZON DR, JUNEAU, AK 99801
LEONARD LEACH, BOX 6017, KETCHIKAN, AK 99901
RONALD LIMBACHER, BOX 3275, FERNDALE, WA 98248
LOREN LUNDQUIST, BOX 244, EASTSOUND, WA 98254
GREG LUTTON, BOX 1924, PETERSBURG, AK 99833
FREDERICK MAGILL, BOX 444, PETERSBURG, AK 99833
BEVERLY MANGUE, 521 REDWOOK DR, VACAVILLE, CA 95687
MICHAEL MANN, BOX 32653, JUNEAU, AK 99803
COLLEEN MARSDEN, BOX 601, METLAKATLA, AK 99926
DAVID MARTIN, BOX 88, PETERSBURG, AK 99833
NICHOLAS MARTIN, BOX 8312, KETCHIKAN, AK 99901
MARTY MARTINEZ, BOX 513, METLAKATLA, AK 99926
BRIAN MATTSON, BOX 1168, PETERSBURG, AK 99833
MORRIS MATTSON, BOX 1168, PETERSBURG, AK 99833
ROD MAY, BOX 303, METLAKATLA, AK 99926
PAUL MENISH, BOX 33, PETERSBURG, AK 99833
CHRISTOPHER MILLER, 605 NE OLD BELFAIR HWY, BELFAIRURG, WA 98528
BRIAN NEWMAN, BOX 893, PETERSBURG, AK 99833
MICHAEL NILSEN, BOX 2069, PETERSBURG, AK 99833
JAMES ODEGAARD, 2309 CEDAR CT, MOUNT VERNON, WA 98273
DENNIS ONEIL, BOX 1083, PETERSBURG, AK 99833
DOMINIC PAPETTI, 3151 WILD MUSTANG PASS, WICKENBURG, AZ 85390
NANCY PAPETTI, BOX T, BELLINGHAM, WA 98227
SALVATORE PAPETTI, BOX T, BELLINGHAM, WA 98227
JOEL PASQUAN, BOX 845, HAINES, AK 99827
LANCE PIHLMAN, BOX 5322, KETCHIKAN, AK 99901
JAMES PORTER, BOX 957, WARD COVE, AK 99928
MARK SALDI, BOX 287, SKAGWAY, AK 99840
JAMES SCUDERO, BOX 493, METLAKATLA, AK 99926
JAMES SCUDERO, BOX 551, METLAKATLA, AK 99926
JERRY SCUDERO, 955 FOREST AVE, KETCHIKAN, AK 99901
ALAN SEE, BOX 99, NASELLE, WA 98638
JEV SHELTON, 1670 EVERGREEN AVE, JUNEAU, AK 99801
BRIAN SIMPSON, 3104 PLYMOUTH DR, BELLINGHAM, WA 98225
RALPH SORENSEN, 222 3RD AVE S, EDMONDS, WA 98020

HERRING ROE—GILLNET

RAY STONER, BOX 394, PETERSBURG, AK 99833
KIMBERLY SVENSON, 104 SHARON DR, SITKA, AK 99835
MIKE SVENSON, 104 SHARON DR, SITKA, AK 99835
ADAM SWANSON, BOX 2151, PETERSBURG, AK 99833
DEREK THYNES, BOX 1624, PETERSBURG, AK 99833
KRISTOFFER THYNES, BOX 193, PETERSBURG, AK 99833
STEVEN THYNES, BOX 193, PETERSBURG, AK 99833
ROLF TORGERSON, 5118 167TH AVE CT, LONGBRANCH, WA 98351
JAY WALLING, 16765 LENA LOOP RD, JUNEAU, AK 99801
FRANK WARFEL, BOX 1512, WRANGELL, AK 99929
JERRY WELCH, BOX 1686, PETERSBURG, AK 99833
NICHOLAS WELCH, BOX 1873, PETERSBURG, AK 99833
TODD WELCH, BOX 1686, PETERSBURG, AK 99833
CHARLES WILLS, BOX 7554, KETCHIKAN, AK 99901
GEORGE WOOD, BOX 902, PETERSBURG, AK 99833
KARSTEN WOOD, BOX 2195, PETERSBURG, AK 99833
MAXIMILIAN WORHATCH, BOX 407, PETERSBURG, AK 99833
ANDY WRIGHT, BOX 1432, PETERSBURG, AK 99833

HERRING ROE, GILLNET, PRINCE WILLIAM SOUND
HEIDI BABIC, BOX 1208, CORDOVA, AK 99574
RUSSELL BABIC, BOX 1833, CORDOVA, AK 99574
JOSEPH BANTA, 6820 TERESA CIR, ANCHORAGE, AK 99516
STEPHEN BARNES, BOX 332, CORDOVA, AK 99574
SCOTT BLAKE, 9910 HILLSIDE DR, ANCHORAGE, AK 99507
MICHAEL BOWEN, 2150 INNES CIR, ANCHORAGE, AK 99515
CARL BURTON, BOX 81, CORDOVA, AK 99574
HARRY CURRAN, BOX 42, CORDOVA, AK 99574
GEORGE DAUBER, 1809 TAYLOR AVE, BELLINGHAM, WA 98225
ROBERT DE.VILLE, 4101 259TH ST NE, ARLINGTON, WA 98223
LINDA ECOLANO, BOX 1593, CORDOVA, AK 99574
SHAWN GILMAN, BOX 223, CORDOVA, AK 99574
LAURIE HONKOLA, 4354 BIRCH RUN DR, ANCHORAGE, AK 99507
JOHN JOHNSON, BOX 1179, CORDOVA, AK 99574
ROBERT KOPCHAK, BOX 1126, CORDOVA, AK 99574
LYLE KRITCHEN, BOX 935, CORDOVA, AK 99574
GORDON LIPSCOMB, BOX 1311, CORDOVA, AK 99574
ELWYN PATTEN, 620 38TH ST, WOODWARD, OK 73801
DANIEL STRICKLAND, 5992 N NODDING AVE, PALMER, AK 99645
GARY TAYLOR, BOX 112241, ANCHORAGE, AK 99511
EARL WIESE, BOX 1981, CORDOVA, AK 99574
ROBERT WIESE, BOX 864, CORDOVA, AK 99574
BETTY YORK, BOX 835, CORDOVA, AK 99574
PETER ZAREMBA, BOX 995, ANACORTES, WA 98221

HERRING ROE, GILLNET, COOK INLET
HUNTER.J.R COOPER, BOX 39341, NINILCHIK, AK 99639
ROBERT CORREIA, BOX 456, CLAM GULCH, AK 99568
CHRIS GARCIA, BOX 203, KENAI, AK 99611
JEFFREY GLOSSER, BOX 39315, NINILCHIK, AK 99639
TODD MOORE, BOX 4152, SOLDOTNA, AK 99669
RAY RODGERS, 5433 W 73RD, ANCHORAGE, AK 99502
CHARLES SEATER, BOX 7552, NIKISKI, AK 99635
DYLAN SEATER, BOX 7552, NIKISKI, AK 99635

HERRING ROE, GILLNET, KODIAK
JOSE AGUILAR, 1315 28TH ST, ANACORTES, WA 98221
PETER ALLAN, BOX 2160, KODIAK, AK 99615
JAMES BAIZE, 36310 SUTHARD BLVD, SOLDOTNA, AK 99669
EVGENY BASARGIN, BOX 1709, HOMER, AK 99603
VASILY BASARGIN, BOX 1423, HOMER, AK 99603
ZAHARY BASARGIN, BOX 991, HOMER, AK 99603
DYLAN BEAN, 11147 WOMENS BAY DR, KODIAK, AK 99615

CHRISTOPHER BERNS, BOX 23, KODIAK, AK 99615
LACEY BERNS, 1620 KRISTIN WAY, MCKINLEYVILLE, CA 95579
RICHARD BLACK, BOX 8833, KODIAK, AK 99615
FREDRICK BOCK, BOX 39829, NINILCHIK, AK 99639
BOB BOWHAY, BOX 187, KODIAK, AK 99615
LEO BROWN, 35717 WALKABOUT RD, HOMER, AK 99603
DANIEL BYRON, BOX 95, PORT LIONS, AK 99550
JEREMY CABANA, BOX 719, HOMER, AK 99603
LEROY CABANA, BOX 49, HOMER, AK 99603
JOSHUA CARDMAN.PEDEN, 34950 MOONRISE ST, HOMER, AK 99603
STACY CASTRO, BOX 8476, KODIAK, AK 99615
CARL CHRISTIANSEN, BOX 779, KODIAK, AK 99615
STEVEN CLARK, BOX C, CHINOOK, WA 98614
GENE COOPER, 1719 35TH PL, ANACORTES, WA 98221
DANIEL CORNELIUS, BOX 1863, KODIAK, AK 99615
ALFRED CRATTY, BOX 1, OLD HARBOR, AK 99643
ANDREW CRAWLEY, BOX 2105, KODIAK, AK 99615
WILLIAM CRAWLEY, BOX 2105, KODIAK, AK 99615
PETER DANELSKI, BOX 2333, KODIAK, AK 99615
PETER DANELSKI, 2069 RIDGE CIR, KODIAK, AK 99615
HARRY DAVIS, 110 EMERALD OAK DR, GALT, CA 95632
LLOYD DAVIS, 48390 INDEPENDENCE AVE, SOLDOTNA, AK 99669
PAUL DELYS, BOX 83797, FAIRBANKS, AK 99708
MMERCE DEPARTMENT OF CO, BOX 110802, JUNEAU, AK 99811
DAVID DIETERS, 4650 BAY BLVD #1302, PORT RICHEY, FL 34668
JONATHAN EDWARDS, BOX 8905, KODIAK, AK 99615
DEWITT FIELDS, BOX 25, KODIAK, AK 99615
DUNCAN FIELDS, BOX 25, KODIAK, AK 99615
WALLACE FIELDS, BOX 1691, KODIAK, AK 99615
ARTHUR GAGNE, 82103 KEITEL ST, INDIO, CA 92201
SIDNEY GIVENS, 12401 BRANDON ST A, ANCHORAGE, AK 99515
BRUCE GOERISCH, 4702 DENTON ST #B, BOISE, ID 83706
HARVEY GOODELL, BOX 3108, KODIAK, AK 99615
STEVEN GRAY, BOX 209, KODIAK, AK 99615
GEROLD GUGEL, BOX 944, HOMER, AK 99603
PETER HANNAH, BOX 647, KODIAK, AK 99615
ERIC HANSEN, BOX 1482, KODIAK, AK 99615
JOREEN HARRIS, BOX 7013, NIKISKI, AK 99635
GEORGE HARTMAN, 412 SARGENT DR, KODIAK, AK 99615
DON HEGWER, BOX 156, SOLDOTNA, AK 99669
PATRICK HOGAN, BOX 1009, KODIAK, AK 99615
WALTER HOK, 331 E 46TH AVE #4, ANCHORAGE, AK 99503
MARGARET HOLM, 305 COPE ST, KODIAK, AK 99615
OLIVER HOLM, BOX 8749, KODIAK, AK 99615
NORMAN HOYT, 19752 LIPPIZAN DR, JACKSONVILLE, FL 33223
DAVID IANI, BOX 549, KODIAK, AK 99615
STEVEN IVANOFF, 1327 MOUNTAIN VIEW DR, KODIAK, AK 99615
TERRY IVANOFF, BOX 8883, KODIAK, AK 99615
CLINT JOHNSON, BOX 909, KODIAK, AK 99615
DAVID JOHNSON, 7916 110TH AVE SE, NEWCASTLE, WA 98056
GARY JOHNSON, BOX 2107, KODIAK, AK 99615
AARON JOLIN, BOX 2022, KODIAK, AK 99615
NICK KATELNIKOFF, BOX 170, OUZINKIE, AK 99644
DILLON KIMPLE, BOX 13, STERLING, AK 99672
GEORGE KIRK, BOX 2796, KODIAK, AK 99615
DAVID KLEPSER, BOX 8946, KETCHIKAN, AK 99901
FRANK KLEPSER, 1108 DUNTON ST, KETCHIKAN, AK 99901
THOMAS KLINKER, 408 NO VIEW AVE, HOMER, AK 99603
WALLE KONING, BOX 5565, CHINIAK, AK 99615
CHARLES KRAMER, BOX 83, PORT LIONS, AK 99550
PAVEL KUZMIN, BOX 1669, KODIAK, AK 99615
ALEXUS KWACHKA, 326 COPE ST, KODIAK, AK 99615
BURDETTE LECHNER, BOX 1616, KODIAK, AK 99615
LUTHER LECHNER, BOX 8538, KODIAK, AK 99615
LUKE LESTER, BOX 553, KODIAK, AK 99615
JOHN LITTLE, 807 S MOUNTAIN AVE, ASHLAND, OR 97520

HERRING ROE—GILLNET

GEORGE LUNDQUIST, BOX 1372, KENAI, AK 99611
GARY MARINCOVICH, 198 LEXINGTON, ASTORIA, OR 97103
STEVEN MATHIEU, 1721 MISSION RD, KODIAK, AK 99615
RAYMOND MAY, BOX 8985, KODIAK, AK 99615
THOMAS MILLER, BOX 1931, KODIAK, AK 99615
MARK MURPHY, 424 SINEX AVE, PACIFIC GROVE, CA 93950
SAMUEL MUTCH, 210 B SHELIKOF, KODIAK, AK 99615
PEGGY NEKEFEROFF, BOX 194, KODIAK, AK 99615
JOHN NEVIN, BOX 2125, KODIAK, AK 99615
KENNETH PARKER, 9577 WEST 5 MILE RD, BRANCH, MI 49402
MICHAEL PATITUCCI, BOX 1511, KODIAK, AK 99615
EDWARD PESTRIKOFF, BOX 56, OLD HARBOR, AK 99643
MITCHELL PESTRIKOFF, BOX 111, OLD HARBOR, AK 99643
CHARLES PETERSON, 1850 THREE SISTERS WAY, KODIAK, AK 99615
DARREN PLATT, BOX 1413, KODIAK, AK 99615
JEFFREY POVELITE, BOX 7, CATHLAMET, WA 98612
JAMES PRYOR, 1012 STELLER WAY, KODIAK, AK 99615
FEODOR REUTOV, BOX 390, KODIAK, AK 99615
MICHELLE RITTENHOUSE, BOX KWP, KODIAK, AK 99615
RUBY ROLLINS, BOX 909, HOMER, AK 99603
TY ROUSE, BOX 2725, KODIAK, AK 99615
PAUL SAUNDERS, BOX 451, CORDOVA, AK 99574
RODNEY SAXTON, BOX 423, TAHOLAH, WA 98587
JAMES SCHAUFF, BOX 8150, KODIAK, AK 99615
KAREN SCHAUFF, BOX 8150, KODIAK, AK 99615
WILLIAM SCHAUFF, BOX 8774, KODIAK, AK 99615
STEVE SCHOONMAKER, BOX 218, KASILOF, AK 99610
PAUL SEASTRAND, BOX 3493, SOLDOTNA, AK 99669
JAMES SHOWALTER, BOX 206, STERLING, AK 99672
ROBERT SMITH, BOX 261, KASILOF, AK 99610
ANN SQUARTSOFF, BOX 63, PORT LIONS, AK 99550
FREDERICK STAGER, BOX 8243, KODIAK, AK 99615
KENYON STIER, 7021 DRIFTWOOD ST, ANCHORAGE, AK 99518
DANIEL STIHL, BOX 3373, KODIAK, AK 99615
A.CARL TAURIAINEN, BOX 8004, NIKISKI, AK 99635
THOMAS TORMALA, BOX 8829, KODIAK, AK 99615
DYER VANDEVERE, BOX 504, KASILOF, AK 99610
RANDALL WALTON, BOX 1950, REDMOND, OR 97756
STEPHEN WEBB, BOX 1127, KASILOF, AK 99610
TONY WESTERN, 53298 LINDGREN CT, KASILOF, AK 99610
JAMES WILLIAMSON, 255 ASPEN DR, SOLDOTNA, AK 99669
WAYNE WILSON, 212 LINWOOD LN, KENAI, AK 99611
JEFFREY YEOMAN, BOX 411, HANA, HI 96713
GERALD YOUEL, BOX 2094, REDMOND, OR 97756
HENRY ZABSKI, 13617 WHIPPET WY W, DELRAY BEACH, FL 33445
BILL ZIMMERMAN, BOX 2261, KODIAK, AK 99615

HERRING ROE & FOOD/BAIT, GILLNET, NELSON ISLAND
MOSES ABRAHAM, BOX 37037, TOKSOOK BAY, AK 99637
PIUS AGIMUK, GEN DEL, TOKSOOK BAY, AK 99637
NOAH AGNUS, BOX 90030, NIGHTMUTE, AK 99690
PAUL AGNUS, BOX 88, CHEFORNAK, AK 99561
FELIX ALBERT, BOX 93, TUNUNAK, AK 99681
GILBERT ALIRKAR, BOX 2453, BETHEL, AK 99559
LEO ALUSKA, BOX 37034, TOKSOOK BAY, AK 99637
PETER ALUSKA, BOX 392, BETHEL, AK 99559
JOHN AMADEUS, BOX 37154, TOKSOOK BAY, AK 99637
CARL AMIK, BOX 111, KIPNUK, AK 99614
NORMAN ANAVER, BOX 235, KIPNUK, AK 99614
JOHN ANDY, BOX 5533, NEWTOK, AK 99559
HARRY ANGAIAK, BOX 46, TUNUNAK, AK 99681
HUBERT ANGAIAK, BOX 2071, BETHEL, AK 99559
PAUL ANGAIAK, BOX 7, TUNUNAK, AK 99681
PETER ANGAIAK, BOX 17, TUNUNAK, AK 99681

PETER ANGAIAK, BOX 23, TUNUNAK, AK 99681
SANCHO ANGAIAK, BOX 17, TUNUNAK, AK 99681
THEODORE ANGAIAK, BOX 81, TUNUNAK, AK 99681
TOMMY ANGAIAK, BOX 11, TUNUNAK, AK 99681
CHARLIE ANTHONY, BOX 90051, NIGHTMUTE, AK 99690
STANLEY ANTHONY, BOX 90017, NIGHTMUTE, AK 99690
STACY ASICKSIK, BOX 62, TUNUNAK, AK 99681
JAMES ASULUK, BOX 37112, TOKSOOK BAY, AK 99637
JOSEPH ASULUK, BOX 37013, TOKSOOK BAY, AK 99637
PETER ASULUK, BOX 37013, TOKSOOK BAY, AK 99637
DAVID BILL, BOX 37052, TOKSOOK BAY, AK 99637
JOSEPH BILL, BOX 37011, TOKSOOK BAY, AK 99637
BERNARD BRUNO, NELSON ISLAND, TOKSOOK BAY, AK 99637
JOSEPH BRUNO, BOX 37148, TOKSOOK BAY, AK 99637
AGNES CARL, BOX 37041, TOKSOOK BAY, AK 99637
CHARLIE CARL, BOX 21, KIPNUK, AK 99614
CYRIL CARL, BOX 37007, TOKSOOK BAY, AK 99637
JOHN CARL, BOX 37032, TOKSOOK BAY, AK 99637
MOSES CARL, BOX 5515, NEWTOK, AK 99559
RAYMOND CARL, BOX 37041, TOKSOOK BAY, AK 99637
HUBERT CHAKUCHIN, BOX 85117, FAIRBANKS, AK 99707
JOHN CHAKUCHIN, BOX 2632, BETHEL, AK 99559
SIMEON CHAKUCHIN, BOX 37113, TOKSOOK BAY, AK 99637
SIMON CHANAR, BOX 37149, TOKSOOK BAY, AK 99637
JIMMY CHARLES, BOX 5502, NEWTOK, AK 99559
LARRY CHARLES, BOX 5505, NEWTOK, AK 99559
BENJAMIN CHARLIE, BOX 37004, TOKSOOK BAY, AK 99637
GREGORY CHARLIE, BOX 35, TUNUNAK, AK 99681
GREGORY CHARLIE, BOX 37025, TOKSOOK BAY, AK 99637
WILLIE CHARLIE, BOX 37017, TOKSOOK BAY, AK 99637
CHARLIE CHIMIUGAK, BOX 37121, TOKSOOK BAY, AK 99637
PAUL CHIMIUGAK, BOX 1267, BETHEL, AK 99559
RICHARD CURTIS, BOX 37065, TOKSOOK BAY, AK 99637
KENNETH DAVIS, 8100 EVANS CIR, ANCHORAGE, AK 99507
JOSE DIAZ.DIAZ, 826 QUEEN ST, BELLINGHAM, WA 98226
DANIEL DOCK, BOX 017, KIPNUK, AK 99614
THOMAS DOCK, BOX 203, TOGIAK, AK 99678
JAY DULL, BOX 90001, NIGHTMUTE, AK 99690
GEORGE ERIK, BOX 56, CHEFORNAK, AK 99561
JOHN EVAN, BOX 73, TUNUNAK, AK 99681
PAUL EVAN, BOX 4, TUNUNAK, AK 99681
RICHARD FELIX, BOX 37005, TOKSOOK BAY, AK 99637
ALEXIE FLYNN, BOX 52, CHEFORNAK, AK 99561
FRANK FLYNN, BOX 61, TUNUNAK, AK 99681
GEORGE GEORGE, 13650 23RD ST, DADE CITY, FL 33525
JAMES GEORGE, BOX 950, NIGHTMUTE, AK 99690
KEITH HENRY, BOX 37006, TOKSOOK BAY, AK 99637
HILARY HOINS, BOX 195, NORDLAND, WA 98358
BOSCO HOOPER, BOX 2662, BETHEL, AK 99559
DAVID HOOPER, BOX 36, TUNUNAK, AK 99681
GEORGE HOOPER, BOX 48, TUNUNAK, AK 99681
JOHN HOOPER, BOX 14, TUNUNAK, AK 99681
ROMMIE HOOPER, BOX 71, TUNUNAK, AK 99681
TOMMY HOOPER, BOX 44, TUNUNAK, AK 99681
HENRY INAKAK, BOX 12, TUNUNAK, AK 99681
JIMMY INAKAK, BOX 12, TUNUNAK, AK 99681
HENRY JACK, 5807 TONGA ST, ANCHORAGE, AK 99507
JOSEPH JAMES, BOX 38, TUNUNAK, AK 99681
MICHAEL JIMMIE, BOX 37127, TOKSOOK BAY, AK 99637
SEAN JIMMIE, BOX 37015, TOKSOOK BAY, AK 99637
SIMEON JIMMIE, BOX 37085, TOKSOOK BAY, AK 99637
EDWARD JOE, BOX 90007, NIGHTMUTE, AK 99690
FRED JOE, BOX 90019, NIGHTMUTE, AK 99690
PAUL JOE, BOX 90007, NIGHTMUTE, AK 99690
BARTHOLOMEW JOHN, BOX 5562, NEWTOK, AK 99559

HERRING ROE & FOOD BAIT—GILLNET

CATHERINE JOHN, BOX 37051, TOKSOOK BAY, AK 99637
LAWRENCE JOHN, BOX 37047, TOKSOOK BAY, AK 99637
MICHAEL JOHN, BOX 5527, NEWTOK, AK 99559
MURPHY JOHN, BOX 5534, NEWTOK, AK 99559
NORMAN JOHN, BOX 37061, TOKSOOK BAY, AK 99637
SIMEON JOHN, BOX 37051, TOKSOOK BAY, AK 99637
THERESA JOHN, 1911 CONGRESS CIRCLE UNIT C, ANCHORAGE, AK 99507
WILLIE JOHN, BOX 204, BETHEL, AK 99559
EVAN JOSEPH, BOX 37021, TOKSOOK BAY, AK 99637
JOHN JOSEPH, BOX 37045, TOKSOOK BAY, AK 99637
BOB JULIUS, BOX 37132, TOKSOOK BAY, AK 99637
MOSES JULIUS, BOX 37144, TOKSOOK BAY, AK 99637
PETER JULIUS, BOX 151, GOODNEWS BAY, AK 99589
PAUL JUMBO, BOX 37086, TOKSOOK BAY, AK 99637
SIMON JUMBO, BOX 90057, NIGHTMUTE, AK 99690
JOHN KAILUKIAK, BOX 37145, TOKSOOK BAY, AK 99637
DAVID KANRILAK, BOX 43, TUNUNAK, AK 99681
GABRIEL KANRILAK, BOX 85, TUNUNAK, AK 99681
LEO KANRILAK, BOX 65, TUNUNAK, AK 99681
VICTOR KANRILAK, BOX 15, TUNUNAK, AK 99681
EVAN KARL, BOX 8, DEERING, AK 99736
JOHN KARL, BOX 37106, TOKSOOK BAY, AK 99637
JOSEPH KARL, BOX 37131, TOKSOOK BAY, AK 99637
WALTER KASSAIULI, BOX 5517, NEWTOK, AK 99559
LARSON KING, BOX 95, MEKORYUK, AK 99630
TOMMY KUSAIAK, BOX 14, CHEFORNAK, AK 99561
PHILLIP KUSAYAK, BOX 22, TUNUNAK, AK 99681
JOHN LAWRENCE, BOX 37015, TOKSOOK BAY, AK 99637
NOAH LAWRENCE, BOX 90037, NIGHTMUTE, AK 99690
DAVID LEWIS, BOX 7, CHEFORNAK, AK 99561
CHARLIE LINCOLN, BOX 37001, TOKSOOK BAY, AK 99637
HARRY LINCOLN, BOX 52, TUNUNAK, AK 99681
JEFFERSON LINCOLN, BOX 37023, TOKSOOK BAY, AK 99637
JOSEPH LINCOLN, BOX 37033, TOKSOOK BAY, AK 99637
NOAH LINCOLN, GEN DEL, TOKSOOK BAY, AK 99637
PETER LINCOLN, BOX 84, TUNUNAK, AK 99681
PETER LINCOLN, BOX 37081, TOKSOOK BAY, AK 99637
JOSEPH MARK, BOX 5532, NEWTOK, AK 99559
MARK MARK, BOX 90032, NIGHTMUTE, AK 99690
LINDGREN MATHLAW, BOX 88, MEKORYUK, AK 99630
FERDINAND MATTHIAS, BOX 90041, NIGHTMUTE, AK 99690
IGNATIUS MATTHIAS, BOX 90004, NIGHTMUTE, AK 99690
DORA MENEGAK, BOX 2654, BETHEL, AK 99559
PAUL MOSES, 7811 CASEY CIR, ANCHORAGE, AK 99507
SIMEON MOSES, BOX 37142, TOKSOOK BAY, AK 99637
BERNARD NEVAK, BOX 37053, TOKSOOK BAY, AK 99637
GEORGE NEVAK, BOX 37053, TOKSOOK BAY, AK 99637
HARRY NEVAK, BOX 5513, NEWTOK, AK 99559
HERBERT OHARA, BOX 40963, SAN FRANCISCO, CA 94140
DANIEL OLRUN, BOX 05, MEKORYUK, AK 99630
STEPHEN OLRUN, BOX 21, MEKORYUK, AK 99630
CHRISTOPHER OSCAR, BOX 3, TUNUNAK, AK 99681
HARRY OSCAR, BOX 541, BETHEL, AK 99559
HERMAN OSCAR, BOX 3, TUNUNAK, AK 99681
ROBERT PANRUK, BOX 61, CHEFORNAK, AK 99561
NANCY PAPETTI, BOX T, BELLINGHAM, WA 98227
ANDY PATRICK, BOX 56, TUNUNAK, AK 99681
FRANK PITKA, BOX 37064, TOKSOOK BAY, AK 99637
PAUL PITKA, BOX 105, TUNUNAK, AK 99681
ROBERT PITKA, BOX 37122, TOKSOOK BAY, AK 99637
TOMMY PITKA, BOX 45, TUNUNAK, AK 99681
CHARLES POST, BOX 90015, NIGHTMUTE, AK 99690
JOSEPH POST, BOX 66, TUNUNAK, AK 99681
ALAN SEE, BOX 99, NASELLE, WA 98638
BRENDA SEE, BOX 99, NASELLE, WA 98638
EDWARD SHAVINGS, BOX 33, MEKORYUK, AK 99630

SAMUEL SHAVINGS, BOX 87, MEKORYUK, AK 99630
HENRY SIMONS, BOX 37071, TOKSOOK BAY, AK 99637
FRANCIS SIPARY, BOX 37102, TOKSOOK BAY, AK 99637
TEDDY SIPARY, BOX 6091, NAPASKIAK, AK 99559
DALE SMITH, BOX 111, MEKORYUK, AK 99630
SIMEON SUNNY, BOX 90033, NIGHTMUTE, AK 99690
WALTER SUOMELA, BOX 3092, HOMER, AK 99603
DEREK THERCHIK, BOX 37022, TOKSOOK BAY, AK 99637
NICK THERCHIK, BOX 37093, TOKSOOK BAY, AK 99637
RAYMOND THERCHIK, 2605 ASPEN HEIGHTS LP, ANCHORAGE, AK 99508
BRYCE THOREEN, 2442 NW MARKET ST #403, SEATTLE, WA 98107
JAMES THOREEN, 2400 NW 80TH ST #111, SEATTLE, WA 98117
DAVID TIM, BOX 37003, TOKSOOK BAY, AK 99637
JAMIN TOM, BOX 5546, NEWTOK, AK 99559
NICK TOM, BOX 5547, NEWTOK, AK 99559
PETE TOM, BOX 8, CHEFORNAK, AK 99561
STANLEY TOM, BOX 5546, NEWTOK, AK 99559
JIMMY TONY, BOX 90031, NIGHTMUTE, AK 99690
CHRISTOPHER TULIK, BOX 90026, NIGHTMUTE, AK 99690
HARRY TULIK, BOX 37143, TOKSOOK BAY, AK 99637
PAUL TULIK, BOX 90016, NIGHTMUTE, AK 99690
PHILLIP TULIK, BOX 90027, NIGHTMUTE, AK 99690
SIMEON TULIK, BOX 90038, NIGHTMUTE, AK 99690
ANDREW USUGAN, BOX 5, TUNUNAK, AK 99681
JOHN WALTER, BOX 24, TUNUNAK, AK 99681
PETER WALTER, BOX 63, TUNUNAK, AK 99681
JOHN WHITE, BOX 37091, TOKSOOK BAY, AK 99637
BARRY WHITMAN, BOX 7, MEKORYUK, AK 99630
MOSES WHITMAN, BOX 7, MEKORYUK, AK 99630
PATRICK WHITMAN, BOX 31, TUNUNAK, AK 99681
SOLOMON WILLIAMS, BOX 75, MEKORYUK, AK 99630

HERRING ROE, GILLNET, SECURITY COVE
DANIEL FARREN, 497 WESTWOOD AVE, HOMER, AK 99603

HERRING ROE, GILLNET, BRISTOL BAY
TREFIM ANDREW, BOX 12, ILIAMNA, AK 99606
CHRISTOPHER ANGASAN, BOX 70131, SOUTH NAKNEK, AK 99670
WALLACE BARTLETT, 3762 GLACIER DR, PITTSBURG, CA 94565
RICHARD ECHUCK, BOX 213, TOGIAK, AK 99678
DANIEL FARREN, 497 WESTWOOD AVE, HOMER, AK 99603
DAVID HILLEY, BOX 1411, DILLINGHAM, AK 99576
WILLIAM JOHNSON, BOX 1178, DILLINGHAM, AK 99576
PETER LOCKUK, BOX 88, TOGIAK, AK 99678
HANS NICHOLSON, 5301 E SHENNUM DR, WASILLA, AK 99654
DAN PAUK, BOX 82, MANOKOTAK, AK 99628
WASSILLIE TUGATUK, BOX 189, MANOKOTAK, AK 99628
BRUCE WHITING, 1302 W MUKILTEO BLVD, EVERETT, WA 98203

HERRING ROE & FOOD/BAIT, GILLNET, NUNIVAK ISLAND
BRADLEY AMOS, BOX 47, MEKORYUK, AK 99630
RAYMOND AMOS, BOX 24, MEKORYUK, AK 99630
TOM AMOS, BOX 74, MEKORYUK, AK 99630
DAVID BILL, BOX 37052, TOKSOOK BAY, AK 99637
ROBERT CLEMENT, 578 CLATSOP ST, ASTORIA, OR 97103
TY CUMMINS, BOX 1402, PETERSBURG, AK 99833
ABRAHAM DAVID, BOX 82, MEKORYUK, AK 99630
JOHN DAVID, BOX 8, MEKORYUK, AK 99630
MONA DAVID, BOX 82, MEKORYUK, AK 99630
KENNETH DAVIS, 8100 EVANS CIR, ANCHORAGE, AK 99507
SAMUEL DAVIS, BOX 83, MEKORYUK, AK 99630
TERRY DON, BOX 2, MEKORYUK, AK 99630
CLIFTON FERGUSON, 3811 NE 157TH AVE, VANCOUVER, WA 98682

HERRING ROE & FOOD BAIT—GILLNET

RUSSELL FLOAT, BOX 64, MEKORYUK, AK 99630
GLENN IVANOFF, BOX 178, BETHEL, AK 99559
HENRY IVANOFF, BOX 65, MEKORYUK, AK 99630
HENRY JACK, 5807 TONGA ST, ANCHORAGE, AK 99507
NORMAN JOHN, BOX 37061, TOKSOOK BAY, AK 99637
PETER JOHN, BOX 5544, NEWTOK, AK 99559
WILLIE JOHN, BOX 204, BETHEL, AK 99559
ALBINA KING, BOX 2371, BETHEL, AK 99559
DEREK KING, BOX 95, MEKORYUK, AK 99630
JEFFREY KING, BOX 95, MEKORYUK, AK 99630
HULTMAN KIOKUN, BOX 1, MEKORYUK, AK 99630
JASON MATHLAW, BOX 272, BETHEL, AK 99559
GARRY MATSON, 92582 ASTOR RD, ASTORIA, OR 97103
SANDRA MEEKS, BOX 1514, PETERSBURG, AK 99833
JEFFREY MEUCCI, BOX 1086, PETERSBURG, AK 99833
HARRY MIKE, BOX 73, MEKORYUK, AK 99630
MABEL MOSES, BOX 877793, WASILLA, AK 99687
TOM NOATAK, BOX 115, MEKORYUK, AK 99630
DANIEL OLRUN, BOX 05, MEKORYUK, AK 99630
EDITH OLRUN, BOX 5, MEKORYUK, AK 99630
LEONARD OLRUN, 1330 W 25TH #2, ANCHORAGE, AK 99503
MARK OLRUN, BOX 71, MEKORYUK, AK 99630
PALMER OLRUN, BOX 18, MEKORYUK, AK 99630
RONALD OLRUN, BOX 46, MEKORYUK, AK 99630
STEPHEN OLRUN, BOX 21, MEKORYUK, AK 99630
STUART OLRUN, BOX 2383, BETHEL, AK 99559
ALAN SEE, BOX 99, NASELLE, WA 98638
BRENDA SEE, BOX 99, NASELLE, WA 98638
EDWARD SHAVINGS, BOX 33, MEKORYUK, AK 99630
EDWARD SHAVINGS, BOX 31, MEKORYUK, AK 99630
HENRY SHAVINGS, 3922 SCENIC VIEW DR, ANCHORAGE, AK 99504
SAMUEL SHAVINGS, BOX 87, MEKORYUK, AK 99630
DALE SMITH, BOX 25, MEKORYUK, AK 99630
JIMMY SMITH, 1901 WALDRON DR, ANCHORAGE, AK 99507
JOHNNY SMITH, 10230 BETULA DR, ANCHORAGE, AK 99507
LUKE SMITH, 2923 LILY ST #A, ANCHORAGE, AK 99508
SAMUEL SMITH, BOX 54, MEKORYUK, AK 99630
VIOLA SMITH, BOX 25, MEKORYUK, AK 99630
CHARLIE SPUD, BOX 37, MEKORYUK, AK 99630
CHARLIE SPUD, BOX 603, HAINES, AK 99827
WALTER SUOMELA, BOX 3092, HOMER, AK 99603
LEWELLYN SWANSON, BOX 536, PETERSBURG, AK 99833
GLEN SZYMONIAK, BOX 345, BARROW, AK 99723
JOBE WESTON, BOX 3234, BETHEL, AK 99559
SAMSON WESTON, BOX 17, MEKORYUK, AK 99630
BARRY WHITMAN, BOX 7, MEKORYUK, AK 99630
JAMES WHITMAN, 2221 MULDOON RD #520, ANCHORAGE, AK 99504
MOSES WHITMAN, BOX 7, MEKORYUK, AK 99630
PATRICK WHITMAN, BOX 31, TUNUNAK, AK 99681
GEORGE WILLIAMS, BOX 57, MEKORYUK, AK 99630
SOLOMON WILLIAMS, BOX 75, MEKORYUK, AK 99630

HERRING ROE & FOOD/BAIT, GILLNET, GOODNEWS BAY

MICHAEL ALAKAYAK, BOX 56, MANOKOTAK, AK 99628
MORRIS ALEXIE, BOX 03, NUNAPITCHUK, AK 99641
CHARLIE ANDREW, BOX 8124, TUNTUTULIAK, AK 99680
WILSON ANDREW, GEN DEL, ATMAUTLUAK, AK 99559
IVAN ARNARIAK, BOX 95, TOGIAK, AK 99678
JACK AYAGALRIA, BOX 919, PALMER, AK 99645
ROBERT AYAGALRIA, BOX 34104, NAPAKIAK, AK 99634
WALTER AYAGALRIA, BOX 07, AKIAK, AK 99552
TOMMY AYOJIAK, BOX 26, GOODNEWS BAY, AK 99589
WALTER AYOJIAK, BOX 026, GOODNEWS BAY, AK 99589
HENRY BAVILLA, BOX 30, PLATINUM, AK 99651

EDNA BEEBE, BOX 35, EEK, AK 99578
DANIEL BERLIN, BOX 158, KASIGLUK, AK 99609
DAVID BERLIN, 7910 LADASA PL, ANCHORAGE, AK 99507
JAMES BERLIN, BOX 118, NUNAPITCHUK, AK 99641
JOHN BERLIN, BOX 152, NUNAPITCHUK, AK 99641
SAMUEL BERLIN, BOX 2735, BETHEL, AK 99559
STANLEY BERLIN, BOX 43, KASIGLUK, AK 99609
GEORGE BLACK, BOX 18, NAPAKIAK, AK 99634
MICHAEL BLACK, BOX 34058, NAPAKIAK, AK 99634
ALBERT BRIGHT, BOX 67, GOODNEWS BAY, AK 99589
ALICE BRIGHT, BOX 5, GOODNEWS BAY, AK 99589
PETER BRINK, BOX 56, KASIGLUK, AK 99609
JESSE BRITTON, BOX 64, QUINHAGAK, AK 99655
CASSIUS BROWN, BOX 5105, KONGIGANAK, AK 99545
JOSEPH BROWN, BOX 5015, KONGIGANAK, AK 99545
VERNON BROWN, BOX 013, EEK, AK 99578
NICK CARTER, BOX 3, EEK, AK 99578
JAMES CHARLES, BOX 8044, TUNTUTULIAK, AK 99680
JESSE CHARLES, BOX 8044, TUNTUTULIAK, AK 99680
WILLIE CHARLES, BOX 83, NUNAPITCHUK, AK 99641
JOHN CHARLIE, BOX 2376, BETHEL, AK 99559
JOSHUA CHARLIE, BOX 1556, BETHEL, AK 99559
RAY CHARLIE, BOX 8064, TUNTUTULIAK, AK 99680
THOMAS CHARLIE, BOX 8064, TUNTUTULIAK, AK 99680
TOM CHARLIE, BOX 8064, TUNTUTULIAK, AK 99680
LARRY CHASE, BOX 1981, BETHEL, AK 99559
ZACHARIAH CHRIS, BOX 8084, TUNTUTULIAK, AK 99680
WILLARD CHURCH, BOX 124, QUINHAGAK, AK 99655
DAVID CLEVELAND, BOX 4074, TWIN HILLS, AK 99576
JOSHUA CLEVELAND, BOX 62, QUINHAGAK, AK 99655
BENJAMIN COOPCHIAK, BOX 251, TOGIAK, AK 99678
DAVID COUPCHIAK, BOX 101, TOGIAK, AK 99678
HELEN COX, 3711 CASPER CT #2, ANCHORAGE, AK 99502
DAVID DAVID, BOX 35, KWETHLUK, AK 99621
GERALD DEMIENTIEFF, BOX 178, KASIGLUK, AK 99609
HENRY DOCK, BOX 215, KIPNUK, AK 99614
FRED DON, BOX 2, MEKORYUK, AK 99630
MELVIN EGOAK, BOX 6511, ATMAUTLUAK, AK 99559
WILLIAM EGOAK, BOX 236, KWETHLUK, AK 99621
RILEY EKAMRAK, 2379 BELL CT #80, MEDFORD, OR 97504
LINCOLN ENOCH, BOX 8033, TUNTUTULIAK, AK 99680
MATTHEW ENOCH, BOX 56, NUNAPITCHUK, AK 99641
JEFFREY EVAN, BOX 44, GOODNEWS BAY, AK 99589
PAVILA EVAN, BOX 8121, TUNTUTULIAK, AK 99680
CHARLES EVANS, BOX 63, QUINHAGAK, AK 99655
JAMES FORBES, BOX 257, TOGIAK, AK 99678
ESTHER FOX, BOX 70, GOODNEWS BAY, AK 99589
RANDY FOX, BOX 4, PLATINUM, AK 99651
LEROY FRIENDLY, BOX 8017, TUNTUTULIAK, AK 99680
HOMER GALILA, BOX 85, GOODNEWS BAY, AK 99589
LESTER GALILA, BOX 90, GOODNEWS BAY, AK 99589
WALTER GALILA, BOX 145, QUINHAGAK, AK 99655
EDWARD GEORGE, BOX 51103, AKIACHAK, AK 99551
JOSEPH GEORGE, BOX 51067, AKIACHAK, AK 99551
RODNEY GOSUK, BOX 237, TOGIAK, AK 99678
JANE GRIFFIN, 1335 S WILLIWAW DR, PALMER, AK 99645
STEVEN HANSEN, BOX 250, RIVERSIDE, WA 98849
KEVIN HARLESS, BOX 98, TOGIAK, AK 99678
JACOB HENRY, BOX 51063, AKIACHAK, AK 99551
KENNETH HENRY, BOX 97, EEK, AK 99578
ROBERT HIMSCHOOT, 3227 RIVERPOINTE CR NE, CEDAR RAPIDS, IA 52411
JERRY IVON, BOX 5103, KONGIGANAK, AK 99545
DANIEL JACKSON, BOX 62, KWETHLUK, AK 99621
IVAN JACOBS, BOX 31, NUNAPITCHUK, AK 99641
FRANK JAMES, BOX 25, PLATINUM, AK 99651

HERRING ROE & FOOD BAIT—GILLNET

NORMAN JAMES, BOX 25, PLATINUM, AK 99651
PETER JENKINS, BOX 6563, ATMAUTLUAK, AK 99559
DAVID JIMMIE, BOX 8006, TUNTUTULIAK, AK 99680
NORMAN JIMMIE, BOX 8067, TUNTUTULIAK, AK 99680
RALPH JIMMIE, BOX 34051, NAPAKIAK, AK 99634
ALLEN JIMMY, BOX 34064, NAPAKIAK, AK 99634
KENNETH JIMMY, BOX 34081, NAPAKIAK, AK 99634
PETER JOSEPH, BOX 8046, TUNTUTULIAK, AK 99680
GERALD KAMEROFF, BOX 34091, NAPAKIAK, AK 99634
RICHARD KAMMEYER, BOX 2274, BETHEL, AK 99559
DAVID KASAK, BOX 74, TOGIAK, AK 99678
ANTHONY KASAYULIE, BOX 29, AKIACHAK, AK 99551
JAMES KASAYULIE, BOX 11, PLATINUM, AK 99651
WILLIE KERNAK, BOX 34035, NAPAKIAK, AK 99634
GARY KILBUCK, BOX 11, PLATINUM, AK 99651
HULTMAN KIOKUN, BOX 1, MEKORYUK, AK 99630
ALBERT KVAMME, BOX 26, TOGIAK, AK 99678
FRANK LOGUSAK, BOX 278, TOGIAK, AK 99678
JACKSON LOMACK, BOX 832, BETHEL, AK 99559
ROSA LUHRS, 3922 DANDILION WINE CIR, ANCHORAGE, AK 99507
ISAAC LUPIE, GEN DEL, TUNTUTULIAK, AK 99680
NICK LUPIE, BOX 8091, TUNTUTULIAK, AK 99680
PETER LUPIE, BOX 8077, TUNTUTULIAK, AK 99680
JOHN MARK, BOX 16, QUINHAGAK, AK 99655
NICHOLAI MARK, BOX 70, QUINHAGAK, AK 99655
WILLIAM MARK, BOX 143, GOODNEWS BAY, AK 99589
NELS MARTIN, BOX 306, TOGIAK, AK 99678
SAMUEL MARTIN, BOX 66, GOODNEWS BAY, AK 99589
LINDGREN MATHLAW, BOX 88, MEKORYUK, AK 99630
FRANK MATTHEW, PITMALLEQ HEIGHTS HOUSE 72, QUINHAGAK, AK 99655
FRANK MATTHEW, BOX 09, QUINHAGAK, AK 99655
BILLY MCCANN, BOX 1924, BETHEL, AK 99559
GEORGE MCCARR, BOX 8028, TUNTUTULIAK, AK 99680
BAVILLA MERRITT, BOX 65, GOODNEWS BAY, AK 99589
JAMES MERRITT, BOX 154, QUINHAGAK, AK 99655
FRANK MILLER, BOX 15, EEK, AK 99578
PETER MILLER, BOX 8065, TUNTUTULIAK, AK 99680
RAYMOND MOORE, BOX TWA, DILLINGHAM, AK 99576
MARK MOYLE, BOX 14, PLATINUM, AK 99651
THOMAS MUTE, BOX 5002, KONGIGANAK, AK 99545
KENNETH NANALOOK, BOX 5, TOGIAK, AK 99678
DANIEL NELSON, BOX 34014, NAPAKIAK, AK 99634
JONATHAN NELSON, BOX 34101, NAPAKIAK, AK 99634
DAVID NICHOLAI, BOX 2603, BETHEL, AK 99559
EDWARD NICHOLAI, GEN DEL, ATMAUTLUAK, AK 99559
MARTIN NICOLAI, BOX 70, KWETHLUK, AK 99621
JAMES NICORI, BOX 41, KWETHLUK, AK 99621
HARRY NOSE, BOX 1787, BETHEL, AK 99559
MARTIN NOSE, BOX 95, AKIACHAK, AK 99551
NOAH NOSE, BOX 520103, BIG LAKE, AK 99652
RANDY NOSE, BOX 51030, AKIACHAK, AK 99551
RAY NOSE, BOX 132, AKIACHAK, AK 99551
ROLAND NOSE, BOX 117, AKIACHAK, AK 99551
RYAN NOSE, BOX 30, AKIACHAK, AK 99551
DANIEL OLRUN, BOX 05, MEKORYUK, AK 99630
DANIEL OLRUN, BOX 46, MEKORYUK, AK 99630
ADOLPH OUYA, BOX 96, GOODNEWS BAY, AK 99589
ALBERT OUYA, BOX 96, GOODNEWS BAY, AK 99589
ARNOLD PAVIAN, BOX 56, TOGIAK, AK 99678
HENRY PAVIAN, BOX 194, TOGIAK, AK 99678
SAMUEL PAVIAN, BOX 208, TOGIAK, AK 99678
HOWARD PAVILLA, GEN DEL, ATMAUTLUAK, AK 99559
JOHN PAVILLA, BOX 34017, NAPAKIAK, AK 99634
MOSES PAVILLA, BOX 6522, ATMAUTLUAK, AK 99559
NICKOLAI PAVILLA, BOX 6587, ATMAUTLUAK, AK 99559
ADOLPH PLEASANT, BOX 51, QUINHAGAK, AK 99655

ANTHONY POULSEN, BOX 154, TOGIAK, AK 99678
CHRIS POULSEN, BOX 938, PETERSBURG, AK 99833
ELENA RATH, BOX 5013, KETCHIKAN, AK 99901
JAMES ROBERTS, BOX 54, GOODNEWS BAY, AK 99589
JOHN ROBERTS, BOX 12, GOODNEWS BAY, AK 99589
ROY ROBERTS, BOX 54, GOODNEWS BAY, AK 99589
WASSILIE ROBERTS, BOX 54, GOODNEWS BAY, AK 99589
WILLIAM ROBERTS, BOX 64, GOODNEWS BAY, AK 99589
JOHN SAMUEL, BOX 48, PLATINUM, AK 99651
PETER SAMUELS, BOX 03, PLATINUM, AK 99651
PERCY SCHOLTZ, BOX 17, GOODNEWS BAY, AK 99589
GEORGE SMITH, #9 2ND ST, TOGIAK, AK 99678
ISHMAEL SMITH, BOX 84, MEKORYUK, AK 99630
JIMMY SMITH, 1901 WALDRON DR, ANCHORAGE, AK 99507
JOHN SMITH, BOX 95, GOODNEWS BAY, AK 99589
LOUIS SMITH, BOX 95, GOODNEWS BAY, AK 99589
LUKE SMITH, 2923 LILY ST #A, ANCHORAGE, AK 99508
VIVA SMITH, BOX 84, MEKORYUK, AK 99630
JOSEPH SPEIN, BOX 131, KWETHLUK, AK 99621
PATRICK SPEIN, BOX 57, LOWER KALSKAG, AK 99626
PETER SPEIN, BOX 78, KWETHLUK, AK 99621
CHARLIE SPUD, BOX 37, MEKORYUK, AK 99630
LARRY STRUNK, BOX 94, QUINHAGAK, AK 99655
GEORGE SWIFT, BOX 368, DILLINGHAM, AK 99576
ANDREW THOMAS, 2850 JANEL AVE, NORTH POLE, AK 99705
PETER TOGIAK, BOX 235, TOGIAK, AK 99678
ALBERT TONIAK, BOX 75, GOODNEWS BAY, AK 99589
LEO WASKEY, BOX 462, BETHEL, AK 99559
MATTHEW WASSILIE, BOX 42, AKIACHAK, AK 99551
SCHOUVILLER WASSILIE, BOX 51104, AKIACHAK, AK 99551
ROGER WASSILLIE, BOX 287, TOGIAK, AK 99678
ISAAC WESTCOAST, 802 N PRICE ST #2, ANCHORAGE, AK 99508
SAMSON WESTON, BOX 17, MEKORYUK, AK 99630
HENRY WHITE, BOX 34018, NAPAKIAK, AK 99634
RAYMOND WHITE, BOX 28, EEK, AK 99578
ROLAND WHITE, BOX 8014, TUNTUTULIAK, AK 99680
ROSEMARY WHITE, 105 LANCE DR # 105H, SITKA, AK 99835
HARRY WILLIAMS, BOX 6094, NAPASKIAK, AK 99559
HENRY WILLIAMS, BOX 05, PLATINUM, AK 99651
SOLOMON WILLIAMS, BOX 75, MEKORYUK, AK 99630

HERRING ROE & FOOD/BAIT, GILLNET, CAPE ROMANZOF

BRANDON AGUCHAK, BOX 133, SCAMMON BAY, AK 99662
JAMES AKERELREA, BOX 163, SCAMMON BAY, AK 99662
ETHAN ALORALREA, BOX 1384, BETHEL, AK 99559
BILLY ANDREWS, BOX 104, CHEVAK, AK 99563
ANDREW AYULUK, BOX 133, CHEVAK, AK 99563
EUGENE AYULUK, BOX 241, CHEVAK, AK 99563
JAMES AYULUK, BOX 138, CHEVAK, AK 99563
JAMES BEATON, BOX 58385, FAIRBANKS, AK 99711
JOSEPH BELL, BOX 185, HOOPER BAY, AK 99604
ROBERTA BELL, BOX 3, SCAMMON BAY, AK 99662
CORNELIUS BLACK, GEN DEL, HOOPER BAY, AK 99604
PETER BOYSCOUT, BOX 127, CHEVAK, AK 99563
DAVID BUNYAN, BOX 231, HOOPER BAY, AK 99604
LEEMON BUNYAN.ANDREW, BOX 443, HOOPER BAY, AK 99604
ELIAS FRIDAY, BOX 162, CHEVAK, AK 99563
PETER FRIDAY, BOX 195, HOOPER BAY, AK 99604
RAYMOND GAUTHIER, BOX 189, TOGIAK, AK 99678
VINCENT GREEN, BOX 36, HOOPER BAY, AK 99604
RAYMOND GUMP, BOX 150, HOOPER BAY, AK 99604
PATRICK HALE, BOX 171, HOOPER BAY, AK 99604
JOHNNY HENRY, BOX 190, SCAMMON BAY, AK 99662
IKE HILL, BOX 76, HOOPER BAY, AK 99604
REUBEN HILL, BOX 210, HOOPER BAY, AK 99604

HERRING ROE & FOOD BAIT—GILLNET

DAMIEN HOELSCHER, BOX 177, HOOPER BAY, AK 99604
NICKY HOELSCHER, BOX 14, HOOPER BAY, AK 99604
LARSON HUNTER, BOX 161, SCAMMON BAY, AK 99662
DION IMGALREA, BOX 207, CHEVAK, AK 99563
CALVIN JOE, BOX 45, HOOPER BAY, AK 99604
GLEN JOE, BOX 102, HOOPER BAY, AK 99604
PAUL JOE, BOX 48, HOOPER BAY, AK 99604
TIMOTHY JOHNSON, BOX 314, MOUNTAIN VILLAGE, AK 99632
AMOS KAGANAK, BOX 106, SCAMMON BAY, AK 99662
CHARLIE KAGANAK, BOX 74, SCAMMON BAY, AK 99662
CLIFFORD KAGANAK, BOX 27, SCAMMON BAY, AK 99662
DAVID KAGANAK, BOX 192, SCAMMON BAY, AK 99662
KIMMIE KAGANAK, BOX 88, SCAMMON BAY, AK 99662
NAAMAN KAGANAK, BOX 35, SCAMMON BAY, AK 99662
SCOTT KAGANAK, BOX 07, SCAMMON BAY, AK 99662
WYBON KAGANAK, BOX 112, SCAMMON BAY, AK 99662
PAUL KAISER, BOX 121, HOOPER BAY, AK 99604
BENJAMIN KNIGHT, BOX 86, HOOPER BAY, AK 99604
RICK KOETJE, 206 STATE AVE, MARYSVILLE, WA 98270
NORBERT LAKE, BOX 135, HOOPER BAY, AK 99604
BOYD LEMAN, 11675 STERLING HWY, NINILCHIK, AK 99639
HARVEY MANN, BOX 32, HOOPER BAY, AK 99604
FELIX MATCHIAN, BOX 153, CHEVAK, AK 99563
MICHAEL MATCHIAN, BOX 228, CHEVAK, AK 99563
VINCENT MATCHIAN, BOX 225, CHEVAK, AK 99563
BERNARD MURRAN, BOX 274, HOOPER BAY, AK 99604
RAPHAEL MURRAN, BOX 188, HOOPER BAY, AK 99604
MYRON NANENG, BOX 1226, BETHEL, AK 99559
ROY NANENG, BOX 422, HOOPER BAY, AK 99604
WILLIAM NANENG, BOX 114, HOOPER BAY, AK 99604
GEORGE NANUK, BOX 306, HOOPER BAY, AK 99604
DANIEL NASH, BOX 5517, CHEVAK, AK 99563
FREDERICK NASH, BOX 122, CHEVAK, AK 99563
XAVIER NASH, BOX 182, CHEVAK, AK 99563
MOSES NIGHT, GEN DEL, HOOPER BAY, AK 99604
PAUL NUKUSUK, BOX 153, HOOPER BAY, AK 99604
DENNIS OBRIEN, BOX 252, HOOPER BAY, AK 99604
BRIAN OLSON, BOX 346, HOOPER BAY, AK 99604
ERIC OLSON, BOX 163, HOOPER BAY, AK 99604
LOUIE P.A.J.BUNYAN, BOX 145, HOOPER BAY, AK 99604
CLIFFORD PANIYAK, BOX 223, CHEVAK, AK 99563
MICHAEL PENNYLEGION, 6364 WOODLYN RD, FERNDALE, WA 98428
JOHN PINGAYAK, BOX 118, CHEVAK, AK 99563
NORMAN PINGAYAK, BOX 101, CHEVAK, AK 99563
JACOB RIVERS, BOX 167, SCAMMON BAY, AK 99662
VAN SCHMITTOU, BOX 425, CRAIG, AK 99921
ISAAC SETON, BOX 20032, KOTLIK, AK 99620
LEEMON SETON, BOX 272, HOOPER BAY, AK 99604
MARVIN SETON, BOX 15, HOOPER BAY, AK 99604
MARY SETON, BOX 197, HOOPER BAY, AK 99604
NORMAN SETON, BOX 67, HOOPER BAY, AK 99604
PETER SETON, BOX 63, HOOPER BAY, AK 99604
RONALD SETON, BOX 333, HOOPER BAY, AK 99604
JOSEPH SLATS, 2916 GUINEVERE PL, FAIRBANKS, AK 99709
ARTHUR SMART, BOX 164, HOOPER BAY, AK 99604
JOSEPH SMART, BOX 28, HOOPER BAY, AK 99604
ALOYSIUS SMITH, BOX 183, HOOPER BAY, AK 99604
AUGUSTINE SMITH, BOX 181, HOOPER BAY, AK 99604
EDGAR SMITH, BOX 354, HOOPER BAY, AK 99604
HENRY SMITH, BOX 292, HOOPER BAY, AK 99604
JANET SMITH, BOX 2194, HOOPER BAY, AK 99604
LOUIS SMITH, BOX 17, HOOPER BAY, AK 99604
RUDOLPH SMITH, GEN DEL, HOOPER BAY, AK 99604
RUDOLPH SMITH, GEN DEL, HOOPER BAY, AK 99604
TEDDY SMITH, BOX 183, HOOPER BAY, AK 99604

STEVEN STONE, BOX 248, HOOPER BAY, AK 99604
JOHN STRONGHEART, BOX 82, ALAKANUK, AK 99554
HARLEY SUNDOWN, BOX 2, SCAMMON BAY, AK 99662
DON TALL, BOX 44, HOOPER BAY, AK 99604
LUKE TALL, BOX 165, HOOPER BAY, AK 99604
MICHAEL TEVE, BOX 167, CHEVAK, AK 99563
PAUL TEVE, GEN DEL, CHEVAK, AK 99563
WILLIAM TINKER, BOX 108, HOOPER BAY, AK 99604
NAAMAN TOMAGANUK, BOX 101, HOOPER BAY, AK 99604
NOEL TOMAGANUK, BOX 77, HOOPER BAY, AK 99604
SILAS TOMAGANUK, BOX 191, HOOPER BAY, AK 99604
ANTHONY ULAK, BOX 29, SCAMMON BAY, AK 99662
FRANCIS ULROAN, BOX 5445, CHEVAK, AK 99563
BENJAMIN UTTEREYUK, BOX 130, SCAMMON BAY, AK 99662
CAROLYN UTTEREYUK, BOX 191, SCAMMON BAY, AK 99662
FELIX WALKER, BOX 181, SCAMMON BAY, AK 99662
STEVEN WALKER, BOX 104, SCAMMON BAY, AK 99662
MARTIN XITCO, 3401 25TH W #524, SEATTLE, WA 98199

HERRING ROE & FOOD/BAIT, GILLNET, NORTON SOUND
MARTHA AARONS, 1730 SHORE DR, ANCHORAGE, AK 99515
RAYMOND ALEXIE, 6700 EILEEN CIR, ANCHORAGE, AK 99507
AXEL ALSTROM, 4961 E ALDER DR, WASILLA, AK 99654
FRANK ALSTROM, BOX 169, ALAKANUK, AK 99554
RAGNAR ALSTROM, BOX 112, ALAKANUK, AK 99554
WALLACE AMAKTOOLIK, BOX 39025, ELIM, AK 99739
JERRINE AMBROSE, BOX 67, SAINT MICHAEL, AK 99659
HOWARD AMOS, 047 AIRPORT RD, MEKORYUK, AK 99630
EDGAR ANAGICK, 4660 REKA DR #D13, ANCHORAGE, AK 99508
MARY ANAGICK, BOX 116, UNALAKLEET, AK 99684
AHMET ARTUNER, 1855 MARINE DR, BELLINGHAM, WA 98226
RHODA ASICKSIK, 8651 FLAMINGO DR, ANCHORAGE, AK 99502
TYSON ASICKSIK, BOX 24, SHAKTOOLIK, AK 99771
DONALD AULIYE, BOX 96, SHAKTOOLIK, AK 99771
CHARLENE AUSTIN, 2221 MULDOON RD #292, ANCHORAGE, AK 99504
CLARA AUSTIN, BOX 110, SAINT MICHAEL, AK 99659
RUSSELL BABIC, BOX 1833, CORDOVA, AK 99574
PATRIK BARR, BOX 526, PORT TOWNSEND, WA 98368
JIM BAUMGART, 210 BAYSIDE PL, BELLINGHAM, WA 98225
DOMINIC BEANS, BOX 5065, PILOT STATION, AK 99650
PALASSA BEANS, BOX 5052, PILOT STATION, AK 99650
TIM BEGUE, 4835 S VIEWMONT AVE, SALT LAKE CITY, UT 84117
FRED BIGSBY, BOX 157, HAINES, AK 99827
ROBERT BLOUGH, BOX 555, HOONAH, AK 99829
CHARLIE BOULDING, BOX 89, MANLEY HOT SPRINGS, AK 99756
JACK BOWMAN, BOX 1076, TEKOA, WA 99033
ELLIOTT BRADLEY, BOX 92, UNALAKLEET, AK 99684
RANSOM BRADLEY, BOX 108, UNALAKLEET, AK 99684
ROY BRADLEY, BOX 67, ELIM, AK 99739
PAUL BRATTON, BOX 15231, FRITZ CREEK, AK 99603
TIERNA BRAVO.BUCHMAYR, BOX 60026, SEATTLE, WA 98160
STEVE BROCK, BOX 1285, NOME, AK 99762
KELVIN BRODERSEN, 1912 KESTREL LN, FAIRBANKS, AK 99709
NOBLE CARLSON, BOX 99C, HOVLAND, MN 55606
GARY CASSIDY, 520 LYLA LN, BELLINGHAM, WA 98225
WILLIAM CHAMBERLAIN, 1806 N WATTS ST, PORTLAND, OR 97217
BILLY CHARLES, BOX 41, EMMONAK, AK 99581
CAROL CHARLES, BOX 177, UNALAKLEET, AK 99684
FRANCES CHARLES, BOX 55, UNALAKLEET, AK 99684
LEO CHARLES, BOX 53048, KOYUK, AK 99753
MILTON CHEEMUK, BOX 59007, SAINT MICHAEL, AK 99659
THOMAS CHEEMUK, BOX 59034, SAINT MICHAEL, AK 99659
VERN CHERNESKI, 5398 S ECHO LAKE DR, WASILLA, AK 99623
GARRETT COFFEY, BOX 71093, STEBBINS, AK 99671

HERRING ROE & FOOD BAIT—GILLNET

ANNETTE COGGINS, BOX 3427, HOMER, AK 99603
JACK COOK, 3901 TAIGA DR, ANCHORAGE, AK 99516
LIA COOK, 3901 TAIGA DR, ANCHORAGE, AK 99516
SCOTT COUGHLIN, 1903 E CALHOUN ST, SEATTLE, WA 98112
CORNELIUS DAN, BOX 101, STEBBINS, AK 99671
HERMES DAN, BOX 71072, STEBBINS, AK 99671
CHARLES DEGNAN, BOX 180, UNALAKLEET, AK 99684
CALEB DOTOMAIN, BOX 231105, ANCHORAGE, AK 99523
ISAIAH DOTOMAIN, BOX 314, STERLING, AK 99672
LINDA DOWNING, 14429 RIVERWALK DR, SUMNER, WA 98390
JOSEPH DRAGSETH, BOX 408, KENAI, AK 99611
TIM EDWARDS, 1024 UNIVERSITY, WALLA WALLA, WA 99362
DUANE EGE, 1647 W 5TH ST, GRAND MARAIS, MN 55604
KIRK EID, 349 W HEMMI RD, BELLINGHAM, WA 98226
GEORGE EMERSON, 3644 GREENWOOD N, SEATTLE, WA 98103
JEFF ERICKSON, BOX 53, PETERSBURG, AK 99833
JEFFREY ERICKSON, BOX 301, UNALAKLEET, AK 99684
LAWRENCE ETAGEAK, BOX 71032, SHAKTOOLIK, AK 99771
RACHEL FAHY, 301 ELLEN CIR, ANCHORAGE, AK 99515
BRENDA FARREN, 497 WESTWOOD AVE, HOMER, AK 99603
JAKE FARREN, 497 WESTWOOD AVE, HOMER, AK 99603
MAGGIE FERRY, 310 E 45TH AVE #C, ANCHORAGE, AK 99503
MICHAEL FILE, BOX 1666, PETERSBURG, AK 99833
VERNON FITCH, 8029 60TH DR NE, MARYSVILLE, WA 98270
CHARLIE FITKA, BOX 59056, SAINT MICHAEL, AK 99659
DAVID FITKA, BOX 52, MARSHALL, AK 99585
ANDREW FOXIE, BLUEBERRY ST #4112, STEBBINS, AK 99671
RUDY FRANULOVICH, BOX 5433, KETCHIKAN, AK 99901
CHARLES FREESE, 111 W 28TH AVE, SPOKANE, WA 99203
PAUL FRIIS.MIKKELSEN, BOX 276, DILLINGHAM, AK 99576
MARGARET GARCIA, 25806 PEPPER BEND LN, KATY, TX 77494
VINCE GIAMMANCO, 9292 E CORRINE DR, SCOTTSDALE, AZ 85260
TRAVIS GOODRICH, BOX 574, FRIDAY HARBOR, WA 98250
GRAHAM GOTTSTEIN, 9433 NE 14TH ST, CLYDEHILL, WA 98004
WILLIAM GRANT, 16203 SE NEWPORT WAY, BELLEVUE, WA 98006
JOSEPH GREGOIRE, HC 89 BOX 8077, TALKEETNA, AK 99676
RONALD HAKALA, 1695 MENDHENHALL PEN RD, JUNEAU, AK 99801
MARGARET HALLERAN, 206 RIVER RD, UNALAKLEET, AK 99684
W HALLERAN, 8622 XEBEC ST NE, CIRCLE PINES, MN 55014
LUDWIG HANSEN, BOX 193, NAKNEK, AK 99633
BRICE HARDY, 214 E KING APT B, NOME, AK 99762
ROBIN HARPER.CAUDILL, BOX 172, UNALAKLEET, AK 99684
BRIAN HARRISON, 1065 LARKSPUR CT, HOMER, AK 99603
CARLA HARTNELL, 615 17TH ST, BELLINGHAM, WA 98225
SCOTT HATLEY, 3187 W ARIMO RD, ARIMO, ID 83214
ANTHONY HAUGEN, BOX 122, UNALAKLEET, AK 99684
ELLSWORTH HAUGEN, BOX 145, UNALAKLEET, AK 99684
GARY HAUGEN, 7707 STANLEY DR, ANCHORAGE, AK 99518
NORMAN HAUGEN, BOX 145, UNALAKLEET, AK 99684
ARTHUR HECKMAN, BOX 5160, PILOT STATION, AK 99650
MARK HENDRICKS, 1719 ANTOINE ST, ARCATA, CA 95521
WAYNE HENRY, BOX 62043, GOLOVIN, AK 99762
ROBERT HEYANO, BOX 1409, DILLINGHAM, AK 99576
LARRY HIGGINS, BOX 106, LA CONNER, WA 98257
HEATHER HOINS, BOX 217, NORDLAND, WA 98358
WILLIAM HONEA, 28022 BUCHANAN RD, SEDRO WOOLLEY, WA 98284
KEVIN HUGHES, BOX 11, CHINOOK, WA 99614
PATRICIA HUHTA, BOX 355, UNALAKLEET, AK 99684
DOMINIC HUNT, BOX 36, EMMONAK, AK 99581
HERMES HUNT, BOX 20011, KOTLIK, AK 99620
ISIDORE HUNT, BOX 20025, KOTLIK, AK 99620
MICHAEL HUNT, 390 S BRAGAW ST #7, ANCHORAGE, AK 99508
LESLIE HUNTER, BOX 50, MARSHALL, AK 99585
LESLIE HUNTER, 4331 VANCE DR #B6, ANCHORAGE, AK 99508
NELSON HYKES, 1812 CINDYLEE LN, ANCHORAGE, AK 99507
ALEXANDER IVANOFF, BOX 68, UNALAKLEET, AK 99684

ALLEN IVANOFF, BOX 73, UNALAKLEET, AK 99684
ALVIN IVANOFF, BOX 13, UNALAKLEET, AK 99684
CURTIS IVANOFF, 4937 MILLS DR, ANCHORAGE, AK 99507
DEAN IVANOFF, BOX 134, UNALAKLEET, AK 99684
GAGE IVANOFF, BOX 235, UNALAKLEET, AK 99684
HARRY IVANOFF, BOX 13, UNALAKLEET, AK 99684
HERBERT IVANOFF, BOX 191ATMAI, UNALAKLEET, AK 99684
JERRY IVANOFF, BOX 102, UNALAKLEET, AK 99684
PAUL IVANOFF, BOX 324, UNALAKLEET, AK 99684
PAUL IVANOFF, BOX 34, UNALAKLEET, AK 99684
SERGEI IVANOFF, BOX 34, UNALAKLEET, AK 99684
STEPHEN IVANOFF, BOX 235, UNALAKLEET, AK 99684
WEAVER IVANOFF, BOX 113, UNALAKLEET, AK 99684
WILLARD IVANOFF, 154 LEXINGTON PL, ASTORIA, OR 97103
MORGAN JACK, BOX 71098, STEBBINS, AK 99671
GEORGE JACKSON, BOX 112, UNALAKLEET, AK 99684
HEATHER JACKSON, BOX 26, SHAKTOOLIK, AK 99771
LYNN JACKSON, BOX 71004, SHAKTOOLIK, AK 99771
WILLIAM JAHN, 8702 MARINE DR, TULALIP, WA 98271
DARLA JEMEWOUK, BOX 39046, ELIM, AK 99739
JOHN JEMEWOUK, BOX 39046, ELIM, AK 99739
HERB JOHNSEN, 175 S HARRINGTON LAGOON RD, COUPEVILLE, WA 98239
BRIAN JOHNSON, BOX 224, UNALAKLEET, AK 99684
BRUCE JOHNSON, BOX 128, UNALAKLEET, AK 99684
FRANK JOHNSON, BOX 117, UNALAKLEET, AK 99684
HARRY JOHNSON, BOX 56, UNALAKLEET, AK 99684
JOAN JOHNSON, BOX 56, UNALAKLEET, AK 99684
KATHERINE JOHNSON, BOX 117, UNALAKLEET, AK 99684
MARLEENE JOHNSON, BOX 58, UNALAKLEET, AK 99684
MERLIN JOHNSON, BOX 233, UNALAKLEET, AK 99684
THOMAS JOHNSON, 90222 YOUNGS RIVER RD, ASTORIA, OR 97103
TRAEGER JOHNSON, BOX 56, UNALAKLEET, AK 99684
WILLIAM JOHNSON, BOX 222, UNALAKLEET, AK 99684
BRIAN KANDOLL, BOX 1363, PETERSBURG, AK 99833
STEVEN KARABACH, 42465 DEER HEIGHTS DR N, DAVENPORT, WA 99122
BARRY KATCHATAG, BOX 143, UNALAKLEET, AK 99684
JOSEPH KATCHATAG, BOX 165, UNALAKLEET, AK 99684
STANTON KATCHATAG, BOX 268, UNALAKLEET, AK 99684
VAN KATCHATAG, BOX 73, SHAKTOOLIK, AK 99771
BENEDICT KATCHEAK, BOX 71038, STEBBINS, AK 99671
BARBARA KEHRBERG, BOX 40, UNALAKLEET, AK 99684
PHILOMENA KEYES, BOX 20170, KOTLIK, AK 99620
JON KINSEY, BOX 1913, HOMER, AK 99603
RONALD KIRK, BOX 71065, STEBBINS, AK 99671
PHILLIP KNISELEY, 2813 KIMBERLIE CT #1, ANCHORAGE, AK 99508
PAUL KOETJE, 21132 MANN RD, MOUNT VERNON, WA 98273
KANDI KOSTENUK, 2814 BROOKS ST #638, MISSOULA, MT 59801
JAMES KOTONGAN, 002 BEACH RD, UNALAKLEET, AK 99684
PATRICK KOTONGAN, BOX 1371, NOME, AK 99762
MAE KOUTCHAK, 3519 AERO AVE #A, ANCHORAGE, AK 99517
WILLIAM KOUTCHAK, BOX 155, UNALAKLEET, AK 99684
JOHN LAMONT, 7051 W WINDSOR DR, WASILLA, AK 99623
BRUCE LAPE, BOX 294, KASILOF, AK 99610
MICHAEL LARSEN, 2020 LAKE HEIGHTS DR #L103, EVERETT, WA 98208
JERRY LEE, 119 CEDAR LN, GATESVILLE, TX 76528
VITO LIBERATI, 88 EDGEWATER PL, PITTSBURG, CA 94565
JERRY LIBOFF, BOX 646, DILLINGHAM, AK 99576
CHARLES LOCKWOOD, BOX 84, UNALAKLEET, AK 99684
GREG LOREE, 11155 BLUE HERON RD, BOW, WA 98232
ROBERT MATHES, BOX 2140, WINDSOR, CA 95492
CRAIG MATTSON, BOX 530, NASELLE, WA 98638
LOIS MCCLELLAN, 1511 CACHE DR, ANCHORAGE, AK 99507
BERNARD MCDANIEL, 21827 SE 1ST, REDMOND, WA 98053
FRANK MCFARLAND, BOX 364, NOME, AK 99762
PAUL MCTAGGART, 420 E HOWELL ST, SEATTLE, WA 98122
GARY MICHEALS, BOX 5041, BELLINGHAM, WA 98227

HERRING ROE & FOOD BAIT—GILLNET

ROGER MIKE, BOX 71078, STEBBINS, AK 99671
CHESTER MILLETT, BOX 353, UNALAKLEET, AK 99684
CATHY MILLETT.BURRESS, 6960 VIBURNUM DR, ANCHORAGE, AK 99507
GEORGE MILNE, BOX 1846, HOMER, AK 99603
TIM MOERLEIN, BOX 298, KASILOF, AK 99610
CHRIS MORSE, 504 E FAIRHAVEN #219-72, BURLINGTON, WA 98233
DAVID MORSE, 10175 TORVANGER RD, BAINBRIDGE ISLAND, WA 98110
THOMAS MUNROE, 3823 CYCLONE DR, BELLINGHAM, WA 98225
JOSEPH MURRAY, BOX 39014, ELIM, AK 99739
JOHN MYERS, 270 SF GOLD CREEK RD, CARLTON, WA 98814
NATHAN NAGARUK, BOX 1286, NOME, AK 99762
PAUL NAGARUK, BOX 31, ELIM, AK 99739
SHELDON NAGARUK, BOX 42, ELIM, AK 99739
EDWARD NAKARAK, BOX 3, UNALAKLEET, AK 99684
GARY NAKARAK, BOX 39082, ELIM, AK 99739
LARRY NAKARAK, BOX 17, UNALAKLEET, AK 99684
LEWIS NAKARAK, BOX 33, SHAKTOOLIK, AK 99771
MORRIS NAKARAK, BOX 39061, ELIM, AK 99739
PERCY NAKARAK, BOX 333, UNALAKLEET, AK 99684
HENRY NANOUK, BOX 43, UNALAKLEET, AK 99684
PATRICK NASH, 193 SALMONBERRY LN, FRIDAY HARBOR, WA 98250
HENRY NASHALOOK, BOX 212, UNALAKLEET, AK 99684
DANIEL NASHOANAK, BOX 71085, STEBBINS, AK 99671
GREG NELSON, 209 97TH AVE #27, LAKE STEVEN, WA 98258
ALEXANDER NIKSIK, TANK FARM RD #6 BOX 59012, SAINT MICHAEL, AK 99659
JOHNNIE NOYAKUK, BOX 414, NOME, AK 99762
ROBERT ODMARK, BOX 7594, KETCHIKAN, AK 99901
TED ODMARK, 3343 BARANOF, KETCHIKAN, AK 99901
REYNOLD OKITKUN, BOX 20104, KOTLIK, AK 99620
JOHN OKTOYAK, BOX 11, EMMONAK, AK 99581
DAVID OLSON, BOX 192, GLENWOOD, NM 88039
MARGARET OLSON, BOX 1798, NOME, AK 99762
PAUL OLSON, 808 DANA DR, SEDRO WOOLLEY, WA 98284
RAYMOND ONEILL, BOX 1095, SOLDOTNA, AK 99669
ERIC OSBORNE, BOX 1761, NOME, AK 99762
TIMOTHY OSMAR, BOX 382, KASILOF, AK 99610
FRED OTTON, BOX 53044, KOYUK, AK 99753
MELVIN OTTON, BOX 53043, KOYUK, AK 99753
VALENTIN OTTOW, 11 BEACH LN, LAKEWOOD, WA 98498
AXEL OYOUMICK, BOX 12, UNALAKLEET, AK 99684
HENRY OYOUMICK, BOX 237, UNALAKLEET, AK 99684
CALVIN PANIPTCHUK, BOX 71091, SHAKTOOLIK, AK 99771
SILAS PANIPTCHUK, BOX 25, SHAKTOOLIK, AK 99771
DOMINIC PAPETTI, 3151 WILD MUSTANG PASS, WICKENBURG, AZ 85390
GEORGE PARKER, 37590 BRANDON LN, ASTORIA, OR 97103
TIM PATTERSON, BOX 164, CHINOOK, WA 98614
BENJAMIN PAYENNA, BOX 981, NOME, AK 99762
MARK PEACOCK, 2308 BIRCH ST, BELLINGHAM, WA 98226
JULIAN PEREZ, 2721 LAKE WHATCOM BLVD, BELLINGHAM, WA 98229
STEVEN PERKINS, BOX 1122, DILLINGHAM, AK 99576
NATE PERRY, BOX 02, SHAKTOOLIK, AK 99771
TERESA PERRY, BOX 02, SHAKTOOLIK, AK 99771
GEORGE PETE, BOX 71026, STEBBINS, AK 99671
JOSEPH PETE, BOX 71037, STEBBINS, AK 99671
DEAN PETERSON, BOX 62032, GOLOVIN, AK 99762
KATHLEEN POOL, BOX 1540, PORT TOWNSEND, WA 98368
JEFFREY POVELITE, BOX 7, CATHLAMET, WA 98612
MARK PRATER, 24 ROY ST #296, SEATTLE, WA 98109
JOHN RAE, BOX 857, KOTZEBUE, AK 99752
JOHN RANTZ, BOX 58, CHIGNIK BAY, AK 99564
CHRIS REITAN, BOX 266, GALENA, AK 99741
THOMAS RIGHTMIER, BOX 6506, SITKA, AK 99835
BRYANT RYAN, BOX 181, UNALAKLEET, AK 99684
LEE RYAN, 1675 CIRCLEWOOD DR, ANCHORAGE, AK 99515
MATT RYAN, 5145 GRAVELINE RD, BELLINGHAM, WA 98226

WILFRED RYAN, 6740 SEQUOIA CIR, ANCHORAGE, AK 99516
CHARLES SACCHEUS, 515 EAST 12TH #8, ANCHORAGE, AK 99501
FRED SAGOONICK, BOX 45, SHAKTOOLIK, AK 99771
GEORGE SAGOONICK, BOX 7, UNALAKLEET, AK 99684
MELANIE SAGOONICK, BOX 195, UNALAKLEET, AK 99684
PALMER SAGOONICK, BOX 27, SHAKTOOLIK, AK 99771
TONIA SAGOONICK, BOX 12, SHAKTOOLIK, AK 99771
LANCE SAMPSON, BOX 62041, GOLOVIN, AK 99762
EDNA SAVETILIK, BOX 14, SHAKTOOLIK, AK 99771
TREVOR SAVETILIK, BOX 108, SHAKTOOLIK, AK 99771
JAMES SCHMIT, 58488 CASH 16, LITCHFIELD, MN 55355
ALAN SEE, BOX 99, NASELLE, WA 98638
BRENDA SEE, BOX 99, NASELLE, WA 98638
STEPHEN SHAPIRO, 11100 HYLA AVE NE, BAINBRIDGE ISLAND, WA 98110
MICHAEL SHERLOCK, 127 N 35TH ST, SEATTLE, WA 98103
RITA SMITH, 1601 E 41ST CT #B, ANCHORAGE, AK 99508
BENJAMIN SOCKPEALUK, BOX 71008, SHAKTOOLIK, AK 99771
MARLIN SOOKIAYAK, BOX 71058, SHAKTOOLIK, AK 99771
ALLEN SOOSUK, 1200 W DIMOND SP 1442, ANCHORAGE, AK 99501
VERNA SOUTHERN, BOX 145, UNALAKLEET, AK 99684
CHARLES SOXIE, BOX 251, UNALAKLEET, AK 99684
JOHN SPANGLER, 3111 S 273RD ST, AUBURN, WA 98001
DAN ST.JOHN, 11 FANNING RD, OAKESDALE, WA 99158
BRIAN STANLEY, BOX 694, CATHLAMET, WA 98612
MARTIN STARR, BOX 631, FRIDAY HARBOR, WA 98250
ROBERT STARR, BOX 331, FRIDAY HARBOR, WA 98250
THOMAS SVENSEN, BOX 274, ASTORIA, OR 97103
JOHN SWANSON, BOX 1546, PETERSBURG, AK 99833
ROBERT SWANSON, BOX 924, PETERSBURG, AK 99833
OSCAR TAKAK, BOX 21, ELIM, AK 99739
TYLER TAKAK, BOX 68, SHAKTOOLIK, AK 99771
WILLIAM TAKAK, BOX 17, SHAKTOOLIK, AK 99771
MARK THOMAS, BOX 1772, GOLD BEACH, OR 97444
ROBIN THOMAS, BOX 397, NOME, AK 99762
AMY THOMPSON, 5952 FARMINGTON RD, FARMINGTON, WA 99128
FRANCIS THOMPSON, BOX 111, SAINT MARYS, AK 99658
KYLE THOMPSON, BOX 111, SAINT MARYS, AK 99658
AMBROSE TOWARAK, BOX 89, UNALAKLEET, AK 99684
CLARENCE TOWARAK, BOX 175, UNALAKLEET, AK 99684
DONALD TOWARAK, BOX 175, UNALAKLEET, AK 99684
ISAIAH TOWARAK, BOX 40, UNALAKLEET, AK 99684
LINDA TOWARAK, BOX 175, UNALAKLEET, AK 99684
MERLE TOWARAK, BOX 273, UNALAKLEET, AK 99684
RAYMOND TOWARAK, BOX 264, UNALAKLEET, AK 99684
VIVA TOWARAK, BOX 26, UNALAKLEET, AK 99684
LORETTA TWETO, BOX 207, UNALAKLEET, AK 99684
PAMELA TWETO, BOX 225, SAINT MARYS, AK 99658
ANDREW UMLAUF, 5060 INGLEWOOD DR, LANGLEY, WA 98260
ALOYSIUS UNOK, 5620 S TAHITI LP, ANCHORAGE, AK 99507
JOHN WALDRON, 1788 SW STREMLER DR, OAK HARBOR, WA 98277
JOSIE WALKER, 561 E EAGLE RIDGE DR, SHELTON, WA 98584
MARY WASKA, 7761 JUGUAR CIR, ANCHORAGE, AK 99502
ALOYSIUS WASULI, BOX 20012, KOTLIK, AK 99620
ROSE WASULI, 5203 CHENA #4, ANCHORAGE, AK 99514
ERIK WEINGARTH, BOX 74, SAINT MARYS, AK 99658
PATRICK WEST, BOX 03, HOVLAND, MN 55606
BRUCE WHITING, 1302 W MUKILTEO BLVD, EVERETT, WA 98203
DOUG WILLIAMS, 3322 E 23RD ST, TUCSON, AZ 85713
GREGORY WILLIE, BOX 143256, ANCHORAGE, AK 99514
JOSEPH WILLIE, BOX 71008, STEBBINS, AK 99671
LEONARD WILLOYA, BOX 93, GOLOVIN, AK 99762
HENRIETTA WILSON, BOX 146, UNALAKLEET, AK 99684
J.LANCE WILSON, 592 E LARUEL RD, BELLINGHAM, WA 98226
JOHN WILSON, BOX 352, UNALAKLEET, AK 99684
ANDY WORHATCH, BOX 614, PETERSBURG, AK 99833

HERRING FOOD / BAIT—PURSE SEINE

BARBARA WORHATCH, 2708 S MERIDIAN #423, PUYALLUP, WA 98373
MARK YERKES, 2856 FAWN DR, LOXAHATCHEE, FL 33470
JON ZUCK, 16140 TERRACEWOOD LN, ANCHORAGE, AK 99516

HERRING FOOD/BAIT, PURSE SEINE, SOUTHEAST
KEN EICHNER, 5166 SHORELINE DR N, KETCHIKAN, AK 99901
BRYAN HOWEY, 410 MARINE ST #4, SITKA, AK 99835
LEROY JOHNS, BOX 1126, SISTERS, OR 97759
SIGURD MATHISEN, BOX 1460, PETERSBURG, AK 99833
JUSTIN PEELER, BOX 184, SITKA, AK 99835
KENNETH PHIPPEN, 312 TILSON ST, SITKA, AK 99835

HERRING FOOD/BAIT, PURSE SEINE, ALASKA PENINSULA
DICK JACOBSEN, BOX 307, SAND POINT, AK 99661
MICHAEL KURTZ, BOX 32265, BELLINGHAM, WA 98228

HERRING FOOD/BAIT, PURSE SEINE, FIXED VESSEL TO 60', KODIAK
DOREECE MUTCH, 210 B SHELIKOF, KODIAK, AK 99615
SAMUEL MUTCH, 210 B SHELIKOF, KODIAK, AK 99615
SAMUEL MUTCH, 210 B SHELIKOF, KODIAK, AK 99615
BARRY SCHAUFF, 316 CENTER ST, KODIAK, AK 99615
DON ZIMMERMAN, BOX 1157, KODIAK, AK 99615

HERRING FOOD/BAIT, OTTER TRAWL, FIXED VESSEL TO 75', KODIAK
MIKE HAGGREN, 1 THIRD ST #105, ASTORIA, OR 97103

HERRING FOOD/BAIT, OTTER TRAWL, FIXED VESSEL TO 70', KODIAK
RICHARD STARR, 1518 REZANOF, KODIAK, AK 99615

HERRING FOOD/BAIT, OTTER TRAWL, FIXED VESSEL TO 60', KODIAK
DANIEL MACDONALD, BOX 5993, BELLINGHAM, WA 98227
PETER MACDONALD, BOX 1062, ANACORTES, WA 98221

HERRING SPAWN ON KELP, HAND PICK, BRISTOL BAY
PETE ABRAHAM, BOX 106, TOGIAK, AK 99678
ALEXIE ACTIVE, BOX 321, TOGIAK, AK 99678
ANECIA ACTIVE, BOX 131, TOGIAK, AK 99678
EDWARD ACTIVE, 1400 E 4TH AVE, ANCHORAGE, AK 99501
KATHERINE ACTIVE, BOX 868, DILLINGHAM, AK 99576
STANLEY ACTIVE, BOX 131, TOGIAK, AK 99678
CARLA AKELKOK, BOX 1245, DILLINGHAM, AK 99576
ALEXIE ALAKAYAK, BOX 43, MANOKOTAK, AK 99628
CHRISTOPHER ALAKAYAK, BOX 62, MANOKOTAK, AK 99628
DENNIS ALAKAYAK, BOX 10, MANOKOTAK, AK 99628
HENRY ALAKAYAK, BOX 25, MANOKOTAK, AK 99628
JEANNE ALAKAYAK, BOX 25, MANOKOTAK, AK 99628
LOUIE ALAKAYAK, BOX 96, MANOKOTAK, AK 99628
MICHAEL ALAKAYAK, BOX 56, MANOKOTAK, AK 99628
NICOLAI ALAKAYAK, BOX 10, MANOKOTAK, AK 99628
PANSY ALAKAYAK, BOX 56, MANOKOTAK, AK 99628
SAM ALAKAYAK, BOX 62, MANOKOTAK, AK 99628
MARY ALEXIE, BOX 43, TOGIAK, AK 99678
MOSES ALEXIE, 2221 MULDOON RD #911, ANCHORAGE, AK 99504
POSEN ALEXIE, BOX 43, TOGIAK, AK 99678
MARGIE ALOYSIUS, BOX 51, ALEKNAGIK, AK 99555
RICHARD AMATUNAK, BOX 206, TOGIAK, AK 99678
JOHN ANDREW, BOX 57, MANOKOTAK, AK 99628
JOSEPH ANDREW, BOX 102, TOGIAK, AK 99678
ANDREW ANDREWS, BOX 254, TOGIAK, AK 99678

MARK ANDREWS, BOX 63, MANOKOTAK, AK 99628
REBECCA ANDREWS, BOX 254, TOGIAK, AK 99678
FREDERICK ANTONE, BOX 144, TOGIAK, AK 99678
JOHN ANTONE, BOX 32, TOGIAK, AK 99678
NORINE ANTONE, BOX 144, TOGIAK, AK 99678
HERBERT APALAYAK, BOX 21, MANOKOTAK, AK 99628
PAVILLA APALAYAK, BOX 21, MANOKOTAK, AK 99628
GEORGE ARKANAKYAK, BOX 3, TOGIAK, AK 99678
RACHEL ARKANAKYAK, BOX 85, TOGIAK, AK 99678
CARRIAN ARNARIAK, 1017 E 20TH #A, ANCHORAGE, AK 99501
EVERETT ARNARIAK, BOX 42, TOGIAK, AK 99678
IVAN ARNARIAK, BOX 95, TOGIAK, AK 99678
JESSIE ARNARIAK, BOX 95, TOGIAK, AK 99678
JULINE ARNARIAK, BOX 95, TOGIAK, AK 99678
LARRY ARNARIAK, BOX 226, TOGIAK, AK 99678
MICKEY ATAKITLIG, BOX 155, TOGIAK, AK 99678
ARLEN AYOJIAK, 8810 ACADIA DR, EAGLE RIVER, AK 99577
BONNIE AYOJIAK, BOX 61, MANOKOTAK, AK 99628
MARTIN AYOJIAK, BOX 132, TOGIAK, AK 99678
MOSES AYOJIAK, BOX 104, TOGIAK, AK 99678
PHYLLIS AYOJIAK, 2921 W 29TH #7B, ANCHORAGE, AK 99517
JACOB BARTMAN, BOX 193, TOGIAK, AK 99678
HENRY BAVILLA, BOX 111, TOGIAK, AK 99678
HENRY BAVILLA, BOX 114, TOGIAK, AK 99678
MARY BAVILLA, BOX 111, TOGIAK, AK 99678
MICHELLE BAVILLA, BOX 162, TOGIAK, AK 99678
DAVID BEACH, 3731 E 74TH AVE, ANCHORAGE, AK 99507
JAMES BINGMAN, BOX 82, DILLINGHAM, AK 99576
BERTHA BLUE, BOX 135, TOGIAK, AK 99678
HAROLD BLUE, BOX 92, TOGIAK, AK 99678
MYRON BLUE, BOX 207, TOGIAK, AK 99678
TYLER BLUE, BOX 303, TOGIAK, AK 99678
JUDY BRITO, BOX 23, TOGIAK, AK 99678
SIRENA BROCKMAN, BOX 177, DILLINGHAM, AK 99576
JOHN BROWN, BOX 16265, GALVESTON, TX 77552
CARRIE BURKS, BOX 366, TOGIAK, AK 99678
MICHAEL BUSEY, 8222 ENDICOTT, ANCHORAGE, AK 99502
CAROLYN CARLOS, BOX 28, TOGIAK, AK 99678
GARY CARLOS, BOX 249, TOGIAK, AK 99678
SEAN CARLOS, BOX 552, DILLINGHAM, AK 99576
ADAM CHYTHLOOK, BOX 2815, SOLDOTNA, AK 99669
CRAIG CHYTHLOOK, 3020 MOOSE MT RD, FAIRBANKS, AK 99709
GUSTY CHYTHLOOK, BOX 986, DILLINGHAM, AK 99576
JOSEPH CHYTHLOOK, BOX 692, DILLINGHAM, AK 99576
MOLLY CHYTHLOOK, BOX 692, DILLINGHAM, AK 99576
ROBIN CHYTHLOOK, BOX 678, DILLINGHAM, AK 99576
DAVID CLEVELAND, BOX 4074, TWIN HILLS, AK 99576
BENJAMIN COOPCHIAK, BOX 94, TOGIAK, AK 99678
BENJAMIN COOPCHIAK, BOX 251, TOGIAK, AK 99678
BOBBY COOPCHIAK, BOX 181, TOGIAK, AK 99678
ERIC COOPCHIAK, BOX 41, TOGIAK, AK 99678
JIMMY COOPCHIAK, BOX 187, TOGIAK, AK 99678
KATHY COOPCHIAK, BOX 94, TOGIAK, AK 99678
LOUISE COOPCHIAK, BOX 317, TOGIAK, AK 99678
MARGIE COOPCHIAK, BOX 222, TOGIAK, AK 99678
RICHARD COOPCHIAK, BOX 51, TOGIAK, AK 99678
TEDDY COOPCHIAK, BOX 84, TOGIAK, AK 99678
THOMAS COOPCHIAK, BOX 243, TOGIAK, AK 99678
DAVID COUPCHIAK, BOX 101, TOGIAK, AK 99678
MICHAEL COUPCHIAK, BOX 134, TOGIAK, AK 99678
HELEN COX, 3711 CASPER CT #2, ANCHORAGE, AK 99502
MMERCE DEPARTMENT OF CO, BOX 110802, JUNEAU, AK 99811
MMERCE DEPARTMENT OF CO, BOX 110802, JUNEAU, AK 99811
BEN DOCK, 12531 HACE STREET, ANCHORAGE, AK 99515
FRANCES DOCK, BOX 203, TOGIAK, AK 99678
HENRY DOCK, BOX 215, KIPNUK, AK 99614

HERRING SPAWN ON KELP—HAND PICK

MINNIE DOCK, BOX 215, KIPNUK, AK 99614

THOMAS DOCK, BOX 203, TOGIAK, AK 99678

JONATHAN DYASUK, BOX 1266, DILLINGHAM, AK 99576

LOUIE DYASUK, BOX 152, TOGIAK, AK 99678

SAMSON DYASUK, BOX 12, TOGIAK, AK 99678

EMMA ECHUCK, BOX 287, TOGIAK, AK 99678

WILLIE ECHUCK, BOX 271, TOGIAK, AK 99678

DOMINICK EKAMRAK, BOX 51101, AKIACHAK, AK 99551

PETER ETUCKMELRA, BOX 64, MANOKOTAK, AK 99628

DANIEL FARREN, 497 WESTWOOD AVE, HOMER, AK 99603

KEITH FAYER, BOX 182, TOGIAK, AK 99678

RODGER FELTON, 323 171ST AVE NE, SNOHOMISH, WA 98290

JOSE FLORES, BOX 153, TOGIAK, AK 99678

DAVID FORBES, BOX 141, TOGIAK, AK 99678

ARLENE FOX, BOX 225, TOGIAK, AK 99678

LEROY FOX, BOX 136, TOGIAK, AK 99678

MARTHA FOX, BOX 136, TOGIAK, AK 99678

ARLINE FRANKLIN, BOX 84, MANOKOTAK, AK 99628

RAYMOND FRANKLIN, BOX 84, MANOKOTAK, AK 99628

PAUL FRIIS.MIKKELSEN, BOX 276, DILLINGHAM, AK 99576

ADRIAN FROST, BOX 229, TOGIAK, AK 99678

DOUGLAS GAMECHUK, BOX 268, TOGIAK, AK 99678

JOHN GAMECHUK, BOX 66, MANOKOTAK, AK 99628

IRENE GAMECHUK.OLES, BOX 76, MANOKOTAK, AK 99628

CHRISTIAN GLOKO, BOX 7, MANOKOTAK, AK 99628

FRANK GLOKO, BOX 52, MANOKOTAK, AK 99628

LOUISE GLOKO, BOX 52, MANOKOTAK, AK 99628

NORMAN GLOKO, BOX 71, MANOKOTAK, AK 99628

ALFRED GOSUK, BOX 261, TOGIAK, AK 99678

ANNIE GOSUK, BOX 73, TOGIAK, AK 99678

ERIC GOSUK, BOX 21, TOGIAK, AK 99678

RODNEY GOSUK, BOX 237, TOGIAK, AK 99678

SAM GOSUK, BOX 177, TOGIAK, AK 99678

STEVEN GOSUK, BOX 21, TOGIAK, AK 99678

NATHANIEL GREEN, BOX 204, TOGIAK, AK 99678

DOROTHY GREENLEY, 7101 WEIMER RD #29, ANCHORAGE, AK 99502

JOHNNY GREENLEY, BOX 295, TOGIAK, AK 99678

ROBERT GREENLEY, BOX 173, TOGIAK, AK 99678

JOHN GUST, BOX 231, TOGIAK, AK 99678

ROBERT HANSEN, BOX TWA, TWIN HILLS, AK 99576

KEVIN HARLESS, BOX 98, TOGIAK, AK 99678

PETER HEYANO, BOX 730, DILLINGHAM, AK 99576

COLYNN ISAACSON, BOX 157, TOGIAK, AK 99678

DONALD ISAACSON, BOX 157, TOGIAK, AK 99678

MARYANNE ISAACSON, BOX 157, TOGIAK, AK 99678

PETER ISAACSON, BOX 157, TOGIAK, AK 99678

CARL ITUMULRIA, BOX 55, MANOKOTAK, AK 99628

ANDREW JORDAN, BOX 98, MANOKOTAK, AK 99628

HENRY KANULIE, BOX 61, TOGIAK, AK 99678

J.P KANULIE, 12431 HACE ST, ANCHORAGE, AK 99515

JACK KANULIE, 5700 LAKE OTIS PARKWAY #D76, ANCHORAGE, AK 99507

MAYA KANULIE, BOX 284, TOGIAK, AK 99678

KAREN KASAK, BOX 246, TOGIAK, AK 99678

LEO KASAK, BOX 301, TOGIAK, AK 99678

NORMAN KASAK, BOX 228, TOGIAK, AK 99678

ROY KASAK, BOX 1507, DILLINGHAM, AK 99576

LAVERN KATCHATAG, BOX 247, TOGIAK, AK 99678

EVAN KINIKALK, BOX 11, TOGIAK, AK 99678

SAMSON KOHUK, BOX 253, TOGIAK, AK 99678

STEPAN KOHUK, BOX 253, TOGIAK, AK 99678

NORTON KONUKPEOK, BOX 172, NEW STUYAHOK, AK 99636

VAMREGAIL KONUKPEOK.ALAKAY, BOX 27, TOGIAK, AK 99678

ANECIA KRITZ, BOX 83, TOGIAK, AK 99678

KRISTY KRITZ, BOX 245, DILLINGHAM, AK 99576

MOSES KRITZ, BOX 83, TOGIAK, AK 99678

ALBERT KVAMME, BOX 291, TOGIAK, AK 99678

MIRTH KVAMME, BOX 277, TOGIAK, AK 99678

DANIEL LAYLAND, BOX 531, HOMER, AK 99603

ALICE LOCKUK, BOX 82, TOGIAK, AK 99678

EPHRAIM LOCKUK, 337 E 4TH APT 312, ANCHORAGE, AK 99501

HERBERT LOCKUK, BOX 194, TOGIAK, AK 99678

PATRICK LOCKUK, BOX 292, TOGIAK, AK 99678

PETER LOCKUK, BOX 88, TOGIAK, AK 99678

ANDREA LOGUSAK, BOX 301, TOGIAK, AK 99678

EVAN LOGUSAK, BOX 216, TOGIAK, AK 99678

FRANK LOGUSAK, BOX 278, TOGIAK, AK 99678

JUNE LOGUSAK, BOX 216, TOGIAK, AK 99678

ERIC LOMACK, BOX 190, MANOKOTAK, AK 99628

MICKEY LOPEZ, BOX 28, DILLINGHAM, AK 99576

MORRIS LOPEZ, BOX 906, DILLINGHAM, AK 99576

ROSA LUHRS, 3922 DANDILION WINE CIR, ANCHORAGE, AK 99507

PAUL MARKOFF, BOX 134, TOGIAK, AK 99678

CLARA MARTIN, BOX 242, TOGIAK, AK 99678

MAX MARTIN, BOX 1038, DILLINGHAM, AK 99576

BERT MAUD, BOX 67, MANOKOTAK, AK 99628

GARY MICHEALS, BOX 5041, BELLINGHAM, WA 98227

BARBARA MOORE, BOX 88, MANOKOTAK, AK 99628

EVON MOORE, BOX 153, MANOKOTAK, AK 99628

HARRY MOORE, BOX 246, TOGIAK, AK 99678

LESTER MOORE, BOX 88, MANOKOTAK, AK 99628

RAYMOND MOORE, BOX TWA, DILLINGHAM, AK 99576

ANUSKA NANALOOK, BOX 12, MANOKOTAK, AK 99628

LEROY NANALOOK, BOX 41, TOGIAK, AK 99678

SHARON NANALOOK, BOX 71, MANOKOTAK, AK 99628

SIDNEY NELSON, 35577 460TH AVE, WINDOM, MN 56101

DARLENE NICHOLAI, BOX 87, TOGIAK, AK 99678

GARY NICHOLAI, BOX 87, TOGIAK, AK 99678

RITA NICHOLAI, BOX 87, TOGIAK, AK 99678

ROBERT NICHOLAI, BOX 87, TOGIAK, AK 99678

ROBERTA NICHOLAI, BOX 87, TOGIAK, AK 99678

CHRIS NICK, BOX 308, TOGIAK, AK 99678

EDWARD NICK, BOX 110, MANOKOTAK, AK 99628

GEORGE NICK, BOX 186, TOGIAK, AK 99678

JOHN NICK, BOX 124, TOGIAK, AK 99678

LLOYD NICK, BOX 252, TOGIAK, AK 99678

LUCY NICK, BOX 53, TOGIAK, AK 99678

MOSES NICK, BOX 26, TOGIAK, AK 99678

RHONDA NICK, BOX 110, MANOKOTAK, AK 99628

SOPHIE NICK, BOX 124, TOGIAK, AK 99678

MATHIAS OCONNELL, BOX 331, DILLINGHAM, AK 99576

FANNY PARKER, BOX 191, TOGIAK, AK 99678

JOHN PARKER, BOX 191, TOGIAK, AK 99678

DANIEL PASQUARIELLO, BOX 1354, DILLINGHAM, AK 99576

SUSAN PASQUARIELLO, BOX 1354, DILLINGHAM, AK 99576

AGNES PAUK, BOX 36, MANOKOTAK, AK 99628

BRETT PAUK, BOX 74, TOGIAK, AK 99678

DAN PAUK, BOX 82, MANOKOTAK, AK 99628

ERNEST PAUK, BOX 192, MANOKOTAK, AK 99628

JEFFREY PAUK, BOX 354, TOGIAK, AK 99678

NATALIA PAUK, BOX 82, MANOKOTAK, AK 99628

TEODORO PAUK, BOX 282, TOGIAK, AK 99678

WILLIAM PAUK, BOX 36, MANOKOTAK, AK 99628

JOEY PAVIAN, BOX 56, TOGIAK, AK 99678

SAMUEL PAVIAN, BOX 208, TOGIAK, AK 99678

CONNIE PEARSON, BOX 512, DILLINGHAM, AK 99576

DAN PEARSON, BOX 512, DILLINGHAM, AK 99576

ISSAC PEARSON, 2512 W 67TH AVE #2, ANCHORAGE, AK 99502

MAXINE PEARSON, 1800 HIGHLAND RD, WALLA WALLA, WA 99362

DEAN PEPER, 3408 ROCKEFELLER AVE, EVERETT, WA 98201

ROY PETERSEN, BOX 31, TOGIAK, AK 99678

HERRING SPAWN ON KELP

GEORGE PLEASANT, BOX 1174, DILLINGHAM, AK 99576
LAURA PLEASANT, BOX TWA, TWIN HILLS, AK 99576
ANTHONY POULSEN, BOX 154, TOGIAK, AK 99678
ROBERT PRITCHARD, BOX 1249, DILLINGHAM, AK 99576
LAVERNA RENFROE, 4904 DE ARMOUN RD, ANCHORAGE, AK 99515
ADOLPH ROEHL, BOX 104, DILLINGHAM, AK 99576
JUDITH RUNYON, BOX 874781, WASILLA, AK 99687
HUGH SCHROEDER, BOX 402, DILLINGHAM, AK 99576
WILBUR SHARP, BOX TWA, TWIN HILLS, AK 99576
BRUCE SKOLNICK, 145 S BOUNDARY ST, SOLDOTNA, AK 99669
BESSIE SMITH, BOX 126, TOGIAK, AK 99678
GEORGE SMITH, #9 2ND ST, TOGIAK, AK 99678
BENJAMIN SNYDER, BOX 44, TOGIAK, AK 99678
JACK SNYDER, BOX 4021, TWIN HILLS, AK 99576
MARIE SNYDER, BOX 45, TOGIAK, AK 99678
WILLIAM SNYDER, BOX 45, TOGIAK, AK 99678
RALPH SORENSEN, BOX 173, DILLINGHAM, AK 99576
LESLIE STAMBAUGH, BOX 604, NAKNEK, AK 99633
DAVID STOUT, 1321 W 80TH AVE, ANCHORAGE, AK 99518
JOHN SUTTON, BOX 52, TOGIAK, AK 99678
ANDREW THOMAS, 2850 JANEL AVE, NORTH POLE, AK 99705
GEORGE THOMAS, 205 E 12TH ST #5, ANCHORAGE, AK 99501
DARRYL THOMPSON, BOX 263, TOGIAK, AK 99678
ESTHER THOMPSON, BOX 263, TOGIAK, AK 99678
JAMES TIKIUN, BOX 131, NUNAPITCHUK, AK 99641
BENJAMIN TINKER, BOX 61, ALEKNAGIK, AK 99555
NICHOLAS TINKER, BOX 26, ALEKNAGIK, AK 99555
NINA TINKER, BOX 26, ALEKNAGIK, AK 99555
SALLY TINKER, BOX 806, DILLINGHAM, AK 99576
THOMAS TINKER, BOX 26, ALEKNAGIK, AK 99555
ANTONE TOGIAK, 1540 RUSSIAN JACK DR #37, ANCHORAGE, AK 99508
DANNY TOGIAK, BOX 192, ALEKNAGIK, AK 99555
DOLLY TOGIAK, BOX 192, ALEKNAGIK, AK 99555
INA TOGIAK, BOX 232, TOGIAK, AK 99678
PETER TOGIAK, BOX 235, TOGIAK, AK 99678
RICHARD TOGIAK, BOX 232, TOGIAK, AK 99678
BILLY TOMMY, BOX 34, TOGIAK, AK 99678
DENNIS TOMMY, BOX TWA, TOGIAK, AK 99678
PETER TOMMY, BOX 34, TOGIAK, AK 99678
ANECIA TOYUKAK, BOX 22, MANOKOTAK, AK 99628
BESSIE TOYUKAK, BOX 30, MANOKOTAK, AK 99628
MIKE TOYUKAK, BOX 22, MANOKOTAK, AK 99628
MOSES TOYUKAK, BOX 30, MANOKOTAK, AK 99628
MICHAEL TREESH, BOX 3491, HOMER, AK 99603
DAVID TUGATUK, BOX 37, MANOKOTAK, AK 99628
WASSILLIE TUGATUK, BOX 189, MANOKOTAK, AK 99628
WASSILLIE TUGATUK, BOX 65, MANOKOTAK, AK 99628
WALTER TUKAYA, BOX 158, TOGIAK, AK 99678
CHRISTOPHER WASSILLIE, BOX 28, TOGIAK, AK 99678
COLTEN WASSILLIE, BOX 217, TOGIAK, AK 99678
ERNEST WASSILLIE, BOX 168, TOGIAK, AK 99678
EVA WASSILLIE, BOX 42, TOGIAK, AK 99678
EVAN WASSILLIE, BOX 42, TOGIAK, AK 99678
JONATHAN WASSILLIE, BOX 217, TOGIAK, AK 99678
LENNY WASSILLIE, BOX 202, TOGIAK, AK 99678
NATHAN WASSILLIE, BOX 308, CHEVAK, AK 99563
ROGER WASSILLIE, BOX 287, TOGIAK, AK 99678
JOHN WESTCOAST, GEN DEL, KENAI, AK 99611
SCOTT WHITE, 5929 10TH ST, ZEPHYRHILLS, FL 33542
ELENA WHYMN, BOX 14, TOGIAK, AK 99678
FREDERICK WHYMN, BOX 14, TOGIAK, AK 99678
WASSILLIE WHYMN, BOX 14, TOGIAK, AK 99678
WASSILLIE WHYMN, BOX 14, TOGIAK, AK 99678
DONALD WINKELMAN, N 3158 CARDINAL RIDGE LN, MERRILL, WI 54452
TOM WOLLAN, BOX 1198, DILLINGHAM, AK 99576
EVELYN YANEZ, BOX 22, TOGIAK, AK 99678

FRANCISCA YANEZ, 2116 FAIRBANKS ST #8, ANCHORAGE, AK 99503
JOSE YANEZ, 6281 GROSS DR, ANCHORAGE, AK 99507
MERCEDES YANEZ, 6281 GROSS DR, ANCHORAGE, AK 99507

HERRING SPAWN ON KELP, POUND, NORTHERN SOUTHEAST

JASPER ALLBRETT, BOX 2223, SITKA, AK 99835
THERESA ALLEN.OLSON, 3009 HALIBUT POINT RD, SITKA, AK 99835
JASON ANDERSEN, BOX 99, SITKA, AK 99835
DONNA ANDERSON, 2420 6TH AVE, KETCHIKAN, AK 99901
KEIRAN BANGS, BOX 26, PETERSBURG, AK 99833
DALE BARTELDS, 301 WORTMAN LP, SITKA, AK 99835
MICHAEL BELL, BOX 849, CRAIG, AK 99921
AARON BISSON, 2633 GLENMORE ST, FERNDALE, WA 98248
GERALD BRAGER, 110 JARVIS ST, SITKA, AK 99835
JOHN BRUCE, BOX 104, ELK, CA 95432
MATTHEW BRYNER, BOX 1642, PETERSBURG, AK 99833
ARLENE CARLE, BOX 32, HYDABURG, AK 99922
CAYDEN CARLE, BOX 1, HYDABURG, AK 99922
JAN CARLE, BOX 1, HYDABURG, AK 99922
JOHN CARLE, BOX 1, HYDABURG, AK 99922
MATTHEW CARLE, BOX 32, HYDABURG, AK 99922
DANIEL CASTLE, 4430 S TONGASS HWY, KETCHIKAN, AK 99901
JENNIFER CASTLE, 4430 S TONGASS AVE, KETCHIKAN, AK 99901
CHARLES CHRISTENSEN, BOX 824, PETERSBURG, AK 99833
OLIVER CHRISTENSEN, BOX 1946, PETERSBURG, AK 99833
STEVEN DAVIS, BOX 1455, PETERSBURG, AK 99833
ARCHIE DEMMERT, BOX 223, KLAWOCK, AK 99925
BRENDA DEMMERT, 19425 27TH AVE NW, SHORELINE, WA 98177
LAWRENCE DEMMERT, 5775 SCHICKLES LN, BELLINGHAM, WA 98226
NICHOLAS DEMMERT, BOX 1132, CRAIG, AK 99921
TROY DENKINGER, 2221 HALIBUT POINT RD, SITKA, AK 99835
MMERCE DEPARTMENT OF CO, BOX 110802, JUNEAU, AK 99811
FORREST DODSON, 263 KATLIAN, SITKA, AK 99835
KEN EICHNER, 5166 SHORELINE DR N, KETCHIKAN, AK 99901
GEORGE ELIASON, 105 SAND DOLLAR DR, SITKA, AK 99835
JORGEN ELIASON, 131 RIGGS RD, SITKA, AK 99835
RICHARD ELIASON, 8475 E GOLD BULLION BLVD, PALMER, AK 99645
ROCKY ERTZBERGER, BOX 298706, WASILLA, AK 99629
BRANNON FINNEY, BOX 1755, PETERSBURG, AK 99833
ERIC GRUNDBERG, BOX 2193, PETERSBURG, AK 99833
MARK HAMMER, BOX 582, COUPEVILLE, WA 98239
BRADLEY HAYNES, 243 W MATTLE RD, KETCHIKAN, AK 99901
GARY HAYNES, 625 SUNSET DR, KETCHIKAN, AK 99901
EDMOND HISAW, BOX 1179, TENINO, WA 98589
CHRIS HOLM, 54 N VALLEY RD, NASELLE, WA 98638
MARY HOLZMAN, BOX 94, SONOITA, AZ 85637
ROGER INGMAN, BOX 1155, SITKA, AK 99835
DAVID JACOBS, 17303 314TH AVE NE, DUVALL, WA 98019
NEIL JENNY, BOX 796, PETERSBURG, AK 99833
JAMES JENSEN, BOX 402, PETERSBURG, AK 99833
JEREMY JENSEN, 2900 JACKSON RD, JUNEAU, AK 99801
MARK JENSEN, BOX 457, PETERSBURG, AK 99833
CYNTHIA JOHANSON, BOX 276, KLAWOCK, AK 99925
JOHN JOHANSON, BOX 276, KLAWOCK, AK 99925
RUDOLPH JOHANSON, 411 FRONT ST, KETCHIKAN, AK 99901
RUDY JOHANSON, BOX 5120, KETCHIKAN, AK 99901
LEROY JOHNS, BOX 1126, SISTERS, OR 97759
MARTIN JOHNSON, 1807 SAWMILL CREEK, SITKA, AK 99835
ANDREW KALK, 415 COLEMAN ST, JUNEAU, AK 99801
DONALD KALK, BOX EXI, JUNEAU, AK 99850
BRIAN KANDOLL, BOX 1363, PETERSBURG, AK 99833
MATTHEW KANDOLL, BOX 2091, PETERSBURG, AK 99833
SCOT KANDOLL, BOX 2154, PETERSBURG, AK 99833
MATTHEW KINNEY, 103 KRAMER AVE, SITKA, AK 99835
SIDNEY KINNEY, 103 KRAMER AVE, SITKA, AK 99835

HERRING SPAWN ON KELP

KERRY KIRKPATRICK, 14329 OTTER WAY, JUNEAU, AK 99801
KURT KVERNVIK, BOX 1081, PETERSBURG, AK 99833
LAUCHLIN LEACH, 2318 NE 105TH ST, SEATTLE, WA 98125
SHANE LOHR, BOX 765, PETERSBURG, AK 99833
KENNETH MADSEN, BOX 918, PETERSBURG, AK 99833
DONNA MARSH, BOX 1421, PETERSBURG, AK 99833
EVAN MARSH, BOX 1421, PETERSBURG, AK 99833
KIRT MARSH, BOX 1421, PETERSBURG, AK 99833
OTIS MARSH, BOX 606, PETERSBURG, AK 99833
RYAN MARSH, 10137 W VIENNA AVE, MILWAUKEE, WI 53222
LAURA MASTRELLA, BOX 1295, HAINES, AK 99827
SIGURD MATHISEN, BOX 1460, PETERSBURG, AK 99833
THOMAS MCALLISTER, 9156 N DOUGLAS HWY, JUNEAU, AK 99802
RODERICK MCCAY, BOX 161, PETERSBURG, AK 99833
WILLIAM MENISH, BOX 877, PETERSBURG, AK 99833
NIKOULAS NEBL, 3828 EVERGREEN AVE, KETCHIKAN, AK 99901
MARK NUGENT, BOX 5382, KETCHIKAN, AK 99901
CHARLES OLSON, 3009 HALIBUT POINT RD, SITKA, AK 99835
DENNIS ONEIL, BOX 1083, PETERSBURG, AK 99833
MEGAN ONEIL, BOX 4, PETERSBURG, AK 99833
KELLY PELLETT, BOX 614, SITKA, AK 99835
MICHAEL PILLING, 14329 OTTER WAY, JUNEAU, AK 99801
CHRISTOPHER PONTS, 3613 CYPRESS WAY, SANTA ROSA, CA 95405
JAMES PORTER, BOX 957, WARD COVE, AK 99928
JAMES QUIGLEY, BOX 80, CRAIG, AK 99921
JOEL RANDRUP, BOX 1231, PETERSBURG, AK 99833
MICHAEL ROMINE, 301 WACHUSETTES ST, SITKA, AK 99835
JOSEPH ROTH, 16169 WATERFALL RD, KETCHIKAN, AK 99901
MARK SALDI, BOX 287, SKAGWAY, AK 99840
TONY SANDERSON, BOX 78, HYDABURG, AK 99922
ANDREW SCUDDER, 531 N 28TH ST, BOISE, ID 83702
BONNIE SCUDDER, 266 S MOBLEY LN, BOISE, ID 83712
BRADFORD SCUDDER, 266 S MOBLEY LN, BOISE, ID 83712
CHARLES SKEEK, BOX 742, PETERSBURG, AK 99833
GEORGE SKEEK, BOX 334, PETERSBURG, AK 99833
KIMBERLY SVENSON, 104 SHARON DR, SITKA, AK 99835
MARTIN SVENSON, 14861 N TONGASS, KETCHIKAN, AK 99901
MIKE SVENSON, 104 SHARON DR, SITKA, AK 99835
ADAM SWANSON, BOX 2151, PETERSBURG, AK 99833
JOHN SWANSON, BOX 1546, PETERSBURG, AK 99833
ROBERT SWANSON, BOX 924, PETERSBURG, AK 99833
TROY THOMASSEN, BOX 152, PETERSBURG, AK 99833
JAMES TISSYCHY, 554 EAST ST, KETCHIKAN, AK 99901
JAMES VAUGHAN, BOX 770, CRAIG, AK 99921
KELVIN VAUGHAN, BOX 1256, CRAIG, AK 99921
JON W.B.RANDRUP, BOX 44, PETERSBURG, AK 99833
LANCE WATKINS, 537 S 39TH ST, BELLINGHAM, WA 98229
LUKE WHITETHORN, BOX 1716, PETERSBURG, AK 99833
RACHEL WILLIAMS, 411 FRONT ST, KETCHIKAN, AK 99901
JOE WILLIS, BOX 43, PETERSBURG, AK 99833
KARSTEN WOOD, BOX 2195, PETERSBURG, AK 99833

HERRING SPAWN ON KELP, POUND, SOUTHERN SOUTHEAST

DONNA ANDERSON, 2420 6TH AVE, KETCHIKAN, AK 99901
BARBI ARMSTRONG, BOX 322, CRAIG, AK 99921
KEIRAN BANGS, BOX 26, PETERSBURG, AK 99833
JAMES BARNES, BOX 45, CRAIG, AK 99921
MICHAEL BELL, BOX 849, CRAIG, AK 99921
JONELLE BJORGE, BOX 664, WRANGELL, AK 99929
DONALD BORDERS, BOX 1423, WARD COVE, AK 99928
LAURIE BRASSFIELD, 3314 226TH PL SW, BRIER, WA 98036
LOGAN BROOKER, 911 2ND ST, DOUGLAS, AK 99824
MATTHEW BRYNER, BOX 1642, PETERSBURG, AK 99833
PETE BURR, BOX 23129, KETCHIKAN, AK 99901

ARLENE CARLE, BOX 32, HYDABURG, AK 99922
CAYDEN CARLE, BOX 1, HYDABURG, AK 99922
ELIZABETH CARLE, BOX 276, KLAWOCK, AK 99925
JADE CARLE, BOX 1, HYDABURG, AK 99922
JAN CARLE, BOX 1, HYDABURG, AK 99922
JOHN CARLE, BOX 1, HYDABURG, AK 99922
MATTHEW CARLE, BOX 32, HYDABURG, AK 99922
ROBERT CARLE, BOX 1253, CRAIG, AK 99921
TAAN CARLE, BOX 1, HYDABURG, AK 99922
LYNETTE CARLSON, BOX 19214, THORNE BAY, AK 99919
DANIEL CASTLE, 4430 S TONGASS HWY, KETCHIKAN, AK 99901
JOHN CHARLES, BOX 87, KLAWOCK, AK 99925
JULIANNE CONNELLY, 22717 LAKEVIEW DR APT A5, MOUNTLAKE, WA 98043
MATTHEW CONNELLY, 1503 S LAKE STICKNEY DR, LYNNWOOD, WA 98087
ALAN COUSTE, 916 1/2 W 7TH ST, PORT ANGELES, WA 98363
JEROME DAHL, BOX 1275, PETERSBURG, AK 99833
ARCHIE DEMMERT, BOX 223, KLAWOCK, AK 99925
CRAIG DEMMERT, 1347 FAIRY CHASM RD, KETCHIKAN, AK 99901
CURTIS DEMMERT, BOX 223, KLAWOCK, AK 99925
DIANNE DEMMERT, 303 SPRUCE ST, KETCHIKAN, AK 99901
GEORGE DEMMERT, 303 SPRUCE ST, KETCHIKAN, AK 99901
JOSEPH DEMMERT, 2724 4TH AVE, KETCHIKAN, AK 99901
JOSEPH DEMMERT, 7802 209TH ST SW, EDMONDS, WA 98026
KARL DEMMERT, BOX 556, CRAIG, AK 99921
LAWRENCE DEMMERT, 5775 SCHICKLES LN, BELLINGHAM, WA 98226
LAWRENCE DEMMERT, 5775 SCHICKLES LN, BELLINGHAM, WA 98226
LINDA DEMMERT, 10645 MISTY LN, JUNEAU, AK 99801
MICHAEL DEMMERT, BOX 391, CRAIG, AK 99921
NICHOLAS DEMMERT, BOX 1132, CRAIG, AK 99921
NICOLE DEMMERT, BOX 180, KLAWOCK, AK 99925
PAULETTE DEMMERT, BOX 133, CRAIG, AK 99921
ROSEANN DEMMERT, BOX 223, KLAWOCK, AK 99925
MMERCE DEPARTMENT OF CO, BOX 110802, JUNEAU, AK 99811
JESS DILTS, BOX 22, HYDABURG, AK 99922
ALISSA DURGAN, BOX 340, CRAIG, AK 99921
JUNE DURGAN, BOX 340, CRAIG, AK 99921
RONALD DURGAN, BOX 340, CRAIG, AK 99921
ROBERT EDENSHAW, BOX 373, HYDABURG, AK 99922
SIDNEY EDENSHAW, BOX 352, HYDABURG, AK 99922
VIOLET EDENSHAW, BOX 73, HYDABURG, AK 99922
KEN EICHNER, 5166 SHORELINE DR N, KETCHIKAN, AK 99901
LYNORA EICHNER, 5166 SHORELINE DR, KETCHIKAN, AK 99901
MITCHELL EIDE, BOX 981, PETERSBURG, AK 99833
AMOS ELIAS, 152 MIDDLEPOINT RD, PORT TOWNSEND, WA 98368
JEFF ERICKSON, BOX 53, PETERSBURG, AK 99833
MICHAEL ERICSON, 1615 ANNIE ST, DALY CITY, CA 94014
ROCKY ERTZBERGER, BOX 298706, WASILLA, AK 99629
MARY EVENS, BOX 886, PETERSBURG, AK 99833
GERALD GAMBLE, 3602 ENTRADA DR NE, OLYMPIA, WA 98506
JULIETTE GARDNER, BOX 23407, KETCHIKAN, AK 99901
PATRICIA GARDNER, BOX 1, CRAIG, AK 99921
PATRICK GARDNER, BOX 1, CRAIG, AK 99921
SHAWN GIBBS, BOX 584, CRAIG, AK 99921
BRIAN GILSON, 3760 ALASKA AVE, KETCHIKAN, AK 99901
ERIC GRUNDBERG, BOX 2193, PETERSBURG, AK 99833
FRED HAMILTON, BOX 661, CRAIG, AK 99921
STEVEN HANSEN, BOX 250, RIVERSIDE, WA 98849
BILLIE HANSON, 8828 GAIL AVE, JUNEAU, AK 99801
BRADLEY HAYNES, 243 W MATTLE RD, KETCHIKAN, AK 99901
GARY HAYNES, 625 SUNSET DR, KETCHIKAN, AK 99901
HAROLD HAYNES, 148 MATTLE RD, KETCHIKAN, AK 99901
GERARD HELGESEN, BOX 34, HYDABURG, AK 99922
PAUL HENRY, 5137 SHORELINE DR, KETCHIKAN, AK 99901
RONALD HENRY, 2417 TONGASS AVE #111-141, KETCHIKAN, AK 99901
PATRICIA HIATT, BOX 6277, KETCHIKAN, AK 99901

HERRING SPAWN ON KELP

BRAYDEN HISAW, BOX 1179, TENINO, WA 98589
EDMOND HISAW, BOX 1179, TENINO, WA 98589
ROSS HOFACRE, BOX 1205, PETERSBURG, AK 99833
ALBERT HOFSTAD, BOX 1030, PETERSBURG, AK 99833
MARK HOFSTAD, BOX 1397, PETERSBURG, AK 99833
CHRIS HOLM, 54 N VALLEY RD, NASELLE, WA 98638
ROGER INGMAN, BOX 1155, SITKA, AK 99835
CLARENCE JACKSON, BOX 301, KAKE, AK 99830
CLARENCE JACKSON, ONE SEA ALASKA PLAZA #300, JUNEAU, AK 99801
GEORGE JACKSON, BOX 6247, SITKA, AK 99835
NEIL JENNY, BOX 796, PETERSBURG, AK 99833
MARK JENSEN, BOX 457, PETERSBURG, AK 99833
SAMUEL JENSEN, BOX 681, PETERSBURG, AK 99833
KURT JILLSON, BOX 9448, KETCHIKAN, AK 99901
CYNTHIA JOHANSON, BOX 276, KLAWOCK, AK 99925
JOHN JOHANSON, BOX 276, KLAWOCK, AK 99925
JORDAN JOHANSON, BOX 276, KLAWOCK, AK 99925
LUCAS JOHANSON, 3825 NE 155 PL #500, LAKE FOREST PARK, WA 98155
MARIE JOHANSON, 8320 5TH AVE NE, SEATTLE, WA 98115
RUDOLPH JOHANSON, 411 FRONT ST, KETCHIKAN, AK 99901
RUDY JOHANSON, BOX 5120, KETCHIKAN, AK 99901
LEROY JOHNS, BOX 1126, SISTERS, OR 97759
STEVEN JOHNS, 1321 CLEVELAND ST, MOUNT VERNON, WA 98273
DONALD KALK, BOX EXI, JUNEAU, AK 99850
BRIAN KANDOLL, BOX 1363, PETERSBURG, AK 99833
MATTHEW KANDOLL, BOX 2091, PETERSBURG, AK 99833
SCOT KANDOLL, BOX 2154, PETERSBURG, AK 99833
LEONARD KATO, BOX 43, KLAWOCK, AK 99925
ROSE KATO, BOX 35, KLAWOCK, AK 99925
KATHY KATO.YATES, BOX 26, KLAWOCK, AK 99925
WILLIAM KEMPERMAN, BOX 19265, THORNE BAY, AK 99919
GREGORY KENDALL, BOX 535, PETERSBURG, AK 99833
KERRY KIRKPATRICK, 14329 OTTER WAY, JUNEAU, AK 99801
KURT KVERNVIK, BOX 1081, PETERSBURG, AK 99833
LAUCHLIN LEACH, 2318 NE 105TH ST, SEATTLE, WA 98125
SHANE LOHR, BOX 765, PETERSBURG, AK 99833
LORENA MACASAET, 918 NW SYCAMORE AVE APT 1, CORVALLIS, OR 97330
DANIEL MAJORS, BOX 5358, KETCHIKAN, AK 99901
STEVEN MANOS, 5224 NE VARCO RD, TACOMA, WA 98422
WILLIAM MANOS, 1566 KEKAULIKE AVE, KULA, HI 96790
BRUCE MARIFERN, BOX 917, PETERSBURG, AK 99833
DONNA MARSH, BOX 1421, PETERSBURG, AK 99833
KIRT MARSH, BOX 1421, PETERSBURG, AK 99833
OTIS MARSH, BOX 606, PETERSBURG, AK 99833
TOM MARSH, BOX 1708, PETERSBURG, AK 99833
NICHOLAS MARTIN, BOX 8312, KETCHIKAN, AK 99901
TYLER MARTIN, BOX 2033, PETERSBURG, AK 99833
MARTY MARTINEZ, BOX 513, METLAKATLA, AK 99926
DONALD MARVIN, BOX 42, KLAWOCK, AK 99925
SHELTON MAVES, BOX 117, CRAIG, AK 99921
ASHON MCCAY, BOX 2001, PETERSBURG, AK 99833
CALEY MCCAY, BOX 161, PETERSBURG, AK 99833
KAYIN MCCAY, BOX 161, PETERSBURG, AK 99833
RODERICK MCCAY, BOX 161, PETERSBURG, AK 99833
GEORGE MCNAMARA, BOX 360, CRAIG, AK 99921
CHRISTOPHER MILLER, BOX 854, PETERSBURG, AK 99833
REBECCA MOOTS, BOX 1291, CRAIG, AK 99921
JOSEPH MORAN, 930 13TH ST, BELLINGHAM, WA 98225
MELYSSA NAGAMINE, BOX 101, CRAIG, AK 99921
NIKOULAS NEBL, 3828 EVERGREEN AVE, KETCHIKAN, AK 99901
JOHN NELSON, 5785 S TONGASS, KETCHIKAN, AK 99901
BRIAN NEWMAN, BOX 893, PETERSBURG, AK 99833
MARK NUGENT, BOX 5382, KETCHIKAN, AK 99901
JARRED OLSON, BOX 1557, PETERSBURG, AK 99833
DENNIS ONEIL, BOX 1083, PETERSBURG, AK 99833
HEATHER ONEIL, BOX 1083, PETERSBURG, AK 99833

MEGAN ONEIL, BOX 4, PETERSBURG, AK 99833
SCOTT ONEIL, BOX 1455, PETERSBURG, AK 99833
DANA OSTROM, 12141 AVENIDA CONSENTIDO, SAN DIEGO, CA 92128
DREW PATTERSON, BOX 897, CRAIG, AK 99921
KATHY PEAVEY, BOX 442, CRAIG, AK 99921
STEVEN PEAVEY, BOX 101, CRAIG, AK 99921
JACK PERATROVICH, BOX 12, KLAWOCK, AK 99925
GEORGE PETERSON, 5785 S TONGASS, KETCHIKAN, AK 99901
BRYAN PHILBROOK, 1124 BLACK BEAR RD, KETCHIKAN, AK 99901
AARON PHILLIPS, BOX 624, PETERSBURG, AK 99833
JEB PHILLIPS, BOX 1253, PETERSBURG, AK 99833
DALE PIHLMAN, BOX 7814, KETCHIKAN, AK 99901
MICHAEL PILLING, 14329 OTTER WAY, JUNEAU, AK 99801
CHRISTOPHER PONTS, 3613 CYPRESS WAY, SANTA ROSA, CA 95405
ALISON QUIGLEY, BOX 80, CRAIG, AK 99921
JAMES QUIGLEY, BOX 80, CRAIG, AK 99921
JOEL RANDRUP, BOX 1231, PETERSBURG, AK 99833
RONALD RECORDS, BOX 1345, CRAIG, AK 99921
MICHAEL ROMINE, 301 WACHUSETTES ST, SITKA, AK 99835
JIMMIE ROSENBRUCH, 8174 KEEGAN STREET, JUNEAU, AK 99801
ADRIAN RUSCH.GUTHRI, BOX 23578, KETCHIKAN, AK 99901
MARK SALDI, BOX 287, SKAGWAY, AK 99840
TONY SANDERSON, BOX 78, HYDABURG, AK 99922
RONALD SCHARNS, BOX 432, PETERSBURG, AK 99833
ROBERT SCHWARTZ, BOX 1533, PETERSBURG, AK 99833
ANDREW SCUDDER, 531 N 28TH ST, BOISE, ID 83702
BRADFORD SCUDDER, 266 S MOBLEY LN, BOISE, ID 83712
MARLENE SHEPARD, BOX 360, CRAIG, AK 99921
BYRON SKINNA, BOX 308, KLAWOCK, AK 99925
BYRON SKINNA, BOX 74, KLAWOCK, AK 99925
WALTER STEVENS, BOX 151, WRANGELL, AK 99929
NAN STORY, 15071 LIZZIE LN, KETCHIKAN, AK 99901
JOSHUA STUBER, 6835 NE 153RD PL APT C101, KENMORE, WA 98028
KIMBERLY SVENSON, 104 SHARON DR, SITKA, AK 99835
MARTIN SVENSON, 14861 N TONGASS, KETCHIKAN, AK 99901
MICHAEL SVENSON, 104 SHARON DR, SITKA, AK 99835
MIKE SVENSON, 104 SHARON DR, SITKA, AK 99835
NELS SVENSON, 104 SHARON DR, SITKA, AK 99835
ADAM SWANSON, BOX 2151, PETERSBURG, AK 99833
JOHN SWANSON, BOX 1546, PETERSBURG, AK 99833
LEWELLYN SWANSON, BOX 536, PETERSBURG, AK 99833
LOGAN SWANSON, BOX 1546, PETERSBURG, AK 99833
ROBERT SWANSON, BOX 924, PETERSBURG, AK 99833
THOMAS SWANSON, 11354 DURLAND NE, SEATTLE, WA 98125
MICHAEL SYRON, 18066 8TH AVE NE, SHORELINE, WA 98155
ANTHONY TAIBER, BOX 1861, PETERSBURG, AK 99833
TYLER THAIN, BOX 2124, PETERSBURG, AK 99833
NYLE THOMAS, BOX 1744, PETERSBURG, AK 99833
R.CRAIG THOMAS, 3933 ALASKA AVE, KETCHIKAN, AK 99901
TROY THOMASSEN, BOX 152, PETERSBURG, AK 99833
DEREK THYNES, BOX 1624, PETERSBURG, AK 99833
KRISTOFFER THYNES, BOX 193, PETERSBURG, AK 99833
STEVEN THYNES, BOX 193, PETERSBURG, AK 99833
JAMES TISSYCHY, 554 EAST ST, KETCHIKAN, AK 99901
CARO TORGESSEN, 507 STEDMAN ST, KETCHIKAN, AK 99901
CHARLIE TRAYLOR, BOX 1381, WRANGELL, AK 99929
CHRISTIAN VAUGHAN, BOX 7621, KETCHIKAN, AK 99901
HOUSTON VAUGHAN, BOX 770, CRAIG, AK 99921
JACQUELINE VAUGHAN, BOX 770, CRAIG, AK 99921
JAMES VAUGHAN, BOX 770, CRAIG, AK 99921
KELVIN VAUGHAN, BOX 1256, CRAIG, AK 99921
JON W.B.RANDRUP, BOX 44, PETERSBURG, AK 99833
ELDON WALKER, 3848 MELROSE ST, JUNEAU, AK 99801
DREW WARE, BOX 1291, PETERSBURG, AK 99833
FRANK WARFEL, BOX 1512, WRANGELL, AK 99929
LANCE WATKINS, 537 S 39TH ST, BELLINGHAM, WA 98229

HERRING SPAWN ON KELP

JUALANI WEIMER, 6886 A LESLIE AVE, JUNEAU, AK 99801
DEBORAH WELKER, BOX 782, CRAIG, AK 99921
ROBERT WELKER, BOX 1247, FORKS, WA 98331
JEFFREY WHICKER, BOX 774, WARD COVE, AK 99928
RACHEL WILLIAMS, 411 FRONT ST, KETCHIKAN, AK 99901
JOE WILLIS, BOX 43, PETERSBURG, AK 99833
CHARLES WILLS, BOX 7554, KETCHIKAN, AK 99901
TITUS WINROD, BOX 1291, CRAIG, AK 99921
KARSTEN WOOD, BOX 2195, PETERSBURG, AK 99833
RANDALL WORTMAN, BOX 271, CRAIG, AK 99921
COLE YOUNG, BOX 922, PETERSBURG, AK 99833

HERRING SPAWN ON KELP, POUND, PRINCE WILLIAM SOUND

MATHEW BABIC, BOX 988, CORDOVA, AK 99574
MICHAEL BABIC, BOX 1853, CORDOVA, AK 99574
VICTORIA BAKER, BOX 600, CORDOVA, AK 99574
CHARLES BAUGHN, BOX 296, CORDOVA, AK 99574
LOUIS BEAUDRY, BOX 2410, MCCALL, ID 83638
DAVID BENTLEY, 39194 CONSER RD NE, ALBANY, OR 97321
LAURIE BERGER, 4230 WORONZOF DR UNIT D, ANCHORAGE, AK 99517
DENNIS BISHOP, BOX 6447, HALIBUT COVE, AK 99603
JOHN BOCCI, BOX 1312, CORDOVA, AK 99574
DENNIS BROWN, HC 60 BOX 226, COPPER CENTER, AK 99573
JAMES BROWN, 1341 OVERHILL DR, FAIRBANKS, AK 99709
JEANNINE BULLER, BOX 1051, CORDOVA, AK 99574
KIP CARROLL, BOX 1173, CORDOVA, AK 99574
RICHARD CASCIANO, BOX 584, CORDOVA, AK 99574
KENNETH CASTNER, BOX 558, HOMER, AK 99603
ELMER CHESHIER, BOX 2264, CORDOVA, AK 99574
LYNN COLE, BOX 910, SISTERS, OR 97759
RICHARD COLE, BOX 910, SISTERS, OR 97759
MARK CULLENBERG, BOX 870855, HOMER, AK 99603
STUART DEAL, 7314 11TH AVE NW, SEATTLE, WA 98117
JANEY DUNDAS, 1375 NE ROSEMONT ST, PRINEVILLE, OR 97754
ROBERT DUNDAS, 30845 WATERLOO RD, LEBANON, OR 97355
DEBORAH ECKLEY, BOX 1274, CORDOVA, AK 99574
ELLIAS ECKLEY, BOX 1274, CORDOVA, AK 99574
RICHARD ECKLEY, BOX 1274, CORDOVA, AK 99574
ROBERT ECKLEY, BOX 1274, CORDOVA, AK 99574
BRENDA EDENS, BOX 641, HOMER, AK 99603
DAVID EDENS, BOX 3456, HOMER, AK 99603
SUSAN ENTSMINGER, HC 72 BOX 800, TOK, AK 99780
KIM EWERS, 615 E WELLS FARGO DR, BROOKSIDE, UT 84782
MICHELE FIGGINS, 62490 ERICKSON RD, BEND, OR 97701
JOYCE FLEMING, 62211 POWELL BUTTE HWY, BEND, OR 97701
WALTER FLEMING, 62211 POWELL BUTTE HWY, BEND, OR 97701
ROBERT FULTZ, 17368 TOAKOANA DR, EAGLE RIVER, AK 99577
MARK GAGER, 130 HIBISCUS DR, PUNTA GORDA, FL 33950
LANNY GILLESPIE, BOX 2312, CORDOVA, AK 99574
JAMES GLENOVICH, 818 17TH ST, BELLINGHAM, WA 98225
CANDACE GREGORY, BOX 1273, CASCADE, ID 83611
MICHELLE HAHN, BOX 1052, CORDOVA, AK 99574
RONALD HAMES, 411 WALNUT ST #6320, GREEN COVE SPRINGS, FL 32043
TOM HENDERSON, BOX 505, KAKE, AK 99830
JAMES HERBERT, BOX 645, HOMER, AK 99603
CURTIS HERSCHLEB, BOX 1622, CORDOVA, AK 99574
JOHN HERSCHLEB, 440 E 56TH AVE #A, ANCHORAGE, AK 99518
KENT HERSCHLEB, 7536 SW 34TH AVE, PORTLAND, OR 97219
LEONARD HERZOG, 916 DELANEY ST, ANCHORAGE, AK 99501
JAMES HESTON, BOX 331, VALDEZ, AK 99686
DAVID HILLSTRAND, 4110 MAIN ST, HOMER, AK 99603
SHILA HOUGH, 3733 BEN WALTERS LN #2, HOMER, AK 99603
JACK HUGHES, BOX 1401, CRESTED BUTTE, CO 81224
HEATHER ISLEIB, 3202 SE 62ND, PORTLAND, OR 97206

JAMES JENSEN, BOX 402, PETERSBURG, AK 99833
RANDALL JOHNSON, 5575 E ROSEBUD CT, WASILLA, AK 99654
CYNTHIA JONES, BOX 1494, LONG BEACH, WA 98631
LISA JONES, 2660 SICILY DR, NEW SMYRNA BEACH, FL 32168
VICTOR JONES, BOX 1831, CORDOVA, AK 99574
WENDELL JONES, BOX 942, CORDOVA, AK 99574
PAUL JOVICK, BOX 1513, CORDOVA, AK 99574
PATRICIA KALLANDER, BOX 2272, CORDOVA, AK 99574
STEVEN KARABACH, 42465 DEER HEIGHTS DR N, DAVENPORT, WA 99122
SUSAN KELLEY, 350 E HYGRADE LN, WASILLA, AK 99654
MARK KING, BOX 965, CORDOVA, AK 99574
RITA KING, BOX 968, TEHACHAPI, CA 93581
SANDRA KING, BOX 965, CORDOVA, AK 99574
ROBERT KOPCHAK, BOX 1126, CORDOVA, AK 99574
SANDRA KYLE, BOX 256, WALLOWA, OR 97885
SCOTT LINDQUIST, BOX 770449, EAGLE RIVER, AK 99577
ANGELA LUCK, BOX 4997, KETCHUM, ID 83340
BENJAMIN LUCK, 605 BROWN AVE, FORT COLLINS, CO 90525
MATTHEW LUCK, BOX 4997, KETCHUM, ID 83340
KEVIN LUPTON, 440 W MEADOW, HAILEY, ID 83333
DANIEL MACDONALD, BOX 5993, BELLINGHAM, WA 98227
THOMAS MARKEY, 517 OVERLOOK CT, SUBLIMITY, OR 97385
CRAIG MATKIN, 2030 MARY ALLEN AVE, HOMER, AK 99603
RODERICK MCCAY, BOX 161, PETERSBURG, AK 99833
KRISTIN MCCUNE, BOX 1093, ENUMCLAW, WA 98022
JOSEPHINE MCLEAN, BOX 213, SELDOVIA, AK 99663
KELLY MCLEAN, 15201 POINT LOUISA RD, JUNEAU, AK 99801
KRISTI MCLEAN, BOX 213, SELDOVIA, AK 99663
THORNTON MCNEAL, BOX 4948, KETCHUM, ID 83340
D.MICHAEL MCNIVEN, BOX 27109, SEATTLE, WA 98165
MARK MEADOWS, 4894 WENDY LN, KELSEYVILLE, CA 95451
WILLIAM MENISH, BOX 877, PETERSBURG, AK 99833
GARY MULLEN, BOX 693, GLENNALLEN, AK 99588
MARK MUNRO, BOX 1971, HOMER, AK 99603
JAMES MYKLAND, BOX 1241, CORDOVA, AK 99574
CHRISTOPHER NERISON, 11021 E 23RD AVE, SPOKANE, WA 99206
MITCHELL NOWICKI, BOX 2232, CORDOVA, AK 99574
GARY OLSEN, 2215 BELAIR, ANCHORAGE, AK 99517
CHARLES OLSON, 3009 HALIBUT POINT RD, SITKA, AK 99835
NEAL OPPEN, BOX 3388, VALDEZ, AK 99686
MICHAEL PARKS, BOX 4332, HOMER, AK 99603
CAROL PECKHAM, 615 E WELLS FARGO DR, BROOKSIDE, UT 84782
THOMAS PETERSON, 10 OLD BRIGGS RD, LEVERETT, MA 1054
MICHAEL PHILLIPS, BOX 194, COPPER CENTER, AK 99573
ROBERT PUDWILL, BOX 1748, CORDOVA, AK 99574
SUSAN RAMLO, BOX 1659, KINGSTON, WA 98346
ROBERT REDMAYNE, 14443 NE 61ST ST, REDMOND, WA 98052
MONIKA REGHETTI, BOX 685, CORDOVA, AK 99574
PAUL REID, BOX 230085, ANCHORAGE, AK 99523
WILLIAM REID, BOX 1234, CORDOVA, AK 99574
JOHN RENNER, BOX 756, CORDOVA, AK 99574
DREWELLEN RENSCHLER, 18523 E PARADA CIR, RIO VERDE, AZ 85263
TIM RENSCHLER, 18523 E PARADA CIR, RIO VERDE, AZ 85263
GENE RILLING, 6314 SUMMERCREST DR, COLUMBIA, MD 21045
THOMAS ROSENTHAL, 1106 2ND ST #106, ENCINITAS, CA 92024
CHRISTOPHER SAAL, 3900 CLAY PRODUCTS DR, ANCHORAGE, AK 99517
RUTH.ANN SCHULTZ, BOX 640, CORDOVA, AK 99574
ELIZABETH SENEAR, BOX 762, CORDOVA, AK 99574
RONALD SHAW, BOX 1350, CORDOVA, AK 99574
WILLIAM SHERMAN, 645 G ST #100, ANCHORAGE, AK 99501
GERALD SMALLWOOD, BOX 453, CORDOVA, AK 99574
BASIL SMITH, 391 COUNTY RD 513, RIENZI, MS 38865
PAUL SWARTZBART, BOX 233, CORDOVA, AK 99574
GARY TAYLOR, BOX 112241, ANCHORAGE, AK 99511
KENNETH THORALL, 1113 N ROGERS RD, WASILLA, AK 99654

HALIBUT FISHING LIST—LONGLINE

GERALD THORNE, BOX 1192, CORDOVA, AK 99574
RYAN THORNE, BOX 2394, CORDOVA, AK 99574
SUE THORNE, BOX 870295, WASILLA, AK 99687
TROY TIRRELL, BOX 600, CORDOVA, AK 99574
BRIAN TUENGE, 325 QUINNELL AVE N, LAKELAND, MN 55043
GILBERT URATA, BOX 518, CORDOVA, AK 99574
MARK VAN, BOX 854, GIRDWOOD, AK 99587
JEFFERY VANDYCK, BOX 473, CORDOVA, AK 99574
THEKLA VONHAGKE, BOX 58, KELLY, WY 83011
OLGA VONZIEGESAR, BOX 15191, FRITZ CREEK, AK 99603
AL WHALEY, 1311 MEDFRA ST, ANCHORAGE, AK 99501
EDWARD WYMAN, BOX 2068, PORT TOWNSEND, WA 98368

HALIBUT, HAND TROLL, STATEWIDE
GARY AULT, BOX 307, HOMER, AK 99603
RICHARD BAGLEY, 2865 WATER GATE WY, KENAI, AK 99611
RAYMOND EVENS, BOX 197, PETERSBURG, AK 99833
JAMES HEILALA, 36640 MCFARLAND DR, SOLDOTNA, AK 99669
JOHN HYLEN, BOX 39350, NINILCHIK, AK 99639
KENNETH MADSEN, BOX 918, PETERSBURG, AK 99833
DAN OGG, BOX 2754, KODIAK, AK 99615

HALIBUT, LONGLINE VESSEL UNDER 60', STATEWIDE
ALFREDO ABOUEID, BOX 26, CHIGNIK LAGOON, AK 99565
JON ABRAHAMSON, BOX 574, WRANGELL, AK 99929
MICHAEL ADAMS, BOX 961, CORDOVA, AK 99574
GRACE ALLAN, BOX 1907, KODIAK, AK 99615
PETER ALLAN, BOX 2160, KODIAK, AK 99615
JEFFREY ALLEN, BOX 3020, TRINIDAD, CA 95570
TRAVIS ALLENSWORTH, BOX 941, SITKA, AK 99835
JANICE ALSUP, 15008 N TONGASS HWY, KETCHIKAN, AK 99901
NORMAN ALSUP, 15008 N TONGASS HWY, KETCHIKAN, AK 99901
MATTHEW ALWARD, 60082 CLARICE WAY, HOMER, AK 99603
AARON ANDERSON, BOX 43, CHIGNIK LAGOON, AK 99565
DARRIN ANDERSON, 3290 S LAKESHORE LP, PALMER, AK 99645
KAVIK ANDERSON, BOX 310, KODIAK, AK 99615
MARK ANDERSON, 49 NORTH STAR LN, FRIDAY HARBOR, WA 98250
RICHARD ANDREW, BOX 7211, KETCHIKAN, AK 99901
LOWELL ANDREWS, BOX 172, TOGIAK, AK 99678
CHRISTOPHER ANGASAN, BOX 70131, SOUTH NAKNEK, AK 99670
RANDY ARSENAULT, BOX 4104, HOMER, AK 99603
FRED ATHORP, BOX 792, WARD COVE, AK 99928
WILLIAM AUGER, BOX 9335, KETCHIKAN, AK 99901
GARY AULBACH, BOX 726, PETERSBURG, AK 99833
DONALD AUS, BOX 151, UNALASKA, AK 99685
HEIDI BABIC, BOX 1208, CORDOVA, AK 99574
KAYLEY BABIC, BOX 1208, CORDOVA, AK 99574
MATHEW BABIC, BOX 988, CORDOVA, AK 99574
JAMES BACON, 3357 S TONGASS HWY, KETCHIKAN, AK 99901
BRAD BADGER, BOX 684, HAINES, AK 99827
JOHN BAHNKE, BOX 912, NOME, AK 99762
ARNOLD BAKKE, BOX 1482, WRANGELL, AK 99929
ROBERT BALDWIN, BOX 1757, PETERSBURG, AK 99833
RICK BALLAS, BOX 352, CORDOVA, AK 99574
FRANK BALOVICH, BOX 1396, SITKA, AK 99835
KENT BARKHAU, 123 RIGGS RD, SITKA, AK 99835
DAVID BARRY, 3980 N DOUGLAS HWY, JUNEAU, AK 99801
DALE BARTELDS, 301 WORTMAN LP, SITKA, AK 99835
CHARLEEN BARTELS, 8044 DAVIDSON AVE, EDNA BAY, AK 99950
DENNIS BARTLETT, BOX 876819, WASILLA, AK 99687
ANDREAN BASARGIN, BOX 1393, HOMER, AK 99603
DIONISY BASARGIN, BOX 2325, HOMER, AK 99603
FILIMON BASARGIN, BOX 2884, HOMER, AK 99603
IVAN BASARGIN, BOX 324, HOMER, AK 99603

KIRIL BASARGIN, BOX 2395, HOMER, AK 99603
MIHEY BASARGIN, BOX 875797, WASILLA, AK 99687
MIRON BASARGIN, BOX 829, HOMER, AK 99603
PETRO BASARGIN, BOX 2126, HOMER, AK 99603
HENRY BAUMGART, 1504 FAIRVIEW, BELLINGHAM, WA 98229
BRANT BAXTER, BOX 1023, OAK HARBOR, WA 98277
KEVIN BEAM, 2309 HALIBUT POINT RD #8, SITKA, AK 99835
NELS BECKER, BOX 240838, DOUGLAS, AK 99824
ROBERT BECKER, BOX 240238, DOUGLAS, AK 99824
DAVID BEEBE, BOX 148, PETERSBURG, AK 99833
ROBERT BEEDLE, BOX 1242, CORDOVA, AK 99574
LINDA BEHNKEN, 123 RIGGS RD, SITKA, AK 99835
NANCY BEHNKEN, 117 JEFF DAVIS ST, SITKA, AK 99835
ANNETTE BELLAMY, BOX 6426, HALIBUT COVE, AK 99603
MARVIN BELLAMY, BOX 6426, HALIBUT COVE, AK 99603
DAVID BENEDICT, 17099 W SHADY POOL CT, SURPRISE, AZ 85387
TOR BENSON, BOX 441, PETERSBURG, AK 99833
CHRISTINE BENTON, BOX 74, ELFIN COVE, AK 99825
HUGH BENTON, BOX 62, ELFIN COVE, AK 99825
JAMES BENTON, BOX 74, ELFIN COVE, AK 99825
CHELSEA BERG, BOX 263, PETERSBURG, AK 99833
ERIC BERGGREN, 1520 SENECA PL, WENATCHEE, WA 98801
BERT BERGMAN, 801 CHARLES #A, SITKA, AK 99835
WILLIAM BERGMANN, BOX 130, PETERSBURG, AK 99833
GARY BERNHARDT, BOX 3203, SITKA, AK 99835
JAMES BERNS, BOX 44, OLD HARBOR, AK 99643
DAVID BESEAU, BOX 966, CRAIG, AK 99921
LARRY BILLMAN, 17198 HILL TOP LN SE, CHATFIELD, MN 55923
PETER BLAKE, BOX 718, CORDOVA, AK 99574
BRIAN BLANKENSHIP, 2166 A HALIBUT POINT RD, SITKA, AK 99835
BRIAN BLANKENSHIP, 4316 VALLHALLA DR, SITKA, AK 99835
ERIC BLANKENSHIP, 1808 EDGECUMBE DR, SITKA, AK 99835
JEFF BLANKENSHIP, 1709 HALIBUT POINT RD #12, SITKA, AK 99835
LISA BLANKENSHIP, 104 CHIRIKOV DR, SITKA, AK 99835
WILLIAM BLOOM, BOX 1283, WRANGELL, AK 99929
DOUGLAS BLUMER, 6058 AZALEA DR, ANCHORAGE, AK 99516
JOHN BOCCI, BOX 1312, CORDOVA, AK 99574
JIM BODDING, 1911 8TH ST, ANACORTES, WA 98221
CORY BODYFELT, 1616 FARMERS LOOP RD, FAIRBANKS, AK 99709
HANS BORVE, 2138 THORNTON RD, FERNDALE, WA 98248
DALE BOSWORTH, BOX 45, PETERSBURG, AK 99833
THOMAS BOTTS, BOX 424, HOONAH, AK 99829
NORMAN BOTZ, BOX 5508, CHINIAK, AK 99615
CHRISTOPHER BOURGEOIS, BOX 1945, CORDOVA, AK 99574
STEVEN BOX, 1512 LING CT, JUNEAU, AK 99801
ELEANOR BOYCE, BOX 83251, FAIRBANKS, AK 99708
KAREN BOYCE, BOX 564, HAINES, AK 99827
LUCINDA BOYCE, 2433 LANTERN ST, CHARLESTON, SC 29414
MARK BRADLEY, 42205 CO RD 136, FIFTY LAKES, MN 56448
TYLER BRAY, 324 ALDER ST, KETCHIKAN, AK 99901
DONALD BRIDGES, BOX 963, KENAI, AK 99611
DONALD BROOKINS, BOX 512, TIRA AMARILLA, NM 87575
RYAN BROUGHTON, BOX 264, SEWARD, AK 99664
SAMUEL BROW, BOX 1161, SOLDOTNA, AK 99669
LEO BROWN, 35717 WALKABOUT RD, HOMER, AK 99603
JOHN BRUCE, BOX 249, POULSBO, WA 98370
WILLIAM BRUN, BOX 212, SELDOVIA, AK 99663
MATTHEW BRYNER, BOX 1642, PETERSBURG, AK 99833
THOMAS BUDD, 1718 EDGECUMBE DR, SITKA, AK 99835
TIM BUNESS, BOX 66, WRANGELL, AK 99929
JOHN BURNS, BOX 83570, FAIRBANKS, AK 99708
CHRISTIAN BUSCHMANN, BOX 898, PETERSBURG, AK 99833
DONALD BYRD, 2701 HALIBUT POINT RD, SITKA, AK 99835
SHARON BYRD, 2701 HALIBUT POINT RD, SITKA, AK 99835
MICHAEL BYRER, BOX 1462, PETERSBURG, AK 99833
DANE CALDWELL, 2305 39TH ST, BELLINGHAM, WA 98229

HALIBUT FISHING LIST—LONGLINE

CASEY CAMPBELL, 16235 HEADLANDS CIR, ANCHORAGE, AK 99516
CARL CARLSON, BOX 44, SAND POINT, AK 99661
HENRY CARLSON, BOX 500, CORDOVA, AK 99574
LYNETTE CARLSON, BOX 19214, THORNE BAY, AK 99919
ANITA CARPENTER, BOX 1970, KODIAK, AK 99615
JOHN CARPENTER, 3215 BENNETT DR, BELLINGHAM, WA 98225
MARC CARREL, BOX 461, CORDOVA, AK 99574
CHRISTOPHER CARROLL, 107 EBERHARDT DR, SITKA, AK 99835
NATASHA CASCIANO, BOX 584, CORDOVA, AK 99574
RICHARD CASCIANO, BOX 584, CORDOVA, AK 99574
BRIAN CASTLE, BOX 243, CRAIG, AK 99921
KEVIN CASTLE, BOX 1110, CRAIG, AK 99921
BRENT CATHEY, BOX 15166, FRITZ CREEK, AK 99603
SCOTT CHADWICK, BOX 2, YAKUTAT, AK 99689
BRYAN CHARTIER, BOX 233, SELDOVIA, AK 99663
DAVID CHARTIER, BOX 153, SELDOVIA, AK 99663
JEVON CHARTIER, BOX 2, SELDOVIA, AK 99663
PAUL CHERVENAK, BOX 1961, KODIAK, AK 99615
ROBERT CHRISTENSEN, 7761 JAGUAR CIR, ANCHORAGE, AK 99502
DAVID CHRISTIANSEN, BOX 2, OLD HARBOR, AK 99643
DAVID CLARK, 507 KATLIAN ST, SITKA, AK 99835
ROBERT CLARK, BOX 95, HOONAH, AK 99829
JOHN CLEAVER, 100 BAHOVEC CT, SITKA, AK 99835
CHARLES CLEMENT, BOX 282, METLAKATLA, AK 99926
CHARLES CLEMENT, 1242 WALDON PT RD BOX 302, METLAKATLA, AK 99926
JARED COCKRUM, 4677 N TONGASS HWY, KETCHIKAN, AK 99901
RUSSELL COCKRUM, 5791 N TONGASS HWY, KETCHIKAN, AK 99901
CHARLES COHEN, BOX 20670, JUNEAU, AK 99802
TRAVIS CONATSER, 2401 SAWMILL CREEK RD, SITKA, AK 99835
JOSHUA CONN, BOX 593, PETERSBURG, AK 99833
DUSTIN CONNOR, BOX 1372, PETERSBURG, AK 99833
TORI CONNOR, BOX 1641, PETERSBURG, AK 99833
WILLIAM CONNOR, BOX 1124, PETERSBURG, AK 99833
WILLIAM COOK, 605 BRANCH LINE RD, YUKON, OK 73099
DANIEL COOPER, 103 KRESTOF DR, SITKA, AK 99835
DOUGLAS CORL, BOX 1570, PETERSBURG, AK 99833
BRUCE CORSON, 205 E DIMOND BLVD #395, ANCHORAGE, AK 99515
GREGORY COWLING, BOX 1295, PETERSBURG, AK 99833
VERNON CRANE, 111 BAHRT CIR, SITKA, AK 99835
RICHARD CURRAN, BOX 1336, SITKA, AK 99835
JOHN CURRY, 444 S STATE ST #409, BELLINGHAM, WA 98225
JULIANNE CURRY, BOX 2182, PETERSBURG, AK 99833
KERRI CURTISS, BOX 1532, PETERSBURG, AK 99833
TROY CURTISS, BOX 1532, PETERSBURG, AK 99833
JEROME DAHL, BOX 1275, PETERSBURG, AK 99833
ALAN DALE, 926 NORDSTROM DR, KETCHIKAN, AK 99901
COLIN DALRYMPLE, 19033 47TH AVE S, SEATTLE, WA 98188
MIKE DALY, 501 CHARTERIS ST #A, SITKA, AK 99835
DUGAN DANIELS, 507 KATLIAN ST, SITKA, AK 99835
TODD DAUGHERTY, BOX 32705, JUNEAU, AK 99802
BRENT DAVIS, BOX 1171, CORDOVA, AK 99574
HERMAN DAVIS, BOX 395, SITKA, AK 99835
HOLLI DAVIS, BOX 1455, PETERSBURG, AK 99833
JASON DAVIS, BOX 962, CORDOVA, AK 99574
L DAVIS, 29793 SEWARD HWY, SEWARD, AK 99664
PATRICK DAVIS, BOX 921566, DUTCH HARBOR, AK 99692
RICHARD DAVIS, 2347 KEVIN CT, JUNEAU, AK 99801
EDWARD DAY, BOX 534, VALDEZ, AK 99686
BRAD DEERING, BOX 12, SAND POINT, AK 99661
GEORGE DEMMERT, 303 SPRUCE ST, KETCHIKAN, AK 99901
JAMES DENNIS, BOX 591, CRAIG, AK 99921
DOUGLAS DEPLAZES, BOX 2923, KODIAK, AK 99615
STUART DEWITT, BOX 117, HAINES, AK 99827
GREG DIERICK, BOX 421, YAKUTAT, AK 99689
CASEY DIGENNARO, 208 PARK ST, SITKA, AK 99835
SHAWN DOCHTERMANN, BOX 866, KODIAK, AK 99615

JAMESZON DOGGETT, 1302 SAWMILL CREEK RD #29, SITKA, AK 99835
ROBERT DOLAN, BOX 1062, PETERSBURG, AK 99833
JOEL DONER, 210 BREE AVE, ANCHORAGE, AK 99515
RONALD DOTSON, 4417 ICHABOD LN, JUNEAU, AK 99801
MATT DOUCETT, BOX 906, CORDOVA, AK 99574
MICHAEL DOUVILLE, BOX 68, CRAIG, AK 99921
HEATH DUNCAN, BOX 533, KASILOF, AK 99610
LAURIE DUNCAN, BOX 4221, SOLDOTNA, AK 99669
PAUL DUNGAN, 57725 ICY BAY DR, HOMER, AK 99603
JOHN DUPREE, BOX 684, PETERSBURG, AK 99833
ESIAH DUSHKIN, BOX 215, KING COVE, AK 99612
BRENNON EAGLE, BOX 576, WRANGELL, AK 99929
KELLAN EAGLE, BOX 576, WRANGELL, AK 99929
RANDALL EASTERLY, BOX 1524, WRANGELL, AK 99929
GAYLE EASTWOOD, BOX 1185, PETERSBURG, AK 99833
JAMES EASTWOOD, BOX 1185, PETERSBURG, AK 99833
RICHARD ECHUCK, BOX 213, TOGIAK, AK 99678
DEBORAH ECKLEY, BOX 1274, CORDOVA, AK 99574
ROBERT ECKLEY, BOX 1274, CORDOVA, AK 99574
DUANE EDELMAN, BOX 153, VALDEZ, AK 99686
DUANE EDWARDS, BOX 2088, NEWPORT, OR 97365
GARY EGERTON, 3278 BROOKS HILL RD, LANGLEY, WA 98260
AJAX EGGLESTON, BOX 1305, HAINES, AK 99827
KEN EICHNER, 5166 SHORELINE DR N, KETCHIKAN, AK 99901
GEORGE ELIASON, 105 SAND DOLLAR DR, SITKA, AK 99835
NICHOLAS ELIASON, 6201 S 41ST ST, LINCOLN, NE 98516
GARRETT ELWOOD, 326 HEATHER RD, EVERETT, WA 98203
MELISSA ENDICOTT, BOX 506, YAKUTAT, AK 99689
NATHANIEL ENDICOTT, BOX 170, YAKUTAT, AK 99689
STEVEN ENGE, BOX 422, PETERSBURG, AK 99833
JARED ERICKSON, BOX 32374, JUNEAU, AK 99803
MICHAEL ERICKSON, BOX 32632, JUNEAU, AK 99803
MIKE ERICKSON, BOX 34363, JUNEAU, AK 99803
CLAYTON ETHERIDGE, BOX 33043, JUNEAU, AK 99803
CHRIS EVENS, BOX 886, PETERSBURG, AK 99833
CRAIG EVENS, BOX 585, PETERSBURG, AK 99833
ERIC EVENS, BOX 1412, PETERSBURG, AK 99833
RAYMOND EVENS, BOX 197, PETERSBURG, AK 99833
TAMARA EVENS, BOX 886, PETERSBURG, AK 99833
JEFFERY FARVOUR, 439 VERSTOVIA AVE, SITKA, AK 99835
ALEXEY FEFELOV, 1083 N LARKSPUR CIR, HOMER, AK 99603
GENE FENNIMORE, BOX 165, WRANGELL, AK 99929
KEVIN FERRELL, 848 GALA LAKE RD, SPOUT SPRING, VA 24593
MICHAEL FICK, 4 LIBERTY LN, CODY, WY 82414
MICHAEL FILE, BOX 1666, PETERSBURG, AK 99833
FORREST FLEENOR, 100 PACIFIC CT, KETCHIKAN, AK 99901
RANDALL FLEENOR, BOX 5521, KETCHIKAN, AK 99901
SILAS FLOR, BOX 396, PETERSBURG, AK 99833
OTTO FLORSCHUTZ, BOX 547, WRANGELL, AK 99929
THOMAS FLYNN, BOX 8036, NIKISKI, AK 99635
DAN FOLEY, BOX 57, GUSTAVUS, AK 99826
BRUCE FOSTER, BOX 46, SAND POINT, AK 99661
LEROY FOX, BOX 136, TOGIAK, AK 99678
CLAYTON FRANKLIN, BOX 62, PETERSBURG, AK 99833
KYLE FRANKLIN, BOX 62, PETERSBURG, AK 99833
ROBERT FREDRICKSON, 392 PEARCE RD, PORT ANGELES, WA 98362
MICHAEL FRICCERO, BOX 2187, KODIAK, AK 99615
GARRETT GABLEHOUSE, 17587 CYPRESS POINT RD, FORT MYERS, FL 33967
BRUCE GABRYS, 10229 BAFFIN ST, EAGLE RIVER, AK 99577
STEVEN GALOVIN, BOX 215, SAND POINT, AK 99661
CHRIS GARCIA, BOX 203, KENAI, AK 99611
IVY GARDNER, BOX 81, SAND POINT, AK 99661
ADAM GERSHFIELD.HOSME, 4502 14TH AVE NW, SEATTLE, WA 98107
DAVE GIBSON, 127 W 7TH ST, JUNEAU, AK 99801
BRIAN GIERARD, BOX 7343, KETCHIKAN, AK 99901
DAVID GIFFORD, BOX 8125, PORT ALEXANDER, AK 99836

HALIBUT FISHING LIST—LONGLINE

JOSEPH GIL, BOX 5, POINT BAKER, AK 99927

JAY GILLMAN, BOX 651, ANACORTES, WA 98221

DARIN GILMAN, BOX 223, CORDOVA, AK 99574

LEE GILPIN, BOX 1511, PETERSBURG, AK 99833

JASON GJERTSEN, 714 ETOLIN ST, SITKA, AK 99835

LOUIE GJOSUND, BOX 3404, HOMER, AK 99603

KURT GOETZINGER, BOX 1268, CORDOVA, AK 99574

DANIEL GOODWIN, 4245 S PINNACLE PEAK DR, WASILLA, AK 99623

MAXIM GOSTEVSKYH, BOX 5151, NIKOLAEVSK, AK 99556

WILLIAM GRANGER, BOX 1162, SOLDOTNA, AK 99669

STEVEN GRAY, BOX 209, KODIAK, AK 99615

BRENDA GREENBANK, 2760 DOUGLAS HWY, JUNEAU, AK 99801

QUINCY GREGG, BOX 20373, JUNEAU, AK 99802

ROGER GREGG, BOX 3, WRANGELL, AK 99929

SEAN GRISS, BOX 2098, PETERSBURG, AK 99833

CARL GRONN, BOX 8686, KODIAK, AK 99615

ERIC GRUNDBERG, BOX 2193, PETERSBURG, AK 99833

MICHAEL GRUNERT, BOX 187, CHIGNIK LAGOON, AK 99565

EVENINGSTAR GRUTTER, 711 ETOLIN ST, SITKA, AK 99835

FABIAN GRUTTER, 711 ETOLIN ST, SITKA, AK 99835

IVAN GRUTTER, 3205 HALIBUT POINT RD, SITKA, AK 99835

CAROLE GUFFEY, 3421 W 31ST AVE, ANCHORAGE, AK 99517

ANTHONY GUGGENBICKLER, BOX 393, WRANGELL, AK 99929

CHRISTOPHER GUGGENBICKLER, BOX 1491, WRANGELL, AK 99929

RICHARD GUHL, 721 SIRSTAD ST, SITKA, AK 99835

MARK GUILLORY, 1612 SAWMILL CREEK, SITKA, AK 99835

WILLIAM GUITARD, BOX 222, UNALASKA, AK 99685

DENNIS GUNDERSEN, BOX 386, SAND POINT, AK 99661

MARTIN GUNDERSEN, BOX 50, SAND POINT, AK 99661

JARL GUSTAFSON, BOX 952, HOMER, AK 99603

GAYLE HAGEN, BOX 2334, SITKA, AK 99835

ROBERT HAGEN, BOX 2334, SITKA, AK 99835

DYLAN HALEY, 500 LINCOLN ST B1, SITKA, AK 99835

JACOB HALLINGSTAD, BOX 295, KAKE, AK 99830

DEAN HALTINER, BOX 443, PETERSBURG, AK 99833

MIKE HAMAR, 303 DISTIN AVE, JUNEAU, AK 99801

FREDERICK HAMILTON, BOX 106, CRAIG, AK 99921

JASON HAMMER, 1013 S DISCOVERY RD, PORT TOWNSEND, WA 98368

MARK HAMMER, 1130 S DICOVERY RD, PORT TOWNSEND, WA 98368

WILLIAM HAMMER, 32 NELSONS LANDING RD, PORT TOWNSEND, WA 98368

ELLEN HANNAN, BOX 243, CRAIG, AK 99921

ERIC HANSEN, BOX 1482, KODIAK, AK 99615

MICHAEL HANSEN, BOX 822, KODIAK, AK 99615

SCOTT HANSEN, 5515 E EVERGREEN ST, MESA, AZ 85205

JAMES HARRIGAN, 1610 DAVIDOFF, SITKA, AK 99835

RAYMOND HARRIS, BOX 1318, SEWARD, AK 99664

KURT HASTINGS, 2097 E MILLMAN RD, LANGLEY, WA 98260

RICHARD HASTINGS, 1308 DINES POINT RD, GREENBANK, WA 98253

CHARLES HAWKS, BOX 93, CRAIG, AK 99921

JAMES HAYDEN, BOX 8085, KODIAK, AK 99615

MURRAY HAYES, 224 GRANT ST, PORT TOWNSEND, WA 98368

DANNY HAYNES, BOX 7036, KETCHIKAN, AK 99901

NINA HEAVENER, BOX 1003, DILLINGHAM, AK 99576

MATTHEW HEGGE, BOX 848, KODIAK, AK 99615

JAMES HEILALA, 36640 MCFARLAND DR, SOLDOTNA, AK 99669

MARK HEILALA, 7715 45TH PL W, MUKILTEO, WA 98275

RANDAL HENDERSON, BOX 1125, PETERSBURG, AK 99833

JAY HENDRICKS, 2001 HUGHES WAY, JUNEAU, AK 99801

DONALD HERNANDEZ, BOX 48, POINT BAKER, AK 99927

JAMES HICKLE, BOX 4325, PALMER, AK 99645

JONATHAN HILL, 2150 HALIBUT POINT ROAD, SITKA, AK 99835

ROBERT HILL, BOX 623, NAKNEK, AK 99633

DAVID HILLEY, BOX 1411, DILLINGHAM, AK 99576

EDMOND HISAW, BOX 1179, TENINO, WA 98589

PETER HITCH, N1010 M35, MENOMINEE, MI 49858

STANLEY HJORT, BOX 828, PETERSBURG, AK 99833

TOM HOBLET, BOX 108, FALSE PASS, AK 99583

MARK HOFMANN, 1042 OBSTRUCTION PASS RD, OLGA, WA 98279

ALBERT HOFSTAD, BOX 1030, PETERSBURG, AK 99833

MARK HOFSTAD, BOX 1397, PETERSBURG, AK 99833

MELINDA HOFSTAD, BOX 1030, PETERSBURG, AK 99833

THOMAS HOGAN, BOX 1648, HOMER, AK 99603

HEATHER HOLCOMB, BOX 206, YAKUTAT, AK 99689

HEIDI HOLCOMB, BOX 114, YAKUTAT, AK 99689

HERB HOLCOMB, BOX 114, YAKUTAT, AK 99689

JAMES HOLCOMB, BOX 206, YAKUTAT, AK 99689

LES HOLCOMB, BOX 143, YAKUTAT, AK 99689

SONYA HOLCOMB, BOX 143, YAKUTAT, AK 99689

JAMES HOLIEN, BOX 443, KLAWOCK, AK 99925

CHRIS HOLM, 54 N VALLEY RD, NASELLE, WA 98638

IVER HOLM, BOX 8938, KODIAK, AK 99615

OLIVER HOLM, BOX 8749, KODIAK, AK 99615

JASON HOLST, 1400 EDGECUMBE DR, SITKA, AK 99835

MARK HOLT, BOX 1218, KODIAK, AK 99615

SEAN HOVIK, BOX 6312, SITKA, AK 99835

COURTNEY HOWARD, 1809 EDGECUMBE DR, SITKA, AK 99835

JAMES HUBBARD, BOX 3302, SEWARD, AK 99664

RHONDA HUBBARD, BOX 3302, SEWARD, AK 99664

SCOTT HUBBARD, BOX 3302, SEWARD, AK 99664

JACK HUGHES, BOX 1401, CRESTED BUTTE, CO 81224

JAMES HUGHES, 507 KATLIAN ST, SITKA, AK 99835

NORMAN HUGHES, BOX 1136, HAINES, AK 99827

DAVID HULIEN, 725 W KYLE WILLIAMS CIR, WASILLA, AK 99654

H.DANIEL HULL, 19300 VILLAGES SCENIC PKWY, ANCHORAGE, AK 99516

ROBERT HUNLEY, BOX 7, MEYERS CHUCK, AK 99903

DON HUSE, BOX 373, PETERSBURG, AK 99833

JIMMY HUTCHENS, 20282 ENGLISH RD, MOUNT VERNON, WA 98274

DAVID IANI, BOX 549, KODIAK, AK 99615

GREGORY INDRELAND, BOX 413, YAKUTAT, AK 99689

ROGER INGMAN, BOX 1155, SITKA, AK 99835

CLIFTON IVANOFF, BOX 8883, KODIAK, AK 99615

DAVID IVANOV, BOX 15316, HOMER, AK 99603

EFSAY IVANOV, 7140 W MOOSE RIDGE CIR, WASILLA, AK 99623

LAVRO IVANOV, 6127 S SCHNEIDER RD, WOODBURN, OR 97071

NESTOR IVANOV, BOX 15316, FRITZ CREEK, AK 99603

CLINTON IVERS, 9620 MUSKET BALL CIR, ANCHORAGE, AK 99507

KEITH IVERS, 2645 MEADOW LARK WAY, ANCHORAGE, AK 99507

WAYNE IVERS, BOX 42, YAKUTAT, AK 99689

NORMAN JACKSON, 835 E SESAME ST, KETCHIKAN, AK 99901

TONY JACKSON, 103 JOHNSON ST, SITKA, AK 99835

SIMON JACOBI, BOX 1065, SITKA, AK 99835

DICK JACOBSEN, BOX 307, SAND POINT, AK 99661

DORA JACOBSON, 3031 HAMILTON ST, JUNEAU, AK 99801

VINCENT JACOBSON, BOX 28, YAKUTAT, AK 99689

STEVEN JAMES, 42423 N CEDAR, BAKER CITY, OR 97814

VERN JAMISON, 1628 NW SUGARMAPLE CT, MCMINNVILLE, OR 97128

STEVE JANGAARD, 5017 168TH PL NW, STANWOOD, WA 98292

HOWARD JANNECK, BOX 298373, WASILLA, AK 99654

VICKI JANNECK, BOX 298373, WASILLA, AK 99623

EDDIE JASPER, 1613 WETMORE AVE, EVERETT, WA 98201

JOSHUA JENKINS, BOX 947, WRANGELL, AK 99929

PETER JENKINS, 2400 TASHA DR, ANCHORAGE, AK 99502

MICHAEL JEWETT, 3220 1ST, KETCHIKAN, AK 99901

NICHOLAS JOHANSON, 1900 W NICKERSON ST #213, SEATTLE, WA 98119

DEVIN JOHNSON, 4202 HALIBUT POINT RD, SITKA, AK 99835

EARLE JOHNSON, 300 PETERSON AVE APT A, SITKA, AK 99835

ERIK JOHNSON, 1339 S WELDONA LN, SUPERIOR, CO 80027

FRITZ JOHNSON, BOX 1129, DILLINGHAM, AK 99576

KAREN JOHNSON, 419 VERSTOVIA AVE, SITKA, AK 99835

KEVIN JOHNSON, 709 MONASTERY ST, SITKA, AK 99835

MARTY JOHNSON, BOX 744, SITKA, AK 99835

MICHAEL JOHNSON, BOX 1344, SITKA, AK 99835

HALIBUT FISHING LIST—LONGLINE

MOSES JOHNSON, 1413 HALIBUT POINT RD, SITKA, AK 99835
PAUL JOHNSON, BOX 1083, SITKA, AK 99835
WILLIAM JOHNSON, BOX 1178, DILLINGHAM, AK 99576
RUSS JOHNSTON, BOX 18071, COFFMAN COVE, AK 99918
KENNETH JONES, BOX 615, CORDOVA, AK 99574
LARRY JONES, BOX 1147, HOMER, AK 99603
MATTHEW JONES, 9146 SKYWOOD LN, JUNEAU, AK 99801
RICHARD KAER, BOX 2054, WRANGELL, AK 99929
DOUGLAS KAINO, 12722 39TH AVE NE, SEATTLE, WA 98125
ALEX KALUGIN, BOX 16, HOMER, AK 99603
DIMIAN KALUGIN, BOX 3884, HOMER, AK 99603
ILESAY KALUGIN, BOX 2727, HOMER, AK 99603
KONDRATY KALUGIN, 1763 N 2ND ST, SILVERTON, OR 97381
STEVE KALUGIN, BOX 4302, HOMER, AK 99603
BRIAN KANDOLL, BOX 1363, PETERSBURG, AK 99833
MATTHEW KANDOLL, BOX 2091, PETERSBURG, AK 99833
SCOT KANDOLL, BOX 2154, PETERSBURG, AK 99833
ERNEST KARRAS, 6370 #2 GLACIER HWY, JUNEAU, AK 99801
NICK KATELNIKOFF, BOX 170, OUZINKIE, AK 99644
HELEN KELLER, BOX 133, WRANGELL, AK 99929
STEVEN KELLER, BOX 133, WRANGELL, AK 99929
WILLIAM KEMPERMAN, BOX 19265, THORNE BAY, AK 99919
CHRIS KEMPF, 36100 BORE TIDE DR, KENAI, AK 99611
GRACIE KENDALL, BOX 945, STERLING, AK 99672
KELSEY KENNEDY, BOX 63, TENAKEE, AK 99841
TIMOTHY KEOHANE, 35555 SPUR HWY #290, SOLDOTNA, AK 99669
JERRY KING, BOX 725, HOONAH, AK 99829
MARK KING, BOX 965, CORDOVA, AK 99574
SANDRA KING, BOX 965, CORDOVA, AK 99574
GEORGE KIRK, BOX 2796, KODIAK, AK 99615
ANDREW KITTAMS, BOX 1544, PETERSBURG, AK 99833
JASON KLEIN, 34 COURTNEY LN, STERLING, CT 6377
DAVID KLEPSER, BOX 8946, KETCHIKAN, AK 99901
KEVIN KLEPSER, BOX 5341, KETCHUM, ID 83340
MELISSA KLEPSER, BOX 8946, KETCHIKAN, AK 99901
DENISE KLINGLER, 603 ETOLIN ST, SITKA, AK 99835
MARK KLINGLER, 603 ETOLIN ST, SITKA, AK 99835
KEITH KLOCKENBRINK, BOX 2261, CORDOVA, AK 99574
WILLIAM KLOCKENBRINK, 18729 110TH AVE CT, PUYALLUP, WA 98374
MICHAEL KNAUSS, BOX 211, SITKA, AK 99835
WILLIAM KNECHT, BOX 259, WRANGELL, AK 99929
ALANA KNIGHT, BOX 1331, PETERSBURG, AK 99833
CASEY KNIGHT, BOX 942, PETERSBURG, AK 99833
CHRIS KNIGHT, BOX 22365, JUNEAU, AK 99802
JOHN KNIGHT, BOX 1133, PETERSBURG, AK 99833
KYLE KNIGHT, BOX 1133, PETERSBURG, AK 99833
MARK KNIGHT, 12620 NEHER RIDGE DR, ANCHORAGE, AK 99516
REBECCA KNIGHT, BOX 1331, PETERSBURG, AK 99833
DARYL KNUTSEN, 12336 434TH AVE SE, NORTH BEND, WA 98045
GILBERT KNUTSON, 231 KATLIAN ST B-12, SITKA, AK 99835
WILL KOGER, 4116 226TH PL NE, ARLINGTON, WA 98223
ADAM KOHNE, BOX 161, YAKUTAT, AK 99689
RANDY KONRAD, HC 60 BOX 2895, HAINES, AK 99827
LEE KRAUSE, BOX 1150, SITKA, AK 99835
RANDY KRAXBERGER, 2832 HANCOCK ST, PORT TOWNSEND, WA 98368
LYLE KRITCHEN, BOX 935, CORDOVA, AK 99574
DAVID KUBIAK, 818 TAGURA ST, KODIAK, AK 99615
ALEX KUDRIN, BOX 229, SAINT PAUL ISLAND, AK 99660
PAVEL KUSNETSOV, BOX 2627, HOMER, AK 99603
ALEXEI KUZMIN, BOX 27, DELTA JUNCTION, AK 99737
ARTEM KUZMIN, BOX 5103, NIKOLAEVSK, AK 99556
DAVID KUZMIN, 16727 LEARY RD, WOODBURN, OR 97071
DIA KUZMIN, BOX 758, DELTA JUNCTION, AK 99737
DOMIAN KUZMIN, BOX 367, DELTA JUNCTION, AK 99737
FADEY KUZMIN, BOX 3009, HOMER, AK 99603
KALLISTRAT KUZMIN, BOX 896, DELTA JUNCTION, AK 99737

KIRIAN KUZMIN, BOX 1520, HOMER, AK 99603
LEONTEY KUZMIN, BOX 1542, DELTA JUNCTION, AK 99737
NIKITA KUZMIN, BOX 1542, DELTA JUNCTION, AK 99737
PAVEL KUZMIN, BOX 1669, KODIAK, AK 99615
SERGI KUZMIN, BOX 264, DELTA JUNCTION, AK 99737
VASILY KUZMIN, 16727 LEARY RD, WOODBURN, OR 97071
VICTOR KUZMIN, BOX 2495, HOMER, AK 99603
VLADIMIR KUZMIN, BOX 772, DELTA JUNCTION, AK 99737
YAKOV KUZMIN, BOX 3433, HOMER, AK 99603
KIRIK KUZNETSOV, BOX 315, HOMER, AK 99603
LAZARO KUZNETSOV, BOX 315, HOMER, AK 99603
CALE LADUKE, BOX 1216, SITKA, AK 99835
MICHELLE LAFRINIERE, BOX 2186, HOMER, AK 99603
BRAD LANGVARDT, BOX 213, SELDOVIA, AK 99663
RANDY LANTIEGNE, 6053 108TH AVE NE, KIRKLAND, WA 98033
MELVIN LARSEN, BOX 33, SAND POINT, AK 99661
ROBIN LARSEN, BOX 264, SAND POINT, AK 99661
DONALD LEACH, 4521 N AUTUMN LN, WASILLA, AK 99623
LEONARD LEACH, BOX 6017, KETCHIKAN, AK 99901
GARY LEASK, BOX 759, WARD COVE, AK 99928
PAMELA LEASK, BOX 759, WARD COVE, AK 99928
NICHOLAS LEATHERMAN, BOX 1204, KODIAK, AK 99615
LUTHER LECHNER, BOX 8538, KODIAK, AK 99615
JOHN LEE, 1300 EDGECUMBE DR, SITKA, AK 99835
CANDICE LEWIS, BOX 2103, VASHON, WA 98070
HAROLD LEWIS, BOX 124, YAKUTAT, AK 99689
TED LEWIS, BOX 2103, VASHON, WA 98070
MARK LIGHT, BOX 132, HAINES, AK 99827
JOHN LINDBERG, BOX KWP, KODIAK, AK 99615
ANTHONY LINDOW, 41633 E LAKE AVE, SOLDOTNA, AK 99669
ERIK LINDOW, 51315 SEA QUEST DR, KENAI, AK 99611
RITA LINDOW, 51315 SEA QUEST DR, KENAI, AK 99611
WILLIAM LINDOW, BOX 1612, CORDOVA, AK 99574
KYLE LINTS, 64900 BERRY PAIL DR, HOMER, AK 99603
ROCKY LITTLETON, BOX 1373, PETERSBURG, AK 99833
RODNEY LITTLETON, BOX 1427, PETERSBURG, AK 99833
HERBERT LOCKUK, BOX 194, TOGIAK, AK 99678
PETER LOCKUK, BOX 88, TOGIAK, AK 99678
FRANK LOGUSAK, BOX 278, TOGIAK, AK 99678
TEAL LOHSE, BOX 2464, CORDOVA, AK 99574
TRAE LOHSE, BOX 2378, CORDOVA, AK 99574
RYELAN LONG, 3233 PENINSULA RD, KODIAK, AK 99615
PETER LONGRICH, BOX 2677, KODIAK, AK 99615
LUKE LUDVICK, 1980 N FINGER COVE DR, PALMER, AK 99645
RONALD LUNDAMO, 657 N POINT HIGGINS RD, KETCHIKAN, AK 99901
TAYLOR LUNDGREN, BOX 216, SAND POINT, AK 99661
JACOB LUNDLI, BOX 632, CORDOVA, AK 99574
GREG LUTTON, BOX 1924, PETERSBURG, AK 99833
DOUGLAS LYLE, BOX 2606, YELM, WA 98597
DYLAN LYON, BOX 332, HOMER, AK 99603
MARCUS LYON, BOX 1070, HOMER, AK 99603
YAKOBI LYON, 50884 MOUNTAIN GLACIER CT, HOMER, AK 99603
JACK LYONS, BOX 527, PETERSBURG, AK 99833
DANIEL MACDONALD, BOX 5993, BELLINGHAM, WA 98227
JOHN MACDONALD, BOX 5993, BELLINGHAM, WA 98227
KENNETH MACK, BOX 182, KING COVE, AK 99612
MARLENE MACK, BOX 176, KING COVE, AK 99612
ROBERT MACK, 12100 WOOWARD DR, ANCHORAGE, AK 99516
KENNETH MADSEN, BOX 918, PETERSBURG, AK 99833
STACEY MADSEN, BOX 918, PETERSBURG, AK 99833
BRUCE MANN, 363 NE 178TH ST, SHORELINE, WA 98155
DAVID MANN, 73 WINWARD DR, BELLINGHAM, WA 98229
MATTHEW MARINKOVICH, BOX 2084, FRIDAY HARBOR, WA 98250
EVAN MARSH, BOX 1421, PETERSBURG, AK 99833
KIRT MARSH, BOX 1421, PETERSBURG, AK 99833
BRIAN MARTENS, 2420 SIXTH AVE, KETCHIKAN, AK 99901

HALIBUT FISHING LIST—LONGLINE

DAVID MARTIN, BOX 468, CLAM GULCH, AK 99568
KYLE MARTIN, BOX 468, CLAM GULCH, AK 99568
OLIN MARTINSEN, 306 WORTMAN LP #B, SITKA, AK 99835
IOSIF MARTISHEV, BOX 1660, HOMER, AK 99603
ANISIFOR MARTUSHEV, 5640 S WHISKEY HILL RD, HUBBARD, OR 97032
DOROFEY MARTUSHEV, BOX 368, HOMER, AK 99603
KIRIL MARTUSHEV, BOX 1939, HOMER, AK 99603
PETR MARTUSHEV, BOX 452, ANCHOR POINT, AK 99556
TROFIM MARTUSHEV, BOX 879298, WASILLA, AK 99687
FEDOS MARTUSHOFF, BOX 865, STERLING, AK 99672
AUDREY MASON, 18540 MC CRARY RD, EAGLE RIVER, AK 99577
BRENT MASON, 18500 UPPER MCCRARY RD, EAGLE RIVER, AK 99577
BRIAN MASON, 19435 UPPER SKYLINE DR, EAGLE RIVER, AK 99577
GARY MASON, 18540 MCCRARY RD, EAGLE RIVER, AK 99577
ANDREW MASSEY, 8492 THUNDER MTN RD #B, JUNEAU, AK 99801
LAURA MASTRELLA, BOX 1295, HAINES, AK 99827
LENORE MATHISEN, BOX 1061, PETERSBURG, AK 99833
SIGURD MATHISEN, BOX 1460, PETERSBURG, AK 99833
JOHN MATSKO, BOX 458, YAKUTAT, AK 99689
CRAIG MATTHEWS, 64615 SHELTON AVE W, HOMER, AK 99603
SHELTON MAVES, BOX 117, CRAIG, AK 99921
NEVIN MAY, 4468 S TONGASS HWY, KETCHIKAN, AK 99901
MICHAEL MAYO, 2808 SAWMILL CREEK RD, SITKA, AK 99835
ASHON MCCAY, BOX 2001, PETERSBURG, AK 99833
KAYIN MCCAY, BOX 161, PETERSBURG, AK 99833
RODERICK MCCAY, BOX 161, PETERSBURG, AK 99833
GLEN MCCORMICK, 6353 PROMINENCE POINTE DR, ANCHORAGE, AK 99516
KARIN MCCULLOUGH, BOX 707, PETERSBURG, AK 99833
CHARLES MCELDOWNEY, BOX 1731, SEWARD, AK 99664
JEFFRY MCENTIRE, BOX 833, HAINES, AK 99827
HOMER MCFADDEN, BOX 1972, LYNNWOOD, WA 98046
JEFFREY MCFADYEN, BOX 592, PETERSBURG, AK 99833
RICHARD MCGAHAN, 54025 KENAI SPUR HWY, KENAI, AK 99611
GARY MCMASTER, 1722 EDGECUMBE DR, SITKA, AK 99835
HAROLD MEDALEN, BOX 821, PETERSBURG, AK 99833
RYAN MEGANACK, BOX 5526, PORT GRAHAM, AK 99603
NIKI MEIER, 2505 NE 168, SHORELINE, WA 98155
RANDY MEIER, BOX 165, KASILOF, AK 99610
CLEO MELLING, 5001 OAKES AVE, ANACORTES, WA 98221
DANIEL MELLING, 5581 HEART LAKE PL, ANACORTES, WA 98221
FRANK MELSETH, BOX 66, SAND POINT, AK 99661
FRITZ MENISH, 1343 MARION ST, ENUMCLAW, WA 98022
PAUL MENISH, BOX 33, PETERSBURG, AK 99833
WILLIAM MENISH, BOX 877, PETERSBURG, AK 99833
JASON MERCULIEF, BOX 122, SAINT PAUL ISLAND, AK 99660
NELSON MERRELL, 1323 GLACIER HWY, JUNEAU, AK 99801
THEODORE MERRELL, 3240 FRITZ COVE RD, JUNEAU, AK 99801
GERALD MERRIGAN, BOX 1065, PETERSBURG, AK 99833
STEVEN MERRITT, BOX 1138, CRAIG, AK 99921
MATTHEW METCALF, 2999 JOSHUA CT, HOLLAND, MI 49424
MICHAEL METTEER, BOX 109, KENAI, AK 99611
BART MEYER, 210 SHOTGUN ALLEY, SITKA, AK 99835
CHAD MICKEL, 10805 N TONGASS HWY, KETCHIKAN, AK 99901
FRANK MILES, BOX 2744, KODIAK, AK 99615
GARRETT MILLER, BOX 1899, WRANGELL, AK 99929
JAMES MILLER, BOX 1184, PETERSBURG, AK 99833
THANE MILLER, BOX 2961, VALDEZ, AK 99686
THOMAS MILLER, BOX 1931, KODIAK, AK 99615
TIMOTHY MILLER, 11900 CANGE ST, ANCHORAGE, AK 99516
GEORGE MILNE, BOX 1846, HOMER, AK 99603
BENNY MITCHELL, 103 DARRIN DR, SITKA, AK 99835
KATHLEEN MOATS, 1720 DOUGLAS HWY, DOUGLAS, AK 99824
EDWARD MONKIEWICZ, 1110 PURTOV ST, KODIAK, AK 99615
JOSHUA MOORE, BOX 2015, PETERSBURG, AK 99833
DAVID MORK, 13420 WINDRUSH CIR, ANCHORAGE, AK 99516

J MORRISON, BOX 2514, SITKA, AK 99835
ROBERT MOSHER, 11985 MENDENHALL LP RD, JUNEAU, AK 99801
ROBERT MOSS, BOX 3428, HOMER, AK 99603
GARY MUEHLBERGER, BOX PPV, KETCHIKAN, AK 99950
NORMAN MULLAN, BOX 92, KODIAK, AK 99615
WESLEY MULLAN, 8117 148TH ST CT E, PUYALLUP, WA 98375
GARY MULLIGAN, 224 MARINE ST #A, SITKA, AK 99835
RICHARD MULLIGAN, 107 SHELIKOF WAY, SITKA, AK 99835
ALICIA MUNYER, 2716 HALIBUT POINT RD #5, SITKA, AK 99835
ALEKSANDRO MURACHEV, BOX 2259, HOMER, AK 99603
SHEILA MURPHY, 524 ROOT ST, PORT TOWNSEND, WA 98368
JOHN MURRAY, 224 OBSERVATORY ST, SITKA, AK 99835
LYLE MYRVOLD, BOX 870181, WASILLA, AK 99687
DONALD NASH, BOX 1167, HAINES, AK 99827
FRANK NEIDIFFER, BOX 1746, PETERSBURG, AK 99833
NICHOLAS NEKEFEROFF, 3416 HALIBUT POINT RD #A, SITKA, AK 99835
ARNOLD NELSON, BOX 85, PORT LIONS, AK 99550
EMIL NELSON, BOX 130, HOMER, AK 99603
HARRY NELSON, BOX 87, PORT LIONS, AK 99550
JAKOB NELSON, BOX 1392, HOMER, AK 99603
JESSIE NELSON, BOX 130, HOMER, AK 99603
PARRY NELSON, BOX 92, KODIAK, AK 99615
ZACHARY NELSON, BOX 1071, HOMER, AK 99603
TODD NEVERS, 712 SIRSTAD ST, SITKA, AK 99835
JOHN NEVIN, BOX 2125, KODIAK, AK 99615
KENNETH NEWMAN, 3457 INSPIRATION LP, WASILLA, AK 99654
GRANT NEWTON, BOX 51, KING COVE, AK 99612
CARINA NICHOLS, BOX 1255, SITKA, AK 99835
RYAN NICHOLS, 305 ISLANDER DR, SITKA, AK 99835
MATT NILSEN, BOX 1463, PETERSBURG, AK 99833
MICHAEL NILSEN, BOX 1084, PETERSBURG, AK 99833
CHARLES NOGGLE, 10724 167TH AVE SE, SNOHOMISH, WA 98290
EVAN NORBISRATH, 3725 S AIRPORT RD, PORT ANGELES, WA 98363
DENNIS NORTHRUP, BOX 1159, WARD COVE, AK 99928
WAYNE NORTHRUP, BOX 1177, WARD COVE, AK 99928
TIMOTHY OCONNOR, BOX 1225, CRAIG, AK 99921
DAVID OEN, BOX 2473, SITKA, AK 99835
ERIC OEN, BOX 2026, SITKA, AK 99835
BAE OLNEY.MILLER, 505 OCAIN ST, SITKA, AK 99835
NICK OLNEY.MILLER, 3006 BARKER ST, SITKA, AK 99835
ANDREW OLSEN, 724 CEDAR ST, EDMONDS, WA 98020
DAVID OLSEN, 724 CEDAR ST, EDMONDS, WA 98020
DUAYNE OLSEN, BOX 1743, KODIAK, AK 99615
GORDON OLSEN, BOX 1884, PETERSBURG, AK 99833
NELSON OOKA, BOX 1218, SEWARD, AK 99664
PETER ORD, 1606 LAURIE LN, JUNEAU, AK 99801
ARTHUR OSBORNE, BOX 240925, DOUGLAS, AK 99824
ALAN OTNESS, BOX 317, PETERSBURG, AK 99833
NELS OTNESS, BOX 366, PETERSBURG, AK 99833
NELS OTNESS, BOX 2058, PETERSBURG, AK 99833
ROBERT OTTO, 1422 REZANOF DR, KODIAK, AK 99615
QUINN PADGETT, 215 MEDORA WAY, EVERETT, WA 98201
RONALD PAINTER, 3901 WOODLAND DR, KODIAK, AK 99615
CASEY PAPE, BOX 625, CORDOVA, AK 99574
ERIC PARKER, BOX 1424, SITKA, AK 99835
WAYNE PARKS, BOX 985, PETERSBURG, AK 99833
PAT PARRISH, BOX 2895, SITKA, AK 99835
DENNIS PARSONS, BOX 204, CRAIG, AK 99921
JOEL PASQUAN, BOX 845, HAINES, AK 99827
MARKO PATITUCCI, BOX 8918, KODIAK, AK 99615
DAN PAUK, BOX 82, MANOKOTAK, AK 99628
JOEY PAVIAN, BOX 56, TOGIAK, AK 99678
JONATHAN PAVLIK, BOX 293, YAKUTAT, AK 99689
DAN PEAVEY, BOX 19228, THORNE BAY, AK 99919
MATTHEW PEAVEY, BOX 442, CRAIG, AK 99921

HALIBUT FISHING LIST—LONGLINE

STEVEN PEAVEY, BOX 101, CRAIG, AK 99921
BRITT PEDICORD, 1809 S PENNSYLVANIA ST, DENVER, CO 80210
ALFRED PEELER, BOX 761, PETERSBURG, AK 99833
MAXWELL PEELER, BOX 761, PETERSBURG, AK 99833
JOANNA PERENSOVICH, 506 BARANOF ST, SITKA, AK 99835
TERRY PERENSOVICH, 506 BARANOF, SITKA, AK 99835
CHRISTOPHER PERRY, BOX 1808, HOMER, AK 99603
DAVID PETERS, 283 WILD ORCHID LN, PORT ANGELES, WA 98362
JOHN PETRABORG, BOX 6067, SITKA, AK 99835
CHARLES PETTICREW, BOX 971, WRANGELL, AK 99929
CAVEN PFEIFFER, 236 OBSERVATORY ST, SITKA, AK 99835
ALEC PFUNDT, BOX 1342, PETERSBURG, AK 99833
BRYON PFUNDT, BOX 1162, PETERSBURG, AK 99833
TERESA PFUNDT, BOX 1342, PETERSBURG, AK 99833
TORIN PFUNDT, BOX 1342, PETERSBURG, AK 99833
AARON PHILLIPS, BOX 624, PETERSBURG, AK 99833
JAMES PHILLIPS, BOX 109, PELICAN, AK 99832
JEB PHILLIPS, BOX 1253, PETERSBURG, AK 99833
JORDAN PHILLIPS, 321 PETERSON AVE, SITKA, AK 99835
PATRICIA PHILLIPS, BOX 109, PELICAN, AK 99832
KENNETH PHIPPEN, 312 TILSON ST, SITKA, AK 99835
CHARLES PIERCY, BOX 1025, WARD COVE, AK 99928
PATRICK PIKUS, BOX 2843, KODIAK, AK 99615
NORMAN PILLEN, 2517 ADDY GIFFORD RD, ADDY, WA 99101
CHARLES PIPER, BOX 15233, FRITZ CREEK, AK 99603
ANDREY POLUSHKIN, BOX 2458, HOMER, AK 99603
DAVID POLUSHKIN, 690 KNIK GOOSE BAY RD #246, WASILLA, AK 99654
ILARION POLUSHKIN, BOX 3466, HOMER, AK 99603
VLADIMIR POLUSHKIN, BOX 879276, WASILLA, AK 99687
CHRISTOPHER PONTS, 3613 CYPRESS WAY, SANTA ROSA, CA 95405
ASHTON POOLE, BOX 2186, HOMER, AK 99603
MICHAEL POOLE, BOX 2186, HOMER, AK 99603
ABRAHAM PORTER, BOX 1018, KENAI, AK 99611
LYNN POTTER, BOX 1472, CORDOVA, AK 99574
ANTHONY POULSEN, BOX 154, TOGIAK, AK 99678
MARK POWERS, 29780 WILSON ST, SOLDOTNA, AK 99669
SANDRA POWERS, 29780 WILSON ST, SOLDOTNA, AK 99669
ROBERT PROULX, BOX 1736, WRANGELL, AK 99929
MICHAEL PRUDEN, 169 NIXON PEAK RD, BOZEMAN, MT 59715
PHILLIP PRYZMONT, BOX 994, NOME, AK 99762
JAMES QUIGLEY, BOX 80, CRAIG, AK 99921
PEGGY RAUWOLF, 7942 S TONGASS HWY, KETCHIKAN, AK 99901
JOZIAH REAR, 1007 HALIBUT POINT RD, SITKA, AK 99835
KENNETH REAR, 118 DARRIN DR, SITKA, AK 99835
SIMEON REAR, 1007 HALIBUT POINT RD, SITKA, AK 99835
THELTON REAR, 1007 HALIBUT POINT RD, SITKA, AK 99835
TOM REDMOND, 44310 PARKWAY, SOLDOTNA, AK 99669
RONALD REED, BOX 1437, PETERSBURG, AK 99833
ALAN REEVES, BOX 741, WRANGELL, AK 99929
DEANNA REEVES, BOX 741, WRANGELL, AK 99929
KATELYN REEVES, BOX 741, WRANGELL, AK 99929
DANA REID, BOX 8935, KODIAK, AK 99615
TYLER REID, BOX 1548, PETERSBURG, AK 99833
MICHAEL REIF, BOX 2346, SITKA, AK 99835
ARMIN REIMNITZ, 9004 191ST PL SW, EDMONDS, WA 98026
MARTY REMUND, BOX 1295, HAINES, AK 99827
KYLE RENNIE, BOX 2298, VALDEZ, AK 99686
DAVID RENTEL, BOX 1424, VALDEZ, AK 99686
ALEXANDER REUTOV, BOX 687, SOLDOTNA, AK 99669
ALIMPI REUTOV, 8537 W CARMEL RD, WASILLA, AK 99623
ANATOLY REUTOV, BOX 595, STERLING, AK 99672
CORNILY REUTOV, BOX 3523, HOMER, AK 99603
DANIEL REUTOV, BOX 466, HOMER, AK 99603
DAVID REUTOV, BOX 3609, HOMER, AK 99603
DIONICI REUTOV, BOX 4251, HOMER, AK 99603
FEODOR REUTOV, BOX 390, KODIAK, AK 99615

FEODORA REUTOV, BOX 4251, HOMER, AK 99603
FOMA REUTOV, BOX 3058, HOMER, AK 99603
GREGORY REUTOV, BOX 2597, HOMER, AK 99603
IONA REUTOV, BOX 873462, WASILLA, AK 99687
IRMIL REUTOV, BOX 1338, HOMER, AK 99603
IVAN REUTOV, BOX 1294, STERLING, AK 99672
IVAN REUTOV, BOX 4092, HOMER, AK 99603
IVONE REUTOV, BOX 5053, NIKOLAEVSK, AK 99556
JULIAN REUTOV, BOX 1887, HOMER, AK 99603
KIPRIAN REUTOV, BOX 46, STERLING, AK 99672
LAVRENTII REUTOV, BOX 1190, HOMER, AK 99603
LAZAR REUTOV, BOX 258, HOMER, AK 99603
MIHEY REUTOV, BOX 2063, HOMER, AK 99603
MIHEY REUTOV, 154 CAMBRIDGE AVE, SILVERTON, OR 97381
NIKIT REUTOV, BOX 46, STERLING, AK 99672
NIKOLAI REUTOV, BOX 2342, HOMER, AK 99603
PAVEL REUTOV, 11110 S RIDGE TOP DR, MOLALLA, OR 97038
PETER REUTOV, BOX 1204, STERLING, AK 99672
SEVEREAN REUTOV, BOX 2230, HOMER, AK 99603
SOFRON REUTOV, BOX 563, HOMER, AK 99603
STEVE REUTOV, BOX 1463, HOMER, AK 99603
TRIFILYI REUTOV, BOX 793, HOMER, AK 99603
VENEDIM REUTOV, BOX 877691, WASILLA, AK 99687
YAKOV REUTOV, BOX 1251, STERLING, AK 99672
WILLIAM RHODES, BOX 268, CRAIG, AK 99921
SPENCER RICHTER, BOX 1011, CRAIG, AK 99921
DWIGHT RIEDERER, 22928 SE 406TH ST, ENUMCLAW, WA 98022
HAROLD ROBBINS, BOX 69, YAKUTAT, AK 99689
PATRICK ROBBINS, BOX 202, YAKUTAT, AK 99689
MARK ROBERTS, BOX 246, PETERSBURG, AK 99833
HENRY ROBINSON, 306 NICOLE DR, SITKA, AK 99835
ALEX RODRIGUEZ, BOX 717, ANCHOR POINT, AK 99556
JOHN ROHR, BOX 2621, HOMER, AK 99603
GARY ROSENBERGER, 2760 DOUGLAS HWY, JUNEAU, AK 99801
TIMOTHY ROSS, BOX 371, YAKUTAT, AK 99689
PAUL ROSTAD, BOX 183, KAKE, AK 99830
SANDY ROSTAD, BOX 183, KAKE, AK 99830
TREVOR ROSTAD, BOX 191, KAKE, AK 99830
ERIC ROSVOLD, BOX 1144, PETERSBURG, AK 99833
KAREN ROSVOLD, BOX 61, PETERSBURG, AK 99833
TY ROUSE, BOX 2725, KODIAK, AK 99615
REVELLE RUSSELL, 60143 LOOKOUT MT LN, HOMER, AK 99603
STEVEN RUSSELL, 3152 WOODY WAY LP, KODIAK, AK 99615
SUSAN RUSSELL, 3152 WOODY WAY LP, KODIAK, AK 99615
BILL SAGER, BOX 202, KING COVE, AK 99612
KENNETH SAGER, BOX 202, KING COVE, AK 99612
MARK SALDI, BOX 287, SKAGWAY, AK 99840
VLADIMIR SANAROV, BOX 2175, HOMER, AK 99603
WILLIAM SANCHEZ, BOX 256, TOGIAK, AK 99678
MARK SAPPINGTON, BOX 302, YAKUTAT, AK 99689
CHRISTOPHER SARGENT, BOX 574, KODIAK, AK 99615
WALTER SARGENT, 1830 MISSION RD, KODIAK, AK 99615
JOARDAN SAVLAND, 6003 LUND ST, JUNEAU, AK 99801
STANLEY SAVLAND, BOX 621, HOONAH, AK 99829
JAMES SCHAUFF, BOX 8150, KODIAK, AK 99615
MART SCHONBERG, 125 SPOTTED FAWN COURT, SEDONA, AZ 86351
PETER SCHONBERG, 75-816F HIONA ST, HOLUALOA, HI 96725
PAUL SCHREIBER, 231 KATLIAN #A10, SITKA, AK 99835
DAVID SCHUCKMAN, BOX 1569, KODIAK, AK 99615
CHARLES SCHULTZ, 16275 POINT LENA LOOP RD, JUNEAU, AK 99801
J.CARLOS SCHWANTES, BOX 2335, SITKA, AK 99835
JOSEPH SCHWANTES, BOX 2674, SITKA, AK 99835
THOMAS SCHWANTES, BOX 1911, KODIAK, AK 99615
MICHAEL SCHWARTZ, BOX 434, PETERSBURG, AK 99833
ROBERT SCHWARTZ, BOX 1533, PETERSBURG, AK 99833
TEAGEN SCHWARTZ, BOX 1533, PETERSBURG, AK 99833

HALIBUT FISHING LIST—LONGLINE

BRENDA SCHWARTZ.YEAGER, BOX 1996, WRANGELL, AK 99929
DAN SCHWEITZER, BOX 1667, PETERSBURG, AK 99833
GEORGE SCOTT, BOX 281, GIRDWOOD, AK 99587
KEVIN SEABECK, 8555 30TH NW, SEATTLE, WA 98117
RONALD SEATER, 1610 LAURIE LN, JUNEAU, AK 99801
JOSEPH SEBASTIAN, BOX 1990, PETERSBURG, AK 99833
CHARLES SEE, BOX 1412, KENAI, AK 99611
JAMES SEE, BOX 281, CRAIG, AK 99921
AARON SEVERSON, BOX 507, PETERSBURG, AK 99833
MARK SEVERSON, BOX 1502, PETERSBURG, AK 99833
JOSEPH SHAISHNIKOFF, BOX 211, UNALASKA, AK 99685
TREVER SHAISHNIKOFF, BOX 131, UNALASKA, AK 99685
NIKITA SHARABARIN, 6363 S ZIMMERMAN RD, AURORA, OR 97002
JON SHENNETT, 1209 HALIBUT POINT RD, SITKA, AK 99835
BILL SHIPP, 2400 NW 80TH ST PMB 268, SEATTLE, WA 98117
GWYNNE SHORT, BOX 1224, PETERSBURG, AK 99833
JOSEPH SHORT, BOX 1224, PETERSBURG, AK 99833
KAYLEIGH SHORT, BOX 1224, PETERSBURG, AK 99833
MATTHEW SHORT, BOX 1224, PETERSBURG, AK 99833
JAMES SIMPSON, BOX 45, HYDER, AK 99923
JOHN SKEELE, 262 KAAGWAANTAAN ST, SITKA, AK 99835
JAY SKORDAHL, 48174 WESTOAK RD, WESTFIR, OR 97492
KELSEY SKORDAHL, 109C LANCE DR, SITKA, AK 99835
LUCAS SKORDAHL, 110 HARBOR MOUNTAIN DR, SITKA, AK 99835
CHRIS SLAUGHTER, BOX 1933, FERNDALE, WA 98248
GARY SLAVEN, BOX 205, PETERSBURG, AK 99833
BRUCE SMITH, BOX 273, GUSTAVUS, AK 99826
CHAD SMITH, BOX 1741, WRANGELL, AK 99929
DANIEL SMITH, BOX 911, WRANGELL, AK 99929
JIM SMITH, BOX 354, SAND POINT, AK 99661
LARRY SMITH, BOX 346, WILLIAMS, OR 97544
MICHAEL SMITH, BOX 1651, WRANGELL, AK 99929
ROBERT SMITH, BOX 251, CORDOVA, AK 99574
SHARIL SMITH, BOX 1741, WRANGELL, AK 99929
SHARON SMITH, BOX 991, PETERSBURG, AK 99833
TANNER SMITH, BOX 1379, WRANGELL, AK 99929
MICHAEL SODERLUND, BOX 2269, MAPLE FALLS, WA 98266
COLE SOMERVILLE, BOX 163, PETERSBURG, AK 99833
DAVID SOMERVILLE, BOX 163, PETERSBURG, AK 99833
TANYA SOMERVILLE, BOX 163, PETERSBURG, AK 99833
WALTER SONEN, BOX 107, SELDOVIA, AK 99663
KENT SORENSEN, BOX 15127, FRITZ CREEK, AK 99603
PAUL SORENSON, 51454 OCEAN ENTRANCE DR, KENAI, AK 99611
PAUL SOUTHLAND, BOX 257, WRANGELL, AK 99929
EVANS SPARKS, 100 DONNA DR, SITKA, AK 99835
EVANS SPARKS, 101 PEACE LN, SITKA, AK 99835
STEVE SPLEEN, BOX 655, SUQUAMISH, WA 98392
THEODORE SQUARTSOFF, BOX 77, OUZINKIE, AK 99644
PHILIP SQUIRES, BOX 1231, KENAI, AK 99611
ROBERT SRAMEK, 192 DIVIDING RIDGE RD, SPRING CITY, TN 37381
FREDERICK STAGER, BOX 8243, KODIAK, AK 99615
MICHAEL STAINBROOK, BOX 2052, PETERSBURG, AK 99833
STEVE STARK, 23077 JOAQUIN RIDGE DR, MURRIETA, CA 92562
SCOTT STEGER, 39039 SHIRLY ST, STERLING, AK 99672
BEVERLY STEVENS, 4071 WARWICK PL, ANCHORAGE, AK 99508
MILTON STEVENS, 4071 WARWICK PL, ANCHORAGE, AK 99508
DANIEL STIHL, BOX 3373, KODIAK, AK 99615
JAMES STROMDAHL, BOX 1326, PETERSBURG, AK 99833
MARY STROMDAHL, BOX 1326, PETERSBURG, AK 99833
RICHARD SUMMERS, BOX 227, CRAIG, AK 99921
MARTIN SVENSON, 14861 N TONGASS, KETCHIKAN, AK 99901
DYLAN SWANBERG, BOX 3053, SITKA, AK 99835
ADAM SWANSON, BOX 2151, PETERSBURG, AK 99833
ERIC SWANSON, BOX 6330, SITKA, AK 99835
JOHN SWANSON, BOX 1546, PETERSBURG, AK 99833

LOGAN SWANSON, BOX 1546, PETERSBURG, AK 99833
KENNETH SWICK, BOX 112, SELDOVIA, AK 99663
JAMES SZYMANSKI, BOX 418, HAINES, AK 99827
ERIC TABER, BOX 2206, KODIAK, AK 99615
ANTHONY TAIBER, BOX 1861, PETERSBURG, AK 99833
JAY TAYLOR, 2820 KENT AVE, CODY, WY 82414
REBECCA TEMPLE, 488 ELDERBERRY DR, HOMER, AK 99603
JEFF THOMAS, 55784 HWY 112, PORT ANGELES, WA 98363
MARK THOMAS, 2249 SELIEF LN, KODIAK, AK 99615
JAY THOMASSEN, BOX 1451, PETERSBURG, AK 99833
MICHELLE THOMASSEN, BOX 286, WRANGELL, AK 99929
TROY THOMASSEN, BOX 152, PETERSBURG, AK 99833
KEVIN THOMET, BOX 3258, KODIAK, AK 99615
DAVID THOMPSON, 303 S WASHINGTON AVE, PRESCOTT, AZ 86303
HAILEY THOMPSON, BOX 3037, KODIAK, AK 99615
KYLE THOMPSON, 303 S WASHINGTON, PRESCOTT, AZ 86303
OMAR THOMPSON, 2425 SALMON CT, KENAI, AK 99611
PETER THOMPSON, BOX 3037, KODIAK, AK 99615
RICHARD THOMPSON, 443 WINDWARD WAY, DAVENPORT, FL 33837
PEDER THORSTENSON, 1660 HALLINAN ST, LAKE OSWEGO, OR 97034
ARTHUR THURN, 2323 G ST, BELLINGHAM, WA 98225
DEREK THYNES, BOX 1624, PETERSBURG, AK 99833
STEVEN THYNES, BOX 193, PETERSBURG, AK 99833
TROY TIRRELL, BOX 600, CORDOVA, AK 99574
RICHARD TOGIAK, BOX 232, TOGIAK, AK 99678
THOMAS TOMRDLE, BOX 698, KENAI, AK 99611
DAVID TOW, BOX 314, PETERSBURG, AK 99833
THOMAS TRAIBUSH, 1300 PEACE PORTAL DR #206, BLAINE, WA 98230
VICTOR TYLER, BOX 96, KENAI, AK 99611
PATRICK TYNER, BOX 541, CRAIG, AK 99921
SIMPLICIO VALLADOLID, BOX 9014, KODIAK, AK 99615
RION VANEK, BOX 39251, NINILCHIK, AK 99639
STEPHEN VANEK, BOX 39103, NINILCHIK, AK 99639
GALEN VANSANT, BOX 1263, CORDOVA, AK 99574
GREGORY VEITEHANS, 210 24TH ST, PORT TOWNSEND, WA 98368
ERIK VELSKO, 780 DAYBREEZE CT, HOMER, AK 99603
MARGRET VERG.IN, 19415 LINDA LN, KASILOF, AK 99610
RAY VERG.IN, 381 SENIOR CT #110, KENAI, AK 99611
RHY VERG.IN, 19415 LINDA LN, KASILOF, AK 99610
YENTI VERG.IN, 381 SENIOR CT #110, KENAI, AK 99611
NICHOLAS VERSTEEG, BOX 1752, PETERSBURG, AK 99833
KEVIN VESEL, BOX 669, SEWARD, AK 99664
DANIEL VICK, BOX 1271, PETERSBURG, AK 99833
STEWART VICK, BOX 1271, PETERSBURG, AK 99833
JEFFREY VILLARMA, 312 SE RIM LN, PORT ORCHARD, WA 98367
DONALD VINBERG, BOX 9032, KODIAK, AK 99615
SCOTT VISSCHER, HC 60 BOX 2842, HAINES, AK 99827
THERESA VISSCHER, HC 60 BOX 2842, HAINES, AK 99827
ROBERT VOLK, BOX 576, PETERSBURG, AK 99833
W.BRADFORD VON.WICHMAN, 2940 MALLARD LN, ANCHORAGE, AK 99508
JASON VONICK, BOX 23007, KETCHIKAN, AK 99901
RIC VRSALOVIC, BOX 113004, ANCHORAGE, AK 99511
GARY WADDLE, BOX 994, SAHUARITA, AZ 85629
MARK WAGNER, BOX 1502, KINGSTON, WA 98346
WILLIAM WALDER, BOX 11, ELFIN COVE, AK 99825
BRIAN WALKER, 3901 SW AUSTIN ST, SEATTLE, WA 98136
DARRELL WALKER, 57060 E END RD, HOMER, AK 99603
PAMELA WALLING, 17285 LENA LOOP RD, JUNEAU, AK 99801
ROGER WALLING, 17285 LENA LP RD, JUNEAU, AK 99801
DOUG WARE, BOX 1291, PETERSBURG, AK 99833
DREW WARE, BOX 1291, PETERSBURG, AK 99833
FRANK WARFEL, BOX 517, WRANGELL, AK 99929
FRANK WARFEL, BOX 1512, WRANGELL, AK 99929
BRIAN WARMUTH, BOX 6382, KETCHIKAN, AK 99901
CAROL WARMUTH, BOX 6382, KETCHIKAN, AK 99901

HALIBUT FISHING LIST—LONGLINE

ADAM WARTMAN, 2144 NW 204TH ST, SHORELINE, WA 98177
STUART WEATHERS, BOX 1734, SITKA, AK 99835
JARED WEEMS, 1341 GLACIER HWY, JUNEAU, AK 99801
JERRY WELCH, BOX 1686, PETERSBURG, AK 99833
TRACY WELCH, BOX 225, PETERSBURG, AK 99833
MIKE WELLS, BOX 1430, VALDEZ, AK 99686
JOHN WEYHMILLER, BOX 98, CRAIG, AK 99921
CHRISTOPHER WHEELER, BOX 232, SELDOVIA, AK 99663
DAVID WHITE, 189 POTTER RD, KETCHIKAN, AK 99901
JAMES WHITETHORN, BOX 94, PETERSBURG, AK 99833
SONJA WHITETHORN, BOX 94, PETERSBURG, AK 99833
BRUCE WHITING, 1302 W MUKILTEO BLVD, EVERETT, WA 98203
GEOFFREY WIDDOWS, BOX 342, YAKUTAT, AK 99689
ROBERT WIEDERSPOHN, BOX 1223, WRANGELL, AK 99929
HANS WIENBERG, BOX 164, SITKA, AK 99835
ADRIENNE WILBER, 705 ETOLIN ST, SITKA, AK 99835
PHILIP WILEY, BOX 219, WHITE BIRD, ID 83554
JOSHUA WILLIAMS, BOX 920913, DUTCH HARBOR, AK 99692
MIKE WILLIAMS, 333 SCHOENBAR RD, KETCHIKAN, AK 99901
RICKEY WILLIAMS, BOX 1321, PETERSBURG, AK 99833
JAMES WILSON, 1201 CALLISTA AVE, VALRICO, FL 33596
RICHARD WILSON, BOX 237, NAKNEK, AK 99633
RILEY WILSON, 17701 SPAIN DR, ANCHORAGE, AK 99516
CHAD WINNOP, 100 KINCROFT WAY #A, SITKA, AK 99835
TERRY WIRTA, BOX 775, PELICAN, AK 99832
ROLAND WIRTH, 612 MONASTERY ST, SITKA, AK 99835
CHARLES WOOD, BOX 383, PETERSBURG, AK 99833
FLOYD WOOD, 8012 GLADSTONE ST, JUNEAU, AK 99801
GEORGE WOOD, BOX 902, PETERSBURG, AK 99833
KARL WOOD, 2922 JACKSON RD, JUNEAU, AK 99801
KARSTEN WOOD, BOX 2195, PETERSBURG, AK 99833
LES WOODWARD, BOX 2059, WRANGELL, AK 99929
ANDY WORHATCH, BOX 614, PETERSBURG, AK 99833
MAXIMILIAN WORHATCH, BOX 407, PETERSBURG, AK 99833
CHRISTOPHER WORLEY, BOX 168, SELDOVIA, AK 99663
RANDALL WORTMAN, BOX 271, CRAIG, AK 99921
ANDY WRIGHT, BOX 1432, PETERSBURG, AK 99833
FRANK WRIGHT, BOX 497, HOONAH, AK 99829
ERIC WYATT, BOX 369, CRAIG, AK 99921
PHILLIP WYMAN, BOX 2507, SITKA, AK 99835
SETH WYMAN, 5024 ROBINWOOD LN, BOW, WA 98232
TODD WYMAN, 2176 HALIBUT POINT RD, SITKA, AK 99835
GRIGORY YAKUNIN, BOX 1513, HOMER, AK 99603
SERGEY YAKUNIN, BOX 5044, NIKOLAEVSK, AK 99556
JOHN YOUNG, 20109 SANDRIDGE RD, LONG BEACH, WA 98631
MARK YOUNG, BOX 2016, SITKA, AK 99835
BRETT ZAENGLEIN, 403 MILLS ST, SITKA, AK 99835
MICHAEL ZENUHIN, 3660 VICTOR POINT RD NE, SILVERTON, OR 97381
KYLE ZIMIN, BOX 387, NAKNEK, AK 99633
BILL ZIMMERMAN, BOX 2261, KODIAK, AK 99615

HALIBUT, POT GEAR VESSEL UNDER 60', STATEWIDE
JIM BODDING, 1911 8TH ST, ANACORTES, WA 98221
AJAX EGGLESTON, BOX 1305, HAINES, AK 99827
JAY GILLMAN, BOX 651, ANACORTES, WA 98221
MATTHEW HEGGE, BOX 848, KODIAK, AK 99615
BRIAN MARTENS, 2420 SIXTH AVE, KETCHIKAN, AK 99901
BAE OLNEY.MILLER, 505 OCAIN ST, SITKA, AK 99835
AARON PHILLIPS, BOX 624, PETERSBURG, AK 99833
PATRICK PIKUS, BOX 2843, KODIAK, AK 99615
JOSEPH SHORT, BOX 1224, PETERSBURG, AK 99833
ADAM SWANSON, BOX 2151, PETERSBURG, AK 99833
PEDER THORSTENSON, 1660 HALLINAN ST, LAKE OSWEGO, OR 97034

HALIBUT, DINGLEBAR TROLL, STATEWIDE
ROBERT HUNLEY, BOX 7, MEYERS CHUCK, AK 99903
JOHN LINDBERG, BOX KWP, KODIAK, AK 99615
RICHARD MULLIGAN, 107 SHELIKOF WAY, SITKA, AK 99835
RYAN NICHOLS, 305 ISLANDER DR, SITKA, AK 99835
LES WOODWARD, BOX 2059, WRANGELL, AK 99929

HALIBUT, MECHANICAL JIG, STATEWIDE
PETER ALLAN, BOX 2160, KODIAK, AK 99615
SHAWN DOCHTERMANN, BOX 866, KODIAK, AK 99615
WAYNE ELLIS, BOX 2135, WRANGELL, AK 99929
DAVID GIFFORD, BOX 8125, PORT ALEXANDER, AK 99836
MARTIN GUNDERSEN, BOX 50, SAND POINT, AK 99661
JARL GUSTAFSON, BOX 952, HOMER, AK 99603
THOMAS HOGAN, BOX 1648, HOMER, AK 99603
DANA REID, BOX 8935, KODIAK, AK 99615
ERIC TABER, BOX 2206, KODIAK, AK 99615
BRIAN WARMUTH, BOX 6382, KETCHIKAN, AK 99901

HALIBUT, LONGLINE VESSEL 60' OR OVER, STATEWIDE
PATRICK BAKER, 18502 85TH AVE W, EDMONDS, WA 98026
WADE BASSI, 14130 236TH NE, WOODINVILLE, WA 98077
ORLANDO BELL, BOX 1850, PETERSBURG, AK 99833
ORLANDO BELL, BOX 1609, PETERSBURG, AK 99833
GARY BOGEN, 8108 224TH SW, EDMONDS, WA 98026
THOMAS BRANSHAW, BOX 571, CORDOVA, AK 99574
BLAKE BURKHOLDER, 11038 CHANNELSIDE DR, GULFPORT, MS 39503
RONALD CAMERON, BOX 5421, BELLINGHAM, WA 98227
BENJAMIN CLAMPITT, 17707 TALBOT RD, EDMONDS, WA 98026
DANIEL DELAURENTIS, BOX 954, STEVENSVILLE, MT 59870
RICHARD DENNIS, 2190 OLD GARDINER RD, SEQUIM, WA 98382
LUDGER DOCHTERMANN, BOX 714, KODIAK, AK 99615
ORLANDO ECHEVERIO, BOX 222, STEVENSVILLE, MT 59870
STEVEN FISH, BOX 6448, SITKA, AK 99835
ADAM HACKETT, 228 LAKEVIEW DR, SITKA, AK 99835
ALEXANDRA HACKETT, 228 LAKEVIEW DR, SITKA, AK 99835
ROCK HARRIS, BOX 534, CORDOVA, AK 99574
JAY HEBERT, BOX 920027, DUTCH HARBOR, AK 99692
MIKE HELLIGSO, 11962 GARA DR, KODIAK, AK 99615
WILLIAM HIATT, 645 NE JOHNS AVE #8, NEOTSU, OR 97364
CHARLES HILL, BOX 573, KODIAK, AK 99615
SEAN HOGLUND, 111 BENCH CREEK RD, TONASKET, WA 98855
KENNETH HOLLAND, BOX 608, KODIAK, AK 99615
ANDREW IVERSEN, 23279 ALDO RD NW, POULSBO, WA 98370
CHANDLER JOHNSON, 11330 S RUSSIAN CREEK RD, KODIAK, AK 99615
MICHAEL JOHNSON, 88836 YOUNGS RIVER RD, ASTORIA, OR 97103
RICHARD JOHNSON, 1414 SE OAK ST, PORTLAND, OR 97214
BLAINE KELLY, BOX 3098, INCLINE VILLAGE, NV 89450
JOSE LANDEROS, BOX 1875, GYPSUM, CO 81637
KEN LANE, 5770 HOMESTEADER RD, DEMING, WA 98244
PETER LOPUSZYNSKI, 16712 NE 151ST PL, WOODINVILLE, WA 98072
JAMES MARTINDALE, 9916 GOLDEN GIVEN RD E, TACOMA, WA 98445
JERRY MATTHEWS, BOX 2543, SITKA, AK 99835
CHRISTOPHER MCFADYEN, BOX 592, PETERSBURG, AK 99833
JOHN MCHENRY, 12509 10TH AVE NW, SEATTLE, WA 98117
SHAWN MCMANUS, 17421 NE 166TH PL, WOODINVILLE, WA 98072
RODNEY MCVICKER, 24411 GRACEY TRAIL LN NE, POULSBO, WA 98370
CLINT MECHAM, 495 GREENS WY, MESQUITE, NV 89027
ALAN NOREIDE, 23842 N 85TH ST, SCOTTSDALE, AZ 85255
LADD NORHEIM, BOX 935, PETERSBURG, AK 99833
TAYLOR NORHEIM, BOX 2146, PETERSBURG, AK 99833
MICHAEL OFFERMAN, 17144 13TH AVE NW, SHORELINE, WA 98177
GARY OLSEN, 8620 139TH AVE SE, SNOHOMISH, WA 98290
MARIUS OLSEN, 10809 CHINIAK DR, KODIAK, AK 99615
PETER OLSEN, 609 NW 51ST ST, SEATTLE, WA 98107

BLACK COD (SABLEFISH)—LONGLINE

CLINT PARKS, 105 BLUE BIRD LN, WHITEHALL, MT 59759
JESSE PAVLIK, BOX 256, YAKUTAT, AK 99689
CHARLES REHDER, BOX 2065, HOMER, AK 99603
SETH ROCKWELL, BOX 3143, SEWARD, AK 99664
KEVIN SATHER, 1900 W NICKERSON #213, SEATTLE, WA 98119
ALBERT SCHMEIL, BOX 164, KODIAK, AK 99615
ZACKARY SCHMEIL, BOX 2863, KODIAK, AK 99615
JORG SCHMEISSER, BOX 1791, KODIAK, AK 99615
KRISTIAN SCHONBERG, BOX 866, ALLYN, WA 98524
RANDALL SHEAR, 3008 NW 59TH, SEATTLE, WA 98107
KOLLYN SMITH, 6425 PUGET BCH RD NE, OLYMPIA, WA 98516
JAMES STEVENS, BOX 8593, KODIAK, AK 99615
AARON SUTTON, BOX 1363, KODIAK, AK 99615
MIMI TOLVA, BOX 2117, HOMER, AK 99603
DUANE TORGESON, 4017 HALIBUT POINT RD, SITKA, AK 99835
RICHARD TURVEY, 5900 BULEBELL DR, ANCHORAGE, AK 99516
COLE WASSON, BOX 356, CORDOVA, AK 99574
WILLIAM WIDING, BOX 1659, EDMONDS, WA 98020
MARK WITMAN, BOX 1536, PETERSBURG, AK 99833

HALIBUT, POT GEAR VESSEL 60' OR OVER, STATEWIDE
BLAKE BURKHOLDER, 11038 CHANNELSIDE DR, GULFPORT, MS 39503
BENJAMIN CLAMPITT, 17707 TALBOT RD, EDMONDS, WA 98026
RODNEY MCVICKER, 24411 GRACEY TRAIL LN NE, POULSBO, WA 98370
KRISTIAN SCHONBERG, BOX 866, ALLYN, WA 98524
RANDALL SHEAR, 3008 NW 59TH, SEATTLE, WA 98107
ROY WILSON, BOX 1648, CORDOVA, AK 99574

SABLEFISH, LONGLINE VESSEL UNDER 60', STATEWIDE
GILA ALLEN, 4998 BIRCH ST, ASTORIA, OR 97103
MARK ANDERSON, 49 NORTH STAR LN, FRIDAY HARBOR, WA 98250
CHERYLL ATHORP, BOX 792, WARD COVE, AK 99928
KARI BAEKKELUND, BOX 1537, PETERSBURG, AK 99833
PETER BAEKKELUND, BOX 1537, PETERSBURG, AK 99833
FRANK BALOVICH, BOX 1396, SITKA, AK 99835
PATRICK BARKER, 603 SAWMILL CREEK RD, SITKA, AK 99835
HAHLEN BARKHAU, 123 RIGGS RD, SITKA, AK 99835
KENT BARKHAU, 123 RIGGS RD, SITKA, AK 99835
RIO BARKHAU, 123 RIGGS RD, SITKA, AK 99835
DAVID BARRY, 3980 N DOUGLAS HWY, JUNEAU, AK 99801
DALE BARTELDS, 301 WORTMAN LP, SITKA, AK 99835
ANDREAN BASARGIN, BOX 1393, HOMER, AK 99603
DIONISY BASARGIN, BOX 2325, HOMER, AK 99603
KIRIL BASARGIN, BOX 2395, HOMER, AK 99603
MIRON BASARGIN, BOX 829, HOMER, AK 99603
NIKITA BASARGIN, BOX 2057, HOMER, AK 99603
HENRY BAUMGART, 1504 FAIRVIEW, BELLINGHAM, WA 98229
JARED BAYNE, BOX 2025, SITKA, AK 99835
TODD BAYNE, BOX 2025, SITKA, AK 99835
KEVIN BEAM, 2309 HALIBUT POINT RD #8, SITKA, AK 99835
NELS BECKER, BOX 240838, DOUGLAS, AK 99824
LINDA BEHNKEN, 123 RIGGS RD, SITKA, AK 99835
NANCY BEHNKEN, 117 JEFF DAVIS ST, SITKA, AK 99835
ALAN BENEDICT, 15818 14TH AVE W, LYNNWOOD, WA 98087
HUGH BENTON, BOX 62, ELFIN COVE, AK 99825
JAMES BENTON, BOX 74, ELFIN COVE, AK 99825
BERT BERGMAN, 801 CHARLES #A, SITKA, AK 99835
DAVID BERNHARDT, BOX 1791, SITKA, AK 99835
BRIAN BLANKENSHIP, 2166 A HALIBUT POINT RD, SITKA, AK 99835
BRIAN BLANKENSHIP, 4316 VALLHALLA DR, SITKA, AK 99835
ERIC BLANKENSHIP, 1808 EDGECUMBE DR, SITKA, AK 99835
JEFF BLANKENSHIP, 1709 HALIBUT POINT RD #12, SITKA, AK 99835
JIM BODDING, 1911 8TH ST, ANACORTES, WA 98221
DALE BOSWORTH, BOX 45, PETERSBURG, AK 99833

CHRISTOPHER BOURGEOIS, BOX 1945, CORDOVA, AK 99574
DONALD BRIDGES, BOX 963, KENAI, AK 99611
RYAN BROUGHTON, BOX 264, SEWARD, AK 99664
CHRISTIAN BUSCHMANN, BOX 898, PETERSBURG, AK 99833
MICHAEL BYRER, BOX 1462, PETERSBURG, AK 99833
DANE CALDWELL, 2305 39TH ST, BELLINGHAM, WA 98229
CASEY CAMPBELL, 16235 HEADLANDS CIR, ANCHORAGE, AK 99516
TYLER CASE, 314 PRICE ST, SITKA, AK 99835
BRIAN CASTLE, BOX 243, CRAIG, AK 99921
DAVID CLARK, 507 KATLIAN ST, SITKA, AK 99835
CHARLES CLEMENT, BOX 282, METLAKATLA, AK 99926
RUSSELL COCKRUM, 5791 N TONGASS HWY, KETCHIKAN, AK 99901
MICHAEL COLEMAN, BOX 2054, SITKA, AK 99835
GREGORY COWLING, BOX 1295, PETERSBURG, AK 99833
VERNON CRANE, 111 BAHRT CIR, SITKA, AK 99835
PATRICK CRENNA, 3486 HALIBUT POINT RD, SITKA, AK 99835
RICHARD CURRAN, BOX 1336, SITKA, AK 99835
COLIN DALRYMPLE, 19033 47TH AVE S, SEATTLE, WA 98188
DEVON DALY, 501 CHARTENS ST, SITKA, AK 99835
LORRAINE DALY, 501 CHARTERIS ST #A, SITKA, AK 99835
MIKE DALY, 501 CHARTERIS ST #A, SITKA, AK 99835
DUGAN DANIELS, 507 KATLIAN ST, SITKA, AK 99835
MARK DANIELSON, BOX 782, SITKA, AK 99835
JASON DAVIS, BOX 962, CORDOVA, AK 99574
L DAVIS, 29793 SEWARD HWY, SEWARD, AK 99664
PATRICK DAVIS, BOX 921566, DUTCH HARBOR, AK 99692
RICHARD DAVIS, 2347 KEVIN CT, JUNEAU, AK 99801
EDWARD DAY, BOX 534, VALDEZ, AK 99686
RODNEY DEVINE, 1325 HIGHLAND VIEW LOOP, REDMOND, OR 99756
FORREST DODSON, 263 KATLIAN, SITKA, AK 99835
MICHAEL DOUVILLE, BOX 68, CRAIG, AK 99921
RAYMOND DOUVILLE, BOX 66, CRAIG, AK 99921
JAMES EASTWOOD, BOX 1185, PETERSBURG, AK 99833
GARY EGERTON, 3278 BROOKS HILL RD, LANGLEY, WA 98260
AJAX EGGLESTON, BOX 1305, HAINES, AK 99827
KEN EICHNER, 5166 SHORELINE DR N, KETCHIKAN, AK 99901
GARRETT ELWOOD, 326 HEATHER RD, EVERETT, WA 98203
STEVEN ENGE, BOX 422, PETERSBURG, AK 99833
CHRIS EVENS, BOX 886, PETERSBURG, AK 99833
ERIC EVENS, BOX 1412, PETERSBURG, AK 99833
DANIEL FALVEY, 123 ANNA DR, SITKA, AK 99835
ALEXEY FEFELOV, 1083 N LARKSPUR CIR, HOMER, AK 99603
MICHAEL FILE, BOX 1666, PETERSBURG, AK 99833
KYLE FRANKLIN, BOX 62, PETERSBURG, AK 99833
ROBERT FREDRICKSON, 392 PEARCE RD, PORT ANGELES, WA 98362
ROD FREW, 12107 NW 8TH AVE, VANCOUVER, WA 98685
TAD FUJIOKA, 214 SHOTGUN ALLEY, SITKA, AK 99835
BRIAN GARMON, 744 NW 12TH, CORVALLIS, OR 97333
LEE GILPIN, BOX 1511, PETERSBURG, AK 99833
JASON GJERTSEN, 714 ETOLIN ST, SITKA, AK 99835
SEAN GRISS, BOX 2098, PETERSBURG, AK 99833
CARL GRONN, BOX 8686, KODIAK, AK 99615
EVENINGSTAR GRUTTER, 711 ETOLIN ST, SITKA, AK 99835
FABIAN GRUTTER, 711 ETOLIN ST, SITKA, AK 99835
IVAN GRUTTER, 3205 HALIBUT POINT RD, SITKA, AK 99835
ANTHONY GUGGENBICKLER, BOX 393, WRANGELL, AK 99929
DYLAN HALEY, 500 LINCOLN ST B1, SITKA, AK 99835
MIKE HAMAR, 303 DISTIN AVE, JUNEAU, AK 99801
JASON HAMMER, 1013 S DISCOVERY RD, PORT TOWNSEND, WA 98368
WILLIAM HAMMER, 32 NELSONS LANDING RD, PORT TOWNSEND, WA 98368
KAI HANSEN, BOX 1008, POINT ARENA, CA 95468
SCOTT HANSEN, 5515 E EVERGREEN ST, MESA, AZ 85205
RAYMOND HARRIS, BOX 1318, SEWARD, AK 99664
JAMES HAYDEN, BOX 8085, KODIAK, AK 99615
MATTHEW HEGGE, BOX 848, KODIAK, AK 99615
JAMES HICKLE, BOX 4325, PALMER, AK 99645

BLACK COD (SABLEFISH)—LONGLINE

JONATHAN HILL, 2150 HALIBUT POINT ROAD, SITKA, AK 99835

PETER HITCH, N1010 M35, MENOMINEE, MI 49858

MARK HOFMANN, 1042 OBSTRUCTION PASS RD, OLGA, WA 98279

CHRIS HOLM, 54 N VALLEY RD, NASELLE, WA 98638

OLIVER HOLM, BOX 8749, KODIAK, AK 99615

SEAN HOVIK, BOX 6312, SITKA, AK 99835

COURTNEY HOWARD, 1809 EDGECUMBE DR, SITKA, AK 99835

JAMES HUBBARD, BOX 3302, SEWARD, AK 99664

JAMES HUGHES, 507 KATLIAN ST, SITKA, AK 99835

DAVID HULIEN, 725 W KYLE WILLIAMS CIR, WASILLA, AK 99654

DON HUSE, BOX 373, PETERSBURG, AK 99833

JIMMY HUTCHENS, 20282 ENGLISH RD, MOUNT VERNON, WA 98274

GREGORY INDRELAND, BOX 413, YAKUTAT, AK 99689

SIMON JACOBI, BOX 1065, SITKA, AK 99835

STEVE JANGAARD, 5017 168TH PL NW, STANWOOD, WA 98292

NICHOLAS JOHANSON, 1900 W NICKERSON ST #213, SEATTLE, WA 98119

EARLE JOHNSON, 300 PETERSON AVE APT A, SITKA, AK 99835

ERIK JOHNSON, 1339 S WELDONA LN, SUPERIOR, CO 80027

PAUL JOHNSON, BOX 1083, SITKA, AK 99835

KENNETH JONES, BOX 615, CORDOVA, AK 99574

DIMITIAN KALUGIN, BOX 1624, HOMER, AK 99603

ILESAY KALUGIN, BOX 2727, HOMER, AK 99603

STEVE KALUGIN, BOX 4302, HOMER, AK 99603

G.KEVIN KAMBAK, BOX 426, SITKA, AK 99835

GAVIN KAMBAK, BOX 426, SITKA, AK 99835

BRIAN KANDOLL, BOX 1363, PETERSBURG, AK 99833

SCOT KANDOLL, BOX 2154, PETERSBURG, AK 99833

MATTHEW KINNEY, 103 KRAMER AVE, SITKA, AK 99835

ANDREW KITTAMS, BOX 1544, PETERSBURG, AK 99833

JASON KLEIN, 34 COURTNEY LN, STERLING, CT 6377

DAVID KLEPSER, BOX 8946, KETCHIKAN, AK 99901

MICHAEL KNAUSS, BOX 211, SITKA, AK 99835

DARYL KNUTSEN, 12336 434TH AVE SE, NORTH BEND, WA 98045

GILBERT KNUTSON, 231 KATLIAN ST B-12, SITKA, AK 99835

RANDY KONRAD, HC 60 BOX 2895, HAINES, AK 99827

LEE KRAUSE, BOX 1150, SITKA, AK 99835

RANDY KRAXBERGER, 2832 HANCOCK ST, PORT TOWNSEND, WA 98368

ALEXANDRE KUSNETSOV, BOX 1719, HOMER, AK 99603

LAURENTI KUSNETSOV, BOX 445, HOMER, AK 99603

PAVEL KUSNETSOV, BOX 2627, HOMER, AK 99603

SAFRON KUSNETSOV, BOX 1719, HOMER, AK 99603

ALEXEI KUZMIN, BOX 27, DELTA JUNCTION, AK 99737

DIA KUZMIN, BOX 758, DELTA JUNCTION, AK 99737

FEKLA KUZMIN, BOX 1671, DELTA JUNCTION, AK 99737

LEONTEY KUZMIN, BOX 1542, DELTA JUNCTION, AK 99737

NIKITA KUZMIN, BOX 1542, DELTA JUNCTION, AK 99737

SERGI KUZMIN, BOX 264, DELTA JUNCTION, AK 99737

VASILY KUZMIN, 16727 LEARY RD, WOODBURN, OR 97071

LAZARO KUZNETSOV, BOX 315, HOMER, AK 99603

CALE LADUKE, BOX 1216, SITKA, AK 99835

JOHN LEE, 1300 EDGECUMBE DR, SITKA, AK 99835

BRETT LISKEY, 46 CEDAR CREEK LN, FT DEFIANCE, VA 24437

TEAL LOHSE, BOX 2464, CORDOVA, AK 99574

RYELAN LONG, 3233 PENINSULA RD, KODIAK, AK 99615

PETER LONGRICH, BOX 2677, KODIAK, AK 99615

DOUGLAS LYLE, BOX 2606, YELM, WA 98597

DYLAN LYON, BOX 332, HOMER, AK 99603

MARCUS LYON, BOX 1070, HOMER, AK 99603

YAKOBI LYON, 50884 MOUNTAIN GLACIER CT, HOMER, AK 99603

DAVID LYONS, BOX 379, SITKA, AK 99835

RICHARD MAHER, BOX 1579, HOMER, AK 99603

MATTHEW MARINKOVICH, BOX 2084, FRIDAY HARBOR, WA 98250

BRIAN MARTENS, 2420 SIXTH AVE, KETCHIKAN, AK 99901

SCOTT MARTIN, BOX 2033, PETERSBURG, AK 99833

DOROFEY MARTUSHEV, BOX 368, HOMER, AK 99603

KIRIL MARTUSHEV, BOX 1939, HOMER, AK 99603

PETR MARTUSHEV, BOX 452, ANCHOR POINT, AK 99556

TROFIM MARTUSHEV, BOX 879298, WASILLA, AK 99687

SHELTON MAVES, BOX 117, CRAIG, AK 99921

MICHAEL MAYO, 2808 SAWMILL CREEK RD, SITKA, AK 99835

CHARLES MCELDOWNEY, BOX 1731, SEWARD, AK 99664

JEFFRY MCENTIRE, BOX 833, HAINES, AK 99827

MONTE MCFARLAND, 4314 VALLHALLA, SITKA, AK 99835

GARY MCMASTER, 1722 EDGECUMBE DR, SITKA, AK 99835

MICHAEL MEINTS, BOX 2402, CORDOVA, AK 99574

FRANK MELSETH, BOX 66, SAND POINT, AK 99661

KATRESE MELVILLE, 4202 HALIBUT POINT RD, SITKA, AK 99835

WILLIAM MENISH, BOX 877, PETERSBURG, AK 99833

NELSON MERRELL, 1323 GLACIER HWY, JUNEAU, AK 99801

MATTHEW METCALF, 2999 JOSHUA CT, HOLLAND, MI 49424

JAMES MILLER, BOX 1184, PETERSBURG, AK 99833

GEORGE MILNE, BOX 1846, HOMER, AK 99603

KATHLEEN MOATS, 1720 DOUGLAS HWY, DOUGLAS, AK 99824

JOSHUA MOORE, BOX 2015, PETERSBURG, AK 99833

GARY MULLIGAN, 224 MARINE ST #A, SITKA, AK 99835

RICHARD MULLIGAN, 107 SHELIKOF WAY, SITKA, AK 99835

ALICIA MUNYER, 2716 HALIBUT POINT RD #5, SITKA, AK 99835

ALEKSANDRO MURACHEV, BOX 2259, HOMER, AK 99603

SHEILA MURPHY, 524 ROOT ST, PORT TOWNSEND, WA 98368

CHRISTINE NAGY, HC 60 BOX 2895, HAINES, AK 99827

DONALD NASH, BOX 1167, HAINES, AK 99827

NICHOLAS NEKEFEROFF, 3416 HALIBUT POINT RD #A, SITKA, AK 99835

RYAN NICHOLS, 305 ISLANDER DR, SITKA, AK 99835

MICHAEL NILSEN, BOX 2069, PETERSBURG, AK 99833

CHARLES NOGGLE, 10724 167TH AVE SE, SNOHOMISH, WA 98290

DAVID OEN, BOX 2473, SITKA, AK 99835

ERIC OEN, BOX 2026, SITKA, AK 99835

DOUGLAS OGILVY, BOX 323, GUSTAVUS, AK 99826

BAE OLNEY.MILLER, 505 OCAIN ST, SITKA, AK 99835

NICK OLNEY.MILLER, 3006 BARKER ST, SITKA, AK 99835

ANDREW OLSEN, 724 CEDAR ST, EDMONDS, WA 98020

DAVID OLSEN, 724 CEDAR ST, EDMONDS, WA 98020

NELSON OOKA, BOX 1218, SEWARD, AK 99664

ARTHUR OSBORNE, BOX 240925, DOUGLAS, AK 99824

ALAN OTNESS, BOX 317, PETERSBURG, AK 99833

NELS OTNESS, BOX 366, PETERSBURG, AK 99833

NELS OTNESS, BOX 2058, PETERSBURG, AK 99833

QUINN PADGETT, 215 MEDORA WAY, EVERETT, WA 98201

CASEY PAPE, BOX 625, CORDOVA, AK 99574

MEGAN PASTERNAK, BOX 830, SITKA, AK 99835

WALTER PASTERNAK, BOX 830, SITKA, AK 99835

MATTHEW PEAVEY, BOX 442, CRAIG, AK 99921

ALFRED PEELER, BOX 761, PETERSBURG, AK 99833

MAXWELL PEELER, BOX 761, PETERSBURG, AK 99833

JOHN PETRABORG, BOX 6067, SITKA, AK 99835

CHARLES PETTICREW, BOX 971, WRANGELL, AK 99929

RICHARD PETTICREW, BOX 971, WRANGELL, AK 99929

BRYON PFUNDT, BOX 1162, PETERSBURG, AK 99833

AARON PHILLIPS, BOX 624, PETERSBURG, AK 99833

DAVID PHILLIPS, BOX 1676, CORDOVA, AK 99574

JAMES PHILLIPS, BOX 109, PELICAN, AK 99832

JEB PHILLIPS, BOX 1253, PETERSBURG, AK 99833

JORDAN PHILLIPS, 321 PETERSON AVE, SITKA, AK 99835

KENNETH PHIPPEN, 312 TILSON ST, SITKA, AK 99835

PATRICK PIKUS, BOX 2843, KODIAK, AK 99615

NORMAN PILLEN, 2517 ADDY GIFFORD RD, ADDY, WA 99101

ANDREY POLUSHKIN, BOX 2458, HOMER, AK 99603

VLADIMIR POLUSHKIN, BOX 879276, WASILLA, AK 99687

ROBERT PROULX, BOX 1736, WRANGELL, AK 99929

MICHAEL PRUDEN, 169 NIXON PEAK RD, BOZEMAN, MT 59715

BLACK COD (SABLEFISH)—LONGLINE

JAMES QUIGLEY, BOX 80, CRAIG, AK 99921
JOZIAH REAR, 1007 HALIBUT POINT RD, SITKA, AK 99835
THELTON REAR, 1007 HALIBUT POINT RD, SITKA, AK 99835
RONALD REED, BOX 1437, PETERSBURG, AK 99833
MARTY REMUND, BOX 1295, HAINES, AK 99827
ALEXANDER REUTOV, BOX 687, SOLDOTNA, AK 99669
ANDREY REUTOV, BOX 2212, HOMER, AK 99603
CORNILY REUTOV, BOX 3523, HOMER, AK 99603
DIONICI REUTOV, BOX 4251, HOMER, AK 99603
ELESEY REUTOV, BOX 1251, STERLING, AK 99672
FEODOR REUTOV, BOX 390, KODIAK, AK 99615
FEODORA REUTOV, BOX 4251, HOMER, AK 99603
IVAN REUTOV, BOX 4092, HOMER, AK 99603
IVONE REUTOV, BOX 5053, NIKOLAEVSK, AK 99556
LAVRENTII REUTOV, BOX 1190, HOMER, AK 99603
LAZAR REUTOV, BOX 258, HOMER, AK 99603
MARK REUTOV, BOX 3523, HOMER, AK 99603
MIHEY REUTOV, BOX 2063, HOMER, AK 99603
SEVEREAN REUTOV, BOX 2230, HOMER, AK 99603
TRIFILYI REUTOV, BOX 793, HOMER, AK 99603
YAKOV REUTOV, BOX 1251, STERLING, AK 99672
DWIGHT RIEDERER, 22928 SE 406TH ST, ENUMCLAW, WA 98022
CALVIN ROBINSON, BOX 2225, SITKA, AK 99835
HENRY ROBINSON, 306 NICOLE DR, SITKA, AK 99835
SIGURD RUTTER, 310 TILSON, SITKA, AK 99835
VLADIMIR SANAROV, BOX 2175, HOMER, AK 99603
WALTER SARGENT, 1830 MISSION RD, KODIAK, AK 99615
STANLEY SAVLAND, BOX 621, HOONAH, AK 99829
MART SCHONBERG, 125 SPOTTED FAWN COURT, SEDONA, AZ 86351
PETER SCHONBERG, 75-816F HIONA ST, HOLUALOA, HI 96725
PAUL SCHREIBER, 231 KATLIAN #A10, SITKA, AK 99835
J.CARLOS SCHWANTES, BOX 2335, SITKA, AK 99835
JOSEPH SCHWANTES, BOX 2674, SITKA, AK 99835
KEVIN SEABECK, 8555 30TH NW, SEATTLE, WA 98117
AARON SEVERSON, BOX 507, PETERSBURG, AK 99833
CAMERON SEVERSON, BOX 2118, PETERSBURG, AK 99833
MARK SEVERSON, BOX 1502, PETERSBURG, AK 99833
BILL SHIPP, 2400 NW 80TH ST PMB 268, SEATTLE, WA 98117
JOSEPH SHORT, BOX 1224, PETERSBURG, AK 99833
JOHN SKEELE, 262 KAAGWAANTAAN ST, SITKA, AK 99835
JAY SKORDAHL, 48174 WESTOAK RD, WESTFIR, OR 97492
KELSEY SKORDAHL, 109C LANCE DR, SITKA, AK 99835
LUCAS SKORDAHL, 110 HARBOR MOUNTAIN DR, SITKA, AK 99835
GARY SLAVEN, BOX 205, PETERSBURG, AK 99833
VOLNEY SMITH, 2318 HALIBUT POINT RD, SITKA, AK 99835
EVANS SPARKS, 100 DONNA DR, SITKA, AK 99835
STEVE STARK, 23077 JOAQUIN RIDGE DR, MURRIETA, CA 92562
ANNA STRICKLAND, 426 ANDREWS ST, SITKA, AK 99835
DYLAN SWANBERG, BOX 3053, SITKA, AK 99835
ADAM SWANSON, BOX 2151, PETERSBURG, AK 99833
JOHN SWANSON, BOX 1546, PETERSBURG, AK 99833
KEITH SWICK, BOX 42, SELDOVIA, AK 99663
KENNETH SWICK, BOX 112, SELDOVIA, AK 99663
JEFF THOMAS, 55784 HWY 112, PORT ANGELES, WA 98363
JAY THOMASSEN, BOX 1451, PETERSBURG, AK 99833
TROY THOMASSEN, BOX 152, PETERSBURG, AK 99833
DAVID THOMPSON, 303 S WASHINGTON AVE, PRESCOTT, AZ 86303
PEDER THORSTENSON, 1660 HALLINAN ST, LAKE OSWEGO, OR 97034
DAVID TOW, BOX 314, PETERSBURG, AK 99833
CHARLES TRIERSCHIELD, BOX 616, SITKA, AK 99835
ERIK VELSKO, 780 DAYBREEZE CT, HOMER, AK 99603
GARY WADDLE, BOX 994, SAHUARITA, AZ 85629
STUART WEATHERS, BOX 1734, SITKA, AK 99835
STEVE WEISSBERG, 455 CHARTERIS ST, SITKA, AK 99835
ADRIENNE WILBER, 705 ETOLIN ST, SITKA, AK 99835

CHAD WINNOP, 100 KINCROFT WAY #A, SITKA, AK 99835
LES WOODWARD, BOX 2059, WRANGELL, AK 99929
ANDY WORHATCH, BOX 614, PETERSBURG, AK 99833
RANDALL WORTMAN, BOX 271, CRAIG, AK 99921
FRANK WRIGHT, BOX 497, HOONAH, AK 99829
PHILLIP WYMAN, BOX 2507, SITKA, AK 99835
SETH WYMAN, 5024 ROBINWOOD LN, BOW, WA 98232
TODD WYMAN, 2176 HALIBUT POINT RD, SITKA, AK 99835
GRIGORY YAKUNIN, BOX 1513, HOMER, AK 99603
PAUL YANAK, 8409 W 2200 S, CEDAR CITY, UT 84720
BRENT YOUNG, 22896 BULSON RD, MOUNT VERNON, WA 98274
JOHN YOUNG, 20109 SANDRIDGE RD, LONG BEACH, WA 98631
MARK YOUNG, BOX 2016, SITKA, AK 99835
CHRIS YSTAD, 104 CHIRIKOV DR, SITKA, AK 99835

SABLEFISH, POT GEAR VESSEL UNDER 60', STATEWIDE

JIM BODDING, 1911 8TH ST, ANACORTES, WA 98221
JEREMY BROWN, 3217 GREEN WOOD AVE, BELLINGHAM, WA 98225
JOHN CLEAVER, 100 BAHOVEC CT, SITKA, AK 99835
BRIAN DAFFORN, 1517 N 80TH ST, SEATTLE, WA 98103
AJAX EGGLESTON, BOX 1305, HAINES, AK 99827
JAY GILLMAN, BOX 651, ANACORTES, WA 98221
CARL GRONN, BOX 8686, KODIAK, AK 99615
MATTHEW HEGGE, BOX 848, KODIAK, AK 99615
BEN LEY, 8316 WINDING RUN RD, ST LOUISVILLE, OH 43071
KAI MALICOAT, BOX 2266, SITKA, AK 99835
JULIAN MANOS, BOX 749, GIRDWOOD, AK 99587
BRIAN MARTENS, 2420 SIXTH AVE, KETCHIKAN, AK 99901
BAE OLNEY.MILLER, 505 OCAIN ST, SITKA, AK 99835
AARON PHILLIPS, BOX 624, PETERSBURG, AK 99833
PATRICK PIKUS, BOX 2843, KODIAK, AK 99615
JOSEPH SHORT, BOX 1224, PETERSBURG, AK 99833
ADAM SWANSON, BOX 2151, PETERSBURG, AK 99833
PEDER THORSTENSON, 1660 HALLINAN ST, LAKE OSWEGO, OR 97034

SABLEFISH, DINGLEBAR TROLL, STATEWIDE

ROBERT ROOD, 6294 NE LARIAT LOOP, BAINBRIDGE ISLAND, WA 98110

SABLEFISH, NET GEAR MAXIMUM VESSEL 50', PRNCE WILLIAM SOUND

JON VANHYNING, BOX 872580, WASILLA, AK 99687

SABLEFISH, FIXED GEAR MAXIMUM VESSEL 90', PRINCE WILLIAM SOUND

DEBORAH ECKLEY, BOX 1274, CORDOVA, AK 99574
THOMAS MANOS, BOX 749, GIRDWOOD, AK 99587

SABLEFISH, FIXED GEAR MAXIMUM VESSEL 60', PRINCE WILLIAM SOUND

NELSON OOKA, BOX 1218, SEWARD, AK 99664
JOHN PALMISANO, 7249 SHADOWBROOK DR, KIRTLAND, OH 44094
ANDREY POLUSHKIN, BOX 2458, HOMER, AK 99603

SABLEFISH, FIXED GEAR MAXIMUM VESSEL 50', PRINCE WILLIAM SOUND

IAN AMERICUS, BOX 2112, CORDOVA, AK 99574
LEO AMERICUS, BOX 2112, CORDOVA, AK 99574
ELI BEEDLE, BOX 2454, SEWARD, AK 99664
JOHN EARLE, BOX 126, GIRDWOOD, AK 99587
MICHAEL GLASEN, BOX 432, CORDOVA, AK 99574
BRITT.MARI HOLLOWAY, BOX 770912, EAGLE RIVER, AK 99577
RODERICK JENSEN, BOX 1614, CORDOVA, AK 99574
KENNETH JONES, BOX 615, CORDOVA, AK 99574

BLACK COD (SABLEFISH)—LONGLINE

VICTOR JONES, BOX 1831, CORDOVA, AK 99574
SANDRA KING, BOX 965, CORDOVA, AK 99574
EROS KUZMIN, BOX 141531, ANCHORAGE, AK 99514
IOSIF KUZMIN, 709 PINTAIL ST, SILVERTON, OR 97381
ANATOLIE LISOV, 407 E SHORE RD, NINE MILE FALLS, WA 99026
MICHAEL MAHONEY, BOX 2416, CORDOVA, AK 99574
CHRISTOPHER MALLORY, BOX 904, CORDOVA, AK 99574
ZENON MARTUSHEV, BOX 1011, HOMER, AK 99603
BRIAN MASON, 19435 UPPER SKYLINE DR, EAGLE RIVER, AK 99577
GARY MASON, 18540 MCCRARY RD, EAGLE RIVER, AK 99577
KRISTA MASON, 20510 DAVID AVE, EAGLE RIVER, AK 99577
SHARRY MILLER, BOX 2961, VALDEZ, AK 99686
THANE MILLER, BOX 2961, VALDEZ, AK 99686
LYLE MYRVOLD, BOX 870181, WASILLA, AK 99687
THOMAS OOKA, BOX 1218, SEWARD, AK 99664
BRITT PEDICORD, 1809 S PENNSYLVANIA ST, DENVER, CO 80210
FEODOR REUTOV, BOX 1388, HOMER, AK 99603
LAVRENTII REUTOV, BOX 1190, HOMER, AK 99603
ONICIFOR REUTOV, BOX 2197, HOMER, AK 99603
BRETT ROTH, 7810 CASEY CIR, ANCHORAGE, AK 99507
JACK SCOBY, BOX 966, SEWARD, AK 99664
GEORGE SCOTT, BOX 281, GIRDWOOD, AK 99587
KARL SKRIFVARS, BOX 770912, EAGLE RIVER, AK 99577
MARTIN SPARGO, 4251 DIMOND WAY, WASILLA, AK 99654
GREG TIPIKIN, 2725 N JENNY ANNE PL, WASILLA, AK 99654
TROY TIRRELL, BOX 600, CORDOVA, AK 99574
KENNETH VLASOFF, 6300 ANDOVER DR, ANCHORAGE, AK 99516
ALEXANDRA VON.WICHMAN, 2940 MALLARD LN, ANCHORAGE, AK 99508
KJERSTI VON.WICHMAN, 2940 MALLARD LN, ANCHORAGE, AK 99508
W.BRADFORD VON.WICHMAN, 2940 MALLARD LN, ANCHORAGE, AK 99508
RIC VRSALOVIC, BOX 113004, ANCHORAGE, AK 99511
TIM WILKIE, BOX 1726, SEWARD, AK 99664
CALISTA WILSON, 17701 SPAIN DR, ANCHORAGE, AK 99516
RILEY WILSON, 17701 SPAIN DR, ANCHORAGE, AK 99516

SABLEFISH, FIXED GEAR MAXIMUM VESSEL 35', PRINCE WILLIAM SOUND

BRYAN ANDERSON, 10809 CRESENT VALLEY DR NW, GIG HARBOR, WA 98332
VICTORIA BAKER, BOX 600, CORDOVA, AK 99574
NATASHA CASCIANO, BOX 584, CORDOVA, AK 99574
RICHARD CASCIANO, BOX 584, CORDOVA, AK 99574
EUGENE DESJARLAIS, 6550 LIMESTONE CIR, ANCHORAGE, AK 99507
ROBERT ECKLEY, BOX 1274, CORDOVA, AK 99574
DUANE EDELMAN, BOX 153, VALDEZ, AK 99686
DENNIS HUTCHINSON, 31805 NE CLEARWATER DR, YACOLT, WA 98675
PETER JENKINS, 2400 TASHA DR, ANCHORAGE, AK 99502
KYLE KING, BOX 956, CORDOVA, AK 99574
MARK KING, BOX 965, CORDOVA, AK 99574
MARK MARTUSHEFF, BOX 223, ANCHOR POINT, AK 99556
DOROFEY MARTUSHEV, BOX 368, HOMER, AK 99603
JAMIE OAKLEY, 2030 PAXSON DR, ANCHORAGE, AK 99504
MICHAEL SOWARDS, 2195 N GUNFLINT TRAIL, WASILLA, AK 99623
PHILLIP STACEY, 12830 OOMIAK CIR, ANCHORAGE, AK 99515
JONATHAN WILKIE, 33354 BEAR LAKE RD, SEWARD, AK 99664

SABLEFISH, LONGLINE, NORTHERN SOUTHEAST

THERESA ALLEN.OLSON, 3009 HALIBUT POINT RD, SITKA, AK 99835
FRANK BALOVICH, BOX 1396, SITKA, AK 99835
DALE BARTELDS, 301 WORTMAN LP, SITKA, AK 99835
MARTIN BEAM, 35628 WHITNAH LN, RICHLAND, OR 97870
RANDALL BEASON, BOX 240552, DOUGLAS, AK 99824
NELS BECKER, BOX 240838, DOUGLAS, AK 99824
ORLANDO BELL, BOX 1850, PETERSBURG, AK 99833
BRIAN BLANKENSHIP, 2166 A HALIBUT POINT RD, SITKA, AK 99835
DALE BOSWORTH, BOX 45, PETERSBURG, AK 99833

LONNIE CHESNUT, BOX 2506, PALMER, AK 99645
STEPHEN CLAYTON, BOX 2476, SITKA, AK 99835
WILLIAM CONNOR, BOX 1124, PETERSBURG, AK 99833
RICHARD CURRAN, BOX 1336, SITKA, AK 99835
DAVID DAPCEVICH, 1720 DOUGLAS HWY, DOUGLAS, AK 99824
RICHARD DAUGHERTY, BOX 34864, JUNEAU, AK 99803
NICHOLAS DAVIS, BOX 234, KAKE, AK 99830
JOHN DUPREE, BOX 684, PETERSBURG, AK 99833
PAUL DUPREE, BOX 684, PETERSBURG, AK 99833
MICHAEL ERB, 16461 ST JAMES CIR, ANCHORAGE, AK 99516
CUB FINNEY, 9951 STEPHEN RICHARDS #46, JUNEAU, AK 99803
STEVEN FISH, BOX 6448, SITKA, AK 99835
ALAN FISHER, 9195 JAMES BLVD, JUNEAU, AK 99801
MARK FITZJARRALD, BOX 22982, JUNEAU, AK 99802
JONATHAN FUHRER, 6828 SHADOWBROOK DR, GOLETA, CA 93117
DAWN GILLMAN, BOX 651, ANACORTES, WA 98221
MARTHA GREBA, 104 JAMESTOWN DR, SITKA, AK 99835
IVAN GRUTTER, 3205 HALIBUT POINT RD, SITKA, AK 99835
JASON HAMMER, 1013 S DISCOVERY RD, PORT TOWNSEND, WA 98368
WILLIAM HAMMER, 32 NELSONS LANDING RD, PORT TOWNSEND, WA 98368
WILLIAM HANKINS, BOX 3261, SEWARD, AK 99664
BRUCE HATTRICK, 631 COOK ST, KETCHIKAN, AK 99901
JAMES HUBBARD, BOX 3302, SEWARD, AK 99664
MATTHEW HUBBARD, BOX 3302, SEWARD, AK 99664
RHONDA HUBBARD, BOX 3302, SEWARD, AK 99664
SCOTT HUBBARD, BOX 3302, SEWARD, AK 99664
GLENDA HUFF, 15717 CRESCENT VALLEY DR NW, GIG HARBOR, WA 98332
KARI JOHNSON, BOX 6448, SITKA, AK 99835
BRIAN KANDOLL, BOX 1363, PETERSBURG, AK 99833
SIDNEY KINNEY, 103 KRAMER AVE, SITKA, AK 99835
DOUGLAS LECHNER, 13101 BAINBRIDGE RD, ANCHORAGE, AK 99516
TARA LEE.MASON, 16526 GLACIER HWY, JUNEAU, AK 99801
ANGELA LUNDA, 19400 BEARDSLEY WAY, JUNEAU, AK 99801
ROSS MARLEY, 308 ISLANDER DR, SITKA, AK 99835
SIGURD MATHISEN, BOX 1460, PETERSBURG, AK 99833
MICHAEL MAYO, 2808 SAWMILL CREEK RD, SITKA, AK 99835
SHERYL MAYO, 2800 SAWMILL CREEK RD, SITKA, AK 99835
JAMES MILLER, BOX 1184, PETERSBURG, AK 99833
JOSHUA MOORE, BOX 2015, PETERSBURG, AK 99833
MARY MURRAY.JENKINS, 2716 HALIBUT POINT RD #33, SITKA, AK 99835
RONALD NYMAN, 2395 AURORA CT, JUNEAU, AK 99801
DAVID OLSEN, 724 CEDAR ST, EDMONDS, WA 98020
ARTHUR OSBORNE, BOX 240925, DOUGLAS, AK 99824
ALAN OTNESS, BOX 317, PETERSBURG, AK 99833
DUSTIN PETERS, BOX 726, WARD COVE, AK 99928
ALEC PFUNDT, BOX 1342, PETERSBURG, AK 99833
AARON PHILLIPS, BOX 624, PETERSBURG, AK 99833
FREDERICK PHILLIPS, 1210 EDGECOMB DR, SITKA, AK 99835
JAMES PHILLIPS, BOX 109, PELICAN, AK 99832
MARTY REMUND, BOX 1295, HAINES, AK 99827
STEPHEN RHOADS, 111 JAMESTOWN DR, SITKA, AK 99835
DWIGHT RIEDERER, 22928 SE 406TH ST, ENUMCLAW, WA 98022
ERIC ROSVOLD, BOX 1144, PETERSBURG, AK 99833
STANLEY SAVLAND, BOX 621, HOONAH, AK 99829
JULIA SCHONBERG, BOX 877, PETERSBURG, AK 99833
MART SCHONBERG, 125 SPOTTED FAWN COURT, SEDONA, AZ 86351
PAUL SCHREIBER, 231 KATLIAN #A10, SITKA, AK 99835
AARON SEVERSON, BOX 507, PETERSBURG, AK 99833
MARK SEVERSON, BOX 1502, PETERSBURG, AK 99833
JEANNE SORENSON, 51454 OCEAN ENTRANCE DR, KENAI, AK 99611
PAUL SORENSON, 51454 OCEAN ENTRANCE DR, KENAI, AK 99611
ALBERT STROM, 4039 29TH AVE W, SEATTLE, WA 98199
DUANE TORGESON, 4017 HALIBUT POINT RD, SITKA, AK 99835
ZAK WASS, BOX 6507, SITKA, AK 99835
MARY WEBER, 5301 BLUEBERRY LN, JUNEAU, AK 99801
PHILIP WILEY, BOX 219, WHITE BIRD, ID 83554

LING COD FISHING LIST—LONGLINE / TROLL

PHILLIP WYMAN, BOX 2507, SITKA, AK 99835
MARK YOUNG, BOX 2016, SITKA, AK 99835

SABLEFISH, LONGLINE VESSEL 60' OR OVER, STATEWIDE
KEVIN ABENA, 1628 LYNDEN WAY, KODIAK, AK 99615
PATRICK BAKER, 18502 85TH AVE W, EDMONDS, WA 98026
WADE BASSI, 14130 236TH NE, WOODINVILLE, WA 98077
ORLANDO BELL, BOX 1609, PETERSBURG, AK 99833
GARY BOGEN, 8108 224TH SW, EDMONDS, WA 98026
THOMAS BRANSHAW, BOX 571, CORDOVA, AK 99574
BLAKE BURKHOLDER, 11038 CHANNELSIDE DR, GULFPORT, MS 39503
BENJAMIN CLAMPITT, 17707 TALBOT RD, EDMONDS, WA 98026
DANIEL DELAURENTIS, BOX 954, STEVENSVILLE, MT 59870
ORLANDO ECHEVERIO, BOX 222, STEVENSVILLE, MT 59870
PETER ERICKSON, BOX 280, BAY CENTER, WA 98527
STEVEN FISH, BOX 6448, SITKA, AK 99835
ADAM HACKETT, 228 LAKEVIEW DR, SITKA, AK 99835
SIGURD HAVERMAN, 20124 GREENWOOD AVE N, SHORELINE, WA 98133
JAY HEBERT, BOX 920027, DUTCH HARBOR, AK 99692
ANDREW IVERSEN, 23279 ALDO RD NW, POULSBO, WA 98370
RICHARD JOHNSON, 1414 SE OAK ST, PORTLAND, OR 97214
BLAINE KELLY, BOX 3098, INCLINE VILLAGE, NV 89450
TIM KNAPP, BOX 144, BOW, WA 98232
CHATHAM LEE, 1300 EDGECUMBE DR, SITKA, AK 99835
PETER LOPUSZYNSKI, 16712 NE 151ST PL, WOODINVILLE, WA 98072
JAMES MARTINDALE, 9916 GOLDEN GIVEN RD E, TACOMA, WA 98445
JERRY MATTHEWS, BOX 2543, SITKA, AK 99835
CHRISTOPHER MCFADYEN, BOX 592, PETERSBURG, AK 99833
BRIAN MCKENNA, 4905 SABAL LAKE CIR, SARASOTA, FL 34238
SHAWN MCMANUS, 17421 NE 166TH PL, WOODINVILLE, WA 98072
RODNEY MCVICKER, 24411 GRACEY TRAIL LN NE, POULSBO, WA 98370
CLINT MECHAM, 495 GREENS WY, MESQUITE, NV 89027
ALAN NOREIDE, 23842 N 85TH ST, SCOTTSDALE, AZ 85255
MICHAEL OFFERMAN, 17144 13TH AVE NW, SHORELINE, WA 98177
GARY OLSEN, 8620 139TH AVE SE, SNOHOMISH, WA 98290
KRISTIAN OLSEN, 5650 24TH AVE NW #617, SEATTLE, WA 98107
PETER OLSEN, 609 NW 51ST ST, SEATTLE, WA 98107
JESSE PAVLIK, BOX 256, YAKUTAT, AK 99689
DAVID PHILLIPS, BOX 1676, CORDOVA, AK 99574
NORMAN PILLEN, 2517 ADDY GIFFORD RD, ADDY, WA 99101
MICHAEL REIF, BOX 2346, SITKA, AK 99835
SETH ROCKWELL, BOX 3143, SEWARD, AK 99664
KEVIN SATHER, 1900 W NICKERSON #213, SEATTLE, WA 98119
JORG SCHMEISSER, BOX 1791, KODIAK, AK 99615
KRISTIAN SCHONBERG, BOX 866, ALLYN, WA 98524
KOLLYN SMITH, 6425 PUGET BCH RD NE, OLYMPIA, WA 98516
JAMES STEVENS, BOX 8593, KODIAK, AK 99615
JEFFERY THELEN, BOX 645, CORDOVA, AK 99574
DUANE TORGESON, 4017 HALIBUT POINT RD, SITKA, AK 99835
RICHARD TURVEY, 5900 BULEBELL DR, ANCHORAGE, AK 99516
GILBERT URATA, BOX 518, CORDOVA, AK 99574
NICHOLAS VERSTEEG, BOX 1752, PETERSBURG, AK 99833
COLE WASSON, BOX 356, CORDOVA, AK 99574
ADAM WESTFALL, 5956 38TH AVE SW, SEATTLE, WA 98126
WILLIAM WIDING, BOX 1659, EDMONDS, WA 98020

SABLEFISH, LONGLINE, SOUTHERN SOUTHEAST
DALE BOSWORTH, BOX 45, PETERSBURG, AK 99833
JOSEPH BURNS, 1011 S POINT HIGGINS RD, KETCHIKAN, AK 99901
MATTHEW CARLE, BOX 32, HYDABURG, AK 99922
WILLIAM CONNOR, BOX 1124, PETERSBURG, AK 99833
JANET ENGLE, BOX 9296, KETCHIKAN, AK 99901
JOHN ENGLE, BOX 9296, KETCHIKAN, AK 99901

KYLE FRANKLIN, BOX 62, PETERSBURG, AK 99833
BRUCE HATTRICK, 631 COOK ST, KETCHIKAN, AK 99901
DANNY HAYNES, BOX 7036, KETCHIKAN, AK 99901
WILLIAM HORWATH, 3515 HAWKINS AVE, KETCHIKAN, AK 99901
JAMES HUBBARD, BOX 3302, SEWARD, AK 99664
ANDREW KITTAMS, BOX 1544, PETERSBURG, AK 99833
WILLIAM MENISH, BOX 877, PETERSBURG, AK 99833
JAMES OLSEN, 14406 24TH AVE SE, MILL CREEK, WA 98012
RONALD OLSON, BOX 123, KLAWOCK, AK 99925
KIMBERLY PETERS, 6482 ROOSEVELT DR, KETCHIKAN, AK 99901
CHARLES PETTICREW, BOX 971, WRANGELL, AK 99929

SABLEFISH, POT GEAR VESSEL 60' OR OVER, STATEWIDE
BLAKE BURKHOLDER, 11038 CHANNELSIDE DR, GULFPORT, MS 39503
BENJAMIN CLAMPITT, 17707 TALBOT RD, EDMONDS, WA 98026
PAUL CLAMPITT, 7721 168TH PL SW, EDMONDS, WA 98026
MICHAEL HANKINS, BOX 249, GERVAIS, OR 97026
WILLIAM HIATT, 645 NE JOHNS AVE #8, NEOTSU, OR 97364
GEORGON LAPHAM, BOX 1478, NEWPORT, OR 97365
RODNEY MCVICKER, 24411 GRACEY TRAIL LN NE, POULSBO, WA 98370
MICHAEL OFFERMAN, 17144 13TH AVE NW, SHORELINE, WA 98177
KRISTIAN SCHONBERG, BOX 866, ALLYN, WA 98524
RANDALL SHEAR, 3008 NW 59TH, SEATTLE, WA 98107
WILLIAM WAHL, 20735 WAGONTIRE WAY, BEND, OR 97701
ROY WILSON, BOX 1648, CORDOVA, AK 99574

SABLEFISH, POT GEAR, SOUTHERN SOUTHEAST
CYNTHIA JOHANSON, BOX 276, KLAWOCK, AK 99925
JOHN JOHANSON, BOX 276, KLAWOCK, AK 99925
MIKE MARQUES, 10 MARINA DR, BELLINGHAM, WA 98229

LING COD, HAND TROLL, STATEWIDE
PATRICK BARKER, 603 SAWMILL CREEK RD, SITKA, AK 99835
PAUL BOOTS, 13137 GULF CIR, ANCHORAGE, AK 99515
BRUCE BOWMAN, HC 60 BOX 227 I, COPPER CENTER, AK 99573
DAN EAMES, 7436 TYRE DR, ANCHORAGE, AK 99502
KEVIN MCNAMEE, BOX 6243, SITKA, AK 99835
CLAYTON STROMQUIST, 1302 SMC #31, SITKA, AK 99835
JOSH WISNIEWSKI, BOX 474, SITKA, AK 99835

LING COD, LONGLINE VESSEL UNDER 60', STATEWIDE
CHARLES BLATTNER, BOX 33916, JUNEAU, AK 99803
HENRY CARLSON, BOX 500, CORDOVA, AK 99574
DAWSON EVENDEN, BOX 244, HAINES, AK 99827
KURT GOETZINGER, BOX 1268, CORDOVA, AK 99574
SCOTT HUBBARD, BOX 3302, SEWARD, AK 99664
H.DANIEL HULL, 19300 VILLAGES SCENIC PKWY, ANCHORAGE, AK 99516
LYLE KRITCHEN, BOX 935, CORDOVA, AK 99574
PAMELA LEASK, BOX 759, WARD COVE, AK 99928
TEAL LOHSE, BOX 2464, CORDOVA, AK 99574
TRAE LOHSE, BOX 2378, CORDOVA, AK 99574
JAMES PHILLIPS, BOX 109, PELICAN, AK 99832
LYNN POTTER, BOX 1472, CORDOVA, AK 99574
ANATOLY REUTOV, BOX 595, STERLING, AK 99672
AVRAAMY REUTOV, BOX 3207, HOMER, AK 99603

LING COD, DINGLEBAR TROLL, STATEWIDE
KALEB ALDRED, BOX 6123, SITKA, AK 99835
RAFE ALLENSWORTH, BOX 862, SITKA, AK 99835
ALAN ANTHONY, 507 KATLIAN ST, SITKA, AK 99835

LING COD / GROUNDFISH FISHING LIST—LONGLINE & TROLL

BERT BERGMAN, 801 CHARLES #A, SITKA, AK 99835
JONATHAN BROUWER, BOX 22927, JUNEAU, AK 99802
ANDY CALLISTINI, 106 NAOMI KANOSH LN, SITKA, AK 99835
DAVID CLARK, 507 KATLIAN ST, SITKA, AK 99835
RONALD CUNNINGHAM, BOX 6114, SITKA, AK 99835
ARNE DAHL, GEN DEL, POINT BAKER, AK 99927
JOSEPH DANIELS, 507 KATLIAN ST, SITKA, AK 99835
RICHARD DAVIS, 2347 KEVIN CT, JUNEAU, AK 99801
CASEY DIGENNARO, 208 PARK ST, SITKA, AK 99835
MATTHEW DONOHOE, BOX 3114, SITKA, AK 99835
RAYMOND DOUVILLE, BOX 66, CRAIG, AK 99921
J DOWNER, BOX 1045, HAINES, AK 99827
JAMES DYBDAHL, BOX 47, HOONAH, AK 99829
DEVON FERNANDEZ, BOX 270, YAKUTAT, AK 99689
ZACHARY FOSS, 1820 EDGECUMBE DR, SITKA, AK 99835
FOREST GERMAN, BOX 6393, SITKA, AK 99835
DAVID GIFFORD, BOX 8125, PORT ALEXANDER, AK 99836
ERIC GRUNDBERG, BOX 2193, PETERSBURG, AK 99833
ANTHONY GUGGENBICKLER, BOX 393, WRANGELL, AK 99929
JOHN HAGEN, BOX 1153, CRAIG, AK 99921
MARK HOFMANN, 1042 OBSTRUCTION PASS RD, OLGA, WA 98279
JASON HOLST, 1400 EDGECUMBE DR, SITKA, AK 99835
ROBERT HUNLEY, BOX 7, MEYERS CHUCK, AK 99903
BENJAMIN JOHNSON, 110 FINN ALLEY, SITKA, AK 99835
BILL JOHNSTON, BOX 134, PETERSBURG, AK 99833
GREGG JONES, 4016 HALIBUT POINT RD, SITKA, AK 99835
ERIC JORDAN, 103 GIBSON PL, SITKA, AK 99835
KARL JORDAN, 101 DONNA DR, SITKA, AK 99835
DAVID KRAUSE, BOX 1065, SITKA, AK 99835
PETER KROVINA, BOX 6027, SITKA, AK 99835
JAMES LANGE, BOX 8114, PORT ALEXANDER, AK 99836
MATTHEW LAWRIE, BOX 6006, SITKA, AK 99835
TAYLOR LECRONE, 1972 HALIBUT POINT RD, SITKA, AK 99835
STANLEY LOPATA, BOX 6004, SITKA, AK 99835
CERIDWEN MALEIN, BOX 3114, SITKA, AK 99835
OLIN MARTINSEN, 306 WORTMAN LP #B, SITKA, AK 99835
ERNEST MATTESON, BOX 6304, SITKA, AK 99835
STEVEN MERRITT, BOX 1138, CRAIG, AK 99921
GARY MULLIGAN, 224 MARINE ST #A, SITKA, AK 99835
CHRISTOPHER NASH, BOX 6493, SITKA, AK 99835
DAVID NASH, 1267 FRITZ COVE RD, JUNEAU, AK 99801
RYAN NICHOLS, 305 ISLANDER DR, SITKA, AK 99835
JONATHAN PAVLIK, BOX 293, YAKUTAT, AK 99689
JOHN PETRABORG, BOX 6067, SITKA, AK 99835
CAVEN PFEIFFER, 236 OBSERVATORY ST, SITKA, AK 99835
CHARLES PIERCY, BOX 1025, WARD COVE, AK 99928
JOSHUA RHOADES, BOX 6211, SITKA, AK 99835
CALEB ROBBINS, BOX 6256, SITKA, AK 99835
ROBERT ROOD, 6294 NE LARIAT LOOP, BAINBRIDGE ISLAND, WA 98110
MAXWELL ROYALL, BOX 18014, COFFMAN COVE, AK 99918
MARK SAPPINGTON, BOX 302, YAKUTAT, AK 99689
TIM SEXTON, BOX 6426, SITKA, AK 99835
JAMES SIMPSON, BOX 45, HYDER, AK 99923
RUSSELL SNELL, BOX 6425, SITKA, AK 99835
SHANE STANLEY, BOX 19531, THORNE BAY, AK 99919
LYNN STEYAART, BOX 545, PETERSBURG, AK 99833
JACOB STRUBBE, BOX 130, SONOITA, AZ 85637
JEFFREY TURNER, 329 KATLIAN ST, SITKA, AK 99835
TRAVIS WHITE, BOX 864, CRAIG, AK 99921
KENNETH WILKINSON, 203 AIRPORT RD #A12, SITKA, AK 99835
DAVID WILLIAMS, 1912 SAWMILL CREEK RD, SITKA, AK 99835
RYAN WILSON, BOX 414, SITKA, AK 99835
WAYNE WINTHER, BOX 505, SITKA, AK 99835
LES WOODWARD, BOX 2059, WRANGELL, AK 99929

LING COD, MECHANICAL JIG, STATEWIDE
NORMAN ALSUP, 15008 N TONGASS HWY, KETCHIKAN, AK 99901
RILEY DOWD, 3519 HARBOR VIEW DR #1, GIG HARBOR, WA 98332
ERIC HOLMLUND, 4416 HALIBUT POINT RD, SITKA, AK 99835
SAFRON KALUGIN, BOX 1921, HOMER, AK 99603
DAVID KRAUSE, BOX 1065, SITKA, AK 99835
FALILEY KUZMIN, BOX 3360, HOMER, AK 99603
SEAN PULLIAM, BOX 2422, YUCCA VALLEY, CA 92286
AVRAAMY REUTOV, BOX 3207, HOMER, AK 99603
CHRISTOPHER REUTOV, BOX 3116, HOMER, AK 99603
VLADIMIR SANAROV, BOX 2175, HOMER, AK 99603

MISC. SALTWATER FINFISH, PURSE SEINE, STATEWIDE
MITCHELL KEPLINGER, BOX 1006, KODIAK, AK 99615

MISC. SALTWATER FINFISH, PURSE SEINE, GOA
SAMUEL MUTCH, 210 B SHELIKOF, KODIAK, AK 99615
ROBERT NELSON, BOX 205, KASILOF, AK 99610

MISC. SALTWATER FINFISH, BEACH SEINE, STATEWIDE
TANYA ABLOWLUK, BOX 525, TELLER, AK 99778

MISC. SALTWATER FINFISH, HAND TROLL, STATEWIDE
PATRICK BARKER, 603 SAWMILL CREEK RD, SITKA, AK 99835
BRUCE BOWMAN, HC 60 BOX 227 I, COPPER CENTER, AK 99573
KELLEY GREEN, BOX 806, NOME, AK 99762
JAIME MOORE, BOX 130, CHIGNIK LAGOON, AK 99565
SARAH SPURLOCK, 208 PARK ST, SITKA, AK 99835
ELDON WALKER, 3848 MELROSE ST, JUNEAU, AK 99801
JOSH WISNIEWSKI, BOX 474, SITKA, AK 99835

MISC. SALTWATER FINFISH, HAND TROLL, GOA
DAVID BECK, BOX 6410, HALIBUT COVE, AK 99603
THOMAS CROTEAU, BOX 2364, SITKA, AK 99835
ALAN DALE, 926 NORDSTROM DR, KETCHIKAN, AK 99901
MICHAEL DOGGETT, 1306 EDGECUMBE DR, SITKA, AK 99835
MICHAEL DUBY, 7220 GLACIER HWY, JUNEAU, AK 99811
BRANDON FINN, 105 LANCE DR APT F, SITKA, AK 99835
BENJAMIN JOHNSON, 110 FINN ALLEY, SITKA, AK 99835
JORDAN MAY, 29941 W NANCY LN, SUTTON, AK 99674
JAMES MCCRACKEN, BOX 691, SEWARD, AK 99664
CHARLES MCELDOWNEY, BOX 1731, SEWARD, AK 99664
STEPHAN REISER, 3328 BARANOF AVE, KETCHIKAN, AK 99901
JOHN ROCK, BOX 21506, JUNEAU, AK 99801
CLAYTON STROMQUIST, 1302 SMC #31, SITKA, AK 99835
KENNETH WILKINSON, 203 AIRPORT RD #A12, SITKA, AK 99835

MISC. SALTWATER FINFISH, LONGLINE VESSEL UNDER 60', STATEWIDE
TIMOFIY ANFILOFEV, BOX 879118, WASILLA, AK 99687
FILARET BASARGIN, BOX 15052, FRITZ CREEK, AK 99603
KIRIL BASARGIN, BOX 2395, HOMER, AK 99603
MIRON BASARGIN, BOX 829, HOMER, AK 99603
NELS BECKER, BOX 240838, DOUGLAS, AK 99824
WILLIAM BRUN, BOX 212, SELDOVIA, AK 99663
WILLIAM CONNOR, BOX 1124, PETERSBURG, AK 99833
PATRICK DAVIS, BOX 921566, DUTCH HARBOR, AK 99692
RODNEY DEVINE, 1325 HIGHLAND VIEW LOOP, REDMOND, OR 99756
DAN DOAK, BOX 677, WRANGELL, AK 99929
JOHN DUPREE, BOX 684, PETERSBURG, AK 99833
ALEXEY FEFELOV, 1083 N LARKSPUR CIR, HOMER, AK 99603

GROUNDFISH FISHING LIST—LONGLINE

DAVID GIFFORD, BOX 8125, PORT ALEXANDER, AK 99836
MATTHEW HEGGE, BOX 848, KODIAK, AK 99615
SEAN HOVIK, BOX 6312, SITKA, AK 99835
JAMES HUBBARD, BOX 3302, SEWARD, AK 99664
ALEXEI KUZMIN, BOX 27, DELTA JUNCTION, AK 99737
DIA KUZMIN, BOX 758, DELTA JUNCTION, AK 99737
DIONICI KUZMIN, BOX 15, DELTA JUNCTION, AK 99737
EROS KUZMIN, BOX 141531, ANCHORAGE, AK 99514
SERGI KUZMIN, BOX 264, DELTA JUNCTION, AK 99737
SILIVERST KUZMIN, BOX 1046, DELTA JUNCTION, AK 99737
ZINON KUZMIN, BOX 873414, WASILLA, AK 99687
ROBIN LARSEN, BOX 264, SAND POINT, AK 99661
MICHAEL LASITER, BOX 5115, NIKOLAEVSK, AK 99556
DOUGLAS LYLE, BOX 2606, YELM, WA 98597
IOSIF MARTISHEV, BOX 2906, HOMER, AK 99603
ANATOLY MARTUSHEV, BOX 879661, WASILLA, AK 99687
MATTHEW MARTUSHEV, BOX 3603, HOMER, AK 99603
SERGEI MARTUSHEV, BOX 1299, HOMER, AK 99603
SIGURD MATHISEN, BOX 1460, PETERSBURG, AK 99833
MICHAEL MAYO, 2808 SAWMILL CREEK RD, SITKA, AK 99835
JAMES MILLER, BOX 1184, PETERSBURG, AK 99833
MIKE MONSON, BOX 1736, KODIAK, AK 99615
DENNIS ONEIL, BOX 1083, PETERSBURG, AK 99833
ALFRED PEELER, BOX 761, PETERSBURG, AK 99833
CHARLES PETTICREW, BOX 971, WRANGELL, AK 99929
DAVID POLUSHKIN, 690 KNIK GOOSE BAY RD #246, WASILLA, AK 99654
PHILLIP PRYZMONT, BOX 994, NOME, AK 99762
LAVRENTII REUTOV, BOX 1190, HOMER, AK 99603
NIKOLAI REUTOV, BOX 2342, HOMER, AK 99603
SEVEREAN REUTOV, BOX 2230, HOMER, AK 99603
TIMON REUTOV, BOX 563, HOMER, AK 99603
WALTER SARGENT, 1830 MISSION RD, KODIAK, AK 99615
STANLEY SAVLAND, BOX 621, HOONAH, AK 99829
MARK SEVERSON, BOX 1502, PETERSBURG, AK 99833
BILL SHIPP, 2400 NW 80TH ST PMB 268, SEATTLE, WA 98117
GARY SLAVEN, BOX 205, PETERSBURG, AK 99833
KEVIN STAFFORD, BOX 210262, AUKE BAY, AK 99821
JOHN SWANSON, BOX 1546, PETERSBURG, AK 99833
THOMAS TRAIBUSH, 1300 PEACE PORTAL DR #206, BLAINE, WA 98230
JOE WILLIS, BOX 43, PETERSBURG, AK 99833
LES WOODWARD, BOX 2059, WRANGELL, AK 99929
FRANK WRIGHT, BOX 497, HOONAH, AK 99829
GRIGORY YAKUNIN, BOX 1513, HOMER, AK 99603

MISC. SALTWATER FINFISH, LONGLINE VESSEL UNDER 60', GOA

KAVIK ANDERSON, BOX 310, KODIAK, AK 99615
TRAVIS ANDERSON, BOX 1623, SITKA, AK 99835
ARNOLD BAKKE, BOX 1482, WRANGELL, AK 99929
ANDREAN BASARGIN, BOX 1393, HOMER, AK 99603
ARTEMON BASARGIN, 52818 OLD EAST END RD, HOMER, AK 99603
DAVID BASARGIN, BOX 1089, HOMER, AK 99603
MIHEY BASARGIN, BOX 875797, WASILLA, AK 99687
NIKITA BASARGIN, BOX 2057, HOMER, AK 99603
BRIAN BLANKENSHIP, 4316 VALLHALLA DR, SITKA, AK 99835
CHARLES BLATTNER, BOX 33916, JUNEAU, AK 99803
DALE BOSWORTH, BOX 45, PETERSBURG, AK 99833
ROBERT CARTER, BOX 2817, KODIAK, AK 99615
TODD CHAPIN, 2417 TONGASS AVE SUITE 111-244, KETCHIKAN, AK 99901
RUSSELL COCKRUM, 5791 N TONGASS HWY, KETCHIKAN, AK 99901
MIKE DALY, 501 CHARTERIS ST #A, SITKA, AK 99835
DUGAN DANIELS, 507 KATLIAN ST, SITKA, AK 99835
PAUL DUPREE, BOX 684, PETERSBURG, AK 99833
DUANE EDELMAN, BOX 153, VALDEZ, AK 99686
ROBERT GELLER, BOX 483, GIRDWOOD, AK 99587

DAVE GIBSON, 127 W 7TH ST, JUNEAU, AK 99801
JAY GILLMAN, BOX 651, ANACORTES, WA 98221
SEAN GRISS, BOX 2098, PETERSBURG, AK 99833
MATTHEW HAFFNER, 18216 PT STEHENS RD, JUNEAU, AK 99801
CLAYTON HAMILTON, BOX 20767, JUNEAU, AK 99802
TIMOTHY HANNON, BOX 47, HAINES, AK 99827
MICHAEL HANSEN, BOX 822, KODIAK, AK 99615
JAMES HAYDEN, BOX 8085, KODIAK, AK 99615
CARL HUMPHREY, BOX 665, PETERSBURG, AK 99833
GREGORY INDRELAND, BOX 413, YAKUTAT, AK 99689
DAVID IVANOV, BOX 15316, HOMER, AK 99603
KENNETH JONES, BOX 615, CORDOVA, AK 99574
CORNILY KALUGIN, 46810 GOLDEN VIEW CIR, HOMER, AK 99603
ILESAY KALUGIN, BOX 2727, HOMER, AK 99603
ANDREW KITTAMS, BOX 1544, PETERSBURG, AK 99833
PETER KROVINA, BOX 6027, SITKA, AK 99835
ALEXANDRE KUSNETSOV, BOX 1719, HOMER, AK 99603
ALEXEI KUZMIN, BOX 27, DELTA JUNCTION, AK 99737
DIMITRY KUZMIN, BOX 2192, HOMER, AK 99603
FADEY KUZMIN, BOX 3009, HOMER, AK 99603
ILIA KUZMIN, BOX 3433, HOMER, AK 99603
LEONTEY KUZMIN, BOX 1542, DELTA JUNCTION, AK 99737
NIKITA KUZMIN, BOX 1542, DELTA JUNCTION, AK 99737
LAZARO KUZNETSOV, BOX 315, HOMER, AK 99603
GREG LUTTON, BOX 1924, PETERSBURG, AK 99833
JOHN MANGUSSO, BOX 240573, DOUGLAS, AK 99824
DAVID MARTISHEV, BOX 1660, HOMER, AK 99603
IOSIF MARTISHEV, BOX 1660, HOMER, AK 99603
TROFIM MARTUSHEV, BOX 879298, WASILLA, AK 99687
LENORE MATHISEN, BOX 1061, PETERSBURG, AK 99833
KENT MCCOLLUM, BOX 2096, PETERSBURG, AK 99833
WILLIAM MENISH, BOX 877, PETERSBURG, AK 99833
THANE MILLER, BOX 2961, VALDEZ, AK 99686
JAMISON MORK, BOX 44, PELICAN, AK 99832
ROBERT MOSHER, 11985 MENDENHALL LP RD, JUNEAU, AK 99801
ALEKSANDRO MURACHEV, BOX 2259, HOMER, AK 99603
NELSON OOKA, BOX 1218, SEWARD, AK 99664
ZACK OSTERHAUS, 641 WEST FARIVIEW AVE #S, HOMER, AK 99603
JONATHAN PAVLIK, BOX 293, YAKUTAT, AK 99689
JAMES PHILLIPS, BOX 109, PELICAN, AK 99832
ANDREY POLUSHKIN, BOX 2458, HOMER, AK 99603
VLADIMIR POLUSHKIN, BOX 879276, WASILLA, AK 99687
ALEXANDER REUTOV, BOX 2272, HOMER, AK 99603
ALEXANDER REUTOV, BOX 687, SOLDOTNA, AK 99669
ANATOLY REUTOV, BOX 595, STERLING, AK 99672
ANDREY REUTOV, BOX 2212, HOMER, AK 99603
CORNILY REUTOV, BOX 3523, HOMER, AK 99603
DIMITRY REUTOV, BOX 2063, HOMER, AK 99603
GEORGE REUTOV, BOX 1276, HOMER, AK 99603
GREGORY REUTOV, BOX 2597, HOMER, AK 99603
MARK REUTOV, BOX 3523, HOMER, AK 99603
MAVRIK REUTOV, BOX 910, HOMER, AK 99603
SOFRON REUTOV, BOX 563, HOMER, AK 99603
TRIFILYI REUTOV, BOX 793, HOMER, AK 99603
YAKOV REUTOV, BOX 1251, STERLING, AK 99672
TIMOTHY ROSS, BOX 371, YAKUTAT, AK 99689
PAUL ROSTAD, BOX 183, KAKE, AK 99830
JOSEPH SAMOILOV, BOX 1832, HOMER, AK 99603
FELEMON SANAROV, BOX 3432, HOMER, AK 99603
VLADIMIR SANAROV, BOX 2175, HOMER, AK 99603
JOSEPH SHORT, BOX 1224, PETERSBURG, AK 99833
ANTHONEY SINE, BOX 32132, JUNEAU, AK 99803
KELSEY SKORDAHL, 109C LANCE DR, SITKA, AK 99835
ROBERT SMITH, BOX 251, CORDOVA, AK 99574
KEVIN STAFFORD, BOX 210262, AUKE BAY, AK 99821

GROUNDFISH FISHING LIST—POT GEAR

JACOB STRUBBE, BOX 130, SONOITA, AZ 85637
TROY THOMASSEN, BOX 152, PETERSBURG, AK 99833
GREG TIPIKIN, 2725 N JENNY ANNE PL, WASILLA, AK 99654
DAVID TROUT, BOX 1094, HAINES, AK 99827
ALEXANDRA VON.WICHMAN, 2940 MALLARD LN, ANCHORAGE, AK 99508
W.BRADFORD VON.WICHMAN, 2940 MALLARD LN, ANCHORAGE, AK 99508
STUART WEATHERS, BOX 1734, SITKA, AK 99835
MIKE WELLS, BOX 1430, VALDEZ, AK 99686
MICHAEL ZENUHIN, 3660 VICTOR POINT RD NE, SILVERTON, OR 97381

MISC. SALTWATER FINFISH, POT GEAR VESSEL UNDER 60', STATEWIDE

MICHAEL ALFIERI, 18120 196TH AVE SE, RENTON, WA 98058
KAVIK ANDERSON, BOX 310, KODIAK, AK 99615
MICHEL BAIN, BOX 920501, DUTCH HARBOR, AK 99692
KEITH BELL, 3712 ROALD AMUNDSEN, ANCHORAGE, AK 99517
BRYCE BUHOLM, 15129 35TH AVE W, LYNNWOOD, WA 98087
MICHAEL BYRER, BOX 1462, PETERSBURG, AK 99833
MICHAEL CLARK, BOX 2009, KODIAK, AK 99615
DANIEL CLOUD, 318 CAROLYN ST, KODIAK, AK 99615
AARON COOK, 69625 NICOLAI CUTOFF ROAD, RAINIER, OR 97048
JAMES CRICHTON, 318 SUNDSTROM LN, FRIDAY HARBOR, WA 98250
PATRICK DAVIS, BOX 921566, DUTCH HARBOR, AK 99692
ROBERT DAVIS, 7704 W OWENS RD, DEAR PARK, WA 99006
STEPHEN DAY, 8830 GLORALEE ST, ANCHORAGE, AK 99502
DUSTAN DICKERSON, BOX 921408, DUTCH HARBOR, AK 99692
MATTHEW DZIEDZIC, 125 ELLA VITA CT, DURANGO, CO 81301
RICKEY FEHST, BOX 920911, DUTCH HARBOR, AK 99692
JACK FOSTER, BOX 254, SAND POINT, AK 99661
MICHAEL GALLIGAN, BOX 1926, FRIDAY HARBOR, WA 98250
TROY GIBSON, 1447 OAK LEAF DR, COLUMBIA, TN 38401
EDWARD GIRARD, BOX 245, SELDOVIA, AK 99663
ROBERT GUNDERSON, 3614 SPRUCE CAPE RD, KODIAK, AK 99615
TRAVIS HALL, BOX 501, HOMER, AK 99603
ROBERT HANSON, 3705 ARCTIC BLVD PMB 2086, ANCHORAGE, AK 99503
MATTHEW HEGGE, BOX 848, KODIAK, AK 99615
WADE HENLEY, 2088 FIRE LANE RD, BELLINGHAM, WA 98229
KEITH HILTY, BOX 873742, WASILLA, AK 99687
JONATHAN HINMAN, BOX 2773, KODIAK, AK 99615
TODD HOPPE, BOX 2589, HOMER, AK 99603
MATTHEW HUTTER, BOX 3543, HOMER, AK 99603
MARK JACKSON, 1442 CHENA RIDGE RD CABIN, FAIRBANKS, AK 99709
DICK JACOBSEN, BOX 307, SAND POINT, AK 99661
NORMAN JOHANNESSEN, BOX 1638, OROVILLE, WA 98844
ROBERT JOHNSON, 305 COPE ST, KODIAK, AK 99615
GARRETT KAVANAUGH, 1533 SAWMILL CIR, KODIAK, AK 99615
RONALD KAVANAUGH, 1533 SAWMILL CIR, KODIAK, AK 99615
ROBIN LARSEN, BOX 264, SAND POINT, AK 99661
BEN LEY, 8316 WINDING RUN RD, ST LOUISVILLE, OH 43071
RYELAN LONG, 3233 PENINSULA RD, KODIAK, AK 99615
SHEA LONG, 3233 PENINSULA RD, KODIAK, AK 99615
DYLAN LYON, BOX 332, HOMER, AK 99603
ROBERT MAGNUSSON, 4150 SWEET RD, BLAINE, WA 98230
JASON MILLER, BOX 1473, PETERSBURG, AK 99833
DAVID MOREY, BOX 1188, SEWARD, AK 99664
PETER NEATON, 59065 MEADOW LANE, HOMER, AK 99603
MIKE NEUNEKER, BOX 52, PETERSBURG, AK 99833
DUKE OGATA, BOX 181, SAND POINT, AK 99661
MINH PHAM, 706 S 104TH ST, SEATTLE, WA 98168
DANNY POWELL, BOX 8953, KODIAK, AK 99615
PHILLIP PRYZMONT, BOX 994, NOME, AK 99762
TREVER SHAISHNIKOFF, BOX 131, UNALASKA, AK 99685
JAMES SMITH, BOX 104, KING COVE, AK 99612
MICHAEL SPOKAS, 3851 FOXTAIL LN, HELENA, MT 59602
JAMES STEVENS, BOX 8593, KODIAK, AK 99615
ABRAHAM SULLIVAN, 17710 TEKLANIKA DR, EAGLE RIVER, AK 99577

JOSHUA TROSVIG, BOX 17911, SEATTLE, WA 98127
ANDREW WHITETHORN, BOX 187, PETERSBURG, AK 99833
KEITH WILLIAMS, 1924 E COLGATE DR, TEMPE, AZ 85283
ANDREW WILSON, BOX 127, KING COVE, AK 99612
DAVID WILSON, BOX 333, SAND POINT, AK 99661
JUSTIN WILSON, BOX 267, KING COVE, AK 99612
JERAMY YOUNG, BOX 806, KODIAK, AK 99615
RONALD ZWAHLEN, BOX 1427, HOMER, AK 99603

MISC. SALTWATER FINFISH, POT GEAR VESSEL UNDER 60', GOA

ALFREDO ABOUEID, BOX 26, CHIGNIK LAGOON, AK 99565
RAME ABOUEID, 5 AIRWAYS RD, CHIGNIK LAGOON, AK 99565
AARON ANDERSON, BOX 43, CHIGNIK LAGOON, AK 99565
RODNEY ANDERSON, BOX 188, CHIGNIK LAGOON, AK 99565
RANDY ARSENAULT, BOX 4104, HOMER, AK 99603
CRAIG BENDIXEN, BOX 36, KING COVE, AK 99612
BRIAN BLONDIN, BOX 1521, KODIAK, AK 99615
JASON BLONDIN, 1415 BARANOF ST, KODIAK, AK 99615
ALBERT CARROLL, 55090 BENJAMIN AVE #1, HOMER, AK 99603
PAUL CLAYTON, 56855 THURSTON DR, HOMER, AK 99603
AARON COOK, 69625 NICOLAI CUTOFF ROAD, RAINIER, OR 97048
JEREMIAH COUSINS, 3080 HOMER SPIT RD, HOMER, AK 99603
DANNY CUMBERLIDGE, BOX 93, SAND POINT, AK 99661
INAR DUSHKIN, BOX 224, ANCHOR POINT, AK 99556
ANDREW FOSTER, BOX 162, SAND POINT, AK 99661
BRUCE FOSTER, BOX 46, SAND POINT, AK 99661
DWAIN FOSTER, BOX 162, SAND POINT, AK 99661
JOHN FOSTER, BOX 225, SAND POINT, AK 99661
STEVEN GALOVIN, BOX 215, SAND POINT, AK 99661
TIMOTHY GERVAIS, BOX 7, RUBY, AK 99768
DEAN GOULD, BOX 124, KING COVE, AK 99612
ROBERT GOULD, BOX 307, KING COVE, AK 99612
STEVEN GOULD, BOX 375, KING COVE, AK 99612
JACOB HANOHANO, BOX 851, KODIAK, AK 99615
CARLIN HOBLET, 11730 SUNCREST CIR, ANCHORAGE, AK 99515
IVAN HOBLET, BOX 62, FALSE PASS, AK 99583
TOM HOBLET, BOX 108, FALSE PASS, AK 99583
ARTHUR HOLMBERG, BOX 78, SAND POINT, AK 99661
CLIFTON IVANOFF, BOX 8883, KODIAK, AK 99615
BERT KUZAKIN, 440 W 123RD AVE, ANCHORAGE, AK 99515
TIM LEVENSON, BOX 1284, KODIAK, AK 99615
RYELAN LONG, 3233 PENINSULA RD, KODIAK, AK 99615
TAYLOR LUNDGREN, BOX 216, SAND POINT, AK 99661
KENNETH MACK, BOX 182, KING COVE, AK 99612
KENNETH MACK, BOX 176, KING COVE, AK 99612
FRANK MILES, BOX 2744, KODIAK, AK 99615
DEREK OSTRANDER, BOX 126, CATHALAMET, WA 98612
ROGER OVERA, 14010 154 AVE SE, RENTON, WA 98059
DALE PEDERSEN, 9218 CAMPBELL TERRACE DR, ANCHORAGE, AK 99502
DEAN PEDERSEN, BOX 877325, WASILLA, AK 99687
EDUARDO PEREZ, BOX 208, KODIAK, AK 99615
PATRICK PIKUS, BOX 2843, KODIAK, AK 99615
MATTHEW RAFFERTY, 39307 SUCHAVIEW RD, HOMER, AK 99603
SHAWNA RITTENHOUSE, BOX KWP, KODIAK, AK 99615
BILL SAGER, BOX 202, KING COVE, AK 99612
HERMAN SAMUELSON, 8 MAIN ST, KING COVE, AK 99612
WALTER SARGENT, 1830 MISSION RD, KODIAK, AK 99615
JAMES SMITH, BOX 104, KING COVE, AK 99612
DALE STANLEY, BOX 7442, KETCHIKAN, AK 99901
IVAN STONOROV, 41046 CRESTED CRANE ST, HOMER, AK 99603
MATTHEW STOVER, BOX 921, HOMER, AK 99603
KENNETH SWICK, BOX 112, SELDOVIA, AK 99663
KILEY THOMPSON, BOX 116, SAND POINT, AK 99661
DONALD VINBERG, BOX 9032, KODIAK, AK 99615
DAVID WILSON, BOX 333, SAND POINT, AK 99661

GROUNDFISH FISHING LIST—TROLL & JIG

BRIAN ZWICK, 801 PETERSON ST, KETCHIKAN, AK 99901

MISC. SALTWATER FINFISH, BEAM TRAWL, STATEWIDE
DONALD SPERL, BOX 1407, PETERSBURG, AK 99833

MISC. SALTWATER FINFISH, BEAM TRAWL, GOA
EUGENE LEE, BOX 1286, PETERSBURG, AK 99833

MISC. SALTWATER FINFISH, DINGLEBAR TROLL, STATEWIDE
CHRISTOPHER HANSON, BOX 2283, SITKA, AK 99835
DAVID KRAUSE, BOX 1065, SITKA, AK 99835
JOHN LINDBERG, BOX KWP, KODIAK, AK 99615
LES WOODWARD, BOX 2059, WRANGELL, AK 99929

MISC. SALTWATER FINFISH, DINGLEBAR TROLL, GOA
CASEY DIGENNARO, 208 PARK ST, SITKA, AK 99835
STANLEY LOPATA, BOX 6004, SITKA, AK 99835
MARK SAPPINGTON, BOX 302, YAKUTAT, AK 99689

MISC. SALTWATER FINFISH, MECHANICAL JIG, STATEWIDE
JEREMY ABENA, BOX 2277, KODIAK, AK 99615
TIMOTHY ABENA, 3103 MILL BAY RD, KODIAK, AK 99615
PETER ALLAN, BOX 2160, KODIAK, AK 99615
NORMAN ALSUP, 15008 N TONGASS HWY, KETCHIKAN, AK 99901
PETER ANDERSON, BOX 37, CHIGNIK, AK 99564
TIMOFIY ANFILOFEV, BOX 879118, WASILLA, AK 99687
DAVID ARDINGER, BOX 1438, KODIAK, AK 99615
ROBERT BARNETT, BOX 274, SAND POINT, AK 99661
KIRIL BASARGIN, BOX 2395, HOMER, AK 99603
BRIAN BLONDIN, BOX 1521, KODIAK, AK 99615
TROY BOUSLEY, BOX 465, SAND POINT, AK 99661
BOB BOWHAY, BOX 187, KODIAK, AK 99615
PATRICK BROWN, BOX 69, SAND POINT, AK 99661
KELLY BROYLES, 7060 BLACKHAWK LN, FOREST HILL, CA 95631
DANIEL BYRON, BOX 95, PORT LIONS, AK 99550
LEONARD CARPENTER, BOX 1970, KODIAK, AK 99615
MATTHEW CARPENTER, BOX 1970, KODIAK, AK 99615
DAVID CHRISTIANSEN, BOX 2, OLD HARBOR, AK 99643
ALFRED CRATTY, BOX 1, OLD HARBOR, AK 99643
CASEY DIGENNARO, 208 PARK ST, SITKA, AK 99835
DONALD EUBANK, BOX 272, SAND POINT, AK 99661
BRUCE FOSTER, BOX 46, SAND POINT, AK 99661
JACK FOSTER, BOX 254, SAND POINT, AK 99661
JOHN GALLIHER, 2933 SPRUCE CAPE RD, KODIAK, AK 99615
HENRY GATES, 1614 LARCH ST, KODIAK, AK 99615
TIMOTHY GERVAIS, BOX 7, RUBY, AK 99768
ROBERT GOULD, BOX 234, KING COVE, AK 99612
ROBERT GOULD, BOX 307, KING COVE, AK 99612
STEVEN GOULD, BOX 375, KING COVE, AK 99612
OMAR GUCER, BOX 1386, HOMER, AK 99603
CHARLES GUNDERSEN, BOX 24, SAND POINT, AK 99661
KIM GUNDERSEN, BOX 148, SAND POINT, AK 99661
MARTIN GUNDERSEN, BOX 50, SAND POINT, AK 99661
JARL GUSTAFSON, BOX 952, HOMER, AK 99603
JAMES HAYDEN, BOX 8085, KODIAK, AK 99615
JOE HINTON, BOX 2543, SEWARD, AK 99664
OLIVER HOLM, BOX 8749, KODIAK, AK 99615
RAYMOND HOLMBERG, BOX 266, SAND POINT, AK 99661
RYAN HOLMBERG, BOX 241, SAND POINT, AK 99661
RON HORTON, BOX 903, CORDOVA, AK 99574
TERRY IVANOFF, BOX 8883, KODIAK, AK 99615

PATRICK J.KEEGAN.MARRS, BOX 6552, SITKA, AK 99835
CHARLES JACKSON, BOX 54, SAND POINT, AK 99661
DICK JACOBSEN, BOX 307, SAND POINT, AK 99661
DAVID JOHANNESSEN, BOX 474, CORDOVA, AK 99574
ROBERT JOHANSEN, BOX 15, SAND POINT, AK 99661
CHRISTOPHER JOHNSON, BOX 151, KODIAK, AK 99615
RONALD JOLIN, BOX 2022, KODIAK, AK 99615
KARL JORDAN, 101 DONNA DR, SITKA, AK 99835
VLADIMIR KALUGIN, BOX 2480, HOMER, AK 99603
DARIUS KASPRZAK, BOX 531, KODIAK, AK 99615
NICK KATELNIKOFF, BOX 170, OUZINKIE, AK 99644
DOMIAN KUZMIN, BOX 367, DELTA JUNCTION, AK 99737
ALEXUS KWACHKA, 326 COPE ST, KODIAK, AK 99615
BRANISLAV LALICH, BOX 2583, HOMER, AK 99603
JOHN LINDBERG, BOX KWP, KODIAK, AK 99615
KENNETH MACK, BOX 182, KING COVE, AK 99612
HAROLD MAGNUSSON, BOX 283, KODIAK, AK 99615
ROBERT MAGNUSSON, 4150 SWEET RD, BLAINE, WA 98230
DAVID MANN, 73 WINWARD DR, BELLINGHAM, WA 98229
JOSHUA MARCHART, 785 WILLOW CR, KODIAK, AK 99615
GABRIEL MCKILLY, BOX 190344, ANCHORAGE, AK 99519
RYAN MEGANACK, BOX 5526, PORT GRAHAM, AK 99603
KODI METZGER, 2725 WILLEYS LAKE RD, CUSTER, WA 98240
PARRY NELSON, BOX 92, KODIAK, AK 99615
GRANT NEWTON, BOX 51, KING COVE, AK 99612
ROBERT NYBERG, BOX 161, SAND POINT, AK 99661
DUKE OGATA, BOX 181, SAND POINT, AK 99661
RAYMOND OGATA, 1980 N FINGER COVE DR, PALMER, AK 99645
CECILIO OROZCO, BOX 2221, KODIAK, AK 99615
MATTHEW OXFORD, BOX 15201, FRITZ CREEK, AK 99603
MATTHEW PEAVEY, BOX 442, CRAIG, AK 99921
EDUARDO PEREZ, BOX 208, KODIAK, AK 99615
DAVID POLUSHKIN, 690 KNIK GOOSE BAY RD #246, WASILLA, AK 99654
VIRGIL PORTER, BOX 73, SAND POINT, AK 99661
COREY POTTER, BOX 1939, KODIAK, AK 99615
PHILLIP PRYZMONT, BOX 994, NOME, AK 99762
RICK QUINT, GEN DEL, SAND POINT, AK 99661
ERIC RANGUETTE, 34760 POPPY WOOD ST, SOLDOTNA, AK 99669
DANA REID, BOX 8935, KODIAK, AK 99615
DAVID REUTOV, BOX 3609, HOMER, AK 99603
GEORGE REUTOV, BOX 1276, HOMER, AK 99603
IONA REUTOV, BOX 873462, WASILLA, AK 99687
JULIAN REUTOV, BOX 1887, HOMER, AK 99603
MICHELLE RITTENHOUSE, BOX KWP, KODIAK, AK 99615
NATHANIEL ROSE, 3011 SPRUCE CAPE RD APT A, KODIAK, AK 99615
JAMES ROTH, BOX 2008, HOMER, AK 99603
VLADIMIR SANAROV, BOX 2175, HOMER, AK 99603
CRAIG SCHLOESSER, BOX 356, ANCHOR POINT, AK 99556
ARTHUR SCHULTZ, 3580 SITKINAK DR, KODIAK, AK 99615
PETER SHURAVLOFF, 28 RED COVE RD, SAND POINT, AK 99661
BRANDON SMITH, BOX 354, SAND POINT, AK 99661
FREDERICK STAGER, BOX 8243, KODIAK, AK 99615
ERIC TABER, BOX 2206, KODIAK, AK 99615
STACEY TOLAR, 1201 EQUINOX WAY, KENAI, AK 99611
MARK WAGNER, BOX 1502, KINGSTON, WA 98346
CHRISTOPHER WENZEL, 3806 W TAPPS DR E, LAKE TAPPS, WA 98391
MONIQUE WILKINSON, 203 AIRPORT DR. UNIT A-12, SITKA, AK 99835
DAVID WILLIAMS, 1912 SAWMILL CREEK RD, SITKA, AK 99835
JOSHUA WILLIAMS, BOX 920913, DUTCH HARBOR, AK 99692
LES WOODWARD, BOX 2059, WRANGELL, AK 99929
CHRISTOPHER WORLEY, BOX 168, SELDOVIA, AK 99663

MISC. SALTWATER FINFISH, MECHANICAL JIG, GOA
ALFREDO ABOUEID, BOX 26, CHIGNIK LAGOON, AK 99565
JOSHUA ADKINS, BOX 8671, KODIAK, AK 99615
JAMES ALPIAK, BOX 8683, KODIAK, AK 99615

GROUNDFISH FISHING LIST—LONGLINE

JAMES ALPIAK, BOX 879320, WASILLA, AK 99687
DAVID BASARGIN, BOX 1089, HOMER, AK 99603
CRAIG BENDIXEN, BOX 36, KING COVE, AK 99612
MARK BLAKESLEE, BOX 2356, KODIAK, AK 99615
BRIAN BLONDIN, BOX 1521, KODIAK, AK 99615
BRANDON BOECK, 13431 CONSTITUTION OR, PALMER, AK 99645
JOHN BOGGS, BOX 1199, KODIAK, AK 99615
JON BOTZ, BOX 5538, KODIAK, AK 99615
STEVEN BRANSON, BOX 451, KODIAK, AK 99615
YIYEON BROWN, BOX 8650, KODIAK, AK 99615
JAMES CARLSEN, 2483 SPRUCE CAPE #6, KODIAK, AK 99615
ROBERT CARTER, BOX 2817, KODIAK, AK 99615
GLENN CROCETTI, 118 BANCROFT DR, KODIAK, AK 99615
BRAD DEERING, BOX 12, SAND POINT, AK 99661
SHAWN DOCHTERMANN, BOX 866, KODIAK, AK 99615
WILLIAM DUSHKIN, BOX 135, SAND POINT, AK 99661
RICHARD EASTLICK, BOX 147, SAND POINT, AK 99661
DUANE EDELMAN, BOX 153, VALDEZ, AK 99686
JONATHAN EDWARDS, BOX 8905, KODIAK, AK 99615
KIM EUFEMIO, 1327 MYLARK LN, KODIAK, AK 99615
MIKE FERRIS, BOX 331, KODIAK, AK 99615
MARTIN GILBERT, BOX 2232, SITKA, AK 99835
DEAN GOULD, BOX 124, KING COVE, AK 99612
DENNIS GUNDERSEN, BOX 386, SAND POINT, AK 99661
WAYNE GUNDERSEN, BOX 89, SAND POINT, AK 99661
CRAIG GUSTAFSON, BOX 8573, KODIAK, AK 99615
THOMAS HAGBERG, BOX 175, ANCHOR POINT, AK 99556
ERIC HANSEN, BOX 1482, KODIAK, AK 99615
JOE HOCHMUTH, 1225 PURTOV AVE #2, KODIAK, AK 99615
ROBERT HOCHMUTH, BOX 74, LARSEN BAY, AK 99624
MATTHEW HOCKEMA, BOX 15386, FRITZ CREEK, AK 99603
IVER HOLM, BOX 8938, KODIAK, AK 99615
ERIC HOLMLUND, 4416 HALIBUT POINT RD, SITKA, AK 99835
JASON HOLST, 1400 EDGECUMBE DR, SITKA, AK 99835
RYAN HORWATH, BOX 465, KODIAK, AK 99615
AARON JOLIN, BOX 2022, KODIAK, AK 99615
GREGG JONES, 4016 HALIBUT POINT RD, SITKA, AK 99835
ERIC JORDAN, 103 GIBSON PL, SITKA, AK 99835
ARTEMIE KALMAKOFF, BOX 286, SAND POINT, AK 99661
ALEXANDER KALUGIN, BOX 1131, HOMER, AK 99603
SAFRON KALUGIN, BOX 1921, HOMER, AK 99603
FALILEY KUZMIN, BOX 3360, HOMER, AK 99603
BRAD LANGVARDT, BOX 213, SELDOVIA, AK 99663
LUTHER LECHNER, BOX 8538, KODIAK, AK 99615
LUKE LESTER, BOX 553, KODIAK, AK 99615
KYLE LINTS, 64900 BERRY PAIL DR, HOMER, AK 99603
IOSIF MARTISHEV, BOX 1660, HOMER, AK 99603
THOMAS MILLER, BOX 1931, KODIAK, AK 99615
JOSHUA MOORE, BOX 2015, PETERSBURG, AK 99833
THOMAS NELSON, BOX 101, PORT LIONS, AK 99550
CLINT PARKS, 105 BLUE BIRD LN, WHITEHALL, MT 59759
ARSENY POLUSHKIN, BOX 62, HOMER, AK 99603
DANIEL REAR, 1007 HALIBUT POINT RD, SITKA, AK 99835
ANDREY REUTOV, BOX 2212, HOMER, AK 99603
AVRAAMY REUTOV, BOX 3207, HOMER, AK 99603
CHRISTOPHER REUTOV, BOX 3116, HOMER, AK 99603
DIMITRY REUTOV, BOX 2063, HOMER, AK 99603
FEODOR REUTOV, BOX 390, KODIAK, AK 99615
GREGORY REUTOV, BOX 2597, HOMER, AK 99603
MAVRIK REUTOV, BOX 910, HOMER, AK 99603
NIKOLAI REUTOV, BOX 2342, HOMER, AK 99603
SEVEREAN REUTOV, BOX 2230, HOMER, AK 99603
VAVIL REUTOV, BOX 809, HOMER, AK 99603
CONNER ROSS, 181 BLACKSTONE ST, SOLDOTNA, AK 99669
WILLIAM SCHAUFF, BOX 8774, KODIAK, AK 99615
ZOSIMA SEREBREKOFF, BOX 753, HOMER, AK 99603

JIM SMITH, BOX 354, SAND POINT, AK 99661
THEODORE SQUARTSOFF, BOX 77, OUZINKIE, AK 99644
CY ST.AMAND, BOX 8650, KODIAK, AK 99615
RHY VERG.IN, 19415 LINDA LN, KASILOF, AK 99610
DONALD VINBERG, BOX 9032, KODIAK, AK 99615
JEFFREY WINEGARDEN, BOX 877315, WASILLA, AK 99687

MISC. SALTWATER FINFISH, LONGLINE VESSEL 90' OR OVER, STATEWIDE
RANDY ADKINS, BOX 423, BURLEY, WA 98322
SHAUN ANDREW, BOX 2058, KODIAK, AK 99615
DENNIS BLACK, 16336 ELIZABETH ST, ANCHORAGE, AK 99516
RICHARD BOYER, 3603 SE 160TH AVE, PORTLAND, OR 97236
MARC CAULEY, 18811 SW READ CT, LAKE OSWEGO, OR 97035
SAM COLLIER, BOX 3259, ALBANY, OR 97321
LYNN DUTSON, 76018 PALMER JUNCTION RD, ELGIN, OR 97827
MICHAEL FITZGERALD, 4062 S MARBLE ST, GILBERT, AZ 85297
RUSSEL FLIPPEN, 3500 W SCENIC DR, BOISE, ID 83703
ELBERT FOTHERGILL, 2930 WESTLAKE AVE N #300, SEATTLE, WA 98109
MARIO GARCIA, 641 W EWING ST, SEATTLE, WA 98119
MARK GUSTAFSON, 23632 HWY 99 #F424, EDMONDS, WA 98026
BRADLEY HALL, BOX 4157, BELLINGHAM, WA 98227
SCOTT HANSEN, 22929 22ND DR SE, BOTHELL, WA 98801
DANIEL HARNDEN, 2625 TRADEWIND DR, LAKE HAVASU CITY, AZ 86403
SCOTT HARNDEN, 2605 BOULEVARD PARK CT SE, OLYMPIA, WA 98501
SIGURD HAVERMAN, 20124 GREENWOOD AVE N, SHORELINE, WA 98133
JUSTIN JOHNSON, 2304 GREEN MOUNTAIN RD, KALAMA, WA 98625
JERRY KENNEDY, 28924 48TH AVE NW, STANWOOD, WA 98292
AARON KENYON, 641 W EWING ST, SEATTLE, WA 98119
BAZ LLOYD, 5079 HARNDEN RD, CASHMERE, WA 98815
JAMES MATTICE, 818 POLK ST S, TACOMA, WA 98444
DENNIS MCKIBBIN, 4502 14TH AVE NW, SEATTLE, WA 98107
BRIAN MOEN, 2930 WESTLAKE AVE N #300, SEATTLE, WA 98109
DEAN PAINE, 76 COTTAGE ST, BAR HARBOR, ME 4609
SCOTT PENNY, 641 W EWING ST, SEATTLE, WA 98119
BRADLY PETEFISH, 4224 E 28TH AVE, SPOKANE, WA 99223
MARIO REYES, 23929 22ND DR SE, BOTHELL, WA 98021
FREDERICK ROMAN, 7824 NE 112TH ST, KIRKLAND, WA 98034
WILLIAM ROTHSCHILD, 16509 ROBINSON RD, SNOHOMISH, WA 98296
REYNALDO RUBALCAVA, 4502 14TH AVE NW, SEATTLE, WA 98107
TIMOTHY SHAPLEY, BOX 1231, WINTHROP, WA 98862
ORVILLE SMITH, 2105 SLEEPY HOLLOW HTS, WENATCHEE, WA 98801
KENNETH TREAT, 720 15TH ST NW, PUYALLUP, WA 98371
CHARLES VELASCO, 23717 SE 227TH ST, MAPLE VALLEY, WA 98038
BRIAN WALKER, 3901 SW AUSTIN ST, SEATTLE, WA 98136
BRUCE WATSON, 55 LAKE HAVASU AVE S STE F311, LAKE HAVASU, AZ 88403
BRIAN WILLIAMS, 6412 72ND ST DR NE, MARYSVILLE, WA 98270

MISC. SALTWATER FINFISH, LONGLINE VESSEL 60' TO 90', STATEWIDE
KRISTIAN SCHONBERG, BOX 866, ALLYN, WA 98524
RANDALL SHEAR, 3008 NW 59TH, SEATTLE, WA 98107
DUANE TORGESON, 4017 HALIBUT POINT RD, SITKA, AK 99835

MISC. SALTWATER FINFISH, LONGLINE VESSEL 60' TO UNDER 90', GOA
STEVEN FISH, BOX 6448, SITKA, AK 99835
MICHAEL OFFERMAN, 17144 13TH AVE NW, SHORELINE, WA 98177

MISC. SALTWATER FINFISH, OTTER TRAWL VESSEL TO 60', STATEWIDE
MICHAEL ALFIERI, 18120 196TH AVE SE, RENTON, WA 98058
JODY COOK, 2115 NW 12TH ST, BATTLE GROUND, WA 98604
MICHAEL GALLIGAN, BOX 1926, FRIDAY HARBOR, WA 98250
ROBERT GUNDERSON, 3614 SPRUCE CAPE RD, KODIAK, AK 99615
ALEX JACKSON, BOX 1221, FRIDAY HARBOR, WA 98250

GROUNDFISH FISHING LIST—TRAWL

DICK JACOBSEN, BOX 307, SAND POINT, AK 99661
NORMAN JOHANNESSEN, BOX 1638, OROVILLE, WA 98844
DEREK OSTRANDER, BOX 126, CATHALAMET, WA 98612
JUAN.CARLOS PENALOZA, 3155 SPRUCE CAPE RD, KODIAK, AK 99615
JOSEPH PURATICH, BOX 272, GIG HARBOR, WA 98335
ROBERT PURATICH, BOX 1223, GIG HARBOR, WA 98335
DAVID WILSON, BOX 333, SAND POINT, AK 99661

MISC. SALTWATER FINFISH, OTTER TRAWL VESSEL UNDER 60', GOA
DWAIN FOSTER, BOX 162, SAND POINT, AK 99661
JOHN FOSTER, BOX 225, SAND POINT, AK 99661
STEVEN GALOVIN, BOX 215, SAND POINT, AK 99661
MATTHEW HEGGE, BOX 848, KODIAK, AK 99615
ARTHUR HOLMBERG, BOX 78, SAND POINT, AK 99661
ROBIN LARSEN, BOX 264, SAND POINT, AK 99661
BEN LEY, 8316 WINDING RUN RD, ST LOUISVILLE, OH 43071
TAYLOR LUNDGREN, BOX 216, SAND POINT, AK 99661
MIKE NEUNEKER, BOX 52, PETERSBURG, AK 99833
DUKE OGATA, BOX 181, SAND POINT, AK 99661
ROGER OVERA, 14010 154 AVE SE, RENTON, WA 98059
DALE PEDERSEN, 9218 CAMPBELL TERRACE DR, ANCHORAGE, AK 99502
RICHARD STARR, 1518 REZANOF, KODIAK, AK 99615
KILEY THOMPSON, BOX 116, SAND POINT, AK 99661
KEITH WILLIAMS, 1924 E COLGATE DR, TEMPE, AZ 85283
JUSTIN WILSON, BOX 267, KING COVE, AK 99612

MISC. SALTWATER FINFISH, OTTER TRAWL VESSEL 60' - 90' STATEWIDE
CHRISTOPHER ALLINSON, 624 VAN WYCK RD, BELLINGHAM, WA 98226
JASON CHANDLER, 569 LETA, KODIAK, AK 99615
ROCKY CHIRRICK, 320 YASEK LP, TOLEDO, OR 97391
KEITH COCHRAN, BOX 616, NEWPORT, OR 97365
JEDEKIAH COHEN, 61870 WARD RD, BEND, OR 97702
CHRISTOPHER COOPER, 24000 HWY 20, PHILOMATH, OR 97370
SAM EADS, BOX 8805, KODIAK, AK 99615
SCOTT JENSEN, 20607 70TH ST SE, SNOHOMISH, WA 98290
RON KEESEE, BOX 648, NEWPORT, OR 97365
MATT MALO, 338 NW 16TH ST, NEWPORT, OR 97365
MIKE MURDOCK, 505 TORDEN LN SE, OLYMPIA, WA 98513
RONALD NAUGHTON, BOX 3210, KODIAK, AK 99615
PATRICK ODONNELL, BOX 3075, KODIAK, AK 99615
JOHN SAVAGE, BOX 189, SOUTH BEACH, OR 97366
DAVE SMITH, BOX 1650, NEWPORT, OR 97365
TOM STAM, BOX 668, SILETZ, OR 97380
TIVEN TEGNER, BOX 253, SILETZ, OR 97380
CHRISTOPHER WILLIAMSON, 928 KRAFT WAY, KODIAK, AK 99615

MISC. SALTWATER FINFISH, OTTER TRAWL VESSEL 60' TO 90', GOA
DYLAN BEAN, 11147 WOMENS BAY DR, KODIAK, AK 99615
LARRY BOYDSTON, 1322 NW DEER DR, TOLEDO, OR 97391
ROBERT LANGDON, 10783 BIRCH CIR, KODIAK, AK 99615
JOHN MCCARTHY, 11555 MIDDLE BAY DR, KODIAK, AK 99615
ROBERT STARR, BOX 1423, KODIAK, AK 99615

MISC. SALTWATER FINFISH, OTTER TRAWL 90' TO 125', STATEWIDE
LUIS ARRUELA, 2816 NW 92ND ST, SEATTLE, WA 98117
BERT ASHLEY, BOX 425, KODIAK, AK 99615
TAYLOR ASHLEY, BOX 425, KODIAK, AK 99615
CLAYTON BARNHART, 741 SE 7TH ST, TOLEDO, OR 97391
STEVEN BEARD, BOX 568, TOLEDO, OR 97391
BRIAN BEAVER, 10 BEAVER HILL LN, MONTESANO, WA 98563
DAVID BETHEL, 2209 PINE TREE RD, LEVENWORTH, WA 98826

CRAIG BOLTON, 59 BIRCH BANKS RD, SAGLERT, ID 83860
STEVE BRANSTITER, 2727 ALASKAN WAY,PIER 69, SEATTLE, WA 98121
SIMON BURN, 951 NE GRANT ST, NEWPORT, OR 97365
JAMES BYINGTON, 2911 65TH AVE CT NW, GIG HARBOR, WA 98335
TIMOTHY CARRIER, 75142 LOST CREEK RD, CLATSKANIE, OR 97016
RICK CLARK, 2480 SW 37TH ST, REDMOND, OR 97756
KURT COCHRAN, BOX 290, SILETZ, OR 97380
GUY COX, 8131 12TH CT SE, LACEY, WA 98503
GUILLERMO CURIEL, 13114 123RD AVE E, PUYALLUP, WA 98374
DAVID DAHL, BOX 11, SOUTH BEND, WA 98586
TAD DALTON, 22120 BRIER RD, BRIER, WA 98036
KEVIN DIXON, BOX 2065, NEWPORT, OR 97365
ANTONIO DONOVO, 14102 NE 2ND ST, BELLEVUE, WA 98007
STEVEN ELLIOTT, 8504 184TH ST SW, EDMONDS, WA 98026
JAKE EVERICH, 3932 WOLVERINE WAY #1, KODIAK, AK 99615
DAN FOGG, 25564 BUCK HORN RIDGE RD, PIONEER, CA 95666
CHRIS FRANULOVICH, 2101 E AVE, ANACORTES, WA 98221
CHARLIE FREEBURG, 120 MOUNTAIN SHIRE LANE, SOMERS, MT 59932
JEFFERY FREESE, BOX 189, LONG BEACH, WA 98631
ED FRENCH, BOX 411, TOLEDO, OR 97391
KEVIN GANLEY, 2200 ALASKAN WAY #420, SEATTLE, WA 98121
MARK GARBRICK, 23920 101ST PL W, EDMONDS, WA 98020
CHARLES GROESBECK, 16663 BEAVER MARSH RD, MT VERNON, WA 98273
ROBERT HARRINGTON, BOX 1862, KODIAK, AK 99615
DANIEL HEES, 17605 DANSVILLE DR, SPRING HILL, FL 34610
MIKE HELLIGSO, 11962 GARA DR, KODIAK, AK 99615
PER HESBERG, 2910 NE KIMILA DR, ALBANY, OR 97321
GABRIEL HOCKEMA, 21520 FLETCHER LN, BENDORT, OR 97701
JOHN HOCKEMA, 1717 LARCH ST, KODIAK, AK 99615
JOHN HOCKEMA, 35425 JULIA LN, SOLDOTNA, AK 99669
TERRY HOPKINS, 554 BLACKSTRAP RD, FALMOUTH, ME 4105
EDWARD HOUSTON, BOX 1074, KODIAK, AK 99615
SCOTT HOVIK, 11701 BELLA COOLA RD, WOODWAY, WA 98020
JAMES HOWARD, 318 W. REZANOF DR, KODIAK, AK 99615
TERRANCE HULSING, 26894 100TH AVE, ONAMIA, MN 56359
STEFAN IANKOV, BOX 761, KODIAK, AK 99615
DAVID JENSEN, 4818 151ST ST SW, EDMONDS, WA 98026
SCOTT JENSEN, 20607 70TH ST SE, SNOHOMISH, WA 98290
CRAIG JENSSEN, 2107 9TH ST, ANACORTES, WA 98221
CHANDLER JOHNSON, 11330 S RUSSIAN CREEK RD, KODIAK, AK 99615
DALE JOHNSON, 333 1ST AVE W, SEATTLE, WA 98119
STEVE JOHNSON, 333 1ST AVE W, SEATTLE, WA 98119
JAMES KASPER, 750 N S LOW RD, SEAL ROCK, OR 97376
RAY KELLISON, 12981 SR 20, COUPEVILLE, WA 98239
TONY KENNEDY, BOX 1634, NEWPORT, OR 97365
KYE KIRKPATRICK, 3527 SW 170TH ST, BURIEN, WA 98166
MIKE LYNCH, 12218 GARA DR, KODIAK, AK 99615
FRANK MANNES, 18525 8TH AVE NW, SHORELINE, WA 98177
STEINAR MANNES, 7215 156TH ST SW, EDMONDS, WA 98026
JEFF MASON, 386 COUNTRY CLUB DR UNIT C, SIMI VALLEY, CA 93065
BRIAN MAVAR, 604 SAINT MARYS DR, ANACORTES, WA 98221
PAUL MCCABE, 11128 WOMENS BAY DR, KODIAK, AK 99615
DANIEL MCCAY, 1563 FRUITLAND DR, BELLINGHAM, WA 98226
MICHAEL MCELHENIE, BOX 8390, KODIAK, AK 99615
BRUCE MCPEAK, 582 A SKAMANIA LANDING, STEVENSON, WA 98648
GARY MINKOFF, 780 BUNKER CK RD, CHEHALIS, WA 98532
BRUCE MORRICE, BOX 234, TOLEDO, OR 97391
CAMILO NETO, 7215 156TH ST SW, EDMONDS, WA 98026
BOI NJARDVIK, 1932 WINNERS CIRCLE, CANTONMENT, FL 32533
TADEUSZ NOGACKI, 421 E HARVARD AVE #2, ANCHORAGE, AK 99501
STEVEN OLSEN, 15409 NE 153RD ST, WOODENVILLE, WA 98072
EDUARDO OREJUELA, 4201 21ST AVE W, SEATTLE, WA 98199
DALE PAGE, BOX 94, BOOTHBAY HARBOR, ME 4538
JAY PEDERSEN, 2200 ALASKAN WAY #420, SEATTLE, WA 98121
CHRISTOPHER PETERSON, 2171 N 122 PL, SEATTLE, WA 98133

GROUNDFISH FISHING LIST—TRAWL

DAVID RICHCREEK, 2026 NW OCEANVIEW DR, NEWPORT, OR 97365
ARIK ROBERTS, BOX 280, BROOKINGS, OR 97415
TIM ROBERTSON, 6392 ADMIRALTY WAY, FREELAND, WA 98249
BRANNAN ROWE, 4201 21ST AVE W, SEATTLE, WA 98199
DON SITTON, BOX 2434, KODIAK, AK 99615
DEAN SLATER, BOX 921007, DUTCH HARBOR, AK 99692
STEVEN SPAIN, BOX 226, SOUTH BEND, WA 98586
MARTIN STAM, 84488 BRISTOW RD, PLEASANT HILL, OR 97455
DAN THALMAN, BOX 8869, KODIAK, AK 99615
WAYNE TIPLER, BOX J, SOUTH BEND, WA 98586
DAVID WILLMORE, BOX 1227, FERNDALE, WA 98248
JOHN WOOD, 11528 SEOLA BEACH DR SW, SEATTLE, WA 98146
BRYAN WRIGHT, BOX 8861, KODIAK, AK 99615
RICHARD WYATT, BOX 129, MONTESANO, WA 98563
FRED YECK, BOX 871, NEWPORT, OR 97365
BARRY YETTER, BOX 31094, BELLINGHAM, WA 98228
MARK ZABLE, BOX 1150, ROCKLAND, ME 4841

MISC. SALTWATER FINFISH, OTTER TRAWL VESSEL 90' TO 125', GOA
JAMIE FAGAN, BOX 2140, KODIAK, AK 99615
GEORGE HUTCHINGS, BOX 8242, KODIAK, AK 99615
MICHAEL O.CALLAGHAN, BOX 1967, KODIAK, AK 99615
JAMIE POTTER, 18160 COTTONWOOD RD PMB 211, SUNRIVER, OR 97707
MATT RAY, BOX 384, NEAH BAY, WA 98357
CURT WATERS, BOX 471, KODIAK, AK 99615

MISC. SALTWATER FINFISH, OTTER TRAWL OVER 125', STATEWIDE
PHILIP BAKER, 1549 BAKER RANCH LN, OAK HARBOR, WA 98277
NORMAN BAKKEN, 11689 E 35TH PLACE, YUMA, AZ 85365
JEFFERY BARNETT, 4201 21ST AVE W, SEATTLE, WA 98199
STUART BARNHART, 26016 NE 227TH ST, BATTLEGROUND, WA 98604
MICHAEL BENESCH, 3141 HARRISON, ASTORIA, OR 97103
DAVID BISHOP, 4201 21ST AVE W, SEATTLE, WA 98119
SCOTT BRYANT, 4201 21ST AVE W, SEATTLE, WA 98199
JOSHUA BUCHAN, 877 HAILEY CT, SAN MARCOS, CA 92078
JAMES BUSKIRK, 161 LOVELL AVE SW, BAINBRIDGE ISLAND, WA 98110
BRYAN CARDINAL, 5003 TEXADA LN, PASCO, WA 99301
DANIEL CARNEY, 380 S AUGUST CIR, WASILLA, AK 99654
JAMES COX, 1148 SAWYER RD, CAPE ELIZABETH, ME 4107
JEFF CRAIN, 13201 47TH PL W, MUKILTEO, WA 98275
PAT DEDMORE, 2025 1ST AVE SUITE 900, SEATTLE, WA 98121
DAN DIETRICH, 5511 134TH ST COURT NW, GIG HARBOR, WA 98332
CHARLES DODGE, 2025 1ST AVE #900, SEATTLE, WA 98121
ACACIO DOMAR, 2233 NW 59TH ST #105, SEATTLE, WA 98107
LUIS DOMAR, 2233 NW 59TH ST #105, SEATTLE, WA 98107
STEVE DOREMUS, 5215 CATOCTIO DR, SAN DIEGO, CA 92115
KEVIN DOYLE, 850 BEECH ST UNIT 1801, SAN DIEGO, CA 92101
PAUL LINDQUIS, 11611 NE ANGLEO DR # 109, VANCOUVER, WA 98684
STEVE DUBOIS, 17812 OLD HWY 99 SW, TENINO, WA 98589
THOMAS DURNAN, 2442 NW MARKET ST #196, SEATTLE, WA 98107
JON EDSON, 19808 PARSONS CREEK RD, SEDRO WOOLLEY, WA 98284
JAMES EGAAS, 18463 NE 196TH PL, WOODINVILLE, WA 98077
DARRIN EKLUND, BOX 128, GIG HARBOR, WA 98335
TOM ELLIS, 2727 ALASKAN WAY PIER 69, SEATTLE, WA 98802
BRANDON ERICKSON, 2025 1ST AVE STE 900, SEATTLE, WA 98121
VERNON ETLICHER, 4211 H AVE, ANACORTES, WA 98221
THORBJORN FINNBOGASON, 1801 FAIRVIEW AVE E #100, SEATTLE, WA 98102
RAYMOND FISCHER, 4201 21ST AVE W, SEATTLE, WA 98199
WILLIAM FITZGERALD, 1801 FAIRVIEW AVE E #100, SEATTLE, WA 98102
JEFFERY GARRISON, 2157 N NORTHLAKE WAY STE 210, SEATTLE, WA 98103
ROLF GRAESDAL, 2025 1ST AVE #900, SEATTLE, WA 98121
ROBERT GRAHAM, 3433 ANTONE WAY, KODIAK, AK 99615
RAYMOND HADDON, 8216 61ST AVE NW, GIG HARBOR, WA 98332
BRIAN HAGEN, BOX 728, SEDRO WOLLEY, WA 98284

BRIAN HALEY, BOX 936, BLACK DIAMOND, WA 98010
PATRICK HALEY, 4201 21ST AVE W, SEATTLE, WA 98199
KIMBREY HAMPTON, 1801 FAIRVIEW AVE E #100, SEATTLE, WA 98102
DAVID HELMERSEN, 1967 HILLVISTA PL, FREELAND, WA 98249
ROBERT HEZEL, 6164 COUNTNER CT, CLINTON, WA 98236
JARL HOGSETH, 4836 SOUNDSIDE DR, GULF BREEZE, FL 32563
PAUL ISON, 7223 224TH ST SW #J11, EDMONDS, WA 98026
KURT JASTAD, BOX 15112, MILL CREEK, WA 98082
KJELL JENSEN, 2025 1ST AVE #900, SEATTLE, WA 98121
JENS JOHNSEN, 2025 1ST AVE #900, SEATTLE, WA 98121
MICHAEL JOHNSON, 4008 FOREST PK CT NW, OLYMPIA, WA 98502
SHAWN KENNY, 2727 ALASKAN WAY PIER 69, SEATTLE, WA 98121
OLE KNOTTEN, 2025 1ST AVE #900, SEATTLE, WA 98121
MICHAEL KRALJEVICH, 6503 146TH ST SE, SNOHOMISH, WA 98296
SCOTT KREY, 19064 10TH AVE NE, POULSBO, WA 98370
ARTHUR KUHR, 11098 CARAMEL CREST COURT, LAS VEGAS, NV 89135
SVEIN LANGAKER, 24025 NEWELLHURST CIR NE, KINGSTON, WA 98346
MARC LASHUA, 2801 WESTERN AVE 135, SEATTLE, WA 98121
MATTHEW LIESKE, 2415 T AVE #208, ANACORTES, WA 98221
RICK LOAN, 3681 N CORGETT WASH CT, TUCSON, AZ 85745
OSCAR LOEWEN, 12084 S SHADOW HILLS CT SE, TURNER, OR 97392
DAVID LONG, 2320 W COMMODORE WAY #200, SEATTLE, WA 98199
GARY LONGAKER, 9210 232 ST SW, EDMONDS, WA 98020
HARALD LONGVANES, 1801 FAIRVIEW AVE E #300, SEATTLE, WA 98102
ELMER LOOSE, BOX 6, ADNA, WA 98522
BRANDON LYNN, 20214 108TH DR SE, SNOHOMISH, WA 98296
MIROSLAW MACIEJSKI, 6421 SPRUCE ST, ANCHORAGE, AK 99507
ROBERT MACKINNON, 23 SPRING ST, CAMDEN, ME 4843
SAM MADEJA, 631 N STEPHANIE ST #365, HENDERSON, NV 89014
NICK MALAHOVSKY, 6515 152ND AVE E, SUMNER, WA 98390
HOWARD MALCOLM, 14069 ERVINE RD, ANACORTES, WA 98221
PAUL MANGAN, 7215 156TH ST SW, EDMONDS, WA 98026
JOHAN MANNES, 8228 234TH ST SW, EDMONDS, WA 98026
DANIEL MARTIN, BOX 1047, LA CENTER, WA 98629
STEVE MAYOR, 2727 ALASKAN WAY PIER 69, SEATTLE, WA 98121
ARTHUR MCARDLE, 111 RATHFARNHAM CIR, ASHEVILLE, NC 28803
WILLIAM MCCARTHEY, 1801 FAIRVIEW AVE E #100, SEATTLE, WA 98102
PATRICK MCGRORTY, 2013 EAST JOHN ST, SEATTLE, WA 98112
ERIN MOORE, 1911 SW CAMPUS DR #131, FEDERAL WAY, WA 98023
JOHN NELSON, 5517 MOOSE MEADOW WAY, DEER PARK, WA 99006
TONY NORG, 520 AABY DR, AUBURN, WA 98001
ROY OLSEN, 760 AUTUMN LN, BELLINGHAM, WA 98226
BRENT PAYLOR, 504 E CYPRESS AVE, GLENDORA, CA 91741
KIETH PENDLETON, 2320 W COMMODORE WAY #200, SEATTLE, WA 98199
LORIN PERRY, 23725 196TH AVE SE, MAPLE VALLEY, WA 98038
JOHN QUANDT, 2025 1ST AVE #900, SEATTLE, WA 98121
MICHAEL REARDON, 4201 21ST AVE W, SEATTLE, WA 98199
LOREN REYNOLDS, BOX 921113, DUTCH HARBOR, AK 99692
REED ROUSAR, BOX 281, FRIDAY HARBOR, WA 98250
SHAWN RUSSELL, 16627 154TH ST SE, MONROE, WA 98272
DANIEL SKAUGE, 2025 1ST AVE #900, SEATTLE, WA 98121
CLAYTON SMITH, 19381 INDIAN SUMMER RD, BEND, OR 97702
DANIEL SORIA, BOX 988, BURLINGTON, WA 98233
PHILLIP SOUTER, C/O OHARA CORP 4315 11TH AVE NW, SEATTLE, WA 98117
FRANCIS ST.CROIX, 160 FRANKLIN ST, HALIFAX, MA 2338
BROOKS STEVENS, 2025 1ST AVE #900, SEATTLE, WA 98121
BRIAN STYKE, 2727 ALASKAN WAY PIER 69, SEATTLE, WA 98121
GLENN SULLIVAN, 15191 GIBRALTER RD, ANACORTES, WA 98221
JAMES SUMMERS, 2415 T AVE #208, ANACORTES, WA 98221
JAMES SUSOL, 2025 1ST AVE #900, SEATTLE, WA 98121
SCOTT SYMONDS, 7388 REMINGTON LN, ANACORTES, WA 98221
JOSE TEIXEIRA, 16124 54TH PL W, EDMONDS, WA 98026
TIMOTHY THOMAS, 2025 1ST AVE #900, SEATTLE, WA 98121
ERIC TOWER, 567 PIONEER TRAIL, TOLEDO, OR 97391
KURT VANBRERO, 2025 1ST AVE #900, SEATTLE, WA 98121
DARIN VANDERPOL, 484 W POLE RD, LYNDEN, WA 98264

GROUNDFISH / OCTOPI / SQUID / DUNGENESS CRAB FISHING LIST

VITTORIO VANONI, 16105 SE 45TH CT, BELLEVUE, WA 98006
FRANK VARGAS, 2025 1ST AVE #900, SEATTLE, WA 98121
BRIAN WEBER, 2025 1ST AVE #900, SEATTLE, WA 98121
ADAM WHITE, 2865 WANDERER LANE, LAKE HAVASU CITY, AZ 86403
ERIC WIECHMANN, 2727 ALASKAN WAY PIER 69, SEATTLE, WA 98121
GREG WRIGHT, BOX 387, BOOTHBAY, ME 4537
SAM WRIGHT, 16059 HIDDEN CREEK LN, ANCHORAGE, AK 99518
DAVID YORK, 10650 E BLANCHE DR, SCOTTSDALE, AZ 85255

MISC. SALTWATER FINFISH, POT GEAR VESSEL 60' + OVER, STATEWIDE
MARK ATKINSON, 5470 SHILSHOLE AVE NW #520, SEATTLE, WA 98107
JACOB BONGEN, 9153 N TREASURE MOUNTAIN DR, TUCSON, AZ 85742
SCOTT CAMPBELL, 3707 E FRATELLO ST, MERIDIAN, ID 83642
CHRISTOPHER CHERNOFF, 3112 BETTLES BAY LOOP, ANCHORAGE, AK 99515
JOSHUA COZBY, 12705 NE 112TH ST, VANCOUVER, WA 98682
DANIEL DELAURENTIS, BOX 954, STEVENSVILLE, MT 59870
SEAN DWYER, 4011 228TH PL SW, MOUNTLAKE TERRACE, WA 98043
MIKE FERRIS, BOX 331, KODIAK, AK 99615
MURRAY GAMRATH, BOX 920031, DUTCH HARBOR, AK 99692
MARK GILES, BOX 127, SELDOVIA, AK 99663
CRAIG GUSTAFSON, BOX 8573, KODIAK, AK 99615
DAVID HARRIS, 2807 S LAKE ROESIGER RD, SNOHOMISH, WA 98290
JAY HEBERT, BOX 920027, DUTCH HARBOR, AK 99692
CHARLES JOHNSON, 8837 SW MARSEILLES DR, BEAVERTON, OR 99615
DAHER JORGE, 3871 STEILACOM BLVD SW #C, LAKEWOOD, WA 98499 JOHN
KORPI, 4005 20TH AVE W, SEATTLE, WA 98199
JOSE LANDEROS, BOX 1875, GYPSUM, CO 81637
OYSTEIN LONE, 3315 150TH PL SE, MILL CREEK, WA 98012
CHAD LOWENBERG, 451 SEXTON RD, SEBASTOPOL, CA 95472
DAVID MARTIN, BOX 2652, HOMER, AK 99603
JAMES MARTINDALE, 9916 GOLDEN GIVEN RD E, TACOMA, WA 98445 JERRY
MATTHEWS, BOX 2543, SITKA, AK 99835
SETH MCCALLUM, BOX 191, PETERSBURG, AK 99833
KERBY MITCHELL, BOX 2161, HOMER, AK 99603
JEFFREY MOREHOUSE, 1605 NW 192ND ST, SHORELINE, WA 98177 JOSEPH
MORRIS, BOX 2487, CHELAN, WA 98816
HERBERT MURRAY, 8615 NE 169TH, KENMORE, WA 98028
DONALD NORTON, BOX 3282, KODIAK, AK 99615
KELLY PAINTER, 4385 YAQUINA BAY RD, NEWPORT, OR 97365
HENRY PERALES, 12712 ADMIRALTY WAY #D101, EVERETT, WA 98204
ROBERT PERKEY, 110 SE DIVISION ST, SUBLIMITY, OR 97385
MICHAEL PERRY, 23 OCOSTA SIXTH ST, ABERDEEN, WA 98520
KYLE POTTER, BOX 944, QUECHEE, VT 5059
CHARLES REHDER, BOX 2065, HOMER, AK 99603
DOUG SHELFORD, 16212 BOTHELL EVERETT HWY #340, MILL CRK, WA 98102
DONALD SPROULE, 1020 W 16TH, ANCHORAGE, AK 99501
BRIAN STELTER, 344 GUNNISON AVE SW, GRAND RAPIDS, MI 49504
CHRISTOPHER STUDEMAN, 1833 DEAN CK RD, REEDSPORT, OR 97467
THOMAS SURYAN, 20126 BALLINGER WY NE PMB 158, SHORELINE, WA 98155
ROBERT SYKES, 9545 DRY GROVE RD, RAYMOND, MS 39154
CHRIS SYLCE, 51053 E END RD, HOMER, AK 99603
RAYMOND TERRY, BOX 46, PETERSBURG, AK 99833
ROBERT THELEN, 637 COUNTY RD 6, MEEKER, CO 81641
BLAKE TUCKER, 46011 SE 134TH ST, NORTH BEND, WA 98045
WADE VEESER, 2001 S 22ND ST, ESCAMABA, MI 49829
WILLIAM WAHL, 20735 WAGONTIRE WAY, BEND, OR 97701
WILLIAM WICHROWSKI, BOX 2462, VALDEZ, AK 99686
JAMES WILSON, 13481 BAYWIND DR, ANCHORAGE, AK 99516
PETER WILSON, 3615 OLYMPUS DR NE, BREMERTON, WA 98310

MISC. SALTWATER FINFISH, POT GEAR VESSEL 60' OR OVER, GOA

KEVIN BUNDY, BOX 2705, KODIAK, AK 99615

JOSHUA COZBY, 12705 NE 112TH ST, VANCOUVER, WA 98682
STEPHEN MILES, BOX 1053, KODIAK, AK 99615
CARL PEDERSEN, BOX 1193, KODIAK, AK 99615
GREG WALLACE, BOX 9041, KODIAK, AK 99615

OCTOPI/SQUID, POT GEAR VESSEL UNDER 60', STATEWIDE
TIMOTHY GERVAIS, BOX 7, RUBY, AK 99768
BRANISLAV LALICH, BOX 2583, HOMER, AK 99603
KENNETH MACK, BOX 176, KING COVE, AK 99612
PATRICK PIKUS, BOX 2843, KODIAK, AK 99615
DONALD VINBERG, BOX 9032, KODIAK, AK 99615
LES WOODWARD, BOX 2059, WRANGELL, AK 99929

OCTOPI/SQUID, MECHANICAL JIG, STATEWIDE
ALEK DYAKANOFF, BOX 7111, KETCHIKAN, AK 99901
SHARON HOLT, BOX 9224, KETCHIKAN, AK 99901
PAMELA LEASK, BOX 759, WARD COVE, AK 99928
ADAM MENGE, 905 NORDSTROM DR, KETCHIKAN, AK 99901
WENDI STICKWAN, BOX 5041, KETCHIKAN, AK 99901
AXEL SVENSON, 283 S POINT HIGGINS, KETCHIKAN, AK 99901

OCTOPI/SQUID, POT GEAR VESSEL 60' OR OVER, STATEWIDE
CHARLES JOHNSON, 8837 SW MARSEILLES DR, BEAVERTON, OR 99615
COREY POTTER, BOX 1939, KODIAK, AK 99615

FRESH WATER FISH, BEACH SEINE, STATEWIDE
KELLEY GREEN, BOX 806, NOME, AK 99762

FRESH WATER FISH, SET GILLNET, STATEWIDE
TIM DEACON, 103 THIRD ST, GRAYLING, AK 99590
DAVID HERBERT, BOX 287, SAINT MARYS, AK 99658
EVAN HUNT, BOX 20025, KOTLIK, AK 99620
CLARENCE JOHNSON, BOX 367, SAINT MARYS, AK 99658
LORRAINE MURPHY, BOX 56, ALAKANUK, AK 99554
JOHN WESTLOCK, BOX 44, EMMONAK, AK 99581

DUNGENESS CRAB, POT GEAR VESSEL UNDER 60', WESTWARD
JEFFREY ALLEN, BOX 3020, TRINIDAD, CA 95570
BRIAN BLONDIN, BOX 1521, KODIAK, AK 99615
JASON BLONDIN, 1415 BARANOF ST, KODIAK, AK 99615
KELLY BROYLES, 7060 BLACKHAWK LN, FOREST HILL, CA 95631
MARK THOMAS, 2249 SELIEF LN, KODIAK, AK 99615

DUNGENESS CRAB, POT GEAR VESSEL UNDER 60', CHIGNIK
ALLEN MITCHELL, 41 STRAWBERRY PT RD, BELLINGHAM, WA 98229

DUNGENESS CRAB, POT GEAR VESSEL UNDER 60', ALASKA PENINSULA
ALFREDO ABOUEID, BOX 26, CHIGNIK LAGOON, AK 99565
BRUCE FOSTER, BOX 46, SAND POINT, AK 99661
ROBIN LARSEN, BOX 264, SAND POINT, AK 99661
DUKE OGATA, BOX 181, SAND POINT, AK 99661
JIM SMITH, BOX 354, SAND POINT, AK 99661

DUNGENESS CRAB, RING NET, SOUTHEAST
MYRON BAKER, BOX 24, POINT BAKER, AK 99927
BRYAN BURGHDUFF, BOX 6462, KETCHIKAN, AK 99901
WES CRASKE, BOX 541, KLAWOCK, AK 99925

DUNGENESS CRAB FISHING LIST

GLEN DUSSEAULT, BOX NKI #11, KETCHIKAN, AK 99950
CHRISTOPHER GUGGENBICKLER, BOX 1491, WRANGELL, AK 99929
BILL JOHNSTON, BOX 134, PETERSBURG, AK 99833
RODNEY SELVIG, BOX 981, MEADOW VISTA, CA 95722
DIETRICK TYLER, BOX 1632, PETERSBURG, AK 99833

DUNGENESS CRAB, RING NET, COOK INLET
JOHN OGLE, BOX 694, ANCHOR POINT, AK 99556

DUNGENESS CRAB, DIVING GEAR, SOUTHEAST
RAYMOND CAMPBELL, 2707 W 18TH AVE, FAIRBANKS, AK 99709
GEORGE DODDINGTON, 3850 YORKSHIRE AVE, EUGENE, OR 97405
MARK JOHNSON, BOX 5644, KETCHIKAN, AK 99901

DUNGENESS CRAB, POT GEAR, COOK INLET
ALBERT ARAKELIAN, BOX 1014, HOMER, AK 99603
RANDY ARSENAULT, BOX 4104, HOMER, AK 99603
DAVE BARKER, 126 E FAIRVEIW AVE, HOMER, AK 99603
BRANT BAXTER, BOX 1023, OAK HARBOR, WA 98277
RONALD BERGLUND, 14450 SE 5TH PL, WILLISTON, FL 32696
GARLAND BLANCHARD, BOX 406, HOMER, AK 99603
TIMOTHY BOWLER, BOX 2980, HOMER, AK 99603
MICHAEL BROOKS, BOX 220727, ANCHORAGE, AK 99522
EVERETT BROWN, 62 DILLARD RD, GLENWOOD, AR 71943
JOHN BURY, 1710 EDMOND ST, WALLA WALLA, WA 99362
LEROY CABANA, BOX 49, HOMER, AK 99603
GEORGE CALLAHAN, 385 LEE DR, HOMER, AK 99603
ROBERT CARLSON, 14401 ELMORE RD, ANCHORAGE, AK 99516
KENNETH CASTNER, BOX 558, HOMER, AK 99603
BARTON CHOW, BOX 2044, HOMER, AK 99603
DOUGLAS COPE, BOX 4053, SOLDOTNA, AK 99669
FRED CURRIER, BOX 3667, HOMER, AK 99603
MICHAEL DEVANEY, 484 KLONDIKE AVE, HOMER, AK 99603
BRAD DICKEY, BOX 2677, HOMER, AK 99603
LEDA DISLER, 3919 WRIGHT ST, HOMER, AK 99603
MICHAEL DISLER, 3919 WRIGHT ST, HOMER, AK 99603
ELROY ERICKSON, BOX 39452, NINILCHIK, AK 99639
MYRTLE ERICKSON, BOX 39452, NINILCHIK, AK 99639
LEONARD FABICH, BOX 1331, HOMER, AK 99603
BRADFORD FAULKNER, BOX 996, HOMER, AK 99603
MIKE HAGGREN, 1 THIRD ST #105, ASTORIA, OR 97103
TODD HOUBREGS, BOX 31, ELMA, WA 98541
SHILA HOUGH, 3733 BEN WALTERS LN #2, HOMER, AK 99603
WESLEY HUMBYRD, 860 WILLOW DR, HOMER, AK 99603
LAVRO IVANOV, 6127 S SCHNEIDER RD, WOODBURN, OR 97071
MERLE KEIM, BOX 832, ANCHOR POINT, AK 99556
DOUG KELLER, 39980 FERNWOOD DR, HOMER, AK 99603
GAVIN KEOHANE, BOX 481, KENAI, AK 99611
JENS KLAAR, HC67 BOX 1261A, ANCHOR POINT, AK 99556
SCOTT KRICK, BOX 875214, WASILLA, AK 99687
DAVID KROM, GENERAL DELIVERY, KODIAK, AK 99615
RUSSELL KUIPERS, BOX 351, ANCHOR POINT, AK 99556
JOHN KVARFORD, 6240 N WELTIN WY, PALMER, AK 99645
DANNY MCLEAN, BOX 351, HOMER, AK 99603
JOHN MCLEAN, BOX 2191, HOMER, AK 99603
FRANCIS MERRIGAN, 7401 E JIM COTTRELL CIR, PALMER, AK 99645
MICHAEL MILLER, BOX 273, SELDOVIA, AK 99663
JACK MONTGOMERY, BOX 1526, HOMER, AK 99603
ROBERT MOSS, BOX 3428, HOMER, AK 99603
LAURENCE NAGY, 2409 5TH AVE, KETCHIKAN, AK 99901
MICHAEL NAKADA, BOX 1838, HOMER, AK 99603
PATRICK NEHER, BOX 15011, FRITZ CREEK, AK 99603
ROBERT NELSON, BOX 205, KASILOF, AK 99610

THOMAS NELSON, BOX 1392, HOMER, AK 99603
JOHN OGLE, BOX 694, ANCHOR POINT, AK 99556
MARY OLSON, 40545 LOFTY LN, HOMER, AK 99603
CHARLES PIPER, BOX 15233, FRITZ CREEK, AK 99603
SANDRA R.A.CHRISTEN, BOX RDO, HOMER, AK 99603
FRANK RICHARDSON, BOX 16, ANCHOR POINT, AK 99556
CRAIG SCHLOESSER, BOX 356, ANCHOR POINT, AK 99556
CHARLES SEVILLE, BOX 26, SELDOVIA, AK 99663
DAVID SMITH, BOX 333, ANCHOR POINT, AK 99556
DAVID SONNEBORN, 2548 DISCOVERY CT, ANCHORAGE, AK 99517
KENT SORENSEN, BOX 15127, FRITZ CREEK, AK 99603
WILLIAM SOWERS, BOX 415, HOMER, AK 99603
CLARK SPRINGER, 1407 BAY AVE, HOMER, AK 99603
GARY SQUIRES, BOX 3444, HOMER, AK 99603
ALEXANDER STUART, BOX 172, HOMER, AK 99603
DOUGLAS STUART, 292 MOUNTAIN VIEW DR, HOMER, AK 99603
SONJA TOBIESSEN, 4800 SNOW CIR, ANCHORAGE, AK 99508
EDWARD TYSON, BOX 401, ANCHOR POINT, AK 99556
WILLIAM WALDORF, 40055 OLD STERLING HWY, ANCHOR POINT, AK 99556
MARY WALLIS, 442 LEE DR, HOMER, AK 99603
MARTIN WHITE, BOX 62, KING SALMON, AK 99613
CHRIS WYTHE, BOX 452, HOMER, AK 99603
HARRY YUTH, BOX 6, SELDOVIA, AK 99663

DUNGENESS CRAB, POT GEAR VESSEL 60' OR OVER, WESTWARD
KENNETH HOLLAND, BOX 608, KODIAK, AK 99615

DUNGENESS CRAB, POT GEAR VESSEL 60' & OVER, ALASKA PENINSULA
ROBERT TRUMBLE, 3705 ARCTIC BLVD PMB 1101, ANCHORAGE, AK 99503

DUNGENESS CRAB, 300 POTS/OR 100% OF MAX, SOUTHEAST
DAVID BEEBE, BOX 148, PETERSBURG, AK 99833
STEVEN BOX, 1512 LING CT, JUNEAU, AK 99801
JARED BRIGHT, BOX 2097, PETERSBURG, AK 99833
CHARLES CLEMENTS, BOX 77, GUSTAVUS, AK 99826
RICHARD DAUGHERTY, BOX 34864, JUNEAU, AK 99803
DANIEL ELLINGSEN, 4266 HALIBUT POINT RD, SITKA, AK 99835
JEFF ERICKSON, BOX 53, PETERSBURG, AK 99833
OTTO FLORSCHUTZ, BOX 547, WRANGELL, AK 99929
CHARLES GADD, BOX 2144, WRANGELL, AK 99929
DAVID GREBE, BOX 71, LAKE CLEAR, NY 12945
RICHARD GREGG, BOX 20669, JUNEAU, AK 99802
BENJAMIN HINDE, BOX 2099, PETERSBURG, AK 99833
JOSEPH JANSSEN, BOX 492, TOK, AK 99780
RONALD JOHNSON, BOX 2232, WRANGELL, AK 99929
DAVID KLEPSER, BOX 8946, KETCHIKAN, AK 99901
PAUL KORCHAK, BOX 1256, PETERSBURG, AK 99833
RYAN LITTLETON, BOX 2143, PETERSBURG, AK 99833
MICHAEL LOCKABEY, BOX 1542, WRANGELL, AK 99929
JACK LYONS, BOX 527, PETERSBURG, AK 99833
CLIFFORD MACDONALD, BOX 575, PETERSBURG, AK 99833
KIRT MARSH, BOX 1421, PETERSBURG, AK 99833
CHARLES MASON, 16526 GLACIER HWY, JUNEAU, AK 99801
PAUL MENISH, BOX 33, PETERSBURG, AK 99833
AARON MILLER, BOX 2144, PETERSBURG, AK 99833
MATT NILSEN, BOX 1463, PETERSBURG, AK 99833
MICHAEL NILSEN, BOX 1084, PETERSBURG, AK 99833
GORDON OLSEN, BOX 1884, PETERSBURG, AK 99833
DENNIS ONEIL, BOX 1083, PETERSBURG, AK 99833
PETER ORD, 1606 LAURIE LN, JUNEAU, AK 99801
LOGAN PADGETT, BOX 205, PETERSBURG, AK 99833
ALFRED PEELER, BOX 761, PETERSBURG, AK 99833
JOEL RANDRUP, BOX 1231, PETERSBURG, AK 99833

DUNGENESS CRAB FISHING LIST

SVEN SAVLAND, BOX 621, HOONAH, AK 99829
RONALD SKEENS, 27720 315TH AVE, WINNER, SD 57580
BRAD SOBJACK, 2422 CRESTLINE DR, BELLINGHAM, WA 98229
DAVID SOMERVILLE, BOX 163, PETERSBURG, AK 99833
RALPH STRICKLAND, BOX 292, PETERSBURG, AK 99833
STACY SUNDBORG, 5115 N DOUGLAS HWY, JUNEAU, AK 99801
TANNER THOMASSEN, BOX 468, WRANGELL, AK 99929
DEREK THYNES, BOX 1624, PETERSBURG, AK 99833
BRYAN TODD, BOX 181, GUSTAVUS, AK 99826
THOMAS TRAIBUSH, 1300 PEACE PORTAL DR #206, BLAINE, WA 98230
ROB TUCKER, BOX 554, TOKELAND, WA 98590
SHAYAR VALANDRO, BOX 210966, AUKE BAY, AK 99821
FRANK WARFEL, BOX 1512, WRANGELL, AK 99929
LUKE WHITETHORN, BOX 1716, PETERSBURG, AK 99833
TOM WICKMAN, BOX 1513, WRANGELL, AK 99929
JOE WILLIS, BOX 43, PETERSBURG, AK 99833
JEFF WOLFE, BOX 381, SITKA, AK 99835
MAXIMILIAN WORHATCH, BOX 407, PETERSBURG, AK 99833
DANIEL ZEIK, BOX 646, PETERSBURG, AK 99833

DUNGENESS CRAB, 225 POTS/OR 75% OF MAX, SOUTHEAST
TODD BAILEY, 511 KENNEDY ST, JUNEAU, AK 99801
DAVID BENITZ, BOX 1535, PETERSBURG, AK 99833
TOR BENSON, BOX 441, PETERSBURG, AK 99833
CLAYTON BRANDA, BOX 8473, KETCHIKAN, AK 99901
THOMAS BRAYTON, 145 BEHRENDS AVE, JUNEAU, AK 99801
DUSTIN CAPLES, BOX 526, PETERSBURG, AK 99833
DAVID COLEMAN, BOX 6082, SITKA, AK 99835
VERNE CRAIG, BOX 1238, PETERSBURG, AK 99833
ERIC DAUGHERTY, BOX 34602, JUNEAU, AK 99803
STUART DEWITT, BOX 117, HAINES, AK 99827
WILLIAM DORN, 11615 SUNDLER RD, HAYDEN, ID 83835
MATTHEW DUDDLES, BOX 490, PETERSBURG, AK 99833
JOHN DUPREE, BOX 684, PETERSBURG, AK 99833
RANDALL EASTERLY, BOX 1524, WRANGELL, AK 99929
MIKE ERICKSON, BOX 34363, JUNEAU, AK 99803
RAYMOND EVENS, BOX 197, PETERSBURG, AK 99833
LYNN EWING, BOX 1335, PETERSBURG, AK 99833
DAN FOLEY, BOX 57, GUSTAVUS, AK 99826
ANDREW FRISKE, 3004 BARKER ST, SITKA, AK 99835
CARSON GRANT, 502 CHARTERES, SITKA, AK 99835
JEFFREY GRIN, BOX 397, WRANGELL, AK 99929
RICHARD HANSON, BOX 991, CLINTON, WA 98236
TERRY HASBROUCK, BOX 486, PETERSBURG, AK 99833
JAKE JABUSCH, BOX 1228, PETERSBURG, AK 99833
JIMMY LEGGETT, 2505 SOUND VIEW DR, LANGLEY, WA 98260
BRIAN MARTENS, 2420 SIXTH AVE, KETCHIKAN, AK 99901
BRIAN MATTSON, BOX 1168, PETERSBURG, AK 99833
PATRICK MCGRATH, BOX 2060, PETERSBURG, AK 99833
PAUL MCINTYRE, BOX 1994, WRANGELL, AK 99929
MARLA MELLING, 5581 HEART LAKE PL, ANACORTES, WA 98221
MATTHEW METCALF, 2999 JOSHUA CT, HOLLAND, MI 49424
DAVID MORK, BOX 1500, WRANGELL, AK 99929
LAWTON PADDOCK, 1415 W 9TH AVE, ANCHORAGE, AK 99501
MARK PETERSON, BOX 302, CHINOOK, WA 98614
BRYON PFUNDT, BOX 1162, PETERSBURG, AK 99833
JONATHAN POWELL, BOX 1733, WRANGELL, AK 99929
STEVE PRUNELLA, BOX 2157, WRANGELL, AK 99929
CHAD RITCHIE, BOX 79, WRANGELL, AK 99929
PETER RODDY, BOX 6436, SITKA, AK 99835
ROBERT SCHWARTZ, BOX 1533, PETERSBURG, AK 99833
BRUCE SORENSON, 47704 175TH ST, CLEAR LAKE, SD 57226
BRIAN STERBA, BOX 812, CLINTON, WA 98236
STEWART VICK, BOX 1271, PETERSBURG, AK 99833

JEFFREY VILLARMA, 312 SE RIM LN, PORT ORCHARD, WA 98367
MICHAEL WALKER, 8479 THUNDER MOUNTAIN RD, JUNEAU, AK 99801
GREGORY WALLACE, 417 MONASTERY ST, SITKA, AK 99835
JESSE WEST, BOX 1786, PETERSBURG, AK 99833
BRETT YOUNG, BOX 1971, WRANGELL, AK 99929
RUDOLF ZIEL, BOX 44, TENAKEE, AK 99841

DUNGENESS CRAB, 150 POTS/OR 50% OF MAX, SOUTHEAST
GARY ADKISON, BOX 873, CRAIG, AK 99921
TRAVIS BANGS, BOX 403, WRANGELL, AK 99929
REED BARBER, HC 60 BOX 6200, HAINES, AK 99827
ROBERT BARCAS, BOX 784, NEW MEADOWS, ID 83654
DOUGLAS BARKER, BOX 813, WRANGELL, AK 99929
ROBERT BRISCOE, 1043 PEACE PORTAL DR, BLAINE, WA 98230
DAVID BROWN, BOX 491, WRANGELL, AK 99929
MICHAEL BUNESS, BOX 217, WRANGELL, AK 99929
JOSHUA CONN, BOX 593, PETERSBURG, AK 99833
DENNY CORBIN, BOX 765, PELICAN, AK 99832
EDWARD CRAWFORD, 370 NE CAMANO DR #375, CAMANO ISLAND, WA 98282
TROY CURTISS, BOX 1532, PETERSBURG, AK 99833
WINSTON DAVIES, BOX 1695, WRANGELL, AK 99929
PAUL DUPREE, BOX 684, PETERSBURG, AK 99833
WAYNE EASTERLY, BOX 335, WRANGELL, AK 99929
STUART EDDY, BOX 2085, PETERSBURG, AK 99833
JAMES EDSON, BOX 1314, PETERSBURG, AK 99833
STEPHEN FARLER, 4223 76TH PL NW, TULALIP, WA 98271
SILAS FLOR, BOX 396, PETERSBURG, AK 99833
OTTO FLORSCHUTZ, BOX 547, WRANGELL, AK 99929
STEVEN FORREST, BOX 308, WRANGELL, AK 99929
GARRETT GABLEHOUSE, 17587 CYPRESS POINT RD, FORT MYERS, FL 33967
GRAHAM GABLEHOUSE, BOX 1344, WRANGELL, AK 99929
DEREK GIBB, BOX 1845, PETERSBURG, AK 99833
STEVEN GILE, BOX 2225, WRANGELL, AK 99929
LEE GILPIN, BOX 1511, PETERSBURG, AK 99833
DINA GREGG, BOX 20373, JUNEAU, AK 99802
RUSSELL GREY, BOX 102, WRANGELL, AK 99929
CHARLES HAMLEY, BOX 2354, WRANGELL, AK 99929
RICHARD HANSON, BOX 991, CLINTON, WA 98236
TYLER JANSSEN, BOX 1982, WRANGELL, AK 99929
MARK JENSEN, BOX 457, PETERSBURG, AK 99833
ANDREW KNIGHT, BOX 1658, PETERSBURG, AK 99833
DEREK KNUDSEN, BOX 2150, PETERSBURG, AK 99833
ROBERT KUNTZ, BOX 455, WRANGELL, AK 99929
JAY LISTER, BOX 469, PETERSBURG, AK 99833
MICHAEL LOCKABEY, BOX 1542, WRANGELL, AK 99929
KREIG LORD, BOX 1995, PETERSBURG, AK 99833
ANGELA LUNDA, 19400 BEARDSLEY WAY, JUNEAU, AK 99801
KENNETH MADSEN, BOX 918, PETERSBURG, AK 99833
TYLER MARTIN, BOX 2033, PETERSBURG, AK 99833
MARC MARTINSEN, BOX 371, PETERSBURG, AK 99833
WAYNE MATHISEN, BOX 671, PETERSBURG, AK 99833
MALIA MCINTYRE, BOX 1994, WRANGELL, AK 99929
CHRISTOPHER MCMURREN, BOX 312, WRANGELL, AK 99929
CLEO MELLING, 5001 OAKES AVE, ANACORTES, WA 98221
DANIEL MELLING, 5581 HEART LAKE PL, ANACORTES, WA 98221
KRISTOPHER MELLING, 710 HADDON RD, ANACORTES, WA 98221
WILLIAM MENISH, BOX 877, PETERSBURG, AK 99833
JOSHUA MIETHE, BOX 2031, WRANGELL, AK 99929
DAWSON MILLER, BOX 2231, WRANGELL, AK 99929
MARK MITCHELL, BOX 80, WRANGELL, AK 99929
JOHN MOLLER, BOX 32425, JUNEAU, AK 99803
KRISTOPHER MORDEN, BOX 32, HAINES, AK 99827
FRANK NEIDIFFER, BOX 1746, PETERSBURG, AK 99833
STEVEN NELZEN, 4352 BAY VIEW CT, HOMER, AK 99603

DUNGENESS CRAB FISHING LIST

DARRYL OLSON, BOX 1304, PETERSBURG, AK 99833
KENNETH OLSON, BOX 1557, PETERSBURG, AK 99833
HELEN OPHEIM, BOX 2118, WRANGELL, AK 99929
MIKEL PAYNE, BOX 1453, PETERSBURG, AK 99833
JULIE PETERSON, BOX 302, CHINOOK, WA 98614
MARK PETERSON, BOX 302, CHINOOK, WA 98614
ERIN PFUNDT, BOX 1162, PETERSBURG, AK 99833
FRED PFUNDT, BOX 233, SOUTHWORTH, WA 98386
PETER RODDY, BOX 6436, SITKA, AK 99835
ROBERT ROONEY, BOX 2179, WRANGELL, AK 99929
HEIDI ROWLAND, BOX 970, WRANGELL, AK 99929
JAMES ROWLAND, BOX 970, WRANGELL, AK 99929
ROBERT RUDE, BOX 641, HAINES, AK 99827
JULIE RUHLE, BOX 1843, PETERSBURG, AK 99833
E.KEVIN SCHADE, 12200 STONE AVE N #34, SEATTLE, WA 98133
DAN SCHWEITZER, BOX 1667, PETERSBURG, AK 99833
RODNEY SELVIG, BOX 981, MEADOW VISTA, CA 95722
WILLIAM SMITH, BOX 103, PETERSBURG, AK 99833
BRANDON SNYDER, 1421 HALIBUT POINT RD, SITKA, AK 99835
NEAL SOETEBER, BOX 1663, WRANGELL, AK 99929
EVANS SPARKS, 101 PEACE LN, SITKA, AK 99835
NAOMI SUNDBERG, BOX 88, GUSTAVUS, AK 99826
JAY TAYLOR, 2820 KENT AVE, CODY, WY 82414
RAYMOND TERRY, BOX 46, PETERSBURG, AK 99833
KENNETH THYNES, 16948 PARK PLACE ST #4, EAGLE RIVER, AK 99577
NICHOLAS VERSTEEG, BOX 1752, PETERSBURG, AK 99833
ROBERT VOLK, BOX 576, PETERSBURG, AK 99833
STEVEN WALLIS, 34586 N CLUE CT, ATHOL, ID 83801
BRUCE WARD, BOX 1501, WRANGELL, AK 99929
DREW WARE, BOX 1291, PETERSBURG, AK 99833
MATTHEW WIEGAND, BOX 1775, PETERSBURG, AK 99833
COLE WILBURN, BOX 240056, DOUGLAS, AK 99824
ZACHARY WORRELL, 155 CORDOVA ST, JUNEAU, AK 99801
DWIGHT YANCEY, BOX 1853, WRANGELL, AK 99929

DUNGENESS CRAB, 75 POTS/OR 25% OF MAX, SOUTHEAST

JAN ADAMSON, BOX 18075, COFFMAN COVE, AK 99918
ROBERT BALDWIN, BOX 1757, PETERSBURG, AK 99833
ROBERT BARCAS, BOX 784, NEW MEADOWS, ID 83654
STACEY BARCAS, BOX 784, NEW MEADOWS, ID 83654
DENNIS BARTLETT, BOX 876819, WASILLA, AK 99687
JOSEPH BELLINA, 14715 BETZ LN, RED BLUFF, CA 96080
CYNTHIA BENITZ, BOX 1535, PETERSBURG, AK 99833
DEVEN BENITZ, BOX 1535, PETERSBURG, AK 99833
KENYATTA BRADLEY, BOX 2, SITKA, AK 99835
KEITH BUEHNER, 1940 NE TAYLOR ST, BEND, OR 97701
JORDAN BUNESS, BOX 634, WRANGELL, AK 99929
MARK BUNESS, 3437 MEANDER WAY, JUNEAU, AK 99801
RICHARD CALLAHAN, 3321 FOSTER AVE, JUNEAU, AK 99801
ERIC CALVIN, 210 BRADY ST, SITKA, AK 99835
DENNIS CAPUA, BOX 21333, JUNEAU, AK 99802
JONATHAN CASTOR, BOX 407, CRAIG, AK 99921
ROXANNE CHRISTENSEN, BOX 1639, FRIDAY HARBOR, WA 98250
HARRY CHURCHILL, BOX 606, WRANGELL, AK 99929
JASON CLAPSHAW, BOX 1780, WARD COVE, AK 99928
JOSHUA COZBY, 12705 NE 112TH ST, VANCOUVER, WA 98682
ELIAS DAUGHERTY, 17216 ANDREANOFF DR, JUNEAU, AK 99801
EMMA DEATS, BOX 20517, JUNEAU, AK 99802
RICHARD DEAVER, 1018 BLVD ST, STURGIS, SD 57785
DANIEL DEBOER, BOX 3960, PALMER, AK 99645
GEORGE DODDINGTON, 3850 YORKSHIRE AVE, EUGENE, OR 97405
TRAVIS DOWDS, 3106 SW 11TH AVE, PORTLAND, OR 97239
DARREN EASTERLY, BOX 407, WRANGELL, AK 99929
DAN EASTON, 17645 POINT LENA LP RD, JUNEAU, AK 99801

AJAX EGGLESTON, BOX 1305, HAINES, AK 99827
JEFFREY ERICKSON, BOX 53, PETERSBURG, AK 99833
RAYMOND ETTEN, BOX 925, WARD COVE, AK 99928
CODY EVANS, BOX 1358, WARD COVE, AK 99928
GREG EWART, 1190 MARTHAS VINYARD CT, VENTURA, CA 93001
DANIEL EWERT, 14760 SHORELINE LN, LAKE PARK, MN 56554
TYSON FICK, 9831 NINE MILE CREEK RD, JUNEAU, AK 99801
GLEN GALLOWAY, 611 ST ANNS, DOUGLAS, AK 99824
TY GRUSSENDORF, 9386 RIVERCOURT WAY, JUNEAU, AK 99801
KEVIN HACK, 1621 TONGASS AVE #100, KETCHIKAN, AK 99901
RICHARD HAERLING, BOX 675, PETERSBURG, AK 99833
HERMAN HAFFNER, 2710 ENGINEERS CUTOFF RD, JUNEAU, AK 99801
MATTHEW HAFFNER, 18216 PT STEHENS RD, JUNEAU, AK 99801
CHARLES HANSON, BOX 619, CRAIG, AK 99921
RAFE HANSON, 612 ETOLIN ST, SITKA, AK 99835
RANDY HOLT, BOX 2853, SEQUIM, WA 98382
JAMES HUBBARD, 74056 RIMROCK LN, IMNAHA, OR 97842
NORMAN HUGHES, BOX 1136, HAINES, AK 99827
EDDIE JASPER, 1613 WETMORE AVE, EVERETT, WA 98201
RICK JEWELL, BOX 715, SEDRO WOOLLEY, WA 98284
DONALD JOHNSON, 1345 PLUG MILL RD, ELMA, WA 98541
MARK JOHNSON, BOX 5644, KETCHIKAN, AK 99901
KENNETH JUDSON, 5875 GLACIER HWY #34, JUNEAU, AK 99801
NORMAN JUDSON, BOX 240931, DOUGLAS, AK 99824
ROBERT JURRIES, BOX 177, CRAIG, AK 99921
DAN KAYSER, BOX 2153, PETERSBURG, AK 99833
STEPHEN KINNEY, 12767 N TONGASS HWY, KETCHIKAN, AK 99901
COLIN KUAMOO, 21 MOHOULI ST, HILO, HI 96720
KURT KVERNVIK, BOX 1081, PETERSBURG, AK 99833
PERRY LEACH, BOX 5534, KETCHIKAN, AK 99901
KAREN LOCKABEY, BOX 1542, WRANGELL, AK 99929
MARKI LOCKHART, BOX 6241, SITKA, AK 99835
ERIC LUNDE, 852 WARREN ST #B, KETCHIKAN, AK 99901
MARCUS LYON, BOX 1070, HOMER, AK 99603
JASON MANNEY, BOX 32265, JUNEAU, AK 99803
OTIS MARSH, BOX 606, PETERSBURG, AK 99833
CHRIS MCDOWELL, 2207 RADCLIFFE RD, JUNEAU, AK 99801
MACLANE MCGRATH, BOX 2060, PETERSBURG, AK 99833
ABRAHAM MCINTYRE, BOX 1994, WRANGELL, AK 99929
ALEC MCMURREN, BOX 1508, PETERSBURG, AK 99833
PATRICK MCMURREN, BOX 12, WRANGELL, AK 99929
CHAD MICKEL, 10805 N TONGASS HWY, KETCHIKAN, AK 99901
LANCE MIETHE, BOX PPV, KETCHIKAN, AK 99950
DAVID MILLER, BOX 2231, WRANGELL, AK 99929
JOY MILLER, BOX 2231, WRANGELL, AK 99929
KYLE MILLER, 2992 RIVERWOOD DR, JUNEAU, AK 99801
STEVEN MIYAKI, 249 ANAMULI ST, KAHULUI, HI 96732
ELMER MORK, BOX 154, WRANGELL, AK 99929
ROBERT MOSHER, 11985 MENDENHALL LP RD, JUNEAU, AK 99801
WAYNE MUSILEK, 8221 S BLACKSBERG MTN RD, STURGIS, SD 57785
MICHAEL NEALSON, 181 DOGWOOD LN, BRINNON, WA 98320
FRANKLIN NEIDIFFER, BOX 1746, PETERSBURG, AK 99833
SCOTT NELSON, BOX 74, TOKELAND, WA 98590
KRISTINE NOROSZ, BOX 805, PETERSBURG, AK 99833
DIANA OLSON, BOX 34595, JUNEAU, AK 99803
RON OPHEIM, BOX 2118, WRANGELL, AK 99929
TERRANCE PARDEE, BOX 296, HAINES, AK 99827
MARK PEDERSEN, 8512 RAINBOW ROW, JUNEAU, AK 99801
DONALD PEELER, BOX 1691, PETERSBURG, AK 99833
CALEB PFUNDT, BOX 1162, PETERSBURG, AK 99833
MARK POWERS, BOX 308, ANGOON, AK 99820
CALEB PURVIANCE, BOX 2003, WRANGELL, AK 99929
LEN RASCHKE, 7595 SAWTELL RD, SHERIDAN, OR 97378
DAVID RAU, 624 PHODORA HGTS RD, LAKE STEVENS, WA 98258
JANEY REED, BOX 1437, PETERSBURG, AK 99833

HAIR CRAB / KING CRAB FISHING LIST

RONALD REED, BOX 1437, PETERSBURG, AK 99833
DONALD RICHARDS, BOX 1764, PETERSBURG, AK 99833
LAUREN ROGERS, BOX 842, WRANGELL, AK 99929
JASON ROONEY, BOX 307, WRANGELL, AK 99929
TERRY ROWLAND, BOX 605, WRANGELL, AK 99929
RODERICK RYLL, BOX 2273, WRANGELL, AK 99929
TERRY SAUNDERS, BOX 4212, PALMER, AK 99645
JOHN SCHADE, 11631 100TH NE 7C, KIRKLAND, WA 98034
ADRIANNE SCHWARTZ, 9183 RIVERWOOD DR, JUNEAU, AK 99801
GEORGE SHAPLEY, BOX 281, CRAIG, AK 99921
JAMES SIMPSON, BOX 45, HYDER, AK 99923
RONALD SIMPSON, BOX 632, PETERSBURG, AK 99833
KYLE SKINNER, BOX 853, PETERSBURG, AK 99833
CHRISTOPHER SNYDER, BOX 8135, KETCHIKAN, AK 99901
TANYA SOMERVILLE, BOX 163, PETERSBURG, AK 99833
KEVIN STELMACH, BOX 621, PETERSBURG, AK 99833
DAVID STEPHAN, BOX 2078, WRANGELL, AK 99929
DAVID STICKLER, BOX 685, HAINES, AK 99827
SCOTT STUART, BOX 212, ANGOON, AK 99820
RIDER SULLIVAN, 106 SUNSET BVLD, BOZEMAN, MT 59715
DEAN TERRY, BOX 46, PETERSBURG, AK 99833
CARLENE THAYER, BOX 33354, JUNEAU, AK 99803
TODD THINGVALL, BOX 375, HOONAH, AK 99829
RICK VERSTEEG, BOX 63, PETERSBURG, AK 99833
DAVID VEST, 82 HIGGINS SPUR RD, KETCHIKAN, AK 99901
JAMES VICK, BOX 613, PETERSBURG, AK 99833
MICHAEL WALKER, 8479 THUNDER MOUNTAIN RD, JUNEAU, AK 99801
FRANK WARFEL, BOX 517, WRANGELL, AK 99929
MARK WEAVER, BOX 1181, PETERSBURG, AK 99833
MARK WETTENGEL, BOX 75, MANLEY HOT SPRINGS, AK 99756
HAROLD WHITTLESY, 2440 E TUDOR RD #171, ANCHORAGE, AK 99507
SHARON WIKAN, BOX 785, PETERSBURG, AK 99833
LUKE WILLIAMS, BOX 1675, HAINES, AK 99827
CHARLES WILLS, BOX 7554, KETCHIKAN, AK 99901
BRADLEY WINGE, BOX 982, HAINES, AK 99827
COLE YOUNG, BOX 922, PETERSBURG, AK 99833

HAIR CRAB, POT GEAR, BERING SEA (VESSEL PERMIT)
REGION FUND COASTAL VILLAGES, 711 H ST #200, ANCHORAGE, AK 99501
FV MAVERICK LLC, 548 SR 401, NASELLE, WA 98638
MARWIN INC, BOX 509, PETERSBURG, AK 99833
MATTSEN FISHERIES INC, 3615 OLYMPIC DRIVE NE, BREMERTON, WA 98310
MGF FISHERIES INC, 18211 85TH PLACE W, EDMONDS, WA 98026
NORTH PACIFIC LLC, 620 6TH ST S, KIRKLAND, WA 98033
OCEAN OLYMPIC LLC, 620 6TH ST S, KIRKLAND, WA 98033
ROYAL VIKING INC, 5303 SHILSHOLE AVE NW, SEATTLE, WA 98107
RSD (OCEAN CAPE) LLC, BOX 12946, MILL CREEK, WA 98052
TAMARAK VENTURES LLC, BOX 7899, KENT, WA 98042
TIME BANDIT LLC, BOX 2270, ASHBURN, VA 20146
TYNES WABEY ENTERP INC, 1212 NW CULBERTSON DR, SEATTLE, WA 98177

KING CRAB, POT GEAR VESSEL UNDER 60', BERING SEA
CHASE GRAY, BOX 153, NOME, AK 99762

KING CRAB, POT GEAR VESSEL UNDER 60', NORTON SOUND
JAMES ABBOTT, BOX 507, NOME, AK 99762
MICHAEL AUKON, BOX 1968, NOME, AK 99762
JOHN BAHNKE, BOX 1873, NOME, AK 99762
JOHN BAHNKE, BOX 912, NOME, AK 99762
LOUIS BUFFAS, BOX 898, NOME, AK 99762
FRANK CARRUTHERS, BOX 1145, NOME, AK 99762
DAVID.D.L EVANS, BOX 1158, NOME, AK 99762
CHASE GRAY, BOX 153, NOME, AK 99762

KELLEY GREEN, BOX 806, NOME, AK 99762
KEVIN GREEN, BOX 806, NOME, AK 99762
DONALD JOHNSON, BOX 1946, NOME, AK 99762
MARTIN LEWIS, BOX 1375, NOME, AK 99762
FRANK MCFARLAND, BOX 364, NOME, AK 99762
JARED MILLER, BOX 1893, NOME, AK 99762
KEANE MOORE, BOX 1213, NOME, AK 99762
KEVIN OLANNA, PO BOX 85066, BREVIG MISSION, AK 99785
ERIC OSBORNE, BOX 1761, NOME, AK 99762
SILAS PANIPTCHUK, BOX 25, SHAKTOOLIK, AK 99771
SCOTT PAYENNA, BOX 1614, NOME, AK 99762
PHILLIP PRYZMONT, BOX 994, NOME, AK 99762
THOMAS SAGOONICK, BOX 71031, SHAKTOOLIK, AK 99771

KING CRAB, POT GEAR VESSEL UNDER 60', NORTON SOUND CDQ, NSED
DAVID.D.L EVANS, BOX 1158, NOME, AK 99762
CHASE GRAY, BOX 153, NOME, AK 99762

RED/BLUE KING CRAB, POT GEAR, SOUTHEAST
TIMOTHY DIMOND, BOX 240692, DOUGLAS, AK 99824
JOHN ETHERIDGE, 5301 BLUEBERRY LN, JUNEAU, AK 99801
ANDREW KITTAMS, BOX 1544, PETERSBURG, AK 99833
CHARLES MASON, 16526 GLACIER HWY, JUNEAU, AK 99801
GARY SLAVEN, BOX 205, PETERSBURG, AK 99833
DEREK THYNES, BOX 1624, PETERSBURG, AK 99833
KARSTEN WOOD, BOX 2195, PETERSBURG, AK 99833

RED/BLUE/BROWN KING CRAB, POT GEAR, SOUTHEAST
ERIC EVENS, BOX 1412, PETERSBURG, AK 99833
JOHN HINCHMAN, 808 EVANS DR, SEDRO WOOLLEY, WA 98284
ANDREW KALK, 415 COLEMAN ST, JUNEAU, AK 99801
JASON KOHLHASE, 10753 HORIZON DR, JUNEAU, AK 99801
ROCKY LITTLETON, BOX 1373, PETERSBURG, AK 99833
CLIFFORD MACDONALD, BOX 575, PETERSBURG, AK 99833
FRANK WARFEL, BOX 1512, WRANGELL, AK 99929

BROWN KING CRAB, POT GEAR, SOUTHEAST
CLYDE CURRY, BOX 572, PETERSBURG, AK 99833
CHRIS EVENS, BOX 886, PETERSBURG, AK 99833
JEREMY JENSEN, 2900 JACKSON RD, JUNEAU, AK 99801
ROBERT LEEKLEY, BOX 217, PETERSBURG, AK 99833
JOSEPH LEWIS, BOX 2603, SITKA, AK 99835
OLE NILSEN, BOX 32676, JUNEAU, AK 99803
BAE OLNEY.MILLER, 505 OCAIN ST, SITKA, AK 99835
NELS OTNESS, BOX 2058, PETERSBURG, AK 99833
JEB PHILLIPS, BOX 1253, PETERSBURG, AK 99833
JON PLACE, 10234 HERON WY, JUNEAU, AK 99801
PETER RODDY, BOX 6436, SITKA, AK 99835
GAINHART SAMUELSON, BOX 449, PETERSBURG, AK 99833

RED/BLUE KING/TANNER CRAB, POT GEAR, SOUTHEAST
TODD DAUGHERTY, BOX 32705, JUNEAU, AK 99802
KEN EICHNER, 5166 SHORELINE DR N, KETCHIKAN, AK 99901
JEREMY JENSEN, 2900 JACKSON RD, JUNEAU, AK 99801
JOHN JENSEN, BOX 681, PETERSBURG, AK 99833
JACK LYONS, BOX 527, PETERSBURG, AK 99833
CHRIS MCDOWELL, 2207 RADCLIFFE RD, JUNEAU, AK 99801
NICK NELSON, 3380 PARK PLACE, JUNEAU, AK 99801
TAYLOR NORHEIM, BOX 2146, PETERSBURG, AK 99833
TAYLOR NORHEIM, BOX 2146, PETERSBURG, AK 99833
NELS OTNESS, BOX 2058, PETERSBURG, AK 99833

KING CRAB / OPILIO CRAB FISHING LIST

KENNETH PHIPPEN, 312 TILSON ST, SITKA, AK 99835
MATTHEW SHORT, BOX 1224, PETERSBURG, AK 99833
TROY THOMASSEN, BOX 152, PETERSBURG, AK 99833
LUKE WHITETHORN, BOX 1716, PETERSBURG, AK 99833
JOE WILLIS, BOX 43, PETERSBURG, AK 99833
AARON WOODROW, 17875 POINT STEPHENS RD, JUNEAU, AK 99801
AARON WOODROW, 17875 POINT STEPHENS RD, JUNEAU, AK 99801
ANDY WRIGHT, BOX 1432, PETERSBURG, AK 99833
FRANK WRIGHT, BOX 497, HOONAH, AK 99829

BROWN KING/TANNER CRAB, POT GEAR, SOUTHEAST

DENNIS BARTLETT, BOX 876819, WASILLA, AK 99687
RICHARD DAUGHERTY, BOX 34864, JUNEAU, AK 99803
ERIC EVENS, BOX 1412, PETERSBURG, AK 99833
DAN FOLEY, BOX 57, GUSTAVUS, AK 99826
JOHN KARUZA, 27 SHOREWOOD DR, BELLINGHAM, WA 98225
ANDREW KITTAMS, BOX 1544, PETERSBURG, AK 99833
PAUL ROSTAD, BOX 183, KAKE, AK 99830
GARY SLAVEN, BOX 205, PETERSBURG, AK 99833
DANIEL VICK, BOX 1271, PETERSBURG, AK 99833

RED/BLUE/BROWN KING/TANNER CRAB, POT GEAR, SOUTHEAST

JOHN BARRY, 800 HALIBUT POINT RD #C, SITKA, AK 99835
ROBERT BECKER, BOX 240238, DOUGLAS, AK 99824
JARED BRIGHT, BOX 2097, PETERSBURG, AK 99833
CHARLES CHRISTENSEN, BOX 824, PETERSBURG, AK 99833
DANIEL CROME, BOX 1010, WESTPORT, WA 98595
RICHARD DAUGHERTY, BOX 34864, JUNEAU, AK 99803
SHANE DROLLINGER, 18131 CHAMPIONS DR, ARLINGTON, WA 98223
CRAIG EVENS, BOX 585, PETERSBURG, AK 99833
RICHARD GREGG, BOX 20669, JUNEAU, AK 99802
RONALD HAKALA, 1695 MENDHENHALL PEN RD, JUNEAU, AK 99801
NATHAN LEASK, 15290 GLACIER HWY, JUNEAU, AK 99801
DAVID LETHIN, BOX 350, CHINOOK, WA 98614
SIGURD MATHISEN, BOX 1460, PETERSBURG, AK 99833
WAYNE MATHISEN, BOX 671, PETERSBURG, AK 99833
AARON MILLER, BOX 2144, PETERSBURG, AK 99833
JAMES MILLER, BOX 1184, PETERSBURG, AK 99833
RODMAN MILLER, BOX 82, SEAVIEW, WA 98644
NORVAL NELSON, 1625 FRITZ COVE RD, JUNEAU, AK 99801
NORVAL NELSON, 800 F ST PARKSHORE CONDOS D1, JUNEAU, AK 99801
MICHAEL NILSEN, BOX 1084, PETERSBURG, AK 99833
YANCEY NILSEN, BOX 1822, PETERSBURG, AK 99833
LADD NORHEIM, BOX 935, PETERSBURG, AK 99833
DENNIS ONEIL, BOX 1083, PETERSBURG, AK 99833
ARTHUR OSBORNE, BOX 240925, DOUGLAS, AK 99824
ERIC ROSVOLD, BOX 1144, PETERSBURG, AK 99833
STANLEY SAVLAND, BOX 621, HOONAH, AK 99829
AARON SEVERSON, BOX 507, PETERSBURG, AK 99833
MARK SEVERSON, BOX 1502, PETERSBURG, AK 99833
JAY THOMASSEN, BOX 1451, PETERSBURG, AK 99833
STEVEN THOMASSEN, BOX 424, WRANGELL, AK 99929
KORY VERSTEEG, BOX 1775, PETERSBURG, AK 99833

KING CRAB, POT GEAR VESSEL 60' OR OVER, DUTCH HARBOR

FREDERICK ALVAREZ, 82 BRANDYWINE LN, CAMANO ISLAND, WA 98282
MARK MEDJO, 7215 156TH ST SW, EDMONDS, WA 98026

KING CRAB, POT GEAR VESSEL 60' OR OVER, BRISTOL BAY

MARK CASTO, 23929 22ND DR SE, BOTHELL, WA 98021
KEITH COLBURN, 2301 FAIRVIEW AVE E #212, SEATTLE, WA 98102

JON FORSYTHE, 11302 4TH AVE NE, TULALIP, WA 98271
MARK GILES, BOX 127, SELDOVIA, AK 99663
JOHN KORPI, 4005 20TH AVE W, SEATTLE, WA 98199
GENE LEDOUX, BOX 495, KODIAK, AK 99615
DENNIS MCKIBBIN, 4502 14TH AVE NW, SEATTLE, WA 98107
CHARLES REHDER, BOX 2065, HOMER, AK 99603

KING CRAB, POT GEAR VESSEL 60' OR OVER, BRISTOL BAY CDQ, YDFDA

DENNIS MCKIBBIN, 4502 14TH AVE NW, SEATTLE, WA 98107

TANNER CRAB, POT GEAR VESSEL UNDER 60', PRINCE WILLIAM SOUND

ARTEMON BASARGIN, 52818 OLD EAST END RD, HOMER, AK 99603
RONALD BLAKE, BOX 1236, CORDOVA, AK 99574
DERRICK BRANSON, BOX 3404, SEWARD, AK 99664
JEFF CHAPPELL, BOX 1343, CORDOVA, AK 99574
WARREN CHAPPELL, BOX 743, CORDOVA, AK 99574
CLIFFORD DEJAX, 35000 JAMES ST, SOLDOTNA, AK 99669
ROBERT GELLER, BOX 483, GIRDWOOD, AK 99587
RON HORTON, BOX 903, CORDOVA, AK 99574
DAVID IVANOV, BOX 15316, HOMER, AK 99603
KENNETH JONES, BOX 615, CORDOVA, AK 99574
ALEXEI KUZMIN, BOX 27, DELTA JUNCTION, AK 99737
DOMIAN KUZMIN, BOX 367, DELTA JUNCTION, AK 99737
ILIA KUZMIN, BOX 3433, HOMER, AK 99603
NIKITA KUZMIN, BOX 1542, DELTA JUNCTION, AK 99737
ZINON KUZMIN, BOX 873414, WASILLA, AK 99687
JOSEPH LINVILLE, BOX 1753, SEWARD, AK 99664
ROBERT LINVILLE, BOX 1771, CORDOVA, AK 99574
ROBERT NELSON, BOX 205, KASILOF, AK 99610
ZACK OSTERHAUS, 641 WEST FARIVIEW AVE #S, HOMER, AK 99603
MAKENA OTOOLE, BOX 1986, CORDOVA, AK 99574
ARSENY POLUSHKIN, BOX 62, HOMER, AK 99603
DIMITRY REUTOV, BOX 2063, HOMER, AK 99603
NIKOLAI REUTOV, BOX 2342, HOMER, AK 99603
SOFRON REUTOV, BOX 563, HOMER, AK 99603
ROBERT SMITH, BOX 251, CORDOVA, AK 99574
JORDAN STOVER, 54545 E END RD, HOMER, AK 99603

TANNER CRAB, RING NET, SOUTHEAST

BRIAN BLANKENSHIP, 4316 VALLHALLA DR, SITKA, AK 99835
MATTHEW BRYNER, BOX 1642, PETERSBURG, AK 99833
PAUL DUPREE, BOX 684, PETERSBURG, AK 99833
IVAN GONZALEZ, BOX 256, HOONAH, AK 99829
JARED GROSS, BOX 1374, WRANGELL, AK 99929
CARL HUMPHREY, BOX 665, PETERSBURG, AK 99833
PAUL MENISH, BOX 33, PETERSBURG, AK 99833
ROBERT MOSHER, 11985 MENDENHALL LP RD, JUNEAU, AK 99801
FRANK NEIDIFFER, BOX 1746, PETERSBURG, AK 99833
ROBERT OLSEN, BOX 1922, PETERSBURG, AK 99833
MIKEL PAYNE, BOX 1453, PETERSBURG, AK 99833
JONATHAN POWELL, BOX 1733, WRANGELL, AK 99929
JAMES ROWLAND, BOX 970, WRANGELL, AK 99929
BRANDON SNYDER, 1421 HALIBUT POINT RD, SITKA, AK 99835
DAVID SOMERVILLE, BOX 163, PETERSBURG, AK 99833
ADAM SWANSON, BOX 2151, PETERSBURG, AK 99833
THOMAS TRAIBUSH, 1300 PEACE PORTAL DR #206, BLAINE, WA 98230
JEFF WOLFE, BOX 381, SITKA, AK 99835
KARSTEN WOOD, BOX 2195, PETERSBURG, AK 99833

TANNER CRAB, POT GEAR, SOUTHEAST

DALE BARTELDS, 301 WORTMAN LP, SITKA, AK 99835
THOMAS BRAYTON, 145 BEHRENDS AVE, JUNEAU, AK 99801
DANIEL CASTLE, 4430 S TONGASS HWY, KETCHIKAN, AK 99901

TANNER / OPILIO CRAB FISHING LIST

JOSHUA COZBY, 12705 NE 112TH ST, VANCOUVER, WA 98682
TROY DENKINGER, 2221 HALIBUT POINT RD, SITKA, AK 99835
TIMOTHY DIMOND, BOX 240692, DOUGLAS, AK 99824
JOHN ETHERIDGE, 5301 BLUEBERRY LN, JUNEAU, AK 99801
ROGER GREGG, BOX 3, WRANGELL, AK 99929
RONALD JOHNSON, BOX 2232, WRANGELL, AK 99929
BRUCE JOYCE, 2280 SW MAYFIELD AVE, PORTLAND, OR 97225
DONALD KALK, BOX EXI, JUNEAU, AK 99850
JASON KOHLHASE, 10753 HORIZON DR, JUNEAU, AK 99801
R LARSON, BOX 580, TOKELAND, WA 98590
MIKE MARQUES, 10 MARINA DR, BELLINGHAM, WA 98229
KIRT MARSH, BOX 1421, PETERSBURG, AK 99833
CHARLES MASON, 16526 GLACIER HWY, JUNEAU, AK 99801
CHARLES MASON, 16526 GLACIER HWY, JUNEAU, AK 99801
RODERICK MCCAY, BOX 161, PETERSBURG, AK 99833
GARRETT MILLER, BOX 1899, WRANGELL, AK 99929
GARRETT MILLER, BOX 1899, WRANGELL, AK 99929
JOEL PASQUAN, BOX 845, HAINES, AK 99827
JUSTIN PEELER, BOX 184, SITKA, AK 99835
WILLIAM PETERSON, BOX 844, JEFFERSON, OR 97352
JORDAN PHILLIPS, 321 PETERSON AVE, SITKA, AK 99835
SETH ROCKWELL, BOX 3143, SEWARD, AK 99664
PETER RODDY, BOX 6436, SITKA, AK 99835
TREVOR ROSTAD, BOX 191, KAKE, AK 99830
DEREK THYNES, BOX 1624, PETERSBURG, AK 99833
DONALD TURNER, BOX 85, HAINES, AK 99827
WILLIAM VELER, BOX 387, HOONAH, AK 99829
JON W.B.RANDRUP, BOX 44, PETERSBURG, AK 99833
FRANK WARFEL, BOX 1512, WRANGELL, AK 99929
A.ERIC WIDMARK, 918 W 95TH ST #16, SEATTLE, WA 98103

TANNER CRAB, POT GEAR VESSEL 60' + OVER, PRINCE WILLIAM SOUND
TEAL LOHSE, BOX 2464, CORDOVA, AK 99574
ROY WILSON, BOX 1648, CORDOVA, AK 99574

TANNER CRAB, POT GEAR VESSEL 60' OR OVER, BERING SEA
JAKOB ANDERSON, 1623 218 PL SW, LYNNWOOD, WA 98036
MARK ATKINSON, 5470 SHILSHOLE AVE NW #520, SEATTLE, WA 98107
WAYNE BAKER, 225 MILL BAY RD, KODIAK, AK 99615
EDWARD BISHOP, 8891 N DAVIS CR, HAYDEN, ID 83835
STAALE BREKKAA, 17403 5TH AVE W, BOTHELL, WA 98012
JON BRUNEAU, 13121 S CAMPBELL RD, ROCKFORD, WA 99301
SCOTT CAMPBELL, 3707 E FRATELLO ST, MERIDIAN, ID 83642
ROBERT CARLTON, 23929 22ND DR SE, BOTHELL, WA 98021
GLENN CASTO, 16120 DUTIGUE RD, SNOHOMISH, WA 98290
MARK CASTO, 23929 22ND DR SE, BOTHELL, WA 98021
DAMIEN CATALA, 1780 LARCH AVE NE #102, ISSAQUAH, WA 98029
KEITH COLBURN, 2301 FAIRVIEW AVE E #212, SEATTLE, WA 98102
MONTGOMERY COLBURN, BOX 4634, INCLINE VILLAGE, NV 89450
STEVEN DAVIDSON, BOX 405, EASTON, WA 98925
SEAN DWYER, 4011 228TH PL SW, MOUNTLAKE TERRACE, WA 98043
MOORE DYE, 10500 NE 184TH ST, BATTLEGROUND, WA 98604
JON FORSYTHE, 11302 4TH AVE NE, TULALIP, WA 98271
MICHAEL FOX, 8117 FREDERICK PL, EDMONDS, WA 98026
MURRAY GAMRATH, BOX 920031, DUTCH HARBOR, AK 99692
MARK GILES, BOX 127, SELDOVIA, AK 99663
DEAN GRIBBLE, 8617 242ND ST SW, EDMONDS, WA 98020
SIGURD HANSEN, 23929 22ND DR SE, BOTHELL, WA 98021
DAVID HARRIS, 2807 S LAKE ROESIGER RD, SNOHOMISH, WA 98290
WILLIAM HIATT, 645 NE JOHNS AVE #8, NEOTSU, OR 97364
MARK ISRAELSON, 1611 SELIEF LN, KODIAK, AK 99615
CURTISS JOHNSON, 332 MEADOW RD, STEVENSVILLE, MT 59870
DAHER JORGE, 3871 STEILACOM BLVD SW #C, LAKEWOOD, WA 98499

JOHN KORPI, 4005 20TH AVE W, SEATTLE, WA 98199
OWEN KVINGE, 15631 ASH WAY APT B 508, LYNN WOOD, WA 98087
GENE LEDOUX, BOX 495, KODIAK, AK 99615
NORMAN LENON, 522 SUT LARSEN WAY, KODIAK, AK 99615
OYSTEIN LONE, 3315 150TH PL SE, MILL CREEK, WA 98012
CHAD LOWENBERG, 451 SEXTON RD, SEBASTOPOL, CA 95472
JAMES MARTINDALE, 9916 GOLDEN GIVEN RD E, TACOMA, WA 98445
MIKAL MATHISEN, 11753 SUNRISE DR NE, BAINBRIDGE ISLAND, WA 98110
SETH MCCALLUM, BOX 191, PETERSBURG, AK 99833
DENNIS MCKIBBIN, 4502 14TH AVE NW, SEATTLE, WA 98107
CASEY MCMANUS, 8717 182ND PL SW, EDMONDS, WA 98026
GERALD MEALS, 710 MISSION RD, KODIAK, AK 99615
MARK MEDJO, 7215 156TH ST SW, EDMONDS, WA 98026
JEFFREY MOREHOUSE, 1605 NW 192ND ST, SHORELINE, WA 98177
JOSEPH MORRIS, BOX 2487, CHELAN, WA 98816
RICHARD MORTON, BOX 1418, MUKILTEO, WA 98275
HERBERT MURRAY, 8615 NE 169TH, KENMORE, WA 98028
DONALD NORTON, BOX 3282, KODIAK, AK 99615
STEIN NYHAMMER, 18504 RIDGEFIELD RD NW, SHORELINE, WA 98177
KELLY PAINTER, 4385 YAQUINA BAY RD, NEWPORT, OR 97365
ROBERT PERKEY, 110 SE DIVISION ST, SUBLIMITY, OR 97385
MICHAEL PERRY, 23 OCOSTA SIXTH ST, ABERDEEN, WA 98520
STERLING PROUT, BOX 8809, KODIAK, AK 99615
CHARLES REHDER, BOX 2065, HOMER, AK 99603
DOUG SHELFORD, 16212 BOTHELL EVERETT HWY 340, MILL CRK, WA 98102
RICHARD SHELFORD, 13002 175TH DR SE, SNOHOMISH, WA 98290
JOSHUA SONGSTAD, 2520 NW PEOPLES CT, BEND, OR 97701
CHRISTOPHER STUDEMAN, 1833 DEAN CK RD, REEDSPORT, OR 97467
TOM SURYAN, 20126 BALLINGER WAY NE PMB 158, SHORELINE, WA 98155
ROBERT SYKES, 9545 DRY GROVE RD, RAYMOND, MS 39154
ROBERT THELEN, 637 COUNTY RD 6, MEEKER, CO 81641
BLAKE TUCKER, 46011 SE 134TH ST, NORTH BEND, WA 98045
WADE VEESER, 2001 S 22ND ST, ESCAMABA, MI 49829
WILLIAM WAHL, 20735 WAGONTIRE WAY, BEND, OR 97701
WILLIAM WICHROWSKI, BOX 2462, VALDEZ, AK 99686
JAMES WILSON, 13481 BAYWIND DR, ANCHORAGE, AK 99516
MICHAEL WILSON, BOX 741, TOLEDO, OR 97391
JOSEPH WRIGHT, 5754 YUKON CHARLIE LP, ANCHORAGE, AK 99502

TANNER CRAB, POT GEAR VESSEL 60' OR OVER, BERING SEA CDQ
SETH MCCALLUM, BOX 191, PETERSBURG, AK 99833
JOSEPH MORRIS, BOX 2487, CHELAN, WA 98816

TANNER CRAB, POT GEAR VESSEL 60' OR OVER, BERING SEA CDQ
MOORE DYE, 10500 NE 184TH ST, BATTLEGROUND, WA 98604
HERBERT MURRAY, 8615 NE 169TH, KENMORE, WA 98028
THOMAS SURYAN, 20126 BALLINGER WAY NE PMB 158, SHORELINE, WA 98155

TANNER CRAB, POT GEAR VESSEL 60' OR OVER, BERING SEA CDQ
GLENN CASTO, 16120 DUTIGUE RD, SNOHOMISH, WA 98290
RICHARD MORTON, BOX 1418, MUKILTEO, WA 98275

TANNER CRAB, POT GEAR VESSEL 60' OR OVER, BERING SEA CDQ
OWEN KVINGE, 15631 ASH WAY APT B 508, LYNN WOOD, WA 98087

TANNER CRAB, POT GEAR VESSEL 60' OR OVER, BERING SEA CDQ
ROBERT CARLTON, 23929 22ND DR SE, BOTHELL, WA 98021
DEAN GRIBBLE, 8617 242ND ST SW, EDMONDS, WA 98020
TANNER CRAB, POT GEAR VESSEL 60' OR OVER, BERING SEA CDQ
WILLIAM HIATT, 645 NE JOHNS AVE #8, NEOTSU, OR 97364
DENNIS MCKIBBIN, 4502 14TH AVE NW, SEATTLE, WA 98107
MICHAEL WILSON, BOX 741, TOLEDO, OR 97391

TANNER / OPILIO / BAIRDI CRAB FISHING LIST

JOSEPH WRIGHT, 5754 YUKON CHARLIE LP, ANCHORAGE, AK 99502

TANNER BAIRDI CRAB, POT GEAR VESSEL TO 120', KODIAK

FRANK ABENA, 2080 BLOOMFIELD RD, SEBASTOPOL, CA 95472
KEVIN ABENA, 1628 LYNDEN WAY, KODIAK, AK 99615
TIMOTHY ABENA, 3103 MILL BAY RD, KODIAK, AK 99615
MARK ALWERT, BOX 8889, KODIAK, AK 99615
WILLIAM ALWERT, BOX 1711, KODIAK, AK 99615
STOSH ANDERSON, BOX 310, KODIAK, AK 99615
BERT ASHLEY, BOX 425, KODIAK, AK 99615
ANDREW BLAIR, BOX 108, FOX ISLAND, WA 98333
JERRY BONGEN, BOX 392, KODIAK, AK 99615
THOMAS BRANSHAW, BOX 571, CORDOVA, AK 99574
KURT COCHRAN, BOX 290, SILETZ, OR 97380
GREGORY COLLINS, BOX 144, HOMER, AK 99603
SHAWN DOCHTERMANN, BOX 866, KODIAK, AK 99615
JAMES EMERSON, BOX 3907, KODIAK, AK 99615
TIMOTHY GERVAIS, BOX 7, RUBY, AK 99768
MARK GLADU, 3829 N ROWEN CIR, MESA, AZ 85207
CRAIG GUSTAFSON, BOX 8573, KODIAK, AK 99615
PAUL HARDER, BOX 48, NAALEHU, HI 96772
KENT HELLIGSO, BOX 319, KODIAK, AK 99615
CHARLES HILL, BOX 573, KODIAK, AK 99615
DOUGLAS HOEDEL, 2111 SORBUS WAY, ANCHORAGE, AK 99508
KENNETH HOLLAND, BOX 608, KODIAK, AK 99615
GEORGE HUTCHINGS, BOX 8242, KODIAK, AK 99615
STOIAN IANKOV, 4531 NW FREMONT ST, CAMAS, WA 98607 CHANDLER
JOHNSON, 11330 S RUSSIAN CREEK RD, KODIAK, AK 99615 CHARLES
JOHNSON, 8837 SW MARSEILLES DR, BEAVERTON, OR 99615 LUKE
LESTER, BOX 553, KODIAK, AK 99615
JOSHUA MIDDLESWORTH, BOX 1164, BIGFORK, MT 59911
TARY MIDDLESWORTH, 22814 FENBY LN, SWAN LAKE, MT 59911
STEPHEN MILES, BOX 1053, KODIAK, AK 99615
SOPHIA NIELSEN, BOX 8525, KODIAK, AK 99615
DANIEL OLSEN, BOX 1743, KODIAK, AK 99615
MARIUS OLSEN, 10809 CHINIAK DR, KODIAK, AK 99615
CARL PEDERSEN, BOX 1193, KODIAK, AK 99615
IAN PITZMAN, 4254 SVEDLUND CIR, HOMER, AK 99603
COREY POTTER, BOX 1939, KODIAK, AK 99615
DANNY POWELL, BOX 8953, KODIAK, AK 99615
KEITH REYNOLDS, 3481 EDS WAY, KODIAK, AK 99615
ALBERT SCHMEIL, BOX 164, KODIAK, AK 99615
JORG SCHMEISSER, BOX 1791, KODIAK, AK 99615
DON SITTON, BOX 2434, KODIAK, AK 99615
ROBERT STEELMAN, BOX 2603, KODIAK, AK 99615
JAY STINSON, BOX 1256, KODIAK, AK 99615
AARON SUTTON, BOX 1363, KODIAK, AK 99615
MARK VICKSTROM, BOX 318, KODIAK, AK 99615
MICHAEL WOODLEY, BOX 1546, KODIAK, AK 99615

TANNER BAIRDI CRAB, POT GEAR VESSEL UNDER 60', KODIAK

JEREMY ABENA, BOX 2277, KODIAK, AK 99615
ALFREDO ABOUEID, BOX 26, CHIGNIK LAGOON, AK 99565
BRADLEY AGA, 3805 E COTTONWOOD WAY, WASILLA, AK 99654
JEFFREY ALLEN, BOX 3020, TRINIDAD, CA 95570
AARON ANDERSON, BOX 43, CHIGNIK LAGOON, AK 99565
KAVIK ANDERSON, BOX 310, KODIAK, AK 99615
MARK ANDERSON, 49 NORTH STAR LN, FRIDAY HARBOR, WA 98250
ADAM BARKER, 126 E FAIRVIEW AVE, HOMER, AK 99603
FILIMON BASARGIN, BOX 2884, HOMER, AK 99603
DYLAN BEAN, 11147 WOMENS BAY DR, KODIAK, AK 99615
JULIAN BEAN, BOX 2813, KODIAK, AK 99615

CHRISTOPHER BERNS, BOX 23, KODIAK, AK 99615
JAMES BERNS, BOX 44, OLD HARBOR, AK 99643
TRAVIS BERNS, BOX 33, OLD HARBOR, AK 99643
BRADFORD BLONDIN, 1412 BARANOF ST, KODIAK, AK 99615
BRIAN BLONDIN, BOX 1521, KODIAK, AK 99615
RONALD BLONDIN, 1412 BARANOF ST, KODIAK, AK 99615
JOHN BOGGS, BOX 1199, KODIAK, AK 99615
JON BOTZ, BOX 5538, KODIAK, AK 99615
NORMAN BOTZ, BOX 5508, CHINIAK, AK 99615
TIMOTHY BOTZ, BOX 5505, CHINIAK, AK 99615
JARED BRIGHT, BOX 2097, PETERSBURG, AK 99833
KELLY BROYLES, 7060 BLACKHAWK LN, FOREST HILL, CA 95631
DANIEL BYRON, BOX 95, PORT LIONS, AK 99550
JAMES CALHOUN, 4360 ANDERSON ST, HOMER, AK 99603
LEONARD CARPENTER, BOX 1970, KODIAK, AK 99615
ROBERT CARTER, BOX 2817, KODIAK, AK 99615
CARMEL CARTY, BOX 2733, KODIAK, AK 99615
WARREN CHAPPELL, BOX 743, CORDOVA, AK 99574
CARL CHRISTIANSEN, 11721 12TH AVE NW, SEATTLE, WA 98177
DAVID CHRISTIANSEN, BOX 2, OLD HARBOR, AK 99643
EMIL CHRISTIANSEN, 8211 DEBARR RD, ANCHORAGE, AK 99504
HAROLD CHRISTIANSEN, BOX 129, OLD HARBOR, AK 99643
KENNETH CHRISTIANSEN, 1849 MARMOT DR, KODIAK, AK 99615
MICHAEL CLARK, BOX 2009, KODIAK, AK 99615
GENE COOPER, 1719 35TH PL, ANACORTES, WA 98221
FRANCIS COSTELLO, BOX 108, KODIAK, AK 99615
ALFRED CRATTY, 3510 EDS WAY, KODIAK, AK 99615
ALFRED CRATTY, BOX 1, OLD HARBOR, AK 99643
DOUGLAS DEPLAZES, BOX 2923, KODIAK, AK 99615
KEN EICHNER, 5166 SHORELINE DR N, KETCHIKAN, AK 99901
JAMES EUFEMIO, BOX 907, KODIAK, AK 99615
LATRINA FELLOWS, 266 E BAYVIEW AVE, HOMER, AK 99603
ROBERT FELLOWS, 266 E BAYVIEW AVE, HOMER, AK 99603
WALLACE FIELDS, BOX 1691, KODIAK, AK 99615
C.DAVID FRANKLIN, 3401 W LAWTON ST, SEATTLE, WA 98199
ROBERT FREEMAN, 5000 OLD GLENN HWY, PALMER, AK 99645
DONALD GALLAGHER, 2216 PADRE BLVD STE B #114, S. PADRE ISD, TX 78597
HARVEY GOODELL, BOX 3108, KODIAK, AK 99615
BURT GRONN, BOX 963, KODIAK, AK 99615
BURT GRONN, BOX 963, KODIAK, AK 99615
COREY GRONN, 3901 WOLVERINE WAY, KODIAK, AK 99615
MICHAEL GRUNERT, BOX 187, CHIGNIK LAGOON, AK 99565
MARILYN GUILMET, BOX 625, KODIAK, AK 99615
ROBERT GUNDERSON, 3614 SPRUCE CAPE RD, KODIAK, AK 99615
MIKE HAGGREN, 1 THIRD ST #105, ASTORIA, OR 97103
PETER HANNAH, BOX 647, KODIAK, AK 99615
JACOB HANOHANO, BOX 851, KODIAK, AK 99615
JAMES HAYDEN, BOX 8085, KODIAK, AK 99615
MATTHEW HEGGE, BOX 848, KODIAK, AK 99615
TAMMY HELMS, 3805 COTTONWOOD WAY, WASILLA, AK 99654
OLIVER HOLM, BOX 8749, KODIAK, AK 99615
BRYAN HORN, 1776 MISSION RD, KODIAK, AK 99615
JAMES HORN, 1776 MISSION RD, KODIAK, AK 99615
STEVEN HORN, 1210 MISSION RD, KODIAK, AK 99615
CLIFTON IVANOFF, BOX 8883, KODIAK, AK 99615
STEVEN IVANOFF, 1327 MOUNTAIN VIEW DR, KODIAK, AK 99615
DAVID IVANOV, BOX 15316, HOMER, AK 99603
MARY JACOBS, BOX 135, OPHIR, OR 97464
RYAN JOHNSON, BOX 2931, KODIAK, AK 99615
RONALD JOLIN, BOX 2022, KODIAK, AK 99615
DARIUS KASPRZAK, BOX 531, KODIAK, AK 99615
NICK KATELNIKOFF, BOX 170, OUZINKIE, AK 99644
PETER KENDRICK, BOX 2798, KODIAK, AK 99615
MITCHELL KEPLINGER, BOX 1006, KODIAK, AK 99615
CHARLES KRAMER, BOX 83, PORT LIONS, AK 99550

TANNER / BAIRDI CRAB / GEODUCK CLAMS FISHING LIST

DAVID KUBIAK, 818 TAGURA ST, KODIAK, AK 99615
DIA KUZMIN, BOX 758, DELTA JUNCTION, AK 99737
DIONICI KUZMIN, BOX 15, DELTA JUNCTION, AK 99737
ILIA KUZMIN, BOX 3433, HOMER, AK 99603
ALEXUS KWACHKA, 326 COPE ST, KODIAK, AK 99615
LUTHER LECHNER, BOX 8538, KODIAK, AK 99615
MARK LEVENSON, BOX 1284, KODIAK, AK 99615
EVERETT LINDHOLM, 415 E PARK DR, ANACORTES, WA 98221
MICHAEL LONGRICH, BOX 730, KODIAK, AK 99615
PETER LONGRICH, BOX 2677, KODIAK, AK 99615
BRETT LOUNSBURY, BOX 8947, KODIAK, AK 99615
LESTER LUKIN, BOX 62, PORT LIONS, AK 99550
DANIEL MACDONALD, BOX 5993, BELLINGHAM, WA 98227
JOE MACINKO, 2625 SPRUCE CAPE RD, KODIAK, AK 99615
MOSES MALUTIN, 914 WILLOW, KODIAK, AK 99615
ERIC MANZER, BOX 1033, CORDOVA, AK 99574
MICHAEL MARTIN, BOX 1275, KODIAK, AK 99615
RAYMOND MAY, BOX 8985, KODIAK, AK 99615
BRIAN MCWETHY, 3836 SUNSET DR, KODIAK, AK 99615
CHARLES MCWETHY, BOX 8552, KODIAK, AK 99615
FRANK MILES, BOX 2744, KODIAK, AK 99615
DANIEL MILLER, BOX 2865, KODIAK, AK 99615
THOMAS MILLER, BOX 1931, KODIAK, AK 99615
JAMES MONROE, BOX 1202, KODIAK, AK 99615
SAMUEL MUTCH, 210 B SHELIKOF, KODIAK, AK 99615
PEGGY NEKEFEROFF, BOX 194, KODIAK, AK 99615
PEGGY NEKEFEROFF, BOX 194, KODIAK, AK 99615
ARNOLD NELSON, BOX 85, PORT LIONS, AK 99550
DANIEL NELSON, BOX 867, KODIAK, AK 99615
ERIK NELSON, BOX 2008, KODIAK, AK 99615
HARRY NELSON, BOX 87, PORT LIONS, AK 99550
PARRY NELSON, BOX 92, KODIAK, AK 99615
THOMAS NELSON, BOX 101, PORT LIONS, AK 99550
JOHN NEVIN, BOX 2125, KODIAK, AK 99615
DAVID OBRIEN, 3700 PUFFIN DR, KODIAK, AK 99615
STEPHEN OBRIEN, BOX 8804, KODIAK, AK 99615
TYLER OBRIEN, 10826 BELLS FLATS RD, KODIAK, AK 99615
KEVIN OLEARY, BOX 1427, KODIAK, AK 99615
CONSTANCE OLSEN, BOX 322, KODIAK, AK 99615
JACOB ORGAN, BOX 58, KODIAK, AK 99615
MARKO PATITUCCI, BOX 8918, KODIAK, AK 99615
KURT PEDERSEN, BOX 2405, KODIAK, AK 99615
EDWARD PESTRIKOFF, BOX 56, OLD HARBOR, AK 99643
CHARLES PETERSON, 1850 THREE SISTERS WAY, KODIAK, AK 99615
DEANA PIKUS, BOX 2843, KODIAK, AK 99615
PATRICK PIKUS, BOX 2843, KODIAK, AK 99615
DARREN PLATT, BOX 1413, KODIAK, AK 99615
ROBERT PLETNIKOFF, BOX 2449, KODIAK, AK 99615
WILLIAM POLSON, BOX 1248, KODIAK, AK 99615
DANA REID, BOX 8935, KODIAK, AK 99615
MICHAEL RESOFF, BOX 911, KODIAK, AK 99615
ALEXANDER REUTOV, BOX 2272, HOMER, AK 99603
GREGORY REUTOV, BOX 2597, HOMER, AK 99603
LAZAR REUTOV, BOX 258, HOMER, AK 99603
VAVIL REUTOV, BOX 809, HOMER, AK 99603
SHAWNA RITTENHOUSE, BOX KWP, KODIAK, AK 99615
NATHANIEL ROSE, 3011 SPRUCE CAPE RD APT A, KODIAK, AK 99615
ERIC ROSVOLD, BOX 1144, PETERSBURG, AK 99833
TY ROUSE, BOX 2725, KODIAK, AK 99615
RICHARD ROZELLE, BOX 5033, AKHIOK, AK 99615
STEVEN RUOTSALAINEN, BOX 2499, KODIAK, AK 99615
CHRISTOPHER SARGENT, BOX 574, KODIAK, AK 99615
WALTER SARGENT, 1830 MISSION RD, KODIAK, AK 99615
BRUCE SCHACTLER, BOX 2254, KODIAK, AK 99615
BARRY SCHAUFF, 316 CENTER ST, KODIAK, AK 99615
WILLIAM SCHAUFF, BOX 8774, KODIAK, AK 99615

RANDALL SHOLL, BOX 681, KODIAK, AK 99615
CALVIN SKONBERG, BOX 2572, KODIAK, AK 99615
FREDERICK STAGER, BOX 8243, KODIAK, AK 99615
DANIEL STIHL, BOX 3373, KODIAK, AK 99615
IVAN STONOROV, 41046 CRESTED CRANE ST, HOMER, AK 99603
IVAN STONOROV, 41046 CRESTED CRANE ST, HOMER, AK 99603
STEVEN SUYDAM, BOX 987, KODIAK, AK 99615
ERIC SWANBERG, BOX 15425, FRITZ CREEK, AK 99603
MARK THOMAS, 2249 SELIEF LN, KODIAK, AK 99615
CHARLES TREINEN, 2054 ARLINGTON DR, ANCHORAGE, AK 99517
DONALD VINBERG, BOX 9032, KODIAK, AK 99615
JERAMY YOUNG, BOX 806, KODIAK, AK 99615
JOSHUA YOUNG, 11531 WOMENS BAY DR, KODIAK, AK 99615
BILL ZIMMERMAN, BOX 2261, KODIAK, AK 99615

GEODUCK CLAMS, DIVING GEAR, SOUTHEAST
JIMMIE ACKERMAN, BOX 544, QUILCENE, WA 98376
JAMES ALEXANDER, BOX 325, CRAIG, AK 99921
KEVIN ANDERSON, 2417 TONGASS STE 111 #186, KETCHIKAN, AK 99901
GEORGE ARCHBOLD, 519 LUPINE WY, OCEANSIDE, CA 92057
JIM AULT, BOX 6583, KETCHIKAN, AK 99901
CORNELIS BAKKER, BOX 5253, KETCHIKAN, AK 99901
DANIEL BAKKER, BOX 282, OLYMPIA, WA 98507
MICHAEL BANGS, BOX 26, PETERSBURG, AK 99833
LAITH BARNHILL, BOX 668, CRAIG, AK 99921
RICHARD BAUDER, BOX 277, SITKA, AK 99835
BRANT BAXTER, BOX 1023, OAK HARBOR, WA 98277
ROGER BERNDT, BOX 652, FRIDAY HARBOR, WA 98250
CLAY BEZENEK, 1617 WATER ST, KETCHIKAN, AK 99901
CHUCK BOOTHMAN, 3356 DALE ST, KETCHIKAN, AK 99901
ANTHONY BOYCE, BOX 5266, KETCHIKAN, AK 99901
HOWARD BRAND, BOX 1546, WARD COVE, AK 99928
CURTIS BROWN, BOX 456, CRAIG, AK 99921
ROBERT CALKINS, BOX 388, MANZANITA, OR 97130
ERIC CALVIN, 210 BRADY ST, SITKA, AK 99835
LYNETTE CARLSON, BOX 19214, THORNE BAY, AK 99919
JEFF CARRIERE, BOX 448, INDIANOLA, WA 98342
TOM CARRUTH, BOX 8641, KETCHIKAN, AK 99901
LAWRENCE CARSON, 15285 N TONGASS HWY, KETCHIKAN, AK 99901
SERGEY CHEPURKO, BOX 1931, PORT ORCHARD, WA 98366
BRETT CLAGGETT, 319 SPRUCE ST, KETCHIKAN, AK 99901
JAY CLIFTON, 3802 HALIBUT POINT RD, SITKA, AK 99835
FOREST COLLINS, BOX 664, CRAIG, AK 99921
AARON CUMMINS, 1010 NEWELL ST, BELLINGHAM, WA 98225
TY CUMMINS, BOX 1402, PETERSBURG, AK 99833
GREG CUSHING, 1217 GEORGESON LP, SITKA, AK 99835
ALAN DALE, 926 NORDSTROM DR, KETCHIKAN, AK 99901
COLLIN DARRAH, 311 33RD AVE E, SEATTLE, WA 98112
KEVIN DAU, BOX 219, CRAIG, AK 99921
GEORGE DODDINGTON, 3850 YORKSHIRE AVE, EUGENE, OR 97405
DANIEL EASLEY, 8415 166TH CT NW, GIG HARBOR, WA 98329
JOHN EASTABROOK, 706 DENNIS ST SE #11, TUMWATER, WA 98501
COREY ELKINS, 14227 OLYMPIC DRIVE SE, OLALLA, WA 98359
JAMES EVANS, 3993 GENTLEBROOK LN #31, BELLINGHAM, WA 98225
STEVEN FRANKLIN, 1138 WOODLAND AVE, KETCHIKAN, AK 99901
R.DALE GARNICK, 1730 MEADE, NORTH BEND, OR 97459
JONATHAN GATCH, 5240 SE NORTH ST, PORT ORCHARD, WA 98367
JODI GOFFINET, BOX 1176, WARD COVE, AK 99928
GREGORY HARRISON, BOX 997, WARD COVE, AK 99928
SCOTT HEITMAN, BOX 1039, WARD COVE, AK 99928
KRISTIAN HERR, 19134 NOLL RD, POULSBO, WA 98370
GEORGE HILL, 4209 NE PARISH LN, POULSBO, WA 98370
JESSE HOYT, BOX 7501, KETCHIKAN, AK 99901
DAVID JACOBS, 17303 314TH AVE NE, DUVALL, WA 98019
ROBERT JURRIES, BOX 177, CRAIG, AK 99921

GEODUCK CLAMS / SHRIMP FISHING LIST

DONALD KAMBEITZ, BOX 147, CRAIG, AK 99921
WILLIAM KEMPERMAN, BOX 19265, THORNE BAY, AK 99919
ANDREW KITTAMS, BOX 1544, PETERSBURG, AK 99833
DAVID KLEIN, 126 MOUNTAIN ASH HTS #A, KETCHIKAN, AK 99901
DAVID KRAUSE, BOX 1065, SITKA, AK 99835
JANUSZ KUNAT, BOX 335, GUSTAVUS, AK 99826
LEO LANDRY, 19020 TRIAL BAY DR, EAGLE RIVER, AK 99577
TREMAINE LAWRENCE, 4168 TIOPI LP, BELLINGHAM, WA 98226
JEREMY LEIGHTON, BOX 1176, WARD COVE, AK 99928
CHRISTOPHER LERVICK, BOX 6534, KETCHIKAN, AK 99901
ANDREW LINDNER, BOX 845, WARD COVE, AK 99928
RODNEY LINTON, 628 E CENTRAL AVE, SUTHERLIN, OR 97479
MATTHEW LORIG, 932 CARLANNA LAKE RD #B-11, KETCHIKAN, AK 99901
JOHN MALOUF, 5191 BORCH ST, KETCHIKAN, AK 99901
DESI MANGINI, 14872 CRESCENT VALLEY RD SE, OLALLA, WA 98359
BRIAN MATTSON, BOX 1168, PETERSBURG, AK 99833
JOEL MCKELLAR, BOX 672146, CHUGIAK, AK 99567
DERRICK MCRAE, 2227 47 ST NW #G201, GIG HARBOR, WA 98335
GARY MICHEALS, BOX 5041, BELLINGHAM, WA 98227
MARK MIKKELSEN, BOX 5235, KETCHIKAN, AK 99901
WILLIAM MILLER, BOX 8131, KETCHIKAN, AK 99901
RYAN MORIN, BOX 8164, KETCHIKAN, AK 99901
JAMES MURRAY, 285 WILCOX LN, CORVALLIS, MT 59828
PHIL NEHL, BOX 1246, WARD COVE, AK 99928
MARK NUGENT, BOX 5382, KETCHIKAN, AK 99901
DANA OSTROM, 12141 AVENIDA CONSENTIDO, SAN DIEGO, CA 92128
MATTHEW PEAVEY, BOX 442, CRAIG, AK 99921
LANCE PIHLMAN, BOX 5322, KETCHIKAN, AK 99901
DAVID POPE, 2417 TONGASS AVE SUITE 111-344, KETCHIKAN, AK 99901
PATRICK QUIGLEY, BOX 80, CRAIG, AK 99921
MARC REYNOLDS, BOX 6824, KETCHIKAN, AK 99901
SPENCER RICHTER, BOX 1011, CRAIG, AK 99921
ERIC RIEMER, BOX 23458, KETCHIKAN, AK 99901
JACOB RODRIGUEZ, BOX 5691, KETCHIKAN, AK 99901
MIKE ROGERS, 5025 DITTO LN, POULSBO, WA 98370
SCOTT SABIN, 120 FIREWEED LN, KENAI, AK 99611
MICHAEL SALTER, 3614 N VILLARD ST, TACOMA, WA 98407
JASON SANDERS, 4747 LAKE TERRELL RD, FERNDALE, WA 98248
RANDY SELNESS, 5312 BLACK LAKE BLVD SW, OLYMPIA, WA 98512
RICK SERIKAKU, 599 SALMONBERRY CIR, KETCHIKAN, AK 99901
SCOTT SINCLAIR, 6615 S 239TH PL #R103, KENT, WA 98032
DALE STANLEY, BOX 7442, KETCHIKAN, AK 99901
SAMUEL SWANSON, 1136 NW CLONINGER CT, SILVERDALE, WA 98383
CURTIS THOMAS, BOX 974, WARD COVE, AK 99928
R.CRAIG THOMAS, 3933 ALASKA AVE, KETCHIKAN, AK 99901
SCOTT THOMAS, BOX 1503, WARD COVE, AK 99928
SCOTT THOMAS, BOX 1503, WARD COVE, AK 99928
JEREMY THUET, 3306 79TH AVE NW, OLYMPIA, WA 98502
DAVID THYNES, BOX 533, PETERSBURG, AK 99833
CHAD TRANI, 11520 JUANITA DR NE, KIRKLAND, WA 98034
LAWRENCE TRANI, 2008 HALIBUT POINT RD, SITKA, AK 99835
GARY TRUMPER, BOX 624, CLOVERDALE, CA 95425
THOMAS TRUMPER, 1940 2ND AVE, KETCHIKAN, AK 99901
ROBERT WALKOFF, 1619 SAWMILL CREEK RD S APT 1, SITKA, AK 99835
IAN WALT, BOX 1372, FRIDAY HARBOR, WA 98250
LARRY WEDVIK, BOX 383, LAKEBAY, WA 98349
GLENN WILBER, BOX 562, CRAIG, AK 99921
RODGER WILBER, BOX 3204, SITKA, AK 99835
CHRISTOPHER WILHELM, BOX 9463, KETCHIKAN, AK 99901
JOHN WILSON, 90 NE NEWKIRK RD, BELFAIR, WA 98528
WILLIAM WOOLDRIDGE, 17010 7TH AVE NW, LAKEBAY, WA 98349
RANDALL WORTMAN, BOX 271, CRAIG, AK 99921
BRIAN ZWICK, 801 PETERSON ST, KETCHIKAN, AK 99901

SHRIMP, OTTER TRAWL, SOUTHEAST
JAMES DICICCO, BOX 1066, SITKA, AK 99835

SHRIMP, OTTER TRAWL, PRINCE WILLIAM SOUND
JON VANHYNING, BOX 872580, WASILLA, AK 99687

SHRIMP, OTTER TRAWL, WESTWARD
CHRISTOPHER JOHNSON, BOX 151, KODIAK, AK 99615
ROBIN LARSEN, BOX 264, SAND POINT, AK 99661

SHRIMP, POT GEAR VESSEL UNDER 60', YAKUTAT
ROBERT BULARD, BOX 241, YAKUTAT, AK 99689
MARK HOFMANN, 1042 OBSTRUCTION PASS RD, OLGA, WA 98279
DONALD PATE, BOX 402, YAKUTAT, AK 99689
CALEB ROBBINS, BOX 6256, SITKA, AK 99835
PATRICK ROBBINS, BOX 202, YAKUTAT, AK 99689

SHRIMP, POT GEAR VESSEL UNDER 60', PRINCE WILLIAM SOUND
NORMAN ALSUP, 15008 N TONGASS HWY, KETCHIKAN, AK 99901
DARRIN ANDERSON, 3290 S LAKESHORE LP, PALMER, AK 99645
RANDY ARSENAULT, BOX 4104, HOMER, AK 99603
DAVE BARKER, 126 E FAIRVEIW AVE, HOMER, AK 99603
PETRO BASARGIN, BOX 2126, HOMER, AK 99603
KORY BLAKE, BOX 1122, CORDOVA, AK 99574
PAUL BOOTS, 13137 GULF CIR, ANCHORAGE, AK 99515
BRUCE BOWMAN, HC 60 BOX 227 I, COPPER CENTER, AK 99573
WESTON BRANSHAW, BOX 2585, VALDEZ, AK 99686
ELLIS BROCK, 19313 INLET VIEW DR, CHUGIAK, AK 99567
ROBERT BROCK, BOX 2258, SEQUIM, WA 98382
LISA BROWN, HC60 BOX 294E, COPPER CENTER, AK 99573
TRACY BROWN, HC60 BOX 294E, COPPER CENTER, AK 99573
TIM CABANA, BOX 201, GIRDWOOD, AK 99587
RYAN CROPPER, 1111 E DOWLING RD, ANCHORAGE, AK 99518
PATRICK DAY, BOX 788, VALDEZ, AK 99686
CLIFFORD DEJAX, 35000 JAMES ST, SOLDOTNA, AK 99669
EUGENE DESJARLAIS, 6550 LIMESTONE CIR, ANCHORAGE, AK 99507
TYLER DILLON, BOX 1326, CORDOVA, AK 99574
BRAD DOMAS, 8931 ELIM ST, ANCHORAGE, AK 99507
MICHAEL DURTSCHI, BOX 1012, GIRDWOOD, AK 99587
DAN EAMES, 7436 TYRE DR, ANCHORAGE, AK 99502
DUANE EDELMAN, BOX 153, VALDEZ, AK 99686
JOHN FORD, 14295 MINORCA COVE, DEL MAR, CA 92014
DOUGLAS FRASHER, BOX 4034, SOLDOTNA, AK 99669
ROBERT GELLER, BOX 483, GIRDWOOD, AK 99587
LARRY GILMAN, BOX 672, WHITTIER, AK 99693
JARL GUSTAFSON, BOX 952, HOMER, AK 99603
DAVID HAMRE, BOX 111492, ANCHORAGE, AK 99511
PATRICK HODGSON, BOX 806, KASILOF, AK 99610
RON HORTON, BOX 903, CORDOVA, AK 99574
PETER JENKINS, 2400 TASHA DR, ANCHORAGE, AK 99502
BRIAN JURENKA, 2630 W RIVER DR, EAGLE RIVER, AK 99577
LYNN KEOGH, 4778 MILLS DR, ANCHORAGE, AK 99508
GAVIN KEOHANE, BOX 481, KENAI, AK 99611
TIMOTHY KEOHANE, 35555 SPUR HWY #290, SOLDOTNA, AK 99669
MARK KNIGHT, 12620 NEHER RIDGE DR, ANCHORAGE, AK 99516
DOMIAN KUZMIN, BOX 367, DELTA JUNCTION, AK 99737
KALLISTRAT KUZMIN, BOX 896, DELTA JUNCTION, AK 99737
NIKITA KUZMIN, BOX 1542, DELTA JUNCTION, AK 99737
SERGI KUZMIN, BOX 264, DELTA JUNCTION, AK 99737
VLADIMIR KUZMIN, BOX 772, DELTA JUNCTION, AK 99737
ZINON KUZMIN, BOX 873414, WASILLA, AK 99687

SHRIMP FISHING LIST—TRAWL / POT GEAR

NICKOLAS LEE, BOX 1822, KENAI, AK 99611
BRENT MASON, 18500 UPPER MCCRARY RD, EAGLE RIVER, AK 99577
BRIAN MASON, 19435 UPPER SKYLINE DR, EAGLE RIVER, AK 99577
MICHAEL MCDANELD, 2021 GUNFLINT TRAIL, WASILLA, AK 99654
DONALD MCKEE, 3655 OLD GLEN HWY #211, PALMER, AK 99645
DAVID MORK, 13420 WINDRUSH CIR, ANCHORAGE, AK 99516
LYLE MYRVOLD, BOX 870181, WASILLA, AK 99687
ROBERT NELSON, BOX 205, KASILOF, AK 99610
NELSON OOKA, BOX 1218, SEWARD, AK 99664
MAKENA OTOOLE, BOX 1986, CORDOVA, AK 99574
KENNETH PARKER, 9577 WEST 5 MILE RD, BRANCH, MI 49402
SARA PARKER, BOX 1986, CORDOVA, AK 99574
LESLIE PEMBERTON, BOX 606, SEWARD, AK 99664
JOSEPH PERSON, BOX 873, ANCHOR POINT, AK 99556
RICHARD PERSON, 24120 RAMBLERS RD, CHUGIAK, AK 99567
DENNIS PETRE, BOX 140054, SALCHA, AK 99714
GREG PETTINGILL, BOX 916, CORDOVA, AK 99574
DILLON POGUE, BOX 2352, KENAI, AK 99611
ANDREY POLUSHKIN, BOX 2458, HOMER, AK 99603
ARSENY POLUSHKIN, BOX 62, HOMER, AK 99603
DAVID POPE, 1031 W 71ST AVE, ANCHORAGE, AK 99518
LYNN POTTER, BOX 1472, CORDOVA, AK 99574
LINDA RAGAN, 5940 GREECE DR, ANCHORAGE, AK 99516
RICHARD RAGAN, 5940 GREECE DR, ANCHORAGE, AK 99516
DAVID RENTEL, BOX 1424, VALDEZ, AK 99686
MICHAEL RENTEL, BOX 33406, JUNEAU, AK 99803
ALIMPI REUTOV, 8537 W CARMEL RD, WASILLA, AK 99623
DIMITRY REUTOV, BOX 2063, HOMER, AK 99603
JOE REUTOV, BOX 44, AURORA, OR 97002
NIKOLAI REUTOV, BOX 2342, HOMER, AK 99603
PELAGIA REUTOV, BOX 2342, HOMER, AK 99603
BRETT ROTH, 7810 CASEY CIR, ANCHORAGE, AK 99507
BRADLEY SAPP, BOX 2543, CORDOVA, AK 99574
JED SAPP, BOX 2543, CORDOVA, AK 99574
GEORGE SCOTT, BOX 281, GIRDWOOD, AK 99587
JOHN.DEWINDT SCOTT, BOX 281, GIRDWOOD, AK 99587
EVELYN SMITH, BOX 877563, WASILLA, AK 99687
SEAN SMITH, BOX 877563, WASILLA, AK 99687
STEVEN SMITH, BOX 877563, WASILLA, AK 99687
PHILLIP STACEY, 12830 OOMIAK CIR, ANCHORAGE, AK 99515
KEVIN STAFFORD, BOX 210262, AUKE BAY, AK 99821
JOHN STELLING, BOX 929, VALDEZ, AK 99686
MILTON STEVENS, 4071 WARWICK PL, ANCHORAGE, AK 99508
DANIEL SWANSON, BOX 652, SOLDOTNA, AK 99669
GREG TIPIKIN, 2725 N JENNY ANNE PL, WASILLA, AK 99654
MICHAEL TOWLE, BOX 2234, CORDOVA, AK 99574
NATHAN TUELLER, BOX 913, GIRDWOOD, AK 99587
KENNETH VLASOFF, 6300 ANDOVER DR, ANCHORAGE, AK 99516
ALEXANDRA VON.WICHMAN, 2940 MALLARD LN, ANCHORAGE, AK 99508
W.BRADFORD VON.WICHMAN, 2940 MALLARD LN, ANCHORAGE, AK 99508
KRISTOPHER WALKER, 39631 GROUSE DR, SOLDOTNA, AK 99669
JOHN WIESE, 4160 EDINBURGH DR, ANCHORAGE, AK 99502
BRETT WILBANKS, 4701 MANYTELL AVE, ANCHORAGE, AK 99516
DUKE WILLIAMS, BOX 872425, WASILLA, AK 99687

SHRIMP, POT GEAR VESSEL UNDER 60', WESTWARD
HAROLD MAGNUSSON, BOX 283, KODIAK, AK 99615
PATRICK PIKUS, BOX 2843, KODIAK, AK 99615
JEFFREY SPENCER, 3367 SPRUCE CAPE RD, KODIAK, AK 99615
THEODORE SQUARTSOFF, BOX 77, OUZINKIE, AK 99644

SHRIMP, BEAM TRAWL, SOUTHEAST
WILLIAM ARMSTRONG, 8215 53RD DR NE, MARYSVILLE, WA 98270
JEFFREY BERG, BOX 890, PETERSBURG, AK 99833

JARED BRIGHT, BOX 2097, PETERSBURG, AK 99833
ANTHONY BYFORD, 4222 PTARMIGAN ST, JUNEAU, AK 99801
ROBERT CHAPMAN, BOX 19261, THORNE BAY, AK 99919
BART CHURCHILL, BOX 1493, WRANGELL, AK 99929
DANIEL COHEN, 985 OCEAN DR, CAPE MAY, NJ 8204
DAN DOAK, BOX 677, WRANGELL, AK 99929
JOHN DUPREE, BOX 684, PETERSBURG, AK 99833
ARNOLD ENGE, BOX 2113, PETERSBURG, AK 99833
CHRISTOPHER FISK, 923 A ST, JUNEAU, AK 99801
OTTO FLORSCHUTZ, BOX 547, WRANGELL, AK 99929
MATTHEW GERRITS, BOX 414, PETERSBURG, AK 99833
LLOYD GILMAN, BOX 878, HAINES, AK 99827
WILLIAM HAMMER, 32 NELSONS LANDING RD, PORT TOWNSEND, WA 98368
DANIEL HICKMAN, BOX 108, PETERSBURG, AK 99833
NELSON JODWAY, BOX 8869, PORT ALEXANDER, AK 99836
ROBERT JOHNSON, BOX 2184, WRANGELL, AK 99929
EUGENE LEE, BOX 1286, PETERSBURG, AK 99833
SAMUEL MARTIN, 985 OCEAN DR, CAPE MAY, NJ 8204
PAUL MCINTYRE, BOX 1994, WRANGELL, AK 99929
MICHAEL MEDALEN, BOX 969, PETERSBURG, AK 99833
KEITH MORK, 111 B ANDREW HOPE, SITKA, AK 99835
DANA OSTROM, 12141 AVENIDA CONSENTIDO, SAN DIEGO, CA 92128
RICHARD PHILLIPS, BOX 522, WRANGELL, AK 99929
JASON ROONEY, BOX 307, WRANGELL, AK 99929
DAVID SHIRRA, BOX 686, BLAINE, WA 98231
TANNER SMITH, BOX 1379, WRANGELL, AK 99929
DONALD SPERL, BOX 1407, PETERSBURG, AK 99833
BRETT STILLWAUGH, BOX 1552, WRANGELL, AK 99929
WALTER STUART, BOX 2196, WRANGELL, AK 99929
THORNE TASKER, 7724 ARLENE ST, ANCHORAGE, AK 99502
WILLIAM TERRY, BOX 362, PETERSBURG, AK 99833
SIGUARD TORGRAMSEN, BOX 1939, WRANGELL, AK 99929
CARL TORMALA, 444 GRAND VIEW DR, SEQUIM, WA 98382
FRANK WARFEL, BOX 517, WRANGELL, AK 99929
AARON WOODROW, 17875 POINT STEPHENS RD, JUNEAU, AK 99801

SHRIMP, BEAM TRAWL, WESTWARD
ROBIN LARSEN, BOX 264, SAND POINT, AK 99661

SHRIMP, POT GEAR, SOUTHEAST
DREW ALLEN, BOX 211122, AUKE BAY, AK 99821
ALLAN ALMQUIST, 308 DEERMOUNT, KETCHIKAN, AK 99901
NORMAN ALSUP, 15008 N TONGASS HWY, KETCHIKAN, AK 99901
BRADLEY ANDERSON, 3112 HALIBUT PT RD, SITKA, AK 99835
ERIC ANDERSON, BOX 23496, KETCHIKAN, AK 99901
PAUL ARRINGTON, BOX 252, WRANGELL, AK 99929
BEN ATWOOD, BOX 583, WARD COVE, AK 99928
RICK AYRES, 73-4392 PUKIAWE ST #A, KAILUA KONA, HI 96740
JOHN BAHRT, BOX 1654, SITKA, AK 99835
DANIEL BALL, BOX 8915, KETCHIKAN, AK 99901
MARGUERITE BARBER, BOX 5076, KETCHIKAN, AK 99901
DOUGLAS BARKER, BOX 813, WRANGELL, AK 99929
TY BARKHOEFER, 103 SCARLETT WAY, SITKA, AK 99835
JAY BARNETT, BOX 2145, PETERSBURG, AK 99833
LANCE BARNETT, BOX 1267, ASTORIA, OR 97103
BRANT BAXTER, BOX 1023, OAK HARBOR, WA 98277
GREGORY BEAM, BOX 1994, SITKA, AK 99835
ROBERT BECKER, BOX 240238, DOUGLAS, AK 99824
ALEXANDER BEHARY, BOX 2041, PETERSBURG, AK 99833
HENRY BLAKE, 119 SE 19TH DR, PENDLETON, OR 97801
HUGHIE BLAKE, BOX 2376, CORDOVA, AK 99574
THOMAS BLAKE, BOX 925, CRAIG, AK 99921
BRIAN BLANKENSHIP, 4316 VALLHALLA DR, SITKA, AK 99835
PAUL BLANKENSHIP, 500 LINCOLN ST #B6, SITKA, AK 99835

SHRIMP FISHING LIST—POT GEAR

VERGIL BOLES, 3415 N BEIGE ST, SPOKANE, WA 99216

CHARLIE BOWER, 20115 GLACIER HWY, JUNEAU, AK 99801

RICHARD BOYCE, BOX 83251, FAIRBANKS, AK 99708

MARK BRADLEY, 218 LAKEVEIW DR, SITKA, AK 99835

LENORD BRADY, BOX 19308, THORNE BAY, AK 99919

JAMES BRAME, BOX 7303, KETCHIKAN, AK 99901

THOMAS BRAYTON, 145 BEHRENDS AVE, JUNEAU, AK 99801

MIKE BRECKON, BOX 2351, FERNDALE, WA 98248

JONATHAN BROUWER, BOX 22927, JUNEAU, AK 99802

LYLE BROWN, 6590 GLACIER HWY #285, JUNEAU, AK 99801

NATHEN BROWN, BOX 90218, ANCHORAGE, AK 99509

TERRY BROWN, 8499 RAINBOW RD, JUNEAU, AK 99801

JAMES BUNN, BOX 9, HYDER, AK 99923

PETE BURR, BOX 23129, KETCHIKAN, AK 99901

THOMAS BUSBY, GEN DEL, HOONAH, AK 99829

RONN BUSCHMANN, BOX 1367, PETERSBURG, AK 99833

ANTHONY BYFORD, 4222 PTARMIGAN ST, JUNEAU, AK 99801

DONALD BYRD, 2701 HALIBUT POINT RD, SITKA, AK 99835

ERIC CALVIN, 210 BRADY ST, SITKA, AK 99835

PAUL CANIK, BOX 1653, PETERSBURG, AK 99833

SONNY CANNON, 3016 S TONGASS, KETCHIKAN, AK 99901

DENNIS CAPUA, BOX 21333, JUNEAU, AK 99802

JAMES CARLE, BOX 1163, CRAIG, AK 99921

JOHN CARLE, BOX 1, HYDABURG, AK 99922

RICHARD CARLE, GEN DEL, BETHEL, AK 99559

KELLY CARLISLE, BOX 1153, GIRDWOOD, AK 99587

ERLING CARLSON, 19136 BIRCH WOOD LOOP RD, CHUGIAK, AK 99567

LYNETTE CARLSON, BOX 19214, THORNE BAY, AK 99919

HENRY CHARTRAND, BOX 1992, SITKA, AK 99835

KENNETH CHRISTIANSEN, 1849 MARMOT DR, KODIAK, AK 99615

RALPH CLARKSON, BOX 2015, PETERSBURG, AK 99833

MICHAEL COLEMAN, BOX 2054, SITKA, AK 99835

JAMES COLIER, BOX 966, WRANGELL, AK 99929

RICHARD COLLINS, 1148 GREEN VALLEY DR, FALLON, NV 89406

JEROD COOK, BOX 1262, PETERSBURG, AK 99833

CASEY COOK.HARRENSTEIN, BOX 6164, SITKA, AK 99835

PATRICK CRENNA, 3486 HALIBUT POINT RD, SITKA, AK 99835

CARL CRUIKSHANK, BOX 390, CRAIG, AK 99921

RICHARD CURRAN, BOX 1336, SITKA, AK 99835

JEROME DAHL, BOX 1275, PETERSBURG, AK 99833

MIKE DALY, 501 CHARTERIS ST #A, SITKA, AK 99835

FRED DAMER, BOX 2001, PETERSBURG, AK 99833

DUGAN DANIELS, 507 KATLIAN ST, SITKA, AK 99835

MARK DANIELSON, BOX 782, SITKA, AK 99835

RICHARD DAUGHERTY, BOX 34864, JUNEAU, AK 99803

TODD DAUGHERTY, BOX 32705, JUNEAU, AK 99802

JIM DAVENPORT, BOX 1925, ABERDEEN, WA 98520

PATRICK DAVIS, BOX 921566, DUTCH HARBOR, AK 99692

PAUL DE.MONTIGNY, BOX 1584, PETERSBURG, AK 99833

LUKE DEMMERT, BOX 125, CRAIG, AK 99921

JACQUELINE DEMONTIGNY, BOX 691, WRANGELL, AK 99929

TONI DEPUE, BOX 842, WRANGELL, AK 99929

STUART DEWITT, BOX 117, HAINES, AK 99827

JAMES DICICCO, BOX 1066, SITKA, AK 99835

BILL DODSON, BOX EDB, EDNA BAY, AK 99950

RAYMOND DOUVILLE, BOX 66, CRAIG, AK 99921

DAVID DOYLE, BOX 4, HYDER, AK 99923

LEONARD DUBBER, BOX 349, HAINES, AK 99827

DONALD DURGAN, BOX 340, CRAIG, AK 99921

RONALD DURGAN, BOX 340, CRAIG, AK 99921

BRENNON EAGLE, BOX 576, WRANGELL, AK 99929

RANDALL EASTERLY, BOX 1524, WRANGELL, AK 99929

WAYNE EASTERLY, BOX 335, WRANGELL, AK 99929

SIDNEY EDENSHAW, BOX 352, HYDABURG, AK 99922

DUANE EDWARDS, BOX 2088, NEWPORT, OR 97365

CLEVELAND EELLS, BOX 853, SITKA, AK 99835

D.JEFFREY EELLS, BOX 1811, OREGON CITY, OR 97045

TYLER EELLS, 114 DARRIN DR2, SITKA, AK 99835

KEN EICHNER, 5166 SHORELINE DR N, KETCHIKAN, AK 99901

WAYNE ELLIS, BOX 2135, WRANGELL, AK 99929

ROBERT EVANS, 113 METLAKATLA NORTH #4, SITKA, AK 99835

ERIC EVENS, BOX 1412, PETERSBURG, AK 99833

LYNN EWING, BOX 1335, PETERSBURG, AK 99833

JUSTIN FAGER, 206 1/2 LAKEVIEW DR, SITKA, AK 99835

FALICIA FARMER, BOX 79, CRAIG, AK 99921

JIM FARMER, BOX 692, CRAIG, AK 99921

TOM FISHER, BOX 1928, WRANGELL, AK 99929

OTTO FLORSCHUTZ, BOX 547, WRANGELL, AK 99929

ROLAND FRANKS, BOX 743, WRANGELL, AK 99929

MARY GEBHARD, 2635 STELLAR WAY, FAIRBANKS, AK 99712

HARRY GIBBS, BOX 457, CRAIG, AK 99921

STEVEN GILE, BOX 2225, WRANGELL, AK 99929

JASON GJERTSEN, 714 ETOLIN ST, SITKA, AK 99835

RICHARD GOTTARDI, BOX 760, HAYFORK, CA 96041

ANTHONY GUGGENBICKLER, BOX 393, WRANGELL, AK 99929

CHRISTOPHER GUGGENBICKLER, BOX 1491, WRANGELL, AK 99929

MARK GUILLAUME, 8300 VALLEY AVE, JUNEAU, AK 99801

ELI HAGEN, BOX 421, CRAIG, AK 99921

JOHN HAGEN, BOX 1153, CRAIG, AK 99921

RICHARD HAGEN, BOX 421, CRAIG, AK 99921

ROBERT HAGEN, BOX 2334, SITKA, AK 99835

TRAVIS HAGEN, BOX 421, CRAIG, AK 99921

KYLE HAGER, BOX 628, MAPLE FALLS, WA 98226

CHARLES HALEY, 500 LINCOLN ST #1B, SITKA, AK 99835

DEAN HALTINER, BOX 443, PETERSBURG, AK 99833

FRED HAMILTON, BOX 661, CRAIG, AK 99921

FREDERICK HAMILTON, BOX 106, CRAIG, AK 99921

JACOB HAND, BOX 2191, CORDOVA, AK 99574

TOMMY HANSON, BOX 234, CRAIG, AK 99921

ALDWIN HARDER, BOX 714, HOONAH, AK 99829

CHARLES HARRIS, BOX 555, PETERSBURG, AK 99833

JEFFREY HAY, BOX 1373, WRANGELL, AK 99929

ROBERT HAYES, BOX 886, WRANGELL, AK 99929

DANNY HAYNES, BOX 7036, KETCHIKAN, AK 99901

GERARD HELGESEN, BOX 34, HYDABURG, AK 99922

RONALD HENRY, 2417 TONGASS AVE #111-141, KETCHIKAN, AK 99901

LYLE HILDE, 505 MONASTERY ST, SITKA, AK 99835

MARK HOFMANN, 1042 OBSTRUCTION PASS RD, OLGA, WA 98279

ERIC HOLMLUND, 4416 HALIBUT POINT RD, SITKA, AK 99835

JASON HOLST, 1400 EDGECUMBE DR, SITKA, AK 99835

STEVEN HOLTON, BOX 277, KLAWOCK, AK 99925

JESSE HOYT, BOX 7501, KETCHIKAN, AK 99901

RICHARD HUDSON, BOX 194, METLAKATLA, AK 99926

JAMES HUGHES, 507 KATLIAN ST, SITKA, AK 99835

NORMAN HUGHES, BOX 1136, HAINES, AK 99827

MAURICE INGMAN, 15008 N TONGASS HWY, KETCHIKAN, AK 99901

ROGER INGMAN, BOX 1155, SITKA, AK 99835

JOSEPH JANSSEN, BOX 492, TOK, AK 99780

J.R. JENSEN, 3022 WOODUCK, JUNEAU, AK 99801

MICHAEL JEWETT, 3220 1ST, KETCHIKAN, AK 99901

GREG JOHNS, BOX 214, KLAWOCK, AK 99925

BRADLEY JOHNSON, BOX 100, MEYERS CHUCK, AK 99903

DONALD JOHNSON, 1345 PLUG MILL RD, ELMA, WA 98541

RONALD JOHNSON, BOX 2232, WRANGELL, AK 99929

RYAN JONES, BOX 1166, SITKA, AK 99835

WILLIAM JONES, BOX 72, KLAWOCK, AK 99925

TIMOTHY JUNE, BOX 672, HAINES, AK 99827

ROBERT JURRIES, BOX 177, CRAIG, AK 99921

RICHARD KAER, BOX 2054, WRANGELL, AK 99929

JOHN KAMPMEIER, BOX 2316, WRANGELL, AK 99929

SHRIMP FISHING LIST—POT GEAR

LESLEY KEATON, 125 MAIN ST #103, KETCHIKAN, AK 99901
WILLIAM KEMPERMAN, BOX 19265, THORNE BAY, AK 99919
MILLARD KENDALL, BOX 476, TOK, AK 99780
PAUL KERBER, BOX 1187, HAINES, AK 99827
WAYDE KING, 8526 N TONGASS, KETCHIKAN, AK 99901
CRAIG KINNEY, 3531 BAILEY BLVD, KETCHIKAN, AK 99901
ANDREW KITTAMS, BOX 1544, PETERSBURG, AK 99833
DAVID KLEPSER, BOX 8946, KETCHIKAN, AK 99901
WILLIAM KNECHT, BOX 259, WRANGELL, AK 99929
GILBERT KNUTSON, 231 KATLIAN ST B-12, SITKA, AK 99835
TODD KORTH, 2154 VIZCAYA CIR, CAMPBELL, CA 95008
KEVIN KRIENER, BOX 537, THORNE BAY, AK 99919
PETER KROVINA, BOX 6027, SITKA, AK 99835
LESTER KUNTZ, BOX 642, WRANGELL, AK 99929
MATTHEW LAWRIE, BOX 6006, SITKA, AK 99835
JOHN LAWS, BOX 523, GARIBALDI, OR 97118
RONALD LEIGHTON, BOX 19414, THORNE BAY, AK 99919
KATHERINE LELO, 8400 35TH AVE SW, SEATTLE, WA 98126
TODD LENIHAN, BOX 6376, SITKA, AK 99835
JOSEPH LINVILLE, BOX 1753, SEWARD, AK 99664
KENNETH MADSEN, BOX 918, PETERSBURG, AK 99833
KENNETH MALONE, 2221 MULDOON RD #96, ANCHORAGE, AK 99504
JAMES MARKER, BOX 267, CRAIG, AK 99921
OTIS MARSH, BOX 606, PETERSBURG, AK 99833
NICHOLAS MARTIN, BOX 8312, KETCHIKAN, AK 99901
SHANE MARTIN, BOX 284, HAINES, AK 99827
MARTY MARTINEZ, BOX 513, METLAKATLA, AK 99926
CHARLES MASON, 16526 GLACIER HWY, JUNEAU, AK 99801
WAYNE MATHISEN, BOX 671, PETERSBURG, AK 99833
JOHN MATSUURA, BOX 7516, KETCHIKAN, AK 99901
SEAN MCCABE, 2106 VINING DR, BELLINGHAM, WA 98226
JON MCGRAW, BOX 552, KLAWOCK, AK 99925
PAUL MCINTYRE, BOX 1994, WRANGELL, AK 99929
PATRICK MCMURREN, BOX 12, WRANGELL, AK 99929
RODNEY MCVICKER, 24411 GRACEY TRAIL LN NE, POULSBO, WA 98370
WILLIAM MENISH, BOX 877, PETERSBURG, AK 99833
DEAN MICHELSON, BOX 81, HYDER, AK 99923
JOSHUA MIETHE, BOX 2031, WRANGELL, AK 99929
LANCE MIETHE, BOX PPV, KETCHIKAN, AK 99950
ROGER MIKKELSEN, BOX 403, WRANGELL, AK 99929
BONNY MILLARD, BOX 210114, AUKE BAY, AK 99821
GARRETT MILLER, BOX 1899, WRANGELL, AK 99929
JOHN MOLLER, BOX 32425, JUNEAU, AK 99803
ROBERT MOSHER, 11985 MENDENHALL LP RD, JUNEAU, AK 99801
CEDAR MULLIGAN, 7635 W WAGONER RD, GLENDALE, AZ 85308
MILES MUNHOVEN, BOX 6335, KETCHIKAN, AK 99901
DAIN MYERS, BOX 19538, THORNE BAY, AK 99919
ARNOLD NATKONG, BOX 203, HYDABURG, AK 99922
DONALD NATKONG, BOX 346, HYDABURG, AK 99922
RANDALL NEIMEYER, BOX 551, METLAKATLA, AK 99926
C.GENE NELSON, BOX 1251, PORT ANGELES, WA 98362
STEVEN NELZEN, 4352 BAY VIEW CT, HOMER, AK 99603
VIRGIL NEYMAN, 3306 HALIBUT POINT RD #5, SITKA, AK 99835
KRAIG NORHEIM, BOX 1152, PETERSBURG, AK 99833
LADD NORHEIM, BOX 935, PETERSBURG, AK 99833
JOHN OAKES, 15202 BIRCH ST, LONG BEACH, WA 98631
CLINT OCONNOR, BOX 112, CRAIG, AK 99921
GORDON OLSEN, BOX 1884, PETERSBURG, AK 99833
DENNIS ONEIL, BOX 1083, PETERSBURG, AK 99833
RON OPHEIM, BOX 2118, WRANGELL, AK 99929
CHRIS OTTESEN, BOX 2011, WRANGELL, AK 99929
PIPPIN OWEN, BOX 152, KLAWOCK, AK 99925
BRADELLE PADON, 740 5TH ST, JUNEAU, AK 99801
WOODY PAHL, BOX 1581, HAINES, AK 99827
AL PATOTZKA, 7220 THIEL CIRCLE, ANCHORAGE, AK 99502
JIM PEACOCK, BOX 284, PORT TOWNSEND, WA 98368

JERRINE PEELER, BOX 1572, WARD COVE, AK 99928
THOMAS PERKINS, BOX 5393, KETCHIKAN, AK 99901
DUSTIN PETERS, BOX 726, WARD COVE, AK 99928
CHARLES PETTICREW, BOX 971, WRANGELL, AK 99929
BURLIN PHILLIPS, 136 E 8TH ST, PORT ANGELES, WA 98362
RICHARD PHILLIPS, BOX 522, WRANGELL, AK 99929
RONALD PHILLIPS, 1500 S COTTEN DR, WASILLA, AK 99654
DONALD PIEPER, 5212 SE JENNINGS AVE, MILWAUKIE, OR 97267
JAMES PORTER, BOX 892, CRAIG, AK 99921
JAMES PROCTOR, BOX 31, GUSTAVUS, AK 99826
JAMES QUIGLEY, BOX 80, CRAIG, AK 99921
MICHAEL QUINN, BOX 210315, AUKE BAY, AK 99821
DANIEL REAR, 1007 HALIBUT POINT RD, SITKA, AK 99835
ALAN REEVES, BOX 741, WRANGELL, AK 99929
RYAN REEVES, BOX 758, WRANGELL, AK 99929
RANDY RICE, 710 N 160TH ST #B112, SHORELINE, WA 98133
DONALD RICHARDS, BOX 1764, PETERSBURG, AK 99833
MICHAEL RIES, 1198 VENTURA NAVIGATOR DR, VENTURA, CA 93001
THOMAS RIGHTMIER, BOX 6506, SITKA, AK 99835
CHAD RITCHIE, BOX 79, WRANGELL, AK 99929
SEAN ROBERTS, BOX 583, WARD COVE, AK 99928
PAUL ROSTAD, BOX 183, KAKE, AK 99830
JOSEPH ROTH, 16169 WATERFALL RD, KETCHIKAN, AK 99901
JAMES ROWLAND, BOX 970, WRANGELL, AK 99929
SIGURD RUTTER, 310 TILSON, SITKA, AK 99835
JOHN SAUNDERS, BOX 528, HAINES, AK 99827
MICHAEL SHAW, BOX 34506, JUNEAU, AK 99803
ALLEN SIFTSOFF, 3306 HALIBUT POINT RD #5, SITKA, AK 99835
JAMES SIMPSON, BOX 45, HYDER, AK 99923
CARL SIMS, BOX 2172, WRANGELL, AK 99929
ALF SKAFLESTAD, BOX 177, HOONAH, AK 99829
WESLEY SLATTERY, 206 W MATTLE RD, KETCHIKAN, AK 99901
ROBERT SMART, BOX 420, NAUKATI BAY, AK 99950
CHAD SMITH, BOX 1741, WRANGELL, AK 99929
DANIEL SMITH, BOX 911, WRANGELL, AK 99929
TANNER SMITH, BOX 1379, WRANGELL, AK 99929
WILLIAM SMITH, BOX 2735, SITKA, AK 99835
CHRISTOPHER SNYDER, BOX 8135, KETCHIKAN, AK 99901
AUSTIN SOLLARS, BOX 32424, JUNEAU, AK 99803
DAVID SOMERVILLE, BOX 163, PETERSBURG, AK 99833
CHRIS SONDIE, BOX 541, CLATSKANIE, OR 97016
DONALD SORRIC, BOX 2296, WRANGELL, AK 99929
EVANS SPARKS, 100 DONNA DR, SITKA, AK 99835
DONALD SPERL, BOX 1407, PETERSBURG, AK 99833
LARS STANGELAND, 222 FRONT ST #600, JUNEAU, AK 99801
MICHAEL STEELE, BOX 19157, THORNE BAY, AK 99919
MICHAEL STEWART, 29520 SE 472ND ST, ENUMCLAW, WA 98022
BRETT STILLWAUGH, BOX 1552, WRANGELL, AK 99929
ZEB STRONG, 3213 S 166TH ST, SEATAC, WA 98188
JAMES STUDLEY, BOX 946, HAINES, AK 99827
TIGER TASKER, 7724 ARLENE ST, ANCHORAGE, AK 99502
LEE TAYLOR, BOX 1077, HAINES, AK 99827
CHARLES TEAL, BOX 1637, WARD COVE, AK 99928
R.CRAIG THOMAS, 3933 ALASKA AVE, KETCHIKAN, AK 99901
WILLIAM THOMAS, BOX 942, HAINES, AK 99827
PALMER THOMASSEN, BOX 608, PETERSBURG, AK 99833
STEVEN THOMASSEN, BOX 742, WRANGELL, AK 99929
RICHARD THOMPSON, 443 WINDWARD WAY, DAVENPORT, FL 33837
LARRY TILLOTSON, BOX 518, WARD COVE, AK 99928
KARL TORGRAMSEN, BOX 1410, WRANGELL, AK 99929
PAUL TORGRAMSEN, BOX 1959, WRANGELL, AK 99929
THOMAS TRAIBUSH, 1300 PEACE PORTAL DR #206, BLAINE, WA 98230
KARL TRAVENSHEK, 92215 FRONT RD, ASTORIA, OR 97103
CHARLIE TRAYLOR, BOX 1381, WRANGELL, AK 99929
ROBERT TROTTER, BOX 455, KLAWOCK, AK 99925
SHAYAR VALANDRO, BOX 210966, AUKE BAY, AK 99821

SHRIMP / SEA CUCUMBER FISHING LIST

MICHAEL VAN.NOTE, BOX 26, HAINES, AK 99827
CHRISTIAN VAUGHAN, BOX 7621, KETCHIKAN, AK 99901
JAMES VAUGHAN, BOX 770, CRAIG, AK 99921
JOHN VERHEY, BOX 2281, WRANGELL, AK 99929
LOUIE WAGNER, BOX 369, METLAKATLA, AK 99926
HOWARD WALCOTT, BOX 15, KLAWOCK, AK 99925
JAY WALLING, 16765 LENA LOOP RD, JUNEAU, AK 99801
DONALD WANG, 392 LOMA DR #201, LOS ANGELES, CA 90017
BRUCE WARD, BOX 1501, WRANGELL, AK 99929
FRANK WARFEL, BOX 1512, WRANGELL, AK 99929
BRIAN WARMUTH, BOX 6382, KETCHIKAN, AK 99901
KELLY WARREN, BOX 472, SITKA, AK 99835
MARSHALL WARREN, BOX 344, GUSTAVUS, AK 99826
RONALD WATSON, 2825 SUNSET HWY, EAST WENATCHEE, WA 98802
LEE WAYNE, BOX 6348, SITKA, AK 99835
STACEY WAYNE, 210 SHOTGUN ALLEY, SITKA, AK 99835
STUART WEATHERS, BOX 1734, SITKA, AK 99835
STEVE WEISSBERG, 455 CHARTERIS ST, SITKA, AK 99835
DONALD WESTLUND, BOX 871, WARD COVE, AK 99928
FRANK WHITE, BOX 1474, HAINES, AK 99827
DUANE WHITSON, BOX 1456, SITKA, AK 99835
EVELYN WIDMYER, BOX 7100, KETCHIKAN, AK 99901
SHERMAN WIGLE, BOX 2038, PETERSBURG, AK 99833
PHILIP WILEY, BOX 219, WHITE BIRD, ID 83554
CHRISTOPHER WILHELM, BOX 9463, KETCHIKAN, AK 99901
DAVID WILLIAMS, 1912 SAWMILL CREEK RD, SITKA, AK 99835
MARK WILLIAMS, BOX 463, HAINES, AK 99827
WILLIAM WILSON, BOX 602, TENAKEE, AK 99841
AVERY WINTER, BOX 563, METLAKATLA, AK 99926
WAYNE WINTHER, BOX 505, SITKA, AK 99835
KURT WOHLHUETER, BOX 1312, PETERSBURG, AK 99833
DAVID WOLTEN, BOX 501, WRANGELL, AK 99929
GREGORY WOOD, BOX 2361, WRANGELL, AK 99929
AARON WOODROW, 17875 POINT STEPHENS RD, JUNEAU, AK 99801
LES WOODWARD, BOX 2059, WRANGELL, AK 99929
CHARLES WOOLSEY, 2309 HALIBUT POINT RD #38, SITKA, AK 99835
MIKE WORTHINGTON, 370 NE CAMANO DR #5-9, CAMANO ISLAND, WA 98282
RANDALL WORTMAN, BOX 271, CRAIG, AK 99921
GUTHRIE ZASTROW, 3930 S TONGASS HWY, KETCHIKAN, AK 99901
GARY ZAUGG, 5825 FALLA CT, KETCHIKAN, AK 99901

SHRIMP, POT GEAR VESSEL 60' OR OVER, PRINCE WILLIAM SOUND
CHRISTINE HITE, BOX 1431, CORDOVA, AK 99574

SEA CUCUMBER, DIVING GEAR, SOUTHEAST
EVAN ADSIT, BOX 80290, FAIRBANKS, AK 99708
JESSE AGNER, BOX 565, PETERSBURG, AK 99833
KALEB ALDRED, BOX 6123, SITKA, AK 99835
JOHN ANDERSON, 2203 HIGHLAND DR, CAMANO ISLAND, WA 98282
KEVIN ANDERSON, 2417 TONGASS STE 111 #186, KETCHIKAN, AK 99901
STEVE ANDERSON, BOX 1144, CRAIG, AK 99921
RYAN ASA, BOX 1134, CORDOVA, AK 99574
BRIAN ASHTON, BOX 406, WRANGELL, AK 99929
DAVID AUSMAN, BOX 9629, KETCHIKAN, AK 99901
RAYMOND BAINES, BOX 75, METLAKATLA, AK 99926
CORNELIS BAKKER, BOX 5253, KETCHIKAN, AK 99901
DANIEL BAKKER, BOX 282, OLYMPIA, WA 98507
HARRY BARNARD, BOX 1682, FORT BRAGG, CA 95437
FRANK BARNES, 2417 TONGASS AVE #111 PMB 135, KETCHIKAN, AK 99901
MARK BARNES, BOX 240535, DOUGLAS, AK 99824
PAUL BARNES, BOX 155, GUSTAVUS, AK 99826
DANIEL BARNETT, 4671 ANSONVILLE RD, NEW MILLPORT, PA 16861
LAITH BARNHILL, BOX 668, CRAIG, AK 99921
RICHARD BAUDER, BOX 277, SITKA, AK 99835

CHRISTOPHER BEAN, BOX 205, PELICAN, AK 99832
DAVID BEEBE, BOX 148, PETERSBURG, AK 99833
ALAN BENITZ, BOX 204, REPUBLIC, WA 99166
BERT BERGMAN, 801 CHARLES #A, SITKA, AK 99835
ROGER BERNDT, BOX 652, FRIDAY HARBOR, WA 98250
DEREK BEZEMER, BOX 885, CRAIG, AK 99921
CHRISTIAN BIAGI, BOX 8965, KETCHIKAN, AK 99901
JAMES BINGMAN, 16229 WATERFALL RD N, KETCHIKAN, AK 99901
BRIAN BITZ, BOX 627, HOONAH, AK 99829
JILL BLACKBURN, 51346 GATES BRIDGE E, GATES, OR 97346
CHRISTOPHER BOOTH, BOX 576, METLAKATLA, AK 99926
DOUGLAS BOOTH, 6068 CHURCHILL CT S, KETCHIKAN, AK 99901
STEVEN BOOTH, BOX 395, METLAKATLA, AK 99926
CHUCK BOOTHMAN, 3356 DALE ST, KETCHIKAN, AK 99901
JOSEPH BORER, 18 MOORE DR N, KETCHIKAN, AK 99901
ANTHONY BOYCE, BOX 5266, KETCHIKAN, AK 99901
JOSEPH BOYLE, 3055 TIMBELINE DR, CORONA, CA 92882
HOWARD BRAND, BOX 1546, WARD COVE, AK 99928
PETER BRANSON, BOX 1259, WRANGELL, AK 99929
CHARLES BREMER, 1122 S POINT HIGGINS, KETCHIKAN, AK 99901
CURTIS BROWN, BOX 456, CRAIG, AK 99921
JEFFREY BROWN, 14244 VIEW MOOR DR, MOUNT VERNON, WA 98273
VICTOR BUCHANAN, BOX 2553, KODIAK, AK 99615
RODNEY BURBA, 63 MATTLE RD, KETCHIKAN, AK 99901
SPENCER BURNFIELD, 561 E EAGLE RIDGE DR, SHELTON, WA 98584
TOM BUTTERBAUGH, 1621 SW JORDEN ST, GRANTS PASS, OR 97526
MICHAEL BYRER, BOX 1462, PETERSBURG, AK 99833
ERIC CALVIN, 210 BRADY ST, SITKA, AK 99835
GEORGE CAMPBELL, BOX 210732, AUKE BAY, AK 99821
RAYMOND CAMPBELL, 2707 W 18TH AVE, FAIRBANKS, AK 99709
ROBERT CAMPBELL, 448 EDGEWOOD AVE, ROCHESTER, NY 14620
EILEEN CANOLA, 111 CYPRESS, SAN FRANCISCO, CA 94110
ROD CAREW, 23711 57TH AVE SE, WOODINVILLE, WA 98072
BRYAN CARLSON, BOX 271, THORNE BAY, AK 99919
LYNETTE CARLSON, BOX 19214, THORNE BAY, AK 99919
MICHAEL CARPENTER, BOX 35, ALBION, CA 95410
MARK CARR, 12507 PRAIRE RIDGE DRIVE EAST, SUMNER, WA 98390
TOM CARRUTH, BOX 8641, KETCHIKAN, AK 99901
DANIEL CASEY, BOX 382, SITKA, AK 99835
PATRICK CASSIN, 1561 CEDAR RIDGE RD, KENDRICK, ID 83537
DANIEL CASTLE, 4430 S TONGASS HWY, KETCHIKAN, AK 99901
JAMES CASTLE, 87 SHOUP ST, KETCHIKAN, AK 99901
SERGEY CHEPURKO, BOX 1931, PORT ORCHARD, WA 98366
LONNIE CHESNUT, BOX 2506, PALMER, AK 99645
CHUCK CHISM, LOUS PLACE, MEYERS CHUCK, AK 99903
RALPH CIANFLONE, 4230 AUBERT DR, PARKDALE, OR 97041
BRETT CLAGGETT, 319 SPRUCE ST, KETCHIKAN, AK 99901
JAY CLIFTON, 3802 HALIBUT POINT RD, SITKA, AK 99835
PATRICK CLIFTON, 1815 SAWMILL CREEK RD, SITKA, AK 99835
BRIAN CLOOSE, 1417 JAY WEST RD, CARLTON, MN 55718
FOREST COLLINS, BOX 664, CRAIG, AK 99921
DUSTIN CONNOR, BOX 1372, PETERSBURG, AK 99833
AARON COOK, BOX 313, METLAKATLA, AK 99926
CHRIS COOK, 961 E AGATE LN, WASILLA, AK 99654
DENNY CORBIN, BOX 765, PELICAN, AK 99832
LYNDEN COTHARY, BOX 5186, KETCHIKAN, AK 99901
DOUGLAS COX, 3507 N E 97TH AVE, VANCOUVER, WA 98661
SCOTT CRAYNE, BOX 1794, WRANGELL, AK 99929
CLAY CULBERT, BOX 553, WRANGELL, AK 99929
RICHARD CURRAN, BOX 1336, SITKA, AK 99835
GREG CUSHING, 1217 GEORGESON LP, SITKA, AK 99835
CHRISTOPHER DABNEY, 2522 TAFT DR, LUMMI ISLAND, WA 98262
ALAN DALE, 926 NORDSTROM DR, KETCHIKAN, AK 99901
COLLIN DARRAH, 311 33RD AVE E, SEATTLE, WA 98112
KEVIN DAU, BOX 219, CRAIG, AK 99921

SEA CUCUMBER FISHING LIST

JAMES DENNIS, BOX 591, CRAIG, AK 99921
RICHARD DENOVA, 620 SAWMILL CREEK RD, SITKA, AK 99835
MICHAEL DENTLER, BOX 9054, KETCHIKAN, AK 99901
MATTHEW DUDDLES, BOX 490, PETERSBURG, AK 99833
ROBERT DUNCANSON, BOX 92, MEYERS CHUCK, AK 99903
DARRELL DURBIN, BOX 179, SEABECK, WA 98380
DANIEL EASLEY, 8415 166TH CT NW, GIG HARBOR, WA 98329
TRAVIS EASLON, BOX 1287, PORT ORFORD, OR 97465
JOHN EASTABROOK, 706 DENNIS ST SE #11, TUMWATER, WA 98501
JAMES EASTWOOD, BOX 1185, PETERSBURG, AK 99833
ROBERT EDENSHAW, BOX 373, HYDABURG, AK 99922
SIDNEY EDENSHAW, BOX 352, HYDABURG, AK 99922
GARRY EDSON, 122 WATER ST, THORNE BAY, AK 99919
KEN EICHNER, 5166 SHORELINE DR N, KETCHIKAN, AK 99901
GEORGE ELIASON, 105 SAND DOLLAR DR, SITKA, AK 99835
COREY ELKINS, 14227 OLYMPIC DRIVE SE, OLALLA, WA 98359
HARLEY ETHELBAH, 86 APPALOOSA LN, BELLINGHAM, WA 98229
MARK EVANOFF, BOX 8612, KETCHIKAN, AK 99901
RICK EVANOFF, 671 ALLEN CT, PLACEVILLE, CA 95667
DANIEL FALVEY, 123 ANNA DR, SITKA, AK 99835
SCOTT FALZERANO, 113 HARBER MT RD #6, SITKA, AK 99835
ORION FENNER, BOX 476, PETERSBURG, AK 99833
TIMOTHY FOLEY, 429 COUNTRY HILL DR, ROSEBURG, OR 97471
STEVEN FORREST, BOX 308, WRANGELL, AK 99929
JAMES FOSTER, BOX 240195, DOUGLAS, AK 99824
AARON FRANCK, BOX 759, ARCATA, CA 95518
STEVEN FRANKLIN, 1138 WOODLAND AVE, KETCHIKAN, AK 99901
RUDY FRANULOVICH, BOX 5433, KETCHIKAN, AK 99901
TERRY GANS, BOX 6583, KETCHIKAN, AK 99901
JONATHAN GATCH, 5240 SE NORTH ST, PORT ORCHARD, WA 98367
THOMAS GEORGE, BOX 1, KLAWOCK, AK 99925
MATTHEW GERRITS, BOX 414, PETERSBURG, AK 99833
DEREK GIBB, BOX 1845, PETERSBURG, AK 99833
BRIAN GIERARD, BOX 7343, KETCHIKAN, AK 99901
DANIEL GLAAB, BOX 6442, SITKA, AK 99835
GLENN GOLLEN, BOX 625, WARD COVE, AK 99928
RICHARD GOUIN, 6662 WELLINGTON LN, BREMERTON, WA 98311
JOSEPH GRIFFIN, 1298 N 62ND AVE, WEST RICHLAND, WA 99353
FABIAN GRUTTER, 711 ETOLIN ST, SITKA, AK 99835
CARTER GUELLER, BOX 1904, PETERSBURG, AK 99833
MICHAEL GUY, 3208 HALIBUT POINT ROAD #14, SITKA, AK 99835
TODD HADFIELD, 8286 GARNET ST, JUNEAU, AK 99801
CHARLES HALEY, 500 LINCOLN ST #1B, SITKA, AK 99835
JEREMY HAMBERGER, 1148 PARK AVE, KETCHIKAN, AK 99901
ERIC HAMILTON, BOX 23022, KETCHIKAN, AK 99901
EDWARD HAMLIN, 65050 S VICTORY RD, SUTTON, AK 99674
JACOB HAMMER, BOX 97, PETERSBURG, AK 99833
JOHN HANNON, 527 ROSEVILLE RIDGE CT, ROSEVILLE, CA 95661
DEL HANSEN, 5194 SHORELINE, KETCHIKAN, AK 99901
GREGORY HARRISON, BOX 997, WARD COVE, AK 99928
KYLE HAWKINS, 2535 WISTERIA, NEW ORLEANS, LA 70122
REID HAWKINS, 6545 HUASNA TOWNSITE RD, ARROYO GRANDE, CA 93420
JOHN HENDRICKS, BOX 5921, KETCHIKAN, AK 99901
GAR HENNING, 8631 AUGUSTA CIR, ANCHORAGE, AK 99504
CRAIG HENTHORNE, BOX 874, WARD COVE, AK 99928
KRISTIAN HERR, 19134 NOLL RD, POULSBO, WA 98370
KEVIN HIERSCHE, 30375 HILLSIDE TERRACE, GOLD BEACH, OR 97444
LYLE HILDE, 505 MONASTERY ST, SITKA, AK 99835
DENNIS HODGSON, 3011 227TH ST CT E, SPANAWAY, WA 98387
PATRICIA HOLLEY, BOX 283, KLAWOCK, AK 99925
ERIC HOLMLUND, 4416 HALIBUT POINT RD, SITKA, AK 99835
TRISTAN HOLMLUND, BOX 1976, PETERSBURG, AK 99833
SHARON HOLT, BOX 9224, KETCHIKAN, AK 99901
KEVIN HONC, 8843 83RD AVE SE, OLYMPIA, WA 98513
JEFFREY HOOD, 320 BAWDEN #302, KETCHIKAN, AK 99901
PAUL HORN, 665 SARGENT CREEK RD, KODIAK, AK 99615

DANIEL HOYT, 7565 S TONGASS HWY, KETCHIKAN, AK 99901
JESSE HOYT, BOX 7501, KETCHIKAN, AK 99901
MATTHEW HUBLOU, 6831 185TH ST SE, SNOHOMISH, WA 98296
CLIFFORD HUDSON, BOX 480, METLAKATLA, AK 99926
MARGARET HUGHES, BOX 6364, SITKA, AK 99835
NORMAN HUGHES, BOX 1136, HAINES, AK 99827
WILLIAM HUGHES, 215 BRADY ST, SITKA, AK 99835
HOWARD HUNTER, BOX 1281, PETERSBURG, AK 99833
JAMES HWANG, BOX 6854, KETCHIKAN, AK 99901
JORGE I.MOLINA.SALAS, 2716 HALIBUT POINT RD #13, SITKA, AK 99835
ROGER INGMAN, BOX 1155, SITKA, AK 99835
CLIFFORD JAMES, BOX 1709, PETERSBURG, AK 99833
SAMUEL JENSEN, BOX 681, PETERSBURG, AK 99833
LUTHER JENSON, BOX 19102, THORNE BAY, AK 99919
BRET JOHNSON, 130 BRYANT ST #204, KETCHIKAN, AK 99901
DANIEL JOHNSON, 1093 S POINT HIGGINS, KETCHIKAN, AK 99901
KEVIN JOHNSON, 4408 26TH AVE SE, LACEY, WA 98503
STANLEY JOHNSON, 108 SEAVIEW DR, SITKA, AK 99835
TIMOTHY JOHNSON, BOX 848, WRANGELL, AK 99929
GREGG JONES, 4016 HALIBUT POINT RD, SITKA, AK 99835
STEPHANIE JURRIES, BOX 177, CRAIG, AK 99921
DONALD KAMBEITZ, BOX 147, CRAIG, AK 99921
DALE KANEN, 9050 ROCKY COVE DR, ANCHORAGE, AK 99507
SUSAN KANEN, BOX 1249, CRAIG, AK 99921
DANIEL KELLY, BOX 1046, SPIRIT LAKE, ID 83869
WILLIAM KEMPERMAN, BOX 19265, THORNE BAY, AK 99919
GREGORY KENDALL, BOX 535, PETERSBURG, AK 99833
PAUL KERBER, BOX 1187, HAINES, AK 99827
ANDREW KITTAMS, BOX 1544, PETERSBURG, AK 99833
DAVID KLEIN, 126 MOUNTAIN ASH HTS #A, KETCHIKAN, AK 99901
DANIEL KNIGHT, BOX 6912, KETCHIKAN, AK 99901
JASON KNUTH, BOX NKI #357, KETCHIKAN, AK 99901
DAVID KRAUSE, BOX 1065, SITKA, AK 99835
JAMES KREUCHER, BOX 306, WRANGELL, AK 99929
ELZBIETA KUNAT, BOX 335, GUSTAVUS, AK 99826
JANUSZ KUNAT, BOX 335, GUSTAVUS, AK 99826
ROBERT KUNTZ, BOX 455, WRANGELL, AK 99929
KURT KVERNVIK, BOX 1081, PETERSBURG, AK 99833
EDWIN LAITY, 1619 LOT 1 SAWMILL CK RD, SITKA, AK 99835
LEO LANDRY, 19020 TRIAL BAY DR, EAGLE RIVER, AK 99577
DENNIS LANHAM, 125 COMMUNITY LN, SEQUIM, WA 99835
BRIAN LAPEYRI, 1551 SPNNIKER RD, VENTURA, CA 93001
ERIC LARSON, BOX 301, PETERSBURG, AK 99833
JOHN LARSON, 5959 S TONGASS HWY, KETCHIKAN, AK 99901
SCOTT LARSON, BOX 365, PETERSBURG, AK 99833
TREMAINE LAWRENCE, 4168 TIOPI LP, BELLINGHAM, WA 98226
JEREMY LEIGHTON, BOX 1176, WARD COVE, AK 99928
FRANK LEON, 1432 MASON ST, SHELTON, WA 98584
ANDREW LINDNER, BOX 845, WARD COVE, AK 99928
SCOTT LISENBURY, 470 MONROE RD, PORT ANGELES, WA 98362
SHANE LOHR, BOX 765, PETERSBURG, AK 99833
MATTHEW LORIG, 932 CARLANNA LAKE RD #B-11, KETCHIKAN, AK 99901
LEWIS LOWERY, BOX 807, WRANGELL, AK 99929
ELI LUCAS, BOX 1634, PETERSBURG, AK 99833
JOHN MALOUF, 5191 BORCH ST, KETCHIKAN, AK 99901
DESI MANGINI, 14872 CRESCENT VALLEY RD SE, OLALLA, WA 98359
DINO MANGINI, 4227 PERRY AVE, BREMBERTON, WA 98310
DAVID MANN, 920 W SESAME ST, KETCHIKAN, AK 99901
CARY MARKHAM, 11506 117TH ST CT E, PUYALLUP, WA 98374
DANIEL MARSDEN, BOX 15, METLAKATLA, AK 99926
CHARLES MARTIN, BOX 2299, WRANGELL, AK 99929
BRADLEY MARTINEZ, BOX 338, METLAKATLA, AK 99926
MARTY MARTINEZ, BOX 513, METLAKATLA, AK 99926
JOHN MATSUURA, BOX 7516, KETCHIKAN, AK 99901
KRISTIE MATTHEWS, BOX WWP, KETCHIKAN, AK 99950
BRIAN MATTSON, BOX 1168, PETERSBURG, AK 99833

SEA CUCUMBER FISHING LIST

SHELTON MAVES, BOX 117, CRAIG, AK 99921
KAYIN MCCAY, BOX 161, PETERSBURG, AK 99833
JON MCGRAW, BOX 552, KLAWOCK, AK 99925
FRANK MCGUIGAN, 31500 PEARL DR, FORT BRAGG, CA 95437
SIDNEY MCGUIRE, 650 STANTON ST, ARROYO GRANDE, CA 93420
DERRICK MCRAE, 2227 47 ST NW #G201, GIG HARBOR, WA 98335
DOUG MCRAE, 3824 41ST ST CT NW, GIG HARBOR, WA 98335
GARY MICHEALS, BOX 5041, BELLINGHAM, WA 98227
MARK MIKKELSEN, BOX 5235, KETCHIKAN, AK 99901
SCOTT MILLER, BOX 1794, SITKA, AK 99835
WILLIAM MILLER, BOX 8131, KETCHIKAN, AK 99901
RICHARD MILNE, BOX 692, QUILCENE, WA 98376
MONTE MITCHELL, 19508 23RD AVE NE, ARLINGTON, WA 98223
MARC MOATS, B0X 3076, SITKA, AK 99835
ROBERT MOMMSEN, BOX 9222, KETCHIKAN, AK 99901
JAMES MORGAN, BOX 6167, SITKA, AK 99835
RYAN MORIN, BOX 8164, KETCHIKAN, AK 99901
ERIC MORROW, 1311 SAW MILL CREEK RD #2, SITKA, AK 99835
SHAWN MUIR, 7327 225TH SW, EDMONDS, WA 98026
PATRICK MULLINS, 3204 VIEWCREST DR NE, BREMERTON, WA 98310
LARRY MUNN, 3492 WILSON RD, OAK HARBOR, WA 98277
SHAWN MURPHY, 1167 JACKSON ST UPPER, KETCHIKAN, AK 99901
JAMES MURRAY, 285 WILCOX LN, CORVALLIS, MT 59828
PAUL MYERCHIN, 3500 BALCHEN DR, ANCHORAGE, AK 99517
DEVIN MYERS, 1215 COLUMBINE, WENATCHEE, WA 98801
MELYSSA NAGAMINE, BOX 101, CRAIG, AK 99921
JOHN NELSON, BOX 242, PORT GAMBLE, WA 98364
PETER JOHNSON, 2417 TONGASS AVE #111-324, KETCHIKAN, AK 99901
NATE NORTON, BOX 5724, KETCHIKAN, AK 99901
MARK NUGENT, BOX 5382, KETCHIKAN, AK 99901
HERBERT OHARA, BOX 40963, SAN FRANCISCO, CA 94140
RICHARD OLIN, BOX 628, METLAKATLA, AK 99926
BRIAN OMANN, 285 BON JON VIEW WAY, SEQUIM, WA 98382
RONALD ONEIL, #53 WWP, KETCHIKAN, AK 99950
RON OPHEIM, BOX 2118, WRANGELL, AK 99929
DANA OSTROM, 12141 AVENIDA CONSENTIDO, SAN DIEGO, CA 92128
JAMES PARROTT, 610 SUNSET DR, KETCHIKAN, AK 99901
CHARLES PARSLEY, BOX 393, HOONAH, AK 99829
DENNIS PARSONS, BOX 204, CRAIG, AK 99921
MICHAEL PAULSEN, 361 MAIN ST, KETCHIKAN, AK 99901
MATTHEW PEAVEY, BOX 442, CRAIG, AK 99921
THEODORE PEELE, BOX 334, HYDABURG, AK 99922
BRYAN PEREZ, BOX 7991, KETCHIKAN, AK 99901
TIMOTHY PEROV, BOX 33321, JUNEAU, AK 99803
ARTHUR PETERSON, BOX 382, NAKNEK, AK 99633
JEB PHILLIPS, BOX 1253, PETERSBURG, AK 99833
DAN PIEPER, 21914 N PEASE HILL RD, COLBERT, WA 99005
LANCE PIHLMAN, BOX 5322, KETCHIKAN, AK 99901
RON PLACE, BOX 468, KLAWOCK, AK 99925
DANIEL PLATT, BOX 1912, FORT BRAGG, CA 95437
DAVID POPE, 2417 TONGASS AVE SUITE 111-344, KETCHIKAN, AK 99901
MATTHEW PRESSLY, 730 PARK AVE, KETCHIKAN, AK 99901
JAMES QUIGLEY, BOX 80, CRAIG, AK 99921
PATRICK QUIGLEY, BOX 80, CRAIG, AK 99921
JOHN RANWEILER, BOX 2118, EL PRADO, NM 87529
RICHARD REID, 15063 LIZZIE LN, KETCHIKAN, AK 99901
ROBERT REID, 506 OCAIN ST, SITKA, AK 99835
MICHAEL REIF, BOX 2346, SITKA, AK 99835
MARC REYNOLDS, BOX 6824, KETCHIKAN, AK 99901
JOSHUA RHOADES, BOX 6211, SITKA, AK 99835
ZACHARY RHOADES, 5847 SUNSET ST, JUNEAU, AK 99801
HAROLD RHODES, BOX 389, NAUKATI BAY, AK 99950
GLEN RICE, ISLAND D, MEYERS CHUCK, AK 99903
JOHN RICE, BOX 18181, COFFMAN COVE, AK 99918
DONALD RICHARDS, BOX 1764, PETERSBURG, AK 99833

SPENCER RICHTER, BOX 1011, CRAIG, AK 99921
ERIC RIEMER, BOX 23458, KETCHIKAN, AK 99901
ANTHONY RIGONI, 3162 JACKSON HEIGHTS, KETCHIKAN, AK 99901
JASON RINAS, BOX 514, WRANGELL, AK 99929
JEFFREY ROBINSON, BOX 633, PETERSBURG, AK 99833
SETH ROCKWELL, BOX 3143, SEWARD, AK 99664
DOUGLAS ROEHR, 513 CANYON DR, SOLANA BEACH, CA 92075
MICHAEL ROMINE, 301 WACHUSETTES ST, SITKA, AK 99835
C.ALAN ROSS, BOX 19376, THORNE BAY, AK 99919
JOSEPH ROTH, 16169 WATERFALL RD, KETCHIKAN, AK 99901
SCOTT SABIN, 120 FIREWEED LN, KENAI, AK 99611
SCOTT SALINE, BOX 3183, SITKA, AK 99835
MICHAEL SALLEE, BOX 7603, KETCHIKAN, AK 99901
MICHAEL SALTER, 3614 N VILLARD ST, TACOMA, WA 98407
JASON SANDERS, 4747 LAKE TERRELL RD, FERNDALE, WA 98248
BRIAN SANTMAN, BOX 363, BEAVER, WA 98305
LLOYD SAVAGE, 3805 HAMPTON DR, ANCHORAGE, AK 99504
JAMES SCANLON, BOX 8861, KETCHIKAN, AK 99901
ROD SCHENK, 2795 LAKE WHATCOM BLVD, BELLINGHAM, WA 98229
BRIAN SCHOLD, 15901 PEACOCK HILL RD SE, OLALLA, WA 98359
FRANZ SCHONBERG, BOX 866, ALLYN, WA 98524
ALEC SCHRAMEK, BOX 124, PETERSBURG, AK 99833
JOE SCHREINER, 63 BLUEBERRY HILL RD, PORT LUDLOW, WA 98365
BRUCE SCHUTTER, BOX 1112, SEWARD, AK 99664
JAMES SCUDERO, BOX 551, METLAKATLA, AK 99926
RANDY SELNESS, 5312 BLACK LAKE BLVD SW, OLYMPIA, WA 98512
RICK SERIKAKU, 599 SALMONBERRY CIR, KETCHIKAN, AK 99901
TORY SHIER, BOX 861, METLAKATLA, AK 99926
BRIAN SHILTS, BOX 367, WRANGELL, AK 99929
KEITH SHIPLEY, BOX 2074, WRANGELL, AK 99929
KELLAN SHOEMAKER, 106 GIBSON PL, SITKA, AK 99835
TERRY SIMPSON, BOX 55, KLAWOCK, AK 99925
SCOTT SINCLAIR, 6615 S 239TH PL #R103, KENT, WA 98032
CLAYTON SMALLEY, BOX 18023, COFFMAN COVE, AK 99918
CHRISTOPHER SMITH, BOX 8053, KODIAK, AK 99615
MICHAEL SMITH, BOX 1027, CRAIG, AK 99921
STEVEN SMITH, BOX 501, BURLEY, WA 98322
TIMOTHY SMITH, BOX 596, STERLING, AK 99672
MICHAEL SODERLUND, BOX 2269, MAPLE FALLS, WA 98266
A.MICHAEL STANDRIDGE, BOX 5783, KETCHIKAN, AK 99901
DALE STANLEY, BOX 7442, KETCHIKAN, AK 99901
MARVIN STICKWAN, BOX 5041, KETCHIKAN, AK 99901
ANDREW STOCK, 1288 COLUMBUS AVE #212, SAN FRANCISCO, CA 94133
BERT STROMQUIST, 106 BAHOVEC ST, SITKA, AK 99835
JOSHUA STUKEY, BOX 1073, CRAIG, AK 99921
SUSAN SUAREZ, BOX 341, SITKA, AK 99835
IGOR SUDARKIN, 2317 183 CT NE, REDMOND, WA 98052
DAVID SULSER, 109 SHARON DR, SITKA, AK 99835
SAMUEL SWANSON, 1136 NW CLONINGER CT, SILVERDALE, WA 98383
DARREN SWEDBERG, BOX 627, CRAIG, AK 99921
ANTHONY TAIBER, BOX 1861, PETERSBURG, AK 99833
KATHRYN TAYLOR, BOX 40201, SAN FRANSCISCO, CA 94140
ROD TAYLOR, 235 ELIZABETH DR, POINT ROBERTS, WA 98281
R.CRAIG THOMAS, 3933 ALASKA AVE, KETCHIKAN, AK 99901
TED THOMASSEN, 702 ETOLIN ST #2, SITKA, AK 99835
JEREMY THUET, 3306 79TH AVE NW, OLYMPIA, WA 98502
DAVID THYNES, BOX 533, PETERSBURG, AK 99833
MICA TOWNSEND.TRANI, BOX 3016, SITKA, AK 99835
CHAD TRANI, 11520 JUANITA DR NE, KIRKLAND, WA 98034
KREG TRANI, 155 RAVINHILL RD, LOPEZ ISLAND, WA 98261
LAWRENCE TRANI, 2008 HALIBUT POINT RD, SITKA, AK 99835
GARY TRUMPER, BOX 624, CLOVERDALE, CA 95425
THOMAS TRUMPER, 32800 NAMLESS LN, FORT BRAGG, CA 95437
THOMAS TRUMPER, 1940 2ND AVE, KETCHIKAN, AK 99901
ROBERT TUCKER, BOX 776, PORT ANGELES, WA 98362

SEA CUCUMBER / CLAMS / SEA URCHIN FISHING LIST

EARL TUTTLE, 1805 ALDER WAY #B, SITKA, AK 99835
ADAM UMSTEAD, 1260 REPUBLICIAN ST #340, SEATTLE, WA 98109
SHAYAR VALANDRO, BOX 210966, AUKE BAY, AK 99821
ROGER VALLION, 1721 EDGECUMBE DR, SITKA, AK 99835
JAMES VAUGHAN, BOX 770, CRAIG, AK 99921
ANTONIJA VENTENBERGS, 311 33RD AVE E, SEATTLE, WA 98112
JOHN VERHEY, BOX 2281, WRANGELL, AK 99929
DAVID VEST, 82 HIGGINS SPUR RD, KETCHIKAN, AK 99901
JOHN VEZINA, BOX 6234, SITKA, AK 99835
SCOTT VORRATH, BOX 281, CORDOVA, AK 99574
CYNTHIA WADE, 197 GRIMES RD, TOLEDO, WA 98591
RALPH WADE, 207 MALLARD LN, TOLEDO, WA 98591
HARRIET WADLEY, BOX 318, CRAIG, AK 99921
LOUIE WAGNER, BOX 672, METLAKATLA, AK 99926
LOUIE WAGNER, BOX 369, METLAKATLA, AK 99926
ELDON WALKER, 3848 MELROSE ST, JUNEAU, AK 99801
IAN WALT, BOX 1372, FRIDAY HARBOR, WA 98250
DREW WARE, BOX 1291, PETERSBURG, AK 99833
LANCE WATKINS, 537 S 39TH ST, BELLINGHAM, WA 98229
QUINN WEBSTER, 3848 MELROSE ST, JUNEAU, AK 99801
LARRY WEDVIK, BOX 383, LAKEBAY, WA 98349
BRADLEY WEIGER, 5840 MERIDIAN RD SE, OLYMPIA, WA 98513
JEFFREY WEIS, BOX 4327, SITKA, AK 99835
STEVE WEISSBERG, 455 CHARTERIS ST, SITKA, AK 99835
DARELL WELK, 100 CASCADE RD, KETCHIKAN, AK 99901
NATHANIEL WELTZIN, BOX 210253, JUNEAU, AK 99801
PAUL WELTZIN, BOX 210253, AUKE BAY, AK 99821
GERALD WENTWORTH, BOX 101, CRAIG, AK 99921
MELINDA WEST, 91494 CAPE ARAGO HWY, COOS BAYON, OR 97420
JEFF WHEELER, 3488 HALIBUT POINT RD, SITKA, AK 99835
KENNETH WIDMYER, BOX 242, EDNA BAY, AK 99950
JOE WILLIS, BOX 43, PETERSBURG, AK 99833
KEVIN WILLMAN, 1311 SAWMILL CREEK RD #15, SITKA, AK 99835
JOHN WILSON, 90 NE NEWKIRK RD, BELFAIR, WA 98528
SCOTT WINNOP, 100 KINCROFT WAY #A, SITKA, AK 99835
DUSTIN WINTER, BOX 532, METLAKATLA, AK 99926
KYLE WOLTJER, BOX 947, CRAIG, AK 99921
KARSTEN WOOD, BOX 2195, PETERSBURG, AK 99833
WILLIAM WOOLDRIDGE, 17010 7TH AVE NW, LAKEBAY, WA 98349
ERIC WYATT, BOX 369, CRAIG, AK 99921
KYLE YOUNG, 102 KNUTSO DR, SITKA, AK 99835
LARRY YOUNG, BOX 922, PETERSBURG, AK 99833
MONTE YOUNG, 2413 SAWMILL CREEK RD, SITKA, AK 99835
TAMAR YOUNG, BOX 8005, PORT ALEXANDER, AK 99836
TYLER ZAUGG, 5833 S TONGASS HWY, KETCHIKAN, AK 99901
BRIAN ZWICK, 801 PETERSON ST, KETCHIKAN, AK 99901

SEA CUCUMBER, DIVING GEAR, STATEWIDE
SHAYNE WESTON, BOX 3238, FRIDAY HARBOR, WA 98250

SEA CUCUMBER, DIVING GEAR, KODIAK
MARK BEARDSLEY, BOX 8776, KODIAK, AK 99615
MARK BLAKESLEE, BOX 2356, KODIAK, AK 99615
CLIFTON IVANOFF, BOX 8883, KODIAK, AK 99615
REUBEN IVANOFF, BOX 8883, KODIAK, AK 99615

CLAMS, SHOVEL, STATEWIDE
JEFFREY ALLEN, BOX 3020, TRINIDAD, CA 95570

SEA URCHIN, DIVING GEAR, SOUTHEAST
KEVIN ANDERSON, 2417 TONGASS STE 111 #186, KETCHIKAN, AK 99901

MIKE ASHMON, 121 SILETZ HWY, LINCOLN CITY, OR 97367
CORNELIS BAKKER, BOX 5253, KETCHIKAN, AK 99901
HARRY BARNARD, BOX 1682, FORT BRAGG, CA 95437
DEREK BECKER, 302 N 4TH AVE, KELSO, WA 98626
DEREK BEZEMER, BOX 885, CRAIG, AK 99921
HENRY BLACKWELL, BOX 815, GUERNEVILLE, CA 95446
CHARLES BREMER, 1122 S POINT HIGGINS, KETCHIKAN, AK 99901
ARMANDO BRIONEZ, 2534 MACKENZIE RD, BELLINGHAM, WA 98226
GARY BROWN, 1107 WESTWOOD AVE #15, WENATCHEE, WA 98801
JOSEPH BUCHL, 10024 CHANNEL DR NW, OLYMPIA, WA 98502
BRET BURNETT, BOX 35793, JUNEAU, AK 99803
MICHAEL CARPENTER, BOX 35, ALBION, CA 95410
TOM CARRUTH, BOX 8641, KETCHIKAN, AK 99901
JAMES CLAYHOLT, BOX 192, MOSS LANDING, CA 95039
ROBERT CORBETT, BOX 6043, KETCHIKAN, AK 99901
JOHN EASTABROOK, 706 DENNIS ST SE #11, TUMWATER, WA 98501
THOMAS EDWARDS, 10617 RIVIERA DR, ANDERSON ISLAND, WA 98303
KEN EICHNER, 5166 SHORELINE DR N, KETCHIKAN, AK 99901
COREY ELKINS, 14227 OLYMPIC DRIVE SE, OLALLA, WA 98359
KIRK EVANOFF, 23341 SHADY LN, FORT BRAGG, CA 95437
MARK EVANOFF, BOX 8612, KETCHIKAN, AK 99901
RICK EVANOFF, 671 ALLEN CT, PLACEVILLE, CA 95667
TIMOTHY FOLEY, 429 COUNTRY HILL DR, ROSEBURG, OR 97471
ISTVAN FUZAK, BOX 1137, CRAIG, AK 99921
JONATHAN GATCH, 5240 SE NORTH ST, PORT ORCHARD, WA 98367
MARK GMEINER, BOX 281, MANCHESTER, CA 95459
BEN GODWIN, 421 W 40TH ST, SAN PEDRO, CA 90732
JEREMY HAMBERGER, 1148 PARK AVE, KETCHIKAN, AK 99901
ERIC HAMILTON, BOX 23022, KETCHIKAN, AK 99901
CHRISTOPHER HARRIS, BOX 1726, WARD COVE, AK 99928
DENNIS HODGSON, 3011 227TH ST CT E, SPANAWAY, WA 98387
JORDAN HOOKS, 8401 EDGEWATER DR, LAKEWOOD, WA 98499
BLAKE JUNTZ, BOX 1334, MENEOCINO, CA 95460
DONALD KAMBEITZ, BOX 147, CRAIG, AK 99921
DAVID KLEIN, 126 MOUNTAIN ASH HTS #A, KETCHIKAN, AK 99901
JEREMY LEIGHTON, BOX 1176, WARD COVE, AK 99928
JIM LEWIS, BOX 711, CRAIG, AK 99921
FRANK MCGUIGAN, 31500 PEARL DR, FORT BRAGG, CA 95437
SIDNEY MCGUIRE, 650 STANTON ST, ARROYO GRANDE, CA 93420
DERRICK MCRAE, 2227 47 ST NW #G201, GIG HARBOR, WA 98335
WILLIAM MILLER, BOX 8131, KETCHIKAN, AK 99901
DOUG MONK, BOX 1227, PORT ANGELES, WA 98362
KURTIS MORIN, BOX 621, WARD COVE, AK 99928
PETER N. JOHNSON, 2417 TONGASS AVE #111-324, KETCHIKAN, AK 99901
DANA OSTROM, 12141 AVENIDA CONSENTIDO, SAN DIEGO, CA 92128
DONALD PADEN, 24414 UNIVERSITY AVE #3, LOMA LINDA, CA 92354
JAN PAYNE, 1862 HAVILLAH RD, TONASKET, WA 98855
JEREMIAH PERCIVAL, BOX 5053, KETCHIKAN, AK 99901
RICHARD POGRE, 712 LAURELWOOD DR, SAN MATEO, CA 94403
DAVID POPE, 2417 TONGASS AVE SUITE 111-344, KETCHIKAN, AK 99901
MATTHEW PRESSLY, 730 PARK AVE, KETCHIKAN, AK 99901
DAVID RUDIE, 2653 FAIRFIELD ST, SAN DIEGO, CA 92110
MICHAEL SALLEE, BOX 7603, KETCHIKAN, AK 99901
BRIAN SANTMAN, BOX 363, BEAVER, WA 98305
ZACHARY SEIBERT, 395 CORRALITIS RD, ARROYO GRANDE, CA 93420
RANDY SELNESS, 5312 BLACK LAKE BLVD SW, OLYMPIA, WA 98512
RICK SERIKAKU, 599 SALMONBERRY CIR, KETCHIKAN, AK 99901
CHRISTOPHER SMITH, BOX 8053, KODIAK, AK 99615
JOHN SPENCER, BOX 412, MYRTLE CREEK, OR 97457
DALE STANLEY, BOX 7442, KETCHIKAN, AK 99901
MICHAEL STEWART, 29520 SE 472ND ST, ENUMCLAW, WA 98022
ANDREW STOCK, 1288 COLUMBUS AVE #212, SAN FRANCISCO, CA 94133
ROD TAYLOR, 235 ELIZABETH DR, POINT ROBERTS, WA 98281
LAWRENCE TRANI, 2008 HALIBUT POINT RD, SITKA, AK 99835
EVAN TRUMPER, 4920 LAUREL DELL RD, UPPER LAKE, CA 95485

SEA URCHIN / SCALLOPS / ROCKFISH FISHING LIST

GARY TRUMPER, BOX 624, CLOVERDALE, CA 95425
THOMAS TRUMPER, 32800 NAMLESS LN, FORT BRAGG, CA 95437
THOMAS TRUMPER, 1940 2ND AVE, KETCHIKAN, AK 99901
SHAYAR VALANDRO, BOX 210966, AUKE BAY, AK 99821
JAMES VAUGHAN, BOX 770, CRAIG, AK 99921
DANIEL VOGL, 1013 CRESTVIEW DR, MILLBRAE, CA 94030
W.BRADFORD VON.WICHMAN, 2940 MALLARD LN, ANCHORAGE, AK 99508
SCOTT VORRATH, BOX 281, CORDOVA, AK 99574
IAN WALT, BOX 1372, FRIDAY HARBOR, WA 98250
SHAYNE WESTON, BOX 3238, FRIDAY HARBOR, WA 98250
CHRISTOPHER YOUNG, BOX 2511, HOMER, AK 99603
JAMES YOUNG, BOX 132, EASTPORT, ME 4631
MEL ZACHARY, 16298 OLD CASPER RAIL RD, FORT BRAGG, CA 95437
ROYCE ZACHARY, 16298 OLD CASPER RAIL RD, FORT BRAGG, CA 95437

SEA URCHIN, DIVING GEAR, STATEWIDE
SAMUEL SWANSON, 1136 NW CLONINGER CT, SILVERDALE, WA 98383

SEA URCHIN, DIVING GEAR, KODIAK
CAROLINA BOY INC, BOX 600, SEAFORD, VA 23696
FORUM STAR LLC, 2025 1ST AVE #900, SEATTLE, WA 98121
FUTURE FISHERIES, 14 HERVEY TICHON AVE, NEW BEDFORD, MA 2740
OCEAN FISHERIES, 3871 STEILACOM BLVD SW STE C, LAKEWOOD, WA 98499
THOMAS MINIO, BOX 8989, KODIAK, AK 99615

SCALLOPS DREDGE, VESSEL OVER 80', FEDERAL WATERS
TOM MINIO, BOX 8989, KODIAK, AK 99615

SCALLOPS DREDGE, VESSEL OVER 80', STATE WATERS
TOM MINIO, BOX 8989, KODIAK, AK 99615
ALASKAN DREAM VENTURES, 8344 MARY ESTHER DR, EAGLE RVR, AK 99577
EWT LLC, 38 HASSEY ST, NEW BEDFORD, MA 2740
WILLIAM J HARRINGTON, BOX 8166, KODIAK, AK 99615

DEMERSAL SHELF ROCKFISH, HAND TROLL, SOUTHEAST
JAMES SIMPSON, BOX 45, HYDER, AK 99923

DEMERSAL SHELF ROCKFISH, LONGLINE VESSEL UNDER 60', SOUTEAST
JASON ANDERSEN, BOX 99, SITKA, AK 99835
WILLIAM AUGER, BOX 9335, KETCHIKAN, AK 99901
JOHN BAHRT, BOX 1654, SITKA, AK 99835
ARNOLD BAKKE, BOX 1482, WRANGELL, AK 99929
FRANK BALOVICH, BOX 1396, SITKA, AK 99835
NELS BECKER, BOX 240838, DOUGLAS, AK 99824
BERT BERGMAN, 801 CHARLES #A, SITKA, AK 99835
BRIAN BLANKENSHIP, 4316 VALLHALLA DR, SITKA, AK 99835
CHARLES BLATTNER, BOX 33916, JUNEAU, AK 99803
DALE BOSWORTH, BOX 45, PETERSBURG, AK 99833
TODD CHAPIN, 2417 TONGASS AVE SUITE 111-244, KETCHIKAN, AK 99901
DAVID CLARK, 507 KATLIAN ST, SITKA, AK 99835
RUSSELL COCKRUM, 5791 N TONGASS HWY, KETCHIKAN, AK 99901
RICHARD CURRAN, BOX 1336, SITKA, AK 99835
ALAN DALE, 926 NORDSTROM DR, KETCHIKAN, AK 99901
MIKE DALY, 501 CHARTERIS ST #A, SITKA, AK 99835
DUGAN DANIELS, 507 KATLIAN ST, SITKA, AK 99835
JULIE DECKER, BOX 2138, WRANGELL, AK 99929
CASEY DIGENNARO, 208 PARK ST, SITKA, AK 99835
DAN DOAK, BOX 677, WRANGELL, AK 99929
MICHAEL DOUVILLE, BOX 68, CRAIG, AK 99921
RAYMOND DOUVILLE, BOX 66, CRAIG, AK 99921
RONALD DURGAN, BOX 340, CRAIG, AK 99921
WILLIAM FARMER, BOX 336, CRAIG, AK 99921
DAVID GIFFORD, BOX 8125, PORT ALEXANDER, AK 99836
DYLAN HALEY, 500 LINCOLN ST B1, SITKA, AK 99835
CHRISTOPHER HANSON, BOX 2283, SITKA, AK 99835

JONATHAN HILL, 2150 HALIBUT POINT ROAD, SITKA, AK 99835
JESSE JESKE, 203 BRADY ST, SITKA, AK 99835
PAMELA LEASK, BOX 759, WARD COVE, AK 99928
BLAIR MARTENS, BOX 485, SITKA, AK 99835
MICHAEL MAYO, 2808 SAWMILL CREEK RD, SITKA, AK 99835
KENNETH MCLEOD, BOX 434, SITKA, AK 99835
ROBERT MEYER, BOX 10, MEYERS CHUCK, AK 99903
ROBERT MOSHER, 11985 MENDENHALL LP RD, JUNEAU, AK 99801
IZAAK NEEDHAM, BOX 6382, SITKA, AK 99835
TIMOTHY OCONNOR, BOX 1225, CRAIG, AK 99921
BAE OLNEY.MILLER, 505 OCAIN ST, SITKA, AK 99835
PAT PARRISH, BOX 2895, SITKA, AK 99835
MATTHEW PEAVEY, BOX 442, CRAIG, AK 99921
ERIC PETERSON, BOX 2976, SITKA, AK 99835
CHARLES PETTICREW, BOX 971, WRANGELL, AK 99929
MARK ROBERTS, BOX 246, PETERSBURG, AK 99833
CALVIN ROBINSON, BOX 2225, SITKA, AK 99835
ANTHONEY SINE, BOX 32132, JUNEAU, AK 99803
KELSEY SKORDAHL, 109C LANCE DR, SITKA, AK 99835
JACOB STRUBBE, BOX 130, SONOITA, AZ 85637
STUART WEATHERS, BOX 1734, SITKA, AK 99835
LES WOODWARD, BOX 2059, WRANGELL, AK 99929
RANDALL WORTMAN, BOX 271, CRAIG, AK 99921
GUTHRIE ZASTROW, 3930 S TONGASS HWY, KETCHIKAN, AK 99901

DEMERSAL SHELF ROCKFISH, DINGLEBAR TROLL, SOUTHEAST
SUSAN YOUNG, BOX 825, PETERSBURG, AK 99833

DEMERSAL SHELF ROCKFISH, MECHANICAL JIG, SOUTHEAST
CASEY DIGENNARO, 208 PARK ST, SITKA, AK 99835
DAVID GIFFORD, BOX 8125, PORT ALEXANDER, AK 99836
SEAN PULLIAM, BOX 2422, YUCCA VALLEY, CA 92286
LES WOODWARD, BOX 2059, WRANGELL, AK 99929

DEMERSAL SHELF ROCKFISH, LONGLINE VESSEL 60' +, SOUTHEAST
STEVEN FISH, BOX 6448, SITKA, AK 99835
WILLIAM LEWIS, BOX 6181, SITKA, AK 99835
DUANE TORGESON, 4017 HALIBUT POINT RD, SITKA, AK 99835

MISC. MARINE INVERTEBRATES, OTHER GEAR, STATEWIDE
THERESA ABBAS, 4011 SHADY LN, JUNEAU, AK 99801
ALASKA SPICE SHOP, 55 HAINES HWY # 846, HAINES, AK 99827
JENNIFER BROWN, BOX 5555, KETCHIKAN, AK 99901
TOMI MARSH, 2417 TONGASS AVE # 111-176, KETCHIKAN, AK 99901
HOPE MERRITT, 1302 SAWMILL CREEK RD #40, SITKA, AK 99835
MICHELLE ROY, BOX 846, HAINES, AK 99827
ALEX THORNE, 834 LINCOLN ST STE 200, SITKA, AK 99835

GLOSSARY OF TERMS

Beach seine. A method of fishing with a small net along the beach.

Brailer. A netted pouch or scoop used for weighing or transferring fish from one place to another.

Carpal tunnel syndrome. Stiffness in the hands and wrists caused by repetitive motion.

Cork line. The cork or Styrofoam part of the net that floats.

Crab pot. A steel and mesh cage that is used to catch crab.

Cork piler. The person who piles the corks onto the deck.

Crew share. The percentage of the catch that the crew is paid.

Deck. The level of the boat where the crew works while fishing.

Deck boss. The person in charge of helping both skipper and crew.

Deck hands. All persons who work on deck besides the skipper.

EPIRB. A radio device that is automatically activated in emergencies, and emits an emergency radio signal to satellites, enabling the Coast Guard to pinpoint, within minutes, the location of a vessel in distress.

Fathom. Unit of measurement, six feet.

Fishing license. An individual license to participate in commercial fishing. The present cost is $200 a year.

Fishing permit. A permanent permit allowing a skipper to catch and sell fish in a specific Alaskan fishing area. It may be sold on the open market. Typical price is about $50,000.

Fish poisoning. An infection caused by a cut being exposed to the bacteria that covers a fish's skin.

Factory trawler. A large ship that catches and processes fish in the remote waters of Alaska. It may have a crew of 100 and extend up to 300 feet long.

Floating processor. A large ship, up to 300 feet long, that only processes fish in the remote waters of Alaska. Unlike a factory trawler, it relies on other boats to supply the fish it processes.

Fish slime. The oozy, slippery, bacteria-laden coating that exists on a fish's scaly skin.

Full share. The amount of the catch paid to crew members with full qualifications.

Gear. Anything related to the net, ropes, fisherman's clothing or fishing supplies.

Galley. The inside part of the boat where the crew lives and eats.

Gillnet. A method of fishing where the fish get caught by their gills in a net.

Greenhorn. An inexperienced fisherman.

Half share. The amount of the catch paid to a less-qualified crew member, who works at a reduced share to gain experience as an apprentice.

Hatch. The space under the deck where the fish are stored.

Haul. The process of fishing and bringing fish aboard.

Knots. Nautical miles, equals 1.15 land miles.

Lead line. The weighted part of the purse seine net that sinks to the ocean bottom.

Lead piler. The person who piles the lead line on a purse seiner.

Longline. A method of fishing that employs baited hooks attached to a mile-long groundline. It's placed on the ocean floor to catch halibut and groundfish.

Pelican release. A spring-loaded snap release for disconnecting the skiff from the boat.

Permit holder. Person who holds a fishing permit.

Pick the anchor. The process of raising the anchor from the bottom of the ocean.

Plunger pole. A long aluminum pole with a cup at the end of it used for hitting the water and scaring salmon or herring into the net. Used by purse seiners.

Power block. A hydraulic wheel that pulls the net out of the water so the crew can stack it on deck. Used by purse seiners.

Purse line. The line that's used to draw up the bottom of the net to trap the fish in a purse seine net.

Purse seining. A method of fishing that involves surrounding the fish with a net, drawing it up with a purse line to form a bowl shape, then hauling the fish aboard.

Rigging. The boom, mast, and all the cables and lines connected to them.

Roe. Fish eggs. Salmon, pollock and herring roe are favorite foods among the Japanese.

Salt-water boil. A red, pimple-like bump that appears on parts of the body continually exposed to wet clothing soaked in salt water.

Scopolamine. Seasickness medication in the form of patches that are stuck behind the ear.

Second skiffman. The skiffman's helper.

Skiff. The small power boat that is used in the purse seine fishing operation.

Skiffman. The person who runs the skiff.

Slime line. The area on a floating processor, factory trawler or cannery where fish are gutted and cleaned.

Skipper. The captain who runs the boat and makes the decisions.

Spring settlement. A bonus paid to fishermen by the canneries in the springtime.

Surimi. Sold as imitation crab meat. It's made from processed pollock and other groundfish.

Survival suit. A neoprene suit that maintains a person's body temperature in ocean waters. It's used in emergencies that force crew members to jump overboard.

Tender. A large boat that services the fishing grounds and buys directly from fishing boats. Equipped with refrigerated tanks, the tender then transports the fish to the cannery or floating processor to be canned, smoked or frozen.

Tophouse. Covered area on the boat's upper deck that houses the boat's steering wheel and navigational equipment.

Trawl. To fish by dragging a long net, similar in shape to a large windsock, behind the boat until it's full.

Troll. To fish by trailing a baited hook and line.

Unload. The process of pulling the fish out of the hatch and either selling them to a tender or to a cannery on the dock.

Web. The light, meshy, netted, nylon, tar-covered portion of the net in which the fish get trapped.

Web piler. The person who piles the web portion of the net on the deck of a purse seiner.

EPILOGUE

Well, there you have it—a no-nonsense look at what the commercial fishing industry is all about. If you decide to fish, it'll be the most difficult—and exciting—job you'll ever have! Not only is fishing a very rewarding job monetarily, but the raw beauty of Alaska is something to be cherished forever!

Fishing in Alaska is an adventure and is also fun. However, it may be a dangerous occupation at times, and shouldn't be taken lightly. Almost every year, people are lost at sea in fishing-related accidents. Most of these incidents are caused by problems encountered in treacherous seas during the harsh winter months—can happen at all times, year round.

With these losses at sea, the United States Coast Guard has been enforcing much stricter safety standards. In fact, in the last few years, the overall safety of the industry has improved dramatically, ensuring a safe work environment for the tens of thousands of commercial fishermen in Alaska. This has been achieved by requiring crew members and skippers to be trained in how to respond to many different at-sea emergencies. They must know how to perform a variety of different safety procedures, and be pre-assigned a specific duty on the boat for each type of possible emergency.

In addition to safety education, all vessels are required to meet safety requirements and must pass a yearly inspection by the U.S. Coast Guard. All vessels are required to have U.S. Coast-Guard-approved survival suits for every person on board. Every boat must also have a USCG-approved life raft (which comes equipped with survival supplies). Also, each vessel must have an EPIRB. This radio device is automatically activated in emergencies, and emits an emergency radio signal to satellites, enabling the Coast Guard to pinpoint, within minutes, the location of a vessel in distress.

Yes, commercial fishing may be dangerous at times, but with the cooperation of the United States Coast Guard and concerned fishermen, the industry is getting safer every year.

As the author of this book, I'll leave the decision about whether you should go fishing to you. But Alaska is something you should experience at least once in your life!

Sincerely,

Mark Maricich

INDEX

INDEX

INDEX

Questions for the Reader:

Since we are continually improving this guide to make it the best that it can be, we rely on comments and suggestions from our readers to help us with our efforts. If you have any comments or suggestions, we'd love to hear them. We'd especially like to hear of your experiences in Alaska, and of your successful job search. If you complete this form and send it to us, we might post your experience on our website at www.AlaskaFishingJobs.com! Also, feel free to send us any non-returnable photos of your Alaska trip.

PLEASE COMPLETE THIS FORM AND SEND IT TO:
KING SALMON COMMUNICATIONS, P.O. BOX 2942, SEAL BEACH, CA 90740
OR E-MAIL US YOUR INPUT AT: contactus@alaskafishingjobs.com

NAME:_____

ADDRESS:_____

PHONE NUMBER:_____ E-MAIL ADDRESS:_____

DATE YOU READ THIS GUIDE:_____

WHAT PART OF THIS GUIDE WAS THE MOST HELPFUL?_____

_____

WHAT PART OF THIS GUIDE NEEDS IMPROVING?_____

_____

WHAT DO YOU THINK OF THE QUALITY OF THIS GUIDE AND ITS

INFORMATION?_____

HOW DID THIS GUIDE HELP YOU TO FIND A JOB IN ALASKA?_____

_____

To order additional copies of this book,
"The Greenhorn's Guide™ to Alaska Fishing Jobs,"
visit our website at
www.AlaskaFishingJobs.com

Thank you and good luck!

www.ingramcontent.com/pod-product-compliance
Lightning Source LLC
Chambersburg PA
CBHW080415270326
41929CB00018B/3039